JavaScript:
The Complete Reference

JavaScript:
The Complete Reference

Thomas Powell
Fritz Schneider

Osborne/**McGraw-Hill**

New York   Chicago   San Francisco
Lisbon   London   Madrid   Mexico City
Milan   New Delhi   San Juan
Seoul   Singapore   Sydney   Toronto

About the Authors

Thomas Powell (tpowell@pint.com) has been involved in the Internet community for over ten years. In the early 1990s he worked at the first internet service provider in Southern California, CERFnet. In 1994, he founded PINT (www.pint.com), a Web development and consulting firm that now provides Web services for numerous major corporations around the United States.

Powell is the author of numerous Web development books including *HTML: The Complete Reference*, *HTML Programmers Reference*, *Web Design: The Complete Reference*, and *Web Site Engineering*. He has written extensively on Web technology in trade publications and is a frequent contributor to *Network World*. Powell is also a member of the Network World Test Alliance.

Thomas Powell teaches Web publishing and development classes for the University of California, San Diego Computer Science department. He also teaches for the UCSD Extension where he and his colleagues founded the Web Publishing program. He holds a B.S. in Math Applied Science from UCLA and an M.S. in Computer Science from UCSD.

Fritz Schneider is a software engineer who has worked in the Internet privacy industry for the last several years. He has a wide variety of Web design and implementation experience, from implementing custom proxy modules for the Apache web server to writing large DHTML applications and database-driven Web sites.

Schneider served as Technical Editor for *HTML: The Complete Reference* and continues to serve as an instructor in HTML, JavaScript, and Web design in general. He holds a B.S. in Computer Engineering from Columbia University and was in the final stage of the completion of his M.S. in Computer Science from UCSD during the time of this writing.

Osborne/**McGraw-Hill**
2600 Tenth Street
Berkeley, California 94710
U.S.A.

To arrange bulk purchase discounts for sales promotions, premiums, or fund-raisers, please contact Osborne/**McGraw-Hill** at the above address. For information on translations or book distributors outside the U.S.A., please see the International Contact Information page immediately following the index of this book.

JavaScript: The Complete Reference

1234567890 2CUS 2CUS 01987654321

ISBN 0-07-219127-9

Publisher Brandon A. Nordin	**Proofreader** Stefany Otis
Vice President & Associate Publisher Scott Rogers	**Indexer** Jack Lewis
Acquisitions Editor Ann Sellers	**Computer Designer** Elizabeth Jang Lauren McCarthy Melinda Moore Lytle
Project Editor Julie M. Smith	
Acquisitions Coordinators Paulina Pobocha Timothy Madrid	**Illustrator** Lyssa Wald Michael Mueller
Technical Editor Pankaj Kamthan	**Series Design** Peter F. Hancik
Copy Editor Carl Wikander	

This book was composed with Corel VENTURA™ Publisher.

Contents

Acknowledgments xxiii

Part 1

Introduction

1 Introduction to JavaScript 3
A First Look at JavaScript 4
Adding JavaScript to HTML Documents 7
    Using the <script> Element. 9
    Event Handlers 13
    Linked Scripts 16
    JavaScript Pseudo-URL 18
    JavaScript Entities 21
JavaScript Applications 25
History of JavaScript 26
Summary 28

2 JavaScript Core Features—Overview 29
Basic Definitions 30
Script Execution Order 30

Case Sensitivity 31
    HTML and Case Sensitivity 32
Whitespace 33
Statements 34
    Semicolons 35
    Blocks 36
Variables 37
Basic Data Types 37
    Weak Typing 38
Composite Types 39
    Arrays 40
    Objects 41
    Expressions 42
    Operators 42
    Operator Precedence 45
Flow Control 45
Loops 47
    Loop Control 48
Functions 49
Input and Output in JavaScript 50
Regular Expressions 53
Comments 54
Summary 55

Part II

Core Language

3   Data Types and Variables 59

Basic Notions 60
Weak Typing 61
Primitive Types 61
    Numbers 61
    Strings 66
    Booleans 71
    Undefined and Null 73
Composite Types 74
    Objects 74
    Arrays 76
Functions 77
    Creating Functions 78
Variables 80
    Identifiers 80
    Variable Declaration 82
    Variable Scope 83
Type Conversion 86
    Type Conversion in the Real World 89
Summary 90

4   Operators, Expressions, and Statements 91

Statement Basics 92
  Semicolons 92
  Blocks 94

Basic Operators 95
  Assignment Operator 95
  Basic Arithmetic Operators 96
  Bitwise Operators 99
  Bitwise Shift Operators 101
  Advanced Assignment Statements 101
  Increment and Decrement 103
  Comparison Operators 105
  Logical Operators 107
  ?: Operator 108
  Comma Operator 110
  void Operator 110
  typeof 111
  Object Operators 112
  Operator Precedence 115

Core JavaScript Statements 118
  if Statements 118
  switch 122
  while Loops 125
  do-while Loops 128
  for Loops 128
  Loop Control with continue and break 129

Object-Related Statements 133
  with Statement 133
  Object Loops Using for...in 134
  Other Statements? 134

Summary 134

5   Functions 137

Function Basics 138
  Parameter Passing 141
  Global and Local Variables 143
  Local Functions 146

Functions as Objects 148
  Function Literals and Anonymous Functions 149
  Static Variables 151
  Advanced Parameter Passing 152

Recursive Functions 154
Using Functions 156
Summary 160

6   Objects 161

Objects in JavaScript 162

Creating Objects 163
    Object Literals 165
Primitive and Reference Types 167
Object Destruction and Garbage Collection 169
Objects as Associative Arrays 170
Object Properties 172
    Instance Properties 172
    Common Object Properties 173
Creating User-Defined Objects 174
    The Prototype Chain 178
    Good Practice in Object Creation 179
JavaScript's Object-Oriented Reality 180
    The Rise of the Object-Oriented Approach 180
Summary 181

7   Array, Date, Math, and Type-Related Objects 183
Array 184
    Accessing Array Elements 185
    Adding and Changing Array Elements 185
    Removing Array Elements 187
    The Length Property 187
    Arrays as Stacks and Queues 190
    Manipulating Arrays 192
    Multidimensional Arrays 198
    Extending Array with Prototype 198
    Issues with Arrays 200
Boolean 201
Date 201
    Creating Dates 202
    Manipulating Dates 203
    Global 207
Math 210
    Random Numbers 213
    Easing Math Computations 213
Number 213
String 214
    Examining Strings 215
    Manipulating Strings 217
    Marking Up Strings as HTML 218
Object Types and Primitive Types 221
Summary 221

8   Regular Expressions 223
The Need for Regular Expressions 224
Introduction to JavaScript Regular Expressions 225
    Creating Patterns 227
RegExp Object 236
    exec() Method 237

RegExp Properties 240
String Methods for Regular Expressions 245
Advanced Regular Expressions 248
Limitations of Regular Expressions 250
Summary 250

Part III

Fundamental Client-Side JavaScript

9   Traditional JavaScript Object Models 253
Object Model Overview 254
The Traditional JavaScript Object Model 256
The Document Object 258
    Accessing Document Elements by Position 264
    Accessing Document Elements by Name 266
    Event Handlers 267
Putting It All Together 269
The Object Models 271
    Netscape 2 271
    Netscape 3 272
    Netscape 4 274
    Netscape 6 280
    Internet Explorer 3 281
    Internet Explorer 4 282
    Internet Explorer 5, 5.5, and 6 288
    Opera, Mozilla, Konqueror, and Other Browsers 289
The Nightmare of Cross-Browser Object Support 289
    A Solution? 290
Summary 290

10   The Standard Document Object Model 293
DOM Flavors 294
Document Trees 295
Accessing Elements 299
    Other Access Properties 305
Creating Nodes 308
Inserting and Appending Nodes 309
    Copying Nodes 311
Deleting and Replacing Nodes 312
    Modifying Nodes 314
Manipulating Attributes 316
The DOM and HTML Elements 317
The DOM and CSS 319
    Inline Style Manipulation 319
    Dynamic Style Using Classes and Collections 325
    Accessing Complex Style Rules 328

The DOM Versus DHTML Object Models 331
 The Power of innerHTML 332
 Document.all[ ] 334
Summary 335

11 Event Handling 337
Basic Event Model 338
 Event Binding in HTML 339
 Event Binding in JavaScript 352
 Firing Events Manually 353
 Return Values 354
Modern Models 356
 Netscape 4 Event Model 357
 Internet Explorer 4 Event Model 362
DOM2 Event Model 368
 Mouse Events 370
 Keyboard Events 370
 Browser Events 370
 UI Events 370
 Mutation Events 371
 Binding Events to Elements 371
 Event Propagation: Bubbling and Capturing 374
 Event Redirection 376
Event Model Issues 376
Summary 377

Part IV

Using JavaScript

12 Controlling Windows and Frames 381
Introduction to the Window Object 382
Dialogs 382
 Alert 382
 Confirm 383
 Prompts 385
Opening and Closing Generic Windows 387
 Window Features 390
 Writing to Windows 395
 DOM Methods and Windows 398
Inter-Window Communication Details 399
Controlling Windows 400
 Moving Windows 400
 Resizing Windows 401
 Scrolling Windows 402
Window Events 404
Frames: A Special Case of Windows 405
 State Management with Frames 409
 Solving Frame Problems: Frame Busting and Building 412

Window Extensions   413
    IE Window Extensions: Modal, Modeless,
       and Pop-up Windows   413
Full-Screen Windows   416
    Netscape Window Extensions: Simulating
       the Browser   417
Summary   418

13   Handling Documents **419**
Historic Document Object Properties   420
    Document Color   420
    Last Modification Date   423
    Location and Related Properties   424
Basic Document Methods   425
Traditional HTML Element Access with Document   427
    document.anchors[ ] and document.links[ ]   428
    document.forms[ ]   429
    document.images[ ]   431
    Object-Related Collections: applets[ ], embeds[ ],
       and plugins[ ]   434
    DHTML-Related Document Collections   435
Document Object Model Redux   436
    Accessing Specific HTML Element Properties   440
DOM Table Manipulation   444
DOM Applied   455
Summary   456

14   Form Handling **457**
The Need for JavaScript Form Checking   458
Form Basics   458
Form Elements   462
    Form Buttons   463
    Text Fields   467
    Checkboxes and Radio Buttons   472
    Hidden Fields   476
    File Uploads   477
    Select Menus   478
    Other Form Elements: Label, Fieldset, and Legend   485
Form Validation   486
    Validation Issues   495
    Keyboard Masking   495
Form Usability and JavaScript   497
    First Field Focus   498
    Labels and Field Selection   498
    Status Messages   499
    Disabling Fields   499
    Read-Only Fields   501
    Keyboard Improvements   502

Dynamic Forms 505

Summary 509

15 Image Effects: Rollovers, Positioning,
and Animation 511

Image Basics 512

Rollover Buttons 516

Extending Rollovers 523

CSS Positioning 525

Netscape 4 Layers 529

Internet Explorer 4 Layers 531

DOM Errors 532

Cross-Browser Layers 532

Applied DHTML 543

Simple Transition 543

Second-Generation Image Rollovers 547

Targeted Rollovers (Take 2) 550

General Animation 552

Practical DHTML 557

Summary 557

16 Navigation and Site Visit Improvements 559

Implementation Issues 560

Pull-Down Menus 561

Complex Menu Systems 564

Quicklinks Pull-Down Menus 565

Other Menu Forms 585

Navigation Assistance with Cookies 592

Cookies in JavaScript 594

Using Cookies for User State Management 598

Cookie Limitations 602

Internet Explorer State Extensions 604

Summary 605

17 Controlling the Browser 607

Browser Detection Basics 608

Browser Sensing Basics: The Navigator Object 608

Browser Detection—An Introduction 610

What to Detect 612

Technology Detection 612

Visual Detection: Screen Object 617

Language Detection 622

Advanced Detection Techniques 622

Microsoft Client Capabilities 623

Browser Detection in Practice 625

Browser Control 625

Location Object 625

History Object 626

Controlling the Status Bar 627
Setting Timeouts 627
Simulating Browser Button Presses 630
Summary 633

Part V

Advanced Topics

18 JavaScript and Embedded Objects 637
Java 638
Including Applets 639
Java Detection 640
Accessing Applets in JavaScript 640
Issues with JavaScript-Driven Applets 644
Accessing JavaScript with Applets 645
Plugins 645
Embedding Plugins 645
MIME Types 646
Detecting Support for MIME Types 647
Detecting Specific Plugins 649
Interacting with Plugins 651
ActiveX 656
Including ActiveX Controls 656
Interacting with ActiveX Controls 658
Summary 661

19 Server-Side JavaScript 663
Server-Side JS Overview 664
Netscape Server-Side JavaScript 664
Creating an Application 665
Server-Side JavaScript Syntax 670
SSJS Objects 670
ASP Overview 672
Methods to Include JavaScript under ASP 673
JavaScript Syntax and ASP 675
Interacting with Server Objects 678
ASP and External Systems 683
Other JavaScript Uses 685
Summary 686

20 JavaScript and XML 687
Overview of XML 688
Valid Documents 692
XML Presentation 695
The DOM and XML 700
Internet Explorer Example 700
Netscape 6 Example 706

Internet Explorer's XML Data Islands 711
Summary 715

Part VI

Real World JavaScript

21   JavaScript Security 719
The JavaScript Security Model 720
    Same-Origin Policy 721
    Data Tainting 723
    Signed Scripts 724
    Fundamentals 725
    Certificates 726
    Creating and Including Signed Scripts 728
    Utilizing Signed Script Privileges 733
    Practical Considerations 738
Security Problems with JavaScript 739
    Bombing Browsers with JavaScript 740
    Deceptive Practices 741
    Developer Responsibility 742
Summary 743

22   Netscape Extensions and Considerations 745
Core Language Issues 746
    JavaScript 1.1 747
    JavaScript 1.2 748
    JavaScript 1.3 748
    JavaScript 1.4 749
    JavaScript 1.5 750
    JavaScript 2.0 750
Browser Issues 751
    Netscape 3 751
    Netscape 4 752
    Netscape 6 756
Summary 757

23   Internet Explorer Extensions and Considerations 759
Core Language Issues 760
    JScript 1.0 762
    JScript 2.0 762
    JScript 3.0 763
    JScript 4.0 764
    JScript 5.0 764
    JScript 5.5 764
Browser Issues 764
    Internet Explorer 3 765
    Internet Explorer 4 765

Internet Explorer 5 769
Internet Explorer 5.5 772
Internet Explorer 6 772
Proprietary Features 773
JScript Features 773
CSS Filters 780
Data Binding 781
Microsoft Office Web Components 782
Dynamic Properties 786
HTML Applications 790
DHTML Behaviors 792
Popup Windows 799
Summary 801

24   JavaScript Practices 803
Errors 804
Debugging 807
Turning on Error Messages 807
Common Mistakes 809
Debugging Techniques 812
Defensive Programming 819
Error Handlers 820
Exceptions 824
Capability and Browser Detection 830
Code Hiding 832
Coding Style 836
Speeding up Your Code 837
Protecting Your Code 838
JavaScript's Place on the Web 840
Summary 841

Part VII

Appendixes

A   Core Syntax Quick Reference 845
Language Fundamentals 846
Language Versions 847
Language Standards Conformance 849
Data Types 849
Primitive Types 849
Type Conversion 852
Composite Types 854
Operators 858
Arithmetic Operators 858
Bitwise Operators 859
Logical Operators 860
Conditional Operator 861

Type Operators 861
Comma Operator 863
Relational Operators 863
Operator Precedence and Associativity 864
Flow Control Constructs 866
Exceptions 869
Regular Expressions 870

B JavaScript Object Reference 875
General References 876
Object Models 876
The Traditional Object Model 878
Netscape 3 879
Internet Explorer 3 879
Netscape 4 880
Internet Explorer 4+ 880
Internet Explorer 5.5+, Netscape 6, and the DOM 881
Core Property Reference 883
Events 883
DOM Properties 892
DOM Methods 894
Other Core Properties 897
Other Core Methods 902
JavaScript Object Reference 907
Generic HTML Element Object (Document Object) 908
a, Anchor, Link (Document Object) 914
abbr (Document Object) 916
acronym (Document Object) 916
ActiveXObject (Built-in/Browser Object) 917
address (Document Object) 917
Anchor (Document Object) 917
applet (Document Object) 917
area (Document Object) 918
Array (Built-in Object) 919
b (Document Object) 921
base (Document Object) 921
basefont (Document Object) 922
bdo (Document Object) 922
big (Document Object) 923
blockquote (Document Object) 923
body (Document Object) 923
Boolean (Built-in Object) 925
br (Document Object) 926
button (Document Object) 926
Button (Document Object) 927
caption (Document Object) 928
center (Document Object) 928
Checkbox (Document Object) 929

cite (Document Object) 930
clientInformation (Browser Object) 930
clipboardData (Browser Object) 930
code (Document Object) 931
col (Document Object) 931
colgroup (Document Object) 932
Components (Browser Object) 932
CSSrule (Document Object) 932
currentStyle (Document Object) 932
dataTransfer (Browser Object) 932
Date (Built-in Object) 933
dd (Document Object) 937
del (Document Object) 937
dfn (Document Object) 938
Dictionary (Built-in Object) 938
dir (Document Object) 938
div (Document Object) 938
dl (Document Object) 939
Document (Document Object) 940
dt (Document Object) 945
em (Document Object) 946
embed (Document Object) 946
Enumerator (Built-in Object) 947
Error (Built-in Object) 948
Event (Browser Object) 949
external (Browser Object) 952
fieldSet (Document Object) 952
File, FileUpload (Document Object) 953
FileSystemObject (Built-in Object) 954
font (Document Object) 954
FileUpload 955
form (Document Object) 955
frame (Document Object) 956
Frame (Browser Object) 957
frameset (Document Object) 957
Function (Built-in Object) 958
Global (Built-in Object) 959
h1, ..., h6 (Document Object) 961
head (Document Object) 961
Hidden (Document Object) 962
History (Browser Object) 962
hr (Document Object) 963
html (Document Object) 963
i (Document Object) 964
iframe (Document Object) 964
Image, img (Document Object) 965
implementation (Document Browser/Object) 967
input (Document Object) 967

ins (Document Object) 968
isindex 968
java (Browser Object) 968
kbd (Document Object) 969
label (Document Object) 969
Layer (Document Browser/Object) 970
legend (Document Object) 972
li (Document Object) 972
link (Document Object) 973
Location (Browser Object) 974
map (Document Object) 975
marquee (Document Object) 975
Math (Built-in Object) 975
menu (Document Object) 977
meta (Document Object) 978
mimeType (Browser object) 978
namespace (Browser object) 979
Navigator (Browser object) 979
netscape (Browser Object) 981
nobr (Document Object) 982
noframes (Document Object) 982
noscript (Document Object) 982
Number (Built-in Object) 982
Object (Built-in Object) 983
object (Document Object) 984
ol (Document Object) 986
optgroup (Document Object) 987
option (Document Object) 987
p (Document Object) 988
Packages (Browser Object) 989
param (Document Object) 989
Password (Document Object) 990
Plugin (Browser Object) 990
popup (Browser Object) 991
pkcs11 (Browser Object) 991
pre (Document Object) 992
q (Document Object) 992
Radio (Document Object) 993
RegExp (Built-in Object) 994
Reset (Document Object) 996
rule, CSSrule (Browser object) 997
runtimeStyle (Document object) 997
samp (Document Object) 998
screen (Browser object) 998
script (Document Object) 999
select (Document Object) 1000
selection (Browser Object) 1001
small (Document Object) 1002

span (Document Object) 1002
strike (Document Object) 1003
String (Built-in Object) 1003
strong (Document Object) 1005
Style (Document/Browser Object) 1005
style (Document Object) 1018
styleSheet (Document Object) 1019
sub (Document Object) 1020
Submit (Document Object) 1021
sun (Browser Object) 1022
sup (Document Object) 1022
table (Document Object) 1022
tbody, thead, tfoot (Document Object) 1024
td, th (Document Object) 1025
Text (Document Object) 1026
textarea (Document Object) 1028
TextRange (Browser Object) 1029
tfoot (Document Object) 1029
th (Document Object) 1029
thead (Document Object) 1029
tr (Document Object) 1029
title (Document Object) 1030
tt (Document Object) 1031
u (Document Object) 1031
ul (Document Object) 1031
userProfile (Browser Object) 1032
var (Document Object) 1033
VBArray (Built-in Object) 1033
Window (Browser Object) 1033
xml (Document Object) 1042

C   Reserved Words 1043

Index 1047

Acknowledgments

B y the time you get to write the acknowledgments of a "Complete Reference" you are usually completely sick and tired of writing. Yet the words of thanks for all those that have helped me produce over 3000 pages in the Complete Reference series flow easily. I'll try not to ramble too much though, and thank things like caffeine, various overplayed CDs, chili dogs, or any of the other necessities of a true tech writer and get right to the point.

First I have to thank my co-author Fritz Schneider. You probably never expected that being my Teaching Assistant at UCSD would lead you to help write a massive book like this. Hopefully, you'll be as proud of the result as I am of you.

Second, once again many of the folks at my Web development firm PINT (www. pint.com) really helped out on the production of the book. Cory Ducker, Marcus Richards, and Reuben Poon helped to ferret out problems with the chapters. Many others helped keep things running smoothly at PINT, especially Maria Defante, Eric Raether, Jimmy Tam, Rob McFarlane, Melinda Serrato, Cathleen Ryan, and Kim Smith. Dan Whitworth escaped most of the work on this book, but I am sure he'll be back for more. Special thanks goes to Reuben Poon for his extra assistance, particularly with Chapter 19. Mine Okano deserves much of the credit for the massive Appendix and site project, and for helping me get rid of my comma deficiency problem. Lastly, to the now dozens of other PINT folks, a heap of thanks for everything you do that helps keeps this place fun.

The students of my past JavaScript classes also deserve some credit for suggesting areas of improvement and examples. I'm very thankful for the fresh eyes of my recent students, particularly Lorraine Chuman, Stuart Baker, Rick Seaman, and Daisy Bhonsle who caught numerous typos and errors.

As always, the folks at Osborne were a pleasure to work with. Paulina, Tim, Julie, and Ann kept Fritz and me busy and appropriately motivated. Of course, many others worked behind the scenes and I pass my thanks on to you.

My friends and family deserve more than the brief mention they get, as they had the hard job of putting up with me when I had such a big task on my plate. Sylvia, your smile in particular makes all the work worth it.

Lastly at this time I must reflect on the day my last book, HTML: The Complete Reference 3rd Edition went to press. That day was the saddest day of my life as I was shocked by the news of the sudden passing of my father Dr. Howard T. Powell. I always admired his passion for sharing his knowledge with the scientific community, and I sorely miss him. I couldn't stop the presses on the last book to add a dedication, so I hope in some sense, Dad, you know this book was one I had to write for you.

Thomas A. Powell
tpowell@pint.com
August 2001

First and foremost, I would like to extend my thanks to my co-author Thomas Powell for his support, confidence, and sage advice over the past several years. His encouragement and experience have helped me grow in innumerable ways as a student, teacher, developer, editor, and writer. As always, Thomas was a pleasure to work with and as helpful, generous, and insightful a co-author as one could imagine.

The staff at Powell Internet (www.pint.com) rendered assistance and expertise throughout the production of this book. My thanks goes out to everyone there, especially to Mine Okano for her assistance with the support site and appendix, and to Reuben Poon for his assistance with Chapter 19.

The folks at Osborne/McGraw-Hill were a pleasure to work with. Paulina Pobocha and Julie Smith kept us in line and focused, despite our best efforts to throw everything off track, as did Timothy Madrid and Ann Sellers. My thanks to everyone at Osborne/ McGraw-Hill, including our eternally patient copy editors.

My personal thanks goes out to all my friends, family, and colleagues for their support over the past six months. In particular, Daniele Micciancio at UCSD exhibited godlike patience and understanding during the course of this project. My friends Tim Stephens, Charles Wood, Pat Woodside, Sharif Khaleel, and Alison Hurley were always there to provide a laugh or twenty when I needed it. Thanks also to Tom Perkin whose desk I commandeered and then proceeded to bury with the computers, notes, charts, and drafts a project like this entails. And finally, my thanks to musicians and coffeemakers everywhere for providing the *aqua vitae* from which everything computer-related ultimately stems.

Fritz Schneider
August 2001

The Complete Reference

JavaScript

Part 1

Introduction

Chapter 1

Introduction to JavaScript

avaScript is the premier client-side scripting language used today on the Web. Its use is widespread in tasks ranging from the validation of form data to the creation of complex user interfaces. Yet the language has capabilities that many of its users have yet to discover. Soon JavaScript will be increasingly used to manipulate the very HTML and even XML documents in which it is contained. When it finally achieves this role, it will become a first class client-side Web technology, ranking alongside HTML, CSS, and, eventually, XML. As such, it will be a language that any Web designer would be remiss not to master. This chapter serves as a brief introduction to the language and how it is included in Web pages.

A First Look at JavaScript

Our first look at JavaScript is the ever-popular "Hello World" example. In this version we will use JavaScript to write the string "Hello World from JavaScript!" into the HTML document to be displayed:

```
<!DOCTYPE HTML PUBLIC "-//W3C//DTD HTML 4.01 Transitional//EN">
<html>
<head>
<title>JavaScript Hello World</title>
</head>
<body>
<h1 align="center">First JavaScript</h1>
<hr>
<script language="JavaScript" type="text/javascript">
    document.write("Hello World from JavaScript!");
</script>
</body>
</html>
```

Notice how the script is intermixed into the HTML document using the **<script>** element that encloses the simple one line script:

```
document.write("Hello World from JavaScript!");
```

Using the **<script>** element allows the browser to differentiate between what is JavaScript and what is regular text or HTML. If we type this example in using a standard text editor, we can load it into a JavaScript-aware Web browser—such as Internet Explorer 3, Netscape 2, Opera 3, or any later version of these browsers—and we should see the result shown in Figure 1-1.

If we wanted to embold the text we could modify the script to output not only some text but also some HTML. However, we need to be careful when the world of

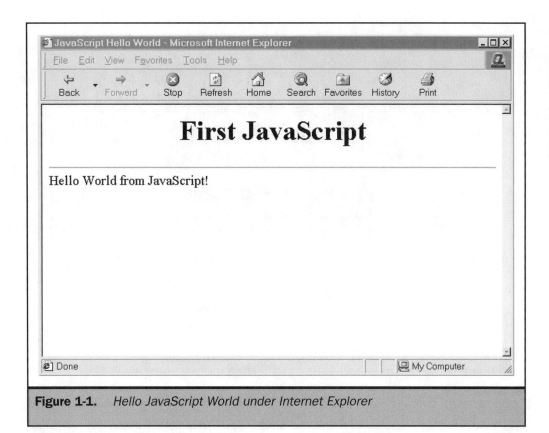

Figure 1-1.   *Hello JavaScript World under Internet Explorer*

JavaScript and the world of HTML intersect—they are two different technologies. For example, consider what happens if we substitute the following **<script>** block in the document, hoping that it would embold the text:

```
<script language="JavaScript" type="text/javascript">
<b>
   document.write("Hello World from JavaScript!");
</b>
</script>
```

Doing so would probably throw an error in our browser window as shown in Figure 1-2. The reason for this is that **<b>** tags are part of HTML, not JavaScript. Because the browser treats everything enclosed in **<script>** tags as JavaScript, it naturally throws an error when it encounters something that is out of place.

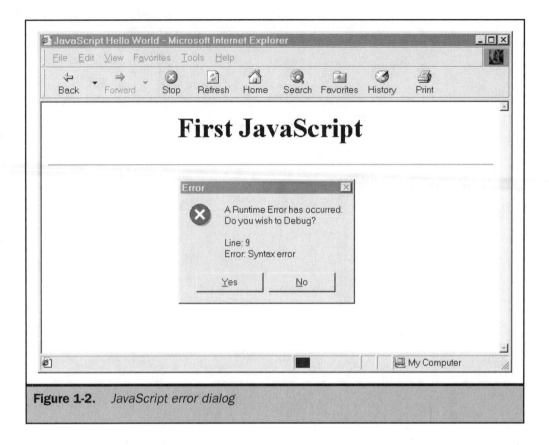

Figure 1-2.   *JavaScript error dialog*

Some browsers unfortunately may not show errors directly on the screen. The reason for this is that JavaScript errors are so commonplace on the Web that error dialogs became a real nuisance for many users, thus leading the browser vendors to suppress errors by default. In the case of Netscape 4.x generation browsers, you can type **javascript:** in the URL bar to view the JavaScript console. In the case of Netscape 6, choose the Tasks menu, then the Tools menu, and enable the JavaScript console. With Internet Explorer you may have to check "Display a notification about every script error," which can be found under the Advanced tab of the dialog displayed when selecting Internet Options. There may be different ways for achieving this in other browsers.

Regardless of whether or not the error was displayed, to output the string properly we either include the **<b>** element directly within the output string, as in:

```
document.write("<b>Hello World</b> from <font
```

or surround **<script>** element itself in a **<b>** element, like this:

```
<b>
<script language="JavaScript" type="text/javascript">
    document.write("Hello World from JavaScript!");
</script>
</b>
```

In this case the **<b>** tag surrounds the output from the JavaScript, which is displayed as boldface text by the browser. This example suggests the importance of understanding the intersection of HTML and JavaScript. In fact, before learning JavaScript, readers should fully understand the subtleties of correct HTML markup, especially given that most scripts will be used to produce HTML markup. Any JavaScript used within malformed HTML documents may act unpredictably, particularly if the script tries to manipulate HTML that is not well formed. A firm understanding of HTML is essential to writing effective scripts.

 Readers looking for more information on correct HTML usage should consult the companion book, HTML: The Complete Reference, *3rd Edition, by Thomas Powell (Osborne/McGraw-Hill, 2001).*

Adding JavaScript to HTML Documents

As suggested by the previous example, the **<script>** element is commonly used to add script to a document. However, there are four standard ways to include JavaScript in an HTML document:

- Within a **<script>** tag
- As a linked file via the **src** attribute of the **<script>** tag
- Within an HTML event handler attribute such as **onclick**
- Via the pseudo-URL **javascript:** syntax referenced by a link

There are other nonstandard ways to include scripts in your page, most commonly with the entity JavaScript. It is also possible to execute JavaScript on the server side by embedding it in an application or even using it to automate common operating system tasks. The use of the language outside the Web browser and HTML documents is extremely uncommon and is not significantly discussed in this book. However, Chapter 19 presents a brief discussion of JavaScript's server-side role. The following section presents the various methods for combining with HTML and JavaScript, and should be studied carefully by all readers before tackling the examples in the rest of the book.

The <script> Element

The primary method of including JavaScript within HTML is by using the **<script>** element. A script-aware browser assumes that all text within the **<script>** tag is to be interpreted as some form of scripting language; by default this is generally JavaScript.

However, it is possible for the browser to support other scripting languages such as VBScript, which is supported by the Internet Explorer family of browsers. Traditionally, the way to indicate the scripting language in use is to specify the **language** attribute for the tag. For example,

```
<script language="JavaScript">

</script>
```

is used to indicate the enclosed content is to be interpreted as JavaScript. Other values are possible; for example,

```
<script language="VBS">

</script>
```

would be used to indicate VBScript is in use. A browser should ignore the contents of the **<script>** element when it does not understand the value of its language attribute.

Tip *Be very careful setting the **language** attribute for <script>. A simple typo in the value will usually cause the browser to ignore any content within.*

According to the W3C HTML syntax, however, the **language** attribute should not be used. Instead, the **type** attribute should be set to indicate the MIME type of the language in use. JavaScript's MIME type is "text/javascript," so you use:

```
<script type="text/javascript">
</script>
```

Practically speaking, the **type** attribute is not as common as the **language** attribute, which has some other useful characteristics, particularly to conditionally set code according to the version of JavaScript supported by the browser (this technique will be discussed in Chapter 24 and illustrated throughout the book). To harness the usefulness of the **language** attribute while respecting the standards of the **<script>** element, using the following would be a good idea:

```
<script language="JavaScript" type="text/javascript">

</script>
```

Note   *Besides using the **type** attribute for **<script>**, you could also specify the script language in use document-wide via the **<meta>** element, as in **<meta http-equiv="Content-Script-Type" content="text/javascript">**. Inclusion of this statement within the **<head>** element of a document would avoid having to put the type attribute on each **<script>** element. However, poor browser support for this approach argues for the continued use of the **language** and **type** attributes together to limit script execution.*

Using the <script> Element

You can use as many **<script>** elements as you like. Documents will be read and possibly executed as they are encountered, unless the execution of the script is deferred for later. (The reasons for deferring script execution will be discussed in a later section.) The next example shows the use of three simple printing scripts that run one after another.

```
<!DOCTYPE HTML PUBLIC "-//W3C//DTD HTML 4.01 Transitional//EN">
<html>
<head>
<title>JavaScript and Script Tag</title>
</head>
<body>
<h1>Ready start</h1>
<script language="Javascript" type="text/javascript">
     alert("First Script Ran");
</script>
<h2>Running...</h2>
<script language="Javascript" type="text/javascript">
     alert("Second Script Ran");
</script>
<h2>Keep running</h2>
<script language="Javascript" type="text/javascript">
     alert("Third Script Ran");
</script>
</h1>Stop!</h1>
</body>
</html>
```

Try this example in various browsers to see how the script runs. With some browsers the HTML is written out as the script progresses, with others not. This difference is an example of how the execution model of JavaScript varies from browser to browser.

Script in the <head>

A special location for the **<script>** element is within the **<head>** tag of an HTML document. Because of the sequential nature of Web documents, the **<head>** is always read in first, so scripts located here are often referenced later on by scripts in the **<body>** of the document. Very often scripts within the **<head>** of a document are used to define variables or functions that may be used later on in the document. The example here shows how the script in the **<head>** defines a function that is later called by script within the **<script>** block in the **<body>** of the document.

```
<!DOCTYPE html public "-//W3C//DTD HTML 4.01 Transitional//EN">
<html>
<head>
<script language="JavaScript" type="text/javascript">
function alertTest()
{
  alert("Danger! Danger! JavaScript Ahead");
}
</script>
</head>
<body>
<h2 align="center">Script in the Head</h2>
<hr>
<script language="JavaScript" type="text/javascript">
 alertTest();
</script>
</body>
</html>
```

Script Hiding

With HTML, browsers tend to print out anything they don't understand on the screen, so it is important to mask code from browsers. One way to do this is to use comments around the script code; for example:

```
<script language="JavaScript" type="text/javascript">
<!--
  put your JavaScript here
//-->
</script>
```

Figure 1-3 shows a Web page viewed by non-JavaScript–supporting browsers without masking.

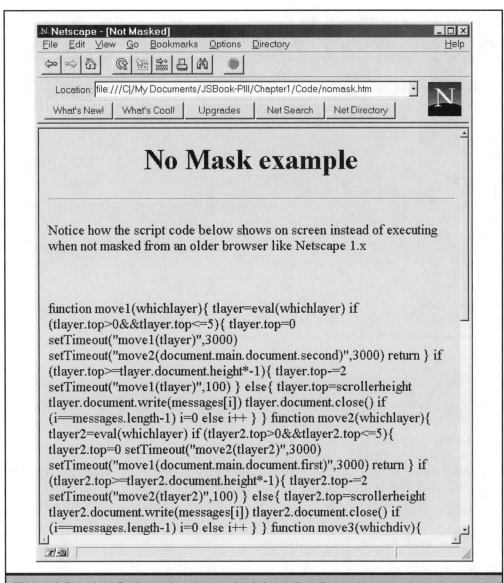

Figure 1-3.   *JavaScript code, not masked, but printed on screen*

Note *This masking technique is similar to the method used to hide CSS markup, except that the final line must include a JavaScript comment to mask out the HTML close comment. The reason for this is that the characters – and > have special meaning within JavaScript.*

The <noscript> Element

When a browser does not support JavaScript or when JavaScript is turned off, you should provide an alternative version or at least a warning message telling the user what happened. The **<noscript>** element can be used to accomplish this very easily. All JavaScript-aware browsers should ignore the contents of **<noscript>** unless scripting is off. The following example illustrates a simple example of this versatile element's use:

```
<!DOCTYPE HTML PUBLIC "-//W3C//DTD HTML 4.01 Transitional//EN">
<html>
<head>
<title>noscript Demo</title>
</head>
<body>
<script language="JavaScript" type="text/javascript">
<!--
      alert("Your JavaScript is on!");
//-->
</script>
<noscript>
      <i>Either your browser does not support JavaScript or it
          is currently disabled.</i>
</noscript>
</body>
</html>
```

Figure 1-4 shows a rendering in three situations: first a browser that does not support JavaScript, then a browser that does support it but has JavaScript disabled, and finally a modern browser with JavaScript turned on.

One interesting use of the **<noscript>** element is to automatically redirect users to a special error page if they do not have scripting enabled in the browser or are using a very old browser. This example shows how it might be done:

```
<!DOCTYPE HTML PUBLIC "-//W3C//DTD HTML 4.0 Transitional//EN">
<html>
<head>
<title>Needs JavaScript</title>
<noscript>
      <meta http-equiv="Refresh" content="0;URL=noscript.htm">
</noscript>
```

```
</head>
<body>
<script language="JavaScript" type="text/javascript">
<!--
 document.write("Congratulations! If you see this you have JavaScript.");
//-->
</script>
<noscript>
   <b>JavaScript required</b><br>
   <p>Read how to <a href="noscript.htm">rectify this problem</a>.
</noscript>
</body>
</html>
```

More information about defensive programming techniques like this one is found in
Chapter 24.

Event Handlers

To make a page more interactive you can add JavaScript commands that wait for a user
to perform a certain action. Typically, these scripts are in response to form actions and
mouse movements. To specify these scripts we set up various event handlers, generally
by setting an attribute of an HTML element to reference a script. We refer to these HTML
attributes collectively as *event handlers*. All of these attributes start with the word "on"—
for example, **onclick**, **ondblclick**, and **onmouseover**. The simple example here shows how
a form button would react to a click:

```
<!DOCTYPE HTML PUBLIC "-//W3C//DTD HTML 4.01 Transitional//EN">
<html>
<head>
<title>JavaScript and HTML Events Example</title>
</head>
<body>
<form>
<input type="button" value="press me"
       onclick="alert('Hello from JavaScript!');">
</form>
</body>
</html>
```

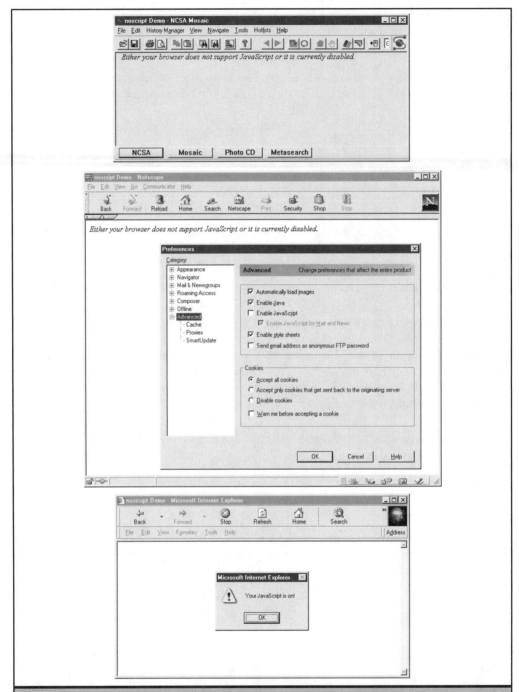

Figure 1-4. Use of <noscript> to handle browsers with no JavaScript

Note *When writing traditional HTML markup, developers would often mix-case the event handlers, for example onClick="". This mixed casing made it easy to pick them out from other markup and had no effect other than improving readability. Remember, these event handlers are part of HTML and are not case sensitive, so onClick, ONCLICK, onclick, or even oNcLiCK are all valid. However, because the eventual movement towards XHTML will require all lowercase, you should lowercase event handlers regardless of the tradition.*

By putting together a few **<script>** tags and event handlers you can start to see how scripts can be constructed. The following example shows how a user event on a form element can be used to trigger a JavaScript defined in the **<head>** of a document.

```
<!DOCTYPE html public "-//W3C//DTD HTML 4.01 Transitional//EN">
<html>
<head>
<script language="JavaScript" type="text/javascript">
<!--
function alertTest( )
{
  alert("Danger! Danger!");
}
//-->
</script>
</head>
<body>
<div align="center">
<form>
<input type="button" name="TestButton"
       value="Don't push me!"
       onclick="alertTest()">
</form>
</div>
</body>
</html>
```

A rendering of the previous example is shown in Figure 1-5.

You may wonder what HTML elements have event handler attributes. Under the HTML 4.0 specification nearly every tag should have most of the core events, such as **onclick**, **ondblclick**, **onkeydown**, **onkeypress**, **onkeyup**, **onmousedown**, **onmousemove**, **onmouseout**, and **onmouseover**, associated with it. For example, even though it might not make much sense, you should be able to specify that a paragraph can be clicked using markup and script like this:

```
<p onclick="alert('Under HTML 4 you can!')">Can you click me</p>
```

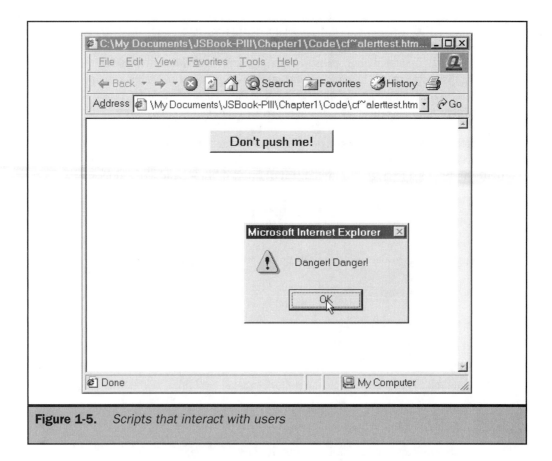

Figure 1-5. *Scripts that interact with users*

Of course many older browsers, even those from the 4.x generation, won't recognize event handlers for many HTML elements, such as a paragraph. Most browsers, however, should understand events such as the page loading and unloading, link presses, form fill-in, and mouse movement. Unfortunately, the degree to which each browser supports events and how they are handled varies significantly. There will be many examples throughout the book examining how events are handled, and an in-depth discussion on browser differences for event handling can be found in Chapter 11.

Linked Scripts

A very important way to include a script in an HTML document is by linking it via the **src** attribute of the **<script>** element. The example here shows how we might put the function from the previous example in a linked JavaScript file:

```
<!doctype html public "-//W3C//DTD HTML 4.01 Transitional//EN">
<html>
<head>
<script language="JavaScript" type="text/javascript"
        src="danger.js">
</script>
</head>
<body>
<div align="center">
<form>
<input type="button" name="TestButton"
        value="Don't push me!"
        onclick="alertTest()">
</form>
</div>
</body>
</html>
```

Notice that the **src** attribute is set to the value "danger.js." This value is a URL path to the external script. In this case, it is in the same directory, but it could just have easily been an absolute URL, such as http://www.javascriptref.com/scripts/danger.js. Regardless of the location of the file, all it will contain is the JavaScript code to run—no HTML or other Web technologies. So in this example the file danger.js should contain the following script:

```
function alertTest( )
{
   alert("Danger! Danger!");
}
```

The benefit of script files that are external is that they separate the logic, structure, and presentation of a page. With an external script it is possible to easily reference the script from many pages in a site and to update only one file to affect many others. Further, a browser can cache external scripts so their use effectively speeds up Web site access by avoiding extra download time spent refetching the same script.

Tip   *Consider putting all the scripts used in a site in a common script directory similar to how images are stored in an images directory. Doing this will ensure proper caching, keep scripts separated from content, and start a library of common code for use in a site.*

While external scripts have many benefits, they are often not used because of potential downsides. First, not all JavaScript-aware browsers support linked scripts. Fortunately, this problem is related mostly to older browsers, specifically Netscape 2 and some Internet Explorer 3 releases. Another challenge with external scripts has to do with browser loading. If an external script contains certain functions referenced later on, particularly those invoked by user activities, programmers must be careful not to allow them to be invoked until they have been downloaded; otherwise error dialogs may be displayed. Lastly, there are just plain and simple bugs when using external scripts. Fortunately, most of the problems with external scripts can be alleviated with the good defensive programming styles demonstrated throughout this book. However, if stubborn errors won't seem to go away and external scripts are in use, a good strategy is to move the code into the HTML file itself.

When using external .js files make sure that your Web server is set up to map the file extension .js to the MIME type text/javascript. Most Web servers have this MIME type set by default, but if you are experiencing problems with linked scripts this could be the cause.

JavaScript Pseudo-URL

In most JavaScript-aware browsers it is possible to invoke a statement using a JavaScript pseudo-URL. A pseudo-URL begins with **javascript:** and is followed by the code to execute. For example, typing **javascript: alert('hello')** directly into the browser's address bar invokes the alert box shown here:

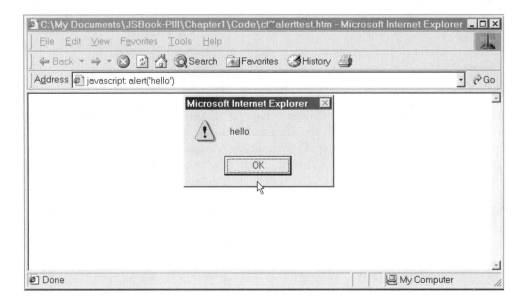

Under Netscape 4 and 6, it is possible to gain access to a JavaScript console by typing in the URL **javascript:** by itself in the address bar. Netscape 6 also provides this access via the Tools submenu of the Tasks menu. Other browsers may not provide such direct access to the console, which can be used for debugging as well as for testing the values of scripts. Examples of the JavaScript console are shown in Figure 1-6.

One very important way to use the JavaScript pseudo-URL is within a link, as demonstrated here.

```
<a href="javascript: alert('hello I am a pseudo-URL script')">Click to invoke</a>
```

When the user clicks the link, the alert is executed, resulting in the dialog box shown here:

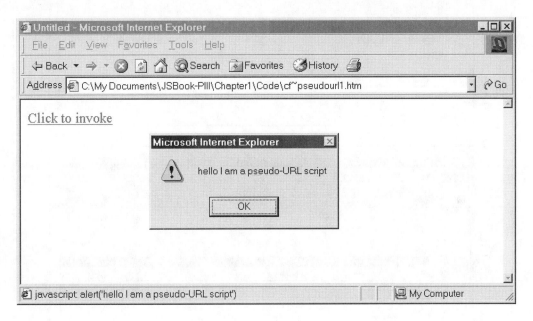

The pseudo-URL inclusion can be used to trigger an arbitrary amount of JavaScript, so

```
<a href="javascript: x=5;y=7;alert('The sum = '+(x+y))">Click to invoke</a>
```

is just as acceptable as invoking a single function or method.

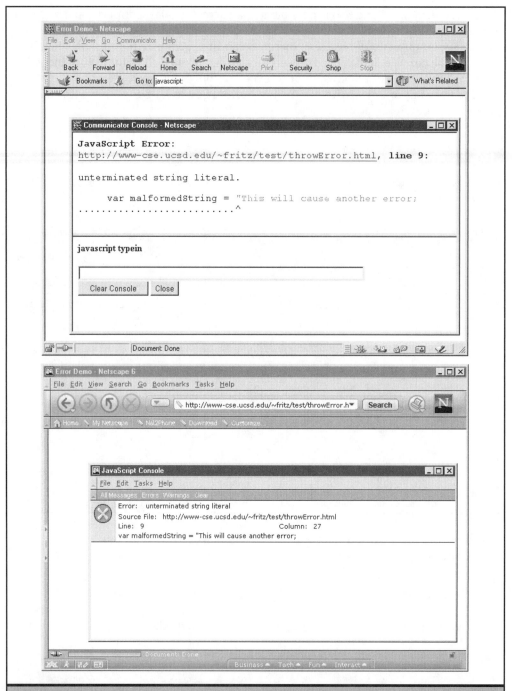

Figure 1-6. *JavaScript console used for debugging and testing*

The JavaScript pseudo-URL does have a problem, of course, when used in a browser that does not support JavaScript. In such cases, the browser will display the link appropriately, but the user will not be able to cause the link to do anything, which would certainly be very frustrating. Designers relying on pseudo-URLs should make sure to warn users by using the **<noscript>** element, as shown here:

```
<noscript>
<b><i>Warning:</i></b> This page contains links that use JavaScript and your browser
either has JavaScript disabled or does not support this technology.</b>
</noscript>
```

While the JavaScript pseudo-URL does have some limitations, it is commonly found in all major implementations of the language. The final method of including JavaScript in a page (to be discussed next) is not nearly as safe and should generally be avoided.

JavaScript Entities

Netscape 3.x and 4.x generation browsers supported a form of script inclusion called *JavaScript entities*. Under HTML an entity is generally used to insert a special character, such as a copyright symbol, and is indicated using the **&*code*;** notation where *code* is either a keyword or a numeric value corresponding to the character's ASCII value. For example, in HTML we would use either **©** or **©** to insert the copyright symbol. Older Netscape browsers also made it possible to use JavaScript within an entity to simulate a form of a macro. JavaScript entities are indicated using a slightly modified entity style, as in

```
&{script};
```

where *script* is some JavaScript identifier or function call. JavaScript entities can be used only within HTML attributes. For example,

```
<body bgcolor="&{pagebgcolor};" >
```

would set the **bgcolor** attribute of the **<body>** element to the value of "pagebgcolor," which would be some JavaScript variable defined elsewhere in the document. However, do not attempt to use these entities outside of an attribute value; for example,

```
<p>Hello, &{username}; !</p>
```

will only produce the text "&{username};" on the screen instead of the value stored in a JavaScript variable called "username."

Generally, JavaScript entities are used in this simple macro fashion to create attribute values at page load-time, but it is possible to have the entity script call a function or perform multiple statements to compute the final attribute value. The code here illustrates the possible uses of JavaScript entities:

```html
<!DOCTYPE HTML PUBLIC "-//W3C//DTD HTML 4.0 Transitional//EN">
<html>
<head>
<title>JavaScript Entities</title>
<script>
var bordersize=5;
var tablecellcolor="#ff0000";
var alignment="center";

function setImage()
  {
   var today = new Date();
   var hours = today.getHours();
   if ((hours > 8) && (hours < 18))
     return 'sun.gif'
   else
     return 'moon.gif';
  }
</script>
</head>
<body>
<table border="&{bordersize};" align="&{alignment};">
<tr>
  <td bgcolor="&{tablecellcolor};">JavaScript Entities!</td>
</tr>
</table>
In the sky now:   <img src="&{setImage()};">
</body>
</html>
```

While JavaScript entities appear useful, they are not supported under standard JavaScript and have never been supported under Internet Explorer. Figure 1-7 shows how different the result of the previous example would be under browsers that support script entities and those that do not.

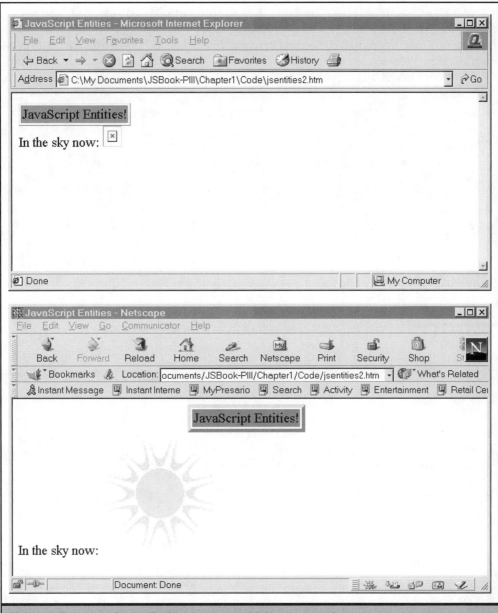

Figure 1-7.   *JavaScript Entities are not widely supported*

While entities may appear enticing, they should not be used since they are not supported by newer JavaScript implementations. To accomplish the same types of tasks, use the **document.write()** method to manually output an HTML element complete with attribute values. The code here illustrates how the previous entity example can be made to work under all browsers.

```
<!DOCTYPE HTML PUBLIC "-//W3C//DTD HTML 4.0 Transitional//EN">
<html>
<head>
<title>JavaScript Without Entities</title>
<script>
var bordersize=5;
var tablecellcolor="#ff0000";
var alignment="center";

function setImage()
  {
    var today = new Date();
    var hours = today.getHours();
    if ((hours > 8) && (hours < 18))
      return 'sun.gif'
    else
      return 'moon.gif';
  }
</script>
</head>
<body>
<script>
 document.write('<table border="'+bordersize+'"
align="'+alignment+'">');
</script>
<tr>
<script>
 document.write('<td bgcolor="'+tablecellcolor+'">JavaScript
Without Entities!</td>');
</script>
</tr>
</table>
In the sky now:
<script>
        document.write('<img src="'+setImage()+'">');
```

```
</script>
</body>
</html>
```

The previous sections have detailed the ways that JavaScript will typically be included within an HTML document. Now, before concluding the chapter, let's take a brief look at what such scripts might do.

JavaScript Applications

JavaScript is quite powerful as a client-side technology, but, like all languages, there are limitations on the types of applications it can be used for. Some common uses of JavaScript include:

- Form validation
- Page embellishments and special effects
- Navigation systems
- Basic mathematical calculations
- Dynamic document generation

Historically, the main reason JavaScript came to be was to perform simple checks of form data before submission to a server-side application, such as a CGI program. This is generally known as *form validation*. Since its beginnings, JavaScript has grown in its usefulness, and for many its primary use now is for page embellishments, such as the ubiquitous "mouseover" or rollover button or various types of page animations. The language actually can be used for much more than merely implementing simple gimmicks, and it has been successfully employed to build sophisticated navigation systems, such as drop-down menus or look-up lists. Also, the language has been employed for basic client-side calculations, such as loan calculators and other applications that may be useful for a Web visitor. However, JavaScript's eventual role will be more significant than all these uses put together. Already, JavaScript is used for simple dynamic documentation manipulation, such as conditional inclusion of code or markup on the basis of browser version, and eventually it will be used to modify a page significantly after load. This concept is often called *Dynamic HTML*, or *DHTML* for short. A large focus of this book, particularly in Chapters 9 and 10, will be to explain the implications of DHTML and the Document Object Model (discussed in the next section) that will power the dynamic Web pages of the future.

While it may be possible to write full-blown applications in JavaScript, most programmers will find the bugs, browser differences, and stability of the language ill-suited for a large application. Remember, it is a scripting language and as such is supposed to be focused in its use. Chapter 2 will present a more complete overview of the use of JavaScript within Web sites and compare it with other technologies, such as CGI, Java, and so on, that could be used. Before concluding the chapter let's take a brief look at the history of JavaScript as it sheds some insight to why the language is the way it is.

History of JavaScript

A study of the evolution of JavaScript is critical for mastering its use, as it can clarify the design motivations for its changes as well as lead to an understanding of its quirks, challenges, and potential as a first-class Web technology. For example, even the name JavaScript itself can be confusing unless you consider its history because, despite the similarity in name, JavaScript has very little to do with Java. In fact, Netscape initially introduced the language under the name LiveScript in an early Beta release of Navigator 2.0 in 1995. Most likely the language was renamed JavaScript because of the industry's fascination with all things Java at the time as well as the potential for the two languages to be integrated to build Web applications. Unfortunately, because of the inclusion of the word "Java" in its name, JavaScript is often thought of as some reduced scripting form of Java. In reality the language as it stands today is only somewhat similar to Java, and syntactically it often has more in common with languages such as C or Perl.

While the name of the language has lead to some confusion among its users, it has been widely adopted by browser vendors. After Netscape introduced JavaScript in version 2.0 of its browser, Microsoft introduced a clone of JavaScript called JScript in Internet Explorer 3.0. Opera also introduced JavaScript support in the 3.x generation of its browser. Many other browsers, including WebTV, also supported various flavors of JavaScript. As time has gone by, each of the major browser vendors has made its own extensions to the language, and the browsers have each supported various versions of JavaScript or JScript. Table 1-1 details the common browsers that support a JavaScript language. The various features of each version of JavaScript are discussed throughout the book, and Appendix B provides information on the support of various features in each version of the language.

Because the specification of JavaScript is changing rapidly and cross platform support is not consistent, you should be very careful with your use of JavaScript with browsers. Since different levels of JavaScript support different constructs, programmers should be careful to create conditional code to handle browser and language variations. Much of this book will deal with such issues, but a concentrated discussion can be found in Chapter 24.

Because each browser originally implemented its own proprietary version of JavaScript, writing code for cross-browser compatibility was a tedious task. To address this issue, a standard form of JavaScript called ECMAScript was specified. While most of the latest browsers have full or close to full support for ECMAScript, the name itself has really yet to catch on with the public, and most programmers tend to refer to the language, regardless of flavor, as simply JavaScript.

Browser Version	JavaScript Support
Netscape 2.x	1.0
Netscape 3.x	1.1
Netscape 4.0-4.05	1.2
Netscape 4.06-4.08, 4.5x, 4.6x, 4.7x	1.3
Netscape 6.x	1.5
Internet Explorer 3.0	JScript 1.0
Internet Explorer 4.0	JScript 3.0
Internet Explorer 5.0	JScript 5.0
Internet Explorer 5.5	JScript 5.5
Internet Explorer 6	JScript 5.6[*]

[*]Still speculative at time of writing, may be renamed JScript 6.0.

Table 1-1. *Browser Versions and JavaScript Support*

Even with the rise of ECMAScript JavaScript can still be challenging to use. ECMAScript is primarily concerned with defining the common statements of the language (such as "if," "for," "while," and so on) as well as the major data types. JavaScript also generally can access a common set of objects related to the browser, such as the window, navigator, history, screen, and others. This collection of objects is often referred to as the *Browser Object Model*, or *BOM* for short. All the browser versions tend to have a different set of objects that make up the BOM, and every new release of a browser seems to include new objects and properties. The BOM finally reached its worst degree of compatibility with the 4.x generation of browsers.

Fortunately, the World Wide Web Consortium (W3C) stepped in to define various objects and interfaces that scripts can utilize to access and manipulate the components of a page in a standardized way. This specification is called the *Document Object Model*, or *DOM* for short. There is some crossover between what is considered BOM and what is DOM, but fortunately in the newer browsers the differences are starting to be ironed out and the three parts of JavaScript are starting to become more well defined. More information on the DOM can be found at http://www.w3.org/DOM as well as in Chapter 10.

When taken together, core JavaScript as specified by ECMAScript, Browser Objects, and Document Objects will provides facilities generally required by a JavaScript programmer. Unfortunately, save the core language, all the various objects available seem to vary from browser to browser and version to version, making correct cross-browser coding a real challenge! A good portion of this book will be spent trying to iron out these difficulties.

Summary

JavaScript has quickly become the premier client-side scripting language used within Web pages. Much of the language's success has to do with the ease with which developers can get started using it. The **<script>** element makes it easy to include bits of JavaScript directly within HTML documents; however, some browsers may need to use comments and the **<noscript>** element to avoid errors. A linked script can further be employed to separate the markup of a page from the script that may manipulate it. While including scripts can be easy, the challenges of JavaScript are numerous. The language is inconsistently supported in browsers, and its tumultuous history has lead to numerous incompatibilities. However, there is hope in sight. With the rise of ECMAScript and the W3C-specified Document Object Model, many of the coding techniques required to make JavaScript code work in different browsers may no longer be necessary.

The Complete Reference

Chapter 2

JavaScript Core Features—Overview

A *scripting language* is a language used to manipulate, customize, or automate the facilities of an existing system. In the case of JavaScript, that system is the Web browser and its associated technologies of HTML, CSS, and XML. JavaScript is a mechanism for presenting the functionality available through the browser to the programmer. Because the Web browser is the host environment, it provides much of the functionality that enables JavaScript to carry out useful tasks. It is for this reason that, although JavaScript provides some very powerful capabilities, the structure of the language itself is relatively simple. Most of JavaScript's power is derived from both the built-in and document objects provided by the browser.

The core features of JavaScript that are introduced in this chapter are the syntax rules to which your scripts must adhere and the basic constructs used to store data and manipulate flow control. Once you understand the basic language mechanics, more advanced features can be tackled somewhat independently, without getting mired in myriad details. C, C++, and Java programmers will find JavaScript's syntax familiar and should be able to quickly pick up its more advanced features.

This chapter is introductory and is meant to provide a quick overview of all JavaScript's core features. Most of the topics will be explored in much greater depth in the chapters to follow. Because much of this material will be familiar to veteran programmers, those with previous experience might wish merely to skim this chapter.

Basic Definitions

Large groups of people sharing a common interest or goal accomplish one thing at the very least: they develop jargon. After spending any significant period of time working with computers, one cannot help but notice that software engineers are particularly fond of the language they use to communicate ideas about programming. The terms employed for discussing programming languages offer a technical vocabulary with which specific ideas can be communicated clearly and concisely.

Here we introduce some programming language terminology that will be used throughout the book. Table 2-1 provides precise definitions for concepts that are often only vaguely understood.

Script Execution Order

JavaScript code found in HTML documents is interpreted line-by-line as it is found in the page. This means that it is a good idea to put function definitions and variable declarations in the document head, enclosed by the **<head>** ... **</head>** tags, if they will be used throughout the page. Certain statements, for example the bodies of functions and actions associated with event handlers, are not immediately executed.

Name	Definition	Examples
Token	The smallest indivisible lexical unit of the language. A contiguous sequence of characters whose meaning would change if separated by a space.	All identifiers and keywords are tokens, as are literals like 3.14 and "This is a string."
Literal	A value found directly in the script.	3.14, "This is a string," [2, 4, 6]
Identifier	The name of a variable, object, function, or label.	x, myValue, userName
Operator	Tokens that perform built-in language operations like assignment, addition, and subtraction.	=, +, -, *
Expression	A group of tokens, often literals or identifiers, combined with operators that can be evaluated to a specific value.	2.0 "This is a string" (x + 2) * 4
Statement	An imperative command. Statements usually cause the state of the execution environment (a variable, definition, or the flow of execution) to change. A program is simply a list of statements.	x = x + 2; return(true); if (x) { alert("It's x");}
Keyword	A word that is a part of the language itself. Keywords may not be used as identifiers.	**while, do, function, var**
Reserved Word	A word that might become a part of the language itself. Reserved words may not be used as identifiers, although this restriction is sometimes not strictly enforced.	**class, const, public**

Table 2-1. *Basic Terminology of Programming Languages*

Case Sensitivity

JavaScript is case-sensitive. This means that capital letters are distinct from their lowercase counterparts. For example, if you use the identifiers **result**, **Result**, and

RESULT in your script, each identifier refers to a separate, distinct variable. Case sensitivity applies to all aspects of the language: keywords, operators, variable names, event handlers, object properties, and so on. All JavaScript keywords are lowercase, so when using a feature like an **if** statement, you need to make sure you type "if" and not "If" or "IF." Because JavaScript uses the "camel-back" naming convention, many methods and properties use mixed casing. For example, the *M* in the name of the **lastModified** property of the **Document** object must be uppercase; using a lowercase *m* will retrieve an undefined value.

The primary implication of case sensitivity is that you should pay close attention to capitals when defining and accessing variables, when using language constructs like **if** and **while**, and when accessing properties of objects. One typo can change the meaning of your whole script and require significant debugging effort.

 One exception to JavaScript's case sensitivity is Internet Explorer 3. In this particular browser, client-side objects and properties are case-insensitive. This exception does not pose a problem for scripts you might write today. It merely means that some older scripts relying on Internet Explorer's case insensitivity might not work in modern browsers.

HTML and Case Sensitivity

The fact that JavaScript is commonly embedded directly in HTML can lead to some confusion. Under HTML 4 and earlier, element and attribute names are case-insensitive. For example, the following two tags are equivalent:

```
<IMG SRC="plus.gif" ALT="Increment x" ONCLICK="x=x+1">
<img src="plus.gif" alt="Increment x" onClick="x=x+1">
```

This is not a problem in itself. The problem comes when novice programmers see HTML event handlers referenced in two different ways (like **ONCLICK** and **onClick** in the previous example) and assume event handlers can be accessed similarly in JavaScript. This is not the case. The corresponding event handler in JavaScript is **onclick**, and it must always be referred to as such. The reason that **ONCLICK** and **onClick** work in HTML is that the browser automatically binds them to the correct **onclick** event handler in JavaScript.

To further illuminate the distinction, consider the following two tags, which are *not* equivalent:

```
<img src="plus.gif" alt="Increment x" onclick="x=x+1">
<img src="plus.gif" alt="Increment x" onclick="X=X+1">
```

The reason they are not equivalent is that the first modifies the variable *x*, while the second modifies *X*. Because JavaScript is case-sensitive, these are two distinct variables.

This illustrates an important aspect of HTML attributes: while the attribute name is not case-sensitive, its *value* may be. The **onclick** HTML attribute is not case-sensitive and so may be written **onClick**, **ONCLICK**, or even **oNcLiCk**. However, because the value to which the **onclick** attribute is set contains JavaScript, you must remember that it *is* case-sensitive.

XHTML, the new W3C recommendation for HTML, requires that element and attribute names be written in lowercase. XHTML solves the problem directly and is the reason that we strongly suggest lowercasing the tags and attributes (especially event handlers) of the HTML in which your scripts are embedded. Although older forms of HTML will undoubtedly remain in existence on the Web for a long time to come, it is generally a good idea to keep current with W3C recommendations.

Whitespace

Whitespace characters are those characters that take up space on the screen without any visible representation. Examples include ordinary spaces, tabs, and linebreak characters. Any sequence of excessive whitespace characters is ignored by JavaScript. For example:

```
x                         =     x +     1;
```

is the same as:

```
x = x + 1;
```

This suggests that the use of whitespace is more for the benefit of the programmer than the interpreter. Indeed, thoughtful use of whitespace to offset comments, loop contents, and declarations results in more readable and hopefully understandable code.

Note   *Because of JavaScript's ambivalence to whitespace and most Web users' frustration with slow download times, some JavaScript programmers choose to "compress" their scripts by removing excess whitespace characters. This practice is often termed* crunching. *Crunching can be performed both manually and with utilities. The value of crunching is questionable. Unless scripts are extremely large, crunching will probably not result in a change in page load-time large enough to be really noticeable by a user.*

Note   *If whitespace crunching is employed, it should be applied only to the code for delivery and not to the original source, as then the benefits of including whitespace for the programmer are lost. However, doing this gives rise to a code management problem, as one now has to deal with multiple copies of virtually the same snippets of code. Further, as the next example illustrates, automation of the whitespace removal process always needs to be carried out with caution.*

The spacing between tokens can be omitted if the meaning is unambiguous. For example:

```
x=x+1;
```

contains no spaces, but is acceptable because its meaning is clear. However, most operations other than simple arithmetic functions will require a space to indicate the desired meaning. Consider the following:

```
s = typeof x;
s = typeofx;
```

The first statement invokes the **typeof** operator on a variable *x* and places the result in *s*. The second copies the value of a variable called *typeofx* into *s*. One space changes the entire meaning of the statement.

As a rule, JavaScript ignores whitespace—but there are exceptions. One is in strings. Whitespace will be preserved in any string enclosed in single or double quotes:

```
var s = "This     spacing   is              p r e s e r v e d.";
```

Experienced programmers might wonder what happens if you include a linebreak directly in a string. The answer involves another of the subtleties of whitespace and JavaScript: *implicit semicolons*.

Statements

Statements are the essence of a language like JavaScript. They are instructions to the interpreter to carry out specific actions. For example, one of the most common statements is an *assignment*. Assignment uses the = operator and places the value on the right-hand side into the variable on the left. For example:

```
x = y + 10;
```

adds **10** to *y* and places the value in *x*. The assignment operator should not be confused with the "is equal to" comparison operator ==, which is used in conditional expressions (discussed later in the chapter). One key issue with statements in a programming language is indicating how they are terminated and grouped.

Semicolons

A semicolon indicates the end of a JavaScript statement. For example, you can group multiple statements on one line by separating them with semicolons:

```
x = x + 1;   y = y + 1;   z = 0;
```

You can also include more complicated or even empty statements on one line:

```
x = x + 1; ;; if (x > 10) { x = 0; }; y = y - 1;
```

This example increments *x*, skips past two empty statements, sets *x* to zero if *x* is greater than **10**, and finally decrements *y*. As you can see, including multiple statements on one line is rather unwieldy, and should be avoided.

Although statements are generally followed by semicolons, they can be omitted if your statements are separated by a linebreak. For example:

```
x = x + 1
y = y - 1
```

is treated as:

```
x = x + 1;
y = y - 1;
```

Of course, if you wish to include two statements on one line, a semicolon must be included to separate them:

```
x = x + 1; y = y - 1
```

The formal rules for implicit semicolon insertion are a bit more complex than the preceding description would lead you to believe. In theory, tokens of a single statement can be separated by a linebreak without causing an error. However, if the tokens on a line without a semicolon comprise a complete JavaScript statement, a semicolon is inserted even if the next line could plausibly be treated as an extension of the first. The classic example is the **return** statement. Because the argument to **return** is optional, placing

return and its argument on separate lines causes the **return** to execute without the argument. For example:

```
return
x
```

is treated as:

```
return;
x;
```

rather than what was probably intended:

```
return x;
```

Therefore, relying on implicit semicolon insertion is a bad idea and poor programming style to boot. This practice should be avoided.

Blocks

Curly braces "{ }" are used to group a list of statements together. In some sense you can think of the braces as creating one large statement. For example, the statements that make up the body of a function are enclosed in curly braces:

```
function add(x, y)
{
   var result = x + y;
   return result;
}
```

If more than one statement is to be executed as the result of a conditional or in a loop, the statements are similarly grouped:

```
if (x > 10)
{
   x = 0;
   y = 10;
}
```

Regardless of their groupings, statements generally need to modify data, which is often in the form of a variable.

Variables

A variable stores data. Every variable has a name, called its *identifier*. Variables are declared in JavaScript using **var**, a keyword that allocates storage space for new data and indicates to the interpreter that a new identifier is in use. Declaring a variable is simple:

```
var x;
```

This statement tells the interpreter that a new variable *x* is about to be used. Variables can be assigned initial values when they are declared:

```
var x = 2;
```

In addition, multiple variables can be declared with one **var** statement if the variables are separated by commas:

```
var x, y = 2, z;
```

You should not use variables without first declaring them, although it is possible to do so in certain cases. Using a variable on the right-hand side of an assignment without first declaring it will result in an error.

Experienced programmers will notice that, unlike C, C++, and Java, there is only one way to declare a variable in JavaScript. This highlights the fact that JavaScript's treatment of variable data types is fundamentally different from many languages, including C, C++, and Java.

Basic Data Types

Every variable has a *data type* that indicates what kind of data the variable holds. The basic data types in JavaScript are strings, numbers, and Booleans. A string is a list of characters, and a string literal is indicated by enclosing the characters in single or double quotes. Strings may contain a single character or multiple characters, including white space and special characters such as "\n" (the newline). Numbers are integers or floating-point numerical values, and numeric literals are specified in the natural way. Booleans take on one of two values: **true** or **false**. Boolean literals are indicated by using **true** or **false** directly in the source code. An example of all three data types follows.

```
var stringData = "JavaScript has strings\n It sure does";
var numericData = 3.14;
var booleanData = true;
```

JavaScript also supports two other basic types: undefined and null. All these data types as well as the details of special characters are discussed in Chapter 3. However, one aspect of JavaScript data types should be briefly mentioned in this overview: weak typing.

Weak Typing

A major difference between JavaScript and other languages you might be familiar with is that JavaScript is *weakly typed*. Every JavaScript variable has a data type, but the type is inferred from the variable's content. For example, a variable that is assigned a string value assumes the string data type. A consequence of JavaScript's automatic type inference is that a variable's type can change dynamically. For example, a variable can hold a string at one point and then later be assigned a Boolean. Its type changes according to the data it holds. This explains why there is only one way to declare variables in JavaScript: there is no need to indicate type in variable declarations.

Being weakly typed is both a blessing and a curse for JavaScript. While weak typing appears to free the programmer from having to declare types ahead of time, it does so at the expense of introducing subtle typing errors. For example, given the following script that manipulates various string and number values we will see type conversion cause potential ambiguities

```
document.write(4*3);
document.write("<br>");
document.write("5" + 5);
document.write("<br>");
document.write("5" - 3);
document.write("<br>");
document.write(5 * "5");
```

The output of this example when included in an HTML document is shown here

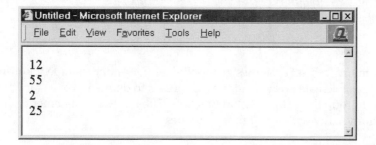

Notice how in the case of addition the result was a string "55" rather than a number 10, while in the other examples the string was converted to a number before output. The reason the addition didn't work is that the plus sign serves two meanings, both as addition and as string concatenation. These types of problems are common in JavaScript and are discussed in Chapters 3 and 4. Fortunately, there are many ways to convert data predictably in JavaScript using methods like **parseFloat()** and to even check the value of a variable using the **typeof** operator. For example,

```
var x = "5";
alert (typeof x);
```

correctly identifies x as a string value, as shown here:

Composite Types

In contrast to primitive types, *composite types* are made up of heterogeneous data. They can include strings, numbers, Booleans, undefined values, null values, and even other composite types. JavaScript supports three composite types: objects, arrays, and functions. In subsequent chapters you will find that arrays and functions are really just special kinds of objects, but we'll ignore the subtleties of JavaScript's object-oriented aspects and just cover the basics for now.

Arrays

An *array* is an ordered set of values grouped together under a single identifier. There are many ways to create arrays, but the simplest is to define it like a standard identifier and then just group the values within brackets. The following statement defines an array called **myArray** with four numeric values

```
var myArray = [1,5,68,3];
```

Arrays can contain arbitrary data items, so a definition like

```
var myArray = ["Thomas", true, 3, -47.6, "x"];
```

is also valid.

A more appropriate way syntactically to define arrays that respects their heritage as objects is to use the keyword **new** to invoke the **Array** object's constructor, as shown here.

```
var myArray = new Array();
```

This defines **myArray** as an array with no particular length. We could easily predetermine the length of the array by passing it a single numeric value. For example,

```
var myArray = new Array(4);
```

defines an array of length 4. We can even populate the array using the explicit constructor style syntax, as shown here:

```
var myArray = new Array(1,5,"Thomas", true);
```

Regardless of how they are defined, the elements of an array are accessed in the same way. To reference a particular piece of the array we must provide an index value within brackets, so given

```
var myArray = new Array(1,5,"Thomas", true);
var x = myArray[2];
var y = myArray[0];
```

the value of *x* would be the string "Thomas" not the number 5, and *y* would be set to the number 1. The reason for this is that arrays in JavaScript are indexed starting from 0. This next script shows both the definition of an array as well as assignments using index values.

```
Var myArray = new Array(4);
myArray[0] = 1;
myArray[1] = 5;
myArray[2] = "Thomas";
myArray[3] = true;
```

As briefly mentioned, arrays are actually objects and have a variety of properties and methods that can be used to manipulate them. These features will be discussed at length later on. However, let's first take at least a brief look at objects in JavaScript.

Objects

Objects can hold any type of data and are the primary mechanism by which useful tasks are carried out. The browser provides a large number of objects for you to use. For example, you can interact with the user using the **Window** object or modify the contents of a Web page with the **Document** object.

Data contained in an object are said to be *properties* of the object. Properties are accessed with the "dot" operator, which is simply a period followed by the property name. The syntax is:

objectname.propertyname

For example, you would access the **lastModified** property of the **Document** object as **document.lastModified**. We have used this notation before when we employed the **write()** method of the **Document** object to output text to the screen:

```
document.write("Hello JavaScript world!")
```

You'll notice that using objects the length of the string to access a particular property can get quite long. By using the keyword **with** we can avoid referencing the full path to an object's property or method:

```
with (document)
{
   write("this is easier ");
   write("than writing out ");
   write("the whole path");
}
```

Besides using built-in objects such as **Document** or **Window**, you can create your own objects using the keyword **new**. The use of **new** was briefly demonstrated with the array examples in the previous section. You can also destroy an object using the keyword **delete**. For example, here we define an array element and then quickly destroy it.

```
var myArray = new Array(4);
myArray[0]="Thomas";
delete myArray[0];
```

At its heart, JavaScript is an object-based language, and everything is derived from the various objects provided by the language or the browser. For example, JavaScript provides objects corresponding to the primitive data types, such as **String**, **Number**, and **Boolean**, which can have methods to operate upon data. More complex data-related objects, such as **Array**, **Math**, and **Date**, are also provided, as are browser-oriented objects such as **Navigator** and **History** and the powerful **Document** object. There is even a generic **Object** that we can use to build our own objects. Details about the process of creating and using objects require significant explanation that can be found in Chapters 4 and 7.

Note *The instances of objects are typically written all lowercase, while the corresponding object type is written with an initial capital. Do not worry about this distinction for the time being— it is discussed in Chapters 4 and 7.*

Expressions

Expressions are an important part of JavaScript and are the building blocks of many JavaScript statements. Expressions are groups of tokens that can be evaluated; for example,

```
var x = 3 + 3
```

is an assignment statement that takes the expression 3+3 and puts the result in the variable *x*. Literals and variables are the simplest kinds of expressions and can be used with operators to create more complex expressions.

Operators

Basic operators include familiar arithmetic symbols: = (assignment), + (addition), - (subtraction or unary negation), * (multiplication), / (division), and % (modulus). All are used here.

```
var x=3, y=6;
x = -x;
```

```
x = y + 2;
x  = y - 1;
x  = y * y;
x  = y  / x;
x = y % 4;
```

In this example, *x* is first assigned -3, then 8, then 5, then 36, then 2, and finally 2 once again. The only basic operator that might cause confusion is the modulus operator. This operator computes the integer remainder resulting from the division of the first operand by the second. For example, because *y* has value **6** at the last line of the previous example, **6 % 4** which is **2** is assigned to *x*.

JavaScript also provides bitwise operators, such as **&** (AND), **|** (OR), **^** (NOT), **~** (Exclusive OR), **<<** (left shift), **>>** (right shift). While bitwise operators will seem familiar to some C programmers, given the high-level nature of JavaScript they seem a little out of place. They are, however, occasionally required in order to use some of the more advanced features provided by modern browsers.

To compare objects, JavaScript provides a rich set of relational operators including **==** (equal to), **!=** (not equal to), **<** (less than), **>** (greater than), **<=** (less than or equal to) and **>=** (greater than or equal to). Using a relational operator in an expression causes the expression to evaluate as true if the condition holds or false if otherwise. So,

$$5 < 10$$

would evaluate as **true** while

$$11 < 10$$

would evaluate as **false**.

Programmers should be very careful with the meanings of = and ==. The first is an assignment operator, while the second is a conditional comparison operator. Mixing the two up is one of the most common mistakes found in JavaScript programs. For example,

```
x = 5;
```

assigns a value to *x*, while

```
x == 5;
```

compares the value of *x* with the literal 5. When these operators are misused within an **if** statement, a frustrating bug occurs.

Once comparisons are made, the logical operators **&&** (AND), **| |** (OR), and **!** (NOT) can be used to create more complex conditionals. For example:

```
if ((x >= 10) && (y < 3))
{
    z = z + 1;
}
```

increments *z* if *x* is greater or equal to 10 and *y* is less than 3.

Given the usefulness of incrementing and decrementing values, JavaScript provides, as do other languages, a shorthand notation. The operator **++** adds one to a value, while **--** subtracts one. So, with

```
var x=4;
x++;
```

the value of *x* at the end of execution is 5.

Note   *There is a subtle difference in the effect of positioning of the **++** or **--** operator before a value or after a value, as discussed in Chapter 4.*

One very useful operator is the string operator (+), which is used to join strings together. The following script

```
document.write("JavaScript is " + "great.");
```

outputs the joined string shown here:

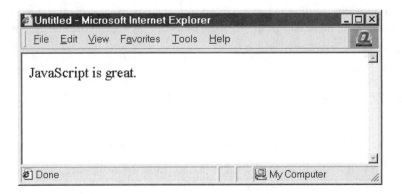

When this operator is used to join string variables to HTML, it is possible to create more complex output.

```
var myName="Thomas";
document.write("Hello <i>"+myName+" </i>");
```

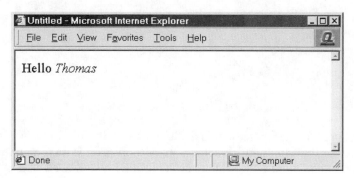

Operator Precedence

When using operators, we must be careful about the order of evaluation. Given that different operators may have stronger precedence than others, the evaluation order may not be what is expected. For example, consider the following:

```
var x = 4 + 5 * 8;
```

Is the value of x set to 72 or to 44? The answer is 44, because the multiplication operator has higher precedence than addition. We can use parentheses to group expressions and force execution a certain way. So, to get the example to set x to 72 we would use

```
var x = (4+5)*8;
```

While this example was very easy, sometimes the order of execution is more ambiguous, so when in doubt add parentheses. The subtleties of all forms of operators are discussed in the first part of Chapter 4.

Flow Control

Statements execute in the order they are found in a script. In order to create useful programs, it is usually necessary to employ *flow control*, code that governs the "flow" of program execution. JavaScript supports conditionals like **if/else** and **switch/case** statements that permit the selective execution of pieces of code. An example of an **if/else** statement is

```
if (x > 10)
{
    x = 0;
}
else
{
    x = x + 1;
}
```

The conditional of an **if** statement is evaluated, and, if the comparison is true and x is indeed greater than 10, then x is set to zero. Otherwise x is incremented. Note that you can use an **if** statement without the corresponding **else** as well as use multiple **if** statements within **else** statements. This can make **if** statements unnecessarily messy, so a **switch** statement might be more appropriate. For example, rather than using a multitude of **if** statements we could use a single **switch** with multiple **case** statements, as shown here:

```
var x=3;
switch (x)
{
  case 1: alert('x is 1');
          break;
  case 2: alert('x is 2');
          break;
  case 3: alert('x is 3');
          break;
  case 4: alert('x is 4');
          break;
  default: alert('x is not 1, 2, 3 or 4');
}
```

In the previous example, the value of x would determine which message was printed, by comparing the value of the variable to the various **case** statements. If no match were found, the **default** statement would be executed. The **break** statement is also used commonly within **switch** to exit the statement once the appropriate choice is found. However, the **break** statement's use is also commonly associated with loops, which are discussed next.

> **Note** *The **switch** statement wasn't introduced into the language until JavaScript 1.2. It should be used carefully to avoid script errors in older browsers.*

Loops

It is often necessary to iterate a number of statements until a particular condition is true. For example, you might wish to perform the same operation on each element of an array until you hit the end of the array. Like many other languages, JavaScript enables this behavior with *loop* statements. Loops continue to execute the body of their code until a halting condition is reached. JavaScript supports **while**, **do/while**, **for**, and **for/in** loops. An example of a **while** loop is

```
var x=0;
while (x < 10)
{
  document.write(x);
  document.write("<br>");
  x = x + 1;
}
document.write("Done");
```

This loop increments *x* continuously while its conditional, *x* less than 10, is **true**. As soon as *x* reaches value 10, the condition is **false**, so the loop terminates and execution continues from the first statement after the loop body, as shown here:

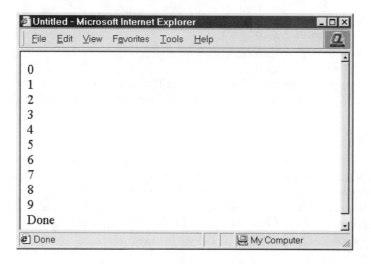

The **do/while** loop is similar to the **while** loop, except that the condition check happens at the end of the loop. This means that the loop will always be executed at least once unless a **break** statement is encountered first.

```
var x=0;
do
 {
   document.write(x);
   x = x + 1;
} while (x < 10)
```

The same loop written as a **for** loop is slightly more compact, because it sets the loop variable, condition check, and increment all in a single line, as shown here:

```
for (x=0; x < 10; x++)
{
   document.write(x);
}
```

One interesting variation of the **for** loop is the **for/in** construct. This construct allows us to loop through the various properties of an object. For example, we could loop through and print the properties of a browser's window object using a **for/in** statement like this:

```
for (var aprop in window)
{
    document.write(aprop)
    document.write("<br>");
}
```

Experienced programmers should welcome this familiar statement, which will make much more sense to others in the context of the discussion of objects in later chapters.

Loop Control

JavaScript also supports statements generally used to modify flow control, specifically **break** and **continue**. These statements act similarly to the corresponding constructs in C and are often used with loops. The **break** statement will exit a loop early, while the **continue** statement will skip back to the loop condition check. In the next example, which writes out the value of x starting from 1, when x is equal to 3 the **continue** statement continues the loop without printing the value. When *x* is equal to 5, the loop is exited using the **break** statement.

```
var x=0;
while (x < 10)
{
   x = x + 1;
   if (x == 3)
     continue;

   document.write("x = "+x);
   if (x == 5)
     break;
}
document.write("Loop done");
```

All forms of statements including flow control and looping are discussed in detail in Chapter 4.

Functions

Functions are used to encapsulate code that performs a specific task. Sometimes functions are defined for commonly required tasks to avoid the repetition entailed in typing the same statements over and over. More generally, they are used to keep code that performs a particular job in one place in order to enhance reusability and program clarity.

JavaScript functions are declared with the **function** keyword, and the statements that carry out their operations are listed in curly braces. Function arguments are listed in parentheses following the function name and are separated by commas. For example:

```
function add(x, y)
{
   var sum = x + y;
   return sum;
}
```

This code declares a function named *add* that adds its arguments together and "returns" the resulting value. The **return** statement tells the interpreter what value the function evaluates to. For example, you can set the value of the function equal to a variable:

```
var result = add(2, 3);
```

The arguments **2** and **3** are passed to the function, the body of the function executes, and the result of their addition, **5**, is placed in the variable *result*.

Besides passing in literal values to a function, it is also possible to pass in variables. For example:

```
var a = 3, b = 5;
var result;
result = add(a,b);
```

Experienced programmers might ask whether it is possible to modify the values of variables that are passed in to functions. The answer is more a piece of advice: *no*. JavaScript supports the idea of passing by value for primitive data types, so the values of the variables *a* and *b* should remain unchanged regardless of what happens in the function **add**. However, other data types, notably objects, can be changed when passed in, and many programmers go around the pass-by-value restriction of JavaScript by using globally defined variables, which is simply poor programming practice.

If you have programmed in other languages before, you will recognize that functions are variously called procedures, subroutines, and methods. The term *method* in JavaScript refers to a function that is contained in an object. As you can see, functions, which are discussed in detail in Chapter 5, are very powerful.

Input and Output in JavaScript

The ability to perform input and output (I/O) is an integral part of most languages. Because JavaScript executes in a host environment like a Web browser, its I/O facilities might be different from what you would expect. For obvious security reasons, plain client-side JavaScript is not usually allowed to read or write files in the local file system. There are exceptions, but these are considerably more advanced and will not be addressed until a later chapter.

I/O, like most useful tasks in JavaScript, is carried out through the objects provided by the browser. Interacting with the user is typically achieved through the **Window** object, several methods of which are described here. One of the most common I/O methods in JavaScript is using the **alert()** method of **Window**, which displays its argument message in a dialog box that includes an OK button. For example:

```
alert("This is an important message!");
```

causes the following dialog box to be presented to the user:

Other forms of dialog with the user include the **confirm()** method, which displays its argument message in a dialog box with both an OK and Cancel button. With the script

```
confirm("Learn JavaScript?");
```

you should see the following window:

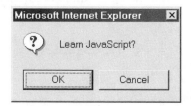

Lastly, we could use the **prompt()** method to collect some data from the user. A prompt displays its argument message in a dialog box and allows the user to enter data into a text field, as illustrated by this example.

```
var answer = prompt("What is your favorite color?","");
```

Note *Despite all the previous methods being part of the **Window** object, you'll note that we did not write* window.alert("hello") *rather just* alert("hello"). *The validity of this shorthand notation is a result of JavaScript's object scoping rules, which are discussed in Chapter 6.*

Another common form of interaction is through the **Document** object. This object provides many ways to manipulate Web pages, the simplest of which are the **write()** and **writeln()** methods. The **write()** method writes its arguments to the current document. The **writeln()** method is identical except that it inserts a linebreak after writing the argument. For example:

```
document.write("This text is not followed by a linebreak. ");
document.writeln("However this uses writeln().");
document.write("So a newline was inserted.");
```

The reason you might not notice any difference if you try this example is that JavaScript outputs to HTML. Recall from Chapter 1 that the intersection between the two languages can provide some frustration for programmers. HTML collapses all newline characters, so a newline won't make any difference at all in output. This feature probably explains why most JavaScript programmers tend to use **document.write()** instead of **document.writeln()**. To show the difference between document.write and document.writeln, you might use the **<pre>** tag around the example, as shown here:

```
<!DOCTYPE HTML PUBLIC "-//W3C//DTD HTML 4.01 Transitional//EN">
<html>
<head>
<title>Write/Writeln Example</title>
</head>
<body>
<pre>
<script>
 document.write("This text is not followed by a linebreak. ");
 document.writeln("However this uses writeln().");
 document.write("So a newline was inserted.");
</script>
</pre>
</body>
</html>
```

The result of this example when used properly in HTML can be seen in Figure 2-1.

In addition to **write()** and **writeln()**, the **Document** object provides powerful features for manipulation of HTML and XML via the Document Object Model. The DOM, which is covered primarily in Chapter 10, can be used to replace or insert text, change formatting characteristics, and write to or read from HTML forms.

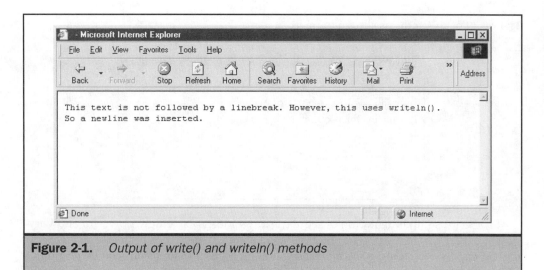

Figure 2-1.   *Output of write() and writeln() methods*

Regular Expressions

The last major functional feature of JavaScript is the regular expression. A regular expression as defined by the **RegExp** is used to handle pattern matching.

```
var country = new RegExp("England");
```

This could have been defined as well using a direct assignment:

```
var country = /England/;
```

Once a regular expression is defined, we can use it to pattern-match and potentially change strings. The following simple example matches a piece of the string in the variable *geographicLocation* and substitutes it for another string.

```
var country = new RegExp("England");
var geographicLocation = "New England";

document.write("Destination for work: "+geographicLocation+"<br>");
geographicLocation = geographicLocation.replace(country, "Zealand");
document.write("Destination for vacation: "+geographicLocation);
```

The result of this script is shown here:

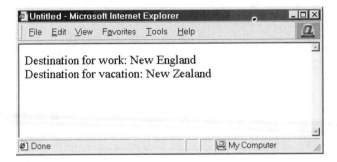

JavaScript's implementation of regular expressions is extremely powerful and very similar to Perl's, so many programmers should be immediately comfortable with JavaScript regular expression facilities. More information on regular expressions can be found in Chapter 8.

Comments

Finally, a very important aspect of good programming style is commenting your code. Commenting allows you to insert remarks and commentary directly in source code, making it more readable to yourself as well as to others. Any comments you include will be ignored by the JavaScript interpreter.

Comments in JavaScript are similar to those in C++ and Java. There are two types of comments: those that run to the end of the current line and those that span multiple lines. Single-line comments begin with a double foreslash (//), causing the interpreter to ignore everything from that point to the end of the line. For example:

```
var count = 10;    // holds number of items the user wishes to purchase
```

Comments spanning multiple lines are enclosed C-style between a slash-asterisk (/*) and asterisk-slash (*/) pair. The following example illustrates both types of comments:

```
/* The function square expects a numeric argument and returns the value squared.
   For example, to square 10 and place the value in a variable called y, invoke it
as follows:
   var y = square(10);
   This function should only be called with numeric arguments!
*/
function square(x)
{
   return x*x;              // multiply x times x, and return the value
}
```

Everything between */* and *\/* is ignored by the interpreter. Note that you *cannot* nest multiline comments. Doing so will cause an error:

```
/* These are
/* nested comments and will
*/
definitely cause an error! */
```

It cannot be stressed enough how important commenting is to writing good code. Comments should add information that is not immediately apparent from the code itself. For example, it is always good style to include a comment for each function you define, detailing the values the function expects, the operation it performs, side effects it might incur, and the type of the value it returns. Complicated statements or loops should always be commented, as should any objects that you create for your own use. In addition, an introductory comment should be included in each script to indicate its purpose and any known bugs or concerns with the code it contains.

Commenting makes code easier for others to understand. Most programmers' worst nightmare is to be assigned to fix or maintain large pieces of uncommented code. You can save your successor hours of work by including your logic and reasoning in the code you write. Professional programmers *always* comment their code, especially in a mercurial environment like the Web.

Commenting also makes code easier for you to understand. Anyone who has spent any significant length of time writing software can tell you about a time they came back to an old piece of code they wrote that completely baffled them. You are not going to remember the details and subtleties of the task at hand forever. If only for your own sake, be sure to include comments in your scripts.

Summary

This chapter provided a brief overview of the basic features of JavaScript, a simple yet powerful Web-oriented scripting language generally hosted within Web browsers. Most of the features of the language are similar to other languages such as C or Java. Common programming constructs such as **if** statements, **while** loops, and functions are found in the language. However, JavaScript is not a simplistic language and it does contain more advanced features, such as composite data types, objects, and regular expressions. The most important part of JavaScript is its use of objects, both user-created and built-in (such as **Window**, **Navigator**, and **Document)**. Most of the book will be spent covering the use of these objects. Experienced programmers might wish to quickly skim the next few chapters, focusing on the subtle differences between JavaScript and other programming languages. However, new programmers should carefully read the next five chapters in order to get a solid foundation to build upon. The next chapter will focus on JavaScript's data types, which can simplify writing scripts if the programmer is careful.

The Complete Reference

Part II

Core Language

The
Complete
Reference

JavaScript

Chapter 3

Data Types
and Variables

The data types a programming language supports are largely dictated by the kind of tasks the language was created to address. For example, a language intended for scientific computation might allow the programmer to create, store, and manipulate floating-point numbers, matrices, and vectors. Although JavaScript is primarily used to manipulate strings in the form of HTML- or XML-based Web pages within a browser, it provides a surprisingly rich set of data types for the programmer. The basic types it supports are numbers, strings, and Booleans. Some more complex types supported are objects, arrays, and functions. Functions, while not normally thought of as data types, are in fact *first-class data types* in JavaScript, meaning they can be assigned to variables and passed as arguments just like any other piece of data. This chapter covers in detail the basic data types and their usage. Functions and composite types, such as objects, are also introduced, but a complete exposition of their capabilities is reserved for Chapters 5 and 6.

Basic Notions

A *variable* can be thought of as a container that holds data. Each variable is known by an *identifier*, a name that refers to the container and allows the program to access and manipulate the data it contains. A *literal* is data that appears directly in the source code, data that is not contained in a variable. The *type* of a variable or literal describes the nature of the data. For example, the type of the literal **3.14** in JavaScript would be *number* and the type of "First Name" would be *string*.

When you *declare* a variable, you tell the interpreter to allocate space to store data. Variables are declared using the **var** keyword with the name of the variable you wish to declare. Although it is good programming practice to declare variables before use, JavaScript allows the implicit declaration of variables by using them on the left-hand side of an assignment. Many programmers use implicit declaration to save time when coding. However, scripts written without variable declarations are significantly harder to read than those that use explicit declarations. The problem with implicit declaration is not merely one of style; we'll see later in the chapter how implicit declaration can also lead to subtle errors involving variable scope.

The following example illustrates basic variable declaration:

```
var pi;
pi = 3.14;
pi = "The ratio of a circle's circumference to its diameter";
```

The first line declares a new (empty) variable with the identifier "pi." The second line places the number literal **3.14** in the container referred to by *pi*. The third line replaces the current contents of *pi* by the given string literal. The type of **3.14** is *number*. The type of the string literal is *string*. The type of *pi* changes! Because it is initially empty, *pi* starts off as *undefined* type. When a number is assigned to it in the second line, its type changes to *number*. When a string is assigned to it in the third line, its type changes to *string*. This example illustrates a very important aspect of JavaScript data types, called "weak typing."

Weak Typing

Most high-level languages, including C and Java, are *strongly typed*. That is, a variable must be declared before it is used, and its type must be included in its declaration. Once a variable is declared, its type cannot change. At the other end of the spectrum are *untyped* languages such as LISP. LISP supports only two primitive data types, atoms and lists. It does not draw any distinction between strings, integers, functions, and other data types. As a *weakly typed* language, JavaScript falls somewhere in between these two extremes. Every variable and literal has a type, but data types are not explicitly declared. Types are inferred from context, and a variable automatically takes on the type of the data it contains. This feature allows a programmer to first assign a number and later a string to the same variable. Attempting to do so in C or Java would cause an error (or in some cases a warning). Type conversion will be covered in greater detail later in the chapter.

Primitive Types

JavaScript supports five primitive data types: number, string, Boolean, undefined, and null. These types are referred to as *primitive types* because they are the basic building blocks from which more complex types are built. Of the five, only number, string, and Boolean are real data types in the sense of actually storing data. Undefined and null are types that arise under special circumstances.

Numbers

Unlike languages such as C and Java, the number type in JavaScript includes both integer and floating-point values. All numbers are represented in IEEE 754-1985 double-precision floating-point format. This representation is 64 bits long, permitting floating-point magnitudes as large as $\pm 1.7976 \times 10^{308}$ and as small as $\pm 2.2250 \times 10^{-308}$. Although JavaScript implementations *should* be able to handle integers with magnitude as large as 2^{53}, simple experimentation shows that this is not always the case. The reason is that for efficiency reasons many JavaScript operators act only on 32-bit values. Because of this, it is generally a good idea to think of integers having an effective range of 2147483647 to -2147483648 (equivalently, $2^{31}-1$ to -2^{31}). More details about these representations can be found at the end of this section.

Numbers in JavaScript are composed of digits followed optionally by a decimal point, more digits, and an optional exponent. The exponent is specified with the letter *e* (which is not case-sensitive) and an optional sign value followed by digits. A leading negative sign to the whole number is also permitted, and although strictly speaking it is a *unary operator*, it can be thought of as part of the number itself.

According to the ECMA-262 grammar, numbers have one of the following three forms (parentheses indicate optional components):

DecimalDigits.(DecimalDigits)(Exponent)

.DecimalDigits(Exponent)

DecimalDigits(Exponent)

According to this grammar, all of the following are valid numbers:

```
10
-2.71
.333333e77
-1.7E12
3.E-5
128e+100
```

while the following are *not* valid numbers:

```
2,717
22e100.5
128e5e10
e10
```

Note that you should *not* include leading zeros in your numbers. The reason is that JavaScript also allows numeric literals to be specified in bases other than 10 (decimal). A leading zero indicates to JavaScript that the literal is in a radix other than 10.

Hexadecimal Literals

Almost all programming languages allow numeric literals to be given in hexadecimal (base-16). JavaScript is no exception. The syntax should be familiar to readers with previous programming experience: a leading zero, followed by the letter *x*, followed by one or more hexadecimal digits. Hexadecimal digits are the numbers zero through nine and letters *A* through *F*, which represent the values zero through fifteen. Neither the *x* in the initial **0x** nor the hexadecimal digits *A* through *F* are case sensitive, though by convention most programmers write *A* through *F* in uppercase and the *x* in lowercase. The following are examples of legal hexadecimal values:

```
0x0
0XF8f00
0x1a3C5e7
```

The optional exponent and decimal digits available for decimal literals are *not* used with hexadecimal notation.

Octal Literals

Although not officially a part of the ECMA-262 specification, almost all JavaScript implementations allow octal (base-8) numeric literals. Octal literals begin with a leading zero and are composed of one or more octal digits. Octal digits are the numbers zero through seven. The following are all valid octal literals:

```
00
0777
024513600
```

As with hexadecimal literals, exponents and fractional digits are not permitted when using octal notation.

Note   *The Opera browser's JavaScript implementations, even up to version 5, do not support octal. Future versions may support this data type, but programmers should be aware of this difference when using octal values.*

Special Values

Numeric data can also take on several special values. When a numeric expression or variable exceeds the maximum representable positive value, it takes on the special value **Infinity**. Likewise, when an expression or variable becomes less than the smallest representable negative value, it takes one the value **-Infinity**. These values are *sticky* in the sense that when one is used in an expression with other normal values or itself, it causes the entire expression to evaluate to its value. For example, **Infinity** minus 100 is still **Infinity**; it does not become a representable number. All **Infinity** values compare equal to each other. Similarly, all **-Infinity** values compare equal.

Although an easier way to get an **Infinity** value is to divide one by zero, the following code demonstrates what happens when you increment the maximum representable positive value.

```
var x = 1.7976931348623157e308;    // set x to max value
x = x + 1e292;         // increment x
alert(x);              // show resulting value to user
```

This code assigns the maximum positive representation to x, increments its least significant digit, and then shows the user the value of x. The result is shown here:

The other important special value is **NaN**, which means "not a number." Numeric data takes on this value when it is the result of an undefined operation. Common examples of operations that result in **NaN** are dividing zero by zero, taking the sine of **Infinity**, and attempting to add **Infinity** to **-Infinity**. The **NaN** value is sticky, but unlike the infinite values it *never* compares equal to anything. Because of this, you must use the **isNan()** method or compare the value to itself to determine if a value is **NaN**. The **isNan()** method returns a Boolean indicating whether the value is **NaN**. This method is so important that it is a property of the global object, so it can be called directly in your scripts. Comparing the value to itself will indicate whether the value is **NaN** because that is the only value that does not compare equal to itself!

The following two conditionals are equivalent:

```
var x = 0 / 0;              // assign NaN to x
if (x != x)                 // check via self-equality
{
// do something
}
if (isNaN(x))               // check via explicit call
{
// do something
}
```

JavaScript 1.1+ and JScript 2.0+ provide easy access to these special numerical values as properties of the **Number** object. These properties are shown in Table 3-1. A complete discussion of functions and constants supported by JavaScript's **Math** object can be found in Chapter 7.

Note   *Division by zero in JavaScript is somewhat consistent with the Calculus. Division of a positive number by zero results in "infinity," division of a negative number by zero results in "negative infinity," and division of zero by zero is "undefined" (NaN). Readers with knowledge of the Calculus will recall this convention with respect to limits and L'Hôpital's rule.*

Property	Value
Number.MAX_VALUE	Largest magnitude representable
Number.MIN_VALUE	Smallest magnitude representable
Number.POSITIVE_INFINITY	The special value **Infinity**
Number.NEGATIVE_INFINITY	The special value **-Infinity**
Number.NaN	The special value **NaN**

Table 3-1. *Properties of the Number Object Relevant to Special Numeric Values*

Issues with Data Representation

Floating-point data representation has some complicated implications and subtle pitfalls. The most important effect to be aware of is that floating-point values can lose precision, especially if the magnitude of the values represented grows very large or becomes very small. Additionally, most integer operations in JavaScript are implemented using only 32 bits, so very large integers will actually lose less significant bits during arithmetic. There are several ways to work around the second limitation, the easiest of which is to use floating point numbers instead of integers if magnitudes are expected to be very large (greater than $2^{31}-1$).

As an example of the loss of precision, consider the following code snippet:

```
var x = .3333;
x = x * 5;
alert(x);
```

One would expect *x* to contain the value **1.6665**. However, the actual result is shown here:

This value will not even compare equal to **1.6665**! This can be a very serious issue for e-commerce applications that need to calculate precise values like sales tax. Significant testing should always be carried out to ensure that your floating-point operations perform as expected.

The reader who intends to carry out serious scientific computation with JavaScript might want to reconsider. Because JavaScript was not intended to be used for numerical analysis, its support for floating-point operations is less refined than that of other languages. Another concern is that because JavaScript runs in an interpreter that runs inside of a Web browser that runs on an operating system, the performance of intensive floating-point calculations is likely to be very poor. At the very least, the reader who intends to carry out such computation should consult a numerical analysis or mathematical programming textbook for further information. A grasp of the intricacies of floating-point arithmetic is fundamental to understanding the inconsistencies and errors that can arise from loss of precision and architectural differences.

Strings

A *string* is simply a piece of text. In JavaScript, a string is a sequence of characters surrounded by single or double quotes. For example,

```
var string1 = "This is a string";
```

defines a string value to be stored in *string1*, as does the code fragment here:

```
var string1 = 'So am I';
```

However, while it is possible to use either single or double quotes with strings, there are some nuances with their use to consider, and these are discussed in the section "Quotes and Strings" later on in the chapter.

Unlike other languages, JavaScript draws no distinction between single characters and strings. So,

```
var oneChar = "s";
```

defines a string of length one. Strings can be thought of as arrays of characters, indexed from zero. Netscape 4+ (but not Internet Explorer) supports this view, allowing strings to be indexed like arrays:

```
var myString = "Strings are like arrays of characters";
var firstLetter = myString[0];
```

However, strings are also associated with a **String** object, so one should not rely too heavily on the view that strings are arrays of characters. A better way to extract characters from strings is to use the **charAt()** method of the **String** object. For example, given the definition of a string "myName":

```
var myName = "Thomas";
```

you could extract the value of the third letter using

```
var thirdletter = myName.charAt(2);
```

The reason for using a value of 2 rather than 3 is that strings are indexed starting from 0. A more complete discussion of this aspect of arrays and their intersection with objects is found later in this chapter.

Beyond reading and setting strings, there are properties that can be read; for example using the string "myName" from before a script like

```
var strlen = myName.length();
```

would set the value of the variable "strlen" to the length of the string, in this case a value of 6. There are also many methods to manipulate strings as well. All of these string specifics, apart from the core data type issues discussed next, will be covered at length in Chapter 7.

Special Characters and Strings

Any alphabetic, numeric, or punctuation characters can be placed in a string, but there are some natural limitations. For instance, the *newline* character is the character that causes output to move down one line on your display. Typing this directly into a string using your ENTER key would result in a string literal like this:

```
var myString = "This is the first line.
This is the second line."
```

which results in a syntax error according to JavaScript's rules for implicit semicolons.

To solve this problem JavaScript, like most other programming languages, makes use of *escape codes*. An escape code (also called escape sequence) is a small bit of text preceded by a backslash ("\") that has special meaning to the interpreter. Escape codes let you include special characters without typing them directly into your string. For example, the escape code for the newline character is **\n**. Using this escape code we can now correctly define the string literal we previously saw:

```
var myString = "This is the first line.\nThis is the second line."
```

This example also illuminates an important feature of escape codes: they are interpreted correctly even when found flush with other characters ("." and "T" in this example). A list of supported escape codes is shown in Table 3-2.

Character Representation

The table of escape codes illustrates the fact that JavaScript supports two different character sets. Current JavaScript implementations support the Unicode character set, which includes nearly every printable character in every language on earth. Browser versions prior to Netscape 6 and Internet Explorer 4 use Latin-1 (ISO8859-1), which is a subset of Unicode. ECMA-262 mandates Unicode support. This distinction will be transparent to most users but can cause problems in a non-English environment. Unless you have a specific reason to use Latin-1, using the Unicode escape code is strongly encouraged.

Escape Code	Value
\b	backspace
\t	tab (horizontal)
\n	linefeed (newline)
\v	tab (vertical)
\f	form feed
\r	carriage return
\"	double quote
\'	single quote
\\	backslash
\OOO	Latin-1 character represented by the octal digits OOO. The valid range is 000 to 377.
\xHH	Latin-1 character represented by the hexadecimal digits HH. The valid range is 00 to FF.
\uHHHH	Unicode character represented by the hexadecimal digits *HHHH*.

Table 3-2.   *Escape Codes*

The following example assigns the string containing the letter *B* to the variables. The only difference between the strings is the character set used to represent the character (that is, they all compare equal):

```
var inLatinOctal = "\102";
var inLatinHex = "\x42"
var inUnicode = "\u0042";
```

More information about character sets and Web technologies can be found at http://www.unicode.org and http://www.w3.org.

Quotes and Strings

Note that there are escape codes for both single and double quotes. If your string is delimited with double quotes, any double quotes within it must be escaped. Similarly, any single quotes in a string delimited with single quotes must be escaped. The reason for this is straightforward: if a quotation mark were not escaped, JavaScript would incorrectly interpret it as the end of the string. The following are examples of validly escaped quotes inside of strings:

```
var string1 = "These quotes \"are\" valid!";
var string2 = 'Isn\'t JavaScript great?';
```

The following strings are *not* valid:

```
var invalid1 = "This will not work!';
var invalid2 = 'Neither 'will this';
```

Strings and HTML

The capability for strings to be delimited with either single or double quotes is very useful when one considers that JavaScript is often found inside HTML attributes like **onclick**. These attributes are themselves quoted, so flexibility with respect to quoting JavaScript strings allows programmers to avoid the laborious task of escaping lots of quotes. The following HTML form button illustrates the principle:

```
<input type="button" onclick="document.write('Thanks for clicking!')">
```

Using unescaped double quotes in the **document.write** would result in the browser interpreting the first such quote as the end of the **onclick** attribute value.

A typical example of the use of escape codes and quoting is found next. Note that the **document.write** method writes the argument string to the browser window but does not automatically insert a newline after the text. HTML automatically "collapses" multiple whitespace characters down to one whitespace. So, for example, including multiple consecutive tabs in your HTML shows up as only one space character. In this example, the **<pre>** tag is used to tell the browser that the text is preformatted and that it should not collapse the whitespaces inside of it. Using **<pre>** allows the tabs in the example to be displayed correctly in the output. The result can be seen in Figure 3-1.

```
<!DOCTYPE HTML PUBLIC "-//W3C//DTD HTML 4.01 Transitional//EN"
"http://www.w3.org/TR/html4/loose.dtd">
<html>
<head>
<title>String Example</title>
</head>
<body>

<pre>
<script language="JavaScript" type="text/javascript">
<!--
document.write("Welcome to Javascript strings.\n");

document.write("This example illustrates nested quotes 'like this.'\n");

document.write("Note how newlines (\\n's) and ");

document.write("escape sequences are used.\n");

document.write("You might wonder, \"Will this nested quoting work?\"");

document.write(" It will.\n");

document.write("Here's an example of some formatted data:\n\n");

document.write("\tCode\tValue\n");

document.write("\t\\n\tnewline\n");

document.write("\t\\\\\tbackslash\n");

document.write("\t\\\"\tdouble quote\n\n");
// -->
</script>
</pre>
</body>
</html>
```

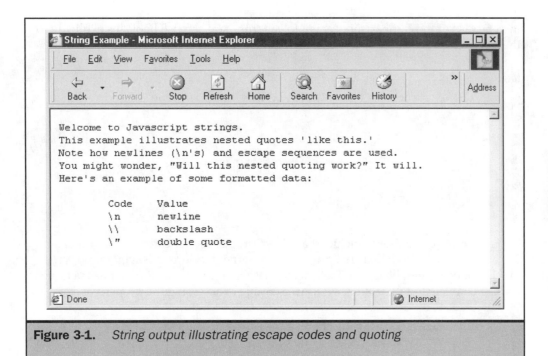

Figure 3-1.   *String output illustrating escape codes and quoting*

Booleans

Booleans derive their name from George Boole, the 19th Century logician who developed the true/false system of logic upon which digital circuits would later be based. With this in mind it should come as no surprise that Booleans take on one of two values: **true** or **false**.

Comparison expressions such as

    x <= y

assume a Boolean value depending upon whether the comparison is true or false. Therefore, the type of the condition of a control structure such as an **if/else** statement is implicitly Boolean. The condition is evaluated and replaced with the Boolean result. For example,

```
if (x == y)
{
   x = x + 1;
}
```

increments *x* if the comparison *x* equal to *y* is **true**. You can use Booleans explicitly to the same effect:

```
var doIncrement = true;
if (doIncrement)          // if doIncrement is true then increment x
{
    x = x + 1;
}
if (true)                 // always increment x
{
    x = x + 1;
}
```

Booleans are commonly included as object properties indicating an on/off state. For example, the **cookieEnabled** property of Internet Explorer's **Navigator** object (**navigator.cookieEnabled**) is a Boolean that has value **true** when the user has persistent cookies enabled and **false** otherwise. An example of accessing the property is

```
if (navigator.cookieEnabled)
{
    alert("Persistent cookies are enabled");
}
else
{
    alert("Persistent cookies are not enabled");
}
```

The result when used in Internet Explorer with persistent cookies enabled is:

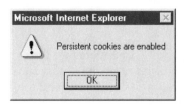

Note *Some Netscape browsers do not support this property so they will always receive the second message ("Persistent cookies are not enabled").*

Undefined and Null

The *undefined* type is used for variables or object properties that either do not exist or have not been assigned a value. The only value an undefined type can have is **undefined**. For example, declaring a variable without assigning it a value,

```
var x;
```

gives *x* the undefined type and value. Accessing a nonexistent object property,

```
var x = String.noSuchProperty;
```

also results in the assignment of **undefined** to *x*.

The **null** value indicates an empty or nonexistent value. It is essentially a placeholder that represents "nothing." Because null is the subject of much confusion, it is best to consider that there are really no null types, only **null** values. In the view of a purist, a *type* is a set of values. The only value the null type can have is **null**. Therefore, one would expect that using the **typeof** operator on a variable holding a **null** value would return **null**. Unfortunately, this is not the case—it returns the **object**. This is because the variable holds a nonexistent (empty) object. To avoid confusion it is best to think of **null** as a value indicating the absence of data.

Distinguishing between undefined and null data can be tricky. JavaScript provides the **null** keyword to enable comparison and assignment of **null** values. Unfortunately, the **undefined** keyword exists only in the most modern browsers. The resolution lies in the fact that **null** and **undefined** values compare equal. So you can check for invalid values by comparing to **null**. For example, the declarations

```
var x;
var y = null;
```

will result in both of the following comparisons evaluating true:

```
if (x == null)
{
// do something
}
if (x == y)
{
// do something
}
```

However, it is important to note that with the previous declarations, the following

```
if (z == null)
{
// do something
}
```

results in a runtime error. The reason is that *z* is not merely undefined, it simply does not exist.

Composite Types

Objects form the basis for all nonprimitive types in JavaScript. An object is a composite type that can contain primitive and composite types. Arrays are objects that have more structure than **Object** (data type) objects. Both are discussed at length in Chapters 6 and 7. In this section we give an introduction to their usage but focus primarily on their characteristics as data types.

Objects

An *object* is a collection that can contain primitive or composite data, including functions and other objects. The members of an object are called *properties*, and member functions are known as *methods*.

Properties are accessed by placing a period and the property name immediately following the object name. For instance, the version information of the browser is stored in the **appVersion** property of the **Navigator** object. One way of accessing this property is

```
alert("Your browser version is: " + navigator.appVersion);
```

The result of which in Internet Explorer 5.5 (domestic US) is

Methods of objects are accessed in the same way but with trailing parentheses immediately following the method name. These parentheses indicate to the interpreter that the property is a method that you want to invoke. The **Window** object has a method named **close**, which closes the current browser window:

```
window.close();
```

If the method takes arguments, the arguments are included in the parentheses in the natural way. We've seen a common example of this usage, the **write** method of the **Document** object:

```
document.write("This text is written to the document.");
```

Built-in Objects

The browser provides several powerful objects for scripts to use. These include browser-specific objects such as **Window**, which contains information about the browser window and current document, and **Navigator**, which contains information about the browser itself. In addition, the browser environment provides numerous objects defined in the JavaScript language that simplify common tasks. Examples of such objects are **Date**, **Math**, and **RegExp**.

An important feature of JavaScript is that each data type is also associated with an object. So there are **String**, **Number**, **Boolean**, **Array**, and even **Object** objects. These objects provide the functionality commonly used to carry out data manipulation tasks for the given type. For example, the **String** object provides methods to extract substrings, replace portions of text, and convert strings to HTML. The relationship between primitive types and their associated objects is a fundamental part of JavaScript and will be examined in greater depth later in this chapter. In fact, most of this book involves discussion of the built-in objects the browsers provide. However you are not limited to using objects defined by the language and the browser: JavaScript allows you to create your own objects.

Creating Objects

Objects are created using the **new** keyword followed by the name of the object and parentheses. The reason for the parentheses is that objects are created using *constructors*, methods that create a fresh instance of an object for you to use. The parentheses tell the interpreter that you want to invoke the constructor method for the given object. The following creates a brand new **String** object:

```
var myString = new String();
```

One nice feature of objects is that you can add properties to them dynamically. For example, to create your own object and populate it with two text fields you might do the following:

```
var myLocation = new Object();
myLocation.city = "San Diego";
myLocation.state = "California";
```

If you are not completely comfortable with the concept of object creation, don't worry. It will be explained at greater length in Chapter 6. The important things to understand at this point are the syntax of how properties are accessed and how objects are declared. In short, you use the **new** operator and then you use the period operation "." to set and access the various properties of the object. One variation of this is the composite type **Array**, which is an object but potentially has different creation and access syntax.

Arrays

An *array* is an ordered list that can contain primitive and complex data types. Arrays are sometimes known as *vectors* or *lists* in other programming languages and are actually **Array** objects in JavaScript. The members of an array are called *elements*. Array elements are numbered starting with zero. That is, each element is assigned an *index*, a non-negative integer indicating its position in the array. You can think of an array as series of boxes labeled 0, 1, 2, and so on. You can place a piece of data into a box, for example box 5, and later retrieve that data by accessing the element at index 5. Individual array elements are accessed by following the array name with square brackets ("[" and "]") containing the desired index. For example, to place a string in array element 5 and then retrieve it you might write:

```
myArray[5] = "Hamburgers are nice, sushi is better.";
var x = myArray[5];
```

Individually setting the values of an array as shown here can be rather tedious, and there are more direct ways to populate an array. Array literals are specified by a comma-separated list of values enclosed in square brackets. The following defines a new array with four numbers and one string:

```
var myArray = [2, 4, 6, 8, "ten"];
```

If you want to define an array but fill it with values later, you can define an empty array in a similar manner:

```
var myArray = [];
```

Because arrays are really **Array** objects, you can use the object syntax to declare a new array:

```
var myArray = new Array();
```

You can then access the array according to the syntax previously discussed.

Because JavaScript is weakly typed, there is no restriction on the type of data that you can place at each index. The first element could be a string, the second an array, the third null, and the fourth a function. Any index into which you have not placed data has the value **undefined**. You need not use array elements in order, although doing so is generally a good idea. And because JavaScript hides the details of memory allocation, the only theoretical upper bound on the maximum index you can address is given by the maximum integer value the browser supports. Practically, however, it is not a good idea to use indices beyond $2^{31}-1$ because of the previously discussed limitations on JavaScript integers.

An important property that all arrays have is **length**. This property is provided by the **Array** object, but it can be used on an array regardless of how it was declared. This property retrieves the index of the next available (unfilled) position at the end of the array. Even if some lower indices are unused, **length** gives the index of the first available slot after the last element. For example,

```
var myArray = [];
myArray[2] = "First element";
myArray[4] = "Last element. There are holes in this array!";
alert("The next available index is: " + myArray.length);
```

shows that the next available index is **5**, even though positions **0**, **1**, and **3** are not used:

One nice feature of arrays is that the **Array** object provides methods similar to those in Perl and Java that allow arrays to be easily used as stacks and queues. Multidimensional arrays are also supported. And as a bonus, a simple trick using objects allows you to create associative arrays much like those in Perl. If you are not sure what these terms mean, not to worry, as they will be discussed in Chapters 6 and 7.

Functions

A *function* is a special type of JavaScript object that contains executable code. A function is called (or *invoked*) by following the function name with parentheses. Functions can take *arguments* (or *parameters*), pieces of data that are *passed* to the function when it is invoked. Arguments are given as a comma-separated list between the parentheses of the function call. The following function call passes two arguments, a string and a number:

```
document.write("The value of pi is: ", 3.14);
```

The call causes the **write** method of the **Document** object to output a string to the current browser window. Function arguments can be any valid piece of data: strings, objects, arrays, nulls, or even other functions.

Creating Functions

Functions are declared with the **function** keyword. The function name is given along with the required parentheses containing the names of the arguments it accepts. The actual code it contains is then specified enclosed in curly braces. This syntax is best shown by example. In the example that follows, two functions are defined and then the second is invoked. When called, the *showSum* function invokes *doSum* to compute the sum of its arguments and then outputs the result.

```
function doSum(x, y)
{
    return x+y;          // compute the sum and return in
}
function showSum(x, y)
{
    var result = doSum(x, y);            // compute the sum
    alert("The sum is: " + result);      // show it to the user
}
showSum(5, 7);                // invoke showSum to add and display 5 + 7
```

The result of this code is:

Experienced programmers will note that neither the return type nor the type of the arguments are specified in a function definition. The reason for this is that JavaScript is weakly typed. Arguments and the values returned by functions may be of any type. This is both a blessing and a curse. It allows the function declaration syntax to remain simple but also allows for the introduction of subtle errors if the types of variables passed to a function are not what it expects.

The **return** keyword, when used inside a function, causes that function to stop executing and "send back" the value of the given expression. In the previous example, the *doSum* function returns the sum of its two arguments while *showSum* returns nothing. In this way, function calls can be used on the right-hand side of an assignment:

```
var result = doSum(10.0, 12.5);
```

The variable *result* now contains **22.5**. The **return** statement is optional in functions that do not return any value.

This example also illustrates a problem with weak typing. Because the **+** operator acts to concatenate strings, the following invocation results in *result* being assigned the string "10.012.5":

```
var result = sum("10.0", "12.5");
```

Weak typing gives the programmer tremendous freedom but can also cause some serious headaches if not used carefully.

In some respects, JavaScript's support of functions is very advanced. Veteran programmers will be pleased to learn that JavaScript supports variadic functions (like C), anonymous functions (like Perl and LISP), and nested functions (like Pascal). Those with less experience will be pleased to learn that these advanced language features are rarely used and that JavaScript's parameter passing is considerably simpler than that of other languages.

Primitive-datatypes passed as arguments are passed by value. This *call-by-value* rule means that the interpreter makes a copy of the function arguments and passes these copies to the function. Any modification made to the arguments inside of the function is actually made to a *copy* of the arguments. This is opposed to *call-by-reference*, which enables functions to modify the "original" data. JavaScript passes composite-types by references, but for the time being we'll ignore this issue.

The following code illustrates call-by-value. A variable is defined and passed to a function that modifies its value. You can see from the results in Figure 3-2 that the original value remains unchanged:

```
function modifyAndPrint(y)
{
   document.writeln("Before modification in the function: ", y);
   y = 5;
   document.writeln("After modification in the function: ", y);
}
var x = 10;
document.writeln("Before calling the function: ", x);
modifyAndPrint(x);
document.writeln("After calling the function: ", x);
```

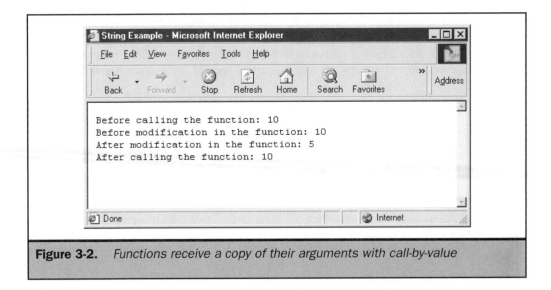

Figure 3-2.   *Functions receive a copy of their arguments with call-by-value*

This example might cause you to wonder: if the argument to *modifyAndPrint* had also been named *x* in the function declaration, could the interpreter keep the two different *x*'s straight? The answer is yes, and the reason is found in JavaScript' s rules for variable scoping.

Variables

Because variables are one of the most important aspects of any programming language, awareness of the implications of variable declaration and reference is key to writing clear, well-behaved code. Variable scoping rules give rise to phenomena like data hiding and can cause subtle bugs if not properly understood. In addition to acquiring a firm grasp on the nuances of JavaScript' s scoping rules, choosing good names for variables is of major importance.

Identifiers

An *identifier* is a name by which a variable or function is known. In JavaScript, any combination of letters, digits, underscores, and dollar signs is allowed to make up an identifier. The only formal restrictions on identifiers are that they must not match any JavaScript reserved words or keywords and that the first character cannot be a digit. Keywords are the words of the JavaScript language, such as **string**, **Object**, **return**, **for**, and **while**. Reserved words are words that might become keywords in the future. You can find a comprehensive list of reserved words and keywords in Appendix E.

Although JavaScript allows you to give a variable a cryptic name like _$0_$, doing so in practice is a bad idea. Using dollar signs in your identifiers is highly discouraged; they are intended for use with code generated by mechanical means and were not supported until JavaScript 1.2. Despite its common use in practice, beginning an identifier with an underscore is also not a good idea. Variables internal to the interpreter often begin with two underscores, so using a similar naming convention can cause confusion.

One of the most important aspects of writing clear, understandable code is choosing appropriate names for your variables. Unreasonably long or incomprehensible identifiers should be avoided. A variable' s name should give some information about its purpose or value that is not immediately apparent from its context. For example, the following identifiers are probably not appropriate:

```
var _ = 10;
var x = "George Washington";
var foobar = 3.14159;
var howMuchItCostsPerItemInUSDollarsAndCents = "$1.25";
```

More apropos might be

```
var index = 10;
var president = "George Washington";
var pi = 3.14159;
var price = "$1.25";
```

You should also use appropriate names for composite types and functions. For example,

```
var anArray = ["Mon", "Tues", "Wed", "Thurs", "Fri"];
```

is a poor choice of identifier for this array. Later in the script it is not at all clear what value *anArray[3]* might be expected to have. Better is

```
var weekdays = ["Mon", "Tues", "Wed", "Thurs", "Fri"];
```

which when later used as *weekdays[3]* gives the reader some idea of what the array contains. Because JavaScript is case-sensitive, *weekdays* and *weekDays* refer to two different variables. For this reason it is not advisable to choose identifiers that closely resemble each other. Similarly, it is not advisable to choose identifiers close to or identical to common objects or properties. Doing so can lead to confusion and even errors.

JavaScript programmers are fond of the camel-back style for variable capitalization. With this convention, each word in a variable name has an initial capital except for the first. For example, a variable holding the text color of the body of the document might be named *bodyTextColor*. Because JavaScript does not have pointers and is not usually used to write very large pieces of software, there is little need for strict naming conventions, such as Hungarian Notation. However, because the camel-back convention is so widely accepted, new programmers are strongly encouraged to adopt its use.

Note	*JavaScript programmers are fond of using very short variable names, like simply the name x, in order to decrease the number of characters that need to be transferred to the client. The reason being that fewer characters to send implies faster download time. Although the end-user might notice some difference in download time for very large scripts, the proliferation of 56k modems, broadband access, and browsers that can handle compressed content (for example, Netscape and Internet Explorer) makes this a dubious practice. When compared to the size of typical images found in Web pages today, the several hundred characters saved by using short variable names is almost inconsequential. In addition, JavaScript stripped of comments and descriptive variable names is very hard to decipher. While this might be a good thing if you do not want anyone reading or understanding your code, this is a very bad thing if anyone else but you is expected to maintain or fix it. The time spent editing scripts for brevity and then trying to figure them out six months down the road might be better spent compressing included images and fine tuning your Web server, operating system, and Internet connection.*

Variable Declaration

As we have seen in numerous examples, variables are declared with the **var** keyword. Multiple variables can be declared at once by separating them with a comma. Variables may also be initialized with a starting value by including an assignment in the declaration. All the following are legal variable declarations:

```
var x;
var a, b, c;
var pi, index = 0, weekdays = ["M", "T", "W", "Th", "F"];
```

In the final declaration *pi* is assigned the **undefined** value, *index* is initialized to zero, and *weekdays* is initialized to a five-element array. Repeatedly declaring a variable has no effect.

One "feature" of JavaScript is implicit variable declaration. When you use an undeclared variable on the left-hand side of an assignment, the variable is automatically declared. The truth of the matter is that implicit declaration is terrible programming style and should never be used. One reason is that readers cannot differentiate an implicit variable declaration from a reference to a variable of the same name in an enclosing scope. Another reason is that implicit declaration creates a global variable even if used inside of a function. Use of implicit declaration leads to sloppy coding style, unintentional variable clobbering, and unclear code. Do not use it.

Variable Scope

The *scope* of a variable is all parts of a program where it is visible. Being visible means that the variable has been declared and is available for use. Undeclared variables are not visible because they do not exist. A variable that is visible everywhere in the program has *global* scope. A variable that is visible only in a specific context—a function for example—has *local* scope. A *context* is the set of defined data that make up the execution environment.

When the browser starts, it creates the global context in which JavaScript will execute. This context contains the definitions of the features of the JavaScript language (the **Array** and **Math** objects, for example) in addition to browser-specific objects like **Navigator**. When a function is invoked, the interpreter creates a new local context for the duration of its execution. All variables declared in the function (including its arguments) exist only within this context. When the function returns, the context is destroyed. So, if you wish to preserve a value across multiple function calls (like a static variable in C), you need to declare a global variable.

When a variable is referenced in a function, the interpreter first checks the local context for a variable of that name. If the variable has not been declared in the local context, the interpreter checks the enclosing context. If it is not found in the enclosing context, the interpreter repeats the process recursively until either the variable is found or the global context is reached. It is important to note that the contexts are checked with respect to the source code and not the current call tree. This type of scoping is called *static scoping* (or *lexical scoping*). In this way, locally declared variables can *hide* variables of the same name that are declared in an enclosing context. The following example illustrates variable hiding:

```javascript
var scope = "global";
function myFunction()
{
 var scope = "local";
 document.writeln("The value of scope in myFunction is: " + scope);
}
myFunction();
document.writeln("The value of scope in the global context is: " + scope);
```

The result is shown in Figure 3-3. The local variable *scope* has hidden the value of the global variable named *scope*. Note that omitting **var** from the first line of *myFunction* would assign the value "local" to the global variable *scope*.

There are some important subtleties regarding variable scope. The first is that each browser window has its own global context. So it is unclear at first glance how to access and manipulate data in other browser windows. Fortunately, JavaScript enables you to do so by providing access to frames and other named windows. The mechanics of cross-window interaction is covered in later chapters, particularly Chapter 12.

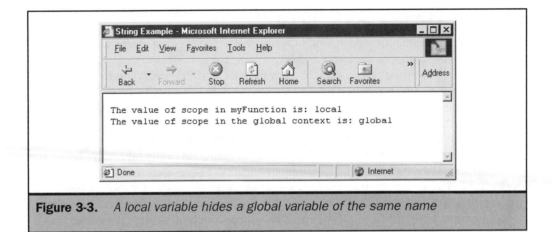

Figure 3-3. *A local variable hides a global variable of the same name*

The second subtlety related to scoping is that, no matter where a variable is declared in a context, it is visible throughout that context. This implies that a variable declared at the end of a function is visible throughout the whole function. However, any initialization that is included in the declaration is only performed when that line of code is reached. The result is that it is possible to access a variable before it is initialized, as in the following example:

```
var scope = "global";
function myFunction()
{
 document.writeln("The value of scope before initialization in myFunction is: ", scope);
 var scope = "local";
 document.writeln("The value of scope after initialization in myFunction
 is: ", scope);
}
document.writeln("The value of scope in the global context is: ", scope);
myFunction();
```

The result is shown in Figure 3-4. Note how *scope* has **undefined** value before it is initialized.

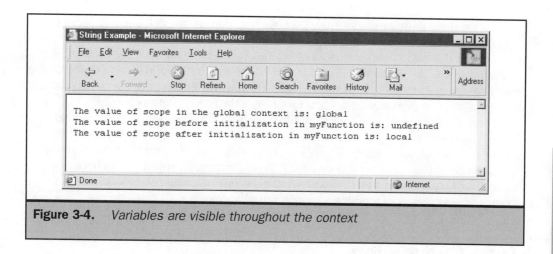

Figure 3-4.   *Variables are visible throughout the context*

The third subtlety has to do with static scoping. Consider the following code:

```
var scope = "global";
function outerFunction()
{
   var scope = "local";
   innerFunction();
}
function innerFunction()
{
   alert("The value of scope is: " + scope);
}
outerFunction();
```

which results in:

This example illustrates a critical aspect of static scoping: the value of *scope* seen in *innerFunction* is the value present in the enclosing the global context: "global." It does not see the value set in *outerFunction*. That value of *scope* is local to that function and not visible outside of it. The correct value for *scope* was found by examination of the enclosing context in the original JavaScript source code. The interpreter can infer the correct value by "static" examination of the program text. Hence the name "static scoping."

If JavaScript used dynamic scoping, the previous example would have printed "local." Dynamic scoping would cause the interpreter to examine the context of the calling function (*outerFunction*) before checking the global context. Dynamic scoping can cause confusion because it is unclear from examining a program which instance of a variable a particular function will see. This is one of many reasons that dynamic scoping is rarely used in modern programming languages.

Type Conversion

One of the most powerful features of JavaScript as well as most dangerous for the sloppy programmer is its automatic *type conversion*. Type conversion is the act of converting data of one type into a different type. It occurs automatically when you change the type of data stored in a variable:

```
var x = "3.14";
x = 3.14;
```

The type of *x* changes from string to number. It also occurs in less obvious ways:

```
var x = "10" - 2;
```

JavaScript knows that subtraction requires two numbers so it converts the string "10" into the number 10, performs the subtraction, and stores the number 8 in *x*. Note that *x*'s type is number.

JavaScript usually converts operands to the correct type before performing an operation. For example,

```
x = "2" - "2"
```

always causes the strings to be converted to numbers before performing the subtraction. One operator that might not work as you would expect is +. The + operator performs addition on numbers but also serves as the concatenation operator for strings. Because string concatenation has precedence over numeric addition, + will be interpreted as string concatenation if any of the operands are strings. For example, both statements

```
x = "2" + "2";
x = "2" + 2;
```

result in the assignment of the string "22" to x. The numeric 2 in the second statement is automatically converted to a string before concatenation is applied.

It was previously mentioned that there is an object provided for each primitive type. These objects provide useful methods for manipulating primitive data. For example, the **String** object provides a method to convert a string to lowercase: **toLowerCase()**. While you can invoke this method on a **String** object:

```
var myStringObject = new String("ABC");
var lowercased = myStringObject.toLowerCase();
```

you can also invoke it on primitive string data:

```
var myString = "ABC";
var lowercased = myString.toLowerCase();
```

The key insight is that JavaScript automatically converts the primitive string *myString* into a **String** object so that the **toLowerCase** method can be invoked. Although it might look odd, the same method can be applied to string literals:

```
var lowercased = "ABC".toLowerCase();
```

JavaScript will automatically convert between objects and primitive types depending upon what is required of the context. **String** objects are converted to string primitives before they are printed. Likewise, a primitive string is converted to a **String** object in order to invoke one of its member methods.

Powerful tools like automatic type conversion need to be used carefully. It is important to know what happens when you convert from one type to another. For example, given the following declarations,

```
var booleanData = true;
var numericData = 3.14;
```

does the following comparison evaluate true or false?

```
numericData >= booleanData
```

Tables 3-3, 3-4, and 3-5 indicate the results of converting between types.

Type	Converted to Boolean
Undefined	false
Null	false
Number	false if 0 or NaN, else true
String	false if string length is 0, else true
Other object	true

Table 3-3. *Result of Conversion to a Boolean*

Two tools that are useful when dealing with mixed types are the **typeof** operator and the === relational operator. The **typeof** operator returns a string indicating the type of its argument. A list of values returned by **typeof** is given in Table 3-6. Note that arrays are really instances of the **Array** object, and, therefore, the **typeof** an array is **object**. The strict equality operator (===) evaluates true only if its two operands are equal and they have the same type. So, for example while

```
true == 1
```

evaluates true because of the primitive conversion rules, the following evaluates false:

```
true === 1
```

Type	Converted to Number
Undefined	NaN
Null	0
Boolean	1 if true, 0 if false
String	the numeric value of the string if it looks like a number, else NaN
Other object	NaN

Table 3-4. *Result of Conversion to a Number*

Type	Converted to a String
Undefined	"undefined"
Null	"null"
Boolean	"true" if true, "false" if false
Number	"NaN," "0," or the string representation of the numeric value
Other object	value of object's **toString()** method if it exists, else "undefined"

Table 3-5. *Result of Conversion to a String*

Type Conversion in the Real World

The reality of most programming tasks is that it is probably better to perform type conversion manually than trust the interpreter to do it for you. One situation when this is definitely the case is when processing user input. User input acquired through use of dialog boxes and HTML forms usually comes in strings. It is often necessary to explicitly convert such data between string and number types to prevent operators like **+** from carrying out the wrong operation (for example, concatenation instead of addition, or

Type	Result
Undefined	"undefined"
Null	"object"
Boolean	"boolean"
Number	"number"
String	"string"
Object	"object"
Function	"function"

Table 3-6. *The String typeof Returns when Called on Data of that Type*

vice versa). JavaScript provides several tools for carrying out explicit type conversion, for example, objects' **toString()** method and the **parseInt()** and **parseFloat()** methods of the **Global** object. These methods are discussed in-depth in later chapters as their applications become more apparent.

Summary

JavaScript provides five primitive data types: **number, string, boolean, undefined,** and **null**. Of the five, **undefined** and **null** are special types that are not used to store data. Support for complex types includes the composite types (objects and arrays) and functions. Arrays and functions are special kinds of objects. Each primitive type is associated with an object that provides methods useful for manipulating that kind of data. Functions are first-class data types, and primitive arguments are passed by value. Scoping for variables is static: if a variable is not found in the execution context in which it is referenced, the interpreter recursively searches enclosing contexts (as defined in the source code) for its value. Because JavaScript is weakly typed, automatic type conversion is performed whenever two unequal data types are operated upon. This feature is powerful but can also lead to ambiguities and subtle errors. Novice JavaScript programmers are always encouraged to define variables in a common place and to keep data types consistent across execution of their scripts. The next chapter discusses how to operate on data values in meaningful ways as well as how to alter program flow.

Chapter 4

Operators, Expressions, and Statements

This chapter provides an overview of the basic building blocks of every script: operators, expressions, and statements. We will take data types introduced in the last chapter and use them either directly as literals or within variables and combine them with simple operators, such as addition, subtraction, and so on, to create expressions. These expressions will in turn be used to form statements—the most basic unit of script execution. The execution of statements will be controlled using conditional logic and loops. For those readers new to programming, after reading this chapter simple scripts should start to make sense. For experienced programmers there should be no surprises in this chapter, because JavaScript is similar to so many other languages: assignment, **if**, **while**, **switch**, and so on are all here. Experienced programmers may only need to skim this chapter.

Statement Basics

A JavaScript program is made up of statements. For example, one of the most common statements is the *assignment*, which has already been seen many times up to this point. The statement here uses the keyword **var** that defines a variable along with the assignment operator to set values for the variables *x* and *y*.

```
var x = 5;
var y = 10;
```

Assignment uses the = operator and places the value on the right-hand side into the variable on the left. For example,

```
x = y + 10;
```

adds **10** to *y* and places the value in *x*, in this case **20**. One key issue with statements in a programming language is indicating how they are terminated and grouped, which will be discussed next.

Semicolons

A semicolon indicates the end of a JavaScript statement. For example, you can group multiple statements on one line by separating them with semicolons:

```
x = x + 1;   y = y + 1;   z = 0;
```

You can also include more complicated or even empty statements on one line:

```
x = x + 1; ;; if (x > 10) { x = 0; }; y = y - 1;
```

This example increments *x*, skips past two empty statements indicated by the semicolon by itself, sets *x* to zero if *x* is greater than **10**, and finally decrements *y*. As you can see, including multiple statements on one line is rather unwieldy and should be avoided.

Although semicolons generally follow statements, they can be omitted if your statements are separated by a line break. The following statements:

```
x = x + 1
y = y - 1
```

are treated the same as:

```
x = x + 1;
y = y - 1;
```

Of course, if you wish to include two statements on one line, a semicolon must be included to separate them:

```
x = x + 1; y = y - 1
```

The formal rules for implicit semicolon insertion are a bit more complex than the previous description would lead you to believe. In theory, tokens of a single statement can be separated by a line break without causing an error. For example, a script like

```
var x
= 5;
x =
x + 1;
alert (x);
```

will actually execute properly and display a value of **6**. However, if the tokens on a line without a semicolon comprise a complete JavaScript statement, a semicolon is inserted even if the next line could plausibly be treated as an extension of the first. This will cause the previous example to throw an error. The classic example is the **return** statement. Because the argument to **return** is optional, placing **return** and its argument on separate lines causes the **return** to execute without the argument. For example,

```
return
x
```

is treated as:

```
return;
x;
```

rather than what was probably intended:

```
return x;
```

For this reason, relying on implicit semicolon insertion is a bad idea and poor programming style to boot. It should be avoided unless you are positive you are aware of all the subtleties of JavaScript's rules for semicolon insertions.

Blocks

Curly braces, "{ }," are used to group a list of statements together. In some sense you can think of the braces as creating one large statement. For example, if more than one statement is to be executed as the result of a conditional or in a loop, the statements are similarly grouped:

```
if (x > 10)
{
    x = 0;
    y = 10;
}
```

One important issue for some programmers is the placement of the curly braces in a block relative to an associated statement. While correct alignment of blocks can certainly improve code readability, the slight differences between

```
if ( x > 10) {
  statements to execute
}
```

and

```
if (x > 10)
{
    statements to execute
}
```

is really more an issue of personal preference than anything else. We have chosen one form to work with in this book, but this is somewhat arbitrary and readers are of course welcome to change examples to fit their favorite formatting style as they type them in.

Statements regardless of their groupings or style generally need to modify data, which is often in the form of variables or literals (discussed in Chapter 3). These values are often combined using operators, which are discussed next.

Basic Operators

JavaScript supports a variety of operators. Some of the operators, like those for arithmetic operations and comparisons, are easy for just about anyone to understand, even those new to programming. Others, like the bitwise **AND** (**&**), increment (**++**), and if/else (**?:**) operators may be less obvious to those who have not programmed before. Fortunately for readers of all levels, JavaScript supports no operators that are unique to the language, and the language mimics C, C++, and Java very closely in its operator support.

Assignment Operator

Probably the most basic operator is the assignment operator (=) that is used to assign one value to another. Typically we use this operator to set a variable to a literal value, for example:

```
var bigPlanetName = "Jupiter";
var distanceFromSun = 483600000;
var visited = true;
```

Generally the assignment operator is used in a one-to-one fashion, but it is possible to perform multiple assignments at once by stringing together the = operator. For example, the statement

```
var x = y = z = 7;
```

sets all three variables to a value of **7**.

Assignments can also be used to set a variable to hold the result of an expression. For example, this script fragment demonstrates how variables can be set to the sum of two literal values as well as a combination of literals and variables:

```
var x = 12 + 5;    // x set to 17
var a, b = 3;
a = b + 2;         // a contains 5
```

A shorthand notation of the assignment operator allows us to combine it with simple arithmetic and bitwise operations (discussed in the section "Advanced Assignment Statements" later in this chapter).

Basic Arithmetic Operators

JavaScript supports all the basic arithmetic operators that readers should be familiar with, including addition (+), subtraction (-), multiplication (*), division (/), and lastly modulus (%), which may be more familiar to some as remainder. Table 4-1 details all these operators and presents examples of each.

> **Note**   *JavaScript itself doesn't directly support any mathematical operations other than the simple ones discussed here, but through the **Math** object there are more than enough methods available to accommodate even the most advanced mathematical calculations. The section entitled "Math" in Chapter 7 provides an overview of these features. Complete syntax can be found in Appendix B.*

Operator	Meaning	Example	Result

+	Addition	var x = 5, y = 7;
		var sum;
		sum = x+y;
			Variable sum contains 12.

-	Subtraction	var x = 5, y = 7;
		var diff1, diff2;
		diff1 = x-y;
		diff2 = y-x;
			Variable diff1 contains –2 while variable diff2 contains 2.

*	Multiplication	var x = 8, y = 4;
		var product;
		product = x*y;
			Variable product contains 32.

/	Division	var x = 36, y = 9, z = 5;
		var div1, div2;
		div1 = x / y;
		div2 = x / z;
			Variable div1 contains 4 while variable div2 contains 7.2.

%	Modulus (remainder)	var x = 24, y = 5, z = 6;
		var mod1, mod2;
		mod1 = x%y;
		mod2 = x%z;
			Variable mod1 contains 4 while variable mod2 contains 0.

Table 4-1.   *JavaScript Basic Arithmetic Operators*

String Concatenation Using +

The addition operator (+) has a different meaning when operating on string values rather than numbers. In its other role, the + operator is used to concatenate two strings together. The following,

```
document.write("JavaScript is " + "great.");
```

results in the string "JavaScript is great" being output to the document. We can use as many string concatenations as we like to form larger strings. Additionally, any combination of variables and literals may be used together, as the following example illustrates.

```
var bookTitle="The Time Machine";
var author="H.G. Wells";
var goodBook = bookTitle + " by " + author;
```

this results in the variable *goodBook* containing the complete string "The Time Machine by H.G. Wells."

One interesting aspect of the string concatenation operator is that it is the same as the addition operator. Given JavaScript's loose typing rules, you might get unexpected results when combining together variables of different types. In general, JavaScript will eventually convert everything to strings when a string value is encountered in conjunction with a + operator. For example,

```
var w = 5;
var x = 10;
var y = "I am string ";
var z = true;
alert(w+x+y+z);
```

displays the following dialog:

Note that because of operator precedence the initial addition precedes properly before the string concatenation is performed. You could force evaluation with appropriate application of parentheses. See the section "Operator Precedence" later in this chapter for a discussion of this issue.

*JavaScript supports a great number of other string operations, but most of these are part of the **String** object, which is discussed in Chapter 7.*

Negation

Another use of the - symbol besides subtraction is to negate a value. As in basic mathematics, placing a minus sign in front of a value will make positive values negative and negative values positive. In this form, it takes only a single value and thus is termed a *unary operator*. The basic use of the unary negation operator is simple as illustrated by these examples:

```
var x = -5;
x = -x;
// x now equals -5
```

Initially, we see the negation used to set the initial value of the variable *x* to negative five. The second application of the negation sets the variable to a positive five.

One important consideration when using this operator is the double application. For example,

```
var x;
x= --5;
```

will result in a value of **4** for *x* rather than a positive **5**, because the double negation is used to specify a decrement (discussed in the section "Increment and Decrement" later in this chapter). Using parentheses can force the negation properly. The script fragment

```
var x;
x=-(-5);
```

will set *x* to a value of **5** as expected.

Arithmetic Nuances

While the previous operators are very simple, there are situations where how they actually function under JavaScript should be understood.

- If any number except 0 is divided by 0, the result will be a value of **Infinity**.
  ```
  alert(5/0);  // displays the value Infinity
  ```
- If 0 is divided by 0, it will produce the value of **NaN** (Not a Number).
  ```
  alert(0/0);   // prints the value NaN
  ```

- Adding or multiplying extremely large numbers together may produce a value of **Infinity**. Conversely, subtracting extremely large numbers may result in a negative infinite value.

```
var reallybig = 1e400 * 1e400;
alert(reallybig);
```

- Once a value becomes **Infinity** or negative **Infinity**, it is not possible to return the value to a normal number. For example, if x contains an infinite value, subtracting 100,000,000 will not produce a regular number.

```
var x = (5/0);   // sets x to infinity
x = x - 100000000;
alert(x);
```

Note *Playing around with extremely large values can be very dangerous. First, what constitutes a value big enough to result in an infinite value may vary with JavaScript implementations. Second, playing with these values may produce errors. While writing this section, we found it was possible to throw exceptions and even crash JavaScript-aware browsers on occasion when playing with values in the extreme ranges.*

Bitwise Operators

JavaScript supports the entire range of bitwise operators that are used to manipulate bit strings. JavaScript will turn any number provided into a 32-bit integer and then into a bit string before performing a bitwise operation on it. As an example, if we were to perform a bitwise **AND** operation on 3 and 5, first the numbers would be converted to bit strings of 00000011 for 3 and 00000101 for 5. We then take the digits and perform an **AND** on them. The truth tables for **AND**, **OR**, and **XOR** (exclusive **OR**) operation on bits is shown in Table 4-2.

First Bit	Second Bit	AND Result	OR Result	XOR Result
0	0	0	0	0
0	1	0	1	1
1	0	0	1	1
1	1	1	1	0

Table 4-2.   *Truth Table for Bitwise Operations*

CORE LANGUAGE

So, given the results specified in Table 4-2, if we **AND** the two bit strings together we get the value shown here:

```
  00000011
& 00000101
  00000001
```

This bit value then converts back to a decimal value of 1. If you try

```
alert(5 & 3);
```

you will see the appropriate result shown here.

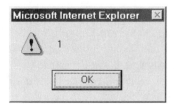

Table 4-3 shows the other operators, complete with the binary intermediary step.

Operator	Description	Example	Intermediate Step	Result
&	bitwise **AND**	3 & 5	00000011 & 00000101 = 00000001	1
|	bitwise **OR**	3 | 5	00000011 | 00000101 = 00000111	7
^	bitwise **XOR** (exclusive **OR**)	3 ^ 5	00000011 ^ 00000101 = 00000110	6
~	bitwise **NOT**	~3	Invert all bits in a number including the first bit which is the sign bit so given ~ 00000011 = 11111100 which is -4	-4

Table 4-3. *JavaScript Logical Bitwise Operators*

The bitwise **not** operator (~) can be a little confusing. Like the other bitwise operators, the **not** (~) converts its operand to a 32-bit binary number first. Next, it inverts the bit string, turning all zeros to ones and all ones to zeros. The result returned looks somewhat confusing if you are not familiar with binary representations of negative numbers. For example, ~**3** returns a value of **-4** while ~**(-3)** returns a value of **2**. An easy way to calculate the result manually is to add 1 to the given value and then flip the sign. This way of writing negative numbers is the *two's complement* representation and is the way most computers represent negative numbers.

Note *It is possible to use any valid number form with a bitwise operator. For example, given the hex value 0xFF that is equivalent to 255, performing a bitwise not (~0xFF) will return a value of –256.*

Bitwise Shift Operators

The bitwise shift operators are similar to the other bitwise operators in that the values operated on are first converted to 32-bit integers, then to their bit representation, then manipulated bitwise, and then converted back. However, rather than performing bitwise logical operations, the shift operators shift the digits in the bitstring in a certain direction and by a number of places, depending on the operator and second operand used.

Bitwise shift operators take two operands. The first is the number to be shifted, and the second specifies the number of bit positions by which the first operand is to be shifted. The direction of the shift operation is controlled by the operator used, << for left and >> for right shift. For example, given a left shift operation of 4 << 3 the number 4 (00000100) will be shifted left three places. Any digits shifted off the left side will be dropped, and the digits to the right will be replaced with zeros. Thus, the result is 00100000, which equals 32.

The various bitwise shift operators are presented in Table 4-4. The difference between the right shifts >> and >>> should be noted: the first operator preserves the sign in the bitstring by copying the left-most bit to the right while the second uses a zero fill, which would not preserve the sign. For non-negative numbers, the zero-fill right shift (>>>) and sign-propagating right shift (>>) actually yield the same result.

Given the high-level nature of JavaScript, the bitwise operators may seem a little out of place. However, they are required in order to use some advanced features such as the **Event** object bitmasks discussed in Chapter 11.

Advanced Assignment Statements

JavaScript contains a shorthand form of an assignment that combines the assignment with the various arithmetic and bitwise operations discussed in the preceding sections. Table 4-5 summarizes these quick assignment forms.

The following section will describe a form of assignment, even more concise than the operators presented here, for use when adding or subtracting one.

Operator	Description	Example	Intermediate Step	Result
<<	Shift Left	4 << 3	00000100 shift to left 3 spots and fill with zeros results in 00100000	32
>>	Shift Right with Sign	-9 >> 2	11110111 shift to the right and copy left-most bit gives 11111110	-3
>>>	Shift Right Zero Fill	32 >>> 3	00100000 shift right 3 spots and fill with zero results in 00000100	4

Table 4-4.   *Bitwise Shift Operators in JavaScript*

Shorthand Assignment	Expanded Meaning	Example

x += y	x = x + y	var x = 5;
		x += 7;
		// x is now 12

x -= y	x = x – y	var x = 5;
		x -= 7;
		// x is now -2

x *= y	x = x * y	var x = 5;
		x *= 7;
		// x is now 35

x /= y	x = x / y	var x = 5;
		x /= 2;
		// x is now 2.5

x %= y	x = x % y	var x = 5;
		x %= 4;
		// x is now 1

Table 4-4.   *JavaScript's Shorthand Assignment Operators*

Shorthand Assignment	Expanded Meaning	Example

x &= y	x = x & y	var x = 5;
		x &= 2;
		// x is now 0

x | = y	x = x | y	var x = 5;
		x | = 2;
		// x is now 7

x ^= y	x = x ^ y	var x = 5;
		x ^= 3;
		// x is now 6

x <<= y	x = x << y	var x = 5;
		x <<= 2;
		// x is now 20

x >>= y	x = x >> y	var x = -5;
		x >>= 2;
		// x is now -2

x >>>= y	x = x >>> y	var x = 5;
		x >>>= 2;
		// x is now 1

Table 4-5.   *JavaScript's Shorthand Assignment Operators* (continued)

CORE LANGUAGE

Increment and Decrement

The **++** operator is used to *increment*—or, simply put, to add 1—to a single operand. For example, with

```
var x=3;
x++;
```

the value of *x* is set to **4**. Of course you could also write the increment portion of the previous example as

```
x=x+1;
```

Similar to the **++** operator is the **--** operator, the *decrement*, which would subtract 1 from a single operand. So,

```
var x=3;
x--;
```

leaves a value of **2** in the variable *x*. Similar to the increment, the decrement could of course be written as:

```
x=x-1;
```

While adding or subtracting 1 from a variable may not seem terribly useful to those readers new to programming, these operators are very important and are found at the heart of looping structures, which are discussed later in this chapter.

Post- and Pre-Increment/Decrement

A subtle nuance of the increment (**++**) and decrement (**--**) is the position of the operator in relation to the operand. When the increment operator appears on the left of the operand, it is termed a *pre-increment*, while if it appears on the right it is a *post-increment*. The importance of the position of the operator is best illustrated by an example. Consider this script:

```
var x=3;
x++;
```

and this one:

```
var x=3;
++x;
```

Both eventually result in a value of **4** in the variable *x*. The question is, when does the increment happen? Given the script

```
var x=3;
alert(x++);
```

you will see:

However, the value of the variable x will be **4**. When given the script

```
var x=3;
alert(++x);
```

the result is more as expected:

And of course the variable x will contain **4** upon conclusion. This example illustrates the subtle differences that can arise simply by when the increment or decrement happens.

 It is not possible to combine post- and pre-increment/decrement syntax together. For example, ++x++ will result in an error rather than adding 2 to the value of x. You should also avoid using post- and pre-increment/decrement more than one time on the same variable in a single expression. Doing so can result in unpredictable behavior.

Comparison Operators

Comparison operators are used to evaluate expressions in order to determine if they are **true** or **false**. Most of JavaScript's comparison operators should be familiar from elementary mathematics or from other programming languages. These operators are summarized in Table 4-6.

A few of these operators warrant further discussion, particularly the equality operators. Consider the common mistake of using a single equal sign (=), which specifies an assignment, rather than a double equal sign (==), which specifies the equality comparison. The following example illustrates this problem in action.

```
var x = 1;
var y = 5;
if (x = y)
 alert("Values are the same");
else
 alert("Values are different");
```

Operator	Meaning	Example	Evaluates
<	Less than	4 < 8	True
<=	Less than or equal to	6 <= 5	False
>	Greater than	4 > 3	True
>=	Greater than or equal to	5 >= 5	True
!=	Not equal to	6 != 5	True
==	Equal to	6 == 5	False
===	Equal to (same type)	5 === '5'	False
!==	Not equal to (same type)	5 !== '5'	True

Table 4-6. *Basic JavaScript Comparison Operators*

In this situation, regardless of the values of the variables, the result will always show that the values are the same.

Even more interesting is the situation of values that do not appear the same but compare as such. For example,

```
alert(5 == "5");
```

returns a **true** value because of JavaScript's type conversion:

Strict equality is handled using the identity operator (===), as shown here. The script

```
alert(5 === "5");
```

displays **false** as expected:

 **Note**   *Identity operators === and !== are not available in Netscape 3 and earlier browsers, though they are available in JavaScript 1.3 and beyond.*

Logical Operators

The various comparison operators described in the previous section result in Boolean values, and the logical operators **&& (AND)**, **|| (OR)**, and **! (NOT)** are useful to combine such values together. A description and example of each logical operator are shown in Table 4-7.

The most common use of the logical operators is when controlling script flow using an **if** statement (see the section "if Statements" later in this chapter for use of logical operators within an **if** statement). The conditional operator (**?:**) discussed next is similar to the **if** statement and can be used to handle simple situations with logical operators.

Operator	Description	Example

&&	Returns true if both logical expressions are true; otherwise returns false.	var x=true, y=false;
		alert(x && y);
		// displays false

||	Returns true if either logical expression is true. If both are false, returns false.	var x=true, y=false;
		alert(x || y);
		// displays true

!	If its single operand is true, returns false; otherwise returns true.	var x=true;
		alert(!x);
		// displays false

Table 4-5.   *JavaScript's Logical Operators*

?: Operator

The **?:** operator is used to create a quick conditional branch. The basic syntax for this operator is

```
(expression) ? true-statement : false-statement;
```

where *expression* is any expression that will evaluate eventually to **true** or **false**, with *true-statement* getting executed if the expression on the left results in **true**, and *false-statement* being run if the expression evaluates **false**. In this example,

```
(x > 5) ? alert("x is greater than 5") : alert("x is less than 5");
```

an alert dialog will be displayed based upon the value of the variable *x*. Contextually, if the conditional expression evaluates **true**, the first statement indicating the value is greater than 5 is displayed; if **false**, the second statement stating the opposite will be displayed.

At first blush, the **?:** operator seems to be simply a shorthand notation for an **if** statement. In fact the previous example could be rewritten in the more readable but less compact **if** style syntax, as shown here:

```
if (x > 5)
  alert("x is greater than 5");
```

```
else
  alert("x is less than 5");
```

Unfortunately, there really isn't such a simple relationship between the two conditional forms. The biggest difference is that the **?:** operator allows only a single statement for the true and false conditions. Thus,

```
( x > 5 ) ? alert("Watch out"); alert("This doesn't work")   :
alert("Error!");
```

doesn't work. In fact, because the **?:** operator is used to form a single statement, the inclusion of the ; anywhere within the expression terminates the statement, and it may ruin it as shown here:

```
( x > 5 ) ? alert("Watch out for the semi-colon! "); : alert("The
last part will throw an error");
```

The use of statement blocks as defined by the { } characters will not improve the situation any either. The code

```
( x > 5 ) ? {alert("using blocks"); alert("doesn't work");} :
{alert("error! "); alert("error!");};
```

will throw errors as well.

Given that the **?:** operator is limited to such single conditional statements and isn't a replacement for the **if** statement, it still can be a useful addition to a JavaScripter's arsenal, as it provides very compact notation. For example, many programmers use it when setting conditional variables indicating browser or object support. Consider this common script:

```
var rolloverallowed;
(document.images) ? rolloverallowed = true : rolloverallowed = false;
```

This compact script sets the variable *rolloverallowed* to **true** or **false** depending on the existence of the **Images[]array** object. For readability you still may prefer **if** statements, but the terseness of this operator does make it useful in larger DHTML-oriented scripts that need to perform a great deal of simple conditional checks.

Comma Operator

The comma operator (,) allows multiple statements to be strung together and executed as one statement. The only value returned for statements strung together with commas is the right-most one. For example, in this assignment, the final assignment will return the value **56** as a side effect; thus, the variable *a* is set to this value:

```
var a,b,c,d;
a = (b='5', c='7', d='56');document.write('a = '+a+' b = '+b+' c = '+c+' d = ' + d);
```

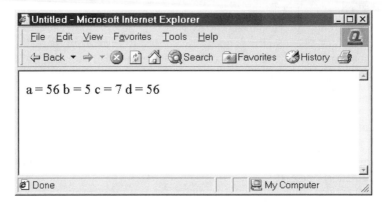

In general commas are rarely used in JavaScript except when separating parameters in method and function calls, as shown here:

```
document.write('Today is sunny.', 'Yes it is.');
myFiddle(5,6,x);
```

Occasionally, commas might also be used in complex looping expressions, as shown here:

```
for (count1 = 1, count2=4; ((count1 + count2) < 10); count1++, count2++)
    document.write("Count1= "+ count1+ " Count2 = "+count2+"<br>");
```

However, the use of the comma operator is really not suggested.

void Operator

The **void** operator specifies an expression to be evaluated without returning a value. For example, take the previous example with the comma operator and void it out:

```
var a,b,c,d;
a = void (b='5', c='7', d='56');
document.write('a = '+a+' b = '+b+' c = '+c+' d = ' + d);
```

In this case the value of *a* will be undefined as shown here:

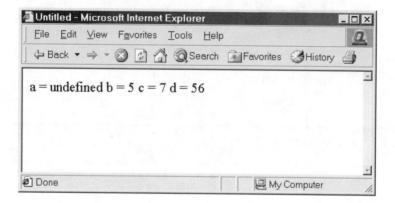

The most common use of the **void** operator is when using the **javascript:** pseudo-URL in conjunction with an HTML event handler attribute, such as **onclick**. Some browsers, notably early versions of Netscape, had problems when script was used in links and threw errors or tried to load another page. To avoid these problems and force a link click to do nothing when scripting is on, use **void** as shown here:

```
<a href="javascript:void (alert('hi!'))">Click me!</a>
```

typeof

The **typeof** operator is used to determine the type of a particular value. The operator returns a string indicating the particular type of the passed expression or variable. The script fragment here shows the basic use of the operator:

```
a = 3;
name = "Howard";
alert(typeof a);        // displays number
alert(typeof name);     // displays string
```

Table 4-8 shows the values returned by **typeof** on the basis of the type of value it is presented.

Type	String Returned by typeof
Boolean	"boolean"
Number	"number"
String	"string"
Object	"object"
Function	"function"
Undefined	"undefined"
Null	"object"

Table 4-6.   *Return Values for* **typeof** *Operator*

The last set of operators to discuss before moving on to statements are the various object operators.

Object Operators

This section provides a very brief overview of various JavaScript object operators. A more complete discussion can be found in Chapter 6. For now, recall from Chapter 3 that an object is a composite data type that contains any number of properties and methods. Each property has a name and a value. The period (.) operator is used to access the various properties of an object; for example,

```
document.lastModified
```

references the **lastModified** property of the **document** object, which contains the date that an HTML document was last modified.

Objects can also be accessed using array bracket operators [ ], as object properties are stored as an associative array. For example,

```
document["lastModified"]
```

is the same as

```
document.lastModified
```

Most often, though, the array operators [ ] will be used to access the elements of arrays. For example, here we define an array called *myArray*:

```
var myArray = [2,4,8,10];
```

To display the individual elements of the array starting from the first position (0), we would use a series of statements like:

```
alert(myArray[0]);
alert(myArray[1]);
alert(myArray[2]);
alert(myArray[3]);
```

In the last example we directly created an **Array** object. We could have also used the **new** operator to do so. For example,

```
var myArray = new Array(2,4,8,10);
```

The **new** operator is used to create an object. It can be used both to create user-defined objects as well as to create instances of built-in objects. For example, consider the following script, which creates a new instance of the **Date** object and places it in the variable *today*.

```
var today = new Date();
alert(today);
```

The result is shown here:

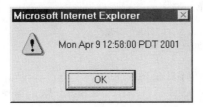

A **new** operator is used in conjunction with a constructor; in this case we used a predefined constructor for the **Date** object. However, as will be discussed in Chapter 6, custom constructors can also be defined.

Given that objects can be created, it could be assumed they could be destroyed. While the **delete** operator doesn't exactly do that, it can be used to remove an object's property. In reality, **delete** is primarily seen in JavaScript when deleting array elements. The following script illustrates its use for this purpose:

```
var myArray = ['1', '3', '78', '1767'];
document.write("myArray before delete = "+myArray);
document.write("<br>");
delete myArray[2];
// deletes third item since index starts at 0
document.write("myArray after delete = "+myArray);
```

Notice here that the third item, "78," is deleted from the array when using the **delete** operation.

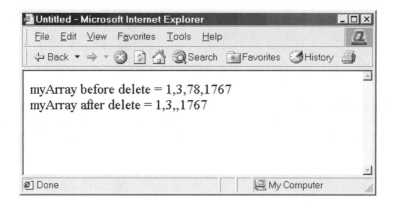

The last operator that is associated with objects is the parentheses "( )". This operator is often used to invoke an object's method. For example, we have already seen the **Document** object's **write()** method:

```
document.write("Hello from JavaScript");
```

In this case we pass a single parameter a string, "Hello from JavaScript," to the **write** method so that it is printed to the HTML document. In general, we can invoke arbitrary object methods as follows:

```
objectname.methodname(optional parameters)
```

We can invoke user-defined functions in a similar manner. For example,

```
mySwap(x,y)
```

would invoke a function called *mySwap*, passing it the values of the variables *x* and *y*.

Operator Precedence

All JavaScript expressions containing the previously discussed operators are evaluated in a predefined order of precedence. This feature is particularly obvious with arithmetic operators and is similar to the evaluation of equations in algebra, where multiplication and division have higher precedence over addition and subtraction. For example, the result of

```
alert(2 + 3 * 2);
```

will be **8** rather than **10**. The reason is that multiplication has higher precedence than addition, so in effect it happens first. Using parentheses **( )** we can group expressions and force their evaluation. For example,

```
alert((2 + 3) * 2);
```

will display **10** rather than **8**.

Of course, operator precedence is not limited to such simple cases. For example, consider the following combination of addition and string concatenation operations:

```
alert(5+6+"Hello");
```

The result will be the string "11Hello" rather than "56Hello." Even though the two instances of + would appear to have the same power, the left to right associativity of the operator results in the first part of the expression being evaluated first. The precedence and associativity of the various operators in JavaScript is presented in Table 4-9.

Precedence	Associativity	Operator	Operator Meaning
Highest	Left to Right	.	Object property access
	Left to Right	[ ]	Array access
	Left to Right	( )	Grouping or function or method call
	Right to Left	++	Increment

Table 4-7. *Precedence and Associativity of JavaScript Operators*

Precedence	Associativity	Operator	Operator Meaning
	Right to Left	--	Decrement
	Right to Left	-	Negation
	Right to Left	~	Bitwise NOT
	Right to Left	!	Logical NOT
	Right to Left	delete	Remove object property or array value
	Right to Left	new	Create object
	Right to Left	typeof	Determine type
	Right to Left	void	Suppress expression evaluation
	Left to Right	*,/,%	Multiplication, Division, Modulus
	Left to Right	+,-	Addition, Subtraction
	Left to Right	+	String Concatenation
	Left to Right	<<	Bitwise left-shift
	Left to Right	>>	Bitwise right-shift with sign
	Left to Right	>>>	Bitwise right-shift with zero fill
	Left to Right	<, <=	Less than, less than or equal to
	Left to Right	>, >=	Greater than, greater than or equal to
	Left to Right	==	Equality
	Left to Right	!=	Inequality
	Left to Right	===	Equality with type checking (Identity)
	Left to Right	!==	Inequality with type checking (Non-identity)

Table 4-9. *Precedence and Associativity of JavaScript Operators* (continued)

Precedence	Associativity	Operator	Operator Meaning
	Left to Right	&	Bitwise AND
	Left to Right	^	Bitwise XOR
	Left to Right	|	Bitwise OR
	Left to Right	&&	Logical AND
	Left to Right	||	Logical OR
	Right to Left	? :	Conditional
	Right to Left	=	Assignment
	Right to Left	*=, /=, %=, +=, -=, <<=, >>=, >>>=, &=, ^=, |=	Assignment in conjunction with preceding operator
Lowest	Left to Right	,	Multiple evaluation

Table 4-9. *Precedence and Associativity of JavaScript Operators* (continued)

Based on this discussion of operator precedence, you might assume that using parentheses could force the evaluation of all the operators discussed so far. However, this isn't always the case. For example, consider the post- and pre-increment/decrement operators. As we saw earlier, the results of

```
var x=3;
alert(++x);
```

and

```
var x=3;
alert(x++);
```

alert a different value because of the difference in when the incrementing happens in relation to the display of the alert dialog. However, if you add parentheses and try to force the incrementing to always happen before the alert is displayed, as shown here,

```
var x=3;
alert((x++));
alert((++x));
```

you won't see any difference. From this example we should at least not underestimate the subtleties of associativity and operator precedence. Now that we have covered all the various operators in JavaScript, it is time to combine these together to create simple statements.

Core JavaScript Statements

JavaScript supports a core set of statements that should be familiar to anyone who has programmed in a modern programming language. These include flow control (**if-else, switch**), loops (**while, do-while, for**), and loop control (**break** and **continue**). JavaScript also supports some object-related statements (**with, for-in**). Readers already familiar with such statements may want to skim this section, focusing only on the more esoteric aspects (particularly the short-circuit evaluation of **if** statements, the differences in **switch** support among versions of JavaScript, endless loop problems and Web browsers, and the use of **break** and **continue** with labels).

if Statements

The **if** statement is JavaScript's basic decision-making control statement. The basic syntax of the **if** statement is

```
if (expression)
   statement;
```

In this case, *expression* is evaluated, and, if the condition is true, the *statement* is executed. Otherwise it moves on to the next statement. For example, given the script fragment here:

```
var x = 5;
if (x > 1)
   alert("X is greater than 1");
alert("moving on ...");
```

the expression evaluates to **true** and prints and displays the message "X is greater than 1" and then displays the second alert dialog afterwards. However, if the value of variable *x* were something like zero, the expression would evaluate to **false**, resulting in skipping the first alert and immediately displaying the second one.

To execute multiple statements with an **if** statement, a block could be used, as shown here:

```
var x = 5;
if (x > 1)
  {
  alert("x is greater than 1.");
  alert("Yes x really is greater than 1.");
  }
alert("moving on ...");
```

Additional logic can be applied with an **else** statement. When the condition of the first statement is not met, the code after the **else** statement will be executed:

```
if (expression)
   statement or block
else
   statement or block
```

Given this syntax, we could expand the previous example as follows:

```
var x = 5;
if (x > 1)
  {
  alert("x is greater than 1.");
  alert("Yes x really is greater than 1.");
  }
else
  {
  alert("x is less than 1.");
  alert("This example is getting old.");
  }

alert("moving on ...");
```

More advanced logic can be added with a combination of **else** and **if** statements; for example:

```
if (expression)
    statement or block
```

```
else if (expression)
    statement or block
else
    statement or block
```

This simple example illustrates how **if** statements might be chained together:

```
var numbertype, x=6;
// substitute x values with -5, 0, and 'test'
if (x < 0)
  {
    numbertype="negative";
    alert("Negative number");
  }
else if (x > 0)
  {
    numbertype="positive";
    alert("Positive number");
  }
else if (x == 0)
  {
    numbertype="zero";
    alert("It's zero.");
  }
else
    alert("Error! It's not a number");
```

As you can see, it is pretty easy to get carried away with complex **if-else** statements. The **switch** statement discussed shortly is a potential alternative to such syntax. However, before moving on we should illustrate a subtlety with the logical expressions used within **if** statements.

Short-Circuit Evaluation

Like many languages, JavaScript may "short circuit" the evaluation of a logical AND (**&&**) or logical OR (**||**) expression. For example, if the first expression of an || operation is **true**, there really is no point in evaluating the rest of the expression, since the expression will completely evaluate to **true** regardless of the other value. Conversely, if the first expression of an **&&** operation evaluates to **false**, there really is no need to continue evaluation since the entire statement will always be **false**. The script here demonstrates the flow of a short-circuit evaluation.

```
document.write("<pre>");
document.writeln("No short circuit evaluation\n");

var age = 31;
if ((document.writeln(" Left expression evaluates"),
    (age >= 13)) &&
    (document.writeln(" Right expression evaluates"),
      (age <= 19)))
   document.writeln("Result: You are a teenager.");
else
  document.writeln("Result: You are not a teenager.");

document.writeln("\n");
document.writeln("With short circuit evaluation\n");

var age = 31;
if ((document.writeln(" Left expression evaluates"),
    (age <= 19)) &&
    (document.writeln(" Right expression evaluates"),
        (age >= 13)))
  document.writeln("Result: You are a teenager.");
else
  document.writeln("Result: You are not a teenager.");
document.write("</pre>");
```

The results of the script are shown in Figure 4-1. Notice how the second part of the script executes only the left half of the logical expression.

Most of the time the subtlety of short-circuit evaluation of logical expressions will not matter to a programmer. However, if the evaluation produces the side effect of modifying a value as well as evaluating to a **true** or **false** value, a subtle error may result because of the short circuit.

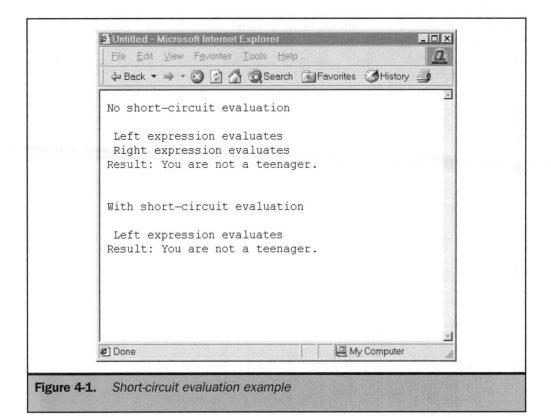

Figure 4-1. *Short-circuit evaluation example*

switch

Starting with JavaScript 1.2, you could use a **switch** statement rather than relying solely on **if** statements for selection. The basic syntax of the **switch** statement is to define an expression to check various cases one by one until a match is found. If nothing matches, a **default** condition will be used. Also **break** statements are typically used to control the execution of the cases. The basic syntax is shown here:

```
switch (expression)
{
  case condition 1: statement(s)
                    break;
  case condition 2: statement(s)
                    break;
  ...
  case condition n: statement(s)
```

```
                    break;
   default: statement(s)
}
```

Consider the following example, which shows how a **switch** statement might be used:

```
var yourGrade='A';
switch (yourGrade)
{
  case 'A': alert("Good job.");
            break;
  case 'B': alert("Pretty good.");
            break;
  case 'C': alert("You passed!");
            break;
  case 'D': alert("Not so good.");
            break;
  case 'F': alert("Back to the books.");
            break;
  default: alert("Grade Error!");
}
```

You could certainly imitate this idea with **if** statements, but consider that the previous case would look something like

```
if (yourGrade == 'A')
 alert("Good job.");
else if (yourGrade == 'B')
  alert("Pretty good.");
else if (yourGrade == 'C')
  alert("You passed!");
else if (yourGrade == 'D')
  alert("Not so good.");
else if (yourGrade == 'F')
  alert("Back to the books.");
else
  alert("Grade error!");
```

Obviously when using numerous **if** statements things can get messy very quickly.

There are a few issues to understand with **switch** statements. First, it is not necessary to use curly braces to create blocks within cases to execute multiple statements. Consider the following example, which demonstrates this:

```javascript
var yourGrade='C';
var deansList = false;
var academicProbation = false;
switch (yourGrade)
{
  case 'A': alert("Good job.");
            deansList = true;
            break;
  case 'B': alert("Pretty good.");
            deansList = true;
            break;
  case 'C': alert("You passed!");
            deansList = false;
            break;
  case 'D': alert("Not so good.");
            deansList = false;
            academicProbation = true;
            break;
  case 'F': alert("Back to the books.");
            deansList = false;
            academicProbation = true;
            break;
  default: alert("Grade Error!");
}
```

The next aspect of **switch** to consider is the fall-through action that may occur. Depending on how you use the **case** statements, it is possible to create multiple situations that match and produce the same result. Consider a rewrite of the previous example that performs similar actions if the grade is "A" or "B" as well as "D" or "F":

```javascript
var yourGrade='B';
var deansList = false;
var academicProbation = false;

switch (yourGrade)
{
  case 'A':
  case 'B': alert("Pretty good.");
```

```
                 deansList = true;
                 break;
  case 'C': alert("You passed!");
                 deansList = false;
                 break;
  case 'D':
  case 'F': alert("Back to the books.");
                 deansList = false;
                 academicProbation = true;
                 break;
  default: alert("Grade Error!");
}
```

The last detail to discuss in relation to **switch** is the use of the **break** statement. Basically, the **break** statement will exit the **switch** statement, finding the nearest enclosing curly brace. We will see the **break** statement again with more detail once we take a look at loops, which are discussed next.

while Loops

Loops are used to perform some action over and over again. The most basic loop in JavaScript is the **while** loop, whose syntax is shown here:

```
while (expression)
    statement or block of statements to execute
```

The purpose of a **while** loop is to execute a statement or code block over and over as long as the expression is **true**. Once the expression becomes **false** or a **break** statement is encountered, the loop will be exited. This script illustrates a basic **while** loop:

```
var count = 0;
while (count < 10)
  {
  document.write(count+"<br>");
  count++;
  }
document.write("Loop done!");
```

In this situation, the value of *count* is initially zero, then the loop enters, the value of *count* is output, and the value is increased. Once *count* reaches 10, the loop exits and executes the statement following the loop body. The output of the loop is shown here:

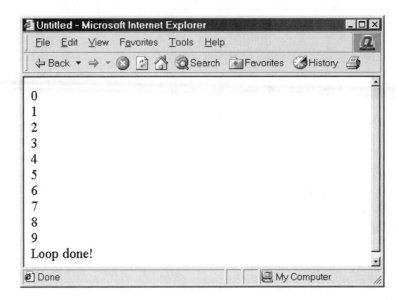

The initialization, loop iteration, and expression can be set up in a variety of ways. Consider this loop that counts downwards from 100 in steps of 10 or more:

```
var count = 100;
while (count > 10)
{
   document.write(count+"<br>");
   if (count == 50)
     count = count - 20;
   else
     count = count - 10;
}
```

One issue with **while** loops is that, depending on the loop test expression, the loop may never actually execute.

```
var count = 0;
while (count > 0)
{
   // do some statements
}
```

Lastly, an important consideration with any loop—a **while** loop or one of the ones discussed in the next sections—is to make sure that the loop eventually terminates. If, for example, we had a slightly different piece of code, we might notice there is no way for the loop to end. The reason is that the expression never becomes **false** since the count becomes smaller and smaller.

```
var count = 0;
while (count < 10)
 {
  document.write("Counting down forever: " + count +"<br>");
  count--;
 }
document.write("Never reached!");
```

In some JavaScript implementations such as Netscape 2 a buggy script like this might actually lock the browser. Today's browsers should respond with one of the messages shown in Figure 4-2, but don't count on it.

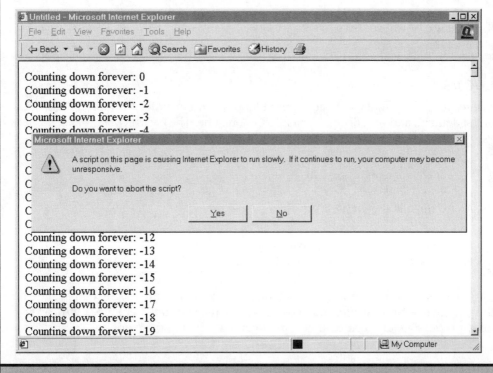

Figure 4-2.   *Modern browsers try to deal with nonterminating scripts*

CORE LANGUAGE

do-while Loops

The **do-while** loop is similar to the **while** loop except that the condition check happens at the end of the loop, meaning that the loop will always be executed at least once unless some **break** is encountered first. The basic syntax of the loop is

```
do
{
statement(s);
}
while (expression);
```

Note the semicolon used at the end of the **do-while** loop.

The example here shows the previous **while** loop counting example rewritten in the form of a **do-while** loop.

```
var count = 0;
do
{
  document.write("Number " + count + "<br>");
  count = count + 1;
} while (count < 10);
```

for Loops

The **for** loop is the most compact form of looping and includes the loop initialization, test statement, and iteration statement all in one line. The basic syntax is

```
for (initialization; test condition; iteration statement)
  looped statement or block
```

An example is shown here:

```
for (var i = 0; i < 10; i++)
  document.write ("Loop " + i + "<br>");
```

The result of this loop would be identical to the first **while** loop example shown in the previous section. As with the **while** loop, by using a statement block with a **for** loop it is possible to execute numerous statements during the loop.

```
document.write("Start the countdown<br>");
for (var i=10; i >= 0; i--)
{
    document.write("<b>"+i+"…</b>");
    document.write("<br>");
}
document.write("Blastoff!");
```

A common problem when using a **for** loop is the accidental placement of the semicolon. For example,

```
for (var i = 0; i< 10; i++);
{
   document.write("value of i="+i+"<br>");
}
document.write("Loop done");
```

will print an output showing what appears to be a single execution of the loop as well as the statement that the loop has finished.

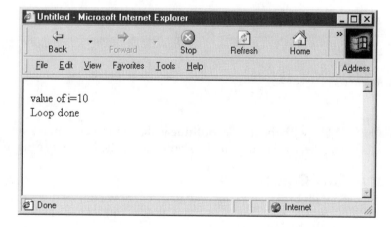

The reason for this is that the semicolon acts as an empty statement for the body of the loop and the block is just executed as normal.

Loop Control with continue and break

The **break** and **continue** statements can be used to control the execution of a loop. The **break** statement, which was briefly introduced with the **switch** statement, is used to exit a loop early, breaking out of the enclosing curly braces. The example here illustrates its use with a **while** loop. Notice how the loop breaks out early once *x* reaches 8:

```
var x = 1;
while (x < 20)
{
   if (x == 8)
      break;  // breaks out of loop completely
   x = x + 1;
   document.write(x+"<br>");
}
```

The **continue** statement, as its name implies, indicates that a loop should continue on. When it's encountered, program flow will move to the loop check expression immediately. The example presented here shows how the **continue** statement is used to skip printing when the index held in variable *x* reaches 8:

```
var x = 1;
while (x < 20)
{
   x = x+1;
   if (x == 8)
     continue;
     // continues loop at 8 without print
   document.write(x+"<br>");
}
```

A potential problem with the use of **continue** is that you have to make sure that iteration still occurs, otherwise it may inadvertently cause the loop to execute endlessly.

Labels and Flow Control

A label can be used with **break** and **continue** to direct flow control more precisely. A label is simply an identifier followed by a colon that is applied to a statement or block of code. The script here shows an example:

```
outerloop:
for (var i = 0; i < 3; i++)
{
```

```
      document.write("Outerloop: "+i+"<br>");
      for (var j = 0; j < 5; j++)
        {
          if (j == 3)
            break outerloop;
          document.write("Innerloop: "+j+"<br>");
        }
  }
  document.write("All loops done"+"<br>");
```

Notice that the outermost loop is labeled "outerloop," and the **break** statement is set to break all the way out of the enclosing loops. Figure 4-3 shows the dramatic difference between the execution of the loop with and without the label.

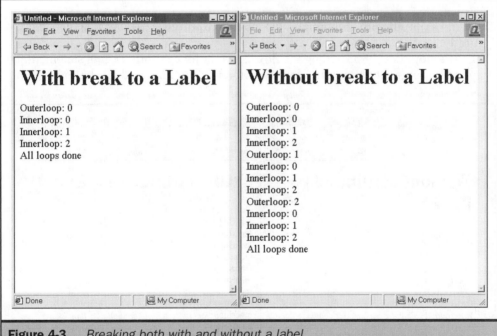

Figure 4-3. *Breaking both with and without a label*

A label can also be used with a **continue** statement. The **continue** statement will cause flow control to resume at the loop indicated by the label. The following example illustrates the use of labels in conjunction with **continue**:

```
outerloop:
for (var i = 0; i < 3; i++)
{
      document.write("Outerloop: "+i+"<br>");
      for (var j = 0; j < 5; j++)
        {
           if (j == 3)
              continue outerloop;
           document.write("Innerloop: "+j+"<br>");
        }
}
document.write("All loops done"+"<br>");
```

The script's output with and without the labeled **continue** statement is shown in Figure 4-4.

Labels stop short of providing the flow control of the notorious **goto** statement, despised by some programmers. However, don't be too surprised if eventually such

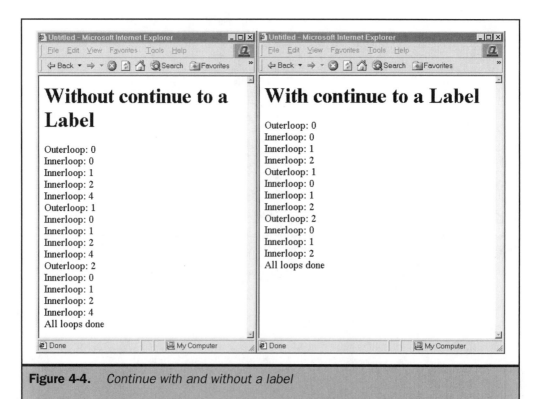

Figure 4-4.   *Continue with and without a label*

a statement is introduced into JavaScript, especially considering that it is already a reserved word (see Appendix C).

Object-Related Statements

The final group of statements to cover is related to the use of both built-in and user-defined objects in JavaScript. A brief introduction to these statements is presented here, while a full-blown discussion of the use of these statements as well as of keywords such as **this** is reserved for Chapters 6 and 7.

with Statement

JavaScript's **with** statement allows programmers to use a shorthand notation when referencing objects. For example, normally to write to an HTML document we would use the **write()** method of the **Document** object:

```
document.write("Hello from JavaScript");
document.write("<br>");
document.write("You can write what you like here");
```

Using a **with** statement we could shorten the reference to the object, as shown here

```
with (document)
{
 write("Hello from JavaScript");
 write("<br>");
 write("You can write what you like here");
}
```

The general syntax of the **with** statement is

```
with (object)
{
   statement(s);
}
```

The **with** statement is certainly a convenience as it avoids having to type the same object names over and over again. However, it can occasionally lead to trouble because you may accidentally reference other methods and properties when inside a **with** statement block.

CORE LANGUAGE

Object Loops Using for...in

Another object-related statement is **for...in**, which is used to loop through the various properties of an object. The basic syntax is

```
for (variablename in object)
   statement or block to execute
```

Consider the following example that prints out the various properties of a Web browser's **Navigator** object.

```
var aProperty;
document.write("<h1>Navigator Object Properties</h1>");
for (aProperty in navigator)
{
  document.write(aProperty);
  document.write("<br>");
}
```

The result when this example is run within Internet Explorer 5 is shown in Figure 4-5.

You might be asking: where did this **Navigator** object come from? Once again, an explanation will be found in the full discussion of objects beginning with Chapter 6, where we will also revisit the **for...in** statement.

Other Statements?

There are actually other statements we might cover, such as error handling statements (for example, **try...catch** and **throw**) and statements that are part of some implementations of JavaScript (for example, Netscape's **import** and **export** statements). We won't talk about these here because they require sophisticated examples or are not part of every version of JavaScript. However, including these more advanced features, the only core statements we have not discussed are related to functions, so let's move on and combine the various core statements we have learned so far into these reusable units of code.

Summary

The last chapter presented data types as the core of the language. This chapter showed how data types could be combined using operators to form expressions. JavaScript supports operators familiar to most programmers, including mathematical (+, -, *, %), bitwise (&, |, ^, <<, >>, >>>), comparison (<, >, ==, ===, !=, >=, <=), assignment (=, +=, -=, *=, /=, %=, <<=, >>=, >>>=, &=, |=, ^=), and logical (&&, ||, !). It also supports less common operators like the conditional operator and string concatenation operator (+).

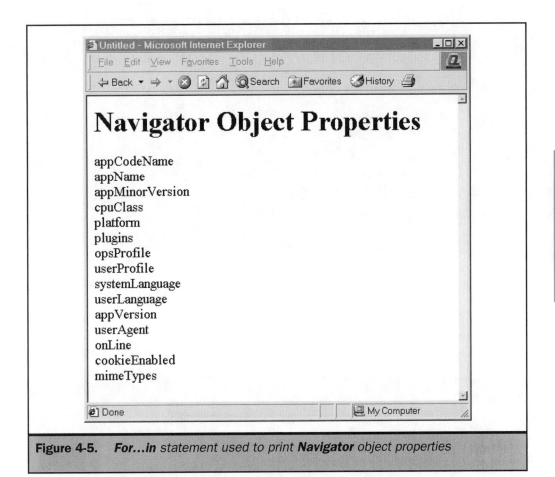

Figure 4-5. *For...in* statement used to print *Navigator* object properties

JavaScript operators are combined with variables and data literals to form expressions. Expressions must be carefully formed to respect precedence of evaluation, and liberal application of parentheses will help avoid any problems. Statements can then be formed from expressions to make up the individual steps of a program. Individual statements are indicated in JavaScript using a semicolon or a return character. Semicolons should always be used to avoid ambiguity and improve script safety. The most common statements are assignment statements, functions, and method calls. These perform the basic tasks of most JavaScripts. Control statements such as **if** and **switch** can alter program flow. A variety of loops can be formed using **while**, **for**, or **do/while** to iterate through code. Further program flow control can be achieved with **break** and **continue**. As larger scripts are built using the constructs presented in this chapter, repetitive code is often introduced. To eliminate redundancy and create more modular programs, functions—the topic of the next chapter—should be employed.

The
Complete
Reference

JavaScript

Chapter 5

Functions

avaScript functions can be used to create script fragments that can be used over and over again. When written properly, functions are *abstract*—they can be used in many situations and are ideally completely self-contained, with data passing in and out through well-defined interfaces. JavaScript allows for the creation of such functions, but many developers avoid writing code in such a fashion and rely instead on global variables and side effects to accomplish their tasks— certainly not the best use of functions. In reality, JavaScript supports all the features necessary to write modular code and even supports some advanced features, such as variable parameter lists. This chapter will present the basics of functions, and the next two chapters will discuss how, underneath it all, the real power of JavaScript comes from objects!

Function Basics

The most common way to define a function in JavaScript is by using the keyword **function**, followed by a unique function name, a list of parameters (that might be empty), and a statement block surrounded by curly braces. The basic syntax is shown below:

```
function functionname(parameter-list)
{
   statements
}
```

A simple function which takes no parameters called *sayHello* is defined here:

```
function sayHello()
{
    alert("Hello there");
}
```

To invoke the function somewhere later in the script, you would use the statement

```
sayHello();
```

Note *Forward references to functions are generally not allowed; in other words you should always define a function before calling it. However, in the same **<script>** element within which a function is defined you will be able to forward-reference a function. This is a very poor practice and should be avoided.*

Very often we will want to pass information to functions to be used in a calculation or which will change the operation the function performs. Data passed to functions, whether in literals or variables, are termed *parameters*, or occasionally *arguments*.

Consider the following modification of the *sayHello* function to take a single parameter called *name*:

```
function sayHello(name)
{
  if (name != "")
   alert("Hello there "+name);
  else
   alert("Don't be shy");
}
```

In this case the function receives a value that determines which output string to display. Calling the function with

```
sayHello("George");
```

results in the alert being displayed:

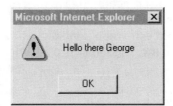

Calling the function either as

```
sayHello("");
```

or simply without a parameter

```
sayHello();
```

will result in the other dialog being displayed:

When you invoke a function that expects arguments without them, JavaScript fills in any arguments that have not been passed with **null** values. This behavior is both useful and extremely dangerous at the same time. While some people might like the ability to avoid typing in all parameters if they aren't using them, the function itself might have to be written carefully to avoid doing something inappropriate with a **null** value. In short it is always good programming practice to carefully check parameters passed in.

Functions do not have to receive only literal values; they can also be passed variables or any combination of variables and literals. Consider the function here named *addThree* that takes three values and displays their result in an alert dialog.

```
function addThree(arg1, arg2, arg3)
{
   alert(arg1+arg2+arg3);
}

var x = 5, y = 7;
addThree(x, y, 11);
```

We might want to extend this function to save the result of the addition; this is easily performed using a **return** statement. The inclusion of a **return** statement indicates that a function should exit and potentially return a value as well. Here the function *addThree* has been modified to return a value:

```
function addThree(arg1, arg2, arg3)
{
   return (arg1+arg2+arg3);
}

var x = 5, y = 7, result;
result = addThree(x,y,11);
alert(result);
```

Functions also can include multiple **return** statements, as shown here:

```
function myMax(arg1, arg2)
{
    if (arg1 >= arg2)
       return arg1;
    else
       return arg2;
}
```

Functions will always return some form of result, regardless of whether or not a **return** statement is included. By default, unless an explicit value is returned, a value of **undefined** will be returned. While the **return** statement should be the primary way that data is returned from a function, parameters can be used as well in some situations.

Note *Sometimes these implicit **return** statements cause problems, particularly when associated with HTML event handlers like **onclick**. Recall from Chapter 4 that the **void** operator can be used to avoid such problems. For example: **<a href="http://www.pint.com" onclick="javascript: void function x()">Press the link</a>**. Using **void** in this manner destroys the returned value, preventing the return value of **x()** from affecting the behavior of the link.*

Parameter Passing

Primitive data types are passed by value in JavaScript. This means that a copy is effectively made of a variable when it is passed to a function, so any manipulation local to the function leaves the original variables untouched. This is best illustrated by an example:

```
function fiddle(arg1)
{
   arg1 = 10;
   document.write("In function fiddle arg1 = "+arg1+"<br>");
}

var x = 5;
document.write("Before function call x = "+x+"<br>");
fiddle(x);
document.write("After function call x ="+x+"<br>");
```

The result of the example is shown here:

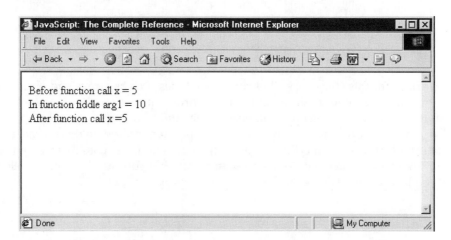

Notice that the function *fiddle* does not modify the value of the variable *x* because it only receives a copy of *x*. However, if composite types such as arrays and objects are used, they are passed by reference rather than value. This means that the function they are passed to can modify the original data because it receives a reference to the data rather than a copy of the value. Consider the following modification of the previous *fiddle* function.

```
function fiddle(arg1)
{
    arg1[0] = "changed";
    document.write("In function fiddle arg1 = "+arg1+"<br>");
}
var x = ["first", "second", "third"];
document.write("Before function call x = "+x+"<br>");
fiddle(x);
document.write("After function call x ="+x+"<br>");
```

In this situation the function *fiddle* can change the values of the array held in the variable *x*, as shown here.

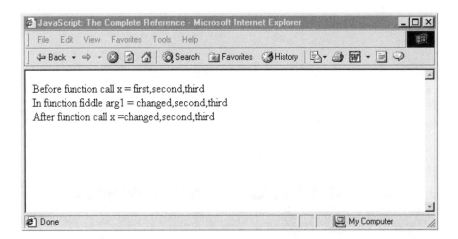

The reason for this is of course that composite types such as arrays and objects are passed by reference rather than value. In other words, a pointer to the object is passed to the function rather than a copy of it. Fortunately, unlike other languages such as C, JavaScript doesn't force the user to worry about pointers or how to de-reference parameters. If you want to modify values within a function, just pass them within an object or use a **return** statement to pass back a new value. Unfortunately, many developers do not use JavaScript this way and instead rely on global variables.

Global and Local Variables

For most JavaScript developers there are only two basic scopes: global and local. A *global variable* is one that is known throughout a document, while a *local variable* is one limited to the particular function it is defined within. For example, in the script here, the variable *x* is defined globally and is available within the function *myFunction*, which both prints and sets its value.

```javascript
// Define x globally
var x = 5;
function myFunction()
{
  document.write("Entering function<br>");
  document.write("x="+x+"<br>");
  document.write("Changing x<br>");

  x = 7;

  document.write("x="+x+"<br>");
  document.write("Leaving function<br>");
}
document.write("Starting Script<br>");
document.write("x="+x+"<br>");
myFunction();

document.write("Returning from function<br>");
document.write("x="+x+"<br>");
document.write("Ending Script<br>");
```

The output of this script is shown here:

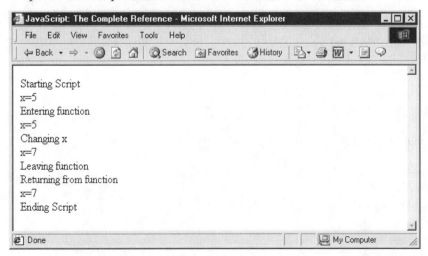

CORE LANGUAGE

Instead of using global variables, we can define local variables that are known only within the scope of the function in which they are defined. For example, in the following script the variable *y* is defined locally within the function *myFunction* and set to the value 5.

```
function myFunction()
{
  var y=5;  // define a local variable

  document.write("Within function y="+y);
}

myFunction();
document.write("After function y="+y);
```

However, outside the function, *y* is undefined so the script will throw an error message:

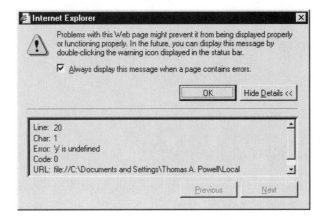

To fix the execution of this script, we can replace the second output statement with a small **if** statement to determine if the variable *y* is defined within the current context, namely the current **Window**:

```
if (window.y)
  document.write("After function y="+y);
else
  document.write("Y is undefined");
```

Notice that in this case the script shows that indeed the variable *y* is undefined in the global space:

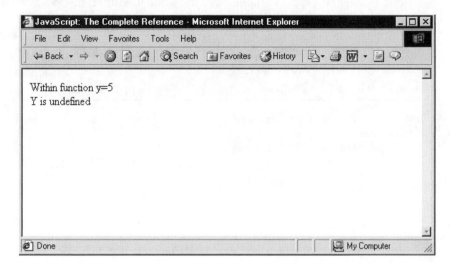

Also note that besides not being passed back to the global scope, the values stored in local variables are not preserved between calls. In other words, any values set locally will be lost if not returned or passed back through referencable parameters. We'll see later in this chapter in the section entitled "Static Variables" how to get around this problem.

Mask Out

Occasionally, the use of similar variable names for both local and global variables creates a potentially confusing situation, often termed a *mask out*. Notice in the example here how both local and global variables named *x* are used:

```
var x = "As a global I am a string";
function maskDemo()
{
 var x = 5;
 document.write("In function maskDemo x="+x+"<br>");
}

document.write("Before function call x="+x+"<br>");
maskDemo();
document.write("After function call x="+x+"<br>");
```

As shown in the output here, the value change made in the function is not preserved, because the local variable effectively masks the global one. As a general rule, when both a local and global variable have the same identifier, the local variable takes precedence.

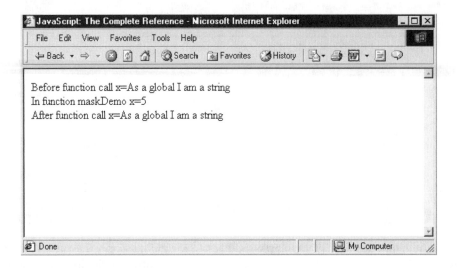

Local Functions

It might also be useful, in addition to limiting a variable's scope to a particular function, to create a function local to a function. This capability is not surprising if you consider that it is possible to create local objects and that functions themselves are objects (as we'll see in the next section, "Functions as Objects"). To create a local function, just declare it within the statement block of the function to which it should be local. For example, the following script shows a function called *testFunction* with two locally defined functions, *inner1* and *inner2*:

```
function testFunction()
{

 function inner1()
  {
    document.write("testFunction-inner1<br>");
  }

 function inner2()
  {
    document.write("testFunction-inner2<br>");
  }
```

```
  document.write("Entering testFunction<br>");
  inner1();
  inner2();
  document.write("Leaving testFunction<br>");

}

document.write("About to call testFunction<br>");
testFunction();
document.write("Returned from testFunction<br>");
```

From within the function it is possible to call these functions as shown above, but attempting to call *inner1* or *inner2* from the global scope results in error messages, as demonstrated here:

```
function testFunction()
{
 function inner1()
  {
    document.write("testFunction-inner1<br>");
  }

 function inner2()
  {
    document.write("testFunction-inner2<br>");
  }
}
inner1();  // this will error because inner1 is local to testFunction
```

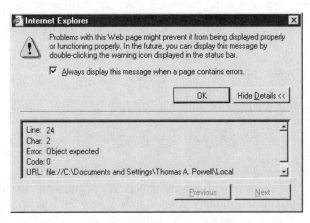

While using local functions provides us with some ability to create stand-alone modules of code, such techniques are rarely seen in JavaScript. Part of the reason is that local (or "nested") functions have been supported only since the 4.x generation of browsers. The other reason, of course, is that most JavaScript programmers do not practice such modular coding styles.

Functions as Objects

As we'll see in the next chapter, in JavaScript just about everything is an object, and functions are no exception. Thus, it is possible to define functions in a much different way than we have seen up until now, by using the keyword **new**. For example, here we define a function and assign it to the variable *sayHello*. Notice that **Function** is capitalized, as we are talking about creating an instance of JavaScript's built-in **Function** object:

```
var sayHello = new Function("alert('Hello there');");
```

Later on we can then use the assigned variable *sayHello* just like a regular function call,

```
sayHello();
```

Because functions are first class data types, the function can even by assigned to another variable and used by that name instead.

```
var sayHelloAgain = sayHello;
sayHelloAgain();
```

To expand the example, we could define a function with a parameter to print out

```
var sayHello2 = new Function("msg","alert('Hello there '+msg);");
```

and call it:

```
sayHello2('Thomas');
```

The general syntax for the **Function()** constructor is

```
var functionName = new Function("argument 1",..."argument n", "statements for
function body");
```

As we have already seen, functions can have zero arguments, so the actual number of parameters to **Function()** will vary. The only thing we have to do is pass, as the final argument, the set of statements that are to execute as the body of the function.

If you have coded JavaScript before, you may not have seen this style of function definition and might wonder what its value is. The main advantage of a declaring function using the **new** operator is that a script can create a function after a document loads.

Note *Since JavaScript 1.2 you can create functions using **new** anywhere in the script; previously you could only define them globally and not within a block such as those associated with **if** statements, loops, or other functions.*

Function Literals and Anonymous Functions

As we have seen in the previous section, defining a function using a **new** operator doesn't give the function a name. A similar way to define a function without a name and then assign it to something is by using a function literal. Function literals use the **function** keyword but without an explicit function name. This process is commonly used when creating methods for user-defined objects. A simple example showing function literals used in this manner is presented here. We have defined a function *simpleRobot* that is used as an object constructor—a function that creates an object. Within the function we have defined three methods that are assigned function literals.

```
function simpleRobot(robotName)
{
    this.name = robotName;
    this.sayHi = function () { alert('Hi my name is '+this.name); };
    this.sayBye = function () { alert('Bye!'); };
    this.sayAnything = function (msg) { alert(this.name+' says '+msg); };
}
```

It is now simple to create an object using the **new** operator in conjunction with our *simpleRobot* constructor function, as shown here:

```
var fred = new simpleRobot("Fred");
```

Invoking the various functions, or more correctly methods, is simply a matter of invoking their names, similar to plain function calls:

```
fred.sayHi();
fred.sayAnything("I don't know what to say");
fred.sayBye();
```

CORE LANGUAGE

The result of the previous example is shown here:

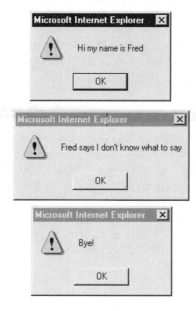

You might wonder why not just use the following **new** style syntax in the constructor function:

```
function simpleRobot (robotName)
{
    this.name = robotName;
    this.sayHi = new Function ("alert('Hi my name is '+this.name); ");
    this.sayBye = new Function ("alert('Bye!'); ");
    this.sayAnything = new Function("msg","alert(this.name+' says '+msg);" );
}
```

The reality is you could, and everything would still operate properly. The only downside to this approach is that it will use substantially more memory, as new function objects are created every time you create a new object.

A similar kind of nameless function doesn't even get assigned a name at any time. An *anonymous function* is one that cannot be further referenced after assignment. For example, we may want to sort arrays in a different manner than what the built-in **sort()** method provides (as we'll see in Chapter 7); in such cases we may pass an anonymous function:

```
var myArray = [2, 4, 2, 17, 50, 8];
myArray.sort( function(x, y)
            {
```

```
         // function statements to do sort
     }
);
```

The creation of an anonymous function is in this case carried out by using a function literal. While the function is accessible to **sort()** because it was passed a parameter, the function is never bound to a visible name, so it is considered anonymous.

Anonymous functions may be confusing, but you probably won't need to use them very often, if at all. Probably the only other place they are used in JavaScript is with event handlers, as shown here:

```html
<!DOCTYPE HTML PUBLIC "-//W3C//DTD HTML 4.01 Transitional//EN">
<html>
<head>
<title>Simple Event and Anonymous Function</title>
</head>
<body>
<form id="form1" name="form1">
<input type="button" id="button1" name="button1" value="Press Me">
</form>

<script>
<!--
window.document.form1.button1.onclick = function () {alert('The button was
pressed!')};
//-->
</script>
</body>
</html>
```

This use of anonymous functions and function literals is demonstrated again in Chapter 11, which covers events in detail.

Static Variables

One interesting aspect of the nature of functions as objects is that you can create static variables that persist beyond function invocations by adding an instance property for the defined function. For example, consider the code here that defines a function *doSum* that adds two numbers and keeps a running sum:

```
function doSum(x, y)
{
    doSum.totalSum = doSum.totalSum + x + y;     // update the running sum
    return(doSum.totalSum);                      // return the current sum
```

```
   }

   // define a static variable to hold the running sum over all calls
   doSum.totalSum = 0;

   document.write("First Call = "+doSum(5,10)+"<br>");
   document.write("Second Call = "+doSum(5,10)+"<br>");
   document.write("Third Call = "+doSum(100,100)+"<br>");
```

The result shown below demonstrates that by using a static variable we can save data between calls of a function.

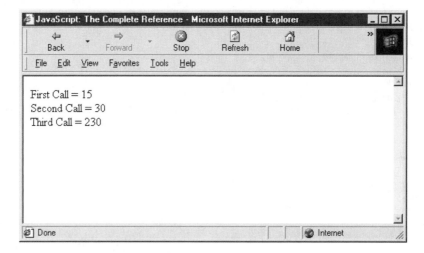

Advanced Parameter Passing

As objects, user-defined JavaScript functions have a variety of properties and methods associated with them. One particularly useful property is the read-only **length** property that indicates the number of parameters the function accepts. For example:

```
function myFunction(arg1,arg2,arg3)
{
  // do something
}
alert("Number of parameters for myFunction = "+myFunction.length);
```

the script would show that *myFunction* takes three parameters. This property shows the defined parameters for a function, so when a function is declared as taking no arguments, a value of **0** is returned for its **length** property.

CORE LANGUAGE

Note *Netscape 4.x and greater browsers also support an **arity** property that contains the same information as **length**. Because this is nonstandard it should be avoided.*

Of course it is possible to vary the number of arguments actually given to a function at any time, and we can even accommodate this possibility by examining the **arguments[]** array associated with a particular function. This array is implicitly filled with the arguments to a function when it is invoked. The following example shows a function, *myFunction*, that has no defined parameters but that is called with three arguments:

```
function myFunction()
{
 document.write("Number of parameters defined = "+myFunction.length+"<br>");
 document.write("Number of parameters passed = "+myFunction.arguments.length+"<br>")
 for (i=0;i<arguments.length;i++)
   document.write("Parameter "+i+" = "+myFunction.arguments[i]+"<br>")
}
myFunction(33,858,404);
```

The result shown here indicates that JavaScript functions are perfectly happy to receive any number of parameters.

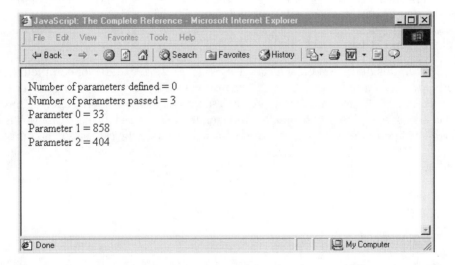

Of course, you may wonder how to put this to use. The following example shows a summation routine that adds any number of arguments passed to it:

```
function sumAll()
{
```

```
    var total=0;

    for (var i=0; i< sumAll.arguments.length; i++)
      total+=sumAll.arguments[i];

    return(total);
}

alert(sumAll(3,5,3,5,3,2,6));
```

Note that this isn't a terribly robust function—if you pass it strings or other data types that shouldn't be added, it will try to sum those as well. We'll see more sophisticated uses of variable parameter functions when we present various JavaScript applications later in the book. We will also see functions used as objects starting in the next chapter. For now let's turn our attention to one final type of special function—the recursive function.

Recursive Functions

A *recursive* function is one that calls itself. While not always the almost efficient, time-wise, way to perform a computation, the elegance of a recursive function is very appealing. Consider the definition of factorial from mathematics, where given a number n,

$$n! = n* (n-1) * (n-2) * \ldots * 1$$

So, given this definition of factorial, 5! = 5 * 4 * 3 * 2 * 1, or 120. For completeness, 0! is defined to be 1, and factorial of negative numbers is not defined. We could write a recursive function to calculate the factorial in a somewhat naïve fashion. Here, the function *factorial* keeps calling itself with smaller and smaller values until the base case of 0 is hit, and which at point the results are returned "upwards" until the calculation is complete.

```
function factorial(n)
{
 if (n == 0)
   return 1;
 else
   return n * factorial(n-1);
}
```

Passing the function a positive value, we see

```
alert(factorial(5));
```

produces the desired result:

However, if a negative value is passed to the function, the recursion will continue indefinitely. Notice the error produced by Internet Explorer in such a case:

A simple **if** statement could be added to the function to avoid such problems. It is also possible to produce a similar error message in some recursive functions simply because the recursion goes on too long, even if the computation is legitimate (will eventually terminate). The reason for this is the overhead incurred by recursive computation, since the suspended functions are held in a function call stack. It is generally fairly straightforward, though not necessarily as elegant, to rewrite a recursive function in an iterative manner. Consider the rewrite of factorial here:

```
function factorial(n)
{
 if (n >= 0)
  {
   var result=1;
   while (n > 0)
    {
      result = result * n;
      n--;
    }
   return result;
  }
 return n;
}
```

In practice, recursive functions are rarely used today in JavaScript within Web pages. For those readers troubled by recursion in computer science or math classes, you've escaped for the moment. However, recursion will make a return later on (Chapter 10) when we consider HTML document tree traversal using the Document Object Model.

Using Functions

Before concluding this chapter we'll take a short detour and talk about the practice of using functions in JavaScript. These tips are suggested as good programming practices and should lead to easier to maintain code.

Define all functions for a script first   The reason for this tip should be obvious: we need to make sure a function is defined and read by a browser before we can invoke it. Secondarily, if we define all the functions that our code will use in one place, it makes functions easier to find.

Name functions well   When naming functions and variables you need to be a little careful. Because functions and variables share the same namespace, you really shouldn't be declaring variables and functions with the same name. It might be a good idea to precede function names with "func" or some other string or letter of your own choosing. So, using such a scheme, if we had a variable named *hello* and wanted to define a function also called *hello*, we would use *funcHello*.

Besides the obvious collision of names, very subtle bugs may slip in when we have similar names, particularly when you consider that functions are created when the document is parsed, while variables are created when the script is run. Notice in the script below how there is a variable as well as a function called *x*.

```
var x = 5;
function x()
{
 alert("I'm a function!");
}
alert(typeof x);
```

You might expect the alert to show *x* to be a **Function** or, more appropriately, an **Object** because it appears to be defined second. However, as you can see here, it is a number:

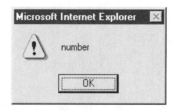

The output makes sense if you consider when the function and variables are actually created. The variable gets created as the script runs, while the function is created as the script is parsed. While this was a contrived example, it illustrates the importance of understanding how things are created in JavaScript.

Consider using linked .js files for functions, but be cautious While many JavaScript programmers like to put functions in external files, we need to make sure that a function is available before calling it. For example, if we have two .js files (*lib1.js* and *lib2.js*), each of which calls functions found in the other, we may have to check to make sure the function is available before calling it. In the main document we would define variables showing the files being loaded as false:

```
var lib1Loaded = false;
var lib2Loaded = false;
```

Then, in each of the loaded documents the last line would set the variables to **true**. Using this scheme we would then make sure to look at the value of the variables *lib1Loaded* or *lib2Loaded* before any functions that are contained in the files are called. For example,

```
if (lib1Loaded)
    doSomething(x,y,z)
```

Most of the time such efforts aren't required, but JavaScript designers should be careful to consider the load order of documents and what happens if certain parts of a script are invoked before an entire document has loaded.

Use explicit return statements Even if your function will not return any values, insert a **return** statement anyway. JavaScript being an interpreted language, keeping the interpreter from having to do any extra work or make any assumptions should produce better running scripts.

Write stand-alone functions As always, we should practice modular design and pass data in to and out from functions using only function arguments, the **return** statement, and data values that are passed by reference. We should avoid side-effects such as changing global values from within functions. Local variables should always be used to perform calculations that are unique to a function, and hidden functions can be used in the same manner to create special-purpose functions that are not needed anywhere else. The value of going through the trouble to create stand-alone functions in this fashion is that such functions can be reused without worry in a variety of situations.

Check arguments carefully   As we have seen, JavaScript doesn't carefully check the number or type of variables passed to a function. It is possible to use *variadic functions*, functions that accept a variable number of arguments, to write very powerful code. However, it is equally possible that doing so will cause a problem." For example, consider this simple function that does no checking:

```
function addTwoNumbers (x,y)
{
  alert (x+y);
}
addTwoNumbers (5);
```

This could be easily rewritten to check for the number of arguments passed:

```
function addTwo (x,y)
{
  if (addTwo.arguments.length == 2)
    alert (x+y);
}
```

Of course, this wouldn't correct a bad function call like

```
addTwo (5,true);
```

which would produce a value of **6**, since **true** would be converted to the integer **1**. If we added type checking into our function, we could solve this problem as shown here:

```
function addTwo (x,y)
{
  if (addTwo.arguments.length == 2)
   {
    if ( (typeof (x) != "number") || (typeof (y) !="number") )
      return;
    else
      alert (x+y);
   }
  return;
}
```

As we can see, to create truly reusable functions that will withstand anything thrown at them, we will have to put in some more effort.

Comment your functions   Consider putting a comment block before a function indicating the name of the function, its purpose, the number and type of parameters accepted, any return values, and any output the function may produce. An example of such a comment block is shown here:

```
/*
   Function customAlert(message,icon,color,buttontext)

   Description: This function creates a custom alert dialog
                with passed message, icon, color and buttontext.

   Input:  message - a string containing message to be displayed
           icon - reference to a GIF or JPEG image to be used on dialog
           color - default color in the form of a hex color
                     string to be used for background. White is used
                     if unspecified
           buttontext - string containing message to be used on
                          dialog button.  Uses the string "ok" if
                          unspecified.

  Output: creates a dialog window relative to the current window
          returns true if successful in creating window, false otherwise
*/
function customAlert(message, icon, color,buttontext)
{
   // function goes here
}
```

Unfortunately, few JavaScript programmers document their functions this way, probably because of the concern of the extra size for download. Of course, we could always have such code stripped down to the bare essentials before delivery, but such practices are still relatively rare.

Good programming of course is not just a matter of correct syntax, but also consistent style. Many may argue about the benefits of one particular coding style over another, but whatever you choose, stick to it. In this chapter we have shown a primarily modular programming that should be familiar to anyone who has programmed in Pascal or C. However, a more modern programming style based upon object usage is also possible and is used in the next chapter.

CORE LANGUAGE

Summary

JavaScript functions are the developer's most basic tool for creating structured reusable code. A function should be designed to be self-contained and pass data in through parameters and back via the **return** statement. In general, most parameters are passed to a function by value, but composite types such as arrays and objects are passed by reference. JavaScript functions are very flexible and a variable number of parameters can be passed to a function. However, some programming caution should be employed, given JavaScript's lax type and parameter checking. Further, to ensure reusable functions, local variables should be declared with the **var** statement to avoid conflicts with global names. Local or hidden functions can also be used to hide calculations internal to a particular function. Complex tasks can be broken up into multiple functions since JavaScript functions can of course call one another. Recursive functions can be used to create elegant solutions that perform calculations by having a function call itself over and over again. While JavaScript functions are very powerful, they are implemented as objects—an even more useful construct discussed in the next chapter.

The Complete Reference

Chapter 6

Objects

Javascript is an object-based language. With the exception of language constructs like loops and relational operators, almost all of JavaScript's features are implemented using objects in one way or another. Objects are used to define composite data types, create functions, manipulate data, and even provide "built-in" language features like the **isNan()** method. Sometimes objects are used explicitly to carry out certain tasks, such as the manipulation of HTML and XML documents using the Document Object Model. Other times the role of objects in the language is less obvious, like the role played by the **String** object during the manipulation of primitive string data.

The preceding chapters gave some insight into how objects are used in common tasks. For example, the fundamental aspects of object creation and automatic type conversion were discussed in Chapter 3. That chapter also briefly discussed how objects could be accessed. This chapter will delve into objects more deeply, presenting the details of user-defined objects. The next chapter begins the lengthy discussion of the structure and use of objects provided by JavaScript itself. Understanding the capabilities of and relationships between objects in JavaScript is essential to grasping the "big picture" of the role of active scripting on the Web, so we first present an overview of things to come.

Objects in JavaScript

Objects in JavaScript fall into four groups:

- *User-defined* objects are custom objects created by the programmer to bring structure and consistency to a particular programming task. This chapter will focus on the creation and use of such objects.

- *Built-in* objects are provided by the JavaScript language itself. These include those objects associated with primitive data types (**String**, **Number**, and **Boolean**), objects that allow creation of user-defined objects and composite types (**Object** and **Array**), and objects that simplify common tasks, such as **Date**, **Math**, and **RegExp**. The capabilities of built-in objects are governed by the ECMA-262 language standard and, to a lesser extent, by the specifications of particular browser vendors. The following two chapters will discuss these types of objects.

- *Browser* objects are those objects not specified as part of the JavaScript language but that most browsers commonly support. Examples of browser objects include **Window**, the object that enables the manipulation of browser windows and interaction with the user, and **Navigator**, the object that provides information about client configuration. Because most portions of browser objects are not governed by any standard, their properties and behavior can vary significantly from browser to browser and from version to version. These types of objects will be discussed throughout the rest of the book and in Chapter 9 particularly.

- *Document* objects are part of the Document Object Model (DOM), as defined by the W3C. These objects present the programmer with a structured interface to

HTML and XML documents. It is these objects that allow JavaScript to manipulate Cascading Style Sheets (CSS) and that allow the realization of Dynamic HTML (DHTML). Access to the document objects is provided by the browser via the **document** property of the **Window** object (**window.document**). An in-depth discussion of the DOM can be found in Chapter 10.

There is some overlap in the four categories of objects. The major reason is that there is no one standard governing how all aspects of JavaScript are supposed to behave. The ECMA-262 standard governs the nuts and bolts of the language itself. The W3C's DOM specification dictates how structured documents like Web pages should be presented to a scripting environment. Browser vendors define access to the user interface as they see fit and even create their own proprietary extensions to the DOM. The result is a chaotic and somewhat confusing set of technologies that come together under the umbrella of "JavaScript."

The good news is that browser vendors have finally settled on a de facto standard for browser objects. This "standard" is more an artifact of historical circumstances and browser wars than the product of a rational design process. This is evidenced by the fact that the **Navigator** object is supported by Opera, Netscape, and Internet Explorer despite obviously deriving its name from Netscape's original Navigator browser. In addition, close examination of the **Navigator** object reveals considerable variation in the support of its properties by the different browser types and versions.

The core details of the browser object model are covered in Chapter 9, and the details of the DOM are found in Chapter 10. Further discussions of browser and DOM capabilities appear throughout the remainder of the book in the context of specific tasks. This chapter is intended to give a solid grounding in the fundamental aspects of object creation and manipulation as well as a comprehensive overview of user-defined and built-in objects.

Creating Objects

We saw in Chapter 4 that objects are created with the **new** operator. This operator causes the given constructor to create a brand-new object. The nature of the object that is created is determined by the particular constructor that is invoked. For example, the **String()** constructor creates **String** objects while the **Array()** constructor creates **Array** objects. For example,

```
var city = new String();
```

creates a new **String** object and places a reference to it in the variable *city*. Because no argument was given to the constructor, *city* is assigned the default value for strings, the empty string. We could have made the example more interesting by passing the constructor an argument specifying an initial value:

```
var city = new String("San Diego");
```

This places a reference to a new **String** object with the value "San Diego" in *city*.

In addition to explaining how to declare built-in objects like **String**s and **Array**s, Chapter 4 also discussed the creation of **Object** objects. These generic objects can be used to create user-defined data types. As with any objects in JavaScript, you can add properties to **Object**s dynamically:

```
var robot = new Object();
robot.name = "Zephyr";
robot.model = "Guard";
robot.hasJetpack = true;
```

You can also add functions dynamically to objects. Recall that functions that are members of objects are called *methods*. The following code extends our example by adding a method to the **robot** object. We first define the function and then add it to the object:

```
function strikeIntruder()
{
    alert("ZAP!");
}
robot.attack = strikeIntruder();
```

Notice that we named the method *attack* even though the function was named *strikeIntruder*. We could have named it anything; the interpreter does not care what identifier we choose to use. When we invoke the method,

```
robot.attack();
```

we get the result:

We could have done this example without even naming the function we called *strikeIntruder*. Recall from Chapter 5 that JavaScript 1.2+ supports function literals. Here we restate our example using this capability:

```
var robot = new Object();
robot.name = "Zephyr";
robot.model = "Guard";
robot.hasJetpack = true;
robot.attack = function()
                {
                      alert("ZAP!");
                };
```

This syntax is more compact and avoids cluttering the global namespace with a function that will be used only as a method of a user-defined object. Because we've also seen how to define number, string, Boolean, and array literals, it should not come as much of a surprise that we can also specify object literals.

Object Literals

Object literals are supported in JavaScript 1.2+. The syntax is a curly braces-enclosed, comma-separated list of property/value pairs. Property/value pairs are specified by giving a property name followed by a colon and then its value. Here we restate our example using both object and function literals:

```
var robot = { name: "Zephyr ",
              model: "Guard",
              hasJetpack: true,
              attack: function() { alert("ZAP!"); }
            };
```

And we can invoke *robot.attack()* with the same result as before.

This example also hints at the robustness of these capabilities. It is perfectly valid to specify nested literals, properties with **null** or **undefined** values, and values that are not literals (that is, values that are variables). The following code illustrates these concepts in an example similar to those we've previously seen:

```
var jetpack = true;
var robot = { name: null,
```

```
                    hasJetpack: jetpack,
                    model: "Guard",
                    attack: function() { alert("ZAP!"); },
                    sidekick: {  name: "Spot",
                                 model: "Dog",
                                 hasJetpack: false,
                                 attack: function() { alert("CHOMP!"); }
                              }
               };
      robot.name = "Zephyr";
```

There is a fair amount going on here that might require explanation. First notice that *robot*'s property *hasJetpack* is set through another variable, *jetpack*. Also note that the *robot.name* is initially set to **null**, but it is later filled in with the appropriate value. The major change is that *robot* contains a nested object called *sidekick*, which also contains four properties, *name*, *model*, *hasJetpack*, and an *attack* method. Invoking *robot.attack()* results in the now-familiar "ZAP!" output. The method call

```
      robot.sidekick.attack();
```

results in:

If the way the **robot** object has been defined in the previous examples seems bulky and inelegant to you, your programming instincts are very good. There is a better way to create your own objects that makes much better use of the object-oriented nature of JavaScript. These examples were given to illustrate the options you have with regard to object definition. A more complete example utilizing the full power of JavaScript objects follows in a later section. However there are a few more details that need mentioning before we proceed. First, understanding the difference between primitive and reference types will help you understand the intricacies of the more advanced sections that follow.

Primitive and Reference Types

All JavaScript data types can be categorized as either primitive or reference types. These two types correspond to the primitive and composite types discussed in Chapter 3. *Primitive types* are the primitive data types number, string, Boolean, undefined, and null. These types are primitive in the sense that they are restricted to a set of specific values. You can think of primitive data as stored directly in the variable itself. *Reference types* are objects, including **Object**s, **Array**s, and **Function**s. Because these types can hold very large amounts of heterogeneous data, a variable containing a reference type does not contain its actual value. It contains a *reference* to a place in memory that contains the actual data.

This distinction will be transparent to you the majority of the time. But there are two situations when you need to pay particular attention to the implications of these types. The first is when you create two or more references to the same object. Consider the following example with primitive types:

```
var x = 10;
var y = x;
x = 2;
alert("The value of y is: " + y);
```

This code behaves as you would expect. Because *x* has a primitive type (number), the value stored in it (**10**) is assigned to *y* on the second line. Changing the value of *x* has no effect on *y* because *y* received a copy of *x*'s value. The result is shown here:

Now consider similar code using a reference type:

```
var x = [10, 9, 8];
var y = x;
x[0] = 2;
alert("The value of y's first element is: " + y[0]);
```

The result might be surprising:

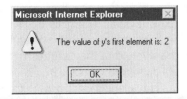

Because arrays are reference types, the second line copies the reference to x's data into y. Both x and y refer to the same data, so changing its value using either variable is naturally visible to both x and y.

Recall from Chapter 5 that arguments to functions are passed by value. Because reference types hold a reference to their actual data, function arguments receive a copy of the reference and can therefore modify the original data. This effect is shown by the following example, which passes two values, a primitive and a reference type, to a function that modifies their data:

```
// declare a reference type (array)
var refType = ["first ", " second", " third"];

// declare a primitive type (number)
var primType = 10;
// declare a function taking two arguments, which it will modify
function modifyValues(x, y)
{
   x[0] = "changed"; // modify the first argument, an array
   y = y - 8; // modify the second, a number
}

// invoke the function
modifyValues(refType, primType);
// print the value of the reference type
document.writeln("The value of refType is: ", refType+"<br>");
// print the value of the primitive type
document.writeln("The value of primType is: ", primType);
```

The result is shown in Figure 6-1. Notice how the value of the reference type changed but the value of the primitive type did not.

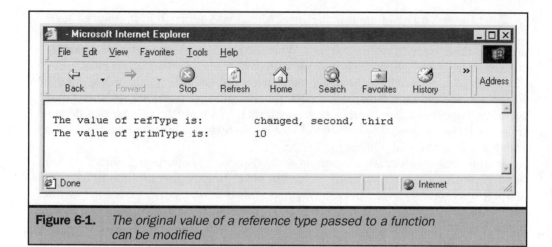

Figure 6-1.   *The original value of a reference type passed to a function can be modified*

Although you should always be aware of the difference between primitive and reference types, references in JavaScript are far less complex than those in other languages. For example, *dereferencing* reference types in order to use their values is of no concern to a JavaScript programmer, because the process is carried out automatically. Further, JavaScript does not have pointers nor does it require the explicit allocation and deallocation of memory.

Object Destruction and Garbage Collection

When you create objects, JavaScript automatically allocates memory for you to use. What actually happens is that the interpreter allocates memory and passes a reference to this new (empty) object to the constructor that was invoked (more on that later). The point is that not only does the interpreter automatically handle allocation of memory it "cleans up" after you as well. This language feature is called *garbage collection*.

Garbage collecting languages keep a watchful eye on your data. When a piece of data is no longer accessible to the program, the space it occupies is reclaimed by the interpreter and returned to the pool of available memory. Data can become inaccessible in a variety of ways. Next is a common example of what might happen with a primitive type:

```
var artist = "Monet was a French Impressionist";
// some other code
artist = "Dali was a Spanish Surrealist";
```

After the second assignment, the string "Monet was a French Impressionist" is no longer accessible. The space it occupies is therefore recycled by the interpreter. The same situation can arise with reference types. When no more references exist for a particular piece of data, its storage space is garbage collected.

The exact details of how the interpreter carries out garbage collection are not really important. The only implementation issue that might cause problems is the fact that Netscape 2 does not reclaim variable memory until the window the variable was declared in is closed. So it is probably not a good idea to use huge amounts of memory if your clients are predominantly Netscape 2 users.

If your code involves large amounts of data, giving the interpreter hints that you are done with specific variables can be useful in keeping the memory footprint of your script to a reasonable level. An easy way to do this is to replace unneeded data with **null**, indicating that the variable is now empty. For example, assuming you had defined a *Book* object:

```
var myBook = new Book();
// assign the contents of War and Peace to myBook
// manipulate your data in some manner
// when you are finished clean up by setting to null
myBook = null;
```

This indicates unequivocally that you are finished with the data referenced by *myBook*. If you have multiple references to the same data, be sure that you set them all to **null**, otherwise the interpreter keeps the data around in case you need it again.

Objects as Associative Arrays

An *associative array* is a structure that allows you to associate data with names. Elements in a normal array are addressed by the integer indicating their index. Elements in an associative array are addressed by names that are strings. JavaScript provides associative arrays as a consequence of the fact that the following two statements are equivalent:

object.property

object["property"]

Associative arrays in JavaScript are merely objects used with the array syntax. We can store values in the array:

```
var customers = new Object();
customers["John Doe"] = "123 Main St., Metropolis, USA";
```

and retrieve it:

```
var address = customers["John Doe"];
```

Storing a string in *customers["John Doe"]* was an arbitrary decision. Data of any type may be placed in an associative array.

Associative arrays are most commonly used when property names are not known until run time. For example, you might have a loop that prompts the user to enter customer names and addresses. The actual storage of the data (inside the loop) might look like:

```
customers[customerName] = customerAddress;
```

where *customerName* is a string and *customerAddress* is arbitrary data, perhaps a user-defined object that stores address information.

In addition to the direct way elements may be accessed, JavaScript's **for/in** construct is perfect for iterating over the elements of associative arrays. The following example loops through all elements of the array we previously defined and prints them out:

```
var customers = new Object();
customers["John Doe"] = "123 Main St., Metropolis, USA";
customers["Jane Cheung"] = "123 Fake St., Vancouver B.C., Canada";
customers["George Speight"] = "145 Baldwin St., Dunedin, NZ";

for (varclient in customers)
{
   document.writeln("The address of client " + client + " is:");
   document.writeln(customers[client]);
   document.writeln("<br><br>");
}
```

Each name that has data associated with it is assigned to *client*, one at a time. This variable is used to access the data in the array. The output of the previous example is shown in Figure 6-2.

CORE LANGUAGE

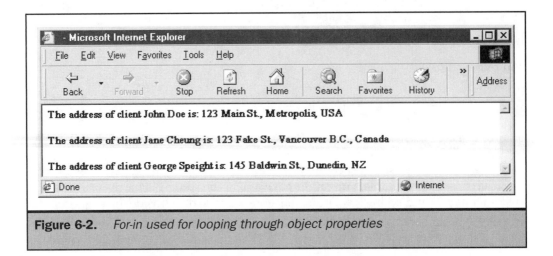

Figure 6-2.   *For-in used for looping through object properties*

Object Properties

We have seen many examples of how properties are accessed and added dynamically to objects. For example, using an object as an associative array allows the programmer to store data in object properties that are defined on-the-fly. The power of the property mechanism in JavaScript is evident, but there remain several aspects of properties that warrant discussion in preparation for a full exposition of JavaScript objects.

Instance Properties

Properties added dynamically to objects in the manner we have seen thus far are called *instance properties*. They have this name because they are only present in the particular instance of the object to which they were added. For example,

```
var myString = new String("Hello world");
myString.simpleExample = true;
```

adds the *simpleExample* property to the specific **String** object *myString*. The property is not added to all other **String** objects. JavaScript does provide the ability to add a property to *all* instances of a particular object through object prototypes. However prototypes are a considerably more advanced language feature and will be discussed along with the details of JavaScript object creation in a section to follow.

You can remove instance properties with the **delete** operator. C++ programmers should note that JavaScript's **delete** is not the same as that of C++. It is used only to remove properties from objects and elements from arrays. The following example illustrates the deletion of an instance property that we add to a **String** object:

```
var myString = new String("hello world");
myString.simpleExample = true;
delete myString.simpleExample;
alert("The value of myString.simpleExample is: " +
myString.SimpleExample);
```

The result is:

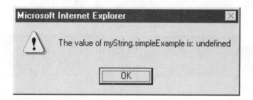

As you can see, the property has **undefined** value just as any nonexistent object property would. Note that you cannot delete *myString* itself. Attempting to do so will silently fail. In general, you can delete only instance properties.

Common Object Properties

When one considers that abstraction and inheritance are two of the primary principles behind object-oriented programming, it should not come as much of a surprise that all JavaScript objects are derived from the **Object** object. This object is the most general kind of object. All other objects are derived from it, according to JavaScript's rules of inheritance. As the "super object," it defines several properties that are common to all its descendants. Some of these properties are listed in Table 6-1. Appendix B provides a description of all the properties of **Object**, including those that are deprecated or proprietary.

Because *all* objects are descendents of **Object**, they all have these properties. For example, you can call the **toString()** method of a **Number** object to retrieve the numeric value it contains as a primitive string. Built-in and user-defined objects often overload the methods **toString()** and **valueOf()** to reflect the specific type of data the object contains. *Overloading* (or *overriding*) replaces default behavior with behavior specific to the descendent object. For example, the **Number** object defines its **valueOf()** method to return a primitive number containing its value. These properties are rarely used in practice but are used extensively by the interpreter to carry out type conversion. They are mentioned here in preparation for the complete discussion of object inheritance to follow.

A property that many objects have (but that is not a part of **Object**) is **length**. Not surprisingly, this property usually contains length information about the data the object contains. What "length" means depends on the type of the object. For example, the **length** of a **String** object holds the number of characters that make up the string. The **length** of the **Frames** object holds the number of frames present in the current Web page.

The fact that different objects can respond in different ways to properties that they all have illustrates one of the beauties of object-oriented programming. When creating

Property	Description
constructor	A read-only reference to the function that served as the object's constructor. Available in JavaScript 1.1.
toString()	A method that converts the object to a primitive string.
valueOf()	A method that returns the value associated with the object. Available in JavaScript 1.1.

Table 6-1. *Properties of the **Object** object*

your own user-defined objects, it is always good to keep the principles of object-oriented design in mind. Robust user-defined objects will overload the **toString()** and **valueOf()** methods they inherit from **Object** to reflect the characteristics of the data they contain.

With these ideas in mind, we are now ready to discuss the details of JavaScript's object-oriented features. A firm grasp on the mechanics of object creation is essential to creating useful user-defined objects.

Creating User-Defined Objects

Java and C++ are *class-based* object-oriented languages. An object's properties are defined by its class, a statically specified description of code and data that each object of that class contains. Instances of a class are called "objects," and objects are created by invoking the constructor function of a particular class. The class-based approach clearly defines object structure and inheritance relationships before an instance of a particular class is created.

JavaScript takes a more dynamic approach. As a *prototype-based* object-oriented language, it does not have classes in the sense of Java and C++. Object instances are created with *constructors*, executable objects (functions) that prepare new instances for use. Every constructor contains an *object prototype* that defines the code and data that each object instance contains. Every aspect of objects is dynamic: new properties can be added at any time to a particular instance, to all instances that share the same prototype, and even to the constructors themselves.

Before delving any deeper, some commentary regarding nomenclature is appropriate. Because everything in JavaScript except primitive data and language constructs is an object, the term "object" is used quite often. It is important to differentiate between a *type* of object, for example the **Array** or **String** object, and an *instance* of an object, for example a particular variable containing an **Array** or **String**. A *type* of object is defined by a particular constructor. All instances created with that constructor are said to have the same "type" or "class." To keep things clear, remember that a constructor and its prototype define a type of object, and objects created with that constructor are instances of that type.

We've seen numerous examples of object creation; for example:

```
var s = new String();
```

This line invokes the constructor for **String** objects, a function named **String()**. JavaScript knows that this function is a constructor because it is called in conjunction with the **new** operator. We can define our own constructor by defining a function:

```
function Robot()
{

}
```

This function by itself does absolutely nothing. However, we can invoke it as a constructor just like we did for **String()**:

```
var guard = new Robot();
```

We have now created an instance of the **Robot** object. Obviously, this object is not particularly useful. More information about object construction is necessary before we proceed.

When a constructor is invoked, the interpreter allocates space for the new object and implicitly passes the object to the function. The constructor can access it using **this**, a special keyword that holds a reference to the new object. We can redefine our constructor to reflect this ability:

```
function Robot()
{
    this.hasJetpack = true;
}
```

We add a new instance property *hasJetpack* to the object being created. Note that all **Robot** objects will have this property because they are all created with the **Robot()** constructor. After creating an object with our constructor, we can access the *hasJetpack* property as one would expect:

```
var guard = new Robot();
var canFly = guard.hasJetpack;
```

Recall how you can pass arguments to constructors to specify an initial value. We can modify our constructor again so that it takes an optional argument and can specify that argument if we wish:

```
function Robot(needsToFly)
{
    if (needsToFly == true)
        this.hasJetpack = true;
    else
        this.hasJetpack = false;
}
// create a Robot with hasJetpack == true
var guard = new Robot(true);
// create a Robot with hasJetpack == false
var sidekick = new Robot();
```

Note that in the previous example we could have explicitly passed in a **false** value when creating the *sidekick* instance. However, by passing in nothing, we implicitly have done so, since the parameter *needsToFly* would be **undefined.** Thus, the **if** statement fails properly.

We can also add methods to the objects we create. One way to do so is to assign an instance variable an anonymous function inside of the constructor. However, there is another way to do so, using the object's prototype.

Every object has a *prototype* property that gives it its structure. The prototype describes the code and data that all objects of that type have in common. We can populate the constructor's prototype with the code and data we want all of our **Robot** objects to possess. We modify our definition to the following:

```
Robot.prototype.hasJetpack = false;
Robot.prototype.doAction = function()
                            {
                                alert("Intruders beware!");
                            };
function Robot(flying)
{
    if (flying == true)
        this.hasJetpack = true;
}
```

Several substantial changes have been made. First, we moved the *hasJetpack* property into the prototype and gave it the default value of **false**. Doing this allows us to remove the **else** clause from the constructor. Second, we added a function *doAction()* to the prototype of the constructor. Every **Robot** object we create now has both properties:

```
var guard = new Robot(true);
var canFly = guard.hasJetpack;
guard.doAction();
```

A question naturally arises: if these two properties are properties of the prototype, how can we access them through an instance of the object? The answer is similar to how the interpreter "finds" global variables from inside of a function. If a property is accessed and the object has no instance property of that name, the object's prototype is checked. If we omit the argument to the **Robot()** constructor and then access the *hasJetpack* property of the object created, the interpreter finds the default value in the prototype. If we pass the constructor **true**, then the default value in the prototype is overridden by the constructor adding an instance variable called *hasJetpack* whose value is **true**.

Prototype methods can refer to the instance they are contained in using **this**. We can redefine our class once again to reflect the new capability:

```
Robot.prototype.hasJetpack = false;
Robot.prototype.actionValue = "Intruders beware!";
Robot.prototype.doAction = function()
{
    alert(this.actionValue);
};
function Robot(flying, action)
{
    if (flying == true)
        this.hasJetpack = true;
    if (action)
        this.actionValue = action;
}
```

We have added a new property to the prototype *actionValue*. This property has a default value that can be overridden by passing a second argument to the constructor. If a value for *action* is passed to the constructor, invoking *doAction()* will show its value rather than the default ("Intruders beware!"). For example,

```
var guard = new Robot(true, "ZAP!");
guard.doAction();
```

results in "ZAP!" being alerted rather than "Intruders beware."

A very important aspect of the prototype is that it is *shared*. That is, there is only one copy of the prototype that all objects created with the same constructor use. An implication of this is that a change in the prototype will be visible to all objects that share it! This is why default values in the prototype are overridden by instance variables and not changed directly. Changing them directly would change the value for *all* objects sharing that prototype. Modifying the prototypes of built-in objects can be very useful. Suppose you need to repeatedly extract the third character of strings. You can modify the prototype of the **String** object so that all strings have a method of your definition:

```
String.prototype.getThirdChar = function()
 {
   return this.charAt(2);
 }
```

You can invoke this method as you would any other built-in **String** method:

```
var c = "Example".getThirdChar();
```

In addition to instance properties and properties of prototypes, JavaScript allows you to define *static properties* (also known as *class properties*). Because constructors are functions, and functions are instances of the **Function** object, you can add properties to constructors. Such properties are static properties. Continuing our example,

```
Robot.isMetallic = true;
```

defines a static property of the **Robot** object by adding an instance variable to the constructor. It is important to remember that static properties exist in only one place, as members of constructors. They are therefore accessed through the constructor rather than an instance of the object. Static properties hold data or code that does not depend on the contents of any particular instance. The **toLowerCase()** method of the **String** object could not be a static method because the string it returns depends on the object on which it was invoked. On the other hand the **PI** property of the **Math** object (**Math.PI**) and the **parse()** method of the **String** object (**String.parse()**) are perfect candidates, because they do not depend on the value of any particular instance. You can see from the way they are accessed that they are, in fact, static properties. The *isMetallic* property we just defined is accessed similarly, as **Robot.isMetallic**, just like C++ or Java.

The Prototype Chain

Inheritance in JavaScript is achieved through prototypes. It is clear that instances of a particular object "inherit" the code and data present in the constructor's prototype. It is also possible to derive a new object type from a type that already exists. Instances of such objects inherit all the properties of their "parent" type in addition to any properties added by the new type. For example, we can define a new object type that inherits all the capabilities of our **Robot** object by "chaining" prototypes:

```
function UltraRobot(extraFeature)
{
    if (extraFeature)
        this.feature = extraFeature;
}
UltraRobot.prototype = new Robot();
UltraRobot.prototype.feature = "Radar";
```

The only new concept in this example is setting **UltraRobot**'s prototype to a new instance of a **Robot** object. **UltraRobot** objects contain the properties of the **UltraRobot** object as well as those of **Robot**:

```
var guard = new UltraRobot("Performs Calculus");
var feature = guard.feature;
var canFly = guard.hasJetpack;
guard.doAction();
```

The way the interpreter resolves property access in this example is analogous to the resolution that was previously discussed. The object's instance properties are first checked for a match, then, if none is found, its prototype is checked. If no match is found in the prototype, the parent prototype is checked, and the process repeats recursively.

This process explains why all objects have certain properties like **toString()**. The **toString()** method is a property of the **Object** prototype. Since all objects are derived from **Object**, invoking **toString()** on any object will eventually make its way "up" the chain of inheritance to **Object**'s **toString()** property. For example, constructors are functions, and functions are instances of the **Function** object, which is derived from **Object**.

Good Practice in Object Creation

The prototype chain explains why it is sometimes a good idea to provide specific properties for user-defined objects that override the behavior of the parent. If a programmer expects the behavior of a property might differ from parent to child, the behavior should be overridden in the child. For example, providing a **toString()** method specific to your user-defined objects to override the functionality of the **toString()** method of **Object** is generally a good idea.

Note that we can achieve all the functionality discussed in this section by creating new instances of **Object**. However, for user-defined objects of any complexity, doing so results in laborious, repetitive code that is far less elegant than the proper use of prototypes and constructors. For anything but short, simple sections of code, utilizing the full capabilities of the JavaScript's object-oriented features is the way to go. Yet for some reason many programmers don't take advantage of these features in JavaScript.

JavaScript's Object-Oriented Reality

Today Object-Oriented Programming (or OOP) is commonly accepted as a good way to structure programs, but rarely is full-blown OOP style used in JavaScript. You might wonder why this is. The language itself does support the principles of Object-Oriented Programming, which have been demonstrated in the examples of this chapter and are summarized here:

- **Abstraction**   An object should characterize a certain abstract idea or task. The object should present an interface to the programmer that provides the features or services one might expect of an object of that type.

- **Encapsulation**   An object should maintain internally the state necessary to characterize its behavior. This data is usually *hidden* from other objects and accessed through the public interface the object provides.

- **Inheritance**   The language should provide the means for specialized objects to be created from more general objects. For example, a general **Shape** object should lend itself to the creation of more specific objects, like **Squares**, **Triangles**, or **Circles**. These specific objects should "inherit" capabilities from their "ancestors."

- **Polymorphism**   Different objects should be able to respond in different ways to the same action. For example, **Number** objects might respond to the operation of addition in the arithmetic sense, while **String** objects might interpret addition as concatenation. Additionally, objects should be allowed to *polymorph* ("change shape") depending upon context.

JavaScript supports all of these principles, and they are clearly present in the language itself; however, in practice they are largely ignored by most programmers writing their own scripts. This lack of OOP programming style in JavaScript is due to the tasks it tends to be used for and the ease of employing other approaches to accomplish those tasks.

The Rise of the Object-Oriented Approach

Writing and maintaining large software systems is a challenging endeavor. Years of research have been spent investigating different approaches to software engineering, with the goal of trying to determine the most effective methodologies for creating high-quality products. In the early days of programming, there wasn't much sophistication in code organization or planning. Most programs were straightforward assembly- or machine-language affairs, written without the aid of anything resembling modern-day software engineering.

As higher-level languages began to evolve, it became clear that code modularization and structured programming were important aspects of any sizeable project. Software requirements continued to increase in complexity, impelling programmers to investigate new approaches to the process of software creation. Object-oriented programming grew out of the idea that software can be thought of as a set of abstract objects interacting with one another. While the object-oriented approach is not a panacea for all problems encountered during software development, it does lend itself to the creation of highly modular, maintainable software.

While JavaScript is itself an object-oriented programming language, the value of using many of its structures is lost to many programmers, because the size and complexity of most scripts are not sufficient to warrant the use of an OOP approach. In fact, the success of the language for many of its users is that it doesn't take a great deal of effort or lines of code to accomplish useful tasks within Web sites. The reality of the language's use reveals that many programmers continue to write straight-line or even "spaghetti" style code, chock full of global variables. The authors of this book will try to introduce more appropriate styles, but will steer clear of a quasi-religious approach pushing one particular software development style over another. While we are clearly fans of object-oriented programming, at this point we would settle for the incorporation of structured programming practices in scripts on the Web.

Summary

JavaScript provides four types of objects: user-defined, built-in, browser, and document. This chapter focused on the creation and use of user defined objects. JavaScript is a prototype-based, object-oriented language. New object instances are created with constructors, objects that initialize the properties of new instances. Every object has a prototype property that reflects the prototype of the constructor used to create it. When an object property is accessed, the interpreter first checks the object's instance properties for the desired name. If it is not found, the properties of the object's prototype are checked. This process repeats recursively until it has worked up the chain of inheritance to the top-level object. Most of the time in JavaScript the creation and management of the objects is straightforward, and programmers are freed such headaches as memory management. While user-defined objects can be used to create much more modular and maintainable scripts, many JavaScript programmers do not really use them, given the simplicity of their scripts. Instead, the various built-in, browser, and document objects are utilized. The next chapter begins the examination of such objects, starting with built-in objects, particularly **Array**, **Math**, **Date**, and **String**.

The
Complete
Reference

Chapter 7

Array, Date, Math, and Type-Related Objects

183

This chapter discusses in more detail the capabilities of JavaScript's built-in objects, particularly **Array**, **Date**, and **Math**. We will also look into the built-in objects related to the primitive types, such as **Boolean**, **Number**, and **String**, as well as the mysterious **Global** object. Notably missing from this chapter is the **RegExp** object, which requires a significant amount of explanation and is the subject of the next chapter. For each object covered in this chapter, the focus will be primarily on those properties most commonly used and supported by the major browsers. The complete list of properties of the built-in objects, including version information and examples, can be found in Appendix B. So let's start our overview of these built-in objects, proceeding in alphabetical order, starting from **Array** and ending in **String**.

Array

Arrays were introduced in Chapter 3 as composite types that store ordered lists of data. Arrays may be declared using the **Array** () constructor. If arguments are passed to the constructor, they are usually interpreted as specifying the elements of the array. The exception is if the constructor is passed a single numeric value. Doing so creates an empty array but sets the array's **length** property to the given value. Three examples of array declaration are

```
var firstArray = new Array();
var secondArray = new Array("red", "green", "blue");
var thirdArray = new Array(5);
```

The first declaration creates an empty array and places a reference to it in *firstArray*. The second declaration creates a new array with the first value equal to "red," the second value equal to "green," and the last value equal to "blue." The third declaration creates a new empty array whose **length** property has value **5**. There is no particular advantage to using this last syntax, and it is rarely used in practice.

JavaScript 1.2+ allows you to create arrays using array literals. The following declarations are functionally equivalent to those of the previous example:

```
var firstArray = [];
var secondArray = ["red", "green", "blue"];
var thirdArray = [,,,,];
```

The first two declarations should not be surprising, but the third looks rather odd. The given literal has four commas, but the values they separate seem to be missing. The interpreter treats this example as specifying five **undefined** values and sets the array's **length** to **5** to reflect this. Sometimes you will see a sparse array with such syntax:

```
var fourthArray = [,,35,,,16,,23,];
```

Fortunately, most programmers stay away from this last array creation method, as it is troublesome to count numerous commas.

The values used to initialize arrays need not be literals. The following example is perfectly legal and in fact very common:

```
var x = 2.0, y = 3.5, z = 1;
var myValues = [x, y, z];
```

Not surprisingly, the first value of *myValues* is set to **2.0**, the second to **3.5**, and the last to **1**.

Accessing Array Elements

Accessing the elements of an array is done using the array name with square brackets and a value. For example, we can define a three-element array like so:

```
var myArray = [1,51,68];
```

Given that arrays in JavaScript are indexed beginning with zero, to access the first element we would specify `myArray[0]`. The following shows how the various elements in the last array could be accessed:

```
var x = myArray[0];
var y = myArray[1];
var z = myArray[2];
```

However, you need to be careful when accessing an element of an array that is not set. For example,

```
alert(myArray[35]);
```

results in the display of an **undefined** value, since this array element is obviously not set. However, if we wanted to set this array element, doing so is quite straightforward.

Adding and Changing Array Elements

The nice thing about JavaScript arrays is that you don't have to allocate more memory explicitly as the size of the array grows. For example, to add fourth value to *myArray*, you would use

```
myArray[3] = 57;
```

You do not have to set array values contiguously, so

```
myArray[11] = 28;
```

is valid as well. However, in this case you start to get a sparsely populated array, as shown by the dialog here that displays the current value of *myArray*:

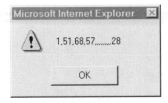

Modifying the values of an array is just as easy. To change the second value of the array, just assign it like this:

```
myArray[1] = 101;
```

Of course, when setting array values, you must remember the distinction between reference and primitive types (made in previous chapters, particularly in Chapter 6). Remember, when you manipulate a variable that has been set equal to a reference type, it modifies the original value as well. For example, consider the following:

```
var firstarray = ["Mars", "Jupiter", "Saturn"]
var secondarray = firstarray;
secondarray[0] = "Neptune";
alert(firstarray);
```

You'll notice, as shown here, that the value in *firstArray* was changed!

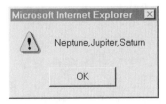

Of course this aspect of reference types is very useful, particularly in the case of parameter passing to functions.

Removing Array Elements

Array elements can be removed using the **delete** operator. This operator sets the array element it is invoked on to **undefined** but does not change the array's **length** (more on this in a moment). For example,

```
var myColors = ["red", "green", "blue"];
delete myColors[1];
alert("The value of myColors[1] is: " + myColors[1]);
```

results in:

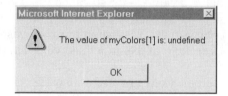

The effect is as if no element had ever been placed at that index. However, the size of the array is actually still three, as shown when you alert the entire array's contents:

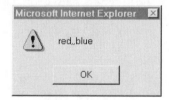

We can also see this by accessing the **length** property of an array like *myColors,* the details of which are discussed next.

The Length Property

The **length** property retrieves the index of the next available (unfilled) position at the end of the array. Even if some lower indices are unused, **length** gives the index of the first available slot after the last element. Consider the following:

```
var myArray = new Array();
myArray[1000] = "This is the only element in the array";

alert(myArray.length);
```

CORE LANGUAGE

Even though *myArray* only has one element at index **1000**, as we see by the alert dialog *myArray.length* that the next available slot is at the end of the array, **1001**.

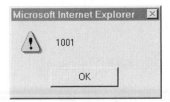

Because of this characteristic of the **length** property, we suggest using array elements in order. Assigning values in a noncontiguous manner leads to arrays that have "holes" between indices holding defined values—the so-called "sparsely populated array" mentioned earlier. Because JavaScript allocates memory only for those array elements that actually contain data, this is not a problem in terms of wasting memory. It merely means that you have to be careful that the undefined values in the "holes" are not accidentally used.

The **length** property is automatically updated as new elements are added to the array. For this reason, **length** is commonly used to iterate through all elements of an array. The following example illustrates array iteration and also a problem that can arise when using an array with "holes:"

```
// define a variable to hold the result of the multiplication
var result = 1;
// define an array to hold the value multiplied
var myValues = new Array();
// set the values
myValues[0] = 2;
myValues[2] = 3;

// iterate through array multiplying each value
for (var index = 0; index < myValues.length; index++)
{
result = result * myValues[index];
}
alert("The value of result is: " + result);
```

As you can see from the result,

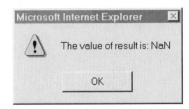

something went very wrong. The expected result was **6**, but we ended up with a value that is not a number (**NaN**). What happened? The array iteration went as expected, but *myValues[1]* was never assigned a value and so remained **undefined**. Attempting to multiply **undefined** by a number results in **NaN** by JavaScript's type conversion rules (see Chapters 3 and 4). The single undefined array element clobbered the entire computation.

Although the previous example is obviously contrived, using arrays with holes requires the programmer to exercise extra caution. We now give a "careful" version of the example, which gives the expected result:

```
var result = 1;
var myValues = new Array();
myValues[0] = 2;
myValues[2] = 3;
for (var index = 0; index < myValues.length; index++)
{
    // check if element is valid or not
    if (myValues[index] != undefined)
    {
        result = result * myValues[index];
    }
}
alert("The value of result is: " + result);
```

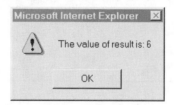

The only difference with this script is that the multiplication has been placed inside of an **if** statement. The **if** statement checks each element for validity and ensures the proper behavior by skipping **undefined** values.

In addition to providing information, the **length** property can be set to perform certain functions. Any indices containing data that are greater than the value assigned to **length** are immediately reset to **undefined**. So, for example, to remove all elements from an array, you could set **length** to zero:

```
var myArray = ["red", "green", "blue"];
myArray.length = 0;
alert("myArray="+myArray);
```

The assignment removes everything from the array by replacing the data at all indices with **undefined**, as if they had never been set. In this case you really aren't going to see much:

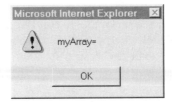

Setting **length** to a value greater than the index of the last valid element has no effect on the array contents, though it will increase the number of undefined slots in the array. Consider, for example, the result of this script.

```javascript
var myArray = ["red", "green", "blue"];
myArray.length = 20;
alert("myArray="+myArray);
```

which is shown here:

You shouldn't bother setting the *length* property directly, since the result of extending an array is usually a sparsely populated array. However, deletion through this method is acceptable. For example, removing the last element in the array with this capability is a bit unwieldy:

```javascript
myArray.length = myArray.length - 1;
```

Newer versions of JavaScript provide a better way to remove the last element with methods the **Array** object provides to simulate stacks and queues.

Arrays as Stacks and Queues

JavaScript 1.2+ and JScript 5.5+ provide methods for treating arrays like stacks and queues. For those readers unfamiliar with these abstract date types, a *stack* is used to store data in *last-in first-out* order, often called LIFO. That is, the first object placed in the stack is the last one retrieved when the stack is read. A *queue* is an abstract data type used to store data in *first-in first-out* order, also called FIFO. Data in a queue is retrieved in the order it was added.

A stack in the form of an array is manipulated using the **push()** and **pop()** methods. Calling **push()** appends the given arguments (in order) to the end of the array and increments the **length** property accordingly. Calling **pop()** removes the last element from the array, returns it, and decrements the **length** property by one. An example of using the properties is as follows. The contents of the array and any values returned are indicated in the comments.

```
var stack = [];            // []
stack.push("first");       // ["first"]
stack.push(10, 20);        // ["first", 10, 20]
stack.pop();               // ["first", 10]        Returns 20
stack.push(2);             // ["first", 10, 2]
stack.pop();               // ["first", 10]        Returns 2
stack.pop();               // ["first"]            Returns 10
stack.pop();               // []                   Returns "first"
```

Of course, you can use **push()** and **pop()** to add data to and remove data from the end of an array without thinking of it as an actual stack.

JavaScript also provides **unshift()** and **shift()** methods. These methods work as **push()** and **pop()** do, except that they add and remove data from the front of the array. Invoking **unshift()** inserts its arguments (in order) at the beginning of the array, shifts existing elements to higher indices, and increments the array's **length** property accordingly. For example,

```
var myArray = [345, 78, 2];
myArray.unshift(4,"fun");
alert(myArray);
```

adds two more elements to the front of the array, as shown here.

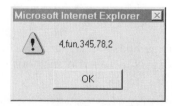

Calling **shift()** removes the first element from the array, returns it, shifts the remaining elements down one index, and decrements **length**. You can think of **shift()**

as shifting each element in the array down one index, causing the first element to be ejected and returned; so, given the previous example, if we called

```
myArray.shift();
```

we would end up with an array containing "fun," 345, 78, and 2. As with **pop()**, invoking **shift()** on an array returns a value that can be used. For example, we could save the value shifted off the array into a variable:

```
var x = myArray.shift();
```

You can use **push()** and **shift()** to simulate a queue. The following example illustrates the principle. We place new data at the end of the array and retrieve data by removing the element at index zero. The contents of the array and any return values are indicated in the comments.

```
var queue = [];
queue.push("first", 10);    // ["first", 10]
queue.shift();              // [10]              Returns "first"
queue.push(20);            // [10, 20]
queue.shift();              // [20]              Returns 10
queue.shift();              // []                Returns 20
```

Even if you never use arrays as stacks or queues, the methods discussed in this section can come in handy to manipulate the contents of arrays. Now let's look at a few more useful array manipulations.

Note   *As mentioned at the start of the chapter, these methods require JavaScript 1.2 or JScript 5.5 or better. Internet Explorer 5 and earlier will not be able to natively use these features. However, using an Array prototype to add our own **pop()** and **push()** methods can fix this problem. See the section entitled "Extending Array with Prototype" later in this chapter.*

Manipulating Arrays

JavaScript provides a wealth of methods for carrying out common operations on arrays. This section provides an overview of these **Array** methods with a brief discussion of some of their quirks.

Concat

The **concat()** method returns the array resulting from appending its arguments to the array on which it was invoked. Given the script,

```
var myArray = ["red", "green", "blue"];
alert(myArray.concat("cyan", "yellow"));
```

the expected larger array is shown here:

Be careful, though; **concat()** does not modify the array in place. Notice the output of this script,

```
var myArray = ["red", "green", "blue"];
myArray.concat("cyan", "yellow");
alert(myArray);
```

which is shown here:

Unlike with the **push()** and **shift()** methods discussed earlier, you will need to save the returned value; for example:

```
var myArray = ["red", "green", "blue"];
myArray = myArray.concat("cyan", "yellow");
```

If any argument to **concat()** is itself an array, it is flattened into array elements. This flattening is not recursive, so an array argument that contains an array element has only its outer array flattened. An example illustrates this behavior more clearly:

```
myArray.concat("pink", ["purple", "black"]);
// Returns ["red", "green", "blue", "pink", "purple", "black"]
myArray.concat("white", ["gray", ["orange", "magenta"]]);
```

```
// Returns ["red", "green", "blue", "white", "gray", ["orange", "magenta"]]
alert(myArray[myArray.length-1]);
// shows orange, magenta
```

*You may notice that arrays are recursively flattened if you output the entire array with an **alert**. However, access the **length** property or the individual elements and it will become apparent that you have nested arrays.*

Join

The **join()** method of JavaScript 1.1+ and JScript 2.0+ converts the array to a string and allows the programmer to specify how the elements are separated in the resulting string. Typically, when you print an array, the output is a comma-separated list of the array elements. You can use **join()** to format the list separators as you'd like:

```
var myArray = ["red", "green", "blue"];
var stringVersion = myArray.join(" / ");
alert(stringVersion);
```

One important thing to note is that the **join()** method will not destroy the array as a side-effect of returning the joined string of its elements. You could obviously do this, if you like, by overriding the type of the object. For example,

```
var myArray = ["red", "green", "blue"];
myArray = myArray.join(" / ");
```

The **join()** method is the inverse of the **split()** method of the **String** object.

Reverse

JavaScript 1.1+ and JScript 2.0+ also allow you to reverse the elements of the array in place. The **reverse()** method, as one might expect, reverses the elements of the array it is invoked on:

```
var myArray = ["red", "green", "blue"];
myArray.reverse();
alert(myArray);
```

CORE LANGUAGE

Slice

The **slice()** method of **Array** (supported since JavaScript 1.2+ JScript 3.0) returns a "slice" (subarray) of the array on which it is invoked. As it does not operate in-place, the original array is unharmed. The method takes two arguments, the *start* and *end* index, and returns an array containing the elements from index *start* up to but not including index *end*. If only one argument is given, the method returns the array composed of all elements from that index to the end of the array. Note that *start* and *end* are allowed to take on negative values. When negative, these values are interpreted as an offset from the end of the array. For example, calling **slice (-2)** returns an array containing the last two elements of the array. More examples of its use are

```
var myArray = [1, 2, 3, 4, 5];
myArray.slice(2);         // returns [3, 4, 5]
myArray.slice(1, 3);      // returns [2, 3]
myArray.slice(-3);        // returns [3, 4, 5]
myArray.slice(-3, -1);    // returns [3, 4]
myArray.slice(-4, 3);     // returns [2, 3]
myArray.slice(3, 1);      // returns []
```

Splice

The **splice()** method, available in JavaScript 1.2+ and JScript 5.5+, can be used to add, replace, or remove elements of an array in place. Any elements that are removed are returned. It takes a variable number of arguments, the first of which is mandatory. The syntax could be summarized as:

```
splice(start, deleteCount, replacevalues);
```

The first argument *start* is the index at which to perform the operation. The second argument is *deleteCount*, the number of elements to delete beginning with index *start*. If *deleteCount* is omitted, all elements from *start* to the end of the array are removed and returned. Any further arguments represented by *replacevalues* (that are comma-separated, if more than one) are inserted in place of the deleted elements.

```
var myArray = [1, 2, 3, 4, 5];
myArray.splice(2, 2);
// myArray = [1, 2, 5]     Returned [3, 4]
```

```
myArray.splice(3);
// myArray = [1, 2, 3]      Returned [4, 5]
myArray.splice(2, 0, 15, 10);
// myArray = [1, 2, 15, 10, 3, 4, 5] Returns []
myArray.splice(1, 2, "red", 22, 7);
// myArray = [1, "red", 22, 7, 4, 5]   Returns [2, 3]
```

Note *There is a bug with the return values of **splice()** in Netscape 4. If a single element is removed, the element itself rather than an array containing the element is returned. In addition, if no elements are removed the method returns nothing instead of the empty array.*

toString and toSource

The **toString()** method returns a string containing the comma-separated values of the array. This method is invoked automatically when you print an array. It is equivalent to invoking **join()** without any arguments. Netscape 4 has an unfortunate bug. When the **<script>** tag has the attribute **language="JavaScript1.2,"** this method includes square brackets in the returned string. Under normal circumstances, the following code,

```
var myArray = [1, [2, 3]];
var stringVersion = myArray.toString();
```

places "1,2,3" in *stringVersion*. But because of the aforementioned bug, under Netscape 4 with the "**JavaScript1.2" language** attribute, the value "[1, [2, 3]]" is assigned to *stringVersion*.

The creation of a string that preserves square brackets is available through the **toSource()** method as of JavaScript 1.3. This allows you to create a string representation of an array that can be passed to the **eval()** function to be used as an array later on. The **eval()** function is discussed in the section entitled "Global" later in this chapter.

Sort

One of the most useful Array methods is **sort()**. Supported since JavaScript 1.1 and JScript 2.0, the **sort()** works much like the **qsort()** function in the standard C library. By default, it sorts the array elements in place according to lexicographic order. It does this by first converting the array elements to string and then sorting them lexiographically. This can cause an unexpected result. Consider the following:

```
var myArray = [14,52,3,14,45,36];
myArray.sort();
alert(myArray);
```

If you run this script you will find that, according that according to this JavaScript sort, 3 is larger than 14! You can see the result here.

The reason for this result is that, from a string ordering perspective, 14 is smaller than 3. Fortunately, the sort function is very flexible and we can fix this. If you want to sort on a different order, you can pass **sort()** a comparison function that determines the order of your choosing. This function should accept two arguments and return a negative value if the first argument should come before the second in the ordering. (Think: the first is "less" than the second.) If the two elements are equal in the ordering, it should return zero. If the first argument should come after the second, the function should return a positive value. (Think: the first is "greater" than the second.) For example, if we wished to perform a numerical sort, we might write a function like:

```
function myCompare(x, y)
{
 if (x < y)
   return -1;
 else if (x === y)
    return 0;
 else
    return 1;
}
```

Then we could use the function in the previous example:

```
var myArray = [14,52,3,14,45,36];
myArray.sort(myCompare);
alert(myArray);
```

Here we get the result that we expect:

If you want to be more succinct, you can use an anonymous function, as described in Chapter 5. Consider this example, which sorts odd numbers before evens:

```
var myArray = [1,2,3,4,5,6];
myArray.sort( function(x, y) {
                      if (x % 2)
                          return -1;
                      if (x % 2 == 0)
                          return 1;
                  }
            );
alert(myArray);
```

The result is shown here:

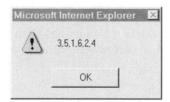

Note that we could make this example more robust by including code that ensures that the even and odd values are each sorted in ascending order.

Multidimensional Arrays

Although not explicitly included in the language, JavaScript supports multidimensional arrays. A *multidimensional array* is an array that has arrays as its elements. For example:

```
var tableOfValues = [[2, 5, 7], [3, 1, 4], [6, 8, 9]];
```

defines a two-dimensional array. Array elements in multidimensional arrays are accessed as you might expect, by using a set of square brackets to indicate the index of the desired element in each dimension. In the previous example, the number **4** is the third element of the second array and so is addressed as *tableOfValues[1][2]*. Similarly, **7** is found at *tableOfValues[0][2]*, **6** at *tableOfValues[2][0]*, and **9** at *tableOfValues[2][2]*.

Extending Array with Prototype

In JavaScript all non-primitive data is derived from the **Object** object, which was discussed in the previous chapter. We should recall that because of this fact we could add new methods and properties to any object we like through object prototypes. For example, we could add a special **display()** method to arrays that alerts the user as to the array contents.

```
function myDisplay()
 {
    if (this.length != 0)
      alert(this.toString());
    else
      alert("The array is empty");
}
Array.prototype.display = myDisplay;
```

We could then print out the value of arrays using our new **display()** method, as illustrated here:

```
var myArray = [4,5,7,32];
myArray.display();
// displays the array values

var myArray2 = [];
myArray2.display();
// displays the string "The array is empty"
```

By using prototypes we can "fix" the lack of **pop()** and **push()** methods in pre-Internet Explorer 5.5 browsers. For example, to add the **pop()** method in older browsers or override safely the built-in **pop()** in newer browsers, we would use:

```
function myPop()
{
  if (this.length != 0)
   {
     var last = this[this.length-1];
      this.length--;
     return last;
    }
}
Array.prototype.pop = myPop;
```

Our own implementation of **push()** is only slightly more complicated and is shown here:

```
function myPush()
{
  var numtopush = this.push.arguments.length;
  var arglist = this.push.arguments;
  if (numtopush > 0)
```

CORE LANGUAGE

```
    {
      for (var i=0; i < numtopush; i++)
        {
          this.length++;
          this[this.length-1] = arguments[i];
        }
    }
}
Array.prototype.push = myPush;
```

We can see that mastery of the ideas from the previous chapter really can come in handy! While our own functions could be used to resolve issues with older browsers, don't think the use of prototypes will solve all your problems with arrays in early versions of JavaScript. Serious deficiencies in array implementations of JavaScript, such as in Netscape 2, probably can't be fixed by prototypes since they may also be lacking. However, if you want to add **push()** and **pop()** support to Internet Explorer 4 or Netscape 3, you'll find this code should do the trick.

Issues with Arrays

JavaScript allows you to use objects as arrays. For example, you can add array elements to a user-defined object:

```
var hybrid = new Object();
hybrid.someVal = "This is an instance property";
hybrid[0] = "This is an array element";
```

This capability can occasionally be useful but should be used with caution. The reason for restraint is that object properties in JavaScript 1.0 share the same internal "slots" as object array values. So our example,

```
var hybrid = new Object();
hybrid.someVal = "This is an instance property";
hybrid[0] = "This clobbers someVal under JavaScript 1.0!";
```

under JavaScript 1.0 replaces the *someVal* property with the string assigned to *hybrid*'s first array position.

There are more troublesome aspects of arrays in JavaScript 1.0: there was no **Array()** constructor, there were no **Array** methods, and user-created arrays did not have the **length** property. The way programmers created arrays in JavaScript 1.0 was to declare a user-defined object and use the array syntax of the object that we previously saw. If you must include support for JavaScript 1.0, creating your own array object is your best bet. It is not all that difficult and doing so might be a good exercise.

Boolean

Boolean is the built-in object corresponding to the primitive Boolean data type. This object is extremely simple. It has no interesting properties of its own. It inherits all of its properties and methods from the generic **Object**. So it has **toSource()**, **toString()**, and **valueOf()**. Out of these, maybe the only method of practical use is the **toString()** method, which returns the string "true" if the value is **true** or "false" otherwise. The constructor takes an optional Boolean value indicating its initial value:

```
var boolData = new Boolean(true);
```

However if you don't set a value with the constructor it will be false by default.

```
var anotherBool = new Boolean();
// set to false
```

Because of some subtleties in JavaScript's type conversion rules, it is almost always preferrable to use primitive Boolean values than **Boolean** objects.

Date

The **Date** object provides a sophisticated set of methods for manipulating dates and times. Working with some of the more advanced methods that **Date** provides can be a bit confusing, unless you understand the relationship between Greenwich Mean Time (GMT), Coordinated Universal Time (UTC), and local time zones. Fortunately, for the vast majority of applications you can assume that GMT is the same as UTC and that your computer's clock is faithfully ticking away GMT and is aware of your particular time zone.

There are several facts to be aware of when working with JavaScript date values:

- JavaScript stores dates internally as the number of milliseconds since the "epoch," January 1st, 1970 (GMT). This is an artifact of the way UNIX systems store their time and can cause problems if you wish to work with dates prior to the epoch in older browsers.

- When reading the current date and time, your script is at the mercy of the client machine's clock. If the client's date or time is incorrect, your script will reflect this fact.

- Days of the week and months of the year are enumerated beginning with zero. So day **0** is Sunday, day **6** is Saturday, month **0** is January, and month **11** is December. Days of the month, however, are numbered beginning with one.

Creating Dates

The syntax of the **Date()** constructor is significantly more powerful than other constructors we have seen. The constructor takes optional arguments permitting the creation of **Date** objects representing points in the past or future. Table 7-1 describes constructor arguments and their results.

Argument	Description	Example
none	Creates object with the current date and time.	var rightNow = new Date();
"month dd, yyyy hh:mm:ss"	Creates object with the date represented by the specified month, day (dd), year (yyyy), hour (hh), minute (mm), and second (ss). Any omitted values are set to zero.	var birthDay = new Date("March 24, 1970"); Date ("March 24, 1970 24:12:59")
milliseconds	Creates object with date represented as the integer number of milliseconds after the epoch.	var someDate = new Date(795600003020);
yyyy, mm, dd	Creates object with the date specified by the integer values year (yyyy), month (mm), and day (dd).	var birthDay = new Date(1970, 2, 24);
yyyy, mm, dd, hh, mm, ss	Creates object with the date specified by the integer values for the year, month, day, hours, minutes, and seconds.	var birthDay = new Date(1970, 2, 24, 15, 0, 0);
yyyy, mm, dd, hh, mm, ss, ms	Creates object with the date specified by the integer values for the year, month, day, hours, seconds, and milliseconds.	var birthDay = new Date(1970, 2, 24, 15, 0, 250);

Table 7-1. *Arguments to the Date() Constructor*

Table 7-1 warrants some commentary. The string version of the constructor argument can be any date string that can be parsed by the **Date.parse()** method. In the syntax of the last two formats, the arguments beyond the year, month, and day are optional. If they are omitted, they are set to zero. The final syntax that includes milliseconds is available only in JavaScript 1.3+.

Note *Because of the ambiguity that arises from representing the year with two digits, you should always use four digits when specifying the year. This can be done using the getFullYear() method discussed later in this section.*

It is important to note that **Date** objects you create are static. They do not contain a ticking clock. **Date** objects are created to be picked apart and manipulated and to assist in formatting dates according to your specific application. If you need to use a timer of some sort, the **setInterval()** and **setTimeout()** methods of the **Window** object are much more appropriate. These other methods are discussed both in Appendix B as well as in later application-oriented chapters. You can, however, calculate the difference between two dates directly:

```
var firstDate = new Date(1995, 0, 6);
var secondDate = new Date(1999, 11, 2);
var difference = secondDate - firstDate;
alert(difference);
```

The result indicates the approximate number of milliseconds elapsed between January 6, 1995 and December 2, 1999:

Converting this to a more usable value isn't difficult and is discussed next.

Manipulating Dates

To hide the fact that **Date** objects store values as millisecond offsets from the epoch, dates are manipulated through the methods they provide. That is, **Date** values are set and retrieved by invoking a method rather than setting or reading a property directly. These methods handle the conversion of millisecond offsets to human-friendly formats and back again for you automatically. The following example illustrates a few of the common **Date** methods:

```
var myDate = new Date();
var year = myDate.getYear();
year = year + 1;
myDate.setYear(year);

alert(myDate);
```

This example gets the current date and adds one year to it. The result is shown here:

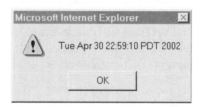

JavaScript provides a comprehensive set of **get** and **set** methods to read and write each field of a date, including **getDate()**, **setDate()**, **getMonth()**, **setMonth()**, **getHours()**, **setHours()**, **getMinutes()**, **setMinutes()**, **getTime()**, **setTime**, and so on. In addition, UTC versions of all these methods are also included: **getUTCMonth()**, **getUTCHours()**, **setUTCMonth()**, **setUTCHours()**, and so forth. One set of methods requires a special comment: **getDay()** and **setDay()**. These are used to manipulate the day of the week that is stored as an integer from **0** (Sunday) to **6** (Saturday). An example that illustrates many of the common **Date** methods in practice is shown here (the results are shown in Figure 7-1):

```
var today = new Date();
document.write("The current date : "+today+"<br>");
document.write("Date.getDate() : "+today.getDate()+"<br>");
document.write("Date.getDay() : "+today.getDay()+"<br>");
document.write("Date.getFullYear() : "+today.getFullYear()+"<br>");
document.write("Date.getHours() : "+today.getHours()+"<br>");
document.write("Date.getMilliseconds() : "+today.getMilliseconds()+"<br>");
document.write("Date.getMinutes() : "+today.getMinutes()+"<br>");
document.write("Date.getMonth() : "+today.getMonth()+"<br>");
document.write("Date.getSeconds() : "+today.getSeconds()+"<br>");
document.write("Date.getTime() : "+today.getTime()+"<br>");
document.write("Date.getTimezoneOffset() : "+today.getTimezoneOffset()+"<br>");
document.write("Date.getYear() : "+today.getYear()+"<br>");
```

A complete list of methods supported by **Date** objects is given in Appendix B.

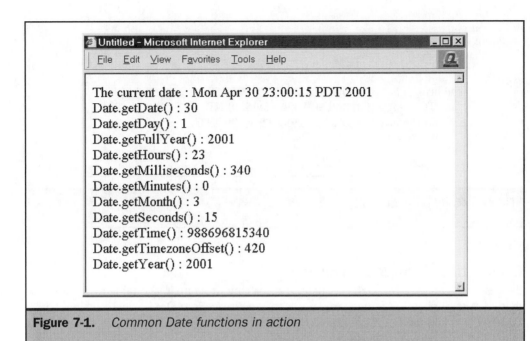

Figure 7-1.   *Common Date functions in action*

Converting Dates to Strings

There are a variety of ways to convert **Date** objects to strings. If you need to create a date string of a custom format, the best way to do so is to read the individual components from the object and piece the string together manually. If you want to create a string in a standard format, **Date** provides three methods to do so. These methods are **toString()**, **toUTCString()**, and **toGMTString()**, and their use is illustrated in the next example. Note that **toUTCString()** and **toGMTString()** format the string according to Internet (GMT) standards, whereas **toString()** creates the string according to "local" time. The result is shown in Figure 7-2.

```
var appointment = new Date("February 24, 1996 7:45");
document.write("toString():", appointment.toString());
document.write("<br>");
document.write("toUTCString():", appointment.toUTCString());
document.write("<br>");
document.write("toGMTString():", appointment.toGMTString());
```

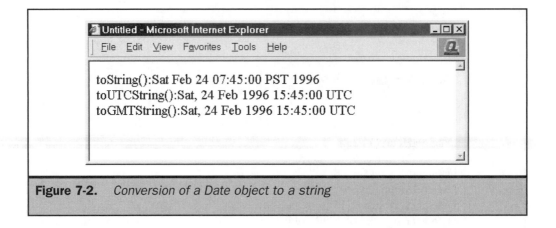

Figure 7-2.   *Conversion of a Date object to a string*

Converting Strings to Dates

Because you can pass the **Date()** constructor a string, it seems reasonable to assume that JavaScript provides a mechanism to convert strings into **Date** objects. It does so through the class method **Date.parse()**, which returns an integer indicating the number of milliseconds between the epoch and its argument. Note that this method is a property of the **Date** constructor, not of individual **Date** instances.

The **parse()** method is very flexible with regard to the dates it can convert to milliseconds (the complete details of the method are found in Appendix B). The string passed as its argument can, naturally, be a valid string of the form indicated in Table 7-1. Also recognized are standard timezones, timezone offsets from GMT and UTC, and the month/day/year triples formatted with "-" or "/" separators as well as month and day abbreviations like "Dec" and "Tues." For example,

```
// Set value = December 14, 1982
var myDay = "12/14/82";
// convert it to milliseconds
var converted = Date.parse(myDay);
// create a new Date object
var myDate = new Date(converted);
// output the date
alert(myDate);
```

creates *myDate* with the correct value shown here:

If you are not sure whether the particular string you wish to convert will be recognized by **Date.parse()**, you need to check the value it returns. If it cannot convert the given string to a date, the method returns **NaN**. For example, the invocation in this example,

```
var myDay = "Friday, 2002";
var invalid = Date.parse(myDay);
```

results in **NaN** because *myDay* does not contain enough information to resolve the date.

Limitations of Date Representations

The nuances of the **Date** object should not be underestimated. Recall that ECMA-262 is the standard governing core JavaScript language features. While most aspects of browser implementations adhere to the specification rigorously, deviation in **Date** object behavior is commonplace. For example, **Date** support in Netscape 2 is atrocious. There are so many bugs that the programmer is advised to avoid all but the simplest date operations on this platform. Netscape 3 is better, but still has problems handling timezones correctly. At the very least, caution should be exercised when manipulating dates in these two versions of Netscape. Internet Explorer 3 does not allow dates prior to the epoch. However, Netscape 4+ and Internet Explorer 4+ can handle dates hundreds and thousands of years before or after the epoch, which should be enough to handle most tasks. Of course using extreme dates such as prior to 1 A.D. or far in the future should be done with caution. Appendix B contains full details on the various **Date** methods and implementation issues.

Global

The **Global** object is a seldom-mentioned object that is a catchall for top-level properties and methods that are not part of any other object. You cannot create an instance of the **Global** object; it is defined in the ECMA-262 standard to be a place for globally accessible, otherwise homeless properties to reside. It provides several essential properties that can be used anywhere in JavaScript. Table 7-2 summarizes its most useful methods. These methods are called directly and are not prefixed with "global." In fact, doing so will result in an error. It is because the methods appear unrelated to any particular object that some documentation on JavaScript refers to these as "global" or built-in functions.

Method	Description	Example

escape()	Takes a string and returns a string where all non-alphanumeric characters, such as spaces, tabs, and special characters, have been replaced with their hexadecimal equivalents in the form %xx.	var aString="O'Neill & Sons";
		// aString = "O'Neill & Sons"
		aString = escape(aString);
		// aString="O%27Neill%20%26%20Sons"

eval()	Takes a string and executes it as JavaScript code.	var x;
		var aString = "5+9";
		x = aString;
		// x contains the string "5+9"
		x = eval(aString);
		// x will contain the number 14

isFinite()	Returns a Boolean indicating whether its number argument is finite.	var x;
		x = isFinite('56');
		// x is true
		x = isFinite(Infinity)
		// x is false

isNaN()	Returns a Boolean indicating whether its number argument is **NaN**.	var x;
		x = isNaN('56');
		// x is False
		x = isNaN(0/0)
		// x is true
		x = isNaN(NaN);
		// x is true

parseFloat()	Converts the string argument to a floating point number and returns the value. If the string cannot be converted, it returns **NaN**. The method should handle strings starting with numbers and peel off what it needs, but other mixed strings will not be converted.	var x;
		x = parseFloat("33.01568");
		// x is 33.01568
		x = parseFloat("47.6k-red-dog");
		// x is 47.6
		x = parseFloat("a567.34");
		// x is NaN
		x = parseFloat("won't work");
		// x is NaN

Table 7-2. *Globally Available Methods*

Method	Description	Example

parseInt()	Converts the string argument to an integer and returns the value. If the string cannot be converted, it returns **NaN**. Like **parseFloat()**, this method should handle strings starting with numbers and peel off what it needs, but other mixed strings will not be converted.	var x;
		x = parseInt("-53");
		// x is -53
		x = parseInt("33.01568");
		// x is 33
		x = parseInt("47.6k-red-dog");
		// x is 47
		x = parseInt("a567.34");
		// x is NaN
		x = parseInt("won't work");
		// x is NaN

unescape()	Takes a hexadecimal string value containing some characters of the form %xx and returns the ISO-Latin-1 ASCII equivalent of the passed values.	varaString="O%27Neill%20%26%20Sons";
		aString = unescape(aString);
		// aString = "O'Neill & Sons"
		aString = unescape("%64%56%26%23"); // aString = "dV&#"

Table 7-2.   *Globally Available Methods* (continued)

Note   *The **Global** object also defines the constants **NaN** and **Infinity** that were used in the examples in Table 7-2. However, similar constants are also provided by the **Number** object discussed later in the chapter.*

The **Global** methods are very useful and will be used in examples throughout the book. Aspiring JavaScript programmers should try to become very familiar with them. One interesting consideration is the escaping of strings provided by **escape()** and **unescape()**. Primarily, we see this done on the Web in order to create URL safe strings. You probably have seen this when working with forms. While these methods would be extremely useful, the ECMAScript specification suggests that **escape()** and **unescape()** should be deprecated

CORE LANGUAGE

in favor of the more aptly named **encodeURI()**, **encodeURIComponent()**, **decodeURI()**, and **decodeURIComponent()**. Their use is illustrated here:

```
var aURLFragment = encodeURIComponent("term=O'Neill & Sons");
document.writeln("Encoded URI Component: "+aURLFragment);
document.writeln("Decoded URI Component: "+decodeURIComponent(aURLFragment));

var aURL = encodeURI("http://www.pint.com/cgi-bin/search?term=O'Neill & Sons");
document.writeln("Encoded URI: "+ aURL);
document.writeln("Decoded URI: "+ decodeURI(aURL));
```

While these methods are part of the specification, programmers are advised to avoid them for the time being until more browsers support them and to rely on **escape()** and **unescape()** instead. A complete documentation of **Global**, including these issues, can be found in Appendix B.

Math

The **Math** object holds a set of constants and methods enabling more complex mathematical operations than the basic arithmetic operators discussed in Chapter 4. You cannot instantiate a **Math** object as you would an **Array** or **Date**. The **Math** object is static (automatically created by the interpreter) so its properties are accessed directly. For example, to compute the square root of **10**, the **sqrt()** method is accessed through the **Math** object directly:

```
var root = Math.sqrt(10);
```

Table 7-3 gives a complete list of constants provided by **Math**. A complete list of mathematical methods is given in Table 7-4.

Property	Description
Math.E	The base of the natural logarithm (Euler's constant e)
Math.LN2	Natural log of 2
Math.LN10	Natural log of 10
Math.LOG2E	Log (base 2) of e
Math.LOG10E	Log (base 10) of e

Table 7-3. *Constants Provided by the Math Object*

Property	Description
Math.PI	Pi (π)
Math.SQRT1_2	Square root of 0.5 (equivalently, one over the square root of 2)
Math.SQRT2	Square root of 2

Table 7-3. *Constants Provided by the Math Object* (continued)

Method	Returns
Math.abs(*arg*)	Absolute value of *arg*
Math.acos(*arg*)	Arc cosine of *arg*
Math.asin(*arg*)	Arc sine of *arg*
Math.atan(*arg*)	Arc tangent of *arg*
Math.atan2(*y*, *x*)	Angle between the x-axis and the point (x, y), measured counterclockwise (like polar coordinates). Note how *y* is passed as the first argument rather than the second.
Math.ceil(*arg*)	Ceiling of *arg* (smallest integer greater than or equal to *arg*)
Math.cos(*arg*)	Cosine of *arg*
Math.exp(*arg*)	*e* to *arg* power
Math.floor(*arg*)	Floor of *arg* (greatest integer less than or equal to *arg*)
Math.log(*arg*)	Natural log of *arg* (log base *e* of *arg*)
Math.max(*arg1*, *arg2*)	The greater of *arg1* or *arg2*
Math.min(*arg1*, *arg2*)	The lesser of *arg1* or *arg2*
Math.pow(*arg1*, *arg2*)	*arg1* to the *arg2* power
Math.random()	A random number in the interval [0,1]
Math.round(*arg*)	The result of rounding *arg* to the nearest integer. If the decimal portion of *arg* is greater than or equal to .5, it is rounded up. Otherwise *arg* is rounded down.

Table 7-4. *Methods Provided by the Math Object*

Method	Returns
Math.sin(*arg*)	Sine of *arg*
Math.sqrt(*arg*)	Square root of *arg*
Math.tan(*arg*)	Tangent of *arg*

Table 7-4. *Methods Provided by the Math Object* (continued)

There are several aspects of the **Math** object that need to be kept in mind. The trigonometric methods work in radians, so you need to multiply any degree measurements by $\pi / 180$ before using them. Also, because of the imprecise characteristic of floating-point operations, you might notice minor deviations from the results you expect. For example, though the sine of π is **0**, the following code:

```
alert(Math.sin(Math.PI));
```

gives the result:

This value is very close to zero, but just large enough to trip up sensitive calculations.

It might seem that **Math** does not provide the capability to compute logarithms in bases other than *e*. Indeed it does not, directly. However the following mathematical identity:

```
loga n = (loge n) / (loge a)
```

can be used to compute logarithms in an arbitrary base. For example, you can compute the log base 2 of 64 as:

```
var x = Math.log(64) / Math.log(2);
```

Random Numbers

Because the **Math.random()** method returns values between zero and one, you must normalize its return value to fit the range of numbers required of your application. An easy way to get random integers in the range *m* to *n* (inclusive) is as follows:

```
Math.round(Math.random() * (n - m)) + m;
```

Generating random numbers in this manner is sufficient for most applications, but if "high quality" randomness is required, a more advanced technique should be used.

Easing Math Computations

When working extensively with the **Math** object, it is often convenient to use the **with** statement. Doing so allows you to use **Math** properties without prefixing them with "Math." The concept is illustrated by the following example (computing the length of a side of a triangle with the Law of Cosines):

```
with (Math)
{
   var a = 3, b = 4, c;
   var angleA = atan(a / b);
   var angleB = atan(b / a);
   var angleC = PI / 2;
   c = pow(a, 2) + pow(b, 2) - 2 * a * b * cos(angleC);
   c = sqrt(c);
}
```

Number

Number is the built-in object corresponding to the primitive number data type. As discussed in Chapter 3, all numbers are represented in IEEE 754-1985 double-precision floating-point format. This representation is 64 bits long, permitting floating-point magnitudes as large as $\pm1.7976\times10^{308}$ and as small as $\pm2.2250\times10^{-308}$. The **Number()** constructor takes an optional argument specifying its initial value:

```
var x = new Number();
var y = new Number(17.5);
```

Table 7-5 lists the special numeric values that are provided as properties of the **Number** object.

Property	Value
Number.MAX_VALUE	Largest magnitude representable
Number.MIN_VALUE	Smallest magnitude representable
Number.POSITIVE_INFINITY	The special value **Infinity**
Number.NEGATIVE_INFINITY	The special value **-Infinity**
Number.NaN	The special value **NaN**

Table 7-5. *Properties of the Number Object*

The only useful method of this object is **toString()**, which returns the value of the number in a string. Of course it is rarely needed, given that generally a number type converts to a string when we need to use it as such.

String

String is the built-in object corresponding to the primitive string data type. It contains a very large number of methods for string manipulation and examination, substring extraction, and even conversion of strings to marked-up HTML. A full description of all **String** methods, including examples, is included in Appendix B. Here we highlight most of them with a focus on those that are most commonly used.

The **String()** constructor takes an optional argument that specifies its initial value:

```
var s = new String();
var headline = new String("Dewey Defeats Truman");
```

Because you can invoke **String** methods on primitive strings, programmers rarely create **String** objects in practice.

The only property of **String** is **length**, which indicates the number of characters in the string.

```
var s = "String fun in JavaScript";
var strlen = s.length;
// strlen is set to 24
```

The **length** property is automatically updated when the string changes and cannot be set by the programmer. In fact there is *no* way to manipulate a string directly. That is, **String** methods do not operate on their data "in place." Any method that would change the value of the string returns a string containing the result. If you want to change the value of the string you must set the string equal to the result of the operation. For example, converting a string to uppercase with the **toUpperCase()** method would require the following syntax:

```
var s = "abc";
s = s.toUpperCase();
// s is "ABC"
```

Invoking *s.toUpperCase()* without setting *s* equal to its result does not change the value of *s*. The following does *not* modify *s*:

```
var s = "abc";
s.toUpperCase();
// s is still "abc"
```

Other simple string manipulation methods such as **toLowerCase()** work in the same way; forgetting this fact is a common mistake made by new JavaScript programmers.

Examining Strings

Individual characters can be examined with the **charAt()** method. It accepts an integer indicating the character to return. Because JavaScript makes no distinction between individual characters and strings, it returns a string containing the desired character. Remember that, like arrays, characters in JavaScript strings are enumerated beginning with zero; so,

```
"JavaScript".charAt(1);
```

retrieves "a." You can also retrieve the numeric value associated with a particular character using **charCodeAt()**. Because the value of "a" in Unicode is **97**, the following statement,

```
"JavaScript".charCodeAt(1);
```

returns **97**.

Conversion from a character code is easy enough using the **fromCharCode()** method. Unlike the other methods, this is generally used with the generic object **String** itself rather than a string instance. For example,

```
var aChar = String.fromCharCode(82);
```

would set the value of the variable *aChar* to **R**. Multiple codes can be passed in by separating them with commas. For example,

```
var aString = String.fromCharCode(68,79,71);
```

would set *aString* to "DOG."

 *You will probably receive a **?** value for any unknown values passed to the fromCharCode() method.*

The **indexOf()** method takes a string argument and returns the index of the first occurrence of the argument in the string. For example,

```
"JavaScript".indexOf("Script");
```

returns **4**. If the argument is not found, **-1** is returned. This method also accepts an optional second argument that specifies the index at which to start the search. When specified, the method returns the index of the first occurrence of the argument at or after the start index. For example,

```
"JavaScript".indexOf("a", 2);
```

returns **3**. A related method is **lastIndexOf()**, which returns the index of the last occurrence of the string given as an argument. It also accepts an optional second argument that indicates the index at which to end the search. For example,

```
"JavaScript".lastIndexOf("a", 2);
```

returns **1**. This method also returns **-1** if the string is not found.

There are numerous ways to extract substrings in JavaScript. The best way to do so is with **substring()**. The first argument to **substring()** specifies the index at which the desired substring begins. The optional second argument indicates the index at which the desired substring ends. The method returns a string containing the substring beginning at the given index up to but not including the character at the index specified by the second argument. For example:

```
"JavaScript".substring(3);
```

returns "aScript," and

```
"JavaScript".substring(3, 7);
```

returns "aScr". The **slice()** method is a slightly more powerful version of **substring()**. It accepts the same arguments as **substring()** but the indices are allowed to be negative. A negative index is treated as an offset from the end of the string.

The **match()** and **search()** methods use regular expressions to perform more complicated examination of strings. The use of regular expressions is discussed in the next chapter.

Manipulating Strings

The most basic operation one can perform with strings is concatenation. Concatenating strings with the + operator should be familiar by now. The **String** object also provides a **concat()** method to achieve the same result. It accepts any number of arguments and returns the string obtained by concatenating the arguments to the string on which it was invoked. For example,

```
var s = "JavaScript".concat(" is", " a", " flexible", " language.");
```

assigns "JavaScript is a flexible language." to the variable *s*, just as the following would:

```
var s = "JavaScript" + " is" + " a" + " flexible" + " language";
```

A method that comes in very useful when parsing preformatted strings is **split()**. The **split()** method breaks the string up into separate strings according to a delimiter passed as its first argument. The result is returned in an array. For example,

```
var wordArray = "A simple example".split(" ");
```

assigns *wordArray* an array with three elements, "A," "simple," and "example." Passing the empty string as the delimiter breaks the string up into an array of strings containing individual characters. The method also accepts a second argument that specifies the maximum number of elements into which the string can be broken. There are some subtle issues with the behavior of **split()**, so reading its full description in Appendix B before use is highly suggested.

Regular expressions, discussed in the next chapter, provide powerful tools for string manipulation and validation. They allow the programmer to specify patterns against which strings are matched and enable the extraction or transformation of those portions of the string that match the pattern. Many **String** methods accept regular expressions as arguments. For example, you can invoke **split()** with a regular expression as a delimiter in order to parse strings that have a complicated structure.

CORE LANGUAGE

Marking Up Strings as HTML

Because JavaScript is commonly used to manipulate Web pages, the **String** object provides a large set of methods that mark strings up as HTML. Each of these methods returns the string surrounded by a pair of HTML tags. For example, the **bold()** method places **<B>** and **</B>** tags around the string it is invoked on; the following,

```
var s = "This is very important".bold();
```

places this string in *s*:

```
<B>This is very important</B>
```

You may wonder how to apply more than one HTML-related method to a string. This is easily accomplished by chaining method invocations. While chained method invocations can appear intimidating, they come in handy when creating HTML markup from strings. For example,

```
var s = "This is important".bold().strike().blink();
```

assigns the following string to *s*:

```
<BLINK><STRIKE><B>This is important</B></STRIKE></BLINK>
```

This displays a blinking, struck-through, bold string when placed in a Web document. Ignoring the fact that such strings are incredibly annoying, the example illustrates how method invocations can be "chained" together for efficiency. It is easier to write the invocations in series than to invoke each on *s*, one at a time. Note how the methods were invoked "inner-first," or, equivalently, left to right.

The various HTML **String** methods correspond to common HTML tags. A complete list of the HTML-related **String** methods can be found in Table 7-6.

Method	Description	Example
anchor(name)	Creates a named anchor specified by the <A> element using the argument name as the value of the corresponding attribute.	var x = "Marked point".anchor("marker"); // <A NAME="marker" Marked point</A>

Table 7-6. *HTML-Related String Methods*

Method	Description	Example
big()	Creates a <BIG> element using the provided string.	var x = "Grow".big(); // <BIG>Grow</BIG>
blink()	Creates a blinking text element enclosed by <BLINK> out of the provided string (despite Internet Explorer's lack of support for the <BLINK> element).	var x = "Bad Netscape".blink(); // <BLINK>Bad Netscape // </BLINK>
bold()	Creates a bold text element indicated by <B> out of the provided string.	var x = "Behold!".bold(); // <B>Behold!</B>
fixed()	Creates a fixed width text element indicated by <TT> out of the provided string.	var x = "Code".fixed(); // <TT>Code</TT>

fontcolor(color)	Creates a <FONT> tag with the color specified by the argument color. The value passed should be a valid hexadecimal string value or a string specifying a color name.	var x =
		"Green".fontcolor("green");
		// <FONT COLOR="green">
		// Green</FONT>
		
		var x =
		"Red".fontcolor("#FF0000");
		// <FONT COLOR="FF0000">
		// Red</FONT>

fontsize(size)	Takes the argument specified by size that should be either in the range 1-7 or a relative +/- value of 1-7 and creates a <FONT> element.	var x = "Change size".font(7);
		// <FONT SIZE="7">Change
		//size</FONT>
		var x = "Change size".font("+1");
		// <FONT SIZE="+1">
		// Change size</FONT>

italics()	Creates an italics element <I>.	var x = "Special".italics(); // <I>Special</I>

Table 7-6. *HTML Related String Methods* (continued)

Method	Description	Example

link(location)	Takes the argument location and forms a link with the \<A\> element using the string as the link text.	var x = "click here".location("http://www.pint.com/");
		// \<A HREF="http://www.pint.com">
		// click here\</A\>

small()	Creates a \<SMALL\> element out of the provided string.	var x = "Shrink".small(); // \<SMALL\>Shrink\</SMALL\>
strike()	Creates a \<STRIKE\> element out of the provided string.	var x = "Legal".strike(); // \<STRIKE\>Legal\</STRIKE\>
sub()	Creates a subscript element specified by \<SUB\> out of the provided string.	var x = "test".sub() // \<SUB\>test\</SUB\>
sup()	Creates a superscript element specified by \<SUP\> out of the provided string.	var x = "test".sup() // \<SUP\>test\</SUP\>

Table 7-6. *HTML Related String Methods* (continued)

Note *You may notice that it is possible to pass just about anything to these HTML methods. For example "bad".fontcolor('junk') will happily create a string containing the markup \<FONT COLOR="junk"\>bad\</FONT\>. No range or type checking related to HTML is provided by these methods.*

Notice in Table 7-6 how these JavaScript methods produce uppercase and even nonstandard markup like **\<BLINK\>** rather than XHTML-compliant tags. In fact, many of the methods like **fontcolor()** create markup strings containing deprecated elements that have been phased out under HTML 4 in favor of CSS-based presentation. Yet given the relatively slow uptake of XHTML and the only-recent adoption of CSS on the Web at large, it is pretty unlikely that the transition away from these elements will happen soon. Fortunately, once this does happen, we are going to have a much better set of HTML-related JavaScript methods than these **String** methods. The Document Object Model will allow us to easily create and manipulate any HTML element, as discussed starting in Chapter 10. Before concluding this chapter it is important to understand one subtle issue concerning type-related objects.

Object Types and Primitive Types

After reading this chapter it should be clear that, as discussed in Chapter 3, each primitive type has a corresponding built-in object. This is not obvious since primitive data values are transparently converted to the appropriate object when one of its properties is accessed. There are two circumstances when you might prefer to declare a variable as a built-in object rather than use the primitive type. The first is if you plan to add instance properties to the object. Because you cannot add instance properties to primitive data, you must declare the variable as the appropriate object if you wish to do so. The second reason is if you wish to pass a reference to the data to a function. Because JavaScript uses call-by-value, a copy of primitive data is passed to function arguments; the function cannot modify the original. Objects, on the other hand, are reference types. Called functions receive a copy of the reference and can therefore modify the original data.

Outside of these two cases, there is no particular reason to prefer the object versions of Boolean, string, or number data over their primitive counterparts. It is highly unlikely that choosing one over the other will have any significant effect on performance or memory usage. The programmer should use whichever one he or she finds most convenient. Examination of real-world scripts on the Web reveals that the vast majority use primitive types.

Summary

Built-in objects are those provided by the JavaScript language itself, such as **Array**, **Boolean**, **Date**, **Math**, **Number**, and **String**. Many of the built-in objects are related to the various data types supported in the language. Programmers will often access the methods and properties of the built-in objects related to the complex data types such as arrays or strings. The **Math** and **Date** objects are commonly used as well in JavaScript applications. However, much of the time the fact that the primitive types are objects— as are everything else in JavaScript including functions—goes unnoticed by JavaScript programmers. Understanding these underlying relationships can make you a better JavaScript programmer. However, if you feel you don't fully comprehend or care about the interconnectedness of it all and just want to use the provided methods and properties of the various built-in objects, you'll still find an arsenal of easy-to-use and powerful features at your disposal. The next chapter takes a look at one very useful aspect of JavaScript: regular expressions.

CORE LANGUAGE

The Complete Reference

Chapter 8

Regular Expressions

M anipulation of textual data is a common task in JavaScript. Checking data entered into forms, creating and parsing cookies, constructing and modifying URLs, and changing the content of Web pages can all involve complicated operations on strings. The suitability of languages with powerful text manipulation capabilities for such Web-related tasks are what make them such popular choices for Web applications. In JavaScript, a *regular expression* allows you to specify patterns of characters and sets of strings without listing them explicitly. Regular expressions, sometimes referred to as *regexps* or *regexes* for brevity, have long been a part of UNIX operating systems. Readers unfamiliar with tools like *grep*, *sed*, *awk*, and *Perl* might find regular expressions odd at first but will soon recognize their utility. If you have ever used the "dir" command in DOS or "ls" in UNIX, chances are you've used "wildcard" characters such as "*" or "?". These are primitive regular expressions! Readers who have worked in more depth with regular expressions, especially with Perl, will find JavaScript regexps very familiar. This chapter is an introduction to JavaScript's **RegExp** object. It covers basic syntax, common tasks, and more advanced applications of regular expressions in your scripts. We start off with very basic regexp syntax and proceed to add more functionality in each section.

The Need for Regular Expressions

Consider the task for validating e-mail addresses in a form submission. The goal is to verify that the given address has the proper format before submitting it to the remote server in order to prevent needless processing of malformed data that result from typos. You might check first to see if the string contains the "@" symbol. Then you might ensure that there is at least one character before and after the "@" and that the string contains at least one period. Then you might check the set of characters after the final period for validity, perhaps against country codes and top-level domains like "org," "com," and "net." Clearly, writing code to check each of these conditions individually by examining the string one character at a time would be very tedious. Now imagine how much more tedious it would be to replace all instances of e-mail addresses in a string with something else. Not only would you have to recognize all valid addresses, but you would have to write the code to remove them and replace them one at a time.

Regular expressions simplify tasks like this considerably by allowing the programmer to specify a pattern against which a string is "matched." The portions of the string that match the given regular expression can be easily located, extracted, or even replaced. This simplifies the recognition and extraction of structured data like URLs, e-mail addresses, phone numbers, and cookies. Just about any type of string data with a predictable format can be operated upon with regular expressions.

Introduction to JavaScript Regular Expressions

Regular expressions were introduced in JavaScript 1.2 and JScript 3.0 with the **RegExp** object, so much of their functionality is available through **RegExp** methods. However, many methods of the **String** object take regular expressions as arguments; so you will see regexps commonly used in both contexts.

Regular expressions are most often created using their literal syntax, in which the characters that make up the pattern are surrounded by slashes ("/" and "/"). For example, to create a regular expression that will match any string containing "http," you might write the following:

```
var pattern = /http/;
```

Flags that alter the interpretation of the pattern can be given immediately following the second slash. For example, to specify that the pattern is to ignore case, the "i" flag is used:

```
var patternIgnoringCase = /http/i;
```

This declaration creates a pattern that will match "http" as well as "HTTP" and "HttP." The common flags used with regular expressions are shown in Table 8-1 and will be illustrated in examples throughout the chapter.

Regular expressions can also be declared using the **RegExp()** constructor. The first argument to the constructor is a string containing the desired pattern. The second

Character	Meaning
i	Case-insensitive.
g	Global match. Find *all* matches in the string, rather than just the first.
m	Multiline matching.

Table 8-1. *Regular Expression Flags*

argument is optional, and contains any special flags for that expression. The two previous examples could equivalently be declared as:

```
var pattern = new RegExp("http");
var patternIgnoringCase = new RegExp("http", "i");
```

The constructor syntax is most commonly used when the pattern to match against is not determined until run time. You might allow the user to enter a regular expression and then pass the string containing that expression to the **RegExp()** constructor.

The most basic method provided by the **RegExp** object is **test()**. This method returns a Boolean indicating whether the string given as its argument matches the given pattern. For example, given the previous declarations we could test

```
pattern.test("HTTP://WWW.W3C.ORG/");
```

which returns **false** because *pattern* matches only strings containing "http." Or we could test using the case-insensitive pattern:

```
patternIgnoringCase.test("HTTP://WWW.W3C.ORG/");
```

which returns **true** because it matches for strings containing "http" while ignoring case. Of course, you won't see much unless you use the returned value:

```
alert(patternIgnoringCase.test("HTTP://WWW.W3C.ORG/"));
```

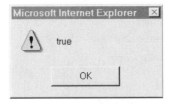

Because of JavaScript's automatic type conversion, you can invoke **RegExp** methods on regular expression literals (just like **String** methods on string literals). For example,

```
/http/i.test("HTTP://WWW.W3C.ORG/");
```

would return **true** as well.

Creating Patterns

Regular expressions use special character sequences to enable the programmer to create complicated patterns. The examples so far have merely checked for the presence of a particular substring in the given string and exhibit none of the powerful capabilities to which we have alluded. Special character sequences in regexps are a lot like escape codes in strings. They provide a special, at times awkward, way to refer to properties of a pattern that would otherwise be difficult to specify. For example, special characters provide a way to indicate that a certain character or set of characters should be repeated a certain number of times or that the string must not contain a certain substring.

Positional Indicators

The first set of special characters can be thought of as *positional indicators*, characters that relate information about the required position of the pattern in the string against which it will be matched. These characters are ^ and $, indicating the beginning and end of the string, respectively. For example:

```
var pattern = /^http/;
```

will match against only those strings beginning with "http." The following returns **false**:

```
pattern.test("The protocol is http");
```

The $ character causes the opposite behavior:

```
var pattern = /http$/;
```

will match only those strings ending with "http." You can use the two positional indicators in concert to ensure an exact match to the desired pattern:

```
var pattern = /^http$/;
```

This regular expression will match only the string "http."

You need to be very careful to employ positional indicators properly when doing matches, as the regular expression may match strings that are not expected.

Escape Codes

Given the syntax of regexp literals, one might wonder how to specify a string that includes slashes, such as "http://www.w3c.org/." The answer is that as with strings, regular expressions use escape codes to indicate problematic characters. Escape codes are specified using a backslash character ("\"). The escape codes used in regular expressions are a superset of those used in strings (there are far more characters with special meaning, like ^ and $, in regexps). These escape codes are listed in Table 8-2.

Code	Matches
\f	Form feed
\n	Newline
\r	Carriage return
\t	Tab
\v	Vertical tab
\/	Foreslash "/"
\\	Backslash "\"
\.	Period "."
*	Asterisk "*"
\+	Plus sign "+"
\?	Question mark "?"
|	Horizontal bar, aka Pipe "|"
\(	Left parenthesis "("
\)	Right parenthesis ")"
\[	Left bracket "["
\]	Right bracket "]"
\{	Left curly brace "{"
\}	Right curly brace "}"
\OOO	ASCII character represented by octal value OOO
\xHH	ASCII character represented by hexadecimal value HH
\uHHHH	Unicode character represented by the hexadecimal value HHHH
\cX	Control character represented by ^X, for example \cH represents CTRL-H

Table 8-2. *Regular Expression Escape Codes*

Using the appropriate escape code, we can now define a regular expression that matches "http://www.w3c.org/":

```
var pattern = /http:\/\/www\.w3c\.org\//;
```

Repetition Quantifiers

Regexp quantifiers allow you to specify the number of times a particular item in the expression can or must be repeated. For now, consider that by "previous item" we mean "previous character." The distinction will become clear later in the chapter. As an example of a repetition quantifier, * (the asterisk) indicates that the previous item may be repeated zero or more times. Any sequence of zero or more repetitions of the previous item can be present in the string against which we will match; for example:

```
var pattern = /ab*c/;
```

This pattern will match any string containing an *a* that is followed immediately by zero or more *b*'s, followed immediately by a *c*. All the following strings will match this expression:

"ac"

"abc"

"abbbbbbbbbbbbbbbbbbbbbbbbbbbc"

"The letters abc begin the alphabet"

Similarly, **+** specifies that the previous character must be repeated one or more times. Given the following declaration:

```
var pattern = /ab+c/;
```

all the following strings match:

"abc"

"abbbbbc"

"The letters abc begin the alphabet"

Note that "ac" does not match because it does not contain at least one *b* between *a* and *c*.

The **?** quantifier indicates that the previous character may be repeated zero times or one time, but no more. For example:

```
var pattern = /ab?c/;
```

matches "ac" and "abc," but not "abbc."

Sometimes you might want to limit the number of matches to a particular value. The curly braces { } are used to indicate the number of matches allowed for the preceding pattern. For example,

```
var pattern = /a*b{5}c/;
```

would specify a pattern of zero or more *a* characters, followed by exactly five *b* characters and then the letter *c*. Of course this particular expression could have also been written as:

```
var pattern = /a*bbbbbc/;
```

Using the curly braces it is possible to get even more specific with the range of character repetition allowed. For example,

```
var pattern = /ab{5,7}c/;
```

would create a regular expression that matched a single *a* followed by between five and seven (inclusive) *b* characters and then the letter *c* while

```
var pattern = /ab{3,}c/;
```

would create an expression to match an *a* followed by three or more letter *b* characters followed by a *c*. The full list of repetition quantifiers is summarized in Table 8-3.

Character	Meaning
*	Match previous item zero or more times
+	Match previous item one time or more
?	Match previous item zero or one times
{m, n}	Match previous item at minimum *m* times, but no more than *n* times
{m, }	Match previous item *m* or more times
{m}	Match previous item exactly *m* times

Table 8-3.   *Repetition Characters for Regular Expressions*

Aggressive Matching

One particularly challenging aspect facing those new to regular expressions is aggressive matching of regular expressions, often termed *greedy* or *maximal* matching because the regular expression will try to match as many characters as possible. A simple way to think about this is that JavaScript will try to match something if at all possible and will match as much as possible. You have to be very specific in order to keep the expression from overmatching results. For example, consider the following statement (noting that **\d** matches any digit character):

```
var pattern = /\d{3}-\d{4}/;
```

This would appear to be an appropriate regular expression to match simple phone numbers of three digits followed by a dash and then four digits. If you try

```
alert(pattern.test("555-2222"));
```

it will return **true**; however, testing of 56533-3454446 will also return **true** as will a variety of other strings that are not in the desired format. This situation can be especially troublesome when using repetition characters. It can be avoided by being very specific in your expression. Using positional identifiers will solve the problem; the following,

```
var pattern = /^\d{3}-\d{4}$/;
```

would match only three digits, a dash, and four digits—nothing else. It is very important to think about the aggressive matching of regular expressions, particularly when talking about groupings and subexpressions.

Grouping and Character Classes

Notice how Table 8-3 indicates that the repetition quantifiers match the "previous item" a certain number of times. In the examples seen so far, the "previous item" has been a single character. However, JavaScript lets you easily group characters together. The simplest way to do so is to use parentheses. Any group of characters surrounded by parentheses is considered a unit with respect to the special regexp operators. For example,

```
var pattern = /a(bc)+/;
```

will match any string containing an *a* followed by one or more repetitions of "bc."

Sometimes it is necessary to match a sequence of characters from a group of possibilities. For example, you might wish to extract a phone number consisting of a contiguous sequence of numbers or a name made up of strictly alphabetic characters.

JavaScript allows you to define character classes by including valid characters between square brackets [ ]. Any character from the class can be matched in the string. For example,

```
var pattern = /[1234567890]/;
```

will match any string containing a number. This format looks like it could get very messy if you desired to set a large group of allowed characters, but luckily JavaScript allows you to use a dash ("–") to indicate a range of values:

```
var pattern = /[0-9]/;
```

This regular expression is the same as the previous example, just written more compactly.

Any time you use the range operator, you specify a range of valid ASCII values. So, for example, you might do this,

```
var pattern = /[a-z]/;
```

to match any lowercase alphabetic character or:

```
var pattern = /[a-zA-Z0-9]/;
```

to match any alphanumeric character. JavaScript allows you to place all the valid characters in a contiguous sequence in a character class, as in the last example. It interprets such a class correctly. However, be careful with these types of pattern matches. Given the previous pattern, the following strings are all valid:

"abc"

"123"

"&*$^a@#%&%"

Only a string like "$%^" would fail because it contains no alphanumeric characters. One shortcoming of the regular expression defined in the previous example is that it does not specify the number of repetitions of characters from the class required for a match. As it is given, the expression matches any string with at least one alphanumeric character. In fact, in order to be useful in most situations, repetition quantifiers are often required. A very simple example that matches a string containing one or more contiguous alphabetic characters is:

```
var pattern = /[a-z]+/;
```

A more complicated example might match a case-insensitive username beginning with an alphabetic character followed by zero or more alphanumeric characters as well as underscores and dashes. The following regular expression defines such a pattern:

```
var pattern = /^[a-z][a-z0-9_-]*/i;
```

This will match for example "m," "m10-120," "abracadabra," and "abra_cadabra" but not "_user" or "10abc." Note how the dash was included in the character class last to prevent it from being interpreted as the range operator.

Square brackets can also be used when describing "negative" character classes, namely classes that specify which characters *cannot* be present. A negative class is specified by placing a carat ("^") at the beginning of the class. For example,

```
var pattern = /[^a-zA-Z]+/;
```

will match any sequence of one or more non-alphabetic characters, for instance "314," "!!%&^," or "__0." For a string to match the preceding expression, it must contain at least one non-alphabetic character.

Commonly used character groups have shorthand escape codes associated with them. A particularly useful notation is the period, which matches *any* character except a newline. For instance,

```
var pattern = /abc..d/;
```

would match "abcx7d" or "abc_-d." Other common classes are **\s**, any whitespace character, **\S**, any non-whitespace character, **\w**, any word character, **\W**, any non-word character, **\d**, any digit, and **\D**, any non-digit. The complete list of character classes is given in Table 8-4.

Character	Meaning
[*chars*]	Any one character indicated either explicitly or as a range between the brackets.
[^*chars*]	Any one character *not* between the brackets represented explicitly or as a range.
.	Any character except newline.

Table 8-4.   *Regular Expression Character Classes*

Character	Meaning
\w	Any word character. Same as [a-zA-Z0-9_].
\W	Any non-word character. Same as [^a-zA-Z0-9_].
\s	Any whitespace character. Same as [\t\n\r\f\v].
\S	Any non-whitespace character. Same as [^ \t\n\r\f\v].
\d	Any digit. Same as [0-9].
\D	Any non-digit. Same as [^0-9].
\b	A word boundary. The empty "space" between a \w and \W.
\B	A word non-boundary. The empty "space" between word characters.
[\b]	A backspace character.

Table 8-4.   *Regular Expression Character Classes* (continued)

Subexpressions

Aside from grouping sequences of characters together as a unit, parentheses in regular expressions induce *subexpressions* on the string operated upon. When a match is successful, parenthesized subexpressions can be referred to individually by using static properties of the **RegExp** object itself. For example, the following script matches a simple pattern of a word followed by a string of digits.

```
var customer = "Alan 555-1212";
var pattern = /(\w+) ([\d-]+)/;
pattern.test(customer);
```

Since the pattern contained parentheses that created two subexpressions, "\w+" and "[\d-]+," we can reference the two substrings they match, "Alan" and "555-1212," individually. Substrings accessed in this manner are numbered from left to right, beginning with $1 and ending typically with $9. For example,

```
var customer = "Alan 555-1212";

var pattern = /(\w+) ([\d-]+)/;
```

```
pattern.test(customer);

alert("$1 = " + RegExp.$1 + "\n$2 = " + RegExp.$2);
```

displays the alert shown here:

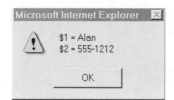

Notice the use of the **RegExp** object itself to access the subexpression components. We'll see more direct access of this object fairly soon, but let's cover one last tool.

According to the ECMA specification, you should be able to reference more than nine subexpressions. In fact, up to 99 should be allowed using identifiers like $10, $11, and so on. At the time of this book's writing, though, no browser supported more than nine.

Alternatives

The final major tool necessary to define useful patterns is " | ," which indicates the logical OR of several items. For example, to match a string that begins with "ftp," "http," or "https," you might write:

```
var pattern = /^(http|ftp|https)/;
```

The following pattern matches any string containing either "abc" or "xyzxyzxyz:"

```
var pattern = /abc|(xyz){3}/;
```

Notice the use of the repetition indicator to avoid having to type out the "xyz" sequence several times. You can see that regular expressions get more terse yet more powerful as we describe all the possible features.

The tools described so far work together to permit the creation of useful regular expressions. It is important to be comfortable interpreting the meaning of regular expressions before delving further into how they are used. Table 8-5 provides some practice examples along with strings they do and do not match. You should make sure you understand each example before proceeding.

Regular Expression	Matches	Does Not Match
/\Wten\W/	" ten "	"ten", "tents"
/\wten\w/	"aten1"	" ten", "1ten "
/\bten\b/	"ten"	"attention", "tensile" "often"
/\d{1,3}\.\d{1,3}\.\ d{1,3}\.\d{1,3}/	"128.22.45.1"	"abc.44.55.42" "128.22.45."
/^(http|ftp|https):\/ \/.*/	"https://www.w3c.org", "http://abc"	"file:///etc/motd" "https//www.w3c.org"
/\w+@\w+\.\w{1,3}/	"president@whitehouse. gov","president@white_ house.us", "root@127.0.0.1"	"president@.gov" "prez@white.house.gv"

Table 8-5. *Some Regular Expression Examples*

RegExp Object

Now that we know how to form regular expressions, it is time to look at how to use them. There are a variety of properties and methods related to the **RegExp** object that can be used to test and parse the results of a regular expression being applied to a piece of data. For example, the simplest **RegExp** method, which we have already seen in this chapter numerous times, is **test()**. This method returns a Boolean value indicating whether the given string argument matches the regular expression. Here we construct a regular expression and then use it to test against two strings:

```
var pattern = new RegExp("a*bbbc", "i");
alert(pattern.test("1a12c"));   // displays false
alert(pattern.test("aaabBbcded")); //displays true
```

Of course, until now we have tended to use statements like

```
var pattern = /a*bbbc/i;
```

to construct a regular expression, but it is important to emphasize by using traditional object creation syntax that regular expressions are normal objects with methods and properties we can use.

A less frequently used method is **compile()**, which replaces an existing regexp with a new one. This method takes the same arguments as the **RegExp()** constructor (a string containing the pattern and an optional string containing the flags) and can be used to create a new expression by discarding an old one:

```
var pattern = /http:.*/i;
// do something with your regexp
pattern.compile("https:.* ", "i");
// replaced the regexp in pattern with new pattern
```

exec() Method

The **RegExp** object also provides a method called **exec()**. The method accepts a string to execute the match against, and it can be written shorthand by directly invoking the name of the regexp as a function. For example, the two invocations in the following example are equivalent:

```
var pattern = /http:.*/;
pattern.exec("http://www.w3c.org/");
pattern("http://www.w3c.org/");
```

The **exec()** method returns an array with a variety of properties. Included are the **length** of the array; **input** that shows the original input string; **index,** which holds the index of the first match; and **lastIndex**, which holds the character after the match, at which point the next search will begin. The script here illustrates the **exec()** method and its returned values:

```
var pattern = /cat/;
var result = pattern.exec("He is a big cat, a fat black cat named Rufus.");

document.writeln("result = "+result+"<br>");
document.writeln("result.length = "+result.length+"<br>");
document.writeln("result.index = "+result.index+"<br>");
document.writeln("result.lastIndex = "+result.lastIndex+"<br>");
document.writeln("result.input = "+result.input+"<br>");
```

The result of the previous example is shown here:

```
result = cat
result.length = 1
result.index = 12
result.lastIndex = 15
result.input = He is a big cat, a fat black cat named Rufus.
```

The array returned may have more than one element if subexpressions are used. For example, the following script has a set of three parenthesized subexpressions that are parsed out in the array separately:

```
var pattern = /(cat) (and) (dog) /;
var result = pattern.exec("My cat and dog are black.");

document.writeln("result = "+result);
document.writeln("result.length = "+result.length);
document.writeln("result.index = "+result.index);
document.writeln("result.lastIndex = "+result.lastIndex);
document.writeln("result.input = "+result.input);
```

As you can see from the result,

```
result = cat and dog ,cat,and,dog
result.length = 4
result.index = 3
result.lastIndex = 15
result.input = My cat and dog are black.
```

the **exec()** method places the entire matched string in element zero of the array returned and any substrings that match parenthesized subexpressions in subsequent elements.

An interesting aspect of the **exec()** method that makes it different from the **match()** method for **String** (discussed later in this chapter) is that that **exec()** performs global searches incrementally. That is, when a regular expression with the global flag is invoked, it finds and returns at most one match. Thus,

```
var pattern = /cat/g;
var result = pattern.exec( "The cat was black. The cat was fat.");
```

will not return an array with multiple matches in it, just the first match. However, it is possible to use this outcome to our advantage. Recall that the method updates the **lastIndex** property of both the array and the **RegExp** object itself to point to the character immediately following the substring that was most recently matched. Subsequent calls to the regexp's **exec()** method begin their search from offset **lastIndex** in the string. If no match is found, **lastIndex** is set to zero. This allows you to loop through each matching substring, obtaining complete information about each match. The use of **exec()** is illustrated in the following example, which matches words in the given string. The result (when used within a <pre>tag) is shown in Figure 8-1.

```
var sentence = "A very interesting sentence.";
var pattern = /\b\w+\b/g;          // recognizes words; global
var token = pattern.exec(sentence);   // get the first match
while (token != null)
{

// if we have a match, print information about it
document.writeln("Matched " + token[0] + " ");
document.writeln("\ttoken.input = " + token.input);
document.writeln("\ttoken.index = " + token.index);
document.writeln("\ttoken.lastIndex = " + token.lastIndex + "\n ");
token = pattern.exec(sentence);    // get the next match
}
```

One caveat when using the **exec()** method: if you stop a search before finding the last match, you need to manually set the **lastIndex** property of the regular expression to zero. If you do not, the next time you use that regexp, it will automatically start matching at offset **lastIndex** rather than at the beginning of the string. Note that the **test()** method obeys **lastIndex** as well, so it can be used to incrementally search a string in the same manner as **exec()**.

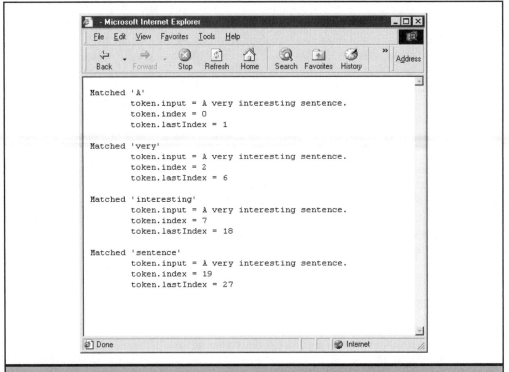

Figure 8-1. *Results of regular expression exec() with the global flag*

RegExp Properties

Examining the internals of regular expression instance objects as well as the static ("class") properties of the **RegExp** object can be helpful when performing complex regexp tasks and during debugging. The instance properties of **RegExp** objects are listed in Table 8-6 and, with a few exceptions, should be familiar to the reader by this point.

Property	Value	Example

global	Boolean indicating whether the global flag ("**g**") was set. This property is ReadOnly.	var pattern = /(cat) (dog)/g;
		pattern.test("this is a cat dog and cat dog");
		document.writeln(pattern.global);
		// prints true

Table 8-6. *Instance Properties of RegExp Objects*

Property	Value	Example
ignoreCase	Boolean indicating whether the case-insensitive flag ("**i**") was set. This property is ReadOnly.	var pattern = /(cat) (dog)/g; pattern.test("this is a cat dog and cat dog"); document.writeln(pattern. ingoreCase); // prints false
lastIndex	Integer specifying the position in the string at which to start the next match. You may set this value.	var pattern = /(cat) (dog)/g; pattern.test("this is a cat dog and cat dog"); document.writeln(pattern. lastIndex); // prints 17
multiline	Boolean indicating whether the multiline flag ("**m**") was set. This property is ReadOnly.	var pattern = /(cat) (dog)/g; pattern.test("this is a cat dog and cat dog"); document.writeln(pattern. multiline); // prints false
source	The string form of the regular expression. This property is ReadOnly.	var pattern = /(cat) (dog)/g; pattern.test("this is a cat dog and cat dog"); document.writeln(pattern.source); // prints (cat) (dog)

Table 8-6.   *Instance Properties of RegExp Objects* (continued)

The **RegExp** object also has static properties that can be very useful. These properties are listed in Table 8-7 and come in two forms. The alternate form uses a dollar sign and a special character and may be recognized by those who are already intimately familiar with regexps. A downside to the alternate form is that it has to be accessed in an associative array fashion. (Using this form will probably confuse those readers unfamiliar with languages like Perl, so it is probably best to just stay away from it.)

One interesting aspect of the static **RegExp** properties is that they are global and therefore change every time you use a regular expression, whether with **String** or **RegExp** methods. For this reason they are the exception to the rule that JavaScript is statically scoped. These properties are *dynamically scoped*—that is, changes are reflected in the **RegExp** object in the context of the calling function, rather than in the enclosing context of the source code that is invoked. For example, JavaScript in a frame that calls a function using regular expressions in a different frame will update the static **RegExp** properties in the *calling* frame, not the frame in which the called function is found. This rarely poses a problem, but it is something you should keep in mind if you are relying upon static properties in a framed environment.

Property	Alternate Form	Value	Example
$1, $2, ..., $9	None	Strings holding the text of the first nine parenthesized subexpressions of the most recent match.	var pattern = /(cat) (dog)/g; pattern.test("this is a cat dog and cat dog"); document.writeln ("$1="+RegExp.$1); document.writeln ("$2="+RegExp.$2); // prints $1= cat $2 = dog
index	None	Holds the string index value of the first character in the most recent pattern match. This property is not part of the ECMA standard, though it is supported widely. Therefore it may be better to use the **length** of the regexp pattern and the **lastIndex** property to calculate this value.	var pattern = /(cat) (dog)/g; pattern.test("this is a cat dog and cat dog"); document.writeln (RegExp.index); // prints 10

Table 8-7. *Static Properties of the RegExp Object*

Property	Alternate Form	Value	Example

input	$_	String containing the default string to match against the pattern.	var pattern = /(cat)(dog)/g;
			pattern.test("this is a cat dog and cat dog");
			document.writeln(RegExp.input);
			// prints "this is a cat dog and cat dog"
			document.writeln(RegExp['$_ ']);

lastIndex	None	Integer specifying the position in the string at which to start the next match. Same as the instance property, which should be used instead.	var pattern = /(cat)(dog)/g;
			pattern.test("this is a cat dog and cat dog");
			document.writeln(RegExp.lastIndex);
			// prints 17

lastMatch	$&	String containing the most recently matched text.	var pattern = /(cat)(dog)/g;
			pattern.test("this is a cat dog and cat dog");
			document.writeln(RegExp.lastMatch);
			// prints "cat dog"
			document.writeln(RegExp['$&']);
			// prints "cat dog"

Table 8-7. *Static Properties of the RegExp Object* (continued)

Property	Alternate Form	Value	Example
lastParen	$+	String containing the text of the last parenthesized subexpression of the most recent match.	var pattern = /(cat) (dog)/g; pattern.test("this is a cat dog and cat dog"); document.writeln (RegExp.lastParen); // prints dog document.writeln (RegExp['$+ ']); // prints "dog"
leftContext	$`	String containing the text to the left of the most recent match.	var pattern = /(cat) (dog)/g; pattern.test("this is a cat dog and cat dog"); document.writeln (RegExp.leftContext); // prints "this is a" document.writeln (RegExp['$` ']); // prints "this is a"
rightContext	$ '	String containing the text to the right of the most recent match.	var pattern = /(cat) (dog)/g; pattern.test("this is a cat dog and cat dog"); document.writeln (RegExp.rightContext); // prints "and cat dog" document.writeln (RegExp['$\' ']); // prints "and cat dog"

Table 8-7. *Static Properties of the RegExp Object* (continued)

| Note | *As shown in Table 8-7, because JavaScript's regular expression engine is modeled after Perl's, you can use "Perlisms" in your regular expressions. For example, referencing **RegExp["$'"]** is the same as **RegExp.leftContext**. However, just because you can do it does not mean that you should. Using Perl syntax in regular expressions will seriously trip up anyone trying to understand your code.* |

String Methods for Regular Expressions

The **String** object provides four methods that utilize regular expressions. The simplest such method is **search()**, which takes a regular expression argument and returns the index of the character at which the first matching substring begins. If no substring matching the pattern is found, **-1** is returned. Consider the following two examples:

```
"JavaScript regular expressions are powerful!".search(/pow.*/i);
"JavaScript regular expressions are powerful!".search(/\d/);
```

The first statement returns **35**, the character index at which the matching substring "powerful!" begins. The second statement searches for a digit and returns **-1** because no numeric character is found.

The second method provided by **String** is also fairly simple. The **split()** method literally splits a string up into substrings and returns them in an array. It accepts a string or regular expression argument containing the delimiter at which the string will be broken. For example,

```
var stringwithdelimits = "10 / 3 / / 4  / 7 / 9";
var splitExp = /[ \/]+/;
myArray = stringwithdelimits.split(splitExp);
```

places 10, 3, 4, 7, and 9 into the first five indices of the array called *myArray*. Of course you could do this much more tersely:

```
var myArray = "10 / 3 / / 4  / 7 / 9".split(/[ \/]+/);
```

Using **split()** with regular expressions allows you the flexibility of ignoring multiple whitespace or delimiter characters. Because regexps are greedy, the regular expression "eats up" as many delimiter characters as it can. See Appendix B for complete details on **String.split()**.

The **replace()** method returns the string resulting from replacing the text matching its first argument (a regular expression) with the second argument (a string). If the **g** flag is not indicated in a regular expression declaration, the method replaces the first occurrence of the expression with the desired text. For example,

```
var s = "Hello. Regexps are fun.";
s = s.replace(/\./, "!");  // replace first period with an exclamation point
alert(s);
```

produces the string "Hello! Regexps are fun." Including the **g** flag will cause the interpreter to perform a global replace, finding and replacing every matching substring. For example,

```
var s = "Hello. Regexps are fun.";
s = s.replace(/\./g, "!");  // replace all periods with exclamation points
alert(s);
```

yield this result: "Hello! Regexps are fun!"

Recall that parenthesized subexpressions can be referred to by number. You can use this capability in **replace()** to reference certain portions of a string. The substrings matched by parenthesized subexpressions are referred to in the replacement string with a dollar sign ("$") followed by the number of the desired subexpression. For example, the following inserts dashes into a hypothetical social security number:

```
var pattern = /(\d{3})(\d{2})(\d{4})/;
var ssn = "123456789";
ssn = ssn.replace(pattern, "$1-$2-$3");
```

The result "123-45-6789" is placed in *ssn*. This technique is called *backreferencing* and can also be used to extract matched subexpressions into an array with the **match()** method.

The final method provided by the **String** object is **match()**. This method takes a single regular expression as an argument and returns an array containing the results of the match. If the given regexp has the global ("**g**") flag, the array returned contains the results of each substring matched. For example,

```
var pattern = /\d{2}/g;
var lottoNumbers = "22, 48, 13, 17, 26";
var result = lottoNumbers.match(pattern);
```

places **22** in *result[0]*, **48** in *result[1]* and so on up to **26** in *result[4]*.

The behavior of **match()** when the expression does not have the global flag is a bit more involved. The method places the character position at which the first match begins in an instance property **index** of the array that is returned. The instance property called **input** is also added and contains the entire original string. The contents of the entire matching substring are placed in the first element (index zero) of the array. The rest of the array elements are filled in with the matching subexpressions, with index *n* holding the value of **$n**. For example,

```
var url = "The URL is http://www.w3c.org/DOM/Activity";
var pattern = /(\w+):\/\/([\w\.]+)\/([\w\/]+)/;
var results = url.match(pattern);
document.writeln("results.input =\t" + results.input);
document.writeln("<br>");
document.writeln("results.index =\t" + results.index);
document.writeln("<br>");
for (var i=0; i < results.length; i++)
  {
  document.writeln("results[" + i + "] =\t" + results[i]);
  document.writeln("<br>");
  }
```

produces the result shown in Figure 8-2. As you can see, all three subexpressions were matched and placed in the array. The entire match was placed in the first element, and the instance properties **index** and **input** reflect the original string (remember, string offsets are enumerated beginning with zero, just like arrays). Note that if **match()** does not find a match, it returns **null**.

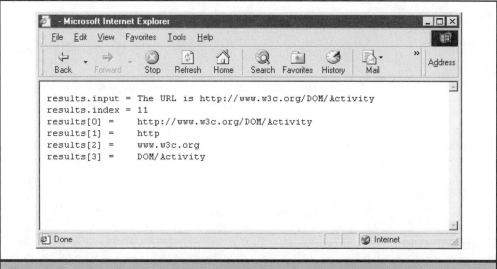

Figure 8-2.   *Results of regular expression match() without the global flag*

Advanced Regular Expressions

There are a few other regular expression tools that are worth spending a little more time on in case you need to perform more advanced string matching. The first is the multiline flag ("**m**"). Setting this flag causes ^ and $ to match the beginning and end of a line, in addition to the beginning and end of a string. You could use this flag to parse text like the following:

```
var text = "This text has multiple lines.\nThis is the second line.\nThe third.";
var pattern = /^.*$/gm;
var lines = text.match(pattern);
document.writeln("Length of lines = "+lines.length);
document.writeln("<br>");
document.writeln("lines[0] = "+lines[0]);
document.writeln("<br>");
document.writeln("lines[1] = "+lines[1]);
document.writeln("<br>");
document.writeln("lines[2] = "+lines[2]);
document.writeln("<br>");
```

which uses the String **method match()** to break the text up into individual lines and places them in the array *lines*. The output of this example is shown here.

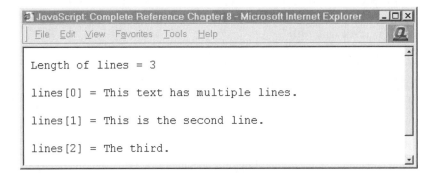

JavaScript also provides more flexible syntax for parenthesized expressions. Using the syntax **(?:)** specifies that the parenthesized expression should not be made available for backreferencing. These are referred to as *non-capturing* parentheses. For example,

```
var pattern = /(?:abc)(def)/;
var text = "abcdef".replace(pattern, "First subexpression: $1");
```

results in the string "First subexpression: def" being placed in *text*. Using normal parentheses without the non-capturing syntax results in "First subexpression: abc" being placed in *text*.

JavaScript allows you to specify that a portion of a regular expression matches only if it is or is not followed by a particular subexpression. The **(?=)** syntax specifies a positive lookahead; it only matches the previous item if it is followed immediately by the expression contained in **(?=)**. The lookahead expression is *not* included in the match. For example, in the following,

```
var pattern = /\d(?=\.\d+)/;
```

pattern matches only a digit that is followed by a period and one or more digits. It matches **3.1** and **3.14159**, but not **3.** or **.3**. Remember that the lookahead expression is not returned by the match, so using **exec()** or **match()** with the preceding example would return **3** in the array when it matches a digit followed by a period and one or more digits. Negative lookahead is achieved with the **(?!)** syntax, which behaves like **(?=)**. It matches the previous item only if the expression contained in **(?!)** does not immediately follow.
For example,

```
var pattern = /\d(?!\.\d+)/;
```

will match **3** but not **3.1** or **3.14**. The negative lookahead expression is also not returned on a match.

You can force a quantifier (*****, **+**, **?**, **{m}**, **{m,}**, **{m,n}**) to be non-greedy by following it with a question mark. Doing this forces the expression to match the *minimum* number of characters rather than the maximum. For example, normally the following,

```
"aaaa".match(/a+/);
```

matches the entire string "aaaa." However, forcing non-greediness,

```
"aaaa".match(/a+?/);
```

will match *a* (under browsers that support these advanced features—for example, Internet Explorer 5.5). Note that Netscape 4's support is incomplete, so it is best to carefully test your code under a variety of browsers before putting it into "the wild."

As we have seen throughout this chapter, there is certainly a lot of power as well as complexity with regular expressions. All JavaScript programmers really should master regexps, as they can aid in common tasks such as form validation. However, before rushing out and adding them to every script, programmers should consider well some of the challenges of using regexps.

Limitations of Regular Expressions

Regular expressions derive their name from the fact that the strings they recognize are (in a formal Computer Science sense) "regular." This implies that there are certain kinds of strings that it will be very hard, if not impossible, to recognize with regular expressions. Luckily, these strings are not often encountered and usually arise only in parsing things like source code or natural language. However, you do need to be very careful when performing form validation with regular expressions on strings like e-mail addresses. Keep in mind the variety of forms such strings can take. Valid e-mail addresses can contain punctuation characters like **!** and **+**, and they can employ IP addresses instead of domain names (like **root@127.0.0.1**). You'll need to do a bit of research and some experimentation to ensure that the regexps you create will be robust enough to match the types of strings you're interested in.

It is important to remember that even the best-crafted regexp cannot test for semantic validity. For example, you might be able to verify that a credit card number has the proper format, but without a database or more complicated server-side functionality, your script has no way to check whether the card is truly valid. Still, associating a syntax checker with forms is a convenient way to catch common errors before submission to the server.

Summary

Regular expressions are the tool that JavaScript provides for matching and manipulating string data. Regular expressions can be created using literal syntax or the **RegExp()** constructor and are used in **String** methods, such as **match()**, **replace()**, **search()**, and **split()**. Regular expression objects also provide **test()**, **match()**, and **compile()** methods for testing, matching, and replacing regexps. Regular expressions themselves are composed of strings of characters along with special escape codes, character classes, and repetition quantifiers. The special escape codes provide the means to include otherwise problematic characters, such as newlines and those characters that have a special meaning in regexps. Character classes provide a way to specify a class or range of characters that a string must or must not draw from. Repetition quantifiers allow you to specify the number of times a particular expression must be repeated in the string in order to match. Regular expressions are at times hard to get right, so they should be crafted with care. Properly used, they provide a very powerful way to recognize, replace, and extract patterns of characters from strings. At this point, the core parts of the language of JavaScript have been covered. It is now time to move on and see how browser and document objects can be applied to create useful applications.

The Complete Reference

JavaScript

Part III

Fundamental Client-Side JavaScript

The Complete Reference

JavaScript

Chapter 9

Traditional JavaScript Object Models

An object model defines the interface to the various aspects of the browser and the document that can be manipulated by JavaScript. In JavaScript, two primary object models are employed—a Browser Object Model (BOM) and a Document Object Model (DOM). The BOM provides access to the various characteristics of a browser, such as the browser window itself, the screen characteristics, the browser history, and so on. The DOM, on the other hand, provides access to the contents of the browser window—namely the document and including the various HTML elements, ranging from anchors to images as well as any text that may be enclosed by such elements. Unfortunately, the division between the DOM and the BOM is at times somewhat fuzzy, and the exact document-manipulation capabilities of different browsers' implementations of JavaScript vary significantly. This section begins our exploration of the use of the various aspects of JavaScript object models that are fundamental to the effective use of the language. We'll begin with an exploration of the traditional, though nonstandardized, object models found in the two major browsers. We'll find that many of the ideas of what is related to the browser and what is related to the document are mixed up in these models. The next chapter will begin our discussion of the W3C standard Document Object Model that provides a standard way to manipulate HTML (or even XML) documents for a variety of languages, including JavaScript. Finally, we will explore the various event models supported by the browser vendors. Readers are encouraged to study these next few chapters carefully, as a complete understanding of the evolution and capabilities of the various object models discussed here is fundamental to understanding the applications found in Part IV of the book.

Object Model Overview

An object model is an interface describing the logical structure of an object and the standard ways in which it can be manipulated. Figure 9-1 presents the "big picture" of all the various aspects of JavaScript, including its object models. There are four primary pieces:

1. The core JavaScript language (data types, operators, statements, and so on)

2. The core objects primarily related to data types (**Date**, **String**, **Math**, and so on)

3. The browser objects (**Window**, **Navigator**, **Location**, and so on)

4. The document objects (**Document**, **Form**, **Image**, and so on)

Up until this point we have focused on primarily the first and second aspects of JavaScript. This part of the language is actually fairly consistent between browser types and versions and corresponds to the features defined by the ECMAScript specification (**http://www.ecma.ch/ecma1/STAND/ECMA-262.HTM**). However, the actual objects with which we can manipulate the browser and document do vary. In Figure 9-1 you'll notice that the Browser Object Model (BOM) and Document Object Model (DOM) appear somewhat intermixed. In fact, in older browser versions there really wasn't much of a distinction between the Browser Object Model and the Document Object Model—it was just one big mess!

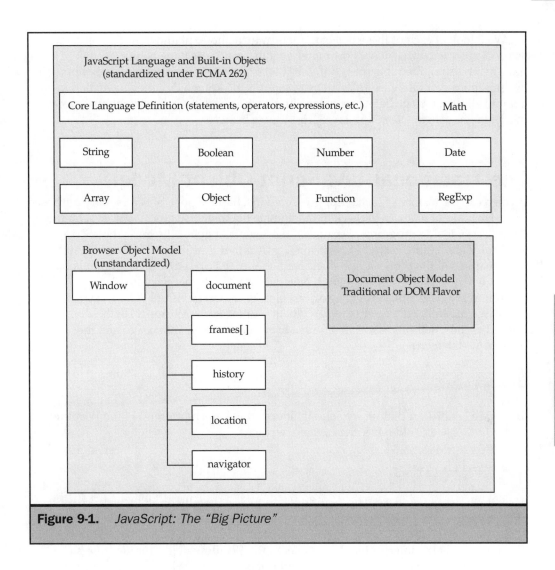

Figure 9-1. *JavaScript: The "Big Picture"*

By studying the history of JavaScript, we can bring some order to the chaos of competing object models. There have been four distinct object models used in JavaScript:

- Traditional JavaScript Object Model (Netscape 2 and Internet Explorer 3)
- Extended Traditional JavaScript Object Model (Netscape 3)
- Dynamic HTML-Flavored Object Models
  - Internet Explorer 4
  - Netscape 4
- Traditional Browser Object Model + Standard DOM (NS6 and IE 5)

We'll look at each of these object models in turn and explain what features as well as problems each introduced. Fortunately, today standards have begun to emerge that have helped straighten this mess out, but it will take some time before JavaScript programmers can safely let go of all browser-specific knowledge they have. Before we get into all that, let's go back to a much simpler time and study the traditional object model that is safe to use in any JavaScript-aware browser.

The Traditional JavaScript Object Model

If you recall the history of JavaScript presented in Chapter 1, one of the primary purposes of the language at first was to check or manipulate the contents of forms before submitting them to server-side programs. Because of these modest goals, the initial JavaScript object model first introduced in Netscape 2 was rather limited, and it focused on the basic features of the browser and document. Figure 9-2 presents the traditional object model, which is pretty similar in both Netscape 2 and Internet Explorer 3.

You might be curious how the various objects shown in Figure 9-2 are related to JavaScript. Well, we've actually used them. For example, **Window** defines the properties and methods associated with a browser window. When we used the JavaScript statement

```
alert("hi");
```

to create a small alert dialog, we actually invoked the **alert()** method of the **Window** object. In fact, we could have just as easily written

```
window.alert("hi");
```

to create the same window. The "window" prefix is generally omitted, because most of the time the interpreter can infer that we are using the current **Window** object. More specifically, the **Window** object is almost always within the scope of your scripts. This means that the interpreter always checks the **Window** object for identifiers (for example, function names) that are used without being explicitly defined in the script.

The containment hierarchy shown in Figure 9-2 should also make sense once you consider a statement like this:

```
window.document.write("<strong>Hi there from JavaScript!</strong>");
```

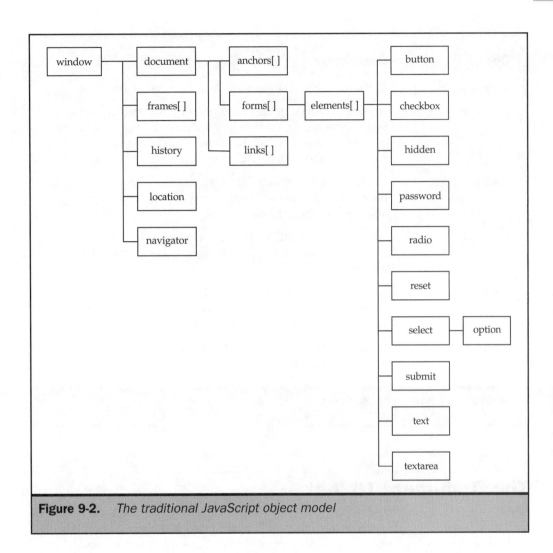

Figure 9-2.   *The traditional JavaScript object model*

This should look like the familiar output statement used to write text to an HTML document. Once again, we added in the "prefix window," this time to call attention to the hierarchy, as we have tended to use just **document.write( )** in our examples. You might be curious about what all the various objects shown in Figure 9-2 do, so in Table 9-1 we present an overview of the traditional browser objects. The bulk of the objects are contained within the **Document** object, so we'll look at that more closely now.

Object	Description
Window	The object that relates to the current browser window.
Document	An object that contains the various HTML elements and text fragments that make up a document. In the traditional JavaScript object model, the **Document** object relates roughly to the HTML **<body>** tag.
Frames[ ]	An array of the frames in the page (if it contains any). Each frame in turn references another **Window** object that may also contain more frames.
History	An object that contains the current window's history list, namely the collection of the various URLs visited by the user recently.
Location	An object that contains the current location of the document being viewed in the form of a URL and its constituent pieces such as protocols, host names, and paths.
Navigator	An object that describes the basic characteristics of the browser, notably its type and version.

Table 9-1. *Overview of Core Browser Objects*

The Document Object

The **Document** object provides access to page elements such as anchors, form fields, and links as well as page properties such as background and text color. We will see that the structure of this object varies considerably from browser to browser and from version to version. Table 9-2 and Table 9-3 list those **Document** properties and methods, respectively, that are the "least common denominator" for the earliest browsers providing a document object model (Netscape 2.0 and Internet Explorer 3.0). For the sake of brevity, some details and **Document** properties will be omitted in the following discussion. Complete information about the **Document** properties can be found in Appendix B.

An examination of Tables 9-2 and 9-3 reveals that the early object model was very primitive. The only parts of a document that could be directly accessed were document-wide properties, links, anchors, and forms. There was no support for the manipulation of text or images, no support for applets or embedded objects, and no way to access

Document Property	Description	HTML Relationship	Writeable in NS?	Writeable in IE?
alinkColor	The color of "active" links—by default red	<body alink="color value">	Only in NS6+	Yes
anchors[ ]	Array of anchor objects in the document	<a name="anchor name"> </a>	No	No
bgColor	The page background color	<body bgcolor="color value">	Yes	Yes
cookie	String giving access to the cookies the browser has for the page	n/a	Yes	Yes
fgColor	The color of the document's text	<body text="color value">	Only in NS6+	Yes
forms[ ]	Array containing the form elements in the document	<form>	No	No
lastModified	String containing the date the document was last modified	n/a	No	No
links[ ]	Array of links in the document	<a href="URL">linked content</a>	No	No
linkColor	The color of unvisited links—by default blue	<body link="color value">	Only in NS6+	Yes
location	String containing URL of the document (deprecated: use document.URL or the **Location** object instead)	n/a	Only in NS6+	Yes
referrer	String containing URL of the document from which the current document was accessed (broken in IE3 and IE4)	n/a	No	No
title	String containing the document's title	<title>Document Title</title>	Only in NS6+	Only in IE4+
URL	String containing the URL of the document	n/a	No	Yes
vlinkColor	The color of visited links—by default purple or dark blue	<body vlink="color value">	Only in NS6+	Yes

Table 9-2.   *Lowest Common Denominator Document Properties*

Method	Description
close()	Closes input stream to the document
open()	Opens the document for input
write()	Writes the argument to the document
writeln()	Writes the arguments to the document followed by a newline

Table 9-3. *Lowest Common Denominator Document Methods*

the presentation properties of most elements. An example showing the various **Document** properties printed for a sample document is presented here:

```
<!DOCTYPE HTML PUBLIC "-//W3C//DTD HTML 4.01 Transitional//EN"
          "http://www.w3.org/TR/html4/loose.dtd">
<html>
<head>
<title>Traditional Document Object Test</title>
<script language="JavaScript" type="text/javascript">
<!--
function showProps()
{
 var i;

document.write("<h1 align='center'>Document Object Properties</h1><hr><br>");
document.write("<h2>Basic Page Properties</h2>");
document.write("Location = "+document.location + "<br>");
document.write("URL = " + document.URL + "<br>");
document.write("Document Title = "+ document.title + "<br>");
document.write("Document Last Modification Date = " + document.lastModified + "<br>");

document.write("<h2>Page Colors</h2>");
document.write("Background Color = " + document.bgColor + "<br>");
document.write("Text Color = " + document.fgColor + "<br>");
document.write("Link Color = " + document.linkColor +"<br>");
document.write("Active Link Color = " + document.alinkColor +"<br>");
```

```
document.write("Visited Link Color = " + document.vlinkColor + "<br>");
if (document.links.length > 0)
 {
    document.write("<h2>Links</h2>");
    document.write("# Links = "+ document.links.length + "<br>");
    for (i=0; i < document.links.length; i++)
        document.write("Links["+i+"]=" + document.links[i] + "<br>");
 }
if (document.anchors.length > 0)
 {
   document.write("<h2>Anchors</h2>");
   document.write("# Anchors = " + document.anchors.length + "<br>");
   for (i=0; i < document.anchors.length; i++)
   document.write("Anchors["+i+"]=" + document.anchors[i] + "<br>");
 }

 if (document.forms.length > 0)
  {
   document.write("<h2>Forms</h2>");
   document.write("# Forms = " + document.forms.length + "<br>");
   for (i=0; i < document.forms.length; i++)
       document.write("Forms["+i+"]=" + document.forms[i].name + "<br>");
  }
}
//-->
</script>
</head>
<body bgcolor="white" text="green" link="red" alink="#ffff00">
<h1 align="center">Test Document</h1>
<hr>
<a href="http://www.pint.com/">Sample link</a>
<a name="anchor1"></a>
<a name="anchor2" href="http://www.javascriptref.com">Sample link 2</a>

<form name="form1"></form>
<form name="form2"></form>
```

```
<hr>
<br><br>
<script>
<!--
//-->
</script>
</body>
</html>
```

An example of the output of the previous example is shown in Figure 9-3.

One thing to note, about this example is that many of the properties will not be set if you do not run this with a document containing forms, links, and so on. Notice the result of the same script on a document with the following simple **<body>** contents:

```
<body>
<h1 align="center">Test 2 Document</h1>
<hr>
<script>
<!--
//-->
</script>
</body>
</html>
```

JavaScript will not instantiate an object for an element that is not present, so notice that you do not have nearly as many properties to view as shown in Figure 9-4. However, you will notice that browsers will tend to define default values for certain types of properties, such as text and link colors, regardless of the presence of HTML elements or attributes.

Although it might not be obvious at first glance, the **Document** object is set up as a *containment hierarchy*. Such a hierarchy is induced by the placement of more specific objects "inside" more general objects. Notice how document-wide properties like link color are available within the **Document** object itself, but to examine form elements one must first access the **forms[]** array found inside of the **Document** object. This sort of containment is characteristic of document object models and is carried to its logical conclusion by later models that present the document as a "tree" reflecting the structure of the original HTML.

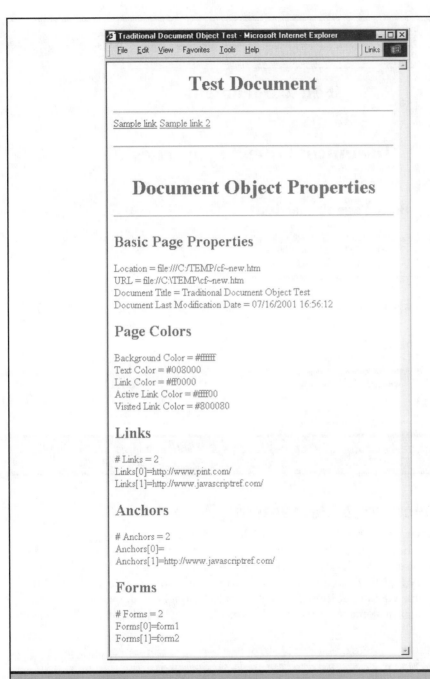

Figure 9-3. Simple Document properties

FUNDAMENTAL
CLIENT-SIDE JAVASCRIPT

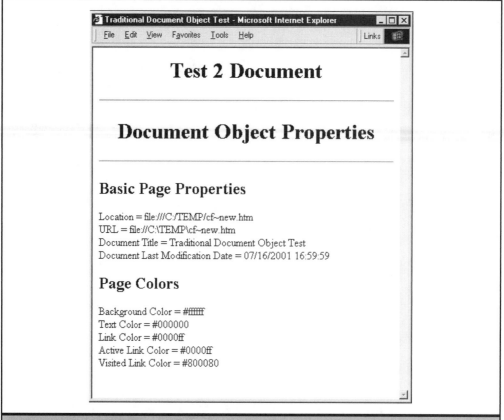

Figure 9-4. *Some Document properties require no HTML elements.*

Accessing Document Elements by Position

When the browser reads an HTML document, JavaScript objects are instantiated for all HTML elements that are scriptable. The number of HTML elements that are scriptable in the first few browsers was fairly limited, but we'll see that in later browsers it is possible to access arbitrary HTML elements. For now, however, let's concentrate on the HTML elements accessible via the traditional JavaScript object model which include anchors, links, forms, and form elements. For example, consider an HTML document like this:

```
<!DOCTYPE HTML PUBLIC "-//W3C//DTD HTML 4.01 Transitional//EN"
        "http://www.w3.org/TR/html4/loose.dtd">
```

```
<html>
<head>
<title>Simple Form</title>
</head>
<body>
<form>
  <input type="text">
</form>
<br><br>
<form>
  <input type="text">
  <br>
  <input type="text">
</form>
</body>
</html>
```

Using the traditional JavaScript object model, we can access the first **<form>** tag using

```
window.document.forms[0]
```

To access the second **<form>** tag, we would use

```
window.document.forms[1]
```

As there are no more **<form>** tags in the document, accessing *window.document.forms[5]* or other values would cause a problem.

If we look again at Figure 9-2, notice that the **forms[ ]** collection also contains an **elements[ ]** collection. This collection contains the various form fields, like text fields, buttons, pull-downs, and so on. Following the basic containment concept, in order to reach the first form element in the first form of the document we would use

```
window.document.forms[0].elements[0]
```

While this array-based access is straightforward, the major downside is that it relies on the position of the HTML tag in the document. If the tags are moved around, the JavaScript might actually break. A better approach is to rely on the name of the object.

Accessing Document Elements by Name

HTML elements in a Web page really should be named to allow scripting languages to easily read and manipulate them. The basic way to attach a unique identifier to an HTML element under HTML 4 is by using the **id** attribute. The **id** attribute is associated with nearly every HTML element.

The point of the **id** attribute is to bind a unique identifier to the element. To name a particular enclosed bolded piece of text "SuperImportant," you could use the markup shown here:

```
<b id="SuperImportant">This is very important.</b>
```

Just like choosing unique variable names within JavaScript, HTML naming is very important. HTML document authors are encouraged to adopt a consistent naming style and to avoid using potentially confusing names that include the names of HTML elements themselves. For example, *button* does not make a very good name for a form button and will certainly lead to confusion in code and may even interfere with scripting language access.

Before HTML 4, the **name** attribute was used instead of **id** to expose items to scripting. For backward compatibility, the **name** attribute is commonly defined for **<a>**, **<applet>**, **<button>**, **<embed>**, **<form>**, **<frame>**, **<iframe>**, **<img>**, **<input>**, **<object>**, **<map>**, **<select>**, and **<textarea>**. Notice that the occurrence of the **name** attribute corresponds closely to the traditional Browser Object Model.

Note *Both **<meta>** and **<param>** support attributes called **name**, but these have totally different meanings.*

Page developers must be careful to use **name** where necessary to ensure backward compatibility with older browsers. Earlier browsers will not recognize the **id** attribute, so use **name** as well. For example, **<a name="link1" id="link1">** would be interpreted, it is hoped, both by older script-aware browsers as well as by the latest standards-supporting browser.

Note *There are some statements in standards documentation that suggest that it is not a good idea to set the **name** and **id** attributes to the same value, but practice shows this appears to be the only way to ensure backward browser-compatibility.*

To access the form defined by

```
<form name="myform" id="myform">
<input type="text" name="username" id="username">
</form>
```

by name in JavaScript, use either

```
window.document.myform
```

or simply

```
document.myform
```

because the **Window** object can be assumed. The field and its value can be accessed in a similar fashion. To access the text field, use *document.myform.username.*

Accessing Objects Using Associative Arrays

Most of the arrays in the **Document** object are associative. That is, they can be indexed with an integer, as we have seen, or with a string denoting the name of the element you wish to access. The name, as we have also seen, is assigned either with HTML's **name** or **id** attribute for the tag. Of course many older browsers will only recognize the setting of an element's name using the **name** attribute. Consider the following HTML:

```
<form name="myForm">
<input name="user" type="text" value="">
</form>
```

You can access the form as *document.forms["myForm"]* or the **elements[ ]** array of the **Form** object to access the field as *document.forms["myForm"].elements["user"]*. Internet Explorer generalizes these associative arrays a bit and calls them *collections*. Collections in IE can be indexed with an integer, with a string, or with the special **item()** method. The **item()** method is used to retrieve a named object from a collection and accepts a string indicating the name of the object to retrieve. For example:

```
document.forms.item("myForm")
```

accesses the previous **Form** object. Internet Explorer collections are discussed in more detail in Chapter 23, but for now just assume that *collection.item("name")* is the same as *collection["name"].*

Event Handlers

The primary way in which scripts respond to user actions is through *event handlers.* An event handler is JavaScript code associated with a particular part of the document and a particular "event." The code is executed if and when the given event occurs at the part of the document to which it is associated. Common events include **Click**, **MouseOver**, and **MouseOut**, which occur when the user clicks, places the mouse over, or moves the mouse away from a portion of the document. These events are commonly associated with form buttons, form fields, images, and links and are used for rollover buttons and tasks like form field validation. It is important to remember that not every object is capable of handling every event. The events an object can handle are largely a reflection of the way the object is most commonly used.

Setting Event Handlers

You have probably seen event handlers before in HTML. The following simple example shows users an alert box when they click the button:

```
<form name="myForm" id="myForm">
<input name="myButton" type="button" value="Click me" onclick="alert('That
tickles!')">
</form>
```

The **onclick** attribute of the input element binds the given code to the button's **Click** event. Whenever the user clicks the button, the browser sends a **Click** event to the **Button** object, causing it to invoke its **onclick** event handler.

How does the browser know where to find the object's event handler? This is dictated by part of the document object model known as the *event model*. An event model is simply set of interfaces and objects that enable this kind of event handling. In most major browsers, an object's event handlers are accessible as properties of the object itself. So instead of using HTML to bind an event handler to an object, we can do it with pure JavaScript. The following code is equivalent to the previous example:

```
<form name="myForm" id="myForm">
<input name="myButton" type="button" value="Click me">
</form>
<script language="JavaScript" type="text/javascript">
<!--
document.myForm.myButton.onclick = new Function("alert('That tickles!')");
// -->
</script>
```

We define an anonymous function containing the code for the event handler and then set the button's **onclick** property equal to it.

Event Models

There is obviously much more to event handlers than we have described here. Both major browsers implement sophisticated event models that allow applications great flexibility when it comes to events. For example, if you have to define the same event handler for a large number of objects, you can bind the handler once to an object higher up the hierarchy rather than binding it to each child individually. A more complete discussion of event handlers is found in Chapter 11.

Putting It All Together

Now that we have seen all the components of the traditional object model, it is time to show how all the components are used together. As we have seen previously using a **name** or **id** it is fairly easy to reference an occurrence of an HTML element that is exposed in the JavaScript object model. For example, given:

```
<form name="myform" id="myform">
<input type="text" name="username" id="username">
</form>
```

we would use

```
document.myform.username
```

to access the field named *username* in this form. But how do you manipulate that tag's properties? The key to understanding JavaScript's object model is that, generally, an HTML element's attributes are exposed as JavaScript object properties. So, given that a text field in HTML has the basic syntax of:

```
<input type="text" name="unique identifier" id="unique identifier"
          size="number of characters" maxlength="number of characters"
          value="default value">
```

then *document.myform.username.name* references the **name** attribute of a text field from our example, *document.myform.username.size* references its displayed screen size in characters, and so on. The following simple example puts everything together and shows how the content of a form field is accessed and displayed dynamically in an alert window by referencing the fields by **name**.

```
<!DOCTYPE HTML PUBLIC "-//W3C//DTD HTML 4.01 Transitional//EN"
          "http://www.w3.org/TR/html4/loose.dtd">
<html>
<head>
<title>Meet and Greet</title>
<script language="JavaScript" type="text/javascript">
<!--
function sayHello()
{
 var theirname = document.myform.username.value;
 if (theirname ! = "")
   alert("Hello "+theirname+"!");
```

```
 else
    alert("Don't be shy.");
}
// -->
</script>
</head>
<body>
<form name="myform" id="myform">
<b>What's your name?</b>
<input type="text" name="username" id="username"  size="20"><br><br>
<input type="button" value="Greet" onclick="sayHello()">
</form>
</body>
</html>
```

Aside from reading the contents of an element with JavaScript, it also is possible, in some cases, to update the contents of certain elements, such as form fields. The following code shows how this might be done:

```
<!DOCTYPE HTML PUBLIC "-//W3C//DTD HTML 4.01 Transitional//EN"
          "http://www.w3.org/TR/html4/loose.dtd">
<html>
<head>
<title>Meet and Greet 2</title>
<script language="JavaScript" type="text/javascript">
<!--
function sayHello()
{
 var theirname = document.myform.username.value;
 if (theirname != "")
   document.myform.response.value="Hello "+theirname+"!";
 else
   document.myform.response.value="Don't be shy.";
}
// -->
</script>
</head>
<body>
<form name="myform" id="myform">
<b>What's your name?</b>
<input type="text" name="username" id="username"  size="20">
<br><br>
<b>Greeting:</b>
```

```
<input type="text" name="response" id="response" size="40">
<br><br>
<input type="button" value="Greet" onclick="sayHello()">
</form>
</body>
</html>
```

One final item to note is that some of the **Document** properties are writeable, while others are not. Notice how the **anchors[ ]**, **forms[ ]**, and **links[ ]** arrays are listed as read-only in Table 9-2. This does not imply that you cannot modify data contained *in* elements of these arrays. Rather, it means that you cannot modify the elements of the arrays themselves. For example, although you can modify data in a particular form, for instance *document.forms[0].userName.value,* you cannot replace the form *forms[0]* with another **Form** object. Because of the containment hierarchy, all interesting information is contained inside each object anyway, so this restriction does not present a problem.

The previous examples simply show how to access elements using an object model. Later on, in Part IV of the book, we'll see how to do something interesting like form checking using these techniques. Now that we understand the basics of using an object model, it is time to take a look at the specific object models supported by the popular Web browsers.

The Object Models

So far, the discussion has focused primarily on the generic features common to all document object models, regardless of browser version. Not surprisingly, every time a new version was released, browser vendors extended the functionality of the **Document** object in various ways. Bugs were fixed, access to a greater portion of the document was added, and the existing functionality was continually improved.

The gradual evolution of document object models is a good thing in the sense that more recent object models allow you to carry out a wider variety of tasks more easily. However it also poses some major problems for Web developers. The biggest issue is that the object models of different browsers evolved in different directions. New proprietary tags were added to facilitate the realization of Dynamic HTML (DHTML), and new, nonstandard means of carrying out various tasks became a part of both Internet Explorer and Netscape. The result is that the brand-new DHTML code a developer writes using the Netscape object model probably will not work in Internet Explorer (and vice versa). The following sections discuss the object models of major browser versions. In particular, we highlight the new features to be found in each and their relevance to common programming tasks.

Netscape 2

The object model of Netscape 2 is that of the basic object model presented earlier in the chapter. It was the first browser to present such an interface to JavaScript, and its capabilities are limited. With these limitations, the main uses of JavaScript in this browser are form validation and very simple page manipulation, such as printing the last date of modification.

Netscape 3

Netscape 3's **Document** object opened the door for the first primitive DHTML-like applications. It exposes more of the document content to scripts by providing the ability to access embedded objects, applets, plugins, and images. This object model is shown in Figure 9-5, and the major additions to the **Document** object are listed in Table 9-4.

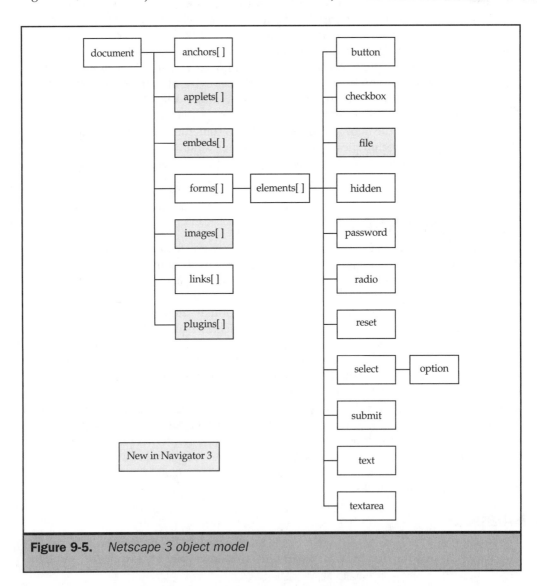

Figure 9-5. *Netscape 3 object model*

Property	Description
applets[ ]	Array of applets (**<applet>** tags) in the document.
domain	String containing the hostname of the Web server from which the document was fetched. Can be changed only to a more general hostname (for instance, www.w3c.org to w3c.org).
embeds[ ]	Array of embedded objects (**<embed>** tags) in the document.
images[ ]	Array of images (**<img>** tags) in the document.
plugins[ ]	Array of plugins installed in the browser.

Table 9-4. *New Document Properties in Netscape 3*

FUNDAMENTAL CLIENT-SIDE JAVASCRIPT

Arguably the most important addition to the **Document** object in this version is the inclusion of the **images[ ]** array. Although most of the properties of each **Image** object are read-only, the **src** property is writeable. This afforded for the first time the ability to change images dynamically in response to user events. A typical application of this capability is *rollover buttons*—buttons that change appearance when the user's mouse is placed over them. Unfortunately, because **Image** objects had no event handlers in this model, rollovers were usually implemented by placing the image inside of an anchor tag; for example:

```
<a href="#"
onmouseover="document.images[0].src='/images/buttonOn.gif'"
onmouseout="document.images[0].src='/images/buttonOff.gif'">
<img src="/images/buttonOff.gif">
</a>
```

Whenever a user's mouse is placed over the link (and thereby over the image), the anchor tag's **onmouseover** event handler swaps images. When the user moves the mouse away from the link, the anchor's **onmouseout** handler swaps the original image back in. Note how the **href** attribute is included in the anchor tag; omitting it may cause the script to fail since the **<a>** tag will not instantiate a **Link** object unless it is properly formed. We'll take an in-depth look at image effects in Chapter 15.

Netscape also made a few additions to its support for forms. The **reset()** method was added to the **Form** object and resets the form upon invocation, regardless of the presence of a reset button. Other, subtler changes were made to the event handlers available for each object. The major addition was the document-wide event handlers **onblur** and **onfocus**. Although these properties are specified in the **<body>** tag of the document, they are actually event handlers for the **Window** object.

More significant additions to the **Window** object were also made. The **History** object was added at this point along with two new properties, **closed** and **opener**. The **window.closed** property indicates if the user has closed that window and helps to avoid using an invalid window. The **window.opener** property lets a "child" window access its "parent," the window containing the JavaScript that created it.

Netscape 4

The document object model of version 4 browsers marks the point at which support for DHTML begins to mature. Outside of swapping images in response to user events, there was little one could do to bring Web pages alive before Netscape 4. Major changes in this version include support for the proprietary **<layer>** tag, additions to Netscape's event model, and the addition of **Style** objects and the means to manipulate them. Figure 9-6 shows the essentials of Netscape 4's object model; the most interesting new properties of the **Document** object are listed in Table 9-5.

DHTML Additions

One of the most important features of Netscape 4's document model is its exposure of stylistic elements to scripts. In fact, the interaction between style sheets and JavaScript under Netscape 4 is so pronounced that Netscape initially termed its style sheet implementation JavaScript Style Sheets (JSSS). Further, if you disable JavaScript under Netscape 4, you will find that style sheets will not work regardless of how they are included.

Under Netscape 4, JavaScript programmers can create or manipulate CSS attributes for every element in the document. It is important to note that this capability is primarily useful for creating or changing stylistic elements *before* the content they apply to is displayed on the screen. Under Netscape 4, the style of most HTML elements cannot be changed once they are displayed. This is very different from the Internet Explorer model discussed later in the chapter.

The new **Document** properties introduced in Netscape 4 that enable manipulation of style are **classes[ ]**, **ids[ ]**, and **tags[ ]**. With JSSS you can access individual tags named using HTML 4's core **id** attribute with the **ids[ ]** property of the **Document** object. The syntax for this is:

document.ids.*idName.propertyName*

where

- *idName* indicates the particular ID you wish to access
- *propertyName* designates the CSS property

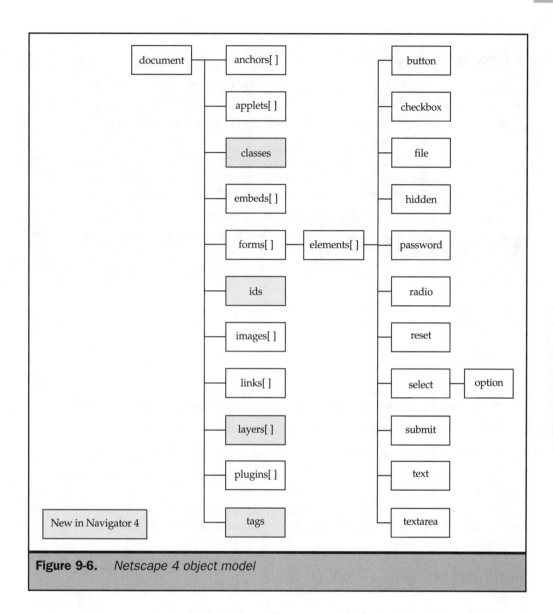

Figure 9-6. *Netscape 4 object model*

For example, to change the size of the element with **id="myHeading"**, you would write

```
document.ids.myHeading.fontSize = "64pt";
```

Property	Description
classes	Creates or accesses CSS style for HTML elements with **class** attributes set.
ids	Creates or accesses CSS style for HTML elements with **id** attributes set.
layers[ ]	Array of layers (**<layer>** tags or positioned **<div>** elements) in the document. If indexed by an integer, the layers are ordered from back to front by z-index (where z-index of 0 is the bottommost layer).
tags	Creates or accesses CSS style for arbitrary HTML elements.

Table 9-5.   *New Document Properties in Netscape 4*

Similarly, to change a particular group of tags identified with **class** attributes, you use the **classes[ ]** property of Netscape 4's **Document** object using the following syntax:

document.classes.*className.tagName.propertyName*

where

- *className* indicates the name of the class you wish to access
- *tagName* is the name of the specific tag in that class that you are interested in
- *propertyName* indicates the particular CSS property to access

Note that if you wish to access the style information for all tags in a particular class, you can use "all" for the *tagName*.

For example, suppose that you have defined two classes in the **<style>** tag called "important" and "codeListing." You could change the color of list items in the "important" class as:

```
document.classes.important.li.color = "red";
```

or the font of all elements with the "codeListing" class as:

```
document.classes.codeListing.all.fontFamily = "monospace";
```

Lastly, the **tags[ ]** property lets you define or manipulate style globally for a particular HTML element. Its syntax is

document.tags.*tagName.propertyName*

where

- *tagName* specifies the HTML element
- *propertyName* indicates the particular CSS property to access

For example, to change the text color of **<h1>** to blue, you might write:

```
document.tags.h1.color = "blue";
```

There are quite a few other aspects of JSSS, but the point is not to cover the syntax in detail. In fact, this discussion is primarily historical in nature. Using this syntax is not encouraged at all. It works only in Netscape 4.x generation browsers. Even hardcore Netscape fanatics didn't give much thought to this syntax, since it affects only the presentation of an HTML element before the element is rendered. For example, consider the following simple JSSS example.

```
<!DOCTYPE HTML PUBLIC "-//W3C//DTD HTML 4.01 Transitional//EN"
         "http://www.w3.org/TR/html4/loose.dtd">
<html>
<head>
<title>Simple Netscape JSSS Example</title>
</head>
<body>
<script language="JavaScript" type="text/javascript">
<!--
  // Danger! Example only works in Netscape 4.x Browsers
  document.tags.h1.color = "blue";
  document.ids.myHeading.fontSize = "64pt";
  document.classes.important.p.backgroundColor = "orange";
  document.classes.important.all.fontStyle = "italic";
// -->
</script>
<h1 class="important">This is an H1 with class important</h1>
<hr>
<p class="important">This is a paragraph with class important</p>
<h2 id="myHeading">This is an H2 with id myHeading</h2>
<p class="important">This is a paragraph with class important</p>
</body>
</html>
```

Note   *The output is shown in Figure 9-7; but remember, if we place the script block after the HTML elements the page presentation will not be modified.*

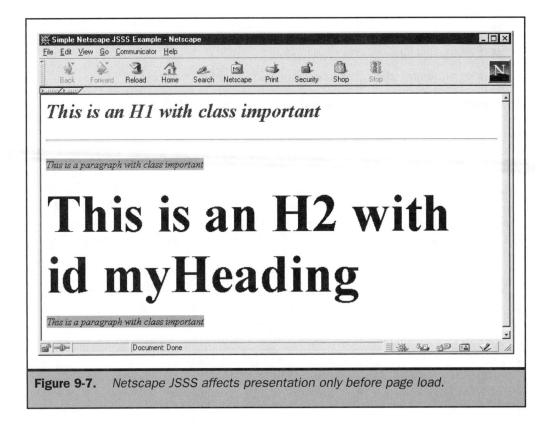

Figure 9-7. *Netscape JSSS affects presentation only before page load.*

One aspect of the Netscape 4.x generation of browsers that is important to understand from a historical perspective is the **Layer** object.

Netscape Layers

Outside of the manipulation of style, Netscape 4 recognizes a new, proprietary HTML tag: **<layer>**. The **<layer>** tag allows you to define content areas that can be precisely positioned, moved, and overlapped as well as rendered hidden, visible, or even transparent. You can write new content to a layer using its **write()** and **writeln()** methods, enabling functionality akin to some of the more advanced features of Internet Explorer. Netscape envisioned this tag as one of the primary foundations upon which DHTML applications would be built. However, the **<layer>** tag never made it into the W3C's HTML standard and was never included by any competing browser vendors. As a result, Netscape abandoned the tag in version 6 of its browser. Thus the **<layer>** tag is available only in Netscape 4.x browsers. It is for this reason that its utility is considered to be fairly limited. Even in the Netscape 4.x browser, the **<div>** element combined with Cascading Style Sheets positioning rules provide very similar capabilities.

However, if you must perform some form of positioning in Netscape 4.x, you may be forced to use a **<layer>** tag or at least manipulate a more standard **<div>** tag with CSS through the **Layer** object. For example, in the script here, a region was positioned using CSS—but to dynamically modify it under Netscape 4.x, you must use the **Layer** object.

```
<!DOCTYPE HTML PUBLIC "-//W3C//DTD HTML 4.01 Transitional//EN"
           "http://www.w3.org/TR/html4/loose.dtd">
<html>
<head>
<title>NS4 Layer Example</title>
<style type="text/css">
<!--
     #div1 { position: absolute;
             top: 200px;
             left: 350px;
             height: 100px;
             width: 100px;
             background-color: orange;}
-->
</style>
</head>
<body>
<h1 align="center">Netscape 4 Layer Example</h1>
<div id="div1">An example of a positioned region</div>
<form>
<input type="button" value="hide"
onclick="document.layers['div1'].visibility='hide'">
<input type="button" value="show"
onclick="document.layers['div1'].visibility='show'">
</form>
</body>
</html>
```

Only the first level of nested layers is available via **document.layers[ ]**, because each layer receives its own **Document** object. To reach a nested layer, you must navigate to the outer layer, then through its **Document** to the nested layer's **layers[ ]** array, and so on. For example, to reach a layer within a layer you might write:

```
var nestedLayer = document.layers[0].document.layers[0].document;
```

Although the use of layers will eventually die off, layers do provide a good way to detect version 4 Netscape browsers. Under Netscape 4, accessing **document.layers** will return the **layers[ ]** array. Under any other browser, accessing **document.layers** will return **undefined**, so you can conveniently check for Netscape 4 like this:

```
if (document.layers) { /*  do something Netscape specific  */ }
```

Window Additions

A tremendous number of new properties were added to the **Window** object in Netscape 4. Included are properties that give information about screen size, height, and width; properties that give information about the configuration of various toolbars in the user's browser; base-64 encoding and decoding methods; methods to move, resize, and offset the screen; and methods to simulate the click of the browser's forward and back buttons.

Event Model Additions

Aside from the addition of new mouse and keyboard event handlers, such as **onmouseup/down** and **onkeyup/down**, Netscape fleshed out its event model in several significant ways. Events in this browser begin at the top of the object hierarchy and "trickle down" to the object upon which they are acting. This traversal allows **Window** and **Document** objects (including **Layer** objects) to perform *captures* that halt or alter the downward "flow" of an event. Event capturing is achieved with the **captureEvents()** method and permits a captured event to be dealt with at the "higher" level—modified, redirected, or simply passed through to continue on its way down the hierarchy. This feature is used to simplify programming pages where numerous lower-level objects like form fields all require the same event handlers. A detailed discussion of Netscape 4 event handling can be found in Chapter 11.

Netscape 6

The release of Netscape 6 marks a new era for Netscape browsers. The main emphasis of this browser is standards compliance, a refreshing change from the ad hoc proprietary document object models of the past. It is backwards compatible with the so-called DOM Level 0, the W3C's DOM standard that incorporates many of the widespread features of older document object models, in particular that of Netscape 3. However, it also implements DOM Level 1 and parts of DOM Level 2, the W3C's object models for standard HTML, XML, CSS, and events. These standard models differ in significant ways from older models and are covered in detail in the next chapter.

Support for nearly all of the proprietary extensions supported by Netscape 4, most notably the **<layer>** tag and corresponding JavaScript object, have been dropped in Netscape 6. This breaks the paradigm that allowed developers to program for older browser versions knowing that such code would be supported by newer versions. Like many aspects of document models, this is both good and bad; older code may not work in Netscape 6, but future code written for this browser will have a solid standards foundation.

Internet Explorer 3

The object model of IE3 is the basic "lowest common denominator" object model presented at the beginning of this chapter. It includes several "extra" properties in the **Document** object not included in Netscape 2, for example the **frames[ ]** array, but for the most part it corresponds closely to the model of Netscape 2. The Internet Explorer 3 object model is shown in Figure 9-8.

For the short period of time when Netscape 2 and IE3 coexisted as the latest versions of the respective browsers, object models were in a comfortable state of unity. It wouldn't last long.

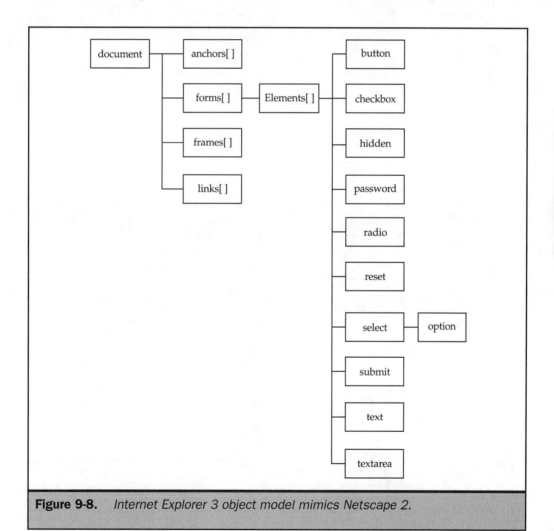

Figure 9-8. *Internet Explorer 3 object model mimics Netscape 2.*

Internet Explorer 4

Like version 4 of Netscape's browser, IE4 lays the foundations for DHTML applications by exposing much more of the page to JavaScript. In fact, it goes much further than Netscape 4 by representing *every* HTML element as an object. Unfortunately, it does so in a manner incompatible with Netscape 4's object model. The basic object model of Internet Explorer 4 is shown in Figure 9-9.

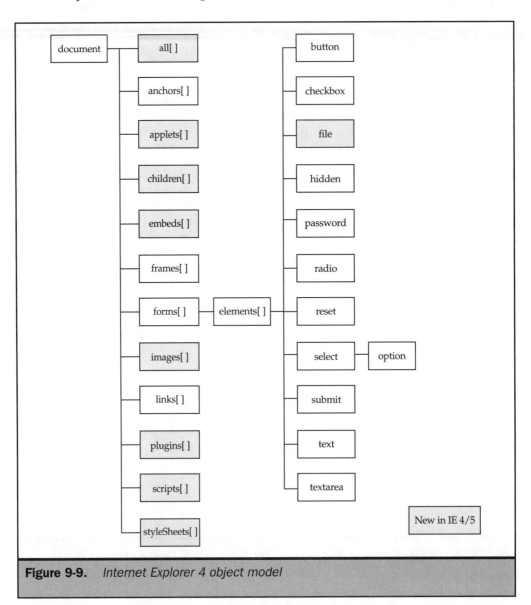

Figure 9-9. *Internet Explorer 4 object model*

Inspection of Figure 9-9 reveals that IE4 supports the basic object model of Netscape 2 and IE3, plus most of the features of Netscape 3 as well as many of its own features. This suggests that code can be written for the set of properties that IE4 and Netscape 3 have in common without too many problems. Table 9-6 lists some important new properties found in IE4. You will notice that Figure 9-9 and Table 9-6 show that IE4 also implements new **Document** object features radically different from those present in Netscape 4. It is in version 4 of the two major browsers where the object models begin their radical divergence.

DHTML Additions

One of the most important new JavaScript features introduced in IE4 is the **document.all[ ]** collection. This array provides access to every element in the document. It can be indexed in a variety of ways and returns a collection of objects matching the index, **id** or **name** attribute provided; for example:

```
// sets variable to the fourth element in the document
var theElement = document.all[3];

// finds tag with id or name = myHeading
var myHeading = document.all["myHeading"];

// alternative way to find tag with id or name = myHeading
var myHeading = document.all.item("myHeading");

// returns array of all <em> tags
var allEm = document.all.tags("EM");
```

Property	Description
all[ ]	Array of all HTML tags in the document
applets[ ]	Array of all applets (**<applet>** tags) in the document
children[ ]	Array of all child elements of the object
embeds[ ]	Array of embedded objects (**<embed>** tags) in the document
images[ ]	Array of images (**<img>** tags) in the document
scripts[ ]	Array of scripts (**<script>** tags) in the document
styleSheets[ ]	Array of **Style** objects (**<style>** tags) in the document

Table 9-6.   *New Document Properties in Internet Explorer 4*

As you can see there are many ways to access the elements of a page, but, regardless of the method used, the primary effect of the **document.all[ ]** collection is that it flattens the document object hierarchy to allow quick and easy access to any portion of an HTML document. The following simple example shows that Internet Explorer truly does expose all the elements in a page; its result is shown in Figure 9-10.

```
<!DOCTYPE HTML PUBLIC "-//W3C//DTD HTML 4.01 Transitional//EN"
          "http://www.w3.org/TR/html4/loose.dtd">
<html>
<head>
<title>Document.All Example</title>
</head>
<body>
<h1>Example Heading</h1>
<hr>
<p>This is a <em>paragraph</em>.  It is only a <em>paragraph.</em></p>
<p>Yet another <em>paragraph.</em></p>
<p>This final <em>paragraph</em> has <em id="special">special emphasis.</em></p>
<hr>
<script language="JavaScript" type="text/javascript">
<!--
 var i, origLength;
 origLength = document.all.length;
 document.write('document.all.length='+origLength+"<br>");
 for (i = 0; i < origLength; i++)
   {
   document.write("document.all["+i+"]="+document.all[i].tagName+"<br>");
   }
// -->
</script>
</body>
</html>
```

Note *The previous example will result in an endless loop if you do not use the* origLength *variable and rely on the **document.all.length** as your loop check. The reason is that the number of elements in the **document.all[ ]** collection will grow every time you output the element you are checking!*

Similar to the trick to detect Netscape 4 through the existence of the **Layer** object, many programmers rely on the existence of **document.all** to detect Internet Explorer browsers and often rely on statements like:

```
if (document.all) { /*  do something IE specific  */ }
```

to deal with browser-specific code.

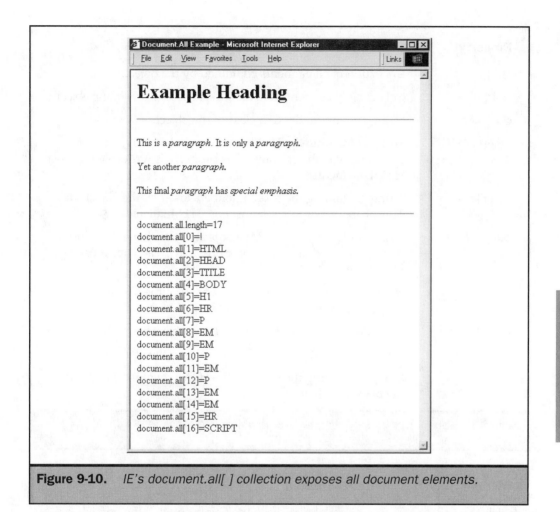

Figure 9-10. *IE's document.all[ ] collection exposes all document elements.*

Once a particular element has been referenced using the **document.all** syntax, you will find a variety of properties and methods associated with it, including the **all** property itself, which references any tags enclosed within the returned tag. Tables 9-7 and 9-8 show some of the more interesting, but certainly not all of these new properties and methods. Note that inline elements will not have certain properties (like **innerHTML**) because by definition their tags cannot enclose any other content.

If Tables 9-7 and 9-8 seem overwhelming, do not worry. At this point you are not expected to fully understand each of these properties and methods. Rather, we list them to illustrate just how far the Netscape and Internet Explorer object models diverged in a very short period of time.

Examination of the new features available in IE4 should reveal that this is the first browser where real DHTML is possible. It provides the means to manipulate style dynamically (after the page has loaded, unlike with Netscape 4) and to insert,

Property	Description
all[ ]	Collection of all elements contained by the object.
children[ ]	Collection of elements that are direct descendents of the object.
className	String containing the CSS class of the object.
innerHTML	String containing the HTML content enclosed by, but not including, the object's tags. This property is writeable for most HTML elements.
innerText	String containing the text content enclosed by the object's tags. This property is writeable for most HTML elements.
outerHTML	String containing the HTML content of the element, including its start and end tags. This property is writeable for most HTML elements.
outerText	String containing the outer text content of the element. This property is writeable for most HTML elements.
parentElement	Reference to the object's parent in the object hierarchy.
style	**Style** object containing CSS properties of the object.
tagName	String containing the name of the HTML tag associated with the object.

Table 9-7. *Some New Properties for Document Model Objects in IE4*

Method	Description
click()	Simulates clicking the object, causing the **onclick** event handler to fire
getAttribute()	Retrieves the argument HTML attribute for the element
insertAdjacentHTML()	Allows the insertion of HTML before, after, or inside the element
insertAdjacentText()	Allows the insertion of text before, after, or inside the element
removeAttribute()	Deletes the argument HTML attribute from the element
setAttribute()	Sets the argument HTML attribute for the element

Table 9-8. *Some New Methods for Document Model Objects in IE4*

modify, and delete arbitrary HTML and text. For the first time, JavaScript can manipulate the structure of the document, changing content and presentation of all aspects of the page as desired. The following example illustrates this feature using Internet Explorer syntax:

```
<!DOCTYPE HTML PUBLIC "-//W3C//DTD HTML 4.01 Transitional//EN"
          "http://www.w3.org/TR/html4/loose.dtd">
<html>
<head>
<title>Document.All Example #2</title>
</head>
<body>
<!-- Only works in Internet Explorer 4 and greater -->
<h1 id="heading1" align="center">DHTML Fun!!!</h1>

<form name="testform" id="testform">
<br><br>
<input type="button" value="Align Left"
onclick="document.all['heading1'].align='left'">
<input type="button" value="Align Center"
onclick="document.all['heading1'].align='center'">
<input type="button" value="Align Right"
onclick="document.all['heading1'].align='right'">
<br><br>
<input type="button" value="Bigger"
onclick="document.all['heading1'].style.fontSize='larger'">
<input type="button" value="Smaller"
onclick="document.all['heading1'].style.fontSize='smaller'">
<br><br>
<input type="button" value="Red"
onclick="document.all['heading1'].style.color='red'">
<input type="button" value="Blue"
onclick="document.all['heading1'].style.color='blue'">
<input type="button" value="Black"
onclick="document.all['heading1'].style.color='black'">
<br><br>
<input type="text" name="userText" id="userText" size="30">
<input type="button" value="Change Text"
onclick="document.all['heading1'].innerText=document.testform.userText.value"><br>
</form>
</body>
</html>
```

As this short introduction demonstrates, there are tremendous possibilities for DHTML in IE4. The examples given here barely scratch the surface of IE's powerful document object model, though they do show how a highly structured DOM might be presented to scripts. Notice how the interface represents each element as a mutable object and that each object has well-defined parent-child inclusion properties. These characteristics foreshadow many of the features of the W3C DOM discussed in the next chapter.

Event Model Additions

IE4 implements an "opposite" event model from that of Netscape 4. Events begin at the bottom of the hierarchy at the object where they occur and "bubble up" through parent objects to the **Window**. Any object along the path from the origin of the event to the "top" of the hierarchy can intercept an event, process it, and cancel it or pass it along up the tree. To complicate matters, the properties of IE4's **Event** object are different from those of Netscape's. We'll see these differences in great detail in Chapter 11.

Internet Explorer 5, 5.5, and 6

The document object model of Internet Explorer 5.x is very similar to that of IE4. New features include an explosive rise in the number of properties and methods available in the objects of the document model and proprietary enhancements allowing the development of reusable DHTML components.

Many of the additions to objects of the document model implement portions of the W3C DOM. These features are significantly less complete than those found in Netscape 6, but they are a step in the right direction. Microsoft has also included numerous properties that build on the existing IE4 object model, making it much more robust and capable of more powerful document manipulation. Also greatly increasing in number are the event handlers added in IE5. As of IE5.5, the browser supports almost 40 different events, ranging from specific mouse and keyboard actions to editing events such as cutting and pasting.

IE5 supports two new features called *DHTML Behaviors* and *HTML Applications*. DHTML Behaviors allow programmers to define reusable DHTML components that can be applied to arbitrary elements. HTML Applications (HTA's) are HTML documents that act more like a real programs than web applications. These features are not yet in widespread use, but might make their way into future W3C standards. We'll discuss both of these technologies in Chapter 23 where we cover proprietary Internet Explorer features.

Internet Explorer 5.5 and 6 continue Microsoft's trend of adding features that work only in its browsers, including new behaviors, new forms of popup windows, scrollbar changes, and so on. However, Internet Explorer 5.5 continues to improve its DOM support, and the pre-release versions of Internet Explorer 6 available at the time of this book's writing suggest that IE6 will be totally CSS1- and DOM1-compliant, but that developers must "switch on" the "standards-compliant mode" by including a valid **<DOCTYPE>**. The browser will be backwards compatible with previous IE document object models in order to preserve the functionality of old code. The question of whether or not further standards will be implemented in IE6 is still up in the air.

Opera, Mozilla, Konqueror, and Other Browsers

Although rarely considered by some Web developers, there are some other browsers that have a small but loyal following in many tech-savvy circles. Most third-party browsers are "strict standards" implementations, meaning that they implement W3C and ECMA standards and ignore most of the proprietary object models of Internet Explorer and Netscape. Some provide support for the basic Netscape 2 and IE3 object models, but most focus their development efforts on the W3C standards. If the demographic for your Web site includes users likely to use third-party browsers (for example, Linux users), it might be a good idea to avoid IE- and Netscape-specific features and use the W3C DOM instead.

The Nightmare of Cross-Browser Object Support

The common framework of the **Document** object shared by Internet Explorer and Netscape dates back to 1996. It might be hard to believe, but in the intervening years there has been very little improvement to the parts of the document object model the major browsers have in common.

As a result, when faced with a non-trivial JavaScript task, Web developers have become accustomed to writing two separate scripts, one for Internet Explorer 4+ and one for Netscape 4+. The IE version usually utilizes the extensive style manipulation capabilities of IE4, often relying on the **document.all[ ]** collection, while the Netscape version relies heavily on the **<layer>** tag and associated **document.layers[ ]** array for similar functionality. Because the object models evolved in such incompatible directions, this process can be tiresome and susceptible to errors and oversights. If the developer does not take care in verifying support for particular features and testing applications with a variety of browsers, he or she might be forced to rewrite pages of code.

Continuing down this road will only make the situation worse. If browser vendors continue to make proprietary extensions document objects, the number of different object models developers must support will continue to increase. How long can the average developer be expected to accommodate the myriad of ways to perform seemingly simple tasks like changing text color, replacing pieces of text, and interacting with browser plugins?

Aside from the tedious nature of writing each piece of JavaScript code multiple times for different browsers, there are other problems with traditional document object models. One major question is how scripts will interact with newer technologies like XML, given the diverse and heterogeneous nature of the traditional models. Are browser wars again going to force developers into maintaining a different piece of JavaScript code for each proprietary object model? Are we to be stuck with a fixed, browser-based interface to each object model regardless of application requirements such as memory footprint, speed, and presentation on alternative media?

It should be clear that the situation with traditional object models is less than optimal. With many developers and users frustrated with incompatibilities in object and events models, the Web is ripe for a change.

A Solution?

Such a change has been proffered by the standards put together by the World Wide Web Consortium in the form of its Document Object Model. The W3C gives a succinct description of the DOM: "It is a platform- and language-neutral interface that will allow programs and scripts to dynamically access and update the content, structure and style of documents, both HTML and XML." This is music to Web developers' ears. Combined with the standardized ways of describing presentation characteristics defined by CSS, the DOM promises a uniform paradigm for creating interactive documents not only for the Web, but for a variety of offline business and technical endeavors as well.

Progress towards realization of this standard is already being made. Netscape has made a firm commitment to implementation of standards, a commitment it is already making good on with Netscape 6. Netscape is also actively supporting several Open Source projects aimed at bringing standards compliance to the browser community. In the year 2001, the Mozilla project is nearing the completion of developing its fully featured standards-based browser. Microsoft is also coming around, promising more DOM features than ever in version 6 of Internet Explorer.

It is interesting to observe that if browser vendors wholeheartedly embrace the W3C DOM, the document models will have come full circle. In the mid-nineties, there was a brief period of time when access to the document was uniform across both major browsers. Version 4 of the browsers marked the beginning of the radical divergence of object models, and there has been little compatibility since. If browser vendors continue to support the W3C DOM, there might be a point in the future when developers have access to a powerful, robust, and standardized interface for the manipulation of structured documents.

Summary

This chapter gives a basic introduction to the traditional document object models. The **Document** object is structured as a containment hierarchy and accessed by "navigating" through general objects to those that are more specific. The most useful **Document** properties are found in associative arrays, like **images[ ]**, which can be indexed by an integer or name when an element is named using an HTML tag's **name** or **id** attribute. Event handlers were introduced as a means to react to user events and may be set with JavaScript or traditional HTML. The main portion of this chapter introduced the specific document object nodels of the major browsers. Netscape 2 and Internet Explorer 3 implement the most basic object model upon which other models are built. Netscape 3 added a few useful new properties, while the bulk of the changes occur in Netscape 4.

Netscape 6 was introduced as a standards-based browser not necessarily supporting all portions of previous models. We saw that Internet Explorer 4 introduced some powerful DHTML applications by exposing all portions of the document to scripts. The IE4 object model was further extended by IE5, and further extensions are likely in IE6. In the course of the chapter, the divergent and incompatible nature of the different object models was stressed, and near the end a possible solution, the W3C DOM, was proposed. The next chapter explains the details of the DOM and why it might revolutionize the way scripts manipulate documents.

Chapter 10

The Standard Document Object Model

In the last chapter we presented the various object models supported by the two major browsers. These object models included objects for the window, documents, forms, images, and so on. We pointed out that these objects correspond to the features of the browser as well as to the features of the HTML document and style sheets. A major problem with browser-based object models is that each vendor decides which features to expose to the programmer and how to do so. To combat the browser incompatibilities discussed in Chapter 9, the W3C came up with a standard that maps between an HTML or XML document and the document object hierarchy presented to the programmer. This model is called the *Document Object Model*, or the DOM for short (**www.w3.org/ DOM**). The DOM provides an application programming interface (API) that exposes the entirety of a Web page (including tags, attributes, style, and content) to a programming language like JavaScript. This chapter explores the basic uses of the DOM, from examining document structure to accessing common properties and methods. We'll see that a key part of DOM mastery is a thorough understanding of HTML and CSS. While the DOM does point towards a future where cross-browser scripting will be less of an issue, we will also see that browser vendors are only just now truly embracing Web standards. As a result, serious bugs abound. This chapter's examples will work in the 5.x generation (or better) of the two major browsers—but some bugs may still exist, so proceed with caution.

Note *The discussion of the DOM really does require that you are comfortable with HTML and CSS. Readers who are not are encouraged to review these topics, for example in the companion book* HTML: The Complete Reference.

DOM Flavors

In order to straighten out the object model mess presented in the last chapter, the W3C has defined three levels of the DOM:

- **DOM Level 0** is roughly equivalent to what the Netscape 3.0 and Internet Explorer 3.0 have supported. We call this DOM the *classic* or *traditional* JavaScript object model. This form of the DOM was presented in the last chapter.

- **DOM Level 1** provides the ability to manipulate all elements in a document through a common set of functions. In DOM Level 1, all elements are exposed and parts of the page can be read and written to at all times. The Level 1 DOM provides capabilities similar to Internet Explorer 4.0's **document.all[ ]** collection, except that it is cross-browser compatible, standardized, and a bit more robust.

- **DOM Level 2** provides further access to page elements primarily related to XML and focuses on combining DOM Level 0 and Level 1 while adding support for style sheet access and manipulation. Support for an event model fusing the concepts of Netscape 4 and Internet Explorer 4 is also included.

Note *At the time of this book's writing, the DOM Level 3 was under consideration. This version of the DOM will improve support for XML, extend Level 2's event model (primarily to support keyboard and device events), and add features to allow content to be exchanged between files (including a load and save feature to exchange documents).*

Another way of looking at the DOM as defined by the W3C is by grouping the pieces of the DOM concept into the following five categories:

- **DOM Core**   Specifies a generic model for viewing and manipulating a marked up document as a tree structure.

- **DOM XML**   Specifies an extension to the core DOM for use with XML. DOM XML addresses the particular needs of XML, such as CDATA Sections, processing instructions, namespaces, and so on.

- **DOM HTML**   Specifies an extension to the core DOM for use with HTML. DOM HTML provides the features used to manipulate HTML documents and utilizes a syntax similar to the traditional JavaScript object models. Basically, this is DOM Level 0 plus the capabilities to manipulate all of the HTML element objects.

- **DOM Events**   Adds event handling to the DOM. These events range from familiar user interface events such as mouse clicks to DOM-specific events that fire when actions occur that modify parts of the document tree.

- **DOM CSS**   Provides the interfaces necessary to manipulate CSS rules programmatically.

In this chapter we will focus primarily on DOM Level 1 and the parts of Level 2 that are available in today's browsers. In other words we will talk about DOM Core, DOM HTML, and DOM CSS. DOM Events will be discussed in Chapter 11. It is important to note that although we will be using JavaScript in this chapter, the DOM specifies a language-independent interface. So, in principle, you can use the DOM in other languages such as C and Java.

The first step in understanding the DOM is to learn how it models an HTML document.

Document Trees

The most important thing to think about with the DOM Level 1 and Level 2 is that you are manipulating a document tree. For example, consider the simple HTML document presented here:

```
<!DOCTYPE HTML PUBLIC "-//W3C//DTD HTML 4.01 Transitional//EN"
        "http://www.w3.org/TR/html4/loose.dtd">
<html>
<head>
<title>DOM Test</title>
</head>
<body>
<h1>DOM Test Heading</h1>
```

```
<hr>
<!-- Just a comment -->
<p>A paragraph of <em>text</em> is just an example</p>
<ul>
    <li><a href="http://www.yahoo.com">Yahoo!</a></li>
</ul>
</body>
</html>
```

When a browser reads this particular HTML document, it represents the document in the form of a tree, as shown here:

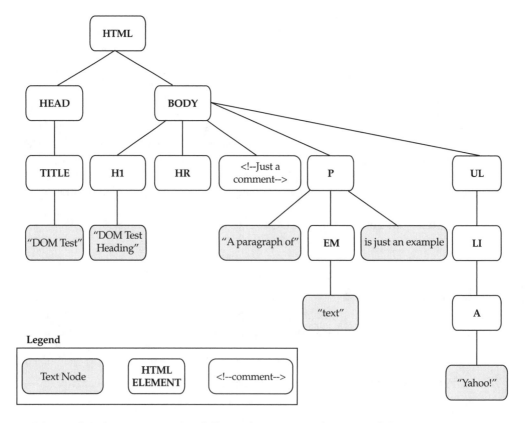

Notice that the tree structure follows the structured nature of the HTML. The **<html>** element contains the **<head>** and **<body>**. The **<head>** contains the **<title>**, and the **<body>** contains the various block elements like paragraphs (**<p>**), headings

(**<h1>**), and lists (**<ul>**). Each element may in turn contain more elements or textual fragments. As we can see, each of the items (or, more appropriately, *nodes*) in the tree correspond to the various types of objects allowed in an HTML or XML document. There are 12 types of nodes defined by the DOM; however, many of these are useful only within XML documents. We'll discuss JavaScript and XML in Chapter 20, so for now the node types we are concerned with are primarily related to HTML and are presented in Table 10-1.

Before moving on, we need to introduce some familiar terminology related to node relationships in an HTML document tree. A *subtree* is part of a document tree rooted at a particular node. The subtree corresponding to the following HTML fragment from the last example,

```
<p>A paragraph of <em>text</em> is just an example</p>
```

Node Type Number	Type	Description	Example
1	Element	An HTML or XML element	<p>...</p>
2	Attribute	An attribute for an HTML or XML element	align="center"
3	Text	A fragment of text that would be enclosed by an HTML or XML element	This is a text fragment!
8	Comment	An HTML comment	<!-- This is a comment -->
9	Document	The root document object, namely the top element in the parse tree	<html>
10	DocumentType	A document type definition	<!DOCTYPE HTML PUBLIC "-//W3C//DTD HTML 4.01 Transitional//EN" "http://www.w3.org/ TR/html4/loose.dtd">

Table 10-1. *DOM Nodes Related to HTML Documents*

is shown here:

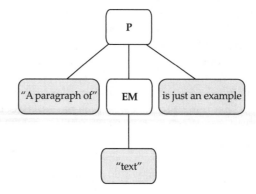

The following relationships are established in this tree:

- The **p** element has three *children*: a text node, the **em** element, and another text node.
- The text node "A paragraph of" is the *first child* of the **p** element.
- The *last child* of the **p** element is the text node "is just an example."
- The *parent* of the **em** element is the **p** element.
- The text node containing "text" is the child of the **em** element, but is *not* a direct descendent of the **p** element.

The nomenclature used here should remind you of a family tree. Fortunately, we don't talk about second cousins, relatives twice removed or anything like that! The diagram presented here summarizes all the basic relationships that you should understand:

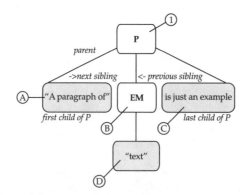

Make sure that you understand that nodes *a*, *b*, and *c* would all consider node 1 to be their parent.

Now that we have the basics down, let's take a look at how we can move around the document tree and examine various HTML elements using JavaScript and the DOM.

Accessing Elements

In moving around the HTML document tree, we can either start at the top of the tree or at an element of our choice. We'll start with directly accessing an element, since the process is a bit easier to understand. Notice in the simple document shown here how the **<p>** tag is uniquely identified by the **id** attribute value of "p1":

```
<!DOCTYPE HTML PUBLIC "-//W3C//DTD HTML 4.01 Transitional//EN"
        "http://www.w3.org/TR/html4/loose.dtd">
<html>
<head>
<title>DOM Test</title>
</head>
<body>
<p id="p1" align="center">A paragraph of
<em>text</em> is just an example</p>
</body>
</html>
```

Because the paragraph is uniquely identified, we can access this element using the **getElementById()** method of the **Document**—for example, by **document.getElementById('p1')**. This method returns a DOM **Element** object. We can examine the object returned to see what type of tag it represents.

```
var currentElement = document.getElementById('p1');
var msg = "nodeName: "+currentElement.nodeName+"\n";
msg += "nodeType: "+currentElement.nodeType+"\n";
msg += "nodeValue: "+currentElement.nodeValue+"\n";
alert(msg);
```

The result of inserting this script into the previous document is shown here:

Notice that the element held in **nodeName** is type **P**, corresponding to the HTML paragraph element that defined it. The **nodeType** is **1**, corresponding to an **Element** object, as shown in Table 10-1. However, notice that the **nodeValue** is **null**. You might have expected the value to be "A paragraph of text is just an example" or a similar string containing the HTML elements themselves. In actuality, an element doesn't have a value. While elements define the structure of the tree, it is *text nodes* that hold most of the interesting values. Text nodes are attached as children of other nodes, so to access what is enclosed by the <p> tags, we would have to examine the children of the node. The various **Node** properties available for doing so are summarized in Table 10-2.

Note DOM **HTMLElement** objects also have a property **tagName** that is effectively the same as the **Node** object property **nodeName**.

DOM Node Properties	Description
nodeName	Contains the name of the node
nodeValue	Contains the value within the node, generally only applicable to text nodes
nodeType	Holds a number corresponding to the type of node, as given in Table 10-1
parentNode	A reference to the parent node of the current object, if one exists
childNodes	Access to the list of child nodes
firstChild	Reference to the first child node of the element, if one exists
lastChild	Points to the last child node of the element, if one exists
previousSibling	Reference to the previous sibling of the node; for example, if its parent node has multiple children
nextSibling	Reference to the next sibling of the node; for example, if its parent node has multiple children
attributes	The list of the attributes for the element
ownerDocument	Points to the HTML **Document** object in which the element is contained

Table 10-2. *DOM Node Properties*

Given the new properties, we can "walk" the given example quite easily. The following is a simple demonstration of walking a known tree structure.

```
<!DOCTYPE HTML PUBLIC "-//W3C//DTD HTML 4.01 Transitional//EN"
         "http://www.w3.org/TR/html4/loose.dtd">
<html>
<head>
<title>DOM Walk Test</title>
</head>
<body>
<p id="p1" align="center">A paragraph of <em>text</em> is just an example</p>

<script language="JavaScript" type="text/javascript">
function nodeStatus(node)
{
  var temp = "";

  temp += "nodeName: "+node.nodeName+"\n";
  temp += "nodeType: "+node.nodeType+"\n";
  temp += "nodeValue: "+node.nodeValue+"\n\n";
  return temp;
}
var currentElement = document.getElementById('p1'); // start at P
var msg = nodeStatus(currentElement);
currentElement = currentElement.firstChild;  // text node 1
msg += nodeStatus(currentElement);
currentElement = currentElement.nextSibling; // em Element
msg += nodeStatus(currentElement);
currentElement = currentElement.firstChild; //  text node 2
msg += nodeStatus(currentElement);
currentElement = currentElement.parentNode; // back to em Element
msg += nodeStatus(currentElement);
currentElement = currentElement.previousSibling; //back to text node 1
msg += nodeStatus(currentElement);
currentElement = currentElement.parentNode; // to p Element
msg += nodeStatus(currentElement);
currentElement = currentElement.lastChild; // to text node 3
msg += nodeStatus(currentElement);
alert(msg);
</script>
</body>
</html>
```

The output of the example is shown in Figure 10-1.

The problem with the previous example is that we knew the sibling and child relationships ahead of time by inspecting the HTML of the example. How do you navigate a structure that you aren't sure of? We can avoid looking at nonexistent nodes by first

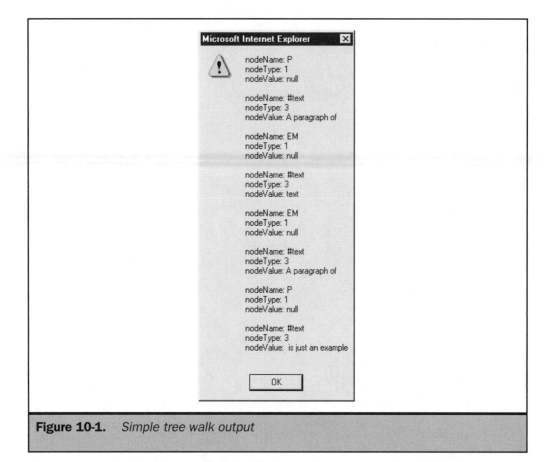

Figure 10-1. *Simple tree walk output*

querying the **hasChildNodes()** method for the current node before traversing any of its children. This method returns a Boolean value indicating whether or not there are children for the current node.

```
if (current.hasChildNodes())
   current = current.firstChild;
```

When traversing to a sibling or parent, we can simply use an **if** statement to query the property in question, for example:

```
if (current.parentNode)
   current = current.parentNode;
```

The following example demonstrates how to walk an arbitrary document. We provide a basic document to traverse, but you can substitute other documents as long as they are well formed:

```
<!DOCTYPE HTML PUBLIC "-//W3C//DTD HTML 4.01 Transitional//EN"
        "http://www.w3.org/TR/html4/loose.dtd">
<html>
<head>
<title>DOM Test</title>
</head>
<body>
<h1>DOM Test Heading</h1>
<hr>
<!-- Just a comment -->
<p>A paragraph of <em>text</em> is just an example</p>
<ul>
    <li><a href="http://www.yahoo.com">Yahoo!</a></li>
</ul>

<form name="testform" id="testform">
Node Name: <input type="text" id="nodeName" name="nodeName"><br>
Node Type: <input type="text" id="nodeType" name="nodeType"><br>
Node Value: <input type= "text" id="nodeValue" name="nodeValue"><br>
</form>
<script language="JavaScript" type="text/javascript">
<!-->
function update(currentElement)
{
  window.document.testform.nodeName.value = currentElement.nodeName;
  window.document.testform.nodeType.value = currentElement.nodeType;
  window.document.testform.nodeValue.value = currentElement.nodeValue;
}

function nodeMove(currentElement, direction)
{
  switch (direction)
    {
     case "previousSibling": if (currentElement.previousSibling)
                                currentElement=currentElement.previousSibling;
                             else
                                 alert("No previous sibling");
                             break;
      case "nextSibling":  if (currentElement.nextSibling)
                                currentElement = currentElement.nextSibling;
                             else
```

FUNDAMENTAL CLIENT-SIDE JAVASCRIPT

```
                               alert("No next sibling");
                               break;
        case "parent":    if (currentElement.parentNode)
                               currentElement = currentElement.parentNode;
                          else
                               alert("No parent");
                          break;
        case "firstChild": if (currentElement.hasChildNodes())
                               currentElement = currentElement.firstChild;
                          else
                               alert("No Children");
                          break;
        case "lastChild":  if (currentElement.hasChildNodes())
                               currentElement = currentElement.lastChild;
                          else
                               alert("No Children");
                          break;
        default: alert("Bad direction call");
      }
   update(currentElement);
   return currentElement;
}
var currentElement = document.documentElement;
update(currentElement);
//-->
</script>
<form>
 <input type="button" value="Parent"
        onclick="currentElement = nodeMove(currentElement,'parent')">
 <input type="button" value="First Child"
        onclick="currentElement = nodeMove(currentElement,'firstChild')">
 <input type="button" value="Last Child"
        onclick="currentElement = nodeMove(currentElement,'lastChild')">
 <input type="button" value="Next Sibling"
        onclick="currentElement = nodeMove(currentElement,'nextSibling')">
 <input type="button" value="Previous Sibling"
        onclick="currentElement = nodeMove(currentElement,'previousSibling')">
 <input type="button" value="Reset to Root"
        onclick="currentElement = document.documentElement;
update(currentElement)">
</form>
</body>
</html>
```

The rendering of this example is shown in Figure 10-2.

Something to be aware of when trying examples like this is that different browsers create the document tree in slightly different ways. Netscape 6 will appear to have more nodes to traverse than Internet Explorer 5 and 5.5. This can cause some headaches if you are using this kind of tree traversal to examine a document. Fortunately, since most programmers tend to use **getElementById()** to retrieve specific nodes, there is usually little need for full-blown tree traversal.

Other Access Properties

In addition to **document.getElementById( )**, there are other methods and properties useful for accessing a specific node in a document. Particularly valuable are the collections provided by the DOM Level 0 to support traditional JavaScript practices.

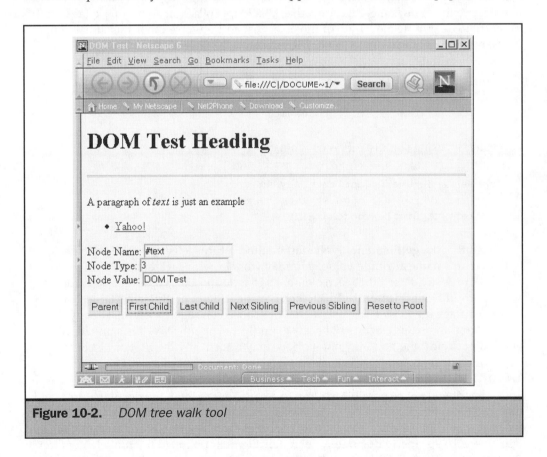

Figure 10-2.   *DOM tree walk tool*

getElementsByName()

Given that many older HTML documents favor the use of the **name** (rather than **id**) attribute with HTML elements like **<form>**, **<input>**, **<select>**, **<textarea>**, **<img>**, **<a>**, **<area>**, and **<frame>**, it is often useful to retrieve these elements by **name**. To do so, use the **getElementsByName()** method of the **Document**. This method accepts a string indicating the name of the element to retrieve; for example:

```
tagList = document.getElementsByName('myTag');
```

Notice that this method can potentially return a list of nodes rather than a single node. This is because the uniqueness of the value in a **name** attribute is not strictly enforced under traditional HTML, so, for example, an **<img>** tag and a **<form>** element might share the same **name**. Like any other JavaScript collection, you can use the **length** property to determine the length of the object list and traverse the list itself using the **item()** method or normal array syntax; for example:

```
tagList = document.getElementsByName('myTag');
for (var i = 0; i < tagList.length; i++)
   alert(tagList.item(i).nodeName);
```

Equivalently, using slightly different syntax:

```
tagList = document.getElementsByName('myTag');
for (var i = 0; i < tagList.length; i++)
   alert(tagList[i].nodeName);
```

Given that the **getElementsByName()** method returns a list of HTML elements with the same **name** attribute value, you may wonder why **getElementById()** does not work this way. Recall that each element's **id** is supposed to be a unique value. In short, permitting **getElementById()** to behave as **getElementsByName()** does would only encourage the loose HTML style that has caused enough problems already. If you do have an invalid document because multiple elements have the same **id**, the **getElementById()** method may not work or may return only the first or last item.

Common Tree Traversal Starting Points

Sometimes it will not be possible to jump to a particular point in the document tree, and there are times when you will want to start at the top of the tree and work down through the hierarchy. There are two **Document** properties that present useful starting points for tree walks. The property **document.documentElement** points to the root element in the document tree. For HTML documents, this would be the **<html>** tag. The second possible starting point is **document.body**, which references the node in the tree corresponding to the **<body>** tag. You might also have some interest in looking at the DOCTYPE definition for the file. This is referenced by **document.doctype**, but this node is not modifiable and really doesn't have much use under DOM Level 1.

Traditional JavaScript Collections

For backwards compatibility, the DOM supports some object collections popular under early browser versions. These values are shown in Table 10-3 and can be referenced numerically (**document.forms[0]**), associatively (**document.forms['myform']**), or directly (**document.myform**). You can also use the **item()** method to access an array index (**document.forms.item(0)**), though this is uncommon and not well supported in older JavaScript so should probably be avoided.

You may notice that Table 10-3 does not include proprietary collections like **embeds[ ]**, **all[ ]**, **layers[ ]**, and so on. The reason is that the main goal of the DOM is to eliminate the reliance of scripts upon proprietary DHTML features. However, as we'll see throughout this book, old habits die hard on the Web.

Generalized Element Collections

The final way to access elements under DOM Level 1 is using the **getElementsByTag Name( )** method of the **Document**. This method accepts a string indicating the HTML tag whose elements should be retrieved—for example, **getElementsByTagName('img')**. This method returns a list of all the tags in the document that are of the type passed as the parameter. While you may find that

```
allParagraphs = document.getElementsByTagName('p');
```

Collection	Description
document.anchors[ ]	A collection of all the anchors in a page specified by **<a name="">** **</a>**
document.applets[ ]	A collection of all the Java applets in a page
document.forms[ ]	A collection of all the **<form>** tags in a page
document.images[ ]	A collection of all images in the page defined by **<img>** tags
document.links[ ]	A collection of all links in the page defined by **<a href="">** **</a>**

Table 10-3. *DOM Level 0 Collections*

works correctly, it is actually more correct to invoke this function as a method of an existing element. For example, to find all the paragraphs within the **<body>** tag you would use:

```
allParagraphs = document.body.getElementsByTagName('P');
```

You can even find elements within other elements. For example, you might want to find a particular paragraph and then find the **<em>** tags within:

```
para1 = document.getElementById('p1');
emElements = para1.getElementsByTagName('EM');
```

We'll see some examples later on that use these methods to manipulate numerous elements at once. For now, let's turn our attention to manipulating the nodes we retrieve from an HTML document.

Creating Nodes

Now that we know how to move around a tree and access its elements, it is time to discuss manipulation of the document tree by creating and inserting nodes. The DOM supports a variety of methods related to creating nodes as a part of the **Document** object, as shown in Table 10-4.

Note   *The DOM Level 1 also supports **document.createCDATASection**(string), **document.createDocumentFragment**(), **document.createEntityReference**(name), and **document.createProcessInstruction**(target,data) but these methods would not be used with typical HTML documents.*

Creating nodes is easy enough if you have a good grasp of HTML. For example to make a paragraph you would use

```
newNode = document.createElement('P');  // creates a paragraph
```

It is just as easy to make text nodes:

```
newText = document.createTextNode("Something to add!");
```

However, we need to join these objects together and insert them somewhere in the document in order to accomplish any interesting tasks. For now they simply sit in memory.

Method	Description	Example
createAttribute (*name*);	Creates an attribute for an element specified by the string *name*. Rarely used with existing HTML elements since they have predefined attribute names that can be manipulated directly.	myAlign = document.createAttribute ("align");
createComment (*string*);	Creates an HTML/XML text comment of the form <!-- *string* --> where *string* is the comment content.	myComment = document.createComment ("Just a comment");
createElement (*tagName*)	Creates an element of the type specified by the string parameter *tagName*.	myHeading = document.createElement ("h1");
createTextNode (*string*)	Creates a text node containing *string*.	newText = document.createTextNode ("Some new text");

Table 10-4. *DOM Methods to Create Nodes*

Inserting and Appending Nodes

The **Node** object supports two useful methods for inserting content, **insertBefore (newChild, referenceChild)** and **appendChild(newChild)**. In the case of **appendChild()**, it is invoked as a method of the node to which you wish to attach a child, and doing so adds the node referenced by *newChild* to the end of its list of children. In the case of the **insertBefore()** method, you specify which child you want to insert *newChild* in front of using *referenceChild*. In practice, you often have to access the parent node of the node you wish to run **insertBefore()** on to acquire the necessary references. Let's see the **appendChild()** method in action, by using it to combine the two nodes that we create.

```
newNode = document.createElement('B');
newText = document.createTextNode("Something to add!");
newNode.appendChild(newText);
```

At this point we would have the HTML fragment:

```
<b>Something to add!</b>
```

We could then add this markup into the document once we have found a convenient place to insert it. For example, we might use

```
current = document.getElementById('p1')
current.appendChild(newNode);
```

to append the bold text fragment to the end of our test paragraph. The following example demonstrates a more complex use of insert and append that places user-entered text before, within, and after a specified element.

Note   *If you have never seen DOM functionality before, you are highly encouraged to try this example yourself. You can type it in manually or find it online at the support site for this book, www.javascriptref.com.*

```
<!DOCTYPE HTML PUBLIC "-//W3C//DTD HTML 4.01 Transitional//EN"
        "http://www.w3.org/TR/html4/loose.dtd">
<html>
<head>
<title>DOM Adding</title>
<script language="JavaScript" type="text/javascript">
function makeNode(str)
{
  var newParagraph = document.createElement("p");
  var newText = document.createTextNode(str);
  newParagraph.appendChild(newText);
  return newParagraph;
}
function appendBefore(nodeId, str)
{
 var node = document.getElementById(nodeId);
 var newNode = makeNode(str);
 if (node.parentNode)
    node.parentNode.insertBefore(newNode,node);
}
function insertWithin(nodeId, str)
{
 var node = document.getElementById(nodeId);
 var newNode = makeNode(str);
 node.appendChild(newNode);
}
function appendAfter(nodeId, str)
{
```

```
    var node = document.getElementById(nodeId);
    var newNode = makeNode(str);

    if (node.parentNode)
    {
        if (node.nextSibling)
            node.parentNode.insertBefore(newNode, node.nextSibling);
        else
            node.parentNode.appendChild(newNode);
    }
}
</script>
</head>
<body>

<h1>DOM Insert and Append</h1>
<hr>
<div style="background-color:#66ff00;">
    <div id="innerDiv" style="background-color:#ffcc00;"></div>
</div>
<hr>
<form id="form1" name="form1">
    <input type="text" id="field1" name="field1">

    <input type="button" value="Before"
 onclick="appendBefore('innerDiv',document.form1.field1.value)">

    <input type="button" value="Middle"
 onclick="insertWithin('innerDiv',document.form1.field1.value)">
    <input type="button" value="After"
 onclick="appendAfter('innerDiv',document.form1.field1.value)">
</form>
</body>
</html>
```

Copying Nodes

Sometimes you won't want to create and insert brand-new elements. Instead, you might use the **cloneNode()** method to make a copy of a particular node. The method takes a single Boolean argument indicating whether the copy should include all children of the node or just the element itself. An example demonstrating cloning and inserting nodes is presented here.

```
<!DOCTYPE HTML PUBLIC "-//W3C//DTD HTML 4.01 Transitional//EN"
        "http://www.w3.org/TR/html4/loose.dtd">
<html>
<head>
<title>Clone Demo</title>
</head>
<body>
<p id="p1">This is a <em>test</em> of cloning</p>
<hr>
<div id="inserthere" style="background-color: yellow">
</div>
<hr>
<script language="JavaScript" type="text/javascript">
function cloneAndCopy(nodeId, deep)
{
 var toClone = document.getElementById(nodeId);
 var clonedNode = toClone.cloneNode(deep);
 var insertPoint = document.getElementById("inserthere");
 insertPoint.appendChild(clonedNode);
}
</script>
<form>
      <input type="button" value="Clone"
             onclick="cloneAndCopy('p1',false)"><br>
      <input type="button" value="Clone Deep"
             onclick="cloneAndCopy('p1',true)">
</form>
</body>
</html>
```

Note *Because of the rules of HTML, empty elements, particularly paragraphs, may not change the visual presentation of the document. The reason is that the browser often minimizes those elements that lack content.*

Deleting and Replacing Nodes

It is often convenient to be able to remove nodes from the tree. The **Node** object supports the **removeChild(child)** method that is used to delete a node specified by the reference *child* that it is passed. For example,

```
current.removeChild(current.lastChild);
```

would remove the last child of the node referenced by the variable *current*. Note that the **removeChild()** method does return the **Node** object that was removed.

Besides deleting a **Node**, you can replace one using the method **replaceChild (newChild, oldChild)**, where *newChild* is the node to replace *oldChild* with. Be careful when using **replaceChild()**, as it will destroy the contents of nodes that are replaced. The following example shows deletion and replacement in action:

```
<!DOCTYPE HTML PUBLIC "-//W3C//DTD HTML 4.01 Transitional//EN"
         "http://www.w3.org/TR/html4/loose.dtd">
<html>
<head>
<title>Delete and Replace Demo</title>
<script language="JavaScript" type="text/javascript">

function doDelete()
{
  var deletePoint = document.getElementById('toDelete');
  if (deletePoint.hasChildNodes())
   deletePoint.removeChild(deletePoint.lastChild);
}
function doReplace()
{
 var replace = document.getElementById('toReplace');
 if (replace)
   {
     var newNode = document.createElement("STRONG");
     var newText = document.createTextNode("strong element");

     newNode.appendChild(newText);
     replace.parentNode.replaceChild(newNode, replace);
   }
}
</script>
</head>
<body>
<div id="toDelete">
 <p>This is a paragraph</p>
 <p>This is <em>another paragraph</em> to delete</p>
 <p>This is yet another paragraph</p>
</div>
<p>
This paragraph has an <em id="toReplace">em element</em> in it.
</p>
<hr>
<form>
```

```
        <input type="button" value="Delete" onclick="doDelete()">
        <input type="button" value="Replace" onclick="doReplace()">
</form>
</body>
</html>
```

Modifying Nodes

Elements really cannot be directly modified, although their attributes certainly can. This may seem strange, but it makes perfect sense when you consider that elements contain text nodes. To effect a change, you really have to modify the text nodes themselves. For example, if you had

```
<p id="p1">This is a test</p>
```

you would use

```
textNode = document.getElementById('p1').firstChild;
```

to access the text node "This is a test" within the paragraph element. Notice how we strung together the **firstChild** property with the method call. Stringing methods and properties together like this helps avoid having to use numerous individual statements to access a particular item. Once the **textNode** has been retrieved we could access its length using its **length** property (which indicates the number of characters it contains), or even set its value using the **data** property.

```
alert(textNode.length);                    // would return 14
textNode.data = "I've been changed!";
```

DOM Level 1 also defines numerous methods to operate on text nodes. These are summarized in Table 10-5.

Method	Description
appendData(*string*)	This method appends the passed *string* to the end of the text node.
deleteData(*offset, count*)	Deletes *count* characters starting from the index specified by *offset*.

Table 10-5. *Text Node Manipulation Methods*

Method	Description
insertData(*offset, string*)	Inserts the value in *string* starting at the character index specified in *offset*.
replaceData(*offset, count, string*)	Replaces *count* characters of text in the node starting from *offset* with corresponding characters from the *string* argument.
splitText(*offset*)	Splits the text node into two pieces at the index given in *offset*. Returns the right side of the split in a new text node and leaves the left side in the original.
substringData(*offset, count*)	Returns a string corresponding to the substring starting at index *offset* and running for *count* characters.

Table 10-5.   *Text Node Manipulation Methods* (continued)

The following example illustrates these methods in use:

```
<!DOCTYPE HTML PUBLIC "-//W3C//DTD HTML 4.01 Transitional//EN"
        "http://www.w3.org/TR/html4/loose.dtd">
<html>
<head>
<title>Text Node Modifications</title>
</head>
<body>
<p id="p1">This is a test</p>

<script language="JavaScript" type="text/javascript">
  var textNode = document.getElementById('p1').firstChild;
</script>

<form>
  <input type="button" value="show"  onclick="alert(textNode.data)">
  <input type="button" value="length" onclick="alert(textNode.length)">
  <input type="button" value="change" onclick="textNode.data = 'Now a new value!'">
  <input type="button" value="append" onclick="textNode.appendData(' added to the end')">
  <input type="button" value="insert" onclick="textNode.insertData(0,'added to the front ')">
  <input type="button" value="delete" onclick="textNode.deleteData(0, 2)">
  <input type="button" value="replace" onclick="textNode.replaceData(0,4,'Zap!')">
  <input type="button" value="substring"
```

```
           onclick="alert(textNode.substringData(2,2))">
  <input type="button" value="split"
         onclick="temp = textNode.splitText(5); alert('Text node
='+textNode.data+'\nSplit Value = '+temp.data)">
</form>
</body>
</html>
```

You should understand that browser support for these methods is spotty. Under Internet Explorer 5 many of these methods will not work, and even under Netscape 6, serious screen redraw problems may occur. In the face of these problems, you can use the "show" button in the example to see what the text node actually contains after an operation.

*After retrieving a text node **data** value, you could always use any of the **String** methods discussed in Chapters 7 and 8 to modify the value and then save it back to the node.*

Lastly, note it is also possible to manipulate the value of **Comment** nodes with these properties and methods. However, given that comments do not influence document presentation, modification is usually not performed this way. You may be tempted to start thinking about modifying comment-masked CSS properties using such a technique, but this is not advisable. We will see later in the chapter, in the section entitled "The DOM and CSS," how the DOM Level 2 provides access to CSS properties.

Manipulating Attributes

At this point you are probably wondering how to create more complex elements complete with attributes. The DOM Level 1 supports numerous attribute methods for elements, including **getAttribute(name)**, **setAttribute(attributename, attributevalue)**, and **removeAttribute(attributeName)**. Under DOM Level 2 there is even a very useful **Node** object method, **hasAttributes()**, that can be used to determine if an element has any defined attributes. We won't go into too much detail here, given the similarity of these methods to those we have already seen. The following example should illustrate attribute manipulation sufficiently:

```
<!DOCTYPE HTML PUBLIC "-//W3C//DTD HTML 4.01 Transitional//EN"
        "http://www.w3.org/TR/html4/loose.dtd">
<html>
<head>
<title>Attribute Test</title>
</head>
<body>
<font id="test" size="2" color="red">Change my attributes!</font>

<script language="JavaScript" type="text/javascript">
```

```
          theElement = document.getElementById('test');
</script>
<form name="testform" id="testform">
Color: <input type="text" id="color" name="color" value="" size="8">
<input type="button" value="Set Color"
onclick="theElement.setAttribute('color',document.testform.color.value)">
<input type="button" value="Remove Color" onclick="theElement.removeAttribute('color')">
<br>
Size:
<select onchange="theElement.setAttribute('size',this.options[this.selectedIndex].text)">
  <option>1</option>
  <option>2</option>
  <option selected>3</option>
  <option>4</option>
  <option>5</option>
  <option>6</option>
  <option>7</option>
</select>
</form>
<script language="JavaScript" type="text/javascript">
  document.testform.color.value = theElement.getAttribute('color');
</script>
</body>
</html>
```

FUNDAMENTAL
CLIENT-SIDE JAVASCRIPT

Note   *The **<font>** tag is generally frowned upon in the emerging CSS-focused Web, but for this demo it was useful since its attributes show visual changes in a dramatic way.*

The DOM and HTML Elements

Now that we have presented both how to create HTML elements as well as how to set and manipulate attributes, it should be clear how very intertwined HTML and JavaScript have become as a result of the DOM. In short, to effectively utilize the DOM you must be an expert in HTML syntax, since many object properties are simply direct mappings to the attributes of the HTML element. For example, the paragraph element under HTML 4.01 has the following basic syntax:

```
<p align="left | center | right | justify"
    id="unique id"
    class="class name"
    style="style rules"
    title="advisory text"
    lang="language code"
    dir="text direction either LTR or RTL">
```

```
    paragraph content
</p>
```

DOM Level 1 exposes most of these attributes, including: **align**, **id**, **className**, **title**, **lang**, and **dir**. DOM Level 2 also exposes **style**, which we'll discuss in the next section. The various event handlers, such as **onclick** and **onmouseover**, are also settable (through mechanisms discussed in the next chapter).

All HTML element interfaces derive from the basic **HTMLElement** object that defines: **id**, **className**, **title**, **lang**, and **dir**. Many HTML elements do not support any other attributes. Such elements are

- **HEAD**
- special: **SUB, SUP, SPAN, BDO**
- font: **TT, I, B, U, S, STRIKE, BIG, SMALL**
- phrase: **EM, STRONG, DFN, CODE, SAMP, KBD, VAR, CITE, ACRONYM, ABBR**
- list: **DD, DT**
- **NOFRAMES, NOSCRIPT**
- **ADDRESS, CENTER**

Beyond the core attributes, the rest of an element's properties follow HTML syntax. In fact, if you are already intimately familiar with HTML, it is fairly easy to guess the DOM properties that correspond to HTML element attributes by following these basic rules of thumb. If the attribute is a simple word value like "align," it will be represented without modification unless the word conflicts with JavaScript reserved words. For example, the **<label>** tag supports the **for** attribute, which would obviously conflict with the **for** statement in JavaScript. To rectify this, often the word "html" is prepended, so in the previous case the DOM represents this attribute as **htmlFor**. In a few other cases, this rule isn't followed. For example, for the **<col>** tag, attributes **char** and **charoff** become **ch** and **chOff** under the DOM Level 1. Fortunately, these exceptions are few and far between. And finally, if the attribute has a two-word identifier such as **tabindex**, it will be represented in the DOM in the standard JavaScript camel-back style, in this case as **tabIndex**.

The only major variation in the HTML-to-DOM mapping is with tables. Given the increased complexity of tables under HTML 4.0, there are numerous methods to create and delete various aspects of tables, such as captions, rows, and cells as well as HTML 4.0 tags like **<tfoot>**, **<thead>**, and **<tbody>**. These are all detailed in Appendix B and are demonstrated in Chapter 13.

Lastly, in order to support traditional JavaScript programming syntax, you will find a number of methods and properties of the **form** element itself as well as the various form field elements like **input**, **select**, **textarea**, and **button**. We'll discuss form manipulation in-depth in Chapter 14.

 Appendix B provides a complete presentation of all HTML elements and properties under DOM Level 1 and 2. For more information on HTML syntax, see the companion book HTML: The Complete Reference *by Thomas Powell (Osborne/McGraw-Hill, 2001), (www.htmlref.com) or visit the W3 site at **www.w3.org/Markup**.*

The DOM and CSS

The last aspect of the DOM standard supported by today's browsers is CSS. DOM Level 2 adds support to manipulate CSS values. DHTML object models, notably Microsoft's, support similar facilities, and, because of the lack of widespread DOM Level 2 support, these capabilities are also mentioned here.

Inline Style Manipulation

The primary way that developers modify CSS values with JavaScript is through the **style** property that corresponds to the inline style sheet specification for a particular HTML element. For example, if you have a paragraph like this:

```
<p id="myParagraph">This is a test</p>
```

you could insert an inline style like this:

```
<p id="myParagraph" style="color: red">This is a test</p>
```

To perform a manipulation with JavaScript DOM interfaces, you would use a script like this:

```
theElement = document.getElementById("myParagraph");
theElement.style.color = "green";
```

As with HTML manipulations, the key concern is how to map the various CSS property names to DOM property names. In the case of CSS, you often have a hyphenated property name like **background-color**, which under JavaScript becomes **backgroundColor**. In general, hyphenated CSS properties are represented as a single word with camel-back capitalization in the DOM. This rule holds for all CSS properties except for **float**, which becomes **cssFloat** because "float" is a JavaScript reserved word. A list of the commonly used CSS1 and CSS2 properties with their corresponding DOM properties is shown in Table 10-6 for reference.

CSS Property	DOM Level 2 Property
background	background
background-attachment	backgroundAttachment
background-color	backgroundColor
background-image	backgroundImage
background-position	backgroundPosition
background-repeat	backgroundRepeat
border	border
border-color	borderColor
border-style	borderStyle
border-top	borderTop
border-right	borderRight
border-left	borderLeft
border-bottom	borderBottom
border-top-color	borderTopColor
border-right-color	borderRightColor
border-bottom-color	borderBottomColor
border-left-color	borderLeftColor
border-top-style	borderTopStyle
border-right-style	borderRightStyle
border-bottom-style	borderBottomStyle
border-left-style	borderLeftStyle
border-top-width	borderTopWidth
border-right-width	borderRightWidth
border-bottom-width	borderBottomWidth
border-left-width	borderLeftWidth
border-width	borderWidth
clear	clear
clip	clip

Table 10-6. *CSS Property-to-DOM Property Mappings*

CSS Property	DOM Level 2 Property
color	color
display	display
float	cssFloat
font	font
font-family	fontFamily
font-size	fontSize
font-style	fontStyle
font-variant	fontVariant
font-weight	fontWeight
height	height
left	left
letter-spacing	letterSpacing
line-height	lineHeight
list-style	listStyle
list-style-image	listStyleImage
list-style-position	listStylePosition
list-style-type	listStyleType
margin	margin
margin-top	marginTop
margin-right	marginRight
margin-bottom	marginBottom
margin-left	marginLeft
overflow	overflow
padding	padding
padding-top	paddingTop
padding-right	paddingRight
padding-bottom	paddingBottom
padding-left	paddingLeft

Table 10-6. *CSS Property-to-DOM Property Mappings* (continued)

CSS Property	DOM Level 2 Property
position	position
text-align	textAlign
text-decoration	textDecoration
text-indent	textIndent
text-transform	textTransform
top	top
vertical-align	verticalAlign
visibility	visibility
white-space	whiteSpace
width	width
word-spacing	wordSpacing
z-index	zIndex

Table 10-6. *CSS Property-to-DOM Property Mappings* (continued)

An example that manipulates many of the common CSS properties is presented here. A sample rendering is shown in Figure 10-3.

```
<!DOCTYPE HTML PUBLIC "-//W3C//DTD HTML 4.01 Transitional//EN"
        "http://www.w3.org/TR/html4/loose.dtd">
<html>
<head>
<title>CSS Inline Rule Scripting</title>
</head>
<body>

<div id="test"> CSS Rules in Action </div>
<hr>

<script language="JavaScript" type="text/javascript">
  theElement = document.getElementById("test");
</script>

<form id="cssForm" name="cssForm">
<strong>Alignment:</strong>
<select onchange="theElement.style.textAlign=this.options[this.selectedIndex].text">
```

```
      <option>left</option>
      <option>center</option>
      <option>right</option>
      <option>justify</option>
</select>
<br><br>
<strong>Font:</strong>
<select onchange="theElement.style.fontFamily=this.options[this.selectedIndex].text">
      <option>sans-serif</option>
      <option selected>serif</option>
      <option>cursive</option>
      <option>fantasy</option>
      <option>monospace</option>
</select>
  
<input type="text" id="font" name="font" size="10" value="Impact">
<input type="button" value="set" onclick="theElement.style.fontFamily =
document.cssForm.font.value">
<br><br>
<strong>Style:</strong>
<select onchange="theElement.style.fontStyle=this.options[this.selectedIndex].text">
      <option>normal</option>
      <option>italic</option>
      <option>oblique</option>
</select>
<strong>Weight:</strong>
<select onchange="theElement.style.fontWeight=this.options[this.selectedIndex].text">
      <option>normal</option>
      <option>bolder</option>
      <option>lighter</option>
</select>
<strong>Variant:</strong>
<select onchange="theElement.style.fontVariant=this.options[this.selectedIndex].text">
      <option>normal</option>
      <option>small-caps</option>
</select>
<br><br>

<strong>Text Decoration</strong>
<select onchange="theElement.style.textDecoration=this.options[this.selectedIndex].text">
      <option>none</option>
      <option>overline</option>
      <option>underline</option>
      <option>line-through</option>
      <option>blink</option>
</select>
<br><br>
```

```html
<strong>Font Size:</strong>
<select onchange="theElement.style.fontSize=this.options[this.selectedIndex].text">
      <option>xx-small</option>
      <option>x-small</option>
      <option selected>small</option>
      <option>medium</option>
      <option>large</option>
      <option>x-large</option>
      <option>xx-large</option>
</select>
  

<input type="text" id="size" name="size" size="3" maxlength="3" value="36">pt   
<input type="button" value="set" onclick="theElement.style.fontSize =
document.cssForm.size.value">
<br><br>
<strong>Color:</strong>
<input type="text" id="fgColor" name="fgColor" size="8" value="yellow">
<input type="button" value="set" onclick="theElement.style.color =
document.cssForm.fgColor.value">
<br><br>
<strong>Background Color:</strong>
<input type="text" id="bgColor" name="color" size="8" value="red">
<input type="button" value="set" onclick="theElement.style.backgroundColor =
document.cssForm.bgColor.value">
<br><br>
<strong>Borders:</strong>
<select onchange="theElement.style.borderStyle=this.options[this.selectedIndex].text">
      <option>none</option>
      <option>dotted</option>
      <option>dashed</option>
      <option>solid</option>
      <option>double</option>
      <option>groove</option>
      <option>ridge</option>
      <option>inset</option>
      <option>outset</option>
</select>
<br><br>
<strong>Height:</strong>
<input type="text" id="height" name="height" value="100" size="3">px   
<strong>Width:</strong>
<input type="text" id="width" name="width" value="100" size="3">px   
<input type="button" value="set" onclick="theElement.style.height =
document.cssForm.height.value; theElement.style.width =
document.cssForm.width.value;">
```

```
<br><br>
<strong>Top:</strong>
<input type="text" id="top" name="top" value="100" size="3">px   
<strong>Left:</strong>
<input type="text" id="left" name="left" value="100" size="3">px   
<input type="button" value="Set"
onclick="theElement.style.position='absolute';theElement.style.top =
document.cssForm.top.value; theElement.style.left = document.cssForm.left.value;">
<br><br>
<strong>Visibility</strong>   
<input type="button" value="show" onclick="theElement.style.visibility='visible'">
<input type="button" value="hide" onclick="theElement.style.visibility='hidden'">
</form>
<hr>
</body>
</html>
```

Dynamic Style Using Classes and Collections

Manipulating style in the fashion of the previous section works only on a single tag at a time. This section explores how you might manipulate style rules in a more complex manner. First, consider the use of CSS **class** selectors. You might have a style sheet with two class rules like this:

```
<style type="text/css">
<!--
.look1  { color: black; background-color: yellow; font-style: normal;}
.look2  { background-color: orange; font-style: italic; }
-->
</style>
```

We might then apply one class to a particular **<p>** tag, like so:

```
<p id="myP1" class="look1">This is a test</p>
```

You could then manipulate the appearance of this paragraph by using JavaScript statements to change the element's **class**. The element's **class** attribute is exposed in its **className** property:

```
theElement = document.getElementById("myP1");
theElement.className = "look2";
```

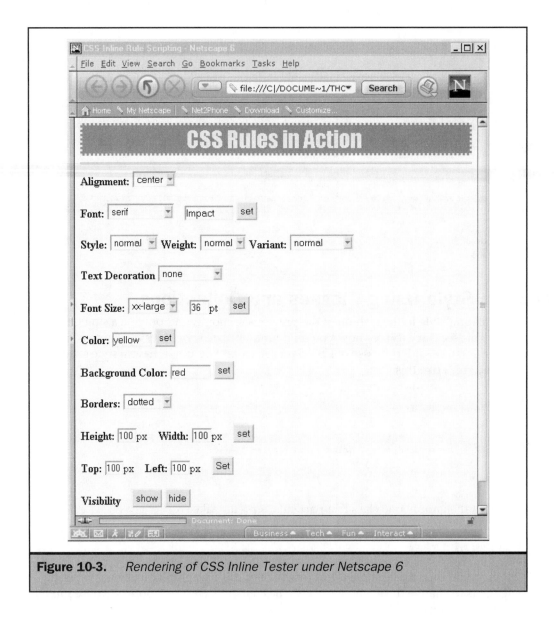

Figure 10-3. *Rendering of CSS Inline Tester under Netscape 6*

The following example shows a simple rollover effect using such DOM techniques:

```
<!DOCTYPE HTML PUBLIC "-//W3C//DTD HTML 4.01 Transitional//EN"
        "http://www.w3.org/TR/html4/loose.dtd">
<html>
```

```
<head>
<title>Class Warfare</title>
<style type="text/css">
<!--
  body    {background-color: white; color: black;}
 .style1 {color: blue; font-weight: bold;}
 .style2 {background-color: yellow; color: red;
          text-decoration: underline;}
 .style3 {color: red; font-size: 300%;}
-->
</style>
</head>
<body>
<p class="style1"
   onmouseover="this.className='style2'"
   onmouseout="this.className = 'style1'">Roll over me</p>
<p>How about
<span class="style1" onmouseover="this.className = 'style2'"
                     onmouseout="this.className = 'style1'">me</span>?</p>
<p> Be careful as dramatic style changes may
<span class="style1"
      onmouseover="this.className = 'style3'"
      onmouseout="this.className = 'style1'">reflow a document</span>
significantly</p>
</body>
</html>
```

FUNDAMENTAL
CLIENT-SIDE JAVASCRIPT

Another way to perform manipulations is by using the **getElementsByTagName()** method and performing style changes on each of the individual elements returned. The following example illustrates this technique by allowing the user to dynamically set the alignment of the paragraphs in the document.

```
<!DOCTYPE HTML PUBLIC "-//W3C//DTD HTML 4.01 Transitional//EN"
        "http://www.w3.org/TR/html4/loose.dtd">
<html>
<head>
<title>Change Style On All Paragraphs</title>
</head>
<body>
<p>This is a paragraph</p>
<p>This is a paragraph</p>
<div>This is not a paragraph</div>
<p>This is a paragraph</p>
<script language="JavaScript" type="text/javascript">
function alignAll(alignment)
{
```

```
      var allparagraphs  = document.body.getElementsByTagName('p');
      for (var i = 0; i < allparagraphs.length; i++)
            allparagraphs.item(i).style.textAlign = alignment;
}
</script>
<form>
<input type="button" value="left align all paragraphs"
       onclick="alignAll('left')">
<input type="button" value="center all paragraphs"
       onclick="alignAll('center')">
<input type="button" value="right align all paragraphs"
       onclick="alignAll('right')">
</form>
</body>
</html>
```

It might seem cumbersome to have to iterate through a group of elements, particularly when you might have set different rules on each. If you are a CSS maven, you may prefer instead to manipulate complex rule sets found in a document-wide or even external style sheet.

Accessing Complex Style Rules

So far, we haven't discussed how to access CSS rules found in **<style>** tags or how to dynamically set linked style sheets. The DOM Level 2 does provide such an interface, but, as of the time of this writing, browser support is not widespread and can be very buggy where it does exist. This section serves only as a brief introduction to some of the more advanced DOM Level 2 bindings for CSS.

Under DOM Level 2, the **Document** object supports the **styleSheets[ ]** collection, which we can use to access the various **<style>** and **<link>** tags within a document. Thus,

```
var firstStyleSheet = document.styleSheets[0];
```

or

```
var firstStyleSheet = document.styleSheets.item(0);
```

retrieves an object that corresponds to the first **<style>** element in the HTML. Its properties correspond to HTML attributes just as have the other correspondences we've seen. The most common properties are shown in Table 10-7.

Note *Under the DOM, when a style is externally linked you cannot modify its rules nor can you change the reference to the linked style sheet to an alternative value. However, you may override them with local rules.*

Property	Description
type	Indicates the **type** of the style sheet, generally "text/css." Read-only.
disabled	A Boolean value indicating if the style sheet is disabled or not. This is settable.
href	Holds the **href** value of the style sheet. Not normally modifiable except under Internet Explorer, where you can dynamically swap linked style sheets.
title	Holds the value of the **title** attribute for the element.
media	Holds a list of the **media** settings for the style sheet, for example, "screen."

Table 10-7. *Style Object Properties*

FUNDAMENTAL CLIENT-SIDE JAVASCRIPT

Under the DOM, the **CSSStyleSheet** object inherits the **StyleSheet** object's features and then adds the collection **cssRules[ ]** that contains the various rules in the style block as well as the **insertRule()** and **deleteRule()** methods. The syntax for **insertRule()** is *theStyleSheet*.**insertRule('ruletext', index)**, where *ruletext* is a string containing the style sheet selector and rules and *index* is the position to insert it in the set of rules. The position is relevant because, of course, these are *Cascading* Style Sheets. Similarly, the **deleteRule()** method takes an *index* value and deletes the corresponding rule, so *theStyleSheet*.**deleteRule(0)** would delete the first rule in the style sheet represented by *theStyleSheet*. Unfortunately, at the time of this writing, Internet Explorer doesn't support these DOM facilities and instead relies on the similar **addRule()** and **removeRule()** methods for its **styleSheet** object.

Accessing individual rules is possible through the **cssRules[ ]** collection or, in Internet Explorer, the nonstandard **rules[ ]** collection. Once a rule is accessed, you can access its **selectorText** property to examine the rule selector, or you can access the **style** property to access the actual set of rules. While the DOM Level 2 provides various methods, such as **getPropertyValue()** and **setProperty()**, to modify rules, it is generally far safer to simply access the **style** object and then the DOM property corresponding to the CSS property in question. For example, *theStyleSheet*.**cssRules** **[0].style.color = 'blue'** would modify (or add) a property to the first CSS rule in the style sheet. Under Internet Explorer, you would use *theStyleSheet*.**rules[0].style.color = 'blue'**. The following script demonstrates the basics of style sheet rule manipulation:

```
<!DOCTYPE HTML PUBLIC "-//W3C//DTD HTML 4.01 Transitional//EN"
        "http://www.w3.org/TR/html4/loose.dtd">
```

```html
<html>
<head>
<title>Style Rule Changes</title>
<style type="text/css">
<!--
  h1   {color: red; font-size: 24pt; font-style: italic; font-family: Impact;}
  p    {color: blue; font-size: 12pt; font-family: Arial;}
  body {background-color: white;}
  strong {color: red;}
  em {font-weight: bold; font-style: normal; text-decoration: underline;}
-->
</style>
</head>
<body>
<h1>CSS Test Document</h1>
<hr>
<p>This is a <strong>test</strong> paragraph.</p>
<p>More <em>fake</em> text goes here.</p>
<p>All done.  Don't need to <strong>continue</strong> this</p>
<hr>
<h3>End of Test Document</h3>

<script language="JavaScript" type="text/javascript">

function modifyRule()
{
   var styleSheet = document.styleSheets[0];
   if (styleSheet.rules)
     styleSheet.cssRules = styleSheet.rules;
   if (styleSheet.cssRules[0])
    {
     styleSheet.cssRules[0].style.color='purple';
     styleSheet.cssRules[0].style.fontSize = '36pt';
     styleSheet.cssRules[0].style.backgroundColor = 'yellow';
    }
}
function deleteRule()
{
   var styleSheet = document.styleSheets[0];
   if (styleSheet.rules)
     styleSheet.cssRules = styleSheet.rules;

   if (styleSheet.cssRules.length > 0) // still rules left
    {
     if (styleSheet.removeRule)
       styleSheet.removeRule(0);
     else if (styleSheet.deleteRule)
```

```
            styleSheet.deleteRule(0);
    }
}

function addRule()
{
    var styleSheet = document.styleSheets[0];
    if (styleSheet.addRule)
       styleSheet.addRule("h3", "color:blue", 4);
    else if (styleSheet.insertRule)
       styleSheet.insertRule("h3 {color: blue;}", 4);
}

</script>
<form>
     <input type="button" value="Enable"
onclick="document.styleSheets[0].disabled=false;">
     <input type="button" value="Disable"
onclick="document.styleSheets[0].disabled=true;">
     <input type="button" value="Modify Rule" onclick="modifyRule()">
     <input type="button" value="Delete Rule" onclick="deleteRule()">
     <input type="button" value="Add Rule" onclick="addRule()">
</form>
</body>
</html>
```

There are a few things to study carefully in the previous example. First, notice how we use conditional statements to detect the existence of particular objects, such as Internet Explorer proprietary collections and methods. Second, notice how in the case of **rules[ ]** versus **cssRules[ ]** we add the collection to simulate correct DOM syntax under Internet Explorer. Lastly, notice how **if** statements are used to make sure that there are still rules to manipulate. You can never be too sure that some designer hasn't changed the rules on you, so code defensively!

Note *You may find that this example does not work well under Netscape 6 or Mozilla. It also may suffer refresh problems because rule-removal may not necessarily be reflected automatically. If you enable or disable rules or refresh a document, you may notice changes.*

The DOM Versus DHTML Object Models

If you found the object collections of the previous chapter easier to follow compared to the DOM, you aren't alone. Many JavaScript programmers have avoided the complexity of the DOM in favor of old-style collections like **document.forms[ ]**, **document.images[ ]** and even proprietary collections like **document.all[ ]**. Interestingly, some proprietary properties like Microsoft's **innerHTML** are actually far easier to use than the DOM. Let's take another look at a few of the 4.x generation browser object models that refuse to die.

The Power of innerHTML

Both Netscape 6 and Internet Explorer 4+ support the nonstandard **innerHTML** property. This property allows easy reading and modification of the HTML content of an element. The **innerHTML** property holds a string representing the HTML contained by an element. Given this HTML markup,

```
<p id="para1">This is a <em>test</em> paragraph.</p>
```

the following script retrieves the enclosed content,

```
var theElement = document.getElementById("para1");
alert(theElement.innerHTML);
```

as shown here:

You can also set the contents of the HTML elements easily with the **innerHTML** property. The following simple example provides a form field to modify the contents of a **<p>** tag. Try running the example and adding in HTML markup. As you will see, it is far easier to add HTML content to nodes using this property than by creating and setting nodes using standard DOM methods.

```
<!DOCTYPE HTML PUBLIC "-//W3C//DTD HTML 4.01 Transitional//EN"
        "http://www.w3.org/TR/html4/loose.dtd">
<html>
<head>
<title>innerHTML Tester</title>
</head>
<body onload="document.testForm.content.value = theElement.innerHTML;">

<p id="para1">This is a <em>test</em> paragraph.</p>
<script language="JavaScript" type="text/javascript">
 var theElement = document.getElementById("para1");
```

```
</script>

<form name="testForm" id="testForm">
Element Content:
 <input type="text" name="content" id="content" size="60">
 <input type="button" value="set" onclick="theElement.innerHTML =
document.testForm.content.value;">
</form>
</body>
</html>
```

innerText, outerText, and outerHTML

Internet Explorer also supports the **innerText**, **outerText**, and **outerHTML** properties. The **innerText** property works similarly to the **innerHTML** property, except that any set content will be interpreted as pure text rather than HTML. Thus, inclusion of HTML markup in the string will not create corresponding HTML elements. Setting **para1.innerText = "test"** will result not in bold text but rather with the string being displayed as "test". The **outerHTML** and **outerText** properties work similarly to the corresponding **inner** properties, except that they also modify the element itself. If you set **para1.outerHTML = "test"**, you will actually remove the paragraph element and replace it with "test". The following example is useful if you would like to play with these properties.

```
<!DOCTYPE HTML PUBLIC "-//W3C//DTD HTML 4.01 Transitional//EN"
        "http://www.w3.org/TR/html4/loose.dtd">
<html>
<head>
<title>inner/outer Tester</title>
</head>
<body onload="document.testForm.content.value = theElement.innerHTML;">
<div style="background-color: yellow">
<br>
<p id="para1">This is a <em>test</em> paragraph.</p>
<br>
</div>
<br><br><hr>
<script language="JavaScript" type="text/javascript">
 var theElement = document.getElementById("para1");
</script>
<form name="testForm" id="testForm">
Element Content:
<input type="text" name="content" id="content" size="60"> <br>
<input type="button" value="set innerHTML"
       onclick="theElement.innerHTML = document.testForm.content.value;">
```

```
<input type="button" value="set innerText"
       onclick="theElement.innerText = document.testForm.content.value;">
<input type="button" value="set outerText"
       onclick="theElement.outerText = document.testForm.content.value;">
<input type="button" value="set outerHTML"
       onclick="theElement.outerHTML = document.testForm.content.value;">
<input type="button" value="Reset" onclick="location.reload()">
</form>
</body>
</html>
```

Document.all[ ]

Like it or not, a great deal of script code has been written for the Internet Explorer object model discussed in the last chapter. Probably the most popular aspect of this model is **document.all[ ]**. This collection contains all the HTML elements in the entire HTML document in read order. Given that many JavaScript applications have been written to take advantage of this construct, you might wonder how it relates to the DOM. In short, it doesn't. The DOM doesn't support such a construct, but it's easy enough to simulate it under DOM-aware browsers. For example, under the DOM, we might use the method **document.getElementsByTagName()** to fetch all elements in a document. We could then set an instance property **document.all** equal to **document.getElementsByTagName("*")** if the **all[ ]** collection did not exist. The following example illustrates this idea:

```
<!DOCTYPE HTML PUBLIC "-//W3C//DTD HTML 4.01 Transitional//EN"
        "http://www.w3.org/TR/html4/loose.dtd">
<html>
<head>
<title>All Test</title>
</head>
<body>
<!-- comment 1 -->
<h1>This is a heading</h1>
<hr>
<p id="test">This is a test.<em>This is just a test</em>!</p>
<a href="http://www.yahoo.com">a link</a>
<p>Another paragraph</p>
<badtag>bad very bad!</badtag>
<script language="JavaScript" type="text/javascript">
  if (!document.all)
    document.all = document.getElementsByTagName("*");
  var msg ="Document.all.length="+document.all.length+"\n";
  for (i = 0; i < document.all.length; i++)
    msg += document.all[i].tagName + "\n";
  alert(msg);
```

```
    alert("Test All: "+document.all['test'].innerHTML);

</script>
</body>
</html>
```

Note that this example really doesn't create a perfectly compatible **all[ ]** collection for Netscape 6 or other DOM-aware browsers, since Microsoft's **all[ ]** collection will include comments and both the start and end tag of an unknown element. The two dialogs presented here show this difference:

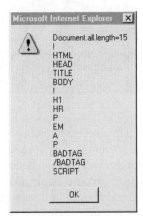
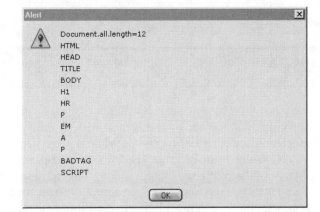

It would be possible to insert the DOCTYPE and comments into our fake **all[ ]** collection, but the bad tag "feature" of Internet Explorer presents a problem. However, as we see in the second **alert()** test shown in Figure 10-4, things aren't quite that bad if you are just looking to preserve your previous scripting efforts in DOM-aware browsers!

Summary

The DOM represents a bright future for JavaScript, where the intersection between script, HTML, and style sheets is cleanly defined. Using the DOM and JavaScript, we are no longer restricted to making minor modifications to a Web page. We can access any tag in a document using methods added to the **Document** object, like **getElementById()**, **getElementsByName()**, and **getElementsByTagName()**. Once elements have been accessed, their attributes and contents can be modified. We can create tags and text fragments on the fly, even going so far as to create a brand new HTML document from scratch. This is the real promise of Dynamic HTML.

Unfortunately, the DOM is not well supported yet. The 6.x generation of browsers has good support for DOM Level 1, but support for CSS manipulations is still a bit buggy. Even when supported by browsers, the DOM presents significant challenges. First,

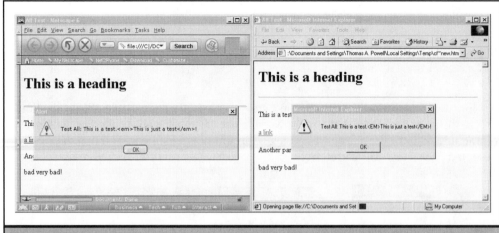

Figure 10-4. *Both Netscape and Internet Explorer with document.all[ ]*

HTML syntax will have to be much more strictly enforced if scripts are to run correctly. The execution of a script using the DOM on a poorly formed document is, in the words of the W3C itself, "unpredictable." Second, JavaScript programmers will have to become intimately familiar with tree manipulations. Given these restrictions, we probably won't see every JavaScript developer making a mad-dash for the DOM, and the old-style objects and access methods will most likely live on for some time. As we work through the practical applications in the next part of the book, we will often see a contrast between the DOM methods presented in this chapter and traditional JavaScript programming methods. However, before presenting these applications we need to cover one last topic—event handling.

Chapter 11

Event Handling

Users can interact with a browser or Web page in a variety of ways. Some actions known as *events* are quite simple, like mouse movements or key presses. Others are a bit more complex, like holding the mouse button and "dragging" an object around the screen or selecting an item from a menu. In the case of a standard Web browser, there are several technologies that contribute to event handling. The most obvious is the browser itself, which defines what type of events are supported and the means for handling them. Second is HTML, which provides the framework of the document objects to which events are "bound." Third is JavaScript itself, which can be used to set, manipulate, and respond to the actions supported by the browser. All of these factors contribute to the *event model*, the portion of the document object model that defines the way in which events are processed by scripts.

As a part of the document object model, the event models of major browsers predictably evolved in separate, incompatible directions. Prior to versions 4 of Internet Explorer and of Netscape's browser, only primitive support for events was available to JavaScript. The type and number of events were restricted, and the manner of their handling was very limited in comparison to modern capabilities. Version 4 browsers added new events and functionality, greatly improving programmer control over many aspects of the event model. However, because of the divergent nature of the version 4 event models, the W3C once again entered the fray by including a standard event model in DOM2. This model extends the DOM to include events, marrying the two incompatible version 4 models to produce a powerful, robust environment for event handling. This chapter begins with the basic event model and how it fits into HTML and JavaScript. The event models of version 4 browsers are discussed and finally the DOM2 event model is introduced.

Basic Event Model

An *event* is some notable action occurring inside the browser to which a script can respond. Events occur when the user clicks the mouse, submits a form, or even moves the mouse over an object in the page. An *event handler* is JavaScript code associated with a particular part of the document and a particular event. The code is executed if and when the given event occurs at the part of the document to which it is associated.

Note
*We refer to the event associated with a handler by omitting the "on" and capitalizing what remains. So, for example, the **Click** event corresponds to the **onclick** handler. We do so in order to draw a distinction between the handler and the event itself.*

Events are not limited to basic user actions like **Click** and **MouseOver**. For example, most browsers support the **Resize** and **Load** events, which fire whenever the user resizes the browser window and when the current document is finished loading. *System events* of this kind are most often employed when JavaScript is used to set up or modify layout characteristics of the page. When the size of the window changes, it is sometimes necessary to change layout properties so the content will fit in the display. The **Load** event is sometimes used to "preload" images from other parts of the site. Once the current page is loaded, the images are forced into the browser cache so that other pages or rollover buttons come up more quickly. Conversely, an **Unload** event might be used to clean things up in a page and clear memory for the next page to be loaded.

Modern event models have a static **Event** object that holds constants and methods used by all events. When an event occurs, a transient instance of the **Event** object is cloned and populated with information about the event. Once mouse location, event type, and other details are stored in the object, it is passed to the relevant handler for processing. The details of this process, which vary according to the model, will be discussed in the following sections. Once an event has been dealt with, the transient object is destroyed and the browser waits for another event to occur. If events occur in rapid succession, they are queued and processed one at a time, in the order they occurred. Serializing execution in this manner reduces some risks associated with multiple threads of execution.

The process of event handling in the basic event model common to all browsers is straightforward. Event handlers are attached to portions of the document using HTML or JavaScript, and, when an event occurs, the browser checks the relevant portion of the document hierarchy for the appropriate handler. If one exists, it is executed. If one does not, nothing happens. The objects at which the event occurs are commonly links, anchors, buttons, forms, and images, but they can also be the document itself (through the **<body>** tag) or even HTML elements you wouldn't expect to receive events (such as paragraphs or tables). Of course, like everything else in JavaScript, not all models support every event for each element in the page. Indeed, the older the browser the less handlers are supported. For cross-browser compatibility, it is important to be aware of which events are supported at which objects.

Event Binding in HTML

HTML supports core *event bindings* for most elements. These bindings are element attributes, like **onclick** and **onmouseover**, that are set equal to the JavaScript that is to be executed when the given event occurs at that object. As the browser parses the page and creates the document object hierarchy, event bindings cause the given JavaScript code to be placed in the event handler for the objects in which they are found. For example, consider the following simple binding that defines a **Click** handler for a link:

```
<a href="http://www.w3c.org/DOM" onclick="alert('Now proceeding
to DOM H.Q.')">Read about the W3C DOM</a>
```

Note   *Although traditional HTML is case-insensitive, XHTML requires lowercase element and attribute names. So while you may see many pages using "onClick" or occasionally "ONCLICK," all lowercase "onclick" is more correct.*

Most of the HTML event attributes cover simple user interaction, such as the click of a mouse button or a key being pressed. A few elements, such as form controls, have some special events associated with them, signaling that the field has received focus from the user or that the form was submitted. The primary event attributes supported in HTML are summarized in Table 11-1.This table includes *intrinsic* (system) events, such as document loading and unloading, which are generally associated with the **<body>** tag.

> **Note**
>
> *In Table 11-1, Internet Explorer 4, 5, and 5.5 and Netscape 4, 4.5, and 4.7 are abbreviated to IE4, IE5, IE5.5, N4, N4.5, and N4.7, respectively. Netscape 6 implements portions of the W3C DOM2 event model and is discussed in a following section. Also,* **most display elements*** *means all elements except <applet>, <base>, <basefont>, <bdo>, <br>, <font>, <frame>, <frameset>, <head>, <html>, <iframe>, <isindex>, <meta>, <param>, <script>, <style>, and <title>.*

Event Attribute	Event Description	Allowed Elements Under HTML 4
onblur	Occurs when an element loses focus, meaning that the user has moved focus to another element, typically either by clicking the mouse on it or tabbing to it.	<a>, <area>, <button>, <input>, <label>, <select>, <textarea> Also <applet>, <area>, <div>, <embed>, <hr>, <img>, <marquee>, <object>, <span>, <table>, <td>, <tr> (Internet Explorer 4, 5, 5.5); <body> (IE 4, 5, and 5.5, N 4 – 4.7); <frameset>, <ilayer>, <layer> (N 4 – 4.7)
onchange	Signals that the form field has lost user focus and its value has been modified during this last access.	<input>, <select>, <textarea>
onclick	Indicates that the element has been clicked.	Most display elements* Also <applet>, <font> (IE 4, 5, 5.5)
ondblclick	Indicates that the element has been double-clicked.	Most display elements* Also <applet>, <font> (IE 4, 5, 5.5)

Table 11-1. *Core Events in the Basic Event Model*

Event Attribute	Event Description	Allowed Elements Under HTML 4
onfocus	Indicates that the element has received focus; namely, that it has been selected for manipulation or data entry.	\<a\>, \<area\>, \<button\>, \<input\>, \<label\>, \<select\>, \<textarea\> Also \<applet\>, \<div\>, \<embed\>, \<hr\>, \<img\>, \<marquee\>, \<object\>, \<span\>, \<table\>, \<td\>, \<tr\> (IE 4, 5, 5.5); \<body\> (N 4 – 4.7, IE 4, 5, 5.5); \<frameset\>, \<ilayer\>, \<layer\> (N 4 – 4.7)
onkeydown	Indicates that a key is being pressed down with focus on the element.	Most display elements* Also \<applet\>, \<font\> (IE 4, 5, 5.5)
onkeypress	Describes the event of a key being pressed and released with focus on the element.	Most display elements* Also \<applet\>, \<font\> (IE 4, 5, 5.5)
onkeyup	Indicates that a key is being released with focus on the element.	Most display elements* Also \<applet\>, \<font\> (IE 4, 5, 5.5)
onload	Indicates the event of a window or frame set finishing the loading of a document or other file.	\<body\>, \<frameset\> Also \<applet\>, \<embed\>, \<link\>, \<script\>, \<style\> (IE 4, 5, 5.5); \<ilayer\>, \<img\>, \<layer\> (N 4– 4.7, IE 4, 5, 5.5)
onmousedown	Indicates the press of a mouse button with focus on the element.	Most display elements* Also \<applet\>, \<font\> (IE 4, 5, 5.5)
onmousemove	Indicates that the mouse has moved while over the element.	Most display elements* Also \<applet\> and \<font\> (IE 4, 5, 5.5)
onmouseout	Indicates that the mouse has moved away from an element.	Most display elements* Also \<applet\>, \<font\> (IE 4, 5, 5.5); \<ilayer\>, \<layer\> (N 4 – 4.7)

Table 11-1. *Core Events in the Basic Event Model* (continued)

Event Attribute	Event Description	Allowed Elements Under HTML 4
onmouseover	Indicates that the mouse has moved over an element.	Most display elements* Also <applet>, <font> (IE 4, 5, 5.5); <ilayer>, <layer> (N 4 – 4.7)
onmouseup	Indicates the release of a mouse button with focus on the element.	Most display elements* Also <applet>, <font> (IE 4, 5, 5.5)
onreset	Indicates that the form is being reset, possibly by the press of a reset button.	<form>
onselect	Indicates the selection of text by the user, typically by highlighting the desired text.	<input>, <textarea>
onsubmit	Indicates that the form is about to be submitted, generally the result of activating a submit button.	<form>
onunload	Indicates that the browser is leaving the current document and unloading it from the window or frame.	<body>, <frameset>

Table 11-1. *Core Events in the Basic Event Model* (continued)

The example shown here illustrates these events in action.

```
<!DOCTYPE html PUBLIC "-//W3C//DTD HTML 4.01 Transitional//EN">
<html>
```

```
<head>
<title>HTML Event Bindings</title>
</head>
<body onload='alert("Event demo loaded")'
      onunload='alert("Leaving demo")'>

<h1 align="center">HTML Event Bindings</h1>
<form onreset='alert("Form reset")'
      onsubmit='alert("Form submit");return false;'>
<ul>
<li>onblur: <input type="text" value="Click into field and then leave"
                 size="40" onblur='alert("Lost focus")'><br><br></li>

<li>onclick: <input type="button" value="Click Me"
                   onclick='alert("Button click")'><br><br></li>

<li>onchange: <input type="text" value="Change this text then leave"
                   size="40" onchange='alert("Changed")'><br><br></li>

<li>ondblclick: <input type="button" value="Double-click Me"
              ondblclick='alert("Button double-clicked")'><br><br></li>
<li>onfocus: <input type="text" value="Click into field"
                   onfocus='alert("Gained focus")'><br><br></li>
<li>onkeydown: <input type="text"
                 value="Press key and release slowly here"size ="40"
                 onkeydown='alert("Key down")'><br><br></li>
<li>onkeypress: <input type="text" value="Type here" size="40"
                   onkeypress='alert("Key pressed")'><br><br></li>
<li>onkeyup: <input type="text" value="Type and release" size="40"
                   onkeyup='alert("Key up")'><br><br></li>
<li>onload:   Alert presented on initial document load.<br><br></li>
<li>onmousedown: <input type="button" value="Click and hold"
                   onmousedown='alert("Mouse down")'><br><br></li>
<li>onmousemove: Move mouse over this<a href=""
onmousemove='alert("Mouse moved")'>link</a><br><br></li>
<li>onmouseout: Position mouse <a href=""
onmouseout='alert("Mouse out")'>here</a> and now leave.<br><br></li>
<li>onmouseover: Position mouse over this <a
href=""onmouseover='alert("Mouse over")'>link</a><br><br></li>
<li>onmouseup: <input type="button" value="Click and release"
                   onmouseup='alert("Mouse up")'><br><br></li>
<li>onreset: <input type="reset" value="Reset Demo"><br><br></li>
<li>onselect: <input type="text" value="Select this text" size="40"
```

```
                            onselect='alert("Selected")'><br><br></li>
<li>onsubmit: <input type="submit" value="Test Submit"><br><br>
<li>onunload: Try to leave document by following this <a
href="http://www.yahoo.com">link</a>.<br><br></li>
</ul>
</form>
</body>
</html>
```

Browsers might support events other than those defined in the HTML 4 specification. Microsoft in particular has introduced a variety of events to capture more complex mouse actions (such as dragging), element events (such as the bouncing of **<marquee>** text); and data-binding events signaling the loading of data. Some of these events are described in more detail in Table 11-2.

Event Attribute	Event Description	Permitted Elements	Compatibility
onabort	Triggered by the user aborting the image load with a stop button or similar effect.	<img>	Netscape 3, 4- 4.7 Internet Explorer 4, 5, 5.5
onafterprint	Fires after user prints document or previews document for printing.	<body>, <frameset>	Internet Explorer 5, 5.5
onafterupdate	Fires after the transfer of data from the element to a data provider, namely a data update.	<applet>, <body>, <button>, <caption>, <div>, <embed>, <img>, <input>, <marquee>, <object>, <select>, <table>, <td>, <textarea>, <tr>	Internet Explorer 4, 5, 5.5

Table 11-2. *Extended Events*

Event Attribute	Event Description	Permitted Elements	Compatibility
onbeforecopy	Fires just before selected content is copied and placed in the user's system clipboard.	`<a>`, `<address>`, `<area>`, `<b>`, `<bdo>`, `<big>`, `<blockquote>`, `<caption>`, `<center>`, `<cite>`, `<code>`, `<custom>`, `<dd>`, `<dfn>`, `<dir>`, `<div>`, `<dl>`, `<dt>`, `<em>`, `<fieldset>`, `<form>`, `<h1>` – `<h6>`, `<i>`, `<img>`, `<label>`, `<legend>`, `<li>`, `<listing>`, `<menu>`, `<nobr>`, `<ol>`, `<p>`, `<plaintext>`, `<pre>`, `<s>`, `<samp>`, `<small>`, `<span>`, `<strike>`, `<strong>`, `<sub>`, `<sup>`, `<td>`, `<textarea>`, `<th>`, `<tr>`, `<tt>`, `<u>`, `<ul>`	Internet Explorer 5, 5.5
onbeforecut	Fires just before selected content is cut from document and added to the system clipboard.	`<a>`, `<address>`, `<applet>`, `<area>`, `<b>`, `<bdo>`, `<big>`, `<blockquote>`, `<body>`, `<button>`, `<caption>`, `<center>`, `<cite>`, `<code>`, `<custom>`, `<dd>`, `<dfn>`, `<dir>`, `<div>`, `<dl>`, `<dt>`, `<em>`, `<embed>`, `<fieldset>`, `<font>`, `<form>`, `<h1>` - `<h6>`, `<hr>`, `<i>`, `<img>`, `<input>`, `<kbd>`, `<label>`, `<legend>`, `<li>`, `<listing>`, `<map>`, `<marquee>`, `<menu>`, `<nobr>`, `<ol>`, `<p>`, `<plaintext>`, `<pre>`, `<rt>`, `<ruby>`, `<s>`, `<samp>`, `<select>`, `<small>`, `<span>`, `<strike>`, `<strong>`, `<sub>`, `<sup>`, `<table>`, `<tbody>`, `<td>`, `<textarea>`, `<tfoot>`, `<th>`, `<thead>`, `<tr>`, `<tt>`, `<u>`, `<ul>`, `<var>`, `<xmp>`	Internet Explorer 5, 5.5

Table 11-2.   *Extended Events* (continued)

Event Attribute	Event Description	Permitted Elements	Compatibility
onbeforepaste	Fires before the selected content is pasted into a document.	<a>, <address>, <applet>, <area>, <b>, <bdo>, <big>, <blockquote>, <body>, <button>, <caption>, <center>, <cite>, <code>, <custom>, <dd>, <dfn>, <dir>, <div>, <dl>, <dt>, <em>, <embed>, <fieldset>, <font>, <form>, <h1> – <h6>, <hr>, <i>, <img>, <input >, <kbd>, <label>, <legend>, <li>, <listing>, <map>, <marquee>, <menu>, <nobr>, <ol>, <p>, <plaintext>, <pre>, <rt>, <ruby>, <s>, <samp>, <select>, <small>, <span>, <strike>, <strong>, <sub>, <sup>, <table>, <tbody>, <td>, <textarea>, <tfoot>, <th>, <thead>, <tr>, <tt>, <u>, <ul>, <var>, <xmp>	Internet Explorer 5, 5.5
onbeforeprint	Fires before user prints document or previews document for printing.	<body>, <frameset>	Internet Explorer 5, 5.5
onbeforeunload	Fires just prior to a document being unloaded from a window.	<body>, <frameset>	Internet Explorer 4, 5, 5.5
onbeforeupdate	Triggered before the transfer of data from the element to the data provider. Might be triggered explicitly, by a loss of focus, or by a page unload forcing a data update.	<applet>, <body>, <button>, <caption>, <div>, <embed>, <hr>, <img>, <input>, <object>, <select>, <table>, <td>, <textarea>, <tr>	Internet Explorer 4, 5, 5.5

Table 11-2. *Extended Events* (continued)

Event Attribute	Event Description	Permitted Elements	Compatibility
onbounce	Triggered when the bouncing contents of a marquee touch one side or another.	\<marquee\>	Internet Explorer 4, 5, 5.5
oncopy	Fires on target when selected content is copied from the document to the clipboard.	\<a\>, \<address\>, \<area\>, \<b\>, \<bdo\>, \<big\>, \<blockquote\>, \<caption\>, \<center\>, \<cite\>, \<code\>, \<dd\>, \<dfn\>, \<dir\>, \<div\>, \<dl\>, \<dt\>, \<em\>, \<fieldset\>, \<form\>, \<h1\> – \<h6\>, \<hr\>, \<i\>, \<img\>, \<legend\>, \<li\>, \<listing\>, \<menu\>, \<nobr\>, \<ol\>, \<p\>, \<plaintext\>, \<pre\>, \<s\>, \<samp\>, \<small\>, \<span\>, \<strike\>, \<strong\>, \<sub\>, \<sup\>, \<td\>, \<th\>, \<tr\>, \<tt\>, \<u\>, \<ul\>	Internet Explorer 5, 5.5
oncut	Fires when selected content is cut from document and added to system clipboard.	\<a\>, \<address\>, \<applet\>, \<area\>, \<b\>, \<bdo\>, \<big\>, \<blockquote\>, \<body\>, \<button\>, \<caption\>, \<center\>, \<cite\>, \<code\>, \<dd\>, \<dfn\>, \<dir\>, \<div\>, \<dl\>, \<dt\>, \<em\>, \<embed\>, \<fieldset\>, \<font\>, \<form\>, \<h1\> – \<h6\>, \<hr\>, \<i\>, \<img\>, \<input\>, \<kbd\>, \<label\>, \<legend\>, \<li\>, \<listing\>, \<map\>, \<marquee\>, \<menu\>, \<nobr\>, \<ol\>, \<p\>, \<plaintext\>, \<pre\>, \<rt\>, \<ruby\>, \<s\>, \<samp\>, \<select\>, \<small\>, \<span\>, \<strike\>, \<strong\>, \<sub\>, \<sup\>, \<table\>, \<tbody\>, \<td\>, \<textarea\>, \<tfoot\>, \<th\>, \<thead\>, \<tr\>, \<tt\>, \<u\>, \<ul\>, \<var\>, \<xmp\>	Internet Explorer 5, 5.5

Table 11-2.   *Extended Events* (continued)

Event Attribute	Event Description	Permitted Elements	Compatibility
ondataavailable	Fires when data arrives from data sources that transmit information asynchronously.	<applet>, <object >	Internet Explorer 4, 5, 5.5
ondatasetchanged	Triggered when the initial data is made available from data source or when the data changes.	<applet>, <object>	Internet Explorer 4, 5, 5.5
ondatasetcomplete	Indicates that all the data is available from the data source.	<applet>, <object>	Internet Explorer 4, 5, 5.5
ondragdrop	Triggered when the user drags an object onto the browser window to attempt to load it.	<body>, <frameset> (window)	Netscape 4 - 4.7

Table 11-2. *Extended Events* (continued)

Event Attribute	Event Description	Permitted Elements	Compatibility
ondragstart	Fires when the user begins to drag a highlighted selection.	\<a>, \<acronym>, \<address>, \<applet>, \<area>, \<b>, \<big>, \<blockquote>, \<body> (document), \<button>, \<caption>, \<center>, \<cite>, \<code>, \<dd>, \<del>, \<dfn>, \<dir>, \<div>, \<dl>, \<dt>, \<em>, \<font>, \<form>, \<frameset> (document), \<h1>, \<h2>, \<h3>, \<h4>, \<h5>, \<h6>, \<hr>, \<i>, \<img>, \<input> \<bd>, \<label>, \<li>, \<listing>, \<map>, \<marquee>, \<menu>, \<object>, \<ol>, \<option>, \<p>, \<plaintext>, \<pre>, \<q>, \<s>, \<samp>, \<select>, \<small>, \<span>, \<strike>, \<strong>, \<sub>, \<sup>, \<table>, \<tbody>, \<td>, \<textarea>, \<tfoot>, \<th>, \<thead>, \<tr>, \<tt>, \<u>, \<ul>, \<var>, \<xmp>	Internet Explorer 4, 5, 5.5
onerror	Fires when the loading of a document or the execution of a script causes an error. Used to trap runtime errors.	\<body>, \<frameset> (window), \<img> (\<link>, \<object>, \<script>, \<style>—Internet Explorer 4)	Netscape 3, 4-4.7 Internet Explorer 4, 5, 5.5
onerrorupdate	Fires if a data transfer has been canceled by the onbeforeupdate event handler.	\<a>, \<applet>, \<object>, \<select>, \<textarea>	Internet Explorer 4, 5, 5.5

Table 11-2. *Extended Events* (continued)

Event Attribute	Event Description	Permitted Elements	Compatibility
onfilterchange	Fires when a page CSS filter changes state or finishes.	Nearly all elements	Internet Explorer 4, 5, 5.5
onfinish	Triggered when a looping marquee finishes.	<marquee>	Internet Explorer 4, 5, 5.5
onhelp	Triggered when the user presses the F1 key or similar help button in the user agent.	Nearly all elements under Internet Explorer 4 only	Internet Explorer 4, 5, 5.5
onmove	Triggered when the user moves a window.	<body>, <frameset>	Netscape 4 - 4.7
onpaste	Fires when selected content is pasted into the document.	<a>, <address>, <applet>, <area>, <b>, <bdo>, <big>, <blockquote>, <body>, <button>, <caption>, <center>, <cite>, <code>, <dd>, <dfn>, <dir>, <div>, <dl>, <dt>, <em>, <embed>, <fieldset>, <font>, <form>, <h1> – <h6>, <hr>, <i>, <img>, <input>, <kbd>, <label>, <legend>, <li>, <listing>, <map>, <marquee>, <menu>, <nobr>, <ol>, <p>, <plaintext>, <pre>, <rt>, <ruby>, <s>, <samp>, <select>, <small>, <span>, <strike>, <strong>, <sub>, <sup>, <table>, <tbody>, <td>, <textarea>, <tfoot>, <th>, <thead>, <tr>, <tt>, <u>, <ul>, <var>, <xmp>	Internet Explorer 5, 5.5

Table 11-2.   *Extended Events* (continued)

Event Attribute	Event Description	Permitted Elements	Compatibility
onreadystatechange	Similar to onload. Fires whenever the ready state for an object has changed.	<applet>, <body>, <embed>, <frame>, <frameset>, <iframe>, <img>, <link>, <object>, <script>, <style>	Internet Explorer 4, 5, 5.5
onresize	Triggered whenever an object is resized. Can only be bound to the window under Netscape as set via the <body> element.	<applet>, <body>, <button>, <caption>, <div>, <embed>, <frameset>, <hr>, <img>, <marquee>, <object>, <select>, <table>, <td>, <textarea>, <tr>	Netscape 4, 4.5 (supports <body> only); Internet Explorer 4 - 5.5
onrowenter	Indicates that a bound data row has changed and new data values are available.	<applet>, <body>, <button>, <caption>, <div>, <embed>, <hr>, <img>, <marquee>, <object>, <select>, <table>, <td>, <textarea>, <tr>	Internet Explorer 4, 5, 5.5
onrowexit	Fires just prior to a bound data source control changing the current row.	<applet>, <body >, <button>, <caption>, <div >, <embed>, <hr>, <img>, <marquee>, <object>, <select>, <table>, <td>, <textarea>, <tr>	Internet Explorer 4, 5, 5.5
onscroll	Fires when a scrolling element is repositioned.	<body>, <div>, <fieldset>, <img>, <marquee>, <span>, <textarea>	Internet Explorer 4, 5, 5.5
onselectstart	Fires when the user begins to select information by highlighting.	Nearly all elements	Internet Explorer 4, 5, 5.5

Table 11-2. *Extended Events* (continued)

Event Attribute	Event Description	Permitted Elements	Compatibility
onstart	Fires when a looped marquee begins or starts over.	<marquee>	Internet Explorer 4, 5, 5.5

Table 11-2. *Extended Events* (continued)

Event Binding in JavaScript

While you can bind event handlers to parts of a document using HTML event attributes, it is sometimes convenient to use JavaScript instead, especially if you wish to harness some of the more advanced event model features. Further, doing so tends to improve the separation between the structure of the document and its logic and presentation. To use JavaScript to set event handlers, it is important to understand that event handlers are accessed as *methods* of the object to which they are bound. For example, to set the **Click** handler of a form button, you set its **onclick** property to the desired code:

```
<form name="myForm" id="myForm">
<input name="myButton" id="myButton" type="button" value="Click me">
</form>
<script language="JavaScript" type="text/javascript">
<!--
document.myForm.myButton.onclick = new Function("alert('Thanks for clicking!')
");
// -->
</script>
```

Note   *The names of event handlers in JavaScript are always all lowercase. This marks one of the few exceptions to the rule that JavaScript properties are named using the "camelback" convention (and reflects XHTML's requirement for lowercased attributes as well).*

Of course, you do not have to use an anonymous function when setting a handler. For example, notice here how we set an **onmouseover** handler to an existing function:

```
<script language="JavaScript" type="text/javascript">
<!--
function rotateImage()
```

```
{
    // Fake contents, but would normally rotate an image
    alert("Rotating the image");
}
// -->
</script>
<img name="myButton" id="myButton" src="image.gif">

<script language="JavaScript" type="text/javascript">
<!--
document.images["myButton"].onmouseover = rotateImage;
// -->
</script>
```

Note *The previous example will not work in Netscape 3.x/4.x generation browsers, as they do not register **MouseOver** events for images, but for links instead. For this reason, when developing for these browsers, images are usually enclosed in links which handle the image rotation.*

Note *Some browsers, Internet Explorer for one, allow you to bind events to objects in highly nonstandard ways. One example of this is the inclusion of **for** and **event** attributes in **<script>** tags under Internet Explorer. Binding events in nonstandard ways should be avoided.*

Regardless of the type of function you use, you do have to make sure to register the event handler after the HTML element has been defined. One way to ensure this is to assign handlers after the document's **onload** handler fires. Another way to ensure this condition is to place the script that assigns the handler after the element in question. Ignoring this condition will cause JavaScript to throw an error since the object you are trying to bind the event to has not been instantiated yet.

Firing Events Manually

You can also invoke event handlers without the user necessarily causing them. For example, to invoke the event handler defined above, you simply call the object's **onmouseover()** method:

```
<form>
<input type="button" value="Trigger Event"
onclick="document.images['myButton'].onmouseover();">
</form>
```

Be careful when using JavaScript to set and invoke event handlers. Because HTML is case-insensitive, some programmers forget that event handler properties in JavaScript are case-sensitive. Trying to set an object's **onClick** property or trying to invoke an object's **onClick()** method will add or invoke an instance property the browser is not aware of. Invoking a non-existent instance property usually causes a runtime error on the page.

You should also be careful when trying to fire events manually as you may also notice that some objects actually contain methods that cause an event to occur. Such methods do not invoke the handler in question; they actually cause the action to immediately happen. For example, the **Form** object contains both **submit()** and **reset()** methods, so both the buttons in

```
<form name="myform" id="myform" onsubmit="return confirm('Send in form
data')" method="get" action="http://www.pint.com">
<input type="button" value="Regular Button with Submit Method"
onclick="document.myform.submit()"><br>
<input type="submit" value="Real Submit Button">
</form>
```

might appear to do the same thing. However, if you try the example, the plain button using the **submit()** method will submit immediately while the other submit button will trigger a submit event.

Return Values

One of the most useful features of event handlers is that their return values can affect the default behavior of the event. For example, clicking a submit button in a form has the default behavior of causing submission of the form. However, if you define a **Submit** handler for the form and the handler returns **false**, the form submission is cancelled. Similarly, the **Click** event on a link usually causes the browser to activate ("follow") the link and load its target. Returning **false** in a **Click** handler for a link will cancel the action and cause the link not to be followed. Table 11-3 lists some useful events and the effect of their return values.

Several examples will make the utility of this capability more clear. Consider the following handler that confirms the user's desire to follow the link:

```
<a href="http://www.w3c.org/" onclick="return confirm('Proceed to W3C?
')">W3C</a>
```

When a user clicks the link, the element's **Click** handler fires and prompts the user with a confirmation box. If the user response is positive ("Yes"), **confirm()** returns **true**, and this value is returned by the handler, causing the browser to proceed. If the user response is negative, **confirm()** returns **false**, and this value is returned by the handler, causing the default action of loading the URL to be cancelled.

Event	Return Value	Effect
Click	false	Radio buttons and check boxes: nothing is set. Submit buttons: form submission canceled. Reset buttons: form is not reset. Links: link is not followed.
DragDrop	false	Drag and drop is cancelled.
KeyDown	false	Cancels the KeyPress events that follow (while the user holds the key down).
KeyPress	false	Cancels the KeyPress event.
MouseDown	false	Cancels the default action (beginning of a drag, beginning selection mode, or arming a link).
MouseOver	true	Causes any change made to the window's *status* or *defaultStatus* properties to be reflected by the browser.
MouseOver	false	Causes any changes to *status* or *defaultStatus* to be ignored until MouseOut.
Submit	false	Cancels form submission.

Table 11-3.   *Common Event Return Values and Their Effect*

Perhaps the most common application of handler return values is in form submission. It is often desirable to validate form data before they are sent to the server in order to catch common typos or invalid data. Consider the following example that validates a single field:

```
<script language="JavaScript" type="text/javascript">
<!--
function validateField(field)
{
   if (field.value == "")
   {
     alert("You must enter a user name");
     field.focus();
     return false;
   }
```

```
    else
        return true;
}
// -->
</script>
<form action="/cgi-bin/login.cgi" onsubmit="return
validateField(this.username)">
Username: <input type="text" name="username" id="username">
<input type="submit" value="Log in">
</form>
```

The event handler is passed a reference to a field in the current form and checks the contents of the username. If the field is empty, an error message is displayed, then a focus event is fired to bring the user back to the empty field, and finally **false** is returned to kill the form submission. If a value is provided, a value of **true** is returned, allowing the form submission to continue. This simple example is used only to illustrate event handlers, return values, and event methods all working together. We'll see many more complex form validation examples in Chapter 13.

Modern Models

The basic event model leaves a lot to be desired. No extra information about the event is passed to the handler, and there is no way to allow event handlers in different parts of the object hierarchy to interact. Modern proprietary models supported in the 4.x generation of browsers correct these shortcomings, albeit in different and incompatible ways. Fortunately, the Level 2 DOM goes even further by merging the proprietary models into one standard and extending its capabilities considerably.

One major difference between version 4+ models and the basic model is the addition of the **Event** object. This object gives event handlers a snapshot of the context in which the event occurred. For example, it includes the screen coordinates of the event, the mouse button that was used (if any), and any modifying keys, such as ALT or CTRL, that were depressed when it occurred.

Another major difference is that events in newer models *propagate* through the document hierarchy. In Netscape 4, events begin at the top of the hierarchy and trickle down to the object at which they occurred, affording enclosing objects the opportunity to modify, cancel, or handle the event. Under Internet Explorer, events begin at the object where they occur and bubble up the hierarchy. Under DOM2, events can trickle down and bubble up, as shown here:

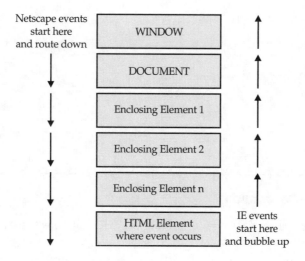

DOM events go either way, but
are usually handled in
"bubble up" fashion

Netscape 4 Event Model

When an event occurs in Netscape 4, the browser creates an **Event** object and passes it
to the handler. Some interesting properties of **Event** objects are listed in Table 11-4.

Now we will illustrate a few details of the Netscape 4.x **Event** object, so you can
get the sense of how events are handled with it. First, if the handler is defined as an
HTML attribute, an **Event** object is passed implicitly and is accessible through the
event identifier. If the handler was defined using JavaScript, the **Event** instance is
passed as an argument to the registered function for the event. For this reason, the
function must declare that it is accepting an argument, though it does not necessarily
have to call it "event." For example, to show the *x* coordinate of a **Click** event attached
to a link, you could use the HTML attribute:

```
<a href="index.html" onclick="alert('Click at ' + event.screenX)
">click me</a>
```

Or you can access the same information when the handler is set with JavaScript:

```
<a href="index.html">click me</a>
<script language="JavaScript1.2" type="text/javascript">
```

```
<!--
function handleIt(e)
{
    alert("Click at " + e.screenX);
}
document.links[0].onclick = handleIt;
// -->
</script>
```

Property	Description
data	Array of strings containing the URLs of objects that were dragged and dropped
modifiers	Bitmask indicating which modifier keys were held down during the event. The bitmask is a bitwise combination of the constants: **ALT_MASK, CONTROL_MASK, META_MASK,** and **SHIFT_MASK** which are static (class) properties of the **Event** object. For example, if the ALT and CTRL keys were depressed, modifiers will have value (**Event.ALT_MASK & Event.CONTROL_MASK).**
pageX	Numeric value indicating the horizontal coordinate where the event occurred
pageY	Numeric value indicating the vertical coordinate where the event occurred
screenX	Numeric value indicating the horizontal coordinate where the event occurred relative to the whole screen
screenY	Numeric value indicating the vertical coordinate where the event occurred relative to the whole screen
target	Reference to the object at which the event occurred
type	String containing the event type (for example, "click")
which	For mouse events, numeric value indicating which mouse button was used (1 is left, 2 middle, 3 right); for keyboard events, the Unicode (numeric) value of the key pressed

Table 11-4.   *Some Instance Properties of Netscape 4's Event Object*

However, note that if a handler bound via HTML invokes a function, the **event** object is not automatically made available to it. It must be passed manually because it is visible only "inside" the HTML event handler attribute. Therefore, the following code will not work as desired under Netscape 4.x browsers:

```
<script language="JavaScript1.2" type="text/javascript">
<!--
function myHandler() {
   alert("Event type: " + event.type);
}
// -->
</script>
<a href="index.html" onclick="myHandler()">click me</a>
```

To fix the example, the **Event** object must be passed manually:

```
<script language="JavaScript1.2" type="text/javascript">
<!--
function myHandler(event) {
   alert("Event type: " + event.type);
}
// -->
</script>
<a href="index.html" onclick="myHandler(event)">click me</a>
```

Event Propagation and Capture

Under Netscape 4.x the **Window, Document,** and **Layer** objects are afforded the opportunity to "capture" events before they are processed by their intended targets. This capability is useful for preprocessing events or defining one handler at a higher level to take the place of multiple handlers at a lower level (for example, for form buttons). Events are captured using the **captureEvents()** method of **Window** and **Document** (and, therefore, also **Layers**, because each layer gets its own **Document** object). The argument to this method is a bitmask indicating which events the object is to capture. Like the constants used with the **modifiers** property, these bitmasks are defined as static properties of the **Event** object. The supported constants, which are case-sensitive, are listed in Table 11-5.

ABORT	ERROR	MOUSEDOWN	RESET
BLUR	FOCUS	MOUSEMOVE	RESIZE
CHANGE	KEYDOWN	MOUSEOUT	SELECT
CLICK	KEYPRESS	MOUSEOVER	SUBMIT
DBLCLICK	KEYUP	MOUSEUP	UNLOAD
DRAGDROP	LOAD	MOVE	

Table 11-5. *Netscape 4.x Event Bitmasks for Event Capture*

To capture all **Click** events at the **Document** level, you could use a script like the one shown here:

```
<!DOCTYPE HTML PUBLIC "-//W3C//DTD HTML 4.01 Transitional//EN">
<html>
<head>
<title>Netscape Click Capture</title>
<script language="JavaScript1.2" type="text/javascript">
<!--
function doClick(e)
{
 alert('doClick');
}
/* check for Nav 4 before trying captureEvents method */
if (document.layers)
   document.captureEvents(Event.CLICK);
document.onclick=doClick;
// -->
</script>
</head>
<body>

<p>Can you click this?</p>
<a href="#">This is a link to nowhere</a>
<form><input type="button" value="press me"></form>
<p>Can you click this?</p>
</body>
</html>
```

Notice the registration of the events using the **captureEvents()** method. To capture more than one event, you should bitwise OR the desired masks together. For example, to capture all **Click**, **DblClick**, and **Blur** events you might use

```
document.captureEvents(Event.CLICK | Event.DBLCLICK | Event.BLUR);
```

Turning off event capture is carried out analogously. You invoke the **releaseEvents()** method of the appropriate object, passing the bitmask of the events to release as the argument. To turn off event capturing of **Blur** and **Click** events at the **Document** level, you use

```
document.releaseEvents(Event.BLUR | Event.CLICK);
```

Because Netscape propagates events top-down, handlers at a higher level always have the opportunity to handle an event before those at a lower level. If you have instructed the **Window** and the **Document** to capture **Click** events, for example, the **Window** will capture the event because it is higher up the document object hierarchy. As a result, Netscape provides a way for handlers to pass the event down along the hierarchy if, after capturing it, it decides that it doesn't want to handle it after all. To let an event proceed along down the hierarchy, a handler invokes the **routeEvent()** method with the event it is processing as the argument. Doing this causes the event to continue down along its course. As an example, consider that you might want to process clicks in a special manner if the user has the ALT key depressed. You might capture it at the **Window** level, examine the **Event**, and pass it along if it is a normal click to be handled by lower-level handlers:

```
function handleClicks(event) {
    if (event.modifiers & Event.ALT_MASK)
    {
            // do something special because they have ALT depressed
    }
    else
       routeEvent(event);
}
window.captureEvents(Event.CLICK);
window.onclick = handleClicks;
```

An occasionally useful aspect of **routeEvent()** is that it returns the value that the handler eventually processing the object returns. Because of this, handlers higher up the hierarchy can keep tabs on what happened to an event after it was passed on. They can modify their behavior according to whether the eventual target returned **true** or **false**.

At times programmers find it necessary to send an event directly to a particular object, skipping down over intervening objects in the hierarchy or "sideways" to an object on another branch. Netscape 4 allows this with use of the **handleEvent()** method. This method is invoked as a property of the object to which the event is to be sent and takes the event itself as an argument. The target object's appropriate event handler is immediately invoked as if it were the original target of the event. For example, to capture all form submissions and send them to the last form on the page for processing, you might use

```
function handleSubmits(event)
{
    document.forms[document.forms.length - 1].handleEvent(event);
}
window.captureEvents(Event.SUBMIT);
window.onsubmit = handleSubmits;
```

Internet Explorer 4 Event Model

In many ways, the event model of Internet Explorer 4+ is more advanced than that of Netscape 4. Because every element in the page is represented as an object under IE4+, a richer, more robust set of elements are capable of generating events. In addition, Microsoft has implemented a wider variety of events that apply to each object.

As with Netscape 4, when an event occurs the browser creates a transient **Event** object and makes it available to the appropriate handler. Unlike Netscape 4, the **Event** instance is not passed to the handler; it is implicitly made available as the global variable **event**. Some properties of the object are listed in Table 11-6.

The flow of events in Internet Explorer is the opposite of Netscape 4. Most events begin at the object at which they occur and bubble up the hierarchy. Bubbling events give the appropriate handler at each level in the hierarchy the opportunity to handle, redirect, or pass the event along up the tree. Some events that have specific, well-defined meanings, such as form submission and receiving focus, do not bubble. The rationale is that such events do not have well-defined semantics at a higher level in the hierarchy, so they should not be propagated up the tree. Bubbling events work their way up the tree, causing the appropriate handler to be invoked at each level in the hierarchy until they reach the top or are cancelled. Non-bubbling events invoke the handler only of the object at which they occur.

Property	Description
srcElement	Reference to the object for which the event is intended
type	String containing the type of event
clientX	Numeric value indicating the horizontal coordinate of the event
clientY	Numeric value indicating the vertical coordinate of the event
screenX	Numeric value indicating the horizontal coordinate of the event relative to the whole screen
screenY	Numeric value indicating the vertical coordinate of the event relative to the whole screen
button	Numeric value indicating the mouse button pressed (primary is 0, but varies from system to system)
keyCode	Numeric value indicating the Unicode value of the key depressed
altKey	Boolean indicating if the ALT key was depressed
ctrlKey	Boolean indicating if the CTRL key was depressed
shiftKey	Boolean indicating if the SHIFT key was depressed
cancelBubble	Boolean indicating whether the event should not bubble up the hierarchy
returnValue	Boolean indicating the return value from the event handler
fromElement	Reference to the element the mouse is moving away from in a MouseOver or MouseOut
toElement	Reference to the element the mouse is moving to during MouseOver or MouseOut

Table 11-6.   *Some Interesting Properties of the IE4+ Event Object*

FUNDAMENTAL CLIENT-SIDE JAVASCRIPT

To illustrate event bubbling in action, consider the following example. The various click handlers are defined for many objects in the hierarchy, and each writes the name of the element to the paragraph below with **id="results"**.

```
<!DOCTYPE HTML PUBLIC "-//W3C//DTD HTML 4.01 Transitional//EN">
<html>
<head>
<title>Event Bubbling Example</title>
</head>
<body onclick="document.all.results.innerHTML += 'At body<br>'">
<table onclick="document.all.results.innerHTML += 'At table<br>'">
<tr onclick="document.all.results.innerHTML += 'At tr<br>'">
<td onclick="document.all.results.innerHTML += 'At td<br>'">
  <p onclick="document.all.results.innerHTML += 'At p<br>'">
Click the<b onclick="document.all.results.innerHTML+='At b<br>'">bold text</b>
      to watch bubbling in action!
  </p>
</td>
</tr>
</table>
<hr>
<p id="results">  </p>
</body>
</html>
```

Clicking the bold text causes a **Click** event to occur that invokes the **onclick** handlers of the **<b>** element and each object above it in the containment hierarchy. The result is shown in Figure 11-1.

You can stop events from propagating up the hierarchy by setting the **cancelBubble** property of the **event** object. This property is **false** by default, meaning that after a handler is finished with it, the event will continue on its way to the next enclosing object in the hierarchy. Setting it to **true** prevents further bubbling after the current handler has finished. For example, you could prevent the event from getting beyond the **<b>** tag in the last example by making this small modification:

```
<b onclick="document.all.results.innerHTML += 'At b<br>';
event.cancelBubble=true;"> bold text</b>
```

A list of handlers supported by Internet Explorer 4 is given in Table 11-7, along with an indication of whether each bubbles up and can be cancelled.

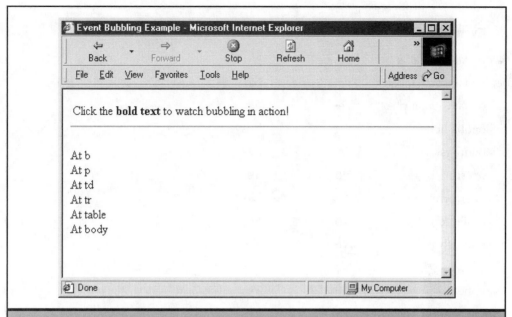

Figure 11-1. *Clicking the bold text causes the Click event to bubble up the hierarchy*

Event Handler	Bubbles?	Cancelable?
onabort	No	Yes
onafterupdate	Yes	No
onbeforeunload	No	Yes
onbeforeupdate	Yes	Yes
onblur	No	No
onbounce	No	Yes
onchange	No	Yes
onclick	Yes	Yes

Table 11-7. *Behavior of Internet Explorer Events*

Event Handler	Bubbles?	Cancelable?
ondataavailable	Yes	No
ondatasetchanged	Yes	No
ondatasetcomplete	Yes	No
ondblclick	Yes	Yes
ondragstart	Yes	Yes
onerror	No	Yes
onerrorupdate	Yes	No
onfilterchange	No	No
onfinish	No	Yes
onfocus	No	No
onhelp	Yes	Yes
onkeydown	Yes	Yes
onkeypress	Yes	Yes
onkeyup	Yes	No
onload	No	No
onmousedown	Yes	Yes
onmouesmove	Yes	No
onmouseout	Yes	No
onmouseover	Yes	Yes
onmouseup	Yes	Yes
onreadystatechange	No	No
onreset	No	Yes
onresize	No	No
onrowenter	Yes	No
onrowexit	No	Yes
onscroll	No	No
onselect	No	Yes

Table 11-7. *Behavior of Internet Explorer Events* (continued)

Event Handler	Bubbles?	Cancelable?
onselectstart	Yes	Yes
onstart	No	No
onsubmit	No	Yes
onunload	No	No

Table 11-7. *Behavior of Internet Explorer Events* (continued)

Events bubble all the way up through the body of the HTML document to the **Document** object, but they do not bubble up to **Window**. Along their course they propagate strictly through objects in the hierarchy that contain them. There is, however, a primitive way to redirect to another object in Internet Explorer 5.5+. Each object has a **fireEvent()** method that transfers the event to that object upon invocation. It takes two arguments, the first is a string denoting the handler to fire and the second is the **event** object itself. The downside of this method is that a new **event** is spawned, so the reference to the original target (*event.srcElement*) is lost during the handoff. The following example illustrates the method:

```
function handleClick()
{
    event.cancelBubble = true;
    document.images[0].fireEvent("onclick", event);
}
```

When set as a **Click** handler, the function above redirects the event to the first image in the page. Remember to cancel the original event before redirecting to another object; failing to do so "forks" the event by allowing it to continue on its way up the hierarchy while adding the new event created by **fireEvent()** to the event queue.

Because of event bubbling and the fact that all parts of the page are scriptable in IE4+, performing event captures as in Netscape 4 is very easy. Simply set the handler at the appropriate level in the hierarchy. For example, to capture clicks at the **Document** level with the function *myHandler*:

```
document.onclick = myHandler;
```

and omit **Click** handlers from lower objects. To unset event capture, simply set the appropriate handler to **null**. For example, to turn off **Click** capturing at the **Document** level:

```
document.onclick = null;
```

FUNDAMENTAL CLIENT-SIDE JAVASCRIPT

Internet Explorer Proprietary Properties

It should be clear from Table 11-5 that Internet Explorer implements a variety of proprietary events over and above those defined in HTML 4. This trend continues in versions 5, 5.5, and 6 to the point where the latest version of IE supports about 50 different events. These events include a slew of new editing events, such as **ondrag**, **ondrop**, **onbeforeprint**, **onafterprint**, **ontextmenu**, **oncopy**, **onpaste**, and on and on. For the sake of brevity and in view of the fact that more proprietary events are being added all the time, the complete list has been omitted here but can be found online at **http://msdn.microsoft.com/workshop/**.

DOM2 Event Model

The W3C describes DOM2 Events as "a platform- and language-neutral interface that gives to programs and scripts a generic event system." It provides a standardized way for scripts to interact with structured documents and does so with a minimum of divergence from previous browser event models. As a result, the DOM Level 2 event model is a hybrid of Netscape 4 and IE4. It builds on the core and HTML aspects of DOM Level 1 to add a robust event model in the DOM. In other words, it requires a fully scriptable Document Object Model (W3C DOM-compliant) to be in place to achieve its functionality.

Events begin their lifecycle at the top of the hierarchy and make their way down to the target object. This is known as the "capture phase" because it mimics the behavior of Netscape 4. During its descent, the event may be pre-processed, handled, or redirected by any intervening object. Once it reaches its target object and the handler (if any) has executed, the object proceeds to make its way back up the hierarchy to the top. This is known as the bubbling phase because of its obvious connections to the model of Internet Explorer 4+. Events bubble up by default but must be explicitly captured on their way down in a manner akin to Netscape 4.

> **Note**
>
> *Netscape 6 is the first browser to implement DOM Level 2. It does not appear that Microsoft plans to fully implement DOM Level 2 in Internet Explorer, most likely because newer versions of their browser support similar capabilities. In the following discussion we include some Netscape 6 features, such as **Event** properties, implemented over and above the DOM Level 2 specification. Netscape-specific extensions are marked as such where they occur, but the vast majority of the discussion applies to DOM Level 2 as well as to Netscape 6.*

Like previous event models, DOM Level 2 defines an **Event** object in a way that provides relevant information to handlers. Some relevant properties of this object are listed in Table 11-8. As with the previous event models presented, not all events will have all the **Event** properties set. Only those properties that are relevant to the particular type of event will be provided. For example, a keyboard event will not set the **button** property.

Property	Netscape specific?	Description
altKey	No	Boolean indicating if the ALT key was depressed during event
bubbles	No	Boolean indicating whether the event bubbles
button	No	Numeric value indicating which mouse button was used (1 for left, 2 middle, 3 right)
cancelable	No	Boolean indicating whether the event can be canceled
charCode	Yes	ASCII value of the key pressed during keypress events
clientX	No	Horizontal coordinate of the event relative to the browser
clientY	No	Vertical coordinate of the event relative to the browser
ctrlKey	No	Boolean indicating if the CTRL key was depressed during event
currentTarget	No	Node the event handler is assigned to
eventPhase	No	Numeric value indicating the phase of the event flow in which this event is being processed (1 for capture, 2 if at the target, 3 for bubble)
keyCode	Yes	ASCII value of the key pressed during keydown and keyup events
metaKey	No	Boolean indicating if the META key was depressed during event
relatedTarget	No	Reference to the node related to the event—for example, on a mouseover it references the node the mouse left; on mouseout it references the node the mouse moved to
screenX	No	Horizontal coordinate of the event relative to the whole screen
screenY	No	Vertical coordinate of the event relative to the whole screen
shiftKey	No	Boolean indicating if the SHIFT key was depressed during event
target	No	Node the event occurred at
type	No	String indicating the type of the event (such as "click")

Table 11-8. *Some Properties of the Netscape 6 and DOM2 Event Object*

Mouse Events

The mouse events defined by DOM2 are those from HTML 4 and DOM0. They are listed in Table 11-9.

Keyboard Events

Surprisingly, DOM Level 2 does not define keyboard events. Keyboard events have been reserved for a future version of the specification. You can see the genesis of the specification in DOM Level 3. Fortunately, because HTML 4 allows **keyup**, **keydown**, and **keypress** events for many elements, you'll find that Netscape 6 supports the basic keyboard events. These events populate the **Event** object with the Netscape-specific keyboard properties in Table 11-6.

Browser Events

DOM2 supports the familiar browser/HTML related events found in all major browsers. The list of these events is found in Table 11-10.

UI Events

Although DOM Level 2 builds primarily on those events found in the HTML 4 specification (and DOM Level 0), it adds a few new "User Interface" (UI) events to round out the field. These events are prefixed with "DOM" to distinguish them from "normal" events. The first is **DOMFocusIn** (with caps!), which corresponds to the traditional **Focus** event but can be applied to any element, not just form fields. This event bubbles and is not cancelable. The second is **DOMFocusOut**, which occurs when the object loses focus. This event bubbles and is not cancelable. The final event

Event	Bubbles?	Cancelable?
click	Yes	Yes
mousedown	Yes	Yes
mouseup	Yes	Yes
mouseover	Yes	Yes
mousemove	Yes	No
mouseout	Yes	Yes

Table 11-9. *Mouse Events Defined in DOM2*

Event	Bubbles?	Cancelable?
load	No	No
unload	No	No
abort	Yes	No
error	Yes	No
select	Yes	No
change	Yes	No
submit	Yes	Yes
reset	Yes	No
focus	No	No
blur	No	No
resize	Yes	No
scroll	Yes	No

Table 11-10. *Browser and HTML Events Defined in DOM2*

is **DOMActivate**, which occurs when the object is activated, for example by a mouse click. This event bubbles and is cancelable. While these new events are rarely used, it is helpful to be aware of them should you encounter them in new scripts.

Mutation Events

Because of the new capabilities for dynamic modification of the document object hierarchy found in DOM-compliant browsers, DOM2 includes events to detect such changes. These events, which are known as *mutation events* because they occur when the document hierarchy changes, are only briefly mentioned here and require a detailed description of the mutation event interface to use effectively. They are listed in Table 11-11. For complete details see the W3C DOM2 event specification at **http://www.w3.org/TR/DOM-Level-2-Events/**

Binding Events to Elements

The easiest way to bind events to elements under DOM Level 2 is to use the HTML attribute-binding technique, which should be familiar by now. Nothing changes for DOM Level 2 when you bind events using HTML save for the restriction that only

Event	Bubbles?	Cancelable?	Description
DOMSubtreeModified	Yes	No	Implementation-dependent; fires when a portion of the node's subtree has been modified
DOMNodeInserted	Yes	No	Fires on a node inserted as the child of another node
DOMNodeRemoved	Yes	No	Fires on a node that has been removed from its parent
DOMNodeRemovedFromDocument	No	No	Fires on a node when it is about to be removed from the document
DOMNodeInsertedIntoDocument	No	No	Fires on a node when it has been inserted into the document
DOMAttrModified	Yes	No	Fires on a node when one of its attributes has been modified
DOMCharacterDataModified	Yes	No	Fires on a node when the data it contains are modified

Table 11-11. *DOM Mutation Events Defined in DOM2*

standard events can be used and the attribute must be supported by the element under HTML 4. One thing to be aware of is that under Netscape 6, event handlers in attributes are still passed an implicit **event** object, so the techniques for attribute binding of handlers for Netscape 4 still apply.

Assigning an event handler using JavaScript is also quite easy. Because DOM Level 2 events are built on top of the DOM Level 1 hierarchy of nodes, you access the desired node using standard DOM techniques rather than navigating a proprietary browser object model. Once the node is located, the event handler is assigned to the appropriate property of the node, as shown in this example:

```
<!DOCTYPE HTML PUBLIC "-//W3C//DTD HTML 4.0 Transitional//EN">
<html>
<head>
<title>DOM 2 Event Test</title>
</head>
<body>
<p>This is just a normal paragraph</p>
<p id="myPara">This is myPara</p>
<p>This is just a normal paragraph</p>

<script language="JavaScript" type="text/javascript">
<!--
function alertUser(event)
{
    alert("Captured a click at: " + event.screenX);
}
document.getElementById('myPara').onclick = alertUser;
// -->
</script>
</body>
</html>
```

Note how the event handler function took an argument *event*. DOM Level 2 dictates that the **Event** instance is passed to the handler as an argument. Although you can name the argument anything you like, the names "event," "evt," and "e" are fairly standard.

Because DOM2 works with the DOM, you can harness its power with your event handlers. For example, to implement a simple text-mode rollover for an object with an **id**="myText", you might write

```
<!DOCTYPE HTML PUBLIC "-//W3C//DTD HTML 4.0 Transitional//EN">
<html>
<head>
<title>Simple DOM Rollover</title>
<script language="JavaScript" type="text/javascript">
<!--
function textOn() { this.style.backgroundColor = "blue"; }
function textOff() { this.style.backgroundColor = "white"; }
// -->
```

```
</script>
</head>
<body>
<p id="myText">This is a test</p>
<script language="JavaScript" type="text/javascript">
<!--
document.getElementById('myText').onmouseover = textOn;
document.getElementById('myText').onmouseout = textOff;
// -->
</script>
</body>
</html>
```

Later versions of Internet Explorer are in various states of compliance with the DOM, and the previous example will work in IE 5 and beyond as well as Netscape 6. However, the more advanced features of DOM Level 2 events require a truly DOM Level 1- and DOM Level 2-compliant browser.

 Opera promises full DOM Level 2 support in the very near future, so this technique is likely to work in very recent versions of Opera as well.

Event Propagation: Bubbling and Capturing

DOM Level 2 provides a new, more powerful way to bind handlers to elements using event listeners. *Event listeners* are event handlers bound to a particular node in the object hierarchy that fire during a particular phase of the event lifecycle. Event listeners are attached to nodes using the **addEventListener()** method. They are removed with **removeEventListener()**. Attaching an event to a node using these methods differs from normal event binding in several respects. First, these methods allow you to specify whether the event will be handled during the capture (down) phase or during the bubbling (up) phase. Events set using traditional techniques fire when the object is the target and during the bubbling phase, if one exists, for that event. Second, these methods allow you to bind multiple handlers for the same event for the same object, a capability previously only available with nonstandard IE5+ methods. And finally, listeners can be bound to text nodes, a capability that was previously unavailable.

The syntax of the listener methods is as follows:

```
node.addEventListener(type, eventHandler, direction)
```

where:

- *node* is the node to which the listener is to be bound
- *type* is a string indicating the event it is to listen for

- *eventHandler* is the function that should be invoked when it fires
- *direction* is a Boolean value indicating whether it should listen during the capture phase (**true**) or bubble phase (**false**)

For example, to register a function *changeColor* as the capture-phase **mouseover** handler for a paragraph with **id="**myText**"** you might write

```
document.getElementById('myText').addEventListener("mouseover", changeColor,
true);
```

To add a bubble phase handler *swapImage*:

```
document.getElementById('myText').addEventListener("mouseover", swapImage,
false);
```

And to remove the first handler (but keep the second), you would invoke:

```
document.getElementById('myText').removeEventListener("mouseover",
changeColor, true);
```

As with more traditional models, DOM Level 2 allows you to cancel events. To cancel the default event behavior you can still return **false** from a handler. You can also use two new methods of the **Event** object: **preventDefault()** and **stopPropagation()**. The **preventDefault()** method has the same effect as returning **false** from the handler. The **stopPropagation()** method halts the flow of the event through the object hierarchy after the current handler finishes. This method can be called during any part of the event's lifecycle but works only for those events that are cancelable; invoking it on an uncancelable event has no effect. An example of the use of these functions that works in Netscape 6 is shown here:

```
Click <a id="myLink" href="index.html">this link</a>
<script language="JavaScript" type="text/javascript">
<!--
function killShiftClicks(event)
{
   if (event.shiftKey)
   {
      event.preventDefault();
      event.stopPropagation();
   }
}
document.addEventListener("click", killShiftClicks, true);
document.getElementById('myLink').onclick = function() { alert("Click got
through!"); };
```

```
// -->
</script>
```

In the example here, the *killShiftClicks()* handler prevents any **Click** events from functioning while the SHIFT key is depressed. It does so by preventing the event's default behavior and halting its propagation through the hierarchy at the very beginning of its lifecycle. Whenever the SHIFT key is depressed when the link is pressed, the user will not see the alert message associated with the link's **Click** handler, because the event will have been halted at the beginning of the capture phase.

 *Listening for events in the capture phase can be tricky business because of the parent-child relationship of nodes in the DOM. The event will be captured only if it is targeted for a node that is in the subtree rooted at the node to which the listener is attached. It is often most convenient to capture events at the **Document** or **Form** object level.*

Default event-behavior cancellations in DOM Level 2 are fundamentally different from those in older models. Once a handler has returned **false** or invoked the event's **preventDefault()** method, it will cancel the event's default behavior no matter what. So if a handler returns **false** or invokes **preventDefault()** and a handler further along the flow returns **true**, the event is still cancelled. This means that you have to be very careful when canceling events under DOM Level 2.

Event Redirection

Every node has a **dispatchEvent()** method that can be invoked to redirect an event to that node. It takes the **Event** object as an argument and returns **false** if any handler associated with the event invokes **preventDefault()** or returns **false**. When redirecting an event in this manner, the node at which the **dispatchEvent()** was invoked becomes the new event target. The browser sends the event along the normal flow down the hierarchy and back up as if the event had really occurred there. You need to be careful that you do not get your events trapped in an endless loop by redirecting them to a part of the document where the handler that dispatched the event is listening. Doing so will send the event back and forth between handlers and quickly crash the browser.

Event Model Issues

Deciding which event mode to use is largely dictated by the browsers your clients are likely to use. For the next few years, it is likely that IE4, IE5, and Netscape 4 will all be fairly widely used. Therefore, it will probably be necessary to write cross-browser event handlers to carry out your tasks. Doing so is not hard if you limit yourself to standard events and straightforward applications. Throughout the remainder of the book you will see examples of cross-browser event handlers used in a variety of tasks.

The future will most probably see the death of the Netscape 4 event model and the rise of DOM Level 2. Whether Microsoft will get on board with full DOM Level 2 compliance remains to be seen; they have invested a lot of time and effort in their proprietary model. Whatever the case, it is certain that programmers will need to accommodate two or three event models in their scripts for the next few years.

Summary

The basic event model of early browsers presents an interface allowing portions of the page to respond dynamically to user events. Version 4 browsers implemented different and incompatible event models to address flexibility and robustness issues in the early models. Netscape 4 sends events to their target from the top down, while Internet Explorer bubbles them from the bottom up. Both browsers make an **Event** object available to handlers, though the manner in which this is accomplished and the structure of the object itself vary from browser to browser.

Netscape 6 is the first browser to implement the DOM2 standard event model. This model builds upon the DOM1 specification to provide the means for events to be bound to nodes in the document hierarchy. Events in this model first move down the hierarchy, allowing themselves to be captured by event listeners. Once they reach their target and its event handler has executed, they bubble back up the hierarchy invoking the corresponding handler at each level. Event propagation can be turned off in DOM2 using the aptly named **stopPropagation()** method, and the default behavior of events can be canceled by returning **false** or with the **preventDefault()** method. As Netscape 6 has emerged on the scene, there are now three major event models (NS4, IE4/5/6, and Netscape 6/DOM2) beyond the traditional JavaScript model that programmers need to be aware of as they build their applications.

FUNDAMENTAL
CLIENT-SIDE JAVASCRIPT

The Complete Reference

JavaScript

Part IV

Using JavaScript

The Complete Reference

JavaScript

Chapter 12

Controlling Windows and Frames

Now it is time to begin to use the syntax and theory we have covered up to this point in the book. Starting from the top of the object hierarchy with **Window**, we will learn how to create a variety of windows, including special dialogs such as alerts, confirmations, and prompts; custom pop-up windows of our own design; and such special types as modal and full-screen windows. We will also show how windows and frames are very closely related. While frames can be troublesome at times and require special scripts to be used properly, it will be shown how useful they can be to store JavaScript variables across page loads. After reading this chapter, you should be able to use JavaScript to start building some of the basic framework required for a JavaScript application.

Introduction to the Window Object

JavaScript's **Window** object represents the browser window (or frame) that a document is displayed in. Every window that is open on the screen can be referenced and manipulated by an instance of this object, though doing so may raise security considerations, particularly if the window is not one your script created. (We'll deal with that issue later, in Chapter 21.) For now, we will always assume we are manipulating only windows of our own creation.

The properties of a particular instance of **Window** might include its size, the amount of chrome (buttons, scrollbars, and so on in the browser frame), its position, and so on. The methods of the **Window** include the creation and destruction of generic windows and the handling of special windows, such as alert, confirmation, and prompt dialogs. Further, as the top object in the JavaScript object hierarchy (aside from the **Global** context), this object contains references to nearly all the objects in JavaScript.

Dialogs

We'll start our discussion of the application of the **Window** object by describing how to create three types of special windows known generically as dialogs. A *dialog box* or simply a *dialog* is a small window in a graphical user interface that "pops-up," requesting some action from a user. The three types of basic dialogs supported by JavaScript directly are alerts, confirms, and prompts. The native implementations of these dialogs are somewhat rudimentary, but (as we'll see in the next section) we can replace these windows with our own.

Alert

The **Window** object's **alert()** method creates a special small window with a short string message and an OK button, as shown here:

Note   *The typical rendering of the alert includes an icon indicating a warning, regardless of the message being presented.*

The basic syntax for alert is

```
window.alert(string);
```

or for shorthand we just use

```
alert(string);
```

as the **Window** object can be assumed.

The string passed as an argument to **alert()** may be a variable, literal, or even the result of an expression. If you pass another type of data it is coerced into a string. All the following examples are valid use of the **alert()** method.

```
alert("Hi there from JavaScript! ");
alert("Hi "+username+" from Javascript");
var messageString = "Hi again!";
alert(messageString);
```

An alert window is *page-modal*, meaning that it receives focus and must be cleared before the user is allowed to continue activity with the page.

Note   *A good use of alert dialogs is for debugging messages. If you are ever in doubt of where a script is executing or what current variables are set at and you don't want to use a debugger, you can use an alert to display useful debugging information. More information on this type of technique is presented in Chapter 24.*

Confirm

The **confirm()** method for the **Window** object creates a window displaying a message for a user to respond to by pressing either an OK button, to agree with the message, or a Cancel button, to disagree with the message. A typical rendering is shown here.

The wording of the confirmation question may influence the usability of the dialog significantly. Many confirmation messages are best answered with a Yes or No button rather than an OK or Cancel button, as shown by the following dialog:

Unfortunately, with the basic JavaScript confirmation method there is no possibility to change the button strings, but it is possible to write your own form of confirmation.

The basic syntax of the **confirm()** method is

```
window.confirm(string);
```

or simply

```
confirm(string);
```

where *string* is any valid string variable, literal, or expression that eventually evaluates to a string value to be used as the confirmation question.

The **confirm()** method returns a Boolean value that indicates whether or not the information was confirmed, **true** if the OK button was pressed and **false** if the window was closed or the Cancel button pressed. This value can be saved to a variable,

```
answer = confirm("Do you want to do this?");
```

or the method call itself can be used within any construct that uses a Boolean expression, such as an **if** statement like the one here:

```
if (confirm("Do you want ketchup on that?"))
  alert("Pour it on!");
else
  alert("Hold the ketchup.");
```

Like the **alert()** method, confirmation dialogs should be browser modal.

The next example shows how the alert and confirm can be used:

```
<!DOCTYPE HTML PUBLIC "-//W3C//DTD HTML 4.01 Transitional//EN"
        "http://www.w3.org/TR/html4/loose.dtd">
<html>
```

```
<head>
<title>JavaScript Power!</title>
<script language="JavaScript" type="text/javascript">
<!--
function destroy()
  {
    if (confirm("Are you sure you want to destroy this page?"))
    {
     alert("What you thought I'd actually let you do that!?");
    }
   else
    {
     alert("That was close!");
    }
  }
// -->
</script>
</head>
<body>
<div align="center">
<h1>The Mighty Power of JavaScript!</h1>
<hr>
<form>
<input type="button" value="Destroy this Page" onclick="destroy()">
</form>
</div>
</body>
</html>
```

Prompts

JavaScript also supports the **prompt()** method for the **Window** object. A prompt window is a small data collection dialog that prompts the user to enter a short line of data, as shown here:

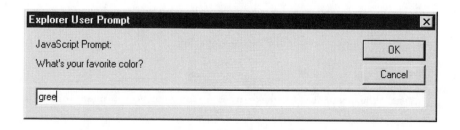

The **prompt()** method takes two arguments. The first is a string that displays the prompt value, and the second is a default value to put in the prompt window. The method returns a string value that contains the value entered by the user in the prompt. The basic syntax is shown here:

```
resultvalue = prompt(prompt string, default value string);
```

Occasionally programmers will use only a single value in the method.

```
result = prompt("What is your favorite color? ");
```

However, in most browsers you should see that a value of **undefined** is placed in the prompt line. You should set the second parameter to an empty string to keep this from happening.

```
result = prompt("What is your favorite color?","");
```

It is important when using the **prompt()** method to understand what is returned back. If the user presses the Cancel button in the dialog or the close box, a value of **null** will be returned. It is always a good idea to check for this. Otherwise, a string value will be returned. Programmers should be careful to convert prompt values to the appropriate type using **parseInt()** or similar methods if they do not want a string value.

The next example shows the **prompt()** method in action.

```
<!DOCTYPE HTML PUBLIC "-//W3C//DTD HTML 4.01 Transitional//EN"
        "http://www.w3.org/TR/html4/loose.dtd">
<html>
<head>
<title>Guru 1.0</title>
<script language="JavaScript" type="text/javascript">
<!--
function askGuru()
  {
   var question = prompt("What is your question o' seeker of knowledge?","")
   if (question != null)
   {
     if (question == "")
       {
        alert("At least you could ask a question.");
       }
     else
       {
        alert("You thought I'd waste my time on your silly questions?");
       }
   }
```

```
   }
   //  -->
   </script>
   </head>
   <body>
   <div align="center">
   <h1>JavaScript Guru 1.0</h1>
   <hr>
   <br>
   <form>
   <input type="button" value="Ask the Guru" onclick="askGuru()">
   </form>
   </div>
   </body>
   </html>
```

If the format of these last three dialogs leaves a little to be desired, we'll see that it is possible to create our own forms of these dialogs; to do so, we first create our own windows.

Opening and Closing Generic Windows

While the **alert()**, **confirm()**, and **prompt()** methods create specialized windows quickly, it is often desirable to open arbitrary windows to show a Web page or the result of some calculation. The **Window** object methods **open()** and **close()** are used to create and destroy a window, respectively.

When you open a window you can set its URL, name, size, and buttons as well as other attributes such as whether or not the window can be resized. The basic syntax of this method is

window.open(*url, name, features, replace***)**

where:

- ■ *url* is a URL that indicates the document to load into the window.

- ■ *name* is the name for the window (which is useful when referencing it later on using the **target** attribute of HTML links).

- ■ *features* is a comma-delimited string that lists the features of the window.

- ■ *replace* is an optional Boolean value (**true** or **false**) that indicates if the URL specified should replace the window's contents or not. This would apply to a window that was already created.

The example of this method,

```
   secondwindow = open("http://www.yahoo.com", "yahoo", "height=300,width=200,
   scrollbars=yes");
```

would open a window to Yahoo with a height of 300 pixels, a width of 200 pixels, and scrollbars, as shown here:

There are a variety of ways programmers create windows, but often links or buttons are used. For example,

```
<a href="#" onclick="javascript: secondwindow = open('http://www.yahoo.com',
'yahoo', 'height=300,width=200,scrollbars=yes');">Open Window</a>

<form>
<input type="button" value="Open Window" onclick="secondwindow =
open('http://www.yahoo.com', 'yahoo', 'height=300,width=200,scrollbars=yes');">
</form>
```

Once a window is open, the **close()** method can be used to close it. For example, the following fragment presents buttons to open and close a window. Notice the use of the *secondwindow* variable that contains the reference to the **Window** object created.

```
<form>
<input type="button" value="Open Window" onclick="window.secondwindow =
window.open('http://www.yahoo.com', 'yahoo',
'height=300,width=200,scrollbars=yes');">
<input type="button" value="Close Window" onclick="if(window.secondwindow)
window.secondwindow.close();">
</form>
```

If, however, the window has been created at some previous time in the current context, you will not see an error regardless of the presence of the window on the screen. This is because the object will probably still remain in the scope chain. Reload the previous example and press the Close button immediately and you should get an error. If, however, you create a window only once, you will not see an error regardless of the presence of the window on the screen, because the object probably will still be in the scope chain. In order to safely close a window you first need to look for the object and then try to close it. Consider the following **if** statement that looks to see if the *secondwindow* variable is instantiated before closing it:

```
if (window.secondwindow)
   secondwindow.close();
```

Do not assume that the **closed** property of the **Window** object will provide any help detecting the status of a window that has not yet been created. While you can also check the status of a window by looking at its **closed** property, which returns a **Boolean** value indicating if the window is closed or not (as shown in the next script), it too requires the object to be defined before access. The following short example shows the safe use of the **Window** methods and properties discussed so far.

```
<form>
<input type="button" value="Open Window" onclick="window.secondwindow =
open('http://www.yahoo.com','example','height=300,width=200,scrollbars=yes')
;">
<input type="button" value="Close Window" onclick="if (window.secondwindow)
window.secondwindow.close(); ">
<input type="button" value="Check Status" onclick="if (window.secondwindow)
alert(window.secondwindow.closed); else alert('Secondwindow undefined');">
</form>
```

You should also be aware that you cannot close windows that you have not created, particularly if your script has not been granted security privileges. Further, you may have a hard time closing the main browser window. If you have a statement like

```
window.close()
```

in the main browser window running the script, you might see a message like

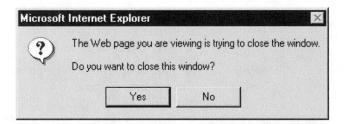

in some browsers, while others without warning may close down the main window (as in the case of Opera) or even the browser (as in very old versions of Netscape).

Window Features

The list of possibilities for the *feature* parameter is quite rich and allows you to set the height, width, scrollbars, and a variety of other window characteristics. The possible values for this parameter are detailed in Table 12-1.

Feature Parameter	Value	Description	Example
alwaysLowered	yes/no	Indicates if window should always be lowered under all other windows. Does have a security risk.	alwaysLowered=no
alwaysRaised	yes/no	Indicates if the window should always stay on top of other windows.	alwaysRaised=no
dependent	yes/no	Indicates if the spawned window is truly dependent on the parent window. Dependent windows are closed when their parents are closed, while others stay around.	dependent=yes
directories	yes/no	Should the directories button on the browser window show?	directories=yes
fullscreen	yes/no	Should the window take over the full screen (IE only)?	fullscreen=yes
height	pixel value	Sets the height of the window, chrome and all.	height=100

Table 12-1.   *Feature Parameter Values for window.open()*

Feature Parameter	Value	Description	Example
hotkeys	yes/no	Indicates whether the hotkeys for the browser (beyond browser-essential ones like Quit) are disabled in the new window.	hotkeys=no
innerHeight	pixel value	Sets the height of the inner part of the window where the document shows.	innerHeight=200
innerWidth	pixel value	Sets the width of the inner part of the window where the document shows.	innerWidth=300
left	pixel value	Specifies where to place the window relative to screen origin. Primarily an IE-specific syntax; use *screeny* otherwise.	left=10
location	yes/no	Specifies if the location bar should show on the window.	location=no
menubar	yes/no	Specifies if the menu bar should be shown or not.	menubar=yes
outerHeight	pixel value	Sets the height of the outer part of the window, including the chrome.	outerHeight=300

Table 12-1.   *Feature Parameter Values for window.open()* (continued)

Feature Parameter	Value	Description	Example
outerWidth	pixel value	Sets the width of the outer part of the window including the chrome.	outerWidth=300
resizable	yes/no	Value to indicate if the user is to be able to resize the window.	resizable=no
screenx	pixel value	Distance left in pixels from screen origin where window should be opened. Netscape oriented syntax (use *left* otherwise).	screenx=100
screeny	pixel value	Distance up and down from the screen origin where window should be opened. Netscape specific syntax (use *top* otherwise).	screeny=300
scrollbars	yes/no	Should scrollbars show?	scrollbars=no
status	yes/no	Should the status bar show?	status=no
titlebar	yes/no	Should the title bar show?	titlebar=yes
toolbar	yes/no	Should the toolbar menu be visible?	toolbar=yes
top	pixel value	IE-specific feature indicating the position of the window from top of the screen; use *sreeny* otherwise.	top=20

Table 12-1.   *Feature Parameter Values for window.open()* (continued)

Feature Parameter	Value	Description	Example
width	pixel value	The width of the window. You may want to use *innerWidth* instead.	width=300
z-lock	yes/no	Specifies if the z-index should be set so that a window can not change its stacking order relative to other windows even if it gains focus.	z-lock=yes

Table 12-1. *Feature Parameter Values for window.open()* (continued)

Note *Typically, in modern JavaScript implementations you can use 1 for "yes" and 0 for "no" for the features using yes/no values. However, for pure backwards compatibility, the yes/no syntax is preferred.*

Oftentimes when using this method you may want to create strings to hold the options rather than to use a string literal. However the features are specified, they should be set one at a time with comma separators and no extra spaces, as, for example:

```
var windowOptions = "directories=no,location=no,width=300,height=300";
var myWindow = open("http://www.yahoo.com", "mywindow", windowOptions);
```

The next example is useful for experimenting with all the various window features that can be set. It also will display the JavaScript string required to create a particular window in a text area so that it can be used in a script.

```
<!DOCTYPE HTML PUBLIC "-//W3C//DTD HTML 4.01 Transitional//EN"
 "http://www.w3.org/TR/html4/loose.dtd">
<html>
<head>
<title>Window Creator</title>
<script language="JavaScript" type="text/javascript">
<!--

function createFeatureString()
{
 var featurestring = "";
 var numelements = document.windowform.elements.length;
```

USING JAVASCRIPT

```
for (var i= 0; i < numelements; i++)
    if ( (document.windowform.elements[i].type == "checkbox")  &&
          (document.windowform.elements[i].checked) )
              featurestring += document.windowform.elements[i].name+"=yes,";

featurestring += "height="+document.windowform.height.value+",";
featurestring += "width="+document.windowform.width.value+",";
featurestring += "top="+document.windowform.top.value+",";
featurestring += "left="+document.windowform.left.value+",";
featurestring += "screenx="+document.windowform.screenX.value+",";
featurestring += "screeny="+document.windowform.screenY.value;
return featurestring;

}
function openWindow()
 {
   var features = createFeatureString();
   var url = document.windowform.windowurl.value;
   var name = document.windowform.windowname.value;
   theNewWindow = window.open(url,name,features);
   if (theNewWindow)
    document.windowform.jscode.value =
"window.open('"+url+"','"+name+"','"+features+"');"
   else
     document.windowform.jscode.value = "Error: JavaScript Code Invalid";
 }

function closeWindow()
{
 if (window.theNewWindow)
  theNewWindow.close();
}
// -->
</script>
</head>
<body>

<form name="windowform" id="windowform">
<h2>Window Basics</h2>
URL: <input type="text" name="windowurl" id="windowurl" size="30" maxlength="300"
value="http://www.yahoo.com"><br>
Window Name: <input type="text" name="windowname" id="windowname" size="30"
maxlength="300" value="secondwindow"><br>
<h2>Size</h2>
Height:     <input type="text" name="height" id="height" size="4" maxlength="4"
value="100">
Width:      <input type="text" name="width" id="width" size="4" maxlength="4"
value="100"><br>
<h2>Position</h2>
```

```
Top:       <input type="text" name="top" id="top" size="4" maxlength="4"
value="100">
Left: <input type="text" name="left" id="left" size="4" maxlength="4" value="100">
(IE)<br><br>
ScreenX:    <input type="text" name="screenX" id="screenX" size="4" maxlength="4"
value="100">
ScreenY:    <input type="text" name="screenY" id="screenY" size="4" maxlength="4"
value="100"> (Netscape)<br>
<h2>Display Features</h2>
Always Lowered: <input type="checkbox" name="alwaysLowered" id="alwaysLowered">
Always Raised: <input type="checkbox" name="alwaysRaised" id="alwaysRaised">
Dependent: <input type="checkbox" name="dependent" id="dependent">
Directories: <input type="checkbox" name="directories" id="directories">
Hotkeys: <input type="checkbox" name="hotkeys" id="hotkeys">
Location: <input type="checkbox" name="location" id="location">
Menubar: <input type="checkbox" name="menubar" id="menubar"><br>
Resizable: <input type="checkbox" name="resizable" id="resizable">
Scrollbars: <input type="checkbox" name="scrollbars" id="scrollbars">
Titlebar: <input type="checkbox" name="titlebar" id="titlebar">
Toolbar: <input type="checkbox" name="toolbar" id="toolbar">
Z-Lock: <input type="checkbox" name="z-lock" id="z-lock">
<br><br>
<input type="button" value="Create Window" onclick="openWindow()">
<input type="button" value="Close Window" onclick="closeWindow()">
<br><br>
<hr>
<h2>JavaScript Window.open Statement</h2>
<textarea name="jscode" id="jscode" rows="4" cols="80"></textarea>
</form>
</body>
</html>
```

Writing to Windows

Up to now, all the examples with windows have used an existing document: either a remote URL like **http://www.yahoo.com** or a local file like "example.htm" to load into the newly created window. We can actually write to windows once they are created either by using the standard **document.write()** method or potentially by manipulating the window with DOM methods. Consider the script here:

```
var myWindow = open('','mywin','height=300,width=300');
myWindow.document.write('Hi there. ');
myWindow.document.write('This is my new window');
myWindow.document.close();
myWindow.focus();
```

which creates a simple window with a sentence of text in it, as shown in Figure 12-1.

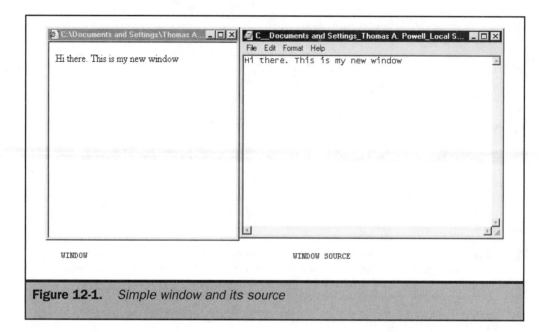

Figure 12-1. *Simple window and its source*

Writing out HTML to the newly created window dynamically is, of course, possible, so you could use something like

```
myWindow.document.writeln("<html><head><title>fun</title></head><body>");
myWindow.document.writeln("<h1>Hi from JavaScript</h1></body></html>");
```

just as easily for your **document.writeln()** statements. The next window creation example shows how the previous "Guru" example implemented with the **alert()** method could be modified to support more customized windows. It is no stretch to create your own form of alerts or other dialogs in a similar fashion, though setting the dialog to be truly modal would take some extra manipulation. (See the section entitled "Window Extensions" later in this chapter for more information.)

```
<!DOCTYPE HTML PUBLIC "-//W3C//DTD HTML 4.01 Transitional//EN"
  "http://www.w3.org/TR/html4/loose.dtd">
<html>
<head>
<title>Guru 1.1</title>
<script language="JavaScript" type="text/javascript">
<!--
```

```
function customAlert(title,message)
{
  var guruWindow=window.open("","","width=300,height=200");
  if (guruWindow != null)
  {
  var windowHTML= "<html><head><title>"+title+"</title></head>";
  windowHTML += "<body bgcolor='black' text='yellow'><h1 align='center'>"
  windowHTML += message + "</h1><hr><center><form>";
  windowHTML += "<input type='button' value='CLOSE' onclick='self.close()'>"
  windowHTML += "</form></center></body></html>";
  guruWindow.document.write(windowHTML);
  guruWindow.focus();
  return;
  }
}
function askGuru()
{
  var question = prompt("What is your question o' seeker of knowledge?","")
  if (question != null)
    {
     if (question == "")
      customAlert("Angry Guru", "You insult me!");
     else
      customAlert("Angry Guru", "Don't waste my time.");
    }
}
//  -->
</script>
</head>
<body>
<div align="center">
<h1>JavaScript Guru 1.1</h1>
<hr>
<form>
<input type="button" value="Ask the Guru" onClick="askGuru()">
</form>
</div>
</body>
</html>
```

The last example would, of course, be useful only to write content to a document as it loaded. However, we can easily use proprietary **Document** objects like **document.all** or the more standard DOM methods to modify windows after load time, as briefly demonstrated in the next section.

DOM Methods and Windows

Traditional document object models require writing dynamic content to the page as it loads. With DOM capabilities we can insert or change HTML in the document at will. The main difference is that you must make sure to use the new window's name when accessing a DOM method or property. For example, if you had a window called *newWindow,* you would use statements like

```
var currentElement = newWindow.document.getElementById("myheading");
```

to retrieve a particular element in the other window. The following simple example shows how information entered in one window can be used to create an element in another window:

```
<!DOCTYPE HTML PUBLIC "-//W3C//DTD HTML 4.01 Transitional//EN"
"http://www.w3.org/TR/html4/loose.dtd">
<html>
<head>
<title>DOM Window Add</title>
<script language="JavaScript" type="text/javascript">
<!--
function domWindowAdd()
{
  var currentElement;
  if ((window.myWindow)  && (myWindow.closed == false))
   {
     var str = document.testForm.textToAdd.value;
     var theString = myWindow.document.createTextNode(str);
     var theBreak = myWindow.document.createElement("BR");

     currentElement = myWindow.document.getElementById('heading1');
     currentElement.appendChild(theString);
     currentElement.appendChild(theBreak);

     myWindow.focus();
   }
}

// Make the window to add to
var myWindow = open('','mywin','height=300,width=300');
myWindow.document.writeln("<html><head><title>fun</title></head><body>");
myWindow.document.writeln("<h1 id='heading1'>Hi from
JavaScript</h1></body></html>");
myWindow.document.close();
myWindow.focus();
// -->
```

```
</script>
</head>
<body>
<h1>DOM Window Interaction</h1>
<form name="testForm" id="testForm">
    <input type="text" name="textToAdd" id="textToAdd" size="30">
    <input type="button" value="Add Text" onclick="domWindowAdd()">
</form>
</body>
</html>
```

This example is simply a reminder of the use of these techniques. See Chapter 10 for a more complete discussion of document manipulation with DOM methods. Before moving on to the methods and events associated with windows, we need to cover one last detail on how windows interact with each other.

Inter-Window Communication Details

For applications that have multiple windows launched, it is especially important to understand the basics of communicating between windows. Normally, we access the methods and properties of the primary window using the object instance named simply *window,* or we even omit the reference. However, if we want to access another window, we could use the name of that window. For example, given a window named "mywindow," we would access its document object using *mywindow.document*. The key to communication between windows is knowing the name of the window and then using that in place of the generic object reference *window*. Of course, there is the important question of how you reference the main window from a created window. The primary way is using the **window.opener** property that references the **Window** object that created the current window. The simple example here shows how one window creates another and each is capable of setting the background color of the other.

```
<!DOCTYPE HTML PUBLIC "-//W3C//DTD HTML 4.01 Transitional//EN"
        "http://www.w3.org/TR/html4/loose.dtd">
<html>
<head>
<title>Window Tester</title>
<script language="JavaScript" type="text/javascript">
<!--
function createWindow()
{
  secondwindow = window.open('','example','height=300,width=200,scrollbars=yes');
  if (secondwindow != null)
    {
```

```
        var windowHTML= "<html><head><title>Second Window</title></head>";
          windowHTML += "<body><h1 align='center'>";
          windowHTML += "Another window!</h1><hr><center><form>";
          windowHTML += "<input type='button' value='Set main red'
onclick='window.opener.document.bgColor=\"red\"'>";
          windowHTML += "<br><input type='button' value='CLOSE'
onclick='self.close()'>";
          windowHTML += "</form></center></body></html>";
          secondwindow.document.write(windowHTML);
          secondwindow.focus();
      }
}
// -->
</script>
</head>
<body>
<form>
<input type="button" value="new window" onclick="createWindow()">
<input type="button" value="set red" onclick="if (window.secondwindow)
{secondwindow.document.bgColor='red';secondwindow.focus();}">
</form>
</body>
</html>
```

Controlling Windows

As we have seen so far, it is easy enough to open and close windows as well as write content to them. There are numerous other ways to control windows; for example, it is possible to bring a window into focus using the **window.focus()** method. Conversely, it is also possible to do the opposite using the **window.blur()** method. This section will demonstrate a few other common window manipulation methods for moving, resizing, and scrolling windows.

Moving Windows

Moving windows around the screen is possible using two different methods: the **window.moveBy()** and **window.moveTo()** methods. The **window.moveBy()** method moves a window a specified number of pixels and has a syntax of

```
windowname.moveBy(horizontalpixels, verticalpixels)
```

where

- *windowname* is the name of the window to move.

■ *horizontalpixels* is the number of horizontal pixels to move the window, where positive numbers move the window to the right and negative numbers to the left.

■ *verticalpixels* is the number of vertical pixels to move the window, where positive numbers moves the window down and negative numbers up.

As an example, given that a window called *myWindow* exists,

```
myWindow.moveBy(100,100);
```

would move the window down 100 pixels and to the right 100 pixels.

If you have a particular position in the screen in mind to move a window to, it is probably better to use the **window.moveTo()** method, which will move a window to a particular x/y coordinate on the screen. The syntax of this method is

windowname.moveTo(*x-coord, y-coord*)

where

■ *windowname* is the name of the window to move.

■ *x-coord* is the screen coordinate on the x-axis to move the window to.

■ *y-coord* is the screen coordinate on the y-axis to move the window to.

So, given the window called *myWindow* is on the screen, the statement

```
myWindow.moveTo(1,1);
```

would move the window to the upper left of the screen.

Resizing Windows

In JavaScript the methods for resizing windows are very similar to the ones for moving them. The method **window.resizeBy(*horizontal, vertical*)** resizes a window by the values given in *horizontal* and *vertical*. Negative values make the window smaller, while positive values make it bigger, as shown by the examples here:

```
myWindow.resizeBy(10,10);   // makes the window 10 pixels taller and wider
myWindow.resizeBy(-100,0);  // makes the window 100 pixels narrower
```

Similar to the **moveTo()** method, **window.resizeTo(*width, height*)** resizes the window to the specified width and height indicated.

```
myWindow.resizeTo(100,100); // make window 100x100
myWindow.resizeTo(500,100); // make window 500x100
```

 Note *In well-behaved JavaScript implementations, it is not possible to resize windows to a very small size, say 1x1 pixels. Such small windows could be used to continuously generate pop-up advertisements or other annoyances without permitting the user the ability to close them.*

Scrolling Windows

Similar to resizing and moving, the **Window** object supports the **scrollBy()** and **scrollTo()** methods, which, respectively, scroll a window *by* a certain number of pixels and *to* a particular pixel location. The following simple examples illustrate how these methods might be used on some window called *myWindow:*

```
myWindow.scrollBy(10,0); // scroll 10 pixels to the right
myWindow.scrollBy(-10,0); // scroll 10 pixels to the left
myWindow.scrollBy(100,100);  // scroll 100 pixels to the right and down
myWindow.scrollTo(1,1); // scroll to 1,1 the origin
myWindow.scrollTo(100,100); // scroll to 100, 100
```

Besides the **scrollTo()** and **scrollBy()** methods, an older method called simply **scroll()** is often used. While this method is supposed to be deprecated, many programmers still use it. The syntax itself is identical to the **scrollBy()** method. The complete syntax for this method can be found in Appendix B.

A complete example presented here can be used to experiment with the various common **Window** methods that we have encountered in this chapter:

```
<!DOCTYPE HTML PUBLIC "-//W3C//DTD HTML 4.01 Transitional//EN"
 "http://www.w3.org/TR/html4/loose.dtd">
<html>
<head>
<title>Common Window Methods</title>
<script language="JavaScript" type="text/javascript">
<!--
var myWindow;
function openIt()
{
 myWindow = open('','mywin','height=300,width=300,scrollbars=yes');
 myWindow.document.writeln("<html><head><title>fun</title></head><body>");
 myWindow.document.writeln("<table bgcolor='#ffcc66' border='1'
 width='600'><tr><td>");
 myWindow.document.writeln("<h1>JavaScript Window
 Methods</h1><br><br><br><br><br><br><br><br><br><br>");
 myWindow.document.writeln("</tr></td></table></body></html>");
 myWindow.document.close();
 myWindow.focus();
}

function moveIt()
```

```
{
 if ((window.myWindow) && (myWindow.closed == false))
    myWindow.moveTo(document.testform.moveX.value,
                 document.testform.moveY.value);
}

function scrollIt()
{
 if ((window.myWindow) && (myWindow.closed == false)) myWindow.scrollTo
 (document.testform.scrollX.value,
 document.testform.scrollY.value);
}

function resizeIt()
{
 if ((window.myWindow) && (myWindow.closed == false))
    myWindow.resizeTo(document.testform.resizeX.value,
document.testform.resizeY.value);
}
// -->
</script>
</head>
<body onload="openIt()">
<h1 align="center">Window Methods Tester</h1>
<hr>
<form name="testform" id="testform">
<input type="button" value="Open Window" onclick="openIt()">
<input type="button" value="Close Window" onclick="myWindow.close()">
<input type="button" value="Focus Window" onclick="if (myWindow)myWindow.focus()">
<input type="button" value="Blur Window" onclick="if (myWindow)
myWindow.blur()">
<br><br>
<input type="button" value="Move Up" onclick="if (myWindow) myWindow.moveBy(0,-10)">
<input type="button" value="Move Left" onclick="if (myWindow)
myWindow.moveBy(-10,0)">
<input type="button" value="Move Right" onclick="if (myWindow)
myWindow.moveBy(10,0)">
<input type="button" value="Move Down" onclick="if (myWindow)
myWindow.moveBy(0,10)"><br>

X: <input type="text" size="4" name="moveX" id="moveX" value="0">
Y: <input type="text" size="4" name="moveY" id="moveY" value="0">
<input type="button" value="Move To" onclick="moveIt()">
<br><br>
<input type="button" value="Scroll Up" onclick="if (myWindow)
myWindow.scrollBy(0,-10)">
<input type="button" value="Scroll Left" onclick="if (myWindow)
myWindow.scrollBy(-10,0)">
<input type="button" value="Scroll Right" onclick="if (myWindow)
myWindow.scrollBy(10,0)">
<input type="button" value="Scroll Down" onclick="if (myWindow)
```

```
myWindow.scrollBy(0,10)"><br>

X: <input type="text" size="4" name="scrollX" id="scrollX" value="0">
Y: <input type="text" size="4" name="scrollY" id="scrollY" value="0">
<input type="button" value="Scroll To" onclick="scrollIt()">
<br><br>
<input type="button" value="Resize Up" onclick="if (myWindow)
myWindow.resizeBy(0,-10)">
<input type="button" value="Resize Left" onclick="if (myWindow)
myWindow.resizeBy(-10,0)">
<input type="button" value="Resize Right" onclick="if (myWindow)
myWindow.resizeBy(10,0)">
<input type="button" value="Resize Down" onclick="if (myWindow)
myWindow.resizeBy(0,10)"><br>
X: <input type="text" size="4" name="resizeX" id="resizeX" value="0">
Y: <input type="text" size="4" name="resizeY" id="resizeY" value="0">
<input type="button" value="Resize To" onclick="resizeIt()">
<br><br>
</form>
</body>
</html>
```

Window Events

The **Window** object supports many events; unfortunately, many of these are proprietary. The safe cross-browser window events include **onblur**, **onerror**, **onfocus**, **onload**, **onunload**, and **onresize** and are detailed in Table 12-2.

Event	Description
onblur	Fires when the window loses focus.
onerror	Rudimentary error handling event fired when a JavaScript error occurs.
onfocus	Fires when the window gains focus.
onload	Fires when the document is completely loaded into the window. *Warning*: Timing of this event is not always exact.
onresize	Event triggered as user resizes the window.
onunload	Triggered when the document is unloaded, such as when following an outside link or closing the window.

Table 12-2. *Common Window Events*

Adding window event handlers can be set through HTML event attributes on the **<body>** element:

```
<body onload="alert('entering window');" onunload="alert('leaving window')">
```

or by registering events through the **Window** object.

```
function sayHi() { alert('hi'); }
function sayBye() { alert('bye'); }
window.onload = sayHi;
window.onunload = sayBye;
```

Internet Explorer and Netscape add numerous events to the **Window** object. A few of the more useful ones are detailed in Table 12-3. A complete listing can be found in Appendix B.

Frames: A Special Case of Windows

A common misunderstanding among Web developers concerns the relationship between frames and windows. From the perspective of HTML and JavaScript, each frame shown on screen is a window that can be manipulated. In fact, when a browser window contains multiple frames, it is possible to access each of the separate window objects through **window.frames[ ]**, which is an array of the individual frames in the

Event	Description
onafterprint	Event triggered after the window is printed.
onbeforeprint	Fires just before the window is printed or print previewed.
onbeforeunload	The event is triggered just before the window unloads. Should happen before the **onunload** event.
ondragdrop	Is triggered when a document is dragged onto a window (Netscape only).
onhelp	Fired when the Help key, generally F1, is pressed.
onresizeend	Fires when the resize process ends; usually the user has stopped dragging the corner of a window.
onresizestart	Fires when the resize process begins; usually the user has started dragging the corner of a window.
onscroll	Fired when the window is scrolled either direction.

Table 12-3. *Useful Extended Window Events*

Window Property	Description
frames[ ]	An array of all the frame objects contained by the current window.
length	The number of frames in the window (should be the same value as **window.frames.length**).
name	The current name of the window. This is both readable and settable since JavaScript 1.1.
parent	A reference to the parent window.
self	A reference to the current window.
top	A reference to the top window. Often the top and the parent will be one and the same—not if **<frame>** elements load documents containing more frames.
window	Another reference to the current window.

Table 12-4. *Common Window Properties Related to Frames*

window. The basic properties useful for manipulating frames are detailed in Table 12-4; notice how many of them are related to the reserved frame names used in HTML.

The major challenge using frames and JavaScript is to keep the names and relationships between frames clear, so that references between frames are formed correctly. Consider a document called **frames.htm** with the following markup:

```
<!DOCTYPE HTML PUBLIC "-//W3C//DTD HTML 4.01 Frameset//EN"
    "http://www.w3.org/TR/html4/frameset.dtd">
<html>
<head>
<title>FrameSet Test</title>
</head>
<frameset rows="33%,*,33%">
      <frame src="framerelationship.htm" name="frame1" id="frame1">
      <frame src="moreframes.htm" name="frame2" id="frame2">
      <frame src="framerelationship.htm" name="frame5" id="frame5">
</frameset>
</html>
```

In this case the window containing this document is considered the parent of the three frames (frame1, frame2, and frame5). While you might expect to use a value like

```
window.frames.length
```

to determine the number of frames in the window, you will probably have to run the script from within a child frame; thus, you would actually use

```
window.parent.frames.length
```

or just

```
parent.frames.length
```

The **parent** property allows a window to determine the parent window. We could also use the **top** property that provides us a handle to the top window that contains all others. This would be written

```
top.frames.length.
```

You do need to be careful, though: unless you have nested frames, the parent and top may actually be one and the same.

To access a particular frame we can use both its name and its position in the array; so

```
parent.frames[0].name
```

would print out the name of the first frame, which in our case is "frame1." We could also access the frame from another child frame using the associate array aspect of an object collection:

```
parent.frame1
```

or even

```
parent.frames["frame1"]
```

Remember that a frame contains a window, so you can use all the **Window** and **Document** methods on what it contains.

The next example shows the way frame names are related to each other. There are three files that are required for this example: two framesets (frames.htm and moreframes.htm) and a document (framerelationship.htm) that contains a script that prints out the self, parent, and top relationships of frames.

Filename: frames.htm

```
<!DOCTYPE HTML PUBLIC "-//W3C//DTD HTML 4.01 Frameset//EN"
"http://www.w3.org/TR/html4/frameset.dtd">
<html>
<head>
<title>FrameSet Test</title>
</head>
<frameset rows="33%,*,33%">
      <frame src="framerelationship.htm" name="frame1" id="frame1">
      <frame src="moreframes.htm" name="frame2" id="frame2">
      <frame src="framerelationship.htm" name="frame5" id="frame5">
</frameset>
</html>
```

Filename: moreframes.htm

```
<!DOCTYPE HTML PUBLIC "-//W3C//DTD HTML 4.01 Frameset//EN"
   "http://www.w3.org/TR/html4/frameset.dtd">
<html>
<head>
<title>More Frames</title>
</head>
<frameset cols="50%,50%">
            <frame src="framerelationship.htm" name="frame3" id="frame3">
            <frame src="framerelationship.htm" name="frame4" id="frame4">
</frameset>
</html>
```

Filename: framerelationship.htm

```
<!DOCTYPE HTML PUBLIC "-//W3C//DTD HTML 4.01 Transitional//EN"
        "http://www.w3.org/TR/html4/loose.dtd">
<html>
<head>
<title>Frame Relationship Viewer</title>
</head>
<body>
<script language="JavaScript" type="text/javascript">
<!--
   var msg="";
   var i = 0;
   msg += "<h2>Window: "+ window.name + "</h2><hr>";
   if (self.frames.length > 0)
     {
         msg += "self.frames.length = " + self.frames.length + "<br>"
```

```
            for (i=0; i < self.frames.length; i++)
               msg += "self.frames["+i+"].name = "+ self.frames[i].name + "<br>";
     }
   else
         msg += "Current window has no frames directly within it<br>";
   msg+="<br>";
   if (parent.frames.length > 0)
     {
        msg += "parent.frames.length = " + parent.frames.length + "<br>"
        for (i=0; i < parent.frames.length; i++)
           msg += "parent.frames["+i+"].name = "+ parent.frames[i].name + "<br>";
     }
   msg+="<br>";
   if (top.frames.length > 0)
     {
        msg += "top.frames.length = " + top.frames.length + "<BR>"
        for (i=0; i < top.frames.length; i++)
           msg += "top.frames["+i+"].name = "+ top.frames[i].name + "<br>";
   }

   document.write(msg);
// -->
</script>
</body>
</html>
```

The relationships you should see using these example files are shown in Figure 12-2.

State Management with Frames

One aspect of frames that can be very useful is the ability to save a variable state across multiple page views. As we saw with windows, it is possible to access the variable space of one window from another; the same holds for frames. Using a special type of frameset, in which a small frame that is hard for a user to notice is used, we can create a space to hold variables across page loads. Consider for example, the frameset in the file stateframes.htm, shown here.

Filename: stateframes.htm

```
<!DOCTYPE HTML PUBLIC "-//W3C//DTD HTML 4.01 Frameset//EN"
"http://www.w3.org/TR/html4/frameset.dtd">
<html>
<head>
<title>State Preserve Frameset</title>
</head>
<frameset rows="99%,*" frameborder="0">
```

```
        <frame src="mainframe.htm" name="frame1" id="frame1" frameborder="0">
        <frame src="stateframe.htm" name="stateframe" id="stateframe"
               frameborder="0" scrolling="no" noresize>
</frameset>
</html>
```

In this case, we have a very small frame called *stateframe* that will be used to save variables across page loads. The contents of mainframe.htm, mainframe2.htm, and stateframe.htm are shown here. Notice how by referencing the *parent* frame we are able to access the hidden frame's variable *username* on any page.

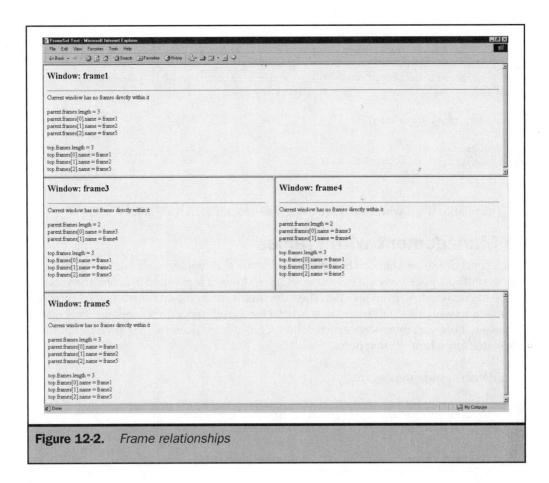

Figure 12-2. *Frame relationships*

Filename: stateframe.htm

```
<!DOCTYPE HTML PUBLIC "-//W3C//DTD HTML 4.01 Transitional//EN"
        "http://www.w3.org/TR/html4/loose.dtd">
<html>
<head><title>Variables</title></head>
<body>
<script language="JavaScript" type="text/javascript">
<!--
var username = "";
// -->
</script>
</body>
</html>
```

Filename: mainframe.htm

```
<!DOCTYPE HTML PUBLIC "-//W3C//DTD HTML 4.01 Transitional//EN"
        "http://www.w3.org/TR/html4/loose.dtd">
<html>
<head>
<title>State Preserve 1</title>
</head>
<body onload="document.testform.username.value = parent.stateframe.username">
<h1 align="center">JS State Preserve</h1>
<form name="testform" id="testform">
<input type="text" name="username" id="username" value="" size="30"
maxlength="60">
<input type="button" value="Save Value"
onclick="parent.stateframe.username
= document.testform.username.value;">
</form>
<div align="center">
    <a href="mainframe2.htm">Next page</a>
</div>
</body>
</html>
```

Filename: mainframe2.htm

```
<!DOCTYPE HTML PUBLIC "-//W3C//DTD HTML 4.01 Transitional//EN"
        "http://www.w3.org/TR/html4/loose.dtd">
<html>
```

```
<head>
<title>State Preserve 2</title>
</head>
<body>
<script language="JavaScript" type="text/javascript">
<!--
if (!(parent.stateframe.username) || (parent.stateframe.username == ""))
  document.write("<h1 align='center'>Sorry we haven't met before</h1>");
else
  document.write("<h1 align='center'>Welcome to the page
"+parent.stateframe.username+"!</h1>");
// -->
</script>
<div align="center">
   <a href="mainframe.htm">Back to previous page</a>
</div>
</body>
</html>
```

While JavaScript can be used to preserve state information and even create something as powerful as a shopping cart, it is not a good idea to use it in this fashion unless you make sure to address script being turned off mid-visit. Also, you may find the easy accessibility of script code a little too open for performing such an important task as preserving state information across pages. Until client-side scripting facilities become more robust, Web programmers probably should rely on traditional state management mechanisms, such as hidden form data, extended URL information, and cookies to maintain state between pages in a site.

Solving Frame Problems: Frame Busting and Building

While frames can be very useful, particularly for state management in JavaScript, they also can cause Web designers significant problems. For example, some sites will put frames around all outbound links, taking away valuable screen real estate. Often site designers will employ a technique called "frame busting" to destroy any enclosing frameset their page may be enclosed within. Doing this is very easy: the following script sets the topmost frame's current location to the value of the page that should not be framed.

```
<script language="JavaScript" type="text/javascript">
<!--
function frameBuster()
{
     if (window != top)
            top.location.href = location.href;
}
window.onload = frameBuster;
```

```
// -->
</script>
```

A related problem to the one solved by frame busting is that of framed windows being displayed outside of their framing context. This occasionally happens when users bookmark a piece of a frameset or launch a link from a frameset into a new window. The basic idea would be to make sure all framed documents were inside of frames by looking at each window's **Location** object, and, if they were not, to dynamically rebuild the frameset document. The script for accomplishing this depends somewhat on the type of frameset employed, so a specific example will not be presented here. However, an example can be found online at the JavaScript Reference Support site (**http://www.javascriptref.com/**).

Window Extensions

Given that the **Window** object is of central importance and really doesn't fall completely under any one standard—DOM or JavaScript—numerous extensions to the object have been made. Most of these are so new and proprietary that they have yet to be adopted by the Web community at large. Some designers have discovered the interesting possibility of creating chromeless windows under IE, and a few have begun to create modal and full-screen windows. This section presents an overview of some of the more useful window extensions made in the two browsers.

IE Window Extensions: Modal, Modeless, and Pop-up Windows

Internet Explorer supports a few special types of windows. The first is the modal window. Like a standard dialog, this more generic window is modal to the page and must be dismissed before moving on. The basic syntax to create a modal dialog is

```
window.showModalDialog(URL of dialog, arguments, features);
```

where

- *"URL of dialog"* is a string containing the URL of the document to display in the dialog.

- *arguments* are any objects or values you wish to pass the modal dialog.

- *features* is a semicolon-separated list of display features for the dialog.

A simple example is shown here:

```
window.showModalDialog("customdialog.htm",window,"dialogHeight: 150px;
dialogWidth: 300px; center: Yes; help: No; resizable: No; status: No;");
```

The **showModalDialog()** method also returns a value. This value can be set in the dialog document by setting that document's **window.returnValue** property. This value will be returned automatically when the dialog has been addressed by the user. This feature allows for the simple creation of **prompt()-** and **confirm()-**style dialogs, which must return a value.

A modeless window is very different from a modal dialog. A modeless window always stays in front of the window that it was created from, even when that window gains focus. A common use is to display Help or other contextually useful information. However, while different in function, a modeless window is syntactically similar to the modal dialog:

```
windowreference = window.showModelessDialog(URL of dialog, arguments, features)
```

A simple example of the syntax to create a modeless window is shown here.

```
myWindow = window.showModelessDialog("customdialog.htm",window,"dialogHeight:
150px; dialogWidth: 300px; center: Yes; help: No; resizable: No; status: No;")
```

The last type of special window form supported by Microsoft is a generic form of pop-up window. Creating a pop-up is very simple: just use the **window.createPopup()**, which takes no arguments and returns a handle to the newly created window.

```
var myPopup = window.createPopup();
```

These windows are created in a hidden state. They are later revealed using the pop-up object's **show()** method and hidden using **hide()**, as shown here.

```
myPopup.show(); // displays created popup
myPopup.hide(); // hides the popup
```

The value of Microsoft's special pop-ups may not be obvious until you consider that you have complete control over their appearance, allowing even the removal of the chrome of the displayed window.

A complete example showing how all these Microsoft-specific windows can be used is shown here.

```
<!DOCTYPE HTML PUBLIC "-//W3C//DTD HTML 4.01 Transitional//EN"
        "http://www.w3.org/TR/html4/loose.dtd">
<head>
<html>
<head>
<title>Special IE Windows</title>
```

```
<script language="JSCRIPT">
<!--
var myPopup = window.createPopup();
function showPopup()
{
    var popupBody = myPopup.document.body;
    popupBody.style.backgroundColor = "#ffff99";
    popupBody.style.border = "solid black 1px";
    popupBody.innerHTML = "Click outside this window to close or press hide
button.";
    myPopup.show(50, 100, 350, 25, document.body);
}

var returnedvalue = "";
function makeModalDialog()
{
 returnedvalue
 =showModalDialog("dialog.htm",window,"status:false;dialogWidth:300px;
 dialogHeight:100px;help:no;status:no;");
 alert(returnedvalue);
}
function makeModelessDialog()
{
 var HTMLoutput = "";

 myModelessDialog =
 showModelessDialog("blank.htm",window,"status:false;dialogWidth:200px;
 dialogHeight:300px;help:no;status:no;");
 modelessBody = myModelessDialog.document.body;
 modelessBody.style.backgroundColor = "#ffcc33"

 HTMLoutput += "<html><head><title>Modeless Dialog</title></head>";
 HTMLoutput += "<body><h1>Important messages in this modeless window</h1><hr>";
 HTMLoutput += "<form><div align='center'><input type='button' value='close'
 onclick='self.close()'>";
 HTMLoutput +="</div></form></body></html>";

 modelessBody.innerHTML = HTMLoutput;
}
// -->
</script>
</head>
<body>
<form name="mainform" id="mainform">
Modal Set Message: <input type="text" id="message" name="message" size="40"
value=""><br>
<input type="button" value="Modal Dialog" onclick="makeModalDialog()">
<input type="button" value="Modeless Dialog" onclick="makeModelessDialog()">
<input type="button" value="Show Popup" onclick="showPopup()">
```

USING JAVASCRIPT

```
<input type="button" value="Hide Popup" onclick="myPopup.hide()">
</form>
</body>
</html>
```

Interested readers are encouraged to visit **http://msdn.microsoft.com** for the latest information on Microsoft extensions to the **Window** object.

Full-Screen Windows

Creating a window that fills up the screen and even removes browser chrome is possible in many browsers. It is possible under 4.x generation browsers and beyond to figure out the current screen size and then create a new window that fits most or all of the available area. In the case of Netscape you may have difficulty covering the entire window because of the way the height and width of the screen are calculated. However, the script presented here should work to fill up the screen in both browsers:

```
<script language="JavaScript1.2" type="text/javascript">
<!--
newwindow=window.open('http://www.yahoo.com','main','height='+screen.height-
2+',width='+screen.width-2+',outerHeight=' + screen.availHeight + ',outerWidth=' +
screen.availWidth+'screenX=0,screenY=0,left=0,top=0,resizable=no');
// -->
</script>
```

The previous "poor man's" script *does* keep the browser chrome and may not *quite* fill up the window. It is possible under 4.x generation browsers to go into a full-screen mode that completely fills the screen. In Internet Explorer it is quite easy and can be done using a JavaScript statement like

```
newWindow=window.open('http://www.yahoo.com', 'main','fullscreen=yes');
```

However, Netscape needs a much more complicated script and will even prompt the user if a security privilege should be granted to go full-screen. A script that works in both browsers is shown here:

```
<script language="JavaScript1.2" type="text/javascript">
<!--
 if (document.layers)
 {
 netscape.security.PrivilegeManager.enablePrivilege('UniversalBrowserWrite');
 window.open('http://www.yahoo.com','newwin','titlebar=no,width=' +
 window.screen.availWidth+',height='+window.screen.availWidth+',screenX=0,screenY=0'
 }
```

```
   else if (document.all) {
      window.open('http://www.yahoo.com', 'newwin', 'fullscreen=yes');
   }
// -->
</script>
```

Note *It is important to remember that many users will not know how to get out of full-screen mode. The key combination* **ALT+F4** *should do the trick on a Windows system. However, users may not know this, so you should provide a Close button or instructions of how to get out of full-screen mode.*

Netscape Window Extensions: Simulating the Browser

While Netscape does not offer quite as many **Window** extensions, it does provide some methods that allow JavaScript programs to simulate various browser activities, such as pressing a particular button. It is even possible to move a window or size a window a certain way. Most of these methods are implemented only in Netscape 4.x, and there is spotty support under 6.x. However, the very useful **window.print()** method has a fair degree of cross-browser support. The next example demonstrates the common browser-button–related **Window** methods:

```
<!DOCTYPE HTML PUBLIC "-//W3C//DTD HTML 4.01 Transitional//EN"
"http://www.w3.org/TR/html4/loose.dtd">
<html>
<head>
<title>Browser Methods</title>
</head>
<body>
<!-- Except for window.print() these will probably not work in IE -->
<h1 align="center">Browser Button Simulator</h1>
<hr>
<form>
<input type="button" value="FIND" onclick="window.find()">
  
<input type="button" value="PRINT" onclick="window.print()">
  
<input type="button" value="FORWARD" onclick="window.forward()">
  
<input type="button" value="BACK" onclick="window.back()">
  
<input type="button" value="HOME" onclick="window.home()">
</form>
</body>
</html>
```

Summary

The **Window** object is probably the most important object in JavaScript beyond the **Document** itself. By using this object you can create and destroy general windows as well as a variety of special purpose windows, such as dialog boxes. It is also possible to manipulate the characteristics of windows using JavaScript and even have windows control each other. The key to all of this is correct naming, for once a window has been found, it can be manipulated with any of the common **Document** methods. Frames were shown to be a special form of window object, and in their case, correct usage was also very much related to naming. While the **Window** object is common to all JavaScript- aware browsers, it also has the most inconsistencies. Many of the new **Window** properties and methods introduced by Microsoft will likely become standard, but for now programmers should be cautious in using them. The next chapter returns to the contents of windows and discusses both traditional and DOM-oriented document manipulation.

The Complete Reference

Chapter 13

Handling Documents

This chapter explores the use of the **Document** object, which can be used to manipulate the HTML document within a window or frame. We begin by studying the **Document** object facilities common to all browsers, as defined in Netscape 2 and 3, such as color properties, **anchors[ ]**, **links[ ]**, and basic methods like **document.write()**. We continue with a discussion of the proprietary features added by the 4.x generation of browsers, including the ability to manipulate arbitrary HTML elements. The chapter concludes with a return to the standard Document Object Model by presenting how common HTML tags can be created and manipulated with DOM facilities supported by modern browsers. A special emphasis is placed on table objects that require careful planning and manipulation. The collections introduced in this chapter, such as **forms[ ]** and **images[ ]**, will be further explored in subsequent chapters.

Historic Document Object Properties

Under the traditional JavaScript object model supported in browsers like Netscape 3, very little of the HTML document within a window is available for manipulation. The primary properties of the **Document** object were related to the basic attributes of the HTML **<body>** tag, such as its background, link, and text colors. Some other basic properties included document modification time, title, and URL. Of course, within the **Document** object there were collections of various HTML elements included in the HTML document, such as anchors, forms, images, and links. Later, under the DOM, we are able to go beyond the predefined collections and access any HTML element. For now let's take a look at the **Document** properties that have historically been supported by all JavaScript-aware browsers.

Document Color

The traditional JavaScript object model supports numerous properties to read and set the color of the document and its text and links. The **Document** properties for accessing page color are shown in Table 13-1. Notice how these properties correspond to the HTML attributes for the **<body>** tag.

Document Object Property	Description
aLinkColor	The color of a link when it is active or pressed specified by <body alink="color"> or often by default red.
bgColor	The background color of the page specified by <body bgcolor="color">.

Table 13-1. *Document Properties Related to Color*

Document Object Property	Description
fgColor	The text color of the document specified by <body text="color">.
linkColor	The color of an unvisited link (when unspecified, usually blue) specified by <body link="color">.
vlinkColor	The visited link color specified by <body vlink="color">, which is by default purple or dark blue.

Table 13-1. *Document Properties Related to Color* (continued)

Of course, under modern HTML specifications, these attributes are deprecated in favor of CSS properties, so one might think that access to them via **Document** properties would be deprecated as well. In fact, while the DOM Level 1 does not support these properties directly, all JavaScript-aware browsers continue to support them and probably will do so for the foreseeable future. A complete example of the use of these color-related properties is presented here, with its rendering in Figure 13-1.

```
<!DOCTYPE HTML PUBLIC "-//W3C//DTD HTML 4.01 Transitional//EN"
        "http://www.w3.org/TR/html4/loose.dtd">
<html>
<head>
<title>Document Color Test</title>
<script language="JavaScript" type="text/javascript">
<!--
function setColors(form)
{
 with (form)
  {
    document.bgColor = backgroundColor.value;
    document.fgColor = textColor.value;
    document.alinkColor = activeLinkColor.value;
    document.linkColor = linkColor.value;
    document.vlinkColor = visitedLinkColor.value;
  }
}
```

```
// -->
</script>
</head>
<body bgcolor="red" text="black" link="blue" alink="yellow" vlink="purple">
<h2>Test Links</h2>
<a href="fakeURL.htm" onclick="return false">Unvisited Link</a><br>
<a href="#" onclick="return false">Click to show active color</a><br>
<a href="#">Visited link</a><br>
<form name="colors" id="colors">
<h2>Page Colors</h2>
Background Color:
<input type="text" name="backgroundColor" id="backgroundColor" value="red"><br>
Text Color:
<input type="text" name="textColor" id="textColor" value="black"><br>
<h2>Link Colors</h2>
Unvisited:
<input type="text" name="linkColor" id="linkColor" value="blue"><br>
Active:
<input type="text" name="activeLinkColor" id="activeLinkColor" value="yellow"><br>
Visited:
<input type="text" name="visitedLinkColor" id="visitedLinkColor" value="purple"><br>
<input type="button" value="set colors" onclick="setColors(this.form)"><br>
</form>
</body>
</html>
```

Note *You may wonder how to manipulate other **<body>** attributes such as **background**. This is left to the DOM or DHTML object models discussed later in the chapter.*

A common use of these properties is to modify color on the basis of user preference or time of day. For example, a page might display one color scheme in the morning and one in the night.

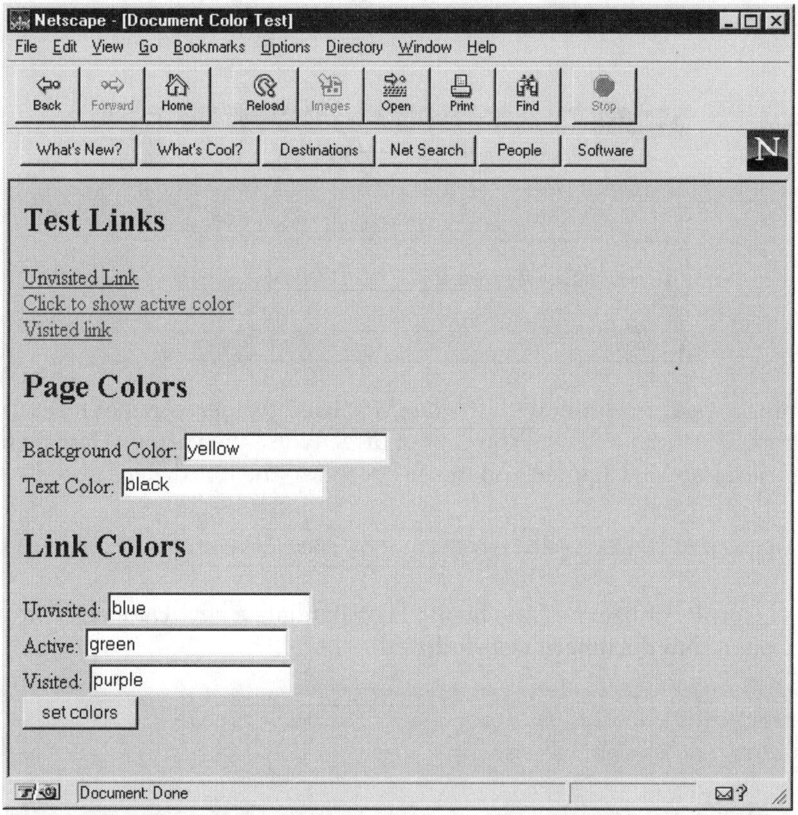

Figure 13-1.   *Rendering of background and color example under Netscape 3*

Last Modification Date

A very useful property of the **Document** object is **lastModified**. This property holds a
string containing the date and time that the document was last modified (saved). This
property can be useful to output the date on which a page was last modified:

```
<script language="JavaScript" type="text/javascript">
<!--
   document.writeln("Document Last Modified: " + document.lastModified);
```

```
//-->
</script>
```

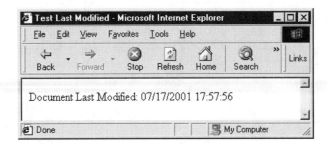

A common misconception with the **lastModified** property is that it returns a **Date** object; in fact, it returns a string. You cannot directly use the various **Date** methods and properties discussed in Chapter 7 on this property, so the following,

```
document.writeln("Last Modified Hour: " + document.lastModified.getHours());
```

throws an error. To utilize the **Date** methods, instantiate a new **Date** object from the string returned from **document.lastModified**:

```
var lastModObj = new Date(document.lastModified);
alert(lastModObj.getHours());
```

The last-modified date is, of course, read-only from the perspective of JavaScript.

Location and Related Properties

The **Document** object supports a few properties related to the location of the document and the HTTP referrer header, including: **document.location**, **document.URL**, and **document.referrer**. The **document.location** property under Netscape 2 is a read-only property holding a text string of the current URL of the document in the browser. Under later browsers from both vendors, **document.location** simply appears to be a pointer to the **window.location** object (discussed in Chapter 17). As a result, you can both read and set this value.

```
alert("Current location: " + document.location);
document.location = "http://www.yahoo.com";        // set new location
```

As a pointer to the actual **Location** object, the **document.location** property can be used to access the **Location** objects' properties, such as **pathname**, **protocol**, **port**, and so on.

```
alert("Current URL protocol: " + document.location.protocol);
// might return http or file
```

Cautious JavaScript developers will want to use the **Location** object directly with **window.location** rather than rely on this common mapping.

The **URL** property of the **Document** object holds a read-only string containing the URL for the current document. It is rarely used because of the availability of **window.location** and **document.location**.

The **referrer** property holds the URL of the referring document—in other words, the URL of the document that contained an activated link pointing to the current document. If there is no referring URL because a user typed in the URL directly or browsed to the file, this property will be blank. The **referrer** property cannot be set.

You may find when experimenting with **document.referrer** on a local system that you do not see a value even when a link is followed. The reason for this is that the HTTP protocol has to be used to reference the file to pass along a referring URL. Upload it to a server and access it using HTTP and you should see the expected result.

This just about does it for the **Document** object's properties—now what about the methods for the object?

Basic Document Methods

Historically the **Document** object supported five methods for controlling output to the document: **clear()**, **close()**, **open()**, **write()**, and **writeln()**. Throughout the book, we have used the **document.write( )** method to output strings to the document. Yet we really haven't used the others at all. Let's take a look at their features to understand why.

First let's address the difference between **document.write(***string***)** and **document.writeln(***string***)**. Both methods take strings and output the passed string to the document. The main difference is that the **writeln( )** method adds a new line character ("\n") to its output while the **write( )** method does not. However, under HTML return or newline characters are ignored (except within certain situations like the **<pre>** tag or within a **<textarea>**), so you may never notice the difference. The following code snippet uses a **<pre>** tag to show the difference between the methods:

```
<pre>
<script language="JavaScript" type="text/javascript">

document.write("This is a write notice it doesn't cause a return even in a pre
```

```
element");
document.writeln("This line will have a line break");
document.writeln("like so.");
document.write("You can always manually use a &lt;br&gt; element to output
<br>breaks to HTML");
</script>
</pre>
```

The result is shown here:

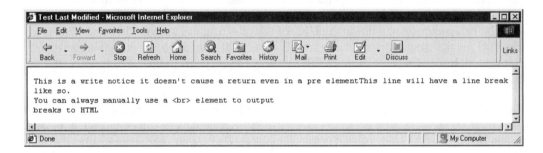

Using the **document.write()** and **writeln()** methods, we have gotten used to writing HTML to documents. However, it can be somewhat time consuming to write these method invocations for a large number of strings, so it is often better to build a string up and then output it all at once, like so:

```
<script language="JavaScript" type="text/javascript">
var str = "";
str += "This is a very long string.";
str += "It has entities like &copy; as well as <b>HTML</b> tags.";
str += "We can even include <pre> various special characters like";
str += "\t \t tabs or even newlines \n \n in our string</pre>";
str += "but remember the rules of HTML may override \t\t\n our efforts";
document.write(str);
</script>
```

It should seem obvious what **clear()**, **open()**, and **close()** do. By their names you would expect **clear()** to clear out the contents of a document and **open()** and **close()** to open and close a document for writing, respectively. The reality is that **document.clear()** is not supported in modern JavaScript browsers, and, in fact, the document is effectively closed for writing using **document.write()** once its output has been displayed. Thus, explicitly opening and closing the document doesn't really do much. However, you might find one use for them when creating content for a document in a new window, as demonstrated by the following simple example:

```
<script language="JavaScript" type="text/javascript">
var mywindow = window.open("","newwin", "height=300,width=300");
mywindow.document.open();
mywindow.document.write("<html><head><title>Test</title></head>");
mywindow.document.write("<body><h1>Hello!</h1></body></html>");
mywindow.document.close();

</script>
```

Note *This example is best tried by loading it over the Web. The reason is that opening a window with URL "" from JavaScript running in a document in the local file system will often show a directory listing rather than a blank document.*

Of course, as you might notice, the **document.open()** and **close()** aren't really required in the example at all! It is hoped that with the rise of a standardized DOM, such unused JavaScript peculiarities will fade away as everything becomes changeable. It might seem that, until this happens, little can be changed in an HTML document after load time. Surprisingly, what was provided under traditional JavaScript object models was quite useful.

Traditional HTML Element Access with Document

JavaScript 1.0 defined three collections of HTML elements for the **Document** object, **anchors[ ], forms[ ]** and **links[ ]**. Later, in browsers like Netscape 3 and Internet Explorer 4 collections like **applets[ ], embeds[ ], images[ ]**, and **plugins[ ]** were made available. Many of these features continue to be supported by the DOM Level 1, and even the ones that are not in the specification will probably continue to be supported by browsers, given their widespread use. Table 13-2 presents an overview of these collections.

Besides the common collections presented in Table 13-2, traditionally the **Document** object also has supported the **title** property, which holds the title of the document as specified by the **<title>** tag within the **<head>** element of an HTML document. Under traditional JavaScript, this property is a read-only string. However, under Internet Explorer 4 and greater as well as Netscape 6, you can set its value. Of course, using the DOM in these browsers you could easily find the **<title>** tag and manipulate it using standard DOM techniques.

Collection Name	Description	Browser Compatibility	DOM Support
anchors[ ]	A collection of all anchors as defined by **<a name="anchorname">...</a>**	Netscape 2+, Internet Explorer 3+	DOM Level 1
applets[ ]	All the Java Applets in the page as defined by the **<applet>** tag	Netscape 3+, Internet Explorer 4+	DOM Level 1
embeds[ ]	All the **<embed>** tags in the page	Netscape 3+, Internet Explorer 4+	No DOM Support
forms[ ]	All forms in a page as set by the **<form>** tag	Netscape 2+, Internet Explorer 3+	DOM Level 1
images[ ]	A collection of all images in the page indicated by the HTML **<img>** tag	Netscape 3+ and Internet Explorer 4+	DOM Level 1
links[ ]	The links in the page defined by tags of the form **<a href="linkdest">...</a>**	Netscape 2+ and Internet Explorer 3+	DOM Level 1
plugins[ ]	Under Internet Explorer, all the **<embed>** tags in the page (synonymous with **embeds[ ]**, the preferred collection) In Netscape, an array of **Plugin** objects representing the plug-ins installed in the browser.	Netscape 3+ and Internet Explorer 4+	No DOM support

Table 13-2.   *Traditional Document Collections*

document.anchors[ ] and document.links[ ]

The first HTML objects we examine in detail are links and anchors and have been accessible since the first versions of JavaScript. In HTML, an anchor is a link that is named—in other words, it serves as a destination for other links, for example to link to a particular part of the page using the "#*anchorname*" URL syntax. Anchors are defined with **<a name="*anchorname*">...</a>**. A link is also defined with the **<a>** tag but contains an **href** attribute setting a link destination—for example: **<a href="http:// www.yahoo.com">click me!</a>**. Of course, it should be evident that a link can be an anchor as well, since **<a name="yahoolink" href="http://www.yahoo.com">** is perfectly valid.

The **anchors[ ]** collection doesn't seem too useful in JavaScript, because you can access its *length* property only using **document.anchors.length**. Other than that, you really can't modify anything although you can read information about the document's anchors with this collection.

The **links[ ]** collection is only slightly more useful. As it is an array, we can of course access its length with **document.links.length**. However, we can also manipulate the URLs within the **href** attributes of each link. **Link** objects under most browsers will have the same properties as the **Location** object has, including: **hash, host, hostname, href, pathname, port, protocol**, and **search**. These properties correspond to the individual portions of a URL, except **href**, which contains the whole URL.

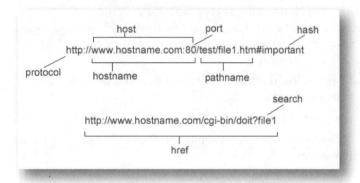

You also can read the **target** property of a link to see the name of the window or frame the link will load into. Also, under Netscape 4 you can read the enclosed text of a link using the **text** property.

The most useful aspect of the **link** property is that you can set the **href** property after the document loads, as shown in this small JavaScript snippet.

```
<a href="http://www.yahoo.com">Test Link</a>
<form>
<input type="button" value="change link"
onclick="document.links[0].href='http://www.google.com'">
</form>
```

JavaScript programmers should be able to dream up many useful applications for this settable property, such as making links act differently depending on user actions, the time of day, return visit, and so on.

 *The <area> tags that make up the links in a client-side image map are also included in a **links[ ]** collection.*

document.forms[ ]

The **forms[ ]** collection contains objects referencing all the **<form>** tags in a document. These can be referenced either numerically or by name. So, **document.forms[0]** would reference the first form in the document, while **document.forms['myform']** or **document.myform** would reference the form named "myform" represented by **<form**

name="myform"> no matter where it occurs in a document. The main properties of an individual **Form** object are related to the attributes of the **<form>** tag and include

- **action** the URL to submit the form to as specified by the **action** attribute. If unspecified, the form will be submitted to the current document location.

- **encoding** the value of the **enctype** attribute, generally *application/x-www-form-urlencoded* unless using a file upload, when it should be *multipart/form-data*. Occasionally, the value may be *text/plain* when using a *mailto:* URL submission.

- **method** the **method** attribute value: either GET or POST. GET is default (though casing may vary).

- **name** the name of the form, if defined.

- **target** the window or frame name within which to display the result of the form submission.

The **Form** object also specifies a **length** property, which corresponds to the number of fields within the form defined by **<input>**, **<select>**, **<textarea>**, and possibly **<button>** in browsers that support this HTML element. Object references to these elements are stored in the **elements[ ]** collection of the **Form** object (to be discussed next). Lastly, the **Form** object supports two methods, **submit()** and **reset()**, which cause the submission and resetting of the form.

Form Elements Collection

The **elements[ ]** collection for each **Form** object is an array containing the various fields in the form, including check boxes, radio buttons, select/option menus, text areas, text fields, password fields, reset buttons, submit buttons, generic buttons, and even hidden fields. Later JavaScript implementations also support file-upload fields. Access to form elements can be performed numerically, (**document.myform.elements[0]**), or by name, (**document.myform.textfield1**). The number of elements in the form is obtained either with **document.formname.length** or **document.formname.elements.length**. The properties of each form field object vary according to their HTML syntax. Let's look at the standard text field to get the idea.

A text field in HTML is defined by **<input type="text" name="*fieldname*" size="*field size in chars*" maxlength="*maxlength of entry in chars*" value="*default text value*">;** so, accordingly, you would expect the properties for a text field object to be **type, name, size, maxlength,** and **value**. Also defined is the property **defaultValue**, which holds the original value, specified by the **value** attribute, since the **value** property of this object will change as the user changes the field. Here is a simple example showing the manipulation of a text field:

```
<!DOCTYPE HTML PUBLIC "-//W3C//DTD HTML 4.01 Transitional//EN"
        "http://www.w3.org/TR/html4/loose.dtd">
```

```
<html>
<head>
<title>Text Field Fun</title>
<script language="JavaScript" type="text/javascript">
function showProps(textfield)
{
 var prop, str="Field Properties\n\n";
 str += "name: "+textfield.name + "\n";
 str += "type: "+textfield.type + "\n";
 str += "size: "+textfield.size + "\n";
 str += "maxLength: "+textfield.maxLength + "\n";
 str += "value: "+textfield.value + "\n";
 str += "defaultValue: "+textfield.defaultValue + "\n";
 alert(str);
}
</script>
</head>
<body>
<form name="myform">
<input type="text" name="field1" size="20" maxlength="30" value="initial
value"><br>
<input type="button" value="Read field"
onclick="alert(document.myform.field1.value)">
<input type="button" value="Write field"
onclick="document.myform.field1.value='Changed!!!'">
<input type="button" value="Show properties"
onclick="showProps(document.myform.field1)">
</form>
</body>
</html>
```

The result of this example is shown in Figure 13-2. What's interesting about this example is that you will see that only some attributes of the text field, like **value** and later **type**, are available in certain versions of Netscape. An in-depth discussion of the nuances of accessing the **Form** object and all of its possible contained elements is presented in Chapter 14, which covers form validation and other JavaScript improvements to forms.

document.images[ ]

Netscape 3 and later Internet Explorer added the **images[ ]** collection to the **Document** object. Obviously, this element contains the images defined by the HTML **<img>** tag.

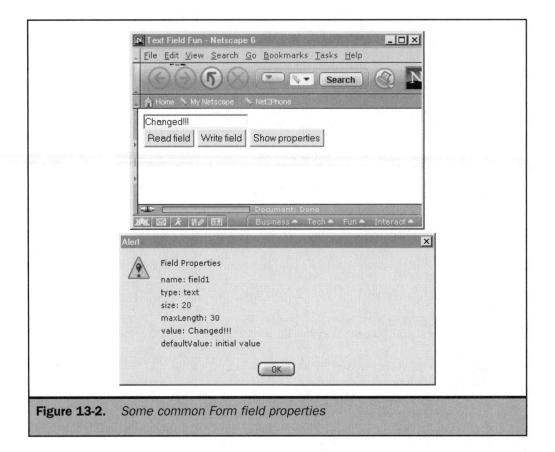

Figure 13-2. *Some common Form field properties*

As with other collections, the **length** property is available, and the various images can be accessed through the collection numerically, (**document.images[0]),** or by name, (**document.images['myimage']**).

Once accessed, the **Image** object supports JavaScript properties related to its HTML attributes, including **border**, **height**, **hspace**, **lowsrc**, **name**, **src**, **vspace**, and **width**. The object also supports the property **complete,** which contains a Boolean value indicating whether the image has completely loaded or not. In Netscape browsers, only the **src** property can be set. All other properties are read-only. Of course, under Microsoft's DHTML model everything tends to be settable. A simple example showing the access of an image is given here, with its rendering in Figure 13-3.

```
<!DOCTYPE HTML PUBLIC "-//W3C//DTD HTML 4.01 Transitional//EN"
        "http://www.w3.org/TR/html4/loose.dtd">
<html>
<head>
<title>Image Fun</title>
<script language="JavaScript" type="text/javascript">
function showProps(theImage)
{
 var prop, str="Image Properties\n\n";
 str += "border: "+theImage.border + "\n";
 str += "complete: "+theImage.complete + "\n";
 str += "height: "+theImage.height + "\n";
 str += "hspace: "+theImage.hspace + "\n";
 str += "lowsrc: "+theImage.lowsrc + "\n";
 str += "name: "+theImage.name + "\n";
 str += "src: "+theImage.src + "\n";
 str += "vspace: "+theImage.vspace + "\n";
 str += "width: "+theImage.width + "\n";
 alert(str);
}
</script>
</head>
<body>
<img src="image1.gif" lowsrc="lowres.gif" name="testimage" width="100"
height="100" border="1" hspace="10" vspace="15">
<br><br>
<form>
<input type="button" value="Show properties"
onclick="showProps(document.testimage)">
<input type="button" value="Swap Image"
onclick="document.testimage.src='image2.gif'">
<input type="button" value="Restore Image"
onclick="document.testimage.src='image1.gif'">
</form>
</body>
</html>
```

We'll explore all these properties again in more detail in Chapter 15, and we'll see how to create a common JavaScript effect called the rollover button using the **Image** object.

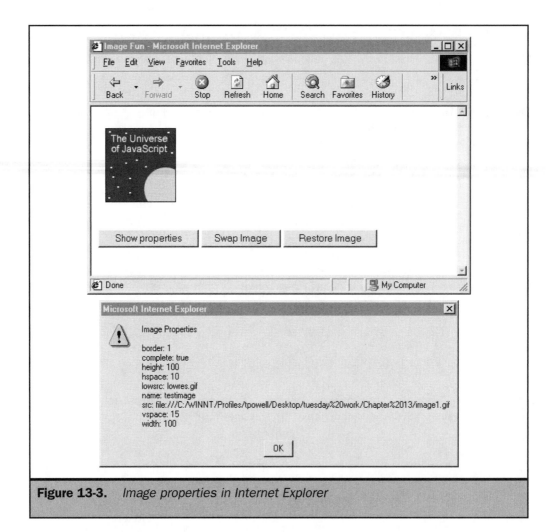

Figure 13-3. *Image properties in Internet Explorer*

Object-Related Collections: applets[ ], embeds[ ], and plugins[ ]

Netscape 3 and Internet Explorer 4 expanded JavaScript access to include object technologies like Java applets and Netscape plugins, which can be accessed with the **applets[ ]** and **embeds[ ]** collection, respectively. The **plugins[ ]** collection is also supported, but while it contains **Plugin** objects that correspond to the plugins installed in Netscape, under Internet Explorer it is just a synonym for the **embeds[ ]** collection. Like the previous collections discussed, **applets[ ]** and **embeds[ ]** contain object references corresponding to the use of the **<applet>** or **<embed>** tag. Thus, the **length** property of the collection can be accessed, and the individual items in the collection can be referenced numerically, (**document.embeds[0]**), or by name, (**document.***myJavaApplet*).

The particular properties and methods supported by included objects are not as consistent as the elements discussed earlier, because they depend greatly on the specific object included. In the case of Java applets, the various public properties and methods of the included applet can be referenced via JavaScript. In the case of embedded objects handled by plugins, the properties and methods available vary from plugin to plugin. This makes sense, since one would expect the features of an included Flash movie to be different than those of, say, an embedded sound file. Readers should look to Chapter 18 for a more complete explanation.

DHTML-Related Document Collections

Given the previous discussion, you would expect that there would be an increasing variety of collections for paragraphs, lists, and on an on in more modern browsers. While this might have seemed likely, things actually degraded into the chaos of DHTML, complete with proprietary collections like **layers[ ]** and **all[ ]**. We'll focus solely on **document.all[ ]**, which serves as a good reminder of the power of the DOM.

Document.all[ ]

Under Internet Explorer, the **all[ ]** collection represents all HTML elements and comments within a document. Like all HTML element collections, it can be used numerically, (**document.all[10]**), or by name, (**document.all['myP11']**), when the element has an **id** attribute set. Named objects in Internet Explorer can all be accessed using the **item** method for **all**: **document.all.item('myP11')**. However, many JavaScript programmers will simply access the object directly by its **id** value (such as *myP11*). You can also use the **tags()** method for **document.all[ ]** to return a list of all tags of a particular type:

```
var allBolds = document.all.tags("B");
```

You can then access the returned collection as any other.

Once an element is found, the question follows: what are its properties? The answer depends on the type of element in question. For example, if *myP1* held a reference to a paragraph element, you could set its alignment under Internet Explorer 4 and greater with *myP1.align*.

```
myP1.align = "center";
```

Other HTML element objects have properties related to their HTML attributes.

While **document.all[ ]** presents a safe and easy way to access HTML elements, many other DHTML-related collections are not so innocuous. In reality, very few of the DHTML-related collections should be used; however, Chapter 15 shows the use of **document.layers[ ]** and **document.all[ ]** to move, show, and hide objects. These facilities are also used in Chapter 16 when presenting navigation menu examples that work in common browsers. Yet the future of JavaScript is not to continue to use all the hacks and workarounds now commonly employed, but instead to migrate to the DOM standard.

Document Object Model Redux

The DOM Level 1 attempts to standardize the JavaScript **Document** object to support the manipulation of arbitrary HTML elements and text objects while at the same time providing support for most commonly supported traditional **Document** properties, collections, and methods. This backwards support is often termed DOM Level 0 and is fairly consistent with what Netscape 3 supported (except JavaScript access to plugins). The **Document** properties supported by DOM Level 1 are presented in Table 13-3.

Document Property or Collection	Description
anchors[ ]	The collection of the anchors defined by **<a name="anchorname">**
applets[ ]	The collection of Java applets in the page defined by the **<applet>** tag.
body	Reference to the object representing the **<body>** tag that contains the visible document.
cookie	A string holding the document's cookie values, if any.
doctype	A reference to the DTD of the document.
documentElement	A reference to the root element of the document. In HTML, this is the **<html>** tag.
domain	The security domain of the document.
forms[ ]	The **<form>** tags in the page.
images[ ]	The collection of images defined by **<img>** tags.
implementation	A reference to an object that can determine markup language feature support for the particular document.
links[ ]	The collection of the links specified by **<a>** and **<area>** tags in the page.
referrer	Holds the referring URL, if any.
title	The title of the document.
URL	A string holding the document's URL.

Table 13-3.   *DOM Level 1 Document Properties and Collections*

Notice in Table 13-3 how the DOM preserves many of the collections discussed previously and adds only a few properties to the mix, such as **body**, **doctype**, and **documentElement**. The only thing missing seems to be **lastModified**; fortunately, browsers continue to support it even though it is not a part of the standard.

As for methods, traditionally the **Document** object supported only **open()**, **close()**, **clear()**, **write()**, and **writeln()**. The DOM Level 1 drops the **clear()** method, which never really had much use anyway. However, beyond the more statically oriented **write()** methods, the DOM provides a variety of methods to dynamically create objects. It adds methods such as **createComment(*data*),** which creates an HTML comment of the form **<!-- *data* -->**, **createElement(*tagName*)**, which creates an HTML element of type *tagName*, and **createTextNode(*data*)**, which creates a text node containing the value of the parameter *data*. There are other DOM "create" methods, but they are not generally useful when working with HTML documents.

We also saw in Chapter 10 that the DOM adds three useful methods for retrieving a location in a document:

- **document.getElementById(*elementId*)**—returns a reference to the object with **id="elementId"**

- **document.getElementsByName(*elementName*)**—returns a list of all HTML element objects with **name="elementName"**

- **document.getElementsByTagName(*tagname*)**—returns a list of all HTML elements of tagname (such as B)

Once we retrieve an object, there are a variety of properties we can examine. For example, recall from Chapter 10 again that every DOM node including an HTML element has a variety of properties related to its position in the document tree, such as **parentNode**, **childNodes**, **firstChild**, **lastChild**, **previousSibling**, and **nextSibling**. There are also numerous methods, such as **insertBefore()**, to add nodes to the document whether they are HTML tags or text nodes. There are also methods to manipulate attributes and values, but doing this is often easier to perform directly, as we'll demonstrate later.

Besides the DOM-defined properties, all elements under HTML 4 and XHTML have in common a core set of properties related to scripting, style sheets, and accessability (**id**, **class**, **style**, and **title**) as well as language usage (**lang** and **dir**). If you put all these together, you get the complete set of properties and methods common to any HTML element represented in JavaScript. Under the DOM this object is called an **HTMLElement**, and its properties and methods are summarized in Table 13-4.

Common HTML Element, Property, or Collection	Description
attributes[ ]	A collection of the attributes for the element, if any.
childNodes[ ]	A collection of the nodes (text nodes, elements, etc.) enclosed within the current HTML element.
className	The value of the **class** attribute.
dir	The text direction of the enclosed text: either *LTR* (left to right) or *RTL* (right to left).
firstChild	A reference to the first node directly enclosed within the current HTML element. This will be the same as *element.childNodes[0]*. Children, of course, can be any type, not just HTML elements.
id	The text string set by the **id** attribute for the element.
lang	The language code for the element set by the **lang** attribute.
lastChild	A reference to the last child in the list of children nodes that are direct decendents of the current HTML element.
nodeName	The name of the HTML element, for example *P*. Same as **tagName**.
nodeValue	The value of the node. This property will be **null** in the case of HTML elements.
nodeType	The numeric code for the node type. In the case of HTML elements, this will always be 1.
nextSibling	A reference to the next DOM node sibling of the current HTML element.
ownerDocument	A reference to the **Document** object containing the current element.
parentNode	A reference to the enclosing HTML element.
previousSibling	A reference to the previous DOM node sibling of the current HTML element.

Table 13-4. *Common DOM Properties for HTML Elements*

Common HTML Element, Property, or Collection	Description
style	Access to the inline style specification for the current element. This is a DOM Level 2 property but is widely supported in DOM1 compliant browsers.
tagName	A reference to the name of the HTML element, such as **OL**. This will be the same as **nodeName** in the case of element nodes.
title	The text string holding the advisory text for the element set by the **title** attribute.

Table 13-4.   *Common DOM Properties for HTML Elements* (continued)

As mentioned in Chapter 10, under the DOM Level 1 all HTML elements also have a variety of useful methods. The more commonly used ones are presented in Table 13-5.

Method Name	Description
appendChild(*newChild***)**	This appends the node in *newChild* as the last child of the current element.
cloneNode(*deep***)**	Makes a copy of the current HTML element. If the parameter *deep* is passed as **true,** the copy made includes all nodes enclosed within the current element.
getAttribute(*name***)**	Returns the attribute *name*. Easier to reference directly via the attribute name when known. For example, if *myP1* holds a paragraph, *myP1.align* would hold its **align** attribute value.
getElementsByTagName(*tagName***)**	Returns a list of elements referenced by *tagName* that are contained within the current element.
hasChildNodes()	This method returns a Boolean value indicating if the current element has children (enclosed elements or text nodes).

Table 13-5.   *Common DOM HTML Element Methods*

USING JAVASCRIPT

Method Name	Description
insertBefore(*newChild, refChild*)	Inserts the node *newChild* into the list of children directly enclosed by the element just before the node referenced by *refChild*.
removeAttribute(*name*)	Removes the attribute named *name*. For example, *myP1.removeAttribute("align")* would delete the **align** attribute for a paragraph called *myP1*. Of course, it might be easier just to assign attributes directly.
removeChild(*oldChild*)	Removes the node specified by *oldChild*.
replaceChild(*newChild, oldChild*)	Replaces the node *oldChild* with *newChild*.
setAttribute(*name, value*)	Sets the attribute *name*. Easier to reference directly via the attribute name itself when known. For example, if *myP1* holds a paragraph, *myP1.align* would holds its **align** attribute value.

Table 13-5.   *Common DOM HTML Element Methods* (continued)

These have been reminders of DOM basics, which have already been covered in Chapter 10.

Accessing Specific HTML Element Properties

As mentioned in Chapter 10, the correlation between HTML attribute names and DOM property names is nearly one to one. For example, the **<body>** tag would be represented by the DOM object **HTMLBodyElement** and would have the generic properties previously discussed plus those specific to the **<body>** element, including: **aLink**, **background**, **bgColor**, **link**, **text**, and **vLink**. Save for the JavaScript "camel-back" style of writing, these are just the attributes for the HTML tag.

To see this, note that paragraphs (**HTMLParagraphElement**) would have only an **align** property beyond the core properties and methods while the **<link>** tag (**HTMLLinkElement**) would have all the common DOM HTML element properties plus **disabled, charset, href, hreflang, media, rel, rev, target,** and **type**. As you can see, all the properties for a given DOM HTML object are closely related to their HTML attributes. Manipulating these attributes is straightforward once the element is accessed using a method like **document.getElementById( )**, as shown here:

```
<p id="myP1">Test Paragraph</p>
<form>
<input type="button" value="align left"
onclick="document.getElementById('myP1').align='left'">
<input type="button" value="align center"
onclick="document.getElementById('myP1').align='center'">
<input type="button" value="align right"
onclick="document.getElementById('myP1').align='right'">
</form>
```

The following more advanced example shows how HTML elements can be added and deleted using a very rudimentary HTML creation tool that employs DOM methods.

```
<!DOCTYPE HTML PUBLIC "-//W3C//DTD HTML 4.01 Transitional//EN"
        "http://www.w3.org/TR/html4/loose.dtd">
<html>
<head>
<title>DOM HTML Editor 0.1</title>
<script language="JavaScript" type="text/javascript">
function addElement()
{
 var choice = document.htmlForm.elementList.selectedIndex;
 var theElement =
document.createElement(document.htmlForm.elementList.options[choice].text);
 var textNode = document.createTextNode(document.htmlForm.elementText.value);
 var insertSpot = document.getElementById('addHere');
 theElement.appendChild(textNode);
 insertSpot.appendChild(theElement);
}

function addEmptyElement(elementName)
{
```

```
  var theBreak = document.createElement(elementName);
  var insertSpot = document.getElementById('addHere');
  insertSpot.appendChild(theBreak);
}
function deleteNode()
{
  var deleteSpot = document.getElementById('addHere');
  if (deleteSpot.hasChildNodes())
   {
    var toDelete = deleteSpot.lastChild;
    deleteSpot.removeChild(toDelete);
   }
}
function showHTML()
{
  var insertSpot = document.getElementById('addHere');
  if (insertSpot.innerHTML)
    alert(insertSpot.innerHTML);
  else
    alert("Not easily performed without innerHTML");
}
</script>
</head>
<body>
<h1 style="text-align: center">Simple DOM HTML Editor</h1>
<br><br>
<div id="addHere" style="background-color: #ffffcc; border: solid;">
 
</div>
<br><br>
<form id="htmlForm" name="htmlForm">
<select id="elementList" name="elementList">
      <option>B</option>
      <option>BIG</option>
      <option>CITE</option>
      <option>CODE</option>
      <option>EM</option>
      <option>H1</option>
```

```
        <option>H2</option>
        <option>H3</option>
        <option>H4</option>
        <option>H5</option>
        <option>H6</option>
        <option>I</option>
        <option>P</option>
        <option>U</option>
        <option>SAMP</option>
        <option>SMALL</option>
        <option>STRIKE</option>
        <option>STRONG</option>
        <option>SUB</option>
        <option>SUP</option>
        <option>TT</option>
        <option>VAR</option>
</select>
<input type="text" name="elementText" id="elementText" value="Default">
<input type="button" value="Add Element" onclick="addElement()">
<br><br>
<input type="button" value="Insert <br>" onclick="addEmptyElement('BR')">
<input type="button" value="Insert <hr>" onclick="addEmptyElement('HR')">
<input type="button" value="Delete Element" onclick="deleteNode()">
<input type="button" value="Show HTML" onclick="showHTML()">
</form>
</body>
</html>
```

It would be easy enough to modify our editor (shown in Figure 13-4) to allow the user to add attributes and apply multiple styles. We'll leave that as an exercise for readers interested in diving into the DOM.

Appendix B contains the complete listing of all HTML-related properties from the DOM Level 1. However, before concluding this chapter, it is time to take a look at one HTML element that continually causes developers trouble—the table.

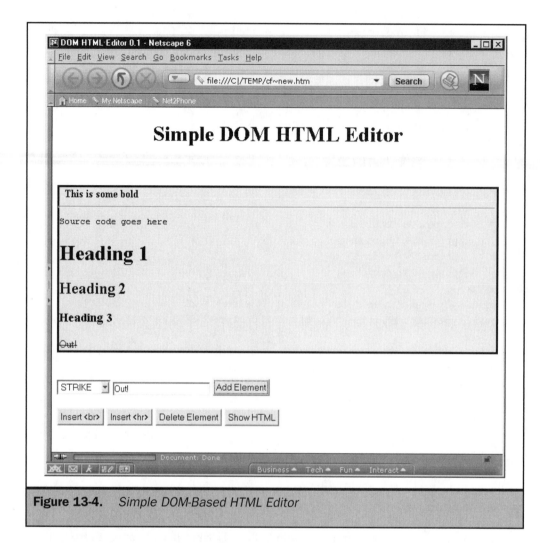

Figure 13-4. Simple DOM-Based HTML Editor

DOM Table Manipulation

The **<table>** tag as defined in HTML has a variety of attributes that have similarly named DOM properties (just as we have seen with all HTML elements). In the case of **<table>,** these properties include: **align**, **bgColor**, **border**, **cellPadding**, **cellSpacing**, and **width**. Within a **<table>** tag, we would expect to possibly find a **<caption>** tag, and one or more table rows defined by the **<tr>** filled with table headers (**<th>**) or data cells (**<td>**). Under HTML 4, tables are extended to support the following structure:

- An opening **<table>** tag.

- An optional caption specified by **<caption> ... </caption>.**

- One or more groups of rows. These might consist of a header section specified by **<thead>,** a footer section specified by **<tfoot>,** and a body section specified by **<tbody>.** Although all these elements are optional, the table must contain at least one row specified by **<tr>.** The rows themselves must contain at least one header or one data cell, specified by **<th>** or **<td>,** respectively.

- One or more groups of columns specified by **<colgroup>,** with individual columns within the group specified by **<col>.**

- A closing **</table>** tag.

Also HTML 4 defines the **frame** attribute for the table, which sets the type of framing the table should have; the **rules** attribute, which sets where the rules (lines) should be placed between rows and columns; and the **summary** attribute, which defines what the table is about for non-visual browsers. The simple example here allows you to play with the common properties for the HTML 4 table element. A sample rendering of this example is shown in Figure 13-5.

```
<!DOCTYPE HTML PUBLIC "-//W3C//DTD HTML 4.01 Transitional//EN"
        "http://www.w3.org/TR/html4/loose.dtd">
<html>
<head>
<title>HTML 4 Table Inspector</title>
</head>
<body>
<table border="1" frame="box" id="testTable">
<caption>Test Table</caption>
<thead>
     <tr>
       <th>Product</th>
       <th>SKU</th>
       <th>Price</th>
     </tr>
</thead>
<tbody>
```

```
<tr>
    <th colspan="3" align="center">Robots</th>
</tr>

<tr>
    <td>Trainer Robot</td>
    <td>TR-456</td>
    <td>$56,000</td>
</tr>
<tr>
    <td>Guard Dog Robot</td>
    <td>SEC-559</td>
    <td>$5,000</td>
</tr>
<tr>
    <td>Friend Robot</td>
    <td>AG-343</td>
    <td>$124,000</td>
</tr>
</tbody>
<tbody>
  <tr>
    <th colspan="3" align="center">Jet Packs</th>
  </tr>

  <tr>
    <td>Economy</td>
    <td>JP-3455E6</td>
    <td>$6,000</td>
  </tr>

  <tr>
    <td>Deluxe</td>
    <td>JP-9999d</td>
    <td>$15,000</td>
  </tr>
</tbody>
<tfoot>
 <tr>
```

```
        <th colspan="3">This has been an HTML 4 table example, thanks for
reading</th>
 </tr>
</tfoot>
</table>
<br clear="all">
<hr>
<br clear="all">
<script language="JavaScript" type="text/javascript">
   var theTable = document.getElementById('testTable');
</script>
<form>
<strong>Alignment:</strong>
      <select onchange="theTable.align = this.options[this.selectedIndex].text;">
            <option>left</option>
            <option>center</option>
            <option>right</option>
      </select>
<strong>Background Color:</strong>
      <select onchange="theTable.bgColor =
this.options[this.selectedIndex].text;">
            <option>white</option>
            <option>red</option>
            <option>blue</option>
            <option>yellow</option>
            <option>orange</option>
            <option>green</option>
            <option>black</option>
      </select>

<strong>Frames:</strong>
      <select onchange="theTable.frame = this.options[this.selectedIndex].text;">
            <option>above</option>
            <option>below</option>
            <option>border</option>
            <option>box</option>
            <option>hsides</option>
            <option>vsides</option>
            <option>lhs</option>
```

```
          <option>rhs</option>
          <option>void</option>
     </select>
<strong>Rules:</strong>
     <select onchange="theTable.rules = this.options[this.selectedIndex].text;">
          <option>all</option>
          <option>cols</option>
          <option>groups</option>
          <option>none</option>
          <option>rows</option>
     </select>
<br><br>
<strong>Border:</strong>
<input type="text" size="2" maxlength="2" value="1" onchange="theTable.border =
this.value;">
<strong>Cell Padding:</strong>
<input type="text" size="2" maxlength="2" value="1" onchange="theTable.cellPadding
= this.value;">
<strong>Cell Spacing:</strong>
<input type="text" size="2" maxlength="2" value="1" onchange="theTable.cellSpacing
= this.value;">
</form>
</body>
</html>
```

Note   *Be aware that even the latest browsers may have spotty support for the values of the*
rules and frame attributes.

The **HTMLTableElement** object also contains shorthand references to its typically
enclosed elements. For example, *tableElement*.**caption** would reference the **<caption>**
tag enclosed by the table referenced via *tableElement*, and *tableElement*.**tHead** and
tableElement.**tFoot** would reference the **<thead>** and **<tfoot>** tags, respectively. The
collection **rows[ ]** provides access to the **<tr>** tags within the table (starting with the
index of 0, like all collections), while the **tBodies[ ]** collection provides access to
the **<tbody>** tags. Within **these objects**, we can also look at their individual **rows[ ]**
collections, which contain the objects pointing to the individual **<tr>** tags within the
corresponding table sub-element. Using our previous example, we might write a small
script to show the values for our previous table.

```
<script language="JavaScript" type="text/javascript">
   var theTable = document.getElementById('testTable');
```

```
    document.writeln("<pre>");
    document.writeln("Overall table rows="+theTable.rows.length);
    document.writeln("Number of tbody tags="+theTable.tBodies.length);
    for (var i = 0; i < theTable.tBodies.length; i++)
      document.writeln("\t tbody["+i+"] number of rows =
"+theTable.tBodies[i].rows.length);

    document.writeln("Rows in tfoot tag="+theTable.tFoot.rows.length);
    document.writeln("Rows in thead tag="+theTable.tHead.rows.length);
    document.writeln("</pre>");
</script>
```

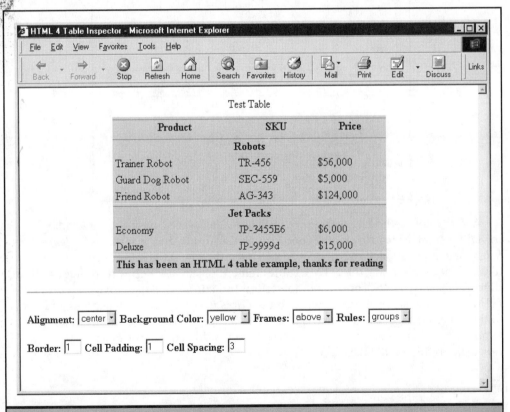

Figure 13-5.   *Inspecting and changing the <table> tag using the DOM*

The output of this script for our sample HTML 4 style table is shown here:

```
HTML 4 Table Inspector - Microsoft Internet Explorer          _ □ ×
File   Edit   View   Favorites   Tools   Help
←          →         ⊗         📄        🏠       🔍      📁     »
Back      Forward    Stop      Refresh   Home    Search Favorites   Links
```

	Test Table	
Product	**SKU**	**Price**
Robots		
Trainer Robot	TR-456	$56,000
Guard Dog Robot	SEC-559	$5,000
Friend Robot	AG-343	$124,000
Jet Packs		
Economy	JP-3455E6	$6,000
Deluxe	JP-9999d	$15,000
This has been an HTML 4 table example, thanks for reading		

```
Overall table rows=10
Number of tbody tags=2
         tbody[0] number of rows = 4
         tbody[1] number of rows = 3
Rows in tfoot tag=1
Rows in thead tag=2
```

A variety of methods are also provided to make up the core pieces of a table, including **createTHead()**, **createTFoot()**, **createCaption()**, and **insertRow(*index*)** where *index* is the numeric value indicating where to insert the row starting from 0. Corresponding to the creation methods, the **HTMLTableElement** object also supports **deleteCaption()**, **deleteTHead()**, **deleteTFoot()**, and **deleteRowIndex(*index*)**. Again given the previous HTML 4 sample table, we could write some scripts to show how to delete and add items to the table. What you will notice is that while it is easy to delete items from the table, to add items is another question. You will need to add some items to a row before much of anything will take place.

```
<script language="JavaScript" type="text/javascript">
   var theTable = document.getElementById('testTable');
</script>
<form name="testForm" id="testForm">
```

```
<input type="text" name="rowtodelete" id="rowtodelete" size="2" maxlength="2"
 value="1">
<input type="button" value="Delete Row" onclick="if (theTable.rows.length > 0)
 theTable.deleteRow(document.testForm.rowtodelete.value)">
<br>
<input type="button" value="Delete <thead>" onclick="theTable.deleteTHead()">
<input type="button" value="Delete <tfoot>" onclick="theTable.deleteTFoot()">
<input type="button" value="Delete <caption>" onclick="theTable.deleteCaption()">

<input type="text" name="rowtoinsert" id="rowtoinsert" size="2" maxlength="2"
 value="1">
<input type="button" value="Insert Row"
onclick="theTable.insertRow(document.testForm.rowtoinsert.value)">

</form>
```

A table row defined by **<tr>** in HTML and by the **HTMLTableRowElement** object under the DOM has its normal HTML attribute-related properties, such as the core attributes (**id**, **class**, **style**, **title**, **lang**, **dir**) and its specific properties like **align**, **bgColor**, **ch**, **chOff** (corresponding to the **charOff** attribute), and **vAlign**. However, there are a few special properties that deserve consideration. For example, **rowIndex** indicates the index of the row in the overall table. The property **sectionRowIndex** indicates the index of the row within a **<tbody>**, **<thead>**, or the **<tfoot>** element it belongs to. Lastly, the **cells[ ]** collection for an **HTMLTableRowElement** is a collection of the cells in the row defined by either **<td>** or **<th>** elements. Within a table row, you can also utilize a few useful methods, including **insertCell(*index*)**, which creates an **HTMLElement** object for a **<td>** tag at a specified column *index* in the row, and **deleteCell(*index*)**, which would obviously remove a cell at a specified *index*.

The actual table cell defined in HTML by the **<td>** tag has few special properties beyond its normal attribute-related ones like **abbr**, **align**, **axis**, **bgColor**, **ch**, **chOff**, **height**, **noWrap**, **rowSpan**, **vAlign**, and **width**. One special property worth mentioning is **cellIndex**, which holds the index of the cell in its current row. This index can be useful to pass to the **insertCell()** and **deleteCell()** methods. The simple example here shows how to manipulate cells:

```
<!DOCTYPE HTML PUBLIC "-//W3C//DTD HTML 4.01 Transitional//EN"
        "http://www.w3.org/TR/html4/loose.dtd">
<html>
<head>
```

```
<title>Table Cell Fun</title>
</head>
<body>
<table id="table1" border="1">
<tr id="row1">
      <td id="cell1">Cell 1</td>
      <td id="cell2">Cell 2</td>
</tr>
<tr id="row2">
      <td id="cell3">Cell 3</td>
      <td id="cell4">Cell 4</td>
</tr>
</table>

<script language="JavaScript" type="text/javascript">
var theTable = document.getElementById("table1");
function doRowInsert(row)
{
   var rowNumber = parseFloat(row);
   if ((rowNumber >= 0) && (rowNumber <= theTable.rows.length))
     theTable.insertRow(rowNumber);
}

function doCellInsert(row,column)
 {
  var rowNumber = parseFloat(row);
  var colNumber = parseFloat(column);
  var numberRowsInTable = theTable.rows.length;
  if ((rowNumber >= 0 ) && (colNumber >= 0))
   {
     if (rowNumber >= numberRowsInTable)
       {
         alert("Can't add beyond defined rows");
         return;
       }
     if (colNumber > theTable.rows[rowNumber].cells.length)
       {
         alert("Can't add more than one beyond columns");
         return;
       }
     theTable.rows[rowNumber].insertCell(colNumber);
```

```
      }
}

function doCellModification(row,column,newValue)
{
  var rowNumber = parseFloat(row);
  var colNumber = parseFloat(column);
  var numberRowsInTable = theTable.rows.length;
  if ((rowNumber >= 0 ) && (colNumber >= 0))
    {
      if (rowNumber >= numberRowsInTable)
        {
          alert("Can't modify cells outside the table");
          return;
        }
      if (colNumber >= theTable.rows[rowNumber].cells.length)
        {
          alert("Can't modify cells outside the table");
          return;
        }
      theTable.rows[rowNumber].cells[colNumber].innerHTML = newValue;
    }
}

function doCellDelete(row,column)
{
    var rowNumber = parseFloat(row);
    var colNumber = parseFloat(column);
    var numberRowsInTable = theTable.rows.length;
    if ((rowNumber >= 0 ) && (colNumber >= 0))
    {
      if (rowNumber >= numberRowsInTable)
        {
          alert("Can't delete beyond defined rows");
          return;
        }
      if (colNumber >= theTable.rows[rowNumber].cells.length)
        {
          alert("Can't delete beyond the column");
          return;
```

```
        }

      theTable.rows[rowNumber].deleteCell(colNumber);
    }
}
</script>
<form name="testForm" id="testForm">

Row #: <input type="text" name="rowtoinsert" id="rowtoinsert" size="2"
maxlength="2" value="1">
<input type="button" value="Insert Row"
onclick="doRowInsert(document.testForm.rowtoinsert.value)"><br>

Row #: <input type="text" name="insertionRow" id="insertionRow" size="2"
maxlength="2" value="0">
Column #: <input type="text" name="insertionColumn" id="insertionColumn" size="2"
maxlength="2" value="0">
<input type="button" value="Insert Cell"
onclick="doCellInsert(document.testForm.insertionRow.value,document.testForm.inser
tionColumn.value)"><br>

Row #: <input type="text" name="modifyRow" id="modifyRow" size="2" maxlength="2"
value="0">
Column #: <input type="text" name="modifyColumn" id="modifyColumn" size="2"
maxlength="2" value="0">
New Contents: <input type="text" name="newContents" id="newContents" size="20"
maxlength="20" value="">
<input type="button" value="Modify Cell Contents"
onclick="doCellModification(document.testForm.modifyRow.value,document.testForm.mo
difyColumn.value,document.testForm.newContents.value)"><br>

Row #: <input type="text" name="deletionRow" id="deletionRow" size="2" maxlength="2"
value="0">
Column #: <input type="text" name="deletionColumn" id="deletionColumn" size="2"
maxlength="2" value="0">
<input type="button" value="Delete Cell"
onclick="doCellDelete(document.testForm.deletionRow.value,document.testForm.deleti
onColumn.value)"><br>
</form>
</body>
</html>
```

The rendering of the previous example is shown in Figure 13-6.

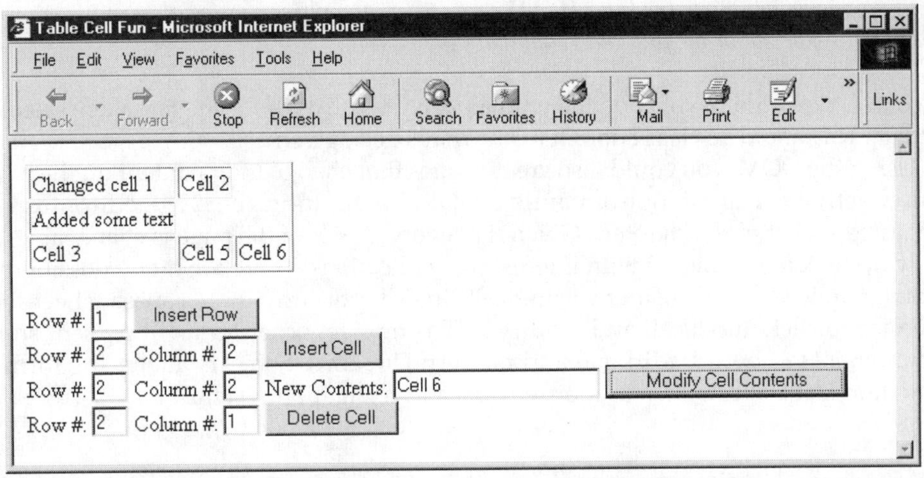

Figure 13-6. *Cell and row manipulation example*

Note *You may have noticed that the HTML table used in the previous example did not include all the tags permitted under HTML 4 (for example there is no **<tbody>**). In most cases, you can get away with using only **<tr>**s and **<td>**s. However, further breaking the HTML "rules" by not closing quotes or tags may produce unpredictable results.*

DOM Applied

You might wonder what to do with the DOM properties. There are numerous applications possible—for example, creating pages that allow the user to dynamically toggle between languages or presentations. This small example demonstrates this idea in a simple form:

```
<form>
Say Hello in:
<select
onchange="document.getElementById('thephrase').firstChild.data =
this.options[this.selectedIndex].value">
        <option value="Hello">English</option>
        <option value="Bonjour">French</option>
        <option value="Hola">Spanish</option>
</select>
</form>

<div id="thephrase">Hello</div>
```

*We could have used the **innerHTML** property commonly supported in most 6.x browsers, but we opted for the full DOM approach here.*

Of course, we could have made the whole page rewrite itself for the language selected, but the idea should be clear enough from what's been given.

Using the DOM, you could also create pages that change their content on the basis of user activity. You might even build a DOM-based, in-page HTML editor (as we suggested earlier in the chapter). Given that every aspect of the page is changeable, it is really up to you to come up with interesting applications. There are many possibilities with dynamic tables. Consider sorting cells in order or providing a spreadsheet-like interface to click into a cell and modify it. The next few chapters will present some common uses of both traditional and modern **Document** objects, including form validation, page effects such as mouseovers, and navigation systems.

Summary

This chapter presented an overview of the **Document** object from the simple traditional object model supported under Netscape 2 and Internet Explorer 3 to the full-blown DOM. Under older models, little was accessible via JavaScript save for anchors, forms, and links. Later, images and embedded media types were added to the mix. Although it was customary for JavaScript-accessible HTML elements to have the **name** attribute, with the rise of the **id** attribute everything became nameable. This development enabled, first with DHTML and later with the DOM, the manipulation of arbitrary HTML and even text elements within a page. While the DHTML object model has provided JavaScript programmers with this power since Internet Explorer 4, the W3C DOM has created a standard way to manipulate HTML objects under all future DOM-compliant browsers. While the DOM standard provides very useful features, its successful use is highly dependent upon the JavaScript programmer's knowledge of HTML, which is the basis of nearly all the standard's properties.

This chapter presented a few basic uses of **Document** properties and methods, such as background color changes and arbitrary element insertion. Because the limited number of canned examples might make it seem that **Document** is not terribly useful, in reality its use is limited only by the imagination of the programmer. The next chapter will take on a common and well-understood use of JavaScript—form validation.

The Complete Reference

Chapter 14

Form Handling

One of the most common uses of JavaScript is for checking the contents of forms before sending them to server-side programs. Commonly known as *form validation*, this use of JavaScript was actually one of the original driving forces behind the development of the language and, as a result, most of the techniques presented in this chapter will work in any implementation of the language. However, while relatively straightforward to implement, JavaScript form validation is not always well implemented, and many details, particularly those related to usability, are often brushed aside. We'll try to present correct usage of form checking as well as the appropriate JavaScript syntax.

The Need for JavaScript Form Checking

It can be quite annoying to fill out a form on a Web site for processing and then wait for it to be sent and processed only to have it come back to complain about malformed data. With JavaScript, we can improve the usability of Web forms by checking the data first before sending on the forms. There are a variety of ways to validate forms using JavaScript. We can look at the fields as they are filled in, or we can check the important fields when a submission is triggered. We can also create a field-mask to keep bad data from even being entered in the first place. We'll see in the next few sections of this chapter how JavaScript can be used to improve the usability of forms, and we'll also find that the correct form design and proper use of HTML form elements and attributes can help even further.

The server also benefits from form validation. Because incomplete or invalid form field entries are caught before submission, the number of interactions the browser will make with the server decreases. This presumably leaves the server free to carry out other work in a more timely fashion, without getting bogged down responding to the majority of common mistakes.

To start our discussion, let's take a look at how to access the **<form>** tag itself using JavaScript.

Form Basics

Traditionally JavaScript provides access to the forms within an HTML document through the **Form** object, which is a child of the **Document** object. As with all **document** objects, the properties and methods of this object correspond to the various features of the HTML element. The basic syntax of the HTML **<form>** tag is summarized here:

```
<form
action="URL to submit form"
enctype="Encoding type for form data"
id="Unique alphanumeric identifier"
method="Method by which to submit form data either GET or POST"
```

```
name="Unique alphanumeric identifier (superceded by id attribute)"
target="Frame target">

HTML form field elements and other markup to structure form

</form>
```

As we have seen already in our discussion of object models, most of the JavaScript properties for the **Form** object should correspond to the attributes of the **<form>** tag. A summary of the most useful properties available from JavaScript's **Form** object is presented in Table 14-1.

Property	Description
action	Holds the value of the **action** attribute indicating the URL to send the form data to on submission.
elements[ ]	An array of the various form element objects.
encoding	Holds the value of the **enctype** attribute, which usually contains the value *application/x-www-form-urlencoded*, *multipart/form-data* or *text/plain*. Superseded by the **enctype** property.
enctype	The DOM-appropriate way to access the **enctype** attribute value.
length	The number of form fields within the **<form>** tag. Should be the same as **elements.length**.
method	The value of the **method** attribute for the **<form>** tag. Should be either *GET* or *POST*.
name	The name of the **<form>** as defined by the **name** attribute for the tag. You should also set the **id** attribute holding the same value.
target	The name of the frame to display the resulting screen after form submission. May hold special frame values, such as a *_blank*, *_parent*, *_self*, or *_top*.

Table 14-1. *Common Form Object Properties*

Forms also have two methods. The **reset( )** method clears the form's fields, similar to pressing a button defined by **<input type="reset">**. The **submit( )** method triggers the submission of the form similar to pressing the button defined by **<input type="submit">**. Given these two events that can be triggered, the **<form>** tag supports the corresponding **onreset** and **onsubmit** event handler attributes. When assigning scripts to these event handlers, if a value of **false** is returned to the handler, the corresponding reset or submit will be cancelled. A **true** value (or no return value) will allow the event to occur normally. Given this procedure, the following form would allow all resets but deny submissions:

```
<form action="sendit.cgi" method="get" onreset="return true"
      onsubmit="return false">
```

 *A troublesome aspect of the **submit( )** method is that it will typically bypass any* ***onsubmit*** *event handling code in place.*

Before moving on to a short example, we need to make sure that we are capable of accessing a form properly. Remember that a page may have multiple forms in it, so naming the form could be useful. To access the first form in an HTML document as defined here,

```
<form name="customerform" id="customerform">
  ...fields...
</form>
```

we might use **window.document.forms[0]**, **window.document.forms['customerform']** or **window.document.customerform**, just as with any other JavaScript collection. Obviously, using a name for our form is preferable to its location in the document, since the **<form>** tag could be moved. While the document itself contains a collection of **<form>** tags, each particular form will contain a collection of form fields that can be referenced by the **elements[ ]** collection. So, in our case, **window.document.customerform. elements[0]** references the first field in the form. We could also iterate through the collection of form fields after examining its **length** property (**window.document. customerform.elements.length**). A shorthand for looking at the number of fields in a form is simply to look at **document.customerform.length** rather than **document. customerform.elements.length**. Before taking a look at how to access the individual types of form fields, we present a brief example to demonstrate the access of the various **Form** object properties and methods.

```
<!DOCTYPE HTML PUBLIC "-//W3C//DTD HTML 4.01 Transitional//EN"
                "http://www.w3.org/TR/html4/loose.dtd">
<html>
```

```
<head>
<title>Form Test</title>
</head>
<body>
<h2 align="center">Test Form</h2>
<form action="http://www.javascriptref.com/cgi-bin/test.cgi"
      method="post" name="testform" id="testform"
      onreset="return confirm('Are you sure?')"
      onsubmit="alert('Not really sending data'); return false">
Name: <input type="text" id="field1" name="field1" size="20"
             value="Joe Smith"><br>
Password: <input type="password" id="field2" name="field2"
                 size="8" maxlength="8"><br>
<input type="reset" value="reset">
<input type="submit" value="submit">
<input type="button" value="Do reset"
       onclick="document.testform.reset()">
<input type="button" value="Do submit"
       onclick="document.testform.submit()">
</form>
<hr>
<h2 align="center">Form Properties</h2>
<script language="JavaScript" type="text/javascript">
<!--
  /* change document.testform to document.forms[0] and
     you will get same result */
  with (document.testform)
   {
     document.write("Action: "+action+"<br>");
     document.write("Encoding: "+encoding+"<br>");
     document.write("Length: "+length+"<br>");
     document.write("Method: "+method+"<br>");
     document.write("Name: "+name+"<br>");
     document.write("Target: "+target+"<br>");
     for (var i=0; i < document.testform.length; i++)
        document.write("Element["+i+"]="+
                      document.testform.elements[i].type+"<br>");
   }
//-->
</script>
</body>
</html>
```

A rendering of the previous example is shown in Figure 14-1.

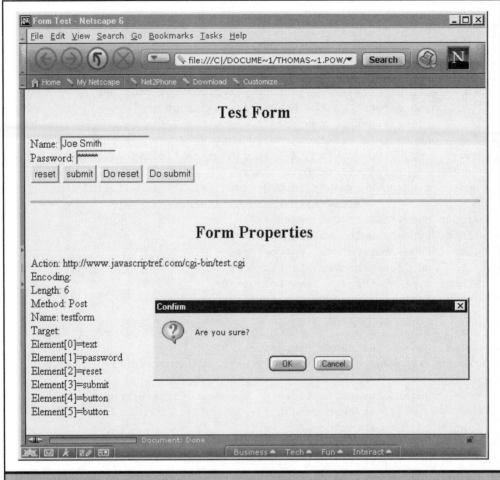

Figure 14-1. Testing basic Form properties and methods

Form Elements

HTML supports a variety of form elements, including single and multiple line text boxes, password fields, radio buttons, checkboxes, pull-down menus, scrolled lists, numerous types of buttons, and hidden fields. This section will present a quick review of each of these constructs and show how JavaScript can be used to access and potentially modify their properties.

Form Buttons

There are three types of basic buttons in HTML: submit, reset, and regular, nondefined function buttons. A fourth type of button is an image button, which is slightly different and will be discussed separately.

All of the basic button types are defined with HTML's versatile **<input>** tag. You would use **<input type="submit">** to create a submit button, **<input type="reset">** to create a reset button, and **<input type="button">** to create a generic button. To define the text that appears on the button, we set the **value** attribute, for example **<input type="button" value="Click me please!">**. We can also define the name of these buttons using the **name** attribute or using the **id** attribute under HTML 4. Like all HTML 4 tags, **<input>** accepts core attributes **id**, **class**, **style**, and **title** as well as language attributes like **lang** and **dir**. Under HTML4, **<input>** also supports attributes to disable the field (**disabled**), set its tabbing order (**tabindex**), and define a keyboard shortcut (**accesskey**). These attributes should not be overlooked as we can use them to improve the look and usability of an HTML button, as demonstrated here:

```
<form>
<input type="button" value="click me" name="button1"
       id="button1" title="please click me, pretty please"
       style="background-color: red; color: white"
       accesskey="c">
</form>
```

Remember that form elements must be defined within a **<form>** tag. While Internet Explorer may let you get away with direct usage of form elements anywhere in a document, browsers enforcing the standard (such as Netscape 6) will not render any form field elements outside a **<form>** tag.

The primary function of a button is to be clicked. This can be invoked with its **click( )** method. Of course, the **onclick** event handler is defined to intercept the event. You can also focus a button using its **focus( )** method and move away from it using its **blur( )** method. Often a browser will highlight a button in some fashion when it has focus—for example, under Internet Explorer a dotted line is placed on the button. Lastly, as we saw in the previous section, reset and submit buttons also trigger form-level reset and submit events. These are generally not caught at the button, but at the **Form** object level through the **onreset** and **onsubmit** event handler attributes for the **<form>** tag. The following simple example shows many of the methods and events for buttons in action.

```
<!DOCTYPE HTML PUBLIC "-//W3C//DTD HTML 4.01 Transitional//EN"
                     "http://www.w3.org/TR/html4/loose.dtd">
<html>
```

```
<head>
<title>Button Tester</title>
</head>
<body>
<form action="http://www.javascriptref.com" method="get"
      name="testform" id="testform"
      onreset="return confirm('Clear fields?')"
      onsubmit="return confirm('Send form?')">
Test Field: <input type="text" value="test information">
<br><br>

<input type="reset" value="clear fields"
       onclick="alert('clicked')">

<input type="submit" value="submit" name="thesubmit"
       id="thesubmit" onclick="alert('clicked')">

<input type="button" value="regular button"
       onclick="alert('clicked')">

<input type="button" value="Focus submit button"
       onclick="document.testform.thesubmit.focus()">

<input type="button" value="Blur submit button"
       onclick="document.testform.thesubmit.blur()">
<input type="button" value="Click the submit button"
       onclick="document.testform.thesubmit.click()">
</form>
</body>
</html>
```

Once again, the most interesting aspect of the previous example would be the **onsubmit** and **onreset** event handlers associated with the **<form>** tag. These event handlers will cancel the action when passed a **false** value and continue the action when given a **true** value. This lends itself well to the form validation schemes presented later in the chapter as well as to the verification of a form reset, as shown in the previous example.

Image Buttons

The simple grey buttons provided by standard HTML form buttons are often not desirable. Some designers add CSS rules to buttons, while others use image buttons.

There are a few ways to create image buttons in HTML. The first is simply to wrap an **<img>** tag within a link and trigger some JavaScript, for example:

```
<a href="javascript:document.myform.submit()"><img
src="images/submit.gif" width="55" height="21" border="0"
alt="Submit"></a>
```

This approach will work in all JavaScript-aware browsers that support javascript: pseudo-URLs. This is the preferred way to create graphical buttons that work under all browsers.

Alternatively, you might desire to use the **<input type="image">** form field. Under HTML such buttons are used to create a more graphical submit button. For example, to create a submission image, you might use

```
<input type="image" name="testbutton" id="testbutton"
       src="../images/button.gif" alt="Submit">
```

Notice the similarity between the use of the **alt** attribute and **src** attribute and that of the HTML **<img>** tag. You also will find that image maps can be used with graphical buttons via the **usemap** and **ismap** attributes. Most of these attributes are scriptable via DOM Level 1 using the corresponding property names, in this case **alt**, **src**, and **useMap**. Notice that **ismap** isn't defined (server-side image maps are rarely used on the Web anymore). Regardless of the use of **usemap** or **ismap** attributes, image-based submit buttons always send an x and y value in during submission, indicating the pixel coordinates of the image clicked. However, despite the definition in the HTML specification, you will find that support for this type of element is lacking in older browsers, and even newer browsers such as Internet Explorer 5 do not seem to properly recognize this element. Instead, use the **<a>** tag with the **<img>** tag to simulate a form button or consider using the HTML 4.0 style buttons described next.

Generalized HTML 4 Buttons

HTML 4 supports the **<button>** tag, which provides the possibility of visually richer buttons. The basic syntax of the **<button>** tag is presented here:

```
<button type="button | return | submit"
            name="button name"
            value="button value during submission">

Button content
</button>
```

Two examples of **<button>** in use are shown here:

```
<button type="submit" name="mybutton">
    <em>Yes sir, I am a submit button!</em>
</button>
<button type="button" name="mybutton2">
    <img src="button.gif" border="0" alt="button! ">
</button>
```

Renderings unfortunately might not be as expected:

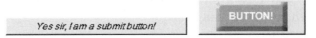

Given the basic syntax and previous example, DOM Level 1 defines the expected properties for the **HTMLButtonElement** object shown in Table 14-2.

Focus and blur events could be caught with **onfocus** and **onblur** event handlers. Click events and methods are also typically supported in browsers. However, despite its inclusion in W3C standards, the **<button>** tag is inconsistently rendered by browsers, so designers should instead opt to use common **<input type="submit">**, **<input type="reset">**, and **<input type="button">** tags or fake the operation of form buttons using links and images (as discussed earlier).

Property	Description
accessKey	Holds the accelerator key string
disabled	Boolean value indicating if field is disabled or not
form	Reference to the enclosing **Form** object
name	Name of the field (also uses id)
tabIndex	Numeric position in the tabbing order as defined by the **tabindex** attribute
type	Indicates the type of the button: "button," "reset," or "submit"
value	The value sent to the server if the form is submitted

Table 14-2.   *DOM Level 1 Properties for <button>*

Text Fields

In HTML forms, there are three types of text fields: single-line text entries, password fields, and multiline text fields called *text areas*. Although they are distinct in JavaScript, the text field objects are so similar that they are generally discussed as one object. We will discuss all these as one as well, but make sure to highlight any differences between the fields.

In HTML a single-line text field is defined by **<input type="text">,** while a password field is defined by **<input type="password">**. Under traditional HTML, both forms of the **<input>** element support the same attributes, as summarized here:

```
<input type="text or password"
       name="unique alphanumeric name for field"
       maxlength="maximum length of field in characters"
       size="display size of field in characters"
       value="default value for the field">
```

HTML 4.0 also adds attributes like **readonly**, which can be set to indicate the field can't be changed; **disabled** to turn off access to the field; **tabindex** to set the tabbing order in the page; and **accesskey** to set an accelerator key binding for the field. Also, as with any other HTML 4 element, we would expect the field to hold core attributes such as **id, class, style, title, lang**, and **dir**.

A few properties do require some brief discussion. First, the **form** property for a text or password field references the **Form** object that element is enclosed within. So, given

```
<form name="myform" id="myform">
  <input type="text" name="field1" id="field1">
</form>
```

the value of **document.myform.field1.form** is the **Form** object named *myform*. Of course, you might wonder about the usefulness of this, since we knew the form name to access the property. In short, it is most useful when a function or object is given some generic form field object without any indication of the form it is enclosed within.

The next property that should be discussed is **defaultValue**. This property holds the string set by the **value** attribute in the original HTML file. So, given **<input type="text" name="testfield" value="First value">**, the value of *testfield*.**defaultValue** would be the string "First value." This will also be held in the property *testfield*.**value**. However, as the user changes the contents of the field, the **value** property will change to whatever is in the field, while the **defaultValue** property will remain constant. The property **value** is settable and, while it might not appear useful to do so, **defaultValue** is also defined to be settable.

In traditional JavaScript as well as under DOM Level 1, all forms of text fields support the **blur( )**, **focus( )**, and **select( )** methods. The **select( )** method does have one important condition in that the field must have content in it to be selected. As far as event handling, **onblur**, **onfocus**, and **onselect** are of course supported. Text fields also support **onchange**, which is fired once a field's content has changed and the field has lost focus, and a variety of keyboard-related events, such as **onkeypress**, **onkeyup**, and **onkeydown**. We'll demonstrate the keyboard event handlers in a moment; for now, we'll examine an example that shows the use of all the text fields and their properties and methods, including both reading and setting values.

```
<!DOCTYPE HTML PUBLIC "-//W3C//DTD HTML 4.01 Transitional//EN"
                      "http://www.w3.org/TR/html4/loose.dtd">
<html>
<head>
<title>Textfield Test</title>
</head>
<body>
<h2 align="center">Test Form</h2>
<form name="testform" id="testform">
Text Field 1: <input type="text" name="text1" size="20"
                      value="Original Value"><br>
Text Field 2: <input type="text" name="text2" size="20"
                      maxlength="20"><br>
<input type="button" value="Check Value"
       onclick="alert(document.testform.text1.value)">
<input type="button" value="Set Value"
       onclick="document.testform.text1.value=
                  document.testform.text2.value">
<input type="button" value="Toggle Disabled"
       onclick="document.testform.text1.disabled=
                  !(document.testform.text1.disabled)">
<input type="button" value="Toggle Readonly"
       onclick="document.testform.text1.readOnly=
                  !(document.testform.text1.readOnly)">
<input type="button" value="Focus"
       onclick="document.testform.text1.focus()">
<input type="button" value="Blur"
       onclick="document.testform.text1.blur()">
<input type="button" value="Select"
       onclick="document.testform.text1.select()">
</form>
<hr>
<h2 align="center">Common Field Properties</h2>
<script language="JavaScript" type="text/javascript">
```

```
<!--
   document.write("defaultValue: " +
          document.testform.text1.defaultValue+"<br>");
   document.write("form: "+document.testform.text1.form+"<br>");
   document.write("form.name: " +
          document.testform.text1.form.name+"<br>");
   document.write("name: "+document.testform.text1.name+"<br>");
   document.write("type: "+document.testform.text1.type+"<br>");
   document.write("value: "+document.testform.text1.value+"<br>");

//-->
</script>
</body>
</html>
```

A rendering of this example is shown in Figure 14-2.

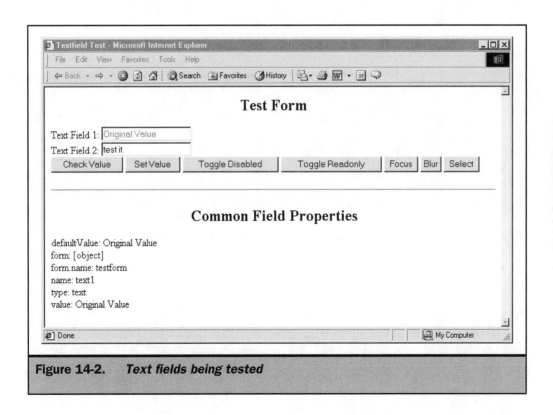

Figure 14-2.   *Text fields being tested*

Under HTML, a multiline text entry field is defined by the **<textarea>** tag. The basic syntax for **<textarea>** is

```
<textarea name="field name" id="field name"
                rows="number of rows"
                cols="number of columns">
Default text for the field
</textarea>
```

Accessing a **<textarea>** tag from JavaScript is similar to accessing a typical text or password field. Traditional JavaScript object models as well as the DOM's **HTMLTextAreaElement** object define two more properties, **rows** and **cols,** corresponding to the similarily named HTML attributes for this object. Also the **type** property will report the field as a *textarea* rather than *text*. Substitute a **<textarea>** tag for **<input type="text">** in the previous example and everything should work as expected.

One interesting aspect of the **<textarea>** tag that bears some discussion is that there is no obvious way to set the maximum amount of content that can be entered in the field. For browsers that support all the core events, such as **onkeypress**, we could easily limit the field, as shown here:

```
<!DOCTYPE HTML PUBLIC "-//W3C//DTD HTML 4.01 Transitional//EN"
                    "http://www.w3.org/TR/html4/loose.dtd">
<html>
<head>
<title>Limited Text Area</title>
</head>
<body>
<form name="myform" id="myform">
Comments:<br>
<textarea name="comments" id="comments" rows="4" cols="40"
onkeypress='return (document.myform.comments.value.length < 100)'>
Will be limited to 100 characters in a compliant browser.
</textarea>
</form>
</body>
</html>
```

Of course, the preceding script will not work in many older browsers because they do not support the **onkeypress** event. A possible work-around to deal with the unlimited field length is to examine the field's **length** when its contents change or at submit time and reduce it to the proper number of characters. The example here illustrates one possible approach to this problem:

```
<!DOCTYPE HTML PUBLIC "-//W3C//DTD HTML 4.01 Transitional//EN"
                    "http://www.w3.org/TR/html4/loose.dtd">
<html>
<head>
<title>Limited Text Area</title>
<script language="JavaScript" type="text/javascript">
<!--
function checkLimit(field, limit)
{
 if (field.value.length > limit)
  {
   alert("Field limited to "+limit+" characters");
   // Change it to the limit
   var revertfield = field.value.slice(0,limit-1);
   field.value = revertfield;
   field.focus();
  }
}
//-->
</script>
</head>
<body>
<form id="myform" name="myform">
Comments:<br>
<textarea id="comments" name="comments" rows="8" cols="40"
 onchange='checkLimit(this, 100)'>

Try entering 10 more characters to pass 100 characters
in this field. Then click outside.
</textarea>
</form>
</body>
</html>
```

Note   *A troublesome aspect of the **<textarea>** element is that the wrapping of text is not supported in a standard way between browsers. The nonstandard **wrap** attribute can be set a value to "soft" to enforce word wrapping in most browsers. Oddly, HTML 4.0 and the DOM do not address this issue, but normal JavaScript object models typically support access to this HTML property. If word wrapping behavior is critical to your application, you will have to address the issue on a browser-by-browser basis.*

Checkboxes and Radio Buttons

Checkboxes and radio buttons ("radios," for short) have much more limited functionality than a text field, and thus there is less to manipulate via JavaScript. In terms of HTML syntax, checkboxes and radio buttons are very similar, and both use the **<input>** tag. The basic HTML syntax for checkboxes and radios follows here:

```
<input type="checkbox or radio"
       name="field name"
       id="field name"
       value="checkbox value"
       checked>
```

The tag also supports common HTML 4 form attributes like **accesskey**, **disabled**, and **readonly**, which act similar to text fields.

There are two attributes related to checkboxes and radios that require some extra discussion. First is the presence of the **checked** attribute, which simply sets the field to be checked by default when the page loads or is reset. Second, the **value** attribute is sent to a server-side program when the field is checked. For example, given **<input type="checkbox" name="testbox" id="testbox" value="green">**, you would have a name-value pair of *testbox=green* transmitted when the field was checked. However, if no **value** attribute is provided, a value of *on* is transmitted instead. The JavaScript properties commonly supported and defined in DOM Level 1 for both checkboxes and radio buttons are shown in Table 14-3.

Property	Description
acccessKey	The accelerator key for the field as defined by the **accesskey** attribute
checked	Boolean value indicating if the field is checked or not
defaultChecked	Boolean value indicating initial checkbox state
disabled	Boolean value indicating if the field is disabled or not
form	Reference to enclosing **Form** object
name	Value of the **name** attribute
type	Holds the type of the field: *checkbox* or *radio*
value	Holds the contents of the **value** attribute

Table 14-3.   *Common Radio and Checkbox properties*

The primary events for the object include **onblur, onclick**, and **onfocus**. You can run **blur(), click(),** and **focus()** methods for checkboxes as well as radios, as will be discussed in a moment.

The main consideration with checkboxes and radios is how they are named. Often checkboxes are given unique names, and thus access to them is similar to other form elements. Given the following,

```
<form name="testform" id="testform">
Mustard: <input type="checkbox" name="mustard" id="mustard">
Ketchup: <input type="checkbox" name="ketchup" id="ketchup">
</form>
```

you would access the two checkboxes via **document.testform.mustard** and **document.testform.ketchup**. However, things change when checkboxes are defined with similar name values or when using radio buttons that required common **name** values in order to maintain the "one choice out of many" functionality. For example, given the following,

```
<form name="testform" id="testform">
Mustard:
<input type="checkbox" name="condiments" id="condiments"
      value="mustard"><br>
Ketchup:
<input type="checkbox" name="condiments" id="condiments"
      value="ketchup"><br>
Mayo:
<input type="checkbox" name="condiments" id="condiments"
      value="mayo"><br>
</form>
```

you would find that **document.testform.condiments** is a collection containing the individual checkboxes. Thus we can find the length of the collection through **document.testform.condiments.length** and even move through elements using array syntax like **document.testform.condiments[1]**. Radio buttons actually must be named this way, so the following,

```
Yes: <input type="radio" name="myradiogroup" id="myradiogroup"
      value="yes">
No: <input type="radio" name="myradiogroup" id="myradiogroup"
      value="no">
Maybe: <input type="radio" name="myradiogroup" id="myradiogroup"
        value="maybe">
```

works properly, while the following

```
Yes: <input type="radio" name="myradiogroup" id="myradiogroup1"
          value="yes">
No: <input type="radio" name="myradiogroup" id="myradiogroup2"
          value="no">
Maybe: <input type="radio" name="myradiogroup" id="myradiogroup3"
          value="maybe">
```

does not, as it fails to preserve the expected "one of many selection" of radio buttons.

Given that with radio or checkbox groups you will have an array of similarly named items, you will have to loop through the collection in order to figure out which item was selected. A complete example showing this as well as other radio and checkbox features is presented here; its rendering appears in Figure 14-3.

```
<!DOCTYPE HTML PUBLIC "-//W3C//DTD HTML 4.01 Transitional//EN"
                 "http://www.w3.org/TR/html4/loose.dtd">
<html>
<head>
<title>Radio/Checkbox Test</title>
<script language="JavaScript" type="text/javascript">
<!--
function showradiovalue(radiogroup)
{
   var numradios = radiogroup.length;

   for (var i = 0; i < numradios; i++)
      if (radiogroup[i].checked)
         alert('Radio '+i+' with value of '+radiogroup[i].value);
}
//-->
</script>
</head>
<body>
<h2 align="center">Test Form</h2>

<form name="testform" id="testform">
<em>Checkbox: </em>
<input type="checkbox" name="check1" id="check1" value="testvalue">
<br><br>
<em>Radio Buttons: </em>
Yes    <input type="radio" name="radiogroup1" id="radiogroup1"
              value="yes">
No     <input type="radio" name="radiogroup1" id="radiogroup1"
              value="no">
```

```
Maybe <input type="radio" name="radiogroup1" id="radiogroup1"
          value="maybe">
<br><br>
<input type="button" value="Click Checkbox"
     onclick="document.testform.check1.click()">
<input type="button" value="Click Radio"
       onclick="document.testform.radiogroup1[0].click()">
<input type="button" value="Focus Checkbox"
       onclick="document.testform.check1.focus()">
<input type="button" value="Blur Checkbox"
       onclick="document.testform.check1.blur()">
<input type="button" value="Checkbox State"
 onclick="alert('Checked?'+document.testform.check1.checked)">
<input type="button" value="Radio State"
      onclick="showradiovalue(document.testform.radiogroup1)">
</form>
<hr>
<h2 align="center"> Field Properties</h2>

<script language="JavaScript" type="text/javascript">
<!--
document.write("checked: " +
    document.testform.check1.checked+"<br>");
document.write("defaultChecked: " +
    document.testform.check1.defaultChecked+"<br>");
document.write("form: " +
    document.testform.check1.form+"<br>");
document.write("form.name: " +
    document.testform.check1.form.name+"<br>");
document.write("name: " +
    document.testform.check1.name+"<br>");
document.write("type: " +
    document.testform.check1.type+"<br>");
document.write("value: " +
    document.testform.check1.value+"<br><br>");
document.write("radiogroup array:" +
    document.testform.radiogroup1+"<br>");

document.write("radiogroup array length:" +
    document.testform.radiogroup1.length+"<br>");

document.write("radiogroup[0].value:" +
    document.testform.radiogroup1[0].value+"<br>");
```

```
//-->
</script>
</body>
</html>
```

Hidden Fields

Hidden form fields are defined using **<input type="hidden">**. The primary goal of this form element is to pass control or state information to a server-side program. The tag will never render on screen, though its name-value pair will be sent during normal form submission. Because it is nonvisual and noninteractive, the HTML syntax of a hidden field is essentially the following:

```
<input type="hidden" name="fieldname" id="fieldname" value="fieldvalue">
```

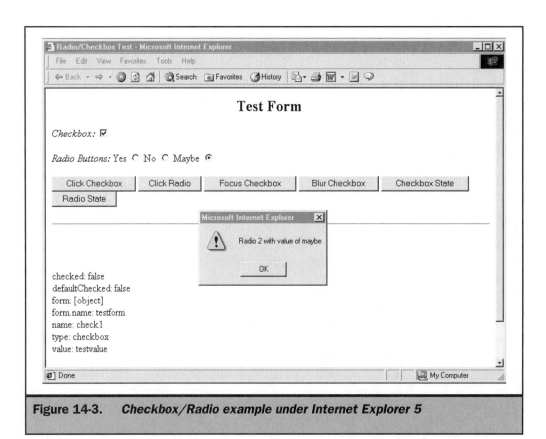

Figure 14-3. *Checkbox/Radio example under Internet Explorer 5*

While it is a part of the **<input>** tag and may support other attributes as defined both by Microsoft and the DOM object **HTMLInputElement,** no other attributes besides **disabled** make sense for this form of the **<input>** tag. The JavaScript properties to manipulate hidden tags are, simply, **disabled, form, id, name,** and **value** (which have been discussed for text fields previously). Hidden fields may not seem terribly useful to some readers, but for many state-preservation tasks they are extremely useful. We'll see some interesting possibilities for this form field when discussing form validation later in the chapter.

File Uploads

The last form of the **<input>** tag is the file upload control as defined by **<input type="file">.** The HTML syntax for the field is

```
<input type="file"
       id="field name"
       name="field name"
       size="field size in chars"
       accept="MIME types allowed for upload">
```

The tag is used to create a file upload field similar to this one in supporting browsers.

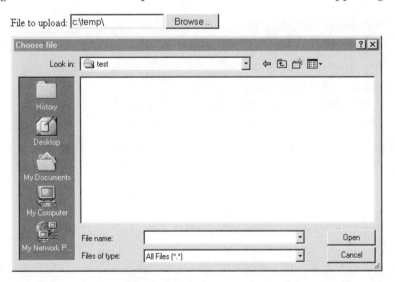

Unfortunately, from JavaScript you have little control over the appearance of the field. You can access all the common properties for the **HTMLInputElement** object, such as **readOnly, disabled, accessKey,** and so on. The only special property for this form of **<input>** is **accept,** which is used to define the allowed MIME types for upload. Unfortunately, given the lack of browser support for this attribute, it seems pointless for **<input type="file">** manipulating.

The main concern with the file upload field is what to do with the files once they are uploaded. Obviously, you would have to have a server-side program to save the file with an appropriate filename to a directory for examination or processing. Doing this is obviously beyond the realm of client-side JavaScript, but server-side technologies (some of which are related to JavaScript, as discussed in Chapter 19) might be useful to perform these tasks. Now that we have covered all forms of the **<input>** tag, it is time to cover the other form elements.

 A common oversight with file upload fields is that in order to work, the form must have method="POST," and the enctype attribute must be set to multipart/form-data.

Select Menus

In HTML the **<select>** element is used to define two forms of pull-down menus. The first and more common is a single-choice menu, often simply called a *pull-down*. The second form of the menu allows for multiple choices to be made and is generally referred to as a *scrolled list*. Under JavaScript we traditionally refer to both tags through one object, simply termed the **Select** object. Under the DOM Level 1, this combination is preserved, but the object is correctly known as the **HTMLSelectElement**.

To begin the discussion, we first present the common single-item pull-down and then the multiple choice item in HTML:

```
<b>Single Robot Choice:</b>
<select name="robot" id="robot">
      <option>Security</option>
      <option>Trainer</option>
      <option>Friend</option>
      <option>Cook</option>
</select>

<br><br>

<b>Multiple Robot Choice:</b>
<select name="robot" id="robot" size="4" multiple >
      <option>Security</option>
      <option>Trainer</option>
      <option>Friend</option>
          <option>Cook</option>
</select>
```

Single Robot Choice: Security

Multiple Robot Choice:

The syntax of the **<select>** tag itself is rather simple and has common HTML form attributes like **disabled**, **readonly**, and **tabindex**. A few important attributes require some discussion. First is **multiple**, the presence of which indicates the menu to be a multiple-select menu. The **size** attribute is also used to show the number of choices that are shown in the field; by default, the value for this attribute is **1** for single-select menus. Of course, as always the JavaScript properties for this HTML element are similar to its HTML attributes and are detailed in Table 14-4. We have left out the common **id**, **className**, **style**, **title**, **dir**, and **lang** properties, since they are common to all HTML elements.

There are two common JavaScript methods that can be performed on a **Select** object, **blur()** and **focus()**. However, three event handlers are commonly used for the object: **onblur**, **onfocus**, and **onchange**. The most useful, **onchange**, is fired whenever a choice in the menu is changed.

Property	Description
disabled	A Boolean value indicating if the field is disabled or not.
form	A reference to the enclosing **Form** object.
length	The number of **<option>** tags within the **<select>**. This is the same value as *selectmenu*.**options.length.**
multiple	A Boolean property indicating if the menu is single choice (**false**) or multiple choice (**true**).
name	The name of the menu as defined by the **name** attribute.
options[ ]	A collection referencing all the **<option>** tags within the **<select>** tag.
selectedIndex	This property holds the index of the currently selected menu choice in the **options[ ]** collection. In the case of *select-multiple* type menus, only the first choice will be held in this property.
size	The number of menu choices showing on the screen by default. The value is **1** in the case of *select-one* type menus.
tabIndex	Holds the value of the **tabindex** attribute indicating the position of the form field in the page's tabbing order.
type	This read-only property shows the type of menu, either *select-one* or *select-multiple*.

Table 14-4.   *Properties for HTMLSelectElement*

Property	Description
value	Holds a string corresponding to the **value** attribute of the selected **<option>** in the menu, or an empty string if the value attribute is undefined. In the case of a *select-multiple* menu, the value holds only the first selected **<option>** value. This property is not DOM Level 0 so is not supported in older browsers. Use the **selectedIndex** property and manually access the **options[ ]** collection to access values for full backwards compatibility.

Table 14-4.   *Properties for HTMLSelectElement* (continued)

The key to using a select menu, be it a single or multiple choice menu, is being able to look through the **options[ ]** for the current value. Given a single choice menu, the currently selected option is held in the **selectedIndex** property and is easily obtained, as demonstrated here.

```
<form>
    <select
     onchange="alert(this.options[this.selectedIndex].value)">
          <option value="value one">Option 1</option>
          <option value="value two">Option 2</option>
          <option value="value three">Option 3</option>
    </select>
</form>
```

However, when the multiple attribute is present you will be forced to loop through the **options[ ]** collection to find all the selected items:

```
<script language="JavaScript" type="text/javascript">
<!--
 function showSelected(menu)
   {
     var i, msg="";
     for (i=0; i < menu.options.length; i++)
      if (menu.options[i].selected)
        msg+="Option "+i+" selected\n";
     if (msg.length == 0)
        msg = "No options selected";
     alert(msg);
   }
```

```
//-->
</script>
<form name="myform" id="myform">
      <select name="myselect" id="myselect" multiple>
            <option value="value one" selected>Option 1</option>
            <option value="value two">Option 2</option>
            <option value="value three" selected>Option 3</option>
            <option value="value four">Option 4</option>
            <option value="value five">Option 5</option>
      </select>
      <br>
      <input type="button" value="Show Selected"
onclick="showSelected(document.myform.myselect)">
</form>
```

Once an option is retrieved you can then read its properties, which are shown in Table 14-5.

Property	Description
defaultSelected	A Boolean property indicating whether the **<option>** is selected by default. This property is **true** only when the **<option>** tag includes the **selected** attribute.
disabled	Boolean value indicating if the field has been disabled.
form	A reference to the enclosing **Form** object.
index	Holds the numeric index of the **<option>** within the **options[ ]** collection.
selected	A Boolean property indicating if the particular **<option>** was chosen in the menu. This property will respect the type of menu, allowing only a single item in a *select-one* menu.
text	The property holds the text within the **<option>** tag. This is often confused with the **value**, since the enclosed text of an **<option>** is sent to a server-side program when the **value** attribute is not used.
value	This property holds the string corresponding to the **value** attribute of the **<option>**.

Table 14-5.   *Properties for HTMLOptionElement*

Select menus are often used as navigation devices. (This feature is discussed in Chapter 16.)

Select Menu Interaction

One interesting possibility with select menus is the ability to affect one pull-down menu's choice with another. Related select menus provide the ability to present a large number of options very quickly to the user. The key to building such menus in JavaScript is understanding how to rewrite or even add new **<option>** values into a menu on the fly. The traditional way to do this in JavaScript is by using the new constructor on the **Option** object to create a new **<option>** to insert into the menu. The constructor syntax is

```
newOption = new Option (optionText, optionvalue);
```

where *optionText* is a string holding the text for the **<option>** and *optionValue* is a string to be used to set the value attribute for the tag. Once created, the **Option** objects can then be inserted into the **options[ ]** collection for a select menu. Of course, you should be careful to delete any unused entries by setting their values to **Null**. The following simple example provides two menus, one with a country and another with a list of cities. The city menu will change dynamically when the user chooses a country.

```
<!DOCTYPE HTML PUBLIC "-//W3C//DTD HTML 4.01 Transitional//EN"
                      "http://www.w3.org/TR/html4/loose.dtd">
<html>
<head>
<title>Related Select Test</title>
<script language="JavaScript" type="text/javascript">
<!--
// create array to hold other menu's options
var cities = new Array(4);
cities["Australia"] =
      ["Sydney", "Melbourne", "Canberra", "Perth", "Brisbane"];
cities["France"] =
      ["Paris", "Lyons", "Nice", "Dijon"];
cities["Japan"] = ["Tokyo", "Kyoto", "Osaka", "Nara"];
cities["New Zealand"] =
      ["Auckland", "Wellington", "Christchurch", "Dunedin",
"Queenstown"];

function removeOptions(optionMenu)
{
  for (i=0; i< optionMenu.options.length; i++)
```

```
        optionMenu.options[i] = null;
}

function addOptions(optionList, optionMenu)
{
 var i=0;
 removeOptions(optionMenu);  // clear out the options
 for (i=0; i < optionList.length; i++)
    optionMenu[i] = new Option(optionList[i], optionList[i]);
}
//-->
</script>
</head>
<body>
<h2>Vacation Chooser</h2>
<form name="testform" id="testform">
Country:
<select name="country" id="country"

onchange="addOptions(cities[this.options[this.selectedIndex].text],
                      document.testform.city)">
      <option selected>Australia</option>
      <option>France</option>
      <option>Japan</option>
      <option>New Zealand</option>
</select>

City:
<select name="city" id="city">
      <option>Sydney</option>
      <option>Melbourne</option>
      <option>Canberra</option>
      <option>Perth</option>
      <option>Brisbane</option>
</select>
</form>
</body>
</html>
```

Internet Explorer as well as DOM Level 1-compliant browsers support the **add(***element,before***)** and **remove(***index***)** methods to more easily work with the list of options in a **<select>** menu. However, note that in the case of the DOM, **add( )** expects the *before* parameter to indicate a particular **HTMLOptionElement** object, while, traditionally, in Internet Explorer, an index value was passed. However, the **remove( )** method works the same. Given the only recent and inconsistent support for these methods, developers are encouraged to use the traditional JavaScript technique shown in the previous example to manipulate the **options[ ]** collection.

*The approach of the previous example will actually work in very old browsers, but the use of array-literal syntax is not supported under older browsers. Interested readers can convert the example to support Netscape 3 or similar level browsers by creating arrays in a more verbose manner, using the **new Array( )** syntax and setting the various elements of the array.*

Option groups

HTML 4 introduces the **<optgroup>** element, which should be used to segment choices or even to create submenus. For example, consider the markup shown here.

```
<select name="robotchooser" id="robotchooser">
    <option>Choose your robot</option>
    <option>-----------------------</option>
    <option>Butler</option>
    <optgroup label="Security Models">
        <option>Man</option>
        <option>K-9</option>
    </optgroup>
    <optgroup label="Friend Models">
        <option>Female</option>
        <option>Male</option>
    </optgroup>
    <option>Trainer</option>
</select>
```

In Netscape 6 or in other browsers that support this tag, you would probably see something like this.

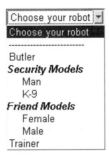

The DOM provides only two properties to manipulate this element via the **HTMLOptGroupElement** object, **disabled** and **label**. The **disabled** property is similar to any other form field, while **label** is obviously used to modify the **label** attribute for the tag. Strangely, unlike with option elements, the DOM does not provide shortcut methods to manipulate **<optgroup>** tags, nor is the **form** property defined. However, given the poor support for this tag in browsers so far, such oversights will probably not be missed.

Other Form Elements: Label, Fieldset, and Legend

HTML 4 defines a few other tags for forms that are primarily related to accessibility improvements and style sheets. For example the **<label>** tag is used to enclose form fields to clearly label them for both style sheets and nonvisual user agents. The following are two examples of the use of the **<label>** tag:

```
<form>
<label>Username:
        <input type="text" id="username" name="username">
</label><br>
<label for="userpassword">Password: </label>
<input type="password" id="userpassword" name="userpassword">
</form>
```

The DOM defines the **HTMLLabelElement** object to access label elements. Besides core properties like **id**, **className**, **style**, and **title**, the object defines **form**, **accessKey**, and **htmlFor**. Notice the use of **htmlFor** for the **for** attribute, in view of the fact that, under JavaScript, **for** is a reserved keyword. We'll see a use for **<label>** later in the chapter to improve form usability.

The **<fieldset>** tag is used to define a grouping around a set of elements. The **<legend>** tag is used within **<fieldset>** to create a label for the grouping. Here is an example of the usage of the two tags.

```
<form>
<fieldset>
<legend>Login Info</legend>
<label>Username: <input type="text" id="username"
name="username"></label><br>
<label for="userpassword">Password: </label>
<input type="password" id="userpassword" name="userpassword">
</fieldset>
</form>
```

Generally a browser will render elements within a **<fieldset>** within a box, as shown here.

From JavaScript we have very limited control over **<fieldset>** and **<legend>**, even from the DOM. Under DOM Level 1, the **HTMLFieldSetElement** object supports only the **form** property beyond its common attributes. The DOM's **HTMLLegendElement** supports **form** as well as **accessKey** and **align,** which correspond to the tag's HTML attributes. Except for possibly clicking a **<fieldset>** to select a particular form field, there is really little to do with this tag interactively.

Now that we have reviewed how to access all types of HTML form elements from JavaScript, it is time to put our knowledge to work by improving form usage through validation, usability improvements, and dynamic forms.

Form Validation

As mentioned numerous times previously, one of the best things you can do in JavaScript is check to make sure that a form is filled in properly. Checking form contents before submission over the network saves server processor cycles as well as the user's time waiting for the network round trip to see if the proper amount of data has been entered into the form. This section will provide an overview of some common techniques for form validation.

The first issue to consider with form validation is when to catch form fill-in errors. There are three possible choices:

- after they happen
- as they happen
- before they happen (prevent them from happening)

Generally, forms tend to be validated just before submission by running a set of validation functions associated with the **onsubmit** event handler. If the fields are in error, a message is displayed and the submission cancelled by returning a **false** value to the handler. If the fields are adequate, the submission continues normally. Consider the small example here that performs a simple check to make sure that something is in a field.

```
<!DOCTYPE HTML PUBLIC "-//W3C//DTD HTML 4.01 Transitional//EN"
                "http://www.w3.org/TR/html4/loose.dtd">
<html>
<head>
```

```
<title>Overly Simplistic Form Validation</title>
<script language="JavaScript" type="text/javascript">
<!--
function validate()
{
  if (document.myform.username.value == "")
    {
        alert('Username is required');
        return false;
    }
  return true;
}
//-->
</script>
</head>
<body>
<form name="myform" id="myform" method="get"
      action="http://www.javascriptref.com"
      onsubmit="return validate()">
Username:
<input type="text" name="username" id="username" size="30">
<input type="submit" value="Submit">
</form>
</body>
</html>
```

The previous example suffers from numerous deficiencies. First off, it really doesn't check the field well. A single space is acceptable using this validation. Second, it is not terribly abstract in that it doesn't work with a generic field. Lastly, the validation doesn't bring the field that is in error into focus. A more complex example correcting all these deficiencies is presented here.

```
<!DOCTYPE HTML PUBLIC "-//W3C//DTD HTML 4.01 Transitional//EN"
                    "http://www.w3.org/TR/html4/loose.dtd">
<html>
<head>
<title>Better Form Validation</title>
<script language="JavaScript" type="text/javascript">
<!--
// define whitespace characters
var whitespace = " \t\n\r";
function isEmpty(s)
{
```

```
    var i;
    if((s == null) || (s.length == 0))
      return true;
    // Search string looking for characters that are not whitespace
     for (i = 0; i < s.length; i++)
     {
      var c = s.charAt(i);
      if (whitespace.indexOf(c) == -1)
         return false;
     }

     // All characters are whitespace.
     return true;
}

function validate()
{
   if (isEmpty(document.myform.username.value))
     {
         alert('Username is required.');
         document.myform.username.focus();
         return false;
     }
   if (isEmpty(document.myform.userpass.value))
     {
         alert('Non-empty password required.');
         document.myform.userpass.focus();
         return false;
     }
   return true;
}
//-->
</script>
</head>
<body>
<form name="myform" id="myform" method="get"
      action="http://www.javascriptref.com"
      onsubmit="return validate()">
Username: <input type="text" name="username" id="username"
                  size="30"><br>
Password: <input type="password" name="userpass" id="userpass"
                  size="8" maxlength="8"><br>
```

```
<input type="submit" value="Submit">
</form>
</body>
</html>
```

Obviously, we might want to expand our validation scheme to be even more abstract so as to avoid repetitive code and address other types of field problems besides checking required fields to make sure that they are not empty. Further checks might indicate if the data entered is correct given what was requested. Common checks include making sure a field is a number, is a number in some range or of some length or form (such as a zip code or US Social Security number), or is something that at least looks like an e-mail address or a credit card number. Many of the checks, particularly the e-mail address and credit card number checks, are not really robust (the form data can really be checked only by making sure that e-mail address or credit card number actually works). We'll present e-mail and numeric checks here as a demonstration of common validation routines in action.

Many forms are used to collect e-mail addresses, and it is nice to ferret out any problems with addresses before submission. Unfortunately, it is difficult to guarantee that addresses are even in a valid form. In general, about the best you can say quickly about an e-mail address is that it is of the form *userid@domain,* where *userid* is a string that may be a single letter or digit and *domain* may be as simple as a top-level domain like "tv" or a more complex domain like mailsystem.javascriptref.com. Because of the variation in e-mail addresses, most validation routines generally look simply for something of the form string@string. The function here would check a passed field to see if it looks like a valid e-mail address.

```
function isEmail(field)
{
  var positionOfAt;
  var s = field.value;
  if (isEmpty(s))
    {
       alert("Email may not be empty");
       field.focus();
       return false;
    }

  positionOfAt = s.indexOf('@',1);
  if ( (positionOfAt == -1) || (positionOfAt == (s.length-1)) )
    {
       alert("E-mail not in valid form!");
       field.focus();
```

```
      return false;
   }
 return true;
}
```

Checking numbers isn't terribly difficult either. You can look for digits and you can even detect if a passed number is within some allowed range. The routines here show a way of doing just that:

```
function isDigit(c)
{
 return ((c >= "0") && (c <= "9"))
}
function isInteger(s)
{
  var i, c;

  if (isEmpty(s))
    return false;
  for (i = 0; i < s.length; i++)
    {
     // Check if all characters are numbers
     c = s.charAt(i);
     if (!isDigit(c))
       return false;
    }
  return true;
}

function isIntegerInRange (s,min,max)
{
  if (isEmpty(s))
    return false;

  if (!isInteger(s))
    return false;
  var num = parseInt (s);
  return ((num >= min) && (num <= max));
}
```

You might also want to use regular expressions (discussed in Chapter 8) to perform field checks. Of course, while not compatible with the very oldest versions of JavaScript, these routines provide an ability to perform complex checks quickly. Consider, for example, the integer check performed here as a regular expression:

```
var reInteger = /^\d+$/
function isInteger (s)
{
  if (isEmpty(s))
     return false;
  return reInteger.test(s);
}
```

A similar effect can be achieved by passing the string data to **parseInt()** and checking whether **NaN** is returned.

The last question is how these routines can be easily added in to work with any form. You might decide to hard-code the entries into the validation function. You also might use an array holding the names of the fields, the type of validation required, and the associated error messages. You would then loop through the array and apply the appropriate validation routine, as shown here:

```
<!DOCTYPE HTML PUBLIC "-//W3C//DTD HTML 4.0 Transitional//EN">
<html>
<head>
<title>Form Check</title>
<script language="JavaScript" type="text/javascript">
<!--
var whitespace = " \t\n\r";
/* Define validations to run */

validations = new Array();
validations[0] = ["document.myform.username", "notblank"];
validations[1] = ["document.myform.useremail", "validemail"];
validations[2] = ["document.myform.favoritenumber", "isnumber"];
function isEmpty(s)
{
  var i;
  if((s == null) || (s.length == 0))
    return true;
  // Search string looking for characters that are not whitespace
  for (i = 0; i < s.length; i++)
    {
       var c = s.charAt(i);
       if (whitespace.indexOf(c) == -1)
             return false;
    }
```

```
    // All characters are whitespace.
    return true;
}

function isEmail(field)
{
  var positionOfAt;
  var s = field.value;
  if (isEmpty(s))
    {
        alert("Email may not be empty");
        field.focus();
        return false;
    }
  positionOfAt = s.indexOf('@',1);
  if ( (positionOfAt == -1) || (positionOfAt == (s.length-1)) )
    {
        alert("E-mail not in valid form!");
        field.focus();
        return false;
    }
  return true;
}

function isDigit(c)
{
  return ((c >= "0") && (c <= "9"))
}

function isInteger(field)
{
  var i, c;
  var s = field.value;
  if (isEmpty(s))
    {
        alert("Field cannot be empty");
        field.focus();
        return false;
    }
  for (i = 0; i < s.length; i++)
    {   // Check if current character is number.
        c = s.charAt(i);
```

```
        if (!isDigit(c))
          {
            alert("Field must contain only digits");
            field.focus();
            return false;
          }
    }

 return true;
}

function validate()
{
  var i;
  var checkToMake;
  var field;

  for (i = 0; i < validations.length; i++)
    {
      checkToMake = validations[i][1];
      field = eval(validations[i][0]);
      switch (checkToMake)
        {
         case 'notblank': if (isEmpty(field.value))
                             {
                               alert("Field may not be empty");
                               field.focus();
                               return false;
                             }
                           break;
         case 'validemail':  if (!isEmail(field))
                                 return false;
                             break;
         case 'isnumber':  if (!isInteger(field))
                               return false;
        }
    }
  return true;
}
//-->
</script>
</head>
```

USING JAVASCRIPT

```
<body>
<form name="myform" id="myform" method="get"
      action="http://www.javascriptref.com"
      onsubmit="return validate()">
Username: <input type="text" name="username" id="username"
                 size="30"><br>
Email: <input type="text" name="useremail" id="useremail"
             size="30" maxlength="30"><br>
Favorite number: <input type="text" name="favoritenumber"
                        id="favoritenumber" size="10"
maxlength="10"><br>
<input type="submit" value="Submit">
</form>
</body>
</html>
```

Another somewhat more elegant possibility is to use hidden form field items and very generic routines. For example, you might define fields like:

```
<input type="hidden" name="fieldname_check"
value="validationroutine_errormessagestring">
```

In this case, we would define hidden form fields for each entry to validate, so to check that a field called *username* is not blank, we might use:

```
<input type="hidden" name="username_check"
value="notblank_Username+must+be+provided">
```

To check for an e-mail address, we might use

```
<input type="hidden" name="email_check"
value="email_Email+must+be+provided+and+well+formed">
```

We would then write a loop to look through forms being submitted for hidden fields and to look for ones in the form of *fieldname_check*. We would then use string routines to strip out the field name and associated error message to use and run the validation. Both of these methods will allow us to abstract our validation to the point where it can work with any form and even be included as an external .js file.

There are a variety of form validation routines that can be used and numerous ways they can be added to a page. However, given the number of people who need to do the same thing, it makes sense to start with a library when making your validation code. For example, take a look at **http://developer.netscape.com/docs/examples/ javascript.html** for some sample scripts. Netscape has provided a form validation collection of code ever since JavaScript 1.0 and also provides regular expression-oriented checks as well.

Validation Issues

Form validation is really a great use of JavaScript, but sometimes it is misused. This section will cover a few of the common issues with validation that should be considered.

- *Performing JavaScript validation when HTML could be used*   Rather than use JavaScript to validate the length of a field, use **maxlength**, or instead of checking a date, provide a pull-down of the possible dates so as to avoid bad entries. The same could be done for typing in state codes or other established items.

- *Providing errors one at a time*   Many people prefer to see all the errors at once, so you could collect each individual error in a string and alert one large dialog showing all the form's errors.

- *Clearly showing fields in error*   Often alerts don't clearly identify the fields that are in error. You might want to consider using the **style** attribute of a field and changing its background color to red or a similar value to indicate its error state. You can also use text fields' **select()** method to highlight problematic inputs.

- *Performing validation redundantly*   Given that fields are validated client-side using JavaScript, there is a question of whether they should be validated server-side as well. Conservative security conscious developers will probably opt for dual validation, but you may add a hidden form field like **<input type="hidden" name="validated" value="false">** and toggle its value to **true** when all fields are OK. Then the server-side program could examine this entry to see if the fields had been pre-validated.

- *Catching errors early*   Waiting until submission is not the best time to catch errors. Some developers will opt instead to catch errors when fields are left using the **onblur** handler. Unfortunately, it doesn't always work as planned because you may get into an endless event loop. If you do use blur and focus triggers, make sure to manage events, including killing their bubble (as discussed in Chapter 11). By using keyboard masks, discussed next, we can go one step further and catch errors before they are made.

Keyboard Masking

JavaScript makes it possible to limit the type of data that is entered into a field as it is typed. This goes along with the strategy of catching errors as they happen rather than waiting for validation later on. The following script could be used in browsers that support a richer event model (discussed in Chapter 11), such as 4.x generation browsers, to force a field to accept only numeric characters:

```
<!DOCTYPE HTML PUBLIC "-//W3C//DTD HTML 4.01 Transitional//EN"
                      "http://www.w3.org/TR/html4/loose.dtd">
<html>
<head>
<title>Numbers Only Field Mask Demo</title>
<script language="JavaScript1.2" type="text/JavaScript">
<!--
function numbersOnly(field, event)
{
 var key,keychar;

 if (window.event)
   key = window.event.keyCode;
 else if (event)
   key = event.which;
 else
   return true;

 keychar = String.fromCharCode(key);

 // check for special characters like backspace
 // then check for the numbers
 if ((key==null) || (key==0) || (key==8) ||
     (key==9) || (key==13) || (key==27) )
   return true;
  else if ((("0123456789").indexOf(keychar) > -1))
         {
            window.status = "";
            return true;
         }
       else
         {
            window.status = "Field excepts numbers only";
            return false;
         }
 }
//-->
</script>
</head>
```

```
<body>
<form name="testform">
Robot Serial Number:
<input type="text" name="serialnumber" size="10" maxlength="10"
       onkeypress="return numbersOnly(this, event)"
       title="Serial number contains only digits">
</form>
</body>
</html>
```

In this script, we detect the key as it is pressed and look to see if we will allow it or not. We could easily vary this script to accept only letters or even convert letters as they "occur" by looking at the key pressed and putting a different one into the field. Of course, don't over-engineer things if you can avoid it. In fully CSS1-compliant browsers, you may find that the **text-transform** property should do the job more simply, as shown here:

```
<form>
Uppercase:      <input type="text" style="text-transform: uppercase"
                       size="30"><br>

Lowercase:      <input type="text" style="text-transform: lowercase"
                       size="30"><br>

Initial Caps: <input type="text" style="text-transform: capitalize"
                       size="30"><br>
</form>
```

The benefit of masking a field is obviously that it avoids having to do heavy validation later on by trying to stop errors before they happen. Of course, you need to let users know that this is happening, both by clearly labeling fields and using advisory text (and even giving an error message, as we did by setting the window status message). You might consider using an alert dialog, but that might be too obtrusive.

Form Usability and JavaScript

There are a variety of form usability improvements that can be made using JavaScript, including focusing fields, automatically moving to other fields once a field is complete, toggling **readOnly** and **disabled** properties, and managing keyboard access, such as accelerators and submission on return key. This section presents an overview of a few of the possibilities with these usability improvements.

First Field Focus

For efficient form use, the user should be able to quickly use the keyboard to enter data in the form. While the tab key can be used to quickly move between fields, you should notice that most browsers will not focus the first field by default, and the user may be forced to click the field before starting keyboard entry. With JavaScript it is fairly easy to focus the first field in a form, and this should improve form entry in a subtle but noticeable way. We might use the **onload** event for the document to trigger the focus of the first field of a form. For example, given a form *testform* and the first field named *firstname*, we would set

```
<body onload="window.document.testform.firstname.focus()">
```

Of course you could write a generic routine to focus the first field of the first form in a field using something like:

```
<script language="JavaScript" type="text/javascript">
function focusFirst()
{
   if ((document.forms.length > 0)  &&
       (document.forms[0].elements.length > 0))
     document.forms[0].elements[0].focus();
}
window.onload=focusFirst;
</script>
```

Labels and Field Selection

While the HTML 4 **<label>** tag is useful to group items in forms for reading by nonvisual browsers, it also could be used with JavaScript to improve form usability. For example, we may desire to relate label actions with field actions. The idea is that when the label receives focus from the user, either by clicking on it or using an accelerator key, the focus should switch to the associated field. The click-select action of the label can easily be simulated using a little bit of JavaScript:

```
<form name="myform" id="myform">
<label onclick="document.myform.firstname.focus()">
 First Name:
 <input type="text" name="firstname" id="firstname">
</label>
</form>
```

In this example, a modern browser will bring the cursor to the associated field when the user clicks on the label by using the **focus()** method on the field. Fortunately, older browsers will just ignore the **<label>** tag as well as the JavaScript on the associated intrinsic event handler attribute.

 You could also write a very generic DOM oriented function to focus the first **<button>**, **<input>**, **<select>**, **<textarea>** *within a* **<label>** *or the value of its* **htmlFor** *property.*

Status Messages

Besides using tool tips as defined by an HTML element's **title** attribute, it may be useful to utilize the status bar to provide information to the user on the meaning and use of various form fields. While the status bar may not be in the primary area of focus for the user, unlike the tool tip it is not transitory and can be set to display a message as long as the field is in focus. We can use the **status** property of the **Window** object to set the status message when a field is focused—for example,

```
<input type="text" size="40" name="name" id="name"
       title="Enter your full name (Required field)"
       onfocus="window.status='Enter your full name (required)';"
       onblur="window.status='';">
```

Disabling Fields

A disabled form field should not accept input from the user, is not part of the tabbing order of a page, and is not submitted with the rest of the form contents. The presence of the HTML 4 attribute **disabled,** as shown here,

```
<input type="text" value="Can't Touch this" name="field1" id="field1" disabled>
```

would be all that's necessary to disable a field under an HTML 4.0-compliant browser. A browser rendering of a disabled field is usually to "gray out" out the field.

JavaScript can be used to turn disabled fields on and off depending on context. The following markup shows how this might be used.

```
<!DOCTYPE HTML PUBLIC "-//W3C//DTD HTML 4.01 Transitional//EN"
                      "http://www.w3.org/TR/html4/loose.dtd">
<html>
<head>
<title>Disabled 1</title>
</head>
<body>
<form name="myform" id="myform">
Color your robot?  
Yes <input type="radio" name="colorrobot" id="colorrobot"
```

```
value="yes" checked
onclick="myform.robotcolor.disabled=false;robotcolorlabel.style.color='black'">
No <input type="radio" name="colorrobot" id="colorrobot"
value="no"
onclick="myform.robotcolor.disabled=true;robotcolorlabel.style.color='gray'">
<br><br>
<label id="robotcolorlabel">
Color:
<select name="robotcolor" id="robotcolor">
    <option selected>Silver</option>
    <option selected>Green</option>
    <option selected>Red</option>
    <option selected>Blue</option>
    <option selected>Orange</option>
</select>
</label>
</form>
</body>
</html>
```

Note *Another way in this example to avoid setting the style of the label would be to disable the* ***<label>*** *itself. However, the approach used works better under most recent versions of Internet Explorer.*

Unfortunately the previous example does not work in Netscape 4 or other browsers that lack full HTML 4 support and vary in their scripting capabilities. However, with JavaScript it is possible to create a more backward-compatible disabling feature, as shown next, but it is less than an ideal approach. In this case, when the field is disabled, it is reset automatically when the user tries to change it. Also, the data will be passed in no matter if the field is disabled or not, so a hidden form field is added that can be relayed to the server to indicate that the field was disabled and can be ignored. This script should work well in all JavaScript-aware browsers, but be aware that it does not change the appearance of fields when they are disabled and does in some sense let the user make a mistake. A less than ideal solution to say the least.

```
<!DOCTYPE HTML PUBLIC "-//W3C//DTD HTML 4.01 Transitional//EN"
    "http://www.w3.org/TR/html4/loose.dtd">
<html>
<head>
<title>Disabled 2</title>
</head>
<body>
```

```
<form name="myform" id="myform">
Color your robot?  
Yes <input type="radio" name="colorrobot" id="colorrobot"
value="yes" checked
onclick="document.myform.robotcolordisabled.value='false'">
No <input type="radio" name="colorrobot" id="colorrobot"
value="no"
onclick="document.myform.robotcolordisabled.value='true'">
<br><br>
<input type="hidden" name="robotcolordisabled"
       id="robotcolordisabled" value="false">
Color:
<select name="robotcolor" id="robotcolor"
 onfocus="currentSelect=document.myform.robotcolor.selectedIndex"
 onchange="if (document.myform.robotcolordisabled.value == 'true')
{document.myform.robotcolor.selectedIndex=currentSelect;
 alert('Field is disabled') }">
    <option selected>Silver</option>
    <option>Green</option>
    <option>Red</option>
    <option>Blue</option>
    <option>Orange</option>
</select>
</form>
</body>
</html>
```

If possible, it is better to redesign a form not to rely on a *disable* function; if required, disabling can be accomplished by use of the HTML 4 **disabled** attributes and JavaScript that either hides a field or clears its value if it is disabled.

Read-Only Fields

Text fields can be set not only to a disabled state but also to read-only status. A read-only text field can be clicked on but not changed. Unlike disabled fields, the values of a read-only field are submitted to the server when a form is submitted. Under HTML 4, it is easy to set a text field to this state simply by including the **readonly** attribute, like so:

```
<input type="text" name="readonlyfield" id="readonlyfield" value="Can't touch
this!?" readonly>
```

Like the **disabled** feature of HTML 4, **readonly** does not degrade well, as older browsers will simply ignore the **readonly** attribute they don't understand, leaving the field modifiable. With JavaScript it is pretty easy to simulate the idea of **readonly** simply by blurring a field as soon as a user tries to select it. The example shown here demonstrates this in action:

```
<form name="myform" id="myform">
Change standard name of robot?  
Yes <input type="radio" name="colorrobot" value="yes" checked
onclick="robotnamereadonly=false;"
No <input type="radio" name="colorrobot" value="no"
onclick="robotnamereadonly=true;document.myform.robotname.value='Robby'">
<br><br>
<script language="JavaScript" type="text/javascript">
<!--
robotnamereadonly=false;
//-->
</script>
Name: <input type="text" name="robotname" id="robotname"
            value="Robby" size="20" maxsize="20"
            onfocus="if (robotnamereadonly) this.blur()">

</form>
```

Keyboard Improvements

If forms are used frequently in a Web site or intranet application, keyboard improvements should be considered, including the previously discussed field masking techniques, accelerator keys, keyboard form submission, and potentially even automatic field movement. Significant improvements can be made if users can focus on data entry rather than moving their hand from keyboard to mouse all the time. However, make sure to test such improvements carefully, as they can also become a source of major frustration for users.

Accesskeys

As we have seen in this chapter, HTML 4.0 introduces the use of the **accesskey** attribute for many form elements. The access key can be used to set an accelerator for a field so that the user can access the field using a key combination, usually ALT + the defined access key. For example,

```
<input type="text" size="40" accesskey="n" name="username" id="username">
```

sets the letter *n* as the accelerator for the field. In a browser such as Internet Explorer that recognizes this attribute, the key combination ALT-N will move the cursor to the field immediately. All other browsers will just ignore the key combination.

The actual key combined with the defined accelerator may vary based on the underlying system. For example, Macintosh users may use COMMAND *instead of* ALT *to activate accelerators. Regardless of the key used the syntax of the accelerator is the same.*

To avoid potential problems with access keys, it is important to make sure to let the user know exactly what keys are used to access fields. In traditional GUI interfaces, the letter of choice is underlined to indicate an accelerator key. For example, the *f* key is used to access the File menu. While this could be used on the Web, there potentially may be users who will consider the underlined letter a link. It is hoped that given the context of the underline and the lack of color, the user will not jump to this conclusion. However, because of this concern, it may be OK to indicate accelerators in another fashion, such as reversing them out. Consider the following potential styles to indicate the accelerator key.

The best approach to indicating accelerators is to use a style sheet. For example, you might define a class *accesskey* in a style sheet using a rule like

```
.accesskey    {text-decoration: underline;}
```

and then reference it later on in the form using a **<span>** tag around the particular letter being used as the accelerator:

```
<span class="accesskey">N</span>ame:
```

Using style sheets will allow you to experiment easily with different styles and will also allow easy removal of the key indications when a browser doesn't support the **accesskey** attribute. It is very important to turn off the key indication, as it would frustrate a user greatly to see an indication of a keyboard shortcut and not have it work.

While it would be a bit difficult to detect if a browser supports keyboard accelerators dynamically using JavaScript, you might make an educated guess about their support. For example, it is known that **accessKey** is supported in Internet Explorer 4 and better as well as Netscape 6. Other DOM-aware browsers probably would also support it. Using a simple object detection routine (discussed in Chapter 17), we might use a small script to add the stylesheet to the head of the HTML document, as shown next. Doing that would address the problem of having older browsers show the accelerator indication.

```
<!- - Use this in the HEAD section of the document only -->
<script language="JavaScript1.2">
<!- -
// detect modern browsers
if ((document.all)  || (document.getElementById))
{
```

```
document.write("<style>");
document.write(".accesskey    {text-decoration: underline;
                               font-weight: bold;}");
document.write("</style>");
}
//- ->
</script>
```

Note *Another potential problem with accelerator keys (besides lack of browser support) is the accidental masking or even overriding of browser accelerator keys. Defining access keys for F, E, C, V, G, A, and H should be avoided as they are defined in one of the two popular browsers.*

Return Keys and Forms

The use of the return key with Web forms is rather troublesome. Sometimes hitting the return key (ENTER) will cause the form to submit wherever the user is within the form—in a fair number of browsers, that is what happens. However, this is not always the case. Some browsers will not submit a form when the return key is pressed unless the form is composed of a single text field.

Many users would like to submit a form by pressing the return key, but generally only at the end of the form. Using JavaScript it is possible to create a hack that makes forms act consistently from browser to browser. The basic idea is that the form elements are in two separate forms. The first form contains the majority of the elements, and the second contains the last element that, after hitting return, should cause the form to submit. When the submission is triggered, the form fields from the first form are copied and sent. The script here illustrates this approach in action.

```
<!DOCTYPE html public "-//W3C//DTD HTML 4.01 Transitional//EN"
                      "http://www.w3.org/TR/html4/loose.dtd">
<html>
<head>
<title>Form Enter Key Hack</title>
<script language="JavaScript" type="text/javascript">
<!--
function duplicateFields()
{
  for (var i = 0; i < document.topForm.elements.length; i++)
   document.bottomForm.elements[i].value =
         document.topForm.elements[i].value;
}
//-->
</script>
```

```
</head>
<body>
<form name="topForm" id="topForm"> action="http://www.javascriptref.com"
method="get">
First Name: <input type="text" name="firstnametemp"
                    id="firstnametemp" value="">
<br><br>
Last Name: <input type="text" name="lastnametemp"
                  id="lastnametemp" value="">
<br>
</form>
<form name="bottomForm" id="bottomForm"> action="http://www.javascriptref.com"
method="get">
      onsubmit="duplicateFields()">
<input type="hidden" name="firstname"  id="firstname" value="">
<input type="hidden" name="lastname" id="lastname" value="">

Phone: <input type="text" name="phone" id="phone" value=""><br><br>
<input type="submit" name="submit" value="submit">
</form>
</body>
</html>
```

While this script does require JavaScript for the form to work, with some
careful sensing and use of **<noscript>** it should be possible to create a fully backward-
compatible implementation of this workaround. Before adding this script to your site,
along with any of the other usability improvements presented in this section, consider
that, unless there is heavy usage on a particular form, it may not be appropriate to go
to such lengths to improve form usage in such a subtle manner.

Dynamic Forms

Before concluding the chapter let's present one final example of how intelligence can
be added to a Web form to make it dynamic. As we have seen throughout the chapter,
it is possible to both read and write form field values; thus, besides checking data and
improving form usage, we should be able to use JavaScript to subtotal orders, calculate
shipping values, and fill in parts of the form dynamically. The following example shows
a simple form that adds up the number of items entered and calculates a subtotal, tax
rate, shipping cost, and grand total. A rendering of the example is shown in Figure 14-4.

```
<!DOCTYPE HTML PUBLIC "-//W3C//DTD HTML 4.01 Transitional//EN"
                      "http://www.w3.org/TR/html4/loose.dtd">
<html>
<head>
<title>Dynamic Form Demo</title>
```

```
<script language="JavaScript" type="text/javascript">
<!--
// set up form variables and constants
var widgetCost = 1.50;
var gadgetCost = 2.70;
var thingieCost = 1.25;
var taxRate = 0.075;
var shippingCost = 0;
function numbersOnly(field, event)
{
 var key,keychar;
 if (window.event)
    key = window.event.keyCode;
 else if (event)
    key = event.which;
 else
    return true;
 keychar = String.fromCharCode(key);
 // check for special characters like backspace
 // then check for the numbers
 if ((key==null) || (key==0) || (key==8) ||
    (key==9) || (key==13) || (key==27) )
    return true;
 else if (("0123456789".indexOf(keychar) > -1))
        {
           window.status = "";
           return true;
        }
      else
        {
           window.status = "Field excepts numbers only";
           return false;
        }
}

function format(value)
{   // format to have only two decimal digits
 var temp =  Math.round(value * 100);
 temp = temp / 100;
 return temp;
}


function calc()
```

```
{
 with (document.myform)
  {
   widgetTotal.value = format(widgets.value * widgetCost);
   gadgetTotal.value = format(gadgets.value * gadgetCost);
   thingieTotal.value = format(thingies.value * thingieCost);
   subtotal.value = format(parseFloat(widgetTotal.value) +
parseFloat(gadgetTotal.value) + parseFloat(thingieTotal.value));
   tax.value = format(subtotal.value * taxRate);

   for (i=0; i < shipping.length; i++)
     if (shipping[i].checked)
         shippingCost = parseFloat(shipping[i].value);
   grandTotal.value = format(parseFloat(subtotal.value) +
                     parseFloat(tax.value) + shippingCost);
  }
}
//-->
</script>
</head>
<body>
<form id="myform" name="myform">

Widgets: <input type="text" name="widgets" id="widgets"
size="2" value="0" onchange="calc()"
onkeypress="return numbersOnly(this, event)"> @ 1.50 each
<input type="text" id="widgetTotal" name="widgetTotal"
       size="5" readonly><br>

Gadgets: <input type="text" name="gadgets" id="gadgets"
size="2" value="0" onchange="calc()"
onkeypress="return numbersOnly(this, event)"> @ 2.70 each
<input type="text" id="gadgetTotal" name="gadgetTotal"
       size="5" readonly><br>

Thingies: <input type="text" name="thingies" id="thingies"
size="2" value="0" onchange="calc()"
onkeypress="return numbersOnly(this, event)"> @ 1.25 each
<input type="text" id="thingieTotal" name="thingieTotal"
       size="5" readonly><br>
<br><br>
<em>Subtotal:</em> <input type="text" id="subtotal"
                    name="subtotal" size="8" value="0" readonly>
<br><br><br>
```

```
<em>Tax:</em> <input type="text" id="tax" name="tax" size="5"
                    value="0" readonly><br>
<br><br>
<em>Shipping:</em>
Next day: <input type="radio" value="12.00" name="shipping"
                id="shipping" checked onclick="calc()">
2-day: <input type="radio" value="7.00" name="shipping"
              id="shipping" onclick="calc()">
Standard: <input type="radio" value="3.00" name="shipping"
                id="shipping" onclick="calc()"><br>
<br><br>
<strong>Grand Total:</strong>
<input type="text" id="grandTotal" name="grandTotal"
      size="8" readonly>
</form>
</body>
</html>
```

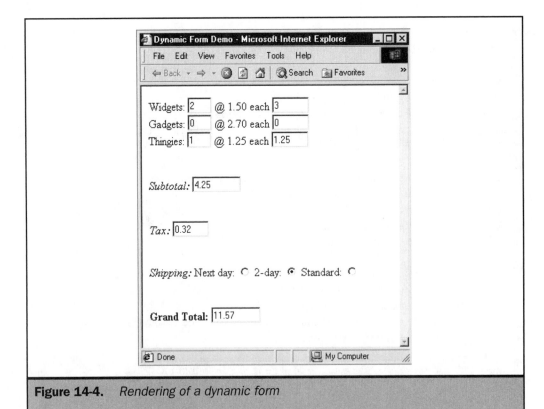

Figure 14-4. *Rendering of a dynamic form*

Note that the previous example uses field masking to avoid excessive checking of form contents and liberal use of the **readonly** attribute to keep users from thinking they can modify calculated fields. Also note that, because of JavaScript's relatively poor numeric formatting, we added in a rudimentary formatting function. Given this basic example, you should see how it is possible to add calculators or other more dynamic form applications to your site.

Summary

Form fields have been accessible via JavaScript since the earliest incarnations of the language. The primary goal in accessing form elements is to validate their contents before submission. However, we also saw in this chapter that usability improvements are possible using very small amounts of code. More complex examples, such as fully dynamic forms, are also possible, and with the DOM, forms can even be more dramatically modified. While many of the examples presented in this chapter are useful for common Web sites, programmers are encouraged to either write their own or build validation libraries to ensure the highest quality form data is submitted. The next chapter will examine another common use of JavaScript—image rollovers and screen animations.

Chapter 15

Image Effects: Rollovers, Positioning, and Animation

In this chapter we explore the use of JavaScript to add flash and sizzle to web pages. Starting first with the basic rollover or mouseover script that toggles images when the user is hovering over them, we then proceed to more complicated rollover forms, including target-based and Cascading Style Sheets (CSS)-based rollovers. The manipulation of CSS-positioned regions is also discussed, with attention given to visibility and positioning issues. Finally, we describe how to create basic animation effects by using timers to move and change positioned objects and text. An emphasis is placed on making all introduced effects as cross-browser compliant as possible.

Image Basics

We begin our discussion by presenting the basics of manipulating an image in a Web page using the HTML **<img>** tag. Starting with Netscape 3 and later adopted by Internet Explorer 4 and the DOM Level 1 standard, the **images[ ]** collection was added to the **Document** object. The collection contains **Image** objects as defined by the **<img>** tag. This collection can be referenced numerically (**document.images[i]**), associatively (**document.images['imagename']**), and directly (**document.imagename**).

Once you access a particular image, you will find that the properties for its object correspond, as expected, to the attributes of the **<img>** tag as defined for HTML 4. An overview of the common properties of the **Image** object (also known as the **HTMLImageElement** under the DOM Level 1) beyond the common **id**, **className**, **style**, and **title** properties is presented in Table 15-1.

Property	Description
align	Indicates the alignment of the image, usually left or right.
alt	The alternative text rendering for the image as set by the **alt** attribute.
border	The border around the image in pixels.
complete	A Boolean value indicating if the image has completely loaded.

Table 15-1. *Image Object Properties*

Property	Description
height	The height of the image defined as a pixel or percentage value.
hspace	The horizontal space around the image.
isMap	Boolean value indicating presence of the **ismap** attribute, which indicates the image is a server-side image map. The **useMap** property is used more often today.
longDesc	The value of the HTML 4 **longdesc** attribute, which provides a more verbose description for the image than the **alt** attribute.
lowsrc	The URL of the "low source" image as set by the **lowsrc** attribute. Under DOM Level 1, this is specified by **lowSrc** property.
name	The value of the **name** attribute for the image.
src	The URL of the image.
useMap	The URL of the client-side image map if the **<img>** tag has a **usemap** attribute.
vspace	The vertical space in pixels around the image.
width	The width of the image in pixels or as a percentage value.

Table 15-1.   *Image Object Properties* (continued)

The traditional **Image** object also supports **onabort**, **onerror**, and **onload** event handlers. The **onabort** handler is invoked when the user aborts the loading of the image, usually by hitting the browser's stop button. The **onerror** handler is fired when an error occurs during image loading. The **onload** handler is, of course, fired once the image has loaded. Under modern browser implementations that support HTML 4 properly, you will also find **onmouseover**, **onmouseout**, **onclick**, and the rest of the core events supported for **Image**. However, under Netscape 3 browsers, these would not be supported. In addition, the **Image** object does not support any methods under traditional JavaScript implementations, such as Netscape 3.

The following example illustrates simple access to the common properties of **Image**. A rendering of the example is shown in Figure 15-1.

```html
<!DOCTYPE HTML PUBLIC "-//W3C//DTD HTML 4.01 Transitional//EN"
         "http://www.w3.org/TR/html4/loose.dtd">
<html>
<head>
<title>JavaScript Image Object Test</title>
</head>
<body>
<img src="sample.gif" width="200" height="100"
name="image1" id="imageI" align="left"
alt="Test Image" border="0">
<br clear="all">
<hr>
<br clear="all">
<h1>Image Properties</h1>
<form name="imageForm" id="imageForm">
    Left:
  <input type="radio" name="align" id="align" value="left" checked
onchange="document.image1.align=this.value">
    Right:
    <input type="radio" name="align" id="align" value="right"
onchange="document.image1.align=this.value"><br>
    Alt:
    <input type="text" name="alt" id="alt"
onchange="document.image1.alt=this.value"><br>
    Border:
    <input type="text" name="border" id="border"
onchange="document.image1.border=this.value"><br>
    Complete:
    <input type="text" name="complete" id="complete"><br>
    Height:
    <input type="text" name="height" id="height"
onchange="document.image1.height=this.value"><br>
    Hspace:
    <input type="text" name="hspace" id="hspace"
onchange="document.image1.hspace=this.value"><br>
    Name:
    <input type="text" name="name" id="name"><br>
    Src:
    <input type="text" name="src" id="src" size="40"
```

```
onchange="document.image1.src=this.value"><br>
    Vspace:
    <input type="text" name="vspace" id="vspace"
onchange="document.image1.vspace=this.value"><br>
    Width:
    <input type="text" name="width" id="width"
onchange="document.image1.width=this.value">
</form>

<script language="JavaScript" type="text/javascript">
<!--
function populateForm()
{
  if ((document.image1)  && (document.image1.complete))
  {
    with (document.imageForm)
      {
        alt.value = document.image1.alt;
        border.value = document.image1.border;
        complete.value = document.image1.complete;
        height.value = document.image1.height;
        name.value = document.image1.name;
        src.value = document.image1.src;
        vspace.value = document.image1.vspace;
        width.value = document.image1.width;
        if (document.image1.align == 'left')
          align[0] = checked;
        else if (document.image1.align == 'right')
          align[1] = checked;
      }
  }
}

window.onload = populateForm;
//-->
</script>
</body>
</html>
```

If you try this example under Netscape 3, you will find that it is not possible to manipulate the properties of the **Image** object, except for the **src** attribute. This leads to the first application of the **Image** object—the ubiquitous rollover button.

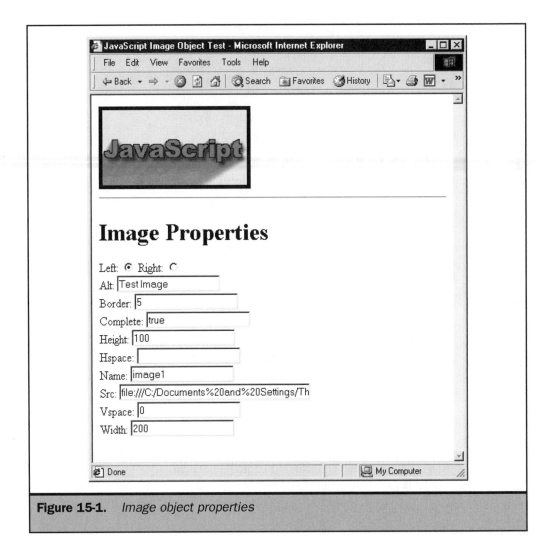

Figure 15-1. *Image object properties*

Rollover Buttons

A common use of JavaScript is for page embellishment. One of the most common embellishments is the inclusion of rollover buttons, a JavaScript feature that has been available since Netscape 3. A *rollover button* is a button that becomes active when the user positions the mouse over it. The button also can have a special activation state when it is pressed. To create a rollover button, you first will need at least two, perhaps even three images, to represent each of the button's states—*inactive*, *active*, and *unavailable*. A simple pair of images for a rollover button is shown here:

To add this rollover image to the page, simply use the **<img>** tag like you normally would. The idea is to swap the image out when the mouse passes over the image and switch back to the original image when the mouse leaves the image. By literally swapping the value of the **src** attribute when the mouse is over the image, you can achieve the rollover effect. With the following,

```
<img src="imageoff.gif" name="myimage" id="myimage">
```

you might be tempted to try

```
<img src="imageoff.gif" name="myimage" id="myimage"
onmouseover="document.myimage.src='imageon.gif'"
onmouseout="document.myimage.src='imageoff.gif'">
```

While this would work in modern browsers, under Netscape 4 you cannot capture **mouseover** events on an image in this way, and in Netscape 3 you can't capture them at all. However, remember that an image can be surrounded by a link, so it is therefore possible to use the **Link** object's event handlers for control purposes. This short example shows how rollovers work from a theoretical standpoint, assuming you had two images called imageon.gif and imageoff.gif.

```
<!DOCTYPE HTML PUBLIC "-//W3C//DTD HTML 4.01 Transitional//EN"
        "http://www.w3.org/TR/html4/loose.dtd">
<html>
<head>
<title>Quick and Dirty Rollovers</title>
<script language="JavaScript" type="text/javascript">
<!--
function mouseOn()
{
 document.image1.src = 'imageon.gif'
}


function mouseOff()
{
  document.image1.src = 'imageoff.gif'
```

```
}
//-->
</script>
</head>
<body>
<a href="#" onmouseover="mouseOn()" onmouseout="mouseOff()">
<img name="image1" id="image1" src="imageoff.gif"
border="0" width="90" height="90"></a>
</body>
</html>
```

While this script will work under Netscape 3 (and better) browsers, you will find that some older JavaScript-enabled browsers, such as Internet Explorer 3 and Netscape 2, do not support access to the **images[ ]** collection. Thus, we should detect for support before trying to modify an image. The easiest way to make sure the user is running a browser that supports the **document.images[ ]** collection is to use a conditional statement:

```
if (document.images)
{
   // do image related code.
}
```

This statement determines whether or not the **document.images** exists. If the object does not exist, **document.images** is **undefined**, so it evaluates to **false** when used in a conditional statement. On the other hand, if the array is not **undefined**, it evaluates to **true** in a conditional statement. You must be sure not to attempt to manipulate **document.images** or an **Image** object unless **document.images** exists, because doing so will cause a runtime error.

Even if the **Image** object is supported, we need to consider whether or not the images that are being used in the rollover effect have been downloaded. If not, the user will see broken images. Thus, we should try to preload images rather than hope that the images are loaded before the mouse rolls over the image. The easiest way to do this is to create an image element and set its source in the **<head>** of a document before the page loads. To create an image, use the object constructor **new**:

```
var variableName = new Image();
```

You should pass in the width and height to the constructor (in reality, it doesn't make much difference, particularly for our simple preloading goal):

```
var imageName = new Image(width, height);
```

Once the object is created, set the **src** property so that the browser *preloads* (downloads before it is actually required) the desired image:

```
variableName.src = "URL of image";
```

A rollover requires two images, so it is often a good idea to create both the *on* and *off* states ahead of time. Be sure to make the images the same size, or you will see some distortion under browsers, like Netscape 3 and 4, that cannot reflow a document easily after page load.

Given this new information, a slightly cleaner version of the last rollover example, with some object checking, is shown here:

```html
<!doctype html public "-//W3C//DTD HTML 4.01 Transitional//EN"
        "http://www.w3.org/TR/html4/loose.dtd">
<html>
<head>
<title>Cleaner Roll Code</title>
<script language="JavaScript" type="text/javascript">
<!--

if (document.images)
{
  // preload images
  var offimage = new Image(90,90);  // for the inactive image
  offimage.src = "imageoff.gif";
  var onimage = new Image(90,90);   // for the active image
  onimage.src = "imageon.gif";
}

function mouseOn()
{
  if (document.images)
    document.images.image1.src = onimage.src;
}

function mouseOff()
{
  if (document.images)
    document.images.image1.src = offimage.src;
}
// -->
</script>
</head>
```

```
<body>
<a href="http://www.pint.com" onmouseover="mouseOn()"
onmouseout="mouseOff()">
<img src="imageoff.gif" name="image1" id="image1" border=
"0" width="90" height="90" alt=""></a>
</body>
</html>
```

This example is closer to what we need. One issue that arises is how to deal with multiple images in a page with generalized rollover code. The key is naming the images in a consistent manner, such as adding the word "On" or "Off" to the end of each named image. We could then automatically compute what image we want by simple evaluation of the name and the appropriate suffix. This is best illustrated in an example:

```
<script language="JavaScript" type="text/javascript">
<!--

if (document.images)
  {
   /* preload images */

   var homeOn = new Image();
   homeOn.src = "homeOn.gif";

   var homeOff = new Image();
   homeOff.src = "homeOff.gif";

   var productsOn = new Image();
   productsOn.src = "productsOn.gif";

   var productsOff = new Image();
   productsOff.src = "productsOff.gif";
  }

function mouseOn(imgName)
{
  if (document.images)
    document[imgName].src = eval(imgName + "On.src");
}

function mouseOff(imgName)
```

```
{
  if (document.images)
    document[imgName].src = eval(imgName + "Off.src");
}
// -->
</script>
```

Later on, somewhere in our HTML file we would have appropriately named the images and links with **onmouseover** and **onmouseout** handlers to trigger the appropriate parts of the script.

```
<a href="home.html" onmouseover="mouseOn('home')"
onmouseout="mouseOff('home')"><img src=
"homeOff.gif" height="50" width="100"  name="home"  id= "home"
    border="0"
alt="Home"></a>
<br>

<a href="products.html" onmouseover="mouseOn('products')"
onmouseout="mouseOff('products')"><img src=
"productsOff.gif" height="50" width="100" name="products" id="products"
    border="0"
alt="Products"></a>
<br>
```

Given such a script, rollovers are limited only by one's capability to copy-paste and keep names correct. However, be careful with too many images in your pages. You are almost doubling your download time with image rollovers! The complete rollover script is shown here.

```
<!doctype html public "-//W3C//DTD HTML 4.01 Transitional//EN"
        "http://www.w3.org/TR/html4/loose.dtd">
<html>
<head>
<title>Rollovers!</title>
<script language="JavaScript" type="text/javascript">
<!--

if (document.images)
 {
  /* preload images */

  var homeOn = new Image();
```

```
      homeOn.src = "homeon.gif";

   var homeOff = new Image();
   homeOff.src = "homeoff.gif";

   var productsOn = new Image();
   productsOn.src = "productson.gif";

   var productsOff = new Image();
   productsOff.src = "productsoff.gif";
   }

function mouseOn(imgName)
{
  if (document.images)
     document[imgName].src = eval(imgName + "On.src");
}

function mouseOff(imgName)
{
  if (document.images)
     document[imgName].src = eval(imgName + "Off.src");
}
// -->
</script>
</head>
<body>
<a href="home.htm" onmouseover="mouseOn('home')"
onmouseout="mouseOff('home')">
<img src="homeoff.gif" name="home" id="home" border=
"0" width="90" height="90" alt=""></a><br>

<a href="products.htm" onmouseover=
"mouseOn('products')" onmouseout="mouseOff('products')">
<img src="productsoff.gif" name="products" id=
"products" border="0" width="90" height="90" alt=""></a><br>
</body>
</html>
```

Because rollovers are so common on Web sites, there are many tools (such as Macromedia's Dreamweaver and Fireworks) that can create the code instantly when provided with two images. Notice that the dialog shown here from Dreamweaver requests the items that we used in our script.

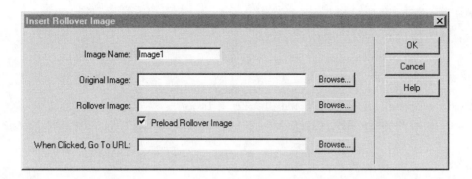

Extending Rollovers

Once the basic rollover is mastered, the next thing to resolve is how to extend the script. Usually the method involves manipulating multiple images at once or improving the rollover to use less bandwidth. For example, rollovers can reveal text or imagery someplace else on the screen as the user moves over a link. A script can be written to reveal a scope note as well as change the state of the link. The following markup and JavaScript illustrate how this would work:

```
<!DOCTYPE HTML PUBLIC "-//W3C//DTD HTML 4.01 Transitional//EN"
        "http://www.w3.org/TR/html4/loose.dtd">
<html>
<head>
<title>Targeted Rollovers</title>
<script language="JavaScript" type="text/javascript">
<!--
/* preload all images */
if (document.images)
   {
      abouton = new Image(147, 29);
      abouton.src = "abouton.gif"
      aboutoff = new Image(147, 29);
      aboutoff.src = "about.gif"

      blank = new Image(130, 127);
      blank.src = "blank.gif"

      description1 = new Image(130, 127);
      description1.src = "description.gif"
   }
```

USING JAVASCRIPT

```
function On(imgName,description)
{
  if (document.images)
    {
      imgOn = eval(imgName + "on.src");
      document.images[imgName].src = imgOn;
      document.images.descriptionregion.src= description.src;
    }
}

function Off(imgName)
{
  if (document.images)
    {
      imgOff = eval(imgName + "off.src");
      document.images[imgName].src = imgOff;
      document.images.descriptionregion.src= "blank.gif";
    }
}
// -->
</script>
</head>
<body>

<a href="about.htm"
   onmouseover="On('about',description1);
   window.status='Company'; return true"
   onmouseout="Off('about');">

<img src="about.gif" border="0" alt="About" name="about" id="about"
     width="159" height="57"></a>
   
<a href="#">
<img src="blank.gif" name="descriptionregion" id="descriptionregion"
     width="328" height="84" border="0" alt=""></a>

</body>
</html>
```

Figure 15-2 shows the rollover code in action.

Generally, designers are encouraged to use rollovers that reveal extra information or to change the look of an object. Imagine rolling over an image of color samples and

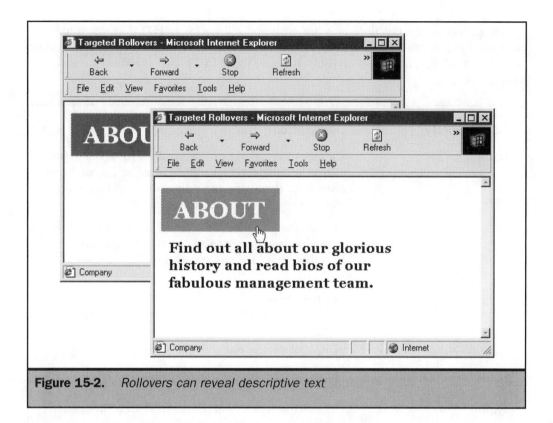

Figure 15-2.   *Rollovers can reveal descriptive text*

USING JAVASCRIPT

having the image of a car change. That's an easy application of rollovers. However, always remember that advanced rollover applications can be troublesome because they require numerous images. Fortunately, using style sheets, lightweight rollover messages can be built, as we'll see later in the chapter in the section "Applied DHTML." For now, let's cover the syntax required to implement more complex CSS-based visual effects.

CSS Positioning

With CSS we have the possibility to modify the look and feel of a Web page in dramatic fashion. With CSS properties, we can control font-sizes (**<h1 style="font-size: 56pt">Test</h1>**), line spacing (**<p style="line-height: 150%">**), and a variety of other formatting properties (**<span style="color: red; text-decoration: underline">**). An important extension made to CSS Level 1 even allows for the positioning of objects on the screen. This extension, known as CSS-P (P obviously for positioning), was quickly adopted by the 4.x generation browsers—despite the incomplete support by these browsers of many CSS properties.

The power of CSS positioning is dramatic and allows for an HTML element to be positioned at any arbitrary pixel coordinate on the screen. Related CSS properties allow for sizing, visibility, and other stylistic changes. Table 15-2 presents a short summary of these properties.

CSS Property	Description
position	Defines the type of positioning used for an element: *static* (default), *absolute, relative, fixed,* or *inherit.* Most often *absolute* is used to set the exact position of an element regardless of document flow.
top	Defines the position of the object from the top of the enclosing region. For most objects, this should be from the top of the content area of the browser window.
left	Defines the position of the object from the left of the enclosing region, most often the left of the browser window itself.
height	Defines the height of an element. With positioned items, a measure in pixels (**px**) is often used, though others like percentage (%) are also possible.
width	Defines the width of an element. With positioned items, a measure in pixels (**px**) is often used.
clip	A clipping rectangle like **clip: rect (*top right bottom left*)** can be used to define a subset of content that is shown in a positioned region as defined by the rectangle with upper-left corner at (*left,top*) and bottom-right corner at (*right,bottom*). Note that the pixel values of the rectangle are relative to the clipped region and not the screen.
visibility	Sets whether an element should be visible. Possible values include *hidden, visible,* and *inherit.*
z-index	Defines the stacking order of the object. Regions with higher **z-index** number values stack on top of regions with lower numbers. Without **z-index**, the order of definition defines stacking, with last object defined the highest up.

Table 15-2.   *Common CSS Properties Related to Positioning*

The following simple example demonstrates some of the CSS rules from Table 15-2 being used to position three regions on the screen. A rendering of this example shown in four different browsers is presented in Figure 15-3.

```
<!DOCTYPE HTML PUBLIC "-//W3C//DTD HTML 4.01 Transitional//EN"
        "http://www.w3.org/TR/html4/loose.dtd">
<html>
<head>
<title>CSS Positioning Basics</title>
<style type="text/css">
<!--
#layer1 {position: absolute;
        top: 40px; left: 120px;
        z-index: 2;
        height: 50px; width: 50px;
        color: white; background-color: blue;}

#layer2 {position: absolute;
        top: 20px; left: 80px;
        z-index: 1;
        height: 150px; width: 150px;
        color: black; background-color: orange;}

#layer3 {position: absolute;
        top: 75px; left: 40px;
        z-index: 3;
        height: 25px; width: 100px;
        color: black; background-color: yellow;}
-->
</style>
</head>
<body>

<div id="layer1">This is layer 1</div>
<div id="layer2">This is layer 2</div>
<div id="layer3">This is layer 3</div>

</body>
</html>
```

A few comments are required for the previous example. First, notice that in the rendering in Figure 15-3 that differences occur visually even in CSS-aware browsers. Most of these differences revolve around the fact that Netscape 4 actually favors a

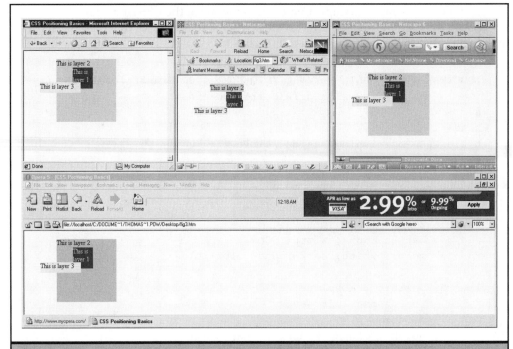

Figure 15-3.   *CSS-positioned regions under Internet Explorer 5, Navigator 4, Netscape 6, and Opera 5.*

proprietary tag **<layer>** over positioned regions. Second, if a browser does not support CSS positioning or the facility is off, the results can be catastrophic, as shown in Figure 15-4. Lastly, notice the heavy use of the **<div>** tag. The **div** element has no particular rendering under standard HTML 4, other than causing a return, since it is a block element. Further, the tag has only the basic meaning of being a grouping of items; thus, it is very useful as a generic container to insert content into and apply style to. While you could bind positioning to other tags, the **<div>** is the safest bet for cross-browser support.

When an arbitrary region is positioned using CSS, we will refer to that region as a *layer*. Do not confuse this nomenclature with the proprietary HTML tag **<layer>**, supported only in Netscape 4. This historically troublesome tag has been phased out, and it won't be a moment too soon before we can stop supporting its syntax, which is discussed next.

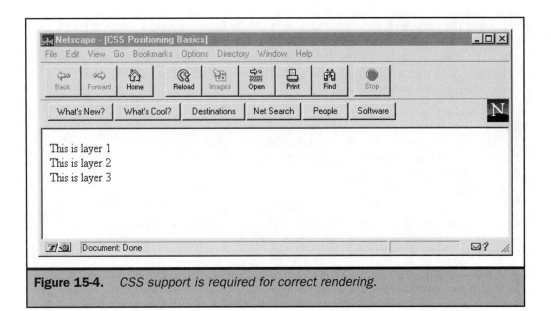

Figure 15-4.   *CSS support is required for correct rendering.*

Netscape 4 Layers

Netscape 4 provides poor support for CSS1. However, it does support the **<layer>** tag, which provides the equivalent of positioned regions in style sheets. For example,

```
<layer name="test" pagex="100" pagey="100" width="100" height="50"
bgcolor="#ffff99">
     This is a layer!
</layer>
```

produces the same region as

```
<div id="test" style="position: absolute; top:
100px; left: 100px; width: 100px; height: 50px; background-color: #ffff99">
     This is a layer!
</div>
```

On the basis of the previous example, you might guess that you have to include both **<div>** and **<layer>** tags in a document in order to achieve proper layout. Fortunately, just before the release of version 4 of its browser, Netscape adopted support for positioned **<div>** tags. Note that this support is actually through a mapping between **<div>** regions and **Layer** objects; in fact, to access a positioned **<div>** object under Netscape 4, you use the **layers[ ]** collection. To demonstrate this, consider that to access a region defined by

```
<div id="region1" style="position: absolute;
top: 100px; left: 100px; width: 100px; height:
100px; background-color: #ffff99">
     I am positioned!
</div>
```

we would use **document.layers['region1']**. However, once it's accessed, we unfortunately cannot modify the **style** property of the region because Netscape 4 does not dynamically reflect changes into the page. Yet we can modify important values, such as position, size, or visibility under Netscape 4. For example, to change the visibility we would use **document.layers['region1'].visibility** and set the property to either *hide* or *show*. The various modifiable aspects of a positioned region map directly to the properties of the **Layer** object. The most commonly used properties for this object are shown in Table 15-3.

Property	Description
background	The URL of the background image for the layer.
bgColor	The background color of the layer.
clip	References the clipping region object for the layer. This object has properties **top**, **right**, **bottom**, and **left** that correspond to normal CSS clipping rectangles as well as **width** and **height**, which can be used similarly to normal **width** and **height** properties in CSS.
document	A reference to the **Document** object of the current layer.
left	The *x*-coordinate position of the layer.
name	The **name** of the layer.

Table 15-3.   *Useful Layer Object Properties*

Property	Description
pageX	The x coordinate of the layer relative to the page.
pageY	The y coordinate of the layer relative to the page.
src	The URL to reference the layer's content when it is not directly set within the **<layer>** tag itself
top	The y coordinate position of the layer.
visibility	References the current visibility of the layer. Values of *show* and *hide* for **<layer>** are equivalent to *visible* and *hidden* under CSS. Later versions of Netscape 4 map the two values so either can be used.
window	Reference the **Window** object containing the layer.
x	The x coordinate value for the layer.
y	The y coordinate value for the layer.
zIndex	Holds the stacking order of the layer.

Table 15-3.   *Useful Layer Object Properties* (continued)

Of course, **<layer>** is a proprietary tag and is not supported outside Netscape 4. In fact, in the 6.x release of the browser, Netscape removed support for this tag. We'll see in the next few sections how Internet Explorer and DOM-compatible browsers access positioned regions.

 *For the best support under Netscape 4 browsers, you may have to rely on **<layer>** syntax in conjunction with positioned **<div>** regions.*

 *Nested layers can add some significant trouble programmatically, and they will require us to look within the **layers[ ]** collection of the current layer to find the required layer.*

Internet Explorer 4 Layers

As mentioned in Chapter 9, Internet Explorer exposes all objects in a page to scripts via the **all[ ]** collection. So, to access a positioned region defined by

```
<div id="region1" style="position: absolute; top: 100px; left: 100px; width:
 100px; height: 100px; background-color: #ffff99">
    I am positioned!
</div>
```

USING JAVASCRIPT

under Internet Explorer 4 (and greater), you would use **document.all['region1']**, or **document.all.region1**, or simply **region1**. Once the particular object was accessed, we would manipulate its presentation using its **Style** object. For example, to set the background color of the region to orange using the CSS property **background-color**, we would use **document.all['region1'].style.backgroundColor = 'orange'** or simply **region1.style.backgroundColor='orange'**. To set visibility, we would use **region1.style.visibility** and set the value to either *visible* or *hidden*.

The mapping of CSS style properties to JavaScript **Style** object properties was presented in Chapter 10, but recall that, in general, you take a hyphenated CSS property and uppercase the first letter of all the hyphen-separated terms except the first. For example, the CSS property **text-indent** becomes **textIndent** under IE and DOM-compatible JavaScript. The next section reflects a slight variation of the scheme presented here, since the standard DOM supports different syntax to access a positioned region. Fortunately, since Internet Explorer 5 and beyond support many DOM features, we can really use either syntax interchangeably.

DOM Errors

Accessing positioned regions under a DOM-compliant browser is nearly as easy as using Internet Explorer's **all[ ]** collection. The primary method is to use **document.getElementById( )**. Given our sample layer called *'region1'*, we would use **document.getElementById('region1')** to retrieve the layer, and then we could set its visibility or other style-related properties via its **Style** object (in a manner similar to how we would do this in Internet Explorer). For example, to hide an object, we would use **document.getElementById('region1').style.visibility='hidden'.** Of course, the question then arises: How do we get and set style properties related to layer positioning in the same way across all browsers? The next section presents one possible solution to this challenge.

Cross-Browser Layers

As we have seen throughout this book, significant differences exist in technology support between the popular Web browsers. For some developers, authoring for one browser (Internet Explorer) or the standard (DOM) has seemed the best way to deal with these differences. However, a better solution is to address cross-browser compatibility head-on and write markup and script that works under any browser capable of producing the intended result. This section explores this approach by creating a cross-browser layer library.

From the previous section, we can see that for layer positioning and visibility we will need to support three different technologies:

- Netscape 4 proprietary **<layer>** tags
- Internet Explorer 4+ **all[ ]** collections with positioned **<div>** tags
- DOM compatible browsers with positioned **<div>** tags

Given this relatively limited set of approaches, we can create a set of JavaScript routines to change visibility and move, modify, size, and set the contents of positioned regions fairly easily. To create such a library, we need to first determine what type of approach a browser supports. The easiest way to do this is by looking at the **Document** object. If we see a **layers[ ]** collection, we know the browser supports Netscape 4 layers. We can look at the **all[ ]** collection to sense if the browser supports Internet Explorer's **all[ ]** collection syntax. Lastly we can look for our required DOM method **getElementById( )** to see if we are dealing with a DOM-aware browser. The following statements show how to set some variables indicating the type of browser we are dealing with:

```
(document.layers) ? layerobject=true : layerobject=false;
(document.all) ? allobject = true: allobject = false;
(document.getElementById) ? dom = true : dom = false;
```

Once we know what kind of layer-aware browser we are dealing with, we might define a set of common functions to manipulate the layers. We define the following layer functions to handle common tasks:

```
function hide(layerName) { }
function show(layerName) { }
function setX(layerName, x) { }
function setY(layerName, y) { }
function setZ(layerName, zIndex) { }
function setHeight(layerName, height) { }
function setWidth(layerName, width) { }
function setClip(layerName, top, right, bottom, left) { }
function setContents( ) { }
```

These are just stubs that we will fill out shortly, but first we will need one special routine in all of them to retrieve positioned elements by name, since each approach does this slightly differently.

```
function getElement(layerName, parentLayer)
{
 if(layerobject)
   {
     parentLayer = (parentLayer) ? parentLayer : self;
     layerCollection = parentLayer.document.layers;
     if (layerCollection[layerName])
       return layerCollection[layerName] ;

     /* look through nested layers */
```

```
      for (i=0; i < layerCollection.length;)
        return(getElement(layerName, layerCollection[i++]));
  }

  if (allobject)
    return document.all[layerName];
  if (dom)
    return document.getElementById(layerName);
}
```

Notice the trouble that the possibility of nested **<layer>** or **<div>** tags under Netscape causes. We effectively have to look through the nested layers recursively until we find the object we are looking for or have run out of places to look.

Once a positioned element is accessed, we can then try to change its style. For example, to hide and show a positioned region we might write:

```
function hide(layerName)
{
   var theLayer = getElement(layerName);
   if (layerobject)
     theLayer.visibility = 'hide';
   else
     theLayer.style.visibility = 'hidden';
}

function show(layerName)
{
   var theLayer = getElement(layerName);
   if (layerobject)
     theLayer.visibility = 'show';
   else
     theLayer.style.visibility = 'visible';
}
```

The other routines are similar and all require the simple conditional detection of the browser objects to work in all layer-capable browsers. Of course, there are even more issues than what has been covered so far. Under Opera browsers, we need to use the **pixelHeight** and **pixelWidth** properties to set the height and width of the layer. In order to detect for the Opera browser, we use the **Navigator** object to look at the user-agent string, as discussed in Chapter 17. Here we set a Boolean value to indicate whether we are using Opera by trying to find the substring "opera" within the user-agent string.

```
opera = (navigator.userAgent.toLowerCase().indexOf('opera') != -1);
```

Once we have detected the presence of the browser, we can write cross-browser routines to set height and width, as shown here:

```
/* set the height of layer named layerName */
function setHeight(layerName, height)
{
  var theLayer = getElement(layerName);

  if (layerobject)
    theLayer.clip.height = height;
  else if (opera)
    theLayer.style.pixelHeight = height;
  else
     theLayer.style.height = height+"px";
}

/* set the width of layer named layerName */
function setWidth(layerName, width)
{
  var theLayer = getElement(layerName);

  if (layerobject)
    theLayer.clip.width = width;
  else if (opera)
    theLayer.style.pixelWidth = width;
  else
    theLayer.style.width = width+"px";
}
```

The same situation occurs for positioning with Opera, as it requires the use of **pixelLeft** and **pixelTop** properties rather than simply **left** and **top** to work. See the complete library for the function for setting position that is similar to the previous example.

We must also take into account some special factors when we write content to a layer. Under Netscape 4, we use the **Document** object methods like **write( )** to rewrite the content of the layer. In Internet Explorer and Netscape 6, we can use the **innerHTML** property. However, under a strictly DOM-compatible browser, life is somewhat difficult, since we would have to delete all children from the region and then create the appropriate items to insert. Because of this complexity and the fact that DOM browsers tend to support **innerHTML,** we punt on this feature. This leaves Opera out, though we wrote the code in such a manner that simply nothing happens rather than an error message being displayed.

```
function setContents(layerName, content)
{
```

USING JAVASCRIPT

```
   var theLayer = getElement(layerName);

  if (layerobject)
    {
      theLayer.document.write(content);
      theLayer.document.close();
      return;
    }

  if (theLayer.innerHTML)
    theLayer.innerHTML = content;
}
```

We skipped presenting a few routines, but their style and usage follow the ones already presented. The complete layer library is presented here:

```
/* layerlib.js: Simple Layer library with basic
   compatibility checking */

/* detect objects */
(document.layers) ? layerobject=true : layerobject=false;
(document.all) ? allobject = true: allobject = false;
(document.getElementById) ? dom = true : dom = false;

/* detect browsers */
opera=navigator.userAgent.toLowerCase().indexOf('opera')!=-1;

/* return the object for the passed layerName value */
function getElement(layerName,parentLayer)
{

 if(layerobject)
   {
     parentLayer = (parentLayer)? parentLayer : self;
     layerCollection = parentLayer.document.layers;
     if (layerCollection[layerName])
       return layerCollection[layerName];
     /* look through nested layers */
     for(i=0; i < layerCollection.length;)
       return(getElement(layerName, layerCollection[i++]));
   }
```

```
  if (allobject)
    return document.all[layerName];

  if (dom)
    return document.getElementById(layerName);
}

/* hide the layer with id = layerName */
function hide(layerName)
{
   var theLayer = getElement(layerName);
   if (layerobject)
     theLayer.visibility = 'hide';
   else
     theLayer.style.visibility = 'hidden';
}

/* show the layer with id = layerName */
function show(layerName)
{
   var theLayer = getElement(layerName);
   if (layerobject)
     theLayer.visibility = 'show';
   else
     theLayer.style.visibility = 'visible';
}

/* set the x-coordinate of layer named layerName */
function setX(layerName, x)
{
   var theLayer = getElement(layerName);
   if (layerobject)
     theLayer.left=x;
   else if (opera)
     theLayer.style.pixelLeft=x;
   else
     theLayer.style.left=x+"px";
}

/* set the y-coordinate of layer named layerName */
```

```
function setY(layerName, y)
{
   var theLayer = getElement(layerName);

   if (layerobject)
     theLayer.top=y;
   else if (opera)
     theLayer.style.pixelTop=y;
   else
     theLayer.style.top=y+"px";
}

/* set the z-index of layer named layerName */
function setZ(layerName, zIndex)
{
   var theLayer = getElement(layerName);

   if (layerobject)
     theLayer.zIndex = zIndex;
   else
     theLayer.style.zIndex = zIndex;
}

/* set the height of layer named layerName */
function setHeight(layerName, height)
{
   var theLayer = getElement(layerName);

   if (layerobject)
     theLayer.clip.height = height;
   else if (opera)
     theLayer.style.pixelHeight = height;
   else
     theLayer.style.height = height+"px";
}

/* set the width of layer named layerName */
function setWidth(layerName, width)
{
  var theLayer = getElement(layerName);

  if (layerobject)
```

```
            theLayer.clip.width = width;
      else if (opera)
            theLayer.style.pixelWidth = width;
      else
            theLayer.style.width = width+"px";
}

/* set the clipping rectangle on the layer named layerName
   defined by top, right, bottom, and left */
function setClip(layerName, top, right, bottom, left)
{
   var theLayer = getElement(layerName);

   if (layerobject)
     {
         theLayer.clip.top = top;
         theLayer.clip.right = right;
         theLayer.clip.bottom = bottom;
         theLayer.clip.left = left;
     }
   else
     theLayer.style.clip = "rect
     ("+top+"px "+right+"px "+" "+bottom+"px "+left+"px )";


}

/* set the contents of layerName to passed content*/
function setContents(layerName, content)
{
   var theLayer = getElement(layerName);

   if (layerobject)
     {
        theLayer.document.write(content);
        theLayer.document.close();
        return;
     }

   if (theLayer.innerHTML)
       theLayer.innerHTML = content;
}
```

We might save this library as "layerlib.js" and then access it in an example document like this one:

```
<!DOCTYPE HTML PUBLIC "-//W3C//DTD HTML 4.01 Transitional//EN"
         "http://www.w3.org/TR/html4/loose.dtd">
<html>
<head>
<title>Cross Browser Layer Tester</title>
<script language="JavaScript1.2" src="layerlib.js"></script>
</head>
<body>

<div id="region1" style="position: absolute; top:
 10px; left: 300px; width: 100px; height:
 100px; background-color: #ffff99; z-index: 10;" >
     I am positioned!
</div>

<div id="region2" style="position: absolute; top:
 10px; left: 275px; width: 50px; height:
 150px; background-color:#33ff99; z-index: 5;">
    Fixed layer at z-index 5 to test z-index
</div>

<br><br><br><br><br><br>
<hr>
<form name="testform" id="testform">

Visibility:
<input type="button" value="show" onclick="show('region1')">
<input type="button" value="hide" onclick="hide('region1')">

<br><br>

X: <input type="text" value="300" name="x" id="x" size="4" >
<input type="button" value="set"
onclick="setX('region1',document.testform.x.value)">

Y: <input type="text" value="10" name="y" id="y" size="4" >
   <input type="button" value="set"
onclick="setY('region1',document.testform.y.value)">
```

```
Z: <input type="text" value="10" name="z" id="z" size="4" >
   <input type="button" value="set"
onclick="setZ('region1',document.testform.z.value)">
<br><br>

Height: <input type="text" value="100" name=
"height" id="height" size="4">
        <input type="button" value="set"
onclick="setHeight('region1',document.testform.height.value)">

Width: <input type="text" value="100" name=
"width" id="width" size="4">
        <input type="button" value="set"
onclick="setWidth('region1',document.testform.width.value)">
<br><br>

Clipping Rectangle:
Top: <input type="text" value=
"0" name="top" id="top" size="4">
Left: <input type="text" value=
"0" name="left" id="left" size="4">
Bottom: <input type="text" value=
"100" name="bottom" id="bottom" size="4">
Right: <input type="text" value="100" name=
"right" id="right" size="4">
<input type="button" value="set"
onclick="setClip('region1',document.testform.top.value,
document.testform.right.value, document.testform.bottom.value,
document.testform.left.value)">

<br><br>
<input type="text" name="newcontent" id=
"newcontent" size="40" value="I am positioned!">
<input type="button" value="set content"
onclick="setContents('region1',document.testform.newcontent.value)">
</form>
</body>
</html>
```

A rendering of the library and example in action is shown in Figure 15-5.

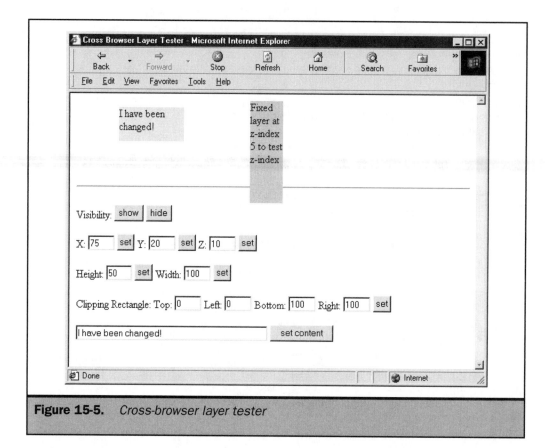

Figure 15-5. *Cross-browser layer tester*

You might encounter problems under Netscape 4 if you position the layer to cover the form elements in the page. You also may encounter a resize bug that causes the page to lose layout on window resize. We can solve the latter problem by adding a somewhat clunky fix that reloads the page every time it is resized. It is presented here for readers to add to their library as a fix for this strictly Netscape 4 problem.

```
/* Reload window in Nav 4 to preserve layout when resized */
function reloadPage(initialload)
{
  if (initialload==true)
    {
      if ((navigator.appName=="Netscape") &&
(parseInt(navigator.appVersion)==4))
        {
```

```
            /* save page width for later examination */
            document.pageWidth=window.innerWidth;
            document.pageHeight=window.innerHeight;

            /* set resize handler */
            onresize=reloadPage;
        }
     }
   else if (innerWidth!=document.pageWidth ||
innerHeight!=document.pageHeight)
        location.reload();
}

/* call function right away to fix bug */
reloadPage(true);
```

In the final examination, the harsh reality of DHTML libraries like the one
presented here is that minor variations under Macintosh browsers and the less common
JavaScript-aware browsers (such as Opera) can ruin everything. The perfect application
of DHTML is certainly not easily obtained, and significant testing is always required.
The next section explores applied DHTML and will show some of these issues in action.

Applied DHTML

This section provides a brief introduction to some other DHTML effects that are
possible using the layer library (layerlib.js). These examples should work under the
common browsers from the 4.x generation on. However, because of bugs with clipping
regions, few of the examples will work under Opera without modification.

Simple Transition

With positioned layers, you can hide and show regions of the screen at any time. Imagine
putting colored regions on-top of content and progressively making the regions smaller.
Doing this would reveal the content in an interesting manner, similar to a PowerPoint
presentation. While we'll see in Chapter 23 that you can create such transitions easily
under Internet Explorer, this effect should work in most modern browsers. The code
for this effect is shown here, and its rendering is shown in Figure 15-6.

```
<!DOCTYPE HTML PUBLIC "-//W3C//DTD HTML 4.01 Transitional//EN"
        "http://www.w3.org/TR/html4/loose.dtd">
<html>
```

```
<head>
<title>Wipe Out!</title>
<style type="text/css">
<!--
.intro { position:absolute;
         left:0;
         top:0;
         layer-background-color:red;
         background-color:red;
         border:0.1px solid red;
         z-index:10; }

#message { position: absolute;
           top: 50%;
           width: 100%;
           text-align: center;
           font-size: 48pt;
           color: green;
           z-index: 1;}
-->
</style>
<script language="JavaScript1.2" src="layerlib.js"></script>
</head>
<body>
<div id="leftLayer" class="intro"></div><div id="rightLayer"
class="intro"></div>

<div id="message">JavaScript Fun</div>

<script language="JavaScript1.2">
<!--
var speed = 20;

/* calculate screen dimensions */
if (window.innerWidth)
  {
    theWindowWidth = window.innerWidth;
    theWindowHeight = window.innerHeight;
  }
else if (document.body)
  {
    theWindowWidth = document.body.clientWidth;
    theWindowHeight = document.body.offsetHeight;
```

```
    }

/* cover the screen with the layers */
  setWidth('leftLayer', parseInt(theWindowWidth/2));
  setHeight('leftLayer', theWindowHeight);
  setX('leftLayer',0);

  setWidth('rightLayer', parseInt(theWindowWidth/2));
  setHeight('rightLayer', theWindowHeight);
  setX('rightLayer', parseInt(theWindowWidth/2));

  clipright = 0;
  clipleft =  parseInt(theWindowWidth/2);


function openIt()
{
   window.scrollTo(0,0)

   clipright+=speed;
   setClip('rightLayer',0,theWindowWidth,
theWindowHeight,clipright);

   clipleft-=speed;
   setClip('leftLayer',0,clipleft,theWindowHeight,0);


   if (clipleft<=0)
       clearInterval(stopIt)
}

function doTransition()
{
  stopIt=setInterval("openIt()",100)
}

window.onload = doTransition

//-->
</script>
</body>
</html>
```

Figure 15-6. *A simple DHTML based page transition*

A point of interest here is the **setInterval(***code, time***)** method of the **Window** object, which is used to perform the animation. The basic use of this method, which is fully presented in Chapter 17, is to execute some specified string *code* every *time* milliseconds. To turn off the interval, you clear its handle, so that if you have *anInterval* **= setInterval ("alert('hi')", 1000),** you would use **clearInterval(***anInterval***)** to turn off the annoying alert.

Second-Generation Image Rollovers

The next example solves a problem with rollovers, again using clipping regions. Recall that the major drawback of rollovers is the heavy download expense required to achieve the effect. For example, for a simple two-state rollover for a menu of eight buttons, you would need a total 16 images, one for each state. If you add a *depressed* state, it rises to 24. Using CSS positioning, it is possible to create a menu of graphic rollover buttons using only two images.

To prepare the effect, first create one large image of all buttons in the menu in their *on* state and one large image of all buttons in their *off* state, as shown here.

In this case, we named these all.gif and allon.gif. Next, create an image map for the image. Now we can use CSS positioning properties to put the two images in the document right on top of each other—except the allon.gif image will be hidden. Next we'll write a script so that as the user passes over the image, a portion of the allon.gif will be revealed. The key is using a clipping path to cut out the area of the image we want to show. Since we used an image map on top of the image, we have the clipping paths already. We used our layer library (layerlib.js) from the previous section to accomplish our task. The code and markup below illustrate the advanced rollovers in action:

```
<!DOCTYPE HTML PUBLIC "-//W3C//DTD HTML 4.01 Transitional//EN"
        "http://www.w3.org/TR/html4/loose.dtd">
<html>
<head>
```

```
<title>Rollovers Generation 2</title>
<style type="text/css">
<!--

 #menu {position: relative }
 #menuoff {position: absolute; top: 0; left: 0; }
 #menuon {position: absolute; top: 0; left: 0; visibility:hidden;}
-->
</style>
<script language="JavaScript1.2" src="layerlib.js"
type="text/javascript"></script>
<script language="JavaScript1.2" type="text/javascript">
<!--
cssRollCapable = (allobject || layerobject || dom) ? 1 : 0;

/* clipRegion object constructor */
function clipRegion(left,top,right,bottom)
{
  this.left = left;
  this.top = top;
  this.right = right;
  this.bottom = bottom;
}


if (cssRollCapable)
  {
    /* create clipping regions */
    var cliparray = new Array();

    cliparray[0] = new clipRegion(3,3,93,33);
    cliparray[1] = new clipRegion(3,41,93,71);
    cliparray[2] = new clipRegion(3,80,93,110);
    cliparray[3] = new clipRegion(3,121,93,151);
  }


function rollover(region,turnon)
{
  /* bailout if not possible for level 2 rollovers */
   if ((!cssRollCapable) || (opera))
     return;

   if (turnon)
```

```
    {
      setClip("menuon", cliparray[region].top,
cliparray[region].right, cliparray[region].bottom,
cliparray[region].left)
      show("menuon");
    }
  else
    hide("menuon");
 }

//-->
</script>
</head>
<body>

<div id="menu">
 <div id="menuoff">
  <img src="alloff1.gif" width="98" height="158" border="0"
usemap="#buttons" alt="">
 </div>
 <div id="menuon">
 <script language="JavaScript1.2" type="text/javascript">
 <!--
    document.write('<img src="allon1.gif" width="95" height=
"158" border="0" usemap="#buttons">');
 //-->
 </script>
 </div>
</div>

<map name="buttons">
<area shape="rect" alt="Button 1" coords="3,3,93,33"
href="javascript:alert('button1');" onmouseover="rollover(0,true)"
onmouseout="rollover(0,false)">
<area shape="rect" alt="Button 2" coords=
"3,41,93,71" href="javascript: alert('button2')"
onmouseover="rollover(1,true)"
onmouseout="rollover(1,false)">
<area shape="rect" alt="Button 3" coords=

"3,80,93,110" href="javascript: alert('button3')"
onmouseover="rollover(2,true)"
onmouseout="rollover(2,false)">
```

```
<area shape="rect" alt="Button 4" coords=
"3,121,93,151" href="javascript
alert('button4')" onmouseover="rollover(3,true)"
onmouseout="rollover(3,false)">
</map>
</body>
</html>
```

Adapting this code for your site should be relatively easy. First, make the two images. Then set up the image map. Next, add the positioning using the **<div>** tags and the style properties provided. If you view the page at this point, you should see only the *off* state image showing. Now add in the JavaScript. The only change would be setting the various clipping regions which is this part of the code:

```
cliparray[0] = new clipRegion(3,3,93,33);
cliparray[1] = new clipRegion(3,41,93,71);
cliparray[2] = new clipRegion(3,80,93,110);
cliparray[3] = new clipRegion(3,121,93,151);
```

Just change the coordinates on the right to match your image map coordinates and add more **cliparray[ ]** entries. Now in the image map, just change the various **<area>** elements to have

```
onmouseover="rollover(3,true)" onmouseout="rollover(3,false)"
```

and you should be in business. The only downside to this script is that it works only in 4.x-generation and better browsers. It also has problems in Opera. However, as written it will degrade gracefully in older browsers, you just won't see the rollover effect.

Targeted Rollovers (Take 2)

We saw earlier in the chapter how a rollover effect might reveal a region on the screen containing a text description. This form of targeted rollover, often called a *dynamic scope note*, can be implemented without CSS by using images, but with the DOM- and CSS-positioned items we may have a much more elegant solution. As an example, look at the code for simple scope notes presented here.

```
<!DOCTYPE HTML PUBLIC "-//W3C//DTD HTML 4.01 Transitional//EN"
        "http://www.w3.org/TR/html4/loose.dtd">
<html>
<head>
<title>CSS Rollover Message</title>
```

```
<style>
<!--
#buttons {position: absolute;
          top: 10px;
          background-color: yellow;
          width: 20%;}

#description {position: absolute;
             top: 10px;
             left: 40%;}
-->
</style>
<script src="layerlib.js" language="JavaScript1.2"></script>
</head>
<body>

<div id="buttons">
<a href="about.htm"
   onmouseover="setContents('description', 'Discover the
   history and management behind the DemoCompany.');"
   onmouseout="setContents('description', ' ')">About</a>

<br><br>

<a href="products.htm"
   onmouseover="setContents('description',
'If you like our domes, you\'ll love our robots!');"
   onmouseout="setContents('description', ' ')">Products</a>
</div>

<div id="description"> </div>

</body>
</html>
```

USING JAVASCRIPT

You can even go beyond this effect by using CSS-based rollovers to make entire buttons out of CSS properties and modify the look. The point here is simply to demonstrate the direction you can take with rollovers.

Note *Without the non-breaking space ( ), you may find that the description layer will collapse under HTML and thus not instantiate the required object for manipulation via JavaScript.*

General Animation

The last example in this chapter presents some very simple animation using JavaScript. In this example we will move an object up and down to particular coordinates as well as left to right. The basic idea will be to figure out the current position of an object and then move the object incrementally around the screen using the **setX( )** and **setY( )** functions in our layer library. First we add simple **getX(***layerName***)** and **getY(***layerName***)** functions that return the coordinates of the layer passed. These routines are shown here.

```
/* return the X-coordinate of the layer named layerName */
function getX(layerName)
{
   var theLayer = getElement(layerName);
   if (layerobject)
     return(parseInt(theLayer.left));
   else
     return(parseInt(theLayer.style.left));
}

/* return the y-coordinate of layer named layerName */
function getY(layerName)
{
   var theLayer = getElement(layerName);

   if (layerobject)
     return(parseInt(theLayer.top));
   else
     return(parseInt(theLayer.style.top));
}
```

Next we need to define some variables to indicate how many pixels to move at a time (*step*) and how quickly to run animation frames (*framespeed*).

```
/* set animation speed and step */
var step = 3;
var framespeed = 35;
```

We should also define some boundaries for our animation so that it doesn't crash into our form controls.

```
/* set animation boundaries */
var maxtop = 100;
```

```
var maxleft = 100;
var maxbottom = 400;
var maxright = 600;
```

Next we'll add routines to move the object in the appropriate direction until it reaches the boundary. The basic idea will be to probe the current coordinate of the object, and if it isn't yet at the boundary, move it a bit closer by either adding or subtracting the value of *step* and then set a timer to fire in a few milliseconds to continue the movement. The function **right( )** is an example of this. In this case, it moves a region called 'ufo' until the right boundary defined by *maxright* is reached.

```
function right()
{
  currentX = getX('ufo');

  if (currentX < maxright)
   {
    currentX+=step;
    setX('ufo',currentX);
    move=setTimeout("right()",(1000/framespeed))
   }
  else
    clearTimeout(move);
}
```

The complete script is shown here with a rendering in Figure 15-7.

```
<!DOCTYPE HTML PUBLIC "-//W3C//DTD HTML 4.01 Transitional//EN"
  "http://www.w3.org/TR/html4/loose.dtd">
<html>
<head>
<title>UFO!</title>
<script language="JavaScript1.2" src="layerlib.js"></script>
<script language="JavaScript1.2" type="text/javascript">
<!--

/* return the X-coordinate of the layer named layerName */
function getX(layerName)
{
   var theLayer = getElement(layerName);
   if (layerobject)
     return(parseInt(theLayer.left));
```

```
      else
        return(parseInt(theLayer.style.left));
}

/* return the y-coordinate of layer named layerName */
function getY(layerName)
{
    var theLayer = getElement(layerName);

    if (layerobject)
      return(parseInt(theLayer.top));
    else
      return(parseInt(theLayer.style.top));
}

 /* set animation speed and step */
 var step = 3;
 var framespeed = 35;

 /* set animation boundaries */
 var maxtop = 100;
 var maxleft = 100;
 var maxbottom = 400;
 var maxright = 600;

 /* move up until boundary */
function up()
{
  var currentY = getY('ufo');
  if (currentY > maxtop)
   {
     currentY-=step;
     setY('ufo',currentY);
     move=setTimeout("up()",(1000/framespeed));
    }
  else
     clearTimeout(move);
}

 /* move down until boundary */
function down()
{

   var currentY = getY('ufo');
```

```
   if (currentY < maxbottom)
    {
     currentY+=step;
     setY('ufo',currentY);
     move=setTimeout("down()",(1000/framespeed));
    }
   else
     clearTimeout(move);
}

/* move left until boundary */
function left()
{
  var currentX = getX('ufo');

  if (currentX > maxleft)
   {
    currentX-=step;
    setX('ufo',currentX);
    move=setTimeout("left()",(1000/framespeed));
   }
   else
     clearTimeout(move);
}

/* move right until boundary */
function right()
{
  var currentX = getX('ufo');
  if (currentX < maxright)
   {
    currentX+=step;
    setX('ufo',currentX);
    move=setTimeout("right()",(1000/framespeed));
   }
   else
     clearTimeout(move);
}
//-->
</script>
</head>
<body background="space_tile.gif">

<div id="ufo" style="position:absolute; left:200px;
```

```
   top:200px; width:241px; height:178px; z-index:1">
<img src="space_ufo.gif" width="148" height="141">
</div>

<form>
   <input type="button" value="up" onclick="up()">
   <input type="button" value="down" onclick="down()">
   <input type="button" value="left" onclick="left()">
   <input type="button" value="right" onclick="right()">
   <input type="button" value="stop" onclick="clearTimeout(move)">
</form>
</body>
</html>
```

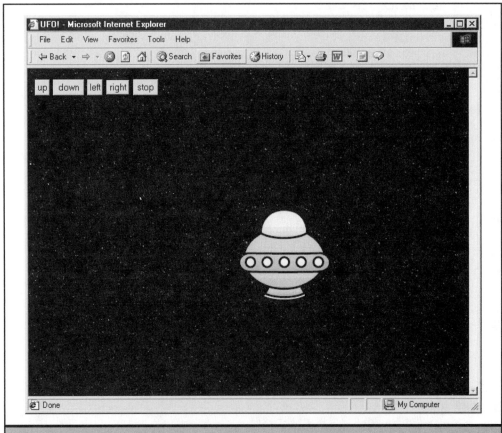

Figure 15-7. *A JavaScript UFO in flight*

We could modify the animation example to move arbitrary regions as well as to move along a path. Yet the question is: *should we*?

Practical DHTML

Practically speaking, many of the effects presented in this chapter should be used with caution. First off, there are many JavaScript bugs associated with positioning objects and manipulating their clipping regions. Careful testing and defensive coding practices (as discussed in Chapter 24) would need to be applied. Second, many of these effects can be created in technologies other than JavaScript. For example, a simple rollover can be created with the CSS **:hover** pseudo-class for the **<a>** tag. As a demonstration, try adding a style rule such as this to your page,

```
<style type="text/css">
<!--
   a:hover     {background-color: yellow; font-weight: bold;}
-->
</style>
```

and you'll see that at least text rollovers require no programming.

Animations raise similar considerations. While you can perform them using JavaScript, you may find that the animations flash or move jerkily. Without significantly complex programming, you won't have perfect animations under JavaScript. However, by using Flash or even simple animated GIFs, you can achieve some very interesting effects—often with far less complexity. If you want to use JavaScript, there are many interesting effects that can be achieved. A few examples are presented at the support site at **www.javascriptref.com** as well as at the numerous JavaScript library sites online, such as DynamicDrive (**www.dynamicdrive.com**).

Summary

This chapter presented some common applications of the **Image** object as well as other visual effects commonly associated with JavaScript. We saw that while many of these effects are relatively easy to accomplish, the scripting and style sheet variations among the browsers require defensive programming techniques to prevent errors from being thrown in browsers that do not support the required technology. DHTML effects, such as animations, visibility, and movement, demonstrated the high degree of effort required to make cross-browser–compliant code. While all the effects demonstrated in this chapter are relatively simple, developers should not necessarily add them to their site. The glitz provided by such scripts is interesting, but there may be little value to the effects beyond eye candy. The next chapter demonstrates how we can take many of the ideas demonstrated in this chapter and adapt them to powerful navigation systems for the purpose of improving a user's site experience.

The
Complete
Reference

Chapter 16

Navigation and Site Visit Improvements

There are numerous ways in which JavaScript can improve the usability of your site. We've already seen some examples in previous chapters covering form validation, window manipulation, and interactive improvements such as layer movement and visibility. But the DHTML capabilities of modern browsers can be used to do more than just implement rollovers and animation; they are often employed to provide the user with GUI-like navigation aids and taskbars. The idea behind such enhancements is that they present the user with an interface to the site that emulates the familiar interface of a typical computer program.

The reality of site navigator enhancement with JavaScript is more complex than you might initially expect. Many site "improvements" turn out to be too unintuitive, bulky, or poorly written to be of much use. In fact often such site enhancement is designed to showcase fancy DHTML effects rather than improve the user experience. Even when implemented with usability in mind, the addition of complex JavaScript to your site can be more of a hassle than it is worth. Doing so increases the amount of work that must be done to accommodate site reorganization or a shift in browser demographics. Writing robust code for site enhancement demands a higher level of skill, knowledge, and testing than writing "plain" HTML. In Web development, simplicity definitely has its merits.

Implementation Issues

Even the simplest DHTML application can be implemented in a variety of ways. The examples in this chapter are by no means the only way to achieve the desired functionality. Stylistic attributes can be defined or linked to in the document header or included inline with the **style** attribute of individual tags. JavaScript code can be linked into a page as an external library or included in the page itself with the help of event handler attributes. It is up to the programmer to choose an approach that is appropriate for the task at hand and addresses the numerous browser bugs that exist.

Because the amount of code involved in many site improvement tasks is often considerable, software engineering considerations should play a role in your design process. Large sites with numerous menus and a large number of pages are much easier to manage when your code is reasonably organized. The amount of time it will take to change entries in a hierarchical menu to reflect a new site organization will largely depend on how the menus were implemented. Making such changes can be a very laborious task if all your code resides inline in each individual page. It is for this reason that DHTML coders for large, professional sites spend almost as much time thinking about ease of use for the *programmer* as they do thinking about utility for the user.

In this chapter we'll take a look at a few of the common JavaScript and DHTML navigation scripts used in Web sites. Seeing how such applications are built will give you insight into some common techniques and tricks, but readers are also encouraged to look at Web sites like **www.dynamicdrive.com** and **www.webreference.com/dhtml** for more examples of JavaScript navigation aids.

Pull-Down Menus

One of the most common navigation aids is the *select* menu. This simple pull-down menu derives most of its functionality from the HTML **<select>** tag. The tag holds a list of **<option>**s that offer navigation or task choices to the user. An event handler bound to the **<select>** tag fires the appropriate action when the user makes a selection, instantly whisking the user to the selected page. A simple example follows.

```
<script language= "JavaScript" type= "text/javascript">
<!--
function redirect(selectObject)
{
        var choice = selectObject.selectedIndex;
        window.location = selectObject.options[choice].value;
}
// -->
</script>
<form method="POST" action="redirector.cgi">
<strong>Site Selector</strong><br>
<select size="1" name="sites" id="sites" onChange="redirect(this)">
<option value="http://www.yahoo.com">Yahoo!</option>
<option value="http://www.google.com">Google</option>
<option value ="http://www.altavista.com">AltaVista</option>
<option value="http://www.goto.com">Goto</option>
</select>

<noscript>
<input type="submit" value="GO">
</noscript>
</form>
```

Pull-downs, like typical application menus, tend to be placed at the top of pages. Although they save a great deal of real estate over conventional navigation bars that show the user all choices at once, they do so by hiding all but one of the links at a time. While this might be perfectly acceptable, it means that there are now two uses for pull-downs: one allowing users to navigate to a page of their choice and the traditional use as a form field. Some users may be confused with the dual purpose if the context of use is not made clear. A pull-down used for navigation should not be placed within a form intended for data entry and it should always be clearly labeled.

Assuming that users understand the use of pull-downs for navigation, there are numerous implementation issues to consider. Notice how the previous example included a "go" button inside of a **<noscript>** to trigger the page load. This button causes submission to a server-side CGI program that deciphers the menu choice and redirects the user appropriately. It is important to include such a button in case a user is visiting the site with a browser where JavaScript is unsupported or disabled. It is often convenient to include a "go" button even if JavaScript is enabled. While automatic page loads are very fast, they can be somewhat of a hair-trigger form of

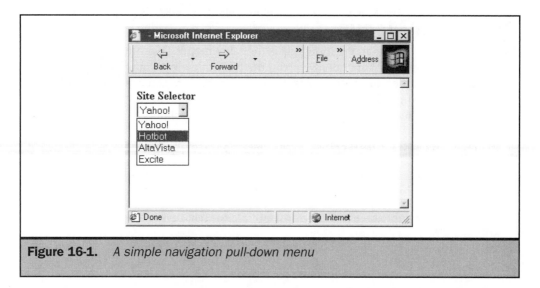

Figure 16-1. *A simple navigation pull-down menu*

navigation. It is very easy for a user to slip up on the mouse, particularly on a long pull-down, and accidentally trigger a page load.

Another problem with pull-downs for navigation has to do with the state in which the menu is left. Often menus include **<option>**s marking divisions between choices or headings indicating the nature of the following options. Consider for example the user pulling the menu down and resting it on a separator. Shouldn't the menu reset to the top like a traditional menu in an application? Most, for some reason, do not. Second, consider a scenario where the user does select a legitimate choice and is sent to a new page. Once at that page the user backs up, only to find the pull-down selecting the choice they just made. Suddenly deciding that the page they had selected was correct they have to either reload the page to reset the pull-down or choose some false choice and try again (try this at home!). The basic problem is that the menu is not reset when the user reloads the page or selects a non-active item like a separator. The following example addresses these problems and adds some cosmetic enhancements.

```
<!DOCTYPE HTML PUBLIC "-//W3C//DTD HTML 4.01 Transitional//EN"
                   "http://www.w3.org/TR/html4/loose.dtd">
<html>
<head>
<title>Select Navigation</title>
<style type="text/css">
<!--
   .nochoice    {color: black;}
   .choice      {color: blue;}
-->
</style>
```

```
<script language="JavaScript" type="text/javascript">
<!--
function redirect(pulldown)
{
   newlocation = pulldown[pulldown.selectedIndex].value;
   if (newlocation != "")
      self.location = newlocation;
}

function resetIfBlank(pulldown)
{
   possiblenewlocation = pulldown[pulldown.selectedIndex].value;
   if (possiblenewlocation == "")
      pulldown.selectedIndex = 0;            // reset to start since no movement
}
//-->
</script>
</head>
<body>
<form name="navForm" id="navForm" action="redirector.cgi">
<b>Favorite Sites:</b>
<select name="menu" id="menu" onchange="resetIfBlank(this)">
<option value="" class="nochoice" selected>Choose your site</option>
<option value="" class="nochoice"></option>
<option value="" class="nochoice">Search Sites</option>
<option value="" class="nochoice">-------------------------</option>
<option value="http://www.yahoo.com" class="choice">Yahoo! </option>
<option value="http://www.hotbot.com" class="choice">HotBot</option>
<option value="http://www.google.com" class="choice">Google</option>
<option value="" class="nochoice"></option>
<option value="" class="nochoice">E-commerce</option>
<option value="" class="nochoice">-------------------------</option>
<option value="http://www.amazon.com" class="choice">Amazon</option>
<option value="http://www.buy.com" class="choice">Buy.com</option>
<option value="" class="nochoice" class="choice"></option>
<option value="" class="nochoice">Demos</option>
<option value="" class="nochoice">-------------------------</option>
<option value="http://www.democompany.com" class="choice">DemoCompany</option>
</select>
<input type="submit" value="go" onclick="redirect(document.navForm.menu); return false">
</form>
<script language="JavaScript" type="text/javascript">
<!--
document.navForm.menu.selectedIndex = 0;
//-->
</script>
</body>
</html>
```

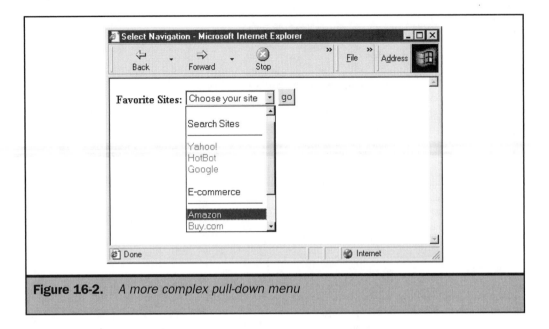

Figure 16-2.   *A more complex pull-down menu*

HTML pull-down menus as navigation devices represent a break from traditional GUI design, so not much is known about their efficacy or usability. However, GUI conventions suggest that pull-down menus with more than 15 items should be discarded in favor of a scrolling list of some sort. You can use **<select>**s with **size** attributes greater than 1 to this effect.

Complex Menu Systems

Implementing complex menu systems in JavaScript requires a high level of skill and knowledge. The process necessitates that the HTML, CSS, event handling, and dynamic manipulation of document objects in your page work together harmoniously under a variety of browsers. With so many interacting technologies, a number of subtle details are often overlooked, particularly with regard to event handling. If not caught during your testing process, these oversights can frustrate your users to the point where they will not return to your site. As with any DHTML task, you should plan on spending a significant amount of time testing your code under a variety of browsers. A malfunctioning menu system is worse than none at all.

The goal of a JavaScript menu is to emulate the functionality of "real" GUIs, such as Windows, MacOS, or Linux's KDE. Pull-down menus provide a convenient and familiar way to provide users with lists of choices. These choices are commonly links to pages with information about your products and company or links that trigger some sort of action in the page. By far the most common use for DHTML menus is for navigation enhancement.

However, some developers are taking the menu concept a step further. Utilizing the full capabilities of modern DOM-compliant browsers, full scale JavaScript DHTML GUIs have been developed. These GUIs feature an entire "desktop" contained in the browser window, complete with menus and windows that can be moved, minimized, scrolled, and even resized. The idea is to present the user with an interface with qualities as similar as possible to those found in Windows and MacOS.

While JavaScript GUIs are too new to make any firm statements about their usefulness, they do have some obvious disadvantages. First, they are usable only by modern browsers. Second, they are far less accessible to users with text or aural Web browsing tools. Third, the whole premise of a JavaScript "desktop" interface is questionable. Is it really necessary to reproduce the functionality of browser windows in JavaScript? Utilizing such a system means that there is a DHTML GUI running inside of a Web browser running inside of an operating system GUI. While this is nothing new (consider Java applets, for example), it is not clear what one gains by using this technology. Despite these concerns, development continues on JavaScript GUI libraries and sites specifically designed to look like a desktop application.

Full-blown Web GUIs are not yet widely accepted, and we'll stay away from such dramatic "all-or-nothing" approaches to JavaScript in this chapter. Instead, we will focus on using JavaScript to augment traditional Web navigation conventions. We start first with the most common navigation enhancement: the "quicklinks" pull-down menu.

Quicklinks Pull-Down Menus

The first incarnation of the pull-down menu system features support for Netscape 4 and 6 as well as Internet Explorer 4+ and makes heavy use of Cascading Style Sheets (CSS) to define presentation characteristics. Although a detailed understanding of Cascading Style Sheets is not required to understand the concepts presented in this chapter, being able to use CSS effectively is of critical importance if you wish to write menus that are pleasing to the eye.

Instead of "hardwiring" each menu into the page as static HTML, it is more useful to use JavaScript to dynamically generate the menus. Doing this facilitates code reuse and clarity and eases page maintenance significantly. In addition, dynamic generation of menus allows the HTML that is generated to be tailored to the specific browser, version, and platform of each user. In this way, we can address the individual quirks and presentation characteristics particular to each client while creating menus that have very similar cross-browser appearance.

To begin our example, we first need to provide the programmer with an interface for adding menu headings and items. The "bookkeeping" data structures used to keep track of the menus as they are being configured do not have to be complicated. They just need to provide a convenient way to store the data until such time as the menus are generated. The primary data structure used in our approach is an associative array, *menus*, which is indexed by the name of the menu (for example, File, Edit, or Help). Each element of the *menus* array is an object that contains the menu name, the menu number, and two arrays, *items* and *actions*. The *items* array contains the text entries that make up the items in the menu. The *actions* array contains the URL or pseudo-URL to invoke when the corresponding menu item is selected.

```
var numMenus = 0;                 // the number of distinct menus defined
var menus = new Object();         // stores the menu data itself
/*  Function addItem: Adds a new item to the menu data structure.
 *
 * Parameters: menuName - the menu heading (a string)
 *             item - text to display in the menu for this item
 *             action - the URL to execute on menu trigger
 */

function addItem(menuName, item, action)
{
   if (!menus[menuName])
    {                          // if a menu with this heading is not yet defined...
     var newMenu = new Object();   // create a new object for it
      newMenu.name = menuName;     // set its name property
      newMenu.num = numMenus++;    // set its menu number

      // create the arrays to hold item/action pairs
      newMenu.items = new Array();
      newMenu.actions = new Array();
      // and add the new menu to the menus associative array
      menus[menuName] = newMenu;
    }

// add the new item to the end of the menu and associate action
   menus[menuName].items.push(item);
   menus[menuName].actions.push(action);
}
function createMenus() {  }             // generates the menus themselves
function createMenuHeadings() {  }      // generates the menu bar
```

How the menus are actually created is browser-dependent, so those functions are left unspecified for the time being. To construct the menus using the functions just defined, you might write the following JavaScript statements:

```
addItem("Products", "Widget", "widgets.html");
addItem("Products", "Robot", "robots.html");
addItem("Products", "Jetpack", "jetpack.html");
addItem("Products", "Snark", "snark.html");
addItem("Corporate", "About Us", "about.html");
```

```
addItem("Corporate", "Contact Info", "contact.html");
addItem("Corporate", "Jobs", "jobs.html");
addItem("Corporate", "Shareholders", "corporate.html");
addItem("Corporate", "Stock Price", "javascript:alert('$2000')");
addItem("Links", "Partners", "partnerlinks.html");
addItem("Links", "Good books", "http://www.amazon.com");
addItem("Links", "W3C", "http://www.w3.org");
```

Three menus are created with a variable number of items in each. Because of the way our menu generation code will be written, the order in which the items and menus are added is the order in which they will appear. So, in this example the menu headings will be "Products," "Corporate," and "Links," in that order. The content of the "Links" menu will be three items: "Partners," "Good books," and "W3C" (ordered from top to bottom). We'll use these later on in an external .js file called menudeclarations.js.

Once the menus have been defined, you might use the following to write the actual menus into the page. The content of **createMenus()** and the significance of the layer comments will be addressed shortly.

```
<body>
<script language="JavaScript" type="text/javascript">
<!--
createMenus();
//-->
</script>
<!-- mainContent layer -->
<!-- rest of page content -->
<!-- end of mainContent layer -->
</body>
```

Now that we have a good way to specify the content of the menus and how they are added to the page, we need to specify how they are generated and how they will actually work. Since DHTML is highly browser-dependent, we do so case-by-case.

Netscape 4-Based Menus

Because of Netscape 4's poor support for HTML and CSS, our implementation must use the proprietary **<layer>** tag. It is hoped that soon we will be able to avoid this type of proprietary implementation, but for now we will show how it is used. We will build the system out of three general kinds of layers. The first type can be thought of as "helper" layers, layers that exist to neatly enclose content or enhance the presentation of the page. Two such layers will be used, one to contain the actual content of the page and one to provide a nice solid background for the menu bar. Enclosing the content of the page in its own layer makes it easy to place a menu over the top of the rest of the page. The second type of layer will be used for items on the menu bar. Because we will want to vary the color of the menu buttons according to user actions, each menu heading on the bar will have its own layer. The final type of layer we will use will be menu layers. Each such layer will enclose the content of one menu, allowing us to independently position, hide, or recolor each menu without affecting adjacent items or text.

The following CSS defines three classes for use with our Netscape 4 menus. In the following examples, we will assume that this code resides in a file called nsmenustyles.css.

```
.menuHeadingNS4 {  padding: 2px 5px 2px 5px;
                   color: white; font-weight: bold;
                   text-decoration: none; }
.menuNS4 {  padding: 2px 5px 2px 5px;
            color: white; font-weight: bold;
            text-decoration: none; }
.menuItemNS4 { text-decoration: none;
               color: darkblue; font-family: sans-serif  }
```

We'll be generating the HTML that these classes are bound to dynamically, but a typical example of the generated HTML is given here for clarity. The background layer will be defined in the following unsurprising manner:

```
<layer name="background" bgcolor="blue" width="95%"
       z-index="0" top="10" left="10" height="21">   </layer>
```

The main content of the page will be included inside of a layer, like this:

```
<layer name="mainContent" z-index="100" bgcolor="white"
       top="50" left="10">Here's the content of the page</layer>
```

Each menu-heading layer will be named *menuHeadingN* where the *N* indicates the menu number to which the heading corresponds:

```
<layer name="menuHeadingN" onmouseout="timeOut = setTimeout('hideMenu(N)', 500)"
width="50" bgcolor="blue" top="10" height="21" left="xxx" z-index="20">
<a class="menuHeadingNS4" href="javascript:showMenu(N)">Menu Name</a>
</layer>
```

There are a few important things to note about this example. First, the **left** attribute will vary from heading to heading because we do not want all the menu headings placed on top of each other (that is, real pixel values will be substituted for *xxx*). They will be spaced about 100 pixels apart. Second, the **onmouseout** attribute of the layer utilizes **setTimeout()**, the reason for which will be discussed shortly. The menus themselves will be defined similar to:

```
<layer class="menuNS4" onmouseover="clearTimeout(timeOut)"
onmouseout="timeOut = setTimeout('hideMenu(N)',500)" visibility="hide"
name="menuN" top="31" left="xxx" bgcolor="lightblue" z-index="0" width="100">
<a class="menuItemNS4" href="action for item 1">Item 1</a><br>
<a class="menuItemNS4" href="action for item 2">Item 2</a><br>
<a class="menuItemNS4" href="action for item 3">Item 3</a><br>
<a class="menuItemNS4" href="action for item 4">Item 4</a><br>
</layer>
```

Note how the menu is named *menuN*. Each of the *N* menus has a corresponding heading layer that activates it, named *menuHeadingN*. Using a regular naming convention makes it easy to correlate menu buttons with the menus themselves and also simplifies the automatic generation of the HTML. This explains why we keep the **num** property of the objects in the *menus* bookkeeping array.

After examining these examples, it should be fairly clear how to write the JavaScript functions referenced in the event handlers. The **showMenu()** function accepts an integer and makes the layer corresponding to its argument visible. The opposite happens when **hideMenu()** is invoked. The only mystery is why timeouts are employed in the event handlers. There are two reasons. The first is that we want to allow for "mouse slippage"— the user's accidental movement of the mouse quickly outside of a menu and then back over it. It can be frustrating if the menu disappears immediately. The second reason is that the Netscape 4 document object model is fairly limited. The easiest way to prevent a menu heading from deactivating when the user moves away from it and onto its corresponding menu is to delay its deactivation. So when the user moves the mouse onto the active menu the deactivation of its heading is cancelled by the **clearTimeout()** method. The code for the required show and hide functions is given here:

```
var timeOut;
// Function showMenu: Accepts an integer indicating which menu to show
function showMenu(which)
{
  document.layers["menuHeading" + which].bgColor = "darkblue";
  document.layers["menu" + which].visibility = "show";
  document.layers["menu" + which].moveAbove(document.layers["mainContent"]);
}
// Function hideMenu: Accepts an integer indicating which menu to hide
function hideMenu(which)
{
  document.layers["menuHeading" + which].bgColor = "blue";
  document.layers["menu" + which].visibility = "hide";
  document.layers["menu" + which].moveBelow(document.layers["mainContent"]);
}
```

> **Note**
>
> *Many Netscape 4 DHTML menu systems available on the Web capture mouse events and examine the screen coordinates to determine the appropriate action. While this technique is useful, we will take the simpler approach found here. As the popularity of Netscape 4 fades, spending large amounts of time writing pixel-specific DHTML code for it becomes an increasingly unattractive proposition. There is plenty of such code available on the Web for the interested reader.*

The only parts of the Netscape 4 system not yet specified are the functions **createMenuHeadings()** and **createMenus()**. For simplicity's sake, we won't do any checking on the length of the strings that make up the menu headings and items. We are making the assumption that they are short enough to fit into the layers as they are defined. You can use the clipping features of the **<layer>** elements to ensure that entries are properly cropped. See, for example, Chapter 22.

The code that generates the **<layer>** elements is included in this full-blown example. We assume that the Netscape 4 styles reside in nsmenustyles.css and that the **addItem()** invocations are as earlier and included in the file menudeclarations.js. We do so in order to conserve space as well as to modularize the code. We have also removed the previously used comments as well to conserve space during the presentation.

```
<!DOCTYPE HTML PUBLIC "-//W3C//DTD HTML 4.01 Transitional//EN"
"http://www.w3.org/TR/html4/loose.dtd">
<html>
<head>
<title>Netscape 4 Menu Example</title>
<link rel="stylesheet" href="nsmenustyles.css" media="screen" type="text/css">
<script language="JavaScript" type="text/javascript">
<!--
var timeout, numMenus = 0;
var menus = new Object();
function showMenu(which)
{
   document.layers["menuHeading" + which].bgColor = "darkblue";
   document.layers["menu" + which].visibility = "show";
   document.layers["menu" + which].moveAbove(document.layers["mainContent"]);   }
function hideMenu(which)
{
  document.layers["menuHeading" + which].bgColor = "blue";
  document.layers["menu" + which].visibility = "hide";
  document.layers["menu" + which].moveBelow(document.layers["mainContent"]);
}
function addItem(menuName, item, action)
{
   if (!menus[menuName])
{
     var newMenu = new Object();
```

```
      newMenu.name = menuName;
      newMenu.num = numMenus++;

      newMenu.items = new Array();
      newMenu.actions = new Array();
      menus[menuName] = newMenu;
   }
   menus[menuName].items.push(item);
   menus[menuName].actions.push(action);
}
function createMenuHeadings()
{
   document.write('<layer name="background" bgcolor="blue" width="95%"
z-index="0" top="10" left="10" height="21">  </layer>');
   for (var menu in menus)
    {
      var theMenu = menus[menu];
      document.write('<layer name="menuHeading' + theMenu.num + '"
onmouseout="timeOut = setTimeout(\'hideMenu(' + theMenu.num + ')\', 500)"
width="80" bgcolor="blue" top="10" height="21" left="' + ((theMenu.num * 100) +
10) + '" z-index="20"><a class="menuHeadingNS4" href="javascript:showMenu(' +
theMenu.num + ')">' + theMenu.name + '</a></layer>');
    }
}
function createMenus()
{
   createMenuHeadings();
   for (var menu in menus)
    {
      var theMenu = menus[menu];
      document.write('<layer class="menuNS4" onmouseover="clearTimeout(timeOut)"
onmouseout="timeOut = setTimeout(\'hideMenu(' + theMenu.num + ')\',500)"
visibility="hide" name="menu' + theMenu.num + '" top="31" left="' + ((theMenu.num
* 100) + 10) + '" bgcolor="lightblue" z-index="0" width="100">');
      for (var i=0; i<theMenu.items.length; i++)
         document.write('<a class="menuItemNS4" href="' + theMenu.actions[i] +
'">' + theMenu.items[i] + '</a><br>');
      document.write('</layer>');
    }
}
//-->
</script>
<script language="JavaScript" type="text/javascript" src="menudeclarations.js">
</script>
</head>
<body onresize="location.href = location.href">
<script language="JavaScript" type="text/javascript">
```

```
<!--
createMenus();
//-->
</script>
<layer name="mainContent" z-index="100" bgcolor="white" top="50" left="10">
<h2>Solvent Solutions Corporation</h2>
<p>We provide solutions. Seriously. Need a gaseous solution of nitrogen and
oxygen? Don't hold your breath waiting for the other guys! We have chemists
online around the clock waiting to take your order. Although we specialize in
solution solutions, we also provide mixtures and compounds upon request. The
staff at Solvent Solutions Incorporated are experts in the arts of decanting and
titration, so send us some email today!
</p>
</layer>
</body>
</html>
```

The page with a menu activated is shown under Netscape 4 in Figure 16-3.

As you can see in Figure 16-3, the appearance of the menu is acceptable but not ideal. You can use CSS, layers, and tables to spruce up the appearance by adding borders, dividers, or texture to the menus. The menu bar appearance can be improved just as easily.

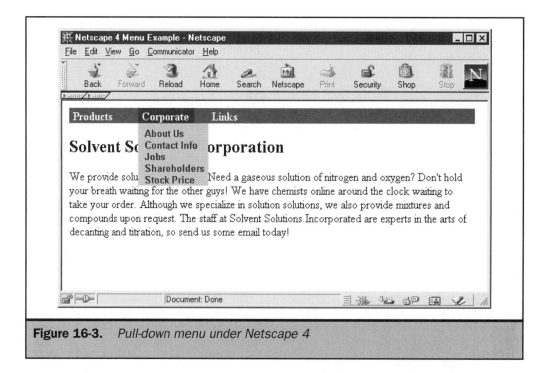

Figure 16-3. *Pull-down menu under Netscape 4*

Internet Explorer Menus

The menus for Internet Explorer 4+ build upon the framework given for Netscape 4. The menu construction functions remain exactly the same, while the DHTML and menu generation routines receive new Explorer-specific code. Major differences include the liberal use of CSS, the utilization of **<div>** elements in place of **<layer>**, and the addition of several new event handlers.

The style definitions for the Internet Explorer menus are given here and are assumed to be in a file called menustyles.css.

```css
.menuBar { background-color: blue;
          border-width: 1px; padding: 2px;
          border-style: solid;
          border-color: black; }
.menuHeading { display: inline; color: white;
              font-weight: bold; margin-left: 6px;
              padding-left: 4px; padding-right: 8px;
              border-style: solid; border-color: blue;
              border-width: 2px; cursor: default;  }
.menu { background: blue;  padding: 0px; margin: 0px;
        border-style: solid; border-width: 2px;
        border-color: lightblue darkblue darkblue lightblue;
        position: absolute; visibility: hidden;
        text-align: left; }
.menuItem { color: white; position: relative; display: block;
            font-style: normal; margin: 0px;
            padding: 2px 15px 2px 10px; font-size: smaller;
            font-family: sans-serif; font-weight: bold;
            text-decoration: none; }
a.menuItem:hover { background-color: darkblue; cursor: default; }
```

Borders are used throughout to give the menus a feeling of depth, but readers should note that different browsers render the same CSS border properties differently, so some variation in appearance should be expected. Additionally, IE 4 does not support all the style rules just given, so it is necessary to accommodate this fact when generating the menus. For example, the *menuItem* class will render correctly as block elements under IE5+ but requires the insertion of **
** tags to render properly in IE 4.

The menu bar is generated as the following HTML:

```html
<div class="menuBar">
...
<a onclick="menuHeadingMouseClick(event, N); return false"
```

```
onmouseout="menuHeadingMouseOut(N)" onmouseover="menuHeadingMouseOver(N)"
class="menuHeading" id="menuHeadingN">Menu Name</a>
...
</div>
```

As with the Netscape code, the *N* in the above HTML corresponds to the menu number the heading is for. There is one **<a>** element per heading, each containing the appropriate menu name and number. Notice the addition of **onmouseover** and **onmouseout** attributes for the menu headings. These functions take advantage of DHTML capabilities not available in Netscape 4 to change menu styles and provide a visual cue to the user.

The HTML making up each menu is generated along the lines of:

```
<div class="menu" id="menuN" onmouseover="clearTimeout(timeOut)"
onmouseout="timeOut = setTimeout('menuHeadingDeactivate(); hideMenu(N)',500)">'
<a class="menuItem" href="action for menu item 1">name for item 1</a>
<a class="menuItem" href="action for menu item 2">name for item 2</a>
<a class="menuItem" href="action for menu item 3">name for item 3</a>
</div>
```

The actual code that is generated will vary slightly to overcome some small bugs in browser presentation.

The function that hides the menu for IE 4+ is extremely simple:

```
function hideMenu(which)
{
    document.all("menu" + which).style.visibility = "hidden";
}
```

The code to show a menu is also easily understandable:

```
function showMenu(which, x, y)
{
    document.all("menu" + which).style.left = x;
    document.all("menu" + which).style.top = y;
    document.all("menu" + which).style.visibility = "visible";
}
```

It accepts a menu number to display along with the screen coordinates of where it goes. The *x* and *y* coordinates are given by the **menuHeadingMouseClick()** function, which is the **onclick** event handler for the menu's heading.

The simplest of the event handlers referenced in the previous HTML are defined as follows:

```
function menuHeadingMouseOver(menuHeading)
{
document.all("menuHeading" + menuHeading).style.borderColor="lightblue darkblue darkblue
lightblue";
}
function menuHeadingMouseOut(menuHeading)
{
    if (activeMenuHeading != -1 && activeMenuHeading == menuHeading)
    {
      timeOut = setTimeout('hideMenu(' + activeMenuHeading +');menuHeadingDeactivate();');
    }
    else
      document.all("menuHeading" + menuHeading).style.borderColor="blue";
}
```

The definition of **menuHeadingMouseOut()** reveals that a global variable *activeMenuHeading* is in use. This variable is used to keep track of which menu heading (and hence which menu) is currently "active," that is, displayed to the user. The value **-1** indicates that no heading is active. The logic behind **menuHeadingMouseOut()** is as follows: if there is an active menu and the user just "moused" out of it, then set a timeout that will deactivate the heading and hide the menu. The timeout is provided to accommodate mouse slippage and the time it takes to move the mouse onto the menu after clicking the heading. If the heading the user moused out of is not active, then simply change its border color back to normal.

The auxiliary functions that change the menu headings to their active and inactive states are shown here:

```
function menuHeadingActivate(menuHeading)
{
    document.all("menuHeading" + menuHeading).style.background = "lightblue";
    document.all("menuHeading" + menuHeading).style.color = "darkblue";
    document.all("menuHeading" + menuHeading).style.borderColor = "darkblue blue
lightblue darkblue";
    activeMenuHeading = menuHeading;
}
function menuHeadingDeactivate()
{
  if (activeMenuHeading != -1)
    {
      document.all("menuHeading" + activeMenuHeading).style.borderColor= "blue";
```

```
        document.all("menuHeading" + activeMenuHeading).style.background = "blue";
        document.all("menuHeading" + activeMenuHeading).style.color = "white";
    }
  activeMenuHeading = -1;
}
```

These functions merely change the appearance of the button and keep track of which button is currently active. Since only one button can be active at a time, **menuHeadingDeactivate()** does not need to be passed any parameters.

Aside from the menu and heading generation routines for IE 4+, the only function we haven't seen is **menuHeadingMouseClick()**, the **onclick** event handler for each menu heading. This function accepts an integer argument indicating which menu heading has been clicked. It also accepts event information so we can calculate where to place the menu. It is defined as follows:

```
function menuHeadingMouseClick(event, which)
{
    menuHeadingActivate(which);
    var x = event.srcElement.offsetLeft;
    var y = event.srcElement.offsetTop + event.srcElement.offsetHeight;
    showMenu(which, x, y);
}
```

It calculates the screen coordinates of the menu heading that was clicked and shows the menu immediately below. Note that because of browser inconsistencies, the actual placement of the menu will vary slightly from browser to browser. This variation is somewhat compensated for in the full version of the code given later.

It is most important to understand how all the parts of the page interact. When the user mouses over a menu heading, its appearance changes. If the heading is clicked, it is shown in an active state and the menu associated with it is displayed. When the user mouses away from an inactive heading its appearance reverts to normal. If the heading moused away from is active, a timer is set to deactivate the heading and hide the menu approximately a half-second in the future. This timer, which is cancelled whenever the user mouses over a menu that is displayed, is designed to allow the user time to reach the menu from the heading. Similarly, when the user moves the mouse off of an active menu, a timer is set that deactivates the active heading and hides the menu when it fires. This timer (actually, the same one) is cancelled if the user places the mouse back over the menu within a half-second or so. This accommodates mouse slippage.

Event handlers bound to layers interacting in this manner are at the heart of pull-down menu development. Once a solid approach like the one earlierss has been ironed out, the majority of the task ahead of you is testing various browsers to ensure that the presentation characteristics of your menus are what you expect. Unfortunately, the appearance often varies considerably from platform to platform and browser to browser. The upcoming full example of this system includes some easy fixes for some browsers. But first we should make sure that the menu system supports Netscape 6 and other DOM-compliant browsers.

DOM Issues and Menus

Because Netscape 6 is a standards-based browser, menus for it can use the same HTML that is generated for IE 4+. The only change that is necessary is in the way that the menu objects are accessed. Netscape 6 supports the DOM standard for retrieving a reference to an element's object: the **getElementById()** method of the **Document** object. Other than one minor change for accessing the **Event** object, the style manipulation code for IE 4+ can be used exactly as is. The ability to use the same (or rather, very similar) code for two different browsers is what standards like the DOM are all about.

Cross-Browser Menus: Putting It All Together

With the addition of browser-detection code, we can fold the three major cases (Netscape 4, IE 4+, and DOM-compatibles such as Netscape 6) into one implementation. The approach taken here is to use **if/else** constructions to take the appropriate action based on what can be discerned about the client's browser. A different approach would be to keep a library for each browser in a separate file and then have the browser detection code write a **<script>** tag into the page that references the appropriate file.

One major omission from the example is a static HTML navigation aid for browsers that do not support DHTML. Also, the script needs a bit more work to make it compatible with Opera. As it stands, it supports IE 4+ and Netscape 4 and 6.

```
<!DOCTYPE HTML PUBLIC "-//W3C//DTD HTML 4.01 Transitional//EN"
"http://www.w3.org/TR/html4/loose.dtd">
<html>
<head>
<title>Pull Down Menu Example</title>
<link rel="stylesheet" href="nsmenustyles.css" media="screen" type="text/css">
<link rel="stylesheet" href="menustyles.css" media="screen" type="text/css">
<script language="JavaScript" type="text/javascript">
<!--
var timeOut = null, numMenus = 0;
var menus = new Object();

var ns4 = false;             // true if the browser supports layers
var ie4 = false;             // true if the browser supports document.all
var otherDOM = false;        // true if ns6
var ie5plus = false;         // true if browser is IE 5+
var adjustSpacing = false;   // true if we need to adjust menu spacing
```

```
var activeMenuHeading = -1;      // holds number of the active menu (heading)

function detectBrowser()
{
  if (document.layers)
      ns4 = true;
    else if (document.all)
{
      ie4 = true;
      if (navigator.userAgent.indexOf("MSIE 4") != -1)
        ie5plus = false;
      else
        ie5plus = true;
      if (((navigator.userAgent.indexOf("MSIE 5.5") == -1) &&
           (navigator.userAgent.indexOf("MSIE 6") == -1)) ||
          (navigator.userAgent.indexOf("Mac") != -1))
        adjustSpacing = true;
    }
  else if (document.getElementById)
    {
      otherDOM = true;
      adjustSpacing = true;
    }
}
function showMenu(which,x,y)
{ // accepts an integer indicating which menu to show and x/y if not ns4
    if (ns4)
     {
      document.layers["menuHeading" + which].bgColor = "darkblue";
      document.layers["menu" + which].visibility = "show";
      document.layers["menu" + which].moveAbove(document.layers["mainContent"]);
     } else if (ie4)
     {
      document.all("menu" + which).style.left = x;
      document.all("menu" + which).style.top = y;
      document.all("menu" + which).style.visibility = "visible";
     }
      else if (otherDOM)
     {
      document.getElementById("menu" + which).style.left = x;
      document.getElementById("menu" + which).style.top = y;
      document.getElementById("menu" + which).style.visibility = "visible";
     }
}
function hideMenu(which)
```

```
{ // accepts an integer indicating which menu to hide

   if (ns4)
    {
     document.layers["menuHeading" + which].bgColor = "blue";
     document.layers["menu" + which].visibility = "hide";
     document.layers["menu" + which].moveBelow(document.layers["mainContent"]);
    } else if (ie4)
    {
     document.all("menu" + which).style.visibility = "hidden";
    }
      else if (otherDOM)
    {
     document.getElementById("menu" + which).style.visibility = "hidden";
    }
}
function addItem(menuName, item, action)
{
   if (!menus[menuName])
    {
      var newMenu = new Object();
      newMenu.name = menuName;
      newMenu.num = numMenus++;
      newMenu.items = new Array();
      newMenu.actions = new Array();
      menus[menuName] = newMenu;
    }
   // IE4 doesn't support push() so add manually
   menus[menuName].items[menus[menuName].items.length] = item;
   menus[menuName].actions[menus[menuName].actions.length] = action;
}
function createMenuHeadings()
{
   if (ns4)
    {
  document.write('<layer name="background" bgcolor="blue" width="95%" z-index="0" top="10"
  left="10" height="21">  </layer>');
    }
   else if (ie4 || otherDOM)
    {
     document.write('<div class="menuBar">');
    }
   for (var menu in menus)
    {
```

```
      var theMenu = menus[menu];
      if (ns4)
        document.write('<layer name="menuHeading' + theMenu.num + '" onmouseout="timeOut =
setTimeout(\'hideMenu(' + theMenu.num + ')\', 500)" width="80" bgcolor="blue" top="10"
height="21" left="' + ((theMenu.num * 100) + 10) + '" z-index="20"><a class="menuHeadingNS4"
href="javascript:showMenu(' + theMenu.num + ')">' + theMenu.name + '</a></layer>');
      else if (ie4 || otherDOM)
        document.write('<a onclick="menuHeadingMouseClick(event, ' + theMenu.num + '); return
false" onmouseout="menuHeadingMouseOut(' + theMenu.num + ')" onmouseover="menuHeadingMouseOver('
+ theMenu.num + ')" class="menuHeading" id="menuHeading' + theMenu.num + '">' + theMenu.name +
'</a>');

    if (adjustSpacing)
      document.write('     ');
  }

 if (ie4 || otherDOM)
    document.write('</div>');
}


function createMenus()
 {
   createMenuHeadings();
   for (var menu in menus)
    {
      var theMenu = menus[menu];
      if (ns4)
        document.write('<layer class="menuNS4" onmouseover="clearTimeout(timeOut)"
onmouseout="timeOut = setTimeout(\'hideMenu(' + theMenu.num + ')\',500)" visibility="hide"
name="menu' + theMenu.num + '" top="31" left="' + ((theMenu.num * 100) + 10) + '"
bgcolor="lightblue" z-index="0" width="100">');
      else if (ie4 || otherDOM)
        document.write('<div class="menu" id="menu' + theMenu.num + '"
onmouseover="clearTimeout(timeOut)" onmouseout="timeOut = setTimeout(\'menuHeadingDeactivate();
hideMenu(' + theMenu.num + ')\',500)">');

      for (var i=0; i<theMenu.items.length; i++)
       {
         if (ns4)
           document.write('<a class="menuItemNS4" href="' + theMenu.actions[i] + '">' +
theMenu.items[i] + '</a><br>');
         else if (ie4 || otherDOM)
            document.write('<a style="width: 110px" class="menuItem" href="' + theMenu.actions[i]
+ '">' + theMenu.items[i] + '</a>');
```

```
        if (ie4 && !ie5plus)
           document.write('<br>');
      }
    if (ns4)
       document.write('</layer>');
    else if (ie4 || otherDOM)
       document.write('</div>');
  }
}
function menuHeadingMouseOver(menuHeading)
{
   if (ie4)
     document.all("menuHeading" + menuHeading).style.borderColor="lightblue darkblue darkblue
lightblue";
   else if (otherDOM)
     document.getElementById("menuHeading" + menuHeading).style.borderColor="lightblue darkblue
darkblue lightblue";
}


function menuHeadingMouseOut(menuHeading)
{
   if (ie4 || otherDOM)
    {
     if (activeMenuHeading != -1 && activeMenuHeading == menuHeading)
       timeOut=setTimeout('hideMenu(' + activeMenuHeading + '); menuHeadingDeactivate();',500);
     else
      {
     if (ie4)
           document.all("menuHeading" + menuHeading).style.borderColor="blue";
     else
           document.getElementById("menuHeading" + menuHeading).style.borderColor="blue";
      }
    }
}


function menuHeadingActivate(menuHeading)
{
   if (ie4)
    {
      document.all("menuHeading" + menuHeading).style.background = "lightblue";
      document.all("menuHeading" + menuHeading).style.color = "darkblue";
      document.all("menuHeading" + menuHeading).style.borderColor = "darkblue blue lightblue
darkblue";
    }
```

```
    else if (otherDOM)
      {
       document.getElementById("menuHeading" + menuHeading).style.background = "lightblue";
       document.getElementById("menuHeading" + menuHeading).style.color = "darkblue";
       document.getElementById("menuHeading" + menuHeading).style.borderColor = "darkblue blue
lightblue darkblue";
      }
       activeMenuHeading = menuHeading;
}


function menuHeadingDeactivate()
 {

   if (activeMenuHeading != -1)
    {
      if (ie4)
       {
        document.all("menuHeading" + activeMenuHeading).style.borderColor= "blue";
        document.all("menuHeading" + activeMenuHeading).style.background = "blue";
        document.all("menuHeading" + activeMenuHeading).style.color = "white";
       }
      else if (otherDOM)
       {
        document.getElementById("menuHeading" + activeMenuHeading).style.borderColor= "blue";
        document.getElementById("menuHeading" + activeMenuHeading).style.background = "blue";
        document.getElementById("menuHeading" + activeMenuHeading).style.color = "white";
       }
      activeMenuHeading = -1;
     }
}


function menuHeadingMouseClick(event, which)
{

   if (activeMenuHeading != -1)
    {
     clearTimeout(timeOut);
     hideMenu(activeMenuHeading);
     menuHeadingDeactivate();
    }
   if (ie4 || otherDOM)
     menuHeadingActivate(which);
   if (event.srcElement)
    {
     x = event.srcElement.offsetLeft;
```

```
      y = event.srcElement.offsetTop + event.srcElement.offsetHeight;
    }
  else if (otherDOM)
    {
      // NS6 specific
      x = document.getElementById("menuHeading" + which).offsetLeft;
      y = document.getElementById("menuHeading" + which).offsetTop +
document.getElementById("menuHeading" + which).offsetHeight;
    }
  if (adjustSpacing)
    {   x += 5; y += 7; }
    showMenu(which, x, y);
}
detectBrowser();
//-->
</script>
<script language="JavaScript" type="text/javascript" src="menudeclarations.js"></script>
</head>
<body onresize="if (ns4) location.href = location.href">
<script language="JavaScript" type="text/javascript">
<!--
createMenus();
//-->
</script>
<layer name="mainContent" z-index="100" bgcolor="white" top="50" left="10">
<h2>Solvent Solutions Corporation</h2>
<p>We provide solutions. Seriously. Need a gaseous solution of nitrogen and
oxygen? Don't hold your breath waiting for the other guys! We have chemists online around the
clock waiting to take your order. Although we specialize in solution solutions, we also provide
mixtures and compounds upon request. The staff at Solvent Solutions Incorporated are experts in
the arts of decanting and titration, so send us some email today!</p>
</layer>
</body>
</html>
```

Sample outputs under Internet Explorer 5 and Netscape 6 are shown in Figures 16-4 and 16-5. Of course, this example is quite a large one to type in. You can find the code for it online at the support site at **www.javascriptref.com**. Before moving on, let's discuss improvements that could be made to our menu system.

Other Improvements

We have emphasized throughout this chapter that the menuing system we have developed is merely one way of achieving the goal. Examination of DHTML menus on the Web reveals a wide variety of implementation techniques and stylistic approaches.

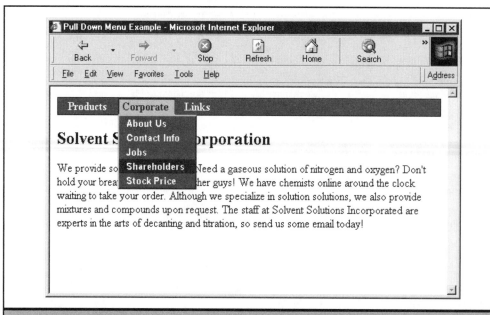

Figure 16-4. Pull-down menu in Internet Explorer 5

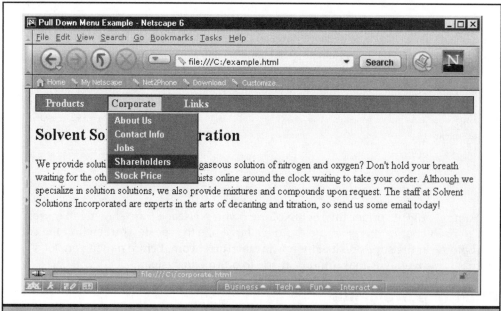

Figure 16-5. Pull-down menu in Netscape 6

Here we list some common variations, improvements, and suggestions for enhancing a basic menu system:

- Images can enhance menu appearance. Using images for buttons and menu backgrounds is commonly employed to avoid the problems presented by different browsers rendering the same CSS differently.

- Clipping can ensure correct appearance. If the user is viewing the page with a low-resolution monitor or with large fonts, making sure that your menu areas are clipped to remove overflow can greatly improve appearance.

- Menu items that can be used to trigger actions other than pseudo-URLs and links are often useful for DHTML applications.

- Carefully written CSS can be used to greatly enhance menu appearance.

- Dynamic repositioning of menus that run outside of the current viewable area is an important feature. Using information about the menu's position and width along with information about the browser **Window** allows you to do so fairly easily.

- Dynamic generation of static navigation aids for non-DHTML browsers is an important usability feature.

- Inclusion of static navigation aids for non-scriptable browsers is also an important feature.

- Careful coordination of the delays associated with menu events can enhance the user's experience.

- Menus can be implemented so that they activate when the user mouses over (rather than clicks) the menu heading.

- Dividers and subheadings can be added to menus in order to group related items.

- Modifying the window's status bar to provide more information when the user mouses over a menu item can improve usability.

A very large improvement we could make to the code is to create a hierarchical menu system, namely one where menu items cascade to reveal even more menus. Of course, while doing this would add some significant complexity to our code, it would also flatten a Web site, allowing a user to reach deep parts of the site easily. Yet before getting carried away and improving menus to support a hierarchical style, you should consider the complexity and the amount of code being generated. Poorly defined menu systems can cause many problems, most notably error dialogs and delays. In fact, generation of a large menu system in JavaScript takes time and may slow a user down.

Other Menu Forms

There are many special menu types in use on the Web today. In this section we mention some of the most popular varieties, but this selection is by no means exhaustive. The DHTML Web sites mentioned in this chapter, particularly **www.dynamicdrive.com**,

www.dhtmlcentral.com, and **www.webreference.com**, are all excellent sources of inspiration and code. We'll present a few examples of what you can find at such sites to get the idea of how other forms of menus can be created.

Remote Control Menus

Remote control menus are simply popup windows that control the behavior of the main browser window. Chapter 12 covered the essentials of manipulation of one window by another, and the same techniques apply here. These types of menus are often useful if you need to present the user with a large number of complex capabilities. Often, screen real estate is at a premium, and a large menu directly in the main content window is inappropriate. You may find it useful to invoke the **focus()** method of the window being controlled after the user performs an action in the control panel. Additionally, windows containing remote control menus are often brought up "naked," that is, without scrollbars, browser buttons, or a location bar. To bring up a window this way, pass the empty string as the third argument to **window.open()**:

```
var remoteControl = window.open(remoteURL, "controlMenu", "");
```

Using a separate window as a menu is not the only way to move menu functionality outside of the main browser window. Slide-in menus are also often appropriate for this task.

Slide-in Menus

A slide-in menu is a layer containing menu items that is partially hidden offscreen, usually to the left. Only a tab or thin vertical slice of the layer remains visible to the user. When the user activates the menu by mousing over or clicking on the exposed portion, the menu slides smoothly onto the page. When the user moves the mouse away from the menu, the layer slides back to its original position offscreen.

The following code illustrates how slide-in menus are usually implemented. The idea is to initially place the layer off the left side of the screen and then incrementally move the menu onto the screen while the mouse is over the menu. A timer wakes the scrolling function up at regular intervals, at which times the menu is moved slightly farther to the right. Once a predefined menu position is reached, the timer is cleared in order to stop the scrolling. When the user moves the mouse away from the menu, the scrolling function is invoked at regular intervals to move the layer back to its original position. Note that your users may find it more convenient if the menu is placed directly on the screen when activated (rather than having it slide in).

Although the following code is written for modern versions of Internet Explorer, you can write cross-browser sliders using the dynamic menu generation techniques found earlier in the chapter.

```
<!DOCTYPE HTML PUBLIC "-//W3C//DTD HTML 4.01 Transitional//EN"
"http://www.w3.org/TR/html4/loose.dtd">
```

```
<html>
<head>
<title>Slide-in menu example</title>
<style type="text/css">
<!--
.menu { background: blue;  padding: 0px; margin: 0px;
        border-style: solid; border-width: 2px;
        border-color: lightblue; position: absolute;
        text-align: left; width: 150px; top: 80px;
        z-index: 100;  }
.menuItem { color: white; position: relative;
            display: block; font-style: normal; margin: 0px;
            padding: 2px 15px 2px 10px; font-size: smaller;
            font-family: sans-serif; font-weight: bold;
            text-decoration: none;  }
a.menuItem:hover { background-color: darkblue }
-->
</style>
<script language="JavaScript" type="text/javascript">
<!--

var leftmost = -120;
var rightmost = 5;
var interval = null;
function scrollRight(menuName)
{
    if (document.all(menuName).style.pixelLeft >= rightmost)
      {     // if the menu is already fully shown stop scrolling
        clearInterval(interval);
            return;
            }
    document.all(menuName).style.pixelLeft += 5;     // else move 5 more pixels
}

function scrollLeft(menuName)
{
    if (document.all(menuName).style.pixelLeft <= leftmost)
      { // if menu is fully retracted stop scrolling
        clearInterval(interval);
        return;
        }
  document.all(menuName).style.pixelLeft -= 5;     // else move 5 more pixels in
}

function startRightScroll(menuName)
{
   clearInterval(interval);
   interval = setInterval('scrollRight("' + menuName + '")', 30);
```

```
}
function startLeftScroll(menuName)
{
  clearInterval(interval);
  interval = setInterval('scrollLeft("' + menuName + '")', 30);
}
//-->
</script>
</head>
<body onload="document.all.slider.style.pixelLeft = leftmost">
<!-- The hidden menu -->
<div class="menu" id="slider" onmouseover="startRightScroll('slider')"
onmouseout="startLeftScroll('slider')">
<h3 class="menuItem"><u>Our Products</u></h3>
<a class="menuItem" href="widgets.html">Widgets</a>
<a class="menuItem" href="swidgets.html">Super Widgets</a>
<a class="menuItem" href="sprockets.html">Sprockets</a>
<a class="menuItem" href="vulcans.html">Vulcans</a>
</div>

<h1>Welcome to our Company</h1>
</body>
</html>
```

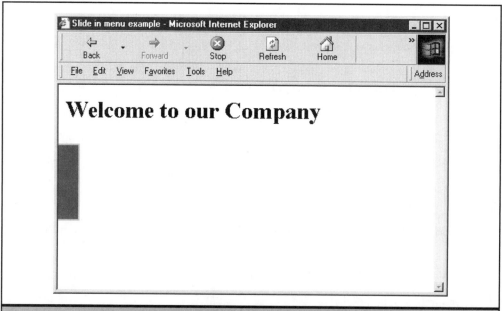

Figure 16-6. *The menu fully retracted to the left*

Figure 16-7.   *The menu fully displayed*

The menu is shown retracted in Figure 16-6 and fully exposed in Figure 16-7. Of course, when deployed live on a site, the exposed portion of the menu should have some indication that the area will react when the user places the mouse over it. Tall, thin images are often used.

Static Menus

If you include menus in a page that has more than one screenful of content, you might consider using static menus. A static menu is one that appears in one place in a browser window at all times, regardless of any scrolling the user might undertake. As you might imagine, implementing a static menu is similar to implementing a "normal" menu, except that the menu must be repositioned whenever the user scrolls. While it is possible to trap scrolling events in some modern browsers, an easy cross-browser implementation of static menus can be achieved with a simple application of **setInterval()**.

The idea is to "wake up" repositioning code at regular (short) intervals. The repositioning code adjusts the position of the menu to some predefined location. The implementation is straightforward. An **onload** handler for the document starts a timer that invokes **makeStatic()** on the menu every 30 milliseconds, and **makeStatic()** accepts the **id** (or layer **name** in Netscape 4) of the element which is to be repositioned. In this example, the "menu" is placed five pixels from the top left of the screen, but this position can be easily changed.

```html
<!DOCTYPE HTML PUBLIC "-//W3C//DTD HTML 4.01 Transitional//EN"
"http://www.w3.org/TR/html4/loose.dtd">
<html>
<head>
<title>Slide-in menu example</title>
<style type="text/css">
<!--
.menu { background: blue;  padding: 0px; margin: 0px; border-style: solid;
        border-width: 0px; border-color: lightblue; color: white;
        position: absolute; text-align: left; width: 150px;  }
-->
</style>
<script language="JavaScript" type="text/javascript">
<!--
var xOff = 5;
var yOff = 5;
function makeStatic(elementName)
{
   if (document.layers)
     {                   // if NS4
       document.layers[elementName].x = window.pageXOffset + xOff;
       document.layers[elementName].y = window.pageYOffset + yOff;
     }
   else if (document.all)
       { // else if IE4+
         document.all(elementName).style.left = document.body.scrollLeft + xOff;
         document.all(elementName).style.top = document.body.scrollTop + yOff;
       }
     else if (document.getElementById)
       {    // else if NS6 or other DOM
         document.getElementById(elementName).style.left = window.pageXOffset + xOff;
         document.getElementById(elementName).style.top = window.pageYOffset + yOff;
       }
}
//-->
</script>
</head>
<body onload="setInterval('makeStatic(\'staticMenu\')',30)">
<layer class="menu" name="staticMenu">

<div class="menu" id="staticMenu">
This is the menu content.
</div>

</layer>
<h1>Welcome to our Company</h1>
<!-- Include more than one screenful of content here -->
<br><br><br><br><br><br><br><br><br><br><br><br><br><br><br><br>
```

```
<br><br><br><br><br><br><br><br><br><br><br><br><br><br><br>
<br><br><br><br><br><br><br><br><br><br><br><br><br><br><br>
<br><br><br><br><br><br><br><br><br><br><br><br><br><br><br>
<br><br><br><br><br><br><br><br><br><br><br><br><br><br><br>
<br><br><br><br><br><br><br><br><br><br><br><br><br><br><br>
<br><br><br><br><br><br><br><br><br><br><br><br><br><br><br>
<br><br><br><br><br><br><br><br><br><br><br><br><br><br><br>
<br><br><br><br><br><br><br><br><br><br><br><br><br><br><br>
<br><br><br><br><br><br><br><br><br><br><br><br><br><br><br>
<br><br><br><br><br><br><br><br><br><br><br><br><br><br><br>
<br><br><br><br><br><br><br><br><br><br><br><br><br><br><br>
<br><br><br><br><br><br><br><br><br><br><br><br><br><br><br>
<br><br><br><br><br><br><br><br><br><br><br><br><br><br><br>
<br><br><br><br><br><br><br><br><br><br><br><br><br><br><br>
<br><br><br><br><br><br><br><br><br><br><br><br><br><br><br>

<h1>Bottom of the page</h1>
</body>
</html>
```

Context Menus

A *context menu* is a special context-specific menu that most programs display when
the right mouse button is pressed. What makes this menu special is that its composition
depends upon the situation in which it is activated. Right-clicking around a Web page
(or on a Mac, holding the button down) is a good way to familiarize yourself with the
concept. In most of the areas of a page, when you right-click you are presented with a
menu with options such as viewing the source file, printing, or moving backwards in
your session history. Right-clicking on an image, however, typically results in a different
menu, perhaps with the option to save the image to your local drive or set the image as
wallpaper for your GUI.

Internet Explorer 5+ allows you to define customized responses to contextual
activations with the **oncontextmenu** event handler associated with the **Document**.
Associating a function with this handler allows you to customize contextual events—
for example, to display a context menu of your own construction. Assuming you have
defined functions **showMyMenu()** and **hideMyMenu()** to display and hide a custom
menu, you might use:

```
document.oncontextmenu = showMyMenu;
document.onclick = hideMyMenu;
```

Hiding your menu when the user clicks normally is an important thing to
remember to implement. Doing so mimics the behavior of the default context menus,
making use of a process that your users are accustomed to seeing. Like any other event

handler, returning **false** from the context menu handler prevents the default action (the display of the default context menu) from occurring.

It is interesting that context menus are often used to attempt to prevent images in the page from being saved to the user's local drive. The typical way a user does this is by right-clicking the image and saving it to disk. Trapping context menu events can prevent naïve users from doing so. For example, you could use a short script like this at the end of an HTML document:

```
<script language="JavaScript" type="text/javascript">
<!--
    function killContext()
    {
    alert("Images should not be copied.");
    return false;
    }
document.oncontextmenu = killContext;
//-->
</script>
```

The reality is that the user can simply disable JavaScript, reload the page, and download the image as usual. Further, using this example might anger the user who expects to see a context menu. We could certainly try to sense if the right-click was on an image or not and improve the script—but the point is the same: disrupting the context menu may confuse or annoy many users. JavaScript should be used to improve a user's visit, not disrupt it.

Navigation Assistance with Cookies

While considered by some users to be harmful, cookies are actually very useful in improving a Web site visit. The main value of cookies comes from the fact that HTTP is a *stateless* protocol. There is no way to maintain connection or user information across multiple requests to the same server by the same client. Netscape addressed this issue in the early stages of the Web with the introduction of cookies. A *cookie* is a small piece of text data set by a Web server that resides on the client's machine. Once it's set, the client automatically returns the cookie to the Web server with each request that it makes. During each transaction, the server has the opportunity to modify or delete any cookies it has already set and also has, of course, the ability to set new cookies. The most common application of this technology is the identification of individual users. Typically, a site will have a user log in and will then set a cookie containing the appropriate username. From that point on, whenever the user makes a request to that particular site, the browser sends the username cookie in addition to the usual information to the server. The server can then keep track of which user it is serving pages to and modify its behavior accordingly. This is how many Web-based e-mail systems "know" that you are logged in.

There are several parts to each cookie, many of them optional. The syntax for setting cookies is:

name=value [; expires=*date*] [; domain=*domain*] [; path=*path*] [; secure]

The tokens enclosed in brackets are optional and may appear in any order. The semantics of the tokens are described in Table 16-1.

Token	Description	Example
name=value	Sets the cookie named *name* to the string *value*.	username=fritz
expires=*date*	Sets the expiration date of the cookie to *date*. The *date* string is given in Internet standard GMT format. To format a **Date** to this specification you can use the **toGMTString()** method of **Date** instances.	expires=Sun, 01-Dec-2002 08:00:00 GMT
domain=*domain*	Sets the domain for the cookie to *domain*, which must correspond (with certain flexibility) to the domain of the server setting the cookie. The cookie will be returned only when making a request of this domain.	domain=www.javascriptref .com
path=*path*	String indicating the subset of paths at the domain for which the cookie will be returned.	path=/users/fritz/
secure	Indicates that the cookie is only to be returned over a secure (HTTPS) connection.	secure

Table 16-1.   *The Tokens That Make Up a Cookie*

Cookies that are set without the *expires* token are called *session cookies*. They derive their name from the fact that they are kept for only the current browser session; they are destroyed when the user quits the browser. Cookies that are not session cookies are called *persistent cookies*, because the browser keeps them until their expiration date is reached, at which time they are discarded.

When a user connects to a site, the browser checks its list of cookies for a match. A match is determined by examination of the URL of the current request. If the domain and path in a cookie match the given URL (in some loose sense), the cookie's *name=value* token is sent to the server. If multiple cookies match, the browser includes each match in a semicolon-separated string. For example, it might return:

```
username=fritz; favoritecolor=green; prefersmenus=yes
```

Be aware that we are glossing over some subtleties with regard to how the browser determines a match. Full details are found at **http://home.netscape.com/newsref/std/cookie_spec.html**. Several RFCs (2109, 2965, and especially 2964) also have bearing on cookie technology, but the Netscape specification is the one widely used.

Cookies in JavaScript

One nice thing about cookies is that nearly every browser in existence with JavaScript support also provides scripts access to cookies. Cookies are exposed as the **cookie** property of the **Document** object. This property is both readable and writeable.

Setting Cookies

When you assign a string to **document.cookie** the browser parses it as a cookie and adds it to its list of cookies. For example:

```
document.cookie = "username=fritz; expires=Sun, 01-Dec-2002 08:00:00 GMT;
path=/home";
```

sets a persistent cookie named *username* with value "fritz" that expires in 2002 and will be sent whenever a request is made for a file under the "/home" directory on the current Web server. Whenever you omit the optional cookie tokens, the browser fills them in automatically with reasonable defaults—for example, the domain of the current URL and path to the current document. It is possible, but not recommended, to set multiple cookies of the same name with differing paths. If you do so, then both values may be returned in the cookie string, and if so you have to check to see if you can tell the difference using their order in the string. Attempting to set cookies for inappropriate domains or paths (for example, domain names other than domains closely related to the current URL) will silently fail.

The cookie parsing routines used by the browser assume that any cookies you set are well formed. The name/value pair must not contain any whitespace characters, commas, or semicolons. Using such characters can cause the cookie to be truncated or even discarded. It is common practice to encode cookie values that might be problematic before setting them in the cookie. The global **escape()** and **unescape()** methods available in all major browsers are usually sufficient for the job. These functions URL-encode and URL-decode the strings that are passed to them as arguments and return the result. Problematic characters such as whitespace, commas, and semicolons are replaced with their equivalent in URL escape codes. For example, a space character is encoded as "%20." The following code illustrates their use:

```
var problemString = "Get rid of , ; and ?";
var encodedString = escape(problemString);
alert("Encoded: " + encodedString + "\n" + "Decoded: " +
unescape(encodedString));
```

When you assign a new cookie value to **document.cookie**, the current cookies are not replaced. The new cookie is parsed and its name/value pair is appended to the list. The exception is when you assign a new cookie with the same name (and same domain and path, if they exist) as a cookie that already exists. In this case, the old value is replaced with the new. For example:

```
document.cookie = "username=fritz";
document.cookie = "username=thomas";
alert("Cookies: " + document.cookie);
```

The result is:

Reading Cookies

As you can see from the previous example, reading cookies is as simple as examining the **document.cookie** string. Because the browser automatically parses and adds any cookies set into this property, it always contains up-to-date name/value pairs of cookies for the current document. The only challenging part is parsing the string to extract the information in which you are interested. Consider the following code:

```
document.cookie = "username=fritz";
document.cookie = "favoritecolor=green";
document.cookie = "jsprogrammer=true";
```

The value of **document.cookie** after these statements are executed is

```
"username=fritz; favoritecolor=green; jsprogrammer=true"
```

If you are interested in the *favoritecolor* cookie, you could manually extract everything after "favoritecolor=" and before "; jsprogrammer=true". However, it is almost always a good idea to write a function that will do this for you automatically.

The following code parses the current cookies and places them in an associative array indexed by *name*. It assumes that the browser is ECMAScript-compliant (nearly all modern browsers are).

```
// associative array indexed as cookies["name"] = "value"
var cookies = new Object();

function extractCookies()
{    // extract current cookies, destroying old value of cookies array
   var name, value;
   var beginning, middle, end;
   for (name in cookies)
     {
     // if there are currently entries in cookies, get rid of them
     cookies = new Object();
     break;
     }
   beginning = 0;     // start at the beginning of the cookie string
   while (beginning < document.cookie.length)
     {
         // find the next equal sign
       middle = document.cookie.indexOf('=', beginning);
         // find the next semicolon
     end = document.cookie.indexOf(';', beginning);
     if (end == -1)     // if no semicolon exists, it's the last cookie...
        end = document.cookie.length;

     // if nothing is in the cookie, blank out its value
     if ( (middle > end) || (middle == -1) )
       {
```

```
          name = document.cookie.substring(beginning, end);
          value = "";
      }
    else
    {  // extract out the name and value
        name = document.cookie.substring(beginning, middle);
        value = document.cookie.substring(middle + 1, end);
    }
    // add cookie to the associative array
    cookies[name] = unescape(value);
    // step over the next space to the beginning of next cookie
    beginning = end + 2;
  }
}
```

Note that invoking **unescape()** on a string that hasn't been **escape()**d will generally not result in any harm. Unescaping affects only substrings of the form %hh where the *h*'s are hex digits.

You might wonder if the extra checking for the equal sign in the previous example is necessary. It is. Consider the following example:

```
document.cookie = "first=value1"
document.cookie = "second=";
document.cookie = "third";
document.cookie = "fourth=value4";
alert("Cookies: " + document.cookie);
```

In Internet Explorer, the output is:

Under Netscape 6, the output is:

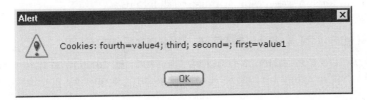

As you can see, it is possible for cookies to exist without explicit values. Additionally, the representation of the cookie named "second" is different under IE and Netscape. Though you should always use complete name/value pairs in the cookies set with JavaScript, some of the cookies the browser has might have been set by a CGI script over which you have no control. Therefore, it is always a good idea to write cookie-reading code to accommodate all possibilities. The **extractCookies()** function given earlier in this section is a good example of the kind of defensive programming tactics that should be employed.

Deleting Cookies

A cookie is deleted by setting a cookie with the same name (and domain and path, if they were set) with an expiration date in the past. Any date in the past should work, but most often programmers use the first second after the epoch in order to accommodate computers with an incorrectly set date. To delete a cookie named "username" that was set without a domain or path token, you would write:

```
document.cookie = "username=nothing; expires=Thu, 01-Jan-1970 00:00:01 GMT";
```

This technique deletes cookies set with a value, but, as previously discussed, some cookies can exist without explicit values. Such cookies require that the equal sign be omitted. For example, the following would define and then immediately delete a cookie without an explicit value:

```
document.cookie = "username";
document.cookie = "username; expires=Thu, 01-Jan-1970 00:00:01 GMT";
```

With defensive programming in mind, you might want to write a **deleteCookie()** function that tries both techniques to delete cookies:

```
function deleteCookie(name)
{
   document.cookie = name + "=deleted; expires=Thu, 01-Jan-1970 00:00:01 GMT";
   document.cookie = name + "; expires=Thu, 01-Jan-1970 00:00:01 GMT";
}
```

Remember that if a cookie was set with path or domain information, you need to include those tokens in the cookie you use to delete it.

Using Cookies for User State Management

Cookies are used to store state information. The kind of information you store in your cookies and what you do with that information is limited only by your imagination. The best applications of cookie technology enhance page presentation or content based on user preference or profile. Functionality critical to the operation of the site is probably not appropriate for cookies manipulated by JavaScript. For example, it is possible to write fully functional "shopping cart" code that stores state information in the client's browser with cookies from JavaScript. However, doing so automatically prevents anyone who chooses to disable JavaScript from using your site.

Some simple applications are discussed briefly in the next few sections. We'll use the **extractCookies()** function defined previously to read cookies.

Redirects

Oftentimes it is useful to send your site's visitors to different pages on the basis of some criterion. For example, first-time visitors might be redirected to an introductory page, while returning users should be sent to a content page. This is easily accomplished:

```
// this script might go in index.html
var cookies = new Object();
// immediately set a cookie to see if they are enabled
document.cookie = "cookiesenabled=yes";

extractCookies();

if (cookies["cookiesenabled"])
  {
    if (cookies["returninguser"])
      {
        location.href = "/content.html";
      }
    else
      {
        var expiration = new Date();
        expiration.setYear(expiration.getYear() + 2);
        // cookie expires in 2 years
        document.cookie = "returninguser=true; expires=" + expiration.toGMTString();
        location.href = "/introduction.html";
      }
  }
```

Note how the script first attempts to set a cookie in order to see if the user has cookies enabled. If not, no redirection is carried out.

One-Time Popups

One-time popup windows are used to present users with information the first time they visit a particular page. Such popups usually contain a welcome message, reminder, special offer, or configuration prompt. An example application targeting a "tip of the day" page that is displayed once per session is shown here:

```javascript
var cookies = new Object();
document.cookie = "cookiesenabled=yes";
extractCookies();
if (cookies["cookiesenabled"] && !cookies["has_seen_tip"])
{
    document.cookie = "has_seen_tip=true";
    window.open("/tipoftheday.html", "tipwindow", "resizable");
}
```

If the user doesn't have cookies enabled we choose not to show the popup window. This prevents users from becoming annoyed by the popup if they frequently load the page with cookies disabled.

Customizations

Cookies provide an easy way to create customized or personalized pages for individual users. The user's preferences can be saved in cookies and retrieved by JavaScript code that modifies stylistic attributes for the page. While CGI scripts often use cookies to customize content, it is usually easier to modify style characteristics in JavaScript. The following example allows the user to select one of three color schemes for the page. While this particular example is rather simplistic, the basic concept can be used to provide very powerful customization features.

```html
<!DOCTYPE HTML PUBLIC "-//W3C//DTD HTML 4.01 Transitional//EN"
"http://www.w3.org/TR/html4/loose.dtd">
<html>
<head>
<title>Customization Example</title>
<script language="JavaScript" type="text/javascript">
<!--
var cookies = new Object();

function extractCookies()
{
    var name, value;
    var beginning, middle, end;
    for (name in cookies)
      {
        cookies = new Object();
        break;
      }
    beginning = 0;
```

```
    while (beginning < document.cookie.length)
      {
        middle = document.cookie.indexOf('=', beginning);
        end = document.cookie.indexOf(';', beginning);

        if (end == -1)
          end = document.cookie.length;
        if ( (middle > end) || (middle == -1) )
          {
           name = document.cookie.substring(beginning, end);
           value = "";
          }
        else
          {
            name = document.cookie.substring(beginning, middle);
            value = document.cookie.substring(middle + 1, end);
          }
        cookies[name] = unescape(value);
        beginning = end + 2;
      }
}
function changeColors(scheme)
{
    switch (scheme)
      {
        case "plain": foreground = "black"; background = "white"; break;
        case "ice": foreground = "lightblue"; background = "darkblue"; break;
        case "green": foreground = "white"; background = "darkgreen"; break;
        default: return;
      }
    if (document.layers)
      { // Nav4 doesn't reflect changes to style after the page is loaded
        // so reload it

        if (pageLoaded)
            location.href = location.href;
        document.tags.body.background = background;
        document.tags.body.color = foreground;
      }
    else
      {
        document.bgColor = background;
        document.fgColor = foreground;
      }
}
function changeScheme(which)
{
```

```
    document.cookie = "cookiesenabled=true";
    extractCookies();
    if (!cookies["cookiesenabled"])
      {
        alert("You need to enable cookies for this demo!");
        return;
      }
    document.cookie = "scheme=" + which;
    changeColors(which);
}
var pageLoaded = false;
extractCookies();
changeColors(cookies["scheme"]);
//-->
</script>
</head>
<body onload="pageLoaded = true">
<h1>Customization Example</h1>
<hr><blockquote> Where a calculator on the ENIAC is equipped with 19,000
vacuum tubes and weighs 30 tons, computers in the future may have only 1,000
vacuum tubes and perhaps only weigh 1.5 tons.</blockquote><em>From Popular
Mechanics, March 1949 issue.</em>
<hr>
<form>
Change color scheme:    
<input type="button" value="Plain" onclick="changeScheme('plain')">
<input type="button" value="Ice" onclick="changeScheme('ice')">
<input type="button" value="Green" onclick="changeScheme('green')">
</form>
</body>
</html>
```

While this example is of limited value, one customization that would be very appropriate would be a system to turn off various facilities. For example, given a site with DHTML menus, it might be nice to present a button to disable the display of DHTML menus in favor of static navigational aids in the event that the user's browser improperly renders the menus or the user just doesn't want the overhead.

Cookie Limitations

Because cookies are useful for such a wide variety of tasks, many developers are tempted to use them for anything and everything they can. While it is a good idea to provide the user with a maximally customizable site, the browser places limitations on the number and size of cookies that you can set. Violating these limitations can have a

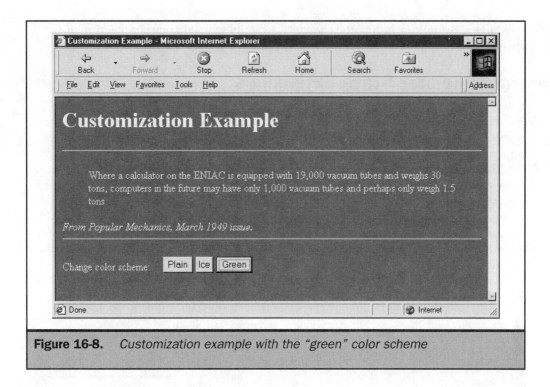

Figure 16-8.   *Customization example with the "green" color scheme*

range of effects from silent failure to full-on browser crashes. You should be aware of the following guidelines:

- The total number of cookies a browser can store at one time is limited to several hundred.
- The total number of cookies a browser can store at one time from one particular site is often limited to 20.
- Each cookie is usually limited to about 4,000 characters.

To get around the limitation of 20 cookies per site, it is often useful to "pack" multiple values into one cookie. Doing so usually requires encoding cookie values in some specific manner that makes it easy to recover the packed values. While this technique increases the size of each cookie, it decreases the total number of cookies required.

One other issue to be aware of is that many users disable cookies for privacy reasons. Because persistent cookies can be set for an arbitrary length of time, advertisers use them to track user browsing habits and product interest. Many people feel that this is an invasion of privacy. For this reason you should use persistent cookies only if you really need them. Before concluding the chapter we should look into one special form of state management supported only by Internet Explorer.

Internet Explorer State Extensions

Internet Explorer 5 includes a new technology called *DHTML Behaviors*. DHTML Behaviors are small components encapsulating specific functionality that can easily be added to a page. One particularly interesting aspect of behaviors is their capacity to store client-side state without the use of cookies.

The **saveHistory** behavior saves the state of the page for when a user returns. Although data saved in this manner persists only during the current browsing session, the storage capacity and ease of use make it a tempting alternative to traditional cookies. To use this feature, you merely include a **<meta>** tag with particular attributes. A **<style>** with a **class** referencing a **behavior:** string permits the storage and retrieval of information. Information on the page that you wish to retain should be given the **class** for which the behavior is defined.

For example, the following document will store any information you enter into the text box and retrieve it when you return to the page.

```
<!DOCTYPE HTML PUBLIC "-//W3C//DTD HTML 4.01 Transitional//EN"
"http://www.w3.org/TR/html4/loose.dtd">
<html>
<head>
<title>DHTML Behavior Example</title>
<meta name="save" content="history">
<style type="text/css">
<!--
.saveHistory {behavior:url(#default#savehistory);}
-->
</style>
</head>
<body>
Enter some text to store:
<input type="text" class="saveHistory" id="persistentInput">
<br>
When you're through, go to a different page and return.
The text will be "as you left it."
</body>
</html>
```

This application is merely the tip of the iceberg. It is possible to store the entire state of the page, up to several hundred kilobytes of data, and retrieve it with a simple binding to DHTML behavior, defined as before. While this technique is highly nonstandard, it seems far preferable to the amount of work involved with the alternatives, for example hooking your site into a large database.

More information about this new technology, including other useful state-storage behaviors, can be found at the Microsoft Developer's Network (**http://msdn.microsoft .com**). Additional discussion about proprietary Microsoft extensions, including DHTML Behaviors, can be found in Chapter 23.

Summary

JavaScript can be used to implement an astonishing array of navigational aids. For example, client-side state information can be saved using the **cookie** property of the **Document** object and may be set for the duration of the browsing session or for an arbitrary length of time. Once set, cookies can be used for customizations such as storing user preference, profile, or identification information. The DHTML features of JavaScript can also be used to create sophisticated navigation schemes, ranging from simple pull-down redirection menu systems to complex CSS-based hierarchical menus. While such menus are quite powerful, Web developers need to take care that they accommodate as large a segment of the browser population as possible. While support for Internet Explorer 4+ is essentially required, providing scripts that work with Netscape 4 and 6 is often desirable as well. Getting the scripts to work in all types of browsers under all conditions, including JavaScript being turned off, requires some significant effort. In the next chapter we'll spend time looking at browser detection and support techniques to help overcome such obstacles.

The Complete Reference

Chapter 17

Controlling the Browser

Given the wide variety of browsers that can hit a public Web site, it would be useful to build pages to suit each user's specific browsing environment. Under most versions of JavaScript, it is possible to detect the user's browser type and version as well as numerous other client-side characteristics, such as screen size, color depth, and support for Java and plugins. Once the characteristics of the user's browser have been detected, it is often possible to improve the user's experience by writing specialized content, redirecting to other locations automatically or after a certain amount of time, or even controlling browser facilities such as navigation history. While many of the techniques presented in this chapter can be very useful, they also lend themselves to the creation of "exclusionary" Web sites. Browser detection and control techniques should improve the use of Web sites for all users, rather than a select few.

Browser Detection Basics

Anyone who has built more than a few Web pages has surely come across some of the numerous differences between browser types and versions. A page that looks perfect on your screen just doesn't look quite the same on your friend's or neighbor's, and sometimes it looks vastly different. The variances range from minor cosmetic inconsistencies, like a small shift of content or container size, to catastrophic situations in which the page causes errors or doesn't render at all.

What's a developer to do when faced with such an unpredictable medium as the Web? Some throw up their hands and just build their site to suit their current browser of choice. If you've ever noticed statements on sites like "This Site best viewed in...", then you have encountered this approach already. Others simplify their site technology to the so-called lowest common denominator. This is the approach that is typically used by the largest of sites, which seem ever focused on continuing to meet the needs of low resolution, CSS- and JavaScript-unaware browsers. Falling somewhere in between these extremes is the more adaptive type of site that modifies itself to suit the browser's needs or indicates to the user their inability to use the site. This "sense and adapt" concept is often termed *browser detection* or *browser sniffing* and is an integral part of JavaScript tasks of any complexity.

Browser Sensing Basics: The Navigator Object

JavaScript's **Navigator** object provides properties that indicate the type of browser and other useful information about the user accessing the page. The most commonly used **Navigator** properties having to do with the browser version are detailed in Table 17-1. Most of these properties relate a piece of the user-agent string that is automatically transmitted to the server by the browser with every request. Note that many of these properties work only in one particular browser type, so developers should stick with the commonly supported **appName**, **appVersion**, and **userAgent** properties.

Property Name	Description	Example Value	Compatibility
appCodeName	Contains the code name of the browser in use.	Mozilla	All JS-aware browsers, but will generally report only as "Mozilla" for historical reasons.
appMinorVersion	The sub-version or upgrades of the browser.	;SP1;	Internet Explorer only.
appName	The official name of the browser.	Microsoft Internet Explorer	All JS-aware browsers, but may not be accurate because Opera and WebTV spoof the value.
appVersion	Contains the version of the browser.	5.0 (Windows; en-US)	All JS-aware browsers, but may contain more information than version, including platform and language type.
userAgent	The complete user-agent value transmitted to the server by the browser.	Mozilla/5.0 (Windows; U; WinNT4.0; en-US; m18) Gecko/20010131 Netscape6/6.01	All JS-aware browsers. There is some question if the browser may spoof a value that is different from what JavaScript reports.
vendor	Indicates the browser vendor.	Netscape6	Netscape 6 and greater only
vendorSub	Indicates the version number of the browser.	6.01	Netscape 6 and greater only

Table 17-1.   *Navigator Properties for Browser Name and Version Detection*

The examination of user-agents for typical browsers reveals a variety of cryptic numbers and abbreviations. Most of these values are rarely used. Rather, the "important" fields, such as major version number and operating system, are extracted and the rest is ignored. For example, when detecting Netscape 6, the important substring is "Netscape 6." Developers usually do not care which particular versions of the browser and rendering engines (for instance, Mozilla or Gecko) went into the release.

Browser Detection—An Introduction

The following simple script shows the basic use of the **Navigator** properties for browser detection. It simply prints the browser name and version values onscreen. An example of the script's rendering in some common browsers is shown in Figure 17-1.

```
<!DOCTYPE HTML PUBLIC "-//W3C//DTD HTML 4.01 Transitional//EN"
                      "http://www.w3.org/TR/html4/loose.dtd">
<html>
<head>
<title>Browser Detect Example</title>
</head>
<body>
<script language="JavaScript" type="text/javascript">
<!--
var browserName = navigator.appName;
var browserVersion = parseFloat(navigator.appVersion);
document.write("Your browser is ", browserName, " ", browserVersion, ".");
// -->
</script>
<noscript>
 Sorry, I can't detect your browser without JavaScript.
</noscript>
</body>
</html>
```

Using a script like the one just given, it is possible to create conditional markup based upon the browser hitting the page. For example, consider the code here, which outputs some browser-specific HTML according to the particular browser in use:

```
<!DOCTYPE HTML PUBLIC "-//W3C//DTD HTML 4.01 Transitional//EN"
                      "http://www.w3.org/TR/html4/loose.dtd">
<html>
<head>
```

```
<title>Browser Detect Example 2</title>
</head>
<body>
<h1>Something Special for Your Browser</h1>
<hr>
<script language="JavaScript" type="text/javascript">
<!--
var browserName = navigator.appName;

if (browserName == "Microsoft Internet Explorer")
   document.write("<marquee>Some IE specific markup!</marquee>");
else if (browserName == "Netscape")
   document.write("<blink>Netscape specific code!</blink>");
else
   document.write("<b>Browser Not Known: Just a bold element!</b>");
// -->
</script>
<hr>
</body>
</html>
```

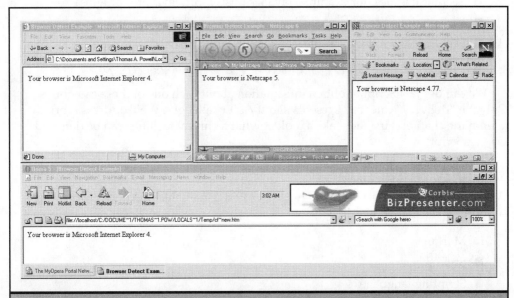

Figure 17-1.   *Browser detection results under Netscape, Internet Explorer, and Opera*

This example will have problems in a stock version of Opera 5, which identifies itself as Internet Explorer by default. Although it identifies itself as Internet Explorer, it obviously is not, so the <marquee> tag is not properly rendered.

There are a few problems using browser detection this way. First, you are making an assumption that the browser will correctly report itself. You may find, in fact, that many obscure browsers will report themselves as Internet Explorer or Netscape because they do not want to be prevented from viewing sites coded to detect the major browser variants. Second, you have to continually check the browser to write out the appropriate markup, littering your page with script code. We'll see later on how we can redirect users or use other techniques to get around this. However, the third problem is the biggest: it is the assumption that simply knowing the browser type and version will be enough to determine what action to take. Developers should not focus on detecting the browser brand and version, but should focus on detecting the capabilities of the browser in use.

What to Detect

When performing browser detection it is important to be aware of the different aspects that affect how your site will be displayed. You can roughly break up the useful detectable information into four categories:

- Technical issues (for example, JavaScript support, Java, and plugins)
- Visual issues (for example, color depth and screen size)
- Delivery issues (for example, connection speed or type)
- User issues (for example, language setting and previous visitor)

We can use JavaScript to obtain information about each one of these categories. Only the "delivery" category presents significant challenges. We'll address it briefly later in the chapter. First let's take a look at what technical facilities can be detected via JavaScript.

Technology Detection

When it comes to browser technology, you would usually like to know the browser's support for the following things:

- Markup
- Style sheets
- Scripting language
- Java
- Object technology (plugins and ActiveX controls)

Markup and style sheets are a bit difficult to detect. You might try to use the DOM to check basic markup support by probing to create a particular object or using the **document.implementation.hasFeature( )** method. This method returns a **Boolean** value if a particular HTML or XML level of binding is supported; for example:

```
var HTMLDOM1 = document.implementation.hasFeature('HTML', '1.0');
// contains true or false indicating HTML binding support
```

Of course few browsers support DOM techniques well enough to really rely on them, and even if they did, such probes really say nothing about the actual support of a particular markup or style facility. In short, just because you can instantiate an HTML element and set some attributes using the DOM doesn't mean those attributes actually do anything in the browser! For now, you will have to rely on your knowledge of browser support for particular versions of HTML or CSS. Fortunately, the other items on our technology list can more easily be addressed from JavaScript.

JavaScript support is probably the easiest technology to detect; if a script doesn't run, this condition implicitly shows that the browser doesn't support JavaScript or that it is turned off. Consider the use of the **<noscript>** tag here with a **<meta>** redirection:

```
<!DOCTYPE HTML PUBLIC "-//W3C//DTD HTML 4.01 Transitional//EN"
                      "http://www.w3.org/TR/html4/loose.dtd">
<html>
<head>
<title>JS Check</title>
<noscript>
<meta http-equiv="Refresh" CONTENT="0; URL=noscript.htm">
</noscript>
</head>
<body>
<script language="JavaScript" type="text/javascript">
<!--
  document.write("This page has JavaScript!");
// -->
</script>
</body>
</html>
```

The user is redirected to a "noscript.htm" page like the one here if they have disabled scripting or have accessed the site with a very old browser.

```
<!DOCTYPE HTML PUBLIC "-//W3C//DTD HTML 4.01 Transitional//EN"
                      "http://www.w3.org/TR/html4/loose.dtd">
<html>
<head>
<title>Error: No JavaScript Support</title>
</head>
<body>
<h1>Error: JavaScript Support Required</h1>
<hr>
<p>Your browser does not appear to support JavaScript or it is turned off.<br>
Please enable JavaScript or upgrade your browser and then return to the page
in question.</p>
<p>If you believe you reached this page in error please contact
<a href="mailto:webmaster@democompany.com">Webmaster</a></p>
</body>
</html>
```

Some developers opt instead to do a positive check: the use of JavaScript, when enabled, redirects the user to a particular page using the **Location** object. For example,

```
<script language="JavaScript" type="text/javascript">
<!--
 window.location="scripton.htm";
// -->
</script>
```

The problem with this approach is that it tends to be used as a single detection point and disrupts the back button facility in the browser. The first technique is a more passive approach and can be easily included on all pages without serious worry.

While it is easy to detect if JavaScript is on or off, what about version or feature support? One way to deal with different versions of JavaScript is to utilize the **language** attribute of the **<script>** tag. Remember that JavaScript-aware browsers will ignore the contents of **<script>** tags with **language** attributes they do not support. Because browsers act in this way, it is possible to create multiple versions of a script for various versions of the language, as in this example:

```
<script language="JavaScript" type="text/javascript">
// JS 1.0 features
</script>


<script language ="JavaScript1.1" type="text/javascript">
// JS 1.1 features
```

```
</script>

<script language="JavaScript1.2" type="text/javascript">
// JS 1.2 features
</script>
```

We could even declare dummy functions or objects to avoid errors using this fall-through method. This technique is illustrated in Chapter 24, yet fall-through code isn't always the best way to do deal with multiple versions of JavaScript. In some cases it is just better to check to see whether it is possible to do something. For example, consider how we dealt with DHTML and image rollovers in Chapter 15 using object detection. We found that, rather than knowing everything about which browsers support what versions of JavaScript, it is probably better just to detect for capabilities by checking whether the appropriate object is available. For example, the script here checks to see if your browser could support rollover images by determining whether the **image[ ]** collection is defined:

```
<script language="JavaScript" type="text/javascript">
if (document.images)
   alert("Rollovers would probably work");
else
   alert("Sorry no rollovers");
</script>
```

When you do object detection, you should go the whole way with it. Far too often in JavaScript, we assume that the existence of one object implies the existence of other objects or the use of a particular browser, but this is not always the case. For example, we might use code like

```
var ie = (document.all) ? true : false;
```

to detect if Internet Explorer is in use. However, does the existence of **document.all** really mean that Internet Explorer is in use? The truth of the matter is that another browser could support **document.all** but not necessarily provide all the features found in Internet Explorer. It might be better to check for each object specifically, so instead we might use

```
var allObject = (document.all) ? true : false;
var getById = (document.getElementById) ? true : false;
```

and so on. In some ways object detection is the best method to use, but it should be used carefully and assumptions shouldn't be made. Remember that probing a property of a nonexistent object throws an error, so first check to see if the object exists.

Java Detection

Detecting Java's availability is fairly easy using the **Navigator** method **javaEnabled( )**. This method returns **true** if Java is available and turned on and **false** otherwise.

```
if (navigator.javaEnabled())
   // do Java stuff or write out <applet> tag
else
   alert("Sorry no Java");
```

You can find out more about Java once you know it is available by accessing a Java applet included in the page. You can even determine what type of Java Virtual Machine is supported. In order to do this, you will have to access the public methods and properties of a Java applet. Interacting with applets is discussed in more detail in Chapter 18.

Plugin Detection

In Netscape 3+ (and Opera 4+) each plugin installed in the browser has an entry in the **plugins[ ]** array of the **Navigator** object. Each entry in this array is a **Plugin** object containing information about the specific vendor and version of the component. A simple detection scheme checks for a plugin's existence using the associative array aspect of JavaScript collections. For example, to look for a Flash plugin, you might write:

```
if (navigator.plugins["Shockwave Flash"])
   alert("You have Flash!");
else
   alert("Sorry no Flash");
```

Of course you need to be careful to use the *exact* name of the particular plugin in which you are interested. It is important to note that different versions of the same plugin can have different names, so you need to carefully check vendor documentation when detecting plugins in this fashion. Also be aware that Internet Explorer defines a faux **plugins[ ]** array as a property of **Navigator**. It does so in order to prevent poorly written Netscape-specific scripts from throwing errors while they probe for plugins. We would need to deal with this cross-browser nuance by checking to make sure we are not using Internet Explorer when doing the **plugins[ ]** array probe, as shown here:

```
if (navigator.appName.indexOf('Microsoft')==-1 ||        // if not a MS browser
    (navigator.plugins && navigator.plugins.length))     // and plugins[] exists
```

```
and has entries
  {
    if (navigator.plugins["Shockwave Flash"])
       alert("You have Flash!");
    else
       alert("Sorry no Flash");
  }
else
    alert("Undetectable: Rely on <object> tag");
```

Fortunately, if Internet Explorer is in use we can rely on the **<object>** tag to install the appropriate object handler if the user allows it. More information about detecting and interacting with objects such as Netscape plugins and Microsoft ActiveX controls can be found in Chapter 18.

Visual Detection: Screen Object

The **Screen** object is available in 4.x (and later) browsers and indicates the basic screen characteristics for the browser. It is actually a child of the **Window** object, although it would seem to make more sense as a parent of **Window** if you think about things logically. The following example shows the common screen characteristics that can be detected in browsers that support the **Screen** object.

```
<!DOCTYPE HTML PUBLIC "-//W3C//DTD HTML 4.01 Transitional//EN"
                    "http://www.w3.org/TR/html4/loose.dtd">
<html>
<head>
<title>Common Screen Properties</title>
</head>
<body>
<h2>Current Screen Properties</h2>
<script language="JavaScript1.2" type="text/javascript">
<!--
if (window.screen)
{
  document.write("Height: "+screen.height+"<br>");
  document.write("Width:"+screen.width+"<br>");
  document.write("Available Height: "+screen.availHeight+"<br>");
  document.write("Available Width: "+screen.availWidth+"<br>");
  document.write("Color Depth: "+screen.colorDepth+"bit<br>");
}
else
  document.write("No Screen object support");
```

```
// -->
</script>
</body>
</html>
```

A rendering of the example is shown here:

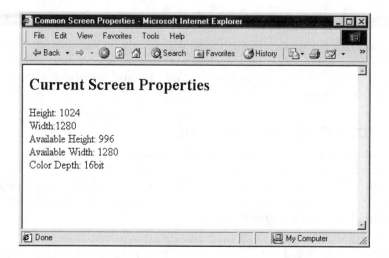

One thing that is rather troublesome with this detection is that the **availHeight** and **availWidth** properties indicate the height and width of the screen minus any operating system chrome rather than, as one might expect, the actual size of the available browser window. In order to detect actual window size you have to use properties of the **Window** object in the case of Netscape. In the case of Internet Explorer, you need to look into the **Document** object and examine the **body** itself. This example shows how you might check this. Notice the use of object detection rather than browser detection in play here:

```
<!DOCTYPE HTML PUBLIC "-//W3C//DTD HTML 4.01 Transitional//EN"
                     "http://www.w3.org/TR/html4/loose.dtd">
<html>
<head>
<title>Available Region Checker</title>
</head>
<body>
<h2>Set to a new size then reload page</h2>
```

```
<hr>
<script language="JavaScript1.2" type="text/javascript">
<!--
    var winWidth = 0;
    var winHeight = 0;

    if (window.innerWidth)
       winWidth = window.innerWidth;
    else if ((document.body) && (document.body.clientWidth))
       winWidth = document.body.clientWidth;

    if (window.innerHeight)
       winHeight = window.innerHeight;
    else if ((document.body) && (document.body.clientHeight))
       winHeight = document.body.clientHeight;

    document.write("Available height = "+winHeight+"<BR>");
    document.write("Available width = "+winWidth+"<BR>");
//-->
</script>
</body>
</html>
```

A typical result is shown here:

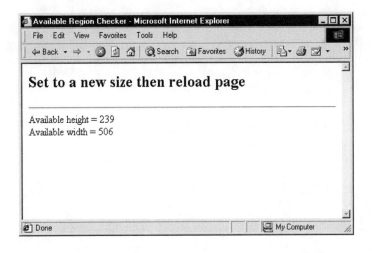

In browsers that permit manipulation of page content and styles at runtime, we can set the size of screen objects such as fonts in a manner appropriate to the current window size. Consider the following example, which works in Internet Explorer 5 and Netscape 6 or later.

```html
<!DOCTYPE HTML PUBLIC "-//W3C//DTD HTML 4.01 Transitional//EN"
                      "http://www.w3.org/TR/html4/loose.dtd">
<html>
<head>
<title>Dynamic Sizing</title>
</head>
<body>

<h1 id="test1" style="font-family: verdana; text-align: center;">Text grows
and shrinks!</h1>

<script language="JavaScript1.2" type="text/javascript">
<!--
function setSize()
{
 if (document.getElementById)
   {
     theHeading = document.getElementById("test1");
     if (window.innerWidth)
        theHeading.style.fontSize = (window.innerWidth / 13)+"px";
     else if ((document.body) && (document.body.clientWidth))
        theHeading.style.fontSize = (document.body.clientWidth / 13)+"px";
   }
}
window.onload = setSize;         // call to set initial size;
window.onresize = setSize;
// -->
</script>
</body>
</html>
```

A typical rendering is shown here, but readers are encouraged to try this example themselves to verify its usefulness.

Under browsers like Internet Explorer that support expressions within CSS rules, we might use something cleaner like this:

```
<h1 style="font-family: verdana; text-align: center;
     font-size: expression(document.body.clientWidth / 13)">
Internet Explorer Font Sizing!</h1>
```

Note *It might be even better to avoid using JavaScript to size objects in CSS and instead rely on relative sizing measurements, like percentage or em values.*

Besides sizing we might also dynamically address color issues on the Web using JavaScript. For example, many designers still use reduced color images that stick to a limited 216-color palette, called the "browser safe" palette, when they might be able to use richer images in many situations. The following code could be used to insert different types of images conditionally:

```
<script language="JavaScript" type="text/javascript">
<!--
 if (window.screen)
   {    // Sense the bit depth...
    if (screen.colorDepth > 8)
       document.writeln('<img src="nonsafecolors.gif">');
    else
       document.writeln('<img src="safecolors.gif">');
   }
else
    document.writeln('<img src="safecolors.gif">');
// -->
</script>
```

USING JAVASCRIPT

```
<!-- Deal with the script off or non-JS aware browsers -->
<noscript>
  <img src="safecolors.gif">
</noscript>
```

Language Detection

The final form of basic detection is to use JavaScript to sense which language the user's browser is set to support. We might use this to send users to a Spanish page if they have the Spanish language set as a preference in their browser. Browsers provide access to this information in slightly different ways. Netscape and Opera use the **window.navigator.language** property, while Internet Explorer relies on **window.navigator.userLanguage** or **window.navigator.systemLanguage**. In the case of Internet Explorer, there is some lack of clarity regarding whether we should pay attention to the operating system language or the browser language. A good guess would be to focus on the browser's language—and it's a good idea to provide links on pages to select other languages in case the detection is incorrect. The following simple example illustrates the use of these properties and could easily be extended using the **Location** object to redirect users to language-specific pages after sensing.

```
var lang = "en-us";
if (window.navigator.language)
  lang = window.navigator.language
else if (window.navigator.userLanguage)
  lang = window.navigator.userLanguage
if (lang == "es")
  document.write("Hola amigo!");
else
  document.write("Hi friend!");
```

Note *There is some concern about the accuracy of the language information available in JavaScript, and some developers suggest looking at the user-agent string to see if anything is specified there as well.*

Advanced Detection Techniques

There are many more tricks we can use for browser detection. For example, we might be able to calculate relative download speed by delivering a set amount of data to the user and timing the transmission. We might also find it useful to add our own properties to the **Navigator** object to keep everything neat and organized. To see some of these techniques implemented, you should take a look at the "Ultimate Browser Sniffer" script developed by Netscape at **http://www.mozilla.org/docs/web-developer/ sniffer/browser_type.html**. Microsoft also has done its part to promote improved browser detection using its client capabilities facility, which is discussed next.

Microsoft Client Capabilities

Microsoft introduced client capabilities detection in Internet Explorer 5 using a default behavior. We'll discuss behaviors in Chapter 23, but for now, take a look at the simple example here; it illustrates Explorer's client capabilities detection, which detects many useful properties, including connection speed.

```
<!DOCTYPE HTML PUBLIC "-//W3C//DTD HTML 4.01 Transitional//EN"
                      "http://www.w3.org/TR/html4/loose.dtd">
<html xmlns:ie>
<head>
<title>IE Specific Browser Detect</title>
<style>
<!--
@media all { IE\:clientCaps {behavior:url(#default#clientCaps)}
}
-->
</style>
</head>
<body>
<ie:clientcaps id="oClientCaps" />
<script language="JSCRIPT" type="text/javascript">
<!--
document.write("<h2>Screen Capabilities</h2>");
document.write("Screen Height: " + oClientCaps.height + "<br>");
document.write("Screen Width: " + oClientCaps.width + "<br>");
document.write("Available Height: " + oClientCaps.availHeight + "<br>");
document.write("Available Width: " + oClientCaps.availWidth + "<br>");
document.write("Color Depth: " + oClientCaps.colorDepth + "bit<br>");
document.write("<h2>Browser Capabilities</h2>");
document.write("Cookies On? " + oClientCaps.cookieEnabled + "<br>");
document.write("Java Enabled? " + oClientCaps.javaEnabled + "<br>");
document.write("<h2>System and Connection Characteristics</h2>");
document.write("Connection Type: " + oClientCaps.connectionType + "<br>");
document.write("CPU: " + oClientCaps.cpuClass + "<br>");
document.write("Platform: " + oClientCaps.platform + "<br>");
document.write("<h2>Language Issues</h2>");
document.write("System Language: " + oClientCaps.systemLanguage + "<br>");
document.write("User Language: " + oClientCaps.userLanguage + "<br>");
// -->
</script>
</body>
</html>
```

A rendering of this example in Internet Explorer 5, as shown in Figure 17-2, shows that nearly every bit of information necessary to customize a site for a user is easily found.

While Explorer's client capabilities make life easier, with the proper amount of scripting we should be able to detect these features under every browser back to Netscape 3 if we make the effort.

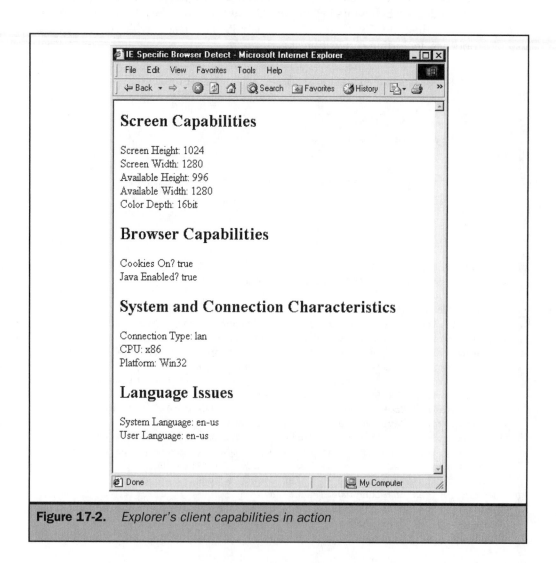

Figure 17-2.   *Explorer's client capabilities in action*

Browser Detection in Practice

There are a few problems using browser detection the way it has been described up to this point. First, you must make sure JavaScript can even be executed; you may want to do some basic browser detection using server-side technologies that look at the user-agent string and then probe more deeply using JavaScript, if it is available. Another problem is that, so far, all the hard detection work is carried out anew for each page the user loads. Ideally, you should save this information to a cookie (see Chapter 16) and then detect only those features that have changed. You will also have to make sure that your detection capabilities are failure-proof by considering all the things that could go wrong: scripting being off, a new browser version hitting the market, and so on. Lastly, you'll have to be a browser capabilities expert, which is difficult to given the number of browsers currently in use. Just counting the major versions of major browsers, there are literally dozens of distinct browsers commonly used, and there is a great deal of information to deal with, especially considering older browsers and the emerging device-based browsers for phones and PDAs. Fortunately, help is out there. Consider looking into browser detection and control software such as Deka (**www.dokoni.com/deka**) and BrowserHawk (**www.browserhawk.com**).

Browser Control

Once we have detected the browser and its various features, we might be interested in trying to control it. Many of these techniques require access to the **Window** object and a few of its lesser-used children. You may have seen a few brief examples of these techniques in this chapter and others, but here we'll take time to introduce these techniques a little more fully. We begin with controlling the browser's current location.

Location Object

The simplest thing we could do might be to send the user automatically to another URL. There are numerous ways to do this in JavaScript, but the best way is to use the **Location** object. The **Location** object is used to access the current location (the URL) of the window. The **Location** object can be both read and replaced, so it is possible to update the location of a page through scripting. Doing this would allow us to create tours and a variety of sophisticated navigation schemes. It is also possible through scripting to update multiple locations at once. Imagine updating multiple framed windows with one button click—this is easily accomplished using the **Location** object. The example here shows how a simple button click can cause a page to load.

```
<form>
<input type="button" value="Go to Yahoo"
```

USING JAVASCRIPT

```
        onclick="window.location='http://www.yahoo.com'">
</form>
```

It is also possible to access parsed pieces of the **Location** object to see where a user is at a particular moment, as shown here

```
alert(window.location.protocol);
// shows the current protocol in the URL
alert(window.location.hostname);
// shows the current hostname
```

The properties of the **Location** object are pretty straightforward for anyone who understands a URL and they are listed in Appendix B. Besides setting the current address, we can also move around in the browser's history list from JavaScript.

History Object

When users press their browser's back or forward button they are navigating the browser's history list. JavaScript provides the **History** object as a way to access the history list for a particular browser window. The **History** object is a read-only array of URL strings that show where the user has been recently. The main methods allow forward and backward progress through the history, as shown here:

```
<a href="javascript: window.history.forward()">Forward</a>
<a href="javascript: window.history.back()">Back</a>
```

 You should be careful when trying to simulate the back button with JavaScript, as it may confuse users who expect links in a page labeled "back" not to act like the browser's back button.

It is also possible to access a particular item in the history list relative to the current position using the **history.go()** method. Using a negative value moves to a history item previous to the current location, while a positive number moves forward in the history list. For example:

```
<a href="javascript: window.history.go(-2)">Back two times</a>
<a href="javascript: window.history.go(3)">Forward 3 times</a>
```

Given that it is possible to read the length of the **history[ ]** array using the **history.length** property, you could easily move to the end of the list using

```
<a href="javascript: window.history.go(window.history.length-1) ">Last Item</a>
```

*If you grant permission to Netscape, you can also access the current, next, and previous URL values from the **History** object. Be aware that this is a serious privacy issue, since it can be used to snoop what pages the user has visited recently.*

Controlling the Status Bar

The status bar is the small text area in the lower left corner of a browser window where messages are typically displayed indicating download progress or other browser status items. It is possible to control the contents of this region with JavaScript. Many developers use this region to display short messages. The benefit of providing information in the status bar is debatable, particularly when you consider the fact that manipulating this region often prevents default browser status information from being displayed— information which many users rely upon.

The status bar can be accessed through two properties of the **Window** object: **status** and **defaultStatus**. The difference between these two properties is how long the message is displayed. The value of **defaultStatus** is displayed any time nothing else is going on in a browser window. The **status** value, on the other hand, is transient and is displayed only for a short period as an event (like a mouse movement) happens. This short example shows some simple status changes as we roll over a link:

```
<a href="http://www.yahoo.com"
    onmouseover="window.status='Don\'t Leave Me!'; return true;"
    onmouseout="window.status=''; return true">
Go to Yahoo!</a>
```

Notice the requirement to return a **true** value from the event handlers, as the browser will kill the status region change without it. Setting the default browser status value is also very easy. Try adding the following to your page:

```
<script language="JavaScript" type="text/javascript">
<!--
defaultStatus='JavaScript is fun!';
//-->
</script>
```

You will have to try status examples outside of page editors like HomeSite, as the status bar may not be visible when using an internal browser to the editor.

Setting Timeouts

The **Window** object supports methods for setting timers that we might use to control the browser. These methods include **setTimeout()** and **clearTimeout()**. The basic idea is to set a timeout to trigger a piece of script to occur at a particular time in the future. The general syntax is

```
timerId = setTimeout(script-to-execute, time-in-milliseconds);
```

where *script-to-execute* is a string holding a function call or other JavaScript statement and *time-in-milliseconds* is the time to wait before executing the specified script fragment. Notice that the **setTimeout()** method returns a handle to the timer that we may save in a variable, as specified by *timerId*. We might then clear the timeout (cancel execution of the function) later on using **clearTimeout(timerId)**. The following example shows how to set and clear a timed event:

```
<!DOCTYPE HTML PUBLIC "-//W3C//DTD HTML 4.01 Transitional//EN"
                      "http://www.w3.org/TR/html4/loose.dtd">
<html>
<head>
<title>5,4,3,2,1...BOOM</title>
</head>
<body>
<h1 align="center">Browser Self-Destruct</h1>
<hr>
<div align="center">
<form>
  <input type="button"
  value="Start Auto-destruct"
  onclick="timer = setTimeout('window.close()', 5000);
alert('Destruction in 5 seconds'); return true">
  <input type="button"
  value="Stop Auto-destruct"
  onclick="clearTimeout(timer); alert('Aborted!'); return true">
</form>
</center>
</body>
</html>
```

Together with the **status** property of the **Window** object, we might use a timer to create the (overly used) scrolling ticker tape effect. Many people like to make use of this effect to market items or draw attention to the status bar. Although this feature may accomplish that goal, it makes it impossible for the user to utilize the status bar to see URLs of the links out of the page. This result degrades the usability of the page significantly. Also, be aware that some ill-behaved scroller scripts may eventually crash a browser because they don't free memory up.

```
<!DOCTYPE HTML PUBLIC "-//W3C//DTD HTML 4.01 Transitional//EN"
                      "http://www.w3.org/TR/html4/loose.dtd">
<html>
<head>
<title>Super Scroller</title>
<script language="JavaScript" type="text/javascript">
<!--
  var message = "Look down in the status bar. It's a JavaScript gimmick. . ."
  var delay = 175;
  var timerID;
  var maxCount = 0;
  var currentCount = 1;

  function scrollMsg()
   {
     if (maxCount == 0)
       maxCount = 3 * message.length;
     window.status = message;
     currentCount++;
     message = message.substring(1, message.length) + message.substring(0,1);
     if (currentCount >= maxCount)
      {
           timerID = 0;
           window.status="";
           return;
      }
       else
           timerID = setTimeout("scrollMsg()", delay);
   }
//-->
</script>
</head>
<body onload="scrollMsg()">
<h1 align="center">The Amazing Scroller</h1>
</body></html>
```

The **setInterval()** and **clearInterval()** methods are supported in later browsers such as the 4.x generation and are used to set a timed event that should occur at a regular interval. We might find that using them is a better way to implement our scroller. Here is an example of the syntax of an interval:

```
<script language="JavaScript" type="text/javascript">
<!--
timer = setInterval("alert('When are we going to get there?')", 10000);
// -->
</script>
```

This example sets an alert that will fire every ten seconds. To clear the interval, you would use a similar method as a timeout:

```
clearInterval(timer);
```

More details on the syntax of intervals and timers can be found in Appendix B.

Simulating Browser Button Presses

Netscape has many methods that allow the developer to fake various browser activities, such as pressing a particular button. Internet Explorer doesn't support very many of these browser control methods, but it supports the most useful one, **window.print()**, which triggers the printing of the page. In Internet Explorer we can, however, use object detection to make an example that will at least not throw an error in non-supporting browsers:

```
<!DOCTYPE HTML PUBLIC "-//W3C//DTD HTML 4.01 Transitional//EN"
                      "http://www.w3.org/TR/html4/loose.dtd">
<html>
<head>
<title>Browser Button Simulator</title>
</head>
<body>
<h1 align="center">Button Simulator</h1>
<hr>
<form>
<input type="button" value="PRINT" onclick="if (window.print) window.print()">
<br><br>
<input type="button" value="FORWARD" onclick="if (window.forward) window.forward()">
<br><br>
<input type="button" value="BACK" onclick="if (window.back) window.back()">
<br><br>
<input type="button" value="HOME" onclick="if (window.home) window.home()">
<br><br>
<input type="button" value="STOP" onclick="if (window.stop) window.stop()">
</form>
</body>
</html>
```

Given that some buttons can be simulated, you might wonder if it is possible to control other aspects of the user's browser such as their preferences. The next section introduces this idea by trying to set the user's default home page using JavaScript.

Preference Setting: Specifying the Home Page

Doing something that may affect the user's browser setup is potentially hazardous, and each browser takes a different approach to this issue. Some just downright disallow it, others require permission, and yet others prompt the user. For example, under Netscape you are required to ask for permission to read and write the values of a user's browser preferences. Take a look at this simple example to see how to set the home page of a user:

```
<!DOCTYPE HTML PUBLIC "-//W3C//DTD HTML 4.01 Transitional//EN"
                      "http://www.w3.org/TR/html4/loose.dtd">
<html>
<head>
<title>Navigator Preference Tester</title>
<script language="JavaScript" type="text/javascript">
<!--
function setHomePage()
{
 if ((window.netscape) && (window.netscape.security))
   {
     netscape.security.PrivilegeManager.enablePrivilege('UniversalPreferencesRead');
     var home = navigator.preference('browser.startup.homepage');
     if (home != 'http://www.pint.com/')
       {

netscape.security.PrivilegeManager.enablePrivilege('UniversalPreferencesWrite');
       navigator.preference('browser.startup.homepage','http://www.pint.com/');
       }
     }
}
// -->
</script>
</head>
<body>
<form>
<input type="button" value="Set Home Page Preference" onclick="setHomePage()">
</form>
</body>
</html>
```

Given the danger involved in setting preferences, when you access the privilege manager from Netscape, you should see a dialog like the one shown here:

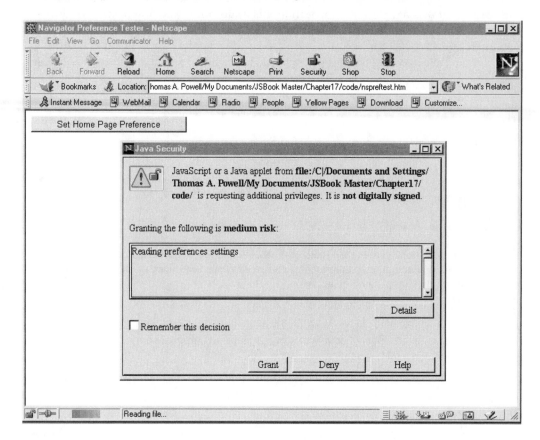

More information on the use of Netscape's privilege manager can be found in Chapter 21.

Internet Explorer uses a very different method to access browser preferences like the home page setting. Under the 5.x release and beyond, you can use a default JavaScript behavior to set the home page:

```
<a href="#"  onclick="HomePage = 'http://www.pint.com';
this.style.behavior='url(#default#homepage)';
this.setHomePage(HomePage);return false">Set PINT to your home page</a>
```

Fortunately, as with Netscape, you will be prompted if you want to do this, so a rogue site can't just slam your current settings without your permission.

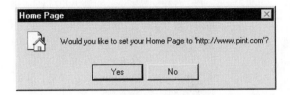

There are similar techniques for setting the user's bookmarks and other preferences, but designers should think twice before taking such drastic control of a user's browsing experience.

Summary

JavaScript's **Navigator** object indicates the type of browser accessing a page as well as many of its characteristics. By using the **Navigator** object, **Screen** object, and a few other **Window** and **Document** properties, we should be able to detect just about everything we would want to control, including: technology usage, screen properties, and user preferences. Using JavaScript, we can then output appropriate page markup or redirect the user to another page using the **Location** object. We can also control the browser in slightly more sophisticated ways, such as moving through a user's history, setting timers, and manipulating the status bar. It is also possible to simulate some browser facilities, such as button presses or preference changes, but there are potential security problems that need to be considered. While browser detection and control techniques can be very useful, there is also a great deal of sophistication involved with their use in a Web site. Developers should make sure to test these approaches well before moving them to a production Web site.

The Complete Reference

JavaScript

Part V

Advanced Topics

The
Complete
Reference

Chapter 18

JavaScript and Embedded Objects

Modern browsers support a plethora of technologies beyond HTML, CSS, and JavaScript. A wide variety of extra functionality is available in the form of browser plugins, ActiveX controls, and Java applets. These technologies provide extended capabilities that can make Web pages appear more like actual applications than marked-up text. Embedded objects provide a natural complement to the limited capabilities of scripting languages like JavaScript.

Embedded objects come in many forms, but the most popular are multimedia in nature. A good example is Macromedia Flash files, which allow designers to add advanced vector graphics and animation to Web sites. Various other types of embedded video, sound, and live audio are also quite popular. Embedded Java applets are often included in pages that require more advanced graphics, network, or processing functionality.

Browsers provide the bridge that facilitates communication between JavaScript and embedded objects. The way this communication is carried out is essentially unstandardized, although browser vendors adhere to their own ad hoc methods, which are in relatively widespread use. Even so, there are numerous concerns when dealing with embedded objects. First, including them makes the assumption that the user's browser has the capability to handle such objects. Second, even if the user does have an appropriate extension installed, many users find embedded objects annoying because they increase download time while only occasionally improving the overall utility of the site. Third, users with older browsers and users on non-Windows platforms are often unable to use embedded objects because of lack of support.

This chapter introduces the way that JavaScript can be used to interact with embedded objects in most major browsers. Serious, complex integration of objects with JavaScript requires more comprehensive information, which can be found at browser and plugin vendor sites.

Java

Many think that JavaScript is a boiled-down form of Java because of the similarity in their names. The fact that JavaScript was originally called "LiveScript" suggests the mistake in drawing such a conclusion. While Java and JavaScript are both object-oriented languages, they are both commonly used on the Web, and the syntax of both resembles the syntax of C, they are in truth very different languages. Java is a class-based object-oriented language, whereas JavaScript is prototype-based. Java is strongly typed, whereas JavaScript is weakly typed. Java is compiled into platform-independent bytecode before execution, while JavaScript source code is generally interpreted directly by the browser. Java programs execute in a separate context called a "sandbox" whereas JavaScript is interpreted in the context of the browser.

This last difference—in execution context—is very important. Java applets are essentially platform-independent, stand-alone programs designed to run in a restricted execution environment. There is a lot of theory that goes into the Java sandbox, but in essence applets run in a "virtual machine" that is somewhat isolated from the user's browser and operating system. This isolation is designed to preserve platform independence as well as the security of the client's machine.

Java applets are most often used to implement applications that require comprehensive graphics capabilities and network functionality. Java packages installed on the client machine provide networking code, graphics libraries, and user interface routines that make it a much more capable language than JavaScript. Common applications include applets that display real-time data downloaded from the Web (for example, stock tickers), interactive data browsing tools, site navigation enhancements, games, and scientific tools that perform calculations or act as visualization tools.

Including Applets

Before delving into the details of applet interaction, a very brief review of how to include applets in your pages is in order. Traditionally, applets are included with the **<applet>** tag. The tag's **code** attribute is then set to the URL of the .class file containing the applet, and the **height** and **width** attributes indicate the shape of the rectangle to which the applet's input and output are confined; for example:

```
<applet code="myhelloworld.class" width="100" height="200"
name=" myHelloWorld" id="myHelloWorld">
<em>Your browser does not support Java!</em>
</applet>
```

Note how the **<applet>** tag's **name** attribute (as well as **id** attribute) is also set. Doing so assigns the applet a convenient handle JavaScript can use to access its internals.

Although the use of **<applet>** is widespread, it has been deprecated under HTML 4. More appropriate is the **<object>** tag. It has a similar syntax:

```
<object classid="java:myhelloworld.class" width="100" height="200"
name="myHelloWorld" id="myHelloWorld">
<em>Your browser does not support Java!</em>
</object>
```

Note *There are some problems with the use of the **<object>** syntax for including applets, the least of which is lack of support in older browsers. We will use the **<applet>** syntax, but you should be aware that it is preferable to use **<object>** whenever possible.*

Initial parameters can be included inside the **<applet>** or **<object>** tag using the **<param>** tag, as shown here:

```
<applet code="myhelloworld.class" width="100" height="200"
name=" myHelloWorld" id="myHelloWorld">
<param name="message" value="Hello world from an initial parameter!">
```

```
<em>Your browser does not support Java!</em>
</applet>
```

Java Detection

Detecting whether the user's browser is Java-enabled is an important first step in working with embedded applets. The contents of the **<applet>** element beyond the **<param>** tags are displayed to the user whenever Java is turned off or unavailable. However, you still need to write your JavaScript so that you do not try to interact with an applet that is not running. The **javaEnabled()** method of the **Navigator** object returns a Boolean indicating whether the user has Java enabled. This method was first made available in IE4 and Netscape 3, the first versions of the browsers that support JavaScript interaction with Java applets. Using a simple **if** statement with this method should provide the most basic Java detection, as shown here:

```
if ( navigator.javaEnabled() )
{
  // do Java related tasks
}
else
  alert("Java is off");
```

Once support for Java is determined, then JavaScript can be used to interact with included applets.

Accessing Applets in JavaScript

The ability to communicate with applets originated with a Netscape technology called LiveConnect that was built into Netscape 3. This technology allows JavaScript, Java, and plugins to interact in a coherent manner and automatically handles type conversion of data to a form appropriate to each. Microsoft implemented the same capabilities in IE4, though not under the name LiveConnect. The low-level details of how embedded objects and JavaScript interact are complicated, unique to each browser, and even vary between different versions of the same browser. The important thing is that no matter what it is called, the capability exists in versions of IE4+ (except under Macintosh) and Netscape 3+ (although early versions of Netscape 6 have some problems).

Applets can be accessed through the **applets[ ]** array of the **Document** object or directly through **Document** using the applet's name. Consider the following HTML:

```
<applet code="myhelloworld.class" width="200" height="50"
name="myHelloWorld" id="myHelloWorld">
<em>Your browser does not support Java!</em>
</applet>
```

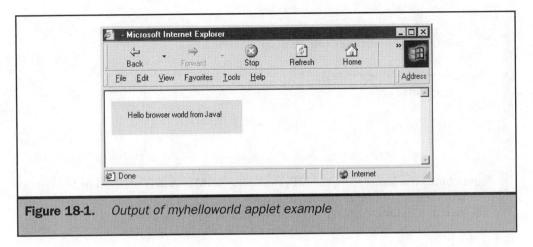

Figure 18-1.   *Output of myhelloworld applet example*

Assuming that this applet is the first to be defined in the document, it can be accessed in all of the following ways, with the last being preferred:

```
document.applets[0]
// or
document.applets["myHelloWorld"]
// or the preferred access method
document.myHelloWorld
```

The Browser Object Model properties of an **Applet** object are listed in Appendix B and consist of an unsurprising assortment of information reflecting the attributes of the HTML **<applet>** tag for which it was defined. The relevant aspect to this JavaScript-Java communication discussion is the fact that all properties and methods of the applet's class that are declared **public** are also available through the **Applet** object. Consider the following Java class definition for the previous **myhelloworld** example. The output (when embedded as before) is shown in Figure 18-1.

```java
import java.applet.Applet;
import java.awt.Graphics;
public class myhelloworld extends Applet
  {
    String message;
    public void init()
    {
        message = new String("Hello browser world from a Java!");
    }
    public void paint(Graphics myScreen)
    {
     myScreen.drawString(message, 25, 25);
```

```
    }
    public void setMessage(String newMessage)
    {
      message = newMessage;
      repaint();
    }
}
```

Now comes the interesting part. Because the **setMessage()** method of the **myhelloworld** class is declared **public**, it is made available in appropriate **Applet** objects. We can invoke it in JavaScript as:

```
document.myHelloWorld.setMessage("Wow. Check out this new message!");
```

Before proceeding further with this example, it is very important to note that applets often require a significant amount of time load. Not only must the browser download the required code, but it also has to start the Java virtual machine and walk the applet through several initialization phases in preparation for execution. It is for this reason that it is never a good idea to access an applet with JavaScript before making sure that it has begun execution. The best approach is to use an **onload** handler for the **Document** object as commonly specified in the **<body>** tag of an HTML document. Because this handler fires only when the document has completed loading, you can use it to set a flag indicating that the applet is ready for interaction. This technique is illustrated in the following example using the previously defined **myhelloworld** applet:

```
<!DOCTYPE HTML PUBLIC "-//W3C//DTD HTML 4.01 Transitional//EN"
        "http://www.w3.org/TR/html4/loose.dtd">
<html>
<head>
<title>Applet interaction example</title>
<script language="JavaScript" type="text/javascript">
<!--
  var appletReady = false;

  function changeMessage(newMessage)
    {
      if (navigator.javaEnabled() == false)
        {
```

```
            alert("Sorry! Java isn't enabled!");
            return;
        }
    if (appletReady)
        document.myHelloWorld.setMessage(newMessage);
    else
        alert("Sorry! The applet hasn't finished loading.");
    }
//-->
</script>
</head>
<body onload="appletReady = true">
<applet code="myhelloworld.class" width="200" height="50"
name="myHelloWorld" id="myHelloWorld">
<em>Your browser does not support Java!</em>
</applet>
<form name="inputForm" id="inputForm">
<input type="text" name="message" id="message">
<input type="button" value="Change Message"
onclick="changeMessage(inputForm.message.value)">
</form>
</body>
</html>
```

The output of this script after changing the message is shown in Figure 18-2.

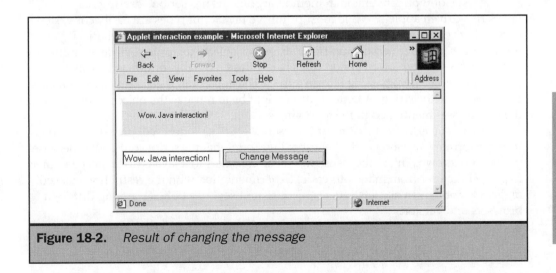

Figure 18-2.   *Result of changing the message*

There are tremendous possibilities with this capability. If class instance variables are declared **public**, they can be set or retrieved as you would expect:

```
document.appletName.variableName
```

Inherited variables are, of course, also available.

Java applets associated with applets defined in **<object>** *tags receive the* **public** *properties and methods just as those defined in* **<applet>** *tags do. However, using* **<object>** *instead of* **<applet>** *is less cross-browser compatible because Netscape 4 does not expose this HTML element to scripts.*

Issues with JavaScript-Driven Applets

Experienced programmers might be asking at this point why one would choose to embed a Java applet alongside JavaScript in a page. One reason might be to avoid having to re-implement code in JavaScript that is readily available in Java. Another reason is that for many people, writing a user interface is easier with HTML/CSS than with Java. If a Web-based interface drives an embedded applet, then changes to the interface can be made without the hassle of recompiling code.

A question that new programmers have sometimes concerns how to know what "hooks" are made available by a particular applet. An easy way to find out is to examine the source code (the .java file) associated with the applet. If it is not available, you can use a **for/in** loop on the appropriate **Applet** object to print out its properties. Anything that is not usually a property of an **Applet** browser object is a part of the interface defined by the applet's class. However, this method is discouraged because it gives you no information about the type of arguments the applet's methods expect.

The issue of type conversion in method arguments has serious bearing on JavaScript-driven applets. While most primitive JavaScript types are easily converted to their Java counterparts, converting complicated objects can be problematic. If you need to pass user-defined or non-trivial browser objects to applets, close examination of each browser's type conversion rules is required. A viable option is to *stringify* the JavaScript object before passing it to an applet. The applet can then manually reconstruct the object from the string. A better option might be to retrieve the objects directly using the Java classes mentioned in the following section.

A final issue is the fact that most browsers' security models will prevent an applet from performing an action at the behest of JavaScript that the script could not otherwise perform on its own. This makes sense when one considers that Java is (in theory) designed to protect the user from malicious code. Experimentation with the restrictions placed on JavaScript-driven applets reveals inconsistent security policies among different browsers and versions.

Accessing JavaScript with Applets

Although it may come as a surprise, it is possible for Java applets to drive JavaScript. Both Internet Explorer and Netscape provide the **netscape** Java package, which defines a family of class libraries for JavaScript interaction. In particular, the **JSObject** class (**netscape.javascript.JSObject**) allows an applet to retrieve and manipulate JavaScript objects in the current page. In addition, it affords an applet the ability to execute arbitrary JavaScript in the browser window as if it were a part of the page. On the HTML side of things, all that is required to enable this functionality is the addition of the **mayscript** attribute to the **<applet>** tag in question. The **mayscript** attribute is a nonstandard security feature used to prevent malicious applets from modifying the documents in which they are contained. Omitting this attribute prevents the applet from crossing over into "browser space."

While this is a powerful capability, Java-driven JavaScript is rarely used in practice. Details about these classes can be found in Java documentation for the specific browsers. Probably the best place to find information is in the LiveConnect examples section of **http://developer.netscape.com**.

Plugins

Browser *plugins* are executable components that extend the browser's capabilities in a particular way. When the browser encounters an embedded object of a type that it is not prepared to handle, the user is given the option to install a plugin that can handle the data (assuming the page is properly written). The plugin consists of executable code for displaying or otherwise processing a particular type of data. In this way, the browser is able to hand special types of data, for example multimedia files, to plugins for processing. Plugins are persistent in the browser in the sense that once installed they remain there unless manually removed by the user. Most browsers come with many plugins already installed, so you may have used them without even knowing. Plugins were introduced in Netscape 2 but are supported, at least HTML–syntax-wise, by most major browsers, including Opera and Internet Explorer 3 and later.

Embedding Plugins

Although never officially a part of any HTML specification, the **<embed>** tag is most often used to include embedded objects for Netscape and Internet Explorer. A Macromedia Flash file might be embedded as follows:

```
http://www.javascriptref.com/examples/ch18/flash.swf
```

The result of loading a page with this file is shown in Figure 18-3.

The most important attributes are **src**, which gives the URL of the embedded object, and **pluginspage,** which indicates to the browser where the required plugin is to be found if it is not installed in the browser. Recall that applets embedded with **<object>** tags are passed initial parameters in **<param>** tags. The syntax of **<embed>** is different in that initial parameters are passed using attributes of the element itself. For instance, in the previous example the **play** attribute tells the plugin to immediately begin playing the specified file.

The **<object>** element is the newer, official way to include embedded objects of any kind in your pages. However, **<object>** is not supported in Netscape browsers prior to version 4, and **<embed>** continues to be supported by new browsers. So it is unlikely that **<object>** will completely supplant **<embed>** any time in the near future. However, **<object>** and **<embed>** are very often used together in order to maximize client compatibility. This technique is illustrated in the later ActiveX section of this chapter.

MIME Types

So how does the browser know what kind of data is appropriate for each plugin? The answer lies in Multipurpose Internet Mail Extension types, or *MIME types* for short. MIME types are short strings of the form *mediatype/subtype*, where the *mediatype* describes the general nature of the data and the *subtype* describes it more specifically.

Figure 18-3. *An embedded Flash file*

For example, GIF images have type *image/gif*, which indicates that the data is an image and its specific format is GIF (Graphics Interchange Format). In contrast, CSS files have type *text/css*, which indicates that the file is composed of plain text adhering to CSS specifications. The MIME major media types are *application* (proprietary data format used by some application), *audio, image, message, model, multipart, text*, and *video*.

Each media type is associated with at most one handler in the browser. Common Web media such as HTML, CSS, plain text, and images are handled by the browser itself. Other media, for example MPEG video and Macromedia Flash, are associated with the appropriate plugin (if it is installed). Keep in mind that a plugin can handle multiple MIME types (for example, different types of video) but that each MIME type is associated with at most one plugin. If one type were associated with more than one plugin, the browser would have to find some way to arbitrate which component actually receives the data.

Detecting Support for MIME Types

Netscape 3+ and Opera 4+ provide an easy way to examine the ability of the browser to handle particular MIME types. The **mimeTypes[ ]** property of the **Navigator** object holds an array of **MimeType** objects. Some interesting properties of this object are shown in Table 18-1.

The browser hands embedded objects off to plugins according to the data that makes up each of these objects. A good way to think about the process is that the browser looks MIME types and filename suffixes up in the **mimeTypes** array to find the **enabledPlugin** reference to the appropriate plugin. The programmer can therefore use the **mimeTypes** array to check whether the browser will be able to handle a particular kind of data.

Property	Description
description	String describing the type of data the MIME type is associated with
enabledPlugin	Reference to the plugin associated with this MIME type
suffixes	Array of strings holding the filename suffixes for files associated with this MIME type
type	String holding the MIME type

Table 18-1.   *Properties of the MimeType Object*

Before delving into this process it might be insightful to see what MIME types your Netscape browser supports. The following code prints out the contents of the **mimeTypes[ ]** array.

```
if (navigator.mimeTypes)
{
document.write("<table><tr><th>Type</th>");
document.write("<th>Suffixes</th><th>Description</th></tr>");
   for (var i=0; i<navigator.mimeTypes.length; i++)
    {
      document.write("<tr><td>" + navigator.mimeTypes[i].type+"</td>");
      document.write("<td>" + navigator.mimeTypes[i].suffixes+"</td>");
      document.write("<td>" + navigator.mimeTypes[i].description
+"</td></tr>");
    }
   document.write("</table>");
}
```

Part of the result in a typical installation of Netscape 4 is shown in Figure 18-4. Of course, you can also access similar information by typing **about:plugins** in Netscape's location bar.

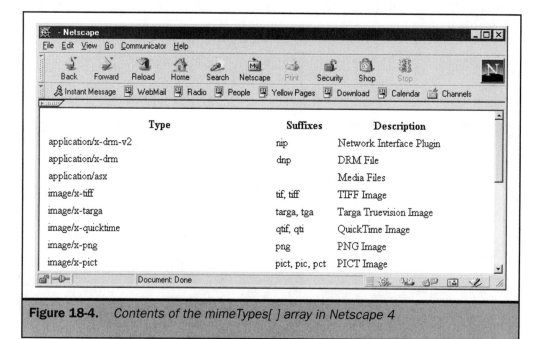

Figure 18-4. *Contents of the mimeTypes[ ] array in Netscape 4*

To detect support for a particular data type, you first access the **mimeTypes** array by the MIME type string in which you are interested. If a **MimeType** object exists for the desired type, you then make sure that the plugin is available by checking the **MimeType** object's **enabledPlugin** property. The concept is illustrated by the following code:

```
if (navigator.mimeTypes && navigator.mimeTypes["video/mpeg"]
    && navigator.mimeTypes["video/mpeg"].enabledPlugin)
   document.write('<embed src="/movies/mymovie.mpeg" width="300"
height="200"></embed>');
else
   document.write('<img src="myimage.jpg" width="300" height="200" alt="My
Widget">');
```

If the user's browser has the **mimeTypes** array and it supports MPEG video (*video/mpeg*) and the plugin is enabled, an embedded MPEG video file is written to the document. If these conditions are not fulfilled, then a simple image is written to the page. Note that the **pluginspage** attribute was omitted for brevity because the code has already detected that an appropriate plugin is installed.

This method of MIME type detection is used when you care only whether a browser supports a particular kind of data. It gives you no guarantee about the particular plugin that will handle it. To harness some of the more advanced capabilities that plugins provide, you often need to know if a specific vendor's plugin is in use. This requires a different approach.

Detecting Specific Plugins

In Netscape 3+ (and Opera 4+) each plugin installed in the browser has an entry in the **plugins[ ]** array of the **Navigator** object. Each entry in this array is a **Plugin** object containing information about the specific vendor and version of the component. Some interesting properties of the **Plugin** object are listed in Table 18-2.

Property	Description
description	String describing the nature of the plugin. Exercise caution with this property because this string can be rather long.
name	String indicating the name of the plugin
length	Number indicating the number of MIME types this plugin is currently supporting

Table 18-2. *Some Interesting Properties of the Plugin Object*

ADVANCED TOPICS

Each **Plugin** object is an array of the **MimeType** objects that it supports (hence its **length** property). You can visualize the **plugins[ ]** and **mimeTypes[ ]** arrays as being cross connected. Each element in **plugins[ ]** refers to one or more elements in **mimeTypes[ ]**. Each element in **mimeTypes[ ]** is referred to by exactly one element in **plugins[ ]**, the element referred to by the **MimeType**'s **pluginEnabled** reference.

You can refer to the individual **MimeType** objects in a **Plugin** element by using double array notation:

```
navigator.plugins[0][2]
```

This example references the third **MimeType** object supported by the first plugin.

Perhaps more useful is to index the plugins by name. For example, to write all the MIME types supported by the Flash plugin (if it exists!), you might write

```
if (navigator.plugins["Shockwave Flash"])
  {
    for (var i=0; i<navigator.plugins["Shockwave Flash"].length; i++)
    document.write("Flash MimeType: " + navigator.plugins["Shockwave
Flash"][i].type + "<br>");
  }
```

Of course, as with all things plugin related, you need to read vendor documentation very carefully in order to determine the *exact* name of the particular plugin in which you are interested.

To illustrate the composition of the **Plugin** object more clearly, the following code prints out the contents of the entire **plugins[ ]** array:

```
for (var i=0; i<navigator.plugins.length; i++)
  {
    document.write("Name: " + navigator.plugins[i].name + "<br>");
    document.write("Description: " + navigator.plugins[i].description + "<br>");
    document.write("Supports: ");
    for (var j=0; j<navigator.plugins[i].length; j++)
      document.write("   " + navigator.plugins[i][j].type);
      // the nonbreaking space included so the types are more readable
    document.write("<br><br>");
  }
```

The results are shown in Figure 18-5.

One thing to be particularly conscious of is that Internet Explorer defines a faux **plugins[ ]** array as a property of **Navigator**. It does so in order to prevent poorly written Netscape-specific scripts from throwing errors while they probe for plugins. Under Internet Explorer, you have some reference to plugin-related data through the **document.embeds[ ]** collection. However, probing for MIME types and other functions

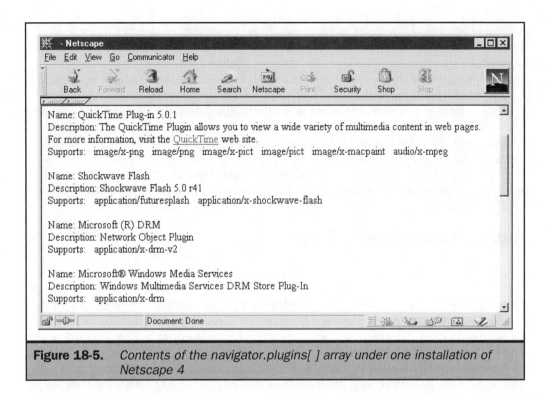

Figure 18-5. *Contents of the navigator.plugins[ ] array under one installation of Netscape 4*

is not supported, since Explorer actually uses ActiveX controls to simulate the function of plugins included via an **<embed>** tag. For more information on using JavaScript with ActiveX, see the section entitled "ActiveX" later in this chapter. For now simply consider that to rely solely on information from **navigator.plugins[ ]** without first doing some browser detection can have some odd or even disastrous consequences.

Interacting with Plugins

By now you might be wondering why one would want to detect whether a specific plugin will be handling a particular MIME type. The reason is that like Java applets, plugins are LiveConnect-enabled in Netscape 3+ and Internet Explorer 4+. This means that plugins can implement a public interface through which they can interact with JavaScript. This capability is most commonly used by multimedia plugins to provide JavaScript with fine-grain control over how video and audio are played. Plugins often make methods available to start, stop, and rewind content as well as to control volume, quality, and size settings. The developer can then present the user with form fields that control the behavior of the plugin through JavaScript.

This capability works in the reverse direction as well. Embedded objects can invoke JavaScript in the browser to control navigation or to manipulate the content of the page.

The more advanced aspects of this technology are beyond the scope of this book, but common aspects include functions that plugins are programmed to invoke when a particular event occurs. Like a JavaScript event handler, the plugin will attempt to invoke a function with a specific name at a well-defined time, for example when the user halts playback of a multimedia file. To prevent namespace collisions with other objects in the page, these methods are typically prefixed with the **name** or **id** attribute of the **<object>** or **<embed>** of the object instance.

As with applets, there remains the issue of how the JavaScript developer knows which methods the plugin provides and invokes. The primary source for this information is documentation from the plugin vendor. But be warned: these interfaces are highly specific to vendor, version, and platform. When using LiveConnect capabilities, careful browser and plugin sensing is usually required.

Refreshing the Plugins Array

Suppose you have written some custom JavaScript to harness the capabilities provided by a specific plugin. When users visit your page without the plugin they are prompted to install it because you have included the proper **pluginspage** attribute in your **<embed>**. Unfortunately, if a user visits your page without the plugin, agrees to download and install it, and then returns to your page, your JavaScript will still not detect that the browser has the required plugin. The reason is that the **plugins[ ]** array needs to be refreshed whenever a new plugin is installed, unless the browser is restarted.

Refreshing the **plugins[ ]** array is as simple as invoking its **refresh()** method. Doing so causes the browser to check for newly installed plugins and to reflect the changes in the **plugins[ ]** and **mimeTypes[ ]** arrays. This method takes a Boolean argument indicating whether the browser should reload any current documents containing an **<embed>**. If you supply **true**, the browser causes any documents (and frames) that might be able to take advantage of the new plugin to reload. If **false** is passed to the method, the **plugins[ ]** array is updated, but no documents are reloaded. A typical example of the method's use is found here:

```
<em>If you have just installed the plugin, please <a
href="javascript:navigator.plugins.refresh(true)"> reload the page with
plugin support</a></em>
```

Of course, this should be presented only to users of Netscape or Opera browsers.

Remember, however, that aside from calling **refresh()** the only way to make a newly installed plugin available is to quit and restart the browser.

Interacting with a Specific Plugin

There are several things to keep in mind when interacting with a specific plugin. The first is that nearly everything that was true of applet interaction remains true for plugins as well. Applets are accessed through the **Document** object, using their **name** or **ID** attribute rather than through the Java interpreter itself. Similarly, data handled by plugins is accessed by the **name** attribute of the **<embed>** tag that includes it rather than through the plugin itself. As with applets, you need to be careful that you do not attempt to access embedded data before it is finished loading. The same technique of using the **Load** handler of the **Document** to set a global flag indicating load completion is often used.

To illustrate interaction with plugins, we show a simple example using a Macromedia Flash file. The first thing to note is that there are two plugin names corresponding to Flash players capable of LiveConnect interaction. They are "Shockwave Flash" and "Shockwave Flash 2.0." Second, consulting Macromedia's documentation reveals that the **<embed>** tag should have its **swliveconnect** attribute set to **true** (though it does not appear to be required for this example).

You can find a list of supported methods at Macromedia's Web site (for example, at **http://www.macromedia.com/support/flash/publishexport/scriptingwithflash/**). The methods we will use in our simple example are **GotoFrame()**, **IsPlaying()**, **Play()**, **Rewind()**, **StopPlay()**, **TotalFrames()**, and **Zoom()**.

The following example controls a small Flash file. There are some problems with the Flash plugin for early versions of Netscape 6, so you should avoid it until support becomes more stable.

```
<!DOCTYPE HTML PUBLIC "-//W3C//DTD HTML 4.01 Transitional//EN"
        "http://www.w3.org/TR/html4/loose.dtd">
<html>
<head>
<title>Simple Flash Control Example (Netscape Only)</title>
<script language="JavaScript" type="text/javascript">
<!--
var pluginReady = false;
var pluginAvailable = false;
if (document.all) alert("Demo for Netscape only");
function detectPlugin()
  {
    // if the appropriate plugin exists and is configured
    // then it is OK to interact with the plugin
    if (navigator.plugins &&
       ((navigator.plugins["ShockwaveFlash"] &&
         navigator.plugins["Shockwave Flash"]["application/x-shockwave-flash"]) ||
        (navigator.plugins["Shockwave Flash 2.0"] &&
         navigator.plugins["Shockwave Flash 2.0"]["application/ x-shockwave- flash"])
        )
        )
        pluginAvailable = true;

    // avoid Netscape 6 for the time being
    if (!document.layers)
```

```
            pluginAvailable = false;
}

function changeFrame(i)
{
    if (!pluginReady || !pluginAvailable)
        return;
    if (i>=0 && i<document.demo.TotalFrames())
        document.demo.GotoFrame(parseInt(i));
        // Function expects an integer, not a string!
}

function play()
{
    if (!pluginReady || !pluginAvailable)
        return;
    if (!document.demo.IsPlaying())
        document.demo.Play();
}

function stop()
{
    if (!pluginReady || !pluginAvailable)
        return;
    if (document.demo.IsPlaying())
        document.demo.StopPlay();
}
function rewind()
{
    if (!pluginReady || !pluginAvailable)
        return;
    if (document.demo.IsPlaying())
        document.demo.StopPlay();
    document.demo.Rewind();
}

function zoom(percent)
{
    if (!pluginReady || !pluginAvailable)
        return;
    if (percent > 0)
        document.demo.Zoom(parseInt(percent));
        // method expects an integer
}
//-->
</script>
</head>
<body onload="pluginReady = true; detectPlugin();">
<embed id="demo" name="demo"
```

```
src="http://www.javascriptref.com/examples/ch18/flash.swf
width="318" height"252"
play="false" loop="false"
pluginspage="http://www.macromedia.com/shockwave/download/index.cgi?P1_Prod_
Version=ShockwaveFlash5" swliveconnect="true"></embed>

<form name="controlForm" id="controlForm">
<input type="button" value="Start" onclick="play()">
<input type="button" value="Stop" onclick="stop()">
<input type="button" value="Rewind" onclick="rewind()"><br>
<input type="text" name="whichFrame" id="whichFrame">
<input type="button" value="Change Frame"
onclick="changeFrame(controlForm.whichFrame.value)"><br>
<input type="text" name="zoomValue" id="zoomValue">
<input type="button" value="Change Zoom"
onclick="zoom(controlForm.zoomValue.value)"> (greater than 100 to zoom out,
less than 100 to zoom in)<br>
</form>
</body>
</html>
```

The example—stopped in the middle of playback and zoomed in—is shown in Figure 18-6.

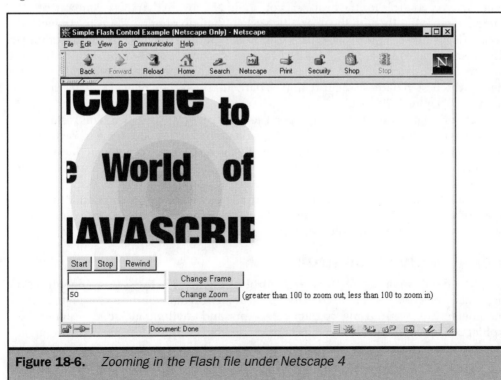

Figure 18-6.   *Zooming in the Flash file under Netscape 4*

There exist far more powerful capabilities than the previous example demonstrates. One particularly useful aspect of Flash is that embedded files can issue Flash commands, using **FSCommand()**, which can then be "caught" with JavaScript by defining an appropriately named function. Whenever an embedded Flash file in a LiveConnect-enabled browser issues an **FSCommand()**, the Flash file crosses over into browser territory to invoke the **name_doFSCommand()** method if one exists. The *name* portion of **name_doFSCommand()** corresponds to the **name** or **id** of the element in which the object is defined. In the previous example, the Flash file would look for **demo_doFS Command()** because the file was included in an **<embed>** with **name** equal to "demo." Common applications include alerting the script when the data has completed loading and keeping scripts apprised of the playback status of video or audio. As with other more advanced capabilities, details about these kinds of *callback functions* can be obtained from the plugin vendors.

ActiveX

Microsoft's response to Netscape plugins is a component technology called ActiveX. Although the functionality provided by ActiveX controls is similar to that provided by plugins, they fit into Microsoft's Component Object Model (COM) and are therefore a much more general type of technology. For example, ActiveX controls can be embedded into Windows applications such as Microsoft Word. Although this section is concerned with ActiveX controls for the browser, you should be aware that these components integrate more tightly with the operating system than do plugins. Once an ActiveX control is installed in the browser, it is essentially granted free reign over the computer. This means that controls can access and change files and configuration data on the host system, obviously creating a very problematic situation from a security standpoint. A deeper discussion of these security issues, particularly as they relate to JavaScript, is found in Chapters 21 and 23.

ActiveX controls are, like plugins, persistent once they are installed. This installation process is often automatic, which is both good and bad. It is good in the sense that it obviates the need to have the user manually install a required component. But it is also a security risk because most users could be easily fooled into accepting the installation of a malicious control.

ActiveX controls are executable code and, therefore, like plugins are built for a specific operating system and platform. One major problem with ActiveX controls is lack of support outside the Internet Explorer for Windows domain.

Including ActiveX Controls

Embedded data intended for ActiveX controls is included in the page using **<object>** elements. The syntax is similar to that of the **<object>** syntax for the inclusion of applets. Parameters are passed using **<param>** elements, and anything included between the **<object>**'s opening and closing tags is processed by non-**<object>**-aware browsers; for example:

```
<object classid="clsid:D27CDB6E-AE6D-11cf-96B8-444553540000"
codebase="http://active.macromedia.com/flash5/cabs/swflash.cab#version=5,0,0,0"
name="demoMovie" id="demoMovie" width="318" HEIGHT="252">
<param name="movie" value="http://www.javascriptref.com/examples/ch18/
flash.swf">
<param name="play" value="true">
<param name="loop" value="false">
<param name="quality" value="high">
<em>Your browser does not support ActiveX!</em>
</object>
```

This example defines an embedded Flash file for use with an ActiveX control. You can tell it is intended for ActiveX by the fact that the **classid** attribute begins with "clsid:". We saw another possibility in a previous section where the **classid** began with "java:". In general, the **classid** attribute specifies the unique identifier of the control for which the data is intended. Values appropriate to each ActiveX control are published by the vendor, but they are also commonly inserted by Web development tools such as Macromedia Dreamweaver (**www.macromedia.com/dreamweaver**).

The final item of note is the **codebase** attribute specifying the version of the ActiveX binary that is required for this particular object. The **classid** and **codebase** attributes serve the function that manual probing of plugins does under Netscape.

By far the best way to ensure the cross-browser compatibility of your pages is to use a combination of ActiveX controls and plugins. To accomplish this, simply use an **<object>** intended for IE/Windows ActiveX controls and include within it an **<embed>** intended for Netscape and IE/Macintosh plugins. The technique is illustrated in the following example:

```
<object classid="clsid:D27CDB6E-AE6D-11cf-96B8-444553540000"
codebase="http://active.macromedia.com/flash5/cabs/swflash.cab#version=5,0,0,0"
name="demoMovie" id="demoMovie" width="318" height="252">
<param name="movie" value="http://www.javascriptref.com/examples/ch18/
flash.swf">
<param name="play" value="true">
<param name="loop" value="false">
<param name="quality" value="high">
<embed src="http://www.javascriptref.com/examples/ch18/flash.swf" width="318"
height="252" play="true" loop="false" quality="high"
pluginspage="http://www.macromedia.com/shockwave/download/index.cgi?P1_Prod_
Version=ShockwaveFlash">
</embed>
</object>
```

Browsers that do not understand **<object>** will see the **<embed>**, whereas browsers capable of processing **<object>** will ignore the enclosed **<embed>**. Using **<object>** and **<embed>** in concert maximizes the possibility that the user will be able to process your content.

ADVANCED TOPICS

Interacting with ActiveX Controls

JavaScript is used to interact with ActiveX controls in a manner quite similar to plugins. There are, however, a few differences. First, there is no equivalent of the **plugins.refresh()** method for ActiveX. Instead, Internet Explorer automatically installs the required control (assuming a well-formed **<object>** element) and immediately makes it available for use. Data handled by a plugin included in an **<embed>** is accessed according to its **name** attribute under the **Document** object. Data handled by ActiveX controls are also accessed under the **Document** object, but according to the **id** attribute of its **<object>** element. You may also have to include the **mayscript** attribute to enable callback functions.

We can rewrite the example in the previous section to utilize either ActiveX or plugins. The code is very similar:

```
<!DOCTYPE HTML PUBLIC "-//W3C//DTD HTML 4.01 Transitional//EN"
        "http://www.w3.org/TR/html4/loose.dtd">
<html>
<head>
<title>Cross-browser Flash Control Example </title>
<script language="JavaScript" type="text/javascript">
<!--
  var dataReady = false;
  var pluginAvailable = false;

function detectPlugin()
{
    if (navigator.plugins &&
        ((navigator.plugins["Shockwave Flash"] &&
          navigator.plugins["Shockwave Flash"]["application/x-shockwave-flash"])
          ||
          (navigator.plugins["Shockwave Flash 2.0"] &&
           navigator.plugins["Shockwave Flash 2.0"]["application/x-shockwave-flash"])
         ))
        pluginAvailable = true;

        // avoid Netscape 6 for the time being
        if (!document.layers && document.getElementById)
          pluginAvailable = false;
        return(pluginAvailable);
}

function changeFrame(i)
{
    if (!dataReady)
       return;
    // Some versions of the ActiveX control don't support TotalFrames,
    // so the check is omitted here. However, the control handles values
```

```
        // out of range gracefully.

        document.demo.GotoFrame(parseInt(i));
}

function play()
{
    if (!dataReady)
        return;
    if (!document.demo.IsPlaying())
      document.demo.Play();
}

function stop()
{
    if (!dataReady)
        return;
    if (document.demo.IsPlaying())
        document.demo.StopPlay();
}

function rewind()
{
    if (!dataReady)
        return;
    if (document.demo.IsPlaying())
        document.demo.StopPlay();
    document.demo.Rewind();
 }
 function zoom(percent)
{
    if (!dataReady)
        return;
    if (percent > 0)
        document.demo.Zoom(parseInt(percent));
}
//-->
</script>
</head>
<body onload="dataReady = true">

<object id="demo" classid="clsid:D27CDB6E-AE6D-11cf-96B8-444553540000"
width="318" height="252"
codebase="http://active.macromedia.com/slash2/cabs/swflash.cab#version=5,0,0,0">
<param name="movie" value="http://www.javascriptref.com/examples/ch18/
flash.swf">
<param name="play" value="false">
<param name="loop" value="false">
<script language="JavaScript" type="text/javascript">
<!--
   if (detectPlugin())
```

```
        {
            document.write('<embed name="demo"
src="http://www.javascriptref.com/examples/ch18/flash.swf"
width="318" height="252"
play="false" loop="false"
pluginspage="http://www.macromdia.comshockwave/download/index.cgi?P1_Prod_
Version=ShockwaveFlash5" swliveconnect="true"></embed>');
        }
    else
        {
            // you can write an image in here in a "real" version
            document.write('Macromedia Flash is required for this demonstration');
        }
//-->
</script>
<noscript>
   JavaScript is required to demonstrate this functionality!
</noscript>
</object>
<form name="controlForm" id="controlForm" onsubmit="return false">
<input type="button" value="Start" onclick="play()">
<input type="button" value="Stop" onclick="stop()">
<input type="button" value="Rewind" onclick="rewind()"><br>
<input type="text" name="whichFrame" id="whichFrame">
<input type="button" value="Change Frame"
onclick="changeFrame(controlForm.whichFrame.value)"><br>
<input type="text" name="zoomValue" id="zoomValue">
<input type="button" value="Change Zoom"
onclick="zoom(controlForm.zoomValue.value)"> (greater than 100 to zoom out,
less than 100 to zoom in)<br>
</form>
</body>
</html>
```

The example script as it stands could use a few improvements. In a production version you might want to write an image in place of the text if the browser doesn't support Flash data. More advanced browser detection is also appropriate to handle clients with spotty plugin functionality (such as Netscape 6).

The previous example might make you wonder if ActiveX controls can do everything plugins can. The answer: yes, and even more. For example, data handled by ActiveX controls can take full advantage of callback functions, so everything that is possible with a plugin is possible with ActiveX. Further, because data destined for ActiveX is embedded in **<object>** elements, it can take full advantage of the **<object>** event handlers defined in HTML 4. Interestingly, there seems to be more robust support for ActiveX in VBScript than in JavaScript. This is most likely a result of the fact that as a Microsoft technology, VBScript is more closely coupled with Microsoft's COM. For more information on ActiveX, see **http://www.microsoft.com/com/tech/activex.asp**.

Summary

Embedded objects provide the means with which you can expand the capabilities of your pages to include advanced processing, network, and multimedia tasks. Web browsers support Java applets and ActiveX controls and/or Netscape plugins. JavaScript can interact with all forms of embedded objects to some degree. For example, JavaScript can access **public** class data of Java applets that are embedded in the page. Conversely, Java applets can even access JavaScript through the special packages provided by browser vendors. Plugins included using the HTML **<embed>** tag are fully supported by Netscape and Opera, and HTML–syntax-wise by Internet Explorer. However, plugin support via JavaScript is limited in Internet Explorer. For example, only Netscape and Opera support the capabilities provided by the **mimeTypes[ ]** and **plugins[ ]** arrays of the **Navigator** object for sensing MIME types and plugins. These arrays can be used to probe for supported MIME types and specific plugins. ActiveX controls are very similar to plugins, but they are a Microsoft-specific technology that is much more integrated with the user's operating system than plugins or Java applets. Interaction with ActiveX controls is carried through the **id** attribute of the **<object>** element in which the data is defined. It is recommended to write cross-browser scripts capable of interacting with both ActiveX controls and plugins or to rely on Java applets instead.

This chapter served as an introduction to what is possible with embedded objects. A large part of ActiveX and plugin capabilities are specific to the browser, vendor, and platform, so the best way to find information about these technologies is from the ActiveX control or plugin vendors themselves. Because of the large number of browser bugs and documentation inconsistencies, oftentimes interaction with embedded objects is best carried out through a JavaScript library written with these subtleties in mind. Many such libraries can be found on the Web.

The bottom line is that ActiveX and plugins provide a way to *enhance* your site, not replace it. Pages should always degrade gracefully, so that they can be used by those on alternative platforms or who choose not to install plugin/ActiveX technology. Sites that *require* a specific plugin or ActiveX control are very frustrating to use for the segment of the population that prefers an operating system and browser configuration other than Windows/Internet Explorer. As we discussed in the last chapter, detection techniques should always be employed to avoid locking users out of sites based upon technology limitations or client differences. However, JavaScript programmers need to be careful— as we have seen in the examples in this chapter, the room for error on the client-side is large. Because of this hassle, many developers prefer to add interactivity on the server-side, so in the next chapter we'll switch gears and look at the use of JavaScript on the Web server.

ADVANCED TOPICS

The
Complete
Reference

JavaScript

Chapter 19

Server-Side JavaScript

When most people think about the JavaScript language, they think about client-side scripting. Many people do not realize that JavaScript can be used in a variety of other contexts as well, including on a Web server. In fact, JavaScript really is just another language in which developers can write Web applications. This chapter will discuss the two main ways JavaScript can be used on the server: Netscape's server-side JavaScript, and the built-in ability for Active Server Pages (ASP) to understand scripts written in JavaScript. We will briefly present how to create an Application for Netscape's server-side JavaScript and how such an application can be used to manipulate objects. We will also show how to perform similar tasks using Active Server Pages written in JavaScript (or, more appropriately, JScript) and how to interact with ASP objects as well as present some common ASP objects available to JavaScript. We'll conclude our discussion with comments on some further uses of JavaScript.

Server-Side JS Overview

Regardless of its form and whether its orientation is to Netscape or Microsoft, the core syntax of server-side JavaScript—variables, data types, expressions, control flow statements, and so on—is the same as client-side JavaScript. This feature makes the transition from writing client-side JavaScript to server-side JavaScript relatively easy. However, there is plenty of room for misunderstanding the difference between code executed on the server and code executed on the client. The main difference, of course, is that the JavaScript code we have studied so far has been interpreted by the Web browser.

In the server-side world, JavaScript will be interpreted or even compiled on the server, with the result delivered to Web browsers as a standard Web document. In most cases, much of the interactivity is performed on the server—just plain HTML is delivered to the browser. Even when JavaScript is delivered to the client for further execution, the interaction between the client side and the server side is very slight. In fact, in most Web applications the tasks carried out by the server and by the client are clearly distinct. This makes sense when you consider the relative strengths and weaknesses of the client and server. For example, having the client talk to a database doesn't make as much sense as having the server carry out the transaction. Similarly, trying to figure out how to implement highly responsive interactive facilities, such as menus or animation, is just as problematic in server-side JavaScript. The truth of such statements will hopefully become crystal clear as we now proceed to give an overview of the two most common server-side JavaScript implementations used today.

Netscape Server-Side JavaScript

Server-side JavaScript (SSJS) is primarily a Netscape technology. While in theory it can be run on other servers, most SSJS implementations are in the form of a NSAPI plugin that comes with the iPlanet server (formerly known as Netscape Enterprise Server) version 4.0 and below. Like any other server-side scripting facility (such as Macromedia/Allaire's ColdFusion, Microsoft's ASP, or PHP), SSJS will execute dynamic requests from the user on the server and perform the required actions before returning information to the client. Because SSJS is a server-side technology and its main function is sending content like HTML to a browser, its output can be displayed in any browser, even those which are not JavaScript aware.

SSJS is based mostly on client-side JavaScript as defined by Netscape. Their Web server, iPlanet, allows developers to write JavaScript to be executed on the server—creating applications. iPlanet Web Server Enterprise Edition 4.1 (SP8) is available for AIX 4.3.3, Compaq TRU64 4.0d,4.0e*-5.1*, HP-Unix 11.0, Linux Red Hat 6.1, Solaris 2.6, 7, 8, and Windows NT 4.0 SP6, so you can develop for any of these platforms using the same language for the client side and server side.

*At the time of this writing, Netscape's newest Web server, **iPlanet Web Server, Enterprise Edition 6.0,** does not support server-side JavaScript. For this reason, the information provided in this chapter is somewhat historical, but it applies to older versions of iPlanet.*

Creating an Application

Unlike many server-side scripting platforms that dynamically interpret scripts, Netscape's SSJS precompiles scripts and HTML code into .web files called Applications. All server-side code must be compiled before execution on the server. SSJS scripts will be placed directly in .htm or .html files or into externally linked .js files. To indicate SSJS in HTML files, code is placed within the **<server>** tag that performs the same function as the **<script>** tag in client-side JavaScript.

Because iPlanet does not interpret code when a request is made for a file, all code must be compiled before requests can be properly handled by the server. A three-step compilation process is required so that iPlanet knows what to do when a request is made for a dynamic page. Web sites are typically split up into separate compiled applications that provide specific functionality. For example, a site for "Demo Company" might have the following applications: About, Products, News, Jobs, and Intranet. These applications would contain all the .htm or .html files and .js files that make up each section.

After you enable SSJS on iPlanet, these three steps are used to create an application:

1. Compile all the server-side code belonging to the application (the specifics will be addressed shortly).

2. Install the application on the server.

3. Start the application using the Application Manager.

Compilation is carried out using the compiler (named **jsac**) which comes as a part of the server. Running **jsac** creates a .web file which you can think of like "a.out" in UNIX or a ".exe" file in Windows.

As our first example, we will create a standard application that displays "Hello World!" Create a new HTML file called hello_world.htm and place the following markup and script inside it:

```
<!DOCTYPE HTML PUBLIC "-//W3C//DTD HTML 4.01 Transitional//EN"
        "http://www.w3.org/TR/html4/loose.dtd">
<html>
<head>
<title>Hello World</title>
</head>
<body>
<server>
   write("Hello World!");
</server>
</body>
</html>
```

Notice how the file contains the **<server>** tag. This tag replaces the **<script>** tag used in client-side JavaScript. For comparison, here is a file that does the same thing as the previous example but is written for client-side JavaScript:

```
<!DOCTYPE HTML PUBLIC "-//W3C//DTD HTML 4.01 Transitional//EN"
        "http://www.w3.org/TR/html4/loose.dtd">
<html>
<head>
<title>Hello World with Client-Side JavaScript</title>
</head>
<body>
<script language="JavaScript" type="text/javascript">
   document.write("Hello World!");
</script>
</body>
</html>
```

Both scripts, we assume, write the familiar line "Hello World!" to the browser window.

But without compilation, if you were to pull up the file hello_world.htm written in SSJS, you would not see the string "Hello World!" but instead the full statement "write('Hello World!');" (shown in Figure 19-1). Remember that SSJS is not an interpreted

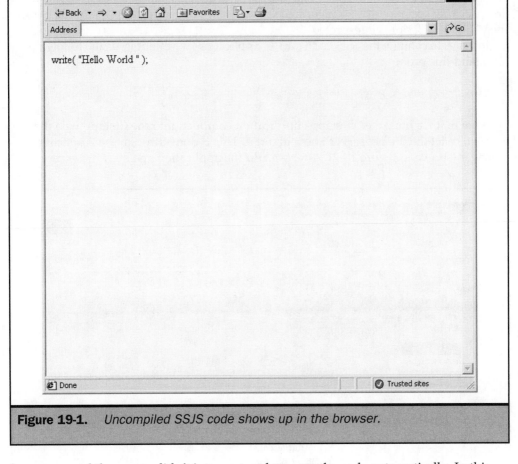

Figure 19-1.   *Uncompiled SSJS code shows up in the browser.*

language, and the server didn't intercept and execute the code automatically. In this case, the iPlanet Web server delivered the file as a normal static Web page, thus the browser receives the code:

```
...

<server>
  write( "Hello World!" );
</server>

...
```

and treats it as it would a normal HTML tag it did not recognize. Because browsers are designed to ignore undefined tags, the browser ignores the **<server>** tag and displays the line "write('Hello World!');". The fact that you actually must compile the script first probably seems a little strange, since, as we have suggested throughout the book, client-side JavaScript is interpreted.

In order to compile the SSJS code into an application, we might issue the following command-line prompt:

```
jsac -o firstapp.web hello_world.htm
```

Now that we have the "firstapp" application compiled into the firstapp.web file, we need to let the iPlanet server know about it. This is done through the Application Manager (shown in Figure 19-2). After we add the application and start it, we can

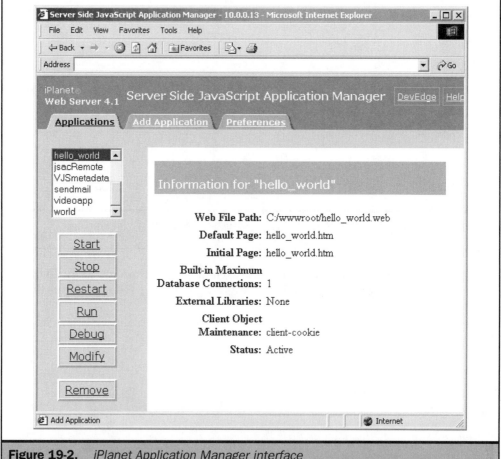

Figure 19-2. *iPlanet Application Manager interface*

access it through the Web. But now, instead of browsing to the file locally as hello_world.htm, we access it through the web server, for example as a URL like **http://127.0.0.1/firstapp/hello_world.htm**. The result is shown in Figure 19-3.

127.0.0.1 is the "local loopback" address; it points to whatever machine you are currently on. If your file is on another server, substitute its domain name or IP address for 127.0.0.1.

Looking closer at the syntax of the URL, notice two things. We are accessing the application named "firstapp," and the file that we would like to retrieve is "hello_world.htm." If we had compiled more files into the "firstapp" application, we could access them in a similar fashion, using their filenames in place of "hello_world.htm"

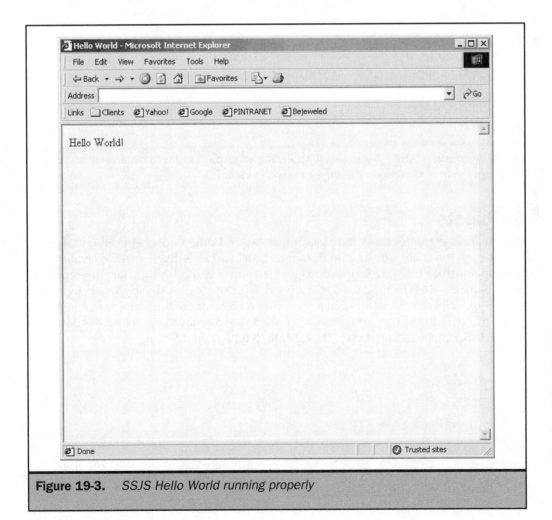

Figure 19-3.   *SSJS Hello World running properly*

Server-Side JavaScript Syntax

Moving from client-side JavaScript to Netscape's SSJS is very simple. The next example builds on the previous "Hello World" example and should be understandable: we demonstrate creating a new variable and populating it with a string, then looping and displaying some text. We also see an example of type conversion from a number to a string. The two differences from client-side JavaScript in the following example are the use of the **<server>** tag instead of the **<script>** tag and the fact that in SSJS the **write()** method is a global function instead of a method of the **Document** object.

```
<server>
var message = "Hello Again!";
for ( var count = -3 ; count < 5 ; count++ )
{
      if ( count >= 0 )
      {
            count = "+" + count;
      }

      write( "<font size=\"" + count + "\">" + message + "<//font><br //>" );
}
</server>
```

When we consider ASP later in the chapter, the example used will be similar but will have more syntax variations than the previous example.

SSJS Objects

Our previous examples show the base similarities and differences between JavaScript executed on the client side and on the server side. Just as with client-side JavaScript, Netscape's server-side JavaScript exposes objects for accomplishing your programming tasks (like the **write()** method used in the previous examples). A side-by-side comparison of CSJS and SSJS objects reveals that a set of core objects for the basic programming tasks exists in both of them. These objects correspond to the core JavaScript objects as defined by ECMAScript, including **Array**, **Date**, **Math**, **Number**, and **String**.

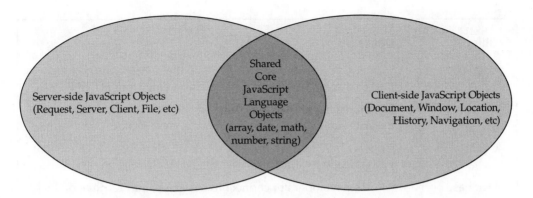

As we already know, in addition to the basic functionality of the core JavaScript language and objects, we need to use browser and document objects to create complete applications. Client-side JavaScript adds objects to interact with Web pages and the client browser. In contrast, SSJS provides support for backend databases, file systems, servers (including mail), and more. The following example creates a new file and writes "Hello World!" to it:

```
<server>
var testFile = new File( "C:/wwwroot/test.txt" );
if ( testFile.open( "w" ) )
{
        testFile.write( "Hello World!" );
}
testFile.close();

write( "This example created the file " + testFile );
</server>
```

Two of the more useful SSJS objects are **Request** and **Database**. The **Request** object is the main gateway between the client and the server. This object grants you access to properties such as **query**, which contains the query string of the requested URL, and methods such as **getPostData()**, which returns data in the body of an HTTP POST request. These are similar to other request-, reading-, and parsing-related functions available in common server-side languages like Perl. The **Database** object allows you to work with a database, either retrieving or submitting data using

Object	Description
Request	Exposes data that the client sends to the server. This includes query strings of the requested URL and data from HTTP POSTs.
Server	Contains information about the server, like the full address of the Web server, the Web server port, current protocol, and so on.
Client	Allows developers to keep client state using cookies, URL-encoded values, etc.
Database	Allows developers to connect to databases and retrieve or maintain data.
File	Exposes the server's file system to developers.
SendMail	Allows developers to send e-mail directly from an application.

Table 19-1.   *Common SSJS Objects and Their Uses*

common SQL (Structured Query Language) statements. Table 19-1 details the most common SSJS objects.

It isn't terribly useful to go over these objects in greater detail, considering that support for this technology appears to be in the process of being phased out. However, interested readers can find more information at Netscape's developer site: **http://developer.netscape.com**. For now, let's turn our attention to a popular and well-supported use of JavaScript on the server, Microsoft's Active Server Pages technology.

ASP Overview

Like Netscape's server-side JavaScript, Microsoft started their own server-side scripting solution: Active Server Pages (ASP for short). ASP is actually somewhat difficult to pin down, and like JavaScript it has a somewhat nebulous definition that is associated more with objects and a programming framework than specific language syntax. In fact, developers wanting to write ASP pages for use in a Web site can write their scripts using any of a multitude of languages, including JavaScript, JScript, VBScript, and even Rexx. Of course, it turns out that Jscript and JavaScript are the most common languages ASP applications are written in and will be the only ones we are concerned with in our discussion of ASP.

Traditionally, ASP is run on Microsoft's IIS Web servers. However, there are other ASP packages, such as Chili!Soft's Chili!ASP, Halcyon Software's Instant ASP, or vWebServer. These ASP servers work with most Web servers on platforms like Linux, Sun Solaris, Apple MacOS, and IBM AIX.

Unlike Netscape's SSJS, ASP pages are interpreted instead of compiled. Because of this, the ASP server needs to know the difference between normal HTML pages and dynamic pages. If the ASP server didn't know, it couldn't tell JavaScript what was intended for processing on the client side and what was intended for execution on the server side. Normal (static) HTML pages retain the .htm or .html extension. Any page that is to be interpreted by the ASP engine needs to have an .asp file extension.

Methods to Include JavaScript *under ASP*

When writing JavaScript for ASP, there are several ways you can tell the server to execute a script: specifying the ASP language as JavaScript when using the <% %> tag, including a script file using a server-side **include**, and using the **<script>** tag with the **runat="server"** attribute. The first two methods are traditional ASP techniques to include server-side scripts on an HTML page. The last is a mostly unused method whose format looks almost the same as client-side scripts.

The most common way to include ASP code in an HTML page is using the <% %> tags. Here is our old favorite, the Hello World example, written in ASP:

```
<%@ LANGUAGE=JavaScript %>
<!DOCTYPE HTML PUBLIC "-//W3C//DTD HTML 4.01 Transitional//EN"
        "http://www.w3.org/TR/html4/loose.dtd">
<html>
<head>
<title>Hello World</title>
</head>
<body>
<%
   Response.write( "Hello World." )
%>
</body>
</html>
```

Those familiar with ASP know that anything between the <% and %> tags are ASP code and will be interpreted by the ASP server.

Another common method for developers to execute code on a server is by including a script with a server-side **include** (or SSI). If the code from the above "Hello World" example is placed in a file named "hello_world.asp," the code can be included in another page using:

```
<!--#include file="hello_world.asp"-->
```

This method allows developers to place common code in a separate file in order to re-use it in other pages. Using this technique makes your code modular and easy to read.

Finally, the least commonly used way to include ASP code on a page is using the **<script>** tag and setting the **runat** attribute to "server":

```
<!DOCTYPE HTML PUBLIC "-//W3C//DTD HTML 4.01 Transitional//EN"
        "http://www.w3.org/TR/html4/loose.dtd">
<html>
<head>
<title>Hello World Again</title>
</head>
<body>
<script language="JavaScript" type="text/javascript" runat="server">
   Response.write( "Hello World!<br />" );
</script>
</body>
</html>
```

As you can see, the only visual difference between this example and the first example is that the delimiters marking ASP code are the **<script> </script>** tags instead of the **<% %>** tag. The benefit of being able to use the **<script>** tag is that you can write your ASP pages with several different languages instead of only one. So you would be able to write parts of the page using VBScript and other parts using JavaScript, using the strengths of each technology to accomplish the tasks for which they are best suited.

Now that you understand the methods used to include ASP script in your code, let's explain why the last method is rarely used. The **<script>** tag, when executed on the server, is processed *first*, before any other parts of the page. This is best illustrated with an example:

```
<!DOCTYPE HTML PUBLIC "-//W3C//DTD HTML 4.01 Transitional//EN"
        "http://www.w3.org/TR/html4/loose.dtd">
<html>
<head>
<title>Hello World Again</title>
</head>
<body>
I am seen first in this file.<br>
<script language="JavaScript" type="text/javascript" runat="server">
   Response.write( "But I am output first on the browser.<br>" );
</script>
</body>
</html>
```

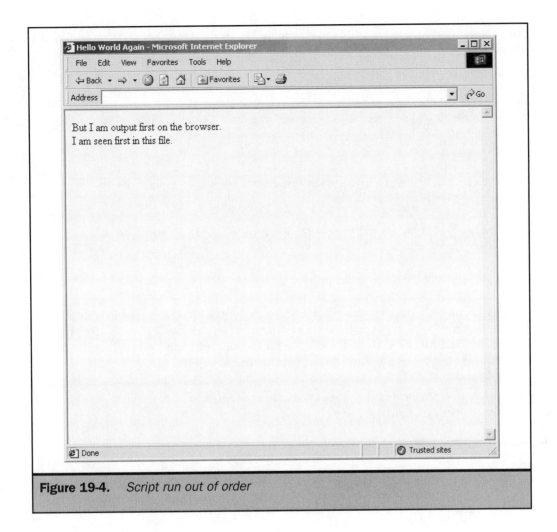

Figure 19-4. *Script run out of order*

Even though the HTML comes before the JavaScript code, when viewing the page in a browser, the output will show the line written with JavaScript *before* the HTML line, as seen in Figure 19-4. We do not recommend using this method because it is very awkward and may lead to confusion about what will actually be written to the browser.

JavaScript Syntax and ASP

Because we have already learned much about writing JavaScript in the previous chapters, we will jump right in and show you an example of an ASP program written with JavaScript. The following code revisits our "Hello World" example (with output

shown in Figure19-5), but it adds some familiar JavaScript language constructs, like **if**, **for**, and **var**:

```
<%
var message = "Hello Again!";
for ( var count = -3 ; count < 5 ; count++ )
{
     if ( count >= 0 )
     {
      // rely on implicit type conversion to get a string like "+3"
     count = "+" + count;
     }
     Response.write( "<font size=\"" + count + "\">" + message +
"<//font><br //>" );
}
%>
```

As you can see from the example, JavaScript's syntax for ASP can be exactly the same as that for the client. In fact, the above code can be rewritten with only two changes to execute on a browser: change the **<% %>** tags to **<script>** tags and replace the call to the **Request** object with the same call to the **Document** object:

```
<script language="JavaScript" type="text/javascript">
var message = "Hello Again!";

for ( var count = -3 ; count < 5 ; count++ )
{
     if ( count >= 0 )
     {
          count = "+" + count;
     }

     document.write( "<font size=\"" + count + "\">" + message +
"<//font><br>" );
}
</script>
```

On the basis of the previous example, it would appear that using server-side JavaScript in ASP pages is the same as using client-side JavaScript, and in fact most of the same rules do apply. For example, variables and objects are case-sensitive; if you were to try to reference and print the variable *Message* to the screen instead of *message*, you would receive an error telling you that *Message* is undefined. However, there are some minor differences between client-side and server-side JavaScript that developers

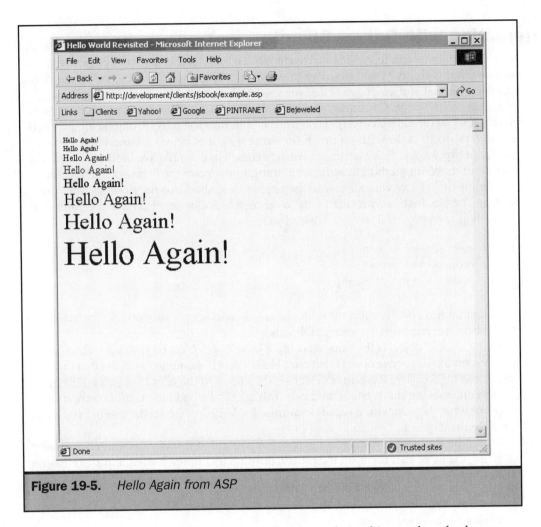

Figure 19-5.   *Hello Again from ASP*

should be aware of. These differences are related mostly to object and method access. The differences are summarized here:

- Methods and properties are *not* case-sensitive. Calling **Response.Write()** or **Response.WrITe()** is equivalent to **Response.write()**.

- Objects are written with the first letter uppercase. Because objects are case-sensitive, objects can be referenced only by their exact name: referencing **response.write()** will not work.

- Methods of objects that do not accept parameters can be called without parentheses. **Response.flush** is equivalent to **Response.flush()**. However, it is recommended that you always use the parentheses for methods to let yourself and others know that you are using a method and not a property.

Interacting with Server Objects

Now that we know *how* to include ASP code written with JavaScript in our pages, what can we do with this ability? Well, from our previous examples we know that we can perform basic operational and language tasks, such as creating variables, looping, and writing something to the page. Of course, as we know, the power of JavaScript is really in the objects, and server-side JavaScript is no different. In the case of ASP, objects are exposed for us to perform tasks with, in much the same way that browsers and client-side JavaScript expose objects for writing client-side code. For example, we used the **Response** object and its **Write** method to write something to the page the browser will receive.

Objects in ASP are very similar to the objects described in a previous section for Netscape's SSJS. Just as with client-side JavaScript, developers also have the ability to create their own objects. Here is a basic object:

```
var car = new Object();
car.make = "Porsche";
car.model = "911 Turbo";
```

Note that this code is valid for both client-side and server-side JavaScript (when the client's browser supports JavaScript **Objects**).

Using an ASP object is the same as using a JavaScript object on the client. Since we've already seen the **Response** object from our "Hello World" example, we'll use that to show how to use objects. The **Response** object sends output to the client (as you might have guessed after seeing the **Write( )** method). Table 19-2 shows some useful methods and describes what they do with a simple example. Table 19-3 presents the useful properties of the **Request** object.

Using the **Request** methods and properties presented thus far, we can create the following example that turns on the buffer, outputs text to the buffer, and then flushes the buffer to the browser:

```
<script language="JavaScript" type="text/javascript" runat="server">
Response.buffer = true;
Response.write( "This comes from the buffer." );
Response.flush();        // Send text to the browser
</script>
```

This is a very simple and not too useful example, but it shows how easy it is to use an ASP object.

There are many other methods, properties, and collections available in the **Response** object, as well as other ASP objects, that can accomplish many more tasks, but an explanation of all of these would be outside the scope of this book. However, as an overview of what's possible, Table 19-4 presents some commonly used objects that are intrinsic to ASP.

Method	Description	Usage
write( )	Outputs data to the client: a browser window, a cookie, etc.	`Response.write("This is displayed in the browser");`
clear( )	Clears anything in the **Buffer** object.	`Response.clear();`
flush( )	Similar to the **Clear( )** method but flushes everything to the client instead of deleting it.	`Response.flush();`
end( )	Flushes anything in the buffer to the client and stops execution of any more statements on the page.	`Response.end();`
redirect( )	Redirects the client to another URL.	`Response.redirect("http://www.democompany.com");`

Table 19-2.   *Response Object Methods*

Property	Description	Usage
CacheControl	Read/write property that lets a proxy server know if it can cache the ASP output.	`Response.CacheControl = "Public";` `Response.CacheControl = "Private";`
Buffer	Controls how and when data is sent to the client. (In IIS 5.0, this is turned on by default).	`Response.Buffer = true;` `Response.Buffer = false;`

Table 19-3.   *Response Object Properties*

Object	Description
Response	Allows you to output to the client and also specify how/when output is sent.
Request	Makes information contained in the HTTP request available. From this object you have access to information such as the query string for the request and any form of information POSTed to a server.
Application	Provides static storage for variables and object references that are available to any page within the application.
Session	This object is created for each visitor. It provides storage for variables and object references available for each specific visitor for the life of the session.
Server	Useful for performing certain server tasks that rely on the specific features on the server, such as connecting to COM objects or URL-encoding strings.
ASPError	New for ASP 3.0, this object provides information about errors that occurr on a page.

Table 19-4. *Commonly used ASP Objects*

One of the more frequently used objects is the **Request** object, which exposes all the information contained in the HTTP request—this includes HTTP header data concerning the browser and user and form variables for HTTP POSTs. Table 19-5 details some useful collections belonging to the **Request** object.

Collection	Description
Form[]	Exposes the data POSTED from an HTML form.
QueryString[]	Exposes data in the query string of the request.
ServerVariables[]	These environmental variables provide information to the HTTP headers.
Cookies[]	Allows developer to set and read cookies from the client's browser.

Table 19-5. *Request Object Collections*

A simple example illustrating the use of the **Request** object is now presented. In this situation, we have provided a small HTML form that submits some data to an ASP page called "respond.asp" using the HTTP POST method.

```
<!DOCTYPE HTML PUBLIC "-//W3C//DTD HTML 4.01 Transitional//EN"
        "http://www.w3.org/TR/html4/loose.dtd">
<html>
<head>
<title>ASP Request Demo</title>
</head>
<body>
<h1>ASP Form</h1>
<form action="respond.asp" method="POST">
Name: <input type="text" name="username" id="username"
size="40"><br>
E-mail:  <input type="text" name="useremail" id="useremail"
size="40"><br>
Page Color: <select name="usercolor" id="usercolor">
                    <option>Red</option>
                    <option>Yellow</option>
                    <option>Orange</option>
                    <option>Light Blue</option>
                    <option>White</option>
            </select>
<br>
<input type="submit" value="send data">
</form>
</body>
</html>
```

The ASP file called "result.asp" is presented here. It parses the incoming data and then builds an HTML page to suit, in this case echoing back the user's name and e-mail address as well as setting the page color based on their choice (see Figure 19-6).

```
<!DOCTYPE HTML PUBLIC "-//W3C//DTD HTML 4.01 Transitional//EN"
        "http://www.w3.org/TR/html4/loose.dtd">
<html>
<head>
<title>ASP Request Result</title>
</head>
<%@ LANGUAGE="JavaScript" %>
<%
```

```
var userColor;
var userName;
var userEmail;

userColor = Request.Form( "userColor" );
userName = Request.Form( "userName" );
userEmail = Request.Form( "userEmail" );
%>

<body bgcolor="<% Response.write( userColor ); %>">
<h1>Hello <%= userName %>
</h1>
<hr>
<p>I've got your email now! It's <% Response.write( userEmail ) %>!</p>
<p>Prepare yourself for my junkmail!</p>
</body>
</html>
```

You may notice that the example application doesn't work well when form fields are not filled out. We could easily add a client-side form validation routine (such as those presented in Chapter 14) to the example. Note that, once again, we have come full-circle to see how client-side JavaScript can work with a server-side application. Before moving on let's briefly present how ASP can be used in a more advanced fashion.

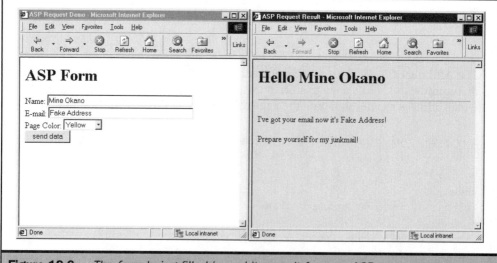

Figure 19-6.   *The form being filled in and its result from an ASP-aware server*

ASP and External Systems

The previous section began to touch on the abilities of using server-side JavaScript to write more complex Web applications, but until the application references external systems, the full capability of ASP is not evident.

Under a Windows Web server environment, the most common way to access some external facility via ASP is through a COM object. COM objects can be anything from custom-written business logic modules to core engines that desktop applications such as Microsoft Office products use. These objects can be referenced by instantiating the object on the server:

```
myObject = Server.CreateObject( ObjectClass );
// call object's method
myObject.method();
// reference object's properties
myObject.property;
```

To demonstrate this type of access, let's take a look at referencing a database using ASP and JavaScript. The following example connects to a (fictitious) SQL database and lists the 50 states. This may be a trivial example, but the power to connect to a database makes possible many things that would otherwise be impossible or very difficult for applications to implement.

```
<%
var objConn;
var objRS;
var strSQL;

//Open up connection to the SQL database
objConn = Server.CreateObject( "ADODB.Connection" );
objConn.ConnectionString = "DRIVER={SQL
Server};SERVER=SQL7;DATABASE=generic_site;";

objConn.Open();

// create a recordset object instance and retrieve the states
objRS = Server.CreateObject( "ADODB.Recordset" );
strSQL = "SELECT * FROM state";
objRS.Open( strSQL, objConn );

//loop through SQL results
while ( !objRS.EOF )
{
    Response.Write( objRS( "state" ) + "<br />" );
```

```
        objRS.MoveNext();
}

objRS.close();
objConn.close();
%>
```

The result of this previous example using an appropriate database is shown in Figure 19-7.

Of course, we have just barely scratched the surface of the power of ASP. The point really isn't to teach ASP but to show that JavaScript syntax is used within it. By

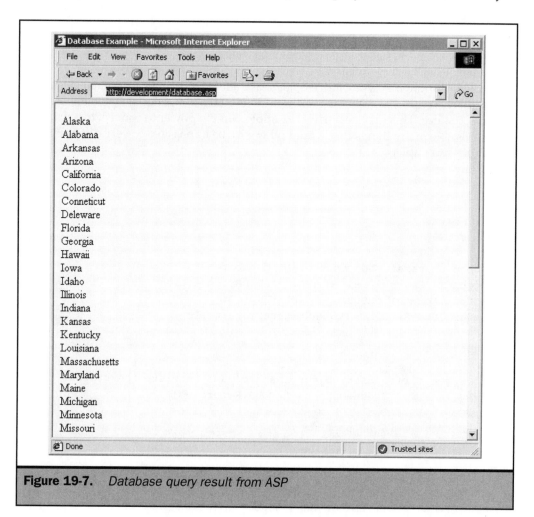

Figure 19-7.   *Database query result from ASP*

learning JavaScript first, you should find that ASP comes more easily. For more information on this technology, visit sites such as **http://www.15seconds.com**, **http://www.asp101.com**, and, of course, **http://msdn.microsoft.com**.

Other JavaScript Uses

JavaScript really is just a computer language like any other such as C, Pascal, C++, or Java. It can be used in a wide variety of ways: in embedded systems, as your own shrink wrapped application, or even as part of a desktop automation environment.

Consider the JavaScript interpreter. The interpreter allows JavaScript code to be executed. Under a Microsoft environment, we can install a JavaScript interpreter on a desktop machine and then script common operating system tasks with JavaScript. A simple example is getting the free space on a drive:

```
freeSpace = GetFreeSpace("c:")
```

You could also embed a JavaScript interpreter in an application. You could use a JavaScript interpreter such as Mozilla's SpiderMonkey (a C-based JavaScript interpreter) or Rhino (a Java-based JavaScript implementation) to embed JavaScript into applications to provide scripting capability with JavaScript for users of the application. This is the whole idea of JavaScript as a *scripting* language, a language which is utilizes existing capabilities to automate or customize aspects of an environment.

Your application could be a Web application or a traditional, non-Web one. When writing an application using C, C++, or Java, you can link your application to the JavaScript engine as a shared resource. In UNIX, this would be a shared library; on Windows, this would be a DLL. You can do things like automate the application with scripts or provide cross-platform functionality by eliminating solutions that rely on the features of a particular platform. You could let power users change the preferences or settings of your program by writing JavaScript scripts to accomplish the task. This would be very similar to writing shell scripts in UNIX.

Although it is possible to use JavaScript outside of traditional server-side and client-side Web applications, the reality is that doing so is very uncommon. JavaScript as a generic scripting language certainly has not made much of an impact in the world of automation or customization, but the potential certainly merits mentioning. Industrious readers might find that JavaScript would work well in automating window manager tasks in UNIX environments, but to our knowledge the practice is not currently in use.

Note *More information about the C-based JavaScript engine can be found at* **http://www.mozilla.org/js/spidermonkey**. *More information about the Java-based JavaScript engine can be found at* **http://www.mozilla.org/rhino**. *More information about the Microsoft interpreters can be found at* **http://msdn.microsoft.com/scripting**.

ADVANCED TOPICS

Summary

In this chapter we showed the two main ways JavaScript is used on the server. Netscape's server-side JavaScript required us to compile, install, and start an application; it provided access to core JavaScript objects, such as **Array**, **Date**, **Math**, **Number**, and **String** as well as server-specific objects such as those that support databases, file systems, and email. Unfortunately, as similar as it may be to client-side JavaScript, SSJS appears to be a dying technology.

Microsoft's Active Server Pages technology, on the other hand, is quite alive and in very widespread use. It supports numerous languages, including Microsoft's JavaScript implementation JScript. We can include JScript in our .asp files (interpreted at delivery time) by using the <% %> tags, by including code with a server-side **include**, or by using the familiar **<script>** tag with a **runat** attribute. Like SSJS, ASP provides access to a variety of useful server objects, such as **Response**, **Request**, **Application**, **Session**, **Server**, and **ASPError**. With these objects, we can perform tasks like writing to the browser, reading client input, and even accessing outside objects to perform such complex tasks as creating graphics or querying databases.

Finally, we saw that—as we have known all along—JavaScript is just a computer language like any other. While it tends to be used on the client side in conjunction with HTML documents, it is not necessarily limited to this domain. However, in some sense it really performs best in such an environment, particularly if you consider how powerful the document and browser objects we have studied are. The next chapter will continue the theme of employing JavaScript outside of its common environment—we'll look at the emerging use of JavaScript to manipulate XML data and documents.

The Complete Reference

Chapter 20

JavaScript and XML

In this chapter we briefly visit the intersection between JavaScript and the Extensible Markup Language (XML). XML has quickly risen to be a favored method of structured data interchange on the Web. Today, many sites exchange XML data feeds or store site content in XML files for later transformation into an appropriate presentation medium such as HTML or WML (Wireless Markup Language). However, client-side use of XML has so far been relatively rare except in the form of specialized languages built with XML, such as XHTML, WML, and SVG. Using JavaScript to manipulate client-side XML is rarer still, at least on public Web sites. Much of this chapter presents examples of XML and JavaScript that are often proprietary, probably bound to change, and almost always buggy. In other words, proceed with optimism but extreme caution.

Overview of XML

To those unfamiliar with XML, it often sounds mysterious and difficult, possibly even requiring esoteric knowledge of writing language grammars. In actuality, writing simple XML documents is fairly easy. For example, suppose that you have a compelling need to define some elements to represent a fast-food restaurant's combination meals, which contain a burger, drink, and fries. How might you do this in XML? You would simply create a file such as burger.xml that contains the following markup:

```xml
<?xml version="1.0" encoding="UTF-8" standalone="yes" ?>
<combomeal>
    <burger>
    <name>Tasty Burger</name>
    <bun bread="white">
        <meat />
        <cheese />
        <meat />
    </bun>
    </burger>
    <fries size="large" />
    <drink size="large">
        Cola
    </drink>
</combomeal>
```

A rendering of this example under Internet Explorer 5.5 is shown in Figure 20-1.

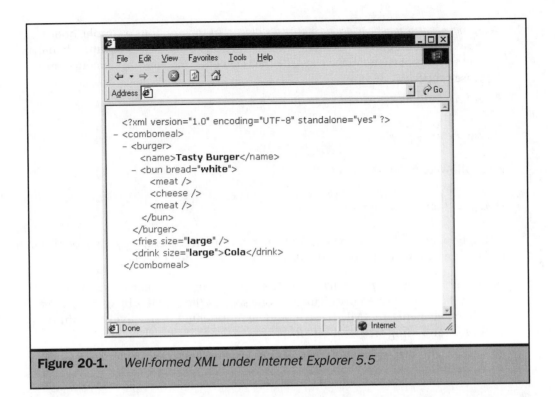

Figure 20-1. *Well-formed XML under Internet Explorer 5.5*

Notice that the browser shows a structural representation of the file, not a screen representation. You'll see how to make this file actually look like something later in the chapter. First, take a look at the document syntax. In many ways, this example— "Fast Food Markup Language" (or FFML, if you like)—looks similar to HTML, but how would you know to name the element **<combomeal>** instead of **<mealdeal>** or **<lunchspecial>**? You don't need to know, because the decision is completely up to you. Simply choose any element and attribute names that meaningfully represent the domain that you want to model. Does this mean that XML has no rules? It has rules, but they are few, simple, and relate only to syntax:

■ *The document must start with the appropriate XML declaration*, as in:

```
<?xml version="1.0" encoding="UTF-8" standalone="yes" ?>
```

or maybe just this:

```
<?xml version="1.0" ?>
```

- *A root element must enclose the entire document.* In the previous example, notice how the **<combomeal>** element encloses all other elements. In addition to the fact that a root element encloses all other elements, the internal elements must close properly.

- *All elements must be closed.*

```
<burger>Tasty
```

is not allowed under XML, but

```
<burger>Tasty</burger>
```

would be allowed. Even when elements do not contain content, they must be closed properly, as discussed in the next rule for a valid XML document.

- *All elements with empty content must be self-identifying, by ending in "/>" instead of the familiar ">".* An empty element is one such as the HTML **
, **<hr>, or **<img>** elements. In XML, these would be represented, respectively, as **
, **<hr />, and **<img src="test.gif" />**.

- Just as with well-written HTML, *all elements must be properly nested.* For example,

```
<outer><inner>ground zero</inner></outer>
```

is correct, whereas this isn't:

```
<outer><inner>ground zero</outer></inner>
```

- *All attribute values must be quoted.* In HTML, quoting is good authoring practice, but it is required only for values that contain characters other than letters (A–Z, a–z), numbers (0–9), hyphens (-), or periods (.). For example, under XML,

```
<blastoff count="10"></blastoff>
```

is correct, whereas this isn't:

```
<blastoff count=10></blastoff>
```

- *All elements must be cased consistently.* If you start a new element such as **<BURGER>**, you must close it as **</BURGER>**, not **</burger>**. Later in the document, if the element is in lowercase, you actually are referring to a new element known as **<burger>**. Attribute names also are case-sensitive.

■ *A valid XML file may not contain certain characters that have reserved meanings.*
These include characters such as **&**, which indicates the beginning of a character
entity, and **<** , which indicates the start of an element name such as **<sunny>**.
These characters must be coded as entities as **&** and **<**, respectively,
or they can occur in a section marked off as character data. In fact, in a basic
standalone XML document this rule is quite restrictive so you must escape all
ampersands (as &), less than symbols (as <), greater than symbols (as
>), apostrophes (as '), and quotation marks (as ").

A document constructed according to the previous simple rules is known as a
well-formed document. Take a look in Figure 20-2 at what happens to a document that
doesn't follow the well-formed rules presented here.

SGML purists might find the notion of *well-formedness* eccentric and somewhat
troubling. Although SGML itself currently is being revised, traditional SGML has
no notion of well-formed documents—that is, documents that are in some sense okay
because they conform to some basic syntax guidelines. Instead of the well-formed
documents criterion, conventional SGML uses the notion of *valid* documents—
documents that adhere to a formally defined document type definition (DTD).
Although this concept also is part of HTML, often it is lost on page authors. For

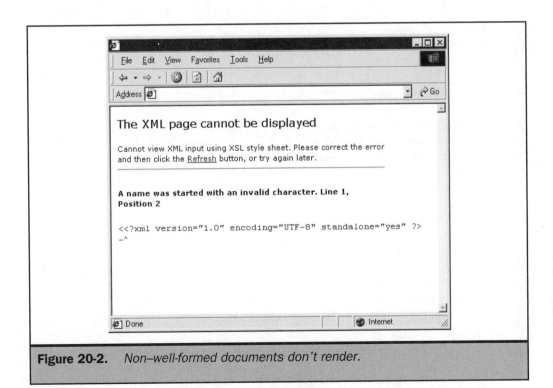

Figure 20-2.   *Non–well-formed documents don't render.*

anything beyond casual applications, defining a DTD and validating documents against that definition are real benefits. XML supports both well-formed and valid documents. The well-formed model, which just enforces the basic syntax, should encourage those not schooled in the intricacies of SGML to begin authoring XML documents, thus making XML as accessible as HTML has been. The validation model is available for applications in which a document's logical structure needs to be verified.

Valid Documents

Most HTML authors are familiar with basic elements and attributes. Now, because of the rising complexity of pages, they are becoming more familiar with the importance of making an HTML document conform to the rules of a DTD, such as HTML 4. As noted in the previous paragraph, a document that conforms to a DTD is said to be *valid*. Unlike most HTML authors, SGML authors normally concern themselves with producing valid documents. Many also concern themselves with writing the DTDs that HTML authors usually take for granted. With the appearance of XML, HTML authors can look forward to mastering a new skill: writing DTDs. The following example illustrates how XML might be used to create some structure for our combo meal example. A definition of the sample language to accomplish this task can be found within the document, although this definition can be kept outside the file as well. The burger2.xml file shown here includes both the DTD and data conforming to the language in the same document:

```
<?xml version="1.0"?>
<!DOCTYPE combomeal [
<!ENTITY cola "Pepsi">
<!ELEMENT combomeal (burger+, fries+, drink+)>

<!ELEMENT burger (name, bun)>
<!ELEMENT name (#PCDATA)>
<!ELEMENT bun (meat+, cheese+, meat+)>
<!ATTLIST bun
        bread (white | wheat) #REQUIRED
>

<!ELEMENT meat EMPTY>
<!ELEMENT cheese EMPTY>

<!ELEMENT fries EMPTY>
<!ATTLIST fries
        size (small | medium | large) #REQUIRED
>
```

```
<!ELEMENT drink (#PCDATA)>
<!ATTLIST drink
        size (small | medium | large) #REQUIRED
>



]>
<!-- the document instance -->
<combomeal>
    <burger>
    <name>Tasty Burger</name>
    <bun bread="white">
        <meat />
        <cheese />
        <meat />
    </bun>
    </burger>
    <fries size="large" />
    <drink size="large">
        &cola;
    </drink>
</combomeal>
```

We could easily have just written the document itself and put the DTD in an external file referencing it using a statement such as:

```
<!DOCTYPE combomeal SYSTEM "combomeal.dtd">
```

at the top of the document after the **<?xml version="1.0">** declaration, and placed the various element, attribute, and entity definitions in the external file combomeal.dtd. Regardless of how it is defined and included, the defined language's meaning is relatively straightforward. A document is enclosed by the **<combomeal>** element, which in turn contains one or more **<burger>, <fries>,** and **<drink>** elements. Each **<burger>** element contains a **<name>** and **<bun>** which in turn contain **<meat />** and **<cheese />** elements. Attributes are defined to indicate the bread type of the bun as well as the size of the fries and drink in the meal.

One nice aspect of using a DTD with an XML file is that the correctness of the document can be checked. For example, adding undefined elements or omitting a required nested element should cause a validating XML parser to reject the document, as shown in Figure 20-3.

ADVANCED TOPICS

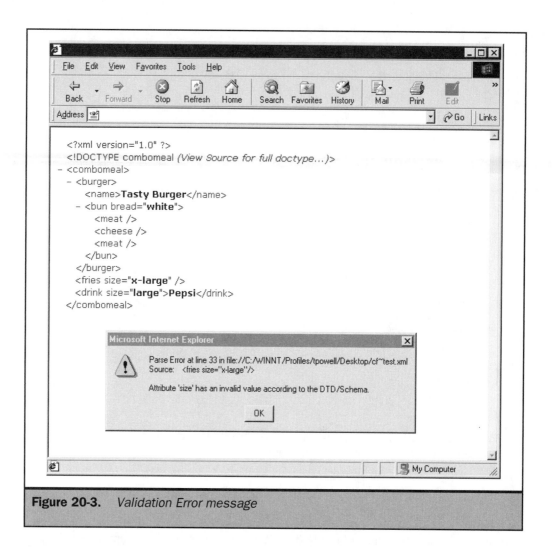

Figure 20-3. *Validation Error message*

Note *At the time of this writing, most browser-based parsers don't necessarily validate the document, but just check to make sure the document is well formed. The IE 5.5 browser snapshot (in Figure 20-3) was performed using an Internet Explorer extension that validates XML documents.*

Writing a DTD might seem like an awful lot of trouble, but without one the value of XML is limited. If you can guarantee conformance to the specification, you can allow automated parsing and exchange of documents. For example, XML could be used to define a newsfeed language which any XML-aware device could utilize. Writing a DTD is going to be a new experience for most HTML authors, and not everybody will want to write one. Fortunately, although not apparent from the DTD rules in this brief example, XML significantly reduces the complexity of full SGML. Turning from the issue of language definitions, a more immediate issue is how to present or manipulate an XML document once it is written.

XML Presentation

XML documents actually have many good uses. First, notice that because XML documents have no predefined presentation, XML forces the separation of content structure from presentation. Many Web developers have embraced the idea of storing Web content in XML format and then transforming it into an appropriate output format such as HTML (with or without CSS), using *Extensible Style Sheet Transformations* (XSLT), or some form of server-side programming. Given the following XML document representing an employee directory, we might wish to convert it into a commonly supported output format like HTML.

```
<?xml version="1.0" encoding="UTF-8" standalone="yes" ?>
<directory>
<employee>
        <name>Fred Brown</name>
        <title>Widget Washer</title>
        <phone>(543) 555-1212</phone>
        <email>fbrown@democompany.com</email>
</employee>

<employee>
        <name>Cory Richards</name>
        <title>Toxic Waste Manager</title>
        <phone>(543) 555-1213</phone>
        <email>crichards@democompany.com</email>
</employee>

<employee>
        <name>Tim Powell</name>
        <title>Big Boss</title>
        <phone>(543) 555-2222</phone>
        <email>tpowell@democompany.com</email>
</employee>

<employee>
        <name>Samantha Jones</name>
        <title>Sales Executive</title>
```

```
        <phone>(543) 555-5672</phone>
        <email>jones@democompany.com</email>
</employee>


<employee>
        <name>Eric Roberts</name>
        <title>Director of Technology</title>
        <phone>(543) 567-3456</phone>
        <email>eric@democompany.com</email>
</employee>


<employee>
        <name>Frank Li</name>
        <title>Marketing Manager</title>
        <phone>(123) 456-2222</phone>
        <email>fli@democompany.com</email>
</employee>
</directory>
```

We might consider creating an HTML table containing each of the individual employee records. For example, an employee represented by

```
<employee>
        <name>Employee's name</name>
        <title>Employee's title</title>
        <phone>Phone number</phone>
        <email>Email address</email>
</employee>
```

might be converted into a table row (**<tr>**) like

```
<tr>
        <td>Employee name</td>
        <td>Employee's title</td>
        <td>Phone number</td>
        <td>Email address</td>
</tr>
```

We can use an XSL style sheet to perform such a transformation. An example XSL stylesheet (staff.xsl) is shown here:

```
<?xml version="1.0"?>
<xsl:stylesheet xmlns:xsl="http://www.w3.org/TR/WD-xsl">
<xsl:template match="/">
    <html>
    <head>
    <title>Employee Directory</title>
    </head>
    <body>
        <h1 align="center">DemoCompany Directory</h1>
    <hr/>
    <table width="100%">
        <tr>
          <th>Name</th>
          <th>Title</th>
          <th>Phone</th>
          <th>Email</th>
        </tr>

        <xsl:for-each select="directory/employee">
        <tr>
          <td><xsl:value-of select="name"/></td>
          <td><xsl:value-of select="title"/></td>
          <td><xsl:value-of select="phone"/></td>
          <td><xsl:value-of select="email"/></td>
        </tr>
        </xsl:for-each>

    </table>
    </body>
    </html>
</xsl:template>
</xsl:stylesheet>
```

Note   *We are sweeping some issues under the rug. The XSLT spec used by most of the Internet Explorer browser family is rather dated. The official namespace for XSLT 1.0 is **http://www.w3.org/XSL/Transform/1.0**, not the URI given above. For more information see **http://www.w3.org/Style/XSL/**.*

We can reference the style sheet from the original XML document by adding

```
<?xml-stylesheet href="staff.xsl" type="text/xsl"?>
```

to the original staff.xml file just below the initial XML declaration. The output of this example in a client-side XSL-aware browser like Internet Explorer 5.5 is shown in Figure 20-4. Of course, we could just as easily have transformed this into HTML on the server-side and not had to worry about using an XSL-aware browser.

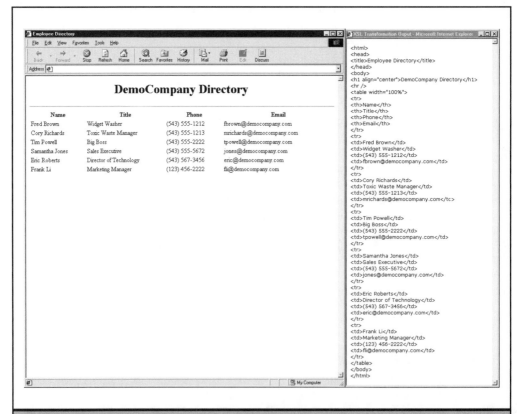

Figure 20-4. *XML document transformed to HTML tables using XSL*

XSL transformations can create all sorts of complex documents complete with embedded JavaScript or style sheets.

It is also possible in 5.x and 6.x generation browsers to directly render XML by applying CSS rules immediately to tags. For example, given the following simple XML file, we might apply a set of CSS rules by relating the sheet using **<?xml-stylesheet href="URL to style sheet " type="text/css"?>,** as shown here:

```
<?xml version="1.0" encoding="UTF-8" standalone="yes" ?>
<?xml-stylesheet href="staff.css" type="text/css"?>
<directory>
<employee>
<name>Fred Brown</name>
<title>Widget Washer</title>
<phone>(543) 555-1212</phone>
<email>fbrown@democompany.com</email>
</employee>
...
</directory>
```

The CSS rules for XML elements are effectively the same as for HTML or XHTML documents, though they do require knowledge of less commonly used properties, such as **display,** to create meaningful renderings. The CSS rule for the previously presented XML document is shown here, and its output under Internet Explorer 5.5 is shown in Figure 20-5.

```
directory {display: block;}
employee {display: block; border: solid; }
name {display: inline; font-weight: bold; width: 200px;}
title {display: inline; font-style: italic; width: 200px;}
phone {display: inline; color: red; width: 150px;}
email {display: inline; color: blue; width: 100px;}
```

This previous discussion is by no means a complete description of XML and related technologies, but is just enough for us to have the necessary background to present some use of XML and JavaScript together for those unfamiliar with the basics of XML. Readers looking for more detailed information on XML might consider sites like **www.xml101.com** and, of course, the W3C XML section (**www.w3.org/XML**).

ADVANCED TOPICS

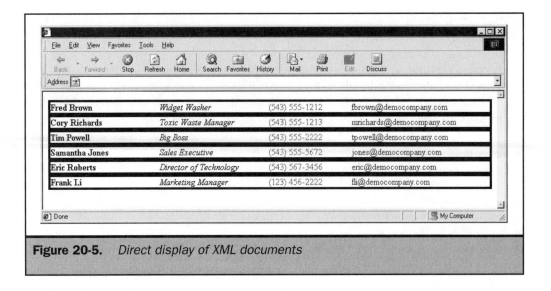

Figure 20-5.   *Direct display of XML documents*

The DOM and XML

Now, considering that we can eventually present XML in a displayable format in a browser, readers may wonder how JavaScript can be used to manipulate the document. In the case of XSL that is applied server side, there is nothing special to consider. The output form would be HTML, and thus we would use standard JavaScript and DOM techniques. However, if the document is delivered natively as XML, you might have a question about how to manipulate the document. Probably you already know the answer—use the DOM!

As discussed in Chapter 10, the DOM represents a document as a tree of nodes, including elements, text data, comments, CDATA sections, and so on. The elements in this tree can be HTML elements, as we have seen so far, or they could be XML elements, including things like our **<burger>** or **<employee>** tags. We could then access these elements and look at them and even modify their contents.

Internet Explorer Example

To demonstrate JavaScript, XML, and the DOM in action, let's use Internet Explorer 5.5 (or better) to load an XML document containing our employee directory and see if we can manipulate it. First, to load in the document, we create an instantiation of Microsoft's XML parser using the JScript-specific **ActiveXObject**. Once the object is created, we load the appropriate XML document into memory. In this case, it is the pure XML file of employee records we saw earlier without style sheets or other references.

```
var xmldoc = new ActiveXObject("Microsoft.XMLDOM");
xmldoc.async = false;
xmldoc.load("staff2.xml");
```

Once it's loaded, we can use the DOM to manipulate it. For example, we can access the root element of the document (**<directory>**) using

```
var rootElement = xmldoc.documentElement;
```

Then, we might alert out its **nodeName** property as shown here:

```
<!DOCTYPE HTML PUBLIC "-//W3C//DTD HTML 4.01 Transitional//EN"
         "http://www.w3.org/TR/html4/loose.dtd">
<html>
<head>
<title>XML Demo</title>
</head>
<body>
<script language="JScript">
 var xmldoc = new ActiveXObject("Microsoft.XMLDOM");
 xmldoc.async = false;
 xmldoc.load("staff2.xml");

 var rootElement = xmldoc.documentElement;
</script>
<form>
<input type="button" value="show node"
onclick="alert(rootElement.nodeName)">
</form>
</body>
</html>
```

We should see this:

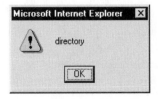

We could further use the DOM properties and methods we are familiar with from Chapter 10. Consider, for example, the following function that deletes the last node:

```
function deleteLastElement()
{
  var rootElement = xmldoc.documentElement;
  if (rootElement.hasChildNodes())
     rootElement.removeChild(rootElement.lastChild);
}
```

Really, the only difference here is the use of the *xmldoc* object that we created to reference the XML document. This takes the place of the **document** which would be a reference to the HTML **Document** object. Otherwise, the manipulations are the same as with HTML.

Given the previous example, we now present a simple demonstration of adding, deleting, and displaying data from an XML file under Internet Explorer 5.0 (or better). The rendering of this example is shown in Figure 20-6.

```
<!DOCTYPE HTML PUBLIC "-//W3C//DTD HTML 4.01 Transitional//EN"
          "http://www.w3.org/TR/html4/loose.dtd">
<html>
<head>
<title>XML Demo</title>
</head>
<body>
<script language="JScript">

/* invoke parser and read in document */
var xmldoc = new ActiveXObject("Microsoft.XMLDOM");
xmldoc.async = false;
xmldoc.load("staff2.xml");

function deleteLastElement()
   {    /* find root element and delete its last child */
   var rootElement = xmldoc.documentElement;
   if (rootElement.hasChildNodes())
   rootElement.removeChild(rootElement.lastChild);
   }

function addElement()
{
  var rootElement = xmldoc.documentElement;

  /* create employee element*/

  var newEmployee = xmldoc.createElement('employee');
```

```
  /* create child elements and text values and append one by one */
  var newName = xmldoc.createElement('name');
  var newNameText = xmldoc.createTextNode(document.myform.namefield.value);
  newName.appendChild(newNameText);
  newEmployee.appendChild(newName);

  var newTitle = xmldoc.createElement('title');
  var newTitleText = xmldoc.createTextNode(document.myform.titlefield.value);
  newTitle.appendChild(newTitleText);
  newEmployee.appendChild(newTitle);

  var newPhone = xmldoc.createElement('phone');
  var newPhoneText = xmldoc.createTextNode(document.myform.phonefield.value);
  newPhone.appendChild(newPhoneText);
  newEmployee.appendChild(newPhone);

  var newEmail = xmldoc.createElement('email');
  var newEmailText = xmldoc.createTextNode(document.myform.emailfield.value);
  newEmail.appendChild(newEmailText);
  newEmployee.appendChild(newEmail);

  /* append completed record to the document */
  rootElement.appendChild(newEmployee);
}

function dump(string)
{
  var currentvalue=document.myform.showxml.value;
  currentvalue+=string;
  document.myform.showxml.value = currentvalue;
}

function display(node)
{
  var type = node.nodeType;
  if (type == 1)
    { // open tag
      dump("\<" + node.tagName);
      // output the attributes if any
      attributes = node.attributes;
      if (attributes)
        {
         var countAttrs = attributes.length;
         var index = 0;
         while(index < countAttrs)
           {
            att = attributes[index];
```

```
        if (att)
            dump(" " + att.name + "=" + att.value);
        index++;
      }
    }
    // recursively dump the children
    if (node.hasChildNodes())
      {
      // close tag
      dump(">\n");
      // get the children
      var children = node.childNodes;
      var length = children.length;
      var count = 0;
      while(count < length)
        {
            child = children[count];
            display(child);
            count++;
        }
      dump("</" + node.tagName + ">\n");
      }
    else
      dump("/>\n");
  }
  else if (type == 3)
    { // if it's a piece of text just dump the text
      dump(node.data+"\n");
    }
}

</script>


<form id="myform" name="myform">
<strong>XML Document:</strong><br>
<textarea id="showxml" name="showxml" rows="10" cols="40"></textarea>
<br><br><br>
Name: <input type="text" name="namefield" id="namefield" size="50"><br>
Title: <input type="text" name="titlefield" id="titlefield" size="30"><br>
Phone: <input type="text" name="phonefield" id="phonefield" size="20"><br>
Email: <input type="text" name="emailfield" id="emailfield" size="20"><br>

<input type="button" value="add record"
onclick="addElement();document.myform.showxml.value='';display
(xmldoc.documentElement)">
```

```
<input type="button" value="delete last record"
onclick="deleteLastElement();document.myform.showxml.value='';display(xmldoc.
documentElement)">

<input type="button" value="redisplay XML document"
onclick="document.myform.showxml.value='';display(xmldoc.documentElement)">
</form>

<script language="JScript">
  /* show initial XML document */
  display(xmldoc.documentElement);
</script>
</body>
</html>
```

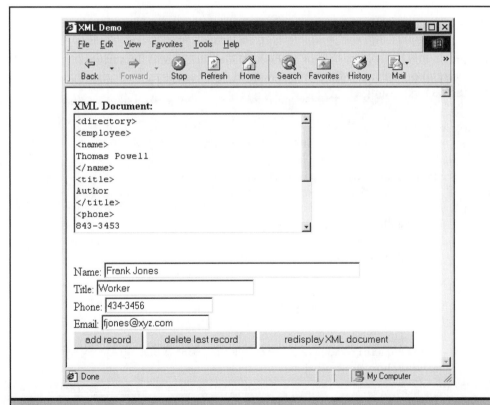

Figure 20-6.   *XML document directly manipulated with JScript and the DOM*

If it seems somewhat clunky to output the XML items manually to the HTML form field, you're right. Microsoft provides a method called Data Binding, discussed later in the chapter, that is much cleaner. The point here was to explicitly show the XML tags during the manipulation. The next examples will work with XML even more directly.

Netscape 6 Example

Nothing is ever easy in the world of emerging standards. Netscape doesn't handle XML in the same fashion as Internet Explorer does. In fact, rather than using HTML and bringing in XML, Netscape 6 seems to adopt the approach of taking XML and bringing in HTML. We present the following approach to demonstrate that, apart from this divergence, the browsers are pretty similar.

The first example shows that, since we are using an XML document rather than an HTML document, we do not require a special **XMLDocument** object; instead we reference the **Document** object just as we would expect. For example, to print out the **nodeName** property of the root element, we would use

```
alert(document.documentElement.nodeName)
```

However, we need to bring in script to the XML document and then trigger it. There is no easy way to do this in XML, so we rely on HTML tags (such as form elements), as shown in this next example:

```
<?xml version="1.0"?>
<?xml-stylesheet href="staff.css" type="text/css"?>

<directory xmlns:html="http://www.w3.org/1999/xhtml"
           xmlns:xlink="http://www.w3.org/1999/xlink">
<employee>
        <name>Fred Brown</name>
        <title>Widget Washer</title>
        <phone>(543) 555-1212</phone>
        <email>fbrown@democompany.com</email>
</employee>

<html:form>
      <html:input type="button" id="test"
      onclick="alert(document.documentElement.nodeName)"
      value="Show Root
 Element"/>
</html:form>
</directory>
```

As with the previous example under Internet Explorer, this will simply display a dialog showing the directory element. Oddly, while you can get this example to work under Internet Explorer, it will display the HTML element rather than directory element! Once again, the browser vendors do things differently.

It is easy enough to adapt our more complex DOM example to Netscape if we can just include the script code in the file. We'll use a linked script to do the trick, using yet another embedded HTML tag like **<html:script src="xmldemo.js" />**. The complete example is shown here:

File:staff3.xml

```
<?xml version="1.0"?>
<?xml-stylesheet href="staff.css" type="text/css"?>

<directory xmlns:html="http://www.w3.org/1999/xhtml"
           xmlns:xlink="http://www.w3.org/1999/xlink">

<html:form id="myform" name="myform">

<html:label>Name: <html:input type="text" name="namefield"
id="namefield" size="50" /></html:label><html:br />
<html:label>Title: <html:input type="text" name="titlefield"
id="titlefield" size="30" /></html:label><html:br />
<html:label>Phone: <html:input type="text" name="phonefield"
id="phonefield" size="20" /></html:label><html:br />
<html:label>Email: <html:input type="text" name="emailfield"
id="emailfield" size="20" /></html:label><html:br />

<html:input type="button" value="add record"
onclick="addElement()" />
<html:input type="button" value="delete last record"
onclick="deleteLastElement()" />
<html:hr />
</html:form>

<employee>
        <name>Fred Brown</name>
        <title>Widget Washer</title>
        <phone>(543) 555-1212</phone>
        <email>fbrown@democompany.com</email>
</employee>
```

```
<employee>
        <name>Cory Richards</name>
        <title>Toxic Waste Manager</title>
        <phone>(543) 555-1213</phone>
        <email>mrichards@democompany.com</email>
</employee>

<employee>
        <name>Tim Powell</name>
        <title>Big Boss</title>
        <phone>(543) 555-2222</phone>
        <email>tpowell@democompany.com</email>
</employee>

<employee>
        <name>Samantha Jones</name>
        <title>Sales Executive</title>
        <phone>(543) 555-5672</phone>
        <email>jones@democompany.com</email>
</employee>

<employee>
        <name>Eric Roberts</name>
        <title>Director of Technology</title>
        <phone>(543) 567-3456</phone>
        <email>eric@democompany.com</email>
</employee>

<employee>
        <name>Frank Li</name>
        <title>Marketing Manager</title>
        <phone>(123) 456-2222</phone>
        <email>fli@democompany.com</email>
</employee>

<html:script src="xmldemo.js" />

</directory>
```

File: xmldemo.js

```
function deleteLastElement()
{

    /* Get list of the employee elements */
    var employeeList = document.getElementsByTagName('employee');
    if (employeeList.length > 0)
      { // find the last employee and delete it
      var toDelete = employeeList.item(employeeList.length-1);
      document.documentElement.removeChild(toDelete);
      }
    else
      alert('No employee elements to delete');
}


function addElement()
{
    var rootElement = document.documentElement;

    var name = document.getElementById('namefield').value;
    var title = document.getElementById('titlefield').value;
    var phone = document.getElementById('phonefield').value;
    var email = document.getElementById('emailfield').value;

    /* create employee element*/
    var newEmployee = document.createElement('employee');


    /* create child elements and text values and
       append one by one */
    var newName = document.createElement('name');
    var newNameText = document.createTextNode(name);
    newName.appendChild(newNameText);
    newEmployee.appendChild(newName);

    var newTitle = document.createElement('title');
    var newTitleText = document.createTextNode(title);
    newTitle.appendChild(newTitleText);
    newEmployee.appendChild(newTitle);
```

ADVANCED TOPICS

```
var newPhone = document.createElement('phone');
var newPhoneText = document.createTextNode(phone);
newPhone.appendChild(newPhoneText);
newEmployee.appendChild(newPhone);

var newEmail = document.createElement('email');
var newEmailText = document.createTextNode(email);
newEmail.appendChild(newEmailText);
newEmployee.appendChild(newEmail);

/* append completed record to the document */
rootElement.appendChild(newEmployee);
}
```

A rendering of this example under Netscape 6 is presented in Figure 20-7.

Note   *The Mozilla and Netscape 6 implementations are very buggy and may require a manual reload to get the demo to work. You also may need to add a JavaScript window reload( ) as well. The demo crashed under some versions of the Mozilla engine but worked under others.*

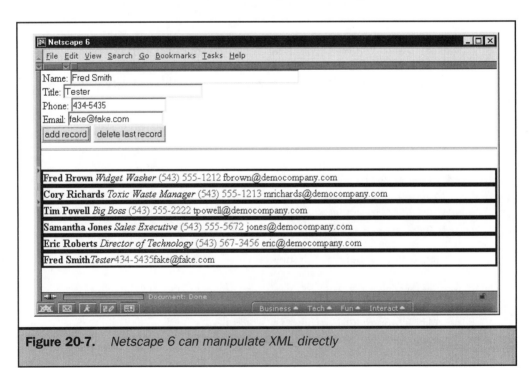

Figure 20-7.   *Netscape 6 can manipulate XML directly*

Internet Explorer's XML Data Islands

Because of the common desire —in many cases need—to embed XML data content into an HTML document, Microsoft introduced a special **<xml>** tag in Internet Explorer 4. The **<xml>** tag is used to create a so-called *XML data island* that can hold XML to be used within the document. Imagine running a query to a database, fetching more data than needed for the page, and then putting it in an XML data island. We may then allow the user to retrieve new information from the data island without going back to the server. To include XML in an HTML document, we can use the **<xml>** tag and enclose the content directly within it:

```
...HTML content...
<xml id="myIsland">
<directory>
<employee>
    <name>Fred Brown</name>
    <title>Widget Washer</title>
    <phone>(543) 555-1212</phone>
    <email>fbrown@democompany.com</email>
</employee>
</directory>
</xml>
...HTML content...
```

Or, we can reference an external file by specifying its URL, like so:

```
<xml id="myIsland" src="staff2.xml"></xml>
```

Once the XML is included in the document, we can bind the XML to HTML elements. While we could write a JavaScript to retrieve the XML elements and write them to HTML elements using the **innerHTML** property, we can use the much simpler method of *data binding*. In the example here, we bind xml data to a table. Notice that we must use HTML 4 style tables to avoid repeating the headings over and over.

```
<!DOCTYPE HTML PUBLIC "-//W3C//DTD HTML 4.01 Transitional//EN"
         "http://www.w3.org/TR/html4/loose.dtd">
<html>
<head>
<title>Employee Directory</title>
</head>
<body>
<xml id="myIsland" src="staff2.xml"></xml>
<h1 align="center">DemoCompany Directory</h1>
```

```
<hr/>
<table width="100%" datasrc="#myIsland">
<thead>
    <tr>
        <th>Name</th>
        <th>Title</th>
        <th>Phone</th>
        <th>Email</th>
    </tr>
</thead>
<tbody>
    <tr>
        <td><span datafld="name"></span></td>
        <td><span datafld="title"></span></td>
        <td><span datafld="phone"></span></td>
        <td><span datafld="email"></span></td>
    </tr>
</tbody>
</table>
</body>
</html>
```

The output of the example is as expected and is shown in Figure 20-8.

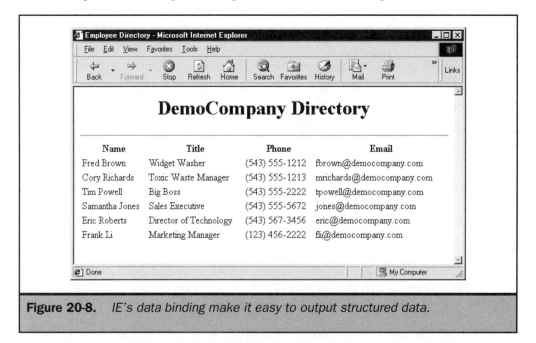

Figure 20-8.   *IE's data binding make it easy to output structured data.*

Now, to manipulate the XML in the data island we just access the element's content by its set **id** value (*myIsland*). We can use the **all[ ]** collection to access the element and assign it to the identifier *xmldoc* (as used in the first IE-related XML example). We can now use this identifier as we have done before. For example, to get the root node, we would access *xmldoc.documentElement*. The add/delete record example is presented here for the final time, written using data binding.

```
<!DOCTYPE HTML PUBLIC "-//W3C//DTD HTML 4.01 Transitional//EN"
          "http://www.w3.org/TR/html4/loose.dtd">
<html>
<head>
<title>Employee Directory</title>
</head>
<body>
<xml id="myIsland" src="staff2.xml"></xml>
<h1 align="center">DemoCompany Directory</h1>
<hr/>
<table width="100%" datasrc="#myIsland">
<thead>
    <tr>
        <th>Name</th>
        <th>Title</th>
        <th>Phone</th>
        <th>Email</th>
    </tr>
</thead>
<tbody>
    <tr>
        <td><span datafld="name"></span></td>
        <td><span datafld="title"></span></td>
        <td><span datafld="phone"></span></td>
        <td><span datafld="email"></span></td>
    </tr>
</tbody>
</table>

<script language="JScript">
/* associate the XML document from the data island */
xmldoc = myIsland;

function deleteLastElement()
{
  /* find root element and delete its last child */
  var rootElement = xmldoc.documentElement;
  if (rootElement.hasChildNodes())
    rootElement.removeChild(rootElement.lastChild);
}
```

```
function addElement()
 {
    var rootElement = xmldoc.documentElement;

    /* create employee element*/
    var newEmployee = xmldoc.createElement('employee');

    /* create child elements and text values and append one by one */
    var newName = xmldoc.createElement('name');
    var newNameText = xmldoc.createTextNode(document.myform.namefield.value);
    newName.appendChild(newNameText);
    newEmployee.appendChild(newName);

    var newTitle = xmldoc.createElement('title');
    var newTitleText = xmldoc.createTextNode(document.myform.titlefield.value);
    newTitle.appendChild(newTitleText);
    newEmployee.appendChild(newTitle);

    var newPhone = xmldoc.createElement('phone');
    var newPhoneText = xmldoc.createTextNode(document.myform.phonefield.value);
    newPhone.appendChild(newPhoneText);
    newEmployee.appendChild(newPhone);

    var newEmail = xmldoc.createElement('email');
    var newEmailText = xmldoc.createTextNode(document.myform.emailfield.value);
    newEmail.appendChild(newEmailText);
    newEmployee.appendChild(newEmail);

    /* append completed record to the document */
    rootElement.appendChild(newEmployee);
 }
</script>
<form id="myform" name="myform">

Name: <input type="text" name="namefield" id="namefield" size="50"><br>
Title: <input type="text" name="titlefield" id="titlefield" size="30"><br>
Phone: <input type="text" name="phonefield" id="phonefield" size="20"><br>
Email: <input type="text" name="emailfield" id="emailfield" size="20"><br>

<input type="button" value="add record" onclick="addElement()">
<input type="button" value="delete last record" onclick="deleteLastElement()">

</form>
</body>
</html>
```

Besides data islands, you will find that Internet Explorer has a very powerful set of tools to interact with XML documents—many of these are based on W3C standards. A few of the objects you would encounter are **XMLDOMDocument**, **XMLDOMNode**, **XMLDOMNodeList**, and **XMLDOMNamedNodeMap**. If you have become familiar with the DOM, you can pretty much guess what these objects, properties, and methods would be (we've already covered them in Chapter 10). As always, see Microsoft's MSDN site for complete information (**msdn.microsoft.com**).

We also saw that Netscape 6 does provide many of the same capabilities, though in a more "standards manner" and without well-distributed documentation. Interestingly enough, both browsers have difficulty with the same problem: how to include XML with other technologies, particularly HTML and scripting languages. Until these not very minor details are worked out, developers should exercise extreme caution mixing XML, JavaScript, HTML, and style sheets. The intersection of these standards seems to still be a very risky area.

Summary

With JavaScript and the DOM, you can directly manipulate the contents of an XML document. This chapter presented a very brief introduction to XML and some examples of how Internet Explorer 5 and Netscape 6 provide for script manipulation of XML. Unfortunately, the two browsers do things in very different ways. Yet even if that were not the case, the actual value of manipulating XML documents client-side has really yet to be tapped by most developers. There are even questions of the usefulness of doing so, quite possibly because of the major bugs that still exist in most browsers. At the time of this book's writing, it appears that in most cases XML documents are being transformed server-side before delivery or are being used as data files to be displayed in an HTML document. Microsoft's approach to dealing with this was the use of XML data islands. We found that JavaScript could play a role there as well.

In the future, direct viewing and manipulation of XML documents will certainly become very important, but for now JavaScript developers should first master the DOM as it relates to HTML before proceeding to interact with XML. In doing so, their experiences should serve them well, since the interaction with and manipulation of documents given in other markup languages will be very similar.

ADVANCED TOPICS

The Complete Reference

Part VI

Real World JavaScript

The Complete Reference

Chapter 21

JavaScript Security

Although everyone agrees that to download and execute programs written by unknown parties is probably a bad idea, most users continue to do so on an alarmingly regular basis. The popularity of the Internet as a software distribution medium has given rise to an unprecedented number of virus-infected and Trojan horse-laden programs that are regularly downloaded and installed by unwary users. This type of security problem is almost always the direct result of bad judgement or carelessness on the part of the user and will probably never go away. However, new challenges are posed by the rise of mobile code such as Java and JavaScript. This code is transferred into the browser and automatically executed during the course of browsing the Web, generally without the user playing any part in the process. Because most users are not aware that Web sites are providing executable code as content, they remain oblivious to these risks. The risk of running malicious code that was once the result only of *explicit* user action is now posed by the more passive act of browsing the Web.

Creating effective security policies for mobile code is an exercise in balancing flexibility and utility against client security. On one hand, users would like to take advantage of the full power of their browser and operating system when running downloaded code. On the other hand, users would like to be protected from leakage or manipulation of data due to malicious or malfunctioning scripts. The simplest policy approach is binary in nature. Downloaded code is either given complete access to the user's environment or run with severe restrictions on the kinds of tasks it can request of the browser and operating system. Such an all-or-nothing policy forces the user to take an extreme position and lacks the flexibility afforded by a finer-grain control over code capabilities.

Browsers take the somewhat more mature approach of limiting JavaScript capabilities to reasonable Web-related tasks within the browser while allowing the user to expand those capabilities under certain conditions. In this chapter we discuss some fundamental aspects of the JavaScript security model as well as the features and problems inherent with its use.

The JavaScript Security Model

The modern JavaScript security model is based upon Java. In theory, downloaded scripts are run by default in a restricted "sandbox" environment that isolates them from the rest of the operating system. Scripts are permitted access only to data in the current document or closely related documents (generally those created by the current document). No access is granted to the local file system, memory space, or networking layer. Containment of this kind is designed to prevent malfunctioning or malicious scripts from wreaking havoc in the user's environment. The reality of the situation, however, is that often scripts are not contained as neatly as one would hope. There are numerous ways that a script can exercise power beyond what you might expect, both by design and by accident.

It is fundamental that there is no reason to trust randomly encountered mobile code, so such code should be executed as if it were hostile. Exceptions are made for authenticated code in the form of signed scripts. Such code is deemed partially trusted and allowed certain extended capabilities with the consent of the user. In addition, scripts can sometimes gain access to otherwise privileged information in other browser windows when the pages are closely related.

Same-Origin Policy

One of the primary JavaScript security policies is what is known as the same-origin policy. The *same-origin policy* prevents scripts loaded from one location from getting or setting properties of a document loaded from a different location. This policy prevents hostile code from one site from "taking over" or manipulating documents from another site. It also prevents hostile code from snooping on user activity occurring in different windows. The list of commonly protected properties is found in Table 21-1. Note that Table 1 lists the minimum amount of protection afforded. Some browser implementations may subject more properties to origin checks. Also note that scripts in layers are subject to origin checks when accessing other layers.

When a script attempts to access protected properties in a different window— for example, using the handle returned by **window.open()**—the browser performs a same-origin check. If the URLs pass the same-origin check, the property can be accessed. If they don't, an error is thrown.

The same-origin check consists of verifying that the URL of the document in the target window has the same "origin" as the calling script. Two documents have the same origin if they were loaded from the same server using the same protocol and port. For example, a script loaded from "http://www.domain.com/dir/page.html"can gain

Object	Properties	Protected From
history	all	reading and writing
image	lowsrc, src	reading and writing
layer	src	reading and writing
location	all except screen coordinates	reading and writing
window	find	invocation
document	anchors[], applets[], cookie, domain, elements[], embeds[], forms[] (and named forms), length, links[], referrer, title, URL, and any objects made available through LiveConnect	reading, writing, and invocation of methods
document	all others	writing

Table 21-1.   *Properties Subject to Origin Check*

access to any objects loaded from www.domain.com using HTTP. Table 21-2 shows the result of attempting to access windows containing various URLs, assuming that the accessing script was loaded from "http://www.domain.com/dir/page.html."

Consider the following example loaded from the local file system:

```
windowHandle = window.open("http://www.google.com", "Snoop Attempt");
var stolenURL = windowHandle.history.current;
```

This access attempt will fail because a local file fails the origin check not only on protocol (file:// versus http://) but on domain as well. The result in Internet Explorer (with scripting-error alerts turned on) is:

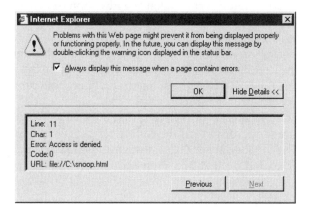

URL of Target Window	Result	Reason
http://www.domain.com/index.html	Success	Same domain and protocol
http://www.domain.com/other1/other2/index.html	Success	Same domain and protocol
http://www.domain.com:8080/dir/page.html	Failure	Different port
http://www2.domain.com/dir/page.html	Failure	Different domain
http://otherdomain.com/	Failure	Different domain
ftp://www.domain.com/	Failure	Different protocol

Table 21-2. *Result of Origin Check of Script at http://www.domain.com/dir/page.html*

There are a few issues to be aware of with regard to origin checks. First, Netscape 3 does not perform origin checks on forms accessed by name (for example, as *windowName.document.formName*). Second, you can set the **domain** property of the document in which your script resides to a more general domain, for example from "www.domain.com" to "domain.com." Doing so causes your script to pass origin checks when accessing URLs at "domain.com" from that point on. And finally, it is very important to note that instance properties of other windows are not protected. So a script at "www.otherdomain.com" can expose a form to any interested scripts by setting it as an instance property of its window:

```
window.exposedForm = document.forms[0];
```

A script of any other origin could then access it (assuming that it has a handle on the window) as:

```
windowHandle.exposedForm
```

The same-origin policy is very important from a user-privacy perspective. Without it, scripts in active documents from arbitrary domains could sit and snoop not only the URLs you visit, but the cookie values for each domain and form entries you make. However, the same-origin policy is far from perfect. Consider that one Web server often hosts numerous sites for unrelated parties. Typically, a URL might look like:

http://www.domain.com/~account/

But a script loaded from

http://www.domain.com/~otheraccount/

would be granted full access to the "http://www.domain.com/~account" pages if they are present in accessible windows. This occurrence might be rare, but it is a serious shortcoming of the same-origin policy.

Data Tainting

In an attempt to permit scripts more flexibility with regard to reading and writing properties in other windows, Netscape 3 included a feature known as data tainting. When enabled, *data tainting* permits scripts in one window to read values in another window, regardless of origin. Programmers have the option of marking properties, objects, and functions as tainted with the aptly named **taint()** method. Doing so prevents the submission of these values or any data derived from them to a server. The user is shown a dialog box that can prevent the submission of tainted values whenever an attempt is made to do so. Most sensitive properties of the browser are tainted by default. If the programmer wishes to allow unfettered submission of a value by scripts from other windows, the **untaint()** method is invoked on the property, object, or function in question. You could also check the status of data tainting with the **Navigator** object's method **taintEnabled()**, which returns a **Boolean** value indicating the state of data tainting.

When enabled, data tainting essentially allows all scripts access to all windows, as long as they do not attempt to send any values derived from other windows to a server, for example as a part of a form submission or URL. While this might seem like a good idea, data tainting was never widely used. One problem is that enabling it requires setting environmental variables in the user's operating system. There are other, deeper problems with this policy that were addressed by better approaches almost immediately, and data tainting consequently became a dead technology, existing only in Netscape 3. It was removed in Netscape 4 and never implemented by other browser vendors. The technology that replaced data tainting in version 4 browsers is known as *signed scripts*, a formidable topic that warrants a complete section of its own.

Signed Scripts

In order to provide some sense of confidence in mobile code, object signing technology was introduced in Internet Explorer 4 and Netscape 4 (IE 3 supported only a primitive form of object signing). Object signing is a technology that provides a digital guarantee of the origin of active content, such as ActiveX controls, plug-ins, Java applets, and JavaScripts. While Java and JavaScript are normally confined to the Java sandbox, signed objects are permitted to request specific extended capabilities, such as access to the local file system and full control over the browser. The idea is that because the origins of the code can be verified, users can grant the program extra capabilities not normally made available to code of questionable origin encountered while browsing.

Code signing goes beyond the binary all-or-nothing model of trust by allowing the user to grant or deny specific types of privileges on a case-by-case basis. This approach seems more robust in the sense that it allows the user to arbitrate privileges from closure of browser windows to full read/write access to the local file system.

As with all things Web-related, the major browser vendors took two different and incompatible approaches to the same idea and gave these approaches different names. Netscape calls its code signing technology *Object Signing*, whereas Microsoft calls its similar technology *Authenticode*. We have and will continue to refer to both technologies as "code signing," since they utilize the same principles to achieve the same goals. One important difference between the technologies is that Netscape supports signed JavaScript code, while Microsoft does not. Both support other types of signed embedded objects, such as applets and objects processed by plug-ins. The fact that Internet Explorer does not support signed JavaScript means that most of the applications using JavaScript found in this section apply only to Netscape 4+. However, as we mentioned, code-signing technology can be applied to applets, ActiveX controls, and plug-ins, so the same concepts are relevant to both browsers. If you need to use signed mobile code in Internet Explorer, the most common approach is to use signed applets or ActiveX controls and, if necessary, to control them using the LiveConnect principles discussed in Chapter 18.

Fundamentals

Understanding the mechanics of signed scripts requires a basic grasp of some ideas from modern cryptography. At the heart of the issue is the notion of public key cryptography. Traditional *private key cryptography* requires that two users wishing to communicate privately share a digital "key" used to scramble their transmissions. Since no other parties know the key, any third party that intercepts their communications cannot "unlock" the encrypted data. *Public key cryptography* uses two keys, one for encryption (think "scrambling") and one for decryption (think "descrambling"). Something encrypted with the "public key" can be decrypted only with the corresponding "private key," and vice versa. This allows an entity to publish its public key so that anyone can encrypt data for it. However, only the entity holding the secret key can unlock the transmissions—the data cannot be recovered with the public key alone. It might be hard to believe that a system can exist where one key scrambles the data and another recovers it, but some nice applications of higher mathematics have made it a reality.

The relevance of public key cryptography is that it enables the use of digital signatures. A *digital signature* is just what it sounds like: a digital "stamp" on a piece of data, for example Java or JavaScript code, that can be used to authenticate its origin. The idea is to have entities like browser vendors, content providers, major corporations, and even individual developers sign any code that requires special privileges. Since users can be guaranteed the origin of a particular piece of code, they can (presumably) make a more informed decision whether to run it or not. For example, you might choose to grant extra privileges to something signed by "Netscape Corporation" but choose to deny them to something signed by "31337@unknown-company-that-might-steal-my-credit-card.com."

In addition to providing *authenticity*, digital signatures guarantee data integrity. *Data integrity* means that you can be sure that the item has not been tampered with since it was signed. Even modifying just one character in a signed object will ruin the integrity of its signature. The idea here is to ensure that code signed by a trusted entity, for example a major corporation, cannot be modified to produce malicious behavior after it is signed.

Digital signatures are based upon public key cryptography used "in reverse." An entity uses its secret key to create a digital signature for an object. Anyone (or any browser, in this context) holding the corresponding public key can then verify that the object was indeed signed by the holder of the secret key, but no one save the secret key holder can generate valid signatures. The important part of this process is how browsers know what entity is associated with what secret key. For example, it is useless to know that a script you have downloaded was signed with a particular secret key without knowing whom that key belongs to. The answer to this problem is that trusted parties known as certification authorities carry out the binding of keys to identities. A *certification authority* (CA) is an independent third party that exists for the sole purpose of verifying the identity of private key holders.

An entity wishing to sign its own scripts (or other objects) creates a public/private key pair and submits the public key to the CA for certification. The CA verifies the identity of the applicant and issues a certificate consisting of the applicant's public key and identifying information signed by the CA's private key. Since all browsers (presumably) come preloaded with the public keys of trusted CAs, they can authenticate any signed code that comes with a certificate. The process works as follows:

1. When a client receives a signed script from some entity, the entity includes its certificate if the client does not yet have it.

2. The client checks the CA signature on the certificate for validity.

3. If the CA signature is valid, the client knows that the public key included in the certificate can be used to authenticate signatures made by the entity identified in the certificate.

4. The signature on the object is then checked with the entity's public key.

To put it more concisely, the authentication process has two distinct steps. The client first authenticates the identity of the signing entity by checking the CA signature on the signer's certificate. Then the client checks the signature on the object itself to make sure that the entity's signature is indeed valid.

Certificates

There are a number of authorities that provide certification services. The most popular are VeriSign (**http://www.verisign.com**) and Thawte (**http://www.thawte.com**); both are now part of the same company. The public keys of these CAs (and others) come built into most browsers. For example, to see a list of CA certificates installed in Netscape 6, from the Tasks menu select Privacy and Security, then Security Manager and click on the Certificates tab on the top and then the Authorities tab on the left. A typical list of CAs in Netscape 6 is shown in Figure 21-1. In Internet Explorer go to the Tools menu and

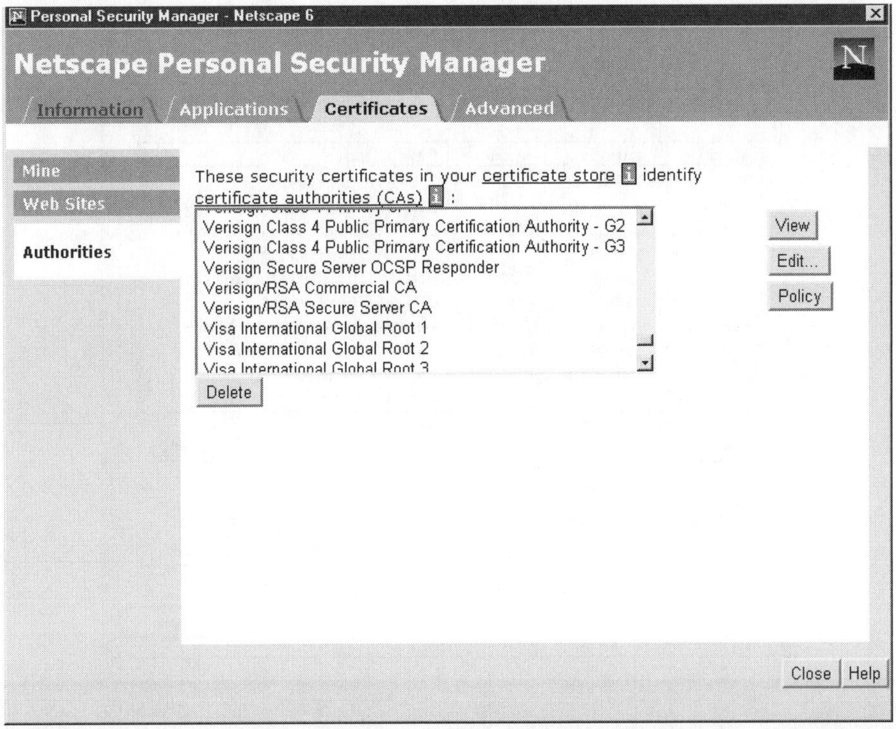

Figure 21-1. *Typical list of Certification Authorities in Netscape 6*

REAL WORLD JAVASCRIPT

select Internet Options and click on the Content tab. Use the Certificates button and then select the "Trusted Certification." A typical list of CAs in Internet Explorer is shown in Figure 21-2, and a typical certificate is shown in Figure 21-3.

Developers commonly purchase individual developer certificates for prices anywhere between fifty and several hundred dollars. These certificates are compatible with most code-signing software and are useful for personal or freelance development. If you are writing scripts for a corporate entity or scripts that will be distributed as part of some official company release, it is more appropriate for your organization to invest in an "official" company-wide certificate. Such certificates cost anywhere from several hundred to several thousand dollars. You can even invest in certificates insured by Lloyd's of London against economic loss due to subversion, but these run in the tens or hundreds of thousands of dollars. Most often, the group or individual responsible for handling SSL certificates (for secure Web servers) for your site can also handle code-signing certificates, since the application process is essentially the same.

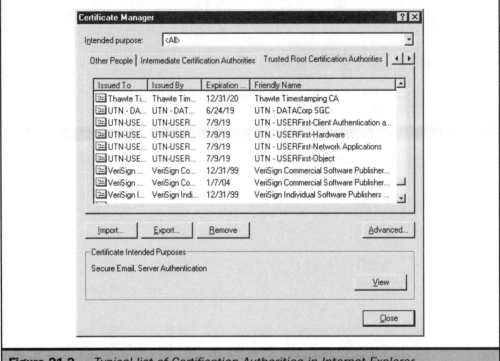

Figure 21-2. *Typical list of Certification Authorities in Internet Explorer*

Creating and Including Signed Scripts

Netscape Signing Tool is the command line program used to create signed scripts and is available for most major platforms including Windows, Linux, and Solaris. You can download it at **http://developer.netscape.com/software/signedobj/jarpack.html**. When used from Windows 9x, you will need to run the tool from the DOS prompt.

If you do not have a certificate or for other reasons would like to use a faux certificate for testing purposes, Signing Tool allows you to do so. Follow these steps to create your own test certificate:

1. Make sure Netscape is not running.

2. Locate the two files key3.db and cert7.db on the machine in which the Signing Tool and Netscape 4+ are installed. They will most likely be located in a subdirectory of the directory in which Netscape or Mozilla is installed. Copy the files into the directory in which Signing Tool is installed (or another directory of your choice, if the path to Signing Tool is included in your environment).

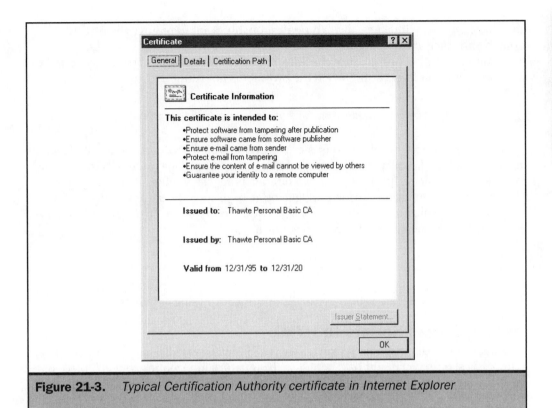

Figure 21-3.   *Typical Certification Authority certificate in Internet Explorer*

3. Type **signtool -G Test -d .**

4. Answer the questions in a reasonable fashion. The "Test" portion of the previous command specifies a nickname for the new certificate, and the second parameter specifies where it should be generated ("." means "in this directory"). If you receive an authentication error, you need to password-protect your certificates. To do so in Netscape 4.x, use the Security button of the browser and then select Passwords. In Netscape 6 use the Tasks menu, then the Password Manager menu, and select Change Personal Security Password. After you have set a password, you will need to recopy the .db files into the directory.

5. Check your certificate by typing: **signtool -l -k Test -d .**

6. Copy cert7.db back to its original location, replacing the original file.

The last step adds your certificate to the list of trusted authorities under Netscape 4 (you will have to import your certificate separately in Netscape 6). This step is necessary because the test certificate hasn't been signed by a real CA, so the browser won't view any objects signed with it as valid. You will probably want to remove the certificate from the browser once you've finished testing.

You can also disable signature checking completely by adding the following line to your JavaScript preferences file when the browser is not running:

```
user_pref("signed.applets.codebase_principal_support", true);
```

The preference file is called prefs.js or preferences.js in UNIX and is usually located in the Netscape or Mozilla installation directory or in ~/.netscape under UNIX. Adding this line allows *any* script to request extended privileges, whether it is signed or not. This feature is often useful during the development process, because you do not have to continually regenerate signatures for files as you modify them. To disable this feature, quit the browser and change the previous line to:

```
user_pref("signed.applets.codebase_principal_support", false);
```

Be sure to disable it before returning to your normal browsing activities!

Binding Signed Scripts to HTML

When you sign a document, a Java Archive (JAR) file is created. This file contains any external .js scripts you might have along with signature information for each piece of JavaScript in your page. The JAR file is linked to any HTML tags in the document that involve JavaScript. There are two important attributes that are used to bind HTML to signatures: **archive** and **id**. The **archive** attribute specifies the JAR file containing the signature of the JavaScript associated with that tag. The **id** attribute specifies the unique name for the element and is used to look up signature information in the JAR file. We'll see how to create the JAR files in a moment, but first let's discuss in a bit more detail how they are bound to HTML.

If a **<script>** tag is used to link in a JavaScript library, the script is stored along with its signature in the JAR file. The **archive** attribute of the element should be set to the appropriate JAR file, but its **src** attribute also needs to be specified so that the browser knows which script to retrieve. For example, to link to an external JavaScript library named myscript.js contained in the file signed.jar, you would write:

```
<script language="JavaScript" type="text/javascript" src="myscript.js"
archive="signed.jar"></script>
```

JavaScript found directly in the page also utilizes the **archive** attribute, but only its signature is stored in the JAR file.

Any JavaScript that is not found in an external library must have its **id** attribute set to a unique value. So, to link signature information found in signed.jar to an inline script you would write:

```
<script language="JavaScript" type="text/javascript"
archive="signed.jar" id="a">
alert("Hello world");
</script>
```

The actual value of the **id** doesn't matter; the important thing is that it needs to be unique, so the browser knows which signature to compare the code against.

Whenever the **archive** attribute is omitted from a **<script>** tag and whenever JavaScript is associated with an event handler, Netscape uses the most recent **archive** attribute found in the page. For example, you might write:

```
<script language="JavaScript" type="text/javascript"
archive="signed.jar" id="a">
alert("Hello world");
</script>
<script language="JavaScript" type="text/javascript" id="b">
alert("I'm also signed");
</script>
<a href="index.html" onclick="alert('So am I!')" id="c">Try me</a>
```

When Netscape sees the first **<script>** it looks up the digital signature for *a* in signed.jar. It compares this signature against the code contained in the tags to validate its authenticity and integrity. When the second **<script>** is parsed, Netscape notes the lack of attribute and uses **signed.jar** as the default. It looks up the signature for *b* in the JAR file and checks the contained code. Finally, the event handler code contained in the **<a>** tag is compared against the digital signature for *c* in **signed.jar**. If all of these scripts are valid, the page is considered "signed."

The important part of the previous example is that every element containing JavaScript was given the required unique **id**. Even elements containing innocuous JavaScript that does not require extended privileges must be signed. Because code signing is an all-or-nothing affair, you will need to include unique **id** attributes for every tag that is associated with JavaScript. The one exception to this rule is JavaScript used with the pseudo-URL syntax. This is the only kind of JavaScript that cannot be signed, and its use should be strictly avoided in signed pages.

Signing Your Code

So, how are JAR files created in the first place? The answer is that the Signing Tool automatically creates them. The Signing Tool will generate the .jar files referenced in the archive attributes of your document as they are signed. To sign your scripts and generate the JAR files follow these steps:

1. Modify your HTML to include the required **id** and **archive** attributes, choosing an appropriate name for the JAR file.

2. Copy the HTML file and any external .js libraries containing JavaScript that must be signed into a subdirectory under the Signing Tool.

3. Run Signing Tool as follows, where *Name* is the nickname of the certificate to use and *dir* is the name of the subdirectory in which your files were placed in step two:

```
signtool -k Name -J dir
```

4. Verify that valid signatures were generated as follows, where *jarfile* is the name of the JAR file referenced in your HTML:

```
signtool -v dir/jarfile.jar
```

5. Copy your files, *including the .jar file*, from the subdirectory to their appropriate place in the Web server file system.

You can use multiple JAR files in the same page to facilitate the reuse of code that changes rarely without having to regenerate signatures for each new page. Additionally, you can use the same JAR files for signatures for JavaScript in multiple HTML files so long as the code contained in the page is exactly the same as the code from which the signatures were generated. More details about the Signing Tool can be found at **http://developer.netscape.com/docs/manuals/signedobj/signtool/signtool.htm**.

Essential Aspects of HTML Bindings

To recap, each **<script>** tag in the page requires:

- An **archive** attribute whose value is the name of the JAR file that contains the script's digital signature. If you do not include an **archive** attribute, Netscape uses the **archive** attribute from an earlier script on the same page.

- Either an **id** attribute whose value is a unique string that associates the script with a digital signature in the JAR file or an **src** attribute that retrieves a script from the JAR file.

Additionally, every element that is associated with JavaScript through an event handler is required to have:

- An **id** attribute whose value is a unique string that associates the script with a digital signature in the JAR file.

- A **<script>** tag with an appropriate **archive** attribute at some previous point in the document so that Netscape knows where the signatures are to be found.

REAL WORLD
JAVASCRIPT

As a final note, you should be aware that scripts served over a secure (HTTPS) connection are automatically considered signed by the certificate of the Web server from which they were retrieved. This feature provides an easy way to use signed scripts without going through the hassle of manual code modification and signing.

Utilizing Signed Script Privileges

As mentioned earlier in the chapter, the JavaScript security model is based on that of Java. This connection is more than just theoretical; the way that signed scripts gain extended capabilities is through interaction with real Java classes included with the browser's virtual machine. Luckily, you don't need to know anything about Java to use them.

A signed script must request the capability to use an extended privilege before it can be used. This request phase gives the user the opportunity to selectively grant and deny different types of capabilities, thereby providing the fine-grain access control mentioned earlier. Privileges are grouped according to their characteristics and must be requested separately. For example, read/write access to the local file system requires requesting a different capability than being able to modify browser window characteristics. These different classes of capabilities are called *targets*, and some of the most useful are listed in Table 21-3. A full list, including macro targets that grant multiple privileges with one request, can be found at **http://developer.netscape.com/docs/ manuals/signedobj/capabilities/01cap.htm**.

Examination of Table 21-3 should scare the living daylights out of you. Signed scripts have the potential to erase your hard drive, read arbitrary files, and even set up a server on your machine. The power that signed scripts can have over your computer is the reason they are granted specific privileges only with the assent of the user.

Target	Provides
UniversalAwtEventQueueAccess	Ability to monitor or intercept mouse and typing events
UniversalBrowserRead	Read access to browser data such as the **History** object
UniversalBrowserWrite	Write access to browser data such as window characteristics
UniversalConnect	Ability to open network connections from the client machine

Table 21-3. *Some Useful Privilege Targets for Signed Scripts*

Target	Provides
UniversalExecAccess	Ability to execute arbitrary programs on the client machine
UniversalExitAccess	Ability to cause browser execution to terminate, effectively quitting the browser
UniversalFileDelete	Ability to delete files on any file system accessible to the user
UniversalFileRead	Ability to read arbitrary files on the client machine
UniversalFileWrite	Ability to modify arbitrary files on the client machine
UniversalListen	Ability to listen for network connections on the client machine, effectively acting as a server
UniversalMulticast	Ability to perform multicast broadcasts over the network from the client machine
UniversalPrintJobAccess	Ability to initiate printing from the browser
UniversalPropertyRead	Ability to read operating system properties of the user environment—for example, the current working directory
UniversalPropertyWrite	Ability to modify properties of the user environment, for example security policy settings
UniversalSendMail	Ability to send e-mail from any e-mail program associated with the browser
UniversalSystemClipboardAccess	Ability to read and write from the desktop clipboard

Table 21-3. *Some Useful Privilege Targets for Signed Scripts* (continued)

To request a privilege, the **enablePrivilege()** method is used. It is invoked through the browser's security monitor as:

```
netscape.security.PrivilegeManager.enablePrivilege("targetName");
```

where *targetName* is the name of the target privilege. For example, to request write access to browser window characteristics, you request the *UniversalBrowserWrite* target:

```
netscape.security.PrivilegeManager.enablePrivilege("UniversalBrowserWrite");
```

If the user has not previously granted your script this privilege, the browser prompts the user as to whether or not it should be granted. A sample of this dialog box in Netscape 4 using a test certificate created with Object Signer is shown in Figure 21-4. The user can examine the signed script's certificate at this time by pressing the Certificate button. The certificate in Netscape 4 is shown in Figure 21-5.

Extended privileges are relinquished using the **disablePrivilege()** method invoked in the same manner as **enablePrivilege()**:

```
netscape.security.PrivilegeManager.disablePrivilege("targetName");
```

Because a user is prompted for confirmation or denial of target access once per session, you can disable, then reenable previously granted privileges at any time without the browser prompting the user again. Disabling privileges as soon as you are done with them is a good idea, because doing so minimizes the possibility of something going awry while your script holds extended access. Remember, the script is signed in the name of you or your company, so even unintentionally malicious behavior can result in undesirable consequences.

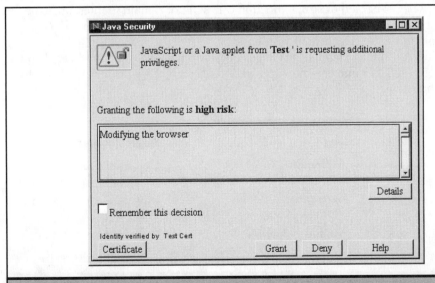

Figure 21-4.   *Dialog box notifying the user of the request for UniversalBrowserWrite*

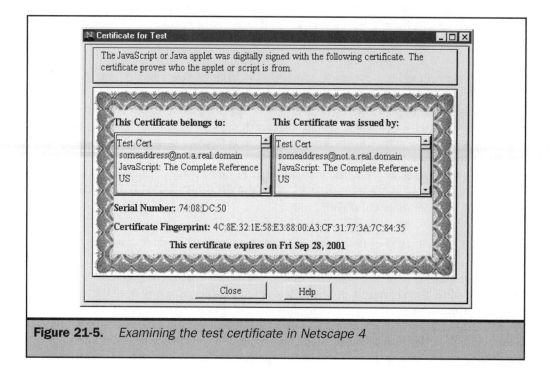

Figure 21-5. *Examining the test certificate in Netscape 4*

One important issue is that granted privileges persist only in the local scope. For example, a privilege enabled during a function call will not remain granted once the function returns. This rarely poses a significant problem, but it is something to keep in mind when planning the structure of your code.

What you do with the extended privileges once you have them depends on the task at hand. Table 21-4 lists some common applications of signed scripts, but the list is by no means exhaustive.

Task	Uses	Target Required
Reading browser preferences	**preference()**	UniversalPreferencesRead
Setting browser preferences	**preference()**	UniversalPreferencesWrite
Modifying window appearance	**Window** properties	UniversalBrowserWrite

Table 21-4. *Common Applications of Signed Scripts*

Task	Uses	Target Required
Capturing events in other windows	**window.enableExternalCapture()**	UniversalBrowserWrite
Closing a window unconditionally	**window.close()**	UniversalBrowserWrite
Moving a window offscreen	**window.moveBy()**, **window.moveTo()**	UniversalBrowserWrite
Creating a window that is always raised, always lowered, or offscreen	**window.open()**	UniversalBrowserWrite
Resizing a window to smaller than 100x100 pixels	**window.resizeBy()**, **window.resizeTo()**	UniversalBrowserWrite
Examining session history	**History**	UniversalBrowserRead

Table 21-4.   *Common Applications of Signed Scripts* (continued)

An example of a signed script that writes out the contents of the normally protected **History** object is shown here:

```
<!DOCTYPE HTML PUBLIC "-//W3C//DTD HTML 4.01 Transitional//EN"
                    "http://www.w3.org/TR/html4/loose.dtd">
<html>
<head>
<title>Signed Script History Example</title>
</head>
<body>
<h2>The sites you've visited</h2>
<script language="JavaScript" type="text/javascript"
archive="signed.jar" id="a">
<!--
netscape.security.PrivilegeManager.enablePrivilege("UniversalBrowserRead");
for (var i=0; i < history.length; i++)
   document.write(history[i] + "<br>");
netscape.security.PrivilegeManager.disablePrivilege("UniversalBrowserRead");
// -->
</script>
</body>
</html>
```

The output in Netscape 6 is shown in Figure 21-6.

For another example, see Chapter 17, where we present an example of using the privilege manager to set a person's home page. For even more information about the capabilities of signed scripts and how they are used, the following Web sites might be helpful:

- http://developer.netscape.com/docs/manuals/communicator/jssec/contents.htm
- http://www.mozilla.org/projects/security/components/jssec.html
- http://developer.netscape.com/viewsource/goodman_sscripts.html

Practical Considerations

The identification process undertaken when a certification request is made of a CA can vary wildly. Personal certificates sometimes require only the submission of a valid e-mail address. Other types of certificates require the submission of proof of incorporation, domain name ownership, or official state and country identification cards. So the guarantee that comes with a CA certificate varies depending upon the type of certificate and CA used. You can even create your own certification authority and issue certificates to yourself or others.

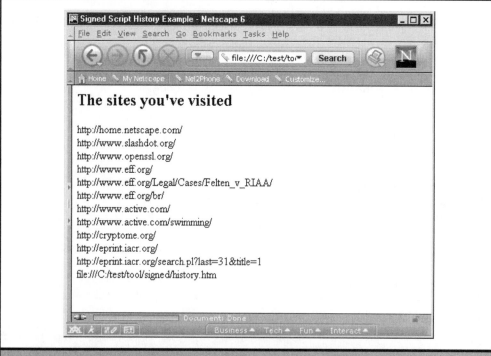

Figure 21-6.   *Using a signed script to access session history information*

In addition, if you think about the signature verification process for a bit, you will realize that *digital signatures do not guarantee anything at all with regard to security.* They merely guarantee that at some point someone with access to the private key signed the given object. They do not guarantee anything at all about the worthiness of the signed object to be run. It is entirely possible for a signed object to contain malicious code, either intentionally or as an oversight. In fact, just months into the new millennium, VeriSign mistakenly issued a certificate for "Microsoft Corporation" to crackers impersonating Microsoft employees. You can read about this unfortunate gaffe in Microsoft Security Bulletin MS01-017.

Developers should realize that for these reasons some users may be unwilling to grant privileges to signed code, no matter what signature it bears. Defensive programming tactics should be employed to accommodate this possibility. For example, it is always a good idea to catch denials of privilege requests. A **try/catch** statement allows you to trap any errors that occur when a block of code is executed. The **try** block encloses the code to be executed, and the **catch** block defines the action to take when an error is thrown. For example, to catch a request denial you might use something like:

```
function doBrowserRead()
{try
{
Netscape.security.PrivilegeManager.enablePrivilege("UniversalBrowserRead");
    } catch (theError)
{alert("This functionality requires that you grant access privileges to
the script.");
      return;
    }
    // do actions that require UniversalBrowserRead
    // ...
netscape.security.PrivilegeManager.disablePrivilege("UniversalBrowserRead");
}
```

Security Problems with JavaScript

JavaScript has a long and inglorious history of atrocious security holes. Fire up your favorite browser, head to your favorite search engine, and search for "JavaScript vulnerability"—you should find thousands of results. Of course, this is not an indication of the exact number of security holes in browsers, but it does give a rough idea of the magnitude of the problem. Such vulnerabilities range from relatively harmless oversights to serious holes that permit access to local files, cookies, or network capabilities.

But security problems with JavaScript are not limited to implementation errors. There are numerous ways in which scripts can affect the user's execution environment without violating any security policies.

Bombing Browsers with JavaScript

The amount of resources a browser is granted on the client machine is largely a function of its operating system. Unfortunately, most operating systems (including Windows 95 and 98) will continue to allocate CPU cycles and memory beyond what may be reasonable for the application. It is all too easy to write JavaScript that will crash the browser, both by design and by accident.

The content of the next several sections is designed to illustrate some of the main problems browsers have with denial of service attacks, with the "service" in this case being access to an operating system that behaves normally. The results will vary from platform to platform, but running any one of these scripts has the potential to crash not only the browser but also your operating system itself.

Infinite Loops

By far the most simplistic (and obvious) way to cause unwanted side effects is to enter an infinite loop, a loop whose exit condition is never fulfilled. Some modern browsers will catch and halt the execution of the most obvious, but seldom would they stop something like:

```
function tag()
{
    you_are_it();
}
function you_are_it()
{
    tag();
}
tag();
```

Infinite loops can arise in a variety of ways but are often unstoppable once they have begun. While most infinite loops eat up cycles performing the same work over and over, some, like the preceding one, have a voracious appetite for memory.

Memory Hogs

One of the easiest ways to crash a browser is to eat up all the available memory. For example, the infamous *doubling string* grows exponentially in size, crashing many browsers within seconds:

```
var adiosAmigo = "Sayanora, sucker.";
while (1)
    adiosAmigo += adiosAmigo;
```

You can also fill up the memory that the operating system has available to keep track of recursive function calls. On many systems, invoking the following code will result in a "stack overflow" or similar panic condition:

```
function recurse()
{
    var x = 1;

    // you can fill up extra space with data which must be pushed
    // on the stack but mostly we just want to call the function
    // recursively
    recurse();
}
```

You can even try writing self-replicating code to eat up browser memory by placing the following in a **<script>** in the document **<head>**:

```
function doitagain()
{
    document.write("<scrip" + "t>doitagain()</scrip"+"t>");
}
doitagain();
```

Using the Browser Functionality

A popular variation on the theme is a script that writes **<frameset>** elements referencing itself, thereby creating an infinite recursion of document fetches. This prevents any user action because the browser is too busy fetching pages to field user interface events.

Similarly, you can open up an endless series of dialog boxes:

```
function askmeagain()
{
    alert("Ouch!");
    askmeagain();
}
```

or continually call **window.open()** until the client's resources are exhausted.

Deceptive Practices

The ease with which developers can send browsers to the grave is only the tip of the iceberg. Often deceptive programming tactics are employed to trick or annoy users in one way or another. One of the most common approaches is to create a small, minimized window and immediately send it to the background by bringing the original window into **focus()**. The secondary window then sets an interval timer that spawns popup ads on a regular basis. The secondary window comes equipped with an event handler that will **blur()** it when it receives focus and an **onunload** handler to respawn it in the unlikely event that the user can actually close it.

In Chapter 23 we discuss a technology found in Internet Explorer 5+ known as "DHTML Behaviors." Behaviors have very powerful capabilities, including the ability to modify browser settings. The simplest example of deceptive use of DHTML Behaviors is attempting to trick a user into changing the default home page of their browser:

```
<a onclick="this.style.behavior='url(#default#homepage)';
this.setHomePage('http://www.somedomain.com')" href="">
Click here to see our list of products</a>
```

Often sites will pop up windows or dialog boxes disguised to look like alerts from the operating system. When clicked or given data, they exhibit all manner of behavior, from initiating downloads of hostile ActiveX controls to stealing passwords.

Possibly the biggest threat comes from developers who have found ways to create unopenable or offscreen windows. Though the authors' karma will undoubtedly suffer for mentioning it, the following code will often help keep a window unseen:

```
window.moveBy(-1000000,-1000000);
```

When combined with an **oncontextmenu** handler, a disabling of the context menu (if you find it), vulnerability sniffing routines, and a popup ad generator, such a window can be exceedingly dangerous, not to mention unbelievably annoying. Variations include having a window attempt to imitate a user's desktop and always stay raised, tiling the desktop with a quilt of banner ads covering all usable space, or playing the ever popular spawning window game, annoying the unsuspecting user by creating more windows mysteriously from offscreen hidden windows.

Developer Responsibility

We have only scratched the surface of the security problems posed by JavaScript and related technologies. By now it should be clear that an unscrupulous programmer could adversely affect the user's execution environment in myriad ways. These are issues that every JavaScript developer should be aware of. Ignoring these problems will not make them go away. Use of any one of these or other questionable tactics is usually a clear indication that the site is up to something dishonest or at least that the programmer cares nothing for the quality of user browsing experience. At the risk of sounding trite, we would advise that it is up to individual developers to use the power afforded by JavaScript in a responsible manner. Abusing this power when writing code for a public Web site is inconsiderate at best, and in some cases downright unethical.

Summary

The JavaScript security model is based on the Java sandbox. Scripts run in a restricted execution environment without access to local file systems, user data, or network capabilities. The *same-origin policy* prevents scripts from one site from reading properties of windows loaded from a different location. The *signed script policy* allows digitally signed mobile code to request special privileges from the user. This technology guarantees code authenticity and integrity, but it does not guarantee functionality or the absence of malicious behavior. Both Netscape and Internet Explorer 4 are capable of using signed code, but Internet Explorer does not support signed JavaScript. Instead, ActiveX controls are commonly utilized to perform privileged operations and are often driven using LiveConnect technology. Code signing involves the acquisition of a certificate from a trusted certification authority and the use of code signing software, for example Netscape's Signing Tool. Digital signatures are bound to JavaScript with **id** attributes in the elements that contain the script. Signatures and externally linked JavaScript libraries are contained in Java Archive (JAR) files that must be published along with the signed code. The browser knows which JAR file to consult when verifying authenticity and integrity through the **archive** attribute of **<script>** elements.

Signed scripts access extended privileges through a Java interface and may be granted or denied access by the user. Although signed scripts can be very useful, many users will refuse to grant them privileges out of well-founded security fears. As a result, signed scripts should always be written in a defensive manner to accommodate this possibility.

JavaScript can be used to wreak havoc on the user's browser and operating system without even violating the security policies of the browser. Simple code that eats up memory or other resources can quickly crash the browser and even the operating system itself. Deceptive programming practices can be employed to annoy or trick the user into actions they might not intend. Because of this, it is up to individual developers to take the responsibility to write clean, careful code that improves the user experience.

Chapter 22

Netscape Extensions
and Considerations

W hile not as common as they were in their heyday, Netscape browsers are still very popular with Web users, second only in deployment to versions of Microsoft Internet Explorer at the time of this writing. Even with its recent decline, Netscape is still an extremely popular browser, particularly with users of non-Windows operating systems, such as Solaris and Linux. Therefore, an awareness of some of the issues and extended capabilities involved with programming for Netscape browsers is often helpful. This chapter discusses some aspects of JavaScript that are particular to Netscape and related browsers such as Mozilla. Since Netscape has been a prime motivator for ECMAScript, some details about ECMAScript versions are included in this chapter as well. A similar treatment for Internet Explorer's JScript and browser extensions follows in Chapter 23.

Core Language Issues

With a few exceptions, Netscape incorporates JavaScript language improvements into major releases of new browser versions. Netscape refers to its implementation of the language as "JavaScript x" where x identifies the language version number. Table 22-1 shows the correspondence between language and browser versions.

JavaScript 1.0, the first JavaScript implementation, was included as a part of Netscape 2 and formed the loose basis for ECMAScript, the standard for the core language features of JavaScript. Other versions of Netscape JavaScript correspond to the ECMAScript standard in varying degrees. The correspondence between Netscape JavaScript and ECMAScript is shown in Table 22-2.

It is sometimes necessary to write JavaScript to accommodate the capabilities of a specific range of browsers. To do so, you need to make sure that you use only language features available in the browsers of interest; for example you will need to avoid using **Number.MAX_VALUE** in Netscape 2 because it was introduced in JavaScript 1.1.

Language Version	Browser Version
JavaScript 1.0	Netscape 2
JavaScript 1.1	Netscape 3
JavaScript 1.2	Netscape 4.0-4.05
JavaScript 1.3	Netscape 4.06-4.7
JavaScript 1.4	None (server-side only)
JavaScript 1.5	Netscape 6, Mozilla 0.9
JavaScript 2.0	Future versions of Netscape and Mozilla

Table 22-1.   *Relationship Between JavaScript Language and Browser Versions*

Netscape Version	Standard Version	Exceptions
JavaScript 1.0–1.2	Very loose conformance to ECMA-262 Edition 1	Many, especially with the **Date** object, and many extra features
JavaScript 1.3	Strict conformance to ECMA-262 Edition 1	Includes some extra features
JavaScript 1.4	Strict conformance to ECMA-262 Edition 1	Includes some extra features
JavaScript 1.5	Strict conformance to ECMA-262 Edition 3	Includes some extra features
JavaScript 2.0	Planned conformance to ECMA-262 Edition 4	Unknown

Table 22-2.   *Relationship Between Netscape JavaScript and ECMAScript*

Complete documentation of which core ECMAScript features are found in which browser and language version can be found in Appendix B. Information about proprietary Netscape extensions can be found later in this chapter. In addition, there are several Web sites that are very useful for researching compliance and the language standards themselves. Netscape maintains its JavaScript reference in the "Documentation" section of **http://developer.netscape.com**. References to the ECMAScript standard are included in the JavaScript portion of the Mozilla project at **http://www.mozilla.org/js/language/**.

In the remainder of this section we will discuss some of the major differences between versions of Netscape's JavaScript. If you are having trouble with one of your scripts under older browsers, you might check for differences in behavior in core language support.

JavaScript 1.1

The majority of new features in Netscape 3 were browser-related—for example, the **applets[ ]** and other **Document** objects and collections mentioned in Chapter 9. The changes from core JavaScript 1.0 include

- Addition of the constants **Number.MAX_VALUE**, **Number.MIN_VALUE**, **Number.NaN**, **Number.POSITIVE_INFINITY**, and **Number.NEGATIVE_ INFINITY**.

- Inclusion of the **prototype** property for all objects, permitting the prototype-based object-oriented features discussed in Chapter 6.

- New methods for **Array**: **sort()**, **join()**, and **reverse()**.
- Addition of the **split()** method and the **String()** constructor to **String**.
- Better type support. Added capability to convert objects to primitive values with the new **valueOf()** method of each object. Addition of the **typeof** and **void** operators.
- Added ability to index arrays with strings (that is, by element name).
- Widespread problem fixes with **isNan()**, **parseFloat()**, and **parseInt()**.

Full documentation of JavaScript 1.1 (and Netscape 3) can be found at **http://home. netscape.com/eng/mozilla/3.0/handbook/javascript/**.

JavaScript 1.2

JavaScript 1.2 (introduced with Netscape 4.x browsers) included massive changes both in the browser capabilities and in core language features.

- Many new **Array** methods: **concat()**, **pop()**, **push()**, **shift()**, **unshift()**, **slice()**, and **splice()**. Fixed bugs with **sort()**.
- Nested functions.
- Many new **String** methods: **charCodeAt()**, **concat()**, **fromCharCode()**, **match()**, **replace()**, **search()**, **slice()**, and **substr()**. Additionally, many behavioral changes to **split()** and **substring()** (see Appendix B).
- Ability to **watch()** and **unwatch()** objects for a change in property values.
- The **eval()** method is now global (rather than a property of each object).
- Ability to use object and array literal notation.
- Addition of the implicitly filled **arguments** property of functions, as well as the **arity** property for **Function** objects.
- Ability to **delete** object properties and array elements.
- Regular expressions (including the **RegExp** object).
- Support for **do/while** and **switch** statements.
- Equality operators do not type-convert before comparison.

A more complete list of new language and browser features for JavaScript 1.2 and Netscape 4.0 can be found at: **http://developer.netscape.com/docs/manuals/ communicator/jsguide/contents.htm**.

JavaScript 1.3

As previously noted, JavaScript 1.3 is the first version of Netscape JavaScript to strictly conform to the ECMAScript standard. In some ways, Netscape JavaScript was "behind" in conformance (even though Netscape "invented" the language), so the behavior of a large number of objects had to be modified in this version. In other ways, Netscape JavaScript was "ahead" in conformance—in the sense that many language features that would be added to later editions of ECMA-262 were already available in Netscape browsers. Regular expression support is one such example: it was first included in the 3rd Edition of ECMA-262, while it was available in Netscape's JavaScript 1.2.

Some major changes in core language features in JavaScript 1.3 are listed here. Note that most of these changes were necessitated for ECMAScript conformance.

- Unicode support. Unicode is used for character representation (rather than Latin-1), so strings may contain Unicode escape sequences.

- The addition of the global **isFinite()** function and **Infinity**, **NaN**, and **undefined** constants.

- Normal equality operators (== and !=) now perform automatic type conversion before comparison (previous versions have a variety of behavior).

- The addition of strict equality operators (=== and !==).

- Changes in **Array** behavior: a numeric parameter to the constructor is interpreted as the initial array length. The **push()** method returns the length of the new array (not the last element). The **splice()** method always returns an array (even if only one element was removed). The **toString()** method returns a comma-separated string of array elements (rather than the literal representation of the array).

- Massive changes to **Date** to bring it into line with ECMA-262.

- The addition of **apply()** and **call()** methods to all functions, and the removal of the implicitly set **arguments.caller** property of each **Function**.

- The inclusion of the **toSource()** method for each object.

- Serious changes to conditionals. Using assignment instead of comparison in a conditional throws an error (rather than silently undergoing conversion to comparison). Additionally, anything with a value other than **undefined** or **null** compares **true** to an object in a conditional.

JavaScript 1.4

JavaScript 1.4 was available only for server-side JavaScript. It never saw the light of day in a browser. It includes some new features, such as the **in** and **instanceof** operators. Aside from changes to LiveConnect behavior, the only interesting aspect of this version is that it is the first implementation of JavaScript that supports **try**/**catch** clauses for exception handling. More about this rare version of JavaScript can be found at **http://developer.netscape.com/docs/manuals/js/core/jsguide14/index.htm**.

JavaScript 1.5

JavaScript 1.5 conforms to ECMA-262 Edition 3, the latest version of the ECMAScript standard. Therefore, many of the changes to core JavaScript in this version were made in accommodation of the standard. Some of the most interesting changes are listed here.

■ Although exception handling with **try/catch** constructs was added in JavaScript 1.4, this is the first browser version of JavaScript where they are available. Runtime errors are also reported as exceptions beginning with this version. For more information about exception handling, see Chapter 24.

■ Constants can be defined with the **const** keyword. It is used in place of **var**, for example, **const x = 10;** places 10 in *x* as an immutable value (try it in Netscape 6!).

■ So-called "getters" and "setters" are supported. These are object methods accessed as properties providing a special value computed at access time. See **http:// developer.netscape.com/docs/manuals/js/core/jsguide15/obj.html#1018325** for more information.

■ Conditional function declarations were added. The questionable practice of declaring functions in the body of a conditional statement was permitted.

■ Enhancements to regular expressions (for example, non-greedy quantifiers, positive/negative look-ahead, and non-capturing parentheses).

■ New methods to improve formatting of numbers, including **toFixed()**, **toPrevision()**, and **toExponential()**.

More information about JavaScript 1.5 can be found at: **http://developer.netscape.com/ docs/manuals/js/core/jsref15/contents.html.**

JavaScript 2.0

Developers at Netscape and other companies are working together with (and as a part of) an ECMA working group to develop the next core version of the JavaScript language. The standard, when finalized, will be known as ECMA-262 Edition 4, but, as usual, Netscape will release its own superset of the language that incorporates extra features that do not make it into the standard. Netscape's JavaScript 2.0 proposal can be found at **http://www.mozilla.org/js/language/es4/index.html**, and some of the major features to expect are briefly outlined here:

■ Explicit class-based object-oriented language features. JavaScript as it stands now is prototype-based.

■ The ability to override operators (similar to C++).

■ More modifiers of properties and variables (for example, **public** and **private**).

■ No distinction between primitive and composite types. Everything will be an object (but primitive types can be simulated).

■ Optional stronger typing and explicit type conversion. Optional distinction between types like integers and floating-point numbers and characters and strings. Additionally, explicit representation of types, for example an 8-bit unsigned integer (**uint8**).

■ Ability to include units in numeric data—for example, to specify a style value of three pixels, you might write **object.style.property = 3_px.**

■ The ability to **include** source files in JavaScript, similar to the **#include** preprocessor directive in C.

These features are just a few of the proposed changes. As you can see, it appears that JavaScript is moving more towards C++ and Java while at the same time retaining key language features. In addition, some Pascal-like syntax is being adopted for type specification. Despite embracing ideas from more traditional languages, the architects developing the specification insist that JavaScript will retain an identity distinct from C++ and Java. Whatever the case, JavaScript 2.0 will clearly be a significant step in the evolution of the language, bringing mature object-oriented features to the client side of the Web.

Browser Issues

A large part of developing robust JavaScript applications is ensuring cross-browser compatibility. You must be aware of which browser supports which features and how to accomplish various DHTML tasks using frequently incompatible object models. This section outlines some of the major proprietary additions to each version of Netscape's browsers. Although much of this information was included in previous chapters as it applied to tasks such as DHTML and form validation, it is often useful to have all this material presented in one place. The goal of this section is to give a rough chronology of features unique to Netscape (and in some cases Netscape and Opera) browsers. Because the divergence in object models is most apparent at the upper levels of the object hierarchy, the proprietary features listed here are primarily those of the **Window**, **Navigator**, and **Document** objects. For proprietary features of other objects, consult the section of Appendix B on the object in question.

Netscape 3

As noted in Chapter 18, Netscape 3 was the first browser to support communication with embedded objects via LiveConnect. Not surprisingly, most of the new proprietary features in this browser are related to Java and plugin interaction with JavaScript. Of course for many JavaScript programmers the main feature that Netscape 3 introduced was the **Image** object that allowed for the "mouseover" technique described in Chapter 15. The most interesting features are listed in Table 22-3.

The ability that Netscape 3+ provides to detect plug-ins and support MIME types was discussed in Chapter 18. Data tainting was mentioned briefly in Chapter 21, but is

New Features	Deprecated Items
MimeType object, **Plugin** object, **navigator.mimeTypes[ ]**, **navigator.plugins[ ]**, **navigator.taintEnabled**, **taint()**, **untaint()**, JavaScript entities	None

Table 22-3. *Major Changes to Proprietary Browser Features in Netscape 3*

not discussed in detail because the technology is obsolete and support for it has been discontinued.

Netscape 4

As discussed in Chapter 9, Netscape 4 was the first version of the browser to support any sort of DHTML capabilities. Therefore, the most significant proprietary aspects of the browser are related to window characteristics, screen characteristics, layers, and event handling. The major proprietary features of Netscape 4 are shown in Table 22-4.

DHTML and Netscape 4

Working with presentation characteristics in Netscape 4 can be very frustrating. One major reason for this is that apparently Netscape used its submission to the W3C known as JSSS (JavaScript Style Sheets) to render markup in Netscape 4. Because the CSS standard was specified when Netscape 4 was nearing completion and JSSS had already been included in the browser, Netscape 4 translates CSS declarations into JSSS in order to render markup. This last-minute (by development standards) inclusion of CSS led to only primitive, buggy support for style sheets, but it is supposed that some support is better than none at all. There are a lot of rumors about what actually happened, but the fact remains that Netscape 4 uses JavaScript to render CSS. You can verify this by running Netscape 4 and noting that CSS rules are not applied to elements when JavaScript is turned off and that it is possible to use JSSS to change the style characteristics of a page.

Regardless of your take on JSSS, a serious problem with Netscape 4 is that CSS properties are not dynamically reflected in the page. That is, although you can manipulate an object's **Style** object before it is displayed on the page, once the element has been displayed, any further changes to its style do not show up. This necessitates keeping some sort of style state and reloading the page when you want the changes to show up. This technique is illustrated in the "Using Cookies for User State Management" section near the end of Chapter 16.

The more popular solution (some would say "problem") is to use Netscape 4's proprietary **<layer>** element. As demonstrated in Chapters 15 and 16, Netscape 4 **<layer>** tags can be dynamically hidden and moved about the screen. This permits a primitive

New Features	Deprecated Items
Layer object, **Screen** object, **window.crypto** object, navigator.language, **navigator.preference()**, **nagivator.savePreferences()**, **window.innerHeight**, **window.innerWidth**, **window.outerHeight**, **window.outerWidth**, **window.screenX**, **window.screenY**, **window.locationbar**, **window.menubar**, **window.personalbar**, **window.scrollbars**, **window.statusbar**, **window.toolbar**, **window.pageXOffset**, **window.pageYOffset**, **window.atob()**, **window.btoa()**, **window.back()**, **window.forward()**, **window.home()**, **document.classes[ ]**, **document.ids[ ]**, **document.layers[ ]**, **document.tags[ ]**, **handleEvent()**, **routeEvent()**, **releaseEvents()**, **captureEvents()**, primitive CSS1 support primarily through Netscape JavaScript Style Sheets (JSSS)	**taint()**, **untaint()**

Table 22-4.   *Major Changes to Proprietary Browser Features in Netscape 4*

sort of DHTML in which layers with different characteristics are manipulated or swapped in and out of visibility to simulate a change in the object's presentation characteristics. Some of the interesting DHTML properties and methods of **Layer** objects are listed in Table 22-5. Note that **z-index** specifies the coordinate in the third dimension (the other two being the height and width of the screen) of the layer. Layers with lower **z-index** values are found below those with higher values.

Layer tags that have their **name** attributes set can be accessed as *document.layers ["name"]* or *document.layers.name*. With the exception of the properties referencing sibling and parent layers (for example, **above**) all the properties in Table 22-5 can be modified dynamically. In addition, because each layer is a **Document** object, it is possible to **open()**, **write()**, and **close()** a layer to dynamically write content to it. The fact that each layer is a **Document** does, however, present a problem. Nested layers must be accessed recursively through each enclosing layer's **Document**, for example as:

```
document.layers.outerLayer.layers.innerLayer
```

For more information about Netscape 4 layers, see Chapter 14 as well as any number of DHTML-focused Web sites, particularly **http://developer.netscape.com/docs/manuals/ communicator/dynhtml/index.htm**.

Property	Description
above, below	Reference to the layer above or below the layer according to the z-index order among all layers in the document (**null** if it is the topmost/bottommost).
siblingAbove, siblingBelow	Reference to the layer above or below the layer according to the z-index order among all layers that share the same parent (**null** if topmost/bottommost).
parentLayer	Reference to layer in which the layer is contained (or to the **Window** object if no such layer exists).
background	String specifying the URL of the background image for the layer.
bgColor	String value indicating the named color or hexadecimal triplet of the layer's background (e.g., "#FF00FF").
clip.bottom, clip.height, clip.left, clip.right, clip.top, clip.width	Numeric values in pixels defining the rectangular clipping area of the layer. Any content outside of this rectangle is not displayed.
left, top, x, y	Numeric or string value indicating the position of the layer. If the layer's **position** attribute is "*absolute*," this placement is relative to the position of the parent (enclosing) layer. Otherwise it is relative to the content surrounding it. String values are used with this property to indicate units other than pixels, for example "25%". Note that x and y are just synonyms for *left* and *top*.
pageX, pageY	Numeric or string value indicating the layer's position relative to the visible page.

Table 22-5. *Interesting DHTML Properties of Netscape 4 Layers*

Property	Description
src	String indicating the URL of the layer's content.
visibility	String indicating whether the layer is visible. A value of *"show"* makes the layer visible, *"hide"* makes it invisible, and *"inherit"* causes it to inherit the visibility property of its parent layer.
zIndex	The relative z-index of the layer (with respect to its siblings).
Load( )	Causes the browser to reload the *src* of the layer.
moveAbove(whichLayer), moveBelow(whichLayer)	Causes the layer to be placed above or below the layer referenced by *whichLayer*.
moveBy(**x, y**)	Moves the layer to an offset of *x* pixels horizontally and *y* pixels vertically from its current position.
moveTo(**x, y**)	Moves the layer to the *x* and *y* coordinates relative to its parent layer (if absolutely positioned) or relative to its surrounding content (if relatively positioned).
moveToAbsolute(**x, y**)	Moves the layer to the *x* and *y* coordinates relative to the visible page.
resizeBy(**x, y**)	Changes the width by *x* pixels and height by *y* pixels relative to its current width and height, effectively changing the clipping rectangle.
resizeTo(**x, y**)	Changes the width to *x* pixels and height to *y* pixels, effectively changing the clipping rectangle.

Table 22-5.   *Interesting DHTML Properties of Netscape 4 Layers* (continued)

Netscape 6

In March 1998 Netscape released to the open source community a cleaned-up version of its browser source code as "Mozilla." Mozilla was the internal code name for Netscape browser products and is derived from "Mosaic killer," a reference to the first popular graphical browsing tool for the Web. Now Mozilla is both a browser and an organization. Mozilla the organization is a nonprofit open source software project dedicated to producing a high-quality, standards-based browser engine free for anyone to use.

The shift of development of "core" browser features into an open source project explains the absence of a Netscape 5. The code that was released as Mozilla was to have formed the basis for Netscape 5. However, Mozilla (the organization) decided it would be better to rewrite most of the browser essentially from scratch, and since future versions of Netscape were to be based on Mozilla (the browser engine), the release of Netscape 5 was cancelled.

Though many of the major contributors to the Mozilla project are Netscape employees (or former employees), the Mozilla source code can be incorporated into any browser release by anyone willing to spend the effort, subject to certain licensing restrictions. This is exactly what Netscape did for Netscape 6. They waited until the Mozilla project had reached sufficient maturity and then incorporated its source code (and that of related open source projects) into a completely new browser and dubbed it Netscape 6. You can picture Netscape taking a "snapshot" of Mozilla (and related) source code at a particular point and forking off on its own development branch. It is for this reason that although Netscape 6 and Mozilla are *not* the same thing, they are very closely related, so often developers speak of Netscape 6 and Mozilla interchangeably.

Netscape 6 marks a stark departure from traditional browser trends. It emphasizes implementation and adherence to W3C and ECMA standards, providing hope that one day standard code can be written once and run equally well on many different platforms and browsers (where have we heard that before?). Although Netscape 6 and Mozilla were greeted with much skepticism, they provide excellent levels of adherence to standards when compared to conformance levels of older browsers. Table 22-6 lists some of the major changes in Netscape 6. Note that unlike the previous tables for Netscape 3 and 4, Table 22-6 does *not* list proprietary features found only in this browser. Rather, it lists the standards it supports. Listing each and every interesting new feature supported is rendered unnecessary by the adherence to W3C standards. The features it supports are implicit in its adherence to each standard.

Examination of Table 22-6 reveals that, unlike with previous browser versions, you can use standard DOM techniques for events and DHTML in Netscape 6. Netscape 6 is also backwards-compatible with Netscape 4 in the sense that it continues to support some proprietary features of the **Window**, **Document**, and **Navigator** objects, such as screen properties and plugin and MIME type sensing. It has also been modified to support a number of Internet Explorer features, notably the **innerHTML** property of element objects. Additionally, it supports DOM Level 0, so the "old" method of event handling will still work, with some minor modifications to take advantage of more advanced

New Features	Deprecated Items
XML 1.0, XHTML 1.0, DOM0, DOM1 (Core and HTML), CSS1, some support of DOM2 and CSS2	everything layer-related, **document.tags[ ]**, **document.ids[ ]**, **document.classes[ ]**

Table 22-6. *Major Changes to Browser Features in Netscape 6*

features. All this is not to say that Netscape 6 is without bugs. Indeed, there are reports of LiveConnect problems and some CSS difficulties. With Mozilla 1/Netscape 6 and unlike with other browsers, you can view the list of current bug reports and fixes; these can be found at **http://www.mozilla.org/bugs/**. If you are having problems with Netscape 6, this is definitely the place to start.

Note *Interested readers can download the Mozilla browser itself from **http://www.mozilla.org**. Development on it continues daily, and although the 1.0 version is slated for release in early 2002, it is a fully functional browser at the time of this writing. Because it is an open source project, interested readers can also write code for the browser, thereby achieving everlasting net.fame.*

Summary

Netscape browsers include a variety of proprietary features. Most prominent are its plugin and MIME type sensing capabilities and Netscape 4's support for the proprietary **<layer>** tag. In addition to new features unique to Netscape browsers, each major version includes a new version of the core JavaScript language. These language versions corresponding to different degrees with the ECMAScript standard, and behavior of core language features such as operators and built-in object methods can vary significantly from version to version. Therefore, it is important to be aware of the differences when writing cross-browser and version-compatible JavaScript. Netscape 6 marks a sharp departure from traditional browser trends. It is based upon the Mozilla open source project and emphasizes standards support over proprietary features. This departure has the lofty goal of creating standardized browser engines so that developers can write one script rather than numerous conditional scripts for each browser version and vendor. While this goal is not likely to be realized any time in the near future, Netscape and Mozilla are taking steps to make it a reality. Until that time, we will have to spend some time learning about the proprietary features specific to each browser. The next chapter delves into the numerous JavaScript extensions made by Microsoft.

Chapter 23

Internet Explorer Extensions and Considerations

W
hile browser demographic statistics vary wildly from survey to survey, one statistic is clear: Microsoft Internet Explorer is hands-down the most widely deployed browser today. As such, it is very useful to be aware of the features available in different versions of this browser. This chapter discusses some aspects of JavaScript that are particular to Internet Explorer and introduces some of the more advanced proprietary features that Microsoft offers as a part of its browser.

Core Language Issues

Like Netscape, Microsoft incorporates JavaScript language improvements into major releases of new browser versions. Unlike Netscape, however, Microsoft refers to its implementation of the language as "JScript" to avoid trademark and licensing issues ("JavaScript" is a trademark of Sun Microsystems). Table 23-1 shows the correspondence between Microsoft language and browser versions. Note that the entry for JScript 5.6/6.0 is marked with an asterisk. This indicates that this entry is entirely speculative. Internet Explorer 6 is currently in public Beta, but Microsoft has not yet released any firm documentation about its JScript implementation.

Different versions of JScript correspond to different degrees with the ECMAScript standard. Table 23-2 lists the relationship between JScript versions and the standard.

The first JScript implementation (JScript 1.0) available in Internet Explorer 3 was essentially a Microsoft clone of Netscape's JavaScript 1.0 found in Netscape 2. However, Internet Explorer 3 was released at roughly the same time as Netscape 3, which included JavaScript 1.1. This led to a "feature lag": Microsoft browsers implemented core language features one "generation" behind those of Netscape. Over time this lag grew smaller and smaller, to the point that the latest releases of the browsers implement essentially the same features set. This is apparent from the fact that Internet Explorer 5.5 and Netscape 6 are both compliant with Edition 3 of the ECMAScript standard. Examining these parallels allows one to draw the rough correspondence between core JavaScript

Language Version	Browser Version
JScript 1.0	Internet Explorer 3.0
JScript 3.0	Internet Explorer 4.0
JScript 5.0	Internet Explorer 5.0
JScript 5.5	Internet Explorer 5.5
JScript 5.6/6.0*	Internet Explorer 6.0

Table 23-1. *Relationship Between JScript Language and Browser Versions*

Microsoft Version	Standard Version	Exceptions
JScript 1.0	Very loose conformance to ECMA-262 Edition 1	Many, and some extra features (even though ECMAScript is based in part on JScript 1.0)
JScript 3.0	Strict conformance to ECMA-262 Edition 1	Includes some extra features
JScript 5.0	Strict conformance to ECMA-262 Edition 1	Includes many extra features
JScript 5.5	Strict conformance to ECMA-262 Edition 3	Includes some extra features
JScript 5.6/6.0*	Likely to be released before ECMA-262 Edition 4 is finalized	Unknown, but unlikely to include many JavaScript 2.0/ ECMAScript Edition 4 features

Table 23-2.   *Relationship Between Microsoft JScript and ECMAScript*

in Netscape and Microsoft browsers found in Table 23-3. Remember, this correspondence is only an approximation, so you should always look up the specific feature you are interested in before making assumptions.

Some would argue that JavaScript 1.1 or 1.2 is a better match for JScript 3.0. While this contention is certainly plausible, the adherence to the ECMAScript standard in JavaScript 1.3 and JScript 3.0 was the chief factor in drawing the correspondence in Table 23-3. Thankfully, there is not as wide a disparity in core language features among browsers as there is in object models.

Language Version	Browser Version	Language Version	Browser Version
JavaScript 1.0	Netscape 2.0	JScript 1.0	Internet Explorer 3.0
JavaScript 1.3	Netscape 4.06	JScript 3.0	Internet Explorer 4.0
JavaScript 1.5	Netscape 6	JScript 5.5	Internet Explorer 5.5

Table 23-3.   *Rough Correspondence Between Netscape and Microsoft JavaScript*

In the remainder of this section we will discuss some of the major differences among versions of JScript. If you are having trouble with one of your scripts under older browsers, this section is a good place to check for when features made it into the language. For example, many developers wonder why their **do/while** loops will not work under IE3. The reason is that this feature was included only starting with JScript 3.0, so it is only found in IE4+. For detailed information regarding language features, consult Microsoft's JScript documentation, available at **http://msdn.microsoft. com/scripting/**.

JScript 1.0

The JScript 1.0 release in Internet Explorer 3.0 was very similar to what Netscape 2.0 supported, and the browser supported almost the exact same object model. However, one huge difference between Netscape and Microsoft existed during this generation of browsers—case sensitivity. JScript 1.0 is not terribly case-sensitive, and you can get away with changing the case of common methods and objects without penalty. This characteristic caused a great deal of confusion for many new JavaScript programmers who used only Internet Explorer. Other than that, the only major concern people should have with JScript 1.0 is that Internet Explorer 3.0 did not support the **src** attribute of the **<script>** tag until the 3.02 release of the browser. The specific nuances of this implementation have more historic interest than utility.

JScript 2.0

Although JScript 2.0 was not originally a part of a browser release, it was made available in later versions of IE3 and included in Microsoft's Internet Information Server (IIS) 1.0. The features new to JScript 2.0 were included in JScript 3.0, so the items listed here are for the most part also new to Internet Explorer 4 (though it implements JScript 3.0).

- The **Array** object. JScript 1.0 did not implement arrays as objects, so you had to use literal notation to create them. The **length** property and the **join()**, **reverse()**, and **sort()** methods were also added in this version.

- Many improvements to functions, including the implicitly filled **arguments[ ]** and **caller** properties as well as the **Function** object.

- Many improvements to numbers, including the **Number** object and its constants **Number.MAX_VALUE**, **Number.MIN_VALUE**, and **Number.NaN** as well as the global constants **NEGATIVE_INFINITY** and **POSITIVE_INFINITY**.

- The **Boolean** object.

- Maturity of objects, which now include the **toString()** and **valueOf()** methods and the **prototype** property (though no **Object** is available in this release).

- The **void** operator.

JScript 3.0

The core language features of this version are ECMAScript-compliant and were
included in IIS 4.0 as well as IE4. You can see from the new features listed here
that this version marks a major release for the language.

- A complete overhaul of **Date** to render it ECMAScript-compliant.

- Regular expressions, including the **RegExp** object.

- New **Array** methods: **concat()** and **slice()**.

- Many new methods for **String**: **concat()**, **fromCharCode()**, **slice()**, **split()**,
  and **substr()**.

- ECMAScript-compliant type conversion.

- The ability to **delete** object properties and array elements.

- New flow control mechanisms, including the **do/while** loop, the ability
  to label statements, and **switch**.

- Further improvements to numbers, including the global **Infinity** and **NaN**
  constants and **isFinite()** method.

- The **Object** object.

- Full support for Unicode.

Microsoft made several proprietary extensions to the language core as well. A brief
overview of these features appears in Table 23-4.

Feature	Description
ActiveXObject object	Allows scripts to open instances of ActiveX components in order to harness extended functionality, for example a spreadsheet or word processor. This feature is discussed in more detail later in the chapter.
Enumerator object	Enables iteration of Microsoft collections similar to **for/in** loops on objects. This object is discussed in more detail later in the chapter.
VBArray object	Permits JavaScript to use "safe" VBScript arrays.
conditional compilation	Allows dynamic definition and execution of code (rather than linear runtime "compilation"). This feature is described in more detail later in the chapter.

Table 23-4.   *Proprietary Extensions to JScript in Version 3.0*

JScript 4.0

This version was never included as part of a browser release. Rather, it was included in Microsoft Visual Studio. However, JScript 4.0 is for all intents and purposes the same as JScript 3.0, just repackaged and renamed for inclusion with another application.

JScript 5.0

Version 5.0 of JScript marks the beginning of support for advanced exception handling. Included is the **try/catch** construct discussed in Chapter 24 and the **Error** object and the **throw** statement for generating custom error conditions. The only other major additions in this version is the **for/in** loop for iterating over object properties and the **instanceof** operator.

JScript 5.5

JScript 5.5 corresponds closely to JavaScript 1.5 and is in compliance with ECMAScript Edition 3. The new features are listed here:

- Improvements to functions, including the implicitly filled **callee** property as well as the **call()** and **apply()** methods. A **length** property was included with a function's **arguments** to indicate the actual number of parameters passed.
- The new **String** method **charCodeAt()**.
- Global **decodeURI()** and **encodeURI()** methods, offering similar functionality to the existing **escape()** and **unescape()**.
- Stack and Queue methods for **Array**: **pop()**, **push()**, **shift()**, and **unshift()**. In addition the **splice()** method was also added.
- Various useful enhancements to regular expressions.
- Numerous global conversion functions, such as **toExponential()**, **toFixed()**, **toPrecision()**, **toTimeString()**, and **toDateString()**.

Browser Issues

Microsoft is the undisputed king of proprietary browser features. More than any other vendor, Microsoft shows continual initiative in bundling new technologies with its browsers. While many critics argue that these new technologies increase Microsoft's domination of the browser market by perpetuating users' reliance upon proprietary Microsoft technologies, the utility of some of Internet Explorer's more advanced features is undeniable. The surprising aspect of these innovations is not in their capabilities or the extent of their integration with the operating system. Indeed, Microsoft has made it clear that increased integration of the Web with Windows and related software products is one of its primary goals. Rather, the surprising aspect of these features is how few developers are aware of their existence.

In this section we briefly discuss some of the new, proprietary features found in each version of Internet Explorer. While some of these features are not, strictly speaking, features of JavaScript itself, they are often close enough in functionality to be of interest to Web developers programming for Internet Explorer. Because of the sheer volume of proprietary features found in newer versions, we have chosen at times to highlight some of the most useful features and to omit some secondary or lesser-used capabilities. Full documentation of Internet Explorer is always available from the Microsoft Developer's Network (MSDN) at **http://msdn.microsoft.com**.

Internet Explorer 3

As the first browser providing JScript support, it is not surprising that Internet Explorer 3 implements only a few proprietary features not found in other browsers. Most notable are support for ActiveX controls and embedded objects signed via Authenticode technology. This browser version also supports the basic LiveConnect functionality discussed in Chapter 18.

There are a few issues to be aware of with IE3. Some early versions apparently have problems loading externally linked JavaScript libraries. Further, certain aspects of IE3's JScript implementation are case-insensitive, so you will need to exercise caution when using very old scripts. Although the shift to newer versions of the browser makes these problems less of a concern, they do rear their heads from time to time.

Internet Explorer 4

The divergence of Document Object Models discussed in Chapter 9 contributed to a large number of the proprietary features in IE4. Because there was no programming language—independent and vendor-neutral standard for how elements were to be exposed to scripts, each vendor implemented its own object model. In addition to proprietary **Document** properties, IE4 implements JScript 3.0, which includes new features that can be categorized somewhere between core language and browser enhancements. Some of these features, which are discussed in depth later in this chapter, really begin to blur the line between an active Web document and a full-blown application. A general overview of the proprietary features introduced in IE4 is given in Table 23-5.

The data binding features of IE4 provide some very powerful capabilities, an overview of which and of the improvements to JScript is included in a following section. A discussion of the Internet Explorer event model can be found in Chapters 9 and 11, and Table 23-6 lists some new proprietary handlers available in IE4. Modal window creation is covered in Chapter 12. While the IE DHTML object model is explicitly covered in Chapter 9 and used throughout the book, Table 23-7 provides a quick summary of some of the most useful proprietary features it provides.

Feature	Description
IE DHTML	The ability to dynamically manipulate documents according to Internet Explorer's document object model.
window.external	Allows scripts to access extended object model features provided by the client machine. For more information, see the MSDN.
IE Event model	Internet Explorer's proprietary event model (event bubbling) as well as proprietary event handlers.
CSS Filters	Offers a variety of nonstandard special effects for fonts and page transitions.
JScript 3.0	The **Enumerator** and **ActiveXObject** objects and conditional compilation, which will be discussed in depth later in this chapter.
Data Binding	Permits HTML elements to be bound to external data sources in order to automate retrieval and update of information without requiring explicit action such as form submission.
scriptlets	Encapsulated JavaScript that can be included in documents as an embedded object.
Modal Windows	The **showModalDialog()** and **showModelessDialog()** methods of **Window** permit the creation of special kinds of popup windows.

Table 23-5.   *Some Proprietary Features Introduced in Internet Explorer 4*

Event Handler	Description
ondragstart	Fires when the user begins to drag an object in the window.
onfilterchange	Fires when an object's CSS Filter transition completes.
onhelp	Fires when the user requests help from the browser, for example by pressing F1 in Windows.
onreadystatechange	Fires when the **readyState** property of an object changes.
onselectstart	Fires when the user starts highlighting or otherwise selecting page content.

Table 23-6.   *Some New IE4+ Event Handlers*

Property	Description
all[ ]	Array of all the elements contained by the object, indexed by **id/name** attribute or number. Most often used as a property of the **Document** as **document.all[ ]**.
children[ ]	Array of the element objects contained by the element, not including text nodes.
clientHeight, clientWidth	Indicates pixel height and width of the content area of the element.
filters[ ]	Array of **Filter** objects set using CSS Filters that are defined for the element. Note that this array is only a property of certain element objects.
innerHTML, outerHTML, innerText, outerText	Strings containing the HTML or text enclosed by (for the **inner** properties) and including (for the **outer** properties) the element.
parentElement	Reference to the element's parent (that is, the object corresponding to the element that encloses the current element).
readyState	Indicates the status of the element's content (for example, whether it has finished loading).
scrollHeight, scrollWidth	Indicates total pixel height and width of the object, regardless of the currently viewable area. Property only of scrollable element objects (for example, the **body**) in IE4 but of almost all element in IE5+.
scrollLeft, scrollTop	Indicates how far (in pixels) the object has been scrolled to the right and down from an offset of zero.
sourceIndex	Indicates the integer index in **document.all[ ]** of the element.
contains()	Accepts a reference to an element object and returns a Boolean indicating whether the argument object is contained (at any nesting depth) in the current element.

Table 23-7.   *Some IE4+ Properties of Element Objects*

Property	Description
getAttribute(), **setAttribute()**	Permits the examination and manipulation of the HTML attributes associated with the current element. Although available in Netscape 6, this feature was for a long time implemented only by IE.
insertAdjacentHTML(), **insertAdjacentText()**	Permits the insertion of HTML or text before, after, and just inside the beginning or end of the current element.
item()	Retrieves a member of a collection by index or **id**. Implemented in Netscape 6, but Netscape 6 does not permit the argument to be an **id**.
removeAttribute()	Removes an HTML element's attribute. Similar to the W3C DOM **removeAttribute()** implemented in Netscape 6.
scrollIntoView()	Forces the page to scroll the element into view.
tags()	Accepts a string indicating an HTML tag and retrieves an array of objects corresponding to that tag in the collection.

Table 23-7. *Some IE4+ Properties of Element Objects* (continued)

One of the most interesting features available in IE4 is its ability to use scriptlets. *Scriptlets* are HTML documents embedded in the page with an **<object>** tag that provides specific functionality—for example, DHTML rollover effects or animation. Scriptlets contain JScript written so as to provide a public interface through which their specific tasks can be carried out. The idea is to facilitate script reusability by encapsulating commonly used functionality in these components. Although scriptlet technology is interesting and often useful, it has been superseded in Internet Explorer 5 by a related technology, DHTML Behaviors. It is for this reason that we do not discuss scriptlets in detail.

One lesser-known capability of IE4+ is the ability to disable instance properties for document objects. By setting the **expando** property of the **Document** object to **false**, any attempt to set instance properties in the document object hierarchy will throw an error.

Internet Explorer 5

Internet Explorer 5 provides even more features that make Web pages act more like applications than documents. A brief outline of some of these powerful features is found in Table 23-8, and a complete discussion of all but HTML+TIME (which is discussed next) appears in a later section.

The HTML+TIME enhancement allows Web pages to become more centered around multimedia content. HTML+TIME provides advanced integration of text, images, audio, and video with HTML and permits synchronization of animation with other media elements on the page.

In addition to the major new technologies listed in Table 23-8, IE5 includes many improvements to the IE document object model. Some of the new proprietary event handlers are listed in Table 23-9, and some new proprietary properties of element objects are listed in Table 23-10.

Feature	Description
HTML+TIME	The Timed Interactive Multimedia Extensions (TIME) is an XML-defined language providing synchronization of sound, video, and other effects in the page.
Dynamic Properties	Permits the assignment of an expression (rather than a static value) as the value of a property. These expressions are dynamically evaluated to reflect the current state of the page.
HTML Applications	HTML Applications (HTAs) are HTML pages (and associated scripts) run on the client as a fully trusted application. They are useful for writing code for Internet Explorer that is not subject to the usual security restrictions associated with untrusted code.
Attached DHTML Behaviors	A powerful technology that allows code performing some predefined action to be bound to tags in the page. Behaviors have a wide range of applications, from automatic modification of style to interacting with the user's browser in a manner similar to signed scripts in Netscape.

Table 23-8.   *Some Proprietary Features Introduced in Internet Explorer 5*

Event Handler	Description
onbeforecopy	Fires before data is copied to the clipboard.
onbeforecut	Fires before data is cut to the clipboard.
onbeforeeditfocus	Fires before an editable object receives focus.
onbeforepaste	Fires before data is pasted from the clipboard.
oncontextmenu	Fires when the user activates a secondary menu; for example, by right-clicking the mouse under Windows.
oncopy	Fires after data is copied to the clipboard.
oncut	Fires after data is cut to the clipboard.
ondrag	Fires after **ondragstart** while the user is dragging the selection across the window.
ondragenter	Fires when an object is dragged over the element.
ondragleave	Fires when an object is dragged out of the element.
ondragover	Fires continuously while an object is being dragged over the element.
ondrop	Fires when a dragged object is released.
onpaste	Fires after the user pastes from the clipboard.
onpropertychange	Fires whenever an object's property changes; for example, when its **Style** object is manipulated.

Table 23-9. *Some New IE5+ Event Handlers*

Property	Description
canHaveChildren	Boolean indicating whether the element can include nested elements (for example, **<img>** cannot).
canHaveHTML	Boolean indicating whether the element can enclose HTML (for example, **<img>** cannot).

Table 23-10. *Some Proprietary Element Object Properties in IE5+*

Property	Description
currentStyle	Reference to the **Style** object defining all style properties for the element, including those not explicitly set by CSS in the page.
runtimeStyle	Reference to the **Style** object defining the runtime style properties for the element. Overrides the normal **style** property.
scopeName	Defines one or more XML namespaces for the element.
uniqueID	A unique **id** property generated by the browser for the element.
applyElement()	Permits the addition of an element as an enclosing parent or enclosed child. Encloses the content of the current element at the outermost child.
clearAttributes()	Removes all attributes from the element.
componentFromPoint()	This method has rather complicated functionality and is used to extract information about the precise location of events.
getAdjacentText()	Retrieves text near the element.
getBoundingClientRect()	Retrieves information about the "bounding rectangle" associated with the element's content.
getClientRects()	Retrieves all bounding rectangles enclosed by the element.
insertAdjacentElement()	Inserts an element at a specific position with respect to the current element.
mergeAttributes()	Allows you to apply the attributes of one element to another.
releaseCapture(), **setCapture()**	Permits the capture and release of some or all mouse events.
removeNode()	Removes a node (and possibly its children) from the document object hierarchy.
replaceAdjacentText(), **replaceNode()**, **swapNode()**	Permits (non-DOM) manipulation of the document object hierarchy.

Table 23-10.   *Some Proprietary Element Object Properties in IE5+* (continued)

Internet Explorer 5 also includes many changes to the IE document object model to bring it partially in line with the W3C DOM. For example, the **getElementById()** and other basic DOM1 HTML methods are available, though this browser is not DOM1-compliant. See Chapter 10 for information about how to use these features.

Internet Explorer 5.5

Although one might expect a minor version like 5.5 to include relatively few new features, this is certainly not the case with IE5.5. Some major new proprietary functionality is listed in Table 23-11, but numerous "under the hood" improvements to object model and core language are included as well. Most noticeable are new DOM-compliant object model features and the adherence of JScript 5.5 to ECMAScript Edition 3.

The ability to create customized popup windows simulates more complicated DHTML menu functionality but with a much cleaner interface than most developers are used to. While this type of feature should be avoided by developers concerned with cross-browser compatibility, as more users switch to new versions of Internet Explorer, these kinds of popup windows will become an increasingly attractive alternative to more complicated DHTML solutions. Popup windows in IE5.5+ are discussed in a following section (and also in Chapter 12).

Internet Explorer 6

While IE6 is in Beta release at the time of this writing, an examination of the current release and Microsoft documentation reveals some of the new features you can expect. Internet Explorer will be fully compliant with CSS1 and DOM1, marking (finally!) a convergence of document object models among major browsers (Internet Explorer 6 and Netscape 6, with Opera soon moving directly to DOM Level 2).

Feature	Description
Popup Windows	The ability to easily create popup windows.
Element DHTML Behaviors	An expanded version of the Attached DHTML Behaviors available in Internet Explorer 5.0. Element Behaviors allow you to define new elements with specific functionality that can be used like standard HTML in your pages.
Printing Customizations	Allows developers extreme flexibility with respect to how pages are printed from the browser, such as automatic document transformations to prepare it for printing, as well as the ability to define custom printing templates.

Table 23-11. *Some Proprietary Features Introduced in IE5.5*

Other improvements include the ability to capture mouse wheel events, support for P3P, and various usability and multimedia (HTML+TIME) enhancements. In addition, developers will be able to create custom "Explorer Bars" for the browser for navigation or content enhancements.

The **onmousewheel** event should include all the standard **Event** properties in addition to the new **wheelDelta** property. This property is used only with **onmousewheel** events and reveals the rotation distance of the wheel button. This will allow you to take specific actions based on how fast or slow the user is moving the mouse wheel.

Currently, it does not appear that Microsoft intends to enable its controversial "Smart Tag" technology in IE6, although there is always the opportunity for many such technologies to be implemented at a later date.

Proprietary Features

From the previous sections it should be abundantly clear that Internet Explorer offers a host of proprietary features to JavaScript developers. In this section we describe some of the most interesting of these features, although our treatment is necessarily less detailed than that which is available from Microsoft directly.

Whether or not these technologies should be used for critical aspects of your site depends upon your target audience. Intranet sites accessed by a uniformly Internet Explorer client population can usually harness these capabilities with relatively few adverse consequences. Public Web sites are another question. Using some of these features for critical site functionality automatically excludes users in non-Windows/ Internet Explorer environments. Whether this is a significant consideration varies, of course, with the specific circumstances and goals of the site. However, usability experts are unanimous in counseling that public Web sites wishing to reach the largest possible target audience should avoid making extensive use of proprietary browser extensions. It is usually more appropriate to implement core functionality using "standard" technology, while using proprietary features to provide enhancements to users with the appropriate browsers.

JScript Features

Although the core language capabilities of JScript have not strayed too far from mainstream JavaScript, Microsoft does implement a few unique features. Some features like collections have been a widely used part of the language for quite some time and have even been adopted into Web standards. Others, like **ActiveXObject**, have traditionally been used on the server side or in scripts embedded in other (non-browser) applications.

Collections

A potentially confusing aspect of the Internet Explorer document object model is its liberal use of collections. A *collection* is a container object holding heterogeneous data that may be accessed by ordinal (that is, by index) or by name. They are often mistaken for arrays because the functionality of the two data types is so similar. For example, the Document Object Model "arrays," such as **document.all** and **document.images**, are actually collections. In addition, the "arrays" of HTML elements found in the W3C DOM are collections as well (**HTMLCollection** objects, to be specific). Although the discussion immediately following applies to Netscape 6 and other DOM browsers, collections are most often used in the context of Internet Explorer document objects, so we focus our discussion here on using collections in Internet Explorer.

Collections are used to hold groups of HTML element objects. For example, **document.all** holds an object for each HTML element (and comment) in the page. There are many ways to access the members of a collection, but they are most often retrieved by name. To retrieve a particular object you use the value of the element's **id** or **name** attribute. All the following syntaxes are valid:

```
collectionName["name"]
collectionName("name")
collectionName.item("name")
collectionName.namedItem("name")          // namedItem() only supported in
Internet Explorer 6+
collectionName.name
```

The interpreter first searches for any member of the collection with **id** matching the given name, then for any member with a matching **name**. If multiple elements match the given name, they are returned as a collection.

Accessing a member by index has similar syntax. Because collection indices are zero-based, you could access the third element of a collection with any of the following:

```
collectionName[2]
collectionName(2)
collectionName.item(2)
```

Note that the *collectionName()* syntax is just shorthand for *collectionName.item()*. We mentioned previously that when accessed by name, a collection returns a collection of members if there are multiple matching elements. In this case, you can combine the two forms of access to select one of the members of the collection returned. For example, if you are interested in the second of multiple items with **name** "myElement," you might write

```
collectionName.item("myElement").item(1);
```

Internet Explorer provides convenient shorthand for this operation. You can pass the index of the item you are interested in as the second parameter to the **item()** method. The following is equivalent to the previous example:

```
collectionName.item("myElement", 1);
```

The other standard properties of collections are **length**, indicating how many members the collection holds, and **tags()**, which accepts a string indicating an HTML tag and returns a collection of all the objects created from that tag. For example, to retrieve a collection of all element objects corresponding to **<p>** tags in the document, you might write

```
var pTags = document.all.tags("p");
```

Some collections, for example the **options** collection of a **Select** object, also have **add()** and **remove()** methods.

The Enumerator Object

Because accessing a collection results in the retrieval of a collection when multiple members share the same **name** or **id**, there is no apparent way to iterate over each member. You might think that a **for/in** loop would work, but unfortunately **for/in** loops were not designed for collections. Instead, Internet Explorer uses an **Enumerator** object. When a collection is passed to the **Enumerator()** constructor, an **Enumerator** instance is created that can be used to step through each item in the collection. Using an object to step through each element has several advantages, most obviously that references to it can be passed around as data in a way that would be impossible otherwise. The methods of **Enumerator** objects are listed in Table 23-12.

Method	Description
atEnd()	Returns a Boolean indicating if the enumerator is at the end of the collection.
item()	Retrieves the current item.
moveFirst()	Moves to the first item in the collection.
moveNext()	Moves to the next item in the collection.

Table 23-12.   *Methods of Enumerator Objects*

Use of an **Enumerator** is illustrated in the following code. The script passes **document.all** to the **Enumerator()** constructor and then uses the resulting object to iterate over all the tags in the page. The result is shown in Figure 23-1.

```
<!DOCTYPE HTML PUBLIC "-//W3C//DTD HTML 4.01 Transitional//EN"
         "http://www.w3.org/TR/html4/loose.dtd">
<html>
<head>
<title>Enumerator Example</title>
</head>
<body>
<h2>Enumerator Example</h2>
<p>Here's some text.</p>
<h3>Tags</h3>
<script language="JScript" text="text/jscript">
<!--
   var element;
   var e = new Enumerator(document.all);
   while (!e.atEnd())
     {
       element = e.item();
       document.write(element.tagName + "<br>");
       e.moveNext();
     }
// -->
</script>
</body>
</html>
```

Conditional Compilation

JScript 3.0 and later versions include conditional compilation features similar to those of the preprocessor in C. Conditional compilation directives permit special environmental variables that give information about the client platform to be tested in conditionals. In addition, these directives can test and set new conditional compilation variables as well as include or exclude code for eventual interpretation. The idea is to use conditional compilation directives to test for specific conditions—for example, a debugging flag or a platform providing extended capabilities—and to modify the code seen by the interpreter accordingly.

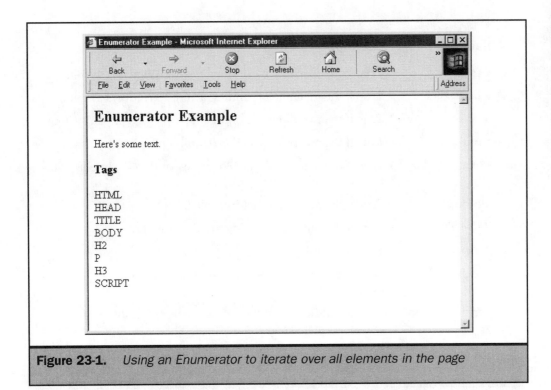

Figure 23-1. *Using an Enumerator to iterate over all elements in the page*

The conditional compilation directives are very simple. All are prefixed with the "@" symbol and have typical preprocessor syntax. The most important syntax is the **if/else** statements, which are straightforward:

```
@if (conditional)
   body
[@elif (conditional)
   body]
...
[@else
   body]
@end
```

The browser provides many predefined variables for use with conditional compilation. These variables are described in Table 23-13. Any conditional compilation variable that is not defined or not **true** behaves as **NaN**.

Variable	Description
@_win32	True if the machine is running a 32-bit Windows system.
@_win16	True if the machine is running a 16-bit Windows system.
@_mac	True if the machine is running an Apple Macintosh system.
@_alpha	True if the machine is a DEC/Compaq Alpha.
@_x86	True if the machine is an x86 processor (that is, Intel 80x86, Pentium, and clones).
@_mc680x0	True if the machine is a Motorola 680x0.
@_PowerPC	True if the machine is a PowerPC processor.
@_jscript	True if JScript is in use (always true).
@_jscript_build	Number indicating the building number of the JScript engine.
@_jscript_version	Number indicating the major and minor JScript version in use. Format is *major.minor* (e.g., 5.5).

Table 23-13. *Conditional Compilation Variables*

You can set and manipulate new variables with identifiers beginning with "@" during conditional compilation. The syntax for setting a variable of this kind is

@set @*identifier* = *value*

The *value* is an expression of other "@" variables, Booleans, numbers, and normal arithmetic and bitwise operators. Strings are not allowed. You can use a variable set this way in future conditional compilation statements or even in "normal" JavaScript. For example,

```
@set @debugging = true
@if (@debugging)
   alert("Debugging is on because the value of @debugging is: " + @debugging);
@end
```

gives the result

REAL WORLD
JAVASCRIPT

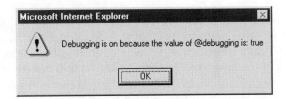

While you can include conditional compilation directives directly in your scripts, as in the previous example, doing so will confuse non-JScript browsers. For this reason it is almost always better to place these directives in comments. Doing so requires two changes to the syntax seen so far. First, you need to begin the comment with an "@" directive and close it with an "@" symbol. You must also use the **@cc_on** directive before any others in order to tell the browser to look for this kind of embedding, for example:

```
/*@cc_on @*/
/*@set @debugging = true@*/
```

Because the processing of conditional compilation directives happens before normal script interpretation, you can use it to selectively enable or disable pieces of code. Consider the following script that defines one of two functions depending upon which version of JScript (if any) is supported:

```
/*@cc_on @*/
/*@if (@_jscript_version >= 5)
function doTask()
        {
            // some code using advanced IE5+ features
        }
@else @*/
function doTask()
{
    // some code using standard browser features
}
/*@end @*/
```

A JScript 3+ browser processes the conditional compilation directives and defines the first *doTask( )* if JScript 5+ is in use. Otherwise, the second definition is used. Browsers not supporting conditional compilation simply ignore everything in the comments and use the second definition as a result.

This technique can be very useful for defining functions that harness advanced platform- or version-specific features but that still degrade gracefully under other browsers. You can expect a more advanced way of addressing these kinds of issues from future versions of the language, but most likely it will not use this syntax or even the conditional compilation model. For the time being, conditional compilation provides an easy way to detect browser capability based on version and platform information.

Other JScript Capabilities

There are numerous JScript capabilities that you might not be aware of. Listed here are some of the most interesting applications and tools that Microsoft provides for JScript. Learn more about these technologies at **http://msdn.microsoft.com/scripting**.

- Remote Scripting—Permits remote procedure calls (RPC) from client-side JScript to server-side JScript in both a synchronous and asynchronous fashion. Client-side scripts make calls through an embedded Java applet to Active Server Pages on the remote server, eliminating the need for traditional interaction via the submission of form data.

- Script Control—Allows you to embed JScript and ActiveX controls in applications.

- Script Host—Integrates JScript support into the Windows operating system, allowing you to automate OS tasks with JScript in a manner similar to shell scripting in UNIX.

- **ActiveXObject** support—Server-side JScript can take advantage of OLE **Automation** objects through the **ActiveXObject** interface to harness services provided by the operating system. For example, you can create a **FileSystemObject** to access and manipulate local drives, folders, and files. Client-side JavaScript can take advantage of these capabilities as well, but only in certain circumstances—for example, when using HTML Applications or when all security features of the browser have been disabled.

CSS Filters

CSS Filters provide a way for developers to add a rich set of visual special effects to their pages without having to resort to embedded multimedia files (such as Flash). These capabilities are available as proprietary CSS (and JavaScript) extensions in systems capable of displaying 256 or more colors that are running IE4+. *Filters* change the static appearance of content in a way that is very similar to the filters provided by graphics manipulation programs such as Photoshop. *Transitions* provide movie-like special effects during page loads, for example, fade-ins and pixelations.

Filters and transitions can be applied to elements through scripts or through the use of static CSS. Specific properties for each filter and transition give the developer a wide range of flexibility over the nature of each effect. For example, they allow the specification of different colors, transition speeds, and even ambient lighting.

While full details of CSS Filters are beyond the scope of this book, the following example illustrates the use of the Xray filter. You can try it yourself by substituting your own image for "myimage.gif." Clicking the image toggles the Xray filter.

```
<script language="JavaScript" type="text/javascript"><!--
function toggleXray( theObject )
{
  // get status of the filter
  var xrayStatus = theObject.filters.item('xray').enabled;
  // toggle the status
  theObject.filters.item('xray').enabled = !xrayStatus;
}
//--></script>
<!-- Place an image on the Web page and manipulate its filter -->
<img src="myimage.gif" id="picture" style="filter:xray" onclick="toggleXray( this )">
```

Using scripts to manipulate filters and transitions can give an almost film-like quality to a Web page. Instead of blasé rollovers from one image to another, JavaScript developers can use transitions such as Fades, Wipes, and RandomDissolves to switch from one image to another.

You can find complete information about CSS Filters at MSDN, currently at **msdn.microsoft.com/library/default.asp?url=/workshop/author/filter/filters.asp**.

Data Binding

Server-side programs such as CGI scripts have traditionally been used to implement data-intensive Web applications, such as pages that allow a user to query or update a large database of information. In the traditional model, form data is submitted to the server-side program, which then parses it, queries the relevant data source, and builds a new page from the result of the query. This new page is then returned to the client, and the process begins anew. Data Binding in Internet Explorer 4+ shifts most of the work to the client-side by providing the ability to bind data sources directly to HTML elements.

In the Data Binding model, a data source is defined at the beginning of the page and then bound to elements (such as the use of the <**span**> tag in tables or form fields) with the proprietary **datasrc** and **datafld** attributes. Through an embedded applet or ActiveX control, the browser automatically handles the retrieval, organization, and presentation of data in the page, a responsibility that was once the domain of server-side scripts. By moving functionality from the server to the client, any further processing of the data—for example, refining search criteria or re-ordering data items—can be carried out in the browser without additional interaction with the server. A wide variety of data sources (Data Source Objects, or DSOs in Microsoft parlance) can be used to supply the data in a fairly interchangeable manner. Most often these DSOs are SQL databases, but they can also be JDBC data sources or even XML or tab-delimited text files.

While a complete discussion of Data Binding is outside the scope of this book, JavaScript programmers in an Internet Explorer environment should be aware that the browser provides a very powerful set of features related to Data Binding. These features are exposed through the document object model, most obviously as the **dataSrc** and **dataFld** properties of element objects. You can dynamically add, modify, and delete data sources from different tags in addition to directly accessing and manipulating the data records themselves. Data source objects have a **recordset** property that can be used to move through, add, and modify records dynamically. Often developers present the user with a list of records and use the **recordset** methods to display and change individual records in response to user actions, for example, by including calls to **recordset** methods in **onclick** handlers of form buttons.

Microsoft Office Web Components

Similar in nature to Data Binding is the process of accessing data objects exposed by various applications, for example Microsoft Office Web Components. These objects are the same ones that desktop applications use to carry out their tasks, so accessing them in Web pages permits many operations that one would normally associate with "real" applications. For example, the **DataSourceControl** object allows scripts to access a wide variety of data sources. It is also possible to place an **Excel** object on your Web page and to insert and manipulate cells in the resulting embedded application just as with a full-blown spreadsheet. Because all of this work is done on the client side, using these features requires that Microsoft Office 2000 or later be installed on the client machine, in addition to Microsoft Office Web Components.

The DataSourceControl Object

By instantiating a **DataSourceControl** object, your scripts can connect to an arbitrary data source, query it, and display the results in the page. The data source can be any valid data source available on the client's machine, most likely defined with Windows' ODBC Data Source Administrator.

The following example illustrates one possibility by connecting to a SQL Server database. The connection information has been omitted for obvious reasons, but you can easily replace the information with values appropriate to your particular environment. As is often the case, VBScript is easier to use for this particular application, so it is utilized liberally in the example. (VBScript is often the scripting language of choice for these kinds of tasks because of its tight coupling with Microsoft's COM.)

```
<!DOCTYPE HTML PUBLIC "-//W3C//DTD HTML 4.01 Transitional//EN"
 "http://www.w3.org/TR/html4/loose.dtd">
<html><head><title>Data Object Example</title></head>
<body>
```

```
<script language="JavaScript" type="text/javascript"><!--
function writeToBrowser(text)
{
     document.write(text);
}
//--></script>
<h2>This is a data binding example</h2>
<!--  The following creates an instance of the DataSourceControl object.
The id attribute is arbitrary (ie, it doesn't have to be "datasource"-->
<object classid="CLSID:0002E530-0000-0000-C000-000000000046"
id="datasource"></object>
<table border="1">
<tr>
<td><b>Product</b></td>
<td><b>Cost</b></td>
</tr>
<script language="vbs" type="text/vbscript">
// connect to a SQL Server database
datasource.ConnectionString =
"DRIVER={SQLServer};SERVER=yourServer;DATABASE=yourDatabase;UID=yourDBUsername;PWD=yourDBPW;"
// add a recordset definition
Set rsd = datasource.RecordsetDefs.AddNew("SELECT product , cost FROM product", 3)
// Obtain the recordset from DataSourceControl's RecordsetDef
Set rs = datasource.DefaultRecordset
product_count = rs.RecordCount
// loop through the resulting query and output product and cost
For i = 0 to product_count - 1
   writeToBrowser( "<tr>" )
   writeToBrowser( "<td>" )
   // enter column 1 data into the next row
   writeToBrowser( rs.Fields( 0 ).value )
   writeToBrowser( "</td>" )
   writeToBrowser( "<td>" )
   // enter column 2 data into the next row
   writeToBrowser( rs.Fields( 1 ).value )
   writeToBrowser( "</td>" )
   writeToBrowser( "</tr>" )
   rs.MoveNext
Next
</script>
</table></body></html>
```

Notice how this example, which is mostly written in VBScript, includes a JavaScript function. This allows the VBScript to call the JavaScript writeToBrowser() *function.*

This script looks very similar to an ASP page that one might write to perform the same task. As with data binding, the only difference between the client-side and server-side implementation is that instead of the server pulling data from a data source, the client does so.

Because the client accesses the data directly, security issues should definitely be carefully considered before using this technique. For example, this technique might be appropriate for an intranet application with trusted clients, but might not be appropriate for deployment on a public Web server. If you are tasked with creating intranet applications that query or update a local database, this technique can be used to reduce server load by moving much of the functionality to the client side.

Spreadsheet Objects

Using the spreadsheet component, you can embed an Excel spreadsheet in a document, complete with most of the functionality of the original application. This feature can be very useful for data-intensive applications that are best carried out inside of a spreadsheet-like interface.

The following simple example shows how to insert data into the spreadsheet, boldface a row, change the color of a row, and even hide part of the spreadsheet. Once again, use of VBScript permits us easy access to the components in question.

```
<!DOCTYPE HTML PUBLIC "-//W3C//DTD HTML 4.01 Transitional//EN"
"http://www.w3.org/TR/html4/loose.dtd">
<html><head><title>Excel Spreadsheet Example</title></head>
<body>
<!-- Create an Excel object in the page -->
<object classid="clsid:0002E510-0000-0000-C000-000000000046" height="50%"
id="product_grid" width="600"></object>

<script language="vbs" type="text/vbscript">
// change the title of the Excel spreadsheet
product_grid.TitleBar.Caption = "This is an Excel spreadsheet object."
// enter data into the cell corresponding to the first row, first column
product_grid.ActiveSheet.Cells( 1 , 1 ).Value = "Products"
//enter data into the cell corresponding to the first row, second column
product_grid.ActiveSheet.Cells( 1 , 2 ).Value = "Cost"
// enter data into the cell corresponding to the second row, first column
product_grid.ActiveSheet.Cells( 2 , 1 ).Value = "Widget"
//enter data into the cell corresponding to the second row, second column
product_grid.ActiveSheet.Cells( 2 , 2 ).Value = "$50"
```

```
// make all the elements of the first row bold
product_grid.Rows( 1 ).Font.Bold = True

//change the background color of the first row
product_grid.Rows( 1 ).Interior.Color = "#999999"

// hide all the columns other than the first one
product_grid.Range(product_grid.Cells( 1 , 3 ), product_grid.Cells( 1 ,
product_grid.Cells.Columns.Count)).EntireColumn.Hidden = true
</script>
</body></html>
```

Almost anything you can do using the Excel desktop program you can do through the **Excel** object. Combining the **Excel** object with the **DataSourceControl** object, you can even pull data from a database directly into an Excel spreadsheet, letting the user modify the information; for example:

```
<!DOCTYPE HTML PUBLIC "-//W3C//DTD HTML 4.01 Transitional//EN"
"http://www.w3.org/TR/html4/loose.dtd">
<html><head><title>Data Object Populating Excel Spreadsheet Example</title></head>
<body>
<h2>This is a DataSourceObject/Excel example.</h2>
<!-- The data source  -->
<object classid="CLSID:0002E530-0000-0000-C000-000000000046"
id="datasource"></object>
<!-- The Excel Object -->
<object classid="clsid:0002E510-0000-0000-C000-000000000046" height="50%"
id="product_grid" width="600"></object>

<script language="vbs" type="text/vbscript">

// ---- Spreadsheet setup
// change the title of the Excel spreadsheet
product_grid.TitleBar.Caption = "This is an Excel spreadsheet object."
// enter heading
product_grid.ActiveSheet.Cells( 1 , 1 ).Value = "Products"
product_grid.ActiveSheet.Cells( 1 , 2 ).Value = "Cost"
// make all the elements of the first row bold
product_grid.Rows( 1 ).Font.Bold = True
//change the background color of the first row
product_grid.Rows( 1 ).Interior.Color = "#999999"
```

```
// hide all the columns other than the first two
product_grid.Range(product_grid.Cells( 1 , 3 ), product_grid.Cells( 1 ,
product_grid.Cells.Columns.Count)).EntireColumn.Hidden = true


// ---- Populate the spreadsheet with data from the database
// connect to a SQL Server database
datasource.ConnectionString =
"DRIVER={SQLServer};SERVER=yourServerName;DATABASE=yourDBName;UID=yourDBUsername;
PWD=yourDBPW;"


// add a recordset definition
Set rsd = datasource.RecordsetDefs.AddNew("SELECT product , cost FROM
product", 3)
// obtain the recordset from DataSourceControl's RecordsetDef
Set record_set = datasource.DefaultRecordset

product_count = rs.RecordCount
// loop through the resulting query and output product and cost
// output into row "i + 2" because we don't want to overwrite the data
already inserted in the header
// get the data from Fields( 0 ) for the first column of the query ("product")
// get the data from Fields( 1 ) for the second column of the query ("cost")
For i = 0 to product_count - 1
   // enter column 1 data into the next row
   product_grid.ActiveSheet.Cells( i + 2 , 1 ).Value = record_set.Fields( 0 ).value
   //enter column 2 data into the next row
   product_grid.ActiveSheet.Cells( i + 2 , 2 ).Value = record_set.Fields( 1 ).value

   rs.MoveNext
Next
</script>
</body></html>
```

Changes that the user makes to the spreadsheet can be saved back into the database in a similar manner. Clearly, these capabilities are very powerful. You can learn more about them, as usual, from MSDN.

Dynamic Properties

In Internet Explorer 5+, the value of an object property is not restricted to constant values. You can set a property equal to any valid JavaScript expression, causing the value to be updated whenever the value of the expression changes. The methods used for dynamic properties are listed in Table 23-14. The first three can be invoked as methods of any object in the document object hierarchy, while the **recalc()** method is a property of the **Document** object.

Dynamic properties are incredibly useful. The most obvious application is to automate the update of style properties, eliminating the need to manually update styles when an event like window resizing occurs. For example, to place a heading exactly a quarter of the way across the screen, no matter how the window is resized, you might use:

```
<h1 style="position: absolute; font-size: 48pt;"
id="myHeading">Dynamic Properties</h1>
<script language="JScript" type="text/jscript">
<!--
document.all("myHeading").style.setExpression("fontSize",
"document.body.clientWidth/6");
// -->
</script>
```

The result before resizing and after resizing is shown in Figure 23-2.

Method	Description
setExpression("*aproperty*", "*expression*")	Sets the *aproperty* property of the object to *expression*.
getExpression("*aproperty*")	Retrieves the expression to which the value of *aproperty* is set.
removeExpression("*aproperty*")	Removes the expression to which the value of *aproperty* is set.
document.recalc(*allExpressions*)	Explicitly forces recalculation of properties set to expressions for the document. *allExpressions* is a Boolean that when **true** forces recalculation of every expression in the document. If **false** or omitted, only those expressions that have changed since the last recalculation are reevaluated.

Table 23-14.   *Dynamic Property Methods for Internet Explorer 5+*

Figure 23-2. *The dynamically positioned heading before resizing*

Dynamic properties are, of course, not limited merely to style. The following example illustrates the automatic updating of the **innerText** property of an element. The *sum* element's **innerText** property is set to an expression summing the values of two form fields. Whenever the values of fields change, the sum is updated. Sample output is shown in Figure 23-3.

```html
<!DOCTYPE HTML PUBLIC "-//W3C//DTD HTML 4.01 Transitional//EN"
         "http://www.w3.org/TR/html4/loose.dtd">
<html>
<head>
<title>Dynamic Properties Example 2</title>
</head>
<body>
<form>
First Number: <input type="text" id="num1" value="0"><br>
Second Number: <input type="text" id="num2" value="0"><br>
Sum: <b id="sum"> </b>
</form>
<script language="JScript" type="text/jscript">
```

```
<!--
document.all("sum").setExpression("innerText",
"parseInt(document.all('num1').value) +
parseInt(document.all('num2').value)");
// -->
</script>
</body>
</html>
```

Many developers find the dynamic properties capability very exciting. It simplifies some aspects of page layout and can be used to implement all sorts of applications. The simple calculator- and spreadsheet-like capabilities hinted at in the previous example are just the tip of the iceberg. In addition, the dynamic properties capability greatly simplifies positioning of the static menus discussed in Chapter 16.

Note *You can set dynamic properties directly in style sheets using the **expression()** syntax. For example: **height: expression(document.body.clientHeight/2)***

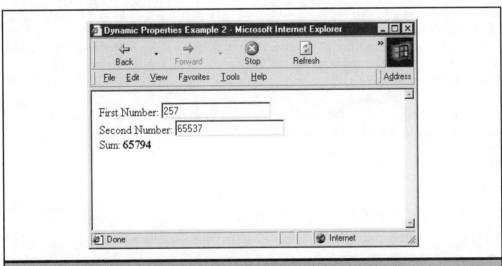

Figure 23-3.   *Using dynamic properties to create a basic calculator*

HTML Applications

HTML Applications (HTAs) allow Web pages to be run like applications on a client's machine. HTAs are normal HTML documents (with associated CSS and JavaScript) renamed with an ".hta" extension. When they are encountered on the Web, the user is prompted with the option to run the file like a normal executable or to save it to disk. Whether saved to disk and then activated or executed directly from the Web, the HTA runs within the context of Internet Explorer. The appearance of the window in which the HTA appears is by default naked (without browser buttons, application menus, and so forth) but can be customized by placing a **\<hta:application\>** element in the document **\<head\>**.

The primary purpose of HTAs is to enable developers to implement complete applications with HTML and its associated technologies. The applications provide their own user interface and are given total access to the client machine. This means that you could write a word processor, spreadsheet, e-mail client, or file utility with an HTML- and CSS-based presentation that uses JavaScript to implement its functionality. You can embed Java applets and ActiveX controls in HTAs as you would in a normal page, and you can use these technologies to carry out operating system and network tasks that would be considerably more complicated or impossible with JavaScript alone.

The following example is a simple text editor. It reads and writes to a file called "test.txt" in the root directory of your C: drive. It doesn't include any error checking and is only intended to demonstrate the basic operation of HTAs. The user is presented with a **\<textarea\>** and two buttons, one that writes the text to the file, and the other that reads the content of the file. You can save the following code as an .hta file and run it from your local drive or from a Web page. Before doing so, be sure that you don't have any important information in C:\TEST.TXT. The output (after typing in some extra text) is shown in Figure 23-4.

```
<!DOCTYPE HTML PUBLIC "-//W3C//DTD HTML 4.01 Transitional//EN"
          "http://www.w3.org/TR/html4/loose.dtd">
<html>
<head>
<title>HTA Example</title>
</head>
<script language="JScript" type="text/jscript">
<!--
// CAREFUL -- no error checking
function readFile()
  {
    var fso, fileHandle, contents;
    fso = new ActiveXObject("Scripting.FileSystemObject");
    fileHandle = fso.OpenTextFile("c:\\test.txt", 1);
    contents = fileHandle.ReadAll();
```

```
    if (contents)
      document.all("fileContents").value = contents;

    fileHandle.close();
 }

function writeFile()
{
    var fso, fileHandle;
    fso = new ActiveXObject("Scripting.FileSystemObject");
    fileHandle = fso.CreateTextFile("c:\\test.txt", true);
    fileHandle.write(document.all("fileContents").value);
    fileHandle.close();
}
//-->
</script>
</head>
<body onload="writeFile()">
<h2>Simple File Editor</h2> Modifying <tt>C:\TEST.TXT</tt>
<form>
<textarea id="fileContents" cols="50" rows="15">
HTAs are powerful.
</textarea>
<br>
<input type="button" value="Read File" onclick="readFile()">    
<input type="button" value="Write File" onclick="writeFile()">
</body>
</html>
```

There are some significant drawbacks to using HTAs. First, they work only under IE5+ in Windows systems. Second, because they are allowed unfettered access to local operating system resources, many users will (for good reason) be reluctant to run them. Note that the browser does warn about HTAs, as shown here:

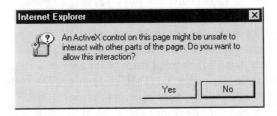

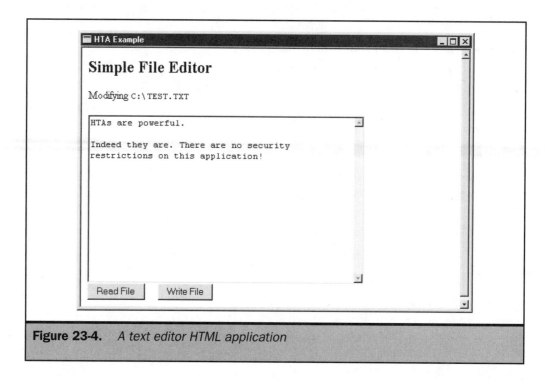

Figure 23-4. *A text editor HTML application*

Despite the fact that the ActiveX controls embedded in many pages users visit on a regular basis have the same capabilities, many users are reluctant to run "executables" like HTAs, even if they can view the source beforehand. There are also some special considerations when using frames with HTAs.

DHTML Behaviors

Behaviors are aimed at moving complex DHTML code out of the page and into smaller, encapsulated, reusable units that serve as the basic building blocks for more complicated applications. Behaviors are a natural outgrowth of the scriptlet capabilities included as a part of Internet Explorer 4. The idea is to encapsulate specific functionality—for example, rollover image swapping or tooltip display—in an HTML Component (HTC) that can be bound to arbitrary elements in a page. HTCs are essentially just separate files containing instance-independent JavaScript code, but in principle Behaviors can be implemented as binaries or VBScript just as easily. However, because this is a book about JavaScript, we naturally focus on HTCs using Microsoft's form of JavaScript, JScript.

At first glance the task of moving DHTML code out of the page itself might seem daunting. After all, it always seems there needs to be some JavaScript in the page, doesn't it? The truth of the matter is that Behaviors allow you (in principle) to move *all* DHTML code, including event handlers, outside of the main document. While there are certainly cases where you will want to include JavaScript directly in the page, you can move most commonly used functionality into HTCs. Customization of Behaviors attached to individual elements is achieved by including an appropriate developer-defined HTML attribute in their tags. Additionally, Internet Explorer comes equipped with numerous and powerful built-in Behaviors that you can use without any coding at all. And, to top it all off, binding Behaviors to elements is incredibly simple. A Behavior can be attached to an element with only one line of JavaScript, or with no JavaScript at all by using an element's CSS bindings.

Excluding scriptlets, there are two kinds of Behaviors available. Internet Explorer 5 supports the original DHTML Behaviors, now referred to as "attached Behaviors." Internet Explorer 5.5 supports an extension of attached Behaviors known as "element Behaviors." The two technologies are not mutually exclusive; rather, each complements the capabilities of the other. The following sections focus primarily on attached Behaviors, but we include a brief discussion of element Behaviors towards the end.

Attaching Behaviors

There are several ways to add a Behavior to an element. The first is by using an element object's **addBehavior()** method. This method accepts a string as an argument indicating the URL of the HTC file that defines the Behavior to add. For example, to attach a rollover Behavior defined in "rollover.htc" to a button with **id** "myButton," you might write

```
document.all("myButton").addBehavior("rollover.htc");
```

You can achieve the same result by setting the **behavior** property of the object's **Style**. For example:

```
document.all("myButton").style.behavior = "rollover.htc";
```

Normally, when binding Behaviors to a large number of elements, the **behavior** extension to the CSS syntax is used. For example, you might assign all your rollover buttons to **class** "rolloverButton" and then attach the HTC to the class with the following CSS:

```
.rolloverButton { behavior:url(rollover.htc) }
```

Because Behaviors are an extension to CSS, you can define them inline as well:

```
<img style="behavior:url(rollover.htc)" src="myimage.gif">
```

To add multiple Behaviors to an element, you can use multiple calls to **addBehavior()**, set multiple space-separated values in the assignment to **style.behavior**, or include multiple **url()** clauses in the style sheet. The following example illustrates the use of multiple **url()**s in the style bindings:

```
.rolloverButton { behavior:url(rolloverr.htc) url(tooltip.htc) }
```

Removing Behaviors

The process of removing a Behavior depends upon how it was added. If the Behavior was added using **addBehavior()**, then the return value of this method is a unique integer that can be passed to **removeBehavior()** in order to remove it. If the Behavior was added using another method, removing it is considerably more complicated. You will most likely need to manually examine the **behaviorUrns** collection of the element in question to determine the **id** of the Behavior you wish to remove. Once determined, you might be able to pass that integer to **removeBehavior()**. A simple example of adding and then immediately removing a Behavior follows.

```
var behaviorIndex = document.all("myButton").addBehavior("rollover.htc");
document.all("myButton").removeBehavior(behaviorIndex);
```

If you need to dynamically remove Behaviors, it is almost always best to add them with calls to **addBehavior()** rather than inline CSS.

Defining Behaviors

HTC files define the public interface, event bindings, and code for a Behavior. These files contain HTML and HTC elements and are saved with an .htc extension. The following example shows the form of a typical HTC file:

```
<public:component>
   <!-- definitions of public properties -->
   <!-- definition of public methods -->
   <!-- definitions binding events at the element to actions in this HTC -->
<script language="JScript" type="text/jscript">
   // code implementing HTC behavior
</script>
</public:component>
```

The **<public:component>** and related elements that we will see shortly are defined by the proprietary XML-based HTC language, so don't worry if you haven't seen them before. You will also notice that some elements will be closed with **"/>"**. Doing this ensures that empty elements are well formed, as required by XML.

Ignoring for the moment the issue of public methods and properties, we first consider how to bind events to code in the HTC. Event binding is carried out with the **<public:attach>** element. Its **event** attribute is set to the event handler you wish to "capture," and its **onevent** attribute is set to the code to execute when the event occurs. For example, to capture **mouseover** events and change the background color of the element, you might define the following HTC:

```
<public:component>
<public:attach event="onmouseover" onevent="activateBackground()"/>
<script language="JScript" type="text/jscript">
<!--
var originalColor;
function activateBackground()
{
   originalColor = style.backgroundColor;
   style.backgroundColor = "yellow";
}
//-->
</script>
</public:component>
```

Notice how the HTC can implicitly access the **Style** object of the element to which it is bound. This is because the scoping rules for HTCs dictate that, if the identifier is not found in the Behavior itself, then the element to which it is attached is the next enclosing scope. If the name cannot be resolved in the element to which it is attached, the **Window** in which the element is defined is checked. Note that you can reference the object to which the Behavior is bound explicitly using the **element** identifier, but there is rarely a need to do so in practice.

To expose a public property to the document containing the element to which the Behavior is bound, a **<public:property>** element is used with the **name** attribute set to the name of the property. For example, you might include the following in your HTC:

```
<public:property name="activeColor"/>
```

Elements to which the Behavior is bound can then set this value by setting an *activeColor* attribute. Assuming the "rollover" **class** is bound to your HTC, you might use:

```
<a href="index.html" class="rollover" activeColor="red">Click me</a>
```

To see how this might be used, we revisit the previous rollover example, this time including an **onload** event handler that sets the *activeColor* if one was not defined in the element:

```
<public:component>
```

```
<public:attach event="onmouseover" onevent="activateBackground()"/>
<public:attach event="onmouseout" onevent="deactivateBackground()"/>
<public:attach event="onload" for="window" onevent="initialize()"/>
<public:property name="activeColor" />
<script language="JScript" type="text/jscript">
<!--
var originalColor;
function activateBackground()
{
    originalColor = style.backgroundColor;
    style.backgroundColor = activeColor;
}
function deactivateBackground()
{
    style.backgroundColor = originalColor;
}
function initialize()
{
    // if the activeColor wasn't specified in an attribute, set it
    if (!activeColor)
        activeColor = "yellow";
}
//-->
</script>
</public:component>
```

There are several new aspects to this HTC. An **onmouseout** handler was attached to revert the background to its original color. In addition, the *activeColor* property was exposed, allowing it to be set as an element's attribute. An **onload** handler for the **Window** object was also specified. This handler invokes *initialize()*, which checks to see if the *activeColor* was specified in the element to which the Behavior is attached. If it wasn't, *activeColor* will not be defined, so it is set to a default value, in this case yellow.

Assuming that this Behavior is included in the file "rollover.htc," we can attach it to elements in a document; for example:

```
<b style="behavior:url(rollover.htc)" activeColor="red">This is red on rollover</b>
<br>
<b style="behavior:url(rollover.htc)">This is yellow on rollover</b>
```

The first **<b>** has an explicitly set *activeColor*, but the second does not. As a result, the second receives the default color, yellow.

HTCs can expose methods as well as properties. Exposing a method is similar to exposing a property, except that a **<public:method>** element is used with **name** set to the name of the function to expose. Once exposed, the function can be invoked as a method of any element to which the Behavior is bound.

Although the capabilities we have discussed so far might seem impressive, they are really only the basic aspects of Behavior definition. There are numerous other features available, including the ability to create custom event handlers and much nicer DHTML effects than we have space for here. After reading this section, you have a solid grounding upon which you can build more advanced DHTML Behavior skills. Interested readers are encouraged to visit Microsoft's MSDN site (**msdn.microsoft.com**) to learn more about what DHTML Behaviors have to offer. But first, it is important to be aware of the Behaviors that come built into the browser by default.

Default Behaviors

Internet Explorer 5+ comes equipped with numerous DHTML Behaviors that can be applied to a wide variety of elements. These Behaviors are listed in Table 23-15.

As you can see, the default Behaviors are more related to browser functionality and state information than to traditional DHTML. The interfaces they expose can be a bit complex, so we will not get into the specifics of each (although an example of saving state information is included at the end of Chapter 16, and browser capabilities were touched upon in Chapter 17).

Default Behaviors are attached to elements like any other Behavior, but the URL employed has the form:

#default#*behaviorName*

where *behaviorName* is the name of the default Behavior you wish to attach. For example, to attach the **userData** Behavior to all form elements, you might use the following in your CSS definitions:

```
form { behavior:url(#default#userData) }
```

Full documentation of default Behaviors can be found at MSDN.

Element Behaviors

Whereas attached Behaviors augment or override the normal behavior of an existing element, element Behaviors are used to define new, customized elements. For instance, you can create your own rollover element, define default Behaviors for it, and include it in your pages as if it were a real part of HTML. You can even use attached Behaviors with new elements created in this fashion.

Creating a custom element is like creating an attached Behavior. An HTC file is created using almost exactly the same syntax as you would use to define an attached

Behavior	Description
anchorClick	Enables the browser to show a browseable navigation "tree" for a Web server. This Behavior can only be attached to **<a>** elements.
anim	Enables interaction with Microsoft's DirectAnimation viewer.
clientCaps	Provides information about the browser and platform—similar to **Navigator** object, but more detailed. Also provides an easy way to install browser components.
download	Downloads a file and invokes a callback function when the download has completed.
homePage	Provides information about the user's starting page. For example, it permits getting, setting, and navigating to the start page.
httpFolder	Enables features that allow browsing of navigation "tree" (folder view).
saveFavorite	Enables the current state of the page to be saved when the page is added to the user's list of "Favorites." Most often attached to a form and very useful for a "login" page.
saveHistory	Enables the current state of the page to be saved for the current browsing session. Whenever the user navigates back to the page, the page will be displayed with the saved state. Most often attached to a form.
saveSnapshot	Enables the current state of the page to be saved when the user saves the page to the local file system.
userData	Permits saving and retrieving large amounts of state information, even across multiple browsing sessions.

Table 23-15.   *Default DHTML Behaviors*

Behavior. However, an element Behavior is imported into the page using XML, and after it has been imported the new element can be used directly in the page without explicit binding to the HTC file. Because the HTC file defines the new element, there is no need to use **addBehavior()** or the CSS syntax used for attached Behaviors; doing so would be redundant. In fact, it is not possible to bind an element Behavior to an element as you would an attached Behavior.

Element Behaviors are tremendously powerful, and well beyond the scope of this book. However, readers with an understanding of XML and the attached Behavior features discussed previously should have little problem creating their own elements. Aside from the highly nonstandard nature of element Behaviors, the only drawback of their use is that they are supported only by Internet Explorer 5.5+. For the time being, it might be advisable to stick with attached Behaviors until browser demographics shift heavily to newer versions of IE.

Behaviors Versus Traditional DHTML

There are two primary advantages that attached Behaviors have over traditional DHTML. The first is that attached Behaviors are easier to add to your pages and are easier to maintain once they have been added. The second is that Behaviors are more encapsulated and reusable than most traditional DHTML applications. While traditional DHTML can certainly be written in a very modular fashion, it is generally far easier to create reusable components using attached Behaviors. In addition, Behaviors are easily used in combination on the same element. This is a feature even well-written traditional code often lacks.

Element Behaviors permit functionality that would otherwise be impossible (or very hard to obtain). The ability to extend your documents with your own custom elements gives you tremendous freedom in design and implementation.

The downside of Behaviors has already been mentioned, namely, that they are a proprietary technology not yet a part of any standard. But, then again, a large number of DHTML applications are written to use proprietary document object models, so Behaviors do not mark all that significant of a departure from traditional trends.

Popup Windows

The final proprietary extension provided by Internet Explorer is the ability to create popup windows using the **createPopup()** method of the **Window** object. This capability was touched upon in Chapter 12, but is included here for completeness.

The behavior of popup windows is a bit odd. The **createPopup()** method accepts no arguments and returns a reference to a window that was created. The newly created popup window is initially empty and hidden and is not immediately given focus. The programmer is responsible for populating the window with content and then displaying it to the user with its **show()** method. The popup menu is then automatically hidden once the user activates another part of the page, for example by right-clicking outside of the popup menu.

The syntax of the **show()** method is

popupWindow.show(*x*, *y*, *width*, *height* [, *relativeTo*])

where *popupWindow* is a reference to a window created with **window.createPopup()** and *x*, *y*, *width*, and *height* specify the horizontal location, vertical location, width, and height of the popup window in pixels. The optional *relativeTo* parameter is a reference to the object to which the *x* and *y* coordinates are relative. If *relativeTo* is omitted then the *x* and *y* coordinates are treated as relative to the upper-left corner of the window.

Creating an example popup window gives us a good excuse to exercise the conditional compilation features mentioned earlier in the chapter. Because popup windows are available only in Internet Explorer 5.5+, one would only be used if supported by the browser. Otherwise, an **alert()** box would be used, although it would probably be better to use a relatively positioned DHTML layer in a "real" application. The popup menu displayed in IE5.5 is shown in Figure 23-5.

```
<!DOCTYPE HTML PUBLIC "-//W3C//DTD HTML 4.01 Transitional//EN"
        "http://www.w3.org/TR/html4/loose.dtd">
<html>
<head>
<title>Popup Window Example</title>
<script language="JScript" type="text/jscript">
<!--
function showPopup()
 {
   /*@cc_on @*/
   /*@if (@_jscript_version >= 5.5)
       var newPopup = window.createPopup();
       newPopup.document.body.style.backgroundColor = "lightblue";
       newPopup.document.body.style.padding = "8";
       newPopup.document.body.innerHTML = "What a <b>wonderful</b> menu!";
       newPopup.show(150, 30, 150, 50, document.all("myButton"));
   @else @*/
       alert("What a boring menu!");
   /*@end @*/
}
// -->
</script>
</head>
<body>
<h2>Popup Example</h2>
<form>
  <input id="myButton" type="button" value="Show the Popup" onclick="showPopup()">
</form>
</body>
</html>
```

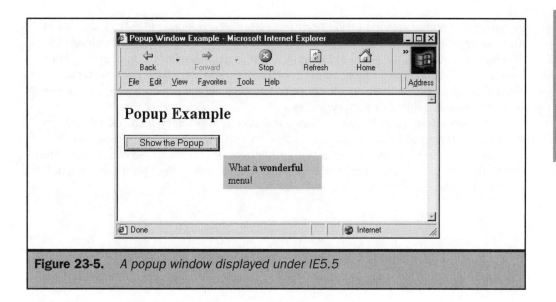

Figure 23-5. *A popup window displayed under IE5.5*

The popup window has a few other useful properties besides **show()**. Its **hide()** method hides it from view and its **isOpen** property returns a Boolean indicating whether the window is currently displayed. A few more examples of IE-specific window features can be found at the end of Chapter 12 and, of course, online at MSDN.

Summary

Microsoft implements its own version of JavaScript called JScript. While the different versions of JScript included in Internet Explorer correspond in varying degrees to versions of Netscape JavaScript, Microsoft has come in line with many standards. JScript 3.0 is compliant with ECMAScript Edition 1 and JScript 5.5 is compliant with ECMAScript Edition 3. However, Microsoft JScript does offer several proprietary features not found in other browsers. For example, conditional compilation allows pieces of code to be selectively included or excluded depending upon platform and JScript version information.

Aside from its proprietary document object model, Internet Explorer comes equipped with a variety of useful features not found in other browsers. Data Binding allows data sources such as SQL databases to be bound to HTML elements and data records to be manipulated with JScript. Dynamic Properties expand the type of values to which document object properties can be set to include expressions that are evaluated dynamically. HTML Applications are HTML documents run as fully trusted applications on the client machine and have access to the full features of the user's operating system. DHTML Behaviors are a powerful technology that allows the encapsulation of specific DHTML functionality into reusable HTML components that can be bound to elements in the page in a variety of ways. Internet Explorer 5.5 also includes support for element Behaviors that permit the definition of entirely new elements that can be used like normal HTML in pages in which they are imported. Version 5.5 also includes support for popup windows, which often provide a convenient way to customize alert or tooltip windows.

Although Internet Explorer provides a wealth of proprietary features, whether these features should be used in a Web site is an important question. Doing so prevents users on non-Windows platforms or with other browsers from using your pages. From a usability perspective, it is highly desirable to include equivalent (or at least partial) functionality for non-Internet Explorer clients.

Chapter 24

JavaScript Practices

In the previous two chapters we covered some of the proprietary issues involving the Netscape and Internet Explorer browsers. While an awareness of the features and quirks of each major browser and version is required to write well-behaved code, it is not a sufficient condition. You need to be able to apply what you know in an effective manner in order to accommodate the needs of your users, fellow programmers, and future script maintainers.

In this chapter we bring to a close our discussion of JavaScript by highlighting some recommended practices for and salient issues regarding JavaScript in the "real world." Our focus is on errors and debugging as well as on writing robust JavaScript that utilizes defensive programming techniques. We also touch on some distribution issues, such as protecting your code and decreasing its download time, and discuss where JavaScript fits into the "big picture" of the Web. The discussion in this chapter condenses many years worth of programming experience into a few dozen pages, so that developers— new ones in particular—can save themselves and their users some headaches by careful consideration of the content presented here.

Errors

Before launching into a discussion of how errors can be found and handled, it is useful to understand the taxonomy of errors found in typical applications. The wide variety of errors that can occur during the execution of a script can be roughly placed into three categories: syntax errors, semantic errors, and runtime errors.

Of the three types of errors, *syntax errors* are the most obvious and are the result of code that somehow violates the rules of the language itself. For example, writing the following:

```
var x = y + * z;
```

is a syntax error because the syntax of the * operator requires two expressions to operate upon, and "y +" does not constitute a valid expression. Another example is:

```
var myString = "This string doesn't terminate
```

because the string literal never terminates.

Syntax errors are generally *fatal* in the sense that they are errors from which the interpreter cannot recover. The reason they are fatal is that they introduce *ambiguity*, which the language syntax is specifically designed to avoid. Sometimes the interpreter can make some sort of assumption about what the programmer intended and can continue to execute the rest of the script. For example, in the case of an unterminated string literal, the interpreter might assume that the string ends at the end of the line.

However, scripts with syntax errors should for all intents and purposes be considered "dead," as they do not constitute a valid program and their behavior can therefore be erratic, destructive, or otherwise anomalous.

Luckily, syntax errors are fairly easy to catch because they are immediately evident when the script is parsed before being executed. You cannot hide a syntax error from the interpreter in any way except by placing it in a comment. Even placing it inside a block that will never be executed, as in:

```
if (false) { x = y + * z }
```

will still result in an error. The reason, as we have stated, is that these types of errors show up during the parsing or compilation of the script, a step that occurs before execution. You can easily avoid syntax errors by turning on error warnings in the browser and then loading the script or by using one of the debuggers discussed later in this chapter.

Errors of the second type, *semantic errors*, occur when the program executes a statement that has an effect that was unintended by the programmer. These errors are much harder to catch because they tend to show up under odd or unusual circumstances and therefore go unnoticed during testing. The most common type of semantic errors are those caused by JavaScript's weak typing; for example:

```
function add(x, y)
{
    return x + y;
}
var mySum = add(prompt("Enter a number to add to five",""), 5);
```

If the programmer intended **add()** to return the numeric sum of its two arguments, then the assignment above is a semantic error in the sense that *mySum* is assigned a string instead of a number. The reason, of course, is that **prompt()** returns a string that causes **+** to act as the string concatenation operator, rather than as the numeric addition operator.

Semantic errors arise most often as the result of interaction with the user. They can usually be avoided by including explicit checking in your functions. For example, we could redefine the **add()** function to ensure that the type and number of the arguments are correct:

```
function add(x, y) {
    if (arguments.length != 2 || typeof(x) != "number" || typeof(y) != "number")
        return(Number.NaN);
    return x + y;
}
```

Alternatively, the **add()** function could be rewritten to attempt to convert its arguments to numbers—for example, by using the **parseFloat()** or **parseInt()** function.

In general, semantic errors can be avoided (or at least reduced) by employing defensive programming tactics. If you write your functions anticipating that users and programmers will purposely try to break them in every conceivable fashion, you can save yourself future headaches. Writing "paranoid" code might seem a bit cumbersome, but doing so enhances code reusability and site robustness (in addition to showcasing your mature attitude towards software development).

In the final category are the *runtime errors*, which are exactly what they sound like: errors that occur while the script is running. These errors result from JavaScript that has the correct syntax but which encounters some sort of problem in its execution environment. Common runtime errors result from trying to access a variable, property, method, or object that does not exist or from attempting to utilize a resource that is not available.

Some runtime errors can be found by examination of source code. For example,

```
window.allert("Hi there");
```

results in a runtime error because there is no **allert()** method of the **Window** object. This example constitutes perfectly legal JavaScript, but the interpreter cannot tell until runtime that invoking **window.allert()** is invalid, because such a method might have been added as an instance property at some previous point during execution.

Other kinds of runtime errors cannot be caught by examination of source code. For example, while the following might appear to be error-free,

```
var products = ["Widgets", "Snarks", "Phasers"]
var choice = parseInt(prompt("Enter the number of the product you are interested in"));
alert("You chose: " + products[choice]);
```

what happens if the user enters a negative value for *choice*? A runtime error indicating the array index is out of bounds. Although some defensive programming can help here,

```
var products = ["Widgets", "Snarks", "Phasers"]
var choice = parseInt(prompt("Enter the number of the product in which you are interested"));
if (choice >= 0 && choice < products.length)
   alert("You chose: " + products[choice]);
```

the reality is that you cannot catch all potential runtime errors before they occur. You can, however, catch them at runtime using JavaScript's error and exception handling facilities, which are discussed later in the chapter.

Debugging

Every programmer makes mistakes, and a large part of becoming a more proficient developer is honing your instincts for finding and rooting out errors in your code. Debugging is a skill that is best learned through experience, and although basic debugging practices can be taught, each programmer must develop an approach that works for him or her. It is because of the individual nature of debugging that most software development groups have a language expert, whether formally or informally designated, to whom elusive problems and anomalies can be taken for resolution. This individual is often a veteran developer with an ability for tracking down problems honed by years of software development experience. Experience is indeed the greatest teacher when it comes to debugging.

Turning on Error Messages

The most basic way to track down errors is by turning on error information in your browser. This is accomplished in Internet Explorer by using the Tools menu, selecting Internet Options, and activating the Advanced tab. Make sure that the "Disable script debugging" box is unchecked and that the "Display a notification about every script error" box is checked, as shown in Figure 24-1.

Netscape 3 shows all JavaScript errors to the user by default, but Netscape 4+ sends them to the JavaScript Console. To view the Console in Netscape 4.x, type **javascript:** in the browser's Location bar. In Netscape 6, use the Tasks menu to open the Tools submenu, and then select "JavaScript Console." By default, the only indication that an error has occurred in Netscape 4 is a message on the status bar:

However, it is possible to configure Netscape 4 to bring up the JavaScript Console whenever an error occurs. To do so follow these steps:

1. Quit the browser.
2. Open the file prefs.js for editing. This file is usually found in the Netscape install directory (or in UNIX, it is often called preferences.js under ~/.netscape).
3. Add the following line to the file:
   user_pref("javascript.console.open_on_error", true);.
4. Save the file and close the editor.

Netscape 6 gives no indication when an error occurs, so you must keep the JavaScript Console open and watch for errors as your script executes.

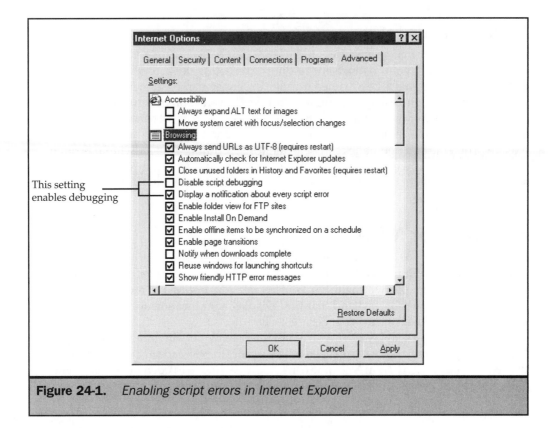

This setting enables debugging

Figure 24-1. *Enabling script errors in Internet Explorer*

Error notifications that show up on the JavaScript Console or through Internet Explorer dialog boxes are the result of both syntax and runtime errors. Loading a file with the syntax error from a previous example,

```
var myString = "This string doesn't terminate
```

results in the error dialog and JavaScript Console messages in Figure 24-2. Loading a file with the runtime error from a previous example,

```
window.allert("Hi there");
```

results in the error dialog and JavaScript Console shown in Figure 24-3.

A very helpful feature of this kind of error reporting is that it includes the line number at which the error occurred. However, you should be aware that occasionally line numbers can become skewed as the result of externally linked files. Most of the

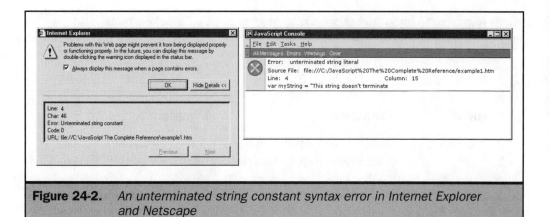

Figure 24-2. *An unterminated string constant syntax error in Internet Explorer and Netscape*

time these error messages are fairly easy to decipher, but some messages are less descriptive than others. It is therefore useful here to explicitly mention some common mistakes.

Common Mistakes

Table 24-1 indicates some common JavaScript mistakes and their symptoms. This list is by no means exhaustive, but it does include the majority of mistakes made by novice programmers. Of this list, errors associated with type mismatches and access to form elements are probably the hardest for beginners to notice, so you should take special care when interacting with forms or other user-entered data.

Using some sort of integrated development environment (IDE) that matches parentheses and that colors your code is often helpful in avoiding syntax errors.

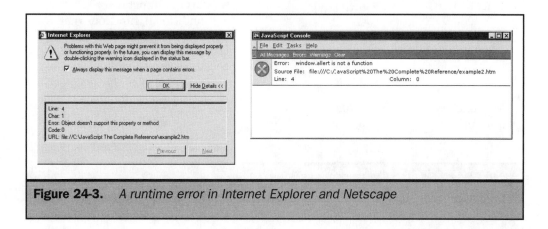

Figure 24-3. *A runtime error in Internet Explorer and Netscape*

Such programs automatically show where parentheses and brackets match and provide visual indications of the different parts of the script. For example, comments might appear in red while keywords appear blue and string literals appear in black.

Mistake	Example	Symptom
Infinite loops	while (*x*<myArray.length) doSomething(myArray[*x*]);	A stack overflow error or a totally unresponsive page.

Using assignment instead of comparison (and vice versa)	if (*x* = 10)
	// or
	var x == 10;
		Clobbered or unexpected values. Some JavaScript implementations automatically fix this type of error. Many programmers put the variable on the right-hand side of a comparison in order to cause an error when this occurs. For example, "if (10 = x)"

Unterminated string literals	var myString = "Uh oh	An "unterminated string literal" error message or malfunctioning code
Mismatched parentheses	if (typeof(*x*) == "number" alert("Number");	A "syntax error," "missing ')'", or "expected ')'" error message
Mismatched curly braces	function mult(*x,y*) { return (*x,y*);	Extra code being executed as part of a function or conditional, functions that are not defined, and "expected '}'", "missing '}'", or "mismatched '}'" error messages
Mismatched brackets	*x*[0 = 10;	"invalid assignment," "expected ']'", or "syntax error" error messages

Table 24-1.   *Common JavaScript Mistakes*

Mistake	Example	Symptom
Misplaced semicolons	if (isNS4 == true); hideLayers();	Conditional statements always being executed, functions returning early or incorrect values, and very often errors associated with unknown properties (as in this example)

Omitted "break" statements	switch(browser)
	{
	case "IE": // IE-specific
	case "NS": // NS-specific
	}
		Statements in the latter part of the **switch** always being executed and very often errors associated with unknown properties

Type errors	var sum = 2 + "2";	Values with an unexpected type, functions requiring a specific type not working correctly, and computations resulting in **NaN**
Accessing undefined variables	var x = variableName;	"*variableName* is not defined" error messages
Accessing non-existent object properties	var x = window.propertyName;	**undefined** values where you do not expect them, computations resulting in **NaN**, "*propertyName* is null or not an object," or "*objectName* has no properties" error messages
Invoking non-existent methods	window.methodName()	"*methodName* is not a function," or "object doesn't support this property or method" error messages
Invoking undefined functions	noSuchFunction();	"object expected" or "*noSuchFunction* is not defined" error messages

Table 24-1. *Common JavaScript Mistakes* (continued)

Mistake	Example	Symptom
Accessing the document before it has finished loading	`<head><script>var myElement=document.all.myElement;</script></head>`	**undefined** values, broken DHTML, and errors associated with nonexistent properties and methods
Accessing a form element rather than its value	`var x = document.myform.myfield;`	Computation resulting in **NaN**, broken DHTML, and form "validation" that always rejects its input

Assuming that detecting an object or method assumes the existence of all other features related to the detected object.	`if (document.layers)`
	`{`
	`  // do Netscape 4 stuff`
	`}`
	`if (document.all)`
	`{`
	`  // do all sorts of IE stuff`
	`}`
		Probably will result in an error message complaining about a nonexistent object or property, because other proprietary objects beyond the detected ones were assumed to be presented and then used.

Table 24-1. *Common JavaScript Mistakes* (continued)

Debugging Techniques

Although turning on error messages and checking for common mistakes can help you find some of the most obvious errors in your code, doing so is rarely helpful in finding logical errors. There are, however, some widespread practices that many developers employ when trying to find the reason for malfunctioning code.

Outputting Debugging Information

One of the most common techniques is to output verbose status information throughout the script in order to verify the flow of execution. For example, a debugging flag might be set at the beginning of the script that enables or disables debugging output included within each function. The most common way to output information in JavaScript is using **alert()**s; for example, you might write something like:

```
var debugging = true;
var whichImage = "widget";
if (debugging)
```

```
        alert("About to call swapImage() with argument: " + whichImage);
    var swapStatus = swapImage(whichImage);
    if (debugging)
        alert("Returned from swapImage() with swapStatus="+swapStatus);
```

and include **alert()**s marking the flow of execution in *swapImages()*. By examining the
content and order of the **alert()**s as they appear, you are granted a window to the
internal state of your script.

Because using a large number of **alert()**s when debugging large or complicated scripts
may be impractical (not to mention annoying), output is often sent to another browser
window instead. Using this technique, a new window is opened at the beginning of the
script, and debugging information is written into the window using its **document.write()**
method. For example, consider the following (erroneous) implementation of the
extractCookie() method from Chapter 16 that has been instrumented with debugging
statements. Of course, you can omit the HTML from the calls to **output()** below; we
included them to ensure correct rendering. Note the **for** loop immediately after the
window.open(). This loop kills some time before writing to the new window in order to
avoid a bug with Internet Explorer that sometimes occurs when you attempt to **write()**
to a newly opened empty window before it is done setting up.

```
var debugging = true;
if (debugging)
{
   var debuggingWindow = window.open("");

   // omitting the name causes a new window to open
   for (var x=0; x<1500000; x++);      // give IE time to open window
   output = debuggingWindow.document.writeln;
   output("<html><head><title>Debugging
Window</title></head><body><pre>");
   // we're going to be writing preformatted info, so include the <pre>
}
var cookies = new Object();     // associative array indexed as cookies["name"] = "value"
function extractCookies()
{ // extract current cookies, destroying old value of cookies array
   if (debugging) output("Beginning extractCookies on:\n" + document.cookie + "\n");
   var name, value, beginning, middle, end;
   beginning = 0;
   while (beginning < document.cookie.length)
    {
```

```
   if (debugging)
      output("Top of the loop (beginning = " + beginning + ")");
   middle = document.cookie.indexOf('=', beginning);
   end = document.cookie.indexOf(';', beginning);
   if (end == -1)
      end = document.cookie.length;
   if ( (middle > end) || (middle == -1) )
    {  // if no equal sign in this cookie...
       if (debugging) output("\tNo value for this cookie");
       name = document.cookie.substring(beginning, end);
       value = "";
    }
   else
    {
       name = document.cookie.substring(beginning, middle);
       value = document.cookie.substring(middle, end);
       if (debugging)
          output("\tExtracted cookie with name='"+name+"' and value='"+value+"'");
    }
   cookies[name] = unescape(value);
   beginning = end + 1;
  }
  if (debugging) output("\nExiting extractCookies()</pre></body></html>")
}
document.cookie = "username=fritz";
document.cookie = "favoritecolor=green";
document.cookie = "debuggingisfun=false";
extractCookies();
alert(cookies["favoritecolor"]);
```

Running this code, it is apparent that there is some sort of error. The following alert is shown:

An examination of the output to the debugging window shown in Figure 24-4 reveals that the reason for this behavior is an extra space in the name of the cookies. Also, it appears as if the equal sign is being included in the value.

Tracing through the source code it looks like the line "beginning = end + 1" is the culprit. It appears as if *beginning* is being set to the character before the name of the next cookie (which is a space) rather than being set to the first character of the cookie name. So we change "beginning = end + 1" to "beginning = end + 2" in hopes that this will solve the problem. Doing so should point *beginning* past the space to the beginning of the cookie name. Running the script with this change results in:

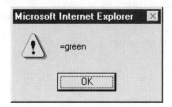

This is definitely progress, but is still incorrect. The debugging output is shown in Figure 24-5.

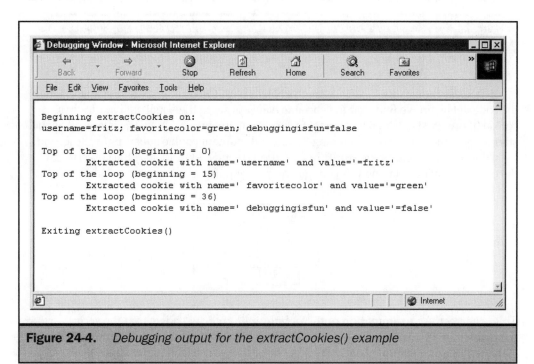

Figure 24-4. *Debugging output for the extractCookies() example*

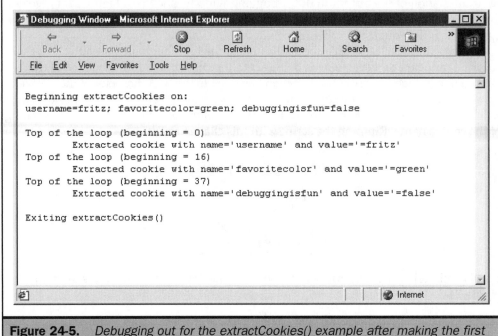

```
Beginning extractCookies on:
username=fritz; favoritecolor=green; debuggingisfun=false

Top of the loop (beginning = 0)
        Extracted cookie with name='username' and value='=fritz'
Top of the loop (beginning = 16)
        Extracted cookie with name='favoritecolor' and value='=green'
Top of the loop (beginning = 37)
        Extracted cookie with name='debuggingisfun' and value='=false'

Exiting extractCookies()
```

Figure 24-5. *Debugging out for the extractCookies() example after making the first correction*

It looks as though we have a similar problem with the cookie value. Tracing through the code yet again we find that the variable *middle* is set to the equal sign in the current cookie (if one exists). When we extract the cookie value into *value*, *middle* is passed as the start of the value substring. Changing "value = document.cookie.substring(middle, end)" to "value = document.cookie.substring(middle + 1, end)" should start the substring at the correct position. Making this change and running the script again results in:

This is correct. An examination of the debugging window shows that the script appears to be functioning correctly, so we can disable debugging. To do so, either the debugging statements can be removed from the script or *debugging* can be set to **false**.

While this example may seem somewhat contrived, it reflects the actual debugging process that went on when **extractCookies()** was written. Using **alert()**s or **write()**s to assist in tracking down problems is a very common technique, but as you can see it requires a bit of work. A better solution is to use a tool designed specifically for the task.

Using a Debugger

A *debugger* is an application that places all aspects of script execution under the control of the programmer. Debuggers provide fine-grain control over the state of the script through an interface that allows you to examine and set values as well as control the flow of execution.

Once a script has been loaded into a debugger, it can be run one line at a time or instructed to halt at certain *breakpoints*. The idea is that once execution is halted, the programmer can examine the state of the variables in order to determine if something is amiss. You can also *watch* variables for changes in their values. When a variable is watched, the debugger will suspend execution whenever the value of the variable changes. This is tremendously useful in trying to track down variables that are mysteriously getting clobbered. Most debuggers also allow you to examine a *trace* of the program, the call tree representing the flow of execution through various pieces of code. And to top it all off, debuggers are often programmed to alert the programmer when a potentially problematic piece of code is encountered. And because debuggers are specifically designed to track down problems, the error messages and warnings they display tend to be more helpful than those of the browser.

Note *Because you can type in **javascript:** pseudo-URLs in the Location bar of Netscape 4 and 6, you can use the browser itself as a primitive debugger. Netscape 4's JavaScript Console also allows you to type in arbitrary statements that are executed within the context of the current document. You can use these capabilities to examine or set values on a page—for example, with **alert()** or assignment statements.*

Clearly, debuggers sound like extremely useful tools. But where can they be found? You have three primary options. The first is the Netscape JavaScript debugger, a Java application that runs on top of Netscape 4.x and is implemented specifically with Netscape JavaScript and the Netscape family of browsers in mind. This debugger has the advantage of accommodating Netscape-centric technologies, like signed scripts and LiveConnect, but has the disadvantage of being a couple of generations out of date (no new version has appeared in the last several years). You can find more information about this free tool at **http://developer.netscape.com/software/jsdebug.html**.

Your second option is Microsoft Script Debugger, a free utility that integrates with Internet Explorer 4+ and is available from **http://msdn.microsoft.com/scripting**. Whenever debugging is turned on and you load a page that has errors, the following dialog is shown in place of the normal error message, allowing you to load the page into the debugger.

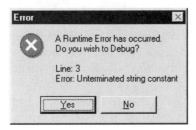

Of course, you can also load a document directly into the debugger without having an error occur. This debugger has the advantage of close coupling with Microsoft's JScript and document object model and is much more current (though still a bit out of date) than Netscape's debugger. A screenshot of Microsoft Script Debugger is shown in Figure 24-6.

The third option you have is to use a commercial development environment. A JavaScript debugger is usually just one small part of such development tools, which

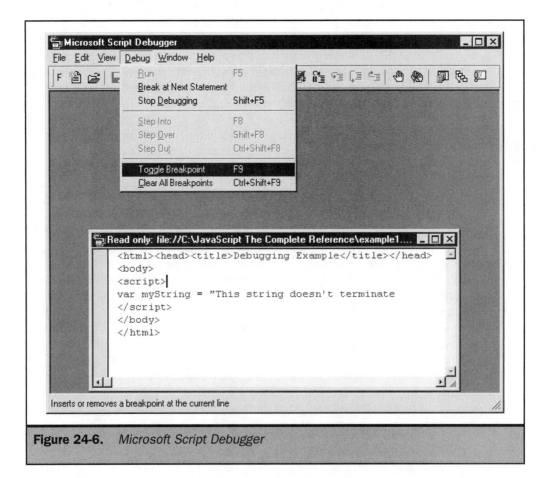

Figure 24-6. *Microsoft Script Debugger*

can offer sophisticated HTML and CSS layout capabilities and can even automate certain aspects of site generation. This option is probably the best choice for professional developers, because chances are you will need a commercial development environment anyway, so you might as well choose one with integrated JavaScript support. A typical example of such an environment is Macromedia's Dreamweaver, available from **http:// www.macromedia.com/software/dreamweaver/** (for purchase or free trial). There are two primary drawbacks to such environments. The first and most obvious is the expense. The second is the fact that such tools tend to emit spaghetti code, so trying to hook your handwritten code into JavaScript or HTML and CSS generated by one of these tools can be tedious.

Defensive Programming

Now that we have covered how you can recognize and track down errors in your code, we turn to techniques you can use to prevent or accommodate problems that might be outside of your direct control.

Defensive programming is the art of writing code that functions properly under adverse conditions. In the context of the Web, an "adverse condition" could be many different things: for example, a user with a very old browser or an embedded object or frame that gets stuck while loading. Coding defensively involves an awareness of the situations in which something can go awry. Some of the most common possibilities you should try to accommodate include:

- Users with JavaScript turned off.
- Users with cookies turned off.
- Embedded Java applets that throw an exception.
- Frames or embedded objects that load incorrectly or incompletely.
- Older browsers that do not support DHTML.
- Older browsers with incomplete JavaScript implementations—for example, those that do not support a specific feature such as the **push()**, **pop()**, and related methods in the **Array** object of versions of Internet Explorer prior to 5.5.
- Browsers with known errors, such as early Netscape browsers with incorrectly functioning **Date** objects.
- Users with third-party, text-based, or aural browsers.
- Users on non-Windows platforms. This is especially important in light of the fact that Internet Explorer for MacOS lags significantly behind Internet Explorer for Windows in terms of functionality.
- Malicious users attempting to abuse a service or resource through your scripts.
- Users who enter typos or other invalid data into form fields or dialog boxes, such as entering letters in a field requiring numbers.

The key to defensive programming is flexibility. You should strive to accommodate as many different possible client configurations and actions as you can. From a coding standpoint, this means you should include HTML (such as **<noscript>**s) and browser sensing code that permit graceful degradation of functionality across a variety of platforms. From a testing standpoint, this means you should always run a script in as many different browsers and versions and on as many different platforms as possible before placing it live on your site.

In addition to accommodating the general issues described above, you should also consider the specific things that might go wrong with your script. If you are not sure when a particular language feature you are using was added to JavaScript, it is always a good idea to check a reference, such as Appendix B of this book, to make sure it is well supported. If you are utilizing DHTML or embedded objects, you might consider whether you have appropriate code in place to prevent execution of your scripts while the document is still loading. If you have linked external .js libraries, you might include a flag in the form of a global variable in each library that can be checked to ensure that the script has properly loaded.

In this section we discuss a variety of techniques you can use for defensive programming. While no single set of ideas or approaches will solve every problem that might be encountered, applying the following principles to your scripts can dramatically reduce the number of errors your clients encounter. Additionally, doing so can also help you solve those errors that are encountered in a more timely fashion. However, at the end of the day, the efficacy of defensive programming comes down to the skill, experience, and attention to detail of the individual developer. If you can think of a way for the user to break your script or to cause some sort of malfunction, this is usually a good sign that more defensive techniques are required.

Error Handlers

Internet Explorer 3+ and Netscape 3+ provide primitive error-handling capabilities through the nonstandard **onerror** handler of the **Window** object. By setting this event handler, you can augment or replace the default action associated with runtime errors on the page. For example, you can replace or suppress the error messages shown in Netscape 3 and Internet Explorer (with debugging turned on) and the output to the JavaScript Console in Netscape 4+. The values to which **window.onerror** can be set and the effects of doing so are outlined in Table 24-2.

*The **onerror** handler is also available for objects other than **Window** in many browsers, most notably the **<img>** and **<object>** elements.*

Value of window.onerror	Effect
null	Suppresses reporting of runtime errors in Netscape 3+.
A function which returns **true**	Executes the function whenever a runtime error occurs and suppresses the normal reporting of runtime errors.
A function which returns **false**	Executes the function whenever a runtime error occurs and reports the error as usual.

Table 24-2. *Effect of Setting window.onerror to Different Values*

Because the display of JavaScript error messages can be unsettling to non-technical users, their display is often suppressed:

```
function doNothing() { return true; }
window.onerror = doNothing;
```

or replaced with a more benign message:

```
function reportError()
{
  alert("Sorry, an error has occurred. As a result, parts of the page might not work properly.");
  return true;
}
window.onerror = reportError;        // replace the default error functionality
window.noSuchProperty();             // throw a runtime error
```

The result in Netscape 6 is shown here:

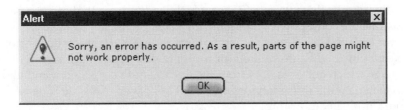

A useful feature of **onerror** handlers is that they are automatically passed three values by the browser. The first argument is a string containing an error message describing the error that occurred. The second is a string containing the URL of the page that generated the error, which might be different from the current page if, for example, the document has frames. The third parameter is a numeric value indicating the line number at which the error occurred.

*Netscape 6 does not currently pass these values to **onerror** handlers. This could be a bug, but it more likely represents a movement towards the exception-handling features described in the next section.*

You can use these parameters to create custom error messages, such as:

```
function reportError(message, url, lineNumber)
{
 if (message && url && lineNumber)        // avoid netscape 6
   alert("An error occurred at "+ url + ", line " + lineNumber + "\nThe error is: " + message);
 return true;
}
window.onerror = reportError;        // assign error handler
window.noSuchProperty();             // throw an error
```

The result of which in Internet Explorer might be:

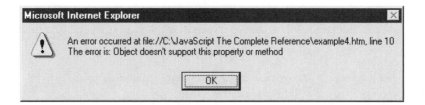

However, a better use for this feature is to add automatic error reporting to your site. You might trap errors and send the information to a new browser window, which automatically submits the data to a CGI or which loads a page that can be used to do so. We illustrate the concept with the following code. Suppose you have a CGI script "submitError.cgi" on your server that accepts error data and automatically notifies the webmaster or logs the information for future review. You might then write the following page which retrieves data from the document that opened it and allows the user to include more information about what happened. This file is named "errorReport.html" in our example:

```
<html>
<head>
<title>Error Submission</title>
<script language="JavaScript" type="text/javascript">
<!--
// fillValues() is invoked when the page loads and retrieves error data from the offending document
function fillValues()
{
  if (window.opener && !window.opener.closed && window.opener.lastErrorURL)
   {
    document.errorForm.url.value = window.opener.lastErrorURL;
    document.errorForm.line.value = window.opener.lastErrorLine;
    document.errorForm.message.value = window.opener.lastErrorMessage;
    document.errorForm.userAgent.value = navigator.userAgent;
   }
}
//-->
</script>
</head>
<body onload="fillValues()">
<h2>An error occurred</h2>
Please help us track down errors on our site by describing in more detail what you were doing when
the error occurred. Submitting this form helps us improve the quality of our site, especially for
users with your browser.
<form id="errorForm" name="errorForm" action="/cgi-bin/submitError.cgi">
The following information will be submitted:<br>
URL: <input type="text" name="url" id="url" size="80"><br>
Line: <input type="text" name="line" id="line" size="4"><br>
Error: <input type="text" name="message" id="message" size="80"><br>
Your browser: <input type="text" name="userAgent" id="userAgent" size="60"><br>
Additional Comments:<br>
<textarea name="comments" value="comments" cols="40" rows="5">
</textarea><br>
<input type="submit" value="Submit to webmaster">
</form>
</body>
</html>
```

The other part of the script is placed in each of the pages on your site and provides
the information that *fillValues()* requires. It does so by setting a handler for **onerror** that

stores the error data and opens "errorReport.html" automatically when a runtime error occurs:

```
var lastErrorMessage, lastErrorURL, lastErrorLine;
// variables to store error data
function reportError(message, url, lineNumber)
{
    if (message && url && lineNumber)
    {
        lastErrorMessage = message;
        lastErrorURL = url;
        lastErrorLine = lineNumber;
        window.open("errorReport.html");
    }
    return true;
}
window.onerror = reportError;
```

When "errorReport.html" is opened as a result of an error, it retrieves the relevant data from the window that opened it (the window with the error) and presents the data to the user in a form. Figure 24-7 shows the window opened as the result of the following runtime error:

```
window.noSuchMethod();
```

The first four form values are automatically filled in by *fillValues()*, and the **<textarea>** shows a hypothetical description entered by the user. Of course, the presentation of this page needs some work (especially under Netscape 4), but the concept is solid.

There are two important issues regarding use of the **onerror** handler. The first is that this handler fires only as the result of runtime errors; syntax errors do not trigger the **onerror** handler and in general cannot be suppressed. The second is that support for this handler is spotty under some versions of Internet Explorer. While IE4.x and 5.5 appear to have complete support, some versions of IE5.0 might have problems.

Exceptions

An *exception* is a generalization of the concept of an error to include any unexpected condition encountered during execution. While errors are usually associated with some unrecoverable condition, exceptions can be generated in more benign problematic situations and are not usually fatal. JavaScript 1.4+ and JScript 5.0+ support exception handling as the result of their movement towards ECMAScript conformance.

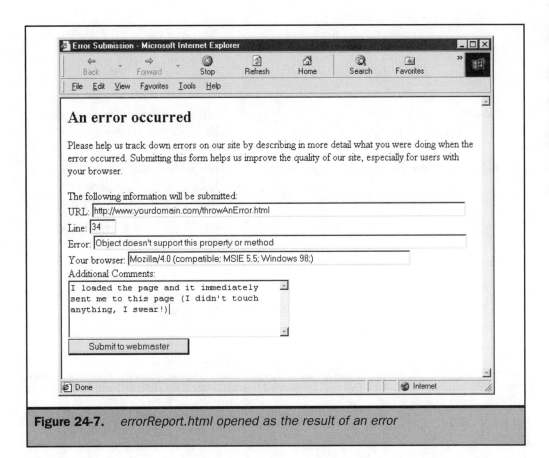

Figure 24-7. *errorReport.html opened as the result of an error*

When an exception is generated, it is said to be *thrown* (or, in some cases, *raised*). The browser may throw exceptions in response to various tasks, such as incorrect DOM manipulation, but exceptions can also be thrown by the programmer or an embedded Java applet. Handling an exception is known as *catching* an exception. Exceptions are often explicitly caught by the programmer when performing operations that he or she knows could be problematic. Exceptions that are *uncaught* are usually presented to the user as runtime errors.

The Error Object

When an exception is thrown, information about the exception is stored in an **Error** object. The structure of this object varies from browser to browser, but its most interesting properties and their support are described in Table 24-3.

Property	IE5?	IE5.5+?	NS6+?	ECMA?	Description
description	Yes	Yes	No	No	String describing the nature of the exception.
fileName	No	No	Yes	No	String indicating the URL of the document that threw the exception.
lineNumber	No	No	Yes	No	Numeric value indicating the line number of the statement that generated the exception.
message	No	Yes	Yes	Yes	String describing the nature of the exception.
name	No	Yes	Yes	Yes	String indicating the type of the exception. ECMAScript values for this property are "EvalError," "RangeError," "ReferenceError," "SyntaxError," "TypeError," and "URIError."
number	Yes	Yes	No	No	Number indicating the Microsoft-specific error number of the exception. This value can deviate wildly from documentation and from version to version.

Table 24-3. *Properties of the Error Object*

The **Error()** constructor can be used to create an exception of a particular type. The syntax is

var *variableName* = new Error(*message*);

where *message* is a string indicating the *message* property that the exception should have. Unfortunately, support for the argument to the **Error()** constructor in Internet Explorer 5 and some very early versions of 5.5 is particularly bad, so you might have to set the property manually, such as:

```
var myException = new Error("Invalid data entry");
myException.message = "Invalid data entry";
```

You can also create instances of the specific ECMAScript exceptions given in the *name* row of Table 24-3. For example, to create a syntax error exception you might write

```
var myException = new SyntaxError("The syntax of the statement was invalid");
```

However, in order to keep user-created exceptions separate from those generated by the interpreter; it is generally a good idea to stick with **Error** objects unless you have a specific reason to do otherwise.

try, catch, and throw

Exceptions are caught using the **try/catch** construct. The syntax is:

try {

   statements that might generate an exception

} catch (theException) {

   statements to execute when an exception is caught

} finally {

   statements to execute unconditionally

}

If a statement in the **try** block throws an exception, the rest of the block is skipped and the **catch** block is immediately executed. The **Error** object of the exception that was thrown is placed in the "argument" to the **catch** block (*theException* in this case, but any identifier will do). The *theException* instance is accessible only inside the **catch** block and should not be a previously declared identifier. The **finally** block is executed whenever the **try** or **catch** block finishes and is used in other languages to perform clean-up work associated with the statements that were tried. However, because JavaScript performs garbage collection, the **finally** block is essentially useless.

Note that the **try** block must be followed by exactly one **catch** or one **finally** (or one of both), so using **try** by itself or attempting to use multiple **catch** blocks will result in a syntax error. However, it is perfectly legal to have nested **try/catch** constructs, as in the following:

```
try {
   // some statements to try
```

```
try {
    // some statements to try that might throw a different exception
} catch(theException) {
    // perform exception handling for the inner try
}
} catch (theException) {
    // perform exception handling for the outer try
}
```

Creating an instance of an **Error** does not cause the exception to be thrown. You must explicitly throw it using the **throw** keyword. For example, with the following,

```
var myException = new Error("Couldn't handle the data");
throw myException;
```

the result in Netscape 6's JavaScript Console is

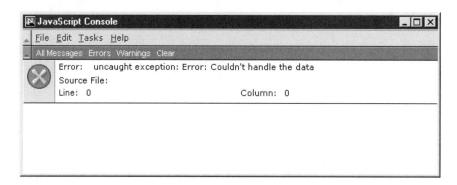

In Internet Explorer 5.5 with debugging turned on, a similar error is reported.

*You can **throw** any value you like, including primitive strings or numbers, but creating and then throwing an **Error** instance is the preferable strategy.*

To illustrate the basic use of exceptions, consider the computation of a numeric value as a function of two arguments (mathematically inclined readers will recognize this as an identity for sine(a + b)). Using previously discussed defensive programming techniques we could explicitly type-check or convert the arguments to numeric values in order to ensure a valid computation. We choose to perform type checking here using exceptions (and assuming, for clarity, that the browser has already been determined to support JavaScript exceptions):

```
function throwMyException(message)
{
  var myException = new Error(message);
  throw myException;
}
function sineOf(a, b)
{
    var result;
    try

    {
        if (typeof(a) != "number" || typeof(b) != "number")
           throwMyException("The arguments to sineOf() must be numeric");
        if (!isFinite(a) || !isFinite(b))
           throwMyException("The arguments to sineOf() must be finite");
        result = Math.sin(a) * Math.cos(b) + Math.cos(a) * Math.sin(b);
        if (isNaN(result))
           throwMyException("The result of the computation was not a number");
        return result;
    } catch (theException) {
        alert("Incorrect invocation of sineOf(): " + theException.message);
    }
}
```

Invoking this function correctly, for example,

```
    var myValue = sineOf(1, .5);
```

returns the correct value, but an incorrect invocation:

```
    var myValue = sineOf(1, ".5");
```

results in an exception, in this case:

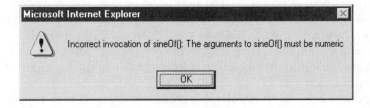

Exceptions in the real world

While exceptions will hopefully be the method of choice for notification of and recovery from problematic conditions in the future, the reality is that they are not well supported by today's Web browsers. To accommodate the non-ECMAScript **Error** properties of Internet Explorer 5 and Netscape 6, you will probably have to do some sort of browser detection in order to extract useful information. While it might be useful to have simple exception handling, such as:

```
try {
   // do something IE or Netscape specific
} catch (theException) {
}
```

that is designed to mask the possible failure of an attempt to access proprietary browser features, the real application of exceptions at the current moment is to Java applets and the DOM.

By enclosing LiveConnect calls to applets and the invocation of DOM methods in **try/catch** constructs, you can bring some of the robustness of more mature languages to JavaScript. However, using exception handling in typical day-to-day scripting tasks is probably still a few years in the future. For the time being, JavaScript's exception handling features are best used in situations where some guarantee can be made about client capabilities—for example, by applying concepts from the following two sections.

Capability and Browser Detection

We've seen some examples of capability and browser detection throughout the book, particularly in Chapter 17, and while we continue to assert that utilizing these techniques is good defensive programming, there remain a few relevant issues to discuss. To clarify terminology in preparation for this discussion, we define *capability detection* as probing for support for a specific object, property, or method in the user's browser. For example, checking for **document.all** or **document.getElementById** would constitute capability detection. We define *browser detection* as determining which browser, version, and platform is currently in use. For example, parsing the **navigator.userAgent** would constitute browser detection.

Often, capability detection is used to infer browser information. For example, we might probe for **document.layers** and infer from its presence that the browser is Netscape 4.x. The other direction holds as well: often capability assumptions are made based upon browser detection. For example, the presence of "MSIE 5.5" and "Windows" in the **userAgent** string might be used to infer the ability to use JavaScript's exception handling features.

When you step back and think about it, conclusions drawn from capability or browser detection can easily turn out to be false. In the case of capability detection, recall from Chapter 18 that the presence of **navigator.plugins** in no way guarantees that a script can probe for support for a particular plugin. Internet Explorer does not support plugin probing, but defines **navigator.plugins[ ]** anyway as a synonym for **document.embeds[ ]**. Drawing conclusions from browser detection can be equally as dangerous. Although Opera has the capability to masquerade as Mozilla or Internet Explorer (by changing its **userAgent** string), both Mozilla and IE implement a host of features not found in Opera.

While it is clear that there are some serious issues here that warrant consideration, it is not clear exactly what to make of them. Instead of coming out in favor of one technique over another, we list some of the pros and cons of each technique and suggest that a combination of both capability and browser detection is appropriate for most applications.

The advantages of capability detection include:

- You are free from writing tedious case-by-case code for various browser version and platform combinations.

- Users with third-party browsers or otherwise alternative browsers (such as text browsers) will be able to take advantage of functionality that they would otherwise be prevented from using because of an unrecognized **userAgent** (or related) string.

- Capability detection is "forward safe" in the sense that new browsers emerging in the market will be supported without changing your code, so long as they support the capabilities you utilize.

Disadvantages of capability detection include:

- The appearance of a browser to support a particular capability in no way guarantees that that capability functions the way you think it does. (Recall **navigator.plugins[ ]** in Internet Explorer).

- The support of one particular capability does not necessarily imply support for related capabilities. For example, it is entirely possible to support **document.getElementById()** but not support **Style** objects.

- The task of verifying each capability you intend to use can be rather tedious.

The advantages of browser detection include:

- Once you have determined the user's browser correctly, you can infer support for various features with relative confidence, without having to explicitly detect each capability you intend to use.

The disadvantages of browser detection include:

- Support for various features often varies widely across platforms, even in the same version of the browser (for example, DHTML Behaviors are not supported in MacOS, even in Internet Explorer 5.5).

- You must write case-by-case code for each browser or class of browsers that you intend to support. As new versions and browsers continue to hit the market, this prospect looks less and less attractive.

- Users with third-party browsers may be locked out of functionality their browsers support simply by virtue of an unrecognized **userAgent**.

- Browser detection is not necessarily "forward safe." That is, if a new version of a browser or an entirely new browser enters the market, you will in all likelihood be required to modify your scripts to accommodate the new **userAgent**.

- There is no guarantee that a valid **userAgent** string will be transmitted.

While the advent of the DOM offers some hope for a simplification of these issues, it will not solve all of these problems. First, DOM-compliant browsers are currently being used by only a minority of the population. Second, DOM support in "DOM-compliant" browsers can be rife with errors and inconsistencies. Third, the vast majority of scripts in existence today are not written for the DOM, and it is unlikely that developer focus will wholeheartedly shift to the DOM in the near future. And, finally, browser vendors such as Microsoft bundle a very large number of proprietary features with the browser, necessitating some sort of detection if they are to be used.

Although this outlook may seem pretty bleak, there are some general guidelines you can follow. Support for proprietary features is probably best determined with browser detection. This follows from the fact that such features are often difficult to capability-detect properly and from the fact that you can fairly easily determine which versions and platforms of a browser support the features in question. Standard features are probably best detected using capabilities. This follows from the assumption that support for standards is relatively useless unless the entire standard is implemented. Additionally, it permits users with third-party standards-supporting browsers the use of such features without the browser vendor having to control the market or have their **userAgent** recognized.

These guidelines are not meant to be the final word in capability versus browser detection. There are some obvious exceptions to the rules, notably that the proprietary **document.layers[ ]** capability is an almost airtight guarantee that Netscape 4 is in use, and therefore that layers are properly supported. Careful consideration of your project requirements and prospective user base also factor into the equation in a very significant way. Whatever your choice, it is important to bear in mind that there is another tool you can add to your defensive programming arsenal for accomplishing the same task.

Code Hiding

Browsers are supposed to ignore the contents of **<script>** tags with **language** attributes that they do not recognize. We can use this to our advantage by including a cascade of **<script>**s in the document, each targeting a particular language version. The **<script>**

elements found earlier in the cascade target browsers with limited capabilities, while those found later in sequence can target increasingly specific, more modern browsers.

The key idea is that there are two kinds of code hiding going on at the same time. By enclosing later scripts with advanced functionality in elements with appropriate **language** attributes (for example, "JavaScript1.5"), their code is hidden from more primitive browsers because these scripts are simply ignored. At the same time, the more primitive code can be hidden from more advanced browsers by replacing the old definitions with new ones found in later tags.

To illustrate the concept more clearly, suppose we wanted to use some DHTML code in the page when DHTML features are supported, but also want to degrade gracefully to more primitive functionality when such support is absent. We might use the following code, which redefines a *writePage()* function to include advanced functionality, depending upon which version of the language the browser supports:

```
<script language="JavaScript">
<!--
function writePage()
{
    // code to output primitive HTML and JavaScript for older browsers
}
// -->
</script>
<script language="JavaScript1.3">
<!--
function writePage()
{
    // code to output more advanced HTML and JavaScript that utilizes DHTML
    // or even the DOM
}
// -->
</script>
<script language="JavaScript">
<!--
    writePage();
    // write out the page according to which writePage is defined
// -->
</script>
```

Because more modern browsers will parse the second **<script>**, the original definition of *writePage()* is hidden. Similarly, the second **<script>** will not be processed by older browsers, because they do not recognize its **language** attribute.

If you keep in mind the guidelines for the **language** attributes given in Table 24-4, you can use this technique to design surprisingly powerful cascades (as will be

language attribute	Supported by
JScript	All scriptable versions of Internet Explorer and Opera 5+
JavaScript	All scriptable versions of Internet Explorer, Opera, and Netscape
JavaScript1.1	Internet Explorer 4+, Opera 3+, and Netscape 3+
JavaScript1.2	Internet Explorer 4+, Opera 3+, and Netscape 4+
JavaScript1.3	Internet Explorer 5+, Opera 4+, and Netscape 4.06+
JavaScript1.5	Opera 5+ and Netscape 6+

Table 24-4. *Support for Value of the language attribute*

demonstrated momentarily). Note that Opera 3 parses any **<script>** with its **language** attribute beginning with "JavaScript."

To glimpse the power that the **language** attribute affords us, suppose that you wanted to include separate code for older browsers—Netscape 4, Netscape 6, and Internet Explorer 4+. You could do so with the following:

```
<script language="JScript">
<!--
   var isIE = true;
   // set a flag so we can differentiate between Netscape and IE later on
// -->
</script>
<script language="JavaScript">
<!--
function myFunction()
{
   // code to do something for older browsers
}
// --></script>
<script language="JavaScript1.2">
<!--
if (window.isIE)
{
   function myFunction()
```

REAL WORLD
JAVASCRIPT

```
    {
        // code to do something specific for Internet Explorer 4+
    }
}
else
{
  function myFunction()
    {
        // code to do something specific for Netscape 4 and others
    }
}
// -->
</script>
<script language="JavaScript1.5">
<!--
function myFunction()
{
    // code to do something specific for Netscape 6 and Opera 5+
}
// -->
</script>
```

We've managed to define a cross-browser function, *myFunction()*, for four different browsers using only the **language** attribute and a little ingenuity! Combined with some simple browser detection, this technique can be very powerful indeed.

 *The **language** attribute is deprecated under HTML 4, so don't expect your pages to validate as strict HTML 4 or XHTML when using this trick. The upside is that all modern browsers continue to support the attribute even though it is no longer officially a part of the language.*

Accommodating Old Browsers

In our exploration of code hiding so far, we have glossed over several important issues that merit attention. First, you should keep in mind that the original purpose of the **language** attribute was to hide code utilizing new language features from older browsers. Therefore, you should make use of this feature whenever appropriate (and not just for cross-browser scripting tricks).

Another important thing to remember is that browsers that are not script-aware will display the contents of **<script>** tags as if they were HTML. Therefore, you should always hide your JavaScript inside HTML comments. Doing so suppresses the messy pages that can result from the JavaScript-as-HTML treatment that **<script>**s receive in very old or text-mode browsers.

And, finally, it is always good style to include **<noscript>**s for older browsers or browsers in which JavaScript has been disabled. Each piece of code in this book should properly have been followed by a **<noscript>** indicating that JavaScript is required or giving alternative HTML functionality for the page. We omitted such **<noscript>**s in most cases for the sake of brevity and clarity, but we would always include them in a document that was live on the Web. We turn our attention now towards general practices that are considered good coding style.

Coding Style

Because of the ease with which JavaScript can be used for a variety of tasks, developers often neglect good coding style in the rush to implement. Doing so often comes back to haunt them when later they are faced with mysterious bugs or code maintenance tasks and cannot easily decipher the meaning or intent of their own code. Practicing good coding habits can reduce such problems by bringing clarity and consistency to your scripts.

While we have emphasized what constitutes good coding style throughout the book, we summarize some of the key aspects in Table 24-5. We cannot stress enough how important good style is when undertaking a large development project, but even for smaller projects good style can make a serious difference. The only (possible) time you might wish to take liberties with coding style is when compressing your scripts for speed.

Aspect of JavaScript	Recommendation
variable identifiers	Use camel-back capitalization and descriptive names that give an indication of what value the variable might be expected to hold. Appropriate variable names are most often made up of one or more nouns.
function identifiers	Use the camel-back capitalization and descriptive names that indicate what operation they carry out. Appropriate function names are most often made up of one or more verbs.
variable declarations	Avoid implicitly declared variables like the plague—they clutter the global namespace and lead to confusion. Always use **var** to declare your variables in the most specific scope possible. Avoid global variables whenever possible.

Table 24-5.   *Recommended Good Coding Habits*

Aspect of JavaScript	Recommendation
functions	Pass values that need to be modified by reference by wrapping them in a composite type. Or, alternatively, return the new value that the variable should take on. Avoid changing global variables from inside functions. Declare functions in the document **\<head>** or in a linked .js library.
constructors	Indicate that object constructors are such by capitalizing the first letter of their identifier.
comments	Use them. Liberally. Complex conditionals should always be commented and so should functions.
indentation	Indent each block two to five spaces further than the enclosing block. Doing so gives visual cues as to nesting depth and the relationship between constructs like **if/else**.
modularization	Whenever possible, break your scripts up into externally linked libraries. Doing so facilitates code reuse and eases maintenance tasks.
semicolons	Use them. Do not rely on implicit semicolon insertion.

Table 24-5.   *Recommended Good Coding Habits* (continued)

Speeding up Your Code

There are a variety of ways in which developers try to decrease the time it takes to download and render their pages. The most obvious is *crunching*, which is the process of removing excess whitespace in files (since it is collapsed or ignored by the browser anyway) and replacing long identifiers with shorter ones. The assumption is that there will be fewer characters to transfer from the server to the client, so download speed should increase proportionally. There are many tools available on the Web that perform crunching, and the capability is often packaged with commercial development studios as well.

Another, better approach is to move the bulk of your code into external .js libraries. Doing so permits the code to be cached by the browser, obviating the need to re-fetch the same JavaScript that would otherwise be included inline in each page.

Protecting Your Code

If you are concerned with people stealing your scripts for use on their own sites, then you probably should not be implementing them in JavaScript. Because of JavaScript's nature as an interpreted language included directly in HTML documents, your users have unfettered access to your source code, at least in the current Web paradigm. While you might be able to hide code from naïve users by placing it in externally linked .js files, doing so will certainly not deter someone intent upon examining or "borrowing" your code. Just because the JavaScript is not included inline in the page does not mean that it is inaccessible. It is very easy to load an external .js library into a debugger or to download it using a text-mode browser like Lynx. You can even telnet to port 80 of the Web server and issue an HTTP request for the file manually.

A partial solution is offered by code *obfuscators*, programs that read in JavaScript (or a Web page) and output a functionally equivalent version of the code that is scrambled (presumably) beyond recognition. Obfuscators are often included with crunchers, but there are numerous standalone obfuscators available on the Web.

To illustrate the technique, we use an obfuscator on the following snippet of HTML and JavaScript:

```
<a href="#" onclick="alert('No one must know this secret!')">This is a secret link!</a>
```

The result of obfuscation is

```
<script>var
enkripsi="$2B`$31isdg$2E$33$32$33$31nobmhbj$2E$33`mdsu$39$36On$31nod$31ltru$31jonv$
31uihr$31rdbsdu$30$36$38$33$2DUihr$31hr$31`$31rdbsdu$31mhoj$30$2B.`$2D"; teks="";
teksasli="";var panjang;panjang=enkripsi.length;for (i=0;i<panjang;i++){
teks+=String.fromCharCode(enkripsi.charCodeAt(i)^1)
}teksasli=unescape(teks);document.write(teksasli);</script>
```

This obfuscated code replaces the original code in your document and, believe it or not, works entirely properly, as shown in Figure 24-8.

There are a few downsides with using obfuscated code. The first is that often the obfuscation increases the size of the code substantially, so obscurity comes at the price of size. Second, although code obfuscation might seem like an attractive route, you should be aware that reversing obfuscation is always possible. A dedicated and clever adversary will eventually be able to "undo" the obfuscation to obtain the original code (or a more tidy functional equivalent) no matter what scrambling techniques you might apply. Still, obfuscation can be a useful tool when you need to hide functionality from naïve or unmotivated snoopers. It certainly is better than relying on external .js files alone.

REAL WORLD
JAVASCRIPT

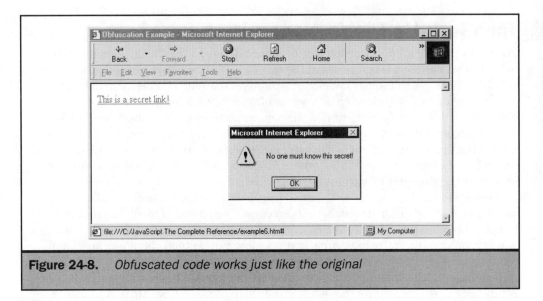

Figure 24-8.   *Obfuscated code works just like the original*

Note   *Many developers refer to obfuscation as "encryption." While doing so is likely to make a cryptographer cringe, the term is in widespread use. It is often helpful to use "encryption" instead of "obfuscation" when searching the Web for these kinds of tools.*

Note   *Microsoft Script Engine 5+ comes with a feature that allows you to encrypt your scripts. Encrypted scripts can be automatically decrypted and used by Internet Explorer 5+. However, this technology is available only for Internet Explorer, so using it is not a recommendable practice.*

Paranoid developers might wish to move functionality that must be protected at all costs into a more appropriate technology, perhaps a plugin, ActiveX control, or Java applet. However, doing so doesn't really solve the problem either, because both binaries and bytecode are successfully reverse-engineered on a regular basis. It does, however, put the code out of reach for the vast majority of Web users.

Probably the best solution is to accept the fact that people will probably peruse, play with, and occasionally reuse parts of your code from time to time. If you feel that you've been seriously burned, for example by someone who sells your code or publishes it for profit, you are most likely protected by the copyright laws in your state, province, or country. You should, however, obtain appropriate legal advice on this issue. At the very least, you might wish to include a copyright notice in your scripts and indicate the acceptable terms under which others can use your code.

Note   *Most JavaScript programmers take a very liberal attitude towards code sharing. This might be the result of the fact that many people learn the language by reading others' code, but, whatever the case, it is definitely true that the majority of JavaScript programmers are happy to share code snippets and tips.*

JavaScript's Place on the Web

We began this book by listing some of the common uses for JavaScript on the Web. Now that you know a lot more about the language's capabilities and limitations, we return to this topic to discuss JavaScript's place on the Web in a bit more detail.

The rise of mobile code such as Java and JavaScript means that developers now have a choice about where they wish the computation in Web applications to take place. Functionality that was once the domain of CGI scripts can now be effectively carried out at either the client or the server side of the Web. There are, however, some natural guidelines for determining where functionality should be placed in order to maximize the strengths of various technologies.

Server-side technology is most often appropriate for data-intensive tasks such as content customization or database interaction. The reasons for this are numerous, but they boil down to security issues, computational power, and bandwidth concerns. Server machines typically have greater processing power than client machines and can be more closely coupled to data sources than can arbitrary clients. Additionally, well-founded security and privacy concerns dictate that access to a content database is probably best achieved by the server rather than the client. Sensitive calculations (especially in financial matters) should always be carried out on the server in order to minimize the risks posed by subversive clients. It would be all too easy to save an "e-commerce" JavaScript application to the local disk and modify its functionality to induce unintended behavior. For example, the price of items or the calculation of sales tax could be modified to give a malicious client the deal of the century. If you must carry out e-commerce–related tasks in client-side JavaScript, it is absolutely essential to include "sanity checking" on the server side to ensure that such malicious behavior cannot occur.

Client-side technologies are most appropriate for non-critical enhancements, such as form validation, minor document or presentation customizations, and creation of navigational aids. The reason that these applications are most often found on the client side is the close coupling of client-side technologies to Web documents themselves. Client-side features are always available to the user and document (once it's loaded in the browser). Server-side features, on the other hand, are unavailable once the document is sent from the server to the client (or, at the least, until the next request). It makes sense that tasks involving a high degree of user interaction are best placed on the client side. Form validation, presentation customization, and use of navigational aids are all tasks that involve significant user interaction. Keeping them on the client speeds things up by obviating the need for time-consuming communication with a server.

JavaScript fits into the server side of the Web by providing the means to automate document generation prior to transmission to the user. It faces a number of related, competing technologies such as Java servlets and other database-driven scripting languages like PHP and ColdFusion. One major advantage of server-side JavaScript over related technologies is the degree to which it is integrated with Windows and Windows Internet Information Server.

JavaScript fits into the client side of the Web as the language of choice for dynamic examination, generation, and manipulation of Web pages. Tremendous browser support and easy access to a page's document object model make any other choice for such tasks downright silly. While related technologies like plugins and ActiveX controls can provide more power than JavaScript scripts, they do so at the cost of increased separation from the browser and document objects and of decreased support.

JavaScript's capabilities continue to increase at a pace more rapid than most developers can keep up with. The W3C DOM facilities provide JavaScript with the unique position of being the most easily used language for manipulation and interaction with XML. JavaScript is also easy to learn and without a doubt, will continue to dominate the client-side scripting market for a long time to come. There is simply no competition even on the farthest horizon.

Summary

JavaScript *syntax errors* are those errors that result from code that does not conform to the rules of the language. Scripts generally can't recover from errors that introduce such ambiguity. On the other hand, *runtime* errors are those errors that occur as the result of attempting to utilize an unavailable resource—for example, the document object model before the page has loaded or an undefined object, property, method, or variable. Runtime errors can be caught on a **Window**-wide level in most modern browser by utilizing that object's **onerror** event handler. Runtime errors can also be caught as a part of JavaScript's more advanced exception-handling features.

Semantic errors occur when a JavaScript statement has an effect unintended by the programmer. Typical debugging techniques such as turning on error messages and outputting verbose status information can be used to track down logical errors, but a better approach is to use a program designed specifically for the task, a *debugger*. Defensive programming can help reduce both runtime and semantic errors.

Code hiding is an important aspect of defensive programming. Code hiding occurs when JavaScript is hidden from a browser that is not able to handle it. Although often carried out by utilizing the **language** attribute of the **<script>** element, it also occurs in more straightforward ways—for example, by commenting out the contents of a **<script>** to prevent old browsers from outputting the script as HTML.

An *exception* is a generalization of an error to include more benign and unexpected conditions, such as those arising from incorrect data types or malfunctioning embedded Java applets. Programmers can create and *throw* their own exceptions by instantiated **Error** objects used in conjunction with the **throw** keyword. Exceptions are *caught* (handled) using the **try/catch** construction, which permits the execution of a specific block of code if an exception occurs while executing the **try** statements.

The
Complete
Reference

JavaScript

Part VII

Appendixes

The Complete Reference

Appendix A

Core Syntax
Quick Reference

Them he syntax of core language features is covered in this section. The data here is intended for use as a quick reference. For a more complete discussion of each item, see the appropriate chapter of the book.

Our conventions will be

- *italicized text* to indicate a key term or phrase and also to indicate a placeholder for some specified grammatical or lexical unit, such as an expression, statement, or sequence of characters.

- **boldfaced text** to indicate language keywords or reserved words.

- [bracketed text] to indicate optional grammatical units. Note that [*unit1*] [*unit2*] permits the absence of *unit1* and *unit2*; or *unit1* followed by *unit2*; or *unit1*; or *unit2*; while [*unit1* [*unit2*]] permits the absence of *unit1* and *unit2*; or *unit1*; or *unit1* followed by *unit2*. The only exception is in the discussion of arrays and objects, which necessitate "real" brackets.

- ... (an ellipsis) to indicate repetition of the previous unit in the natural way.

- ⊗ indicates a generic operator.

> **Note**   *You can find the full specification for the language at **www.ecma.ch**, currently at **http://www.ecma.ch/ecma1/STAND/ecma-262.htm**.*

Language Fundamentals

The following points are core principles of JavaScript:

- Excess white space is ignored when outside of a regular expression literal or string.

- Statements are terminated with a semicolon.

- Automatic semicolon insertion on lines with complete statements.

- Data are weakly typed.

- References to identifiers are resolved using lexical (static) scoping. The one exception to this is class properties of the **RegExp** object, which are dynamically scoped.

- Indices are enumerated beginning with zero.

- Three kinds of objects are available: built-in objects, host (browser) objects, and user-defined objects.

- Object oriented features are prototype-based (*not* class-based in its current incarnation).

- Source code is interpreted.

- Comments use C++ inline comment style "//" or C-style block comment "/* */".

- I/O is limited in most cases to interaction with Web documents and the user (no local filesystem or network access by default).

Language Versions

Standard Version	Description
ECMAScript Edition 1	First standardized version of JavaScript, based loosely on JavaScript 1.0 and JScript 1.0.
ECMAScript Edition 2	Standard version correcting errors within Edition 1 (and some minor improvements).
ECMAScript Edition 3	More advanced language standard based on ECMAScript Edition 2. Includes regular expressions and exception handling. In widespread use.
ECMAScript Edition 4	New standard still unfinished at the time of this writing. Expected perhaps in 2002.

Table A-1.   *Standard Versions of JavaScript*

Language Version	Browser Version
JavaScript 1.0	Netscape 2
JavaScript 1.1	Netscape 3
JavaScript 1.2	Netscape 4.0–4.05
JavaScript 1.3	Netscape 4.06-4.7
JavaScript 1.4	None
JavaScript 1.5	Netscape 6, Mozilla 0.9
JavaScript 2.0	Future versions of Netscape and Mozilla

Table A-2.   *Correspondence Between Netscape Language and Browser Versions*

Language Version	Browser Version
JScript 1.0	Internet Explorer 3.0
JScript 3.0	Internet Explorer 4.0
JScript 5.0	Internet Explorer 5.0
JScript 5.5	Internet Explorer 5.5
JScript 5.6/6.0 (speculative)	Internet Explorer 6.0

Table A-3. *Correspondence Between Microsoft Language and Browser Versions*

Language Version	Browser Version	Language Version	Browser Version
JavaScript 1.0	Netscape 2.0	JScript 1.0	Internet Explorer 3.0
JavaScript 1.3	Netscape 4.06	JScript 3.0	Internet Explorer 4.0
JavaScript 1.5	Netscape 6	JScript 5.5	Internet Explorer 5.5

Table A-4. *Approximate Correspondence Between Netscape and Microsoft Implementations*

Netscape Version	Standard Version	Exceptions
JavaScript 1.0-1.2	Very loose conformance to ECMA-262 Edition 1	Many, especially with the **Date** object, and many extra features
JavaScript 1.3	Strict conformance to ECMA-262 Edition 1	Includes some extra features
JavaScript 1.4	Strict conformance to ECMA-262 Edition 1	Includes some extra features
JavaScript 1.5	Strict conformance to ECMA-262 Edition 3	Includes some extra features
JavaScript 2.0	Planned conformance to ECMA-262 Edition 4	Unknown

Table A-5. *Relationship Between Netscape JavaScript and ECMAScript*

Language Standards Conformance

Microsoft Version	Standard Version	Exceptions
JScript 1.0	Very loose conformance to ECMA-262 Edition 1	Many, and some extra features
JScript 3.0	Strict conformance to ECMA-262 Edition 1	Includes some extra features
JScript 5.0	Strict conformance to ECMA-262 Edition 1	Includes many extra features
JScript 5.5	Strict conformance to ECMA-262 Edition 3	Some minor exceptions (for example, does not include the **in** operator), includes some extra features
JScript 5.6/6.0 (speculative)	Likely to be released before ECMA-262 Edition 4 is finalized	Unknown, but unlikely to include many JavaScript 2.0/ECMAScript Edition 4 features

Table A-6.   *Relationship Between Microsoft JScript and ECMAScript*

Data Types

JavaScript's data types are broken down into *primitive* and *composite* types. Primitive types hold simple values and are passed to functions by value. Composite types hold heterogeneous data (primitive and/or composite values) and are passed to functions by reference. JavaScript is *weakly typed*.

Primitive Types

Five primitive types are defined, only three of which can hold useful data.

Type	Description	Values	Literal Syntax
Boolean	Takes on one of two values. Used for on/off, yes/no, or true/false values and conditionals.	**true, false**	**true**, **false**
null	Has only one value. Indicates the absence of data.	**null**	**null**
number	Includes both integer and floating-point types. 64-bit IEEE 754 representation. Integer ops usually carried out using only 32 bits.	Magnitudes as large as $\pm 1.7976 \times 10^{308}$ and as small as $\pm 2.2250 \times 10^{-308}$. Integers considered to have a range of $2^{31}-1$ to -2^{31} for computational purposes.	Decimal values (including exponent), hexadecimal, octal (nonstandard)
string	Zero or more Unicode (Latin-1 prior to Netscape 6 / IE4) characters.	Any sequence of zero or more characters.	Single- or double-quote delimited.
undefined	Has only one value and indicates that data has not yet been assigned. For example, *undefined* is the result of reading a nonexistent object property.	**undefined**	**undefined** (IE5.5+/NS6+/ECMA3) as a property of **Global**. Previously not available.

Table A-7. *Primitive JavaScript Data Types*

Numeric Constants

Infinity (property of **Global**), **NaN** (property of **Global**),
**Number.NEGATIVE_INFINITY, Number.POSITIVE_INFINITY,
Number.NaN, Number.MAX_VALUE, Number.MIN_VALUE**

Table A-8.   *Useful Numeric Constants*

Escape Code	Value
\b	backspace
\t	tab (horizontal)
\n	linefeed (newline)
\v	tab (vertical)
\f	form feed
\r	carriage return
\"	double quote
\'	single quote
\\	backslash
\OOO	Latin-1 character represented by the octal digits OOO. The valid range is 000 to 377.
\xHH	Latin-1 character represented by the hexadecimal digits HH. The valid range is 00 to FF.
\uHHHH	Unicode character represented by the hexadecimal digits *HHHH*

Table A-9.   *String Escape Codes*

Type Conversion

Type conversion is automatically carried out (see later section in this Appendix on relational operators for more information).

Boolean converted to	Result
number	1 if **true**, 0 if **false**
string	"true" if **true**, "false" if **false**
object	A **Boolean** object whose **value** property is **true** if true, or **false** if false

Table A-10. *Result of Type Conversion of Primitive Boolean Data*

Null converted to	Result
Boolean	**false**
number	0
string	"null"
object	Impossible. A **TypeError** exception is thrown.

Table A-11. *Result of Type Conversion of Null Data*

Number converted to	Result
Boolean	**false** if value is **0** or **NaN**, otherwise **true**
string	string representing the number (including special values)
object	A **Number** object whose **value** property is set to the value of the number

Table A-12. *Result of Type Conversion of Primitive Number Data*

String converted to	Result
Boolean	**false** if given the empty string (i.e., a string of length zero), **true** otherwise.
number	Attempts to parse the string as a numeric literal (e.g., "3.14" or "-Infinity") to obtain the value. If parsing fails, **NaN**.
object	A **String** object whose **value** property is set to the value of the string.

Table A-13. *Result of Type Conversion of Primitive String Data*

Undefined converted to	Result
Boolean	**false**
number	**NaN**
string	"undefined"
object	Impossible. A **TypeError** exception is thrown.

Table A-14. *Result of Type Conversion of Undefined Data*

Description	Details
String methods	toExponential(), toFixed(), toPrecision() for conversion to numbers
Global methods	parseInt(), parseFloat() for converting strings to numbers
Object methods	toString(), valueOf() (retrieves the primitive value associated with the object)
constructors	Use the **String()** and **Number()** constructors

Table A-15. *Manual Type Conversion Techniques*

Composite Types

The most generic composite type from which all other composite types are derived is the **Object**. An **Object** is an unordered set of properties that may be accessed using the dot operator:

> *object.property*

equivalently:

> *object*["*property*"]

In case the property is a function (method), it make be invoked as:

> *object.method*()

Static (or *class*) properties are accessed through the constructor:

> *Object.property*

Object Creation

> [**var**] *instance* = **new** *Constructor*(*arguments*);

Places a reference to a new instance of the object created by the constructor in the variable *instance*. The *arguments* accepted vary from object to object.

Instance Properties

> *instance.property* = *value;*
>
> *instance.property*

The first assignment adds a new property to the object which *instance* references (but not other objects of that type). The second syntax shows that instance properties are accessed as normal properties.

The "this" statement

The **this** statement refers to the "current" object—that is, the object inside of which **this** is used. Its syntax is:

> **this**.*property*

and it is typically used inside of a function (for example, to access the function's **length** property) or inside of a constructor (in order to access the new instance being created). Used in the global context, **this** refers to the current **Window**.

ECMAScript Built-in Objects

Table 16 lists the ECMAScript built-in objects. These objects are part of the language itself, as opposed to *host* (or *browser*) objects that are provided by the browsers. Note that you cannot instantiate **Global** or **Math** objects. The **Global** object is not even explicitly addressable. It is defined as the outermost enclosing scope (so its properties are always addressable). The **Math** object provides its functionality in the form of static methods (for example, **Math.PI**).

Object	Description
Array	Provides an ordered list data type and related functionality
Boolean	Object corresponding to the primitive Boolean data type
Date	Facilitates date- and time-related computation
Error	Provides the ability to create a variety of exceptions (and includes a variety of derived objects, such as **SyntaxError**)
Function	Provides function-related capabilities such as examination of function arguments
Global	Provides universally available functions for a variety of data conversion and evaluation tasks
Math	Provides more advanced mathematical features than those available with standard JavaScript operators
Number	Object corresponding to the primitive number data type
Object	Generic object providing basic features (such as type-explicit type conversion methods) from which all other objects are derived
RegExp	Permits advanced string matching and manipulation
String	Object corresponding to the primitive string data type

Table A-16. *JavaScript Built-in Objects*

Property	Description
decodeURI(*encodedURI*)	URI-decodes the string *encodedURI* and returns the result
decodeURIComponent (*uriComponent*)	URI-decodes the encodeURIComponent-encoded string *uriComponent* and returns the result
encodeURI(*string*)	URI-encodes the string *string* (not including legal URI characters) and returns the result
encodeURIComponent(*string*)	URI-encodes the string *string* (including legal URI characters) and returns the result
escape(*string*)	URL-encodes *string* and returns the result
eval(*x*)	Executes the string *x* as if it were JavaScript source code
Infinity	The special numeric value **Infinity**
isFinite(*x*)	Returns a Boolean indicating whether *x* is finite (or results in a finite value when converted to a number)
isNaN(*x*)	Returns a Boolean indicating whether *x* is **NaN** (or results in **NaN** when converted to a number)
NaN	The special numeric value **NaN**
parseInt(*string* [, *base*])	Parses *string* as a base-*base* number (10 is the default unless *string* begins with "0x") and returns the primitive number result (or **NaN** if it fails)
parseFloat(*string*)	Parses *string* as a floating-point number and returns the primitive number result (or **NaN** if it fails)
undefined	Value corresponding to the primitive **undefined** value (this value is provided through **Global** because there is no **undefined** keyword)
unscape(*string*)	URL-decodes *string* and returns the result

Table A-17.   *Properties of the Global Object*

Array Literals

Array literals are used with the following syntax (the brackets are "real" brackets and do not indicate optional components):

> [*element1, element2, …*]

Each *elementN* is optional, so you may use an array with "holes" in it, such as:

```
var myArray = ["some data", , 3.14, true ];
```

Although not strictly a literal, you can also use the **Array()** constructor:

var *variable* = **new Array**(*element1, element2, …*);

But be aware that if only one numeric argument is passed, it is interpreted as the initial value for the **length** property.

Function Literals

Function literals are used with the following syntax:

> **function** ([*args*]) { *statements* }

where *args* is a comma-separated list of identifiers for the function arguments, and *statements* is zero or more valid JavaScript statements.

Although not strictly a literal, the **Function()** constructor can also be used:

new Function(["*arg1*", ["*arg2*"], … ,] "*statements*");

The *argN*'s are the names of the parameters the function accepts, and *statements* is the body of the function. For example:

```
var myHello = new Function("name," "alert('Hello there' + name)");
```

Object Literals

Object literals are used with the following syntax:

> { [*prop1*: *val1* [, *prop2*: *val2*, …]] }

For example:

```
var myInfo = {
    city: "San Diego",
    state: "CA" ,
    province: null,
    sayHi = function() { alert("Hello there") }
}
```

Regular Expression Literals

Regular expression literals (actually **RegExp** literals) have the following syntax:

lexplflags

where *exp* is a valid regular expression, and *flags* is zero or more regular expression modifiers (for example, "gi" for global and case-insensitive).

Although not strictly a literal, the **RegExp()** constructor can be used:

new RegExp("*exp*" [, "*flags*"])

Operators

Operators are used to perform calculations with, to manipulate, and to compare data. The operators available in JavaScript are defined by ECMAScript and therefore (in principle) have identical behavior across all platforms and browsers.

Note　*We take some liberty with the following categorization of operators. The following categories (and placement of operators) do not strictly reflect the ECMAScript operator organization, but we believe that the following groupings make the operators easier to understand.*

Arithmetic Operators

Arithmetic operators operate on numbers, with one exception: + as string concatenation.

Operator	Self-assignment Operator	Operation
+	+=	Addition (also functions as string concatenation)
-	-=	Subtraction
*	*=	Multiplication
/	/=	Division
%	%=	Modulus (the integer remainder when the first operand is divided by the second)

Table A-18.　*Binary (Two-Operand) and Self-Assignment Arithmetic Operators*

Operator	Description
++	Auto-increment (increment the value by one and store)
--	Auto-decrement (decrement the value by one and store)

Table A-19. *Pre/Postfix Arithmetic Operators*

Operator	Description
+	Has no effect on numbers but causes non-numbers to be converted into numbers
-	Negation (changes the sign of the number or converts the expression to a number and then changes its sign)

Table A-20. *Unary (One Operand) Arithmetic Operators*

Bitwise Operators

Bitwise operators operate upon integers in a bit-by-bit fashion. Most computers store negative numbers using their two's complement representation, so you should exercise caution when performing bit operations on negative numbers.

Operator	Self-assignment Operator	Description
<<	<<=	Bitwise left-shift the first operand by the number of bits given by the value of the second operand, zero filling "vacated" bit positions
>>	>>=	Bitwise right-shift the first operand by the number of bits given by the value of the second operand, sign filling the "vacated" bit positions

Table A-21. *Binary and Self-Assignment Bitwise Operators*

APPENDIXES

Operator	Self-assignment Operator	Description
>>>	>>>=	Bitwise right-shift the first operand by the number of bits given by the value of the second operand, zero filling "vacated" bit positions
&	&=	Bitwise AND
|	|=	Bitwise OR
^	^=	Bitwise XOR (exclusive OR)

Table A-21..   *Binary and Self-Assignment Bitwise Operators* (continued)

Operator	Description
~	Bitwise negation

Table A-22.   *Unary Bitwise Operator*

Logical Operators

Logical operators operate upon Boolean values and are used to construct conditional statements. Logical operators are short-circuited in JavaScript, meaning that once a logical condition is guaranteed, none of the other sub-expressions in a conditional expression are evaluated. They are evaluated left to right.

Operator	Description
&&	Logical AND
||	Logical OR

Table A-23.   *Binary Logical Operators*

Operator	Description
!	Logical negation

Table A-24. *Unary Logical Operator*

Conditional Operator

The conditional operator is a ternary operator popular among C programmers.
Its syntax is:

$(\; expr1 \; ? \; expr2 : expr3 \;)$

where *expr1* is an expression evaluating to a Boolean, and *expr2* and *expr3* are
expressions. If *expr1* evaluates **true** then the expression takes on the value *expr2*,
otherwise it takes on the value *expr3*.

Type Operators

Type operators generally operate on objects or object properties.

Operator	Description
instanceof	Evaluates **true** if the first operand is an instance of the second operand. The second operand must be an object (for example, a constructor).
in	Evaluates **true** if the first operand (a string) is the name of a property of the second operand. The second operand must be an object (for example, a constructor).

Table A-25. *Binary Type Operators*

Operator	Description
delete	If the operand is an array element or object property, the operand is removed from the array or object.
new	Creates a new instance of the object given by the constructor operand.
typeof	Evaluates to a string indicating the type of the object (see Table 27).
void	Effectively **undefine**s the value of its expression operand.

Table A-26. *Unary Type Operators*

Type	Result of typeof
Boolean	"boolean"
null	"object"
number	"number"
string	"string"
undefined	"undefined"
Function	"function"
Object (built-in or user defined)	"object"
Object (browser or other host)	Implementation dependent, but something like "[Object: *ObjectType*]" where *ObjectType* is the type of object. For example, "[Object: Navigator]"

Table A-27. *Result of Invoking typeof on Different Data Types*

Also included in the type operators is the property-accessing operator. To access a property *property* of an object *object*, the following two syntaxes are equivalent:

object.property

object["*property*"]

Note that the brackets above are "real" brackets (they do not imply an optional component).

Comma Operator

The comma operator allows multiple statements to be carried out as one. The syntax of the operator is

statement1, statement2 [, *statement3*] ...

If used in an expression, its value is the value of the last statement.

Relational Operators

Relational operators are binary operators that compare two like types and evaluate to a Boolean indicating whether the relationship holds. If the two operands are not of the same type, type conversion is carried out so that the comparison can take place (see the next section for more information).

Operator	Description
<	Evaluates **true** if the first operand is less than the second
<=	Evaluates **true** if the first operand is less than or equal to the second
>	Evaluates **true** if the first operand is greater than the second
>=	Evaluates **true** if the first operand is greater than or equal to the second
!=	Evaluates **true** if the first operand is not equal to the second
==	Evaluates **true** if the first operand is equal to the second
!==	Evaluates **true** if the first operand is not equal to the second (and they have the same type)
===	Evaluates **true** if the first operand is equal to the second (and they have the same type)

Table A-28.   *Binary Relational Operators*

APPENDIXES

Type Conversion in Comparisons

The interpreter carries out the following steps in order to compare two different types:

1. If both of the operands are strings, compares them lexicographically.

2. Converts both operands to numbers.

3. If either operand is **NaN**, returns **undefined** (which in turn evaluates to **false** when converted to a Boolean).

4. If either operand is infinite or zero, evaluates the comparison using the rules that **+0** and **-0** compare **false** unless the relation includes equality, that **Infinity** is never less than any value, and that **-Infinity** is never more than any value.

5. Compares the operands numerically.

Note that using the strict equality (===) or inequality (!==) operator on operands of two different types will always evaluate **false**.

Lexicographic Comparisons

The lexicographic comparisons performed on strings adhere to the following guidelines. Note that a string of length n is a "prefix" of some other string of length n or more if they are identical in their first n characters. So, for example, a string is always a prefix of itself.

- If two strings are identical, they are equal (note that there are some very rare exceptions when two strings created using different character sets might not compare equal, but this almost never happens).

- If one string is a prefix of the other (and they are not identical) then it is "less than" the other. (For example, "a" is less than "aa".).

- If two strings are identical up to the nth (possibly 0th) character, then the character at position $(n + 1)$ is examined. (For example, the third character of "abc" and "abd" would be examined if they were to be compared.)

- If the numeric value of the character code under examination in the first string is less than that of the character in the second string, the first string is "less than" the second. (The relation "1" < "9" < "A" < "Z" < "a" < "z" is often helpful for remembering which characters are "less" than others.)

Operator Precedence and Associativity

JavaScript assigns a precedence and associativity to each operator so that expressions will be well-defined (that is, the same expression will always evaluate to the same value). Operators with higher precedence evaluate before operators with lower precedence. Associativity determines the order in which identical operators evaluate.

Given the expression,

a ⊗ b ⊗ c

a left-associative operator would evaluate

(a ⊗ b) ⊗ c

while a right-associative operator would evaluate

a ⊗ (b ⊗ c)

Precedence	Associativity	Operator	Operator Meanings
Highest	Left	., [ ], ()	Object property access, array or object property access, parenthesized expression
	Right	++, —, -, ~, !, **delete**, **new**, **typeof**, **void**	Pre/Post increment, Pre/post decrement, arithmetic negation, bitwise negation, logical negation, removal of a property, object creation, getting data type, **undefine** a value
	Left	*, /, %	Multiplication, Division, Modulus
	Left	+, -	Addition (arithmetic) and concatenation (string), Subtraction
	Left	<<, >>, >>>	Bitwise left-shift, bitwise right-shift, bitwise right-shift with zero fill

Table A-29.   *Precedence and Associativity of JavaScript Operators*

Precedence	Associativity	Operator	Operator Meanings
	Left	<, <=, >, >=, in, instanceof	Less than, less than or equal to, greater than, greater than or equal to, object has property, object is an instance of
	Left	==, !=, ===, !===	Equality, inequality, equality (with type checking), inequality (with type checking)
	Left	&	Bitwise AND
	Left	^	Bitwise XOR
	Left	|	Bitwise OR
	Left	&&	Logical AND
	Left	||	Logical OR
	Right	? :	Conditional
	Right	=	Assignment
	Right	*=, /=, %=, +=, -=, <<=, >>=, >>>=, &=, ^=, |=	Operation and self-assignment
Lowest	Left	,	Multiple evaluation

Table A-29. *Precedence and Associativity of JavaScript Operators* (continued)

Flow Control Constructs

The following flow control constructions are available in JavaScript, the first of which is a building block for simplifying the grammar of other constructions.

Block Statements

While not really a flow control construct, the block statement allows many statements to be treated as one by enclosing them in curly braces:

```
{
    statements
}
```

where *statements* is composed of zero or more valid JavaScript statements. Statements can always be grouped like this, as the body of a loop or function, or directly in the script, although a block only has its own local scope for functions.

The "with" Statement

```
with ( objectExpression )
    statement
```

The object that *objectExpression* evaluates to is placed at the front of the scope chain while *statement* executes. Statements in *statement* can therefore utilize methods and properties of this object without explicitly using the property-accessing operator.

Functions

Primitive types are passed to functions by value. Composite types are passed by reference. Functions have their own local scope. Static scoping is employed.

```
function identifier( [ arg1 [, arg2 [, ... ] ] ] ) {
    statements
}
```

From within a function you can return a value using the **return** statement:

```
return [expression];
```

If *expression* is omitted, the function returns **undefined**.

You can check how many arguments a function expects by accessing its **length** property:

identifier.**length**

The argument values, in addition to being placed in the declared parameters upon invocation, are accessible via the **arguments[ ]** array. This array holds the actual values passed to the function, so it may hold a different number of arguments than the function expects.

Conditionals
The following conditionals are supported:

- **if** (*expression*) *statement*
- **if** (*expression*) *statement* **else** *statement*
- **if** (*expression*) *statement* **else if** (*expression*) *statement* ...
- **if** (*expression*) *statement* **else if** (*expression*) *statement* ... **else** *statement*
- **switch** (*expression*) {

case *val1*: statement
[**break;**]
case *val2*: statement
[**break;**]
...
default: statement
}

Loops
The following loops are all supported:

- **for** ([*initStatement*] ; [*logicalExpression*] ; [*iterationStatement*]) *statement*
- **for** ([**var**] *variable* **in** *objectExpression*) *statement*
- **while** (*expression*) *statement*
- **do** *statement* **while** (*expression*);

Labeled statements—"break" and "continue"
Statements can be labeled using:

- *label*: *statement*

Jump to labeled statements in a block using either of the following:

- **break** *label*;
- **continue** *label*;

Otherwise:

- **break** exits the loop, beginning execution following the loop body
- **continue** skips directly to the next iteration ("top") of the loop

Exceptions

You can catch programmer-generated and runtime exceptions, but you cannot catch JavaScript syntax errors. You may instantiate any of the exceptions in Table 30, but interpreter-generated exceptions are usually of type **Error**.

"Throw"

> **throw** *value*;

The *value* can be any value, but is generally an **Error** instance.

"Try," "catch," and "finally"

```
try {
  statementsToTry
} catch ( e ) {
  catchStatements
} finally {
  finallyStatements
}
```

Exception Object	Description
Error	Generic exception
EvalError	Thrown when **eval()** is used incorrectly
RangeError	Thrown when a number exceeds the maximum allowable range
ReferenceError	Thrown on the rare occasion that an invalid reference is used
SyntaxError	Thrown when some sort of syntax error has occurred at runtime—note that "real" JavaScript syntax errors are not catchable
TypeError	Thrown when an operand has an unexpected type
URIError	Thrown when one of **Global**'s URI-related functions is used incorrectly

Table A-30. *JavaScript Exception Objects*

The **try** block must be followed by either exactly one **catch** block or one **finally** block (or one of both). When an exception occurs in the **catch** block, the exception is placed in *e* and the **catch** block is executed. The **finally** block executes unconditionally after **try/catch**.

Regular Expressions

Regular expression flags are used when creating expressions. Escape codes are used to match certain problematic characters.

Character	Meaning
i	Case-insensitive
g	Global match. Find *all* matches in the string, rather than just the first.
m	Multiline matching.

Table A-31. *Regular Expression Flags*

Character	Meaning
*	Match previous item zero or more times
+	Match previous item one time or more
?	Match previous item zero or one time
{m, n}	Match previous item at minimum *m* times, but no more than *n* times
{m, }	Match previous item *m* or more times
{m}	Match previous item exactly *m* times

Table A-32. *Regular Expression Repetition Quantifiers*

Character	Meaning
[*chars*]	Any one character indicated either explicitly or as a range between the brackets
[^*chars*]	Any one character *not* between the brackets represented explicitly or as a range
.	Any character except newline
\w	Any word character. Same as [a-zA-Z0-9_]
\W	Any non-word character. Same as [^a-zA-Z0-9_]
\s	Any whitespace character. Same as [\t\n\r\f\v]
\S	Any non-whitespace character. Same as [^ \t\n\r\f\v]
\d	Any digit. Same as [0-9]
\D	Any non-digit. Same as [^0-9]
\b	A word boundary. The empty "space" between a \w and \W.
\B	A word non-boundary. The empty "space" between word characters.
[\b]	A backspace character

Table A-33.   *Regular Expression Character Classes*

Code	Matches
\f	Form feed
\n	Newline
\r	Carriage return
\t	Tab
\v	Vertical tab
\/	Foreslash "/"
\\	Backslash "\"

Table A-34.   *Regular Expression Escape Codes*

Code	Matches
\.	Period "."
*	Asterisk "*"
\+	Plus sign "+"
\?	Question mark "?"
\		Vertical bar, aka Pipe "	"
\(	Left parenthesis "("
\)	Right parenthesis ")"
\[	Left bracket "["
\]	Right bracket "]"
\{	Left curly brace "{"
\}	Right curly brace "}"
\OOO	ASCII character represented by octal value OOO
\xHH	ASCII character represented by hexadecimal value HH
\uHHHH	Unicode character represented by the hexadecimal value HHHH
\cX	Control character represented by ^X; for example \cH represents CTRL-H

Table A-34.   *Regular Expression Escape Codes* (continued)

Feature	Description
(?:*expr*)	Non-capturing parentheses. Does not make the given parenthesized subexpression *expr* available for backreferencing.
(?=*expr*)	Positive lookahead. Forces the previous item to match only if it is followed by a string that matches *expr*. The text that matched *expr* is not included in the match of the previous item.

Table A-35.   *Advanced Regular Expression Features*

Feature	Description
(!*expr*)	Negative lookahead. Forces the previous item to match only if it is not followed by a string matching *expr*. The text that did not match *expr* is not included in the match of the previous item.
?	Non-greedy matching. Forces the immediately preceding repetition quantifier to match the minimum number of characters required.

Table A-35.   *Advanced Regular Expression Features* (continued)

Property	Value
$1, $2, ..., $9	Strings holding the text of the first nine parenthesized subexpressions of the most recent match.
index	Holds the string index value of the first character in the most recent pattern match. This property is not part of the ECMA standard, though it is supported widely. Therefore it may be better to use the **length** of the **regexp** pattern and the **lastIndex** property to calculate this value.
input	String containing the default string to match against the pattern.
lastIndex	Integer specifying the position in the string at which to start the next match. Same as the instance property, which should be used instead.
lastMatch	String containing the most recently matched text.
lastParen	String containing the text of the last parenthesized subexpression of the most recent match.
leftContext	String containing the text to the left of the most recent match.
rightContext	String containing the text to the right of the most recent match.

Table A-36.   *Static Properties of the RegExp Object*

Appendix B

JavaScript Object Reference

This appendix provides a reference for objects available in JavaScript, including their properties, methods, event handlers, and support under Netscape and Internet Explorer.

General References

The following sites serve as useful references for more in-depth information than we have room to include here:

- **www.javascriptref.com**   The support site for this book. Features an extended online reference along with examples.

- **msdn.microsoft.com**   The Microsoft Developer's Network. In particular, this URL: **http://msdn.microsoft.com/library/default.asp?url=/workshop/author/dhtml/dhtml.asp** is (currently) the link for Microsoft's DHTML documentation. Under it you can find the DHTML Reference, a list of Internet Explorer-supported objects and their properties and methods.

- **developer.netscape.com**   Netscape's Developer site where you can find JavaScript documentation for Netscape browsers.

- **developer.irt.org/script/script.htm**   A JavaScript FAQ that, while it occasionally contains erroneous information, is usually a good source of information.

Object Models

An *object model* defines the interface used by scripts to examine and manipulate structured information, for example an HTML document. An object model also defines the composition and characteristics of its constituent parts as well as how they may be operated upon. The "big picture" of the JavaScript object models is shown in Figure B-1.

There are four kinds of objects available in JavaScript:

- **User-defined** objects are created by the programmer and therefore are not subject to any standards and are *not* discussed in this appendix. These objects are *not* shown in Figure B-1.

- **Built-in objects** are provided for common tasks such as regular expression and date manipulation, as well as tasks associated with JavaScript's data types. These objects are governed by the ECMAScript standard (ECMA-262) and are fairly consistent across browsers.

- **Browser objects** are part of the Browser Object Model (BOM), the totality of non–Built-in objects available in a particular browser. These objects provide the ability to examine and manipulate the browser itself, including the size and shape of its windows and its configuration information. These objects do not fall under any standard but often adhere to ad hoc structural norms that have evolved over the years.

- **Document objects** represent the elements of the HTML (or XML) document that is currently loaded by the browser. Traditionally, different browsers have implemented different features and interfaces for manipulation of document objects, but recently these objects have been standardized by the W3C Document Object Model.

As you can see from Figure B-1, the document object model falls under the umbrella of the objects provided by the browser. For this reason, early document object models were highly

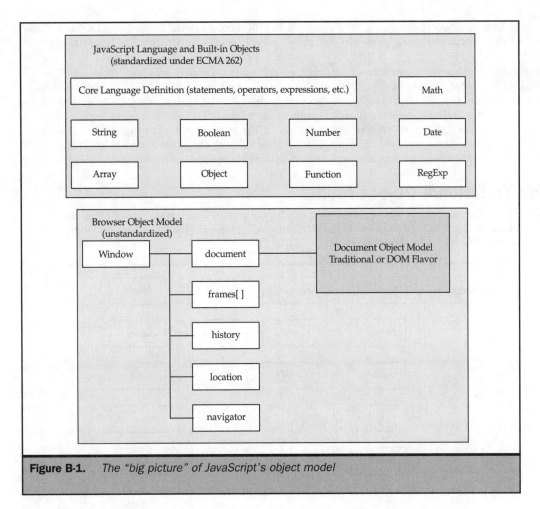

Figure B-1.   *The "big picture" of JavaScript's object model*

browser-specific, in fact so intertwined with the BOMs that there is really little use trying to specify the two separately.

This section contains a general reference and basic review of the different browser/ document object models that exist in major versions of Netscape and Internet Explorer.

It is important to understand the semantics of the document object model diagrams that follow. Browser objects are usually given with the first letter capitalized (for example, **Location**) and are accessed using lowercase versions of their names in JavaScript. The object names in the document object model, for example **checkbox**, indicate that an object corresponding to an element of that type (in this case **<input type="checkbox">**) is made accessible to scripts at that location in the object hierarchy, if it occurs in the document. It does not imply that there is an object accessible by the identifier "document.forms[0].checkbox."

The contents of the collections are generally objects of the given type, for example **Frame** objects are found in the **frames[ ]** collection. In traditional models, however, document objects are not normally instantiated by the programmer. Rather, they are automatically created by the browser to reflect an occurrence of the given element in the document. In the W3C DOM you can instantiate objects corresponding to elements, but this task is carried out through DOM methods such as **document.createElement()**, and only rarely through a constructor like **Image()**.

Note

*The manner in which document objects are referred to has evolved over time. For example, the contents of the **links[ ]** collection are thought of as **Link** objects in traditional models while they are now more often thought of as **\<a\>** element objects created by an occurrence of an **\<a href="..."\>** tag in the document. To complicate matters, the official DOM name for a member of the **links[ ]** collection is an **HTMLAnchorElement** object. The important thing to remember is that although these names may vary, they all refer to the same thing: an object that is accessible to JavaScript that corresponds to an instance of a particular HTML element in the document.*

The Traditional Object Model

This is the basic object model common to all scriptable browsers. It was implemented in Netscape 2 and Internet Explorer 3 and is shown in Figure B-2. This model has only limited support for events (no bubbling).

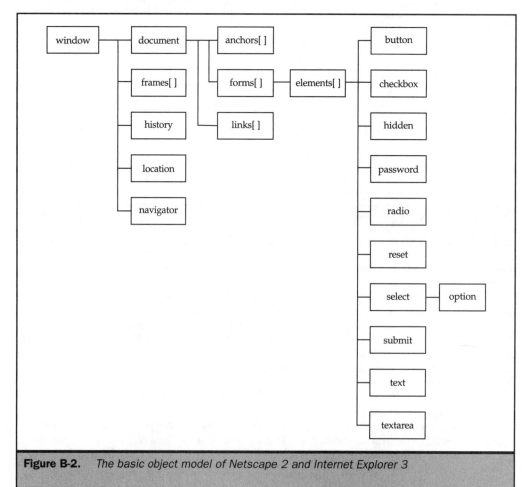

Figure B-2. *The basic object model of Netscape 2 and Internet Explorer 3*

Netscape 3

Netscape 3 makes more parts of the page available to scripts and includes for the first time the ability to dynamically manipulate images through its **images[ ]** collection. Also scriptable are Java applets (via the **applets[ ]** collection and LiveConnect features), and embedded objects. This browser also provides MIME type and plugin sensing. Its object model is shown in Figure B-3.

Internet Explorer 3

The model of Internet Explorer 3 is essentially that of the traditional object model and is shown in Figure B-4.

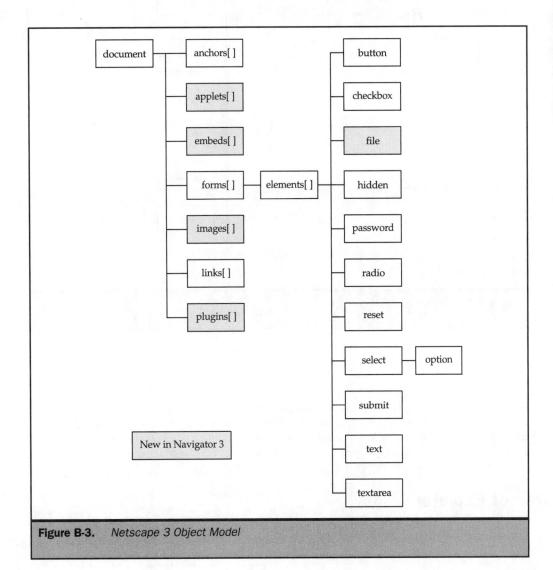

Figure B-3.   *Netscape 3 Object Model*

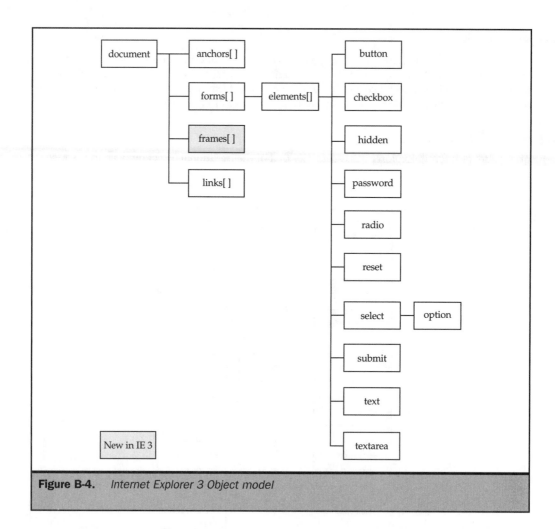

Figure B-4.   *Internet Explorer 3 Object model*

Netscape 4

Netscape 4 adds the first primitive DHTML capabilities by exposing the proprietary **<layer>** element to scripts. This browser also has a more robust event model where events begin at the top of the hierarchy and trickle down to the target element, affording intervening objects the opportunity to handle or redirect the event. While it might appear that dynamic manipulation of style is possible, most parts of the page will not reflect changes to their style once the page has been loaded.

This model is shown in Figure B-5.

Internet Explorer 4+

Internet Explorer 4 marks the point at which DHTML capabilities begin to come of age. This browser exposes all parts of the page to scripts through the **all[ ]** collection. The event model

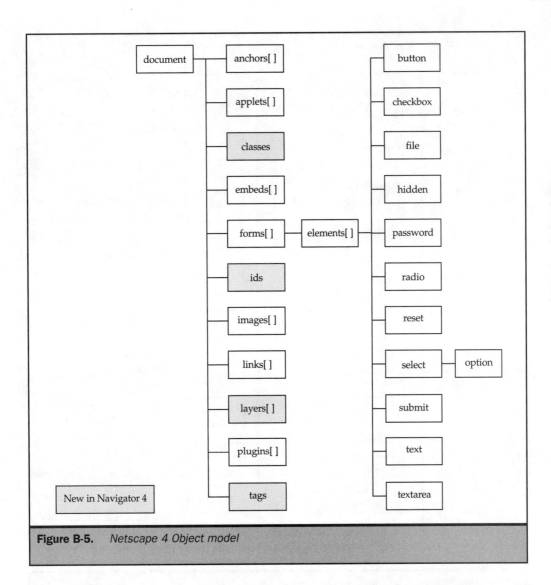

Figure B-5.   *Netscape 4 Object model*

features event bubbling, where events begin their life cycle at the element at which they occur and bubble up the hierarchy, affording intervening elements the opportunity to handle or redirect the event. This model is shown in Figure B-6.

Although later versions of Internet Explorer add a tremendous amount of new features, the core aspects of the IE document object model remain essentially the same.

Internet Explorer 5.5+, Netscape 6, and the DOM

Support for DOM properties and methods matures gradually in versions of Internet Explorer but occurs all at once in Netscape with version 6. Netscape 6 keeps the so-called DOM0 document objects, basically those found in the traditional model, and adds support for W3C DOM methods.

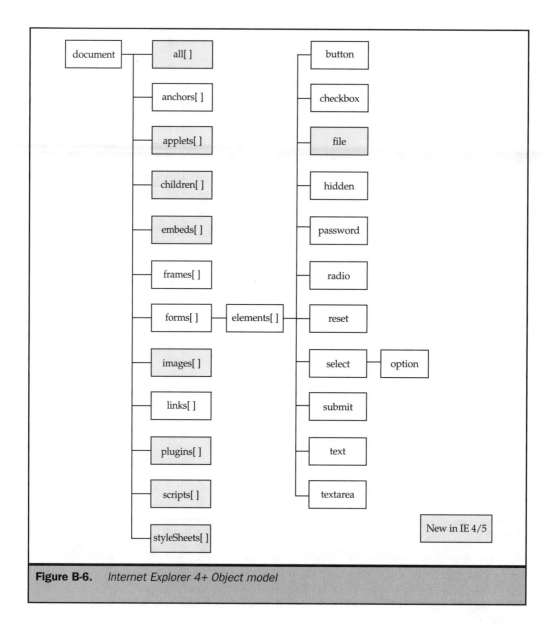

Figure B-6.   *Internet Explorer 4+ Object model*

Internet Explorer 5.5 provides decent support for parts of the DOM as well, and Internet Explorer 6 claims to be DOM-compliant, although both 5.5 and 6.0 still provide the model of IE4 for backwards compatibility.

In this modern model all parts of the page are scriptable, and the document is represented as a tree. Access to elements and attributes is standardized, as are a core set of properties and methods for document objects that largely reflect their corresponding element's HTML 4 attributes.

Core Property Reference

This section details a number of core properties that many objects have in common. Included are event handlers and DOM methods that have the same meaning for all document objects, in addition to some "core" properties commonly found in element objects. When one of these properties for a particular object has characteristics that differ from the norm, its deviation is noted in the reference section for that object.

Events

Event handlers are JavaScript code that are associated with an object and that "fire" in response to a user or system event on that object. Document objects typically support numerous event handlers encompassing a wide range of user actions in addition to intrinsic or system events that occur in response to a browser or DOM event such as the page completing loading. Some browser objects, most notably **Window**, also support a variety of handlers that allow it to process events for any document it contains, for example if the window is made up of multiple frames.

HTML 4 Events

The standard HTML 4 events are listed here. According to the event model of Internet Explorer 4+, some events may be cancelled and some events bubble up the hierarchy. The behavior of each of the HTML 4 events under Internet Explorer 4+ is indicated along with its associated handler (for example, the behavior of the **blur** event is given with the **onblur** handler).

- **onblur**   Fires when an element loses focus, meaning that the user has moved focus to another element, typically either by clicking or tabbing away. In IE4+ does not bubble and is not cancelable.

- **onchange**   Fires when a form field loses focus and its value was changed while it had focus. In IE4+ does not bubble but is cancelable.

- **onclick**   Fires when an element is clicked. In IE4+ bubbles and is cancelable.

- **ondblclick**   Fires when an element is double-clicked. In IE4+ bubbles and is cancelable.

- **onfocus**   Fires when an element receives focus, typically when it has been selected for manipulation or data entry by a click or tab. In IE4+ does not bubble and is not cancelable.

- **onkeydown**   Fires when the user presses a key and the element has focus. In IE4+ bubbles and is cancelable.

- **onkeypress**   Fires when the user presses or holds down a key (an alphanumeric key in Internet Explorer) and the element has focus. In IE4+ bubbles and is cancelable.

- **onkeyup**   Fires when the user releases a key and the element has focus. In IE4+ bubbles but is not cancelable.

- **onload**   Fires when the element has completed loading. In IE4+ does not bubble and is not cancelable.

- **onmousedown**   Fires when the mouse button is pressed and the element has focus. In IE4+ bubbles and is cancelable.

- **onmousemove**   Fires when the mouse is moved and the cursor is over the element. In IE4+ bubbles but is not cancelable.

- **onmouseout**   Fires when the user moves the mouse away from the element. In IE4+ bubbles but is not cancelable.

- **onmouseover** Fires when the user moves the mouse over the element. In IE4+ bubbles and is cancelable.

- **onmouseup** Fires when the mouse button is released and the element has focus. In IE4+ bubbles and is cancelable.

- **onreset** Fires when the form is reset, often the result of the user pressing a reset button. In IE4+ does not bubble but is cancelable.

- **onselect** Fires when text or other content is selected by the user, typically by highlighting text with the mouse. In IE4+ does not bubble but is cancelable.

- **onsubmit** Fires just prior to the submission of the form. In IE4+ does not bubble but is cancelable.

- **onunload** Fires just prior to the unloading of the object (for example, when following a link to another page). In IE4+ does not bubble and is not cancelable.

DOM Events

DOM2 supports the standard HTML4 events. Their behavior under the DOM2 event model is given in the following table.

Event	Bubbles?	Cancelable?
abort	Yes	No
blur	No	No
change	Yes	No
click	Yes	Yes
error	Yes	No
focus	No	No
load	No	No
mousedown	Yes	Yes
mouseup	Yes	Yes
mouseover	Yes	Yes
mousemove	Yes	No
mouseout	Yes	Yes
reset	Yes	No
resize	Yes	No
scroll	Yes	No
select	Yes	No
submit	Yes	Yes
unload	No	No

DOM2 also supports document mutation events that occur on portions of the document tree and GUI events that permit arbitrary elements to have an equivalent to the **onfocusin/onfocusout** handlers defined for form fields. These events should be bound using standard DOM methods, as support for the corresponding event handler properties is nonexistent. The mutation events are listed in the following table.

Event	Bubbles?	Cancelable?	Description
DOMFocusIn	Yes	No	Fires on a node when it receives focus.
DOMFocusOut	Yes	No	Fires on a node when it loses focus.
DOMSubtreeModified	Yes	No	Implementation-dependent; fires when a portion of the node's subtree has been modified.
DOMNodeInserted	Yes	No	Fires on a node inserted as the child of another node.
DOMNodeRemoved	Yes	No	Fires on a node that has been removed from its parent.
DOMNodeRemovedFromDocument	No	No	Fires on a node when it is about to be removed from the document.
DOMNodeInsertedIntoDocument	No	No	Fires on a node when it has been inserted into the document.
DOMAttrModified	Yes	No	Fires on a node when one of its attributes has been modified.
DOMCharacterDataModified	Yes	No	Fires on a node when the data it contains are modified.

Netscape Extended Events

The following events are not part of any standard, but are supported by Netscape browsers.

- **onabort** Fires when the loading of the element is cancelled before completion.
- **ondragdrop** Fires when something has been dragged onto the object and dropped.
- **onerror** Fires when a runtime error occurs at the element.
- **onmove** Fires when the user or a script moves the window or frame (Netscape 4 only).
- **onpaint** The meaning of this handler is unclear. Possibly related to XUL functionality. Netscape 6 only.

- **onresize**   Fires when the object is about to be resized (for example, just after the user has resized the window).

- **onscroll**   Fires when a scrollable object has been repositioned (Netscape 6 only).

Internet Explorer Extended Events

The following events are not part of any standard, but are supported by Internet Explorer. According to the event model of Internet Explorer 4+, some events may be cancelled and some events bubble up the hierarchy. The behavior of each of these extended events under Internet Explorer 4+ is indicated along with its associated handler (for example, the behavior of the **abort** event is given with the **onabort** handler).

- **onabort**   Fires when the loading of the object is cancelled before completion. In IE4+ does not bubble but is cancelable.

- **onactivate**   Fires when the object is set as the active element. In IE4+ bubbles but is not cancelable.

- **onafterprint**   Fires immediately after the object is printed (or previewed). In IE4+ does not bubble and is not cancelable.

- **onafterupdate**   Fires on a databound object after successfully updating the associated data in the data source object. In IE4+ bubbles but is not cancelable.

- **onbeforeactivate**   Fires immediately before the object is set as the active element. In IE4+ bubbles and is cancelable.

- **onbeforecopy**   Fires on the source object just before the selection is copied to the system clipboard. In IE4+ bubbles and is cancelable.

- **onbeforecut**   Fires on the source object before the selection is cut from the document to the clipboard (or deleted from the document). In IE4+ bubbles and is cancelable.

- **onbeforedeactivate**   Fires immediately before the **activeElement** is changed from the current object to another object in the parent document. In IE4+ bubbles and is cancelable.

- **onbeforeeditfocus**   Fires before the element receives focus for editing. In IE4+ bubbles and is cancelable.

- **onbeforepaste**   Fires on the target object before the selection is pasted from the system clipboard. In IE4+ bubbles and is cancelable.

- **onbeforeprint**   Fires on the object before its associated document prints or previews for printing. In IE4+ does not bubble and is not cancelable.

- **onbeforeunload**   Fires prior to a page being unloaded (just before the **unload** handler). In IE4+ does not bubble but is cancelable.

- **onbeforeupdate**   Fires on a databound object just before updating the associated data in the data source object. In IE4+ bubbles and is cancelable.

- **onbounce**   Fires on an alternating **<marquee>** just prior to the contents reaching one side of the window. In IE4+ does not bubble but is cancelable.

- **oncellchange**   Fires when data changes in the data provider. In IE4+ bubbles but is not cancelable.

- **oncontextmenu**   Fires when the user clicks the right mouse button on the object, opening the context menu. In IE4+ bubbles and is cancelable.

■ **oncontrolselect**   Fires just prior to the object being selected. In IE4+ bubbles and is cancelable.

■ **oncopy**   Fires on the object when the user copies it (or a selection that includes it) to the system clipboard. In IE4+ bubbles and is cancelable.

■ **oncut**   Fires on the object when the user cuts it (or a selection that includes it) to the system clipboard. In IE4+ bubbles and is cancelable.

■ **ondataavailable**   Fires when data arrives from asynchronous data source objects. In IE4+ bubbles but is not cancelable.

■ **ondatasetchanged**   Fires when the data set exposed by a data source object changes. In IE4+ bubbles but is not cancelable.

■ **ondatasetcomplete**   Fires to indicate that all data is available from the data source object. In IE4+ bubbles but is not cancelable.

■ **ondeactivate**   Fires when the **activeElement** is changed from the current object to another object in the parent document. In IE4+ bubbles but is not cancelable.

■ **ondrag**   Fires on an object continuously as it is being dragged. In IE4+ bubbles and is cancelable.

■ **ondragend**   Fires on an object being dragged when the object is released at the end of a drag operation. In IE4+ bubbles and is cancelable.

■ **ondragenter**   Fires on an object that is a valid drop target as the user drags an object into it. In IE4+ bubbles and is cancelable.

■ **ondragleave**   Fires on an object that is a valid drop target as the user drags an object out of it. In IE4+ bubbles and is cancelable.

■ **ondragover**   Fires on an object that is a valid drop target continuously as the user drags an object over it. In IE4+ bubbles and is cancelable.

■ **ondragstart**   Fires on the object about to be dragged when the user begins a drag operation. In IE4+ bubbles and is cancelable.

■ **ondrop**   Fires on an object when something is dropped on it at the end of a drag operation. In IE4+ bubbles and is cancelable.

■ **onerror**   Fires when a runtime error occurs in or at the object. In IE4+ does not bubble but is cancelable.

■ **onerrorupdate**   Fires on a databound object when an error occurs while updating the associated data in the data source object. In IE4+ bubbles but is not cancelable.

■ **onfilterchange**   Fires when a the object's CSS Filter changes state or completes a transition. In IE4+ does not bubble and is not cancelable.

■ **onfinish**   Fires on a **<marquee>** when looping is complete. In IE4+ does not bubble but is cancelable.

■ **onfocusin**   Fires on an element just prior to it receiving focus (before the **focus** event). In IE4+ bubbles but is not cancelable.

■ **onfocusout**   Fires for the current element with focus, immediately after moving focus to another element. In IE4+ bubbles but is not cancelable.

■ **onhelp**   Fires when the user presses the F1 key while the browser is the active window. In IE4+ bubbles and is cancelable.

- **onlayoutcomplete**   Fires when the print or print preview layout process finishes filling the current **LayoutRect** object with content from the source document. In IE4+ bubbles and is cancelable.

- **onlosecapture**   Fires when the object loses universal mouse capture. In IE4+ does not bubble and is not cancelable.

- **onmouseenter**   Fires when the user moves the mouse pointer into the object. (Different from **onmouseover** because the **mouseenter** event does not bubble). In IE4+ does not bubble and is not cancelable.

- **onmouseleave**   Fires when the user moves the mouse pointer outside the boundaries of the object. (Different from **onmouseout** because the **mouseleave** event does not bubble). In IE4+ does not bubble and is not cancelable.

- **onmousewheel**   Fires when the mouse wheel button is rotated. In IE4+ bubbles and is cancelable.

- **onmove**   Fires when the object moves. In IE4+ bubbles but is not cancelable.

- **onmoveend**   Fires when the object stops moving. In IE4+ bubbles but is not cancelable.

- **onmovestart**   Fires just prior to the object starting to move. In IE4+ bubbles and is cancelable.

- **onpaste**   Fires on the object into which the user is pasting data from the clipboard. In IE4+ bubbles and is cancelable.

- **onpropertychange**   Fires when a property of the object changes. In IE4+ does not bubble and is not cancelable.

- **onreadystatechange**   Fires when the **readyState** of the object changes. In IE4+ does not bubble and is not cancelable.

- **onresize**   Fires when the size of the object is about to change (for example, just after the user has resized the window). In IE4+ does not bubble and is not cancelable.

- **onresizeend**   Fires when the user finishes changing the dimensions of the object in a selection. In IE4+ does not bubble and is not cancelable.

- **onresizestart**   Fires when the user begins to change the dimensions of the object in a selection. In IE4+ does not bubble but is cancelable.

- **onrowenter**   Fires to indicate that the current row has changed in the data source and new data values are available on the object. In IE4+ bubbles but is not cancelable.

- **onrowexit**   Fires just before the data source control changes the current row in the object. In IE4+ does not bubble but is cancelable.

- **onrowsdelete**   Fires when rows are about to be deleted from the recordset. In IE4+ bubbles but is not cancelable.

- **onrowsinserted**   Fires just after new rows are inserted in the current recordset. In IE4+ bubbles but is not cancelable.

- **onscroll**   Fires on a scrollable object when the user repositions the scrollbox on the scroll bar. In IE4+ does not bubble and is not cancelable.

- **onselectionchange**   Fires whenever the selection state of a document changes. In IE4+ does not bubble and is not cancelable.

- **onselectstart**   Fires when the object is being selected. In IE4+ bubbles and is cancelable.

- **onstart** Fires on **<marquee>** elements at the beginning of every loop. In IE4+ does not bubble and is not cancelable.

- **onstop** Fires when the user clicks the Stop button or leaves the Web page. In IE4+ does not bubble and is not cancelable.

Netscape Event Methods

captureEvents(eventMask) Instructs the object of which it was invoked as a method (**Layer**, **Window**, or **Document**) to capture the events given in *eventMask*. Note that you must still manually set the appropriate handler of the object, for example **document.onunload**, to the function that it is to execute when the event occurs. The *eventMask* argument is a bitmask of static properties of the **Event** object, and these properties are given in the table that follows. For example, to capture **submit** and **reset** events at the **Document** you might write:

```
document.captureEvents(Event.SUBMIT & Event.RESET);
```

ABORT	ERROR	MOUSEDOWN	RESET
BLUR	FOCUS	MOUSEMOVE	RESIZE
CHANGE	KEYDOWN	MOUSEOUT	SELECT
CLICK	KEYPRESS	MOUSEOVER	SUBMIT
DBLCLICK	KEYUP	MOUSEUP	UNLOAD
DRAGDROP	LOAD	MOVE	

handleEvent(event) Fires the event handler of the object according to the **Event** instance *event* that was passed as an argument. This method is invoked in order to redirect the *event* to the object it was invoked as a method of. For example, an **onsubmit** handler for a form could pass the **submit** event to the first form on the page as:

```
<form onsubmit="document.forms[0].handleEvent(event)">…</form>
```

Supported in N4 (JavaScript 1.2).

releaseEvents(eventMask) Instructs the object of which it was invoked as a method (**Layer**, **Window**, or **Document**) to stop capturing the events given in *eventMask*. After using this method you do not have to reset the object's event handlers that were released, because the object will cease to capture the events, even if it has a handler defined. The *eventMask* is a bitmask of static properties defined in the **Event** object given in the table for **captureEvents()** given just previously in this section. For example, to cease capture of **error** and **click** events at the **Document** level you would use:

```
document.releaseEvents(Event.ERROR & Event.CLICK);
```

Supported in N4+ (JavaScript 1.2+).

routeEvent(event) Passes the **Event** instance *event* along normally down the object hierarchy for processing. This method is used by a **Layer**, **Window**, or **Document** to elect not to handle the specific event. For example, if the event was captured and after examination determined not to be of interest, this method is invoked to pass the event on down the hierarchy for (possibly) other handlers to processes. Supported in N4+ (JavaScript 1.2+).

Internet Explorer Event Methods

attachEvent(whichHandler, theFunction)   Attaches the function *theFunction* as a handler specified by the string *whichHandler*. The *whichHandler* argument specifies the name of the event handler that is to execute *theFunction* upon firing. For example, to attach *myHandler* as an **onclick** handler for the **Document,** you would write:

```
document.attachEvent("onclick", myHandler);
```

Handlers attached using this method are executed after any handler that was set as an HTML attribute or directly into the appropriate **on-**property of the object. Multiple handlers can be attached using this method, but no guarantee is made as to their order of execution. This method returns a Boolean indicating whether the attachment was successful. Supported in IE5+ (JScript 5.0+).

detachEvent(whichHandler, theFunction)   Instructs the object to cease executing the function *theFunction* as a handler of the type given in the string *whichHandler*. This method is used to detach handlers applied to objects using **attachEvent()**. For example, to detach the function *myHandler* that was attached as an **onclick** handler for the **Document** (using **attachEvent()**), you would use:

```
document.detachEvent("onclick", myHandler);
```

Supported in IE5+ (JScript 5.0+).

fireEvent(handler [, event])   Causes the event handler given by the string *handler* of the object to fire. If an **Event** instance is supplied as the *event* parameter, the **Event** instance passed to the target object's *handler* reflects the properties of *event*. This method returns **true** or **false** depending upon whether the event was eventually cancelled. Events created in this manner follow the normal bubbling and cancellation rules for the event created. This method is used to redirect an event to a new target (or to create a brand new event at that target) by invoking it as a method of that target. For example, to fire the **onclick** handler of the first image on the page, you might write:

```
document.images[0].fireEvent("onclick");
```

Note that the **srcElement** of the **Event** instance created is set to the object of which this method was invoked, whether the *event* parameter was supplied or not. Supported in IE5.5+ (JScript 5.5+).

releaseCapture()   Disables universal mouse event capturing that was enabled using **setCapture()**. If this method is invoked as a method of the **Document**, whichever element that is currently capturing all mouse events will cease to do so. You can, of course, invoke this function as a method of the object that is capturing to the same effect. However the ability to invoke it on the **Document** frees the programmer from determining exactly which element is currently capturing. Invoking this method when no element is universally capturing mouse events has no effect. Supported in IE5+ (JScript 5.0+).

setCapture([containerCapture])   Causes all mouse events that occur in the document to be sent to this object. The **srcElement** of the **Event** instance will always reflect the original target of the event, but all other handlers and bubbling are bypassed. In Internet Explorer 5.5+ you can specify *containerCapture* to be **false**, which causes mouse events contained by the element to function normally. However, mouse events outside the element are still unconditionally captured. This method is used to direct all mouse events to an object when that object could not otherwise capture them. For example, if there are elements whose mouse events need to be captured but those elements are not the children of the object, you need to use this method because bubbling events from the other elements would not reach it. Note that capturing is automatically disabled when the user scrolls the page, gives focus to another window, uses a dialog box, or activates a context menu. For this reason, it is always a good idea to set the **Document's onlosecapture** handler to re-enable capture if you wish to keep it on. Supported in IE5+ (JScript 5.0+).

DOM2 Event Methods

These DOM event methods are back-referenced in the "JavaScript Object Reference" section later in this appendix. They are placed in this location because they are common to many (if not all) nodes. The full specification can be found at **http://www.w3.org/DOM/**.

addEventListener(whichEvent, handler, direction)   Instructs the object to execute function *handler* when an event of the type given in the string *whichEvent* (for example, "click") occurs. The *direction* parameter is a Boolean indicating whether the handler should be fired in the capture phase (**true**) or bubbling phase (**false**). Multiple handlers for the same event can be attached by using this method multiple times. Listeners (event handlers) can be bound to text nodes as well as element nodes. Supported in N6+ (JavaScript 1.5+), DOM2.

dispatchEvent(event)   Causes the **Event** instance *event* to be processed by the appropriate handler of the object that this function was invoked as a method of. This method returns **false** if any handler that eventually processes the *event* returns **false** or invokes **preventDefault()**. The node at which this method was invoked becomes the new target of *event*. This method is used to redirect an event to another node in the tree. Supported in N6+ (JavaScript 1.5+), DOM2.

preventDefault()   When invoked in a handler has the effect of canceling the default action associated with the event. Calling this method is the same as returning **false** from a handler. Note that in DOM2 once a handler has returned **false** or invoked this method, the default action associated with the event will not occur, no matter what value other handlers that process the event return. Supported in N6+ (JavaScript 1.5+), DOM2.

removeEventListener(whichEvent, handler, direction)   Removes the function *handler* as a handler for the event given in the string *whichEvent* (for example, "click") for the phase given by the Boolean *direction*. Note that *direction* must correspond to the value passed as the third parameter to **addEventListener()** when the handler was originally attached to the object. Supported in N6+ (JavaScript 1.5+), DOM2.

stopPropagation()   When invoked in an event handler, halts the normal propagation of the event after the current handler completes execution. This method works only for those events that are cancelable. Supported in N6+ (JavaScript 1.5+), DOM2.

DOM Properties

The DOM properties a node will have are largely a reflection of the attributes the corresponding element is permitted under HTML 4. However, there are many properties that are common to all elements, in particular the core HTML properties **dir**, **id**, **lang**, **title**, and **class** (named **className** in the DOM because "class" is a JavaScript reserved word). Additionally, all nodes have DOM properties that permit the traversal and manipulation of the document tree.

These DOM properties are back-referenced in the "JavaScript Object Reference" section later in this appendix. They are placed in this location because they are common to many (if not all) nodes. This list is not exhaustive, but encompasses the vast majority of properties used in typical tasks. The full specification can be found at **http://www.w3.org/DOM/**.

attributes[ ]   Collection of attributes for the element. This property is supported in IE5+ (JScript 5.0+), N6+ (JavaScript 1.5+), and DOM1. This property is ReadOnly.

childNodes[ ]   Collection of child nodes. This property is supported in IE5+ (JScript 5.0+), N6+ (JavaScript 1.5+), and DOM1. This property is ReadOnly.

className   String holding the name of the CSS **class** bound to the element. The **class** is usually set with the **class** HTML attribute, but of course may also be set by a script. A class name might be used by a stylesheet to associate style rules to multiple elements at once. For example, it might be desirable to associate a special class name called "important" with all elements that should be rendered with a yellow background. Because class values are not unique to a particular element, **<em class="important">** could be used as well as **<p class="important">** in the same document. While it is theoretically possible to have multiple values for the **class** by separating them by white space—for example, "important special"—support for this technique is limited. This property is supported in IE4+ (JScript 3.0+), N6+ (JavaScript 1.5+), and DOM1.

dir   String holding the text direction of text enclosed by the element. The accepted values under the HTML 4.01 specification are "ltr" (left to right) and "rtl" (right to left). This attribute is commonly used to override whatever direction a user agent sets by using it with the **<bdo>** element:

```
<bdo dir="rtl">Napoleon never really said "Able was I ere I saw Elba."</bdo>
```

Internet Explorer 5.5 supports **dir** for the **<bdo>** element, but Netscape 6 does not. Setting this value for other block-level elements might produce right-aligned text, but usually will not change the actual direction of the text flow. This property is supported in IE5+ (JScript 5.0+), N6+ (JavaScript 1.5+), and DOM1.

firstChild   Reference to the first child node of the element, if one exists (**null** otherwise). This property is supported in IE5+ (JScript 5.0+), N6+ (JavaScript 1.5+), and DOM1. This property is ReadOnly.

id   String holding the unique alphanumeric identifier for the element. Commonly assigned using the **id** HTML attribute and used as the target for **getElementById()**. This unique identifier is not only important for scripting, but also for binding of CSS as well. This property is supported in IE4+ (JScript 3.0+), N6+ (JavaScript 1.5+), and DOM1.

lang   String holding the language code for the content the element encloses. Corresponds to the **lang** HTML attribute. For a full list of valid values, see RFC 1766 (**http://www.ietf.org/rfc/**

rfc1766.txt?number=1766), which describes language codes and their formats. This property is supported in IE4+ (JScript 3.0+), N6+ (JavaScript 1.5+), and DOM1.

lastChild   Reference to the last child node of the element, if one exists (**null** otherwise). This property is supported in IE5+ (JScript 5.0+), N6+ (JavaScript 1.5+), and DOM1. This property is ReadOnly.

nextSibling   Reference to the next sibling of the node—for example, if its parent node has multiple children. This property is supported in IE5+ (JScript 5.0+), N6+ (JavaScript 1.5+), and DOM1. This property is ReadOnly.

nodeName   String containing the name of the node (the name of the tag to which the object corresponds, for example "H1"). This property is supported in IE5+ (JScript 5.0+), N6+ (JavaScript 1.5+), and DOM1. This property is ReadOnly.

nodeType   Number holding the node type as given in the following table (for DOM1 HTML). This property is supported in IE5+ (JScript 5.0+), N6+ (JavaScript 1.5+), and DOM1. This property is ReadOnly.

Node Type Number	Type	Description	Example
1	Element	An HTML or XML element.	\<p>...\</p>
2	Attribute	An attribute for an HTML or XML element.	align="center"
3	Text	A fragment of text that would be enclosed by an HTML or XML element	This is a text fragment!
8	Comment	An HTML comment	\<!-- This is a comment -->
9	Document	The root document object, namely the top element in the parse tree	\<html>
10	DocumentType	A document type definition	\<!DOCTYPE HTML PUBLIC "-//W3C//DTD HTML 4.01 Transitional//EN" "http://www.w3.org/TR/html4/loose.dtd">

nodeValue   String containing the value within the node (usually only applicable to text nodes). This property is supported in IE5+ (JScript 5.0+), N6+ (JavaScript 1.5+), and DOM1.

ownerDocument   Reference to the **Document** object in which the element is contained. This property is supported in IE5+ (JScript 5.0+), N6+ (JavaScript 1.5+), and DOM1. This property is ReadOnly.

parentNode   Reference to the parent node of the current object, if one exists (**null** otherwise). This property is supported in IE5+ (JScript 5.0+), N6+ (JavaScript 1.5+), and DOM1. This property is ReadOnly.

previousSibling   Reference to the previous sibling of the node, for example if its parent node has multiple children. This property is supported in IE5+ (JScript 5.0+), N6+ (JavaScript 1.5+), and DOM1. This property is ReadOnly.

style   A reference to the inline **Style** object for the element. This object contains properties corresponding almost directly to CSS style attributes. For a complete list of these properties, see the **Style** object in the reference section. This property is supported to various degrees by Netscape 4 (very spotty), Netscape 6+ (good support), Internet Explorer 3 (spotty and defined only for some elements), Internet Explorer 4 (better, defined for all objects), Internet Explorer 5 (good support), and Internet Explorer 5.5+ (reliable support). It is a part of DOM2.

tagName   String containing the name of the tag to which the object corresponds. For example, "H1". This property is supported in IE5.5+, N6+, and DOM1.

title   String containing the advisory text for the element, often rendered as a tooltip in modern browsers when the mouse is placed over the object. This property can also be used to provide information for future document maintainers as to the meaning of the element and its enclosed content. In some cases, such as the **<a>** element, the **title** attribute can provide additional help in bookmarking. This property can be very useful in facilitating automatic index generation for documents. This property is supported in IE4+ (JScript 3.0+), N6+ (JavaScript 1.5+), and DOM1.

DOM Methods

These DOM methods are back-referenced in the "JavaScript Object Reference" section later in this appendix. They are placed in this location because they are common to many (if not all) nodes. This list is not exhaustive, but encompasses the vast majority of methods used in typical tasks. The full specification can be found at **http://www.w3.org/DOM/**.

appendChild(newChild)   Appends *newChild* to the end of the node's **childNodes[ ]** list and returns a reference to the inserted node. Supported in IE5+ (JScript 5.0+), N6+ (JavaScript 1.5+), and DOM1 (Core).

appendData(data)   Appends the string *data* to the end of the text node. Supported in IE6+ (JScript 5.6/6.0+), N6+ (JavaScript 1.5+), and DOM1 (Core).

blur()   Removes focus from the element. Support began in IE3+ (JScript 1.0+) and N2+ (JavaScript 1.0+), but support for specific elements varies and is therefore noted with the element itself. DOM1 (HTML). See also **blur()** in "Other Core Methods" section that follows.

click()   Simulates a user mouse click at the object. In older browsers, this method does not invoke the **onclick** handler of the object. This method does not bring the clicked element into focus, so if this is required it must be done manually using the **focus()** method. Although supported for form elements in almost all browsers, support for all elements didn't mature until IE4+ (JScript 3.0+), N6+ (JavaScript 1.5+). DOM1.

cloneNode(cloneChildren)   Clones the node and returns the new clone. If the Boolean *cloneChildren* is **true**, the returned node will include the recursively constructed subtree of clones of the node's children (and their child, and their children...). Supported in IE5+ (JScript 5.0+), N6+ (JavaScript 1.5+), and DOM1 (Core).

createAttribute(name)   Returns a new attribute node of name given by string *name*. Method of the **Document** object. Supported in IE6+ (JScript 5.6/6.0+), N6+ (JavaScript 1.5+), and DOM1 (Core).

createComment(data)   Return a new comment node with text content given by the string *data*. Method of the **Document** object. Supported in IE6+ (JScript 5.6/6+), N6+ (JavaScript 1.5+), and DOM1 (Core).

createElement(tagName)   Returns a new element node corresponding to the string *tagName*, for example "P." Method of the **Document** object. Supported in IE4+ (JScript 3.0+), N6+ (JavaScript 1.5+), and DOM1 (Core).

createTextNode(data)   Returns a new text node with text content given by the string *data*. Method of the **Document** object. Supported in IE5+ (JScript 5.0+), N6+ (JavaScript 1.5+), and DOM1 (Core).

deleteData(offset, count)   Deletes *count* characters starting from index *offset* in the text node. Supported in IE6+ (JScript 5.6/6.0+), N6+ (JavaScript 1.5+), and DOM1 (Core).

focus()   Gives focus to the element. Support began in IE3+ (JScript 1.0+) and N2+ (JavaScript 1.0+), but support for specific elements varies and is therefore noted with the element itself. DOM1 (HTML). See also **focus()** in "Other Core Methods" section that follows.

getAttribute(name)   Returns a string containing the value of the attribute specified by the string *name*. If no such attribute is found, Internet Explorer returns **null** while more standard implementations return the empty string (IE 6+ should return the empty string). Note that Internet Explorer may return attribute values as Booleans or numbers if they appear to be such (for example, if the value is "true" or "10"). Internet Explorer supports a nonstandard optional second parameter that when set to **1** (or **true**) causes the method to perform a case-sensitive attribute search. When this second parameter is **2** the method returns the property exactly as it was set in the source document (the case is not changed). Supported in IE4+ (JScript 3.0+), N6+ (JavaScript 1.5+), DOM1 (Core).

getAttributeNode(name)   Returns the attribute node corresponding to the attribute given in the string *name*. If no such node exists, **null** is returned. Supported in IE6+ (JScript 5.6/6.0+) , N6+ (JavaScript 1.5+), DOM1.

getElementById(id)   Returns the element with **id** or **name** equal to the string *id*. Returns **null** if no such element exists. Method of the **Document** object. Supported in IE5+ (JScript 5.0+), N6+ (JavaScript 1.5+), and DOM1 (HTML).

getElementsByName(name)   Retrieves a collection of elements with **id** or **name** attributes equal to the string *name*. Should not be relied upon to return elements with the corresponding **id**, but many implementations will. Method of the **Document** object. Supported in IE5+ (JScript 5.0+), N6+ (JavaScript 1.5+), DOM1 (HTML).

getElementsByTagName(tagname)   Retrieves a collection of element nodes corresponding to the tag given in the string *tagname*. A value of "*" for *tagname* retrieves all tags. Supported in IE5+ (JScript 5.0+), N6+ (JavaScript 1.5+), and DOM1 (Core).

hasAttribute(name)   Returns a Boolean indicating if the attribute given in the string *name* is defined (either explicitly or with a default value) for the node. Supported in N6+ (JavaScript 1.5+), DOM2 (Core).

hasAttrbutes()   Returns a Boolean indicating if any attributes are defined for the node. Supported in N6+ (JavaScript 1.5+), DOM2 (Core).

hasChildNodes()   Returns a Boolean indicating if the node has child nodes. Supported in IE5+ (JScript 5.0+), N6+ (JavaScript 1.5+), and DOM1 (Core).

insertBefore(newChild, refChild)   Inserts node *newChild* in front of *refChild* in the **childNodes** list of *refChild*'s parent node. Returns a reference to the newly inserted node. Supported in IE5+ (JScript 5.0+), N6+ (JavaScript 1.5+), and DOM1 (Core).

insertData(offset, string)   Inserts the string *string* into the text node at character index *offset*. Supported in IE6+ (JScript 5.6/6.0+), N6+ (JavaScript 1.5+), and DOM1 (Core).

isSupported(feature [, version])   Returns a Boolean indicating whether the feature given in the string *feature* is supported. If the string *version* is given, the method returns a Boolean indicating whether version *version* of the *feature* is supported. For example, to check for DOM1 HTML support, you might use *nodeReference*.**isSupported("HTML", "1.0")**. For a list of potential values see **www.w3.org/TR/DOM-Level-2-Core/introduction.html#ID-Conformance**. Supported in N6+ (JavaScript 1.5+), DOM2 (Core).

normalize()   Recursively merges text nodes in the subtree rooted at this element to achieve a "normal" form where there are no adjacent text nodes. This method is useful if tree manipulations have left fragmented text nodes throughout the tree and you need a "clean" view of the tree. Supported in IE6 + (JScript 5.5+), N6+ (JavaScript 1.5+), DOM1 (Core).

removeAttribute(name)   Removes attribute corresponding to the string *name* from the node. Supported in IE4+ (JScript 3.0+) for most nodes, IE5+ (JScript 5.0+) for almost all, IE6+ (JScript 5.6/6.0+) for all nodes, N6+ (JavaScript 1.5+), and DOM1 (Core).

removeAttributeNode(attribute)   Removes the attribute node given by the node *attribute* and returns the removed node. Supported in IE6+ (JScript 5.6/6.0+), N6+ (JavaScript 1.5+), DOM1 (Core).

removeChild(oldChild)   Removes *oldChild* from the node's children and returns a reference to the removed object. Supported in IE5+ (JScript 5.0+), N6+ (JavaScript 1.5+), and DOM1 (Core).

replaceChild(newChild, oldChild)   Replaces the node's child node *oldChild* with node *newChild* and returns a reference to the child replaced. Supported in IE5+ (JScript 3.0+), N6+ (JavaScript 1.5+), and DOM1 (Core).

replaceData(offset, count, string)   Replaces *count* characters of the text node starting at index *offset* with the corresponding number of characters from the string *string*. Supported in IE6+ (JScript 5.6/6.0+), N6+ (JavaScript 1.5+), and DOM1 (Core).

setAttribute(name, value)   Sets a new attribute for the node with name given by the string *name* and value given by the string *value*. If an attribute of this name already exists, it is replaced. Supported in IE4+ (JScript 3.0+), N6+ (JavaScript 1.5+), DOM1 (Core).

setAttributeNode(newAttr)   Adds the attribute node *newAttr*. If an attribute with the same name is already present, it is replaced and the method returns the replaced attribute node. Otherwise, it returns **null**. Supported in IE5+ (JScript 5.6/6.0+), N6+ (JavaScript 1.5+), DOM1 (Core).

splitText(offset)   Splits the text node into two pieces at character position *offset*. A new text node containing the right half of the text is returned and the corresponding text is removed from the node. Supported in IE5+ (JScript 5.0+), N6+ (JavaScript 1.5+), and DOM1 (Core).

substringData(offset, count)   Returns a string corresponding to the substring beginning at character index *offset* and running for *count* characters. Supported in IE6+ (JScript 5.6/6.0+), N6+ (JavaScript 1.5+), and DOM1.

Other Core Properties

These properties are back-referenced in the "JavaScript Object Reference" section later in this appendix. They are placed in this location because they are common to many objects, although they are for the most part nonstandard. General guidelines on support are often supplied, but specific support information for these properties is found for each object in the "JavaScript Object Reference" section. The reason for this is that, unlike DOM properties, these properties are often added to different objects in different versions, rather than in one large batch as is done for DOM compliance. The DOM properties included in this section are primarily those that have a long pre-DOM history and are not related to tree manipulation.

accessKey   Single character string indicating the key, which when used in combination with ALT (or other key in non-Windows operating systems) gives the element focus. When this key is used, the element is automatically scrolled into focus (if it is offscreen). Corresponds to the **accesskey** attribute. Supported in IE4+ (JScript 3.0+), N6+ (JavaScript 1.5+), DOM1 (HTML). Note that support under Netscape 6 may be spotty.

align   String specifying the alignment of the element with respect to the surrounding content. Typical values are "left," "right," "center," and "justify" for horizontal alignment or "bottom," "middle," and "top" for vertical alignment.

all[ ]   Collection of elements contained by the element, including nodes for unknown tags and comments. Accessed as you normally would access a collection (by array syntax with an index or name, associative array syntax, or directly by name). The name in the case of this collection is the **id** or **name** attribute of the element. This collection supports the **namedItem()**, **tags()**, and **urns()** methods in addition to **item()** (all described in the following section). Supported in IE4+ (JScript 3.0+).

behaviorUrns[ ]   A collection of DHTML Behaviors attached to the node, represented by their URNs. If no Behaviors are attached to the node(s), the empty collection is returned whenever this property is accessed. Supported in IE5+ (JScript 5.0+).

canHaveChildren   Boolean indicating whether the element can have child nodes (for example, **<img>** cannot). Supported in IE5+ (JScript 5.0+). This property is ReadOnly.

canHaveHTML   Boolean indicating whether the element can enclose HTML markup (for example, **<img>** cannot). Supported in IE5.5+ (JScript 5.5+). This property is ReadOnly.

children[ ]   Collection of child nodes. This is IE's pre-DOM equivalent of **childNodes[ ]**. The **childNodes[ ]** collection is standard, but this collection is available in IE4. Supported in IE4+ (JScript 3.0+). This property is ReadOnly.

clientHeight   Numeric value indicating the height of the element's content area in pixels. This value is often useful for determining the height of the content area of the browser window (as a property of the document **<body>**). Supported in IE4+ (JScript 3.0+). This property is ReadOnly.

clientLeft   Numeric value indicating difference between the **offsetLeft** property and the beginning of the element's content area, in pixels. While this property could be used to determine the vertical border width of the element, there are really no other uses for it. To find the left pixel position of an element, use **offsetLeft**. Supported in IE4+ (JScript 3.0+). This property is ReadOnly.

clientTop   Numeric value indicating difference between the **offsetTop** property and the beginning of the element's content area, in pixels. While this property could be used to determine the horizontal border width of the element, there are really no other uses for it. To find the top pixel position of an element, use **offsetTop**. Supported in IE4+ (JScript 3.0+). This property is ReadOnly.

clientWidth   Numeric value indicating the width of the element's content area in pixels. This value is often useful for determining the width of the content area of the browser window (as a property of the document **<body>**). Supported in IE4+ (JScript 3.0+). This property is ReadOnly.

contentEditable   String determining whether the content of the element is editable. Values are "inherit," "true," or "false." A value of "inherit" means that it will inherit the **contentEditable** property of its parent (this value is the default). This property is useful for making table data cells editable. Elements with **disabled** set to **true** are not editable, no matter what value this property has. Corresponds to the **contenteditable** attribute. Supported in IE5.5+ (JScript 5.5+).

currentStyle   Reference to a **Style** object that reflects the style characteristics of the element as specified by global and inline styles, and style set through HTML attributes. Differs from the **style** property because the **style** property reflects only inline style, not global or linked styles. Includes all styles that are applied, event those that result from presentation-related markup. This object is useful for examining global (default) styles but is updated asynchronously, so its values might lag during page loading or complex style manipulations that result in screen updates. Supported in IE5+ (JScript 5.0+). This property is ReadOnly.

dataFld   String specifying which field of a given data source is bound to the element. Corresponds to the **datafld** attribute. Supported in IE4+ (JScript 3.0+).

dataFormatAs   String indicating how the element treats data supplied to it. Values are "text" (the default), "html," or "localized-text." Useful primarily with data binding. Corresponds to the **dataformatas** attribute. Supported in IE4+ (JScript 3.0+).

dataSrc   String containing the source of data for data binding. Corresponds to the **datasrc** attribute. Supported in IE4+ (JScript 3.0+).

disabled   Boolean indicating whether the element is disabled. Disabled elements are grayed out and do not respond to events. Corresponds to the **disabled** attribute. Supported in IE4+ (JScript 3.0+), though not scriptable for many elements until IE5.5+ (JScript 5.5+).

filters[ ]   Collection of Microsoft CSS Filters that have been applied to the object. See Microsoft documentation, currently at **msdn.microsoft.com/library/default.asp?url=/workshop/author/ filter/filters.asp**. Supported in IE4+ (JScript 3.0+).

height   Specifies the height in pixels of the object. Corresponds to the **height** attribute (in general).

hideFocus   Boolean indicating whether the object gives a visible cue when it receives focus (for example, the "focus rectangle" that appears around a focused form element). If **true**, the element does not give a cue. Supported in IE5.5+ (JScript 5.5+).

innerHeight   Numeric value indicating the height of the element's content area in pixels. Supported in N4+ (JavaScript 1.2+).

innerHTML   String holding the HTML content enclosed within the element's tags. Supported in IE4+ (JScript 3.0+), N6+ (JavaScript 1.5+).

innerText   String holding the text enclosed by the element's tags. This text is not interpreted as HTML, so setting it to a value like "Important" will result in "Important" being displayed, rather than "Important" with boldfaced font. Supported in IE4+ (JScript 3.0+).

innerWidth   Numeric value indicating the width of the element's content area in pixels. Supported in N4+ (JavaScript 1.2+).

isContentEditable   Boolean indicating whether the user can edit the contents of the element. Use the **contentEditable** property if you wish to change this value. Supported in IE5.5+ (JScript 5.5+). This property is ReadOnly.

isDisabled   Boolean indicating if the user can interact with the object. To change this value, use the **disabled** property. Supported in IE5.5+ (JScript 5.5+). This property is ReadOnly.

isMultiLine   Not currently implemented.

isTextEdit   Boolean indicating if a **TextRange** object can be created using the object. Supported in IE4+ (JScript 3.0+). This property is ReadOnly.

language   String indicating the scripting language in use, for example "JScript." Has no real meaning outside of **<script>** elements, although it can be used to explicitly instruct IE to treat the element's event handlers as consisting of a particular scripting language. Corresponds to the **language** attribute. Supported in IE4+ (JScript 3.0+).

localName   String indicating the "local" XML name for the object. See W3C information on XML Namespace. Supported in N6+ (JavaScript 1.5+). This property is ReadOnly.

namespaceURI   String indicating the XML Namespace URI for the object. See W3C information on XML Namespace. Supported in N6+ (JavaScript 1.5+). This property is ReadOnly.

APPENDIXES

offsetHeight   Numeric value indicating the height of the element in pixels, relative to its parent. Usually a good indication of the element's actual height (give or take a few pixels for border and margin on different platforms). See Microsoft's documentation, currently at **msdn.microsoft.com/library/default.asp?url=/workshop/author/om/measuring.asp** for more information. Supported in IE4+ (JScript 3.0+), N6+ (JavaScript 1.5+). This property is ReadOnly.

offsetLeft   Numeric value indicating the pixel offset of the left edge of the element, relative to its **offsetParent** (usually the innermost enclosing block element). See Microsoft's documentation, currently at **msdn.microsoft.com/library/default.asp?url=/workshop/author/om/measuring.asp** for more information. Supported in IE4+ (JScript 3.0+), N6+ (JavaScript 1.5+). This property is ReadOnly.

offsetParent   Reference to the object relative to which the **offsetHeight/Left/Top/Width** is calculated. Usually the block element in which the current element is enclosed (for example, unenclosed elements would be relative to the **<body>**). This property is often useful when calculating the position of an element on the screen. For example, you can recursively follow this property up the enclosure chain (until you hit **null**) and sum the **offsetTop/Left** properties. The exact behavior of this property can vary from browser to browser (as it is unstandardized). Supported in IE4+ (JScript 3.0+), N6+ (JavaScript 1.5+). This property is ReadOnly.

offsetTop   Numeric value indicating the pixel offset of the top edge of the element, relative to its **offsetParent** (usually the innermost enclosing block element). See Microsoft's documentation, currently at **msdn.microsoft.com/library/default.asp?url=/workshop/author/om/measuring.asp** for more information. Supported in IE4+ (JScript 3.0+), N6+ (JavaScript 1.5+). This property is ReadOnly.

offsetWidth   Numeric value indicating the width of the element in pixels, relative to its parent. Usually a good indication of the element's actual width (give or take a few pixels for border and margin on different platforms). See Microsoft's documentation, currently at **msdn.microsoft.com/library/default.asp?url=/workshop/author/om/measuring.asp** for more information. Supported in IE4+ (JScript 3.0+), N6+ (JavaScript 1.5+). This property is ReadOnly.

outerHeight   Numeric value indicating the total height in pixels of the element (including borders, margins, scrollbars, and so on). Supported in N4+ (JavaScript 1.2+).

outerHTML   String holding the HTML content enclosed within the element's tags, including the element's tags themselves. Supported in IE4+ (JScript 3.0+).

outerText   String holding the text enclosed by the element's tags, including the element's tags themselves. This value is not interpreted as HTML, so setting it to "Important" will replace the element with the text "Important," but it will not be rendered boldfaced. Supported in IE4+ (JScript 3.0+).

outerWidth   Numeric value in pixels indicating the total width in pixels of the element (including borders, margins, scrollbars, and so on). Supported in N4+ (JavaScript 1.2+).

parentElement   Reference to the object's parent element in the document object hierarchy (or **null** if the node is the topmost). This is IE's pre-DOM equivalent of **parentNode**. Supported in IE4+ (JScript 3.0+), ReadOnly.

parentTextEdit   Reference to the innermost container element outside of the current object that is capable of creating a **TextRange** containing the current element. If no such container exists, this property is **null**. Supported in IE4+ (JScript 3.0+). This property is ReadOnly.

prefix   String indicating the "prefix" XML name for the object. See W3C information on XML Namespace. Supported in N6+ (JavaScript 1.5+). This property is ReadOnly.

readyState   String containing the current state of the object. Values include "uninitialized," "loading," "loaded," "interactive" (not finished loading but able to respond to user actions), and "complete." Objects progress through each of these states until they have completed loading, though some objects may skip some intermediate steps (for example, pass from "uninitialized" directly to "complete"). This property is very useful in determining whether an element has completed loading. However, you should always make sure the object exists in the **Document** before attempting to read this property (otherwise a runtime error will be thrown because you would be attempting to read a property of an object not yet defined). Note that an **<object>**'s **readyState** is given by the integers 0 through 4 (with the same meaning). Supported in IE4+ (JScript 3.0+) for some elements, and IE5+ (JScript 5.0+) for almost all elements. This property is available for frames only as of IE5.5+ (JScript 5.5+). This property is ReadOnly.

recordNumber   Numeric value indicating the record number of the data set from which the element was generated (used in data binding). Supported in IE4+ (JScript 3.0+). This property is ReadOnly.

runtimeStyle   Reference to a **Style** object that reflects the current (runtime) style characteristics of the element. This object has precedence over the object in the **style** property. This object is used to guarantee that your styles will be reflected in the page in an IE5+ environment. Supported in IE5+ (JScript 5.0+).

scopeName   String containing the "local" XML name for the object. See W3C documentation on XML Namespace. Supported in IE5+ (JScript 5.0+). This property is ReadOnly.

scrollHeight   Numeric value indicating the total height in pixels of the inside of the object's content area, no matter how much of the object is displayed onscreen. Supported in IE4+ (JScript 3.0+) for some objects, IE5+ (JScript 5.0+) for most. This property has poor support under MacOS. This property is ReadOnly.

scrollLeft   Numeric value indicating the distance in pixels from the left edge of the object to the leftmost edge of the object that is currently displayed—in other words, how many pixels to the right the object is scrolled. This property has meaning only for scrollable objects; for all others, this property is always zero. Supported in IE4+ (JScript 3.0+) for some objects, IE5+ (JScript 5.0+) for most.

scrollTop   Numeric value indicating the distance in pixels from the top edge of the object to the topmost edge of the object that is currently displayed—in other words, how many pixels down the object is scrolled. This property only has meaning for scrollable objects; for all others, this property is always zero. Supported in IE4+ (JScript 3.0+) for some objects, IE5+ (JScript 5.0+) for most.

scrollWidth   Numeric value indicating the total width in pixels of the inside of the object's content area, no matter how much of the object is displayed on screen. Supported in IE4+ (JScript 3.0+) for some objects, IE5+ (JScript 5.0+) for most. This property has poor support under MacOS. This property is ReadOnly.

sourceIndex   Number indicating the index of the element in the **document.all[ ]** collection. Useful for gaining access to adjacent elements on the page. Supported in IE4+ (JScript 3.0+). This property is ReadOnly.

style   Reference to a **Style** object that contains the inline style characteristics of the element. This object is the standard way in which scripts manipulate the style of objects. Supported in IE4+ (JScript 3.0+), primitive nonstandard support in N4 (JavaScript 1.2+), supported in N6+ (JavaScript 1.5+), DOM2. See documentation for the **Style** object.

tabIndex   Numeric value indicating the tab order for the object. Elements with positive values for this property are tabbed to in order of increasing **tabIndex** (before any others). Elements with zero for this property (the default) are tabbed to in the order they occur in the document source. Elements with negative values are not tabbed to at all. Supported in IE4+ (JScript 3.0+) some objects, IE5+ (JScript 5.0+) for most,. N6+ (JavaScript 1.5+), DOM1 (HTML).

tagUrn   String containing the URN of the XML Namespace for the object. See Microsoft and W3C XML Namespace documentation. Supported in IE5+ (JScript 5.0+) but is unsupported in MacOS.

uniqueID   Reading this string property automatically generates a unique **id** attribute for the node that can be used to access it via standard methods. Note that it does not replace the current **id** if one is set. The value generated is consistent across accesses to this property (unless the page is reloaded). This property allows you to manipulate otherwise unknown elements or to gain finer-grain access to individual elements with the same **id** or **name**. Supported in IE5+ (JScript 5.0+) but is unsupported in MacOS. This property is ReadOnly.

width   Specifies the width of the object in pixels. Corresponds to the **width** attribute (in general).

Other Core Methods

These methods are back-referenced in the "JavaScript Object Reference" section later in this appendix. They are placed in this location because they are common to many objects, although they are for the most part nonstandard. General guidelines on support are often supplied, but specific support information for these methods is found for each object in the "JavaScript Object Reference" section. The reason for this is that, unlike most DOM methods, these methods are often added to different objects in different versions, rather in one large batch, as is done for DOM compliance. The DOM methods included in this section are primarily those that have a long pre-DOM history and are not related to tree manipulation.

addBehavior(url)   Binds the attached behavior referenced in the string *url* to the element. For default behaviors, *url* has the form "#default#behaviorName." For binary behaviors (those behaviors which are implemented as binary objects in the page), *url* has the form "#id," which references the **id** of the behavior **<object>**. Returns an identifier that can later be used to detach the behavior. Supported in IE5+ (JScript 5.0+) but not available in MacOS.

applyElement(newElement [, where])   "Applies" one element to another by enclosing one within the other. If the string *where* is omitted or "outside," the object referenced by *newElement* becomes the parent of the current element. Equivalent to adding the tags of the node *newElement* just outside of the current element's tags. If *where* is "inside," *newElement* becomes the only child of the current element and encloses all of the current element's children. Equivalent to adding the tags of the node *newElement* just inside of the current element's tags. The *newElement* object is often a new node created by **document.createElement()**. Supported in IE5+ (JScript 5.0+).

blur()   Causes the element to lose focus. Often used to send a **Window** into the background. Although supported in all major browsers since for some elements, support for all elements began to mature in IE5+ (JScript 5.0+) and N6+ (JavaScript 1.5+), DOM1.

clearAttributes()   Clears all HTML attributes from the element except those that are essential (**id**, **style**, etc.). Supported in IE5+ (JScript 5.0+).

click()   Simulates a user mouse click at the object. In older browsers, this method does not invoke the **onclick** handler of the object. This method does not bring the clicked element into focus, so if this is required it must be done manually using the **focus()** method. Although supported for form elements in almost all browsers, support for all elements didn't mature until IE4+ (JScript 3.0+), N6+ (JavaScript 1.5+), DOM1.

componentFromPoint(x, y)   Returns a string that gives information about the pixel coordinate (*x,y*) in the client window with respect to the current element. The string returned may have one of the values in the next Table. The return value specifies whether the coordinate is inside of the element (""), outside of the element ("outside"), or a part of the various scrolling mechanisms that may be displayed for the element.

Return Value	Component at the given coordinate
""	Component is inside the client area of the object.
"outside"	Component is outside the bounds of the object.
"scrollbarDown"	Down scroll arrow is at the specified location.
"scrollbarHThumb"	Horizontal scroll thumb or box is at the specified location.
"scrollbarLeft"	Left scroll arrow is at the specified location.
"scrollbarPageDown"	Page-down scroll bar shaft is at the specified location.
"scrollbarPageLeft"	Page-left scroll bar shaft is at the specified location.
"scrollbarPageRight"	Page-right scroll bar shaft is at the specified location.
"scrollbarPageUp"	Page-up scroll bar shaft is at the specified location.
"scrollbarRight"	Right scroll arrow is at the specified location.
"scrollbarUp"	Up scroll arrow is at the specified location.
"scrollbarVThumb"	Vertical scroll thumb or box is at the specified location.
"handleBottom"	Bottom sizing handle is at the specified location.
"handleBottomLeft"	Lower-left sizing handle is at the specified location.
"handleBottomRight"	Lower-right sizing handle is at the specified location.

Return Value	Component at the given coordinate
"handleLeft"	Left sizing handle is at the specified location.
"handleRight"	Right sizing handle is at the specified location.
"handleTop"	Top sizing handle is at the specified location.
"handleTopLeft"	Upper-left sizing handle is at the specified location.
"handleTopRight"	Upper-right sizing handle is at the specified location.

This method is often used with events to determine where user activity is taking place with respect to a particular element and to take special actions based on scrollbar manipulation. Supported in IE5+ (JScript 5.0+).

contains(element)   Returns a Boolean indicating if the object given in *element* is contained within the current element. Often useful for determining appropriate actions in event handlers. Supported in IE4+ (JScript 3.0+).

dragDrop()   Initiates a drag event (firing the **ondragstart** handler if it exists in the process). Returns **true** if the drag completed successfully or **false** if it was cancelled. Supported in IE5.5+ (JScript 5.5+).

focus()   Causes the element to receive focus. While this method has been supported by some objects (mostly form fields) since very early browsers, support in arbitrary elements didn't begin to mature until IE5+ (JScript 5.0+) and N6+ (JavaScript 1.5+), DOM1.

getAdjacentText(where)   Returns the string of text corresponding to the text string at position *where*, with respect to the current node. The *where* parameter is a string with the following values:

Value of *where*	String returned
"beforeBegin"	Text immediately preceding element's opening tag (back to but not including first element encountered).
"afterBegin"	Text immediately following the element's opening tag (up to but not including the first nested element).
"beforeEnd"	Text immediately preceding the element's closing tag (back to but not including the closing tag of the last enclosed element).
"afterEnd"	Text immediately following element's closing tag (up to but not including the first following tag).

There is no standard DOM method that mimics this behavior. Instead, you must examine the **previousSibling, firstChild, lastChild**, or **nextSibling** (in order corresponding to the values of *where* above) and extract the string manually from their text node(s). Supported in IE5+ (JScript 5.0+).

getBoundingClientRect()   Retrieves a **TextRectangle** object with properties **top, bottom, left, right** indicating the pixel values of the rectangle in which the element's content is enclosed. These values are relative to the top left of the client window. Supported in IE5+ (JScript 5.0+).

getClientRects( )   Retrieves a collection of **TextRectangle** objects (each with properties **top, bottom, left, right**) that give the pixel coordinates of all bounding client rectangles contained within the object. For example, a paragraph of text might have one **TextRectangle** per line, depending upon how wide each line of text is. Supported in IE5+ (JScript 5.0+).

getExpression(propertyName)   Retrieves the string giving the dynamic property expression for the property named in the string *propertyName*. Commonly used as a method of element nodes and **Style** objects. Used for reading dynamic expressions. Supported in IE5+ (JScript 5.0+).

insertAdjacentElement(where, element)   Inserts the element object given in *element* adjacent to the current element in the position given by the string *where*. Supported in IE5+ (JScript 5.0+). The possible values for *where* are

Value of *where*	Effect
"beforeBegin"	Inserts immediately before the object
"afterBegin"	Inserts after the start of the object but before all other content
"beforeEnd"	Inserts immediately before the end of the object, after all other content
"afterEnd"	Inserts immediately after the end of the object

insertAdjacentHTML(where, text)   Inserts the HTML given in string *text* adjacent to the current element according to the string *where*. See table under **insertAdjacentElement()** for the meaning of this parameter. The *text* is parsed and added to the document tree. Supported in IE5+ (JScript 5.0+).

insertAdjacentText(where, text)   Inserts the text given in string *text* adjacent to the current element according to the string *where*. See table under **insertAdjacentElement()** for the meaning of this parameter. The *text* is not parsed as HTML. Supported in IE5+ (JScript 5.0+).

item(index [, subindex])   If *index* is a string, retrieves the object with **id** or **name** attribute corresponding to *index*. If multiple such items exist, a collection is returned. If the number parameter *subindex* is specified, the element at index *subindex* of the collection of elements with **id** or **name** matching *index* is returned. If *index* is a number, retrieves the object at index *index* in the collection. If no element is found, **null** is returned. Invoked as a method of a collection, and often the "item" is omitted, for example, **document.all('myElement')**. Supported in IE4+ (JScript 3.0+), N6+ (JavaScript 1.5+), DOM1.

mergeAttributes(source [, preserve])   Merges all attributes, styles, and event handlers from the element node *source* into the current element. In IE5, ReadOnly attributes (for example, **id**) are not merged. In IE5.5 you can merge all attributes (including **id** and **name**) by passing a **false** value for *preserve*. Supported in IE5+ (JScript 5.0+).

namedItem(name)   Retrieves an object with **id** or **name** attribute corresponding to the string *name*. If multiple such elements exist, a collection is returned. If no such elements exist, **null** is returned. Invoked as a method of a collection, for example, **document.all[ ]**. Supported in IE6+ (JScript 5.6/6.0+), N6+ (JavaScript 1.5+), DOM1.

removeBehavior(id)   Removes the DHTML attached Behavior associated with *id* (previously returned by **attachBehavior()**) from the element. Returns a Boolean indicating if it was successful. Supported in IE4+ (JScript 3.0+) but not available in MacOS.

removeExpression(propertyName)   Removes the dynamic property expression for the property named in the string *propertyName*. Commonly used as a method of element nodes and **Style** objects. Used for removing dynamic expressions. Returns a Boolean indicating if it was successful. Supported in IE5+ (JScript 5.0+).

replaceAdjacentText(where, text)   Replaces the text at position *where* relative to the current node with the text (non-HTML) string *text*. Possible values for *where* include

Value of *where*	Effect
"beforeBegin"	Replaces text immediately before the object (back to but not including first tag or end tag encountered)
"afterBegin"	Replaces text the start of the object but before all other enclosed content (up to but not including first opening tag)
"beforeEnd"	Replaces text immediately before the end of the object, after all other content (back to but not including last tag or closing tag)
"afterEnd"	Replaces text immediately after the element's closing tag (up to but not including the next tag)

Supported in IE5+ (JScript 5.0+).

replaceNode(newNode)   Replaces the current node with *newNode* in the document object hierarchy. The replaced node is returned. Supported in IE5+ (JScript 5.0+).

scrollIntoView([alignToTop])   Immediately scrolls the object into the viewable area of the window. If *alignToTop* is **true** or omitted, the top of the object is aligned with the top of the window (if possible). Otherwise, if *alignToTop* is **false**, the object is scrolled so that the bottom of the object is aligned with the bottom of the viewable window. Supported in IE4+ (JScript 3.0+).

setActive()   Sets the object as the active object without giving it focus. Supported in IE5.5+ (JScript 5.5+).

setExpression(property, expression [, language])   Sets the expression given in the string *expression* as the dynamic expression for the property indicated by the string *property*. The optional *language* parameter specifies which scripting language the *expression* is written in, for example "VBscript" (JScript is the default). Commonly used as a method of element nodes and **Style** objects. Used for setting dynamic expressions. Supported in IE5+ (JScript 5.0+).

swapNode(node)   Exchanges the location of the object with the object given in *node* in the document object hierarchy. Returns the object it was invoked as a method of. Supported in IE5+ (JScript 5.0+).

tags(tagName)   Retrieves a collection of elements that correspond to the string *tagName*, for example "P" for paragraphs. If no such elements exist, **null** is returned. This function is invoked as a method of a collection, for example **document.all[ ]**. Supported in IE4+ (JScript 3.0+).

urns(urn)   Retrieves a collection of all elements to which the behavior given by the string *urn* is attached. If no such elements exist, **null** is returned. This function is generally invoked as a method of a collection, for example **document.all[ ]**. Supported in IE5+ (JScript 5.0+).

JavaScript Object Reference

This section lists the JavaScript objects as well as their properties, methods, and support. The object entries include all or some of the following information:

- ■ **Child Of** Indicates the parent of the object for browser objects. Document objects in general may be children of each other, so this field is not used.

- ■ **Constructor**   Describes the syntax and semantics of the object's constructor, if the object may be instantiated.

- ■ **Properties**   Lists the properties the object provides and their support in various browsers. Also includes any standards that may apply to each property. Many "core" properties, such as those defined by the DOM, have complete descriptions in the preceding sections, and are marked as such.

- ■ **Methods**   Lists the methods the object provides and their support in various browsers. Also includes any standards that may apply to each. Many "core" methods, such as those defined by the DOM, have complete descriptions in preceding sections, and are marked as such.

- ■ **Event Handlers**   Lists the event handlers that may be bound to the object. A description of each handler can be found in the preceding section entitled "Events."

- ■ **Support**   Indicates the browsers that support the object as well as any standards that apply to it. The browser version indicates the first version in which the object was scriptable.

- ■ **Notes**   Gives other relevant information for the object, such as pitfalls, incompatibilities, and bugs.

When describing methods and properties, the attributes shown here are sometimes used.

Attribute	Description
DontEnum	The method or property will not be enumerated in a **for/in** loop. By default, methods are not enumerated. Event handlers are also not enumerated in Netscape.
ReadOnly	The property value is read-only and may not be changed.
Static	The property or method is a static (class) property of the object. Such properties and methods are accessed through their constructor rather than through an instance. For example, all properties of the **Math** object are Static, so are accessed as **Math**.*property*.

*The names of document objects corresponding to HTML elements are, in general, case-insensitive. So "p" is equivalent to "P" when using DOM-related methods like **getElementsByTagName()** and **createElement()**. However, XHTML favors lowercase element names, while current DOM implementations favor uppercase.*

Properties and methods with descriptions marked with an asterisk (*) have more verbose descriptions in the preceding sections.

 *We include documentation for standard HTML document objects but omit those that are nonstandard, such as **bgsound** and **nobr**. Such objects typically have the properties and methods listed in the Generic HTML Element Object found at the beginning of this section and possibly others defined by the browser vendors. For more information consult the MSDN or other vendor documentation.*

Generic HTML Element Object (Document Object)

Generic HTML elements have the form described here. This list of properties, methods, and event handlers are common to almost all HTML element objects and are, in fact, the *only* properties, methods, and event handlers defined for a large number of very basic elements, such as <b>, <i>, and <u>. Elements that back-reference this list may have more specific version information regarding support for particular properties and methods. For example, although **blur()** is not available until IE5 for most elements, it is available for form fields in IE3 and IE4. In addition, some properties do not have a well-defined meaning for particular objects, even though the properties may be defined for them.

Each of these objects corresponds to an occurrence of an HTML element on the page. Access to one of these objects is achieved through standard DOM methods like **getElementById()**.

Properties

- **accessKey** Single character string indicating the hotkey that gives the element focus.* (IE4+)
- **all[ ]** Collection of elements enclosed by the object.* (IE4+)
- **align** String specifying the alignment of the element, for example "left."* This property is defined only for display elements such as **b**, **big**, **cite**, and so on. (IE4+)
- **attributes[ ]** Collection of attributes for the element.* (IE5+, N6+, DOM1, ReadOnly)
- **begin** Sets or retrieves delay before timeline begins playing the element. See MSDN. (IE5.5+, SMIL)
- **behaviorUrns[ ]** Collection of DHTML Behaviors attached to the node.* (IE5+)
- **canHaveChildren** Boolean indicating whether the element can have child nodes.* (IE5+, ReadOnly)
- **canHaveHTML** Boolean indicating whether the element can enclose HTML markup.* (IE5.5+, ReadOnly)
- **childNodes[ ]** Collection of child nodes of the object.* (IE5+, N6+, DOM1, ReadOnly)
- **children[ ]** Collection of child nodes. This is IE's pre-DOM equivalent of **childNodes[ ]**.* (IE4+, ReadOnly)
- **className** String holding value of the CSS **class**(es) the element belongs to.* (IE4+, N6+, DOM1)

- **clientHeight**   Numeric value indicating the height of the element's content area in pixels.* (IE4+, ReadOnly)
- **clientLeft**   Numeric value indicating the difference between the **offsetLeft** property and the beginning of the element's content area, in pixels.* (IE4+, ReadOnly)
- **clientTop**   Numeric value indicating the difference between the **offsetTop** property and the beginning of the element's content area, in pixels.* (IE4+, ReadOnly)
- **clientWidth**   Numeric value indicating the width of the element's content area in pixels.* (IE4+, ReadOnly)
- **contentEditable**   String determining whether the element's content is editable.* (IE5.5+)
- **currentStyle**   Reference to the **Style** object reflecting all styles applied to the element, including global (default) style.* (IE5+, ReadOnly)
- **dir**   String holding the text direction of text enclosed by the element.* (IE5+, N6+, DOM1)
- **disabled**   Boolean indicating whether the element is disabled (grayed out). (IE4+)
- **document**   An undocumented reference to the **Document** in which the element is contained. (IE4+)
- **filters[ ]**   Collection of Microsoft CSS Filters applied to the element.* (IE4+)
- **firstChild**   Reference to the first child node of the element, if one exists (**null** otherwise).* (IE5+, N6+, DOM1, ReadOnly)
- **hasMedia**   Boolean indicating whether the element is an HTML+TIME media element. (IE5.5+, ReadOnly)
- **hideFocus**   Boolean indicating whether the object gives a visible cue when it receives focus.* (IE5.5+)
- **id**   String holding the unique alphanumeric identifier for the element.* (IE4+, N6+, DOM1)
- **innerHTML**   String holding the HTML content enclosed within the element's tags.* (IE4+, N6+)
- **innerText**   String holding text enclosed within the element's tags.* (IE4+)
- **isContentEditable**   Boolean indicating if the user can edit the element's contents.* (IE5.5+, ReadOnly)
- **isDisabled**   Boolean indicating if the user can interact with the object.* (IE5.5+, ReadOnly)
- **isMultiLine**   Not currently in use.
- **isTextEdit**   Boolean indicating if a **TextRange** object can be created using the object.* (IE4+, ReadOnly)
- **lang**   String holding language code for the content the element encloses.* (IE4+, N6+, DOM1)
- **language**   String indicating the scripting language in use.* (IE4+)
- **lastChild**   Reference to the last child node of the element, if one exists (**null** otherwise).* (IE5+, N6+, DOM1, ReadOnly)
- **localName**   String indicating the "local" XML name for the object.* (N6+, ReadOnly)
- **namespaceURI**   String indicating the XML Namespace URI for the object.* (N6+, ReadOnly)

- **nextSibling**   Reference to next sibling of the node, for example if its parent has multiple children.* (IE5+, N6+, DOM1, ReadOnly)

- **nodeName**   String containing name of the node, the name of the tag to which the object corresponds. For example, "H1".* (IE5+, N6+, DOM1, ReadOnly)

- **nodeType**   Number holding the node type as given earlier in this appendix. For example, element nodes have node type **1**.* (IE5+, N6+, DOM1, ReadOnly)

- **nodeValue**   String containing value within the node (or **null** if no value).* (IE5+, N6+, DOM1)

- **offsetHeight**   Numeric value indicating the height of the element in pixels.* (IE4+, N6+, ReadOnly)

- **offsetLeft**   Numeric value indicating the pixel offset of the left edge of the element, relative to its **offsetParent**.* (IE4+, N6+, ReadOnly)

- **offsetParent**   Reference to the object relative to which the **offsetHeight/Width/Left/Top** is calculated.* (IE4+, N6+, ReadOnly)

- **offsetTop**   Numeric value indicating the pixel offset of the top edge of the element, relative to its **offsetParent**.* (IE4+, N6+, ReadOnly)

- **offsetWidth**   Numeric value indicating the width of the element in pixels.* (IE4+, N6+, ReadOnly)

- **outerHTML**   String holding the HTML content enclosed within (and including) the element's tags.* (IE4+)

- **outerText**   String holding the text enclosed by (and including) the element's tags.* (IE4+)

- **ownerDocument**   Reference to the **Document** in which the element is contained.* (IE5+, N6+, DOM1, ReadOnly)

- **parentElement**   Reference to the node's parent. This is IE's pre-DOM equivalent of **parentNode**. (IE4+)

- **parentNode**   Reference to the parent of the object (or **null** if none exists).* (IE4+, N6+, DOM1, ReadOnly)

- **parentTextEdit**   Reference to the innermost container element outside of the current object that is capable of creating a **TextRange** containing the current element.* (IE4+, ReadOnly)

- **prefix**   String containing the "prefix" XML name for the object.* (N6+, ReadOnly)

- **previousSibling**   Reference to previous sibling of the node, for example if its parent node has multiple children.* (IE5+, N6+, DOM1, ReadOnly)

- **readyState**   String containing the current state of the object.* (IE4+, ReadOnly)

- **recordNumber**   Numeric value indicating the record number of the data set from which the element was generated.* (IE4+, ReadOnly)

- **runtimeStyle**   Reference to the **Style** object that reflects the current (runtime) style characteristics of the element.* (IE5+)

- **scopeName**   String containing the XML scope for the object.* (IE5+, ReadOnly)

- **scrollHeight**   Numeric value indicating the total height in pixels of the element's content area, no matter how much is displayed on screen.* (IE4+, ReadOnly)

- **scrollLeft**   Numeric value indicating the distance in pixels from the left edge of the object to the leftmost edge of the object that is currently displayed.* (IE4+)

- **scrollTop**   Numeric value indicating the distance in pixels from the top edge of the object to the topmost edge that is currently displayed.* (IE4+)

- **scrollWidth**   Numeric value indicating the total width in pixels of the object's content area, no matter how much is displayed on screen.* (IE4+, ReadOnly)

- **sourceIndex**   Number indicating the index of the element in the **document.all[ ]** collection.* (IE4+, ReadOnly)

- **style**   Reference to the inline **Style** object for the element.* (IE4+, N4+, DOM2)

- **syncMaster**   Specifies whether time container must synchronize with the element. See MSDN. (IE5.5+, SMIL)

- **tabIndex**   Numeric value indicating the tab order for the object.* (IE4+)

- **tagName**   String containing the name of the tag to which the object corresponds. For example, "H1".* (IE5.5+, N6+, DOM1)

- **tagUrn**   String containing the URN of the XML Namespace for the object.* (IE5+)

- **timeContainer**   Sets or retrieves the type of timeline associated with the element. See MSDN. (IE5.5+, SMIL)

- **title**   String containing advisory text for the element.* (IE4+, N6+, DOM1)

- **uniqueID**   An autogenerated unique **id** for this element.* (IE5+, ReadOnly)

Methods

- **addBehavior(url)**   Attaches the DHTML Behavior referenced by string *url* to the element.* (IE5+)

- **addEventListener(whichEvent, handler, direction)**   Instructs the object to execute the function *handler* whenever an event of type given in the string *whichEvent* (for example, "click") occurs. The *direction* is a Boolean specifying the phase in which to fire, **true** for capture or **false** for bubbling.* (N6+, DOM2)

- **appendChild(newChild)**   Appends *newChild* to end of the node's **childNodes[ ]** list.* (IE5+, N6+, DOM1 Core)

- **applyElement(newElement [, where])**   "Applies" one element to another by enclosing one within the other. If *where* is omitted or has value "outside," the object referenced by *newElement* becomes the parent of the current element. Otherwise, *newElement* becomes the only child of the current element, enclosing all of the current elements children.* (IE5+)

- **attachEvent(whichHandler, theFunction)**   Attaches the function *theFunction* as a handler specified by the string *whichHandler*, for example "onclick."* (IE5+)

- **blur( )**   Removes focus from the element.* (IE5+ for most elements. For form fields N2+ or N3+ and IE3+ or IE4+ and DOM1, listed specifically for each object)

- **clearAttributes( )**   Clears all nonessential HTML attributes from the element (leaves **id**, **dir**, etc.).* (IE5+)

- **click( )**   Simulates a mouse click at the object.* (IE4+)

- **cloneNode(cloneChildren)**   Clones the node and returns the new clone. If *cloneChildren* is **true**, the returned node includes the recursively constructed subtree of clones of the node's children.* (IE5+, N6+, DOM1 Core)

- **componentFromPoint(x, y)**   Returns a string giving information about the pixel coordinates (*x,y*) in the client window with respect to the current element. See extended description.* (IE5+)

- **contains(element)**   Returns a Boolean indicating if the object given in *element* is contained within the element.* (IE4+)

- **detachEvent(whichHandler, theFunction)**   Instructs the object to cease executing the function *theFunction* as a handler given the string *whichHandler*, for example "onclick."* (IE5+)

- **dispatchEvent(event)**   Causes the **Event** instance *event* to be processed by the object's appropriate handler. Used to redirect events.* (N6+, DOM2)

- **dragDrop( )**   Initiates a drag event at the element.* (IE5.5+)

- **fireEvent(handler [, event])**   Causes the event handler given by the string *handler* to fire. If an **Event** instance was passed as *event*, the new event created reflects the properties of *event*.* (IE5.5+)

- **focus( )**   Gives focus to the element.*

- **getAdjacentText(where)**   Returns a string corresponding to the text string at position *where*. See extended description.* (IE5+)

- **getAttribute(name)**   Returns a string containing the value of the attribute specified in the string *name* or **null** if it does not exist.* (IE4+, N6+, DOM1 Core)

- **getAttributeNode(name)**   Returns the attribute node corresponding to the attribute in the string *name*.* (IE6+, N6+, DOM1 Core)

- **getBoundingClientRect( )**   Retrieves a **TextRectangle** with properties **top, bottom, left, right** indicating the pixel values of the rectangle in which the element's content is enclosed. (IE5+)

- **getClientRects( )**   Retrieves a collection of **TextRectangle** objects which give the pixel coordinates of all bounding rectangles contained in the element.* (IE5+)

- **getElementsByTagName(tagname)**   Retrieves a collection of elements corresponding to the tag given in string *tagname*. A value of "*" retrieves all tags.* (IE5+, N6+, DOM1 Core)

- **getExpression(propertyName)**   Retrieves the string giving the dynamic property expression for the property/attribute named *propertyName*.* (IE5+)

- **hasAttribute(name)**   Returns a Boolean indicating if the attribute given in string *name* is defined for the node (explicitly or by default).* (N6+, DOM2 Core)

- **hasAttributes( )**   Returns a Boolean indicating if any attributes are defined for the node.* (N6+, DOM2 Core)

- **hasChildNodes( )**   Returns a Boolean indicating if the node has children.* (IE5+, N6+, DOM1 Core)

- **insertAdjacentElement(where, element)**   Inserts the element object *element* next to the current element according to the string *where*. See extended description.* (IE5+)

- **insertAdjacentHTML(where, text)**   Inserts HTML given in string *text* adjacent to the current element according to string *where*. See full description.* (IE5+)

- **insertAdjacentText(where, text)**   Inserts the text given in string *text* adjacent to the current element according to the string *where*. See full description.* (IE5+)

- **insertBefore(newChild, refChild)**   Inserts node *newChild* in front of *refChild* in the **childNodes[ ]** list of *refChild*'s parent node.* (IE5+, N6+, DOM1 Core)

- **isSupported(feature [, version])**   Returns a Boolean indicating whether feature and version given in the argument strings are supported.* (N6+, DOM2 Core)

- **mergeAttributes(source [, preserve])**   Merges all attributes, styles, and event handlers from the element node *source* into the current element. See full description.* (IE5+)

- **normalize( )**   Recursively merges adjacent text nodes in the subtree rooted at this element.* (IE6+, N6+, DOM1 Core)

- **releaseCapture( )**   Disables universal mouse event capturing at that object.* (IE5+)

- **removeAttribute(name)**   Removes attribute corresponding to string *name* from the node.* (IE4+, N6+, DOM1 Core)

- **removeAttributeNode(attribute)**   Removes the attribute node given by node *attribute* and returns the removed node.* (IE6+, N6+, DOM1 Core)

- **removeBehavior(id)**   Removes the DHTML Behavior associated with *id* (previously returned by **attachBehavior()**) from the element. (IE4+)

- **removeChild(oldChild)**   Removes *oldChild* from the node's children and returns a reference to the removed node.* (IE5+, N6+, DOM1 Core)

- **removeEventListener(whichEvent, handler, direction)**   Removes function *handler* as a handler for the event given in the string *whichEvent* (for example, "click") for the phase given by the Boolean *direction*.* (N6+, DOM2)

- **removeExpression(propertyName)**   Removes dynamic property expression for the property given in the string *propertyName*.* (IE5+)

- **replaceAdjacentText(where, text)**   Replaces text near the current node with the string *text* according to *where*. See full description.* (IE5+)

- **replaceChild(newChild, oldChild)**   Replaces the node's child node *oldChild* with node *newChild*.* (IE5+, N6+, DOM1 Core)

- **replaceNode(newNode)**   Replaces the current node with *newNode*.* (IE5+)

- **scrollIntoView([alignToTop])**   Causes the object to be immediately scrolled into the viewable area of the window.* (IE4+)

- **setActive( )**   Sets the object as the active object without giving it focus.* (IE5.5+)

- **setAttribute(name, value)**   Sets a new attribute for the node with name and value given by the string arguments.* (IE4+, N6+, DOM1 Core)

- **setAttributeNode(newAttr)**   Adds the attribute node *newAttr* (replacing and returning any attribute node with the same *name*).* (IE5+, N6+, DOM1 Core)

- **setCapture([containerCapture])**   Causes all mouse events occurring in the document to be sent to this object.* (IE5+)

- **setExpression(property, expression [, language])**   Sets the expression given in string *expression* as the dynamic expression for the property given in string *property*. (IE5+)

- **swapNode(node)**   Exchanges the location of the object with *node* in the object hierarchy.* (IE5+)

- **unwatch(property)**   Removes the watchpoint on the property given in the string *property*. (N4+)

- **watch(property, handler)**   "Watches" the property given in string *property* and invokes the function *handler* whenever its value changes. The *handler* is passed the name of the property, the old value, and the value to which it is being set. Any value the function returns is interpreted as the new value for the property. (N4+)

Event Handlers

```
onactivate onbeforeactivate onbeforecopy onbeforecut onbeforedeactivate
onbeforepaste onblur onclick oncontextmenu oncontrolselect oncopy oncut
ondblclick ondeactivate ondrag ondragend ondragenter ondragleave ondragover
ondragstart ondrop onfocus onfocusin onfocusout onhelp onkeydown onkeypress
onkeyup onlosecapture onmousedown onmouseenter onmouseleave onmousemove
onmouseout onmouseover onmouseup onmousewheel onmove onmoveend onmovestart
onpaste onpropertychange onreadystatechange onresize onresizeend
onresizestart onselectstart ontimeerror
```

Support

With the exception of the object scriptable under traditional models (**Form**, **Image**, and so on), most elements become scriptable in Internet Explorer 4+, Netscape 6+, and DOM1.

a, Anchor, Link (Document Object)

In traditional models, there was a separate object for **<a>** elements that specified a **name** property (called an **Anchor**) and one that specified an **href** property (called a **Link**). This nomenclature is somewhat outdated, and with the rise of the DOM there is no distinction. Modern browsers typically mesh **Anchor** and **Link** into a more appropriate object, which corresponds to any **<a>** element on the page, and fill in the **Anchor**- or **Link**-related properties if they are defined. In the following list we note explicitly those properties and methods that are available only in **Anchor** or **Link** in traditional models (Netscape 2-4, IE3).

Access to these objects is achieved through standard DOM methods like **getElementById()**. However, you can also access those **<a>** elements with **name** attribute set through the **anchors[ ]** collection of the **Document**, and those elements with **href** attribute through the **links[ ]** collection.

Properties

This object has the following properties in addition to those in the Generic HTML Element Object listed at the beginning of this section.

- **accessKey**   Single character string indicating the hotkey that gives the element focus.* (IE4+, N6+, DOM1)

- **charset**   String indicating the character set of the linked document. (IE6+, N6+, DOM1)

- **coords**   String defining the coordinates of the object, used with the **shape** attribute. However, there is no default functionality. (IE6+, N6+, DOM1)

- **dataFld**   String specifying which field of a data source is bound to the element.* (IE4+)

- **dataFormatAs**   String indicating how the element treats data supplied to it.* (IE4+)
- **dataSrc**   String containing the source of data for data binding.* (IE4+)
- **disabled**   Boolean indicating whether the element is disabled (grayed out). (IE4+, DOM1)
- **hash**   String holding the portion of the URL in the **href** following the hash mark (#). Defined for **Link** in traditional models. (IE3+, N2+)
- **host**   String holding the domain name and port portion of the URL in the **href**. Defined for **Link** in traditional models. (IE3+, N2+)
- **hostname**   String holding the domain name portion of the URL in the **href**. Defined for **Link** in traditional models. (IE3+, N2+)
- **href**   String holding the value of the **href** attribute, the document to load when the link is activated. Defined for **Link** in traditional models. (IE3+, N2+, DOM1)
- **hreflang**   String indicating the language code of the linked resource. (N6+, IE6+, DOM1)
- **media**   String indicating the media of the link. Currently unsupported. (DOM1)
- **name**   String containing the value of the **name** attribute. Defined for **Anchor** in traditional models. (IE3+, N4+, DOM1, ReadOnly)
- **nameProp**   String holding the filename portion of the URL in the **href**. (IE5+)
- **pathname**   String holding the path and filename portion of the URL in the **href** (including the leading slash). Defined for **Link** in traditional models. (IE3+, N2+)
- **port**   String holding the port number portion of the URL in the **href**. Defined for **Link** in traditional models. (IE3+, N2+)
- **protocol**   String holding the protocol portion of the URL in the **href**. Defined for **Link** in traditional models. (IE3+, N2+)
- **protocolLong**   String holding the full name of the protocol used in the URL in the **href**. Defined for **Link** in traditional models. (IE4+, ReadOnly)
- **rel**   String holding the value of the **rel** property of the element. Used to specify the relationship between documents, but currently ignored by most browsers. (IE4+, N6+, DOM1)
- **rev**   String holding the value of the **rel** property of the element. Used to specify the relationship between documents, but currently ignored by most browsers. (IE4+, N6+, DOM1)
- **search**   String holding the portion of the URL in the **href** following the question mark (aka the search string). Defined for **Link** in traditional models. (IE3+, N2+)
- **shape**   String defining the shape of the object. (IE6+, N6+, DOM1)
- **tabIndex**   Numeric value indicating the tab order for the object.* (IE4+, N6+, DOM1)
- **target**   Specifies the target window for a hypertext source link referencing frames. (IE3+, N2+, DOM1)
- **text**   String specifying the text enclosed by the **<a></a>** tags. Defined for **Anchor** in traditional models. (N4+, ReadOnly)
- **type**   Specifies the media type in the form of a MIME type for the link target. (IE6+, N6+, DOM1)
- **urn**   Defines a URN for a target document. (IE4+)

■ **x**   The *x* coordinate of an **Anchor**, in pixels, relative to the left edge of the document. (N4, ReadOnly)

■ **y**   The *y* coordinate of an **Anchor**, in pixels, relative to the top edge of the document. (N4, ReadOnly)

Methods

This object has the methods listed in the Generic HTML Element Object found at the beginning of this section, in addition to the following:

■ **blur( )**   Removes focus from the element. (IE4+, N6+, DOM1)

■ **handleEvent(event)**   Causes the **Event** instance *event* to be processed by the appropriate handler of the object.* (N4 only)

■ **focus( )**   Gives the element focus. (IE4+, N6+, DOM1)

Event Handlers

This object has the event handlers listed in the Generic HTML Element Object found at the beginning of this section, in addition to the following:

```
onafterupdate onbeforeeditfocus onbeforeupdate onerrorupdate
```

Support

Supported in Internet Explorer 3+, Netscape 2+, DOM1.

abbr (Document Object)

This object corresponds to an **<abbr>** (abbreviation) element in the document. It has the properties, methods, and events listed in the Generic HTML Element Object given at the beginning of this section.

Support

Supported in IE4+, N6+, DOM1.

acronym (Document Object)

This object corresponds to an **<acronym>** element in the document. It has the properties and methods listed in the Generic HTML Element Object found at the beginning of this section.

Event Handlers

```
onactivate onbeforeactivate onblur oncontrolselect ondeactivate ondrag
ondragend ondragenter ondragleave ondragover ondragstart ondrop onfocus
onkeydown onkeypress onkeyup onmouseenter onmouseleave onmove onmoveend
onmovestart onreadystatechange onresizeend onresizestart onselectstart
ontimeerror
```

Support

Supported in IE4+, N6+, DOM1.

ActiveXObject (Built-in/Browser Object)

The **ActiveXObject** object provides access to extended operating system or application functionality by permitting the instantiation of Automation objects. These objects are often Microsoft Office components or Windows operating system features. For full documentation of this object see Microsoft's documentation at MSDN.

Support

Supported in IE3+ (JScript 1.0+).

Notes

This is *not* an ECMAScript object. It is a proprietary Microsoft built-in object.

address (Document Object)

This object corresponds to an **<address>** element in the document. It has the properties, methods, and events listed in the Generic HTML Element Object found at the beginning of this section.

Support

Supported in IE4+, N6+, DOM1.

Anchor (Document Object)

See entry for the **a** object.

applet (Document Object)

An **applet** object corresponds to an **<applet>** (Java applet) element in the document. Access to this object is achieved through standard DOM methods (for example, **getElementById()**) or through the **applets[ ]** collection of the **Document**.

Properties

This object has the following properties, in addition to those in the Generic HTML Element Object found at the beginning of this section. It will also have any public properties exposed by the class.

- **align** String specifying the alignment of the element, for example "left."* (IE4+, N6+, DOM1)
- **alt** String specifying alternative text for the applet. (N6+, DOM1)
- **altHtml** String specifying alternative text for the applet. (IE4+)
- **archive** String containing a comma-separated list of URIs giving classes required by the applet that should be preloaded. (N6+, DOM1)
- **code** String containing the URL of the Java applet's class file. (IE4+, N6+, DOM1)
- **codeBase** String containing the base URI for the applet. (IE4+, N6+, DOM1)
- **dataFld** String specifying which field of a data source is bound to the element.* (IE4+)
- **dataFormatAs** String indicating how the element treats data supplied to it.* (IE4+)
- **dataSrc** String containing the source of data for data binding.* (IE4+)
- **height** String specifying the height in pixels of the object. (IE4+, N6+, DOM1)

- **hspace** String specifying the horizontal margin to the left and right of the applet. (IE4+, N6+, DOM1)

- **name** String holding the **name** attribute of the element. (IE4+, N6+, DOM1)

- **src** String specifying the URL of the applet. Nonstandard and should be avoided. (IE4+)

- **object** String containing the name of the resource which contains a serialized representation of the applet. Either **code** or **object** is used, but not both. (N6+, DOM1)

- **vspace** String specifying the vertical margin above and below the applet. (IE4+, N6+, DOM1)

- **width** Specifies the width of the object in pixels. (IE4+, N6+, DOM1)

Methods

This object has the methods listed in the Generic HTML Element Object found at the beginning of this section. It will also have any public methods exposed by the applet.

Event Handlers

```
onactivate onbeforeactivate onbeforecut onbeforedeactivate onbeforeeditfocus
onbeforepaste onblur oncellchange onclick oncontextmenu oncontrolselect
oncut ondataavailable ondatasetchanged ondatasetcomplete ondblclick
ondeactivate onfocus onfocusin onfocusout onhelp onkeydown onkeypress
onkeyup onload onlosecapture onmousedown onmouseenter onmouseleave
onmousemove onmouseout onmouseover onmouseup onmousewheel onmove onmoveend
onmovestart onpaste onpropertychange onreadystatechange onresize onresizeend
onresizestart onrowenter onrowexit onrowsdelete onrowsinserted onscroll
```

Support

Supported in Internet Explorer 4+, Netscape 3+, DOM1.

area (Document Object)

This object corresponds to an **<area>** (client-side image map area) element in the document. Access to this object is achieved through standard DOM methods (for example, **getElementById()**) or through the **links[ ]** array of the **Document**.

Properties

This object has the following properties, in addition to those in the Generic HTML Element Object found at the beginning of this section.

- **accessKey** Single character string indicating the hotkey that gives the element focus.* (IE4+, N6+, DOM1)

- **alt** String defining text alternative to the graphic. (IE4+, N6+, DOM1)

- **coords** String defining the (comma-separated) coordinates of the object, used with the **shape** attribute. (IE6+, N6+, DOM1)

- **hash** String holding the portion of the URL in the **href** following the hash mark (#). (IE3+, N3+)

- **host** String holding the domain name and port portion of the URL in the **href**. (IE3+, N3+)

- **hostname**   String holding the domain name portion of the URL in the **href**. (IE3+, N3+)
- **href**   String holding the value of the **href** attribute, the document to load when the link is activated. (IE3+, N3+, DOM1)
- **noHref**   Boolean indicating that no hyperlink exists for this area. (IE3+, N6+, DOM1)
- **pathname** String holding the path and file name portion of the URL in the **href** (including the leading slash). Defined for **Link** in traditional models. (IE3+, N2+)
- **port**   String holding the port number portion of the URL in the **href**. (IE3+, N3+)
- **protocol**   String holding the protocol portion of the URL in the **href**. (IE3+, N3+)
- **search**   String holding the portion of the URL in the **href** following the question mark (aka the search string). (IE3+, N3+)
- **shape**   String defining the shape of the object, usually "default" (entire region), "rect" (rectangular), "circle" (circular), or "poly" (polygon). (IE4+, N6+, DOM1)
- **tabIndex**   Numeric value indicating the tab order for the object.* (IE4+, N6+, DOM1)
- **target**   Specifies the target window for a hypertext source link referencing frames. (IE3+, N3+, DOM1)
- **x**   The *x* coordinate of the link in pixels, relative to the left edge of the document. (N4, ReadOnly)
- **y**   The *y* coordinate of the link in pixels, relative to the top edge of the document. (N4, ReadOnly)

Methods

This object has the methods listed in the Generic HTML Element Object found at the beginning of this section, in addition to the following:

- **handleEvent(event)**   Causes the **Event** instance *event* to be processed by the appropriate handler of the object.* (N4 only)

Event Handlers

```
onactivate onbeforeactivate onbeforecopy onbeforecut onbeforedeactivate
onbeforeeditfocus onbeforepaste onblur onclick oncontextmenu oncontrolselect
oncopy oncut ondblclick ondeactivate ondrag ondragend ondragenter
ondragleave ondragover ondragstart ondrop onfocus onfocusin onfocusout
onhelp onkeydown onkeypress onkeyup onlosecapture onmousedown onmouseenter
onmouseleave onmousemove onmouseout onmouseover onmouseup onmousewheel
onmove onmoveend onmovestart onpaste onpropertychange onreadystatechange
onresizeend onresizestart onselectstart ontimeerror
```

Support

Supported in Internet Explorer 3+, Netscape 3+, DOM1.

Array (Built-in Object)

Arrays store ordered lists of heterogeneous data. Data is stored at indices enumerated beginning with zero which are accessed using the array access ([ ]) operator. Allocation of array memory is handled by the interpreter, so there is no need to explicitly resize arrays to accommodate more data. In addition, arrays are permitted to be sparse, that is, to have "holes" consisting of an arbitrary number of unused indices. Any index that has not been assigned data has value **undefined**, and the highest index addressable is usually 2^{32} -**1**. JavaScript arrays are one-dimensional, but since array elements can be of any type, multidimensional arrays are supported as arrays with elements that are arrays.

You can explicitly remove a value from an array using the **delete** operator, but there is no way to destroy an array other than by setting the variable that holds its reference to **null**.

Constructor

> **var** *instanceName* = **new** Array([*val1* [, *val2* [, *val3* ...]]]);

where the comma-separated values are treated as initial values for array indices **0**, **1**, **2**, and so on. The exception is if a single numeric parameter is supplied, in which case the array's **length** property is set to this value.

Properties

- **constructor**   Reference to the constructor object which created the object. (IE4+ (JScript 2.0+), N3+ (JavaScript 1.1+), ECMA Edition 1)

- **length**   Numeric value indicating the next empty index at the end of the array (not the number of elements in the array). Setting this property to a value less than its current value will **undefine** any elements with index >= **length**. (IE4+ (JScript 2.0+), N3+ (JavaScript 1.1+), ECMA Edition 1)

- **prototype**   Reference to the object's prototype. (IE4+ (JScript 2.0+), N3+ (JavaScript 1.1+), ECMA Edition 1)

Methods

- **concat([item1 [, item2 [, ...]]])**   Appends the comma-separated list of items to the end of the array and returns the new array (it does not operate on the array in place). If any item is an array, its first level is flattened (that is, the item's elements are appended each as a separate element). (IE4+ (JScript 3.0+), N4+ (JavaScript 1.2+), ECMA Edition 1)

- **join([separator])**   Returns the string obtained by concatenating all the array's elements. If the string *separator* is supplied, *separator* will be placed between adjacent elements. The *separator* defaults to a comma. (IE4+ (JScript 2.0+), N3+ (JavaScript 1.1+), ECMA Edition 1)

- **pop( )**   Removes the last element of the array and returns it. (IE5.5+ (JScript 5.5+), N4+ (JavaScript 1.2+), ECMA Edition 3)

- **push([item1 [, item2 [, ...]]])**   Appends the parameters (in order) to the end of the array and returns the new **length**. (IE5.5+ (JScript 5.5+), N4+ (JavaScript 1.2+), ECMA Edition 3)

- **reverse( )**   Reverses the order of the elements (in place). (IE4+ (JScript 2.0+), N3+ (JavaScript 1.1+), ECMA Edition 1)

- **shift( )**   Removes the first element from the array, returns it, and shifts all other elements down one index. (IE5.5+ (JScript 5.5+), N4+ (JavaScript 1.2+), ECMA Edition 3)

- **slice(begin [, end])**   Returns a new array containing the elements from index *begin* up to but not including index *end*. If *end* is omitted, all elements to the end of the array are extracted. If *end* is negative, it is treated as an offset from the end of the array. (IE4+ (JScript 3.0+), N4+ (JavaScript 1.2+), ECMA Edition 3)

- **sort([compareFunc])**   Sorts the array in place in lexicographic order (see Appendix A). The optional argument *compareFunc* is a function that can change the behavior of the sort. It will be passed two elements and should return a negative value if the first element is less than the second, a positive value if the second is less than the first, or zero if they are equal. (IE4+ (JScript 2.0+), N3+ (JavaScript 1.1+), ECMA Edition 1)

- **splice(start, howMany [, item1 [, item2 [, ...]]])**   Removes *howMany* elements from the array beginning at index *start* and replaces the removed elements with the *itemN* arguments (if passed). An array containing the deleted elements is returned. (IE5.5+ (JScript 5.5+), N4+ (JavaScript 1.2+), ECMA Edition 3)

- **toString( )**   Returns a string containing the comma-separated list of elements. (IE4+ (JScript 2.0+), N3+ (JavaScript 1.1+), ECMA Edition 1)

- **unshift([item1 [, item2 [, ...]]])**   Inserts the items (in order) at the front of the array, shifting existing values up to higher indices. (IE5.5+ (JScript 5.5+), N4+ (JavaScript 1.2+), ECMA Edition 3)

- **valueOf( )**   Same as **toString()**. (IE4+ (JScript 2.0+), N3+ (JavaScript 1.1+), ECMA Edition 1)

Support
Supported in IE4+ (JScript 2.0+), N3+ (JavaScript 1.1+), ECMAScript Edition 1.

Notes
In Netscape 4.0-4.05 (JavaScript 1.2) a single numeric parameter to the constructor is added the single array element—it is not treated as an initial value for **length**.

b (Document Object)

This object corresponds to a **<b>** (bold weight text) element in the document. It has the properties, methods, and events listed in the Generic HTML Element Object found at the beginning of this section.

Support
Supported in IE4+, N6+, DOM1.

base (Document Object)

This object corresponds to a **<base>** (base URL indicator) element in the document. Access to this object is achieved through standard DOM methods (for example, **getElementById()**). However, because this element is found in the document head, you might need to use **document. documentElement.getElementsByTagName()** or a similar method to achieve access to it.

Properties
This object has the following properties, in addition to those in the Generic HTML Element Object found at the beginning of this section.

- **href**   String holding the URL relative to which all relative URLs on the page are fetched. (IE4+, N6+, DOM1)

APPENDIXES

■ **target**   String holding the name of the target window or frame for all links on the page. (IE4+, N6+, DOM1)

Methods

This object has those methods listed in the Generic HTML Element Object found at the beginning of this section.

Event Handlers

    onlayoutcomplete onmouseenter onmouseleave onreadystatechange

Support

Supported in Internet Explorer 4+, Netscape 6+, DOM1.

basefont (Document Object)

This object corresponds to a **<basefont>** (default font) element in the document. Access to this object is achieved through standard DOM methods (for example, **getElementById()**). However, because this element is found in the document head, you might need to use **document. documentElement.getElementsByTagName()** or a similar method to achieve access to it.

Properties

This object has the following properties, in addition to those in the Generic HTML Element Object found at the beginning of this section.

■ **color**   String holding the default text color for the page. (IE4+, N6+, DOM1)

■ **face**   String holding a comma-separated list of one or more default font names. (IE4+, N6+, DOM1)

■ **size**   String holding the default font size (HTML 1-7 or relative +n/-n syntax). (IE3+, N6+, DOM1)

Methods

This element has the methods listed in the Generic HTML Element Object found at the beginning of this section.

Event Handlers

    onlayoutcomplete onmouseenter onmouseleave onreadystatechange

Support

Supported in Internet Explorer 4+, Netscape 6+, DOM1.

bdo (Document Object)

This object corresponds to an **<bdo>** (bidirectional override) element in the document. Access to this object is achieved through standard DOM methods (for example, **getElementById()**). It has the properties and methods listed in the Generic HTML Element Object found at the beginning of this section.

Event Handlers

This object has the event handlers listed in the Generic HTML Element Object found at the beginning of this section, in addition to the following:

```
onafterupdate oncellchange onerrorupdate onfilterchange onscroll
onselectstart
```

Support

Supported in Internet Explorer 5+, Netscape 6+, DOM1.

big (Document Object)

This object corresponds to a **<big>** (large font) element in the document. It has the properties, methods, and events listed in the Generic HTML Element Object found at the beginning of this section.

Support

Supported in Internet Explorer 4+, Netscape 6+, DOM1.

blockquote (Document Object)

This object corresponds to a **<blockquote>** element in the document. Access to this object is achieved through standard DOM methods (for example, **getElementById()**).

Properties

This object has the following property, in addition to those in the Generic HTML Element Object found at the beginning of this section.

- **cite**   String containing the URI of a reference for the quote. (IE6+, N6+, DOM1)

Methods

This element has the methods listed in the Generic HTML Element Object found at the beginning of this section.

Support

Supported in Internet Explorer 4+, Netscape 6+, DOM1.

body (Document Object)

This object corresponds to the **<body>** element in the document. Access to this object is achieved through standard DOM methods (for example, **getElementById()**).

Properties

This object has the following properties, in addition to those in the Generic HTML Element Object found at the beginning of this section.

■ **aLink**   String specifying the color of active links. (IE4+, N6+, DOM1)

■ **background**   String specifying the URL of an image to use as a background for the document. (IE4+, N6+, DOM1)

■ **bgColor**   String specifying the background color of the document. (IE4+, N6+, DOM1)

■ **bgProperties**   String specifying other background properties for the document. When it has the value "fixed," the background image is fixed and will not scroll. (IE4+)

■ **bottomMargin**   Sets the bottom margin for the entire body of the page (in pixels) and overrides the default margin. (IE4+)

■ **leftMargin**   Sets the left margin for the page in pixels, overriding the default margin. (IE4+)

■ **link**   String specifying the color of unvisited links. (IE4+, N6+, DOM1)

■ **noWrap**   Boolean indicating whether the browser automatically performs wordwrapping. (IE4+)

■ **rightMargin**   Sets the right margin for the page in pixels, overriding the default. (IE4+)

■ **scroll**   String specifying whether scroll bars are visible. Values are "yes," "no," and "auto." (IE4+)

■ **text**   String specifying the text color for the document. (IE3+, N6+, DOM1)

■ **topMargin**   Sets the top margin for the document in pixels, overriding the default. (IE4+)

■ **vLink**   String specifying the color of visited links. (IE4+, N6+, DOM1)

Methods

This object has the following methods, in addition to those in the Generic HTML Element Object found at the beginning of this section.

■ **createControlRange( )**   Creates a **controlRange** object for the document and returns a reference to it. (IE5+)

■ **createTextRange( )**   Creates a **TextRange** object for the document and returns a reference to it.

■ **doScroll([action])**   Scrolls the top of the body of the document into view. If *action* is specified it must be one of several predetermined strings, such as "left" or "right," that give fine-grain control over scroll bar actions. See MSDN for complete details. (IE5+)

■ **pause( )**   Pauses the timeline on the document (related to HTML+TIME). See MSDN. (IE5+)

■ **resume( )**   Resumes the timeline on the document (related to HTML+TIME). See MSDN. (IE5+)

Event Handlers

```
onactivate onafterprint onbeforeactivate onbeforecut onbeforedeactivate
onbeforepaste onbeforeprint onbeforeunload onclick oncontextmenu
oncontrolselect oncut ondblclick ondeactivate ondrag ondragdrop ondragend
ondragenter ondragleave ondragover ondragstart ondrop onerror onfilterchange
onfocusin onfocusout onkeydown onkeypress onkeyup onload onlosecapture
```

onmousedown onmouseenter onmouseleave onmousemove onmouseout onmouseover
onmouseup onmousewheel onmove onmoveend onmovestart onpaste onpropertychange
onreadystatechange onresizeend onresizestart onscroll onselect onselectstart
onunload

Support

Supported in Internet Explorer 4+, Netscape 6+, DOM1.

Boolean (Built-in Object)

Boolean is the container object for the primitive Boolean data type. It is not, however, recommendable to use **Boolean** objects unless you have a good reason for doing so. The reason is that any object that is not **undefined** or **null** is converted to the **true** primitive Boolean value when used in a conditional. This means that a **Boolean** object instance with value **false** will evaluate **true** in a conditional, not **false** as you might expect. It is therefore important to remember to use this object's **valueOf()** method to extract the appropriate primitive Boolean value of **Boolean** objects in conditionals.

Constructor

> var *instanceName* = **new** Boolean(*initialValue*);

where *initialValue* is data that will be converted into a Boolean, for example a string, primitive Boolean value, or number. If *initialValue* is **false**, **null**, **NaN**, **undefined**, **0**, the empty string, or if *initialValue* is omitted, the newly created object has value **false**. Otherwise, the initial value is **true**.

Properties

- **constructor**   Reference to the constructor object which created the object. (IE4+ (JScript 2.0+), N3+ (JavaScript 1.1+), ECMA Edition 1)
- **prototype**   Reference to the object's prototype. (IE4+ (JScript 2.0+), N3+ (JavaScript 1.1+), ECMA Edition 1)

Methods

- **toString( )**   Returns the string version of the value, either "true" or "false." (IE4+ (JScript 2.0+), N3+ (JavaScript 1.1+), ECMA Edition 1)
- **valueOf( )**   Returns the primitive Boolean value of the object. (IE4+ (JScript 2.0+), N3+ (JavaScript 1.1+), ECMA Edition 1)

Support

Supported in IE3+ (JScript 1.0+), N3+ (JavaScript 1.1+), ECMAScript Edition 1.

Notes

Versions of Netscape prior to 4.06 (and language versions prior to JavaScript 1.3) convert **Boolean** objects with value **false** to the primitive **false** in conditionals. Modern implementations convert such objects to **true**.

APPENDIXES

br (Document Object)

This document object corresponds to a **
** (linebreak) element in the document. Access to this object is achieved through standard DOM methods (for example, **getElementById()**).

Properties

This object has the following property, in addition to those in the Generic HTML Element Object found at the beginning of this section.

■ **clear**   String specifying how the element flows with surrounding text. Typical values are "left," "right," or "all." (IE4+)

Methods

This element has the methods listed in the Generic HTML Element Object found at the beginning of this section.

Event Handlers

 onlayoutcomplete onlosecapture onreadystatechange

Support

Supported in Internet Explorer 4+, Netscape 6+, DOM1.

button (Document Object)

This object corresponds to a **<button>** element in the document. It does not correspond to an occurrence of **<input type="button">** (see **Button** immediately following). Access to this object is achieved through standard DOM methods (for example, **getElementById()**) or more commonly through the **elements[ ]** array of the form it is contained in (if any).

Properties

This object has the following properties, in addition to those in the Generic HTML Element Object found at the beginning of this section.

■ **accessKey**   Single character string indicating the hotkey that gives the element focus.*
(IE4+, N6+, DOM1)

■ **dataFld**   String specifying which field of a data source is bound to the element.* (IE4+)

■ **dataFormatAs**   String indicating how the element treats data supplied to it.* (IE4+)

■ **dataSrc**   String containing the source of data for data binding.* (IE4+)

■ **disabled**   Boolean indicating whether the element is disabled (grayed out).
(IE4+, N6+, DOM1)

■ **form**   Reference to the **Form** in which the button is contained, if one exists.
(IE4+, N6+, DOM1, ReadOnly)

■ **name**   String holding the **name** attribute of the element. (IE4+, N6+, DOM1)

■ **tabIndex**   Numeric value indicating the tab order for the object.* (IE4+, N6+, DOM1)

- **type**   String indicating the type of the button, either "button," "reset," or "submit." (IE4+, N6+, DOM1)
- **value**   String containing the text of the **value** attribute of the button. (IE4+, N6+, DOM1)

Methods
This element has the methods listed in the Generic HTML Element Object found at the beginning of this section.

Event Handlers

```
onactivate onafterupdate onbeforeactivate onbeforecut onbeforedeactivate
onbeforeeditfocus onbeforepaste onbeforeupdate onblur onclick oncontextmenu
oncontrolselect oncut ondblclick ondeactivate ondrag ondragend ondragenter
ondragleave ondragover ondragstart ondrop onerrorupdate onfilterchange
onfocus onfocusin onfocusout onhelp onkeydown onkeypress onkeyup
onlosecapture onmousedown onmouseenter onmouseleave onmousemove onmouseout
onmouseover onmouseup onmousewheel onmove onmoveend onmovestart onpaste
onpropertychange onreadystatechange onresize onresizeend onresizestart
onselectstart ontimeerror
```

Support
Supported in Internet Explorer 4+, Netscape 6+ (**<button>**s are *not* supported in Netscape 4), DOM1.

Button (Document Object)
This object corresponds to an **<input type="button">** element in the document. It does not correspond to an occurrence of **<button>** (see **button** immediately preceding). Access to this object is achieved through standard DOM methods (for example, **getElementById()**) or more commonly through the **elements[ ]** array of the form it is contained in.

Properties
This object has the following properties, in addition to those in the Generic HTML Element Object found at the beginning of this section.

- **accessKey**   Single character string indicating the hotkey that gives the element focus.* (IE4+, N6+, DOM1)
- **align**   String specifying the alignment of the element, for example "left."* (IE4+, N6+, DOM1)
- **controllers**   Related to XPConnect functionality. See **mozilla.org**. (N6+)
- **dataFld**   String specifying which field of a data source is bound to the element.* (IE4+)
- **dataFormatAs**   String indicating how the element treats data supplied to it.* (IE4+)
- **dataSrc**   String containing the source of data for data binding.* (IE4+)
- **defaultValue**   String holding the original value of the **value** attribute. (IE4+)
- **disabled**   Boolean indicating whether the element is disabled (grayed out). (IE4+, N6+, DOM1)

- **form**   Reference to the **Form** in which the button is contained. (IE3+, N2+, DOM1, ReadOnly)
- **name**   String holding the **name** attribute of the element. (IE3+, N2+, DOM1)
- **size**   String indicating the width of the button in pixels. (IE4+, N6+, DOM1)
- **tabIndex**   Numeric value indicating the tab order for the object.* (IE4+, N6+, DOM1)
- **type**   String indicating the type of the field, "button." (IE4+, N3+, DOM1, ReadOnly)
- **value**   String containing the text of the **value** attribute of the button. (IE3+, N2+, DOM1)

Methods

This object has the following methods, in addition to those in the Generic HTML Element Object found at the beginning of this section.

- **blur( )**   Causes the button to lose focus. (IE3+, N2+, DOM1)
- **click( )**   Simulates a click on the button. (IE3+, N2+, DOM1)
- **focus( )**   Gives the button focus. (IE3+, N2+, DOM1)
- **handleEvent(event)**   Causes the **Event** instance *event* to be processed by the appropriate handler of the object.* (N4 only)

Support

Supported in Internet Explorer 3+, Netscape 2+, DOM1.

caption (Document Object)

This object corresponds to a **<caption>** (table caption) element in the document. Access to this object is achieved through standard DOM methods like **getElementById()** or through the **<table>** it is enclosed within.

Properties

This object has the following properties, in addition to those in the Generic HTML Element Object found at the beginning of this section.

- **align**   String specifying the alignment of the element, for example "top" or "left."* (IE4+, N6+, DOM1)
- **vAlign**   String specifying the vertical alignment of the element ("bottom" or "top"). (IE4+)

Methods

This element has the methods listed in the Generic HTML Element Object found at the beginning of this section.

Support

Supported in Internet Explorer 4+, Netscape 6+, DOM1.

center (Document Object)

This object corresponds to a **<center>** (centered text) element in the document. It has the properties, methods, and events listed in the Generic HTML Element Object found at the beginning of this section.

Support

Supported in Internet Explorer 4+, Netscape 6+, DOM1.

Checkbox (Document Object)

This object corresponds to an **<input type="checkbox">** element in the document. Access to this object is achieved through standard DOM methods (for example, **getElementById()**) or more commonly through the **elements[ ]** array of the form it is contained in.

Properties

This object has the following properties, in addition to those in the Generic HTML Element Object found at the beginning of this section.

- **accessKey**   Single character string indicating the hotkey that gives the element focus.* (IE4+, N6+, DOM1)
- **align**   String specifying the alignment of the element, for example "left."* (N6+, DOM1)
- **controllers**   Related to XPConnect functionality. See **mozilla.org.** (N6+)
- **checked**   Boolean indicating whether the checkbox is checked. (IE3+, N2+, DOM1)
- **dataFld**   String specifying which field of a data source is bound to the element.* (IE4+)
- **dataSrc**   String containing the source of data for data binding.* (IE4+)
- **defaultChecked**   Boolean indicating if the checkbox was checked by default. (IE3+, N2+, DOM1)
- **defaultValue**   String containing the original value of the checkbox's **value** attribute. (IE3+)
- **disabled**   Boolean indicating whether the element is disabled (grayed out). (IE4+, N6+, DOM1)
- **form**   Reference to the **Form** in which the button is contained, if one exists. (IE3+, N2+, DOM1, ReadOnly)
- **height**   The height in pixels of the checkbox. (IE5+)
- **name**   String holding the **name** attribute of the element. (IE3+, N2+, DOM1)
- **size**   String indicating the width in pixels. (IE3+, N6+, DOM1)
- **status**   Boolean indicating whether the checkbox is currently selected. (IE4+)
- **tabIndex**   Numeric value indicating the tab order for the object.* (IE4+, N6+, DOM1)
- **type**   String indicating the type of the field, "button." (IE3+, N3+, DOM1, ReadOnly)
- **value**   String containing the text of the **value** attribute. (IE3+, N2+, DOM1)
- **width**   The width in pixels of the checkbox. (IE5+)

Methods

This object has the following methods, in addition to those in the Generic HTML Element Object found at the beginning of this section.

- **blur( )**   Causes the button to lose focus. (IE3+, N2+, DOM1)
- **click( )**   Simulates a click on the button. (IE3+, N2+, DOM1)
- **focus( )**   Gives the button focus. (IE3+, N2+, DOM1)

■ **handleEvent(event)**   Causes the **Event** instance *event* to be processed by the appropriate handler of the object.* (N4 only)

Event Handlers

```
onactivate onafterupdate onbeforeactivate onbeforecut onbeforedeactivate
onbeforeeditfocus onbeforepaste onbeforeupdate onblur onclick oncontextmenu
oncontrolselect oncut ondblclick ondeactivate ondrag ondragend ondragenter
ondragleave ondragover ondragstart ondrop onerrorupdate onfilterchange
onfocus onfocusin onfocusout onhelp onkeydown onkeypress onkeyup
onlosecapture onmousedown onmouseenter onmouseleave onmousemove onmouseout
onmouseover onmouseup onmousewheel onmove onmoveend onmovestart onpaste
onpropertychange onreadystatechange onresize onresizeend onresizestart
onselectstart ontimeerror
```

Support
Supported in Internet Explorer 3+, Netscape 2+, DOM1.

cite (Document Object)

This object corresponds to a **<cite>** (citation) element in the document. It has the properties, methods, and events listed in the Generic HTML Element Object found at the beginning of this section.

Support
Supported in Internet Explorer 4+, Netscape 6+, DOM1.

clientInformation (Browser Object)

The **clientInformation** object is just a synonym for the browser's **Navigator** object. Microsoft provides it in IE4+ in order not to use Netscape's "Navigator" name, although, of course, IE still supports the **Navigator** object directly. You should avoid using **clientInformation** and opt for **Navigator** instead, since it is far more cross-browser compatible.

clipboardData (Browser Object)

The **clipboardData** object provides an interface for interacting with Windows' system clipboard.

Properties
None.

Methods

■ **clearData([dataFormat])**   Removes all data from the clipboard unless the string *dataFormat* is specified as "Text," "URL," "File," "HTML," or "Image," in which case only data of that kind is cleared. (IE5+ Windows)

■ **getData(dataFormat)**   Gets data of the specified format from the clipboard and returns it as a string (of text, HTML, or a URL). (IE5+ Windows)

■ **setData(dataFormat, data)**   Attempts to place the data given in string *data* (either text, HTML, or a URL) into the clipboard according to the data type specified in the string *dataType* (either Text, URL, File, HTML, or Image). Returns a Boolean indicating whether it was successful. (IE5+ Windows)

Support
Internet Explorer 5+ for Windows.

code (Document Object)

This object corresponds to a **<code>** (code listing) element in the document. It has the properties and methods events listed in the Generic HTML Element Object found at the beginning of this section.

Support
Supported in Internet Explorer 4+, Netscape 6+, DOM1.

Event Handlers

```
onbeforeactivate onbeforecopy onbeforecut onbeforepaste onclick
oncontextmenu oncopy oncut ondblclick ondrag ondragend ondragenter
ondragleave ondragover ondragstart ondrop onfocusin onfocusout onhelp
onkeydown onkeypress onkeyup onlosecapture onmousedown onmouseenter
onmouseleave onmousemove onmouseout onmouseover onmouseup onmousewheel
onpaste onpropertychange onreadystatechange onresize onselectstart
ontimeerror
```

col (Document Object)

This object corresponds to a **<col>** (table column) element in the document. Access to this object is achieved through standard DOM methods like **getElementById()** or through the **<table>** it is enclosed within.

Properties
This object has the following properties, in addition to those in the Generic HTML Element Object found at the beginning of this section.

■ **align**   String specifying the horizontal alignment of the element, for example "left." (IE4+, N6+, DOM1)

■ **ch**   String specifying the alignment character for the column. This property/attribute is generally not supported by browsers but is provided in case programmers wish to implement the functionality themselves. (IE6+, N6+, DOM1)

■ **chOff**   String specifying the offset of the first occurrence of the alignment character for the column. This property/attribute is generally not supported by browsers but is provided in case programmers wish to implement the functionality themselves. (IE6+, N6+, DOM1)

■ **span**   Integer indicating the number of columns in the group or spanned by the column. (IE4+, N6+, DOM1)

- **vAlign**   String specifying the vertical alignment of the column data (for example, "top"). (IE4+, N6+, DOM1)
- **width**   Specifies the width of the column in pixels. (IE4+, N6+, DOM1)

Methods

This element has the methods listed in the Generic HTML Element Object found at the beginning of this section.

Event Handlers

```
onlayoutcomplete onreadystatechange
```

Support

Supported in Internet Explorer 4+, Netscape 6+, DOM1.

colgroup (Document Object)

This object corresponds to a **<colgroup>** (table column group) element in the document. Access to this object is achieved through standard DOM methods like **getElementById()**. This object has structure identical to **col**.

Support

Supported in Internet Explorer 4+, Netscape 6+, DOM1.

Components (Browser Object)

This object provides XPConnect functionality that permits the access and manipulation of XPCOM objects with JavaScript in Netscape 6. See documentation at **mozilla.org**.

CSSrule (Document Object)

See **rule** object.

currentStyle (Document Object)

A read-only **Style** object that reflects all styles that are applied to the element, regardless of where their definitions are. Because the normal **Style** object reflects only inline style set with the **style** attribute, it does not reflect style set by default or through externally linked stylesheets. This object *does*, and is updated dynamically as the styles applied to the element change.

Support

Internet Explorer 5+.

dataTransfer (Browser Object)

The **dataTransfer** object provides properties and methods that give the programmer a great deal of control over how data is transferred from one object to another during drag-and-drop operations. This object is usually accessed as a property of an **event** instance involving a drag-related event.

In order to properly harness the capabilities of this object, you need to adhere to specific guidelines defining what actions must be carried out by the source and target objects' event handlers. Because the discussion is somewhat involved, the details of this object are omitted here and given at the support site (**www.javascriptref.com**).

Support
Internet Explorer 5+ for Windows.

Date (Built-in Object)

The **Date** object provides a wide variety of methods for manipulating dates and times. It is important to remember that **Date** instances do not contain a "ticking clock" but rather hold a static date value. Internally, the date is stored as the number of milliseconds since the epoch (midnight of January 1, 1970 UTC). This accounts for the prominent role of milliseconds in many **Date** methods.

Milliseconds, seconds, minutes, hours, and months are enumerated beginning with zero; so, for example, December is month 11. Days are enumerated beginning with 1. Years should always be given using four digits. Modern implementations permit years as much as several hundred thousand years in the past or future, although older implementations often have trouble handling dates before 1970. Many implementations have trouble handling dates before 1 AD.

Note that Universal Coordinated Time (UTC) is the same as Greenwich Mean Time (GMT).

Constructor

> **var** *instanceName* = **new** Date( );
> **var** *instanceName* = **new** Date(*milliseconds*);
> **var** *instanceName* = **new** Date(*stringDate*);
> **var** *instanceName* = **new** Date(*year, month, day* [, *hrs* [, *mins* [, *secs* [, *ms*]]]]);

The first constructor syntax creates a new **Date** instance holding the current date and time. The second syntax creates an instance holding the date given by the number of milliseconds given in the numeric *milliseconds* argument. The third syntax attempts to create an instance by converting the string *stringDate* into a valid date using the **parse()** method (see below). The fourth syntax creates an instance according to its numeric arguments. If the optional parameters are omitted, they are filled with zero.

Properties

- **constructor**   Reference to the constructor object which created the object. (IE4+ (JScript 2.0+), N3+ (JavaScript 1.1+), ECMA Edition 1)

- **prototype**   Reference to the object's prototype. (IE4+ (JScript 2.0+), N3+ (JavaScript 1.1+), ECMA Edition 1)

Methods

- **getDate( )**   Returns a numeric value indicating the day of the month (1-based). (IE3+ (JScript 1.0+), N2+ (JavaScript 1.0+), ECMA Edition 1)

- **getDay( )**   Returns a numeric value indicating the day of the week (0 for Sunday, 1 for Monday, and so on). (IE3+ (JScript 1.0+), N2+ (JavaScript 1.0+), ECMA Edition 1)

■ **getFullYear( )**   Returns a numeric value indicating the four-digit year. (IE4+ (JScript 3.0+), N4.06+ (JavaScript 1.3+), ECMA Edition 1)

■ **getHours( )**   Returns a numeric value indicating the hours since midnight (0-based). (IE3+ (JScript 1.0+), N2+ (JavaScript 1.0+), ECMA Edition 1)

■ **getMilliseconds( )**   Returns a numeric value indicating the number of milliseconds (0-999). (IE4+ (JScript 3.0+), N4.06+ (JavaScript 1.3+), ECMA Edition 1)

■ **getMinutes( )**   Returns a numeric value indicating the number of minutes (0-59). (IE4+ (JScript 3.0+), N2+ (JavaScript 1.0+), ECMA Edition 1)

■ **getMonth( )**   Returns a numeric value indicating the number of months since the beginning of the year (0-11; 0 is January). (IE3+ (JScript 1.0+), N2+ (JavaScript 1.0+), ECMA Edition 1)

■ **getSeconds( )**   Returns a numeric value indicating the number of seconds (0-59). (IE3+ (JScript 1.0+), N2+ (JavaScript 1.0+), ECMA Edition 1)

■ **getTime( )**   Returns a numeric value indicating the number of milliseconds since the epoch. Dates before the epoch return a negative value indicating the number of milliseconds before the epoch. (IE3+ (JScript 1.0+), N2+ (JavaScript 1.0+), ECMA Edition 1)

■ **getTimezoneOffset( )**   Returns a numeric value indicating the difference in minutes between the local time and the UTC. Positive values indicate the local time is behind UTC (for example, in the United States) and negative values indicate the local time is ahead of UTC (for example, in India). (IE3+ (JScript 1.0+), N2+ (JavaScript 1.0+), ECMA Edition 1)

■ **getUTCDate( )**   Returns a numeric value indicating the day of the month (1-based) using UTC. (IE4+ (JScript 3.0+), N4.06+ (JavaScript 1.3+), ECMA Edition 1)

■ **getUTCDay( )**   Returns a numeric value indicating the day of the week (0 for Sunday, 1 for Monday, and so on) according to UTC. (IE4+ (JScript 3.0+), N4.06+ (JavaScript 1.3+), ECMA Edition 1)

■ **getUTCFullYear( )**   Returns a numeric value indicating the four-digit year according to UTC. (IE4+ (JScript 3.0+), N4.06+ (JavaScript 1.3+), ECMA Edition 1)

■ **getUTCHours( )**   Returns a numeric value indicating the hours since midnight (0-based) according to UTC. (IE4+ (JScript 3.0+), N4.06+ (JavaScript 1.3+), ECMA Edition 1)

■ **getUTCMilliseconds( )**   Returns a numeric value indicating the number of milliseconds (0-999) according to UTC. (IE4+ (JScript 3.0+), N4.06+ (JavaScript 1.3+), ECMA Edition 1)

■ **getUTCMinutes( )**   Returns a numeric value indicating the number of minutes (0-59) according to UTC. (IE4+ (JScript 3.0+), N4.06+ (JavaScript 1.3+), ECMA Edition 1)

■ **getUTCMonth( )**   Returns a numeric value indicating the number of months since the beginning of the year (0-11; 0 is January) according to UTC. (IE4+ (JScript 3.0+), N4.06+ (JavaScript 1.3+), ECMA Edition 1)

■ **getUTCSeconds( )**   Returns a numeric value indicating the number of seconds (0-59) according to UTC. (IE4+ (JScript 3.0+), N4.06+ (JavaScript 1.3+), ECMA Edition 1)

■ **getYear( )**   Deprecated. Use **getFullYear()** instead. Returns the current year minus 1900 or in some cases a four digit year if the year is greater than 1999. (IE3+ (JScript 1.0+), N2+ (JavaScript 1.0+), ECMA Edition 1)

■ **getVarYear( )**   Returns the VT_DATE corresponding to the object. For use with interaction with COM or VBScript, but in general should be avoided. (IE4+ (JScript 3.0+))

- **parse(stringDate)**   Attempts to parse the date given in the string *stringDate* and if successful returns the number of milliseconds of the date relative to the epoch. Valid strings are given in Table 1 of Chapter 7 but in general can be any common representation of a date, for example "month/day/year," "month day, year," or "month day, year hh:mm:ss." Unambiguous shorthand (for example, "Dec" for December) is permitted. If the date cannot be parsed, **NaN** is returned. (IE3+ (JScript 1.0+), N2+ (JavaScript 1.0+), ECMA Edition 1, Static)

- **setDate(dayOfMonth)**   Sets the day of the month (1-based) in local time as given by the numeric parameter *dayOfMonth*. (IE4+ (JScript 3.0+), N2+ (JavaScript 1.0+), ECMA Edition 1)

- **setFullYear(year [, month [, day]])**   Sets the date to the year given in the numeric argument *year* in local time. If the numeric parameters *month* and *day* are passed, the month (0-based) and day of the month (1-based) are set as well. If *month* is greater than 11, the year is incremented accordingly. If *day* is greater than the number of days in the month, the month is incremented accordingly. (IE4+ (JScript 3.0+), N4.06+ (JavaScript 1.3+), ECMA Edition 1)

- **setHours(hours [, mins [, secs [, ms]]])**   Sets the hours (0-based) to the numeric argument given in *hours* in local time. If the optional parameters are passed, the minutes, seconds, and milliseconds are set accordingly. If any of the parameters is greater than the normal range of values, the date is adjusted accordingly (for example, 60 seconds increments the minutes by one and sets the seconds to zero). (IE4+ (JScript 3.0+), N2+ (JavaScript 1.0+), ECMA Edition 1)

- **setMilliseconds(ms)**   Sets the milliseconds (0-based) to the numeric argument *ms* in local time. If *ms* is greater than 999, the seconds are adjusted accordingly. (IE4+ (JScript 3.0+), N4.06+ (JavaScript 1.3+), ECMA Edition 1)

- **setMinutes(minutes [, secs [, ms]])**   Sets the minutes (0-based) to the numeric argument *minutes* in local time. If numeric arguments *secs* and *ms* are supplied, the seconds and milliseconds are set to these values. If any argument is greater than the normal range, appropriate values are incremented accordingly (for example, if *secs* is 60, the minute is incremented by one and the seconds set to zero). (IE3+ (JScript 1.0+), N2+ (JavaScript 1.0+), ECMA Edition 1)

- **setMonth(month [, day])**   Sets the month (0-based) to the numeric argument *month* in local time. If the numeric argument *day* is supplied, the day of the month (1-based) is set accordingly. If either value is outside of the expected range, the date is adjusted accordingly (for example, if *month* is 12 the year is incremented and the month is set to zero). (IE3+ (JScript 1.0+), N2+ (JavaScript 1.0+), ECMA Edition 1)

- **setSeconds(seconds [, ms])**   Sets the seconds (0-based) to the numeric argument *seconds* in local time. If numeric argument *ms* is supplied, the milliseconds (0-based) are set accordingly. If either value is outside the expected range, the date is adjusted accordingly (for example, if *ms* is 1000, then the seconds are incremented and milliseconds set to 0). (IE3+ (JScript 1.0+), N2+ (JavaScript 1.0+), ECMA Edition 1)

- **setTime(ms)**   Sets the date to the date given by the number of milliseconds since the epoch given in *ms*. Negative values of *ms* specify dates before the epoch. (IE3+ (JScript 1.0+), N2+ (JavaScript 1.0+), ECMA Edition 1)

- **setUTCDate(dayOfMonth)**   Sets the day of the month (1-based) in UTC as given by the numeric parameter *dayOfMonth*. (IE4+ (JScript 3.0+), N4.06+ (JavaScript 1.3+), ECMA Edition 1)

■ **setUTCFullYear(year [, month [, day]])**   Sets the date to the year given in the numeric argument *year* in UTC. If the numeric parameters *month* and *day* are passed, the month (0-based) and day of the month (1-based) are set as well. If *month* is greater than 11, the year is incremented accordingly. If *day* is greater than the number of days in the month, the month is incremented accordingly. (IE4+ (JScript 3.0+), N4.06+ (JavaScript 1.3+), ECMA Edition 1)

■ **setUTCHours(hours [, mins [, secs [, ms]]])**   Sets the hours (0-based) to the numeric argument given in *hours* in UTC. If the optional parameters are passed, the minutes, seconds, and milliseconds are set accordingly. If any of the parameters is greater than the normal range of values, the date is adjusted accordingly (for example, 60 seconds increments the minutes by one and sets the seconds to zero). (IE4+ (JScript 3.0+), N4.06+ (JavaScript 1.3+), ECMA Edition 1)

■ **setUTCMilliseconds(ms)**   Sets the milliseconds (0-based) to the numeric argument *ms* in UTC. If *ms* is greater than 999, the seconds are adjusted accordingly. (IE4+ (JScript 3.0+), N4.06+ (JavaScript 1.3+), ECMA Edition 1)

■ **setUTCMinutes(minutes [, secs [, ms]])**   Sets the minutes (0-based) to the numeric argument *minutes* in UTC. If numeric arguments *secs* and *ms* are supplied, the seconds and milliseconds are set to these values. If any argument is greater than the normal range, appropriate values are incremented accordingly (for example, if *secs* is 60, the minute is incremented by one and the seconds set to zero). (IE4+ (JScript 3.0+), N4.06+ (JavaScript 1.3+), ECMA Edition 1)

■ **setUTCMonth(month [, day])**   Sets the month (0 based) to the numeric argument *month* in UTC. If the numeric argument *day* is supplied, the day of the month (1-based) is set accordingly. If either value is outside of the expected range, the date is adjusted accordingly (for example, if *month* is 12, the year is incremented and the month is set to zero). (IE4+ (JScript 3.0+), N4.06+ (JavaScript 1.3+), ECMA Edition 1)

■ **setUTCSeconds(seconds [, ms])**   Sets the seconds (0-based) to the numeric argument *seconds* in UTC. If numeric argument *ms* is supplied, the milliseconds (0-based) are set accordingly. If either value is outside the expected range, the date is adjusted accordingly (for example, if *ms* is 1000, then the seconds are incremented and milliseconds set to 0). (IE4+ (JScript 3.0+), N4.06+ (JavaScript 1.3+), ECMA Edition 1)

■ **setYear(year)**   Deprecated. Use **setFullYear()** instead. Sets the year to the numeric value *year* in local time. The *year* parameter must be the desired year minus 1900. Do not use this method. (IE3+ (JScript 1.0+), N2+ (JavaScript 1.0+), ECMA Edition 1)

■ **toGMTString( )**   Deprecated. Use **toUTCString()** instead. Returns the string representation of the date relative to GMT. (IE3+ (JScript 1.0+), N2+ (JavaScript 1.0+), ECMA Edition 1)

■ **toLocaleString( )**   Returns the date converted to a string formatted according to local conventions as defined by the operating system. For example, the U.S. uses month/day/year whereas Europe uses day/month/year. The return value is not to be used for computation, but rather for display to the user. (IE3+ (JScript 1.0+), N2+ (JavaScript 1.0+), ECMA Edition 1)

■ **toString( )**   Returns the date as a string. (IE4+ (JScript 2.0+), N3+ (JavaScript 1.1+), ECMA Edition 1)

■ **toUTCString( )**   Returns the date formatted as a string according to UTC. (IE4+ (JScript 3.0+), N4.06+ (JavaScript 1.3+), ECMA Edition 1)

- **UTC(year, month, day [, hours [, mins [, secs [, ms]]]])**   Returns a numeric value indicating the number of milliseconds between the epoch and the date given by the numeric parameters. Any parameters outside of their expected range cause the date to be adjusted accordingly. (IE3+ (JScript 1.0+), N2+ (JavaScript 1.0+), ECMA Edition 1, Static)

- **valueOf( )**   Returns a numeric value indicating the number of milliseconds difference between the date and the epoch. (IE4+ (JScript 2.0+), N3+ (JavaScript 1.1+), ECMA Edition 1)

Support

Supported in IE3+ (JScript 1.0+), N2+ (JavaScript 1.0+), ECMAScript Edition 1.

Notes

The **Date** object is seriously broken in older browsers. The authors suggest avoiding its use except in the most basic tasks in browsers earlier than IE4 and Netscape 4.

dd (Document Object)

This object corresponds to a **<dd>** (definition in a definition list) element in the document. It has the properties, methods, and events listed in the Generic HTML Element Object found at the beginning of this section.

Support

Supported in Internet Explorer 4+, Netscape 6+, DOM1.

del (Document Object)

This object corresponds to a **<del>** (deletion modification) element in the document. Access to this object is achieved through standard DOM methods (for example, **getElementById()**).

Properties

This object has the following properties, in addition to those in the Generic HTML Element Object found at the beginning of this section.

- **cite**   String containing the URL of the reference for the modification. (IE6+, N6+ DOM1)
- **dateTime**   String containing the date the modification was made. (IE6+, N6+, DOM1)

Methods

This element has the methods listed in the Generic HTML Element Object found at the beginning of this section.

Event Handlers

```
onblur ondrag ondragend ondragenter ondragleave ondragover ondragstart
ondrop onfocus onkeydown onkeypress onkeyup onreadystatechange onselectstart
ontimeerror
```

Support

Supported in Internet Explorer 4+, Netscape 6+, DOM1.

dfn (Document Object)

This object corresponds to a **<dfn>** (term definition) element in the document. It has the properties, methods, and events listed in the Generic HTML Element Object found at the beginning of this section.

Support

Supported in Internet Explorer 4+, Netscape 6+, DOM1.

Dictionary (Built-in Object)

The **Dictionary** object is a rarely used Microsoft-specific object that permits the creation of associative arrays. Because this capability is easily simulated using **Object**s, programmers rarely use **Dictionary**. For full documentation of this object see Microsoft's documentation at MSDN.

Notes

This is *not* an ECMAScript object. It is a proprietary Microsoft built-in object.

dir (Document Object)

This object corresponds to a **<dir>** (directory listing) element in the document. Access to this objects is achieved through standard DOM methods (for example, **getElementById()**).

Properties

This object has the following property, in addition to those in the Generic HTML Element Object found at the beginning of this section.

- **compact**   Boolean indicating whether the listing should be rendered compactly. (IE6+, N6+, DOM1)

Methods

This element has the methods listed in the Generic HTML Element Object found at the beginning of this section.

Event Handlers

This object has the event handlers listed in the Generic HTML Element Object found at the beginning of this section.

Support

Supported in Internet Explorer 4+, Netscape 6+, DOM1.

div (Document Object)

This object corresponds to a **<div>** (block container) element in the document. Access to this object is achieved through standard DOM methods (for example, **getElementById()**).

Properties

This object has the following properties, in addition to those in the Generic HTML Element Object found at the beginning of this section.

- **align**   String specifying the alignment of the element. (IE4+, N6+, DOM1)
- **dataFld**   String specifying which field of a data source is bound to the element.* (IE4+)
- **dataFormatAs**   String indicating how the element treats data supplied to it.* (IE4+)
- **dataSrc**   String containing the source of data for data binding.* (IE4+)
- **noWrap**   Boolean indicating whether the browser should not carry out word wrapping. (IE4+, N6+, DOM1)

Methods

This object has the following method, in addition to those in the Generic HTML Element Object found at the beginning of this section.

- **doScroll([action])**   Scrolls the top of the block into view. If *action* is specified it must be one of several predetermined strings, such as "left" or "right," which give fine-grain control over scroll bar actions. See MSDN for complete details. (IE5+)

Event Handlers

This object has the event handlers listed in the Generic HTML Element Object found at the beginning of this section, in addition to the following:

```
onafterupdate onbeforeeditfocus onbeforeupdate onerrorupdate onfilterchange
onlayoutcomplete onscroll
```

Support

Supported in Internet Explorer 4+, Netscape 6+, DOM1.

dl (Document Object)

This object corresponds to a **<dl>** (definition list) element in the document. Access to this object is achieved through standard DOM methods (for example, **getElementById()**).

Properties

This object has the following property, in addition to those in the Generic HTML Element Object found at the beginning of this section.

- **compact**   Sets a Boolean value indicating whether the list should be compacted by removing extra space between list objects. (IE4+, N6+, DOM1)

Methods

This element has the methods listed in the Generic HTML Element Object found at the beginning of this section.

Event Handlers

```
onactivate onbeforeactivate onbeforecopy onbeforecut onbeforedeactivate
onbeforepaste onblur onclick oncontextmenu oncontrolselect oncopy oncut
ondblclick ondeactivate ondrag ondragend ondragenter ondragleave ondragover
```

ondragstart ondrop onfocus onfocusin onfocusout onhelp onlayoutcomplete onlosecapture onmousedown onmouseenter onmouseleave onmousemove onmouseout onmouseover onmouseup onmousewheel onmove onmoveend onmovestart onpaste onpropertychange onreadystatechange onresize onresizeend onresizestart onselectstart ontimeerror

Support

Supported in Internet Explorer 4+, Netscape 6+, DOM1.

Document (Document Object)

The **Document** provides access to the contents of the HTML document currently loaded. In early browsers, this was primarily a browser object because there was no standard governing its structure. With the rise of the DOM, this object has become standardized, although modern browsers continue to provide a multitude of proprietary features.

HTML elements in the page are represented as objects under the **Document**. Each such element object has properties and methods derived from a variety of sources. The most obvious of these are proprietary browser features, but elements also inherit properties and methods from the DOM **Node** interface, the DOM **HTMLElement** definition, and possibly more specific DOM objects. While the specific origin of a property is often not particularly important so long as the property is well supported, the reader should be aware that the structure of each element object is derived from a variety of sources.

The collections contained within the **Document** are in general read-only, although specific elements of the collections are often mutable.

Child Of

Window

Properties

- **activeElement**   Reference to the element object which currently has focus. (IE4+, ReadOnly)
- **alinkColor**   String containing the color of activated links. (IE3+, N2+, DOM0)
- **all[ ]**   Collection of all elements and comments in the document.* (IE4+)
- **anchors[ ]**   Collection of **Anchor** objects in the page (corresponds to **<a name="...">...</a>**). (IE3+, N2+, DOM1, ReadOnly)
- **applets[ ]**   Collection of **Applet** objects in the page (corresponds to **<applet>** elements). (IE4+, N3+, DOM1, ReadOnly)
- **attributes[ ]**   Collection of attributes for the element.* (N6+, DOM1, ReadOnly)
- **bgColor**   String containing the background color of the document. (IE3+, N2+, DOM0)
- **body**   Reference to the **<body>** element object of the document. (IE3+, N6+, DOM1)
- **charset**   String containing the character set of the document. (IE4+)
- **characterSet**   String containing the character set of the document. (N6+, DOM1)
- **childNodes[ ]**   Collection of child nodes of the object.* (IE5+, N6+, DOM1, ReadOnly)
- **classes[ ]**   Deprecated. Accesses style properties for CSS classes. See Chapter 9. (NS4 only)

- **cookie**   String holding the cookies the browser has for the domain of the document. Values set into this property are automatically parsed as cookies by the browser. (IE3+, N2+, DOM1)

- **defaultCharset**   String containing the client's default character set. (IE4+, ReadOnly)

- **designMode**   String specifying whether design mode is *on* or *off*. When *on*, the user can double-click or otherwise activate an object and edit its HTML. Only used when IE is being used as a component. (IE5+)

- **dir**   String holding the text direction of text enclosed in the document.* (IE5+, N6+, DOM0)

- **doctype**   Reference to the **DocumentType** object for the document. (IE6+, N6+, DOM1)

- **documentElement**   Reference to the root node of the document object hierarchy. (IE5+, N6+, DOM1)

- **domain**   String containing the domain name from which the document was fetched. Can be set to a more general domain in order to work around the same origin policy. (IE4+, N3+, DOM1)

- **embeds[ ]**   Collection of all **Embed** objects in the document (corresponds to **<embed>** elements). (IE4+, N3+, ReadOnly)

- **expando**   Boolean dictating whether instance properties can be added to the object. (IE4+)

- **fgColor**   String containing the font color for the document. (IE3+, N2+, DOM0)

- **fileCreatedDate**   String containing the date the document was created. (IE4+, ReadOnly)

- **fileModifiedDate**   String containing the date the document was modified. (IE4+, ReadOnly)

- **fileSize**   Integer indicating the file size of the document in bytes. (IE4+, ReadOnly)

- **firstChild**   Reference to the first child node of the element, if one exists (**null** otherwise).* (IE5+, N6+, DOM1, ReadOnly)

- **forms[ ]**   Collection of **Forms** in the document (**<form>** elements). (IE3+, N2+, DOM1, ReadOnly)

- **frames[ ]**   Collection of **Frames** in the document (**<frame>** and **<iframe>** elements). (IE4+, ReadOnly)

- **height**   Specifies the height in pixels of the document's content, including the parts which might be scrolled offscreen. (N4+, ReadOnly)

- **ids[ ]**   Deprecated. Accesses style properties by **id** attribute. See Chapter 9. (NS4 only)

- **images[ ]**   Collection of **Images** in the document (**<img>** elements). (IE4+, N3+, DOM1, ReadOnly)

- **implementation**   Object with method **hasFeature(feature, level)** that returns a Boolean indicating if the browser supports the feature given in the string *feature* at the DOM level passed in the string *level*. Valid values for *feature* are: CSS, Events, HTML, HTMLEvents, MouseEvents, Range, StyleSheets, Views, and XML. Valid values for *level* are DOM levels, for example "1.0" or "2.0." The values returned by the method are often inaccurate because of spotty browser support for DOM functionality. (IE6+, N6+, DOM1)

- **lastChild**   Reference to the last child node of the element, if one exists (**null** otherwise).* (IE5+, N6+, DOM1, ReadOnly)

- **lastModified**   String containing the date the document was last modified. (IE3+, N2+, DOM0, ReadOnly)

- **layers[ ]**   Deprecated. Array of **Layer**s in the document (**<layer>** elements). Note that Netscape also places **<div>**s in this array as well. (NS4 only)

- **linkColor**   String containing the color of links in the document. (IE3+, N2+, DOM0)

- **links[ ]**   Collection of **Link**s in the document (**<a href="...."></a>** elements). (IE3+, N2+, DOM1, ReadOnly)

- **localName**   String indicating the "local" XML name for the object.* (N6+, ReadOnly)

- **location**   A **Location** object containing the URL of the document. Should not be set. (IE2+, N3+)

- **media** String containing the media for which the document is intended. (IE5.5+)

- **mimeType**   String containing information about the type of the document (*not* usually a real MIME type!). (IE5+, ReadOnly)

- **namespaces[ ]**   Collection of XML **namespace** objects for the document. (IE5.5+, ReadOnly)

- **namespaceURI**   String indicating the XML Namespace URI for the document.* (N6+, DOM1, ReadOnly)

- **nextSibling**   Reference to next sibling of the node—for example, if its parent has multiple children.* (N6+, DOM1, ReadOnly)

- **nodeName**   String containing name of node, the name of the tag to which the object corresponds. The value is "#document" in Netscape.* (N6+, DOM1, ReadOnly)

- **nodeType**   Number holding the node type as given earlier in this appendix, **9** for the **Document**.* (N6+, DOM1, ReadOnly)

- **nodeValue**   String containing value within the node (or **null** if no value).* (N6+, DOM1, ReadOnly)

- **ownerDocument**   Reference to the **Document** in which the element is contained (**null** in this case).* (N6+, DOM1, ReadOnly)

- **parentNode**   Reference to the parent of the object (**null** in this case).* (N6+, DOM1, ReadOnly)

- **parentWindow**   Reference to the **Window** that contains the document. (IE4+, ReadOnly)

- **plugins[ ]**   Collection of **Plugin** objects installed in the browser. In Internet Explorer, this is a synonym for the **embeds[ ]** collection. (IE4+, N4+, ReadOnly)

- **prefix**   String containing the "prefix" XML name for the object.* (N6+, DOM1, ReadOnly)

- **previousSibling**   Reference to previous sibling of the node—for example, if its parent node has multiple children.* (N6+, DOM1, ReadOnly)

- **protocol**   String containing the protocol used to retrieve the document (its full name, not "http"). (IE4+)

- **readyState**   String containing the current state of the object.* (IE4+, ReadOnly)

- **referrer**   String containing the URL of the referring document. (IE3+, N2+, DOM1, ReadOnly)

- **scripts[ ]**   Collection of **script** objects in the document (**<script>** elements). (IE4+, ReadOnly)

- **security**   String containing information about the document's certificate. (IE5.5+, ReadOnly)
- **selection**   Reference to the **selection** object representing the currently selected text. (IE4+, ReadOnly)
- **styleSheets[ ]**   Collection of **styleSheets** in the document (**<style>** elements). (IE4+, N6+, ReadOnly)
- **tags[ ]**   Deprecated. Accesses style properties for HTML tags. See Chapter 9. (NS4 only)
- **title**   String containing the title of the object (the **<title>** content). (IE3+, N2+, DOM1)
- **URL**   String containing the URL of the document; traditionally an alias for **location.href**. (IE4+, N2+, DOM1)
- **URLUnencoded**   A URL-decoded version of the **URL** property. (IE5.5+, ReadOnly)
- **vlinkColor**   String holding the color of visited links. (IE3+, N2+, DOM0)
- **width**   Specifies the width of all the document's content in pixels (including any parts that might be scrolled offscreen). (N4+, ReadOnly)
- **XMLDocument**   Reference to the top-level node of the XML Document Object Model exposed by the document. (IE5+, ReadOnly)
- **XSLDocument**   Reference to the XSL document object for the document. (IE5+, ReadOnly)

Methods

- **addEventListener(whichEvent, handler, direction)**   Instructs the object to execute the function *handler* whenever an event of type given in the string *whichEvent* (for example, "click") occurs. The *direction* is a Boolean specifying the phase in which to fire, **true** for capture or **false** for bubbling.* (N6+, DOM2)
- **appendChild(newChild)**   Appends *newChild* to end of the node's **childNodes[ ]** list.* (IE5+, N6+, DOM1)
- **attachEvent(whichHandler, theFunction)**   Attaches the function *theFunction* as a handler specified by the string *whichHandler*, for example "onclick."* (IE5+)
- **captureEvents(eventMask)**   Instructs object to capture the events given in the bitmask *eventMask*.* (N4+)
- **clear( )**   Supposedly clears the document of content but in reality crashes the browser or does nothing. This method should not be used. (IE3+, N2+)
- **cloneNode(cloneChildren)**   Clones the node and returns the new clone. If *cloneChildren* is **true**, the returned node includes the recursively constructed subtree of clones of the node's children.* (IE5+, N6+, DOM1)
- **close( )**   Closes output stream to the document and displays written content. (IE3+, N2+, DOM1)
- **contextual(context1 [, context2 ...] style)**   Deprecated. See Netscape documentation. (N4 only)
- **createAttribute(name)**   Returns a new attribute node of a name given by string *name*.* (IE6+, N6+, DOM1)

- **createComment(data)**   Returns a new comment node with text content given by string *data*.* (IE6+, N6+, DOM1)

- **createElement(tagName)**   Returns a new element object corresponding to the string *tagName* (for example, "P").* (IE4+, N6+, DOM1)

- **createEventObject([eventObj])**   Creates and returns a new **Event** instance to pass to **fireEvent()**. If the **Event** instance *eventObj* is supplied, its properties are cloned into the new event. Otherwise, they must be manually filled. (IE5.5+)

- **createStyleSheet([url [, index]])**   Creates a new **styleSheet** object from the stylesheet at the URL found in string *url* and inserts it into the document at index *index*. If *url* is omitted, an empty stylesheet is added. If *index* is omitted, the new stylesheet is placed at the end. (IE4+)

- **createTextNode(data)**   Returns a new text node with value given by the string *data*.* (IE5+, N6+, DOM1)

- **detachEvent(whichHandler, theFunction)**   Instructs the object to cease executing the function *theFunction* as a handler given the string *whichHandler*—for example, "onclick."* (IE5+)

- **dispatchEvent(event)**   Causes the **Event** instance *event* to be processed by the object's appropriate handler. Used to redirect events.* (N6+, DOM2)

- **elementFromPoint(x, y)**   Returns the element object found at the pixel location (*x,y*) in the document. (IE4+)

- **execCommand(command [, UIFlag][, parameter])**   Permits nonstandard operations on the document. See Microsoft documentation. (IE4+)

- **fireEvent(handler [, event])**   Causes the event handler given by the string *handler* to fire. If an **Event** instance was passed as *event*, the new event created reflects the properties of *event*.* (IE5.5+)

- **focus( )**   Gives focus to the document and causes its **onfocus** handler to fire. (IE5.5+)

- **getElementById(id)**   Returns the element with **id** (or **name**) equal to the string *id* or **null** if it does not exist.* (IE5+, N6+, DOM1)

- **getElementsByName(name)**   Retrieves a collection of elements with **id** (or **name**) equal to string *name*.* (IE5+, N6+, DOM1)

- **getElementsByTagName(tagname)**   Retrieves a collection of elements corresponding to the tag given in string *tagname*. A value of "*" retrieves all tags.* (IE5+, N6+, DOM1)

- **getSelection( )**   Returns any text currently selected by the user. (N4+)

- **hasAttributes( )**   Returns a Boolean indicating if any attributes are defined for the node.* (N6+, DOM2)

- **hasChildNodes( )**   Returns a Boolean indicating if the node has children.* (IE5+, N6+, DOM1)

- **insertBefore(newChild, refChild)**   Inserts node *newChild* in front of *refChild* in the **childNodes**[ ] list of *refChild*'s parent node.* (IE5+, N6+, DOM1)

- **isSupported(feature [, version])**   Returns a Boolean indicating whether feature and version given in the argument strings are supported.* (N6+, DOM2)

- **normalize( )**   Recursively merges adjacent text nodes in the subtree rooted at this element.* (IE6+, N6+, DOM1)

- **open([mimeType [, replace]])**   Opens the document for writing. Using this method is usually unnecessary. The *mimeType* string specifies the type of data that will be written, and *replace* is an optional Boolean that when **true** replaces the document in the browser's history rather than creating a new entry. (IE3+, N2+, DOM1)

- **queryCommandEnabled, queryCommandIndeterm, queryCommandState, queryCommandSupported, queryCommandValue**   These methods permit nonstandard operations on the document. See Microsoft documentation. (IE4+)

- **recalc([forceAll])**   Forces reevaluation of dynamic properties in the document. If *forceAll* is **true**, then all dynamic properties are reevaluated (not just those that have changed). (IE5+)

- **releaseCapture( )**   Disables universal mouse event capturing in the document.* (IE5+)

- **releaseEvents(eventMask)**   Instructs object to stop capturing the events given in the bitmask *eventMask*.* (N4+)

- **removeChild(oldChild)**   Removes *oldChild* from the node's children and returns a reference to the removed node.* (IE5+, N6+, DOM1)

- **removeEventListener(whichEvent, handler, direction)**   Removes function *handler* as a handler for the event given in the string *whichEvent* (for example, "click") for the phase given by the Boolean *direction*.* (N6+, DOM2)

- **replaceChild(newChild, oldChild)**   Replaces the node's child node *oldChild* with node *newChild*.* (IE5+, N6+, DOM1)

- **routeEvent(event)**   Passes the **Event** instance *event* along normally down the hierarchy. Used to decline to handle an event.* (N4+)

- **setActive( )**   Sets the document as the current element without giving it focus. (IE5.5+)

- **write(str1 [, str2 ...])**   Writes the text arguments to the document. (IE3+, N2+, DOM1)

- **writeln(str1 [, str2 ...])**   Writes the text arguments to the document followed by a newline at the end of the output. (IE3+, N2+, DOM1)

Event Handlers

```
onactivate onafterupdate onbeforedeactivate onbeforeeditfocus onbeforeupdate
oncellchange onclick oncontextmenu oncontrolselect ondataavailable
ondatasetchanged ondatasetcomplete ondblclick ondragstart onerrorupdate
onhelp onkeydown onkeypress onkeyup onmousedown onmousemove onmouseout
onmouseover onmouseup onpropertychange onreadystatechange onrowenter
onrowexit onrowsdelete onrowsinserted onselectionchange onselectstart onstop
```

Support
Supported in IE3+ (JScript 1.0+), N2+ (JavaScript 1.0+), DOM.

dt (Document Object)
This object corresponds to a **<dt>** (term definition in a definition list) element in the document. Access to this object is achieved through standard DOM methods like **getElementById()**.

Properties

This object has the following property, in addition to those in the Generic HTML Element Object found at the beginning of this section.

- **noWrap**   Boolean indicating whether the browser should not word wrap the item. (IE4+)

Methods

This element has the methods listed in the Generic HTML Element Object found at the beginning of this section.

Support

Supported in Internet Explorer 4+, Netscape 6+, DOM1.

em (Document Object)

This object corresponds to an **<em>** (emphasized text) element in the document. It has the properties, methods, and events listed in the Generic HTML Element Object found at the beginning of this section.

Support

Supported in Internet Explorer 4+, Netscape 6+, DOM1.

embed (Document Object)

This document object corresponds to a (nonstandard) **<embed>** (embedded object) element in the document. Access to these objects is achieved through standard DOM methods (for example, **getElementById()**) or through the **embeds[ ]** array of the **Document**.

Properties

This object has the following properties, in addition to those in the Generic HTML Element Object found at the beginning of this section. It will also have any properties exposed by the plugin used to handle the data (see plugin vendor documentation).

- **height**   Integer specifying the height in pixels of the embedded object. (IE4+, N6+)
- **hidden**   Boolean indicating whether the object is hidden (invisible). (IE4+, N6+)
- **name**   String holding the **name** attribute of the element. (IE4+, N6+)
- **palette**   String specifying the color palette to use for the object (for example, "foreground"). (IE4+ Windows, ReadOnly)
- **pluginspage**   String specifying the URL of the page that contains information about the required plugin, in case it is not installed. (IE4+, N6+, ReadOnly)
- **src**   String specifying the URL of the embedded object. (IE4+, N6+)
- **type**   String specifying the MIME type of the object. (N6+)
- **units**   String specifying the units ("em" or "px") for the height and width of the object. (IE4+)
- **width**   Specifies the width of the object in pixels. (IE4+, N6+)

Methods

This element has the methods listed in the Generic HTML Element Object found at the beginning of this section. It also has any methods exposed by the plugin used to handle the data (consult plugin vendor documentation).

Event Handlers

```
onactivate onbeforeactivate onbeforecut onbeforedeactivate onbeforepaste
onblur onclick oncontextmenu oncontrolselect oncut ondblclick ondeactivate
onfocus onfocusin onfocusout onhelp onload onlosecapture onmousedown
onmouseenter onmouseleave onmousemove onmouseout onmouseover onmouseup
onmousewheel onmove onmoveend onmovestart onpaste onpropertychange
onreadystatechange onresize onresizeend onresizestart onscroll
```

Support

Supported in Internet Explorer 4+, Netscape 3+ (primitive support—only for those properties and methods exposed by the plugin handling the data).

Enumerator (Built-in Object)

Instances of this proprietary Microsoft object are used to iterate over items in a collection. Since collection items in Internet Explorer are not enumerated in **for/in** loops and are not otherwise directly accessible, you will need to use this object to ensure proper iteration over all items in a collection.

Constructor

> **var** *instanceName* = **new** Enumerator(*collection*);

The constructor returns a new **Enumerator** instance that can be used to iterate over all the items in the collection given by *collection*. Typical values for *collection* are **document.all** and collections returned by methods like **getElementsByTagName()**.

Properties

None.

Methods

- ■ **atEnd( )**   Returns a Boolean indicating if the current item is the last one in the collection. (IE4+)
- ■ **item( )**   Returns the current item or **undefined** if the collection is empty. (IE4+)
- ■ **moveFirst( )**   Resets the current item in the collection to the first item. (IE4+)
- ■ **moveNext( )**   Moves the current item to the next item in the collection. (IE4+)

Support

Supported in IE4+ (JScript 3.0+).

Notes

This is *not* an ECMAScript object. It is a proprietary Microsoft built-in object.

Error (Built-in Object)

Whenever a runtime error occurs, the interpreter creates an **Error** instance that can be caught by the programmer. This object gives information about the error that occurred, including a description of the problem and the line number at which the error occurred. **Error** objects may also be instantiated by the programmer in order to create custom exceptions that can be **thrown**.

There are actually several types of error objects, but each is derived from the basic **Error** object and all have identical structure. The other error objects are **EvalError**, **RangeError**, **ReferenceError**, **SyntaxError**, **TypeError**, and **URIError** and browsers compliant with ECMAScript Edition 3 should provide constructors for all six, in addition to **Error** itself. Note, however, that programmers are encouraged to use the **Error** object and to leave the six "native error" types to be used exclusively by the interpreter.

Constructor

>   **var** *instanceName* = **new** Error(*message*);

The *message* string defines the text associated with the error and is often displayed to the user. Note that creating an **Error** does not cause it to be thrown; you need to use the **throw** statement explicitly.

Properties

- **constructor**   Reference to the constructor object that created the object. (IE5+ (JScript 5.0+), N6+ (JavaScript 1.5+), ECMA Edition 3)
- **description**   String describing the nature of the exception or error. (IE5+ (JScript 5.0+))
- **fileName**   String indicating the URL of the document that threw the exception. (N6+ (JavaScript 1.5+))
- **lineNumber**   The number of the line that generated the exception. (N6+ (JavaScript 1.5+))
- **message**   String describing the nature of the exception or error. (IE5.5+ (JScript 5.5+), N6+ (JavaScript 1.5+), ECMA Edition 3)
- **name**   String containing the type of the error, for example "Error," "URIError," or "SyntaxError." (IE5.5+ (JScript 5.5+), N6+ (JavaScript 1.5), ECMA Edition 3)
- **number**   Numeric value indicating the Microsoft-specific error number of the exception. Experimentation shows that this value very often deviates from Microsoft's documentation, so it should be used with great caution. (IE5+ (JScript 5.0+))
- **prototype**   Reference to the object's prototype. (IE5+ (JScript 5.0+), N6+ (JavaScript 1.5+), ECMA Edition 3)

Methods

- **toString( )**   Returns the error string corresponding to the error. (IE5+ (JScript 5.0+), N6+ (JavaScript 1.5+), ECMA Edition 3)

Support

Supported in IE5+ (JScript 5.0+), N6+ (JavaScript 1.5+), ECMAScript Edition 3.

Notes

Support for this object is spotty under Internet Explorer 5.0. For this reason the authors suggest restricting its use to ECMAScript Edition 3-compliant browsers, such as Internet Explorer 5.5+ and Netscape 6+.

Event (Browser Object)

An instance of the **Event** object is made available to event handlers in two different ways. In IE, the instance is implicitly set as a **Window** property called **event**, so it can be accessed throughout the document simply as *event*. In Netscape and under DOM2, the **Event** is available as *event* in handlers bound to elements via HTML attributes. Handlers bound using Netscape or DOM methods or by setting the appropriate property with JavaScript are passed the **Event** instance as an argument.

Not all properties are defined for every event; for example, **Event** instances corresponding to keyboard events do not include mouse position properties.

Properties

- **ABORT, BLUR, CHANGE, CLICK, DBLCLICK, DRAGDROP, ERROR, FOCUS, KEYDOWN, KEYPRESS, KEYUP, LOAD, MOUSEDOWN, MOUSEMOVE, MOUSEOUT, MOUSEOVER, MOUSEUP, MOVE, RESET, RESIZE, SELECT, SUBMIT, UNLOAD**   Bitmasks corresponding to each event for use with Netscape's event capturing functions. (N4+, Static)

- **ALT_MASK, CTRL_MASK, META_MASK, SHIFT_MASK**   Bitmasks corresponding to each key. (N4+, Static)

- **altKey**   Boolean indicating whether the ALT key was depressed during the event. (IE4+, N6+, DOM2)

- **altLeft**   Boolean indicating if the left ALT key was depressed during the event. (IE5.5+ Windows NT 4 and 2000 only)

- **boundElements[ ]**   Provides Data Binding related functionality. See Microsoft documentation. (IE4+)

- **bookmarks[ ]**   Provides Data Binding related functionality. See Microsoft documentation. (IE4+)

- **bubbles**   Boolean indicating if the event bubbles. (N6+, DOM2)

- **button**   Integer indicating which mouse buttons were pressed during the event. In IE the values are 0 (no buttons), 1 (left button), 2 (right button), 3 (left and right), 4 (middle), 5 (left and middle), 6 (right and middle), or 7 (all three). Behavior will vary under IE in MacOS. In Netscape 6 the values are 1 (primary mouse button), 2 (middle button), or 3 (right button). (IE4+, N6+, DOM2)

- **cancelable**   Boolean indicating if the event is cancelable. (N6+, DOM2)

- **cancelBubble**   Boolean indicating whether the event should bubble any higher in the object hierarchy once the current handler is done executing. (IE4+, N6+)

- **charCode**   ASCII value of the key pressed during keyboard-related events. (N6+)

- **clientX**   The *x* coordinate in pixels of the mouse pointer position relative to the client area of the browser window. Does not factor in user scrolling in IE. (IE4+, N6+, DOM2, ReadOnly in Netscape)

- **clientY**   The *y* coordinate in pixels of the mouse pointer position relative to the client area of the browser window. Does not factor in user scrolling in IE. (IE4+, N6+, DOM2, ReadOnly in Netscape)

- **contentOverflow**   Boolean indicating whether the document contains extra content after processing the current **LayoutRect** object. Only included for **onlayoutcomplete** events. (IE5.5+, ReadOnly)

- **ctrlKey**   Boolean indicating whether the CTRL key was pressed during the event. (IE4+, N6+, DOM2, ReadOnly in Netscape)

- **ctrlLeft**   Boolean indicating if the left CTRL key was depressed during the event. (IE5.5+ Windows NT 4 and 2000 only)

- **currentTarget**   Reference to the element whose handler is currently processing the event. (N6+, DOM2, ReadOnly)

- **data**   Array of strings containing the URLs of objects that were dragged and dropped. (N4, ReadOnly)

- **dataFld**   Provides Data Binding related functionality. See Microsoft documentation. (IE4+)

- **dataTransfer**   A **dataTransfer** object providing functionality for drag-and-drop events. (IE5+)

- **eventPhase**   Numeric value indicating the current phase the event is in (1 for capture, 2 for at its target, 3 for bubbling). (N6+, DOM2, ReadOnly)

- **fromElement**   Reference to the object from which activation or the mouse pointer is exiting. (IE4+)

- **keyCode**   Contains an integer representing the Unicode value of the key (for keyboard events). The value is ASCII in Netscape 6. (IE4+, N6+, ReadOnly in Netscape)

- **layerX**   The horizontal position in pixels of the cursor relative to the layer in which the event occurred. If the event is **resize**, this value holds the width of the object. In Netscape 6 this value is relative to the object according to which the target element of the event is positioned (for example, the **<body>**). (N4+, ReadOnly)

- **layerY**   The vertical position in pixels of the cursor relative to the layer in which the event occurred. If the event is **resize**, this value holds the height of the object. In Netscape 6 this value is relative to the object according to which the target element of the event is positioned (for example, the **<body>**). (N4+, ReadOnly)

- **metaKey**   Boolean indicating if the meta key was pressed during the event. (N6+, DOM2, ReadOnly)

- **modifiers**   Bitmask indicating which modifier keys were held down during the event. The bitmask is a bitwise combination of the static properties **ALT_MASK**, **CONTROL_MASK**, **META_MASK**, and **SHIFT_MASK**. (N4, ReadOnly)

- **nextPage**   Provides print template related functionality. See Microsoft documentation. (IE5.5+)

- **offsetX**   The *x* coordinate in pixels of the mouse with respect to the target object of the event. (IE4+)

■ **offsetY** The y coordinate in pixels of the mouse with respect to the target object of the event. (IE4+)

■ **pageX** Horizontal position in pixels where the event occurred with respect to the page. (N4+, ReadOnly)

■ **pageY** Vertical position in pixels where the event occurred with respect to the page. (N4+, ReadOnly)

■ **propertyName** String containing the name of the property that fired an **onpropertychange** event. (IE5+)

■ **qualifier** Provides Data Binding related functionality. See Microsoft documentation. (IE4+)

■ **reason** Provides Data Binding related functionality. See Microsoft documentation. (IE4+)

■ **recordset** Provides Data Binding related functionality. See Microsoft documentation. (IE4+)

■ **relatedTarget** Reference to the node related to the event. For example, on a **mouseover** it references the node the mouse left; on **mouseout** it references the node the mouse moved to. (N6+, DOM2, ReadOnly)

■ **repeat** Boolean indicating whether the key is continually repeating during **onkeydown** events. (IE5+)

■ **returnValue** Boolean dictating the return value of the event handler (takes precedence over **return** statements). (IE4+)

■ **saveType** String holding the clipboard type ("HTML" or "TEXT") during an **oncontentsave**. (IE5.5+)

■ **screenX** Horizontal position in pixels where the event occurred with respect to the whole screen. (N4+, IE4+, DOM2, ReadOnly in Netscape)

■ **screenY** Vertical position in pixels where the event occurred with respect to the whole screen. (N4+, IE4+, DOM2, ReadOnly in Netscape)

■ **shiftKey** Boolean indicating whether the SHIFT key was depressed during the event. (IE4+, N6+, DOM2, ReadOnly in Netscape)

■ **shiftLeft** Boolean indicating if the left SHIFT key was depressed during the event. (IE5.5+ Windows NT 4 and 2000 only)

■ **srcElement** Reference to the element object that is the target of the event. (IE4+)

■ **srcFilter** String containing the name of the CSS Filter which caused the **onfilterevent** to fire. (IE4+ but appears to be broken)

■ **srcUrn** String containing the URN of the DHTML Behavior that fired the event. (IE5+)

■ **target** Reference to the object at which the event occurred. (N4+, DOM2, ReadOnly)

■ **timeStamp** Time the event occurred, in milliseconds since the epoch. (N6+, ReadOnly)

■ **toElement** Reference to the object towards which the user is moving the mouse (for example, during **onmouseout**). (IE4+)

■ **type** String containing the event type (for example, "click"). (N4+, IE4+, DOM2, ReadOnly in Netscape)

■ **view** Apparently a reference to the window or frame which encloses the object at which the event occurs. (N6+, DOM2, ReadOnly)

- **which**   For mouse events, numeric value indicating which mouse button was used (1 is left, 2 middle, 3 right); for keyboard events, the Unicode (numeric) value of the key pressed. (N4, ReadOnly)
- **x**   Same as **layerX** in Netscape. In IE, the x coordinate in pixels of the mouse pointer relative to the target element's parent. (N4, IE4+, ReadOnly in Netscape)
- **y**   Same as **layerY**. In IE, the y coordinate in pixels of the mouse pointer relative to the target element's parent. (N4, IE4+, ReadOnly in Netscape)

Methods

- **preventDefault( )**   Prevents the default action associated with the event from occurring. (N6+, DOM2)
- **stopPropagation( )**   Prevents further propagation of the event through the object hierarchy. (N6+, DOM2)

Notes

You can set most properties of **Event** instances in Netscape if you have the UniversalBrowserWrite privilege. Also, most IE properties listed above are read-only in IE4, but mutable in IE5+.

external (Browser Object)

This object provides methods for interacting with the operating system or other applications. It is primarily used when IE is being used as a component. Some sample applications are adding items to Windows' desktop, modification of the user's bookmarks, and saving form data for use with IE's form autocompletion.

For full details about this object see Microsoft's documentation. The **external** object is available in IE4+, but only for Windows.

fieldSet (Document Object)

This object corresponds to a **<fieldset>** (form field grouping) element in the document. Access to this object is achieved through standard DOM methods like **getElementById()**.

Properties

This object has the following property, in addition to those in the Generic HTML Element Object found at the beginning of this section.

- **form**   Reference to the **Form** in which the element is contained. (IE6+, DOM1)

Methods

This element has the methods listed in the Generic HTML Element Object found at the beginning of this section.

Event Handlers

This object has the event handlers listed in the Generic HTML Element Object found at the beginning of this section, in addition to the following:

```
onbeforeeditfocus onfilterchange
```

Support

Supported in Internet Explorer 4+, Netscape 6+, DOM1.

File, FileUpload (Document Object)

This object corresponds to an **<input type="file">** element in the document. Access to this object is achieved through standard DOM methods (for example, **getElementById()**) or more commonly through the **elements[ ]** array of the form it is contained in.

Properties

This object has the following properties, in addition to those in the Generic HTML Element Object found at the beginning of this section.

- **accessKey**   Single character string indicating the hotkey that gives the element focus.* (IE4+, N6+, DOM1)
- **controllers**   Related to XPConnect functionality. See **mozilla.org**. (N6+)
- **defaultValue**   String containing the original value of the **value** attribute. (IE4+)
- **disabled**   Boolean indicating whether the element is disabled (grayed out). (IE4+, N6+, DOM1)
- **form**   Reference to the **Form** in which the button is contained. (IE4+, N3+, DOM1, ReadOnly)
- **name**   String holding the **name** attribute of the element. (IE4+, N3+, DOM1)
- **size**   String indicating the width in pixels. (IE4+, N6+, DOM1)
- **tabIndex**   Numeric value indicating the tab order for the object.* (IE4+, N6+, DOM1)
- **type**   String indicating the type of the field, "button." (IE4+, N3+, DOM1, ReadOnly)
- **value**   String containing the filename. (IE4+, N3+, DOM1, ReadOnly)
- **width**   The width in pixels of the input area. (IE4+)

Methods

This object has the following methods, in addition to those in the Generic HTML Element Object found at the beginning of this section.

- **blur( )**   Causes the button to lose focus. (IE4+, N3+, DOM1)
- **focus( )**   Gives the button focus. (IE4+, N3+, DOM1)
- **handleEvent(event)**   Causes the **Event** instance *event* to be processed by the appropriate handler of the object.* (N4 only)
- **select( )**   Selects the text entered as input (the filename). (IE4+, N6+, DOM1)

Event Handlers

```
onactivate onafterupdate onbeforeactivate onbeforecut onbeforedeactivate
onbeforeeditfocus onbeforepaste onbeforeupdate onblur onclick oncontextmenu
oncontrolselect oncut ondblclick ondeactivate ondrag ondragend ondragenter
ondragleave ondragover ondragstart ondrop onerrorupdate onfilterchange
```

```
onfocus onfocusin onfocusout onhelp onkeydown onkeypress onkeyup
onlosecapture onmousedown onmouseenter onmouseleave onmousemove onmouseout
onmouseover onmouseup onmousewheel onmove onmoveend onmovestart onpaste
onpropertychange onreadystatechange onresize onresizeend onresizestart
onselectstart ontimeerror
```

Support

Supported in Internet Explorer 4+, Netscape 3+, DOM1.

FileSystemObject (Built-in Object)

This object provides access to the local filesystem to scripts in an IE/Windows environment (subject, of course, to security restrictions). For full documentation of this object see Microsoft's documentation at MSDN.

Notes

This is *not* an ECMAScript object. It is a proprietary Microsoft built-in object.

font (Document Object)

This object corresponds to a **<font>** element in the document. Access to this object is achieved through standard DOM methods (for example, **getElementById()**).

Properties

This object has the following properties, in addition to those in the Generic HTML Element Object found at the beginning of this section.

- **color**   String holding the default text color for the page. (IE4+, N6+, DOM1)
- **face**   String holding a comma-separated list of one or more default font names. (IE4+, N6+, DOM1)
- **size**   String holding the default font size (HTML 1-7 or relative +n/-n syntax). (IE3+, N6+, DOM1)

Methods

This element has the methods listed in the Generic HTML Element Object found at the beginning of this section.

Event Handlers

```
onactivate onbeforeactivate onbeforecut onbeforedeactivate onbeforepaste
onblur onclick oncontextmenu oncontrolselect oncut ondblclick ondeactivate
ondrag ondragend ondragenter ondragleave ondragover ondragstart ondrop
onfocus onfocusin onfocusout onhelp onkeydown onkeypress onkeyup
onlayoutcomplete onlosecapture onmousedown onmouseenter onmouseleave
onmousemove onmouseout onmouseover onmouseup onmousewheel onmove onmoveend
```

onmovestart onpaste onpropertychange onreadystatechange onresize onresizeend onresizestart onselectstart ontimeerror

Support
Supported in Internet Explorer 4+, Netscape 6+, DOM1.

FileUpload
See **File**.

form (Document Object)
This object corresponds to a **<form>** element in the document and is known as a **Form** in traditional models. Standard DOM methods can be used to access this object but more often the **forms[ ]** array of the **Document** is used.

Properties
This object has the following properties, in addition to those in the Generic HTML Element Object found at the beginning of this section.

- **acceptCharset**   String specifying a list of character encodings for input data that must be accepted by the server processing the form. (IE5+, N6+, DOM1)
- **action**   String containing the URL to which the form will be submitted. (IE3+, N2+, DOM1)
- **autocomplete**   String specifying whether form autocompletion is "on" or "off." See MSDN. (IE5+)
- **elements[ ]**   A collection, in source order, of all fields (controls) in the form. (IE3+, N2+, DOM1, ReadOnly)
- **encoding**   String specifying the MIME type of submitted form data. (IE3+, N2+)
- **enctype**   String specifying the MIME type of submitted form data. (N6+, DOM1)
- **length**   The number of entries in the **elements[ ]** collection (the number of fields of the form). (IE3+, N2+, DOM1, ReadOnly)
- **method**   String indicating the HTTP method used to submit the form data, either "get" or "post." (IE3+, N2+, DOM1)
- **name**   String holding the **name** attribute of the form. (IE3+, N2+, DOM1)
- **target**   String indicating the name of the window or frame in which the results of the form submission should be shown. (IE3+, N2+, DOM1)

Methods
This object has the following methods, in addition to those in the Generic HTML Element Object found at the beginning of this section.

- **handleEvent(event)**   Causes the **Event** instance *event* to be processed by the appropriate handler of the object.* (N4 only)
- **reset( )**   Resets all form fields to their original values. (IE4+, N3+, DOM1)
- **submit( )**   Causes form submission to occur. (IE3+, N2+, DOM1)

APPENDIXES

- **tags(tagName)** Retrieves a collection of contained elements that have tags equal to string *tagName*. (IE4+)
- **urns(urn)** Retrieves collection of all elements to which the behavior given by string *urn* is attached.* (IE5+)
- **handleEvent(event)** Causes the **Event** instance *event* to be processed by the appropriate handler of the object.* (N4 only)

Event Handlers

```
onactivate onbeforeactivate onbeforecopy onbeforecut onbeforedeactivate
onbeforeeditfocus onbeforepaste onblur onclick oncontextmenu oncontrolselect
oncopy oncut ondblclick ondeactivate ondrag ondragend ondragenter
ondragleave ondragover ondragstart ondrop onfocus onfocusin onfocusout
onhelp onkeydown onkeypress onkeyup onlosecapture onmousedown onmouseenter
onmouseleave onmousemove onmouseout onmouseover onmouseup onmousewheel
onmove onmoveend onmovestart onpaste onpropertychange onreadystatechange
onreset onresize onresizeend onresizestart onselectstart onsubmit
ontimeerror
```

Support

Supported in Internet Explorer 3+, Netscape 2+, and DOM1.

frame (Document Object)

This object corresponds to a **<frame>** element in the document. It does not correspond to the **Frame** object (of which the entries in **document.frames[ ]** are composed). The distinction is that this object corresponds to an instance of the **<frame>** tag in the document whereas **Frame** corresponds to the **Window** object in which the frame's content actually appears.

Standard DOM methods are used to access this object.

Properties

This object has the following properties, in addition to those in the Generic HTML Element Object found at the beginning of this section.

- **allowTransparency** Boolean specifying whether the background of the frame can be transparent (can be set to any color). (IE5.5+)
- **borderColor** String specifying the color of the border around the frame. (IE4+)
- **contentDocument** Reference to the **Document** that corresponds to the content of this frame. (N6+, ReadOnly)
- **contentWindow** Reference to the **Window** that corresponds to this frame. (IE5.5+, ReadOnly)
- **dataFld** String specifying which field of a data source is bound to the element.* (IE4+)
- **dataSrc** String containing the source of data for data binding.* (IE4+)
- **frameBorder** String containing "0" (no border) or "1" (show border). (IE4+, N6+, DOM1)

- **longDesc**   String containing the URI of a long description for the frame (for nonvisual browsers). (IE6+, N6+, DOM1)
- **marginHeight**   String specifying the vertical margins, in pixels. Overridden by CSS properties. (IE4+, N6+, DOM1)
- **marginWidth**   String specifying the horizontal margins, in pixels. Overridden by CSS properties. (IE4+, N6+, DOM1)
- **name**   String holding the **name** attribute of the frame. (IE4+, N6+, DOM1)
- **noResize**   Boolean indicating whether the user cannot resize the frame. (IE4+, N6+, DOM1)
- **scrolling**   String specifying whether the frame should have scrollbars, either "yes," "no," or "auto." (IE4+, N6+, DOM1)
- **src**   String giving the URL of the frame's contents. (IE4+, N6+, DOM1)

Methods
This element has the methods listed in the Generic HTML Element Object found at the beginning of this section.

Event Handlers

```
onactivate onafterupdate onbeforedeactivate onbeforeupdate onblur
oncontrolselect ondeactivate onerrorupdate onload onmove onmoveend
onmovestart onresize onresizeend onresizestart
```

Support
Supported in Internet Explorer 4+, Netscape 6+, DOM1.

Frame (Browser Object)

This object corresponds to the (sub)window in which a frame's contents are displayed. It is not a **<frame>** element but is rather created as the result of one. Access to this object is achieved through the **window.frames[ ]** collection.

This object has an identical structure to **Window**.

Support
Supported in Internet Explorer 3+, Netscape 2+.

frameset (Document Object)

This object corresponds to a **<frameset>** element in the document. Access to this object is achieved through standard DOM methods (for example, **getElementById()**).

Properties
This object has the following properties, in addition to those in the Generic HTML Element Object found at the beginning of this section.

- **border**   String or integer indicating the number of pixels to use for the border between frames. (IE4+)

- **borderColor**   String indicating the color of the border. (IE4+)
- **cols**   Comma-separated string of column widths for the frames. This string is composed of pixel values, percentage values, and * values. (IE4+, N6+, DOM1)
- **frameBorder**   String specifying whether to show borders around the frames ("1" for yes, "0" for no). (IE4+)
- **frameSpacing**   String indicating the number of pixels apart to place the frames. (IE4+)
- **name**   String holding the name attribute of the element. (IE4+, N6+)
- **rows**   Comma-separated string of row heights for the frames. This string is composed of pixel values, percentage values, and * values. (IE4+, N6+, DOM1)

Methods

This element has the methods listed in the Generic HTML Element Object found at the beginning of this section.

Event Handlers

```
onactivate onafterprint onbeforedeactivate onbeforeprint onbeforeunload
onblur oncontrolselect ondeactivate onfocus onload onmove onmoveend
onmovestart onresizeend onresizestart onunload
```

Support

Supported in Internet Explorer 4+, Netscape 6+, DOM1.

Function (Built-in Object)

Function is the object from which JavaScript functions are derived. Functions are first-class data types in JavaScript, so they may be assigned to variables and passed to functions as you would any other piece of data. Functions are, of course, passed by reference.

The **Function** object provides properties that convey useful information during the execution of the function (for example, the **arguments[ ]** array) as well as statically (for example, the **length** property).

Constructor

var *instanceName* = **new** Function([*arg1* [, *arg2* [, ...]] ,] *body*);

The *body* parameter is a string containing the text that makes up the body of the function. The optional *argN*'s are the names of the formal parameters the function accepts. For example:

```
var myAdd = new Function("x", "y", "return x + y");
var sum = myAdd(17, 34);
```

Properties

- **arguments[ ]**   An implicitly filled and implicitly available (directly usable as "arguments" from within the function) array of parameters that were passed to the function. (IE4+ (JScript 2.0+), N3+ (JavaScript 1.1+), ECMA Edition 1)

- **arguments.callee**   Deprecated. Reference to the current function. (N4)

- **arguments.caller**   Deprecated. Reference to the function that invoked the current function. (N3)

- **arguments.length**   The number of arguments that were passed to the function. (IE4+ (JScript 2.0+), N3+ (JavaScript 1.1+), ECMA Edition 1)

- **arity**   Deprecated. Numeric value indicating how many arguments the function expects. (N4+)

- **caller**   Reference to the function that invoked the current function or **null** if called from the global context. (IE4+ (JScript 2.0+), N3, N4)

- **constructor**   Reference to the constructor object which created the object. (IE4+ (JScript 2.0+), N3+ (JavaScript 1.1+), ECMA Edition 1)

- **length**   The number of arguments the function expects to be passed. (IE4+ (JScript 2.0+), N3+ (JavaScript 1.1+), ECMA Edition 1)

- **prototype**   Reference to the object's prototype. (IE4+ (JScript 2.0+), N3+ (JavaScript 1.1+), ECMA Edition 1)

Methods

- **apply(thisArg [, argArray])**   Invokes the function with the object referenced by *thisArg* as its context (so references to **this** in the function reference *thisArg*). The optional parameter *argArray* contains the list of parameters to pass to the function as it is invoked. (IE5.5+ (JScript 5.5+), N4.06+ (JavaScript 1.3+), ECMA Edition 3)

- **call(thisArg [, arg1 [, arg2 [, ...]]])**   Invokes the function with the object referenced by *thisArg* as its context (so references to **this** in the function reference *thisArg*). The optional parameters *argN* are passed to the function as it is invoked. (IE5.5+ (JScript 5.5+), N4.06+ (JavaScript 1.3+), ECMA Edition 3)

- **toString( )**   Returns the string version of the function source. The body of built-in and browser objects will be "[native code]". (IE4+ (JScript 2.0+), N3+ (JavaScript 1.1+), ECMA Edition 1)

- **valueOf( )**   Returns the string version of the function source. The body of built-in and browser objects will be "[native code]". (IE4+ (JScript 2.0+), N3+ (JavaScript 1.1+), ECMA Edition 1)

Support

Supported in IE4+ (JScript 2.0+), N3+ (JavaScript 1.1+), ECMAScript Edition 1.

Global (Built-in Object)

The **Global** object provides methods and constants that can be used freely anywhere in your scripts. **Global** is defined to be the globally enclosing context, so this object cannot be instantiated or even directly accessed; its properties and methods are always within the scope of an executing script. Its sole purpose is as a catch-all for globally available methods and constants.

Constructor

None. This object cannot be instantiated because it defines the global context.

Properties

- **Infinity**   Constant holding the numeric value **Infinity**. (IE4+ (JScript 3.0+), N4.06+ (JavaScript 1.3+), ECMA Edition 1)

- **NaN**   Constant holding the numeric value **NaN** (not a number). (IE4+ (JScript 3.0+), N4.06+ (JavaScript 1.3+), ECMA Edition 1)

- **undefined**   Constant holding the value **undefined**. (IE5.5+ (JScript 5.5+), N4.06+ (JavaScript 1.3+), ECMA Edition 1)

Methods

- **decodeURI(encodedURI)**   URI-decodes the string *encodedURI* and returns the decoded string. (IE5.5+ (JScript 5.5+), N6+ (JavaScript 1.5+), ECMA Edition 3)

- **decodeURIComponent(encodedURI)**   URI-decodes the string *encodedURI* and returns the decoded string. (IE5.5+ (JScript 5.5+), N6+ (JavaScript 1.5+), ECMA Edition 3)

- **encodeURI(uri)**   URI-encodes the string *uri*, treating *uri* as a full URI. Legal URI characters (for example, the "://" after the protocol) are not encoded. Returns the encoded string. (IE5.5+ (JScript 5.5+), N6+ (JavaScript 1.5+), ECMA Edition 3)

- **encodeURIComponent(uriComponent)**   URI-encodes the string *uriComponent* and returns the encoded string. All potentially problematic characters (for example, "/" and "?") are encoded. (IE5.5+ (JScript 5.5+), N6+ (JavaScript 1.5+), ECMA Edition 3)

- **escape(string)**   URI-encodes *string* and returns the encoded string. Using the newer **encodeURIComponent()** is preferable. (IE3+ (JScript 1.0+), N2+ (JavaScript 1.0+))

- **eval(string)**   Executes *string* as JavaScript. (IE3+ (JScript 1.0+), N2+ (JavaScript 1.0+), ECMA Edition 1)

- **isFinite(value)**   Returns a Boolean indicating if the numeric argument *value* is finite. Returns **false** if *value* is **NaN**. (IE4+ (JScript 3.0+), N4.06+ (JavaScript 1.3+), ECMA Edition 1)

- **isNaN(value)**   Returns a Boolean indicating if the numeric argument *value* is **NaN**. (IE4+ (JScript 3.0+), N3+ (JavaScript 1.1+), ECMA Edition 1)

- **parseFloat(string)**   Parses *string* as a floating point number and returns its value. If *string* cannot be converted, **NaN** is returned. (IE3+ (JScript 1.0+), N2+ (JavaScript 1.0+), ECMA Edition 1)

- **parseInt(string)**   Parses *string* as an integer and returns its value. If *string* cannot be converted, **NaN** is returned. (IE3+ (JScript 1.0+), N2+ (JavaScript 1.0+), ECMA Edition 1)

- **unescape(encodedString)**   URI-decodes *encodedString* and returns the decoded string. Using the newer **decodeURIComponent()** method is preferable. (IE3+ (JScript 1.0+), N2+ (JavaScript 1.0+))

Support

Supported in IE3+ (JScript 1.0+), N2+ (JavaScript 1.0+), ECMAScript Edition 1.

h1, ..., h6 (Document Object)

This object corresponds to an **<h***n***>** (heading level *n*) element in the document. Access to this object is achieved through standard DOM methods (for example, **getElementById()**).

Properties

This object has the following property, in addition to those in the Generic HTML Element Object found at the beginning of this section.

■ **align**   String specifying the alignment of the element, for example "left."*
(IE4+, N6+, DOM1)

Methods

This element has the methods listed in the Generic HTML Element Object found at the beginning of this section.

Event Handlers

This object has the event handlers listed in the Generic HTML Element Object found at the beginning of this section.

Support

Supported in Internet Explorer 4+, Netscape 6+, DOM1.

head (Document Object)

This object corresponds to the **<head>** element in the document. Access to this object is achieved through standard DOM methods, but because it is not found in the **<body>** you will probably have to use a method of **document.documentElement** to retrieve it (or **document.all** in IE).

Properties

This object has the following property, in addition to those in the Generic HTML Element Object found at the beginning of this section.

■ **profile**   String containing a white space-separated list of URIs giving data properties and legal values. (IE6+, N6+, DOM1)

Methods

This element has the methods listed in the Generic HTML Element Object found at the beginning of this section.

Event Handlers

```
onlayoutcomplete onreadystatechange
```

Support
Supported in Internet Explorer 4+, Netscape 6+, DOM1.

Hidden (Document Object)

This object corresponds to an occurrence of a hidden form field (**<input type="hidden"...>**) in the document. This object can be accessed using standard DOM methods or through the **Form** element which contains it (via the **elements[ ]** array or by **name**).

The structure of this object is identical to the structure of the **Text** object (except that it does not have a **select()** method), so see the reference for **Text** for details.

Event Handlers

```
onactivate onafterupdate onbeforedeactivate onbeforeeditfocus onbeforeupdate
oncontrolselect ondeactivate onerrorupdate onfocus onlosecapture onmove
onmoveend onmovestart onpropertychange onreadystatechange onresizeend
onresizestart ontimeerror
```

Support
Supported in Internet Explorer 3+, Netscape 2+, DOM1.

History (Browser Object)

The browser keeps an array of recently visited URLs in the **History** object and provides script the means to navigate to them. This enables scripts to mimic the behavior of the browser's "Forward" and "Back" buttons as well as the ability to jump to the nth URL in the browser's history.

Netscape 2 keeps track of history information on a window-wide level while later versions of Netscape keep an individual history for each frame, so these methods should be employed with caution in older browsers. Individual entries in the history array can be accessed as **history[i]** using signed scripts in Netscape but are otherwise unavailable for privacy reasons. Internet Explorer's functionality is exactly like using the browser's "Forward" and "Back" buttons.

Child Of
Window.

Properties

- **current**   The current URL in the history. Requires UniversalBrowserRead. (N3+, ReadOnly)
- **length**   The number of entries in the history list. Essentially useless. (IE3+, N2+, ReadOnly)
- **next**   The next URL in the history. Requires UniversalBrowserRead. (N3+, ReadOnly)
- **previous**   The previous URL in the history. Requires UniversalBrowserRead. (N3+, ReadOnly)

Methods

- **back( )**   Causes the browser to move one URL back in its history. (IE3+, N2+)

- **forward( )**   Causes the browser to move one URL forward in its history. (IE3+, N2+)
- **go(where)**   If *where* is an integer, loads the URL at that offset from the current page in the history. For example, **go(-2)** moves back two steps in the history. If *where* is a string, the first entry in the history list containing *where* in its URL or document title is loaded.

Support
Supported in IE3+ (JScript 1.0+), N2+ (JavaScript 1.0+).

hr (Document Object)

This object corresponds to an **<hr>** (horizontal rule) element in the document. Access to this object is achieved through standard DOM methods (for example, **getElementById()**).

Properties
This object has the following properties, in addition to those in the Generic HTML Element Object found at the beginning of this section.

- **align**   String specifying the alignment of the element, for example "left."*
(IE4+, N6+, DOM1)
- **color**   String specifying the color of the rule. (IE4+)
- **noShade**   Boolean indicating that the rule is not to be shaded. (IE4+, N6+, DOM1)
- **size**   String specifying the size (height) of the rule in pixels. (IE4+, N6+, DOM1)
- **width**   String specifying the width of the rule in pixels. (IE4+, N6+, DOM1)

Methods
This element has the methods listed in the Generic HTML Element Object found at the beginning of this section.

Event Handlers

```
onactivate onbeforeactivate onbeforecut onbeforedeactivate onbeforepaste
onblur onclick oncontextmenu oncontrolselect oncopy oncut ondblclick
ondeactivate ondrag ondragend ondragenter ondragleave ondragover ondragstart
ondrop onfocus onfocusin onfocusout onhelp onkeydown onkeypress onkeyup
onlayoutcomplete onlosecapture onmousedown onmouseenter onmouseleave
onmousemove onmouseout onmouseover onmouseup onmousewheel onmove onmoveend
onmovestart onpaste onpropertychange onreadystatechange onresize onresizeend
onresizestart onselectstart ontimeerror
```

Support
Supported in Internet Explorer 4+, Netscape 6+, DOM1.

html (Document Object)

This object corresponds to the **<html>** element in the document. Access to this object is achieved through standard DOM methods, most often as the child of **document.documentElement**.

Properties

This object has the following property, in addition to those in the Generic HTML Element Object found at the beginning of this section.

- ■ **version**   String containing the DTD version for the document. (IE6+, N6+, DOM1)

Methods

This element has the methods listed in the Generic HTML Element Object found at the beginning of this section.

Event Handlers

```
onlayoutcomplete onmouseenter onmouseleave onreadystatechange
```

Support

Supported in Internet Explorer 4+, Netscape 6+, DOM1.

i (Document Object)

This object corresponds to an **<i>** (italics) element in the document. It has the properties, methods, and events listed in the Generic HTML Element Object found at the beginning of this section.

Support

Supported in Internet Explorer 4+, Netscape 6+, DOM1.

iframe (Document Object)

This object corresponds to an **<iframe>** (inline frame) element in the document. Access to this object is achieved through standard DOM methods (for example, **getElementById()**).

Properties

This object has the following properties, in addition to those in the Generic HTML Element Object found at the beginning of this section.

- ■ **align**   String specifying the alignment of the element, for example "left."* (IE4+, N6+, DOM1)
- ■ **allowTransparency**   Boolean specifying whether the background of the frame can be transparent (can be set to any color). (IE5.5+)
- ■ **border**   String or integer indicating the width of the border around the frame. (IE4+)
- ■ **contentDocument**   Reference to the **Document** that corresponds to the content of this frame. (N6+, ReadOnly)
- ■ **contentWindow**   Reference to the **Window** that corresponds to this frame. (IE5.5+, ReadOnly)
- ■ **dataFld**   String specifying which field of a data source is bound to the element.* (IE4+)
- ■ **dataSrc**   String containing the source of data for data binding.* (IE4+)
- ■ **frameBorder**   String containing "0" (no border) or "1" (show border). (IE4+, N6+, DOM1)
- ■ **height**   String specifying the height of the frame in pixels. (IE4+, N6+, DOM1)

- **hspace**   Integer indicating the horizontal margin for the frame in pixels. (IE4+)
- **longDesc**   String containing the URI of a long description for the frame (for nonvisual browsers). (IE6+, N6+, DOM1)
- **marginHeight**   String specifying the vertical margins, in pixels. Overridden by CSS properties. (IE4+, N6+, DOM1)
- **marginWidth**   String specifying the horizontal margins, in pixels. Overridden by CSS properties. (IE4+, N6+, DOM1)
- **name**   String holding the **name** attribute of the frame. (IE4+, N6+, DOM1)
- **scrolling**   String specifying whether the frame should have scrollbars, either "yes," "no," or "auto." (IE4+, N6+, DOM1)
- **src**   String giving the URL of the frame's contents. (IE4+, N6+, DOM1)
- **vspace**   Integer indicating the vertical margin for the frame in pixels. (IE4+)
- **width**   String specifying the width of the frame in pixels. (IE4+, N6+, DOM1)

Methods

This element has the methods listed in the Generic HTML Element Object found at the beginning of this section.

Event Handlers

This object has the event handlers listed in the Generic HTML Element Object found at the beginning of this section.

Support

Supported in Internet Explorer 4+, Netscape 6+, DOM1.

Image, img (Document Object)

An **Image** object corresponds to an **<img>** element in the document. This object exposes properties that allow the dynamic examination and manipulation of images on the page. Access to an **Image** object is often achieved through the **images[ ]** collection of the **Document**, but the modern **getElementById()** method provided by the DOM can of course also be used.

Constructor

   var *instanceName* = **new** Image([*width, height*]);

A new **Image** is created and returned with the given *width* and *height*, if specified. This constructor is useful for preloading images by instantiating an **Image** and setting its **src** earlier in the document than it is needed.

Properties

This object has the following properties, in addition to those in the Generic HTML Element Object found at the beginning of this section.

- **align**   String specifying the alignment of the element, for example "left."* (IE4+, N6+, DOM1)
- **alt**   String containing the alternative text for the image. Corresponds to the **alt** attribute of the **<img>**. (IE4+, N6+, DOM1)

- **border**   Numeric value indicating the border width in pixels of the image. (IE4+, N3+, DOM1, ReadOnly in Netscape 3-4)

- **complete**   Boolean indicating whether the image has finished loading. (IE4+, N3+, ReadOnly)

- **dataFld**   String specifying which field of a data source is bound to the element.* (IE4+)

- **dataSrc**   String containing the source of data for data binding.* (IE4+)

- **dynsrc**   String indicating the URL of the video clip or VRML file to display in the element. (IE4+)

- **fileCreatedDate**   String containing the date the image was created if it can be determined, or the empty string otherwise. (IE4+, ReadOnly)

- **fileModifiedDate**   String containing the date the image was last modified if it can be determined, or the empty string otherwise. (IE4+, ReadOnly)

- **fileSize**   Numeric value indicating the size in bytes of the image (if it can be determined). (IE4+, ReadOnly)

- **fileUpdatedDate**   String containing the date the image was last updated if it can be determined, or the empty string otherwise. (IE4+, ReadOnly)

- **height**   Specifies the height in pixels of the image (IE4+, N3+, DOM1, ReadOnly in Netscape 3-4)

- **hspace**   Specifies the horizontal margin for the image in pixels. (IE4+, N3+, DOM. ReadOnly in versions of Netscape before 6)

- **isMap**   Boolean indicating if the image is a server-side image map. (IE4+, N6+, DOM1)

- **longDesc**   String specifying a URL for a longer description of the image. (IE6+, N6+, DOM1)

- **loop**   Integer indicating the number of times the image is to loop when activated. (IE4+)

- **lowSrc**   String specifying a URL for a lower resolution image to display. (N6+, DOM1)

- **lowsrc**   String specifying a URL for a lower resolution image to display. (IE4+, N3+)

- **name**   String holding the **name** attribute of the element. (IE4+, N3+, DOM1, ReadOnly in Netscape 3-4)

- **nameProp**   String indicating the name of the file given in the **src** attribute of the **<img>**. Does not include protocol, domain, directory, or other information. (IE5+, ReadOnly)

- **protocol**   String containing the full name of the protocol portion of the URL of the **src** attribute of the **<img>**. (IE4+, ReadOnly)

- **src**   String containing the URL of the image. (IE4+, N3+, DOM1)

- **start**   String indicating when the video associated with the image with the **dynsrc** property/attribute should begin playing. Values are "fileopen," the default, which begins playback when the file loads, or "mouseover," which begins when the user mouses over it. (IE4+, DOM2)

- **style**   Reference to the inline **Style** object for the element.* (IE4+, N4+, DOM2)

- **useMap**   String containing URL to use as a client-side image map. (IE4+, N6+, DOM1)

- **vspace**   Specifies the vertical margin for the image in pixels. (IE4+, N3+, DOM1, ReadOnly in Netscape 3-4)

- **width**   Specifies the width of the object in pixels. (IE4+, N3+, DOM1, ReadOnly in Netscape 3-4)

Methods

This object has the following method, in addition to those in the Generic HTML Element Object found at the beginning of this section.

- ■ **handleEvent(event)** Causes the **Event** instance passed to be processed by the appropriate handler of the layer.* (N4 only)

Event Handlers

```
onabort onactivate onafterupdate onbeforeactivate onbeforecopy onbeforecut
onbeforedeactivate onbeforepaste onbeforeupdate onblur onclick oncontextmenu
oncontrolselect oncopy oncut ondblclick ondeactivate ondrag ondragend
ondragenter ondragleave ondragover ondragstart ondrop onerror onerrorupdate
onfilterchange onfocus onfocusin onfocusout onhelp onkeydown onkeypress
onkeyup onload onlosecapture onmousedown onmouseenter onmouseleave
onmousemove onmouseout onmouseover onmouseup onmousewheel onmove onmoveend
onmovestart onpaste onpropertychange onreadystatechange onresize onresizeend
onresizestart onselectstart ontimeerror
```

APPENDIXES

Support

Supported in Internet Explorer 4+, Netscape 3+, DOM1.

implementation (Document Browser/Object)

Contains information about the DOM technologies the browser supports.

Child Of

Document.

Properties

None.

Methods

- ■ **hasFeature(feature [, version])**   Returns a Boolean indicating if the browser supports the feature specified by the string *feature* at the DOM level given in string *level*. Valid values for *feature* are CSS, Events, HTML, HTMLEvents, MouseEvents, Range, StyleSheets, Views, and XML. Valid values for *level* are DOM levels, for example "1.0" or "2.0." The values returned by the method are often inaccurate because of spotty browser support for DOM functionality. (IE6+, N6+, DOM1)

Support

Supported in Internet Explorer 6+, Netscape 6+, DOM1.

input (Document Object)

This object corresponds to an **<input>** element in the document. The type of the input field is set by the **type** attribute and includes "text," "password," "checkbox," "radio," "submit," "reset," "file," "hidden," "image," and "button." Traditional models drew a distinction between **<input>**

elements with different **type** attributes and called them by the **type** value (for example, **Text**, **Password**, or **Radio)**. With the rise of the DOM, this distinction is no longer quite as clearly defined, but for historical reasons we list each type under its **type** attribute. The exception is "image," which has most of the properties of **Button** (in addition to **Image** under Internet Explorer). Full details of **Image** are available at the support site.

Access to these objects is achieved through standard DOM methods, or more commonly through the **elements[ ]** array of the **Form** in which the **<input>** is enclosed.

Support

The generic **<input>** element is supported in Internet Explorer 4+, Netscape 6+, and DOM1. However support for specific types of **<input>**s was available in much earlier versions.

ins (Document Object)

This object corresponds to an **<ins>** (insertion modification) element in the document. Access to this object is achieved through standard DOM methods (for example, **getElementById()**).

Properties

This object has the following properties, in addition to those in the Generic HTML Element Object found at the beginning of this section.

- ■ **cite**   String containing the URL of the reference for the modification. (IE6+, N6+ DOM1)
- ■ **dateTime**   String containing the date the modification was made. (IE6+, N6+, DOM1)

Methods

This element has the methods listed in the Generic HTML Element Object found at the beginning of this section.

Event Handlers

```
onactivate onbeforedeactivate onblur oncontrolselect ondeactivate onfocus
onmove onmoveend onmovestart onreadystatechange onresizeend onresizestart
ontimeerror
```

Support

Supported in Internet Explorer 4+, Netscape 6+, DOM1.

isindex

The HTML element <isindex> is deprecated thus so is its corresponding JavaScript object. See MSDN, W3C DOM, or **developer.netscape.com** for more information about the properties it supplies. Briefly, they are **form** (a reference to the enclosing **Form**) and **prompt** (the prompt string).

java (Browser Object)

See **Packages**.

kbd (Document Object)

This object corresponds to a **<kbd>** (keyboard input) element in the document. It has the properties and methods listed in the Generic HTML Element Object found at the beginning of this section.

Support

Supported in Internet Explorer 4+, Netscape 6+, DOM1.

Event Handlers

```
onactivate onbeforeactivate onbeforecut onbeforedeactivate onbeforepaste
onblur onclick oncontextmenu oncontrolselect oncut ondblclick ondeactivate
ondrag ondragend ondragenter ondragleave ondragover ondragstart ondrop
onfocus onfocusin onfocusout onhelp onkeydown onkeypress onkeyup
onlosecapture onmousedown onmouseenter onmouseleave onmousemove onmouseout
onmouseover onmouseup onmousewheel onmove onmoveend onmovestart onpaste
onpropertychange onreadystatechange onresize onresizeend onresizestart
onselectstart ontimeerror
```

label (Document Object)

This object corresponds to a **<label>** (form field label) element in the document. Access to this object is achieved through standard DOM methods (for example, **getElementById()**).

Properties

This object has the following properties, in addition to those in the Generic HTML Element Object found at the beginning of this section.

- ■ **accessKey**   Single character string indicating the hotkey that gives the element focus.*
  (IE4+, N6+, DOM1)
- ■ **dataFld**   String specifying which field of a data source is bound to the element.* (IE4+)
- ■ **dataFormatAs**   String indicating how the element treats data supplied to it.* (IE4+)
- ■ **dataSrc**   String containing the source of data for data binding.* (IE4+)
- ■ **form**   Reference to the **Form** the label is enclosed within. (IE4+, N6+, DOM1)
- ■ **htmlFor**   String containing the identifier of the object the label is for.
  (IE4+, N6+, DOM1)

Methods

This element has the methods listed in the Generic HTML Element Object found at the beginning of this section.

Event Handlers

```
onactivate onafterupdate onbeforeactivate onbeforecut onbeforedeactivate
onbeforepaste onbeforeupdate onblur onclick oncontextmenu oncontrolselect
```

APPENDIXES

onecut ondblclick ondeactivate onerrorupdate onfocus onfocusin onfocusout
onhelp onkeydown onkeypress onkeyup onlosecapture onmousedown onmouseenter
onmouseleave onmousemove onmouseout onmouseover onmouseup onmousewheel
onmove onmoveend onmovestart onpaste onpropertychange onreadystatechange
onresize onresizeend onresizestart ontimeerror

Support
Supported in Internet Explorer 4+, Netscape 6+, DOM1.

Layer (Document Browser/Object)

Layer objects correspond to **<layer>** or **<ilayer>** elements and are supported in Netscape 4 only. This object was deprecated in favor of the standard **<div>** element which provides very similar functionality.

Properties

- **above**   Reference to the **Layer** above the current layer according to the z-index order among all layers in the document (**null** if the current layer is topmost). (N4)

- **background**   String specifying the URL of the background image for the layer. (N4)

- **below**   Reference to the **Layer** below the current layer according to the z-index order among all layers in the document (**null** if the current layer is the bottommost). (N4)

- **bgColor**   String value indicating the named color or hexadecimal triplet of the layer's background color (e.g., "#FF00FF"). (N4)

- **clip.bottom, clip.height, clip.left, clip.right, clip.top, clip.width**   Numeric (pixel) values defining the rectangular clipping area of the layer. Any content outside of this rectangle is not displayed. (N4)

- **document**   Reference to the **Document** object of the layer. This is a full-featured **Document** object, complete with the **images[ ]** and related collections. Often used to **write()** content to a layer. (N4, ReadOnly)

- **left**   Pixel value indicating x coordinate of the left edge of the layer. If the layer's **position** attribute is "absolute," this placement is relative to the origin of its parent (enclosing) layer. Otherwise this placement is relative to the content surrounding it. You may use string values with this property to indicate units other than pixels, for example "25%." (N4)

- **name**   The value of the **name** or **id** attribute for the layer. (N4, ReadOnly)

- **pageX**   Numeric or string value indicating the layer's horizontal position relative to the visible page. (N4)

- **pageY**   Numeric or string value indicating the layer's vertical position relative to the visible page. (N4)

- **parentLayer**   Reference to **Layer** in which the current layer is contained (or to the **Window** object if no such layer exists). (N4)

- **siblingAbove**   Reference to the **Layer** above the current layer according to the z-index order among all layers that share the same parent as the current layer. **null** if it is the topmost. (N4)

- **siblingBelow**   Reference to the **Layer** below the current layer according to the z-index order among all layers that share the same parent as the current layer, **null** if it is the topmost. (N4)

- **src**   String indicating the URL of the layer's content. (N4)

- **top**   Pixel value indicating *y* coordinate of the top edge of the layer. If the layer's **position** attribute is "absolute," this placement is relative to the origin of its parent (enclosing) layer. Otherwise this placement is relative to the content surrounding it. You may use string values with this property to indicate units other than pixels, for example "25%." (N4)

- **visibility**   String indicating whether the layer is visible. A value of "show" makes the layer visible, "hide" makes it invisible, and "inherit" causes it to inherit the visibility property of its parent layer. (N4)

- **window**   Reference to the window or frame containing the layer. (N4, ReadOnly)

- **x**   Synonym for **left**. (N4)

- **y**   Synonym for **top**. (N4)

- **zIndex**   The relative z-index of the layer (with respect to its siblings). (N4)

Methods

- **captureEvents(eventMask)**   Instructs layer to capture the events given in the bitmask *eventMask*.* (N4)

- **handleEvent(event)**   Causes the **Event** instance to be processed by the appropriate handler of the layer.* (N4)

- **load( )**   Causes the browser to reload the src of the layer. (N4)

- **moveAbove(whichLayer)**   Causes the layer to be placed above the **Layer** referenced by *whichLayer*. (N4)

- **moveBelow(whichLayer)**   Causes the layer to be placed below the **Layer** referenced by *whichLayer*. (N4)

- **moveBy(x, y)**   Moves the layer *x* pixels horizontally and *y* pixels vertically from its current position. (N4)

- **moveTo(x, y)**   Moves the layer to the *x* and *y* coordinates relative to its parent layer (if absolutely positioned) or relative to its surrounding content (if relatively positioned). (N4)

- **moveToAbsolute(x, y)**   Moves the layer to the *x* and *y* coordinates relative to the visible page. (N4)

- **releaseEvents(eventMask)**   Instructs layer to stop capturing the events given in the bitmask *eventMask*.* (N4)

- **resizeBy(dWidth, dHeight)**   Grows or shrinks the layer by the number of pixels given in the arguments. Negative values cause the layer to shrink. (N4)

- **resizeTo(width, height)**   Resizes the layer to the size in pixels given by the arguments. (N4)

- **routeEvent(event)**   Passes the **Event** instance *event* along normally down the hierarchy. Used to decline to handle an event.* (N4)

Event Handlers

onmouseover onmouseout onload onfocus onblur

legend (Document Object)

This object corresponds to a **<legend>** (fieldset caption) element in the document. Access to this object is achieved through standard DOM methods (for example, **getElementById()**).

Properties

This object has the following properties, in addition to those in the Generic HTML Element Object found at the beginning of this section.

- **accessKey**   Single character string indicating the hotkey that gives the element focus.* (IE4+, N6+, DOM1)
- **align**   String specifying the alignment of the element, for example "left."* (IE4+, N6+, DOM1)
- **dataFld**   String specifying which field of a data source is bound to the element.* (IE4+)
- **dataFormatAs**   String indicating how the element treats data supplied to it.* (IE4+)
- **dataSrc**   String containing the source of data for data binding.* (IE4+)
- **form**   Reference to the **Form** in which the element is enclosed. (IE4+, N6+, DOM1)

Methods

This element has the methods listed in the Generic HTML Element Object found at the beginning of this section.

Event Handlers

This object has the event handlers listed in the Generic HTML Element Object found at the beginning of this section, in addition to the following:

onafterupdate onbeforeupdate onerrorupdate

Support

Supported in Internet Explorer 4+, Netscape 6+, DOM1.

li (Document Object)

This object corresponds to a **<li>** (list item) element in the document. Access to this object is achieved through standard DOM methods (for example, **getElementById()**).

Properties

This object has the following properties, in addition to those in the Generic HTML Element Object found at the beginning of this section.

- **type**   String indicating the type of bullet to be used, for example "disc," "circle," or "square" for unordered lists. (IE4+, N6+, DOM1)
- **value**   Integer indicating the item number for this item. (IE4+, N6+, DOM1)

Methods

This element has the methods listed in the Generic HTML Element Object found at the beginning of this section.

Event Handlers

This object has the event handlers listed in the Generic HTML Element Object found at the beginning of this section, in addition to the following:

 `onlayoutcomplete`

Support

Supported in Internet Explorer 4+, Netscape 6+, DOM1.

link (Document Object)

This object corresponds to a **<link>** (externally linked file) element in the document. For information about the traditional **Link** object (corresponding to a **<a href=""></a>**), see the entry for **a**. Access to this object is achieved through standard DOM methods (for example, **getElementById()**).

Properties

This object has the following properties, in addition to those in the Generic HTML Element Object found at the beginning of this section.

- **charset**   String indicating the character set of the linked document. (IE6+, N6+, DOM1)
- **disabled**   Boolean indicating whether the element is disabled (grayed out). (IE4+, N6+, DOM1)
- **href**   String holding the value of the **href** attribute, the document to load when the link is activated. Defined for **Link** in traditional models. (IE3+, N2+, DOM1)
- **hreflang**   String indicating the language code of the linked resource. (N6+, IE6+, DOM1)
- **media**   String indicating the media the linked document is intended for. (N6+, DOM1)
- **rel**   String holding the value of the **rel** property of the element. Used to specify the relationship between documents, but currently ignored by most browsers. (IE4+, N6+, DOM1)
- **rev**   String holding the value of the **rev** property of the element. Used to specify the relationship between documents, but currently ignored by most browsers. (IE4+, N6+, DOM1)
- **target**   Specifies the target window for a hypertext source link referencing frames. (IE4+, N6+, DOM1)
- **type**   String specifying the advisory content type . (IE4+, N6+, DOM1)

Methods

This element has the methods listed in the Generic HTML Element Object found at the beginning of this section.

Event Handlers

```
onload onreadystatechange
```

Support

Supported in Internet Explorer 4+, Netscape 6+, DOM1.

Location (Browser Object)

The **Location** object provides access to URLs and pieces of URLs in a convenient fashion. Assigning a string to a **Location** object causes the browser to automatically parse the string as a URL, update the object's properties, and set the string itself as the **href** property of the object. While most browsers will automatically reflect changes to any property of this object, it is safer to assign the new, complete URL to the **href** attribute or the object itself to ensure that changes are properly reflected by the browser.

Properties

- **hash**   String containing the portion of the URL following the hash mark (#), if it exists. (IE3+, N2+)

- **host**   String containing the host name and port of the URL (although some implementations do not include the port). (IE3+, N2+)

- **hostname**   String containing the host name (domain name). (IE3+, N2+)

- **href**   String containing the entire URL. (IE3+, N2+)

- **pathname**   String containing the path (directory) portion of the URL. Always at least "/". (IE3+, N2+)

- **port**   String containing the port number (if one was specified). (IE3+, N2+)

- **protocol**   String containing the protocol and trailing colon (for example, "http:"). (IE3+, N2+)

- **search**   String containing the portion of the URL after the filename (including the "?" delimiter if it was specified). (IE3+, N2+)

Methods

- **assign(url)**   Assigns the URL in the string *url* to the object (just like assigning *url* to the object). (IE3+, N2+)

- **reload(forceGET)**   Reloads the URL in the current object. The Boolean *forceGET* parameter (when **true**) supposedly forces the browser to bypass cache and refetch the document, but experimentation shows that this feature can hardly ever be relied upon. (IE4+, N3+)

- **replace(url)**   Loads the URL given in the string *url* over the current one found in the object. That is, the new URL replaces the old in the browser's history (rather than creating a new entry). (IE4+, N3+)

Support

Supported in IE3+ (JScript 1.0+), N2+ (JavaScript 1.0+).

map (Document Object)

This object corresponds to a **<map>** (client-side image map) element in the document. Access to this object is achieved through standard DOM methods like **getElementById()**.

Properties

- **areas[ ]**   Collection of **area**s enclosed by the object. (IE4+, N6+, ReadOnly)
- **name**   String holding the name of the image map (for use with **usemap**). (IE4+, N6+)

Methods

This element has the methods listed in the Generic HTML Element Object found at the beginning of this section.

Event Handlers

```
onbeforeactivate onbeforecut onbeforepaste onclick oncut ondblclick ondrag
ondragend ondragenter ondragleave ondragover ondragstart ondrop onfocusin
onfocusout onhelp onkeydown onkeypress onkeyup onlosecapture onmousedown
onmouseenter onmouseleave onmousemove onmouseout onmouseover onmouseup
onmousewheel onpaste onpropertychange onreadystatechange onscroll
onselectstart
```

Support

Supported in Internet Explorer 4+, Netscape 6+, DOM1.

marquee (Document Object)

This object corresponds to a (nonstandard) **<marquee>** element in the document. Access to this object is achieved through standard DOM methods like **getElementById()**. See documentation at the support site for full details.

Support

Supported in Internet Explorer 4+.

Math (Built-in Object)

The **Math** object provides constants and methods that permit more advanced mathematical calculations than JavaScript's native arithmetic operators. All trigonometric methods treat values as radians, so you need to multiple any degree values by **Math.PI/180** before passing them to one of these functions.

All properties and methods of this object are static (class properties), so they are accessed through **Math** itself rather than an object instance.

Properties

- **E**   Numeric value containing the base of the natural logarithm (Euler's constant *e*). (IE3+ (JScript 1.0+), N2+ (JavaScript 1.0+), ECMA Edition 1, Static, ReadOnly)

- **LN2** Numeric value containing the natural logarithm of 2. (IE3+ (JScript 1.0+), N2+ (JavaScript 1.0+), ECMA Edition 1, Static, ReadOnly)

- **LN10** Numeric value containing the natural logarithm of 10. (IE3+ (JScript 1.0+), N2+ (JavaScript 1.0+), ECMA Edition 1, Static, ReadOnly)

- **LOG2E** Numeric value containing the logarithm base 2 of *e*. (IE3+ (JScript 1.0+), N2+ (JavaScript 1.0+), ECMA Edition 1, Static, ReadOnly)

- **LOG10E** Numeric value containing the logarithm base 10 of *e*. (IE3+ (JScript 1.0+), N2+ (JavaScript 1.0+), ECMA Edition 1, Static, ReadOnly)

- **PI** Numeric value of pi (π). (IE3+ (JScript 1.0+), N2+ (JavaScript 1.0+), ECMA Edition 1, Static, ReadOnly)

- **SQRT1_2** Numeric value containing the square root of one-half. (IE3+ (JScript 1.0+), N2+ (JavaScript 1.0+), ECMA Edition 1, Static, ReadOnly)

- **SQRT2** Numeric value containing the square root of two. (E3+ (JScript 1.0+), N2+ (JavaScript 1.0+), ECMA Edition 1, Static, ReadOnly)

Methods

- **abs(arg)** Returns the absolute value of *arg*. (IE3+ (JScript 1.0+), N2+ (JavaScript 1.0+), ECMA Edition 1, Static)

- **acos(arg)** Returns the arc cosine of *arg*. (IE3+ (JScript 1.0+), N2+ (JavaScript 1.0+), ECMA Edition 1, Static)

- **asin(arg)** Returns the arc sine of *arg*. (IE3+ (JScript 1.0+), N2+ (JavaScript 1.0+), ECMA Edition 1, Static)

- **atan(arg)** Returns the arc tangent of *arg*. (IE3+ (JScript 1.0+), N2+ (JavaScript 1.0+), ECMA Edition 1, Static)

- **atan2(y, x)** Returns the angle between the *X* axis and the point (*x*, *y*) in the Cartesian coordinate system, measured counterclockwise (like polar coordinates). Note how *y* is passed as the first argument rather than the second. (IE3+ (JScript 1.0+), N2+ (JavaScript 1.0+), ECMA Edition 1, Static)

- **ceil(arg)** Returns the ceiling of *arg* (the smallest integer greater than or equal to *arg*). (IE3+ (JScript 1.0+), N2+ (JavaScript 1.0+), ECMA Edition 1, Static)

- **cos(arg)** Returns the cosine of *arg*. (IE3+ (JScript 1.0+), N2+ (JavaScript 1.0+), ECMA Edition 1, Static)

- **exp(arg)** Returns *e* to *arg* power. (IE3+ (JScript 1.0+), N2+ (JavaScript 1.0+), ECMA Edition 1,Static)

- **floor(arg)** Returns the floor of *arg* (the greatest integer less than or equal to *arg*). (IE3+ (JScript 1.0+), N2+ (JavaScript 1.0+), ECMA Edition 1, Static)

- **log(arg)** Returns the natural logarithm of *arg* (log base *e* of *arg*). (IE3+ (JScript 1.0+), N2+ (JavaScript 1.0+), ECMA Edition 1, Static)

- **max(arg1, arg2)** Returns the greater of *arg1* or *arg2*. (IE3+ (JScript 1.0+), N2+ (JavaScript 1.0+), ECMA Edition 1, Static)

- **min(arg1, arg2)** Returns the lesser of *arg1* or *arg2*. (IE3+ (JScript 1.0+), N2+ (JavaScript 1.0+), ECMA Edition 1, Static)

- **pow(arg1, arg2)** Returns *arg1* to the *arg2* power. (IE3+ (JScript 1.0+), N2+ (JavaScript 1.0+), ECMA Edition 1, Static)

- **random()** Returns a random number in the interval **[0,1]**. (IE3+ (JScript 1.0+), N3+ (JavaScript 1.1+), ECMA Edition 1, Static)

- **round(arg)** Returns the result of rounding *arg* to the nearest integer. If the decimal portion of *arg* is greater than or equal to **.5**, it is rounded up. Otherwise *arg* is rounded down. (IE3+ (JScript 1.0+), N2+ (JavaScript 1.0+), ECMA Edition 1, Static)

- **sin(arg)** Returns the sine of *arg*. (IE3+ (JScript 1.0+), N2+ (JavaScript 1.0+), ECMA Edition 1, Static)

- **sqrt(arg)** Returns the square root of *arg*. (IE3+ (JScript 1.0+), N2+ (JavaScript 1.0+), ECMA Edition 1, Static)

- **tan(arg)** Returns the tangent of *arg*. (IE3+ (JScript 1.0+), N2+ (JavaScript 1.0+), ECMA Edition 1, Static)

Support

IE3+ (JScript 1.0+), N2+ (JavaScript 1.0+), ECMA Edition 1

Notes

If the argument to one of **Math**'s methods cannot be converted to a number, **NaN** is generally returned.

menu (Document Object)

This object corresponds to a **<menu>** (menu list) element in the document. Access to this object is achieved through standard DOM methods (for example, **getElementById()**).

Properties

This object has the following property, in addition to those in the Generic HTML Element Object found at the beginning of this section.

- **compact** Boolean indicating whether the list should be compacted by removing extra space between list objects. (IE6+, N6+, DOM1)

Methods

This element has the methods listed in the Generic HTML Element Object found at the beginning of this section.

Event Handlers

This object has the event handlers listed in the Generic HTML Element Object found at the beginning of this section.

Support

Supported in Internet Explorer 4+, Netscape 6+, DOM1.

meta (Document Object)

This object corresponds to a **<meta>** element in the document. Access to this object is achieved through standard DOM methods (for example, **getElementById()**), but you might have to use **document.documentElement.getElementsByTagName()** or a similar method because multiple **<meta>** tags are found in the document head.

Properties

This object has the following properties, in addition to those in the Generic HTML Element Object found at the beginning of this section.

- **charset**   Sets the character set used to encode the object. (IE4+, N6+, DOM1)
- **content**   Specifies the character set used to encode the document. (IE4+, N6+, DOM1)
- **httpEquiv**   String holding the HTTP header name. (IE4+, N6+, DOM1)
- **name**   String holding the name attribute of the element. (IE4+, N6+, DOM1)
- **scheme**   String containing the scheme to use to interpret the value of the header. (IE6+, N6+, DOM1)

Methods

This element has the methods listed in the Generic HTML Element Object found at the beginning of this section.

Event Handlers

```
onlayoutcomplete
```

Support

Supported in Internet Explorer 4+, Netscape 6+, DOM1.

mimeType (Browser object)

Instances of **mimeType** objects are accessed through the array **navigator.mimeTypes[ ]** or through a **Plugin** object. They provide basic information regarding the MIME types the browser and its plugins can handle as well as on what types and filename suffixes are associated with each **Plugin**.

Examination of the **navigator.mimeTypes[ ]** array permits the programmer to determine whether a particular MIME type is supported and, if so, to extract information about the **Plugin** that handles it. Examination of a **Plugin** object permits the programmer to extract information about the plugin as well as determine what MIME types it is currently configured to handle.

Properties

- **description**   String containing a human-friendly description of the MIME type. (N3+, ReadOnly)
- **enabledPlugin**   Reference to the **Plugin** object that handles this MIME type. If this MIME type is not associated with a **Plugin**, this property is **null**. (N3+, ReadOnly)

- **suffixes**   String containing a comma-separated list of filename extensions (for example, "mid, wav, mp3") that are commonly associated with this MIME type. (N3+, ReadOnly)

- **type**   String containing the actual MIME type of the object in *mediatype/subtype* format, for example "image/gif." (N3+, ReadOnly)

Methods

None.

Support

Netscape 3+ (JavaScript 1.1+).

Notes

Verifying the existence of a particular MIME type in the **mimeTypes[ ]** array is not a guarantee that the browser can handle the data; you also need to check the **mimeType** object's **enabledPlugin** property.

namespace (Browser object)

The **namespace** object allows you to import a DHTML Element Behavior (custom tag) dynamically, that is, during or after the page load. Its capabilities are outside of the scope of this book, but its methods are fairly straightforward. See Microsoft documentation.

Support

Internet Explorer 5.5+ in Windows.

Navigator (Browser object)

The **Navigator** object makes information about the client browser available to JavaScript. This object is most commonly used for "browser detection," but also contains a wealth of detail about the user's configuration, language of preference, and operating system. Although the **Navigator** object was originally implemented in Netscape Navigator (hence the name), it is supported by most major browsers and has become the de facto standard for accessing configuration information. The entire **Navigator** object is ReadOnly.

Properties

- **appCodeName**   String containing the code name of the browser, for example "Mozilla." (IE3+, NS2+, ReadOnly)

- **appMinorVersion**   String containing the browser's minor version value. (IE4+, ReadOnly)

- **appName**   String containing the name of the browser, for example "Internet Explorer" or "Netscape." (IE3+, NS2+, ReadOnly)

- **appVersion**   String containing the browser's version information. (IE3+, NS2+, ReadOnly)

- **browserLanguage**   String containing the language code of the browser or the operating system. IE4 returns the language of the browser while IE5+ returns the language of the operating system. It does *not* reflect changes made by the user to the browser's language setting. (IE4+, ReadOnly)

■ **cookieEnabled**   Boolean indicating whether persistent cookies are enabled. Does not indicate whether session cookies are enabled. (IE4+, N6+, ReadOnly)

■ **cpuClass**   String indicating the CPU of the client computer. Typical values include "x86," "68K," "Alpha," "PPC" (PowerPC), or "Other." (IE4+, ReadOnly)

■ **language**   String indicating the language code of the browser, for example "en-US." (NS4+, ReadOnly)

■ **mimeTypes[ ]**   Array of **MimeType** objects indicating which MIME types the browser supports. This property is defined in IE5.5, but appears empty. This array can be directly indexed to check for support for a particular MIME type, for example as "if (navigator.mimeTypes['video/mpeg'] && navigator.mimeTypes['video/mpeg'].pluginEnabled)..."(NS2+, ReadOnly)

■ **onLine**   Boolean indicating whether the user is in global offline mode. Global offline mode allows IE to browse local (possibly downloaded) pages while not connected to the network. (IE4+, ReadOnly)

■ **oscpu**   String containing operating system (and sometimes CPU) information, for example "Win98."(N6+, ReadOnly)

■ **platform**   String containing the operating system for which the browser was compiled. Typical values include "Win32," "Win16," "MacPPC," Mac68K," and "SunOS." Under unusual circumstances, could be different from the actual operating system the client is using. (IE4+, N4+, ReadOnly)

■ **plugins[ ]**   In Netscape, an array of **Plugin** objects installed in the browser. Indexed by integer or string referring to the name a plugin. Each **Plugin** is itself an array of **mimeType** objects. The **plugins** array provides the **refresh(reloadDocs)** method that causes newly installed plugins to be reflected in the array. When invoked with *reloadDocs* as **true**, reloads all the **<embed>**s in the window (in order to take advantage of a newly installed plugin). In IE this collection is a synonym for **document.embeds[ ]**, so it cannot be used for plugin detection. (IE4+, N3+, ReadOnly)

■ **product**   String containing the name of the "product," in Netscape 6 the name of its engine, "Gecko." (N6+, ReadOnly)

■ **productSub**   String containing the version information about the "product," apparently the build date string (for example, "20010131"). (N6+, ReadOnly)

■ **systemLanguage**   String containing the language edition of the client's operating system, for example "en-us." (IE4+, ReadOnly)

■ **userAgent**   String containing the value of the HTTP *User-Agent* header the browser sends. This property is most commonly used for browser detection and includes much of the information found in other properties of **Navigator** (for example, language information). (IE3+, N2+, ReadOnly)

■ **userLanguage**   String containing the language code of the user's "natural" language as defined in the operating system specific (Windows) setting. (IE4+, ReadOnly)

■ **userProfile**   Reference to the **userProfile** object for the browser. (IE3+, ReadOnly)

■ **vendor**   String containing browser vendor information, for example "Netscape6." (N6+, ReadOnly)

■ **vendorSub**   String containing vendor version information, for example "6.01." (N6+, ReadOnly)

Methods

- **javaEnabled( )**   Returns a Boolean indicating whether Java is enabled. (IE4+, N3+)
- **preference(preferenceName [, value])**   Invoked by signed scripts with the appropriate privileges to get and set browser preferences. The *preferenceName* is a string containing the name of the preference to be set or gotten. If *value* is given, the preference *preferenceName* is set to *value*. If *value* is omitted, the current value of *preferenceName* is returned. Reading privileges requires the UniversalPreferencesRead privilege. Writing preferences requires UniversalPreferencesWrite. See the following table for potential values for *preferenceName* and *value*. (N4+)
- **savePreferences( )**   Invoked by signed scripts to save the current browser preferences. These preferences are saved to the local file prefs.js (or preferences.js in UNIX). Note that the preferences are saved automatically before quitting the browser. This method requires the UniversalPreferencesWrite privilege. (N4+)
- **taintEnabled( )**   Returns a Boolean indicating whether data tainting is enabled. Data tainting is used to prevent scripts from passing private information to remote servers but is no longer a supported technology. (IE5.5+, N3 only) Why this method is supported in IE5.5 is unknown; perhaps Microsoft intends to resurrect this technology. Whatever the case, support is very poor, so its use should be avoided.

To do this...	Set this preference...	To this value...
Automatically load images	general.always_load_images	**true** or **false**
Enable Java	security.enable_java	**true** or **false**
Enable JavaScript	javascript.enabled	**true** or **false**
Enable stylesheets	browser.enable_style_sheets	**true** or **false**
Enable SmartUpdate	Autoupdate.enabled	**true** or **false**
Accept all cookies	network.cookie.cookieBehavior	**0**
Accept only cookies that get sent back to the originating server	network.cookie.cookieBehavior	**1**
Disable cookies	network.cookie.cookieBehavior	**2**
Warn before accepting cookies	network.cookie.warnAboutCookies	**true** or **false**

Support
Supported in IE3+, N2+.

netscape (Browser Object)

See **Packages**.

r (Document Object)

This object corresponds to a (nonstandard) **<nobr>** (text rendered without linebreaks) element in the document. Access to this object is achieved through standard DOM methods (for example, **getElementById()**). See MSDN or the support site for complete details.

Support

Supported in IE4+.

noframes (Document Object)

This object corresponds to a **<noframes>** (content for agents without frame support) element in the document. It has the properties and methods listed in the Generic HTML Element Object found at the beginning of this section.

Event Handlers

 onreadystatechange

Support

Supported in Internet Explorer 4+, Netscape 6+, DOM1.

noscript (Document Object)

This document object corresponds to a **<noscript>** (content for browsers that do not support scripting) element in the document. It has the properties and methods listed in the Generic HTML Element Object found at the beginning of this section.

Event Handlers

 onreadystatechange

Support

Supported in Internet Explorer 4+, Netscape 6+, DOM1.

Number (Built-in Object)

Number is the container object for the primitive number data type. The primary use of this object is accessing its methods for number formatting and using its static (class) properties, which define useful numeric constants.

Constructor

var *instanceName* = **new** Number(*initialValue*);

where *initialValue* is a number or a string which will be converted to a number. Omitting *initialValue* creates a **Number** with value zero.

Properties

- **MAX_VALUE** Constant holding the largest possible numeric value that can be represented. (IE4+ (JScript 2.0+), N3+ (JavaScript 1.1+), ECMA Edition 1, Static, ReadOnly)
- **MIN_VALUE** Constant holding the smallest possible numeric value that can be represented. (IE4+ (JScript 2.0+), N3+ (JavaScript 1.1+), ECMA Edition 1, Static, ReadOnly)
- **NaN** Constant holding the value **NaN**. (IE4+ (JScript 2.0+), N3+ (JavaScript 1.1+), ECMA Edition 1, Static, ReadOnly)
- **NEGATIVE_INFINITY** Constant holding the value **-Infinity**. (IE4+ (JScript 2.0+), N3+ (JavaScript 1.1+), ECMA Edition 1, Static, ReadOnly)
- **POSITIVE_INFINITY** Constant holding the value **Infinity**. (IE4+ (JScript 2.0+), N3+ (JavaScript 1.1+), ECMA Edition 1, Static ReadOnly)
- **prototype** Reference to the object's prototype. (IE4+ (JScript 2.0+), N3+ (JavaScript 1.1+), ECMA Edition 1)

Methods

- **toExponential([fracDigits])** Returns a string holding the number in exponential notation. If specified, only the number of digits given in *facDigits* will be used after the decimal point. (IE5.5+ (JScript 5.5+), N6+ (JavaScript 1.5+), ECMA Edition 3)
- **toFixed([fracDigits])** Returns a string holding the number in fixed-point notation. If specified, only the number of digits given in *fracDigits* will be used after the decimal point. (IE5.5+ (JScript 5.5+), N6+ (JavaScript 1.5+), ECMA Edition 3)
- **toPrecision([numDigits])** Returns a string holding the number in fixed-point or exponential notation rounded to the number of digits after the decimal point given in *numDigits*. (IE5.5+ (JScript 5.5+), N6+ (JavaScript 1.5+), ECMA Edition 3)
- **toLocaleString( )** Returns a string holding the value of the number formatted according to local (operating system) conventions. (IE5.5+ (JScript 5.5+), N6+ (JavaScript 1.5+), ECMA Edition 3)
- **toString([radix])** Returns the number as a string in base *radix* (defaults to **10**). (IE4+ (JScript 2.0+), N3+ (JavaScript 1.1+), ECMA Edition 1)
- **valueOf( )** Returns the primitive number value of the object. (IE4+ (JScript 2.0+), N3+ (JavaScript 1.1+), ECMA Edition 1)

Support
Supported in IE3+ (JScript 1.0+), N3+ (JavaScript 1.1+), ECMAScript Edition 1.

Notes
To use **Number** methods on number literals, use a space between the literal and the dot operator. For example, "3.14159265 **.toExponential**()."

Object (Built-in Object)

Object is the basic object from which all other objects are derived. It defines methods common to all objects that are often overridden to provide functionality specific to each object type. For

...ple, the **Array** object provides a **toString()** method that functions as one would expect an array's **toString()** method to behave.

This object also permits the creation of user-defined objects and instances are quite often used as associative arrays.

Constructor

var *instanceName* = **new** Object( );

This statement creates a new (generic) object.

Properties

- **prototype**   The prototype for the object. This object defines the properties and methods common to all objects of this type. (IE4+ (JScript 3.0+), N3+ (JavaScript 1.1+), ECMA Edition 1)

Methods

- **toSource( )**   Returns a string containing a JavaScript literal that describes the object. (N4.06+ (JavaScript 1.3+))

- **toString( )**   Returns the object a string, by default "[object Object]". Very often overridden to provide specific functionality. (IE4+ (JScript 3.0+), N2+ (JavaScript 1.0+), ECMA Edition 1)

- **unwatch(property)**   Disables watching of the object's property given by the string *property*. (N4+ (JavaScript 1.2+))

- **valueOf( )**   Returns the primitive value associated with the object, by default the string "[object Object]". Often overridden to provide specific functionality. (IE4+ (JScript 3.0+), N3+ (JavaScript 1.1+), ECMA Edition 1)

- **watch(property, handler)**   Sets a watch on the object's property given in string *property*. Whenever the value of the property changes, the function *handler* is invoked with three arguments: the name of the property, the old value, and the new value it is being set to. The *handler* can override the setting of the new value by returning a value, which is set in its place. (N4+ (JavaScript 1.2+))

Event Handlers
None.

Support
Supported in IE4+ (JScript 3.0+), N2+ (JavaScript 1.0+), ECMAScript Edition 1.

object (Document Object)

This object corresponds to an **<object>** (embedded object) element in the document. Access to this object is achieved through standard DOM methods like **getElementById()**.

Properties

This object has the following properties, in addition to those in the Generic HTML Element Object found at the beginning of this section. It will also have any properties exposed by the embedded object (for example, public java class variables).

- ■ **align**   String specifying the alignment of the element, for example "left."*
  (IE4+, N6+, DOM1)
- ■ **alt**   Sets a text alternative to the object. (IE6+)
- ■ **altHtml**   Sets the optional alternative HTML script to execute if the object fails to load.
  (IE4+, WriteOnly)
- ■ **archive**   Sets a character string that can be used to implement your own archive
  functionality for the object. See Microsoft or DOM documentation. (IE6+, N6+, DOM1)
- ■ **BaseHref**   Retrieves a string of the URL where the object tag can be found. (IE3+)
- ■ **border**   Sets the width of the border to draw around the object. (IE6+, N6+, DOM1)
- ■ **classid**   String containing the class identifier of the object. Used with Java applets or
  ActiveX controls. (IE3+)
- ■ **code**   Sets the URL of the file containing the compiled Java class. Using **classid** and
  codebase is far more common. (IE4+, N6+, DOM1)
- ■ **codeBase**   Sets the URL of the embedded object. (IE3+, N6+, DOM1)
- ■ **codeType**   Sets the MIME type for the object. (IE3+, N6+, DOM1)
- ■ **data**   Sets the URL that references data intended for the object. (IE3+, DOM1)
- ■ **dataFld**   String specifying which field of a data source is bound to the element.* (IE4+)
- ■ **dataFormatAs**   String indicating how the element treats data supplied to it.* (IE4+)
- ■ **dataSrc**   String containing the source of data for data binding.* (IE4+)
- ■ **declare**   Sets a character string that can be used to implement your own **declare**
  functionality for the object. There is none by default. (IE6+, N6+, DOM1)
- ■ **form**   Reference to the form that the object is embedded in or **null** otherwise.
  (IE4+, N6+, DOM1)
- ■ **height**   Specifies the height in pixels of the object. (IE3+, N6+, DOM1)
- ■ **hspace**   Sets the horizontal margin for the object. (IE3+, N6+, DOM1)
- ■ **name**   String holding the **name** attribute of the element. (IE4+, N6+, DOM1)
- ■ **standby**   Sets a character string that can be used to implement your own **standby**
  functionality for the object. There is no functionality by default. (IE6+, N6+, DOM1)
- ■ **tabIndex**   Numeric value indicating the tab order for the object.* (IE4+, N6+, DOM1)
- ■ **type**   Specifies the MIME type for the data the object uses. (N6+, IE6+, DOM1)
- ■ **useMap**   Sets the URL, often with a bookmark extension (#name), to use as a client-side
  image map. (IE6+, N6+, DOM1)
- ■ **vspace**   Sets the vertical margin for the object. (IE3+, N6+, DOM1)
- ■ **width**   Specifies the width of the object in pixels. (IE3+, N6+, DOM1)

Methods

This element has the methods listed in the Generic HTML Element Object found at the beginning of this section. It will also have any methods exposed by the embedded object.

Event Handlers

```
onactivate onbeforedeactivate onbeforeeditfocus onblur oncellchange onclick
oncontrolselect ondataavailable ondatasetchanged ondatasetcomplete
ondblclick ondeactivate ondrag ondragend ondragenter ondragleave ondragover
ondragstart ondrop onerror onfocus onkeydown onkeypress onkeyup
onlosecapture onmove onmoveend onmovestart onpropertychange
onreadystatechange onresize onresizeend onresizestart onrowenter onrowexit
onrowsdelete onrowsinserted onscroll onselectstart
```

Support

Supported in IE4+, N6+, DOM1.

ol (Document Object)

This object corresponds to an **<ol>** (ordered list) element in the document. Access to these objects is achieved through standard DOM methods (for example, **getElementById()**).

Properties

This object has the following properties, in addition to those in the Generic HTML Element Object found at the beginning of this section.

- ■ **compact** Boolean indicating whether the list should be compacted by removing extra space between list objects. (IE4+, N6+, DOM1)
- ■ **start** Sets the starting number or letter, for example 3 or "C". Often used in conjunction with the **type** property. (IE4+, N6+, DOM1)
- ■ **type** Sets the style of list numbering: "1" for numbers, "a" for lowercase letters, "A" for uppercase letters, or "i" or "I" for uppercase or lowercase roman numerals. (IE3+, N6+, DOM1)

Methods

This element has the methods listed in the Generic HTML Element Object found at the beginning of this section.

Event Handlers

This object has the event handlers listed in the Generic HTML Element Object found at the beginning of this section, in addition to the following:

```
onlayoutcomplete
```

Support

Supported in Internet Explorer 4+, Netscape 6+, DOM1.

optgroup (Document Object)

This object corresponds to an **<optgroup>** (option grouping within a **<select>**) element in the document. Access to this object is achieved through standard DOM methods (for example, **getElementById()**).

Properties

This object has the following properties, in addition to those in the Generic HTML Element Object found at the beginning of this section.

- **disabled**   Boolean indicating whether the element is disabled (grayed out). (IE4+, N6+, DOM1)
- **label**   String that sets the label for the option group. (IE6+, N6+, DOM1)

Methods

This element has the methods listed in the Generic HTML Element Object found at the beginning of this section.

Event Handlers

None.

Support

Supported in IE6+, N6+, DOM1.

option (Document Object)

This object corresponds to an **<option>** element in the document. Such elements are found enclosed by **<select>** form fields. Access to this object is achieved through standard DOM methods (for example, **getElementById()**) or through the **options[ ]** array of the **select** object in which it is enclosed.

Constructor

> **var** *instanceName* = **new** Option(*text* [, *value*]);

Creates a new **option** element which can then be added to the **options[ ]** array of the enclosing **select**. This method of creating **option**s is deprecated; you should use standard DOM methods instead.

Properties

- **dataFld**   String specifying which field of a data source is bound to the element.* (IE4+)
- **dataFormatAs**   String indicating how the element treats data supplied to it.* (IE4+)
- **dataSrc**   String containing the source of data for data binding.* (IE4+)
- **defaultSelected**   Boolean indicating if this option is the default. (IE3+, N2+, DOM1, ReadOnly)
- **disabled**   Boolean indicating whether the element is disabled (grayed out). (IE4+, N6+, DOM1)

- **form**   Reference to the **Form** in which the element is contained. (IE3+, N2+, DOM1, ReadOnly)
- **index**   The index of the option in the enclosing **select**. (IE3+, N2+, DOM1, ReadOnly)
- **label**   The alternate text for the option as specified in the **label** attribute. (N6+, DOM1)
- **selected**   Boolean indicating if the element is selected. (IE3+, N2+, DOM1)
- **text**   String containing the text enclosed by the element. (IE3+, N2+, DOM1)
- **value**   String containing the value of the element's **value** attribute. (IE3+, N2+, DOM1)

Methods

This element has the methods listed in the Generic HTML Element Object found at the beginning of this section.

Event Handlers

```
onlayoutcomplete onlosecapture onpropertychange onreadystatechange
onselectstart ontimeerror
```

Support

Supported in IE3+, N2+, DOM1.

p (Document Object)

This document object corresponds to a **<p>** (paragraph) element in the document. Access to this object is achieved through standard DOM methods (for example, **getElementById()**).

Properties

This object has the following property, in addition to those in the Generic HTML Element Object found at the beginning of this section.

- **align**   String specifying the alignment of the element, for example "left."*
(IE4+, N6+, DOM1)

Methods

This element has the methods listed in the Generic HTML Element Object found at the beginning of this section.

Event Handlers

This object has the event handlers listed in the Generic HTML Element Object found at the beginning of this section, in addition to the following:

```
onlayoutcomplete
```

Support

Supported in IE4+, N6+, DOM1.

Packages (Browser Object)

Netscape provides access to the public interface of Java classes through the **Packages** object. Commonly used classes (**java**, **netscape**, and **sun**) are available through this object and also as top-level objects themselves. To access a Java class installed on the client machine, access the fully qualified Java class name through this object. For example, to instantiate a Java **Frame** object, you would use:

```
var myFrame = new Packages.java.awt.Frame();
```

See a book on Java or Netscape's Java and LiveConnect documentation for more information.

Properties

Every Java class and property defined in the client's Java implementation is available as a property of this object. The most commonly used classes are found in the **java**, **netscape**, and **sun** packages. Classes are accessed using their fully qualified class name as a property, for example **Packages.java.awt.Frame**.

Methods

Every public method of every Java class is available by accessing its fully qualified name.

Support

Supported in N3+ (JavaScript 1.1+).

param (Document Object)

This object corresponds to an occurrence of a **<param>** element (initial parameter to an embedded object) in the document. This object can be accessed using standard DOM methods like **getElementById()**.

Properties

This object has the following properties, in addition to those in the Generic HTML Element Object found at the beginning of this section.

- **name**   String holding the name of the parameter. (IE4+, N6+, DOM1)
- **type**   String indicating the type of the value when **valueType** is "ref." (IE6+, N6+, DOM1, ReadOnly after object has loaded)
- **value**   String containing the value of the parameter. (IE6+, N6+, DOM1, ReadOnly after object has loaded)
- **valueType**   String giving more information about how to interpret **value**, usually "data," "ref," or "object." (IE6+, N6+, DOM1, ReadOnly after object has loaded)

Methods

This element has the methods listed in the Generic HTML Element Object found at the beginning of this section.

Event Handlers

None.

Support

Supported in Internet Explorer 4+, Netscape 6+, DOM1.

Password (Document Object)

This object corresponds to an occurrence of a password input field (**<input type="password"...>**) in the document. This object can be accessed using standard DOM methods or through the **Form** element which contains it (via the **elements[ ]** array or by **name**).

The structure of this object is identical to the structure of the **Text** object, so see the reference for **Text** for details.

Event Handlers

```
onactivate onafterupdate onbeforeactivate onbeforecut onbeforedeactivate
onbeforeeditfocus onbeforepaste onbeforeupdate onblur onchange onclick
oncontextmenu oncontrolselect oncut ondblclick ondeactivate ondrag ondragend
ondragenter ondragleave ondragover ondragstart ondrop onerrorupdate
onfilterchange onfocus onfocusin onfocusout onhelp onkeydown onkeypress
onkeyup onlosecapture onmousedown onmouseenter onmouseleave onmousemove
onmouseout onmouseover onmouseup onmousewheel onmove onmoveend onmovestart
onpaste onpropertychange onreadystatechange onresize onresizeend
onresizestart onselect onselectstart ontimeerror
```

Support

Internet Explorer 3+, Netscape 2+, DOM1.

Plugin (Browser Object)

Each **Plugin** object corresponds to a plugin installed in the browser. Such objects are available through the **enabledPlugin** property of **mimeType** objects or through the **navigator.plugins[ ]** array. Each **Plugin** provides information about the plugin, such as its description, the MIME types it handles, and its name. This object is used to determine whether the browser supports a specific plugin and version. Each **Plugin**, in addition to having the properties defined below, is an array of **mimeType** objects representing the MIME types that the plugin handles for the browser.

Access to page content handled by a plugin (for example, an **<embed>** element), including properties made available via LiveConnect, is carried out using the **document.embeds[ ]** array or by fetching a reference to the object using standard DOM techniques.

Although Internet Explorer provides plugin support and LiveConnect functionality, **Plugin** objects are only available in Netscape.

Properties

- **description**   String containing a human-friendly description of the plugin. (N3+, ReadOnly)
- **filename**   String containing the filename of the plugin on the local disk. (N3+, ReadOnly)
- **length**   The number of **mimeType** objects contained in the object (the length of its array content). Equivalently, the number of MIME types the plugin is currently handling. (N3+, ReadOnly)

■ **name**   String specifying the name of the plugin, for example "Shockwave Flash." Carefully consult plugin vendor documentation to find the exact name of the plugin(s) in which you are interested. (N3+, ReadOnly)

Methods
None.

Support
Netscape 3+ (JavaScript 1.1+).

Notes
In order to ensure that a particular plugin is handling a particular MIME type, it is not sufficient to check for the existence of the **Plugin** object in which you are interested. You must also check to ensure that the **Plugin** is currently handling the appropriate MIME type, for example:

```
if (navigator.plugins['Some Player'] && navigator.plugins['Some
Player']['video/mpeg'])
```

See also the **plugins[ ]** property of the **Navigator** object.

popup (Browser Object)

A **popup** is a stripped-down **Window** object created using IE's **createPopup()** method. Popup windows are created initially hidden and without content; the programmer is responsible for writing content to it and rendering it visible.

Properties

■ **document**   Reference to the window's **Document** (initially empty). (IE5.5+)
■ **isOpen**   Boolean indicating if the window is open. (IE5.5+)

Methods

■ **hide( )**   Hides the window. (IE5.5+)
■ **show(x, y, width, height [, relativeTo])**   Renders the window visible at screen coordinates (*x,y*) relative to the desktop. The size of the window is given in the pixel arguments *width* and *height*. The *relativeTo* parameter is a reference to an object relative which the *x* and *y* coordinates will be interpreted. (IE5.5+)

Support
Supported in IE5.5+.

pkcs11 (Browser Object)

Object implementing PKCS #11 cryptographic functionality. See documentation at **www.mozilla.org**. Supported in Netscape 6+.

pre (Document Object)

This object corresponds to a **<pre>** (preformatted text) element in the document. Access to this object is achieved through standard DOM methods (for example, **getElementById()**).

Properties

This object has the following property, in addition to those in the Generic HTML Element Object found at the beginning of this section.

■ **width**   Specifies the width of the object in pixels. (IE6+, N6+, DOM1)

Methods

This element has the methods listed in the Generic HTML Element Object found at the beginning of this section.

Event Handlers

This object has the event handlers listed in the Generic HTML Element Object found at the beginning of this section.

Support

Supported in Internet Explorer 4+, Netscape 6+, DOM1.

q (Document Object)

This object corresponds to a **<q>** (quote) element in the document. Access to this object is achieved through standard DOM methods (for example, **getElementById()**).

Properties

This object has the following property, in addition to those in the Generic HTML Element Object found at the beginning of this section.

■ **cite**   String containing the URL that serves as a reference for the quote. (IE6+, N6+, DOM1)

Methods

This element has the methods listed in the Generic HTML Element Object found at the beginning of this section.

Event Handlers

```
onactivate onbeforedeactivate onblur oncontrolselect ondeactivate ondrag
ondragend ondragenter ondragleave ondragover ondragstart ondrop onfocus
onhelp onkeydown onkeypress onkeyup onmove onmoveend onmovestart
onreadystatechange onresizeend onresizestart onselectstart ontimeerror
```

Support

Internet Explorer 4+, Netscape 6+, DOM1.

Radio (Document Object)

This object corresponds to an **<input type="radio">** form input field. Access to this object is achieved through standard DOM methods or through the enclosing **Form** (via its **elements[ ]** array or by **name**). The preferable way of accessing this object is through the **Form** element because many **radio** elements have the same **name** attribute.

Properties

- **accessKey**   Single character string indicating the hotkey that gives the element focus.* (IE4+, N6+, DOM1)

- **align**   String specifying the alignment of the element, for example "left."* (IE4+, N6+, DOM1)

- **alt**   String containing alternative text for the button (for browsers incapable of rendering buttons). (N6+, DOM1)

- **checked**   Boolean indicating whether the button is currently checked. (IE3+, N2+, DOM1)

- **controllers**   Related to XPConnect functionality. See **mozilla.org** for documentation. (N6+, ReadOnly)

- **dataFld**   String specifying which field of a data source is bound to the element.* (IE4+)

- **dataFormatAs**   String indicating how the element treats data supplied to it.* (IE4+)

- **dataSrc**   String containing the source of data for data binding.* (IE4+)

- **defaultChecked**   Boolean indicating if the button is checked by default (i.e., whether its **checked** attribute was specified). (IE3+, N2+, DOM1)

- **defaultValue**   String containing the initial value of the button's **value** attribute. (IE3+, N6f+, DOM1)

- **disabled**   Boolean indicating whether the element is disabled (grayed out). (IE4+, N6+, DOM1)

- **form**   Reference to the **Form** in which the button is contained. (IE3+, N2+, DOM1, ReadOnly)

- **name**   String holding the **name** attribute of the element. (IE3+, N2+, DOM1, ReadOnly)

- **selectionEnd**   The meaning of this property is unclear. (N6+)

- **selectionStart**   The meaning of this property is unclear. (N6+)

- **status**   Boolean indicating if the button is selected. (IE4+)

- **tabIndex**   Numeric value indicating the tab order for the object.* (IE4+, N6+, DOM1)

- **type**   String containing the **type** of the input, in this case "radio." (IE4+, N3+, DOM1, ReadOnly)

- **value**   The **value** attribute of the button. (IE3+, N2+, DOM1)

Methods

- **blur( )**   Removes focus from the element.* (IE3+, N2+, DOM1)

- **click( )**   Simulates a mouse click at the object.* (IE3+, N2+, DOM1)

- **focus( )**   Gives focus to the element.* (IE3+, N2+, DOM1)

- **handleEvent(event)**   Passes the **Event** *event* to be handled by the object.* (N4 only)

Event Handlers

```
onactivate onafterupdate onbeforeactivate onbeforecut onbeforedeactivate
onbeforeeditfocus onbeforepaste onbeforeupdate onblur onclick oncontextmenu
oncontrolselect oncut ondblclick ondeactivate ondrag ondragend ondragenter
ondragleave ondragover ondragstart ondrop onerrorupdate onfilterchange
onfocus onfocusin onfocusout onhelp onkeydown onkeypress onkeyup
onlosecapture onmousedown onmouseenter onmouseleave onmousemove onmouseout
onmouseover onmouseup onmousewheel onmove onmoveend onmovestart onpaste
onpropertychange onreadystatechange onresize onresizeend onresizestart
onselectstart ontimeerror
```

Support

Internet Explorer 3+, Netscape 2+, DOM1.

RegExp (Built-in Object)

Instances of **RegExp** objects hold regular expression patterns and provide the properties and methods that enable their use on strings. In addition, each window has a **RegExp** object that provides static (class) properties giving information about the most recent match that was executed. These properties are dynamically scoped.

Constructor

> **var** *instanceName* = **new** RegExp(*expr* [, *flags*]);

where *expr* is a string containing a regular expression (for example, "abc.*") and *flags* is an optional string denoting the flags for the expression (for example, "gi").

Properties

- **$1, $2, ... $9**   The $*n* property contains the string corresponding to the *n*th parenthesized subexpression of the most recently executed match. (IE4+ (JScript 3.0+), N4+ (JavaScript 1.2+), Static, ReadOnly)

- **global**   Boolean indicating whether the global flag ("g") was used to create the regular expression. (IE5.5+ (JScript 5.5+), N4+ (JavaScript 1.2+), ECMA Edition 3, ReadOnly)

- **ignoreCase**   Boolean indicating whether the case-insensitive flag ("i") was used to create the regular expression. (IE5.5+ (JScript 5.5+), N4+ (JavaScript 1.2+), ECMA Edition 3, ReadOnly)

- **index**   Integer indicating the character position where the first successful match begins (during the most recently executed match). (IE4+ (JScript 3.0+), Static, ReadOnly)

- **input**   Holds the string upon which the most recent regular expression match was conducted. This property is not automatically filled in N6. (IE4+ (JScript 3.0+), N4+ (JavaScript 1.2+), Static)

- **multiline**   Boolean indicating whether the multiline flag ("m") was used to create the regular expression. (IE5.5+ (JScript 5.5+), N4+ (JavaScript 1.2+), ECMA Edition 3, ReadOnly)

■ **lastIndex**   Integer specifying the character index of the string at which the next match will begin. Used during global matching. (IE4+ (JScript 3.0+), N4+ (JavaScript 1.2+), ECMA Edition 3)

■ **lastMatch**   String containing the last matched characters of the most recent match. (IE5.5+ (JScript 5.5+), N4+ (JavaScript 1.2+), Static, ReadOnly)

■ **lastParen**   String containing the last matched parenthesized subexpression (of the most recent match). (IE5.5+ (JScript 5.5+), N4+ (JavaScript 1.2), Static, ReadOnly)

■ **leftContext**   Substring up to but not including the beginning of the most recently matched text (of the most recently executed match). (IE5.5+ (JScript 5.5+), N4+ (JavaScript 1.2), Static, ReadOnly)

■ **prototype**   Reference to the object's prototype. (IE4+ (JScript 3.0+), N4+ (JavaScript 1.2+), ECMA Edition 3)

■ **rightContext**   Substring following (but not including) the most recently matched text. (IE5.5+ (JScript 5.5+), N4+ (JavaScript 1.2), ECMA Edition 3, Static, ReadOnly)

■ **source**   String containing the text that makes up the pattern (excluding any slashes used to define it and the flags). (IE4+ (JScript 3.0+), N4+ (JavaScript 1.2), ECMA Edition 3, ReadOnly)

Methods

■ **compile(expr [, flags])**   Compiles the regular expression *expr* with flags *flags* in the object. Used to replace an expression with a new one. (IE4+ (JScript 3.0+), N4+ (JavaScript 1.2), ECMA Edition 3)

■ **exec(str)**   Executes a match against the string *str* and returns an array containing the results. If no match was made, **null** is returned. If *str* is omitted, the contents of **RegExp.input** is used as *str*. The resulting array has the entire match in element zero, and any matched subexpressions at subsequent indices. It also has instance properties **input** (which holds the string on which the match was executed), **index** (which holds the index of the beginning of the match in the input string), and in IE **lastIndex** (which holds the index of the first character following the match). (IE4+ (JScript 3.0+), N4+ (JavaScript 1.2), ECMA Edition 3)

■ **test(str)**   Returns a Boolean indicating whether the regular expression matches a part of the string *str*. (IE4+ (JScript 3.0+), N4+ (JavaScript 1.2), ECMA Edition 3)

■ **toString( )**   Returns the string corresponding to the regular expression, including enclosing slashes and any flags that were used to define it. (IE4+ (JScript 3.0+), N4+ (JavaScript 1.2), ECMA Edition 3)

Support

Supported in IE4+ (JScript 3.0+), N4+ (JavaScript 1.2+), ECMAScript Edition 3.

Notes

For a list of special regular expression characters, see Appendix A.

Reset (Document Object)

This object corresponds to an **<input type="reset">** form input field. Access to this object is achieved through standard DOM methods or through the enclosing **Form** (via its **elements[ ]** array or by **name**). Note that all **Form**s have a **reset()** method that can be directly invoked.

Properties

- **accessKey** Single character string indicating the hotkey that gives the element focus.* (IE4+, N6+, DOM1)
- **align** String specifying the alignment of the element, for example "left."* (IE4+, N6+, DOM1)
- **alt** String containing alternative text for the button (for browsers incapable of rendering buttons). (N6+, DOM1)
- **controllers** Related to XPConnect functionality. See mozilla.org. (N6+)
- **dataFld** String specifying which field of a data source is bound to the element.* (IE4+)
- **dataFormatAs** String indicating how the element treats data supplied to it.* (IE4+)
- **dataSrc** String containing the source of data for data binding.* (IE4+)
- **defaultValue** String containing the initial value of the button's **value** attribute. (IE3+, N6+, DOM1)
- **disabled** Boolean indicating whether the element is disabled (grayed out). (IE4+, N6+, DOM1)
- **form** Reference to the **Form** containing the button. (IE3+, N2+, DOM1, ReadOnly)
- **name** String holding the **name** attribute of the element.
- **selectionEnd** The meaning of this property is unclear. (N6+)
- **selectionStart** The meaning of this property is unclear. (N6+)
- **tabIndex** Numeric value indicating the tab order for the object.* (IE4+, N6+, DOM1)
- **type** String containing the **type** of the input, in this case "reset." (IE4+, N3+, DOM1, ReadOnly)
- **value** The **value** attribute of the button. (IE3+, N2+, DOM1)

Methods

- **blur( )** Removes focus from the element.* (IE3+, N2+, DOM1)
- **click( )** Simulates a mouse click at the object.* (IE3+, N2+, DOM1)
- **createTextRange( )** Creates a **TextRange** object for examination or manipulation of the button's text. A better cross-browser solution is to use standard **String** methods on the field's **value**. (IE4+)
- **focus( )** Gives focus to the element.* (IE3+, N3+, DOM1)
- **handleEvent(event)** Passes the **Event** *event* to be handled by the object.* (N4 only)

Event Handlers

```
onactivate onbeforeactivate onbeforecut onbeforedeactivate onbeforeeditfocus
onbeforepaste onblur onclick oncontextmenu oncontrolselect oncut ondblclick
ondeactivate ondrag ondragend ondragenter ondragleave ondragover ondragstart
ondrop onfilterchange onfocus onfocusin onfocusout onhelp onkeydown
onkeypress onkeyup onlosecapture onmousedown onmouseenter onmouseleave
onmousemove onmouseout onmouseover onmouseup onmousewheel onmove onmoveend
onmovestart onpaste onpropertychange onreadystatechange onresize onresizeend
onresizestart onselectstart ontimeerror
```

Support

Internet Explorer 3+, N2+, DOM1.

rule, CSSrule (Browser object)

Instances of **rule** objects correspond to CSS rules found in the **styleSheet** object, and are accessed through the **cssRules[ ]** or **rules[ ]** collections of that object. An easy way to manipulate **rule** objects is to manipulate the appropriate portion of their **style** property.

Properties

■ **cssText**   String containing the text of the rule. (N6+, IE5 MacOS only, DOM2)

■ **parentStyleSheet**   Reference to the **styleSheet** object in which the rule is defined. (N6+, IE5 MacOS only, DOM2, ReadOnly)

■ **readOnly**   Boolean indicating if the stylesheet in which the rule is defined was loaded from an external file. (IE4+, ReadOnly)

■ **selectorText**   String containing the selector portion of the rule. (IE4+, N6+, DOM2, ReadOnly)

■ **style**   Reference to the **Style** object that defines the style properties of the selector. Changing this object is reflected in any elements bound by the rule. (IE4+, N6+, DOM2)

■ **type**   Integer indicating the type of rule: 0 (unknown), 1 (normal style rule), 2 (@charset rule), 3 (@import rule), 4 (@media rule), 5 (@font-face rule), 6 (@page rule). (N6+, DOM2)

Methods

None.

Notes

The official DOM2 name for this object is **cssRule**. DOM2 defines other, unimplemented features for certain kinds of **rule**s.

runtimeStyle (Document object)

A **Style** object that has precedence over the normal **Style** object for the element. Because the normal **Style** object reflects only inline style set with the **style** attribute, it does not reflect style set by default or through externally linked stylesheets. This object *does,* and permits you to modify style values without the changes being reflected into the element's inline style or **styleSheet** objects which might exist.

Support

Internet Explorer 5+.

samp (Document Object)

This object corresponds to a **<samp>** (code sample) element in the document. It has the properties, methods, and events listed in the Generic HTML Element Object found at the beginning of this section.

Support

Supported in Internet Explorer 4+, Netscape 6+, DOM1.

screen (Browser object)

The **screen** object makes information about the client's display capabilities available to JavaScript.

Properties

- **availHeight**   Integer specifying the height of the user's screen minus any operating system chrome (such as the Windows taskbar). (IE4+, N4+, ReadOnly)

- **availLeft**   Integer indicating the x coordinate of the first pixel on the left side of the screen that is not occupied by an operating system object. (N4+, ReadOnly)

- **availTop**   Integer indicating the y coordinate of the first pixel at the top of the screen that is not occupied by an operating system object. (N4+, ReadOnly)

- **availWidth**   Integer specifying the width of the user's screen minus any operating system chrome. (IE4+, N4+, ReadOnly)

- **bufferDepth**   Specifies the number of bits per pixel to use for colors in the offscreen bitmap buffer. Valid values are zero (the default), -1 (use the **colorDepth** value), or a power of two up to 32. (IE4+)

- **colorDepth**   The number of bits per pixel used for colors. (IE4+, N4+, ReadOnly)

- **height**   The vertical resolution of the screen in pixels. (IE4+, N4+, ReadOnly)

- **fontSmoothingEnabled**   Boolean indicating whether the user has font smoothing enabled in Windows. (IE4+, ReadOnly)

- **pixelDepth**   The number of bits per pixel used for colors. (N4+, ReadOnly)

- **updateInterval**   Integer indicating how often the screen should be repainted in milliseconds. Defaults to zero but can be set to larger values if there is a lot of repainting going on that should be buffered. (IE4+)

- **width**   The horizontal resolution of the screen in pixels. (IE4+, N4+, ReadOnly)

Methods

None.

Support

Supported in IE4+, N4+.

script (Document Object)

This object corresponds to a **<script>** element in the document. Access to this object is achieved through standard DOM methods (for example, **getElementById()**) or in Internet Explorer through **document.scripts[ ]**. While examination of source code is easily carried out by examining the text nodes enclosed by this object (DOM) or its **innerText** property (IE), self-modifying code can lead to anomalous behavior.

Properties

This object has the following properties, in addition to those in the Generic HTML Element Object found at the beginning of this section.

- **charset** String specifying the character set used to encode the script. (IE6+, N6+, DOM1)

- **defer** Boolean indicating whether execution of the script is deferred. Used to indicate to the browser that the script is not going to generate any content for the document and so its parsing and execution may be deferred to speed up document rendering. (IE4+, N6+, DOM1)

- **event** In IE, this string specifies the handler the script is for, for example "onclick()," and is used in conjunction with **htmlFor**. Using this property for that purpose is not recommended, as it is nonstandard, although the W3C has reserved this property for future use (probably to implement similar functionality). In Netscape, this property is useless. (IE4+, N6+, DOM1)

- **htmlFor** In IE, this string specifies the object which the script is for, and is used in conjunction with the **event** property/attribute. This property corresponds to the **for** attribute. Using this property to bind events is not recommended at the current time because it is nonstandard, although the W3C has reserved this property for future use (probably to implement similar functionality). This property is useless in Netscape 6+. (IE4+, N6+, DOM1)

- **src** String holding the URL of the external script. (IE4+, N6+, DOM1)

- **text** String holding the contents of the script. (IE4+, N6+, DOM1)

- **type** String holding the value of the **type** attribute, the MIME type of the script. (IE4+, N6+, DOM1)

Methods

This element has the methods listed in the Generic HTML Element Object found at the beginning of this section.

Event Handlers

```
onload onpropertychange onreadystatechange
```

Support

Supported in Internet Explorer 4+, Netscape 6+, DOM1.

select (Document Object)

This object corresponds to a **<select>** element in the document. Access to this object is achieved through standard DOM methods (for example, **getElementById()**) or through the **Form** in which it is contained (via the **elements[ ]** array or by **name**).

Properties

This object has the following properties, in addition to those in the Generic HTML Element Object found at the beginning of this section.

- **dataFld**   String specifying which field of a data source is bound to the element.* (IE4+)
- **dataFormatAs**   String indicating how the element treats data supplied to it.* (IE4+)
- **dataSrc**   String containing the source of data for data binding.* (IE4+)
- **disabled**   Boolean indicating whether the element is disabled (grayed out). (IE4+, N6+, DOM1)
- **form**   Reference to the **Form** in which the element is contained. (IE3+, N2+, DOM1, ReadOnly)
- **length**   Integer indicating the number of **option**s in the selection list. (IE3+, N2+, DOM1)
- **multiple**   Boolean indicating if multiple **option**s may be selected. (IE4+, N6+, DOM1)
- **name**   String holding the **name** attribute of the element. (IE3+, N2+, DOM1)
- **options[ ]**   Collection of **option**s contained by this element. IE supplies methods with this array, so see **options.add()** and **options.remove** below. (IE3+, N2+, DOM1)
- **selectedIndex**   Integer indicating the index in the **options[ ]** collection of the option which is currently selected or -1 if none is. If multiple options are selected, the index of the first one is returned. (IE3+, N2+, DOM1)
- **size**   Integer indicating the **size** attribute of the select, the number of options which are visible at one time. (IE4+, N6+, DOM1)
- **sourceIndex**   Number indicating the index of the element in the **document.all[ ]** collection.* (IE4+, ReadOnly)
- **tabIndex**   Numeric value indicating the tab order for the object.* (IE4+, N6+, DOM1)
- **type**   String containing the type of the select, either "select-one" or "select-multiple." (IE4+, N3+, DOM1, ReadOnly)
- **value**   String containing the **value** of the currently selected option. (IE4+, N6+, DOM1)

Methods

This element has the methods listed in the Generic HTML Element Object found at the beginning of this section.

- **add(element, before)**   Adds the **option** referenced by the *element* to the list of options before the **option** referenced by *before*. If *before* is **null**, it is added at the end of the list. (N6+, DOM1) Under IE, *before* is an optional index at which to insert the new element (shifting the rest of the options up one index). (IE5.5+—but functionality might change to be DOM-compliant in IE6, so be careful using this method in IE)

- **blur( )**   Removes focus from the element.* (IE3+, N2+, DOM1)
- **focus( )**   Gives focus to the element.* (IE4+, N2+, DOM1)
- **options.add(element [, index])**   Adds the **option** referenced by *element* to the **options[ ]** collection at index *index* (if specified), shifting the other options up one index. If *index* is not specified, the new option is added to the end of the list. (IE4+)
- **options.remove(index)**   Removes the option at index *index* and shifts the remaining options down one index. (IE4+)
- **remove(index)**   Removes the option at index *index* from the list of **options**. (IE5.5+, N6+, DOM1)

Event Handlers

```
onactivate onafterupdate onbeforeactivate onbeforecut onbeforedeactivate
onbeforeeditfocus onbeforepaste onbeforeupdate onblur onchange onclick
oncontextmenu oncontrolselect oncut ondblclick ondeactivate ondragenter
ondragleave ondragover ondrop onerrorupdate onfocus onfocusin onfocusout
onhelp onkeydown onkeypress onkeyup onlosecapture onmousedown onmouseenter
onmouseleave onmousemove onmouseout onmouseover onmouseup onmousewheel
onmove onmoveend onmovestart onpaste onpropertychange onreadystatechange
onresize onresizeend onresizestart onselectstart
```

Support
Supported in Internet Explorer 3+, Netscape 2+, DOM1.

selection (Browser Object)

This object represents the active selection, as defined by the user highlighting a block of the document. Selections can also be created by script by invoking the **select()** method of a **TextRange** object.

Child Of
Document

Properties

- **type**   String indicating the type of selection. Either "none" (if there is no selected content), "text" (if the selected content is text/element content), or "control" (if the selected content is a control select—one in which the selected object can be resized). (IE4+, ReadOnly)
- **typeDetail**   The name of the selection, most often not defined. (IE5.5+, ReadOnly)

Methods

- **clear( )**   Clears the contents of the selection. (IE4+)
- **createRange( )**   Creates a **TextRange** out of the selection and returns a reference to the new object. Or if the selection is a control selection, creates a **controlRange** collection. (IE4+)

■ **createRangeCollection( )**   Same as **createRange()** in IE, although other JScript implementations may return a collection of **TextRange** objects created from the selection. (IE5.5+)

■ **empty( )**   Cancels the current selection. (IE4+)

Support
Supported in IE4+.

small (Document Object)

This object corresponds to a **<small>** (small text) element in the document. It has the properties, methods, and events listed in the Generic HTML Element Object found at the beginning of this section.

Support
Supported in Internet Explorer 4+, Netscape 6+, DOM1.

span (Document Object)

This object corresponds to a **<span>** (inline container) element in the document. Access to this object is achieved through standard DOM methods (for example, **getElementById()**).

Properties
This object has the following properties, in addition to those in the Generic HTML Element Object found at the beginning of this section.

■ **dataFld**   String specifying which field of a data source is bound to the element.* (IE4+)

■ **dataFormatAs**   String indicating how the element treats data supplied to it.* (IE4+)

■ **dataSrc**   String containing the source of data for data binding.* (IE4+)

Methods
This object has the following method, in addition to those in the Generic HTML Element Object found at the beginning of this section.

■ **doScroll([action])**   Scrolls the top of the body of the document into view. If *action* is specified it must be one of several predetermined strings, such as "left" or "right," which give fine-grain control over scroll bar actions. See MSDN for complete details. (IE5+)

Event Handlers
This object has the event handlers listed in the Generic HTML Element Object found at the beginning of this section, in addition to the following:

```
onafterupdate onbeforeeditfocus onbeforeupdate onerrorupdate
```

Support
Internet Explorer 4+, Netscape 6+, DOM1.

strike (Document Object)

This object corresponds to a **<strike>** (struck-through text) element in the document. It has the properties, methods, and events listed in the Generic HTML Element Object found at the beginning of this section.

Support

Supported in Internet Explorer 4+, Netscape 6+, DOM1.

String (Built-in Object)

String is the container object for the primitive string data type. It supplies methods for the manipulation of strings in addition to those which create HTML markup from plain text. When manipulating string, remember that like all JavaScript indices, the enumeration of character positions begins with zero.

Constructor

var *instanceName* = **new** String(*initialValue*);

where *initialValue* is a string. Omitting *initialValue* creates a **String** where value is the empty string ("").

Properties

- **length**   Integer indicating the number of characters in the string.
- **prototype**   Reference to the object's prototype. (IE4+ (JScript 2.0+), N3+ (JavaScript 1.1+), ECMA Edition 1)

Methods

- **anchor(name)**   Returns the string marked up as an HTML anchor (**<a name="*name*">***string value***</a>**). (IE3+ (JScript 1.0+), N2+ (JavaScript 1.0+), ECMA Edition 1)
- **big( )**   Returns the string marked up as big HTML text (**<big>***string value***</big>**). (IE3+ (JScript 1.0+), N2+ (JavaScript 1.0+))
- **blink( )**   Returns the string marked up as blinking HTML text (**<blink>***string value***</blink>**). (N2+ (JavaScript 1.0+)
- **bold( )**   Returns the string marked up as bold HTML text (**<bold>***string value***</bold>**). (IE3+ (JScript 1.0+), N2+ (JavaScript 1.0+))
- **charAt(position)**   Returns a string containing the character at index *position* in the string. The empty string is returned if *position* is out of range. (IE3+ (JScript 1.0+), N2+ (JavaScript 1.0+), ECMA Edition 1)
- **charCodeAt(position)**   Returns an unsigned integer representing the Unicode value of the character at index *position*. If *position* is out of range, **NaN** is returned. (IE5.5+ (JScript 5.5+), N4+ (JavaScript 1.2+), ECMA Edition 1)
- **concat(string2 [, string3 [, ...]])**   Returns the string obtained by concatenating the current string value with *string2*, *string3*, ... (IE4+ (JScript 3.0+), N4+ (JavaScript 1.2+), ECMA Edition 1)

■ **fixed( )**   Returns the string marked up as fixed-width HTML text (**<tt>***string value***</tt>**). (IE3+ (JScript 1.0+), N2+ (JavaScript 1.0+))

■ **fontcolor(theColor)**   Returns the string marked up as colored HTML according to the string *color* (**<font color="***theColor***">***string value***</font>**). (IE3+ (JScript 1.0+), N2+ (JavaScript 1.0+))

■ **fontsize(theSize)**   Returns the string marked up according to the HTML font size given in *theSize* (**<font size="***theSize***">***string value***</font>**). HTML font sizes are 1 through 7, or relative +/- 1-6. (IE3+ (JScript 1.0+), N2+ (JavaScript 1.0+))

■ **fromCharCode(char0 [, char1 [, ...]])**   Creates a string from the given characters. The arguments *char0, char1,* ... are Unicode numbers corresponding to the desired characters. (IE4+ (JScript 3.0+), N4+ (JavaScript 1.2+), ECMA Edition 1, Static)

■ **indexOf(searchString [, startIndex])**   Returns the index of the first occurrence of *searchString* in the string. If *startIndex* is specified, then the first occurrence after index *startIndex* is returned. If *searchString* is not found, -1 is returned. (IE3+ (JScript 1.0+), N2+ (JavaScript 1.0+), ECMA Edition 1)

■ **italics( )**   Returns the string marked up as italicized HTML text (**<i>***string value***</i>**). (IE3+ (JScript 1.0+), N2+ (JavaScript 1.0+))

■ **lastIndexOf(searchString [, startIndex])**   Returns the index of the last occurrence of *searchString* in the string. If *startIndex* is specified, the index of the last occurrence starting at index *startIndex* or before is returned. If *searchString* is not found, -1 is returned. (IE3+ (JScript 1.0+), N2+ (JavaScript 1.0+), ECMA Edition 1)

■ **link(theHref)**   Returns the string marked up as an HTML link to the string *theHref* (**<a href="***theHref***">***string value***</a>**). (IE3+ (JScript 1.0+), N2+ (JavaScript 1.0+))

■ **match(regexp)**   Executes a regular expression match with the regular expression *regexp* and returns an array of results. If no match is found, **null** is returned. Otherwise, the returned array is exactly like that returned by **RegExp.exec()**. (IE4+ (JScript 3.0+), N4+ (JavaScript 1.2+), ECMA Edition 3)

■ **replace(regexp, replacement)**   Returns the string obtained by executing a match with the regular expression *regexp* on the string and then replacing each piece of matching text with the string *replacement*. In IE5.5 and N4.06+ *replacement* can be a function (see full description at support site). (IE3+ (JScript 1.0+), N4+ (JavaScript 1.2+), ECMA Edition 3)

■ **search(regexp)**   Executes a regular expression match with regular expression *regexp* and returns the index of the beginning of the matching text in the string. If no match is found, -1 is returned. (IE4+ (JScript 3.0+), N4+ (JavaScript 1.2+), ECMA Edition 3)

■ **slice(start [, end])**   Returns a new string containing the substring from index *start* up to but not including index *end*. If *end* is omitted, the substring returned runs to the end of the string. If *start* or *end* is negative, it is treated as an offset from the end of the string. (IE4+ (JScript 3.0+), N2+ (JavaScript 1.0+), ECMA Edition 3)

■ **small( )**   Returns the string marked up as small HTML text (**<i>***string value***</i>**). (IE3+ (JScript 1.0+), N2+ (JavaScript 1.0+))

■ **split([separator [, limit]])**   Returns the array of strings obtained by splitting the string at each occurrence of *separator* (which may be a string or regular expression). The *separator* is not included in the array returned. If no *separator* is given, the string is split into an array of strings holding its individual characters. If the integer *limit* is given, only the first *limit* parts are placed in the array. See support site for more information. (IE4+ (JScript 3.0+), N3+ (JavaScript 1.1+), ECMA Edition 1)

- **strike( )**   Returns the string marked up as struck-through HTML text (**<strike>***string value***</strike>**). (IE3+ (JScript 1.0+), N2+ (JavaScript 1.0+))

- **sub( )**   Returns the string marked up as subscript HTML text (**_{***string value***}**). (IE3+ (JScript 1.0+), N2+ (JavaScript 1.0+))

- **substr(start [, length])**   Returns a new string containing a substring of length *length* beginning at index *start*. If *length* is not given, the substring returned runs to the end of the string. See support site for more details. (IE4+ (JScript 3.0+), N2+ (JavaScript 1.0+))

- **substring(start [, end])**   Returns a new string containing the substring running from index *start* up to but not including index *end*. If *end* is not given, the substring runs to the end of the string. If *start* is greater than *end*, the values are swapped. See support site for more details. (IE3+ (JScript 1.0+), N2+ (JavaScript 1.0+), ECMA Edition 1)

- **sup( )**   Returns the string marked up as superscript HTML text (**^{***string value***}**). (IE3+ (JScript 1.0+), N2+ (JavaScript 1.0+))

- **toLowerCase( )**   Returns the string converted to all lowercase. (IE3+ (JScript 1.0+), N2+ (JavaScript 1.0+), ECMA Edition 1)

- **toUpperCase( )**   Returns the string converted to all uppercase. (IE3+ (JScript 1.0+), N2+ (JavaScript 1.0+), ECMA Edition 1)

Support

Supported in IE3+ (JScript 1.0+), N2+ (JavaScript 1.0+), ECMAScript Edition 1.

Notes

This object does not operate on values in place. That is, when manipulating a **String** with one of its methods, the method returns the result of the operation. It does not change the value of the **String** which it was invoked as a method of. You can, of course, use self-assignment to this effect. For example, "mystring = mystring.toUpperCase()."

The methods of this object available in early browsers can vary, so checking the support for particular methods before using them is advisable.

strong (Document Object)

This object corresponds to a **<strong>** (strong emphasis) element in the document. It has the properties, methods, and events listed in the Generic HTML Element Object found at the beginning of this section.

Support

Supported in Internet Explorer 4+, Netscape 6+, DOM1.

Style (Document/Browser Object)

The **Style** object permits the examination and manipulation of an element's inline (those defined with the **style** HTML attribute) style definitions. The most common way it is accessed is as a property of the element object, for example as *myElement.style*. If you need to manipulate the appearance of an object on screen, this is the primary object that is used.

This object does not provide access to styles defined in **<style>** or **<link>**ed stylesheets; to access such style rules, use the **styleSheet** object found in **Document.styleSheets[ ]**. You can also access a **<style>** element directly by fetching it using standard DOM methods (like **getElementById()**), but this is generally not necessary.

Properties

■ **cssText** String containing the CSS definition. (IE4+, N6+, ReadOnly)

The properties of the **Style** object that correspond to CSS attributes are listed in the following Table, along with their support. (The following table is partially composed of Microsoft documentation). See a good reference on CSS for a more complete description of the style attributes, but be aware that most of the properties contain strings (with the exception of certain Microsoft-specific properties such as those that are **pixel-** and **pos-**related, which contain integers). It is always a good idea to set these properties to strings (and not numbers) and to specify units of measure (for example "100px" or "20em") where appropriate. And finally, note that many of the Netscape 6-only properties listed in Table B-1 will be implemented in Internet Explorer 6.

Style Attribute	Corresponding Property	Support	Description
accelerator	accelerator	IE5+	Sets or retrieves a string that indicates whether the object contains an accelerator key.
None	align	N4	Sets or retrieves the alignment of the text.
background	background	IE4+, N6+	Sets or retrieves (up to) the five separate background properties of the object.
background-attachment	backgroundAttachment	IE4+, N6+	Sets or retrieves how the background image is attached to the object within the document.
background-color	backgroundColor	IE4+, N4+	Sets or retrieves the color behind the content of the object.
background-image	backgroundImage	IE4+, N4+	Sets or retrieves the background image of the object.
background-position	backgroundPosition	IE4+, N6+	Sets or retrieves the position of the background of the object.
background-position-x	backgroundPositionX	IE4+	Sets or retrieves the x coordinate of the backgroundPosition property.
background-position-y	backgroundPositionY	IE4+	Sets or retrieves the y coordinate of the backgroundPosition property.

Table B-1. *CSS Attributes Exposed in the Style Object*

Style Attribute	Corresponding Property	Support	Description
background-repeat	backgroundRepeat	IE4+, N6+	Sets or retrieves how the backgroundImage property of the object is tiled.
behavior	behavior	IE5+	Sets or retrieves the location of the DHTML Behaviors.
border	border	IE4+, N6+	Sets or retrieves the properties to draw around the object.
border-bottom	borderBottom	IE4+, N6+	Sets or retrieves the properties of the bottom border of the object.
border-bottom-color	borderBottomColor	IE4+, N6+	Sets or retrieves the color of the bottom border of the object.
border-bottom-style	borderBottomStyle	IE4+, N6+	Sets or retrieves the style of the bottom border of the object.
border-bottom-width	borderBottomWidth	IE4+, N4+	Sets or retrieves the width of the bottom border of the object.
border-collapse	borderCollapse	N6+	Sets or retrieves a value that indicates whether the row and cell borders of a table are joined in a single border or detached as in standard HTML.
border-color	borderColor	IE4+, N4+	Sets or retrieves the border color of the object.
border-left	borderLeft	IE4+, N6+	Sets or retrieves the properties of the left border of the object.
border-left-color	borderLeftColor	IE4+, N6+	Sets or retrieves the color of the left border of the object.
border-left-style	borderLeftStyle	IE4+, N6+	Sets or retrieves the style of the left border of the object.
border-left-width	borderLeftWidth	IE4+, N4+	Sets or retrieves the width of the left border of the object.
border-right	borderRight	IE4+, N6+	Sets or retrieves the properties of the right border of the object.
border-right-color	borderRightColor	IE4+, N6+	Sets or retrieves the color of the right border of the object.
border-right-style	borderRightStyle	IE4+, N6+	Sets or retrieves the style of the right border of the object.
border-right-width	borderRightWidth	IE4+, N4+	Sets or retrieves the width of the right border of the object.

Table B-1. *CSS Attributes Exposed in the Style Object* (continued)

Style Attribute	Corresponding Property	Support	Description
border-spacing	borderSpacing	N6+	Sets or retrieves the width of the spacing between table cells.
border-style	borderStyle	IE4+, N4+	Sets or retrieves the style of the left, right, top, and bottom borders of the object.
border-top	borderTop	IE4+, N6+	Sets or retrieves the properties of the top border of the object.
border-top-color	borderTopColor	IE4+, N6+	Sets or retrieves the color of the top border of the object.
border-top-style	borderTopStyle	IE4+, N6+	Sets or retrieves the style of the top border of the object.
border-top-width	borderTopWidth	IE4+, N4+	Sets or retrieves the width of the top border of the object.
border-width	borderWidth	IE4+, N6+	Sets or retrieves the width of the left, right, top, and bottom borders of the object.
bottom	bottom	IE5+, N6+	Sets or retrieves the bottom position of the object in relation to the bottom of the next positioned object in the document hierarchy.
caption-side	captionSide	N6+	Sets or retrieves the position of the table caption.
clear	clear	IE4+, N4+	Sets or retrieves whether the object allows floating objects on its left side, right side, or both, so that the next text displays past the floating objects.
clip	clip	IE4+, N6+	Sets or retrieves which part of a positioned object is visible.
color	color	IE4+, N4+	Sets or retrieves the color of the text of the object.
float	cssFloat	N6+	Sets or retrieves the content wrapping behavior of the element.
cursor	cursor	IE4+, N6+	Sets or retrieves the type of cursor to display as the mouse pointer moves over the object.
direction	direction	IE5+, N6+	Sets or retrieves the reading order of the object.

Table B-1.   *CSS Attributes Exposed in the Style Object* (continued)

Style Attribute	Corresponding Property	Support	Description
display	display	IE4+, N4+	Sets or retrieves whether the object is rendered.
empty-cells	emptyCells	N6+	Sets or retrieves whether table cells without content are displayed.
font	font	IE4+, N6+	Sets or retrieves up to the six separate font properties of the object.
font-family	fontFamily	IE4+, N4+	Sets or retrieves the name of the font used for text in the object.
font-size	fontSize	IE4+, N4+	Sets or retrieves the size of the font used for text in the object.
font-size-adjust	fontSizeAdjust	N6+	Sets or retrieves size adjustment of the font.
font-stretch	fontStretch	N6+	Sets or retrieves how much the characters are stretched or compressed..
font-style	fontStyle	IE4+, N4+	Sets or retrieves the font style of the object as italic, normal, or oblique.
font-variant	fontVariant	IE4+, N6+	Sets or retrieves whether the text of the object is in small capital letters.
font-weight	fontWeight	IE4+, N4+	Sets or retrieves the weight of the font of the object.
height	height	IE4+, N6+	Sets or retrieves the height of the object.
layout-flow	layoutFlow	IE5.5+	Sets or retrieves the direction and flow of the content in the object.
layout-grid	layoutGrid	IE5+	Sets or retrieves the composite document grid properties that specify the layout of text characters.
layout-grid-char	layoutGridChar	IE5+	Sets or retrieves the size of the character grid used for rendering the text content of an element.

Table B-1. *CSS Attributes Exposed in the Style Object* (continued)

Style Attribute	Corresponding Property	Support	Description
layout-grid-line	layoutGridLine	IE5+	Sets or retrieves the gridline value used for rendering the text content of an element.
layout-grid-mode	layoutGridMode	IE5+	Sets or retrieves whether the text layout grid uses two dimensions.
layout-grid-type	layoutGridType	IE5+	Sets or retrieves the type of grid used for rendering the text content of an element.
left	left	IE4+, N6+	Sets or retrieves the position of the object relative to the left edge of the next-positioned object in the document hierarchy.
letter-spacing	letterSpacing	IE4+, N6+	Sets or retrieves the amount of additional space between letters in the object.
line-break	lineBreak	IE5+	Sets or retrieves line-breaking rules for Japanese text.
line-height	lineHeight	IE4+, N4+	Sets or retrieves the distance between lines in the object.
list-style	listStyle	IE4+, N6+	Sets or retrieves up to three separate listStyle properties of the object.
list-style-image	listStyleImage	IE4+, N6+	Sets or retrieves which image to use as a list-item marker for the object.
list-style-position	listStylePosition	IE4+, N6+	Sets or retrieves how the list-item marker is drawn relative to the content of the object.
list-style-type	listStyleType	IE4+, N4+	Sets or retrieves the predefined type of the line-item marker for the object.
margin	margin	IE4+, N6+	Sets or retrieves the width of the top, right, bottom, and left margins of the object.
margin-bottom	marginBottom	IE4+, N4+	Sets or retrieves the height of the bottom margin of the object.

Table B-1. *CSS Attributes Exposed in the Style Object* (continued)

Style Attribute	Corresponding Property	Support	Description
margin-left	marginLeft	IE4+, N4+	Sets or retrieves the width of the left margin of the object.
margin-right	marginRight	IE4+, N4+	Sets or retrieves the width of the right margin of the object.
margin-top	marginTop	IE4+, N4+	Sets or retrieves the height of the top margin of the object.
max-height	maxHeight	N6+	Sets or retrieves the maximum height of the element.
max-width	maxWidth	N6+	Sets or retrieves the maximum width of the element.
min-height	minHeight	N6+	Sets or retrieves the minimum height for an element.
min-width	minWidth	N6+	Sets or retrieves the minimum width for an element.
orphans	orphans	N6+	Sets or retrieves the minimum number of lines of a paragraph to display a the bottom of a page when performing page wrapping.
outline	outline	N6+	Sets or retrieves up to the three outline properties.
outline-color	outlineColor	N6+	Sets or retrieves the color of the outline around the element.
outline-style	outlineStyle	N6+	Sets or retrieves the outline style of the outline around the element.
outline-width	outlineWidth	N6+	Sets or retrieves the width of the outline around the element.
overflow	overflow	IE4+, N6+	Sets or retrieves a value indicating how to manage the content of the object when the content exceeds the height or width of the object.
overflow-x	overflowX	IE5+	Sets or retrieves how to manage the content of the object when the content exceeds the width of the object.

Table B-1.   *CSS Attributes Exposed in the Style Object* (continued)

Style Attribute	Corresponding Property	Support	Description
overflow-y	overflowY	IE5+	Sets or retrieves how to manage the content of the object when the content exceeds the height of the object.
padding	padding	IE4+, N6+	Sets or retrieves the amount of space to insert between the object and its margin or, if there is a border, between the object and its border.
padding-bottom	paddingBottom	IE4+, N4+	Sets or retrieves the amount of space to insert between the bottom border of the object and the content.
padding-left	paddingLeft	IE4+, N4+	Sets or retrieves the amount of space to insert between the left border of the object and the content.
padding-right	paddingRight	IE4+, N4+	Sets or retrieves the amount of space to insert between the right border of the object and the content.
padding-top	paddingTop	IE4+, N4+	Sets or retrieves the amount of space to insert between the top border of the object and the content.
@page	page	N6+	Sets or retrieves the page orientation for printing.
page-break-after	pageBreakAfter	IE4+, N6+	Sets or retrieves a value indicating whether a page break can occur after the object.
page-break-before	pageBreakBefore	IE4+, N6+	Sets or retrieves a string indicating whether a page can occur before the object.
page-break-inside	pageBreakInside	N6+	Sets or retrieves a string indicating whether a page break can occur inside the object.
None	pixelBottom	IE4+	Sets or retrieves the bottom position of the object.
None	pixelHeight	IE4+	Sets or retrieves the height of the object.

Table B-1. *CSS Attributes Exposed in the Style Object* (continued)

Style Attribute	Corresponding Property	Support	Description
None	pixelLeft	IE4+	Sets or retrieves the left position of the object.
None	pixelRight	IE4+	Sets or retrieves the right position of the object.
None	pixelTop	IE4+	Sets or retrieves the top position of the object.
None	pixelWidth	IE4+	Sets or retrieves the width of the object.
None	posBottom	IE4+	Sets or retrieves the bottom position of the object in the units specified by the bottom attribute.
None	posHeight	IE4+	Sets or retrieves the height of the object in the units specified by the height attribute.
position	position	IE4+, N6+	Sets or retrieves the type of positioning used for the object.
None	posLeft	IE4+	Sets or retrieves the left position of the object in the units specified by the left attribute.
None	posRight	IE4+	Sets or retrieves the right position of the object in the units specified by the right attribute.
None	posTop	IE4+	Sets or retrieves the top position of the object in the units specified by the top attribute.
None	posWidth	IE4+	Sets or retrieves the width of the object in the units specified by the width attribute.
quotes	quotes	N6+	Sets or retrieves the characters to replace quotation marks with (for example, "' '")
right	right	IE5+, N6+	Sets or retrieves the position of the object relative to the right edge of the next positioned object in the document hierarchy.

Table B-1. *CSS Attributes Exposed in the Style Object* (continued)

Style Attribute	Corresponding Property	Support	Description
ruby-align	rubyAlign	IE5+	Sets or retrieves the position of the ruby text specified by the **rt** object.
ruby-overhang	rubyOverhang	IE5+	Sets or retrieves the position of the ruby text specified by the **rt** object.
ruby-position	rubyPosition	IE5+	Sets or retrieves the position of the ruby text specified by the **rt** object.
scrollbar-3dlight-color	scrollbar3dLightColor	IE5.5+	Sets or retrieves the color of the top and left edges of the scroll box and scroll arrows of a scroll bar.
scrollbar-arrow-color	scrollbarArrowColor	IE5.5+	Sets or retrieves the color of the arrow elements of a scroll arrow.
scrollbar-base-color	scrollbarBaseColor	IE5.5+	Sets or retrieves the color of the main elements of a scroll bar, which include the scroll box, track, and scroll arrows.
scrollbar-darkshadow-color	scrollbarDarkShadowColor	IE5.5+	Sets or retrieves the color of the gutter of a scroll bar.
scrollbar-face-color	scrollbarFaceColor	IE5.5+	Sets or retrieves the color of the scroll box and scroll arrows of a scroll bar.
scrollbar-highlight-color	scrollbarHighlightColor	IE5.5+	Sets or retrieves the color of the top and left edges of the scroll box and scroll arrows of a scroll bar.
scrollbar-shadow-color	scrollbarShadowColor	IE5.5+	Sets or retrieves the color of the bottom and right edges of the scroll box and scroll arrows of a scroll bar.
scrollbar-track-color	scrollbarTrackColor	IE5.5+	Sets or retrieves the color of the track element of a scroll bar.
size	size	N6+	Sets or retrieves the dimensions of the page for printing.
float	styleFloat	IE4+	Sets or retrieves on which side of the object the text will flow.

Table B-1. *CSS Attributes Exposed in the Style Object* (continued)

Style Attribute	Corresponding Property	Support	Description
table-layout	tableLayout	IE5+, N6+	Sets or retrieves a string that indicates whether the table layout is fixed.
text-align	textAlign	IE4+, N4+	Sets or retrieves whether the text in the object is left-aligned, right-aligned, centered, or justified.
text-align-last	textAlignLast	IE5.5+	Sets or retrieves how to align the last line or only line of text in the object.
text-autospace	textAutospace	IE5+	Sets or retrieves the autospacing and narrow space width adjustment of text.
text-decoration	textDecoration	IE4+, N4+	Sets or retrieves whether the text in the object has blink, line-through, overline, or underline decorations.
None	textDecorationBlink	IE4+	Sets or retrieves a Boolean value that indicates whether the object's textDecoration property has a value of "blink."
None	textDecorationLineThrough	IE4+	Sets or retrieves a Boolean value indicating whether the text in the object has a line drawn through it.
None	textDecorationNone	IE4+	Sets or retrieves the Boolean value indicating whether the textDecoration property for the object has been set to none.
None	textDecorationOverline	IE4+	Sets or retrieves a Boolean value indicating whether the text in the object has a line drawn over it.
None	textDecorationUnderline	IE4+	Sets or retrieves whether the text in the object is underlined.
text-indent	textIndent	IE4+, N4+	Sets or retrieves the indentation of the first line of text in the object.

Table B-1.   *CSS Attributes Exposed in the Style Object* (continued)

Style Attribute	Corresponding Property	Support	Description
text-justify	textJustify	IE5+	Sets or retrieves the type of alignment used to justify text in the object.
text-kashida-space	textKashidaSpace	IE5.5+	Sets or retrieves the ratio of kashida expansion to white space expansion when justifying lines of text in the object.
text-overflow	textOverflow	IE6+	Sets or retrieves a value that indicates whether to render ellipses(...) to indicate text overflow.
text-transform	textTransform	IE4+, N4+	Sets or retrieves the rendering of the text in the object.
text-underline-position	textUnderlinePosition	IE5.5+	Sets or retrieves the position of the underline decoration that is set through the textDecoration property of the object.
top	top	IE4+, N6+	Sets or retrieves the position of the object relative to the top of the next-positioned object in the document hierarchy.
unicode-bidi	unicodeBidi	IE5+, N6+	Sets or retrieves the level of embedding with respect to the bidirectional algorithm.
vertical-align	verticalAlign	IE4+, N6+	Sets or retrieves the vertical alignment of the object.
visibility	visibility	IE4+, N6+	Sets or retrieves whether the content of the object is displayed. Values are "collapse," "hidden," or "visible."
white-space	whiteSpace	IE4+, N4+	Sets or retrieves a value that indicates whether lines are automatically broken inside the object.

Table B-1. *CSS Attributes Exposed in the Style Object* (continued)

Style Attribute	Corresponding Property	Support	Description
widows	widows	N6+	Sets or retrieves the minimum number of lines of a paragraph to display at the top of a page when performing page wrapping.
width	width	IE4+, N4+	Sets or retrieves the width of the object.
word-break	wordBreak	IE5+	Sets or retrieves line-breaking behavior within words, particularly where multiple languages appear in the object.
word-spacing	wordSpacing	IE4+, N6+	Sets or retrieves the amount of additional space between words in the object.
word-wrap	wordWrap	IE5.5+	Sets or retrieves whether to break words when the content exceeds the boundaries of its container.
writing-mode	writingMode	IE5.5+	Sets or retrieves the direction and flow of the content in the object.
z-index	zIndex	IE4+, N6+	Sets or retrieves the stacking order of positioned objects.
zoom	zoom	IE5.5+	Sets or retrieves the magnification scale of the object.

Table B-1.   *CSS Attributes Exposed in the Style Object* (continued)

Methods

- **borderWidths(top, right, bottom, left)**   Sets the borders for the element according to its string arguments. (N4 only)
- **getAttribute(name)**   Returns a string containing the value of the attribute specified in the string *name* or **null** if it does not exist.* (IE4+, N6+, DOM1 Core)
- **getExpression(propertyName)**   Retrieves the string giving the dynamic property expression for the property/attribute named *propertyName*.* (IE5+)

- **margins(top, right, bottom, left)**   Sets the margins for the element according to its string arguments. (N4 only)

- **paddings(top, right, bottom, left)**   Sets the padding for the element according to its string arguments. (N4 only)

- **removeAttribute(name)**   Removes the attribute corresponding to string *name* from the node.* (IE4+, N6+, DOM1 Core)

- **removeExpression(propertyName)**   Removes dynamic property expression for the property given in the string *propertyName*.* (IE5+)

- **setAttribute(name, value)**   Sets a new attribute for the node with name and value given by the string arguments.* (IE4+, N6+, DOM1 Core)

- **setExpression(property, expression [, language])**   Sets the expression given in string *expression* as the dynamic expression for the property given in string *property*. (IE5+)

Support
Internet Explorer 4+, primitive support in Netscape 4, good support in Netscape 6+, DOM2, CSS1, CSS2.

style (Document Object)
This object corresponds to an occurrence of a **<style>** element in the page. It is not the **Style** object that defines stylistic characteristics for each element. The proper way to manipulate the stylesheets found on the page is through the array of **styleSheet** objects found in **Document.styleSheets[ ]**. You can also access the **styleSheet** object corresponding to a **<style>** element using its **sheet** (Netscape 6+) or **styleSheet** (IE4+) property.

Access to **<style>** objects is carried out through normal DOM methods like **getElementById()**. Most of the properties found in objects corresponding to **<style>** elements are generic element properties.

Properties
This object has the following properties, in addition to those in the Generic HTML Element Object found at the beginning of this section.

- **disabled**   Boolean indicating whether the element is disabled (grayed out). (IE4+, N6+, DOM1)

- **media**   String containing the value of the element's **media** attribute, if one was defined. (IE4+, N6+, DOM1 HTML)

- **sheet**   Reference to the **styleSheet** object corresponding to the element. (N6+, ReadOnly)

- **styleSheet**   Reference to the **styleSheet** object corresponding to the element. (IE4+, ReadOnly)

- **type**   String containing the value of the **type** attribute for the stylesheet. Usually "text/css." (IE4+, N6+, DOM1)

Methods
This element has the methods listed in the Generic HTML Element Object found at the beginning of this section.

Event Handlers

```
onerror onreadystatechange
```

Support
Supported in Internet Explorer 4+, Netscape 6+, DOM1.

styleSheet (Document Object)

Each stylesheet used in the document has a corresponding **styleSheet** object in the **Document.styleSheets[ ]** collection (in load order). While **<style>** objects represent actual **<style>** elements in the page, **styleSheet** objects present the programmer with an interface with which the rules contained in each stylesheet can be examined and manipulated in a regular fashion. All stylesheets visible in the document are reflected as **styleSheet** objects, but inline style defined with the HTML **style** attribute is not. If you want to modify the style of a particular object, you should use the object's **style** or **runtimeStyle** property to access its **Style** or **runtimeStyle** object, which can then be directly manipulated.

It is important to notice that access to the individual **rule**s of a stylesheet is achieved in different ways in Netscape/DOM2 and in Internet Explorer. Netscape 2 uses the standard DOM2 collection **cssRules[ ]**, whereas Internet Explorer uses the nonstandard **rules[ ]** collection. In addition, different methods are used to add and delete rules.

Properties

- **cssRules[ ]** Collection of **rule** objects defined by the stylesheet. (IE5+ MacOS only, N6+, DOM2, ReadOnly)

- **cssText** String containing the rules defined by the stylesheet. Manipulating **rule** objects is preferable to modifying this property. (IE5+)

- **disabled** Boolean indicating whether the stylesheet is disabled. (IE4+, N6+, DOM2)

- **href** String containing the value of the **href** attribute, if the stylesheet was included using a **<link>** element. (IE4+, N6+, DOM2)

- **id** String holding the unique alphanumeric identifier for the element.* (IE4+, DOM2)

- **imports[ ]** Array of **styleSheet** objects corresponding to stylesheets included in the current stylesheet using **@import**. (IE4+, ReadOnly)

- **media** String holding the **media** attribute of the stylesheet. (IE4+, N6+, DOM2)

- **ownerNode** Reference to the top-level node in the document in which the stylesheet is defined. (N6+, DOM2, ReadOnly)

- **ownerRule** Reference to the **rule** object which included the stylesheet, if it was included with @import. Essentially useless because Netscape 6 does not reflect @import'd stylesheets as **styleSheet** objects. (N6+, DOM2, ReadOnly)

- **owningElement** Reference to the element in which the stylesheet was defined, for example a **<style>** or **<link>** object. (IE4+, ReadOnly)

- **pages[ ]** Array of **rule** objects corresponding to @page rules. (IE5.5+, ReadOnly)

- **parentStyleSheet**   If the stylesheet was @import'd, this property is a reference to the **styleSheet** object for the element in which it was @import'd. Otherwise **null**. (IE4+, N6+, DOM2, ReadOnly)

- **readOnly**   Boolean indicating if the stylesheet originated from an external file, for example if it was included with a **<link>** or @import. Does not really mean that it is read-only. (IE4+, ReadOnly)

- **rules[ ]**   Collection of **rule** objects defined by the stylesheet. (IE4+, ReadOnly)

- **title**   String containing **title** attribute of the element in which the stylesheet was defined. (IE4+, N6+, DOM2)

- **type**   String containing the value of the **type** attribute of the element in which the stylesheet was defined. Usually "text/css." (IE4+, N6+, DOM2)

Methods

- **addImport(url [, index])**   Adds an @import rule to the stylesheet and imports the stylesheet referenced by the string *url*. If *index* is specified, the new rule is inserted at that index in the **rules[ ]** collection. Otherwise, it is appended to the end. Returns the index at which the rule was added. (IE4+)

- **addRule(selector, value [, index])**   Inserts a new rule with selector given in string *selector* and value given in string *value*. The *value* should not include the curly braces you would normally use, and it is a semicolon-separated list of values. If *index* is specified, the new **rule** is inserted at that position in the **rules[ ]** collection, otherwise it is appended to the end. For example, "addRule('.important','color:red;font-weight:bold')." (IE4+)

- **deleteRule(index)**   Removes the **rule** at index *index* in the **cssRules[ ]** collection. (N6+, DOM2)

- **insertRule(rule, index)**   Adds the rule given in string *rule* to the **cssRules[ ]** collection at index *index*. To add the rule to the end use the **length** property of **cssRules** for *index*. The *rule* string should be exactly as you would normally specify a CSS rule, for example "insertRule('.important { color:red; font-weight: bold }', 0)." (N6+, DOM2)

- **removeRule(index)**   Removes the **rule** at index *index* in the **rules[ ]** collection. (IE4+)

Support

Internet Explorer 4+, Netscape 6+, DOM2.

Notes

At the time of this writing, Microsoft's documentation of this object's properties was incorrect.

sub (Document Object)

This object corresponds to a **<sub>** (subscript) element in the document. It has the properties, methods, and events listed in the Generic HTML Element Object found at the beginning of this section.

Support

Supported in Internet Explorer 4+, Netscape 6+, DOM1.

Submit (Document Object)

This object corresponds to an **<input type="submit">** form button. Access to this object is achieved through standard DOM methods or through the enclosing **Form** (via its **elements[ ]** array or by **name**). Note that all **Form**s have a **submit()** method that can be directly invoked.

Properties

This object has the following properties, in addition to those in the Generic HTML Element Object found at the beginning of this section.

- **accessKey**   Single character string indicating the hotkey that gives the element focus.* (IE4+, N6+, DOM1)
- **align**   String specifying the alignment of the element, for example "left."*
- **alt**   String containing alternative text for the button (for browsers incapable of rendering buttons). (N6+, DOM1)
- **controllers**   Related to XPConnect functionality. See **mozilla.org.** (N6+)
- **dataFld**   String specifying which field of a data source is bound to the element.* (IE4+)
- **dataFormatAs**   String indicating how the element treats data supplied to it.* (IE4+)
- **dataSrc**   String containing the source of data for data binding.* (IE4+)
- **defaultValue**   String containing the initial value of the button's **value** attribute. (IE3+, N6+, DOM1)
- **disabled**   Boolean indicating whether the element is disabled (grayed out). (IE4+, N6+, DOM1)
- **form**   Reference to the **Form** containing the button. (IE3+, N2+, DOM1, ReadOnly)
- **name**   String holding the **name** attribute of the element. (IE3+, N2+, DOM1)
- **selectionEnd**   The meaning of this property is unclear. (N6+)
- **selectionStart**   The meaning of this property is unclear. (N6+)
- **tabIndex**   Numeric value indicating the tab order for the object.* (IE4+, N6+, DOM1)
- **type**   String containing the **type** of the input, in this case "submit." (IE4+, N3+, DOM1, ReadOnly)
- **value**   The **value** attribute of the button. (IE3+, N2+, DOM1)

Methods

This object has the following methods, in addition to those in the Generic HTML Element Object found at the beginning of this section.

- **blur( )**   Removes focus from the element.* (IE3+, N2+, DOM1)
- **click( )**   Simulates a mouse click at the object.* (IE3+, N2+, DOM1)
- **createTextRange( )**   Creates a **TextRange** object for examination or manipulation of the button's text. A better cross-browser solution is to use standard **String** methods on the field's **value**. (IE4+)
- **focus( )**   Gives focus to the element.* (IE3+, N2+, DOM1)
- **handleEvent(event)**   Passes the **Event** *event* to be handled by the object.* (N4 only)

Event Handlers

```
onactivate onbeforeactivate onbeforecut onbeforedeactivate onbeforeeditfocus
onbeforepaste onblur onclick oncontextmenu oncontrolselect oncut ondblclick
ondeactivate ondrag ondragend ondragenter ondragleave ondragover ondragstart
ondrop onfilterchange onfocus onfocusin onfocusout onhelp onkeydown
onkeypress onkeyup onlosecapture onmousedown onmouseenter onmouseleave
onmousemove onmouseout onmouseover onmouseup onmousewheel onmove onmoveend
onmovestart onpaste onpropertychange onreadystatechange onresize onresizeend
onresizestart onselectstart ontimeerror
```

Support

Internet Explorer 3+, Netscape 2+, DOM1.

sun (Browser Object)

See **Packages**.

sup (Document Object)

This object corresponds to a **<sup>** (superscript) element in the document. It has the properties, methods, and events listed in the Generic HTML Element Object found at the beginning of this section.

Support

Supported in Internet Explorer 4+, Netscape 6+, DOM1.

table (Document Object)

This object corresponds to a **<table>** element in the document. Access to this object is achieved through standard DOM methods (for example, **getElementById()**).

Properties

This object has the following properties, in addition to those in the Generic HTML Element Object found at the beginning of this section.

- **align**   String specifying the alignment of the element, for example "left."*
  (IE4+, N6+, DOM1)
- **background**   String containing the URL of the background image for the table. (IE4+)
- **bgColor**   String containing the background color for the table. (IE4+, N6+, DOM1)
- **border**   String specifying the width of the border to draw around the table.
  (IE4+, N6+, DOM1)
- **borderColor**   String specifying the color of the border. (IE4+)
- **borderColorDark**   String specifying the dark border color for 3D borders. (IE4+)
- **borderColorLight**   String specifying the light border color for 3D borders. (IE4+)
- **caption**   Reference to the **caption** object for this table. (N6+, DOM1)

- **cellPadding**   String specifying the space between the cell wall and the content. (IE4+, N6+, DOM1)
- **cellSpacing**   String specifying the space between adjacent cells. (IE4+, N6+, DOM1)
- **cells[ ]**   Collection of all the cells in the table. (IE5+)
- **cols**   Integer specifying the number of columns in the table. (IE4+)
- **dataFld**   String specifying which field of a data source is bound to the element.* (IE4+)
- **dataFormatAs**   String indicating how the element treats data supplied to it.* (IE4+)
- **dataPageSize**   Integer indicating the "page" size for the table (used with data binding). (IE4+)
- **dataSrc**   String containing the source of data for data binding.* (IE4+)
- **frame**   String specifying how the table will be framed. Values are above, below, hsides, lhs, rhs, vsides, box, and border. (IE4+, N6+, DOM1)
- **height**   Specifies the height of the table. (IE4+, N6+)
- **rows[ ]** Collection of **tr**s (table rows) in the table. (IE4+, N6+, DOM1, ReadOnly)
- **rules**   String specifying how to draw dividers between cells in the table. Values are none, groups, rows, cols, or all. (IE4+, N6+, DOM1)
- **summary**   String containing a summary of the table. (IE6+, N6+, DOM1)
- **tBodies[ ]**   Collection of all **tbody** objects in the table. (IE4+, N6+, DOM1, ReadOnly)
- **tFoot**   Reference to the **tfoot** object for the table. (IE4+, N6+, DOM1)
- **tHead**   Reference to the **thead** object for the table. (IE4+, N6+, DOM1)
- **width**   Specifies the width of the table. (IE4+, N6+, DOM1)

Methods

This object has the following methods, in addition to those in the Generic HTML Element Object found at the beginning of this section. This object also provides methods for moving forward and backward through "pages" of data when Data Binding is in use. See the support site or MSDN for more information.

- **createCaption( )**   Creates a new **caption** object for the table if none exists and returns a reference to it. If a **caption** already exists, a reference to it is returned. (IE4+, N6+, DOM1)
- **createTFoot( )**   Creates a new **tfoot** object for the table if none exists and returns a reference to it. If a **tfoot** already exists, a reference to it is returned. (IE4+, N6+, DOM1)
- **createTHead( )**   Creates a new **thead** object for the table if none exists and returns a reference to it. If a **thead** already exists, a reference to it is returned. (IE4+, N6+, DOM1)
- **deleteCaption( )**   Deletes the table's **caption**. (IE4+, N6+, DOM1)
- **deleteRow(index)**   Deletes the row at index *index* from the table. (IE4+, N6+, DOM1)
- **deleteTFoot( )**   Deletes the **tfoot** object from the table. (IE4+, N6+, DOM1)
- **deleteTHead( )**   Deletes the **thead** object from the table. (IE4+, N6+, DOM1)
- **insertRow([index])**   Creates a new **tr** at index *index* (pushing the current occupant up one index) and returns a reference to the new **tr**. If *index* is omitted, the new row is placed at the end of the table. (IE4+, N6+, DOM1)

Event Handlers

This object has the event handlers listed in the Generic HTML Element Object found at the beginning of this section, in addition to the following:

```
onfilterchange onscroll
```

Support

Supported in Internet Explorer 4+, Netscape 6+, DOM1.

tbody, thead, tfoot (Document Object)

This object corresponds to a **<thead>**, **<tfoot>**, or **<tbody>** element in the document. Access to these objects is achieved through standard DOM methods (for example, **getElementById()**). The **tbodies[ ]** collection of **table** objects provides access to **tbody** objects and the **tHead** and **tFoot** properties of a **table** can be used to access **thead** and **tfoot** objects.

Properties

This object has the following properties, in addition to those in the Generic HTML Element Object found at the beginning of this section.

- **bgColor**   String specifying the background color of the section. (IE4+, N6+, DOM1)
- **ch**   String containing the alignment character. (IE6+, N6+, DOM1)
- **chOff**   String containing the offset at which the alignment character should be placed. (IE6+, N6+, DOM1)
- **rows[ ]**   Collection of rows (**<tr>** tags) contained within this section. (IE4+, N6+, DOM1, ReadOnly)
- **vAlign**   String specifying the vertical alignment of the cells, for example "top." (IE4+, N6+, DOM1)

Methods

This object has the following methods, in addition to those in the Generic HTML Element Object found at the beginning of this section.

- **deleteRow(index)**   Deletes the row at index *index* from the section. (IE4+, N6+, DOM1)
- **insertRow([index])**   Creates a new **tr** at index *index* (pushing the current occupant up one index) and returns a reference to the new **tr**. If *index* is omitted the new row is placed at the end of the section. (IE4+, N6+, DOM1)

Event Handlers

```
onactivate onbeforeactivate onbeforecut onbeforedeactivate onbeforepaste
onblur onclick oncontextmenu oncontrolselect oncut ondblclick ondeactivate
ondrag ondragend ondragenter ondragleave ondragover ondragstart ondrop
onfocus onfocusin onfocusout onhelp onkeydown onkeypress onkeyup
onlosecapture onmousedown onmouseenter onmouseleave onmousemove onmouseout
onmouseover onmouseup onmousewheel onmove onmoveend onmovestart onpaste
```

onpropertychange onreadystatechange onresizeend onresizestart onselectstart
ontimeerror

Support
Supported in Internet Explorer 4+, Netscape 6+, DOM1.

td, th (Document Object)

This object corresponds to a **<th>** or **<td>** element in the document. Access to this object is
achieved through standard DOM methods (for example, **getElementById()**) or through the **cells[ ]**
collection of a **tr** object.

Properties

This object has the following properties, in addition to those in the Generic HTML Element
Object found at the beginning of this section.

- **abbr**   String giving an abbreviation for header cells. (IE6+, N6+, DOM1)
- **align**   String specifying the alignment of the element, for example "left."*
  (IE4+, N6+, DOM1)
- **axis**   String containing a comma-delimited list of categories for table headers.
  (IE6+, N6+, DOM1)
- **background**   String containing the URL of the background image for the cell. (IE4+)
- **bgColor**   String specifying the background color of the cell. (IE4+, N6+, DOM1)
- **border**   String specifying the width of the border to draw around the cell. (IE4+, N6+, DOM1)
- **borderColor**   String specifying the color of the border. (IE4+)
- **borderColorDark**   String specifying the dark border color for 3D borders. (IE4+)
- **borderColorLight**   String specifying the light border color for 3D borders. (IE4+)
- **cellIndex**   Integer indicating the index of the cell in its row's **rows[ ]** collection.
  (IE4+, N6+, DOM1, ReadOnly)
- **ch**   String containing the alignment character. (IE6+, N6+, DOM1)
- **chOff**   String containing the offset at which the alignment character should be placed.
  (IE6+, N6+, DOM1)
- **colSpan**   Integer indicating how many columns are spanned by this cell. (IE4+, N6+, DOM1)
- **headers**   String specifying a comma-separated list of **id** attributes of cells that provide
  header information for the current cell. (IE6+, N6+, DOM1)
- **height**   Specifies the height of the cell. (IE4+, N6+, DOM1)
- **noWrap**   Boolean that indicates if word wrapping in the cell is suppressed.
  (IE4+, N6+, DOM1)
- **rowSpan**   Integer indicating how many rows the cell spans. (IE4+, N6+, DOM1)
- **scope**   Specifies which group of cells the current header provides information for.
  (IE6+, N6+, DOM1)

- **vAlign**   String specifying the vertical alignment of the cell data, for example "top." (IE4+, N6+, DOM1)
- **width**   Specifies the width of the cell. (IE4+, N6+, DOM1)

Methods

This element has the methods listed in the Generic HTML Element Object found at the beginning of this section.

Event Handlers

This object has the event handlers listed in the Generic HTML Element Object found at the beginning of this section, in addition to the following:

```
onbeforeeditfocus onfilterchange
```

Support

Supported in Internet Explorer 4+, Netscape 6+, DOM1.

Text (Document Object)

This object corresponds to a text input field (**<input type="text">**) element in the document. This object can be accessed using standard DOM techniques or through its enclosing **Form** (via the **elements[ ]** collection or by **name**).

Remember that the string entered into the input box is accessed through the **value** property of this object.

Properties

This object has the following properties, in addition to those in the Generic HTML Element Object found at the beginning of this section.

- **accessKey**   Single character string indicating the hotkey that gives the element focus.* (IE4+, N6+, DOM1)
- **controllers**   Related to XPConnect functionality. See **mozilla.org**. (N6+)
- **dataFld**   String specifying which field of a data source is bound to the element.* (IE4+)
- **dataFormatAs**   String indicating how the element treats data supplied to it.* (IE4+)
- **dataSrc**   String containing the source of data for data binding.* (IE4+)
- **defaultValue**   String containing the original **value** attribute for the element (does not reflect changes made by the user or script). (IE3+, N2+, DOM1, ReadOnly)
- **disabled**   Boolean indicating whether the element is disabled (grayed out). (IE4+, N6+, DOM1)
- **form**   Reference to the **Form** in which the element is contained. (IE3+, N2+, DOM1, ReadOnly)
- **maxLength**   Integer indicating the maximum number of characters the field can contain. (IE4+, N6+, DOM1)
- **name**   String holding the **name** attribute of the element. (IE3+, N2+, DOM1, ReadOnly)

- **readOnly**   Boolean indicating if the field is read-only. Like **disabled**, but a read-only field appears normal (not grayed out). (IE4+, N6+, DOM1)
- **selectionEnd**   The meaning of this property is unclear. (N6+)
- **selectionStart**   The meaning of this property is unclear. (N6+)
- **size**   Integer indicating the width of the field in characters. Defaults normally to about 20. (IE4+, N6+, DOM1)
- **tabIndex**   Numeric value indicating the tab order for the object.* (IE4+, N6+, DOM1)
- **textLength**   Related to XUL functionality. See **mozilla.org** for more information. (N6+)
- **type**   String containing the value of the **type** attribute, for example "text," "hidden," or "password." (IE3+, N3+, DOM1)
- **value**   String containing the text found in the field. (IE3+, N2+, DOM1)

Methods

This object has the following methods, in addition to those in the Generic HTML Element Object found at the beginning of this section.

- **blur( )**   Removes focus from the element.* (IE3+, N2+, DOM1)
- **createTextRange( )**   Creates a **TextRange** object for examination or manipulation of the input's text. A better cross-browser solution is to use standard **String** methods on the field's **value**. (IE4+)
- **focus( )**   Gives focus to the element.* (IE3+, N2+, DOM1)
- **handleEvent(event)**   Causes the **Event** *event* to be handled by the element.* (N4 only)
- **select( )**   Selects the text contents of the field. Useful for permitting the user to quickly delete large amounts of text or for drawing attention to a particular piece of text. (IE3+, N2+, DOM1)

Event Handlers

```
onactivate onafterupdate onbeforeactivate onbeforecut onbeforedeactivate
onbeforeeditfocus onbeforepaste onbeforeupdate onblur onclick oncontextmenu
oncontrolselect oncut ondblclick ondeactivate ondrag ondragend ondragenter
ondragleave ondragover ondragstart ondrop onerrorupdate onfilterchange
onfocus onfocusin onfocusout onhelp onkeydown onkeypress onkeyup
onlosecapture onmousedown onmouseenter onmouseleave onmousemove onmouseout
onmouseover onmouseup onmousewheel onmove onmoveend onmovestart onpaste
onpropertychange onreadystatechange onresize onresizeend onresizestart
onselectstart ontimeerror
```

Support

Internet Explorer 3+, Netscape 2+, DOM1.

textarea (Document Object)

This object corresponds to a text area input field (**<textarea>**) element in the document. This object can be accessed using standard DOM techniques or through its enclosing **Form** (via the **elements[ ]** collection or by **name**).

Remember that the text entered into the text box is accessed through the **value** property of this object.

Properties

- **accessKey**   Single character string indicating the hotkey that gives the element focus.* (IE4+, N6+, DOM1)

- **cols**   Integer holding the number of columns of the input area. (IE4+, N6+, DOM1)

- **controllers**   Related to XPConnect functionality. See **mozilla.org**. (N6+)

- **dataFld**   String specifying which field of a data source is bound to the element.* (IE4+)

- **dataFormatAs**   String indicating how the element treats data supplied to it.* (IE4+)

- **dataSrc**   String containing the source of data for data binding.* (IE4+)

- **defaultValue**   String holding the initial value of the **value** attribute (does not reflect changes made by the user). (IE3+, N2+, DOM1, ReadOnly)

- **disabled**   Boolean indicating whether the element is disabled (grayed out). (IE4+)

- **form**   Reference to the **Form** in which the textarea is embedded. (IE3+, N2+, DOM1, ReadOnly)

- **name**   String holding the **name** attribute of the element. (IE3+, N2+, DOM1)

- **readOnly**   Boolean indicating if the field is read-only. Like **disabled**, but a read-only field appears normal (not grayed out). (IE4+, N6+, DOM1)

- **rows**   Integer holding the number of rows of the input area. (IE4+, N6+, DOM1)

- **status**   Indicates whether the textarea is selected. (IE4+)

- **tabIndex**   Numeric value indicating the tab order for the object.* (IE4+, N6+, DOM1)

- **type**   String containing the type of the field, in this case "textarea." (IE3+ , N3+, DOM1, ReadOnly)

- **value**   String holding the text currently in the textarea. (IE3+, N2+, DOM1)

- **wrap**   String specifying how word wrapping is to be performed. Values are "hard"(carriage returns are added to the text), "soft" (wrapped but no returns added, the default), or "none." (IE4+)

Methods

- **blur( )**   Removes focus from the element.* (IE3+, N2+, DOM1)

- **createTextRange( )**   Creates a **TextRange** object for examination or manipulation of the textarea's text. A better cross-browser solution is to use standard **String** methods on the textarea's **value**. (IE4+)

- **focus( )**   Gives focus to the element.* (IE3+, N2+, DOM1)

- **handleEvent(event)**   Causes the **Event** *event* to be handled by the element.* (N4 only)

- **select( )**   Causes the contents of the text area to be selected (highlighted). (IE3+, N2+, DOM1)

Event Handlers

This object has the event handlers listed in the Generic HTML Element Object found at the beginning of this section, in addition to the following:

```
onafterupdate onbeforeeditfocus onbeforeupdate onchange onerrorupdate
onfilterchange onscroll onselect
```

Support

Supported in Internet Explorer 3+, Netscape 2+, DOM1.

TextRange (Browser Object)

An instance of this object is created by invoking **createTextRange()** as a method of the **body**, a **button**, or a form field. **TextRange** objects permit the programmer to examine and manipulate the text found in these elements as well as any HTML they contain. For full documentation of this object see MSDN or the support site.

Support

Internet Explorer 4+.

tfoot (Document Object)

See **tbody**.

th (Document Object)

See **td**.

thead (Document Object)

See **tbody**.

tr (Document Object)

This object corresponds to a **<tr>** element in the document. Access to this object is achieved through standard DOM methods (for example, **getElementById()**) or through the **rows[ ]** collection of a **table** element.

Properties

This object has the following properties, in addition to those in the Generic HTML Element Object found at the beginning of this section.

- **bgColor**   String specifying the background color of the row. (IE4+, N6+, DOM1)
- **border**   String specifying the width of the border to draw around the row. (IE4+, N6+, DOM1)
- **borderColor**   String specifying the color of the border. (IE4+)
- **borderColorDark**   String specifying the dark border color for 3D borders. (IE4+)
- **borderColorLight**   String specifying the light border color for 3D borders. (IE4+)

APPENDIXES

- **cells[ ]**   Collection of cells (**td** and **th** elements) in the row. (IE4+, N6+, DOM1)
- **ch**   String containing the alignment character. (IE6+, N6+, DOM1)
- **chOff**   String containing the offset at which the alignment character should be placed. (IE6+, N6+, DOM1)
- **rowIndex**   Integer indicating the index of the current row in its parent **table**'s **rows[ ]** array. (IE4+, N6+, DOM1, ReadOnly)
- **sectionRowIndex**   Integer indicating the index of the current row in its parent container's **rows[ ]** array. A container is either a **thead**, **tbody**, or **tfoot**. (IE4+, N6+, DOM1)
- **vAlign**   String specifying the vertical alignment of the cells, for example "top." (IE4+, N6+, DOM1)

Methods

This object has the following methods, in addition to those in the Generic HTML Element Object found at the beginning of this section.

- **deleteCell(index)**   Deletes the cell at index *index*. (IE4+, N6+, DOM1)
- **insertCell(index)**   Inserts a new cell at index *index* (or at the end if *index* is -1) and returns a reference to the new **td**. (IE4+, N6+, DOM1)

Event Handlers

This object has the event handlers listed in the Generic HTML Element Object found at the beginning of this section, in addition to the following:

```
onbeforeeditfocus onfilterchange
```

Support

Supported in Internet Explorer 4+, Netscape 6+, DOM1.

title (Document Object)

This object corresponds to the **<title>** element in the document head. You can access this property in most versions of IE through **document.all[ ]** or through **getElementById()**, but you cannot do so in browsers that strictly conform to the DOM (like Netscape 6). The reason is that the **<title>** element is not a part of the body of the document, it is part of the head. You will need to access the **<title>** through a node higher up the object hierarchy, (like **<html>**), for example by:

```
var titleObj = document.documentElement.getElementsByTagName('title').item(0);
```

Properties

This object has the following property, in addition to those in the Generic HTML Element Object found at the beginning of this section.

- **text**   String containing the title of the document, the text enclosed by the **<title></title>** tags. (IE4+, N6+, DOM1)

Methods

This element has the methods listed in the Generic HTML Element Object found at the beginning of this section.

Event Handlers

 `onlayoutcomplete onreadystatechange`

Support

Internet Explorer 4+, Netscape 6+, DOM1.

Notes

Most implementations provide access to the title string through **Document.title**.

tt (Document Object)

This object corresponds to a **<tt>** (teletype font) element in the document. It has the properties, methods, and events listed in the Generic HTML Element Object found at the beginning of this section.

Support

Supported in Internet Explorer 4+, Netscape 6+, DOM1.

u (Document Object)

This object corresponds to a **<u>** (underlined) element in the document. It has the properties, methods, and events listed in the Generic HTML Element Object found at the beginning of this section.

Support

Supported in Internet Explorer 4+, Netscape 6+, DOM1.

ul (Document Object)

This object corresponds to a **<ul>** (unordered list) element in the document. Access to these objects is achieved through standard DOM methods (for example, **getElementById()**).

Properties

This object has the following properties, in addition to those in the Generic HTML Element Object found at the beginning of this section.

- **compact** Boolean indicating whether the list should be compacted by removing extra space between list objects. (IE4+, N6+, DOM1)
- **type** Sets the style of list bulleting: "disc," "square," or "circle." (IE3+, N6+, DOM1)

Methods

This element has the methods listed in the Generic HTML Element Object found at the beginning of this section.

Event Handlers

This object has the event handlers listed in the Generic HTML Element Object found at the beginning of this section, in addition to the following:

```
onlayoutcomplete
```

Support

Supported in Internet Explorer 4+, Netscape 6+, DOM1.

userProfile (Browser Object)

This object allows scripts to read and set user profile information. Such information is entered by the user in the "My Profile" section under the "Content" tab of the "Internet Options" menu in IE's "Tools" list.

The "vCard" user profile attributes that you can read and set with this object can be found at the support site, and include information about the user's physical address, gender, contact information, and so on. The reality of these attributes is that their use is extremely uncommon. The only attribute that might occasionally be used is "vCard.Homepage," but even this is very rare.

Because the user is prompted whether to permit each action, requests for reading and setting profile data are queued and then processed in batch fashion. This improves the user experience by requiring only one prompt for a group of related requests.

Although the **userProfile** object might seem like a great way to get data from the user, the number of users who have taken the time to fill out their profile information is essentially zero. For this reason, this object is pretty useless.

Properties

None.

Methods

- **addReadRequest(attribute)**   Adds an entry to the queue for read requests for the vCard property given in the string *attribute*. Returns a Boolean indicating if the request could be added. (IE4+)

- **clearRequest( )**   Clears all requests from the read-request queue to clear the way for a new set of requests. (IE4+)

- **doReadRequest(usageCode [, partyName][, domain][, path])**   Causes the read request queue to be processed, displaying the *partyName* as extra information about the party requesting the access and using the integer *usageCode* to notify the user how the information will be used. Values for *usageCode* are 0–12, and their semantics can be found at the support site. The user can selectively grant or deny access to the information requested for each item in the queue. The *domain* and *path* strings specify other domains and paths of parties that will receive the information (in addition to the current URL). (IE4+)

- **getAttribute(attribute)**   Returns a string containing the value of the vCard property specified by the string *attribute*. Access to this attribute should be requested first using **addReadRequest()** and **doReadRequest()**. Returns **null** if the attribute value is not available or has been denied. (IE4+)

■ **setAttribute(attribute, value)**   Attempts to set the attribute given in the string *attribute* to the value in string *value*. (IE4+)

Support
Internet Explorer 4+.

Notes
Using this object requires that users have filled out their profile information in their browser, a very unlikely condition.

var (Document Object)

This object corresponds to an occurrence of a **<var>** element (variable declaration) in the document. It has the properties and methods listed in the Generic HTML Element Object found at the beginning of this section.

Event Handlers

```
onactivate onbeforeactivate onbeforecut onbeforedeactivate onbeforepaste
onblur onclick oncontextmenu oncontrolselect oncut ondblclick ondeactivate
ondragend ondragenter ondragleave ondragover ondragstart ondrop onfocus
onfocusin onfocusout onhelp onkeydown onkeypress onkeyup onlosecapture
onmousedown onmouseenter onmouseleave onmousemove onmouseout onmouseover
onmouseup onmousewheel onmove onmoveend onmovestart onpaste onpropertychange
onreadystatechange onresizeend onresizestart onselectstart ontimeerror
```

VBArray (Built-in Object)

This object provides access to VBScript safe arrays. For full documentation of this object, see Microsoft's documentation at MSDN.

Notes
This is *not* an ECMAScript object. It is a proprietary Microsoft built-in object.

Window (Browser Object)

This top-level object contains properties and methods that permit the examination and manipulation of a browser window. Access to a window's frames, document, events, and other features are all achieved through this object. If a window has frames, each frame is itself a **Window** object accessed via the **window.frames[ ]** array. This simplifies the organization of nested frames.

The **Window** is always in the context of client-side JavaScript, so its properties and methods can usually be accessed without the "window." prefix. One place you'll need to be careful, though, is in event handlers. Because event handlers are bound to the **Document**, a **Document** property with the same name as a **Window** property (for example, **open**) will mask out the **Window** property. For this reason, you should always use the full "window." syntax when addressing **Window** properties in event handlers.

Because each browser window (and frame) has its own **Window** object, you can access a function or variable in another window by accessing it as a **Window** property. For example, if a variable named "page" is defined in a window you have a reference to, you would access it as *windowHandle.page*. It is always a good idea to verify that the window reference you have and the data you are accessing are valid before using this technique.

Properties

- **clientInformation**   Contains information about the browser configuration. (IE4+)

- **clipboardData**   Provides access to the OS's clipboard. (IE5+)

- **closed**   Boolean indicating whether the user has closed the window. (IE4+, N3+, DOM0, ReadOnly)

- **Components**   This object provides XPConnect functionality that permits the access and manipulation of XPCOM objects with JavaScript. See documentation at **mozilla.org.** (N6+)

- **crypto**   Provides access to Netscape's cryptographic methods. See documentation at Netscape or **mozilla.org** for more information. (N4+)

- **defaultStatus**   String containing the default message for the browser's status bar. (IE3+, N2+)

- **dialogArguments**   Value containing the parameter specified in the second parameter of **showModelDialog()** or **showModelessDialog()**. (IE4+, ReadOnly)

- **dialogHeight**   The height of the window if it was created with **showModelDialog()** or **showModelessDialog()**. Units are in **em** in IE4 or pixels otherwise. (IE4+)

- **dialogLeft**   The *x* coordinate of the left edge of the window if it was created with **showModelDialog()** or **showModelessDialog()**. Units are in **em** in IE4 or pixels otherwise. (IE4+)

- **dialogTop**   The *y* coordinate of the top edge of the window if it was created with **showModelDialog()** or **showModelessDialog()**. Units are in **em** in IE4 or pixels otherwise. (IE4+)

- **dialogWidth**   The width of the window if it was created with **showModelDialog()** or **showModelessDialog()**. Units are in **em** in IE4 or pixels otherwise. (IE4+)

- **directories**   Object with property **visible** which is a Boolean indicating if Netscape 6's "directories" button is visible. Requires UniversalBrowserWrite to set. (N6+)

- **document**   Reference to the **Document** contained in the window. (IE3+, N2+, DOM0)

- **event**   The **Event** instance that IE makes implicitly available to event handlers. (IE4+)

- **external**   Reference to the **external** object providing extended functionality. (IE4+)

- **frameElement**   Reference to the **Frame** in which the window is contained. (IE5.5+ Windows, ReadOnly)

- **frames[ ]**   Collection of frames contained within the window. (IE3+, N2+, DOM0)

- **history**   Reference to the browser's **History** object. (IE3+, N3+, DOM0)

- **innerHeight**   Numeric value indicating height of the window's content area in pixels.* (N4+)

- **innerWidth**   Numeric value indicating the width of the window's content area in pixels.* (N4+)

- **length**   The number of frames contained in the window. (IE3+, N2+, DOM0, ReadOnly)

■ **location**   Reference to the **Location** object holding data about the document currently loaded in the window. (IE3+, N2+, DOM0)

■ **locationbar**   Object with property **visible**, a Boolean indicating if the browser's location bar is currently visible. Requires UniversalBrowserWrite to set. (N4+)

■ **menubar**   Object with property **visible**, a Boolean indicating if the browser's menu bar is currently visible. Requires UniversalBrowserWrite to set. (N4+)

■ **name**   String holding the **name** attribute of the window or frame. Useful for using JavaScript to determine which frame it is currently executing within or with the **target** attribute of links. (IE3+, N2+, DOM0)

■ **navigator**   Reference to the browser's **Navigator** object. (IE3+, N6+ (top level object in earlier versions), DOM0)

■ **offscreenBuffering**   Boolean indicating whether content is buffered before being sent to the screen. Can also take on the value "auto" in IE which permits the browser to choose. (NS4 only, IE4+)

■ **opener**   Reference to the **Window** which opened the current window. (IE3+, N3+, DOM0)

■ **outerHeight**   Numeric value indicating the total height of the window in pixels.* (N4+)

■ **outerWidth**   Numeric value indicating the total width in pixels of the window.* (N4+)

■ **pageXOffset**   Indicates how far to the right (in pixels) the window is currently scrolled. (N4+)

■ **pageYOffset**   Indicates how far down (in pixels) the window is currently scrolled. (N4+)

■ **parent**   Reference to the **Window** or **Frame** which is the parent of the current frame. (IE3+, N2+, DOM0, ReadOnly)

■ **personalbar**   Object with property **visible**, a Boolean indicating if the browser's personal bar is currently visible. Requires UniversalBrowserWrite to set. (N4+)

■ **pkcs11**   Object that provides cryptographic functionality (implementing PKCS #11). See mozilla.org for more information. (N6+)

■ **prompter**   Provides XPConnect functionality. See **mozilla.org** for more information. (N6+)

■ **returnValue**   The value returned by the window (or to be returned by the window) if it was created using **showModalDialog()**. (IE4+)

■ **screen**   Reference to the browser's **Screen** object. (IE4+, N6+ (top level object in N4), DOM0)

■ **screenLeft**   Integer indicating the x coordinate in pixels of the left edge of the client area of the browser window. (IE5+, ReadOnly)

■ **screenTop**   Integer indicating the y coordinate in pixels of the top edge of the client area of the browser window. (IE5+, ReadOnly)

■ **screenX**   Integer indicating the x coordinate of the left edge of the browser window, relative to the entire screen. Setting this property requires UniversalBrowserWrite. (N4+)

■ **screenY**   Integer indicating the y coordinate of the top edge of the browser window, relative to the entire screen. Setting this property requires UniversalBrowserWrite. (N4+)

■ **scrollX**   Integer indicating how far (in pixels) the window is scrolled to the right. (N6+, ReadOnly)

■ **scrollY** Integer indicating how far (in pixels) the window is scrolled down. (N6+, ReadOnly)

■ **scrollbars** Object with property **visible**, a Boolean indicating if the browser's scroll bars are currently visible. Requires UniversalBrowserWrite to set. (N4+)

■ **self** Reference to the current **Window**. (IE3+, N2+, DOM0)

■ **sidebar** Permits XPConnect functionality. See **mozilla.org** for more information. (N6+)

■ **status** String containing the text currently displayed in the browser's status bar. (IE3+, N2+, DOM0)

■ **statusbar** Object with property **visible**, a Boolean indicating if the browser's status bar is currently visible. Requires UniversalBrowserWrite to set. (N4+)

■ **toolbar** Object with property **visible**, a Boolean indicating if the browser's tool bar is currently visible. Requires UniversalBrowserWrite to set. (N4+)

■ **top** Reference to the top **Window** in the document object hierarchy. Useful for accessing the enclosing **Window** from frames. (IE3+, N2+, DOM0, ReadOnly)

■ **window** Reference to the current **Window**. (IE3+, N2+, DOM0, ReadOnly)

Methods

■ **alert(message)** Pops up an alert dialog box with text *message* and an "OK" button. (IE3+, N2+, DOM0)

■ **addEventListener(whichEvent, handler, direction)** Instructs the window to execute the function *handler* whenever an event of type given in the string *whichEvent* (for example, "click") occurs. The *direction* is a Boolean specifying the phase in which to fire, **true** for capture or **false** for bubbling.* (N6+, DOM2)

■ **atob(string)** Base64-encodes *string* and returns the encoded string. (N4 only)

■ **attachEvent(whichHandler, theFunction)** Attaches the function *theFunction* as a handler specified by the string *whichHandler*, for example "onclick."* (IE5+)

■ **back()** Causes the browser to load the previous URL in the top-level window's history. (N4+, DOM0)

■ **blur( )** Removes focus from the element.* (IE4+, N2+, DOM0)

■ **btoa(string)** Base64-decodes *string* and returns the decoded string. (N4 only)

■ **captureEvents(eventMask)** Instructs object to capture the events given in the bitmask *eventMask*.* (N4+)

■ **clearInterval(intervalID)** Cancels the interval *intervalID* (previously returned by **setInterval**). (IE4+, NS4+, DOM0)

■ **clearTimeout(timeoutID)** Cancels the timeout *timeoutID* (previously returned by **setTimeout**). (IE3+, N2+, DOM0)

■ **close( )** Closes the window (subject to user approval in most browsers). (IE3+, N2+, DOM0)

■ **confirm(message)** Displays a confirmation dialog box with text *message* and "OK" and "Cancel" buttons. Returns **true** if the user selects "OK" or **false** otherwise. (IE3+, N2+, DOM0)

■ **createPopup([vArgs])** Creates a popup window (initially hidden and empty) and returns a reference to the new **popup** object. The argument *vArgs* is not currently in use. (IE5.5+)

■ **detachEvent(whichHandler, theFunction)**   Instructs the window to cease executing the function *theFunction* as a handler given the string *whichHandler*, for example "onclick."* (IE5+)

■ **disableExternalCapture( )**   Disables capturing of external events by scripts in the windows. Only used with signed scripts. (N4+)

■ **enableExternalCapture( )**   Enables script in the window to capture events in other windows, no matter what their origin. Once this method is invoked, the script can listen in on other windows' events using their **captureEvents()** method. This method requires UniversalBrowserWrite.

■ **execScript(expression, language)**   Executes the string *expression* as script in the language given in string *language* (for example, "JScript"). (IE4+)

■ **focus( )**   Gives focus to the window.* (IE4+, N3+, DOM0)

■ **forward( )**   Causes the browser to load the next URL in the top-level window's history. (N4+)

■ **home( )**   Causes the browser to load the user's preferred home page. (N4+, DOM0)

■ **moveBy(x, y)**   Moves the window *x* pixels horizontally and *y* pixels vertically from its current position. Moving it outside of the screen requires UniversalBrowserWrite in Netscape. (IE4+, N4+)

■ **moveTo(x, y)**   Moves the window to the absolute screen coordinates (*x, y*). (IE4+, N4+)

■ **navigate(url)**   Loads the URL given in string *url* into the window. (IE3+)

■ **open(url, name [, features] [, replace])**   Opens up a new window to the location given in string *url* with name given in string *name*. Returns a reference to the new window. The string *features* specifies which window features (for example, scrollbars) the new window will have. IE permits *replace*, a Boolean specifying whether the new URL replaces the existing URL (if the window already exists) in the window's history or if it is added as a new entry. If the *features* parameter is specified, any features not listed in it default to being turned off. The *features* string is a comma-separated list of "*feature=value*" entries where *feature* is any feature listed in Table B-2 and *value* is either "yes," "no," 1, or 0, controlling whether the feature is used. Using yes/no is the preferred strategy. Some features require UniversalBrowserWrite in Netscape. See full description at support site. (IE3+, N2+, DOM0)

■ **print( )**   Causes a print dialog to appear, prompting the user with printing options. (IE5+, N4+, DOM0)

■ **prompt(message [, default])**   Causes a dialog to appear with text *message* and a text entry field initially filled with the string *default*. If *default* is omitted, "undefined" is used. Returns the string entered by the user or **null** if the user cancels or closes the dialog. (IE3+, N2+, DOM0)

■ **releaseEvents(eventMask)**   Instructs window to stop capturing the events given in the bitmask *eventMask*.* (N4+)

■ **removeEventListener(whichEvent, handler, direction)**   Removes function *handler* as a handler for the event given in the string *whichEvent* (for example, "click") for the phase given by the Boolean *direction*.* (N6+, DOM2)

■ **resizeBy(dWidth, dHeight)**   Grows or shrinks the window by the number of pixels given in the arguments. Negative values cause the window to shrink. The window is resized along its bottom and right edges. Netscape requires UniversalBrowserWrite to shrink the window to smaller than 100 pixels or larger than the size of the screen. (IE4+, N4+)

- **resizeTo(width, height)**   Resizes the window to the size in pixels given by the arguments. The *height* and *width* give the size of the entire window, including chrome. Netscape requires UniversalBrowserWrite to shrink the window to smaller than 100 pixels or larger than the size of the screen. (IE4+, N4+)

- **routeEvent(event)**   Passes the **Event** instance *event* along normally down the hierarchy. Used to decline to handle an event.* (N4+)

- **scroll(x, y)**   Deprecated. Scrolls the pixel location (*x,y*) to the upper-left corner of the window. (IE4+, N3+)

- **scrollBy(dX, dY)**   Scrolls the window *dX* pixels horizontally and *dY* pixels vertically. (IE4+, N4+)

- **scrollTo(x, y)**   Scrolls the window to the given coordinates. (IE4+, N4+)

- **setActive( )**   Sets the window to be the active window but does not give it focus. (IE5.5+)

- **setCursor(type)** Changes the cursor to the type given in string *type*. Valid values are: alias, auto, cell, context-menu, copy, count-down, count-up, count-up-down, crosshair, default, e-resize, grab, grabbing, help, move, n-resize, ne-resize, nw-resize, pointer, s-resize, se-resize, spinning, sw-resize, text, w-resize, and wait. The result of this method will vary from platform to platform. (N6+)

- **setInterval(toExecute, ms [, arg1 [, arg2 ...]])**   Starts an interval timer that executes *toExecute* every *ms* milliseconds (on a continual basis). Returns an integer identifying the interval timer (so it can later be canceled). If *toExecute* is a string, the optional arguments found after *ms* are not used and *toExecute* is reevaluated upon every invocation so that it can reference variables that might change between intervals. If *toExecute* is a reference to a function, the optional parameters *argN* are passed to it on every invocation. These optional parameters are not available in IE; instead, IE takes an optional third argument that is a string specifying which language to execute *toExecute* as (for example, "JScript"). Note that IE4 supports only string arguments for *toExecute*, so passing a string for this value is the preferred strategy. (IE4+, N4+)

- **setResizable(isResizable)**   Deprecated. Sets whether the window is resizable according to its Boolean argument. Behavior of this method varies wildly across platforms. (N4 only)

- **setTimeout(toExecute, ms [, arg1 [, arg2 ...]])**   Executes *toExecute ms* milliseconds in the future. Returns an integer identifying the timer (so it can later be canceled). If *toExecute* is a string, the optional arguments found after *ms* are not used and *toExecute* is reevaluated upon every invocation so that it can reference variables that might change between intervals. Netscape 4+ permits *toExecute* to be referenced to a function, and if it is, the optional parameters *argN* are passed to it on every invocation. IE5 also permits *toExecute* to be a function reference, but these optional parameters are not available; instead, IE takes an optional third argument that is a string specifying which language to execute *toExecute* as (for example, "JScript"). Passing a string for *toExecute* is the preferred strategy. (IE3+, N2+)

- **setZOptions(position)**   Deprecated. Fixes the *z*-index of the window to a particular value. If *position* is "alwaysRaised," the window will appear above all other windows at all times. If it is "alwaysLowered," the window will appear below all other windows at all times. If it is "z-lock," the window's stacking position is fixed, that is, it does not rise above other windows when activated. This method requires the UniversalBrowserWrite privilege. (N4 only)

■ **showHelp(url [, contextID])**   Launches a help window that loads the *url*. The second parameter specifies a context ID that is used to indicate the initial help position in the document. See Microsoft documentation for Microsoft HTML Help and Winhelp. (IE4+)

■ **showModalDialog(url [, arguments][, features])**   Creates a dialog box that keeps focus and must be addressed before any other action can occur in the browser. The *url* specifies the URL of the document to display and *arguments* defines the value set in the new window's **dialogArguments** property. Returns the value of the **returnValue** property of the new window when it closes. The *features* string is a semicolon-separated list of the "*feature:value*" entries of the features listed in Table B-3 (for example, "help:yes;center:yes"), as provided by Microsoft's documentation. (IE4+)

■ **showModelessDialog(url [, argument][, features])**   Creates a dialog box that stays on top of any other browser windows. The *url* specifies the URL of the document to display and *argument* is a string that defines the value set in the new window's **dialogArguments** property. Returns a reference to the new window. The *features* string is a semicolon-separated list of the "*feature:value*" entries of the features listed in Table B-3 (for example, "help:yes;center:yes"), as provided by Microsoft's documentation. (IE4+)

■ **sizeToContent( )**   Resizes the window so that all of its contents are visible. (N6+)

■ **stop( )**   Halts loading of the page. (N4+, DOM0)

Feature Parameter	Value	Description	Example
alwaysLowered	yes/no	Indicates if window should always be lowered under all other windows. Does have a security risk.	alwaysLowered=no
alwaysRaised	yes/no	Indicates if the window should always stay on top of other windows.	alwaysRaised=no
dependent	yes/no	Indicates if the spawned window is truly dependent on the parent window. Dependent windows are closed when their parents are closed, while others stay around.	dependent=yes
directories	yes/no	Should the directories button on the browser window show?	directories=yes
fullscreen	yes/no	Should the window take over the full screen? (IE only)	fullscreen=yes
height	pixel value	Sets the height of the window, chrome and all.	height=100
hotkeys	yes/no	Indicates if the hotkeys for the browser (beyond browser-essential ones like Quit) should be disabled in the new window.	hotkeys=no

Table B-2.   *Possible Values for the feature Entries in the features Argument to* **window.open( )**

Feature Parameter	Value	Description	Example
innerHeight	pixel value	Sets the height of the inner part of the window where the document shows.	innerHeight=200
innerWidth	pixel value	Sets the width of the inner part of the window where the document shows.	innerWidth=300
left	pixel value	Specifies where relative to the screen origin to place the window. IE-specific syntax; use *screeny* for Netscape.	left=10
location	yes/no	Specifies if the location bar should show on the window.	location=no
menubar	yes/no	Specifies if the menu bar should be shown or not.	menubar=yes
outerHeight	pixel value	Sets the height of the outer part of the window, including the chrome.	outerHeight=300
outerWidth	pixel value	Sets the width of the outer part of the window, including the chrome.	outerWidth=300
resizable	yes/no	Value to indicate if the user is to be able to resize the window.	resizable=no
screenx	pixel value	Distance left in pixels from screen origin where window should be opened. This is Netscape's syntax; use *left* in IE.	screenx=100
screeny	pixel value	Distance up and down from the screen origin where window should be opened. This is Netscape's syntax; use *top* in IE.	screeny=300
scrollbars	yes/no	Should scrollbars show?	scrollbars=no
status	yes/no	Should the status bar show?	status=no
titlebar	yes/no	Should the title bar show?	titlebar=yes
toolbar	yes/no	Should the toolbar menu be visible?	toolbar=yes
top	pixel value	IE-specific feature to indicate position down from the top corner of the screen to position the window; use screeny for Netscape.	top=20
width	pixel value	The width of the window. You may want to use innerWidth instead.	width=300
z-lock	yes/no	Specifies if the z-index should be set so that a window can not change its stacking order relative to other windows even if it gains focus.	z-lock=yes

Table B-2.   *Possible Values for the feature Entries in the features Argument to* **window.open()**

Feature:Value	Description
dialogHeight:Height	Sets the height of the dialog window.
dialogLeft:XPos	Sets the left position of the dialog window relative to the upper-left corner of the desktop.
dialogTop:YPos	Sets the top position of the dialog window relative to the upper-left corner of the desktop.
dialogWidth:Width	Sets the width of the dialog window.
center:{ yes | no | 1 | 0 | on | off }	Specifies whether to center the dialog window within the desktop. The default is yes.
dialogHide:{ yes | no | 1 | 0 | on | off }	Specifies whether the dialog window is hidden when printing or using print preview. This feature is only available when a dialog box is opened from a trusted application. The default is no.
edge:{ sunken | raised }	Specifies the edge style of the dialog window. The default is raised.
help:{ yes | no | 1 | 0 | on | off }	Specifies whether the dialog window displays the context-sensitive Help icon. The default is yes.
resizable:{ yes | no | 1 | 0 | on | off }	Specifies whether the dialog window has fixed dimensions. The default is no.
scroll:{ yes | no | 1 | 0 | on | off }	Specifies whether the dialog window displays scrollbars. The default is yes.
status:{ yes | no | 1 | 0 | on | off }	Specifies whether the dialog window displays a status bar. The default is yes for untrusted dialog windows and no for trusted dialog windows.
unadorned:{ yes | no | 1 | 0 | on | off }	Specifies whether the dialog window displays the border window chrome. This feature is only available when a dialog box is opened from a trusted application. The default is no.

Table B-3.   *Possible Values for Parts of the features Argument to **showModalDialog** and **showModelessDialog***

APPENDIXES

Event Handlers

```
onactivate onafterprint onbeforeactivate onbeforeprint onbeforeunload onblur
oncontrolselect ondeactivate ondragdrop onerror onfocus onhelp onload onmove
onmoveend onmovestart onresize onresizeend onresizestart onscroll onunload
```

xml (Document Object)

This object corresponds to a **<xml>** (XML data island) element in the document. Access to these objects is achieved through standard DOM methods (for example, **getElementById()**). See the support site or MSDN for more details. Chapter 20 also contains examples that use the **<xml>** tag and its JavaScript object.

Support

Internet Explorer 5+.

The Complete Reference

Appendix C

Reserved Words

A ll languages, including JavaScript, have numerous reserved words that cannot be used as variable names, function names, or any other form of identifiers without causing some problem. If one of these reserved words is used as a user-defined identifier, such as a variable or function name, it should result in a syntax error. For example,

```
var for="not allowed";
document.write("Variable = "+for);
```

declares a variable called "for," which is obviously a JavaScript keyword used for looping. You might expect some form of error to occur, and older browsers will throw an error such as the one shown here from Navigator 3:

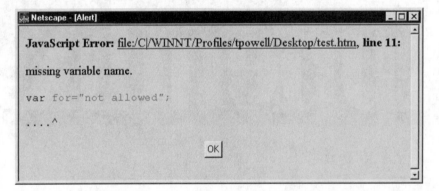

However, newer browsers may not show any form of error at all when a reserved word is used; they will simply ignore the code. Even worse, the actual warning or type of error that results from using a reserved word varies from browser to browser as do the particular reserved words. For example, use a value of "goto" instead of "for" in the previous example and it should work in many browsers, including Internet Explorer.

Generally speaking, reserved words are reserved from use because they already have a defined meaning in some variant of JavaScript or a related technology. Reserved words generally are categorized in three types:

1. Language keywords

2. Future reserved words

3. Words such as object names or related technology keywords

Table C-1 lists the words in the first two categories.

Beyond these well-known reserved words, there are other words that may have problems under future versions of JavaScript. While the words shown in Table C-2 may not actually be reserved in a future version of JavaScript, they should be avoided just to be safe.

abstract	else	instanceof	switch
Boolean	enum	int	synchronized
break	export	interface	this
byte	extends	long	throw
case	false	native	throws
catch	final	new	transient
char	finally	null	true
class	float	package	try
const	for	private	typeof
continue	function	protected	val
debugger	goto	public	var
default	if	return	void
delete	implements	short	volatile
do	import	static	while
double	in	super	with

Table C-1.   *Reserved Words in JavaScript*

The third category of dangerous identifiers includes names of intrinsic JavaScript objects, functions, and data types. Words like **String**, **parseInt**, **document**, and so on are included in this category. There are far too many of these "dangerous" identifier names to list, but consider anything in Appendix A or Appendix B to be a JavaScript identifier and inappropriate for other use.

exclude	namespace
get	set
include	use
as	is

Table C-2.   *Potential JavaScript 2.0 Reserved Words*

Future versions of JavaScript will certainly add more support for object-oriented programming principles as well as increase support for interaction with HTML, XML, and CSS. Therefore, JavaScript programmers should avoid any words specific to these languages, such as "head," "body," "frame," and so on. While many of these words might be safely used, less generic identifiers ought to be used instead, both to future-proof code and to avoid bad programming style.

Index

Symbols

($) character, positional indicators, 227
(!) NOToperators, 107–108
(" ") double quotes, using with strings, 66
(%) modulus operator, 96
<% %> tag, including ASP code with, 673
(' ') single quotes, using with strings, 66
"( )" parenthesis operator, 114
(*) modification operator, 96
(+) addition operator
    example of use, 96
    using with string values instead
      of numbers, 97
(++)increment operators, 103–105
(,) comma operator, 110
(-) subtraction operator, 96
(-) unary operators
    negating values with, 98
    number types and, 62
(--) decrement operator, 103–105

(/) division operator, 96
(/) character (escape codes), 227–228
(;) semicolons, ending statements with,
    35–36, 92–94
(<<) Shift Left, bitwise shift operators, 102
(=) assignment operators
    common use of, 34
    overview of, 95–96
    using with var keyword, 92
(==) equals operator, 34, 105
(===) identity operators, 107
(>>) Shift Right bitwise shift operators, 102
(>>>) Shift Right Zero Fill bitwise shift
    operators, 102
(?:) operator, 108–109
([]) square brackets, defining character
    classes, 232
(^) XOR, bitwise operator, 99–101
(^) character, positional indicator, 227
(~) NOT bitwise operator, 100–101

(&), AND bitwise operator, 99–101
(&&) AND operators
    combining Boolean values with,
        107–108
    short-circuit evaluations and,
        120–121

A

<a>, document object, 914–916
<abbr>, document object, 916
abstraction, object-oriented
    programming and, 180
accesskey attribute, 502–504
<acconym>, document object, 916
Active Server Pages (ASP), 672–673
    interacting with server objects,
        678–682
    JavaScript methods in, 673–675
    JavaScript syntax in, 675–677
    using with external systems, 683–685
ActiveX controls, 656–660
    including, 656–657
    interacting with, 658–660
ActiveXObject, browser/built-in
    object, 917
addBehavior( ) method, 793–794
addEventListener( ) method, 374
addition operator (+)
    example of use, 96
    using with string values instead
        of numbers, 97
<address>, document object, 917
advanced, regular expressions, 248–249,
    872–873
alert( ) method
    dialogs and, 382–383
    I/O and, 50
    outputting debugging information
        with, 812–817
all[ ] collection, 334–335, 435, 531–532
<anchor>, document object, 914–916
anchors[ ] collection, 428–429
AND (&), bitwise operator, 99–101
AND (&&) operators

combining Boolean values with,
    107–108
short-circuit evaluations and,
    120–121
animation, DHTML, 552–557
anonymous functions, 150–151
<applet>, document object, 639,
    644, 917–918
applets[ ] collection, 434–435
applications
    DOM, 455–456
    JavaScript, 25–26
appName property, Navigator
    properties, 608–609
appVersion property, Navigator
    properties, 608–609
archive attribute, 730, 732
<area>, document object, 918–919
arguments. *see* parameters (arguments)
arithmetic operators, 96–99
    binary and self-assignment, 858
    Infinity and NaN values, 98–99
    list of basic, 96
    negation, 98
    pre/postfix, 859
    string concatenation using (+), 97–98
    unary, 859
Array, built-in objects, 184–200
    accessing elements, 185
    adding/changing elements, 185–186
    extending with prototypes, 198–200
    issues with use of, 200
    manipulating, 192–198
    manipulating, concat( ) method,
        192–194
    manipulating, join( ) method, 194
    manipulating, reverse( ) method, 194
    manipulating, slice( ) method, 195
    manipulating, sort( ) method,
        196–198
    manipulating, splice( ) method,
        195–196
    manipulating, toString( ) method,
        toSource( ) method, 196
    multidimensional, 198
    overview of, 184–185, 919–921

removing elements, 187
treating like stacks and queues, 190–192
using length property with, 187–190
Array( ) constructor, 184
array literals, 857
array operators ([]), 112–113
arrays, 76–77
compared with collections, 773–774
elements and indexes of, 76
overview of, 40–41
ASP. *see* Active Server Pages (ASP)
assignment operators (=)
common use of, 34
overview of, 95–96
using with var keyword, 92
associative arrays, 170–172
attributes. *see* properties
authenticity, digital signatures and, 725
Authenticode, 724

B

<b>, document object, 921
<base>, object, 921–922
<basefront>, document object, 922
<bdo>, document object, 922–1283
Behaviors. *see* DHTML Behaviors
<big>, object, 923
bitwise operators, 99–101, 859–860
bitwise shift operators, 101
block statement, 867
<blockquote>, object, 923
blocks, 36–37, 94–95
blur( ) method, 463
<body>, document object, 420–421, 923–925
BOM (Browser Object Model), 27, 254
Boole, George, 71
Boolean, built-in object, 201, 925
Boolean data
as primitive datatype, 37–38, 71–72
type conversion, 852

, document object, 926
break statements, 129–133

label and flow control, 130–133, 868
loop control with, 48–49, 129–130
using with switch statements, 46, 122–123
breakpoints, debuggers and, 817
browser control, 625–644
controlling status bar, 627
History object, 626–627
Location object, 625–626
preference settings, 631–633
setting timeouts, 627–630
simulating browser button presses, 630–633
browser detection, 608–625
advanced options, 622–623
defensive programming and, 830–832
detecting if browser is Java-enabled, 640
IE, 611–612
language detection, 622
Microsoft client capabilities, 623–624
Netscape, 609–612
Opera, 611–612
overview, 608
in practice, 625
pros/cons of, 831–832
technology detection, 612–617
visual detection, 617–622
Browser Object Model (BOM), 27, 254
browser objects. *see* objects, browser
browser sniffing. *see* browser detection
BrowserHawk, 625
browsers. *see also* by type
accommodating older versions, 835–836
alternatives to IE and Netscape, 289
browser events, DOM Level 2, 370
crashing, 740–741
cross-browser compatibility and, 289–290
as JavaScript object category, 162
list of core browser objects, 258
support for JavaScript, 26–27
bubbling, DOM2 event handling, 374

built-in objects. *see also* objects, built-in
  as composite datatype, 75
  as JavaScript object category, 162
  overview of, 184
<button>, document object,
  465–466, 926–927
Button, document object, 927–928
buttons, form elements, 463–466
  HTML4 buttons, 465–466
  image buttons, 464–465
  overview of, 463–464
  properties, 466

C

C, C++ languages, 174, 685
call-by-reference, 79
call-by-value rule, 79–80
capability detection
  pros/cons of, 831
  tools for, 830
<caption>, object, 448, 928
captureEvents( ) method, Netscape 4,
  359–361
CAs. *see* certification authorities (CAs)
Cascading Style Sheets. *see* CSS (Cascading
  Style Sheets)
case sensitivity
  HTML and, 32–33
  JavaScript and, 31–32
catch, exceptions, 827, 869–870
cells, DOM table manipulation, 451–455
<center>, document object, 928–929
certification authorities (CAs)
  certification process using, 726–728
  identification process with, 738–739
  list of, 727
  services providing, 726–727
CGI scripts, 840
character
  classes, 231–234, 871
  escape codes (/), 227–228
  positional indicators, 227
  sets supported by JavaScript, 68
charAt( ) method, 215

<checkbox>, document object, 929–930
checkboxes and radio buttons, 472–476
  events and methods of, 473
  naming, 473–474
  properties of, 472
  syntax of, 472
<cite>, document object, 930
class-based object-oriented languages, 174
class selectors, CSS, 325
clear( ) method, 426
clearInterval( ) method, 629
clearTimeout( ) method, 569, 627–628
Click events, 267
click( ) method, 463
client-side JavaScript
  compared with ASP, 676–677
  moving to SSJS from, 670
client-side scripting, vs. server side Web
  technologies, 840–841
clientInformation, browser object, 930
clipboardData, browser object, 930–931
cloneNode( ) method, 311–312
close( ) method, 388–389, 426–427
code
  hiding, 832–836
  protecting, 838–839
  sharing, 839
  speed of writing, 837
  style, 836–837
<code>, document object, 931
code obfuscators, 838–839
code signing. *see* signed scripts
<col>, document object, 931–932
<colgroup>, document object, 932
collections
  compared with arrays, 773–774
  JScript, 773–775
  properties of, 775
collections, document, 307–308
  all[ ] collection, 334–335, 435, 531–532
  anchors[ ] collection, 428–429
  applets[ ] collection, 434–435, 640
  DHTML-related collections, 435
  DOM-supported, 307–308, 331–332,
    436–437
  embeds[ ] collection, 434–435

forms[ ] collection, 429–431
images[ ] collection, 431–434
links[ ] collection, 428–429
list of traditional, 428
plugins[ ] collection, 434–435, 616–617
styleSheets[ ] collection, 328
color, document properties for, 420–423
COM. *see* Component Object Model (COM)
comma operator (,), 110, 863
comments
functions, 159
multiple line (*/), 54–55
overview of, 54–55
single line (//), 54–55
comparison operators, 105–107
compile( ) method, 237
Component Object Model (COM)
accessing external facilities, 683
ActiveX controls and, 656
integration of VBScript with, 782
Components, browser object, 932
composite datatypes, 39–45, 74–80, 854–858
arrays, 40–41, 76–77, 857
ECMAScript built-in objects, 855
expressions, 42
functions, 77–80, 857
functions, creating, 78–80
functions, overview of, 77–78
objects, 41–42, 74–76, 854, 857
objects, built-in, 75
objects, creating, 75–76
operator precedence, 45
operators, 42–45
regular expression literals, 858
concat( ) method
manipulating arrays, 192–194
manipulating strings, 217
conditional compilation, 776–780
conditional operators, 861, 868
confirm( ) method, 51, 383–385
constants, of Math object, 210–211
constructors, object creation with, 75, 163, 174

context menus, 591–592
continue statements, 129–133
label and flow control, 130–133, 868
loop control with, 48–49, 129–130
cookies
defined, 592
JavaScript, deleting, 598
JavaScript, reading, 595–598
JavaScript, setting, 594–595
limitations of, 602–603
session and persistent cookies, 594
user state management, 598–602
user state management, customizations, 600–602
user state management, one-time popups, 599–600
user state management, redirects, 599
Coordinated Universal Time (UTC), 201
core features, JavaScript. *see* JavaScript, core features
core statements. *see* statements, core
createMenuHeadings( ) method, 570
createMenus( ) method, 570
createsPopup( ) method, 799
cross-browser compatibility, 289–290
cross-browser layers, 532–543
defining common functionality, 533–543
technologies supported, 532–533
testing, 542
cross-browsers menus, 577–583
crunching scripts, 33
cryptography, 725–726
CSS (Cascading Style Sheets), 319–331
dynamic styles using classes and collections, 325–328
filters, 780–781
inline styles, 319–325
mapping CSS properties to DOM properties, 320–322
MIME types for, 647
Netscape Navigator 4.0 and, 752
pull-down menus and, 565
rules, 326
rules, for complex styles, 328–331
rules, for XML elements, 699

CSS positioning (CSS-P), 525–532
    DOM, 532
    examples, 527–529
    IE 4 layers, 531–532
    Netscape 4 layers, 529–531
    properties, 526
CSSrule, browser object, 997
curly brackets {}
    grouping statements with, 36–37, 94
    specifying number of matches
        with, 230
currentStyle, document object, 932

D

data binding, 711–712, 781–782
data, form validation, 489
data integrity, digital signatures and, 725
data representation, floating point, 65–66
data tainting, 723–724
data types, 60–90
    primitive, 37–39, 850
    related concepts, 60–61
    type conversion, 86–90
    type conversion, manually, 89–90
    type conversion, to Boolean, 88
    type conversion, to number, 88
    type conversion, to string, 89
    variables, 80–86
    variables, declaring, 82
    variables, identifiers, 80–82
    variables, scope, 83–86
    weak typing and, 38–39, 61
Database objects, SSJS, 671
DataSourceControl object, Microsoft Office
    Web Components, 782–784
dataTransfer, browser object, 932–933
Date, built-in object, 201–210
    creating dates with Date( )
        constructor, 202–203
    manipulating, 203–207
    manipulating, converting
        strings to, 206
    manipulating, converting
        to strings, 205–206

manipulating, limitations of date
    representations, 207
    overview of, 201, 933–937
Date( ) constructor, 202–203
Date( ) method, 424
Date.parse( ) method, 203
<dd>, document object, 937
debugger applications, 817–819
debugging, 807–819
    alert dialogs and, 383
    common mistakes, 809–812
    outputting information, 812–817
    using debugger applications,
        817–819
    using error messages, 807–809
deceptive programming, 741–742
decrement(—) operators, 103–105
default statements, 46
defensive programming, 819–836. *see also*
    programming practices
    capability and browser detection,
        830–832
    code hiding, 832–836
    error handlers, 820–824
    exceptions, 824–830
    overview, 819–820
Deka, browser detection and control, 625
<del>, document object, 937
delete operator
    deleting array elements, 113–114
    destroying objects with, 42
    removing array elements with, 187
denial of service attacks, 740–741
developer responsibility, 742–743
<dfn>, document object, 938
DHTML Behaviors, 792–799
    attaching, 793–794
    compared with traditional
        DHTML, 799
    defaults, 797–798
    defining, 794–797
    elements, 797–799
    IE 5, 603–604
    IE 6, 288
    removing, 794

DHTML (Dynamic HTML), 543–557
    adding to IE 4, 283–288
    adding to Netscape 4, 274–278
    compared with DHTML
        Behaviors, 799
    compared with DOM, 331–335
    compared with DOM, document.all[ ],
        334–335
    compared with DOM, innerHTML,
        332–333
    compared with DOM, innerText,
        outerText, and outerHTML,
        333–334
    document.all[ ] collection, 435
    dynamic Web pages and, 25
    general animation, 552–557
    learning by example, 560
    menu techniques and styles, 583–585
    Netscape Navigator 4.0 features
        supporting, 752–755
    page-based transitions, 543–547
    practicality of, 557
    second-generation image rollovers,
        547–550
    targeted rollovers, 550–551
    Web site references materials for,
        585–586
DHTML-Flavored Object Models. *see*
    Internet Explorer (IE) 4.0; Netscape
    Navigator 4.0
dialogs, 382–387
    alert( ) method, 382–383
    confirm( ) method, 383–385
    prompt( ) method, 385–387
Dictionary, built-in object, 938
digital signatures, 725–726, 739
<dir>, document object, 938
disabled attributes, HTML, 499–501
dispatchEvent( ) method, 376
<div>, document object
    cross-browser compatibility and, 528
    Netscape support for, 530
    overview of, 938–939
division operator (/), 96
<dl>, document object, 939–940
DLLs, Microsoft Windows, 685

do-while loops
    example of, 48
    overview of, 128
Document, document object, 940–945
Document Object Model. *see* DOM
    (Document Object Model)
Document objects, 258–269. *see also*
    objects, document
    accessing elements by name, 266–267
    accessing elements by
        position, 264–265
    accessing using arrays, 267
    containment hierarchy of, 262
    event handlers, 267–268
    Form object as child of, 458
    function of, 258
    as JavaScript object category, 162–163
    methods, 260
    properties, 259, 263–264
    properties, early browsers, 259
    properties, example, 260–262
    properties, HTML elements, 264
    properties, simple, 263
Document objects, handling documents,
    420–456
    basic methods, 425–427
    DOM, applications of, 455–456
    DOM, HTML element properties,
        437–443
    DOM, HTML methods, 439–440
    DOM, Level 1 properties and
        collections, 436–437
    DOM, methods supported by, 437
    DOM, table manipulation, 444–455
    historic properties, 420–425
    historic properties, color, 420–423
    historic properties, last modification
        date, 423–424
    historic properties, location-related,
        424–425
    HTML element access, 427–435
    HTML element access, anchors and
        links collections, 428–429
    HTML element access,
        DHTML-related collections, 435

HTML element access, forms
collection, 429–431
HTML element access, images
collection, 431–434
HTML element access, object-related
collections, 434–435
document trees, DOM, 295–299
document type definitions. *see* DTDs
(document type definitions)
document.all[ ] collection
capability detection with, 830
DHTML and, 334–335, 435
IE 4 and, 284–285
document.anchors[ ] collection, 428–429
document.applets[ ] collection,
434–435, 640
document.cookie, 594–596
document.embeds[ ] collection, 434–435
document.forms[ ] collection, 429–431
elements[ ] collection of, 430–431
<form> tags, 429–430
document.getElementById( ),
299–305, 437, 532
document.getElementByName( ), 437
document.getElementByTagName( ), 437
document.images[ ] collection, 431–434
document.layers, 830
document.links[ ] collection, 428–429
document.location, 423–424
document.plugins[ ] collection, 434–435
document.referrer, 13: 6–425
document.URL, 423–424
document.write( ) method, 395
DOM (Document Object Model), 294–336
accessing elements, 299–308
accessing elements, collections,
307–308
accessing elements,
document.getElementById( ),
299–305
accessing elements,
getElementsByName( ), 306
accessing elements, HTML
properties, 440–443

accessing elements, node
properties, 300
accessing elements, tree walking,
301–304, 306–307
accessing position regions, 532
applications, 455–456
BOM and, 254
browser and capability detection
with, 832
capabilities, 398–399
categories of, 295
CSS, 319–331
CSS, complex style rules, 328–331
CSS, dynamic styles using classes
and collections, 325–328
CSS, inline styles, 319–325
CSS, mapping CSS properties to
DOM properties, 320–322
DHTML, document.all[ ], 334–335
DHTML, innerHTML, 332–333
DHTML, innerText, outerText, and
outerHTML, 333–334
DHTML object models, 331–335
document objects in, 162–163
dynamic Web pages and, 25
HTML, element properties, 13:
19–439
HTML, elements, 317–319
HTML, methods and, 439–440
manipulating attributes, 316–317
manipulating document trees,
295–299
menu systems, 577
methods supported by, 437
nodes, copying, 311–312
nodes, creating, 308–309
nodes, deleting, 312–314
nodes, inserting, 309–311
nodes, modifying, 314–316
object models and, 881–882
table manipulation, 444–455
W3C specification, 27, 290
windows and, 398–399
XML, 700–711
XML, IE example, 700–706

XML, Netscape 6 example, 706–710
XML, overview of, 700
DOM (Document Object Model), Level 0
 access properties supported, 305
 W3C definition, 294
DOM (Document Object Model), Level 1
 element attributes supported, 316
 HTML elements and, 318
 properties and collections, 436–437
 properties for <button>, 466
 support for node creation, 308
 W3C definition, 294
DOM (Document Object Model),
 Level 2, 368–376
 binding events to elements, 371–374
 browser events, 370
 event propagation, 374–376
 event redirection, 376
 HTML elements and, 318
 keyboard events, 370
 mouse events, 370
 mutation events, 371
 overview, 368–369
 properties, 369
 support for CSS styles, 328
 UI events, 370–371
 W3C definition, 294
dot operator, accessing object
 properties with, 41
double quotes (" "), using with strings, 66
Dreamweaver, 522, 819
<dt>, document object, 945–946
DTDs (document type definitions)
 using with XML, 693–695
 valid documents and, 692
 valid documents vs. well formed
  documents, 691–692
dynamic documents, 25
dynamic forms, 505–509
Dynamic HTML. see DHTML
 (Dynamic HTML)
dynamic properties, IE 5, 786–789
dynamic scope notes, 550

E

e-mail addresses, collecting via form
 validation, 489–490
ECMA standards, 289
ECMAScript
 as composite datatypes, 855
 corresponding to JavaScript
  versions, 746
 cross-browser compatibility
  with, 26–27
ECMAScript versions
 corresponding to JavaScript, 848
 corresponding to JScript, 849
elements
 DOM, 299–308
 DOM, collections, 307–308
 DOM, document.getElementById( ),
  299–305
 DOM, getElementsByName( ), 306
 DOM, Level 2, 376
 DOM, node properties, 300
 DOM, tree walking, 301–304
 DOM, tree walking starting
  points, 306–307
 event attributes associated with,
  340–352
 members of arrays, 76
 XML, 690, 699
elements[ ] collection, for forms, 430–431
else statements, 119–120. see also if
 statements
<em>, document object, 946
<embed>, document object, 645, 946–947
embedded objects, 638–661
 ActiveX controls, including, 656–657
 ActiveX controls, interacting with,
  658–660
 Java applets, accessing in JavaScript,
  640–644
 Java applets, compared with
  JavaScript, 638–639
 Java applets, detecting if browser is
  Java-enabled, 640
 Java applets, driving JavaScript, 645

Java applets, issues with
  JavaScript-driven applets, 644
Java applets, using, 639–640
plugins, detecting specific, 649–651
plugins, detecting support for MIME
  types, 647–649
plugins, embedding, 645–646
plugins, interacting with, 651–656
plugins, MIME types and, 646–647
embeds[ ] collection, 434–435
enablePrivilege( ) method, 734–735
encapsulation, object-oriented
  programming and, 180
encryption, vs. obfuscation, 839
Enumerator, built-in object, 775–776,
  947–948
equals operator (==), 34, 105
Error, built-in object, 825–827, 948–949
Error( ) constructor, 826
errors. *see also* exceptions; form validation
  categories, 804–806
  common, 809–812
  error catching options, form
    validation, 486
  error handlers, 820–824
  error messages, 807–809
escape codes
  regular expression pattern creation
    and, 227–228
  regular expressions, 871–872
  strings, 851
  using with special characters, 67–68
escape( ) method, 208
eval( ) method, 208
event attributes, HTML, 340–352
event binding
  DOM Level 2, 371–374
  for elements, 339
  HTML, 339–352
  JavaScript, 352–353
event handlers
  defined, 338
  event models and, 268
  function of, 267–268
  IE 4, 365–367, 766
  IE 5, 770

for Image objects, 513
invoking, 353–354
JavaScript, 352
overview of, 13–16
return values and, 354–356
setting, 268
event handling, 338–377
  basic model, 338–356
  basic model, event binding in HTML,
    339–352
  basic model, event binding in
    JavaScript, 352–353
  basic model, firing events manually,
    353–354
  basic model, return values, 354–356
  DOM2 model, 368–376
  DOM2 model, binding events to
    elements, 371–374
  DOM2 model, browser events, 370
  DOM2 model, event propagation,
    374–376
  DOM2 model, event redirection, 376
  DOM2 model, keyboard events, 370
  DOM2 model, mouse events, 370
  DOM2 model, mutation events, 371
  DOM2 model, overview, 368–369
  DOM2 model, properties, 369
  DOM2 model, UI events, 370–371
  IE 4 model, 362–368
  IE 4 model, event handlers, 365–367
  IE 4 model, overview, 362
  IE 4 model, properties, 363–365
  IE 4 model, proprietary
    properties, 368
  issues with, 376–377
  Netscape 4 model, 357–362
  Netscape 4 model, event propagation
    and capture, 359–362
  Netscape 4 model, overview, 357–358
  Netscape 4 model, properties, 358–359
  types of models for, 338
event listeners, 374
event models
  event handlers and, 268
  IE 4 and, 288
  Netscape 4 and, 280

Event objects
    DOM2, 368
    IE 4, 362
    Netscape 4, 357
events, 883–889
    common window events, 404–405
    defined, 338
    DOM, 884–885
    DOM, Level 2 binding to elements,
        371–374
    DOM, Level 2 propagation, 374–376
    DOM, Level 2 redirection, 376
    DOM, methods, 891
    extended window events, 405
    HTML events, 405, 883–884
    IE, 886–889, 890–891
    Netscape, 885–886, 889–890
    simple and complex, 338
Events, browser object, 949–952 i
Excel spreadsheets, embedding, 784–786
exceptions, 824–830. *see also* errors
    Error object and, 825–827
    finally, 869
    overview of, 824–825
    try, catch, and throw, 827–829,
        869–870
    working with, 830
exec( ) method, 237–240
expressions
    evaluating with if statements, 118
    order of precedence for, 115–118
    overview of, 42
    using comparison operators for
        true/false evaluations, 105
Extended Traditional JavaScript Object
    Model. *see* Netscape Navigator 3.0
Extensible Markup Language. *see* XML
    (Extensible Markup Language)
Extensible Style Sheet Transformations
    (XSLT). *see* XSLT (Extensible Style Sheet
    Transformations)
Extensible Style Sheets (XSL), 696–698
extensions, 413
      IE extensions, modal, 413–414
      IE extensions, modeless, 414

    IE extensions, pop-up, 414–416
    Netscape extensions, 417
external, browser object, 952

F

fatal errors, 804
feature parameters, window.open( ),
    390–395
fields, of forms
    disabling, 499–501
    first field focus, 498
    read-only fields, 501–502
    selecting, 498–499
    validating, 487–489
<fieldset>, 485–486, 952–953
fieldSet, document object, 485–486,
    952–953
File, object, 953–954
File:staff3.xml, 707–708
FileSystemObject, built-in object, 954
FileUpload, object, 477–478, 953–954
File:xmldemo.js, 709–711
filters, CSS, 780–781
finally, exceptions, 869–870
fireEvent( ) method, 367
first-class data types, 60
flags, regular expressions, 225, 870
floating point data representation, 65–66
flow control
    block statement, 867
    break and continue statements, 868
    conditionals, 868
    controlling with break/continue
        statements, 130–133
    functions, 867
    loops, 868
    overview of, 45–47
    with statement, 867
focus( ) method, 463, 498
<font>, document object, 954–955
for-in loops, 172
for loops, 48, 128–129
for...in statements, 48, 134

<form>, document object, 458–462
    accessing <form> tags, 265
    attributes of, 459
    <form> tag, 458–462
    forms[ ] collection, 429–430
    methods, 460–462
    overview of, 955–956
    properties, 459
    syntax of, 458–459
form handling, 458–509
    dynamic forms, 505–509
    elements, 462–486
    elements, checkboxes and radio
      buttons, 472–476
    elements, fieldset, 485–486
    elements, file uploads, 477–478
    elements, form buttons, 463–466
    elements, hidden fields, 476–477
    elements, labels, 485
    elements, legends, 487
    elements, select menus, 478–485
    elements, text fields, 467–471
    Form objects, 458–462
    Form objects, <form> tag, 458–462
    Form objects, methods, 460–462
    Form objects, properties, 459
    usability, 497–505
    usability, disabling fields, 499–501
    usability, first field focus, 498
    usability, keyboard improvements,
      502–505
    usability, labels and field selection,
      498–499
    usability, read-only fields, 501–502
    usability, status messages, 499
    validation, 486–497
    validation, applying routines to any
      form, 491–495
    validation, checking data, 489
    validation, checking fields, 487–489
    validation, checking numbers, 490
    validation, collecting e-mail
      addresses, 489–490
    validation, error catching
      options, 486
    validation, issues with, 495

    validation, keyboard masking,
      495–497
    validation, using regular
      expression, 490–491
form validation, 486–497
    applying routines to any form,
      491–495
    checking data, 489
    checking fields, 487–489
    checking numbers, 490
    collecting e-mail addresses, 489–490
    defined, 458
    error catching options, 486
    issues, 495
    JavaScript applications and, 25
    keyboard masking, 495–497
    using regular expression, 490–491
formatting properties, controlling
  with CSS, 525
forms[ ] collection, 429–431
    elements[ ] collection of, 430–431
    <form> tags, 429–430
frame attribute, DOM table
  manipulation, 445
Frame, browser object, 957
frame busting, 412–413
<frame>, document object, 956–957
frames, 405–413
    properties, 406
    relationships, 410
    state management, 409–412
    troubleshooting, 412–413
<frameset>, object, 957–958
FSCommand( ) method, 656
full-screen windows, 416–417
Function, built-in object, 958–959
function keyword, 49, 78, 138
functions, 77–80, 138–148
    anonymous, 150–151
    checking arguments, 158–159
    commenting, 159
    creating, 78–80
    defining with new keyword, 148–149
    flow control and, 867
    function literals and, 149–150, 857
    global and local variables, 143–146

invoking or calling, 77
local, 146–148
naming, 156–157
as object methods, 164
overview, 49–50, 77–78
parameter passing, 141–142, 152–154
parameters and arguments of,
     138–140
recursive, 154–156
return statements of, 141, 157
static variables and, 150–151
syntax of, 138
use of linked .js files with, 157
using variables and literals with, 140
writing stand-alone, 157

G

garbage collection, 169–170
get methods, for dates, 204
getElementById( ) method, 577
getElementsByName( ) method, 306
getElementsByTagName( ) method,
     307, 327
GIF (Graphics Interchange Format), 647
Global, built-in object, 207, 208–210,
     959–961
global scope, 83
global variables, 143–146
     defined, 143
     mask out and, 145–146
     use with functions, 143–145
GMT (Greenwich Mean Time), 201
Graphics Interchange Format (GIF), 647
greedy matching, 231
Greenwich Mean Time (GMT), 201
grouping, regular expressions and,
     231–234

H

hanldeEvent( ) method, 362
<head>, document object, 30, 961–962
Hello World example, 4–7
hexadecimal literals, 62–63

hidden fields, form elements, 476–477
Hidden, object, 962
hidden windows, show( ) and hide( )
     methods and, 414
hide( ) method, 414
hideMenu( ) method, 569
History object, browser object, 626–627,
     962–963
<hn>, document object, 961
<hr>, document object, 963
HTAs (HTML Applications), 288, 790–792
HTCs (HTML Components), 792–797
HTML Applications (HTAs), 288, 790–792
HTML Components (HTCs), 792–797
<html>, document object, 963–964
HTML (Hypertext Markup Language)
     adding JavaScript, using event
          handlers, 13–16
     adding JavaScript, using JavaScript
          entities, 21–25
     adding JavaScript, using JavaScript
          pseudo-URLs, 18–21
     adding JavaScript, using linked
          scripts, 16–18
     adding JavaScript, using <script>
          element, 7–13
     button types, 463–464
     case sensitivity and, 32–33
     converting XML to, 695–696
     elements, accessing specific
          properties, 440–443
     elements, anchors[ ] collection,
          428–429
     elements, DHTML-related
          collections, 435
     elements, DOM and, 317–319,
          438–440
     elements, forms[ ] collection, 429–431
     elements, images[ ] collection,
          431–434
     elements, links[ ] collection, 428–429
     elements, object-related collections,
          434–435
     elements, overview of, 908–915
     event binding in, 339–352
     form validation and, 495

forms and, 460
strings and, 69–71, 218–220
valid documents vs. well formed
documents, 691–692
HTML (Hypertext Markup Language) 4.0
disabled attribute, 499–501
<fieldset> tag, 485–486
form buttons, 465–466
keyboard improvements, accesskey
attribute, 502–504
keyboard improvements, return
keys, 504–505
<label> tag, 485, 498–499
<legend> tag, 485–486
<optgroup> element, 484–485
readonly attributes, 501–502
HTMLButtonElement, 466
HTMLElement object, 318
HTMLImageElement, 512
HTMLOptionElement, 481
HTMLSelectElement, 479–480
HTMLTableElement object, 448. *see also*
table manipulation, DOM
HTTP (Hypertext Transfer Protocol), 592
Hypertext Markup Language. *see* HTML
(Hypertext Markup Language)

I

<i>, document object, 964
id attribute, 266, 269, 731–732
IDE (integrated development
environment), 809
identifiers
defined, 60
of variables, 37
identity operators (===), 107
IE. *see* Internet Explorer (IE)
if statements, 118–122
if...else, 119–120
if...else example, 46
short-circuiting AND/OR
expressions, 120–122
<iframe>, object, 964–965
<ilayer>, document object, 970–972

image buttons, 464–465
image effects, 512–557
cross-browser layers, 532–543
cross-browser layers, defining
common functionality, 533–543
cross-browser layers, technologies
supported, 532–533
CSS positioning, 525–532
CSS positioning, DOM errors, 532
CSS positioning, examples, 527–529
CSS positioning, IE 4 layers, 531–532
CSS positioning, Netscape 4 layers,
529–531
CSS positioning, properties, 526
DHTML effects, 543–557
DHTML effects, general animation,
552–557
DHTML effects, page-based
transitions, 543–547
DHTML effects, practicality of, 557
DHTML effects, second-generation
image rollovers, 547–550
DHTML effects, targeted rollovers,
550–551
Image objects, <img> tag, 512
Image objects, properties, 512–516
rollover buttons, 516–525
rollover buttons, examples of,
517–523
rollover buttons, extending, 523–525
rollover buttons, uses of, 516
images[ ] collection, 431–434, 512
<img>, document object
defining Image objects with, 512
event handlers for, 513
image buttons, 465
Image objects, 512
images[ ] collection, 431–432
overview of, 965–967
properties, 512–516
implementation, document object, 967
increment (++) operators, 103–105
indexes, assigning array elements to, 76
indexOf( ) method, 216
infinite loops, denial of service attacks, 740
Infinity values, 63–64, 98–99

inheritance
        object-oriented programming
            and, 180
        through prototypes, 178–179
inline styles, CSS, 319–325
innerHTML
        DHTML, 332–333
        vs. DOM approach, 456
        XML and, 711
innerText, DHTML, 333–334
<input>, object, 463–464, 967–968
input/output (I/0), JavaScript
    facilities for, 50–53
<input type="file">, 477
<input type="hidden">, 476
<input type="password">, 467
<input type="text">, 467
ins, document object, 968
instance properties
        overview of, 172–173
        RegExp objects, 240–241
integrated development environment
    (IDE), 809
inter-window communication, 399–400
Internet Explorer (IE)
        adding events to Window object, 405
        browser detection, 611–612
        browser language detection, 622
        browsers corresponding to
            JavaScript versions, 848
        browsers corresponding to Netscape
            versions, 848
        error handling in, 820
        extensions, 414–416
        object signing technology, 724
        plugin support in, 645
        support for windows, 413
        tools based on W3C standards, 715
        use of JScript by, 26–27
        viewing error messages in dialog
            boxes of, 808
        XML data islands, 711–715
Internet Explorer (IE) 3.0
        case insensitivity in, 32
        new features in, 765
        object model, 281, 879–880

Internet Explorer (IE) 4.0
        adding DHTML, 283–288
        adding event models, 288
        CSS positioning, 531–532
        Data Binding model, 781–782
        event handling, 362–368
        event handling, event handlers,
            365–367
        event handling, overview, 362
        event handling, properties, 363–365
        event handling, proprietary
            properties, 368
        menu systems, 573–577
        new features in, 765–768
        new properties and methods, 286
        object model, 282–288, 881
Internet Explorer (IE) 5.0
        client capabilities detection in,
            623–624
        DHTML Behaviors, 603–604
        DOM model of, 288
        dynamic properties in, 786–789
        new features in, 769–772
        object model, 881–882
Internet Explorer (IE) 5.5
        client capabilities detection in,
            623–624
        DOM model of, 288
        example using DOM with XML,
            700–706
        new features in, 772
        well formed XML under, 689
Internet Explorer (IE) 6.0
        client capabilities detection in,
            623–624
        DOM model of, 288
        new features in, 772–773
Internet Explorer (IE), extensions, 760–802
        browser issues, IE 3, 765
        browser issues, IE 4, 765–768
        browser issues, IE 5, 769–772
        browser issues, IE 5.5, 772
        browser issues, IE 6, 772–773
        CSS filters, 780–781
        data binding, 781–782
        DHTML Behaviors, 792–799

DHTML Behaviors, attaching, 793–794
DHTML Behaviors, compared with traditional DHTML, 799
DHTML Behaviors, defaults, 797–798
DHTML Behaviors, defining, 794–797
DHTML Behaviors, elements, 797–799
DHTML Behaviors, removing, 794
dynamic properties, 786–789
HTML applications, 790–792
JScript features, 773–780
JScript features, collections, 773–775
JScript features, conditional compilation, 776–780
JScript features, Enumerator object, 775–776
JScript features, list of other capabilities, 780
language issues, corresponding JScript versions to browser versions, 760
language issues, corresponding JScript versions to ECMAScript versions, 761
language issues, corresponding Netscape versions to IE versions, 761
language issues, JScript 1.0, 762
language issues, JScript 2.0, 762
language issues, JScript 3.0, 763
language issues, JScript 4.0, 764
language issues, JScript 5.0, 764
language issues, JScript 5.5, 764
Microsoft Office Web Components, 782–786
Microsoft Office Web Components, DataSourceControl object, 782–784
Microsoft Office Web Components, spreadsheet objects, 784–786
modal, 413–414
modeless, 414
popup windows, 799–801

iPlanet servers, 664–665
creating applications, 665–669
objects, 670–672
overview of, 665
syntax, 670
isFinite( ) method, 208
isindex, object, 968
isNaN( ) method, 208

J

JAR (Java Archive) files, 730
Java
as class-based object-oriented language, 174
detecting browser technology, 616
Java applets
accessing in JavaScript, 640–644
compared with JavaScript, 638–639
detecting if browser is Java-enabled, 640
driving JavaScript with, 645
issues with JavaScript-driven applets, 644
using, 639–640
Java Archive (JAR) files, 730
java, built-in object, 989
javaEnabled( ) method, 640
JavaScript, 4–28
accessing Java applets, 640–644
adding to HTML documents, 7–25
adding to HTML documents, using event handlers, 13–16
adding to HTML documents, using JavaScript entities, 21–25
adding to HTML documents, using JavaScript pseudo-URLs, 18–21
adding to HTML documents, using linked scripts, 16–18
adding to HTML documents, using <script> element, 7–13
applications, 25–26
for ASP, 673–675
basic definitions, 30–31
compared with Java applets, 638–639

corresponding to ECMAScript
    versions, 848
detecting browser technology,
    613–616
driving Java applets with, 645
event binding in, 352–353
Hello World example, 4–7
history of, 26–28
interpreters, 685
issues with JavaScript-driven
    applets, 644
language fundamentals, 846
Netscape browsers corresponding to
    versions of, 847–848
object models. *see* object models
overview of entities, 21–25
recommended practices. *see*
    programming practices
reserved words, 1044–1046
security. *see* security
standard versions, 847
support for, 834
versions, corresponding to browser
    versions, 746
versions, corresponding to
    ECMAScript versions, 746
versions, JavaScript 1.1, 747–748
versions, JavaScript 1.2, 748
versions, JavaScript 1.3, 748–749
versions, JavaScript 1.4, 749
versions, JavaScript 1.5, 750
versions, JavaScript 2.0, 750–751
viewing error messages in console,
    807–808
JavaScript, core features
    basic data types, 37–39
    basic data types, overview of, 37–38
    basic data types, weak typing
        and, 38–39
    case sensitivity, 31–33
    comments, 54–55
    composite data types, 39–45
    composite data types, arrays, 40–41
    composite data types, expressions, 42
    composite data types, objects, 41–42
composite data types, operator
    precedence, 45
composite data types,
    operators, 42–45
flow control, 45–47
functions, 49–50
input/output, 50–53
loops, 47–49
loops, loop control, 48–49
loops, types of, 47–48
regular expressions, 53–54
script execution order, 30
statements, grouping into blocks,
    36–37
statements, overview of, 34–35
statements, terminating with
    semicolons, 35–36
variables, 37
white space characters, 33–34
JavaScript Style Sheets (JSSS), 752
join( ) method, 194
.js files
    mapping to text/javascript
        MIME type, 18
    using with functions, 157
JScript
    ASP and, 664, 672
    corresponding to ECMAScript
        versions, 849
    DOM and XML and, 705
    Microsoft browsers corresponding to
        versions of, 848
    proprietary features, 773–780
    proprietary features, collections,
        773–775
    proprietary features, conditional
        compilation, 776–780
    proprietary features, Enumerator
        object, 775–776
    proprietary features, list of other
        capabilities, 780
    support for, 834
    versions, corresponding Netscape
        versions to IE versions, 761
    versions, corresponding to browser
        versions, 760

versions, corresponding to
ECMAScript versions, 761
versions, JScript 1.0, 762
versions, JScript 2.0, 762
versions, JScript 3.0, 763
versions, JScript 4.0, 764
versions, JScript 5.0, 764
versions, JScript 5.5, 764
js.libraries, 837
JSObject class, 645
JSSS (JavaScript Style Sheets), 752

K

<kbd>, document object, 969
keyboard events, DOM Level 2, 370
keyboard improvements, 502–505
accesskey attribute, 502–504
return keys, 504–505
keyboard masking, 495–497
Konqueror, W3C and ECMA standards
and, 289

L

<label>, document object, 485, 498–499,
969–970
labels
controlling with break/continue
statements, 130–133
form elements and, 485
forms and, 498–499
language detection, browsers, 622
last-in-first-out (LIFO) order, 190–191
last modification date property, Document
objects, 423–424
lastIndexOf( ) method, 216
lastModified property, 423–424
<layer>, document object
implementing menus using, 567
Netscape 4 and, 278–280, 752–753
overview of, 970–972
properties, 530–531
using instead of CSS position, 528,
529–531

layers
cross-browser, 532–543
cross-browser, defining common
functionality, 533–543
cross-browser, technologies
supported, 532–533
IE 4, 531–532
layer library (layerlib.js), 543
Netscape 4, 529–531
<legend>, document object, 972
legends, 487
length property, 187–190
of arrays, 77
indicating numbers of parameters a
function accepts, 152
iterating array elements, 187–189
removing array elements with,
189–190
of strings, 214–215
<li>, document object, 972–973
LIFO (last-in-first-out) order, 190–191
<link>, document object, 914–916, 973–974
linked scripts, 16–18
links[ ] collection, 428–429
literals
defined, 60
hexadecimal and octal, 63
using with functions, 140, 149–150
LiveConnect. *see* JavaScript
local functions, 146–148
local scope, of variables, 83
local variables, 143–146
defined, 143
mask out and, 145–146
use with functions, 143–145
Location, browser object, 625–626, 974
location-related properties, Document
objects, 424–425
logical bitwise operators, 100
logical operators, 107–108, 860–861
loops
controlling with break/continue
statements, 129–130
do-while loops, 128
flow control and, 868
loop control, 48–49

overview of, 47–49
types, 47–48
while loops, 125–127

M

Macromedia Dreamweaver, 522, 819
Macromedia Fireworks, 522
Macromedia Flash file
    embedding, 645
    interacting with plugins, 653–656
    MIME types for, 647
<map>, document object, 975
markup, detecting browser
  technology, 613
<marquee>, document object, 975
mask out, 145–146
match( ) method, 246–247
Math, built-in object, 210–213
    constants of, 210–211
    erasing math computations, 213
    methods of, 211–212
    overview of, 975–977
    random numbers, 213
Math.random( ) method, 213
maximal matching, regular expression
  pattern creation and, 231
maxlength, 495
memory hogs, 740–741
<menu>, document object, 977
menu systems, 564–585
    cross-browsers menus, 577–583
    DOM, 577
    IE 4, 573–577
    list of enhancements, 585
    menu types, context menus, 591–592
    menu types, remote control
      menus, 586
    menu types, slide-in menus, 586–589
    menu types, static menus, 589–591
    Netscape 4, 567–573
    quicklinks pull-down menus,
      565–567
<meta>, document object, 978
methods

accessing, 74
accessing event handlers as, 352–353
checkboxes and radio buttons, 473
core, 902–907
Document object, 260, 425–427
DOM, 437, 439–440, 450–451, 894–897
Enumerator object, 775
Form object, 460–462
HTML-related string, 218–220
IE 4, 286
Math object, 211–212
object functions and, 164
<select> tag, 479
text fields, 467–469
Microsoft Active Server Pages. *see* Active
  Server Pages (ASP)
Microsoft client capabilities, browser
  detection, 623–624
Microsoft Component Object Model (COM).
  see Component Object Model (COM)
Microsoft Internet Explorer. *see* Internet
  Explorer (IE)
Microsoft Office Web Components,
  782–786
    DataSourceControl object, 782–784
    spreadsheet objects, 784–786
Microsoft Script Debugger, 817
Microsoft Windows, 685
Microsoft Word, 656
MIME (Multipurpose Internet Mail
  Extension) types. *see* Multipurpose
  Internet Mail Extension (MIME) types
mimeType, browser object, 978–979
mimeTypes[ ] array, 647–649
modal windows, 413
modeless window, 414
modification operator (*), 96
modulus operator (%), 96
mouse events, DOM Level 2, 370
MouseOut events, 267–268
MouseOver events, 267
mouseover scripts, 512. *see also*
  rollover buttons
Mozilla
    bugs in, 710
    as organization and as browser, 756

SpiderMonkey, 685
W3C and ECMA standards and, 289
MPEG, MIME types for, 647
multidimensional arrays, 198
multiline flag ("m"), 248
Multipurpose Internet Mail Extension
(MIME) types
detecting support for, 647–649
mapping .js files to text/javascript
MIME type, 18
using with plugins, 646–647
mutation events, DOM Level 2, 371

N

name attribute
getElementsByName( ) and, 306
HTML elements and, 266, 269
namespace, browser object, 979
naming functions, 156–157
NaN values, 64, 98–99
navigation, 560–605
cookie limitations, 602–603
cookies for user state management,
598–602
cookies for user state management,
customizations, 600–602
cookies for user state management,
one-time popups, 599–600
cookies for user state management,
redirects, 599
cookies in JavaScript, deleting, 598
cookies in JavaScript, reading,
595–598
cookies in JavaScript, setting,
594–595
IE 5 DHTML Behaviors, 603–604
JavaScript applications and, 25
learning DHTML by example, 560
menu systems, 564–585
menu systems, cross-browsers
menus, 577–583
menu systems, DOM, 577
menu systems, IE 4, 573–577

menu systems, list of enhancements
for, 585
menu systems, Netscape 4, 567–573
menu systems, quicklinks pull-down
menus, 565–567
menu types, context menus, 591–592
menu types, remote control
menus, 586
menu types, slide-in menus, 586–589
menu types, static menus, 589–591
pull-down menus, 561–564
Navigator, browser object
browser detection properties of,
609–612
javaEnabled( ) method of, 640
overview of, 979–981
negation, arithmetic operators and, 98
netscape, built-in object, 989
Netscape JavaScript Debugger, 817
Netscape Navigator
adding events to Window object, 405
browser detection, 608–612
browser language detection, 622
browsers corresponding to versions
of JavaScript, 847–848
error handling, 820
extensions, 417
introduces JavaScript, 26–27
Microsoft browsers corresponding to
versions of, 848
MIME type support in, 647
object signing technology, 724
plugin detection, 649
plugin support in, 645
Netscape Navigator 2.0, 271–272
Netscape Navigator 3.0
background and color
properties in, 423
data tainting in, 723
new features in, 751–752
object model, 879
origin checks in, 723
overview of, 272–274
Netscape Navigator 4.0
adding DHTML, 274–278
adding event models, 280

adding <layer> tags, 278–280
adding Window objects, 280
CSS positioning, 529–531
event handling, 357–362
event handling, event propagation
    and capture, 359–362
event handling, overview, 357–358
event handling, properties, 358–359
menu systems, 567–573
new features in, 752–755
object model, 880
overview of, 274–280
problems with nested <layer> and
    <div> tags, 534
use of <layer> tag instead of
    positioning, 528, 529–531
zooming in Flash file of, 655
Netscape Navigator 6.0
    bugs in, 710
    DOM/XML integration, 706–710
    DOM2 and, 368
    Mozilla and, 756
    new features in, 756–757
    object model, 280, 881–882
    problems with Flash file in, 653
Netscape Navigator, extensions, 746–758
    browser issues, Netscape 3, 751–752
    browser issues, Netscape 4, 752–755
    browser issues, Netscape 6, 756–757
    language issues, corresponding
        JavaScript versions to browser
        versions, 746
    language issues, corresponding
        JavaScript versions to
        ECMAScript versions, 746
    language issues, JavaScript 1.1,
        747–748
    language issues, JavaScript 1.2, 748
    language issues, JavaScript 1.3,
        748–749
    language issues, JavaScript 1.4, 749
    language issues, JavaScript 1.5, 750
    language issues, JavaScript 2.0,
        750–751
Netscape Signing Tool. *see* Signing Tool
new keyword

creating objects with, 42, 75
defining functions with, 148–149
new operator, creating objects with, 113, 163
<nobr>, document object, 982
nodes, DOM
    copying, 311–312
    creating, 308–309
    deleting, 312–314
    HTML documents and, 297
    inserting, 309–311
    modifying, 314–316
    node properties, 300
    text node manipulation methods,
        314–315
<noframes>, document object, 982
<noscript>, document object, 982
<noscript> elements, 12–13
NOT (~), bitwise operator, 100–101
NOT (!) operators, 107–108
NSAPI plugin, for iPlanet server, 664–665
null datatype, 38, 852
null values, 73–74, 140
Number, built-in object, 213–214, 982–983
number datatype, 61–66
    data representation issues, 65–66
    hexadecimal literals, 62–63
    octal literals, 63
    special values, 63–65
    type conversion, 852
numbers, form validation, 490
numeric constants, 851

O

obfuscators, 838–839
Object, built-in object, 854, 983–984
object collections
    DOM-supported, 307–308
    DOM-supported vs. traditional,
        331–332
<object>, document object, 639, 644,
    984–986
object literals, 857
    syntax of, 165
    using, 165–166

object models, 252–291
cross-browser compatibility and,
289–290
Document objects, 258–269
Document objects, accessing
elements by name, 266–267
Document objects, accessing
elements by position, 264–265
Document objects, accessing using
arrays, 267
Document objects, event handlers
for, 267–268
Document objects, methods, 260
Document objects, properties, 259,
263–264
IE 3, 281
IE 4, 282–288
IE 4, adding DHTML to, 283–288
IE 4, adding event models, 288
IE 4, new properties and
methods, 286
IE 5, 5.5, and 6, 288
list of types, 255
Netscape 2, 271–272
Netscape 3, 272–274
Netscape 4, 274–280
Netscape 4, adding DHTML, 274–278
Netscape 4, adding event models, 280
Netscape 4, adding <layer> tags,
278–280
Netscape 4, adding Window
objects, 280
Netscape 6, 280
other browsers, 289
primary components, 252
traditional model, overview, 256–258
traditional model, using, 269–271
object models, reference , 876–907
event methods, DOM, 891
event methods, IE, 890–891
event methods, Netscape, 889–890
events, 883–889
events, DOM, 884–885
events, HTML 4, 883–884
events, IE, 886–889
events, Netscape, 885–886

IE 3, 879–880
IE 4+, 881
IE 5 +, Netscape 6, and DOM,
881–882
information resources, 876
methods, core, 902–907
methods, DOM, 894–897
Netscape 3, 879
Netscape 4, 880
properties, core, 897–902
properties, DOM, 892–894
traditional model, 878
types of, 876–878
object operators, 112–115
Object-Oriented Programming, 180–181
object prototypes, 174, 198–200
object-related collections, 434–435
object signing technology, 724. *see also*
signed scripts
objects, 74–76, 162–182
as associative arrays, 170–172
built-in, 75
categories of, 162–163
creating, 75–76, 163–166
functions (methods) of, 164
garbage collection and, 169–170
object literals and, 165–166
Object-Oriented Programming and,
180–181
overview of, 41–42
primitive and reference types,
167–169
properties, 172–174
properties, common object, 173–174
properties, instance, 172–173
properties, methods and, 74
user-defined, 174–179
user-defined, good practices, 179
user-defined, inheritance through
prototypes, 178–179
user-defined, overview of, 174–178
objects, ASP, 680
objects, browser
ActiveXObject, 917
clientInformation, 930
clipboardData, 930–931

Components, 932
CSSrule, 997
dataTransfer, 932–933
Events, 949–952 i
external, 952
Frame, 957
History object, 962–963
Location, 974
mimeType, 978–979
namespace, 979
Navigator, 979–981
popup, 991
rule, 997
screen, 998–999
selection, 1001–1002
Style, 1005–1018
TextRange, 1029
userProfile, 1032–1033
Window objects, 1033–1041
objects, built-in
ActiveXObject, 917
objects, built-in
arrays, 919–921
Boolean, 925
Date, 933–937
Dictionary, 938
Enumerator, 947–948
Error, 948–949
FileSystemObject, 954
Function, 958–959
Global, 959–961
java, 989
Math, 975–977
netscape, 989
Number, 982–983
Object, 983–984
Packages, 989
RegExp, 994–995
String, 1003–1005
sun, 989
VBArray, 1033
objects, document
<a>, 914–916
<abbr>, 916
<acconym>, 916
<address>, 917

<anchor>, 914–916
<applet>, 917–918
<area>, 918–919
<b>, 921
<basefront>, 922
<bdo>, 922–1283
<body>, 923–925

, 926
<button>, 926–927
Button, 927–928
<center>, 928–929
<checkbox>, 929–930
<cite>, 930
<code>, 931
<col>, 931–932
<colgroup>, 932
currentStyle, 932
<dd>, 937
<del>, 937
<dfn>, 938
<dir>, 938
<div>, 938–939
<dl>, 939–940
Document, 940–945
<dt>, 945–946
<em>, 946
<embed>, 946–947
fieldSet, 952–953
<font>, 954–955
<form>, 955–956
<frame>, 956–957
<head>, 961–962
<h*n*>, 961
<hr>, 963
<html>, 963–964
HTML elements, 908–915
<i>, 964
<ilayer>, 970–972
<img>, 965–967
implementation, 967
ins, 968
<kbd>, 969
<label>, 969–970
<layer>, 970–972
<legend>, 972
<li>, 972–973

<link>, 914–916, 973–974
<map>, 975
<marquee>, 975
<menu>, 977
<meta>, 978
<nobr>, 982
<noframes>, 982
<noscript>, 982
<object>, 984–986
<ol>, 986
<optgroup>, 987
<option>, 987–988
<p>, 988
<param>, 989–990
Password, 990
<pre>, 992
<q>, 992
<radio>, 993–994
reset, 996–997
runtimeStyle, 997–998
<samp>, 998
<script>, 999–1000
<select>, 1000–1001
<small>, 1002
<span>, 1002
<strike>, 1003
<strong>, 1005
<style>, 1018–1019
Style, 1005–1018
<sub>, 1020
submit, 1021–1022
<sup>, 1022
<table>, 1022–1024
<tbody>, 1024–1025
<td>, 1025–1026
<text>, 1026–1027
<textarea>, 1028–1029
<tfoot>, 1024–1025
<th>, 1025–1026
<thread>, 1024–1025
<title>, 1030–1031
<tr>, 1029–1030
<tt>, 1031
<u>, 1031
<ul>, 1031–1032
<xml>, 1042

objects, general
<base>, 921–922
<big>, 923
<blockquote>, 923
<caption>, 928
File, 953–954
FileUpload, 953–954
<frameset>, 957–958
Hidden, 962
<iframe>, 964–965
<input>, 967–968
isindex, 968
pkcs11, 991
Plugin, 990–991
styleSheet, 1019–1020
var, 1033
objects, SSJS, 670–672
octal literals, 63
<ol>, document object, 986
one-time popup windows, 599–600
onerror handler, 820–824
onmouseout event handler, 521
onmouseover event handler, 521
onreset event handler, 463–464
onsubmit event handler, 463–464, 486
open( ) method, 387–388, 426–427
Opera
browser detection, 534, 611–612
browser language detection, 622
cross-browser support for
positioning, 534–535
detecting specific plugins, 649
lack of support for octal literals, 63
MIME type support in, 647
plugin support in, 645
use of JavaScript by, 26
W3C and ECMA standards and, 289
operators, 42–45, 95–118
arithmetic operators, 96–99, 858–859
arithmetic operators, Infinity and
NaN values, 98–99
arithmetic operators, list of basic, 96
arithmetic operators, negation, 98
arithmetic operators, string
concatenation using (+), 97–98
assignment operators (=), 95–96

bitwise operators, 43, 99–101, 859–860
bitwise shift operators, 101
comma operator, 110
comma operators, 863
comparison operators, 43, 105–107
conditional operators, 861
increment (++)/decrement(—) operators, 103–105
list of basic, 42–43
logical operators, 44, 107–108, 860–861
object operators, 112–115
?: operator, 108–109
precedence and associativity of, 45, 115–118
precedents and associativity, 864–866
relational operators, 863–864
shorthand assignment operators, 101–103
type operators, 861–863
typeof operator, 111–112
void operator, 110–111
<optgroup>, document object, 987
<optgroup> element, 484–485
<option>, document object, 987–988
OR (|), bitwise operator, 99–101, 235
OR (||) operators, 107–108, 120–121
origin checks. *see* same-origin policy
outerHTML, 333–334
outerText, DHTML, 333–334

P

<p>, document object, 988
Packages, built-in object, 989
page-based transitions, DHTML, 543–547
page embellishments, 25
<param>, document object, 639, 989–990
parameters (arguments)
    advanced passing, 152–154
    checking, 158–159
    of functions, 77, 138–140
    passing, 141–142
parenthesis operator "( )", 114

parse( ) method, 206
parseFloat( ) method, 208
parseInt( ) method, 209
Password, document object, 990
password text fields, 467
pattern matching
    aggressive matching, 231
    escape codes, 227–228
    grouping and character classes, 231–234
    OR (|) operator, 235
    positional indicators, 227
    RegExp objects and, 53
    repetition characters, 229–230
    subexpressions, 234–235
persistent cookies, 594
pkcs11, object, 991
Plugin, object, 990–991
plugins, 645–656
    detecting specific, 649–651
    embedding, 645–646
    interacting, 651–656
    MIME types, 646–647
    support for MIME types, 647–649
plugins[ ] array, 649–652
plugins[ ] collection, 434–435, 616–617
polymorphism, object-oriented programming and, 180
pop( ) method, 191
popup, browser object, 991
popup windows, 799–801
positional indicators, pattern matching and, 227
positioning, CSS, 525–532
    DOM, 532
    examples, 527–529
    IE 4 layers, 531–532
    Netscape 4 layers, 529–531
    properties, 526
post-increment/decrement, 104–105
<pre>, document object, 992
pre-increment/decrement, 104–105
precedence, of operators, 45, 115–118, 864–866
preference settings, browsers, 631–633
preventDefault( ) method, 375–376

primitive datatypes, 61–74, 61–74
    Booleans, 71–72, 71–72
    numbers, 61–66, 61–66
    numbers, data representation issues, 65–66, 65–66
    numbers, hexadecimal literals, 62–63, 62–63
    numbers, octal literals, 63
    numbers, special values, 63–65, 63–65
    objects corresponding to, 221
    reference types and, 167–169
    strings, 66–71, 66–71
    strings, character representation, 68–69, 68–69
    strings, HTML and, 69–71, 69–71
    strings, overview of, 66–67, 66–67
    strings, quotes and, 69
    strings, special characters and, 67–68, 67–68
    undefined and null, 73–74, 73–74
private key cryptography, 725
programming practices, 804–841
    code protection, 838–839
    code, speed of, 837
    code, style of, 836–837
    debugging, common mistakes, 809–812
    debugging, outputting information for, 812–817
    debugging, using debugger applications, 817–819
    debugging, using error messages, 807–809
    defensive programming, browser detection, 830–832
    defensive programming, code hiding, 832–836
    defensive programming, error handlers, 820–824
    defensive programming, exceptions, 824–830
    defensive programming, overview of, 819–820
    errors, categories of, 804–806
    server-side vs. client side Web technologies and, 840–841

prompt( ) method, 51, 385–387
properties, 172–174
    accessing object, 74
    checkbox and radio button, 472
    common object, 173–174
    core, 897–902
    CSS positioning, 526
    Document object, 259, 263–264, 420–425
    Document object, color, 420–423
    Document object, last modification date, 423–424
    Document object, location-related, 424–425
    DOM, 316–317, 892–894
    Event objects, DOM2, 369
    Event objects, IE 4, 363
    Event objects, Netscape 4, 357–359
    form buttons, 466
    Form objects, 459
    HTML, 13: 19–439
    IE 4, 286
    Image objects, 512–516
    instance, 172–173, 172–173
    Layer objects, 530–531
    object, 41, 172–174
    Object object, 174
    <select> tag, 479–480
    text fields, 467
    XML, 690
prototypes
    inheritance through, 178–179
    object-oriented languages and, 174
pseudo-URLs, invoking JavaScript statements, 18–21
public key cryptography, 725
pull-down menus, 561–564
    example code for, 562–564
    placement and implementation of, 561–562
    quicklinks pull-down menus, 565–567
    select menu and, 560
push( ) method, 191, 192

Q

<q>, document object, 992
queues, 192
quicklinks pull-down menus, 565–567
quotes, 69

R

radio buttons. *see* checkboxes and
    radio buttons
<radio>, document object, 993–994
random numbers, 213
read-only fields, 501–502
readonly attributes, 501–502
recommended practices. *see*
    programming practices
recursive functions, 154–156
redirects, using cookies, 599
reference types, primitive types and,
    167–169
RegExp, built-in object, 236–240
        exec( ) method, 237–240
        handling pattern matching with, 53
        instance properties, 240–241
        overview of, 994–995
        static properties, 242–244
regular expression literals, 858
regular expressions
        advanced, 248–249
        advanced features, 872–873
        character classes, 871
        escape codes, 871–872
        examples, 236
        flags, 225, 870
        form validation, 490–491
        limitations of, 250
        need for, 224
        overview of, 53–54
        pattern matching, aggressive
            matching, 231
        pattern matching, escape codes,
            227–228
        pattern matching, grouping and
            character classes, 231–234
        pattern matching, OR (|) operator, 235

pattern matching, positional
    indicators, 227
pattern matching, repetition
    characters, 229–230
pattern matching, subexpressions,
    234–235
RegExp object, static properties of, 873
RegExp objects, exec( ) method,
    237–240
RegExp objects, instance properties,
    240–241
RegExp objects, static properties,
    242–244
    repetition quantifiers, 870
    strings and, 225, 245–247
relational operators, 863–864
releaseEvents( ) method, 361
remote control menus, 586
removeBehavior( ) method, 794
removeChild( ) method, 312–313
removeEventListener( ) method, 374
repetition characters, 229–230
repetition quantifiers, regular
    expressions, 870
replace( ) method, 246
Request methods, ASP, 678
Request objects, SSJS, 671, 680
reserved words, JavaScript, 1044–1046
reset, document object, 996–997
reset( ) method, 460
Response object, ASP
        methods, 679
        properties, 679
return keys, keyboard improvements,
    504–505
return keyword, 78
return statements
        functions and, 140–141
        semicolons (;) and, 35–36
        using explicit, 157
        using with functions, 49–50
return values, 354–356
reverse( ) method, 194
Rhino, 685
rollover buttons, 516–525

DHTML, second-generation image rollovers, 547–550
DHTML, targeted rollovers, 550–551
examples, 517–523
extending, 523–525
revealing descriptive text with, 525
uses, 516
root elements, XML, 690
routeEvent( ) method, 361
rows, DOM table manipulation, 451–455
rules
   browser object, 997
   XML (Extensible Markup Language), 689–691
runtime errors, 806, 809
runtimeStyle, document object, 997–998

S

same-origin policy, 721–723
<samp>, document object, 998
scope, of variables, 83–86
screen, browser object, 617–622, 998–999
<script>, document object
   code hiding and, 832–836
   comments for hiding, 10–11
   identifying script elements from text or HTML, 4
   including ASP code with, 674
   including script elements within HTML, 7–9
   overview of, 999–1000
   signed scripts, 732
   using multiple script elements, 9
   using within <head> tags, 10
script execution order, 30
scripting languages
   defined, 30
   JavaScript as, 685
scrollBy() method, 402
scrollTo() method, 402
search( ) method, 245–247
security, 720–743
   certification process, 726–728, 738–739

cryptography fundamentals, 725–726
data tainting, 723–724
same-origin policy, 721–723
signed scripts, 728–733
signed scripts, accessing history information with, 738
signed scripts, binding to HTML, 730–731, 732–733
signed scripts, common applications, 736–737
signed scripts, Netscape Signing Tool and, 728–730
signed scripts, overview of, 724–725
signed scripts, privilege targets for, 733–735
signed scripts, signing code, 731–732
vulnerabilities, 739–743
vulnerabilities, deceptive programming and, 741–742
vulnerabilities, denial of service attacks, 740–741
vulnerabilities, developer responsibility and, 742–743
<select>, document object
   defining pull-down menus with, 478
   methods, 479
   navigational aids and, 561
   overview of, 1000–1001
   properties of, 479–480
select menus, 478–485
   interaction, 482–484
   as navigational aid, 561
   option groups, 484–485
   single-item pull down menus, 478–480
selection, browser object, 1001–1002
semantic errors, 805–806
semicolons (;), ending statements with, 35–36, 92–94
server-side includes (SSI), 673–674
server-side JavaScript (SSJS), 664–686
   ASP, interacting with server objects, 678–682
   ASP, JavaScript methods in, 673–675
   ASP, JavaScript syntax in, 675–677
   ASP, overview of, 672–673

ASP, using with external systems, 683–685
Netscape version, creating applications, 665–669
Netscape version, objects of, 670–672
Netscape version, overview of, 664–665
Netscape version, syntax of, 670
other uses of, 685
overview of, 664
server-side scripting
technologies for, 665
vs. client side Web technologies, 840–841
session cookies, 594
set methods, for dates, 204
setInterval( ) method, 203, 629
setTimeout( ) method, 203, 627–628
SGML, 691–692
shared libraries, UNIX, 685
Shift Left (<<), bitwise shift operators, 102
shift( ) method
treating arrays as queues, 192
treating arrays as stacks, 191–192
Shift Right (>>), bitwise shift operators, 102
Shift Right Zero Fill (>>>), bitwise shift operators, 102
shorthand assignment operators, 101–103
show( ) method, 414
showMenu( ) method, 569
showModalDialog( ) method, 414
signed scripts, 728–733
accessing history information, 738
binding to HTML, 730–731, 732–733
common applications, 736–737
Netscape Signing Tool, 728–730
overview, 724–725
privilege targets, 733–735
signing code, 731–732
Signing Tool
creating JAR files, 731–732
creating test certificate with, 728–730
single-line text fields, 467
single quotes (' '), using with strings, 66

site navigation. *see* navigation
slice( ) method
examining strings, 217
manipulating arrays, 195
slide-in menus, 586–589
<small>, document object, 1002
sort( ) method, 196–198
<span>, document object, 1002
special characters, 67–68
special effects, pages, 25
SpiderMonkey, Mozilla, 685
splice( ) method, 195–196
split( ) method, 217, 245
spreadsheet objects, Microsoft Office Web Components, 784–786
SQL statements, SSJS objects and, 672
square brackets ([]), defining character classes, 232
src attributes, of <script> element, 16–17
SSI (server-side includes), 673–674
SSJS. *see* server-side JavaScript (SSJS)
stacks, treating arrays as, 190–192
storing data in last-in-first-out (LIFO) order, 190–191
using push( ) and pop( ) methods with, 191
using unshift( ) and shift( ) methods with, 191–192
stand-alone functions, 157
state management, using frames for, 409–412
stateless protocols, HTTP, 592
statements, 34–37, 92–95
core, 118–133
core, continue/break statements, 129–133
core, do-while loops, 128
core, for loops, 128–129
core, if statements, 118–122
core, switch statements, 122–125
core, while loops, 125–127
grouping into blocks, 36–37, 94–95
object-related, 133–130
object-related, for...in statements, 134
object-related, other examples, 134

object-related, with statement, 133
overview of, 34
terminating with semicolons, 35–36, 92–94
static menus, 589–591
static properties, RegExp objects, 242–244, 873
static scoping (lexical scoping), of variables, 83
static variables, 150–151
status bar, in browser windows, 627
status messages, 499
stopPropagation( ) method, 375
<strike>, document object, 1003
String, built-in object, 214–220
  examining, 215–217
  HTML-related methods of, 219–220
  manipulating, 215–217
  marking up as HTML, 218–220
  overview of, 214–215, 1003–1005
string concatenation, 97–98
strings, 66–71
  as basic data type, 37
  character representation, 68–69
  converting dates to, 205–206
  converting to dates, 206
  escape codes, 851
  HTML, 69–71
  methods utilizing regular expressions, 245–247
  overview, 66–67
  quotes, 69
  special characters, 67–68
  type conversion, 853
<strong>, document object, 1005
strongly typed languages, vs. weakly typed, 61
Style, browser object, 1005–1018
<style>, document object, 328, 1018–1019
style objects, CSS, 329
style sheets, 613
styleSheet, object, 1019–1020
styleSheets[ ] collection, 328
<sub>, document object, 1020
submit, document object, 1021–1022
submit( ) method, 460

substring( ) method, 216
subtraction operator (-), 96
subtrees, 297
sun, built-in object, 989
<sup>, document object, 1022
switch statements, 122–125
  issues with use of, 124–125
  switch/case, 46
  using instead of if statements, 122–123
syntax errors, 804–805
system events, 338

T

<table>, document object
  inspecting and changing using DOM, 449
  overview of, 1022–1024
  properties of, 444–445
table manipulation, DOM, 444–455
  defining rows and cells, 451–455
  frame attribute for, 445
  methods for, 450–451
  referencing enclosed elements, 448–450
  table properties, 444–448
taint( ) method, 723
targets, for signed scripts, 733–734
<tbody>, document object, 1024–1025
<td>, document object, 1025–1026
technology detection, 612–617
test( ) method, 226
<text>, document object, 1026–1027
text fields, form elements, 467–471
  methods of, 467–469
  multiline text entry fields, 470–471
  properties of, 467
  types of, 467
text node manipulation methods, 314–315
<textarea>, document object, 470–471, 1028–1029
TextRange, browser object, 1029
<tfoot>, document object, 1024–1025
<th>, document object, 1025–1026

Thawte, certification authorities, 726
<thread>, document object, 1024–1025
throw, exceptions, 828–829, 869
timeouts, setting, 627–630
<title>, document object, 1030–1031
tokens, cookies and, 593
toLowerCase( ) method, 215
toSource( ) method, 196
toString( ) method
    manipulating arrays, 196
    as property of Object prototype, 179
    returning number values in a
        string, 214
toUpperCase( ) method, 215
<tr>, document object, 1029–1030
traces, debuggers and, 817
Traditional Browser Object Model and
    standard DOM. *see* Internet Explorer
    (IE) 5.0; Netscape Navigator 6.0
Traditional JavaScript Object Model.
    see also Internet Explorer (IE) 3.0;
    Netscape Navigator 2
        overview, 256–258
        using, 269–271
tree structure, HTML documents, 296–299
tree walking, 301–304
    output of, 302
    starting points, 306–307
    tool for, 305
try, exceptions, 827, 869–870
<tt>, document object, 1031
type conversion, 86–90, 852–853
    automatic, 86–88
    of Boolean data, 88, 852
    manually, 89–90, 853
    of NULL data, 852
    of number data, 88, 852
    of string data, 853
    of unidentified data, 853
type, of variable or data, 60. *see also*
    data types
type operators, 861–863
typeof operator, 111–112

U

<u>, document object, 1031
UI events, DOM Level 2, 370–371
<ul>, document object, 1031–1032
unary operators (-)
    negating values with, 98
    number types and, 62
undefined datatype, 38
undefined values, 73–74, 141, 187
unescape( ) method, 209
unidentified datatypes, 853
UNIX
    shared libraries, 685
    use of regular expressions in, 224
unshift( ) method, 191–192
untaint( ) method, 724
untyped languages, 61
user-defined objects, 174–179
    good practices, 179
    inheritance through prototypes,
        178–179
    as JavaScript object category, 162
    overview, 174–178
user state management, with cookies,
    598–602
    customizations, 600–602
    one-time popups, 599–600
    redirects, 599
userAgent property, Navigator properties,
    608–609
userProfile, browser object, 1032–1033
UTC (Coordinated Universal Time), 201

V

valid documents, XML, 692–695
validation. *see* form validation
validation error message, 694
var keyword, 37, 82, 92
var, object, 1033
variables, 80–86
    declaring, 60, 82
    defined, 60

.entifiers, 80–82
    overview of, 37
    scope, 83–86
    using with functions, 140
variadic functions, 158
VBArray, built-in object, 1033
VBScript, integration with COM, 782
vectors, 76. *see also* arrays
VeriSign, certification authorities, 726
versions, JavaScript, 847
video, MIME types for, 647
void operator, 110–111

W

W3C. *see* World Wide Web
    Consortium (W3C)
weakly typed languages
    JavaScript as, 61
    pro/cons of, 38–39
well formed XML
    defined, 691
    in IE 5.5, 689
while loops
    example of, 47
    overview of, 125–127
white space characters, 33–34
Window objects
    browser control, History object,
        626–627
    browser control, Location object,
        625–626
    browser control, setting timeouts,
        627–630
    browser control, status bar, 627
    as browser object type, 1033–1041
    close( )method, 388–389
    dialogs, alert( ) method, 382–383
    dialogs, confirm( ) method, 383–385
    dialogs, prompt( ) method, 385–387
    DOM capabilities, 398–399
    events, 404–405
    extensions, 413
    feature parameters, 390–395
    frames, properties, 406

frames, relationships, 410
    frames, state management with,
        409–412
    frames, troubleshooting, 412–413
    full-screen, 416–417
    IE extensions, modal, 413–414
    IE extensions, modeless, 414
    IE extensions, pop-up, 414–416
    inter-window communication,
        399–400
    moving, 400–401
    Netscape 4 and, 280
    Netscape extensions, 417
    open( ) method, 387–388
    properties and methods of, 382
    resizing, 401–402
    scrolling, 402–404
    writing to, 395–397
window.blur( ) method, 400
window.createPopup( ) method, 414
window.focus( ) method, 400
window.moveBy( ) method, 400–401
window.moveTo() method, 400–401
Window.navigator.language property, 622
window.onerror, 820–824
window.open. *see* open( ) method
window.opener property, 399–400
window.print( ) method, 417, 630
window.resizeBy( ) method, 401
window.resizeTo( ) method, 401
Wireless Markup Language) (WML), 688
with statement, 133, 867
WML (Wireless Markup Language), 688
World Wide Web Consortium (W3C)
    browsers and, 289
    DOM specification of, 27, 290
    DOM2 and, 368
    IE tools based on, 715
write( ) method, 52–53, 425–426
writeln( ) method, 52–53, 425–426

X

XML data islands, IE, 711–715
<xml>, document object, 711, 1042

XML (Extensible Markup Language),
688–715
    DOM, 700–711
    DOM, IE example, 700–706
    DOM, Netscape 6 example, 706–710
    IE's XML data islands, 711–715
    overview, 688–695
    overview, examples, 688–689
    overview, rules, 689–691
    overview, valid documents, 692–695
    presentation, converting to HTML,
      695–696
    presentation, direct display, 700
    presentation, separating content
      from, 695
    presentation, using XSL style sheets
      for transformations, 697–699

XMLDOMDocument, 715
XMLDOMNamedNodeMap, 715
XMLDOMNode, 715
XMLDOMNodeList, 715
XOR (^), bitwise operator, 99–101
XSL (Extensible Style Sheets), 696–698
XSLT (Extensible Style Sheet
  Transformations), 711–715
    transforming XML into HTML
      with, 696–698, 696–698
    transforming XML with, 695

Z

z-index, 753

INTERNATIONAL CONTACT INFORMATION

AUSTRALIA
McGraw-Hill Book Company Australia Pty. Ltd.
TEL +61-2-9417-9899
FAX +61-2-9417-5687
http://www.mcgraw-hill.com.au
books-it_sydney@mcgraw-hill.com

CANADA
McGraw-Hill Ryerson Ltd.
TEL +905-430-5000
FAX +905-430-5020
http://www.mcgrawhill.ca

**GREECE, MIDDLE EAST,
NORTHERN AFRICA**
McGraw-Hill Hellas
TEL +30-1-656-0990-3-4
FAX +30-1-654-5525

MEXICO (Also serving Latin America)
McGraw-Hill Interamericana Editores S.A. de C.V.
TEL +525-117-1583
FAX +525-117-1589
http://www.mcgraw-hill.com.mx
fernando_castellanos@mcgraw-hill.com

SINGAPORE (Serving Asia)
McGraw-Hill Book Company
TEL +65-863-1580
FAX +65-862-3354
http://www.mcgraw-hill.com.sg
mghasia@mcgraw-hill.com

SOUTH AFRICA
McGraw-Hill South Africa
TEL +27-11-622-7512
FAX +27-11-622-9045
robyn_swanepoel@mcgraw-hill.com

**UNITED KINGDOM & EUROPE
(Excluding Southern Europe)**
McGraw-Hill Education Europe
TEL +44-1-628-502500
FAX +44-1-628-770224
http://www.mcgraw-hill.co.uk
computing_neurope@mcgraw-hill.com

ALL OTHER INQUIRIES Contact:
Osborne/McGraw-Hill
TEL +1-510-549-6600
FAX +1-510-883-7600
http://www.osborne.com
omg_international@mcgraw-hill.com